Communications
in Computer and Information Science   298

Salvatore Greco   Bernadette Bouchon-Meunier
Giulianella Coletti   Mario Fedrizzi
Benedetto Matarazzo   Ronald R. Yager (Eds.)

Advances in Computational Intelligence

14th International Conference
on Information Processing and Management
of Uncertainty in Knowledge-Based Systems
IPMU 2012
Catania, Italy, July 9-13, 2012
Proceedings, Part II

 Springer

Volume Editors

Salvatore Greco
University of Catania, Italy
E-mail: salgreco@unict.it

Bernadette Bouchon-Meunier
University Pierre et Marie Curie, Paris, France
E-mail: bernadette.bouchon-meunier@lip6.fr

Giulianella Coletti
University of Perugia, Italy
E-mail: coletti@dmi.unipg.it

Mario Fedrizzi
University of Trento, Italy
E-mail: mario.fedrizzi@unitn.it

Benedetto Matarazzo
University of Catania, Italy
E-mail: matarazz@unict.it

Ronald R. Yager
IONA College, New Rochelle, NY, USA
E-mail: ryager@iona.edu

ISSN 1865-0929   e-ISSN 1865-0937
ISBN 978-3-642-31714-9   e-ISBN 978-3-642-31715-6
DOI 10.1007/978-3-642-31715-6
Springer Heidelberg Dordrecht London New York

Library of Congress Control Number: Applied for

CR Subject Classification (1998): I.2, H.3, F.1, H.4, I.5, I.4, C.2

© Springer-Verlag Berlin Heidelberg 2012
This work is subject to copyright. All rights are reserved, whether the whole or part of the material is
concerned, specifically the rights of translation, reprinting, re-use of illustrations, recitation, broadcasting,
reproduction on microfilms or in any other way, and storage in data banks. Duplication of this publication
or parts thereof is permitted only under the provisions of the German Copyright Law of September 9, 1965,
in its current version, and permission for use must always be obtained from Springer. Violations are liable
to prosecution under the German Copyright Law.
The use of general descriptive names, registered names, trademarks, etc. in this publication does not imply,
even in the absence of a specific statement, that such names are exempt from the relevant protective laws
and regulations and therefore free for general use.

Typesetting: Camera-ready by author, data conversion by Scientific Publishing Services, Chennai, India

Printed on acid-free paper

Springer is part of Springer Science+Business Media (www.springer.com)

Preface

We are glad to present the proceedings of the IPMU 2012 conference (International Conference on Information Processing and Management of Uncertainty in Knowledge-Based Systems) held in Catania, Italy, during July 9–13, 2012. The IPMU conference is organized every two years with the focus of bringing together scientists working on methods for the management of uncertainty and aggregation of information in intelligent systems. This conference provides a medium for the exchange of ideas between theoreticians and practitioners in these and related areas. This was the 14th edition of the IPMU conference, which started in 1986 and has been held every two years in the following locations in Europe: Paris (1986), Urbino (1988), Paris (1990), Palma de Mallorca (1992), Paris (1994), Granada (1996), Paris (1998), Madrid (2000), Annecy (2002), Perugia (2004), Paris (2006), Malaga (2008), Dortmund (2010). Among the plenary speakers of past IPMU conferences there are three Nobel Prize winners: Kenneth Arrow, Daniel Kahneman, Ilya Prigogine.

The program of IPMU 2012 consisted of six invited talks together with 258 contributed papers, authored by researchers from 36 countries, including the regular track and 35 special sessions. The invited talks were given by the following distinguished researchers: Kalyanmoy Deb (Indian Institute of Technology Kanpur, India), Antonio Di Nola (University of Salerno, Italy), Christophe Marsala (Université Pierre et Marie Curie, France), Roman Slowinski (Poznan University of Technology, Poland), Tomohiro Takagi (Meiji University, Japan), Peter Wakker (Erasmus University, The Netherlands). Michio Sugeno received the Kampé de Fériet Award, granted every two years on the occasion of the IPMU conference, in view of his eminent research contributions to the handling of uncertainty through fuzzy measures and fuzzy integrals, and fuzzy control using fuzzy systems.

The success of such an event is mainly due to the hard work and dedication of a number of people and the collaboration of several institutions. We want to acknowledge the help of the members of the International Program Committee, the additional reviewers, the organizers of special sessions, and the volunteer students. All of them deserve many thanks for having helped to attain the goal of providing a balanced event with a high level of scientific exchange and a pleasant environment. A special mention is deserved by Silvia Angilella, Salvatore Corrente, Fabio Rindone, and Giuseppe Vaccarella, who contributed greatly to the organization of the conference and especially to the review process.

We acknowledge the use of the EasyChair conference system for the paper submission and review. We would also like to thank Alfred Hofmann and Leonie Kunz, and Springer, for providing continuous assistance and ready advice whenever needed.

May 2012

Salvatore Greco
Bernadette Bouchon-Meunier
Giulianella Coletti
Mario Fedrizzi
Benedetto Matarazzo
Ronald R. Yager

Organization

Conference Committee

General Chair

Salvatore Greco — University of Catania, Italy

Co-chairs

Giulianella Coletti — University of Perugia, Italy
Mario Fedrizzi — University of Trento, Italy
Benedetto Matarazzo — University of Catania, Italy

Executive Directors

Bernadette Bouchon-Meunier — LIP6, Paris, France
Ronald R. Yager — Iona College, USA

Special Session Organizers

Alessandro Antonucci
Michal Baczynski
Edurne Barrenechea
Sebastiano Battiato
Jan Bazan
Abdelhamid Bouchachia
Humberto Bustine
David Carfi
Davide Ciucci
Jesus Chamorro
Giulianella Coletti
Didier Coquin
Alfredo Cuzzocrea
Giovanni Battista
  Dagnino
Didier Dubois
Fabrizio Durante
Zied Eloudi
Macarena Espinilla
Gisella Facchinetti
Javier Fernandez
Tommaso Flaminio
Giovanni Gallo

Roberto Ghiselli
  Ricci
Karina Gibert
Giovanni Giuffrida
Michel Grabisch
Przemyslaw
  Grzegorzewski
Maria Letizia Guerra
Francisco Herrera
Balasubramaniam
  Jayaram
Janusz Kacprzyk
Cengiz Kahraman
Cristophe Labreuche
Ioana Leustean
Edwin Lughofer
Enrico Marchioni
Nicolas Marin
Luis Martinez
Pedro Melo-Pinto
Radko Mesiar
Enrique Miranda
Antonio Moreno

Moamar Sayed
  Mouchaweh
Guillermo
  Navarro-Arribas
Vesa Niskanen
Miguel Pagola
Olga Pons
Ana Pradera
Anca Ralescu
Daniel Sanchez
Miquel Sanchez-Marré
Rudolf Seising
Andrzej Skowron
Dominik Slezak
Hung Son Nguyen
Carlo Sempi
Luciano Stefanini
Eulalia Szmidt
Marco Elio Tabacchi
Vicenc Torra
Gracian Trivino
Lionel Valet
Aida Valls

International Program Committee

J. Aczel (Canada)
J. Bezdek (USA)
P. Bonissone (USA)
G. Chen (China)
V. Cross (USA)
B. De Baets (Belgium)
T. Denoeux (France)
M. Detyniecki (France)
A. Di Nola (Italy)
D. Dubois (France)
F. Esteva (Spain)
J. Fodor (Hungary)
S. Galichet (France)
P. Gallinari (France)
M.A. Gil (Spain)
F. Gomide (Brazil)
M. Grabisch (France)
S. Grossberg (USA)
P. Hajek
   (Czech Republic)

L. Hall (USA)
F. Herrera (Spain)
K. Hirota (Japan)
F. Hoffmann (Germany)
J. Kacprzyk (Poland)
A. Kandel (USA)
J. Keller (USA)
F. Klawonn (Germany)
E.P. Klement (Austria)
L. Koczy (Hungary)
V. Kreinovich (USA)
R. Kruse (Germany)
H. Larsen (Denmark)
M.-J. Lesot (France)
T. Martin (UK)
J. Mendel (USA)
R. Mesiar (Slovakia)
S. Moral (Spain)
H.T. Nguyen (USA)
S. Ovchinnikov (USA)

G. Pasi (Italy)
W. Pedrycz (Canada)
V. Piuri (Italy)
O. Pivert (France)
H. Prade (France)
A. Ralescu (USA)
D. Ralescu (USA)
M. Ramdani (Maroc)
E. Ruspini (Spain)
S. Sandri (Brasil)
M. Sato (Japan)
G. Shafer (USA)
P. Shenoy (USA)
P. Sobrevilla (Spain)
M. Sugeno (Japan)
E. Szmidt (Poland)
S. Termini (Italy)
I.B. Turksen (Canada)
S. Zadrozny (Poland)

We thank the precious support of all the referees, which helped to improve the scientific quality of the papers submitted to the conference:

Daniel Abril
Tofigh Allahviranloo
Cecilio Angulo
Alessandro Antonucci
Luca Anzilli
Raouia Ayachi
Michal Baczynski
Valentina Emilia Balas
Rosangela Ballini
Adrian Ban
Mohua Banerjee
Carlos D. Barranco
Sebastiano Battiato
Jan Bazan
Benjamin Bedregal
Gleb Beliakov
Nahla Ben Amor
Sarah Ben Amor
Alessio Benavoli

Ilke Bereketli
Veronica Biazzo
Isabelle Bloch
Fernando Bobillo
Andrea Boccuto
Gloria Bordogna
Silvia Bortot
Imen Boukhris
Juergen Branke
Werner Brockmann
Antoon Bronselaer
Matteo Brunelli
Alberto Bugarín
Humberto Bustince
Tomasa Calvo
Domenico Candeloro
Andrea Capotorti
Marta Cardin
Fabrizio Caruso

Bice Cavallo
Nihan Çetin Demirel
Emre Cevikcan
Mihir Chakraborty
Davide Ciucci
Lavinia Corina Ciungu
Vincent Clivillé
Giulianella Coletti
Dante Conti
Didier Coquin
Giorgio Corani
Chris Cornelis
Miguel Couceiro
Pedro Couto
Alfredo Cuzzocrea
Nuzillard Danielle
Bernard De Baets
Gert De Cooman
Yves De Smet

Guy De Tre
Roberto De Virgilio
Tufan Demirel
Glad Deschrijver
Sébastien Destercke
Luigi Di Gaetano
Irene Diaz
József Dombi
Michael Doumpos
Antonio Dourado
Józef Drewniak
Didier Dubois
Fabrizio Durante
Antonin Dvorak
Krzysztof Dyczkowski
Susana Díaz
Zied Elouedi
Mujde Erol Genevois
Macarena Espinilla
Gisella Facchinetti
Salvatore Federico
Michele Fedrizzi
Javier Fernandez
Juan Fernandez-Sanchez
Valentina Ferretti
José Rui Figueira
Tommaso Flaminio
Vito Fragnelli
Camilo Franco
Robert Fullér
Marek Gagolewski
Giovanni Gallo
Luis Garmendia
George Georgescu
Brunella Gerla
Karina Gibert
Angelo Gilio
Silvio Giove
Lluis Godo
Fernando Gomide
Michel Grabisch
Przemyslaw
   Grzegorzewski
Jerzy Grzymala-Busse
Maria Letizia Guerra

Manuel Gómez-Olmedo
Robert Hable
Allel Hadjali
Xingxing He
Gernot Herbst
Francisco Herrera
Shoji Hirano
Michal Holcapek
Eyke Huellermeier
Dusan Husek
Julia Inthorn
Masahiro Inuiguchi
David Isern
Alessio Ishizaka
Vladimir Janis
Jouni Jarvinen
Piotr Jaworski
Balasubramaniam
   Jayaram
Radim Jirousek
Özgür Kabak
Janusz Kacprzyk
Cengiz Kahraman
Martin Kalina
Erich Peter Klement
Anna Kolesarova
Beata Konikowska
Tomas Kroupa
Pavol Král'
Pierre Kunsch
Christophe Labreuche
Fabio Lamantia
Fabrizio Lanzafame
Eric Lefevre
Karim Lidouh
Pawan Lingras
Weiru Liu
Carlos Lopez-Molina
Maite Lopez-Sanchez
Lorenzo Di Silvestro
Edwin Lughofer
Lina Mallozzi
Maddalena Manzi
Enrico Marchioni
Jean-Luc Marichal

Ricardo Alberto
   Marques Pereira
Christophe Marsala
Arnaud Martin
Luis Martinez
Murakami Masayuki
Andres R. Masegosa
Sebastià Massanet
Tom Matthé
Jorma K. Mattila
Denis Maua'
Gilles Mauris
Brice Mayag
Gaspar Mayor
Angelo Mazza
Juan Miguel Medina
David Mercier
Radko Mesiar
Enrico Messina
Enrique Miranda
Pedro Miranda
Javier Montero
Ignacio Montes
Susana Montes
Jacky Montmain
Serafin Moral
Antonio Moreno
Masayuki Mukunoki
Francesco Musolino
Kazuaki Nakamura
Juan Carlos Nieves
Satoshi Nishiguchi
Vesa Niskanen
Carles Noguera
Vilem Novak
Piotr Nowak
Hannu Nurmi
Annamaria Olivieri
Wassila Ouerdane
Krzysztof Pancerz
Endre Pap
Pere Pardo
Ana Passuello
Daniel Paternain
Simon Petitrenaud

David Picado Muino
Olivier Pivert
Olga Pons
Henri Prade
Ana Pradera
Mahardhika Pratama
Giovanni Puglisi
Antonio Punzo
Barbara Pękala
Anca Ralescu
Fahimeh Ramezani
Daniele Ravì
Mohammad Rawashdeh
Renata Reiser
Magdalena Rencova
Silja Renooij
Hana Rezankova
Angela Ricciardello
Maria Rifqi
J. Tinguaro Rodríguez
Rosa M. Rodríguez
Antoine Rolland
Nils Rosemann
Rafael Rumi
Nobusumi Sagara
Antonio Salmeron

Giuseppe Sanfilippo
Jose Santamaria
José Antonio Sanz
  Delgado
Moamar
  Sayed-Mouchaweh
Florence Sedes
Rudolf Seising
Carlo Sempi
Jesus Serrano-Guerrero
Prakash Shenoy
Marek Sikora
Andrzej Skowron
Damjan Skulj
Dominik Slezak
Zdenko Sonicki
Luca Spada
Anna Stachowiak
Ivana Stajner-Papuga
Daniel Stamate
Luciano Stefanini
Jaroslaw Stepaniuk
Martin Stepnicka
Marcin Szczuka
Miquel Sànchez-Marrè
Marco Elio Tabacchi

Settimo Termini
Vicenc Torra
Joan Torrens
Krzysztof Trawinski
Gracian Trivino
Alessandra Trunfio
Mayumi Ueda
Ziya Ulukan
Alp Ustundag
İrem Uçal Sarı
Lionel Valet
Aida Valls
Arthur Van Camp
Linda Van Der Gaag
Barbara Vantaggi
Jirina Vejnarova
Thomas Vetterlein
Maria-Amparo Vila
Doretta Vivona
Marcin Wolski
Yu-Lung Wu
Slawomir Zadrozny
Calogero Zarba
Pawel Zielinski
Michele Zito

Table of Contents – Part II

40th Anniversary of the Measures of Fuzziness

SPS11 Uncertainty in Profiling Systems and Applications

Handling Uncertainty with Copulas

Formal Methods to Deal with Uncertainty of Many-Valued Events

Linguistic Summarization and Description of Data

Fuzzy Implications: Theory and Applications

Sensing and Data Mining for Teaching and Learning

Theory and Applications of Intuitionistic Fuzzy Sets

Approximate Aspects of Data mining and Database Analytics

Fuzzy Setting: Fuzziness of General Information

Doretta Vivona[1] and Maria Divari[2]

[1] Sapienza Universitá di Roma, Dip. SBAI, v.A. Scarpa n.16, 00161 Roma, Italy
doretta.vivona@uniroma1.it
[2] Sapienza Universitá di Roma, v.Borgorose n.15, 00189 Roma, Italy
maria.divari@alice.it

Abstract. The aim of this paper is to give, on the fuzzy setting, a definition of fuzziness for the information without probability or fuzzy measure (general information).

Moreover, we present a class of measures of fuzziness, solving a system of functional conditions coming from the properties of fuzziness.

1 Introduction

Many authors have introduced the definition of fuzziness in crisp and fuzzy setting [2, 4, 5]. Instead, we would present a definition of fuzziness for information without probability or fuzzy measure, called general information.

After the sect.2 devoted to some preliminaries, in sect.3 we propose this definition taking into account some implications for a given information J.

For example, we think that the quality of information μ_J, the quality of transmission τ_J and the quality of the reception ρ_J can have an effect on fuzziness of the information, taking into account some parametres which have not been considered so far as elements influencing fuzziness.

Some properties of fuzziness introduced above, allow us to propose a system of functional conditions [1]. Solving this system, we get a class of fuzziness for the information $J(F)$ in sect.4. Sect.5 is devoted to the conclusions.

2 Preliminaries

Let Ω be an abstract space and $\mathcal{F}$ the σ-algebra of all not empty fuzzy sets F [8, 6, 7], such that $(\Omega, \mathcal{F})$ is a measurable space.

In [3] we considered the *measure of general information* as a map

$$J(\cdot) : \mathcal{F} \to [0, +\infty]$$

such that:

(i) $F' \supset F \Rightarrow J(F') \leq J(F)$,
(ii) $J(\emptyset) = +\infty$, $J(\Omega) = 0$.

Also in [3] fixed J, we have proposed that two fuzzy sets are $J-independent$ if, being $F_1 \cap F_2 \neq \emptyset$,

(iii) $J(F_1 \cap F_2) = J(F_1) + J(F_2)$.

S. Greco et al. (Eds.): IPMU 2012, Part II, CCIS 298, pp. 1–3, 2012.
© Springer-Verlag Berlin Heidelberg 2012

3 Definition of Fuzziness for General Information

Having fixed an information J, we take three increasing functions:

$$\mu_J, \tau_J, \rho_J : \mathcal{F} \to [0,1]$$

called *quality of information, quality of transmission,* and *quality of the reception,* respectively, such that:

a) $\mu_J(\emptyset) = \tau_J(\emptyset) = \rho_J(\emptyset) = 0$,
b) $\mu_J(\Omega) = \tau_J(\Omega) = \rho_J(\Omega) = 1$,
c) $F' \subset F \Rightarrow \mu_J(F') \leq \mu_J(F), \quad \tau_J(F') \leq \tau(F), \quad \rho_J(F') \leq \rho_J(F)$.

Now, we consider a function

$$\Phi\left(\mu_J(F), \tau_J(F), \rho_J(F)\right) : [0,1] \times [0,1] \times [0,1] \to [0,1] \tag{1}$$

with the following properties:

I) $\Phi(0,0,0) = 0$,
II) $\Phi(1,1,1) = 1$,
III) $\Phi(x',y',z') \leq \Phi(x,y,z), \quad x' \leq x, \quad y' \leq y, \quad z' \leq z$,
with: $x = \mu_J(F), \ y = \tau_J(F), \ \rho_J(F) = z, \ x' = \mu_J(F'), \ y' = \tau_J(F'),$
$\rho_J(F') = z'$.

We express the natural properties of fuzziness FN_J of information J through the function Φ (1) putting:

$$FN_J(F) = 1 - \Phi\left(\mu_J(F), \tau_J(F), \rho_J(F)\right). \tag{2}$$

Infact, fixed F, we suppose that if the quality of information is max $(\mu_J(F) = 1)$, the quality of transmission is max $(\tau_J(F) = 1)$ and the quality of reception is max $(\rho_J(F) = 1)$, then fuzziness is null: $FN_J(E) = 0$.

On the other hand, if the quality of information, the quality of transmission and the quality of reception are all null $\mu_J(F) = \tau_J(F) = \rho_J(F) = 0$, we suppose that fuzziness is max: $FN_J(F) = 1$.

Moreover, fuzziness $FN_J(F)$ is decreasing with respect to the three variables μ_J, τ_J, ρ_J because they are themselves monotone.

Taking into account (2) and $[(I) - (III)]$, the properties of the fuzziness FN_J can be written in the following way:

I*) $FN_J(1,1,1) = 0$,
II*) $FN_J(0,0,0) = 1$,
III*) $FN_J(x',y',z') \geq FN_J(x,y,z), \quad x' \leq x, \quad y' \leq y, \quad z' \leq z$,
with the same notations of (III).

4   Solution of the Problem

In this paragraph we are looking for the solutions of system of functional conditions for the function Φ seen above: $[(I^*) - (III^*)]$.

It is easy to prove the following propositions:

Proposition 1. *A class of solutions of the system* $[(I^*) - (III^*)]$ *is*

$$\Phi_h(x, y, z) = h^{-1} \left(h(x) \wedge [h(y) \cdot h(z)] \right) ,$$

where h is any strictly decreasing function with $h(0) = 1$ and $h(0) = 1$.

Proposition 2. *A class of solutions of the system* $[(I^*) - (III^*)]$ *is*

$$\Phi_k(x, y, z) = k^{-1} \left(k(x) \vee [k(y) \cdot k(z)] \right) ,$$

where k is any strictly decreasing function with $k(0) = 1$ and $k(1) = 0$.

5   Conclusion

In this paper, we present a first idea on fuzziness FN_J for information depending on the quality of information μ_J, the quality of transmission τ_J and the quality of the reception ρ_J: from (2), we have recognized that possible expressions are:

$$FN_J(F) = 1 - h^{-1} \left(h(\mu_J(F)) \cdot \left[h(\tau_J(F)) \wedge h(\rho_J(F)) \right] \right),$$

and

$$FN_J(F) = 1 - h^{-1} \left(h(\mu_J(F)) \cdot \left[h(\tau_J(F)) \vee h(\rho_J(F)) \right] \right),$$

where $h : [0, 1] \to [0, 1]$ is any decreasing function with $h(0) = 1, h(1) = 0$.

Having fixed information J, it could be interesting to characterize fuzziness FN_J, when it is conditioned by an event which is not linked to its transmission.

References

[1] Aczél J.: Functional equations and their applications. Academic Press (1966)
[2] Ebanks, B.R.: On measures of fuzziness and Their representations. J. Math. An. Appl. 94, 24–37 (1983)
[3] Benvenuti, P., Vivona, D., Divari, M.: A General Information for Fuzzy Sets. In: Bouchon-Meunier, B., Zadeh, L.A., Yager, R.R. (eds.) IPMU 1990. LNCS, vol. 521, pp. 307–316. Springer, Heidelberg (1991)
[4] Couso, I., Gil, P., Montes, S.: Measures of fuzziness and Information Theory. In: Proc. IPMU 1996, pp. 501–505 (1996)
[5] DeLuca, A., Termini, S.: A definition of non probabilistic entropy in the setting of fuzzy sets theory. Inform. and Control 20, 301–312 (1972)
[6] Klir, G.J., Folger, T.A.: Fuzzy sets, Uncertainty, and Information. Prentice-Hall International editions (1988)
[7] Kosko, B.: Fuzzy Thinking: The New Science of Fuzzy Logic, Hyperion Eds. (1993)
[8] Zadeh, L.A.: Fuzzy sets. Inf. and Control 8, 338–353 (1965)

A Probabilistic View of De Luca
and Termini's Entropy

José A. Herencia

Dpto. de Informática y A. N., Universidad de Córdoba, Spain
jaherencia@uco.es

Abstract. We consider two usual aspects associated to a fuzzy subset
of a finite set. First, the "nonprobabilistic entropy" defined by De Luca
and Termini. Second, the representation of the fuzzy set as a consonant evidence or, equivalently, as a possibility or a necessity (i. e., as a
special kind of basic probability assignment or its equivalent associated
fuzzy measures). Maintaining the definition of De Luca and Termini, an
alternative (probabilistic) view is proposed such that it becomes a "probabilistic entropy": the entropy of an alternative random set associated to
the fuzzy set. This is a dissonant evidence, whose belief and plausibility
are also characterized as special cases of fuzzy measures.

Keywords: Entropy, Fuzzy set, Random set, Probability, Possibility,
Necessity, Evidence, Plausibility, Belief, Fuzzy measure.

1 Introduction

The incertitude due to randomness, considered as a mathematical problem by
Fermat and Pascal, originated the "theory of probability", initially described by
Laplace and further studied and developed under different points of view ("frequency" by Venn and von Mises, "logic" by Keynes and Carnap or "subjective"
by De Finetti and Savage). Mathematically, they are different interpretations of
the "axiomatic" theory of probability given by Kolmogorov. The entropy, defined
by Shannon [17], measures the degree of incertitude associated to a probability
distribution (or, equivalently, the information obtained when the result of a random experiment is known).

The determination of an element in a set may be himself imprecise or fuzzy
(because the set does not have sharp boundaries, not depending of the result
of a random experiment). In this sense, Zadeh introduced the concept of "fuzzy
set" [23] (and the resulting "possibility theory" [24]), which has proven to be
a very useful tool in order to deal with this other kind of incertitude. De Luca
and Termini [4] defined a "nonprobabilistic entropy" to measure the degree of
fuzziness of a fuzzy set.

During several years, some authors (e.g. [12–14, 21]) discarded the mathematical treatment of any kind of incertitude different to the probability. Nowadays,

S. Greco et al. (Eds.): IPMU 2012, Part II, CCIS 298, pp. 4–14, 2012.
© Springer-Verlag Berlin Heidelberg 2012

different uncertain aspects like fuzziness, vagueness, possibility, ambiguity, non-specificity, dissonance, confusion, etc. (e.g. [6, 7, 9, 10]) are commonly accepted and studied together with the probability.

The "evidence theory" (Dempster [5] and Shafer [16]) provides a common frame to which the probability and possibility (or fuzziness) belong as particular cases. An evidence may be defined by three equivalent functions: the "basic probability assignment (BPA) or mass function", the "belief" and the "plausibility". The last two functions are particular cases of "fuzzy measures" (Sugeno [18]). In this paper, we restrict ourselves to the evidences (highlighting the special cases of probability and possibility). Nevertheless, other kinds of fuzzy measures (e.g., the capacities, the representable measures, etc.) are studied and classified ([3, 11, 22] ...).

In Section 2, we fix the notation and schematize the principal aspects used in the paper, among the notions considered above.

In spite of the difference between probability and fuzziness (which may occur alone or together in real phenomena), in this paper we consider an alternative representation of fuzzy sets (like a kind of evidence different to a possibility, called here the "probabilistic-fuzzy" evidence) such that the De Luca and Termini's "nonprobabilistic entropy" becomes the Shannon's "probabilistic entropy" of a random set. This is made in Section 3, where we characterize the BPA, belief and plausibility of this alternative kind of evidence.

Finally, in Section 4, some remarks about the "probabilistic-fuzzy evidence" are considered.

2   Preliminaries and Notation

We use the finite set $X = \{x_1, x_2, \ldots, x_n\}$ as universe of discourse. Its [crisp] power set 2^X is denoted $\mathcal{P}(X)$. For any $A \in \mathcal{P}(X)$, we consider its **cardinal** $|A|$ and its **complementary set** $A' := X \setminus A$.

2.1   Fuzzy Measures

A **fuzzy measure** g on X [18] is any increasing ($A \subseteq B \Rightarrow g(A) \leq g(B)$) map $\mathcal{P}(X) \to [0, 1]$ such that $g(\emptyset) = 0$ and $g(X) = 1$. Given any fuzzy measure g on X, its **dual fuzzy measure** g' is defined by: $g'(A) := 1 - g(A')$, $\forall A \subseteq X$ and g is an **autodual** fuzzy measure when $g' = g$. Obviously, $g'' = g$ for any fuzzy measure g.

Let $\lambda \in (-1, \infty)$. A fuzzy measure g on X is called λ**-additive** [19] if whenever $A, B \subseteq X$ and $A \cap B = \emptyset$ then

$$g(A \cup B) = g(A) + g(B) + \lambda g(A)g(B) \tag{1}$$

In the case $\lambda = 0$, g is called simply additive. Then, it is a probability, as we see below.

2.2 Probability and Entropy

Kolmogorov defined a **probability** p on X like an additive fuzzy measure:

$$\forall A, B \in \mathcal{P}(X), \ p(A \cup B) = p(A) + p(B) - p(A \cap B) \tag{2}$$

The probability p is determined by its **probability distribution**: $p_i := p(\{x_i\})$, $\forall i = 1, 2, \ldots, n$. Indeed, for any $A \in \mathcal{P}(X)$, the additivity (2) implies that $p(A) = \sum_{x_i \in A} p_i$. Therefore $\sum_{i=1}^{n} p_i = 1$ and any probability p is an autodual fuzzy measure.

Let us assume that a probability q is given on the set $Y = \{y_1, y_2, \ldots, y_k\}$ by the distribution $q_j = q(\{y_j\})$, $\forall j = 1, 2, \ldots, k$. If q is **independent** of p (on X) then the **product probability** is defined on the set $X \times Y$ by: $r(\{(x_i, y_j)\}) := p_i q_j$, $\forall i = 1, 2, \ldots, n$; $\forall j = 1, 2, \ldots, k$.

The **Shannon's entropy** [17] of the probability p is defined as:

$$H(p) := -\sum_{i=1}^{n} p_i log_2 p_i \tag{3}$$

For the product probability, we have:

$$H(r) = H(p) + H(q) \tag{4}$$

2.3 Fuzziness and Its Measure

A **fuzzy subset** of X [23] is a map $\mu : X \to [0, 1]$ which assigns to any element $x_i \in X$ its **degree of membership** $\mu_i = \mu(x_i)$. For any $\alpha \in [0, 1]$, the α-**cut** of μ is the crisp set $\{x_i \in X : \mu_i \geq \alpha\}$. The fuzzy set μ is called **normal** when $\max\{\mu_i : i = 1, 2, \ldots, n\} = 1$ and it is called **subnormal** when $\max\{\mu_i : i = 1, 2, \ldots, n\} < 1$. We note $\mathcal{F}(X) = [0, 1]^X$ the fuzzy power set of X.

Associated to any normal fuzzy subset of X, a fuzzy measure Π on X, called **possibility** [24], is defined by:

$$\forall A \in \mathcal{P}(X), \ \Pi(A) = \max\{\mu_i : x_i \in A\} \tag{5}$$

Obviously, the following condition is fulfilled:

$$\forall A, B \in \mathcal{P}(X), \ \Pi(A \cup B) = \max\{\Pi(A), \Pi(B)\} \tag{6}$$

Any fuzzy measure Π fulfilling (6) is called a **possibility**. Then Π determines its **possibility distribution** $\pi_i := \Pi(\{x_i\})$, $(\forall i = 1, 2, \ldots, n)$, which is a normal fuzzy set, from what can be obtained by: $\Pi(A) = \max\{\pi_i : x_i \in A\}$, $\forall A \in \mathcal{P}(X)$.

The dual fuzzy measure N of any possibility Π is called a **necessity**. It is characterized by the fulfillment of the following property:

$$\forall A, B \in \mathcal{P}(X), \ N(A \cap B) = \min\{N(A), N(B)\} \tag{7}$$

De Luca and Termini [4] measure the degree of fuzziness of the fuzzy set μ via its **"nonprobabilistic entropy"**, defined as:

$$d(\mu) := -\sum_{i=1}^{n} (\mu_i log_2 \mu_i + (1 - \mu_i) log_2 (1 - \mu_i)) \tag{8}$$

2.4 Evidence: BPA, Belief and Plausibility

The Dempster-Shafer [5, 16] **evidence theory** considers a **random set** or **basic probability assignment (BPA)** on X as any map $m : \mathcal{P}(X) \to [0, 1]$ fulfilling the two following conditions: $m(\emptyset) = 0$ and $\sum_{A \in \mathcal{P}(X)} m(A) = 1$. The **focal elements** of m are the subsets $B \subseteq X$ such that $m(B) > 0$. Associated to any BPA m, the dual fuzzy measures **belief** Bel and **plausibility** Pl are defined ($\forall A \subseteq X$) by:

$$Bel(A) := \sum_{B \subseteq A} m(B), \qquad Pl(A) := \sum_{B \cap A \neq \emptyset} m(B) \tag{9}$$

Conversely, from the fuzzy measure Bel, its only BPA m may be obtained ($\forall A \subseteq X$) by: $m(A) = \sum_{B \subseteq A} (-1)^{|A \backslash B|} Bel(B)$. Therefore, the three functions m, Bel and Pl result equivalent. They contain the same information, called an **evidence** on X.

The probability is the particular case of evidence where all the focal elements are unitary sets: $p_i = m(\{x_i\})$, $\forall i = 1, 2, \ldots, n$. In this case we have: $p = Bel = Pl$. Among all the evidences on X, these "**probabilistic evidences**" are the only fulfilling the following three equivalent conditions:

1. All the focal elements of m are unitary sets.
2. Pl is a probability; that is, it fulfills (2). Then, we note $Pl = p$.
3. $Bel = Pl$.

The possibility is the particular case of evidence where the focal elements are nested. It is called a "**consonant evidence**" or "**possibilistic evidence**". In this case, $Bel = N$ (necessity), $Pl = \Pi$ (possibility) and $\pi_i = \sum_{x_i \in A} m(A)$, $\forall i = 1, 2, \ldots, n$. Among all the evidences on X, these are the only fulfilling the following three equivalent conditions:

1. The focal elements of m are nested (then, we will denote it by m_F).
2. Pl is a possibility; that is, it fulfills (6). Then, it is noted $Pl = \Pi$.
3. Bel is a necessity; that is, it fulfills (7). Then, it is noted $Bel = N$.

This is the usual form to interpret a normal fuzzy subset μ of X (cf., e.g., [1]): like a possibility distribution (where $\pi_i = \mu_i$: the possibility assigned to each element is identified with its degree of membership) or its equivalent consonant evidence (whose focal elements are the α-cuts of μ). In order to detail more this equivalence, let us use the indices (i), indicating that the indices i have been permuted such that the focal elements of the consonant BPA m belong to the following chain of subsets: $\{x_{(1)}\} \subset \{x_{(1)}, x_{(2)}\} \subset \{x_{(1)}, x_{(2)}, x_{(3)}\} \subset \cdots \subset \{x_{(1)}, x_{(2)}, \ldots, x_{(n-1)}\} \subset X$. More specifically, we have ($\forall i = 1, \ldots, n$):

$$m(\{x_{(1)}, x_{(2)}, \ldots, x_{(i)}\}) = m_i \quad \text{with} \quad m_i \geq 0, \ \sum_{i=1}^{n} m_i = 1 \qquad (10)$$

Then, the plausibility associated to m is a possibility, given by the following distribution:

$$\pi_{(i)} = m_i + m_{i+1} + \ldots + m_n \qquad (11)$$

In other terms, we have the normal fuzzy set $\mu : X \to [0,1] : x_{(i)} \mapsto \pi_{(i)}$.

Conversely, given any normal fuzzy subset of X by $\mu(x_i) = \pi_i, \forall i$, we order the indices (i) such that $1 = \pi_{(1)} \geq \pi_{(2)} \geq \ldots \geq \pi_{(n)} \geq 0$. Then, the following consonant BPA is associated to μ:

$$m(\{x_{(1)}, x_{(2)}, \ldots, x_{(i)}\}) = \pi_{(i)} - \pi_{(i+1)}, \quad \text{where} \ \pi_{(n+1)} := 0 \qquad (12)$$

3 A Probabilistic View: Fuzzy Sets as Dissonant Evidences

3.1 De Luca-Termini's Measure of Fuzziness as Probabilistic Entropy

The De Luca and Termini's Entropy (8) may be expressed as:

$$d(\mu) := -\sum_{i=1}^{n} H_i(\xi_i) \quad \text{with} \quad H_i(\xi_i) = \mu_i log_2 \mu_i + (1 - \mu_i) log_2 (1 - \mu_i) \qquad (13)$$

$H_i(\xi_i)$ is the Shannon's entropy (3) of a Bernoulli random variable with success probability μ_i. Therefore, $d(\mu)$ is the Shannon's entropy of a random variable $\xi = (\xi_1, \xi_2, \ldots, \xi_n)$, defined as the product of n independent Bernoulli random variables with success probability $\mu_1, \mu_2, \ldots, \mu_n$. From now on, we note $\nu_i := 1 - \mu(x_i)$ the respective failure probability.

The purpose of this paper is to interpret this random variable ξ as an alternative representation of the fuzzy set μ (including its characterization as a special kind of dissonant evidence). Under this interpretation (already proposed in [8]), the fuzzy set μ is equivalent to a random set to which the element x_i belongs with probability μ_i (and so, it does not belong with probability ν_i) and the membership of each x_i is independent of the membership of any other x_j.

3.2 Representation of a Fuzzy Set by the BPA m_{PF}

According to the previous reasoning, μ is represented by a BPA defined by:

$$m_{PF}(A) := \prod_{x_i \in A} \mu_i \prod_{x_j \notin A} \nu_j \quad (\forall A \subseteq X) \qquad (14)$$

The condition "μ is normal" is then equivalent to "$m_{PF}(\emptyset) = 0$".

In (11), the fuzzy set μ is obtained from its associated consonant BPA m via the formula

$$\mu(x_i) = \sum_{x_i \in A} m(A) \tag{15}$$

This formula may be applied from any BPA. In fact, (15) is called the *covering function* in the **falling shadows theory** [20], where all the random sets which determine μ via (15) are considered.

In this way, we also apply (15), interpreting μ_i like the probability that x_i belong to the random set given by m_{PF}, thus obtaining μ from m_{PF}: $\mu(x_i) = \sum_{x_i \in A} m_{PF}(A) = \sum_{B \in \mathcal{P}(\{x_i\}')} m_{PF}(\{x_i\} \cup B) = \mu_i \prod_{j \neq i}(\mu_j + \nu_j) = \mu_i$.

Let us notice that $\sum_{A \in \mathcal{P}(X)} m_{PF}(A) = \prod_{i=1}^{n}(\mu_i + \nu_i) = 1$ and that (15) may also be applied when $m_{PF}(\emptyset) \neq 0$. In this case, μ is subnormal and $m_{PF}(\emptyset) = \prod_{j=1}^{n} \nu_j$. In conclusion, we have:

Proposition 1. *Any fuzzy set μ may be represented by the probability m_{PF} defined by (14) on $\mathcal{P}(X)$. Moreover, m_{PF} is a BPA on X if and only if μ is normal.*

3.3   Characterization of the "Probabilistic-Fuzzy" Evidences

We call **"probabilistic-fuzzy evidence"** the evidence given by the BPA m_{PF} (so called "probabilistic-fuzzy BPA"). Accordingly, we call "probabilistic-fuzzy belief" to the belief Bel_{PF} associated to m_{PF} and "probabilistic-fuzzy plausibility" to the plausibility Pl_{PF} associated to m_{PF} via (9). Now we obtain the properties which characterize these mass, belief and plausibility functions associated to this special kind of evidences.

Theorem 1. *A BPA m on X is a "probabilistic-fuzzy BPA" (as defined in (14)) if and only if*

$$m(A) = \prod_{x_i \in A} m_i \prod_{x_j \notin A} n_j \quad \forall A \in \mathcal{P}(X), \tag{16}$$

where $m_i := \sum_{x_i \in B} m(B)$, $n_i := \sum_{x_i \notin B} m(B)$.

PROOF: This condition expresses the fulfillment of definition (14), where the probability m in $\mathcal{P}(X)$ coincides with the product of its n marginal probabilities, when we consider the projections $\varphi_i : \mathcal{P}(X) \to \{0,1\}$ given $(\forall i = 1, 2, \ldots, n)$ by:

$$\varphi_i(A) := \begin{cases} 1, & \text{if } x_i \in A \\ 0, & \text{if } x_i \notin A \end{cases}$$

where $m_i = prob(\varphi_i = 1)$, $n_i = prob(\varphi_i = 0)$ ∎

Lemma 1. *Let Bel be the belief function (9) of a BPA m defined on X. Then m is a "probabilistic-fuzzy evidence" (as defined in (14)) if and only if $\exists q_1, q_2, \ldots, q_n \in [0,1]$ such that*

$$Bel(B) = \prod_{x_j \notin B} q_j, \quad \forall B \in \mathcal{P}(X) \tag{17}$$

Proof: The "probabilistic-fuzzy belief" Bel_{PF} is given ($\forall B \in \mathcal{P}(X)$) by: $Bel_{PF}(B) = \sum_{A \subseteq B} \left(\prod_{x_i \in A} \mu_i \prod_{x_j \notin A} \nu_j \right) = \prod_{x_j \notin B} \nu_j \sum_{A \subseteq B} \left(\prod_{x_i \in A} \mu_i \prod_{x_k \in B \setminus A} \nu_k \right) = \prod_{x_j \notin B} \nu_j \prod_{x_i \in B} (\mu_i + \nu_i) = \prod_{x_j \notin B} \nu_j$. Therefore, Bel_{PF} fulfills (17) for $q_i = \nu_i, \forall i = 1, 2, \ldots, n$.

Conversely, for any Bel fulfilling (17), we can obtain its BPA m as follows: $m(A) = \sum_{B \subseteq A} (-1)^{|A \setminus B|} \prod_{x_j \notin B} q_j$. Taking the set $A = \{x_{i_1}, x_{i_2}, \ldots, x_{i_h}\}$, and its subsets $B = A, B = A \setminus \{x_{i_k}\}, B = A \setminus \{x_{i_k}, x_{i_p}\}$, etc. we have: $m(A) = \prod_{x_j \notin A} q_j - \left(\prod_{x_j \notin A} q_j \right)$

$(q_{i_1} + q_{i_2} + \ldots + q_{i_h}) + \left(\prod_{x_j \notin A} q_j \right) (q_{i_1} q_{i_2} + q_{i_1} q_{i_3} + \ldots + q_{i_{h-1}} q_{i_h}) - \ldots$

$+ (-1)^{|A|} \left(\prod_{x_j \notin A} q_j \right) q_{i_1} q_{i_2} \cdots q_{i_h} = \left(\prod_{x_j \notin A} q_j \right) (1 - q_{i_1})(1 - q_{i_2}) \cdots (1 - q_{i_h})$

$= \prod_{x_j \notin A} q_j \prod_{x_i \in A} (1 - q_i)$. Therefore, m belongs to the m_{PF} kind, for the fuzzy set $\mu_i = 1 - q_i, \forall i = 1, 2, \ldots, n$ ∎

Theorem 2. *The belief function Bel is a "probabilistic-fuzzy belief" if and only if*

$$Bel(A \cap B)Bel(A \cup B) = Bel(A)Bel(B), \quad \forall A, B \in \mathcal{P}(X) \tag{18}$$

Proof: If Bel is a "probabilistic-fuzzy belief" then, according to the previous lemma, we have:

$$Bel(A \cap B)Bel(A \cup B) = \left(\prod_{x_i \in A \setminus B} q_i \prod_{x_k \in B \setminus A} q_k \prod_{x_j \notin A \cup B} q_j \right) \left(\prod_{x_j \notin A \cup B} q_j \right)$$

$$= \left(\prod_{x_k \in B \setminus A} q_k \prod_{x_j \notin A \cup B} q_j \right) \left(\prod_{x_i \in A \setminus B} q_i \prod_{x_j \notin A \cup B} q_j \right) = Bel(A)Bel(B).$$

Conversely, if Bel fulfills (18), we prove by induction on the cardinal $|X| = n$ that (17) holds. The case $n = 1$ is trivial: $Bel(\emptyset) \in [0, 1]$ is the value q_1 (and $Bel(X) = 1$.) Let us now assume that, for $|X| = n$, the fulfillment of (18) implies the existence of $q_1, q_2, \ldots, q_n \in [0, 1]$ such that $Bel(B) = \prod_{x_j \notin B} q_j$, for any $B \subseteq X = \{x_1, x_2, \ldots, x_n\}$. Then, we obtain the same implication for the set $Y = \{x_1, x_2, \ldots, x_n, y\}$, (with cardinal $n + 1$) applying (18) to the subsets $A \cup \{y\}$ and $B \cup \{y\}$, for any $A, B \in \mathcal{P}(X)$:

$$Bel((A \cap B) \cup \{y\})Bel(A \cup B \cup \{y\}) = Bel(A \cup \{y\})Bel(B \cup \{y\}).$$

Then we can use the induction hypothesis with the function $\gamma : \mathcal{P}(X) \to [0, 1]$ defined by $\gamma(B) := Bel(B \cup \{y\})$, assuming that $\exists q_1, q_2, \ldots, q_n \in [0, 1]$ s. t. $\gamma(B) = \prod_{x_j \notin B} q_j$. Now, we apply (18) to the sets X and $B \cup \{y\}$, with $B \in \mathcal{P}(X)$, obtaining: $Bel(B) = Bel(X)Bel(B \cup \{y\})$, $\forall B \in \mathcal{P}(X)$. Noting $q_{n+1} := Bel(X)$ and using the definition of γ we conclude that Bel verifies (17) ∎

Theorem 3. *The plausibility function Pl is a "probabilistic-fuzzy plausibility" if and only if, $\forall A, B \in \mathcal{P}(X)$*

$$Pl(A \cup B) + Pl(A \cap B) - Pl(A \cup B)Pl(A \cap B) = Pl(A) + Pl(B) - Pl(A)Pl(B) \tag{19}$$

Proof: Pl is a "probabilistic-fuzzy plausibility" if and only if its belief Bel satisfies (18). This is true if and only if, $\forall A, B \in \mathcal{P}(X)$, we have:

$$Pl(A \cup B) + Pl(A \cap B) - Pl(A \cup B)Pl(A \cap B) =$$

$$1 - Bel(A' \cap B') + 1 - Bel(A' \cup B') - [1 - Bel(A' \cap B')][1 - Bel(A' \cup B')] =$$

$$1 - Bel(A' \cap B')Bel(A' \cup B')$$

Applying (18), this is equal to: $1 - Bel(A')Bel(B') = 1 - [1 - Pl(A)][1 - Pl(B)] = Pl(A) + Pl(B) - Pl(A)Pl(B)$ ∎

Corollary 1.   *1. The plausibility Pl is a "probabilistic-fuzzy plausibility" if and only if, $\forall A, B \in \mathcal{P}(X)$ such that $A \cap B = \emptyset$*

$$Pl(A \cup B) = Pl(A) + Pl(B) - Pl(A)Pl(B) \tag{20}$$

2. For any fuzzy subset μ of X, the "probabilistic-fuzzy plausibility" Pl_{PF} defined via (14) fulfills: $\forall x_i \in X$, $Pl_{PF}(x_i) = \mu_i$

PROOF:

1. (19) implies trivially (20). The converse may be proved by simple calculations.
2. In Lemma 1 we established the condition (17) with $q_i = \nu_i = 1 - \mu_i$. Therefore, $\forall x_i \in X$, $Bel_{PF}(X \backslash \{x_i\}) = \nu_i$ and then $Pl_{PF}(x_i) = \mu_i$ ∎

4   Concluding Remarks

Corollary 1 states that:

1. The "probabilistic-fuzzy plausibility" Pl_{PF} is the "limit" case, with $\lambda = -1$, of the λ-additive fuzzy measures (1).
2. For unitary subsets (or singletons) of X, the "probabilistic-fuzzy plausibility" Pl_{PF} coincides with the possibility Π.

Nevertheless, Π and Pl_{PF} are different for other subsets of X. In fact, $\Pi(A \cup B)$ (resp. $Pl_{PF}(A \cup B)$) is obtained from the corresponding values for A and B via the t-conorm *maximum* (resp. *product* or *probabilistic sum*). So, the usual "possibilistic" representation of a fuzzy set differs from the "probabilistic-fuzzy" representation proposed in this paper. This is the only kind of evidence fulfilling the following three equivalent conditions:

1. The BPA m is a product probability (14), which is equivalent to (16).
2. Bel fulfills (18).
3. Pl fulfills (19), which is equivalent to (20).

Other aspects concerning both representations of a fuzzy set are considered below.

4.1 Considering Subnormal Fuzzy Sets

The representation of a normal fuzzy set μ (interpreted as a possibility distribution) by a consonant BPA is made via the formulae (11)-(12) and the corresponding necessity and possibility are given by (9). Then, the following equivalent conditions are fulfilled: $m(\emptyset) = 0 \Leftrightarrow Pl(X) = 1 \Leftrightarrow Bel(\emptyset) = 0 \Leftrightarrow \mu(x_{(1)}) = 1$.

These formulae may also be applied to any subnormal fuzzy set. Nevertheless, in this case:

1. m is a probability on $\mathcal{P}(X)$, but not a BPA because $m(\emptyset) = 1 - \mu(x_{(1)}) \neq 0$.
2. Bel is an increasing function such that $Bel(X) = 1$, but it is not a fuzzy measure because $Bel(\emptyset) = 1 - \mu(x_{(1)}) > 0$.
3. Pl is an increasing function such that $Pl(\emptyset) = 0$, but it is not a fuzzy measure because $Pl(X) = \mu(x_{(1)}) < 1$.

A similar situation happens when we represent a subnormal fuzzy set μ by a "probabilistic-fuzzy" BPA via (14) and we calculate the corresponding belief and plausibility via (9). As we indicated in Proposition 1, m_{PF} is a BPA on X if and only if μ is normal. In the same way, Theorems 1, 2 and 3 are true considering that:

1. m_{PF} is a probability on $\mathcal{P}(X)$, but it is not a BPA because $m_{PF}(\emptyset) = \nu_1\nu_2 \cdots \nu_n > 0$.
2. Bel_{PF} is an increasing function such that $Bel_{PF}(X) = 1$, but it is not a fuzzy measure because $Bel_{PF}(\emptyset) = \nu_1\nu_2 \cdots \nu_n > 0$.
3. Pl_{PF} is an increasing function such that $Pl_{PF}(\emptyset) = 0$, but it is not a fuzzy measure because $Pl_{PF}(X) = 1 - \nu_1\nu_2 \cdots \nu_n < 1$.

4.2 Comments and Open Questions

The "probabilistic-fuzzy" representation of a fuzzy set is fully motivated by the definition of the De Luca-Termini's entropy (8). In addition, the hypothesis of independence between the different elements x_i plays a central role in the characterization of the "probabilistic-fuzzy" BPA m_{PF} (14). Therefore, in order to justify and complete the study of this proposal, the following aspects are considered for future research:

– To obtain some theoretical property or some practical application of m_{PF}. In this sense, we consider the following interpretation, based upon the fact that the α-cuts are the only focal elements when we represent a fuzzy set μ by a consonant BPA: we may define, for any $(\alpha_1, \ldots, \alpha_n) \in [0,1]^n$, the sets $A_{(\alpha_1,\ldots,\alpha_n)} := \{x_i \in X : \mu(x_i) \geq \alpha_i\}$. Considering the uniform probability distribution in $[0,1]^n$ and the map $\chi : [0,1]^n \rightarrow \mathcal{P}(X) : (\alpha_1, \ldots, \alpha_n) \mapsto A_{(\alpha_1,\ldots,\alpha_n)}$ we obtain precisely the random set m_{PF}.
– To use the BPA m_{PF} (or other similar BPA) in order to interpret in a probabilistic way some measures of fuzziness different to the De Luca-Termini's

entropy (8). For example, associated to the Renyi's and Vajda's probabilistic quadratic entropies, the following measures of fuzziness have been respectively defined: $H_{BP}(\mu) := \frac{1}{1-\alpha} \sum_{i=1}^{n} log\left(\mu_i^{\alpha} + (1 - \mu_i)^{\alpha}\right)$ (where $\alpha > 0, \alpha \neq 1$) by Bhandari and Pal [2] and $H_{QE}(\mu) := \sum_{i=1}^{n} \mu_i(1 - \mu_i)$ by Pal and Bezdek [15]. Nevertheless, we cannot directly extend our results in these cases because neither Renyi's nor Vajda's quadratic entropy fulfill (4).

- To study the representations obtained avoiding or weakening the hypothesis of independence of the elements x_i (respect to its membership in a random set).

References

1. Baldwin, J., Martin, T.P., Pilsworth, B.: Fril-Fuzzy and Evidential Reasoning in Artificial Intelligence. John Wiley & Sons Inc., London (1995)
2. Bhandari, D., Pal, N.R.: Some new information measures for fuzzy sets. Information Sciences 67, 209–228 (1993)
3. Banon, G.: Distinction between several subsets of fuzzy measures. Fuzzy Sets and Systems 5, 291–305 (1980)
4. De Luca, A., Termini, S.: A definition of a nonprobabilistic entropy in the setting of fuzzy sets theory. Inform. and Control 20, 301–312 (1972)
5. Dempster, A.P.: Upper and Lower Probabilities Induced by a Multivalued Mapping. Annals of Mathematical Statistics, 325–339 (1967)
6. Dubois, D., Prade, H.: On several representations of an uncertain body of evidence. In: Gupta, M.M., Sanchez, E. (eds.) Fuzzy Information and Decision Processes, pp. 167–181. North-Holland, Amsterdam (1982)
7. Dubois, D., Prade, H.: Fuzzy sets, probability and measurement. European Journal of Operational Research 40, 135–154 (1989)
8. Herencia, J.A.: Representación de conjuntos difusos mediante evidencias disonantes. In: Proc. of the ESTYLF 2000, Sevilla, Spain, pp. 241–246 (2000)
9. Klir, G.J.: Where do we stand on measures of uncertainty, ambiguity, fuzziness, and the like? Fuzzy Sets and Systems 24, 141–160 (1987)
10. Klir, G.J., Ramer, A.: Uncertainty in Dempster-Shafer theory: A critical reexamination. Int. J. Gen. Syst. 18, 155–166 (1990)
11. Lamata, M., Moral, S.: Classification of fuzzy measures. Fuzzy Sets and Systems 33, 243–253 (1989)
12. Lindley, D.: Scoring rules and the inevitability of probability. Internat. Statist. Review 50, 1–26 (1982)
13. Lindley, D.: The Probability Approach to the Treatment of Uncertainty in Artificial Intelligence and Expert Systems. Statistical Science 2, 3–44 (1987)
14. Natvig, B.: Possibility versus Probability. Fuzzy Sets and Systems 10, 31–36 (1983)
15. Pal, N.R., Bezdek, J.C.: Measuring fuzzy uncertainty. IEEE Trans. Fuzzy Syst. 2, 107–118 (1994)
16. Shafer, G.: A mathematical theory of Evidence. Princeton University Press, Princeton (1976)
17. Shannon, C.E.: The mathematical theory of communication. Bell System Tech. 27, 379–423, 623–656 (1948)
18. Sugeno, M.: Theory of Fuzzy Integrals and its Applications. Ph. D. Thesis. Tokio Inst. of Technology (1974)

19. Sugeno, M., Terano, T.: A model of learning based on fuzzy information. Kybernetes 6, 157–166 (1977)
20. Tan, S.K., Wang, P.Z., Stanley Lee, E.: Fuzzy Set Operations Based on the Theory of Falling Shadows. J. Math. Anal. App. 174, 242–255 (1993)
21. Tribus, M.: Commemts on Fuzzy sets, fuzzy algebra and fuzzy statistics. Proc. IEEE 67, 1168 (1979)
22. Verdegay-López, J.F.: Tratamiento de la incertidumbre mediante medidas difusas. In: Algunos aspectos del tratamiento de la Información en Inteligencia Artificial, pp. 155–172. Publicaciones de la Universidad de Granada (1991)
23. Zadeh, L.A.: Fuzzy sets. Information and Control 8, 338–353 (1965)
24. Zadeh, L.A.: Fuzzy sets as a basis for a theory of possibility. Fuzzy Sets and Systems 1, 3–28 (1978)

A Briefing on Fuzziness and Its Measuring

Enric Trillas and Daniel Sánchez

European Centre for Soft Computing
Edificio Científico-Tecnológico, 33600 Mieres, Asturias, Spain
{enric.trillas,daniel.sanchezf}@softcomputing.es

Abstract. The paper poses, but not answers completely, some questions concerning the measures of fuzziness. For instance, if the sharpened order gives the only poset with which it has sense the measuring of the fuzziness, and if the measurement of either a intersection, or a union, of fuzzy sets is functionally expressible.

1 Introduction

After fuzzy sets were introduced by Lotfi A. Zadeh in 1965, one of the most remarkable concepts that newly arose is that of measuring the fuzziness of a fuzzy set, introduced in [3] in 1972. Such a new concept was reasonably unknown, and not available, before the importance and usefulness of fuzzy sets started to be taken into account.

Although a lot of papers related to the measures of fuzziness, or 'fuzzy entropies', and its applications, did appear since 1972 [3], some basic conceptual problems remain to be studied, and this paper only tries to discuss on some of them. The current briefing is not a conclusive one, it is just inquisitive.

2 Fuzziness and Measure

There is no object or element x in any known universe of discourse of which it can be stated 'x is fuzziness', with the single exception of x=fuzziness, with which it only appears the principle of identity in the form 'fuzziness is fuzziness'. That is the linguistic term 'fuzziness' cannot be considered a predicate, but just a word that, coming from the term 'fuzzy' (indeed a predicate), reflects a concept under which it can be said that something that *is* fuzzy *has*, or *shows*, fuzziness.

A fuzzy object showing fuzziness does show it either equally, or more, or less than other object. For instance, of two copies of the same picture one can be fuzzier than the other. Analogously, any crisp set will show less fuzziness than any proper fuzzy set since, in fact, crisp sets cannot show fuzziness at all as they are the prototypes of the concept 'crispness', the opposite of 'fuzziness'. Such variability in the fuzzy condition shows that fuzziness $(= F)$ can be considered like a quantity distributed on the set of all fuzzy sets in a universe of discourse X. Thus the question that arises is, *how can fuzziness be measured?*

Let X be a set where a quantity Q is shown by its elements, and let X be endowed with a preorder $\leq_Q$ (a reflexive and transitive relation). Let $(L, \leq)$ be a poset. It is

S. Greco et al. (Eds.): IPMU 2012, Part II, CCIS 298, pp. 15–24, 2012.
© Springer-Verlag Berlin Heidelberg 2012

supposed that $\leq_Q$ comparatively reflects the quantity Q each two elements show. That is, $x \leq_Q y$ expresses that x shows less Q than y. This relation is the less it can be known to compare how elements x, y show Q, and what follows can be seen as a 'minimal' definition of measure. A measure of the elements in X respect to Q and $(L, \leq)$ is a mapping $m : X \rightarrow L$, such that:

1. If $x \leq_Q y$, then $m(x) \leq m(y)$
2. If $(X, \leq_Q)$ at least has a minimal x_0, and $(L, \leq)$ also has minimals, then $m(x_0)$ is one of these minimals (the minimum provided it exists).
3. If $(X, \leq_Q)$ at least has a maximal x_1, and $(L, \leq)$ also has maximals, then $m(x_1)$ is one of these maximals (the maximum provided it exists).

A measure m is a way to state up to which extent elements x show Q. Notice that,

- Axiom 1 is essential. Provided that once it is known $x \leq_Q y$, it were not clear if the values $m(x)$ and $m(y)$ always verify either $m(x) \leq m(y)$, or $m(x) \geq m(y)$, or both values are not comparable under $\leq$, the measure will be confusing for what refers the growing of Q. What (1) shows is that m grows with the growing of Q in X, something that, of course, can happen in several ways.
- Axioms (2) and (3) show that minimals and maximals do have, respectively, a kind of lowest and a kind of biggest measure.
- Were $(L, \leq)$ a totally ordered set, the measure also orders the measures of not $\leq_Q$-comparable objects. This is the case when the measure takes its values in the real line, that is, when the measure is numerical as they are, for instance, the so-called 'fuzzy measures' defined in the poset $(P(X), \subseteq)$ whose minimum is $\emptyset$, and whose maximum is X, as mappings $m : P(X) \rightarrow [0, 1]$, such that,
  a) If $A \subseteq B$, then $m(A) \leq m(B)$.
  b) $m(X) = 1$
  c) $m(\emptyset) = 0$,

Example 1. Let $\mathbb{P}(X)$ be the boolean algebra of subsets of a universe X, Q=uncertainty, and with $A \leq_Q B$ iff $A \subseteq B$, a mapping $g_\lambda : \mathbb{P}(X) \rightarrow [0, 1]$, with $\lambda > -1$ is called a Sugeno's λ-measure provided g verifies,

a $g_\lambda(X) = 1$
b If $A \cap B = \emptyset$, then $g_\lambda(A \cup B) = g_\lambda(A) + g_\lambda(B) + \lambda \cdot g_\lambda(A) \cdot g_\lambda(B)$.

It is easy to prove that $A \subset B$ implies $g_\lambda(A) \leq g_\lambda(B)$, and that

$$g_\lambda(A') = \frac{1 + g_\lambda(A)}{1 - \lambda \cdot g_\lambda(A)},$$

with which $g_\lambda(\emptyset) = 0$. Hence, these measures are fuzzy measures and, obviously, with $\lambda = 0$ are just probabilities, with $\lambda < 0$ are sub-additive measures, and with $\lambda > 0$ are super-additive measures. The concept of a λ-measure offers a wide family of measures with subfamilies that can grow additively, sub-additively, and super-additively. Hence, with $\lambda \neq 0$, λ-measures could be adequate for magnitudes very different from length, surface, volume, and randomness.

To measure the fuzziness quantity F in $[0,1]^X$, it is necessary to know when two fuzzy sets μ and σ are linked in the form $\mu \leq_F \sigma$, that is, μ shows less fuzziness than σ. Of course, if μ is crisp, it should be $\mu \leq_F \sigma$ for any actual fuzzy set σ in $[0,1]^X$. Hence, the crisp sets are the minimals in $([0,1]^X, \leq_F)$, and if $E : X \rightarrow R^+$ is going to be taken as a measure of fuzziness it, at least, should verify,

1. If $\mu \leq_F \sigma$, then $E(\mu) \leq E(\sigma)$
2. If $\mu \in \{0,1\}^X$, then $E(\mu) = 0$.

Then, to state that E is a measure of fuzziness it yet lacks to know if there are maximal elements in $([0,1]^X, \leq_F)$. At this respect it is necessary to make mathematically specific what can it be understood by the relation $\leq_F$. Of course, the relation $\leq_F^{-1}$ can be read as 'fuzzier than'.

3   Additional Laws for the Measure of Fuzziness

The Occam's Razor (*never add more entities than those that are necessary*), does be completed by Karl Menger's addition, '*Nor less than those allowing to reach something significative*'. Since the last two laws for E seem insufficient for going ahead, let us try to conjecture if some other laws can be added to the definition and, in the first place, if maximal fuzzy sets under $\leq_F$ can be found before specifying $\leq_F$. What follows is just a sequence of conjectures that could help to select those maximal fuzzy sets.

(i) μ is crisp if and only if μ' (its complementary set) is also crisp. Hence, if E is a measure of fuzziness it is $E(\mu) = E(\mu')$, for all $\mu \in \{0,1\}^X$. If $\mu \in [0,1]^X - \{0,1\}^X$, it is also $\mu' \in [0,1]^X - \{0,1\}^X$. Hence, the pseudo-complement has a separate behavior between fuzzy and crisp sets.

(ii) A non strictly necessary way of preserving (1) *is to define* $E(\mu) = E(\mu')$, $\forall \mu \in [0,1]^X$ as *the third axiom* for E, that simply states that both μ and $\mu' = N_\varphi \circ \mu$ (with $N_\varphi = \varphi^{-1}(1 - \varphi)$ a strong negation given by the order-automorphism φ of the unit interval) do show the same amount of fuzziness. This axiom cannot be considered surprising at all. It establishes a kind of symmetry for the amount of fuzziness. Notice that with $\varphi = id$, the axiom is $E(\mu) = E(1 - \mu)$, $\forall \mu \in [0,1]^X$.

(iii) The strong character of N_φ ($N_\varphi \circ N_\varphi = id$), makes of it a *symmetry* in $[0,1]^X$, under which $\mu_0 \rightarrow \mu_1$, $\mu_1 \rightarrow \mu_0$, $\mu_r \rightarrow \mu_{N_\varphi(r)}$ (with μ_r the fuzzy set constantly $r \in (0,1)$, that is, $\mu_r(x) = r$ for all $x \in X$).

Since $N_\varphi(r) = r \in (0,1)$ holds if and only if $r = \varphi^{-1}(1/2)$, *the fixed point of the symmetry is the fuzzy set* $\mu_{\varphi^{-1}(1/2)}$, constantly equal to $\varphi^{-1}(1/2)$. When $\varphi = id$, the fixed point of $N_{id}(x) = 1 - x$, is 0.5. Let us look at figures 1(a) and 1(b), this last obtained by folding 1(a) under the line $\mu_{\varphi^{-1}(1/2)}$. In both figures appear the fuzzy sets μ and μ', and it is shown that it is $\mu \leq \mu_{\varphi^{-1}(1/2)}$ below $\varphi^{-1}(1/2)$, and $\mu \geq \mu_{\varphi^{-1}(1/2)}$ on the other side.

(iv) If μ is crisp it is never $\mu = \mu'$ and it is $\mu \leq \mu'$ iff $\mu = \mu_0 = \mu_\emptyset$, the empty set. But, if $\mu \in [0,1]^X - \{0,1\}^X$, it is $\mu \leq \mu' = \varphi^{-1}(1 - \varphi(\mu)) \Leftrightarrow \mu \leq \mu_{\varphi^{-1}(1/2)}$, that is,

  $- \mu = \mu' \Leftrightarrow \mu = \mu_\varphi^{-1}(1/2)$

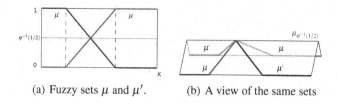

(a) Fuzzy sets μ and μ'.   (b) A view of the same sets

Fig. 1. Illustration of the fixed point of symmetry with two fuzzy sets

– μ is self-contradictory iff $\mu \leq \mu_\varphi^{-1}(1/2)$

In the crisp case, only the empty set is self-contradictory. The crisp sets
– $\{x \in X; \mu(x) \leq \mu'(x)\} = \{x \in X; \mu(x) \leq \varphi^{-1}(1/2)\}$
– $\{x \in X; \mu(x) \geq \mu'(x)\} = \{x \in X; \mu(x) \geq \varphi^{-1}(1/2)\}$

give a partition of X thanks to the 'separation' element $\mu_{\varphi^{-1}(1/2)}$. Notice that if $\mu \in \{0,1\}^X$, the second is the set $A = \{x \in X; \mu(x) = 1\}$, and the first is $\{x \in X; \mu(x) = 0\} = A'$. All that can conduct to accept that the constant fuzzy set $\mu_{\varphi^{-1}(1/2)}$ is the only showing the greatest fuzziness, that is, to take as the *fourth axiom*,

$$\text{For all } \mu \in [0,1]^X : \mu \leq_F \mu_{\varphi^{-1}(1/2)}, \text{ and } E(\mu) \leq E(\mu_{\varphi^{-1}(1/2)}).$$

If σ is crisp, and $\mu \leq_F \sigma$, it follows $E(\mu) \leq E(\sigma) = 0$, and $E(\mu) = 0$. The existence of such a $\mu \in [0,1]^X$ depends on a concrete definition for $\leq_F$. Can $\leq_F$ be specifically defined in such a way that crisp sets are its minimals, and $\mu_{\varphi^{-1}(1/2)}$ its maximum?

4   The Set $[0,1]^X/_{\equiv_F}$

The binary relation, $\mu \equiv_F \sigma \Leftrightarrow \mu \leq_F \sigma \& \sigma \leq_F \mu$, can be understood as '$\mu$ is *equally fuzzy* than σ'. Provided $\leq_F$ is a preorder, that is, $\leq_F$ verifies

– $\mu \leq_F \mu$, for all $\mu \in [0,1]^X$ (reflexivity)
– If $\mu \leq_F \sigma \& \sigma \leq_F \lambda$, then $\mu \leq_F \lambda$ (transitivity),

$\equiv_F$ is an equivalence giving the quotient-set $[0,1]^X/\equiv_F$ constituted by the classes $[\mu]_F = \{\sigma \in [0,1]^X; \mu \equiv_F \sigma\}$ of equally-fuzzy fuzzy sets. If μ is crisp, $[\mu]_F$ is the class of those fuzzy sets not showing fuzziness at all, and to know if it contains non-crisp fuzzy sets we should wait to have a concrete definition of $\leq_F$. Up to this moment, the only that can be stated is that $\{0,1\}^X$ is included in one of the classes in $[0,1]^X/\equiv_F$.

If $E : [0,1]^X \to \mathbb{R}^+$ is a measure of fuzziness verifying axioms 1 and 2, from $\mu \equiv_F \sigma \Leftrightarrow \mu \leq_F \sigma \& \sigma \leq_F \mu$, follows $E(\mu) \leq E(\sigma)$ and $E(\sigma) \leq E(\mu)$, or $E(\mu) = E(\sigma)$. That is, E is *constant in each one of the classes* in the quotient set. Additionally, defining

$$[\mu]_F \leq_F^* [\sigma]_F \Leftrightarrow \mu \leq_F \sigma,$$

it is easy to prove that $([0,1]^X/_{\equiv_F}, \leq_F^*)$ is a poset, and then the mapping $\Phi : [0,1]^X \to [0,1]^X/_{\equiv_F}, \Phi(\mu) = [\mu]_F$, verifies

1) $\mu \leq_F \sigma \Rightarrow \Phi(\mu) \leq_F^* \Phi(\sigma)$
2) If $\mu \in \{0,1\}^X$, $\Phi(\mu)$ is the class including the crisp sets,

that could be taken as a *qualitative* measure of fuzziness, naturally linked to $\leq_F$.

Given a numerical measure of fuzziness $E : [0,1]^X \rightarrow \mathbb{R}^+$, it can be introduced the relation

$$\mu \leq_E \sigma \Leftrightarrow E(\mu) \leq E(\sigma),$$

that is bigger than $\leq_F$, since $\mu \leq_F \sigma \Rightarrow E(\mu) \leq E(\sigma) \Leftrightarrow \mu \leq_E \sigma :\leq_F \subset \leq_E$. Notice that, for all μ, σ in $[0,1]^X$ it should be either $\mu \leq_E \sigma$, or $\sigma \leq_E \mu$, as $\mathbb{R}^+$ is totally ordered. Provided

- $\leq_F = \leq_E$, it can be said that E *perfectly* reflects fuzziness.
- $\leq_F \subseteq \leq_E$, it can be said that E *partially* reflects fuzziness,

and it should be pointed out that since $\leq_E$ enjoys the character of a 'total' relation, the first case does be rare. Notwithstanding, in the last non-numerical case, with Φ it is obviously $\leq_F = \leq_\Phi$: Φ perfectly reflects the fuzziness.

It is not an actual problem to agree that $\leq_B = \leq_F^{-1}$ reflects that σ is less crisp, or less boolean, than μ : $\mu \leq_B \sigma \Leftrightarrow \sigma \leq_F \mu$. Hence, from $\mu \leq_B \sigma$ follows $1 - E(\mu) \leq 1 - E(\sigma)$. That is, $B = 1 - E$ could be taken as a measure of crispness, or booleanity, for which the maximals under $\leq_B$ are the crisp sets, and the minimum or less crisp fuzzy set is $\mu_{\varphi^{-1}(1/2)}$. Notice that $\equiv_F = \leq_F \cap \leq_F^{-1} = \leq_B^{-1} \cap \leq_B := \equiv_B$, and then $[0,1]^X/_{\equiv_F} = [0,1]^X/_{\equiv_B}$. Although with different interpretation, the classes of fuzziness are coincidental with the classes of crispness, hence, *both concepts are not essentially different.*

5   Specifying $\leq_F$

In the former section, relation $\leq_F$ is not specified. The only known proposal of $\leq_F$ having the maximum $\varphi^{-1}(1/2)$, and the minimals $\{0,1\}^X$, is that introduced in [3] with the name 'Sharpened order', and defined by

$$\mu \leq_S \sigma \Leftrightarrow min(\varphi^{-1}(1/2), \mu(x)) \leq min(\varphi^{-1}(1/2), \sigma(x)) \& max(\varphi^{-1}(1/2), \mu(x)) \geq$$

$$\geq max(\varphi^{-1}(1/2), \sigma(x)),$$

Notice that if σ is crisp and it is $\mu \leq_S \sigma$, not only μ is also crisp but it is $\mu = \sigma$. Hence, in the set $[0,1]^X/_{\equiv_S}$ the class containing the crisp sets only contains them, that is, if σ is crisp then $[\sigma]_S = \{0,1\}^X$.

Obviously, the 'sharpened' relation $\leq_S$ is a *partial order* that reduces to the pointwise identity in the case of crisp sets. Consequently, $\leq_S$ is a proper relation between fuzzy sets, not known before the introduction of fuzzy sets. The poset $([0,1]^X, \leq_S)$ is of course not totally ordered since there are many pairs of fuzzy sets that are not comparable under $\leq_S$. It is also clear that $\mu_{\varphi^{-1}(1/2)}$ is the maximum, and that the crisp sets are the minimals in that poset. Nevertheless, and although it seems intuitively clear *it is an open problem* *to prove whether $\leq_S$ is, or it is not, the only poset in $[0,1]^X$ having those minimals and maximum.*

The following functions $E : [0,1]^X \to \mathbb{R}^+$ are some of the most known measures of fuzziness verifying axioms 1, 2, and 4 with $\leq_F=\leq_S$:

- $E_1(\mu) = \frac{1}{\varphi^{-1}(1/2)} \cdot \underset{x\in X}{Sup}\, \min(\mu(x), N_\varphi(\mu(x)))$. If μ is continuous and $\varphi = id$, it is
  $E_1^*(\mu) = 2 \cdot \underset{x\in X}{Max}\, \min(\mu(x), 1-\mu(x))$.
- $E_2(\mu) = \frac{1}{[\varphi^{-1}(1/2)]^2} \cdot \underset{x\in X}{Sup}(\mu(x) \cdot N_\varphi(\mu(x)))$. If μ is continuous and $\varphi = id$, it is
  $E_2^*(\mu) = 4 \cdot \underset{x\in X}{Max}[\mu(x) \cdot (1-\mu(x))]$.
- With μ finite, $\mu = a_1/x_1 + ... + a_n/x_n$, $E_3(\mu) = -k\sum_{i=1}^n[a_i l_n a_i + (1-a_i)l_n(1-a_i)]$, with $k > 0$ a constant (De Luca-Termini).
- With μ finite, $E_4(\mu) = \sum_{i=1}^n \min(a_i, 1-a_i) / \sum_{i=1}^n \max(a_i, 1-a_i)$ (Kosko)
- Also for finite fuzzy sets, a large class of measures is given by $E_5(\mu) = \sum_{i=1}^n w(x_i) \cdot F(\mu(x_i))$ (Trillas & Riera), with $w : X \to \mathbb{R}^+$ a weight function, and F such that $F(0) = 0$, non-decreasing in $[0,1/2]$, and non-increasing in $[1/2,1]$. For instance, with

$$F(x) = \begin{cases} x, & \text{if } x \in [0,1/2] \\ 1-x, & \text{if } x \in [1/2,1], \end{cases} \text{ and } w(x_i) = 1/n\ (1 \leq i \leq n), \text{ it is:}$$

$$E_5^*(\mu) = \frac{1}{n}\left[\sum_{a_i\leq 1/2} a_i + \sum_{a_i>1/2}(1-a_i)\right].$$

Once accepted as an axiom that the fuzzy sets μ and μ' do have the same measure of fuzziness, and although there is no $\mu \equiv_S \mu'$, it also seems difficult to believe that μ and one of its antonyms $\mu^a = \mu \circ \alpha$ (with $\alpha : X \to X$, a symmetry in X) can have different measures of fuzziness. As it is always $\mu' \leq \mu^a$ (but not $\mu' \leq_S \mu^a$) μ' is a limiting case of antonym, and provided it were taken

$$E(\mu) = E(\mu^a), \tag{1}$$

the former axiom $E(\mu) = E(\mu')$ could be seen as a particular case of (1). Anyway, it is not clear that (1) can be generally stated. For instance,

- If $X = [0,10]$, $E(\mu) = E_1(\mu) = 2\underset{x\in X}{Max}\, \min(\mu(x), 1-\mu(x))$, and

$$\mu(x) = \begin{cases} 1, 0 \leq x \leq 2 \\ 2-x/2, 2 \leq x \leq 4 \text{ it is,} \\ 0, 4 \leq x \leq 10 \end{cases}$$

$$\mu^a(x) = \mu(10-x) = \begin{cases} 1, 8 \leq x \leq 10 \\ x/2 - 3, 6 \leq x \leq 8 \ , \\ 0, 0 \leq x \leq 6 \end{cases}$$

By taking into account $\mu' = 1 - \mu$, and $\mu^{a'} = 1 - \mu^a$ it is respectively obtained $E(\mu) = 0.5$, $E(\mu') = 0.5$, and $E(\mu^a) = 0.5$.

– With the same X, μ, μ', μ^a, and $1 - \mu^a$, but with $E_2(\mu) = 4\underset{x \in X}{Max}[\mu(x)(1 - \mu(x))]$, it is $E(\mu) = E(\mu') = 1$, but $E(\mu^a) = 2(= E(\mu_{1/2}))$.
– With the before mentioned measure E_5^*, since μ^a will come from a permutation of $\{x_1, ..., x_n\}$, it is clear that it will be $E_5^*(\mu) = E_5^*(\mu^a)$. But the situation can abruptly change with E_5 having some weight $w(x_i)$ different from $1/n$.

Remark 1. It should be pointed out that *axiom 3* cannot hold for all negations. For instance, if with E_1 and E_2 do hold $E(\mu) = E(\mu')$ for any concrete N_φ, with E_3 and E_4 $E(\mu) = E(\mu')$ only holds for $\mu' = 1 - \mu$. The same remark holds for $E(\mu) = E(\mu^a)$ that depends on the symmetry $\alpha : X \to X$ with which $\mu^a = \mu \circ \alpha$ is obtained.

6 The Concept of Fuzzy Algebra

A fuzzy algebra is built up on the set $[0, 1]^X = \{\mu; \mu : X \to [0, 1]\}$, once it is partially ordered by the pointwise relation of inclusion.

$$\mu \le \sigma \Leftrightarrow \mu(x) \le \sigma(x), \forall x \in X,$$

that gives the equality $\mu = \sigma \Leftrightarrow \mu \le \sigma \& \sigma \le \mu \Leftrightarrow \mu(x) = \sigma(x)$, $\forall x \in X$. With $\mu_0(x) = 0$, and $\mu_1(x) = 1$, for all $x \in X$, it is $\mu_0 \le \mu \le \mu_1$, for all $\mu \in [0, 1]^X$.

Definition 1. *A basic fuzzy algebra (BFA) is a four-tuple $([0, 1]^X, \cdot, +, ')$, with $\cdot, + : [0, 1]^X \times [0, 1]^X \to [0, 1]^X$, and $' : [0, 1]^X \to [0, 1]^X$, verifying*

1. $\mu \cdot \mu_0 = \mu_0 \cdot \mu = \mu_0$, $\mu + \mu_0 = \mu_0 + \mu = \mu$, *for all* $\mu \in [0, 1]^X$
2. $\mu \cdot \mu_1 = \mu_1 \cdot \mu = \mu$, $\mu + \mu_1 = \mu_1 + \mu = \mu_1$, *for all* $\mu \in [0, 1]^X$
3. $\mu_0' = \mu_1$, $\mu_1' = \mu_0$
4. *If $\mu \le \sigma$, then:*
    – $\mu \cdot \lambda \le \sigma \cdot \lambda$, $\lambda \cdot \mu \le \lambda \cdot \sigma$, *for all* $\lambda \in [0, 1]^X$
    – $\mu + \lambda \le \sigma + \lambda$, $\lambda + \mu \le \lambda + \sigma$, *for all* $\lambda \in [0, 1]^X$
    – $\sigma' \le \mu'$
5. *If $\mu, \sigma \in \{0, 1\}^X$, then, $\mu \cdot \sigma$, $\mu + \sigma$, and μ' are in $\{0, 1\}^X$, and:*
    – $\mu \cdot \sigma = min(\mu, \sigma)$
    – $\mu + \sigma = max(\mu, \sigma)$
    – $\mu' = 1 - \mu$

From this definition, it follows

a) $\mu \cdot \sigma \le min(\mu, \sigma) \le max(\mu, \sigma) \le \mu + \sigma$
b) The only BFAs that are lattices are $([0, 1]^X, min, max, ')$. These fuzzy algebras are De Morgan Algebras. No BFA is an ortholattice. Hence, no BFA is a Boolean algebra.
c) Neither commutativity, nor associativity, nor distributivity, nor duality,... , are supposed to hold.

The operations $\cdot$ (*intersection* or *and*), $+$ (*union* or *or*), and $'$ (*pseudo-complement*, *negation*, or *not*), can be or not *functionally expressible* (FE).

- The *and* is FE if it exist $F : [0,1] \times [0,1] \to [0,1]$, such that $(\mu, \sigma)(x) = F(\mu(x), \sigma(x))$, $\forall x \in X$.
- The *or* is FE if it exists $G : [0,1] \times [0,1] \to [0,1]$, such that $(\mu + \sigma)(x) = G(\mu(x), \sigma(x))$, $\forall x \in X$.

Obviously, $F \leq min \leq max \leq G$. A particular and important case is when $F = T$ is a continuous t-norm, and $G = S$ is a continuous t-conorm.

- The *not* is FE if it exists $N : [0,1] \to [0,1]$, such that $\mu'(x) = N(\mu(x))$, $\forall x \in X$. The negation is *strong* if $(\mu')' = \mu'' = \mu$, for all $\mu \in [0,1]^X$, and if it is FE then it should be $N(N(a)) = a$, $\forall a \in [0,1]$. Strong negations are characterized by $N = N_\varphi = \varphi^{-1} \circ (1 - \varphi)$, with an order-automorphism φ of the unit interval $([0,1], \leq)$, that is not unique. Strong negations do have a unique fixed point $N(n) = n \in (0,1)$, given by $n = \varphi^{-1}(1/2)$. Hence, $\mu'_{\varphi^{-1}(1/2)} = \mu_{\varphi^{-1}(1/2)}$. Of course, if N is a strong negation, it is N continuous, and $N = N^{-1}$.
- The FE algebras $([0,1]^X, T, S, N_\varphi)$ are called *Standard* Fuzzy Algebras, in which commutativity and associativity of $\cdot$ and $+$ hold.

7 Measures and Algebras

This section only tries to pose a question whose answer does not seem trivial, that of the *possible functional expressibity* of $E(\mu \cdot \sigma)$, $E(\mu + \sigma)$, and $E(\mu')$. Given a BFA $([0,1]^X, \cdot, +, ')$ and under the *working hypothesis* that $E : [0,1]^X \to [0,1]$:

1) *Are there functions* $F : [0,1] \times [0,1] \to [0,1]$, *s.t.* $E(\mu \cdot \sigma) = F(E(\mu), E(\sigma))$?
   a) $E(\mu_0 \cdot \mu_1) = E(\mu_0) \Rightarrow F(0,0) = 0$.
   b) $E(\mu_{\varphi^{-1}(1/2)} \cdot \mu_0) = E(\mu_0 \cdot \mu_{\varphi^{-1}(1/2)}) = E(\mu_0) \Rightarrow F(0,1) = F(1,0) = 0$.
   c) $E(\mu_0 \cdot \sigma) = E(\sigma \cdot \mu_0) = E(\mu_0) \Rightarrow F(0, E(\sigma)) = F(E(\sigma), 0) = 0$, for all $\mu, \sigma \in [0,1]^X \Rightarrow F(0,a) = F(a,0) = 0$, for all $a \in [0,1]$.
   d) If $\cdot$ is commutative, $E(\mu \cdot \sigma) = E(\sigma \cdot \mu)$, for all μ, σ in $[0,1]^X \Rightarrow F(a,b) = F(b,a)$, for all a, b in $[0,1]$.
   e) *Provided it is* $\cdot = min$, $E(\mu_{\varphi^{-1}(1/2)} \cdot \mu_{\varphi^{-1}(1/2)}) = E(\mu_{\varphi^{-1}(1/2)}) \Rightarrow F(1,1) = 1$
   f) *Provided it is* $\cdot = min$, $E(\mu \cdot \mu) = E(\mu) = F(E(\mu), E(\mu))$, allowing to take $F = min$. Nevertheless, if for instance is $E = E_1^*$, with $X = \{x_1, x_2, x_3\}$, $\mu = 0.7|x_1 + 0.6|x_2 + 1|x_3$, $\sigma = 0.8|x_1 + 0.8|x_2 + 0.9|x_3$, follows

$$E_1^*(\mu \cdot \sigma) = 0.8, \ E_1^*(\mu) = 0.8, \ E_1^*(\sigma) = 0.4,$$

and $F(0.8, 0.4) = min(0.8, 0.4) = 0.4 \neq E_1^*(\mu \cdot \sigma)$. Hence, $F = min$ cannot be generally taken, and it remains the doubt concerning the functional expressibility of the 'entropy' of the intersection of fuzzy sets,
2) *Are there functions* $G : [0,1] \times [0,1] \to [0,1]$, *s.t.* $E(\mu + \sigma) = G(E(\mu), E(\sigma))$?
   a) $E(\mu_0 + \mu_1) = E(\mu_1) \Rightarrow G(0,0) = 0$
   b) $E(\mu_1 + \sigma) = E(\sigma + \mu_1) = E(\mu_1) \Rightarrow G(0, E(\sigma)) = G(E(\sigma), 0) = 0 \Rightarrow G(0,a) = G(a,0) = 0$, for all a in $[0,1]$.
   c) Obviously, if $+$ is commutative, so it does G be commutative.

d) $E(\mu_0 + \mu_{\varphi^{-1}(1/2)}) = E(\mu_{\varphi^{-1}(1/2)} + \mu_0) = E(\mu_{\varphi^{-1}(1/2)}) \Rightarrow G(0,1) = G(1,0) = 1$,
that is *incompatible with* (b).

e) *Provided it is* $+ = max$, $E(\mu_{\varphi^{-1}(1/2)} + \mu_{\varphi^{-1}(1/2)}) = E(\mu_{\varphi^{-1}(1/2)}) \Rightarrow G(1,1) = 1$

f) *Provided it is* $+ = max$, $E(\mu + \mu) = E(\mu) \Rightarrow G(a,a) = a$, for all a in $[0,1]$,
allowing to take $G = max$ that, nevertheless, is not compatible with (b).

Hence, $G = max$ cannot be generally taken, and it also remains the doubt concerning
the functional expressivity of the 'entropy' of the union of fuzzy sets.

3) *Are there functions* $H : [0,1] \rightarrow [0,1]$, *such that* $E(\mu') = H(E(\mu))$?

a) If μ is crisp, μ' is crisp. Hence, $E(\mu) = E(\mu') = 0$, if $\mu \in \{0,1\}^X \Rightarrow H(0) = 0$.

b) $\mu'_{\varphi^{-1}(1/2)} = N_\varphi \circ \mu_{\varphi^{-1}(1/2)} \Rightarrow H(1) = 1$.

Hence, it could be taken $H = id$, like it was done in the third axiom in section **??**.
For example, it is clear that with E_1^* it is always $E_1^*(\mu) = E_1^*(1 - \mu)$. But with E_5,
and by taking adequate weights $w(x_i)$ and a function F, it is clear that not always
can be $E_5(\mu) = E_5(1 - \mu)$.

Obviously, the axiom $E(\mu) = E(\mu')$ restricts the measures E that can be taken.

Remark 2. Since $\mu(x) = 0$ implies $\mu'(x) = 1$, and $\mu(x) = 1$ implies $\mu'(x) = 0$, it cannot
be neither $\mu \leq_S \mu'$ nor $\mu' \leq_S \mu$. That is, μ and μ' are not comparable under $\leq_S$.

8 Conclusion

Actually, the concept of a measure of fuzziness, as it was introduced in 1972 by Aldo
DeLuca and Settimo Termini [3], is a new idea in Science since the concept of 'fuzziness' was not directly applicable to crisp sets, at least before they were viewed as very
particular fuzzy sets.

The only aim of this paper is to present some not too much technical and general
reflections on both 'fuzziness' and its measuring. For such a goal, it is looked at 'fuzziness' as a quantity only properly shown by fuzzy sets, like they are for instance the
length of segments, the area of surfaces, and the volume of solids.

Like in the case of any quantity, and before trying to introduce what can be considered to be a measure of it, it is necessary (or, at least, it is a 'scientifically sane' tactics)
to recognize two empirical relations of *equality* and *ordering*, in the sense of being
able to know when a fuzzy set shows the same fuzziness than another, as well as being
able to know when the first shows less fuzziness than the second. After these relations
are more or less empirically introduced and some general laws or axioms a measure
of fuzziness does fulfill are tried to be conjectured, the mathematical analysis of such
measures can start.

Once some possible justifications for the axioms of the measures of fuzziness are
taken into account, one of the main aspects the paper considers is the question of the
'sharpened order' introduced by DeLuca-Termini, in the sense of debating if it is a good
enough strategy to represent the ordering introduced among fuzzy sets by its inherent
fuzziness. What actually remains open is if it is the only ordering with which the fuzzy
set constantly equal to the fixed point of the negation is its maximum, and the crisp sets
are its minimal elements.

Another question the paper considers is the problem of the possible functional expressibility of the measures of an intersection, a union, and a pseudo-complement of

fuzzy sets, respectively. Although no general conclusion is reached, it rather seems that in general the answer is negative. In the case of the negation it seems that the only acceptable solution is to take the identity of the measure of a fuzzy set and its pseudo-complement, something that as it is previously justified, can be taken as an axiom for the measures of fuzziness.

Although the aim of the authors only lies in offering some conjectures on what the measuring of the quantity 'fuzziness' is based, unfortunately no safe conclusions are reached in the paper. Nevertheless, we wish the arguments presented will be a starting point for a further, more technical and conclusive study.

References

1. Alcalde, C., Burusco, A., Fuentes-González, H.: Ambiguity and fuzziness measures defined on the set of closed intervals in (0,1). Information Sciences 177, 1687–1698 (2007)
2. Banks, E.: On measures of fuzziness and their representations. Journal of Mathematical Analysis and Applications 4, 24–37 (1983)
3. De Luca, A., Termini, S.: A definition of a nonprobabilistic entropy in the setting of fuzzy sets theory. Information and Control 20, 301–312 (1972)
4. De Luca, A., Termini, S.: Entropy of l-fuzzy sets. Information and Control 24, 55–73 (1974)
5. Dombi, J., Porkoláb, L.: Measures of fuzziness. Annales Uni. Sci. Budapest, Sect. Comp. 12, 69–78 (1991)
6. Emptoz, H.: Nonprobabilistic entropies and indetermination measures in the setting of fuzzy sets theory. Fuzzy Sets and Systems 5, 307–317 (1981)
7. Knopfmacher, J.: On measures of fuzziness. J. Math. Analysis and Applications 49, 529–534 (1975)
8. Kosko, B.: Fuzzy entropy and conditioning. Information Sciences 40, 165–174 (1986)
9. Kosko, B.: Fuzziness vs. probability. Int. J. General Systems 11, 211–240 (1990)
10. Kuznetsov, V., Kuznetsova, E.: Types of concept fuzziness. Fuzzy Sets and Systems 96(2), 129–138 (1998)
11. Pardo-Llorente, L.: Medidas de nitidez e información para sucesos difusos. Estadística Española 90, 11–20 (1981) (in Spanish)
12. Trillas, E., Alsina, C.: Sur les mesures di degrée de flou. Stochastica III-1, 81–84 (1979)
13. Trillas, E., Riera, T.: Entropies in finite fuzzy sets. Information Sciences 15, 159–168 (1978)
14. Trillas, E., Sanchiz, C.: Sobre entropías de conjuntos borrosos deducidas de métricas. Estadística Española 82-83, 17–26 (1979) (in Spanish)
15. Ventre, A., Weber, S.: Evaluations of fuzzy sets based on orderings and measures. Stochastica XI-1, 35–44 (1987)
16. Wang, W.J., Chiu, C.H.: Entropy and information energy for fuzzy sets. Fuzzy Sets and Systems 108, 333–339 (1999)
17. Weber, S.: Measures of fuzzy sets and measures of fuzziness. Fuzzy Sets and Systems 13, 247–251 (1984)
18. Yager, R.: On the measure of fuzziness and negation. part i: Membership in the unit interval. Int. J. of General Systems 5, 221–229 (1979)

Measures of Fuzziness under Different Uses of Fuzzy Sets

Daniel Sánchez and Enric Trillas

European Centre for Soft Computing
Edificio Científico-Tecnológico, Mieres, Asturias, Spain
{daniel.sanchezf,enric.trillas}@softcomputing.es

Abstract. In this paper we discuss on the relationship between fuzziness and its measuring on the one side, and the possible uses of fuzzy sets on the other side. We conclude that the usual axioms and measures of fuzziness disregard the commensurability assumption and view the fuzzy set as a collection of fuzzy singletons. We propose new axioms and a relation "less fuzzy than" for a conjunctive view of fuzzy sets under the commensurability assumption. We show that a measure of fuzziness previously introduced by the authors comply with our proposal.

1 Introduction

As we discussed in [7], *fuzziness* is a concept that can be only attributed to, and hence arises with, fuzzy sets. As pointed out by G.J. Klir in chapter 8 of [3], *"The question of how to measure fuzziness is one of the fundamental issues of fuzzy set theory."*. However, for that purpose it is first necessary to know what we mean by fuzziness. Different statements about fuzziness can be found in the literature. Among others:

1. "... a global measure of the "indefiniteness" of the situation of interest" (De Luca and Termini, [2]),
2. " ... how ill defined is the boundary of the [fuzzy] set", and "... the average ambiguity/difficulty in making a decision whether an element belongs to a set or not" (Pal and Bezdek, [3], Chapter 9),
3. "... represents the uncertainty ... with respect to the corresponding crisp set" [8]
4. Lack of distinction between a fuzzy set and its Zadeh-complement [9]

All these definitions have in common that they refer to *fuzziness* as an intrinsic property of fuzzy sets as abstract mathematical objects, without taking into account what kind of information a fuzzy set is representing. However, in practical applications, the measurement of fuzziness is intended to give us some insight into the information represented by a fuzzy set, and here lies the usefulness of these measures. To the best of our knowledge, the relationship between interpretation of fuzzy sets and fuzziness has not been discussed before in the literature.

S. Greco et al. (Eds.): IPMU 2012, Part II, CCIS 298, pp. 25–34, 2012.
© Springer-Verlag Berlin Heidelberg 2012

Our claim in this paper is that the interpretation of the information represented by a fuzzy set and its use have an influence on the notion of fuzziness and the axioms that a measure of fuzziness should verify. We shall point out that, in our view, the usual axioms for measures of fuzzy sets correspond to a view of a fuzzy set as the union of a collection of mutually-independent *fuzzy singletons*[1], but are debatable for other interpretations. We also propose alternative axioms, an alternative to the sharpened order, and an alternative measure of fuzziness for the case of fuzzy sets used in a conjunctive way, having a finite number of different membership degrees (finite level set), with no restrictions about the support (may be finite or not). In addition, we make some reflections about the role of fuzziness in the case of fuzzy sets viewed as possibility distributions (disjunctive use).

2   A Different View on Fuzziness

2.1   Measures of Fuzziness

In order to measure the fuzziness it is necessary to know when one fuzzy set is less fuzzy than another. The sharpened order $\leq_S$ is proposed in [2] as[2]:

$$\mu \leq_S \sigma \Leftrightarrow min(0.5, \mu(x)) \geq min(0.5, \sigma(x)) \& max(0.5, \mu(x)) \leq max(0.5, \sigma(x)),$$

for μ, σ fuzzy subsets of a crisp set X. Notice that $\mu \leq_S \sigma$ means μ is less sharpened and, hence *more fuzzy* than σ. The poset $([0,1]^X, \leq_S)$ is of course not totally ordered since there are many pairs of fuzzy sets that are not comparable under $\leq_S$. On the contrary, measures of fuzziness provide a total order. There is a wide agreement in the literature about the definition of measures of fuzziness as functions $E : [0,1]^X \to R^+$ satisfying the following axioms:

P1: $E(\mu) = 0$ iff μ is a crisp set
P2: $E(\mu)$ attains its maximum value iff $\mu(x) = 0.5 \ \forall x \in X$
P3: If $\mu \leq_S \sigma$ then $E(\mu) \geq E(\sigma)$
P4: $E(\mu) = E(\mu')$ where $\mu'(x) = 1 - \mu(x) \ \forall x \in X$.

P1-P3 were already proposed by De Luca and Termini in [2]. Additional axioms have been proposed, like the *valuation property*:

P5: $E(\mu \cup \sigma) + E(\mu \cap \sigma) = E(\mu) + E(\sigma)$.

---

[1] In this paper, we use the term "fuzzy singleton" meaning "a fuzzy set whose support is a singleton"; the same term has been employed with this and other different meanings in the literature.

[2] This definition is dependent on a fuzzy negation and its fixed point in general. We assume in this paper the standard negation of fuzzy sets is employed, and hence the fixed point is 0.5.

2.2   A Criticism to Axioms P2 and P3

There is an implicit idea underlying the different approaches to fuzziness and its measuring in the literature: *the membership of each element contributes individually to the global fuzziness of the fuzzy set.* This is evident for example in the definition of entropy measures, in which the value of the measure is obtained as the aggregation *for all elements* of some suitable function applied to the memberships (see *Theorem E* about the characterization of measures of fuzziness satisfying P1-P5 in [4]); it is also evident in the notion of sharpened order that underlies axiom P3 [2].

This is so important and undisputed in the existing approaches to fuzziness that, once recognized that the most fuzzy degree in $[0, 1]$ is 0.5 when considering the standard negation, it is recognized as an axiom that the (only) fuzzy set which has the greatest fuzziness among those with support X is the constant fuzzy set $\sum_{x \in X} 0.5/x$ (axiom P2). This axiom is assumed in all the works about fuzziness and measures of fuzziness, with the single exception (to the best of our knowledge) of our proposal in [1], that we shall explain in section 3.

The criticism to axiom P2 (and consequently P3) in [1] concerns two main questions that, as we shall see, are interrelated: *what information is being represented by means of the fuzzy set?* and, *what does fuzziness mean with respect to that information?* Regarding the first, it is well known that fuzzy sets are abstract mathematical objects that can be interpreted in several different ways, and therefore can be employed for representing different types of knowledge. It is not the same to use a fuzzy set for representing a possibility distribution in a disjunctive fashion (e.g. "John is *tall*") that using a fuzzy set in a conjunctive way (e.g. "The languages I speak are *1/Spanish + 0.9/English + 0.3/French*"). In the first case, the height of John is a single number and the fuzzy set *tall* (that we assume to be defined) assigns to each possible height the *possibility* that it is the actual height of John. That is, we are representing our actual lack of information about the height of John, which is in fact a singleton. On the contrary, in the second case, *all the languages in the set are languages that I speak for sure*, and the membership represents some additional information that could be, for instance, the degree to which I would say that I can speak that specific language. In this case, there is no lack of information being represented, but the information is fuzzy. Notice that this is independent from the membership function, e.g., the same fuzzy set can be also employed in a disjunctive way for representing lack of information like, for instance, "The first language that John spoke was *1/Spanish + 0.9/English + 0.3/French*"; in this case, we are using the fuzzy set in order to represent our imperfect knowledge about the first language that John spoke, indicating that we give maximum possibility that it was Spanish, we are less convinced that it was English, and the less convincing alternative among those we are considering is French.

However, in our view, none of these interpretations justify axioms P2 and P3.

– In the case of fuzzy sets as possibility distributions, the possible height of John is much more clear if we have as information $1/180 + 0.5/170$ (it seems that 180 is a better choice) that if we have $1/180 + 1/170$. That is, the fact that the fuzzy set representing our information is closer to a crisp set does not guarantee that the information is more clear/less ambiguous, or that there is less uncertainty, or that it is easier to make a decision. In the case of fuzzy sets as possibility distributions, what is important is *specificity* (related to cardinality) and not *distance to a fuzzy set*.

- In the case of fuzzy sets representing elements that verify a certain concept there is also a problem, which is related to the *commensurability assumption* of fuzzy sets: if $\mu_A(x) = \mu_A(y) = \alpha$ then y is as A as x. This means that, when determining whether x and y are in A or not, we don't have to make a decision about each one but a *single decision* that will imply both x and y, that can be stated as: *if the membership of an object is α, is that element in the set?* In other words, the contribution of a membership degree is the same despite the amount of elements having that membership. That is, fuzziness should not be influenced by cardinality. In this sense, when used in a conjunctive way, the fuzzy sets α/x and $\alpha/x_1 + \alpha/x_2 + \cdots + \alpha/x_p$ with $p \geq 2$ are *equally fuzzy*. To put it in other words, in this case is not the individual elements that matters, but the α-cuts and their associated degrees, and the problem in this case is how difficult is to choose an α-cut as representative of the fuzzy set. Notice that this is not strange if we consider that, as we stated in [7], fuzziness and crispness are not essentially different concepts, and for anyone it is very clear that crispness is not affected by cardinality at all: all crisp sets (including $\emptyset$) are equally crisp, despite their cardinality (just consider $\alpha = 1$ in our previous example).

The question is, is there any interpretation of a fuzzy set under which axioms P2 and P3 make sense? In our view, they are valid only in those cases in which taking a decision about whether an element x belongs to a set is *completely independent* from taking the same decision for another element y. This assumption of independence is pointed out for instance in Chapter 9 of [3] when interpreting the fuzzy entropy of De Luca and Termini as Shannon's entropy. However, under the commensurability assumption, this seems to imply that instead of a conjunctive fuzzy set, we are seeing the information as a collection of mutually-independent *fuzzy singletons*, i.e., instead of $\mu = \sum_{x_i \in X} \mu(x_i)/x_i$, with $X = \{x_1, \ldots, x_n\}$ we have a collection of mutually-independent fuzzy singletons $\{\mu_i(x_i)/x_i \mid 1 \leq i \leq n\}$ (this interpretation comes from the assumption of independence of memberships and the fact that $\mu = \cup_{1 \leq i \leq n} \mu_i$). Assuming that the decision about whether $\mu_i = \{x_i\}$ or $\mu_i = \emptyset$ is independent for each $i \in \{1, \ldots, n\}$, then the global difficulty of making a decision can be calculated as the aggregation of the difficulties for each fuzzy singleton.

In our view, this is the case for instance in the example posed in [2], in which there is a set of sensory units, each one in charge of detecting the presence of a value 1 or 0 meaning white or black. The collection of values reported by the set of units form a certain detected pattern. If the units by some reason are able to detect a grey level, represented by a degree in $[0, 1]$, we have a fuzzy pattern for which we may be interested in measuring fuzziness as the distance to a crisp pattern. In this example, *sensory units are assumed to be independent from each other*, each unit u_i providing a fuzzy set of the form $\mu_i = \mu_i(u_i)/u_i$, so in order to determine the fuzziness of the pattern it is acceptable under this assumption to consider the fuzziness contributed by each unit and to aggregate that information into a final fuzziness measure.

Let us remark that from an abstract point of view (without taking into account the use of the fuzzy set), axioms P2 and P3 also make sense in the context of defining for each fuzzy set a "distance" or "deviation" from its corresponding, closest crisp set or, similarly, from the complement. This is clear for example in the proposals by Kosko [6], Yager [9], and Kaufmann [5]. However, our claim after the previous discussion is that, depending on the use of the fuzzy set, this distance is not always a suitable way to measure indefiniteness, uncertainty, or difficulty of making a decision about what is the best crisp representative of the information expressed by the fuzzy set, and hence a different set of axioms and measures for those cases are necessary.

3   Measuring Fuzziness for Fuzzy Sets under a Conjunctive View

We focus in this section in the case of conjunctive fuzzy sets and the idea of fuzziness as the difficulty associated to making a decision about whether an α-cut is a good representative of the fuzzy set or not. As discussed in the previous section, we consider that this difficulty is related solely to the set of membership degrees of the fuzzy set, and not to the cardinality of the (crisp) sets of elements having a certain membership.

3.1   A Random-Set View

Let μ be a fuzzy set on a finite set X and let $\Lambda(\mu)$ be the set of membership degrees in the support of μ plus $\{1\}$ in case μ is not normalized, i.e., $\Lambda(\mu) = \{\mu(x) \mid x \in supp(\mu)\} \cup \{1\}$. Let $\Lambda(\mu) = \{\alpha_1, \ldots, \alpha_k\}$ with $1 = \alpha_1 > \alpha_2 > \cdots > \alpha_k > 0$ and let us denote $0 = \alpha_{k+1} \notin \Lambda(\mu)$. From μ we can obtain a random set having as focal elements the α-cuts of μ with $\alpha \in \Lambda(\mu)$ with a basic probability assignment $m_\mu(\mu_{\alpha_i}) = \alpha_i - \alpha_{i+1}$.

This basic probability assignment will be the basis of our approach to define a binary relation "less fuzzy than" between fuzzy sets. For each α_i, $m(\mu_{\alpha_i})$ can be seen as the probability that taking a value α at random in $(0, 1]$ we will have $\mu_\alpha = \mu_{\alpha_i}$. We shall consider that the difficulty when making a decision about which is the best crisp set for representing the information given by the fuzzy set is directly related to the distribution given by m: as we have the mass assigned by m to less focal elements with higher values, the decision becomes easier. In the particular case of crisp sets we have $\Lambda(\mu) = \{1\}$ and $m(\mu_1) = 1$, hence every choice of α leads to the same result and the decision is not difficult at all. The most difficult case is when we have $m(\mu_{\alpha_i}) = 1/k \ \forall 1 \leq i \leq k$, i.e., the probability is equally distributed among all possibilities.

3.2   A New Relation $\leq_F$

In order to introduce an order between fuzzy sets in terms of fuzziness, let us define an analogous to the sharpened order for probability distributions. Let p_1 and p_2 be two probability distributions on two finite sets Y and Z respectively. Let us consider without losing generality that $|Y| = |Z| = K$ (elements with probability 0 can be added when necessary).

Let us repeat iteratively the following procedure: if there is $(y, z) \in (Y, Z)$ such that $p_1(y) = p_2(z)$ then eliminate y and z from Y and Z respectively. Notice that once eliminated, y and z are not considered in further iterations, so if there is another pair (y, z') such that $p_1(y) = p_2(z')$, we don't eliminate z' unless there is another y' with $p_1(y') = p_2(z')$, etc. Let Y_e and Z_e be the elements eliminated from Y and Z respectively. It is $|Y_e| = |Z_e| = K_e \leq K$ and $\sum_{y \in Y_e} p_1(y) = \sum_{z \in Z_e} p_2(z) = \alpha \leq 1$. Let $N = K - K_e$, $Y' = Y \backslash Y_e$, $Z' = Z \backslash Z_e$, and let $\beta = 1 - \alpha$. Then p_1 is less p-sharpened than p_2, noted $p_1 \leq_{pS} p_2$ iff there exists a bijection $\psi : Y' \to Z'$ such that for every $y \in Y'$ we have $p_1(y) \leq p_2(\psi(y))$ when $p_1(y) \geq \beta/N$ and $p_1(y) \geq p_2(\psi(y))$ otherwise.

The idea behind this definition is the following: elements with the same probability present the same degree of difficulty and are equally likely when making a decision, so they are not considered in the comparison. On the basis of the rest of information, a probability assignment is preferred to another if the remaining probability β/N is more p-sharpened (less equally distributed).

On this basis, we introduce a binary relation $\leq_F$ ("less fuzzy than") as follows: let us consider two fuzzy sets μ and σ with corresponding mass assignments m_μ and m_σ. Then, $\mu \leq_F \sigma$ iff $m_\mu \geq_{pS} m_\sigma$.

Example 1. Let $\mu = 1/x_1 + 0.75/x_2 + 0.5/x_3 + 0.25/x_4$ and let $\sigma = 0.7/x_2 + 0.4/x_4$. Then $Y_\mu = \{\mu_1, \mu_{0.75}, \mu_{0.5}, \mu_{0.25}\}$ and let $Z_\sigma = \{\sigma_1, \sigma_{0.7}, \sigma_{0.4}, \{x_1\}\}$ (where the set $\{x_1\}$ verifies $m_\sigma(\{x_1\}) = 0$ and is introduced just to have $|Y_\mu| = |Z_\sigma|$; notice that any set $X^* \subset X$ such that $m_\mu(X^*) = 0$ could have been employed for this purpose). Also $m_\mu(\mu_1) = m_\mu(\mu_{0.75}) = m_\mu(\mu_{0.5}) = m_\mu(\mu_{0.25}) = 0.25$, $m_\sigma(\sigma_1) = m_\sigma(\sigma_{0.7}) = 0.3$, $m_\sigma(\sigma_{0.4}) = 0.4$, and $K = 4$. There are no pairs to eliminate so $\beta = 1$ and $N = 4$ and it is easy to see that for any $\psi : Y_\mu \to Z_\sigma$ we have $m_\mu \geq_{pS} m_\sigma$ and hence $\mu \leq_F \sigma$.

Example 2. Let $\mu = 1/x_1 + 0.8/x_2 + 0.7/x_3$ and let $\sigma = 1/x_1 + 0.9/x_2 + 0.8/x_3 + 0.1/x_4$. Then we consider $Y_\mu = \{\mu_1, \mu_{0.8}, \mu_{0.7}, \{x_2\}\}$ and $Z_\sigma = \{\sigma_1, \sigma_{0.9}, \sigma_{0.8}, \sigma_{0.1}\}$. It is $m_\mu(\mu_1) = 0.2$, $m_\mu(\mu_{0.8}) = 0.1$, $m_\mu(\mu_{0.7}) = 0.7$, and $m_\mu(\{x_2\}) = 0$. It is also $m_\sigma(\sigma_1) = 0.1$, $m_\sigma(\sigma_{0.9}) = 0.1$, $m_\sigma(\sigma_{0.8}) = 0.7$, and $m_\sigma(\sigma_{0.1}) = 0.1$, and $K = 4$. We eliminate $\mu_{0.8}$ and σ_1 since they have the same probability (notice that we don't eliminate neither $\sigma_{0.9}$ nor $\sigma_{0.1}$ despite they have the same probability than $\mu_{0.8}$, since once we eliminate one pair, the elements of the pair are not considered for further eliminations). We also eliminate the elements $\mu_{0.7}$ and $\sigma_{0.8}$ since both have probability 0.7. Hence, $Y'_\mu = \{\mu_1, \{x_2\}\}$, $Z'_\sigma = \{\sigma_{0.9}, \sigma_{0.1}\}$, $K_e = 2$, $N = 2$, $\alpha = 0.1 + 0.7 = 0.8$, and $\beta = 1 - 0.8 = 0.2$. Then, for any $\psi : Y'_\mu \to Z'_\sigma$ we have $m_\mu \geq_{pS} m_\sigma$ since Z'_σ equidistributes β ($m_\sigma(\sigma_{0.9}) = m_\sigma(\sigma_{0.1}) = 0.1 = \beta/N$), and hence $\mu \leq_F \sigma$.

The fuzziness relation $\leq_F$ is somehow similar (but inverse) to the sharpened relation in that we split the collection of values of the probability distributions (after elimination of pairs with the same probability) into two sets, in this case those above and below the value β/N. For values above β/N, the higher the value, the most the distribution differs from being equally distributed. Below β/N it is the contrary, i.e., the lower the value, the most is the departure from being equally distributed. However, this relation does not capture the notion of distance to a crisp set, but that of informativeness of μ via m_μ for determining a crisp representative. The following example shows that it is possible to have $\mu \neq \sigma$ with $m_\mu \geq_{pS} m_\sigma$ (and hence $\mu \leq_F \sigma$) and $\mu \leq_S \sigma$.

Example 3. Let μ of example 1 and $\sigma = 0.5/x_1 + 0.5/x_2 + 0.5/x_3 + 0.5/x_4$. Let us define $Z_\sigma = \{\sigma_1, \sigma_{0.5}, \{x_1\}, \{x_2\}\}$ where $m_\sigma(\{x_1\}) = m_\sigma(\{x_2\}) = 0$ are again introduced just to have $|Y_\mu| = |Z_\sigma|$. Also $m_\mu(\mu_1) = m_\mu(\mu_{0.75}) = m_\mu(\mu_{0.5}) = m_\mu(\mu_{0.25}) = 0.25$, $m_\sigma(\sigma_1) = m_\sigma(\sigma_{0.5}) = 0.5$, and $N = 4$. Again, for any $\psi : Y_\mu \to Z_\sigma$ we have $m_\mu \geq_{pS} m_\sigma$ whilst obviously $\sigma \leq_S \mu$.

It is also immediate that we can find fuzzy sets that are incomparable under relation $\leq_F$, just consider $\mu = 1/x_1 + 0.6/x_2$ and $\sigma = 1/x_1 + 0.95/x_2 + 0.3/x_3$. In this case, let us consider $Y_\mu = \{\mu_1, \mu_{0.6}, \{x_2\}\}$, $Z_\sigma = \{\sigma_1, \sigma_{0.95}, \sigma_{0.3}\}$, $N = 3$. Then $m_\mu(\mu_1) = 0.4$, $m_\mu(\mu_{0.6}) = 0.6$, $m_\mu(\{x_2\}) = 0$, $m_\sigma(\sigma_1) = 0.05$, $m_\sigma(\sigma_{0.95}) = 0.65$, and $m_\sigma(\sigma_{0.3}) = 0.3$. Then, above $1/3$ we have probabilities 0.6 and 0.4 in the case of μ and only 0.65 in the case of σ, so it is not possible to define ψ so that $\leq_{pS}$ holds.

It is easy to show that the binary relation $\equiv_F$ induced by this relation is an equivalence relation. In addition, in the set of fuzzy subsets of a certain $X = \{x_1, \ldots, x_n\}$, the fuzziest fuzzy set (maximal element) is unique up to permutations of degrees among elements, and is given by the following formula:

$$\mu = \sum_{i \in \{1, \ldots, n\}} (i/K)/x_i$$

with $K = n + 1$, being $\Lambda(\mu) = \{i/K \mid i \in \{1, \ldots, n\}\} \cup \{1\} = \{i/K \mid i \in \{1, \ldots, K = n+1\}\}$ and $\alpha_i - \alpha_{i+1} = 1/K \ \forall \alpha_i \in \Lambda(\mu)$. Notice that μ is never a normalized fuzzy set and $supp(\mu) = X$, i.e., degrees 1 and 0 are not considered in this maximal fuzzy set.

3.3   Measure

Now, axioms for a measure of fuzziness of fuzzy sets under conjunctive use are P1 and P4 plus P2' and P3' as follows:

P2': $E(\mu)$ attains its maximum value in $X = \{x_1, \ldots, x_n\}$ iff

$$\mu = \sum_{i \in \{1, \ldots, n\}} (i/(n+1))/x_i.$$

P3': If $m_\mu \leq_{pS} m_\sigma$ (hence $\mu \geq_F \sigma$) then $E(\mu) \geq E(\sigma)$

Figure 1 helps to understand the difference between $P2$ and $P2'$. The set μ has the maximal fuzziness under $P2$ since, viewed as a collection of independent fuzzy singletons of the form $0.5/x_i$, each singleton has maximum fuzziness. However, from a conjunctive point of view, there are only two possible choices for this set with probability assignment 0.5 respectively: either $\mu = X$ or $\mu = \emptyset$. The choice of the best crisp representative is much more difficult for σ since there are five different possible candidate sets, corresponding to the α-cuts of levels 1 ($\emptyset$), 0.8, 0.6, 0.4, and 0.2 respectively, and all of them have the same probability assignment 0.2.

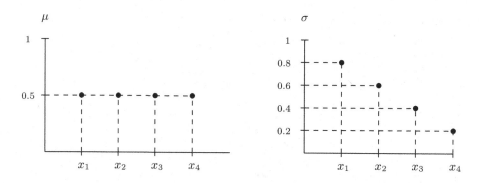

Fig. 1. Fuzzy sets with maximal fuzziness on $X = \{x_1, \ldots, x_4\}$ under $P2$ (μ) and $P2'$ (σ)

In [1] we introduced an entropy measure as follows:

$$Ent(\mu) = - \sum_{\alpha_i \in \Lambda(\mu)} m_\mu(\mu_{\alpha_i}) \ln m_\mu(\mu_{\alpha_i})$$

i.e., the Shannon's functional applied to the mass assignment m_μ. Some properties we showed in [1] are:

- $Ent(\mu) = 0$ iff μ is a crisp set (P1).
- $Ent(\mu) = Ent(\mu')$ when using the standard negation (P4).
- Let us define fuzzy sets $\mu_1, \ldots, \mu_n$ as follows: $\mu_i(x_j) = \mu(x_j)$ iff $i = j$, and 0 otherwise. Then $\mu = \bigcup_{1 \leq i \leq n} \mu_i$, $\mu_i \cap \mu_j = \emptyset \ \forall i \neq j$, and

$$d(\mu) = \sum_{1 \leq i \leq n} Ent(\mu_i) \tag{1}$$

where $d(\mu)$ is the entropy of μ as introduced by De Luca and Termini in [2]. This result is coherent with our previous discussion about axiom P2 as considering a collection of independent fuzzy sets when calculating entropy, instead of a single fuzzy set.

It is easy to show that $\mu \leq_F \sigma$ implies $Ent(\mu) \leq Ent(\sigma)$ (P3') since, as it is a well known property of Shannon's functional, the more the probability is equally distributed, the greater the entropy. By the same reason, P2' holds. As in the case of the sharpened order and classical entropy measures, the reciprocal is not always true, as Ent introduces a total order between fuzzy sets.

4 Conclusions

The usual axioms for measures of fuzziness are well-suited for a specific interpretation/use of fuzzy sets for representing information, in which decisions about membership of each element are independent from the decision taken for others. In this view, the fuzzy set can be better viewed as a collection of fuzzy singletons, or a fuzzy set for which the commensurability assumption is disregarded. For other uses, alternative axioms and measures have to be proposed.

In the case of conjunctive fuzzy sets, the decision about membership involves not individual elements but alpha-cuts. The difficulty in determining which alpha-cut is a better representative of the fuzzy set leads to a new relation between fuzzy sets in terms of fuzziness, different from the sharpened order. A measure that comply with these ideas is discussed here, which was introduced in [1]. In the case of fuzzy sets as possibility distributions, it is specificity and not fuzziness that matters regarding the difficulty in taking a crisp decision, being mainly related to cardinality rather than to measures of fuzziness.

Notice that the measure of fuzziness in section 3.3 has the single requirement that the set of membership degrees (level set) of the fuzzy set is finite. However, there is no restriction about cardinality, so the definition is valid and can be employed for fuzzy sets with infinite, even non-numerable, support, provided the level set is finite.

The definition of $\leq_F$ is just one possibility that is coherent with the idea of measuring departure from equidistribution behind Shannon's functional. It remains open the question whether other relations reflecting the idea of "less fuzzy than" can be defined for conjunctive use of fuzzy sets, and accompanied with suitable measures.

Let us also remark that, if we restrict our study to fuzzy singletons, then $\mu \leq_F \sigma$ iff $\mu \geq_S \sigma$ and hence $P2 = P2'$ and $P3 = P3'$.

Acknowledgements. This work has been partially supported by the Spanish Government under project TIN2009-08296, and by the Andalusian Government (Junta de Andalucía, Consejería de Innovación, Ciencia y Empresa) under project P07-TIC-03175 "Representación y Manipulación de Objetos Imperfectos en Problemas de Integración de Datos: Una Aplicación a los Almacenes de Objetos de Aprendizaje".

References

1. Delgado, M., Martín-Bautista, M.J., Sánchez, D., Vila, M.A.: A probabilistic definition of a nonconvex fuzzy cardinality. Fuzzy Sets and Systems 126(2), 41–54 (2002)
2. DeLuca, A., Termini, S.: A definition of a nonprobabilistic entropy in the setting of fuzzy sets theory. Information and Control 20, 301–312 (1972)
3. Dubois, D., Prade, H. (eds.): Fundamentals of Fuzzy Sets. Kluwer Academic Publishers (2000)
4. Ebanks, B.R.: On measures of fuzziness and their representations. J. Math. Anal. and Appl. 94, 24–37 (1983)
5. Kaufmann, A.: Introduction to the Theory of Fuzzy Subsets, vol. I. Academic Press, New York (1975)
6. Kosko, B.: Fuzzy entropy and conditioning. Information Sciences 40, 165–174 (1986)
7. Trillas, E., Sánchez, D.: A briefing on fuzziness and its measuring. In: IPMU 2012 (submitted, 2012)
8. Wang, H., Lee, S., Kim, J.: Quantitative Comparison of Similarity Measure and Entropy for Fuzzy Sets. In: Huang, R., Yang, Q., Pei, J., Gama, J., Meng, X., Li, X. (eds.) ADMA 2009. LNCS (LNAI), vol. 5678, pp. 688–695. Springer, Heidelberg (2009)
9. Yager, R.R.: On the measure of fuzziness and negation. Part I: Membership in the unit interval. Int. J. of General Systems 5, 221–229 (1979)

(= (+ Intelligence ?) Wisdom)

Anett Hoppe[1], Stefan Haun[1], Julia Inthorn[2],
Andreas Nürnberger[1], and Michael Dick[3]

[1] Data and Knowledge Engineering Group,
Faculty of Computer Science, Otto-von-Guericke-University, Germany
http://www.findke.ovgu.de
[2] Department for Ethics and History of Medicine
University Medical Center Goettingen
http://www.egmed.uni-goettingen.de
[3] Institute for Research and Development of Collaborative Processes
School of Applied Psychology
University of Applied Sciences and Arts Northwestern Switzerland
http://www.fhnw.ch/aps/ifk

Abstract. The concept of wisdom has been a term of reflection since the first philosophical definition attempts by Aristotle (384 BC – 322 BC). Different religions and sciences offered possible properties and facets of wisdom – without ever coming to an agreement on how to define the term. As especially cognitive sciences provided new insights during the last decades the time might have come for a revised, more conclusive definition or at least modelization of wisdom, using and integrating the insights of different disciplines out of humanities, cognitive and natural science to create a common base for further interdisciplinary research. Furthermore, we discuss possible measures that are able to cover a least fundamental properties of wisdom including its vague aspects.

1 Introduction

In Stanislaw Lem's story "Altruizine, or A True Account of How Bonhomius the Hermetic Hermid Tried to Bring About Universal Happiness, and What Came over it", published in the collection Cyberiads (1965-1967), there exists a machine as a digital model of everything that exists in the cosmos. "Properly programmed, it will provide us with an exact simulation of the Highest Possible Level of Development, which we can then question and thereby obtain the Ultimate Answers!" This creature – "man or robot, what does it matter really, whether one thinks with metal or with protoplasm?" exists on the "H.P.L.D." – the Highest Possible Level of Development – it is "a machine able literally to contain the Universe Itself within its innumerable memory banks". But this machine knows that on its H.P.L.D. there is nothing to do in the cosmos. All the machine wishes "is to be left alone to meditate among my many theostats and deiodes..." [1]

Throughout psychological specialist lecture of the last decades, wisdom is the human competence, that has been studied as so-called "peak performance" [2],

S. Greco et al. (Eds.): IPMU 2012, Part II, CCIS 298, pp. 35–43, 2012.
© Springer-Verlag Berlin Heidelberg 2012

the highest level of human excellence. Simultaneously, the behavior shown by Lem's H.P.L.D-machines opposes the common prospect of a wise person – of someone who gets involved and leads people with advice. So are those machines actually wise – or just an unlimited database full of universal knowledge? And what does it need more than data storage and some reasoning?

The work at hand examines the concept of wisdom throughout different domains. Mainly we try to provide a fusion of the last decade's findings in cognitive science with the concepts and models used in information/computer science. As we think, as already argued in [3] that the commonly used modelizations of wisdom in our domain do not correspond with the ones suggested by psychological research. In the first part, we give a brief summary on current insights into wisdom. The following section takes a closer look on intelligence which – as argued in Section 4 – we believe to be, in contrast to most former approaches, an important sub-part of wisdom. Section 5 reviews other possible constituents of wisdom, apart from intelligence. We finish by a reflection on how wisdom might get ascertainable in a mathematical way and what challenges are to defeat along the way.

2   Review of Wisdom Theories

The psychologist Robert Sternberg lists three approaches to understanding wisdom, philosophical, implicit-theoretical and explicit-theoretical approaches [4,5].

Philosophical approaches. Very early analysis of the concept of wisdom can be found in the Platonic dialogues. Plato offered three different senses of wisdom: wisdom as (a) sophia, which is found in those who seek a contemplative life in search of truth; (b) phronesis, which is the kind of practical wisdom shown by statesmen and legislators; and (c) episteme, which is found in those who understand things from a scientific point of view [6,7,8]. In his Ethics Aristotle "distinguishes five conditions ("states") by which truth is obtained: art, scientific knowledge, practical wisdom (phronesis), philosophic wisdom (sophia), intuitive reason." ([9], p. 67)

Implicit-Theoretical Approaches. When searching "for an understanding of people's folk conceptions of what wisdom is, "the goal is not to provide a "psychologically true" account of wisdom, but rather an account that is true with respect to people's beliefs, whether these beliefs are right or wrong." [5] In early studies multidimensionally scaled ratings of pairs of words potentially related to wisdom have been analyzed by Clayton [10]. The earliest terms that were scaled were ones such as experienced, pragmatic, understanding, and knowledgeable.

Explicit-Theoretical Approaches. Looking for a formal theory of wisdom has been a broad research program in psychology in the last decades of the 20th century. Perhaps the most known proposal was "Baltes's longstanding program of research on intellectual abilities and aging" [5]. E. g. in [2] adult participants were given "life-management problems such as "A fourteen-year-old girl is pregnant. What should she, what should one, consider and do?" and "A fifteen-year-old girl wants to marry soon. What should she, what should one, consider and do?" This same problem might be used to measure the pragmatics of intelligence, about which Baltes has written at length. Baltes and Smith tested a five-component model of wisdom on participants' protocols in answering these and other questions, based on a notion of wisdom as expert knowledge about fundamental life matters" [11] "or of wisdom as good judgment and advice in important but uncertain matters of life" [12].

Besides the theories, Sternberg already cited in his book, there are two more to cite that gained importance in the community of cognitive science during the last decade. One is his own "Balance Theory of Wisdom" [13], the other the "3-dimensional Wisdom Scale" introduced by M. Ardelt [14]. Both enhanced the Baltes' view of wisdom as an "expert knowledge system" [15] with additional criteria.

Sternberg put an emphasis on the need for balance in a wise personality – balance between interpersonal, intrapersonal and extrapersonal interests, balance between short-term and long-term needs, balance between the adaption to existing environments and the shaping of new environments – besides the successful application of intelligence and creativity [13].

Ardelt introduces wisdom as a three-fold entity, composed of three abilities: the cognitive ability (the ability to acquire correct knowledge about life's mechanisms), the reflective ability (the ability for critical reflection on those mechanisms and oneself), and the affective ability (the ability to feel sympathetic and compassionate emotion for other beings) [14].

3   Review of Intelligence Theories

It is difficult to define this term (fuzzy concept) that is mostly used in the public as a mental ability of humans to learn and apply knowledge to manipulate the environment or to reason and to abstract thinking. However, the concept means different things to different people and therefore there are plenty of various suggestions to define intelligence. Some of these definitions include abilities as computing, communicating, decision-making, problem-solving, learning rules etc. These factors do also indicate artificial intelligence. Other definitions cover factors like mental speed, general knowledge, creativity, and memory.

In earlier times the traditional idea of a single concept of intelligence was replaced by several competing multi-faceted theories. [16] cites three complex system theories of intelligence – the "Triarchic Model" [17,18,19], the "Theory of Multiple Intelligences" [20] and the "Bioecological Model" [21].

According to R.J. Sternberg, an intelligent being has to implement three interacting aspects of intelligence. The internal aspect comprises all mental skills of information processing that yield to intelligent behavior, including certain knowledge acquisition components, performance components and metacomponents he already presented in an earlier work (see [22]). The second aspect enfolds the practical implementation of the internal dimension in real-world contexts. The third, the experiential aspect, enables human beings to use former experience to process novel and unfamiliar information and automize procedures.

In 1985, H. Gardner introduced a multi-fold theory, splitting up intelligence in at least eight sub-types of intelligence that are mutually independent: logical, spatial, linguistic, interpersonal, naturalist, kinaesthetic, musical and intrapersonal. He never said that there is a limit of "intelligences" but perhaps it seems to be to difficult to add more and more complex intelligences. A more process-oriented and developmental approach was represented by the Bioecological Model [21], accordingly intelligence is a "function of the interactions between innate potential abilities, environmental context, and internal motivation." [16].

4   On "Intelligence + X"

The DIKW-model (see Fig. 1[23]), basing wisdom on a hierarchy composed of data, information and knowledge, has been well-respected in information and computer science for the last two decades. An alternative view, using intelligence as a foundation, was first introduced by R.V. Mayorga [24]. He suggests that wisdom requires, additional to the analytical abilities that intelligence demands, a wise being must provide the skill of synthesis (see Equations 1 and 2).

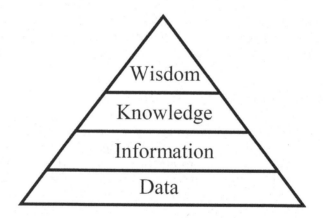

Fig. 1. The Information (or Knowledge) Pyramid: assumed relations between data, information, knowledge and wisdom [3]

$$Intelligence : Analysis \rightarrow Action \tag{1}$$

$$Wisdom : Analysis + Synthesis \rightarrow Action \tag{2}$$

Mayorga's version is a rather simplified one, considering the already cited notions from cognitive sciences. But it proposes a starting point for further reflections on how computer science could use the concept of (computational) intelligence as a base for (computational) wisdom.

It is, in our opinion, an approach that is also supported by the recent theories cited from cognitive sciences. Especially Sternberg supports this point of view in his book "Wisdom, Intelligence, and Creativity Synthesized", by representing the three concepts as overlapping circles, wisdom having conjunct areas with both, intelligence and creativity, but also an area on its own, the "X" we intend to explore in the following.

The parallel might not be as obvious for Ardelt's "3-dimensional wisdom scale". We remind the three parts: cognitive component, reflective component and affective component. As a matter of fact, the extensional view gets apparent the easiest, when using Sternberg's three-fold definition of intelligence as a reference. The three dimensions he names (internal, external and experiential aspect) can be partly mapped on Ardelt's vision of wisdom. So we find the cognitive dimension of wisdom represented by the internal aspect of intelligence - the ability to acquire (correct) knowledge. (It is to be kept in mind, that there might, however, be a important difference between general and wisdom-related types of knowledge.) Ardelt's reflective component can not be directly mapped, there might be parts that belong to the internal level, e.g. theoretical musings about moral questions, large parts in contrast can be assigned to the experiential level that represents the capitalization of knowledge/experiences to novel situations. The external aspect elicited by Sternberg, is not a actual part of the model Ardelt promotes, but her claim for wisdom to be an applied capability becomes apparent in one of her later works [15]:

"Wisdom cannot necessarily be found in what a person says but is expressed through an individual's personality and *conduct* in life."[1]

"But one cannot "have" wisdom without *being* wise."

We skip further reflections on the "Berlin Wisdom Paradigm" as it focusses mostly on the definition of wisdom-related knowledge and thus, helps to understand just *one* fraction of wisdom, the rather intellectual one. The studies conducted are meanwhile not concerned with the search for an exhaustive definition of wisdom.

5 On the Possible X

Our target is to explore the mostly uncharted territories of this ?, and to try and understand the intertwined mix of components that supercharge simple(!) rational behavior into trusting wisdom.

While a map for our ? doesn't exist yet, the disciplines of Cognitive Science have already briefly visited some of its regions, and laid out a general plan that can be usefully employed in our exploration. Some of the local attractions:

---

[1] Italics introduced by author.

5.1   Long-Term Evaluation

Often the most sounding decisions are ridiculed by time and circumstances. Wisdom has the irksome property of being a property that should be decided upon well in advancéd, but can only be judged far later. Intelligent decision are often not required to be farseeing – after all, who can blame anyone for unintended consequences – while what we demand from wisdom is the ability to capture barely a glimpse of the present in order to predict the future.

5.2   Later Onset

Persons of wisdom are rarely young. The other positive properties of mind (intelligence, creativity) can be expressed at any age, within bounds related to age itself, while wisdom is often associated with old age and contentment. Learnable or innate, nature or nurture, wisdom needs to mature and refine with time, patience and examples – no-one is born wise, not even the Dalai Lama.

5.3   Present in Action

It is generally true that wise persons are usually not action bound. Examples do exist, but are wide and far apart, even including in the list the likes of Ghandi, whose action credits consist mostly in motionless protests. This may have something to do with the previously mentioned relationship between wisdom and old age, but a surprising and counterintuitive statement about wisdom is that it almost always implies action. Not necessarily direct action though — the typical wise person modality being counselling. Intelligence can be found busy in theoretical matters, wisdom always gets his hands dirty. The village eldest is consulted on the community's course of action, the doctor discusses with patients and colleagues about therapies and moral dilemmas in life-or-death choices, the great wise thinkers are appreciated for their thoughts, but consulted for their ability of channeling visionary strategies (or should they? Have we lately and ultimately forgot the power of wisdom in real life applications?)

5.4   On Moral Grounds

The word moral, briefly mentioned above, is worthy of a separate treatment as one of the main features of wisdom. Whereas already discussed as the art of balanced decision taking, it is not yet reviewed on how the framework of moral values can contribute or redirect wise decision taking. In fact, many historical examples of wisdom include moral dilemmas and how wise thinking and reframing dissolved them – if wise action is not even said to often enough contradict common knowledge and current social values for a better problem solution.

5.5   Imprecise and Aside

The intelligent approach to problems can often be described in term of optimisation: in a nod to rationality, the best solution within the given framework and external constraint. Wisdom is markedly different: a wise solution often requires reframing, changes of scenery and more generally lateral thinking. The reason for the shift can be more than just one of method. Wisdom's imprecision serves well one of its main features of distinction — being concerned more with the happiness of the actors involved, be they three brothers sharing a number of camels or the whole earth population, than with the solution of a problem by itself. Obviously the term happiness here has to be taken more in a rational agent-like context than in a constitutional right fashion. Once again, wisdom has a moral stance toward the fellow human beings, and by extension toward the ecosystem.

6   Relation to Fuzzy Measures

An inherent fuzziness is introduced to (computational) wisdom when using intelligence as a basic contributing factor. All approaches to computational intelligence suffer from the difficulty to measure, model and implement the need to adjust to various environments, to interpret and act upon input in a correct way. A conceptualization of wisdom will add additional complexity (amongst others the above described components) to this already fuzzy context.

We propose to frame a combinatorial measure for the degree of wisdom that is inherent an inspected situation and activity. Therefore, measures for all the above named components shall be integrated in some kind of weighted belief function. Already established measurements if existent should be used or, if necessary, new ones created. This involves highly inter-disciplinary work that includes especially the fields of cognitive sciences for adequate measurements of the specific abilities of the mind. First steps were made with the above review on intelligence theories, further inquiry on the basic notions of creativity (e.g. [25],[5],[26]) and affect (e.g. [27] are to be done.

The weights in this measuring function might be obtained experimentally, some hints might be given, again, by empirical research that already produced some findings about correlations of some of the named factors and wisdom, for example the relation between intelligence and creativity to wisdom, researched in [5]; or to spirituality as in [28]).

The parameters as well as the weights of this function are influenced by a set of complex and highly dynamic conjunctures and processes.

The part of knowledge acquisition and implementation is already covered in the notion of intelligence, the boundary between general knowledge and wisdom-related knowledge might, once more be ill-defined and, moreover, highly context-dependent. A decision appearing to be wise in one set of circumstances might appear fundamentally foolish in another environmental or personal context. Besides, as outcomes sometimes are not clearly to be seen right away, a wise decision might also include not only a correct model of the current context, but also a correct mental simulation of the possible outcomes and consequences on the needs of other beings. It is to be researched, if it is sufficient use a static objective function on the current state of the system or if more sophisticated, probably simulation including approaches are needed.

7   Conclusion

Starting with a critic on the currently used modelization of wisdom in the infor-mation/computer science context in [3], we continued our reflections on wisdom as a human peak performance. The work at hand examines a alternative ap-proach, proposing to base the concept of wisdom on the human skill set referred to as intelligence. It contains a review of the necessary, inter-disciplinary foun-dations and definitions to support this new theory, muses about possibly still missing features for a wholistic view on wisdom and give a short evaluation on next steps and possible difficulties.

References

1. Lem, S.: The Cyberiad. Fables for the Cybernetic Age. The Seabury Press, New York (1974)
2. Baltes, P., Smith, J.: Toward a psychology of wisdom and its ontogenesis. Wisdom: Its Nature, Origins, and Development 1, 87–120 (1990)
3. Hoppe, A., Seising, R., Nürnberger, A., Wenzel, C.: Wisdom-the blurry top of human cognition in the dikw-model? In: Proceedings of the EUSFLAT Conference, vol. 1, pp. 584–591 (2011)
4. Sternberg, R.: Why schools should teach for wisdom: The balance theory of wisdom in educational settings. Educational Psychologist 36, 227–245 (2001)
5. Sternberg, R.: Wisdom, intelligence, and creativity synthesized. Cambridge Univ. Pr. (2003)
6. Robinson, D.: Aristotle's psychology. Columbia University Press (1989)
7. Robinson, D.: Wisdom through the ages. Wisdom: Its Nature, Origins, and Devel-opment 1, 13–24 (1990)
8. Labouvie-Vief, G.: Wisdom as integrated thought: Historical and developmental perspectives. Wisdom: Its Nature, Origins, and Development 1, 52–83 (1990)
9. Osbeck, L., Robinson, D.: Philosophical theories of wisdom. A Handbook of Wis-dom: Psychological Perspectives 1, 61–83 (2005)
10. Clayton, V.: Erikson's theory of human development as it applies to the aged: Wisdom as contradictive cognition. Human Development 18, 119–128 (1975)
11. Smith, J., Baltes, P.: Wisdom-related knowledge: Age/cohort differences in re-sponse to life-planning problems. Developmental Psychology 26(3), 494 (1990)
12. Baltes, P., Staudinger, U.: The search for a psychology of wisdom. Current Direc-tions in Psychological Science 2, 75–81 (1993)
13. Sternberg, R.: The balance theory of wisdom. The Jossey-Bass Reader on the Brain and Learning 1, 133 (2008)
14. Ardelt, M.: Empirical assessment of a three-dimensional wisdom scale. Research on Aging 25, 275 (2003)
15. Ardelt, M.: Wisdom as expert knowledge system: A critical review of a contem-porary operationalization of an ancient concept. Human Development 47, 257–285 (2004)
16. Davidson, J., Downing, C.: Contemporary models of intelligence. Handbook of Intelligence 1, 34–49 (2000)
17. Sternberg, R.: Beyond iq: A triarchic theory of human abilities (1985)
18. Sternberg, R.: The triarchic mind: A new theory of human intelligence. Penguin Books New York (1989)

19. Sternberg, R.: The triarchic theory of intelligence. Guilford Press (1997)
20. Gardner, H.: Frames of mind: The theory of multiple intelligences. Basic books (1985)
21. Ceci, S.: On intelligence: A bioecological treatise on intellectual development. Harvard Univ. Pr. (1996)
22. Sternberg, R.: Intelligence, information processing, and analogical reasoning: The componential analysis of human abilities (1977)
23. Ackoff, R.L.: From data to wisdom. Journal of Applied Systems Analysis 16, 3–9 (1989)
24. Mayorga, R.: Towards computational sapience (wisdom): A paradigm for sapient (wise) systems. In: International Conference on Integration of Knowledge Intensive Multi-Agent Systems, pp. 158–165. IEEE (2003)
25. Sternberg, R.: Handbook of creativity. Cambridge Univ. Pr. (1999)
26. Boden, M.: Dimensions of creativity. The MIT Press (1996)
27. Russell, J.: A circumplex model of affect. Journal of Personality and Social Psychology 39, 1161 (1980)
28. Jeste, D., Ardelt, M., Blazer, D., Kraemer, H., Vaillant, G., Meeks, T.: Expert consensus on characteristics of wisdom: A delphi method study. The Gerontologist 50, 668–680 (2010)

Evaluating Decisions: Characteristics, Evaluation of Outcome and Serious Games

Julia Inthorn[2], Stefan Haun[1], Anett Hoppe[1],
Andreas Nürnberger[1], and Michael Dick[3]

[1] Data and Knowledge Engineering Group,
Faculty of Computer Science, Otto-von-Guericke-University, Germany
http://www.findke.ovgu.de
[2] Department for Ethics and History of Medicine
University Medical Center Goettingen
http://www.egmed.uni-goettingen.de
[3] Institute for Research and Development of Collaborative Processes
School of Applied Psychology
University of Applied Sciences and Arts Northwestern Switzerland
http://www.fhnw.ch/aps/ifk

Abstract. The characteristics of decisions and the evaluation of their outcome are highly complex. In this paper, we first give a short analysis of different types of decisions such as long-term and short-term decisions or dilemmas by discussing different scenarios and examples. We identify characteristics of decisions and give a short account of the usually quite complex decision scenarios involved and the high uncertainty of long-term predictions. We introduce serious games as a tool for evaluation of decisions through simulation. By using serious games long-term effects of decisions can be evaluated and known measurement criteria for short-term decision can be transformed to support long-term decisions.

1 Introduction

Experience shows that decisions do not always have the consequences we expect. Most people know situations where they felt their decision was wrong but in the end where glad about that decision. Take the student Hans for example who decided to go hiking—with a bad consciousness—instead of learning for his exams and learned later on that the exams were postponed. When circumstances change the consequences of decisions might change as well. This makes decisions the more difficult the longer they will have consequences. Especially long-term effects of decisions are difficult to assess and to be taken into account. Long term effects of our decisions and actions often collide with what we want right now. Though the knowledge of the positive long term effects of a healthy diet and enough exercise are well known this knowledge is usually not what motivates an individual's decision. When we are hungry we need to decide between the options we have and none of them might be healthy. And we might prefer an evening on the sofa instead of running through the rain. Though our decisions

S. Greco et al. (Eds.): IPMU 2012, Part II, CCIS 298, pp. 44–51, 2012.
© Springer-Verlag Berlin Heidelberg 2012

are reasonable in a short-term perspective they need to be seen in a different light in a long-term perspective.

In order to contribute to a better understanding of long-term effects of decisions first basic characteristics of decision-making situations need to be analyzed. We focus on two main characteristics here, the difference between long-term and short-term decsions and dilemma situations.

2 Long Term and Short Term Decisions

The example already sheds some light on the difference between long-term and short-term decisions and their consequences. Short-term decisions are usually characterized by an immediate problem and choosing between the currently available solutions to that problem. The evaluation of the decisions runs along the same criteria as the reasoning within the decision-making process itself. The solutions are compared with regard to all relevant aspects and under a specific evaluation scheme that might weight the different aspects. The best decision in such a situation is the one for the best solution.

When we evaluate different short term decision-making processes they might vary in quality as well. If given good solutions are unknown, the evaluation criteria are not valid or important aspects of the decision were forgotten, a short term decision can take the wrong way. Long term decision-making processes can be quite similar to short term decision processes with only more possible consequences to consider.

Coming back to the example of food the short term decision might be between a canteen, a role from the local bakery or a chocolate bar from the vending machine. One person might only consider costs, time and taste as different dimensions of the decision and take the chocolate while another person also takes social aspects into account and joins a group to the canteen. Some long term decisions, like which bank to choose for the best loan for your new car, can have a similar structure. One chooses between similar options using specific measuring criteria like the lowest interest rate. However, some long term decisions need to be characterized in a different way. These decisions do not take the evaluation of different solutions to a problem as the starting point, but the analysis of the problem, which, in a broader context, might bring up a variation of the possible solutions or a shift in the evaluation criteria. By this new possibilities, adaptation to a changing environment or the change of circumstances by the decision itself are anticipated within the decision-making process and thus change the decision. In the food example a long term decision might be to bring (healthy) food from home to the office for lunch. A person, who is deciding to do that, needs to change his habits and transfer the question of lunch into the morning. But not all decisions need to be transformed into a long term decision. Therefore the philosopher Robert Nozick sees the ability to know when a long term decision is called for as one of the characteristics of wisdom [15]. The analysis shows that the situation of a decision can be reframed by an agent.

A story that illustrates aspects of wisdom goes as follows:

> A father—on his dying bed—told his three sons how to share the inheritance: The oldest should get one half, the second oldest one third and the youngest one ninth of the total of 17 camels. The three sons did not know how to divide this odd number without killing one or more camels. In their despair a man came along with a camel which he generously gave to the three sons. Having 18 camels at hand, the sons could easily assign nine camels to the oldest, six camels to the second oldest and two camels to the youngest. After the transaction, the wanderer took his camel and went on.

The wanderer made wise decisions in two aspects: First, he had the attitude to help the sons solving their problem and willingly give—or at least lend—his camel to reach this goal. Second, he realized that the parts do not sum up to one, but to $\frac{17}{18}$, leaving his camel after the transaction. One may argue that, after the second realization, not much altruism is needed to help the sons. Still, one must be willing to take care of the problem at all. This example also shows the dynamics of wisdom: once the problem is solved, it is now knowledge and seeing a similar problem we may employ the same solution, leaving us only with the necessity of intelligence to realize that a similar situation occurs. The *wise* part of the decision cannot be repeated.

3   The Structure of Dilemmas

Dilemmas make decision processes even more complex, especially in combination with long-term effects. In the following, we discuss specific scenarios and propose a characterization of typical (ethical) dilemmas.

Classical dilemma situations can be characterized as decision-making situations of a specific type. As examples we discuss typical dilemmas from hospital settings where a doctor has to decide in a given situation.

1. In the first scenario there is a young woman who has had anorexia nervosa for a long time. She is in hospital for jet another treatment. She refuses this treatment but asks for palliative care instead. She tells the doctor that she knows that she will die without treatment but that she would like to put an end to her suffering and that the doctor should not force her to be treated (see [1]). The doctor sees a dilemma here. He wants to and could save the patient's life on the one hand side but on the other hand side he wants to respect the patient's wishes and autonomy.

2. In the second scenario there is an old patient who cannot communicate his wishes anymore due to dementia. The doctor diagnoses cancer that would need aggressive therapy. The chances of curing the patient are only around 30%. Should the doctor decide pro or against the treatment? On the one hand side it might add some more life years for the patient. On the other hand side the side effects of the treatment are severe and might harm the patient more without any therapeutic effect.

3. In the third scenario the patient has a different cultural background than the doctor. The patient's prognosis is bad. The doctor is told by a relative that the patient should not be told about his diagnosis because it will cause too much stress for the patient and it would not be done within their culture. Here the doctor is torn between truth telling as a value that is founded in his own cultural understanding of what is good for a patient and the idea of tolerance towards other cultural values.

In all three scenarios the doctor has to face a decision where he has to choose between the given options, he cannot decide to do both or neither of them. The structure of the decision situation does not allow further alternatives. The choice may be brought up by himself or imposed on him by the world (see [19]).

Another common property of the dilemmas is that both options, the doctor has, have severe negative side effects. This can be seen as the second characteristic of a dilemma: For the person who has to decide none of the available options is fully positive [11]. In the scenarios all options have or could have a massive negative impact on the patient. Though the doctor is forced to decide in this situation he might still have a bad consciousness about having harmed his patient in this or that way. This might be different to other decisions because we feel that negative effects of a decision and harming someone need to be considered more intensely than positive effects. Therefore when dealing with dilemmas in practice we find mechanisms installed to support decision-making in cases of dilemmas, examples are ethical committees in hospitals for dilemmas in patient treatment or special responsibilities or laws for dilemmas around welfare.

The third characteristic of moral dilemmas can be described or reframed as dilemmas between conflicting values [19]. Scenario 1 is a conflict between beneficience and autonomy, scenario 2 can be reframed as a conflict between beneficience and non-maleficience and scenario 3 is a conflict between truth telling and acceptance of cultural pluralism. The doctor might wish to change the whole situation into a situation where this dilemma can be transformed into an easier decision.[1] Other typical examples of classical moral dilemmas are if torture should be allowed to save the life of many people, if a hijacked airplane can be shot down with all passengers killed in order to save even more lives, if one is allowed to tell a lie in order to prevent harm.[2]

Ethical theories have developed many different answers to these questions and come to different solutions. Prominent approaches are the, just to name a few:

1. utilitarian approaches [5,12,18]
2. deontological approach [10]
3. virtue ethics approach [3]
4. Justice as fairness approach [16]
5. Pragmatic approach [8]

---

[1] The basic principles of medical ethics were developed by Beauchamp and Childress [4]

[2] Walzer named this type of dilemma the problem of dirty hands. [21]

While some ethicists like Kant think a moral dilemma should be solvable within ethical theory others think dilemmas are inherent to moral reasoning. In practice a dilemma situation usually feels different to other decision situations because of above characteristics.

4   Evaluating through Simulation: A Task for Serious Games

One of the intrinsic problems in the evaluation of long-term decisions is the need for a wide temporal horizon. Consequences stemming from the complex interactions usually involved in ethical dilemmas can present themselves at a later stage without any explicitly premonitory sign. From the early inception of Computer Science, simulations have been one of the tools of choice to evaluate a complex system, thanks to their time compression ability in the limited domain. The evolution of graphic capabilities, the sharp increase in computational power and the development of highly interconnected networks has determined the birth of a family of specific simulation tools geared exactly toward the measurement of the consequences of individual and collective actions, the so-called Serious Games. Serious Games are policy education, exploration, and management tools aimed at the development of skills relative to the management of complex/problematic situations using high end state of the art computer simulation techniques. Born out of the simulation game industry of the eighties, Serious Games, a term in use since 1970 [2], rose to prominence in 2000s, with an important meeting held in Washington in 2003[3] in which the main sectors for the development of serious games as learning tools were singled out as hospitals, high schools, and parks management. And in fact, as of today, the medical industry has been seen as one of the main benefiters from its implementation, both as a cost cutting measure against more complex and realistic simulation and as a cost-cutter measures in order to reduce errors in medical procedures and improve health care decisions [7]. In 2005 Zyda [24] gave the now standard definition of Serious Games as "a mental contest, played with a computer in accordance with specific rules that uses entertainment to further government or corporate training, education, health, public policy, and strategic communication objectives." In this spirit we think Serious Games would make a great tool to help in evaluating long term decisions, especially considering the flexibility in timeline management and the tree exploration possibilities opened by the availability of huge storage memory and massively parallel machines. With few exceptions, Serious Games usually describe a closed-time situation, the actions of the players are carried out in a semi-static, episodic and accessible environment (following Russel and Norvig classification, [17]), and the discretionality of action is usually fairly comparable during the game, by this betraying their roots in boardgames and positional wargames; but simple modifications can be applied to existing routines to give Serious Games, for example, the ability of reducing players' ability of acting on

---

[3] Serious Games Initiative Meeting, February 5 and 6, 2003, Wilson Center, Washington.

variables in a time-dependent manner, to simulate the effects of time, or to end the game not just after the usual episodic end, but in a different point in the timeline, maybe correlated to the number/quality/difficulty of decisions.

A wise agent, in the spirit of our Wisdom project can be partnered in specific points in the game timeline, in a prompting role dependent on the exploration tree's position and content. The evaluation phase can be carried out assigning different utility functions once again connected to the timeline. Such modifications don't increase complexity, are easily implementable using the tools already at disposal and the bent on long-term strategies could be rolled back in more traditional settings in order to increase awareness of extended consequences (e.g. in environmental policies) or learning of long term-skills (once again in healthcare applications).

5   Evaluating Decisions

Most measuring instruments have in common that they assess subjective and/or objective static values that can be used to described the current situation. For example in health care based on health related factors of quality of life. This measure of the subjective outcome of a treatment can help patients as well as doctors to improve their decision-making processes by taking factors into account that are most relevant for the patient and his quality of life. The different measures focus on different aspects of life quality. All measures have been criticized for a lack of validity. The dimensions of the measure usually do not encompass the holistic view patients have on their life quality (see for example [14]). Despite this critique the measures manage to cover many more dimensions of long term effects than earlier variables did. But the question remains what meaning the statistical deterioration in social contacts after a special treatment like a tracheostoma has for an individual patient and her decision.

The example of measuring quality of life in medicine shows that the evaluation of long term effects needs to be done on different levels, and to consider different normative systems for the evaluation. Subjective well being of a patient differs from quantitative objective variables like life expectancy after treatment. The norms to prolong life or to promote life quality might lead into a dilemma as sketched above. Measurement results of long term effects can only guide decisions if their underlying norms are made transparent.

Going back to the examples of long- and short-term decisions and dilemmas, serious games can help to improve existing measuring instruments. In health care most measuring instruments have in common that they assess subjective and/or objective health related factors of quality of life by using static values that can be used to describe the current situation. Examples for objective factors are 5-year survival rate based on the current diagnosis and known statistical outcome of therapies (see scenario 2 in Section 3). Currently new measurement tools are developed to assess subjective parameters of quality of life [13,6,22,9,23,20], they encompass dimensions such as work, social contacts or family. This measure of the subjective outcome of a treatment can help patients as well as doctors to improve their decision-making processes by taking factors into account that are most relevant for the patient and his quality of life. The different measures focus on different aspects of life quality. All measures have been criticized for a lack of validity. The dimensions of the measure usually do not encompass the holistic view patients have on their life quality (see for example [14,20]). Despite this critique the measures manage to cover many more dimensions of long term effects than earlier variables did. But the question remains what meaning the statistical deterioration in social contacts after a special treatment like a tracheostoma has for an individual patient and her decision.

The example of measuring quality of life in medicine shows that the evaluation of long term effects needs to be done on different levels, and to consider different normative systems for the evaluation. Subjective well being of a patient differs from quantitative objective variables like life expectancy after treatment. The norms to prolong life or to promote life quality might lead into a dilemma as sketched above. Serious games can help to restructure decision-making processes in scenarios like the ones in health care settings. The overall aim would be to gain a better understanding how to avoid dilemmas and encompass long term effects into decision-making. Serious games could be used to learn to encompass late-term effects of decisions and plan decisions within a given time line.

6   Conclusion

Based on the discussions given above, we propose the following strategy as a starting point to derive measures for the quality of long term decisions.

One way to obtain useful features allowing us to measure long-term effects might be to simulate and analyze different decisions with long-term effects for their facets and extract especially those that seem to have influence on the long-term effects. Based on these facets we might be able to derive a measure for the quality of long-term decision based on a simple extension of a existing, so far only short-term-oriented measure. The resulting measure could then be evaluated using existing knowledge bases of known cases and belonging prior decisions and iteratively refined.

Ideally, the proposed strategy will derive facets that define a mapping between the properties a good long-term decision and the properties of wise behaviour identified by—especially in the health care area—ethical values as anaylzed in psychological studies [18] and philosophical discussions [4]. Thus, the evaluation of decisions might cover perspectives of ethics on long term effects like the way the decision was conducted, who is involved in the decision and whose evaluation criteria were especially valuable (see the discussion in Section 5 above). This should hold especially in dilemma situations (see Section 3 above) and thus might provide interesting insides in decision-making processes of responsible, possibly even "wise" experts. Due to the highly uncertain and vague properties involved, we expect that especially fuzzy based measures will prove to be useful.

References

1. Fall und Kommentar: Behandlungsabbruch bei Anorexie? EthikMed 22(2), 131–132 (2010)
2. Abt, C.C.: Serious games [by] Clark C. Abt. Viking Press, New York (1970)
3. Aristotele: Nicomachean ethics. In: The Complete Works of Aristotle, vol. I & II, Princeton University Press, Princeton (1984)
4. Beauchamp, T.L., Childress, J.F.: Principles of Biomedical Ethics, 6th edn. Oxford University Press, Oxford (2008)
5. Bentham, J.: An Introduction to the Principles of Morals and Legislation. Clarendon Press, Oxford (1907)
6. Bergner, M., Bobbit, R.A., Carter, W.B., Gilson, S.B.: The sickness impact profile: development and final revision of a health state measurement. Med. Care 46, 787–805 (1981)
7. Blesius, C.R.: Serious games: applications in the medical domain. In: GACET 2011 Proceedings. Fridericiana Editrice Universitaria (2011)
8. Dewey, J.: Ethics, vol. 7. Southern Illinois University Press, Carbondale (1932/1985)
9. Hickey, M.A., Bury, G., O'Boyle, C.A., Bradley, F., O'Kelly, F.D., Shannon, W.: A new short form individual quality of life measure (SEIQoL-DW): application in a cohort of individuals with HIV/AIDS. BMJ 313, 29–33 (1996)
10. Kant, I.: Kritik der praktischen Vernunft. Meiner, Hamburg (1788/2003)
11. Marcus, R.B.: Moral Dilemmas and Consistency. The Journal of Philosophy 77, 121–136 (1980)
12. Mill, J.S.: Utilitarianism. Oxford University Press, Oxford (1861)
13. Neudert, C., Wasner, M., Borasio, G.D.: Patients' assessment of quality of life instruments: a randomised study of SIP, SF-36 and SEIQoL-DW in patients with amyotrophic lateral sclerosis. Journal of the Neurological Sciences 191, 103–109 (2001)
14. Neudert, C., Wasner, M., Borasio, G.D.: Individual Quality of Life is not Correlated with Health-Related Quality of Life or Physical Function in Patients with Amyotrophic Lateral Sclerosis. Journal of Palliative Medicine 4, 551–557 (2004)
15. Nozick, R.: What is Wisdom and Why Do Philosophers Love it So? In: The Examined Life, pp. 267–278. Touchstone Press, New York (1989)
16. Rawls, J.: A Theory of Justice. Harvard University Press, Cambridge (1971) (revised edition 1999)
17. Russell, S., Norvig, P.: Intelligent Agents. In: Artificial Intelligence: A Modern Approach, 2nd edn., pp. 31–52. Prentice-Hall, Englewood Cliffs (2003)
18. Singer, P.: Practical Ethics, 2nd edn., New York (1993)
19. Sinnott-Armstrong, W.: Moral Dilemmas. Basil Blackwell, Oxford (1988)
20. Tsuchiya, A.: The ethical qaly: Ethical issues in healthcare resource allocations. Health Expectations 2(4), 277–278 (1999)
21. Walzer, M.: Political Action: The Problem of Dirty Hands. Philosophy and Public Affairs 2(2), 160–180 (1973)
22. Ware, J.E., Sherbourne, C.D.: A 36-item short-form health survey (SF-36), conceptual framework and item selection. Med. Care 30, 473–483 (1992)
23. WHO: Quality of life (whoqol) - bref. (2004)
24. Zyda, M.: From visual simulation to virtual reality to games. Computer 38, 25–32 (2005)

Measures of Observables and Measures of Fuzziness

Rudolf Seising

European Centre for Soft Computing
Edificio de Investigación
Calle Gonzalo Gutiérrez Quirós S/N
33600 Mieres, Asturias, Spain
Rudolf.seising@softcomputing.es

Abstract. The key aims of modern scientific work have generally been to find relationships between observed phenomena, construct mathematical formulas that describe these relationships, take measurements of the observables, and define axioms using terms that are as exact as possible. In many circumstances, the exactness of observed phenomena is limited – or can only be measured with less than perfect accuracy. However, another problem arises if the concepts of a scientific theory do not fit with the picture that scientists use to understand their observations and experimental results. How to deal with such situations is a question that has intrigued many scientists and philosophers. In the 20th century two scientific theories appeared that change scientist's views from classical to non-classical and on what is measurable: quantum mechanics and fuzzy set theory. This paper focuses on these developments.

Keywords: Philosophy of Science, Measurement, Quantum Mechanics, Probability Theory, Fuzzy Set Theory.

1 Introduction

Since the very beginnings of modern science, the key aims of scientific work have generally been to find relationships between observed phenomena, construct mathematical formulas that describe these relationships, take measurements of the observables, and define axioms using terms that are as exact as possible. However, in many circumstances, the exactness of observed phenomena is limited – or can only be measured with less than perfect accuracy. How to deal with such situations is a question that has intrigued many scientists and philosophers and until the 20th century there was just one mathematical tool in use to handle this: probability theory and statistics.

Two revolutionary developments in 20th century science gave rise to new views into the concept of measurement: 1) Quantum mechanics (QM) in the first third of the 20th century and 2) Fuzzy Sets and Systems (FSS) in the 1960s.

In QM a basic change took place in the relationship between the exact scientific theory of physics and the phenomena observed in basic experiments. Systems of QM do not behave like systems of classical theories in physics – their elements are not particles and they are not waves, they are different.

S. Greco et al. (Eds.): IPMU 2012, Part II, CCIS 298, pp. 52–61, 2012.
© Springer-Verlag Berlin Heidelberg 2012

This change led to a new mathematical conceptual fundament in physics and moreover, to the fact that there is a gap between the observed phenomena and the measurements of observables on the one hand and the objects of the mathematical theory on the other hand. This change led to new concepts to describing uncertainty that is different from classical probabilities.

In FSS Lotfi A. Zadeh found "a radically different kind of mathematics, the mathematics of fuzzy or cloudy quantities which are not describable in terms of probability distributions" ... "for coping with the analysis of systems [...] which are generally orders of magnitude more complex than man-made systems" – e.g. biological systems. ([1], p. 857) He introduced new mathematical entities that "are not classes or sets in the usual sense of these terms, since they do not dichotomize all objects into those that belong to the class and those that do not" and "these concepts relate to situations in which the source of imprecision is not a random variable or a stochastic process but rather a class or classes which do not possess sharply defined boundaries." ([2], p. 29)

However, the two revolutionary new theories resulted in different mathematical concepts to describe uncertainty in science and the both are also in no accordance with classical probabilities. A new question arose from that fact: Are fuzzy sets suitable concepts to describe quantum mechanical findings?

In section 2 we will consider the case of uncertainty in QM and in section 3 we look to the history of Menger's "micro geometry" as a historical link between QM and FSS. In section 4 we will consider the continuation to Fuzzy measures. A brief outlook concludes the paper.

2   Quantum Mechanics and Measurement

QM became the new fundamental theory of physics in the 20th century but it confronted scientists with epistemological problems. Classical physics was built up of the well-known "pictures" of position and momentum in point mechanics and wave mechanics respectively. In QM these classical "pictures" behave complementary, and that means in particular that within only one of the both pictures we can't picture the essential relations of subatomic things completely. Therefore, some physicists argued that classical images or symbols are inadmissible and incorrect to picture the essential relations of subatomic things.

The epistemological change with the emergence of QM took place in the relationship between theoretical physics and the phenomena observed in basic experiments. The new theoretical objects of QM do not behave like theoretical objects of classical physics, they do not have real counterparts, they do not correspond to particles and they do correspond to waves, they are different. The new theoretical fundament in physics was introduced by Werner Heisenberg, Niels Bohr and others. The properties of the objects of QM and the concept of their state are not comparable with those of the objects in Newton's mechanics or Maxwell's electrodynamics.

2.1   Theoretical Objects, States and Probabilities

In physical theory the *state* of an object consists of all the probability distributions of all the object's properties that are formally possible in this theory. We use probability distributions instead of sharp values because of measurement errors. We can determine *states* of objects by the results of the measurements; it is also possible to receive results for all observables simultaneously (e.g. position and momentum). Therefore, in classical physics all probability distributions for observables of all formally possible properties are marginal probability distributions of the unique probability distribution of the object's state.

States of quantum mechanical objects (QM objects) are different as we cannot measure their values for all observables simultaneously (e.g. position and momentum). There is no classical probability space that comprises such events in which all variables have a certain value simultaneously.

However, we can experiment with subatomic things in order to measure a position value, and we can also experiment with these things in order to measure their momentum value. Though we cannot conduct both experiments simultaneously and thus are not able to get either sharp values (or probability distributions resp.) for the same point in time respectively. However, we can predict the outcomes of experiments at this point in time. Since predictions are targeted on future events, we cannot valuate them with logical values "true" or "false", but with probabilities.

As a consequence Heisenberg argued that every concept has a meaning only in terms of the experiments used to measure it. Consequently we must agree that things that cannot be measured really have no meaning in physics. Thus, for instance, the path of a particle has no meaning beyond the precision with which it is observed. Therefore, Heisenberg said that such concepts as orbits of electrons do not exist in nature unless and until we observe them. He took as meaningless the sorts of metaphysical speculations about the "true nature of reality" that, according to Heisenberg, betrayed their metaphysical nature by divorcing questions of truth from more concrete issues of what is observed: It is possible to ask whether there is still concealed behind the statistical universe of perception a 'true' universe in which the law of causality would be valid. But such speculation seems to us to be without value and meaningless, for physics must confine itself to the description of the relationship between perceptions. ([19], p. 197)

QM lacked the features previously found in physics, such as the vividness and perceptibility as well as the measurability of state variables. A function in the Hilbert space, which is infinitely-dimensional by definition, is not descriptive and interpreting it as "probability amplitude" does not offer any real possibility of perceiving a classical physical property of the real object represented in this way or of measuring the corresponding classical physical quantity.

Because there is no joint probability distribution for all observables the QM object's state function embodies the probabilities of all properties of the object, but it delivers no joint probability distribution for all the properties. Therefore, a radically different kind of probabilities was needed.

Already in 1926 the mathematician Max Born established a new and abstract approach to picture the essential relations of QM objects when he proposed an interpretation of this non-classical peculiarity of QM – the quantum mechanical wave function is a "probability-amplitude": The absolute square of its value equals the probability of it having a certain position or a certain momentum if we measure the position or momentum respectively. The higher the probability of the position value, the lesser that of the momentum value and vice versa. [3, 4] Heisenberg said then that we should not even try to imagine this new concept!

In 1932, John von Neumann published the *Mathematical Foundations of Quantum Mechanics* [5], in which he defined the quantum mechanical wave function, which Born has defined as the state function of a QM object, as a one-dimensional subspace of an abstract Hilbert space. With Born's probabilistic interpretation Neumann could claim that the absolute square of the quantum mechanical state function equals the probability density function of it having a certain position or a certain momentum in the position or momentum representation of the wave function respectively.

2.2   Quantum Probabilities

After the establishment of QM as a new physical theory, some approaches were put forward to achieve a new logic and later also a new – and of course non-classical – "probability theory" to handle quantum mechanical propositions that are predictions because they are targeted on future events. We cannot valuate them with the logical values of "true" or "false", but use values in-between that have been called (quantum) probabilities.

In 1936 Garett Birkhoff and John von Neumann proposed the introduction of a "quantum logic", as the lattice of quantum mechanical propositions is not distributive and therefore not Boolean [6] and in 1963 George W. Mackey attempted to provide a set of axioms for the propositional system of predictions of the outcomes of experiments. He was able to show that this system is an orthocomplemented partially ordered set. [7]

In these so-called "logico-algebraic approaches", the "probabilities" of evaluating the predictions of properties of a QM object do not satisfy Andreij Kolmogorov's classical axioms of probability theory. They are not additive and, due to their non-distributivity, it is indicated that the logico-algebraic structure of QM is not a Boolean lattice and therefore it is more complicated than that of the classical probability space as it was defined by Kolmogorov. [8]

Also in the 1960s, Patrick Suppes discussed the "probabilistic argument for a non-classical logic of quantum mechanics" [9, 10]. He introduced the concept of a "quantum mechanical σ-field" as an "orthomodular partial ordered set" covering the classical σ-fields as substructures. Then, in the 1980s, a "quantum probability theory" was proposed and developed by Stanley Gudder and Imre Pitowski [11, 12].

These developments regarding a theory of probabilistic structures of QM became very complex, as the reader can also see e.g. in [13]. It is an open question whether it is beneficial to use fuzzy sets instead of probabilities or "quantum probabilities" for an interpretation of QM. Without mentioning this explicitly the Viennese mathematician Karl Menger was one of the first scientists who went this way.

3   Statistical Metrics in Micro Geometry

Menger, who immigrated into the USA in1937, was one of the first to begin laying the groundwork for the development of scientific methods dealing with uncertainties in theoretical concepts of scientific theories instead of exact concepts. He never abandoned the framework of classical mathematics, particularly classical probability theory but extended its boundaries. He extended the theory of metric spaces in the direction of probabilistic concepts; in 1942 he considered the *distance function* $\Pi(x; p, q)$ *of p* and *q,* which bears the meaning of the *probability* that the points *p* and *q* have a distance $\leq x$. Then he introduced the term "statistical metric: A *statistical metric* is "a set *S* such that with each two elements ('points') *p* and *q* of *S,* a probability function $\Pi(x; p, q)$ is associated satisfying the following conditions:

1. $\Pi(0; p, p) = 1$.   2. If $p \neq q$, then $\Pi(0; p, q) < 1$.
3. $\Pi(x; p, q) = \Pi(x; q, p)$ 4. $T[\Pi(x; p, q), \Pi(y; q, r)] \leq \Pi(x+y; p, r)$

where $T[\alpha, \beta]$ is a function defined for $0 \leq \alpha \leq 1$ and $0 \leq \beta \leq 1$ such that

(a) $0 \leq T(\alpha, \beta) \leq 1$.   (b) T is non-decreasing in either variable.
(c) $T(\alpha, \beta) = T[\beta, \alpha]$.   (d) $T(1, 1) = 1$.
(e) If $\alpha > 0$, then $T(\alpha, 1) > 0$."

([14], p. 535f)

Condition 4, the "triangular inequality" of the statistical metric *S* implies the following inequality for all points *q* and all numbers *x* between 0 and *z*:

$$\Pi(z; p, r) \geq \text{Max } T[\Pi(x; p, q), \Pi(z-x; q, r)].$$

In this paper Menger used the term *triangular norm* (*t-norm*) for the first time to indicate the function *T*.

In 1951 Menger introduced a new notation Δab for the non-decreasing cumulative distribution function, associated with every ordered pair (a, b) of elements of a set *S* and he wrote: "The value $\Delta_{ab}(x)$ may be interpreted as the probability that the distance from *a* to *b* be < *x*." ([15], p. 226.) Much more interesting is the following text passage: "We call *a* and *a'* *certainly-indistinguishable* if $\Delta_{aa'}(x) = 1$ for each $x > 0$. Uniting all elements which are certainly indistinguishable from each other into identity sets, we decompose the space into disjoint sets *A, B,* ... We may define Δ_{AB} $(x) = \Delta_{ab}(x)$ for any *a* belonging to *A* and *b* belonging to *B*. (The number is independent of the choice of a and b.) The identity sets form a perfect analog of an ordinary metric space since they satisfy the condition[1]

If $A \neq B$; then there exists a positive *x* with $\Delta_{ab}(x) < 1$."

In the same year Menger addressed the difference between the mathematical continuum and the physical continuum. Regarding *A, B,* and *C* as elements of a

---

[1] In his original paper Menger wrote ">". I thank E. P. Klement for this correction.

continuum, he referred to a claim of the French mathematician and philosopher Henri Poincaré, "that only in the mathematical continuum do the equalities $A = B$ and $B = C$ imply the equality $A = C$. In the observable physical continuum, 'equal' means 'indistinguishable', and $A = B$ and $B = C$ by no means imply $A = C$. »The raw result of experience may be expressed by the relation $A = B$, $B = C$, $A < C$, which may be regarded as the formula for the physical continuum.« According to Poincaré, physical equality is a non-transitive relation." ([16], p. 178.)

Menger suggested a realistic description of the equality of elements in the physical continuum by associating with each pair (A, B) of these elements the probability that A and B will be found to be indistinguishable. He argued: "For it is only very likely that A and B are equal, and very likely that B and C are equal – why should it not be less likely that A and C are equal? In fact, why should the equality of A and C not be less likely than the inequality of A and C?" ([16], p. 178.) To solve "Poincaré's paradox" Menger used his concept of probabilistic relations and geometry: For the probability $E(a, b)$ that a and b would be equal he postulated:

(1) $E(a, a) = 1$ for every a; $E(a, b) = E(b, a)$,   for every a and b;
(2) $E(a, b) \cdot E(b, c) \leq E(a, c)$,   for every a, b, c.

If $E(a, b) = 1$, then he called a and b *certainly equal*. (In this case we obtain the ordinary equality relation.) "All the elements which are certainly equal to a may be united to an 'equality set', A. Any two such sets are disjoint unless they are identical." ([16], p. 179.)

In addition to studies of well-defined sets, he called for a theory to be developed in which the relationship between elements and sets is replaced by the probability that an element belongs to a set; in a French paper and in contrast to ordinary sets, he called these entities "ensembles flous" ([17], p. 226). Later, Menger used the English term "hazy set" and to elucidate the contrast he referred to conventional sets as "rigid sets." [18].

In 1966 he proposed the application of his findings on statistical metrics to the problem of the "physical continuum" [18].[2] "In his *Dernières Pensées*, Poincaré had suggested defining the physical continuum as a system S of elements, each pair of said elements being linked together by a chain of elements from S such that every element of the chain is indistinguishable from the following element. Menger clearly recognized that the difficulty of using his term *ensemble flou* lay in the fact that the individual elements had to be identified. Since this was simply not possible, he suggested combining the *ensemble flou* with a geometry of "lumps," since lumps were easier to identify and to differentiate from each other than points. Lumps could assume a position between indistinguishability and apartness, which would be the condition of overlapping. It was irrelevant whether the primitive (i. e., undefined) concepts of a theory were characterized as points and probably indistinguishable or as lumps and probably overlapping. Of course, all of this depended on the conditions that these simple concepts had to fulfil, but the properties stipulated in the two cases

---

[2] For more details see chapter II in [19].

could not be identical. I believe that the ultimate solution of problems of micro geometry may well lie in a probabilistic theory of hazy lumps. The essential feature of this theory would be that lumps would not be point sets; nor would they reflect circumscribed figures such as ellipsoids. They would rather be in mutual probabilistic relations of overlapping and apartness, from which a metric would have to be developed." ([18]: p. 233).

Menger never envisaged a mathematical theory of loose concepts that differs from probability theory. When he compared his "micro geometry" with the theory of fuzzy sets – he wrote "In a slightly different terminology, this idea was recently expressed by Bellman, Kalaba and Zadeh under the name fuzzy set." ([18, p 232)] – He did not see that the "slight difference" between "degrees" (fuzziness) and "probabilities" is a difference not just in terminology but in the meaning of the concepts.

4   From Probability Measures to Measures of Fuzziness

In my research work on the history of the theory of FSS, I could show that Zadeh established this new mathematical theory in 1964/65 to bridge the gap that reflects the fundamental inadequacy of conventional mathematics to cope with the analysis of complex systems [20]. In the second part of the paper at hand I would like to start historical work on "40 years of Measures of Fuzziness" and here it is my intention to show very briefly that this development has origins in thinking that came from QM.

4.1   From Quantum Mechanics to Fuzzy Sets and Systems

The first scientists who tried to establish measures of fuzziness were the Italian physicists Settimo Termini and Aldo de Luca. The both have moved to cybernetics in the late 1960s. Termini was introduced to Zadeh's paper on "Fuzzy Sets" [21] by Eduardo Caianiello, another Italian physicist who founded the *Laboratorio di Cibernetica del CNR* in Naples, Italy in 1968, and Termini joined this institute in the following year. Termini and de Luca looked into Zadeh's idea of fuzzy sets and they also studied the 1969-paper "Modified concepts of logic, probability, and information based on generalized continuous characteristic function" and the book *Knowing and guessing* by the Japanese physicist's Satoshi Watanabe's who built an information theory based on quantum mechanics [22, 23]. Termini recalled in my interview: "All these things together created the milieu in which Aldo and I thought that it could be worthwhile to attempt to "measure fuzziness". [...] "The very important thing was the truth functionality of fuzzy sets. It was very appealing that there was a way of approaching the representation of uncertainty in a truth functional way." [...] "However, it was important having ways of controlling this uncertainty, and this should appear clearly by just looking to some properties of fuzzy sets. In a sense it should be something that each fuzzy set carries with it, independently from any other things.

In 1972 the two proposed "the introduction of a 'measure of the degree of fuzziness' or 'entropy' of a generalized set" [24], "starting from the information provided by a fuzzy set, although all the tools of probability had been defined." Looking for the new concept's properties they introduced the "sharpened order" as the base of the theory of "measures of fuzziness" and it was immediately clear that these ways of measuring how much fuzzy is a fuzzy set are entropies." [25]

When the Spanish mathematician Enric Trillas saw Zadeh's paper "Fuzzy Sets" [21] for the first time in 1974 he "got a kind of brain's flash, since I linked the ideas in this paper with my former reading on Menger's hazy sets", he recalled in my interview." He "was unable to think on 'membership' as something different to the probability of belonging to a crisp set", he said, and : "In that time, mathematicians and logicians were not interested in the phenomenon of imprecision, even more, linguistic imprecision was considered out of any mathematical importance, as something dangerous and, consequently, to be avoided. As far as I know, before 1965 no mathematician thought on modelling linguistic imprecision. Nevertheless, between the end of 1974 and mid 1975, I did believe on this possibility." Then, he started his work on de Luca's and Termini's fuzzy entropies, "by trying to obtain new mathematical models of them. For example, models coming from numerical distances." He also studied the relationships between fuzzy entropies and a new concept of the so-called "fuzzy integral" that was introduced by Michio Sugeno, jointly with Teresa Riera, Nadal Batle, Concha Sanchiz, and Claudi Alsina [29].

Fuzzy Measures and Fuzzy Integrals. The Japanese physicist and engineer Michio Sugeno left his position as a researcher in nuclear industry in the late 1960's. As a research associate in control engineering at Tokyo Institute of Technology he became interested in artificial intelligence particularly, in game-playing systems and consequently in problems of decision making under uncertainty. In my interview he said: "We make a decision by evaluating the scores of our possible states caused by an unknown opponent's decision. The scores are given in many ways and often they are associated with multi-attributes. In those days, the probabilistic evaluation of states was popular where an opponent's move was assumed probabilistic. The probabilistic evaluation was naturally based on the probability expectation. However I could never believe that a human player makes a decision on a board game based on probabilities. More precisely, I did not think that a human player performs calculations such as addition and multiplication. Instead, a human player only makes comparisons which are related with max- min-operations in fuzzy sets theory." [30] He started his analytical research to contribute to fuzzy set theory studying an integral form based on max-min-operations, i.e., comparisons. He wondered: "How can we define a measure for such an integral form?" Because the property of additivity seemed to be too strong, he reduced the integral form to monotonicity. He recalled: "I put the adjective 'fuzzy' to this monotone measure simply because max-min-operations were used in its integral form as in fuzzy sets; this naming was later found to be not adequate. More precisely, I should have called it 'monotone measure' or even 'non-additive measure'. I found that the monotonicity of the fuzzy measure well fits the calculations of max-min." Sugeno gave a mathematical foundation to this "fuzzy integral ", later it was called "Sugeno integral", at first in a Japanese journal in 1972 and in 1974 he wrote the doctor thesis "Theory of Fuzzy Integrals and its Applications. [30, 31, 32]

5   Conclusion

When George Klir and Zhenyuang Wang introduced fuzzy measure in their book *Fuzzy Measure Theory* in 1992 they wrote: "After more than 50 years of the existence and steady development of the classical measure theory, the additivity property of classical measures became a subject of controversy. Some mathematicians felt that additivity is too restrictive in some application contexts. It is too restrictive to capture adequately the full scope of measurement. While additivity characterizes well many types of measurements under idealized, error-free conditions, it is not fully adequate to characterize most measurements under real, physical conditions, when measurement errors are unavoidable. Moreover, some measurements, involving, for example, subjective judgements or nonrepeatable experiments, are intrinsically nonadditive." ([33], p. 2-3)

Coming back to Heisenberg's point that things that cannot be measured really have no meaning in physics we have to ask: 1) Can these things be fuzzy-measured? And 2) Do fuzzy measured things have a meaning in physics?

Heisenberg had written his reasoning in 1927 [19]. As a physicist he thought on physical measurements; he never thought on mathematical measure theory. Furthermore, Kolmogorov published his axioms of probability measure theory five years later [8]. This foundation became standard in mathematical probability theory and sometimes it is called "classical". As we showed in section 2.2, the first non-classical probabilities – "quantum probabilities" – appeared in the 1960's, but "the earliest challenge to classical measure theory" was the set function "capacity" that was introduced in 1954 by the French mathematician Gustave Choquet [34]. Capacities are (with respect to the set inclusion) continuous and monotonic set functions that associate with each subset a real number. Capacities are nonadditive and therefore similar to the Sugeno integral and the both are fuzzy measures. Nowadays many other fuzzy measures have been defined (see e.g. [34, 38]). Looking for fuzzy measures to model uncertainties in QM, i.e. uncertainties of the used concepts' meaning, is still work with good prospects!

Acknowledgments. I thank Michio Sugeno, Settimo Termini and Enric Trillas for the willingness to be interviewed. Work leading to this paper was partially supported by the *Foundation for the Advancement of Soft Computing* Mieres, Asturias (Spain).

References

1. Zadeh, L.A.: From Circuit Theory to System Theory. Proc. IRE 50(5), 856–865 (1962)
2. Zadeh, L.A.: Fuzzy Sets and Systems. In: Fox, J. (ed.) System Theory, Microwave Res. Inst. Symp. Series XV, pp. 29–37. Polytechnic Press, Brooklyn (1965)
3. Born, M.: Zur Quantenmechanik der Stoßvorgänge. Z. F. Physik. 37, 86–867 (1926)
4. Born, M.: Das Adiabatenprinzip in der Quantenmechanik. Z. F. Physik. 40, 167–191 (1926)
5. von Neumann, J.: Mathematical Foundations of Quantum Mechanics. Princeton Univ. Press, Princeton (1955)
6. Birkhoff, G., von Neumann, J.: The Logic of Quantum Mechanics. Annals of Mathematics, Series 2 37, 823 (1936)

7. Mackey, G.W.: Mathematical Foundations of Quantum Mechanics. W. A. Benjamin, New York (1963)

8. Kolmogorov, A.: Foundations of the Theory of Probability, 2nd edn. Chelsea, New York (1956); Grundbegriffe der Wahrscheinlichkeitsrechnung. Julius Springer, Berlin (1933)

9. Suppes, P.: Probability Concepts in Quantum Mechanics. Phil. of Sci. 28, 378–389 (1961)

10. Suppes, P.: The Probabilistic Argument for a Non-Classical Logic of Quantum Mechanics. Philosophy of Science 33, 14–21 (1966)

11. Gudder, S.P.: Quantum Probability. Academic Press, San Diego (1988)

12. Pitowski, I.: Quantum Probability - Quantum Logic. LNP, p. 321. Springer, Berlin (1989)

13. Seising, R. (guest ed.): Special Issue: Fuzzy and Quantum Systems. Int. J. of General Systems 40(1), 1–9 (2011)

14. Menger, K.: Statistical Metrics. Proc. Natl. Acad. Sci., U.S.A. 28, 535–537 (1942)

15. Menger, K.: Probabilistic geometry. Proc. Natl. Acad. Sci. 37, 226–229 (1951)

16. Menger, K.: Probabilistic Theories of Relations. Proc. Natl. Acad. Sci. 37, 178–180 (1951)

17. Menger, K.: Ensembles flous et fonctions aléatoires. Comptes Rendus Académie des Sciences 37, 226–229 (1951)

18. Menger, K.: Geometry and Positivism. A Probabilistic Microgeometry. In: Menger, K. (ed.) Selected Papers in Logic and Foundations, Didactics, Economics, pp. 225–234. D. Reidel Publ. Comp, Dordrecht (1979)

19. Heisenberg, W.: Über den anschaulichen Inhalt der quantentheoretischen Kinematik und Mechanik. Zeitschrift für Physik. 43, 172–198 (1927)

20. Seising, R.: The Fuzzification of Systems. In: The Genesis of Fuzzy Set Theory and Its Initial Applications - Its Development to the 1970s. Springer, Berlin (2007)

21. Zadeh, L.A.: Fuzzy Sets. Information and Control 8, 338–353 (1965)

22. Watanabe, S.: Modified concepts of logic, probability, and information based on generalized continuous characteristic function. Information and Control 15, 1–21 (1969)

23. Watanabe, S.: Knowing and guessing. John Wiley & Sons, New York (1969)

24. Termini, S.: Interview with R. Seising. Newsletter Philosophy and Soft Computing 2(2), 7–14 (2010), http://www.eusflat.org/research_wg_phil/Newsletter_Phil_3.pdf

25. de Luca, A., Termini, S.: A Definition of a Nonprobabilistic Entropy in the Setting of Fuzzy Sets Theory. Information and Control 20(4), 301–312 (1972)

26. Trillas, E.: Interview with R. Seising. Newsletter Philosophy and Soft Computing 2(1), 7–11 (2009), http://www.eusflat.org/research_wg_phil/Newsletter_Phil_1.pdf

27. Sugeno, M.: Interview with R. Seising. Newsletter Philosophy and Soft Computing 6(1) (to appear, 2012)

28. Sugeno, M.: Fuzzy Measure and Fuzzy Integral. Transactions of the Society of Instrument and Control Engineers 8(2), 218–226 (1972) (Japanese)

29. Sugeno, M.: Theory of Fuzzy Integrals and its applications. Ph. D. Diss., Tokyo (1974)

30. Klir, G., Wang, Z.: Fuzzy measure Theory. Plenum Press, New York (1992)

31. Choquet, G.: Theory of capacities. Annales de l'institut Fourier, tome 5, 131–295 (1954)

32. Garmendia, L.: The Evolution of the Concept of Fuzzy Measure. Studies in Computational Intelligence (SCI) 5, 185–200 (2005)

33. Zi-Xiao, W.: Fuzzy measures and Measures of Fuzziness. J. Math. Analysis and Appl. 104(2), 589–601 (1984)

34. Mesiar, R.: Fuzzy Measures and Integration. Fuzzy Sets and Systems 156(3), 365–370 (2005)

35. Dombi, J., Porkoláb, L.: Measures of Fuzziness. Ann. Univ. Sci. Budapest, Sect. Comp. 12, 69–78 (1991)

A Few Remarks on the Roots of Fuzziness Measures

Marco Elio Tabacchi[1,2] and Settimo Termini[1,3]

[1] Dipartimento di Matematica ed Informatica - Università degli Studi di Palermo, Italy
[2] Istituto nazionale di ricerche Demopolis, Trapani, Italy
[3] European Center for Soft Computing, Mieres (Asturias), Spain
marcoelio.tabacchi@unipa.it, termini@math.unipa.it

Abstract. In the forty years from the introduction of Fuzzy Entropy, fuzziness measures has been employed in many different fields pertaining both hard and soft sciences, from medicine to art, from engineering to linguistics. If we look back at the road traveled, we can safely state that on of the main reasons for this enduring presence, and maybe the most underrated, is the truly uniqueness of the concept of fuzziness. Far from a reminiscence, this consideration is more of a projection on the future of fuzziness: we strongly believe that the innovation implicit in the concept, while having sometime hindered in the past its perception as a powerful paradigm and tool for the hard science community, will maintain fuzziness measures topical and relevant. New developments of Fuzzy Sets Theory such as Computing with Words, will need new ways of measuring, and new fuzzy measures.

Keywords: Fuzziness, Measures of Fuzziness, Fuzzy Entropy.

1 Introduction

Forty years have passed since the first publication of DeLuca and Termini "A definition of a nonprobabilistic entropy in the setting of fuzzy sets theory" [1], and from then on many cunning ways of measuring the inherent fuzziness in our perception of the world have been devised. Countless examples in medicine, artificial vision, control and pattern recognition, plus the huge number of related papers that each year are submitted to Fuzzy conferences such as this one have demonstrated the flexibility of this tool and its ability to capture aspects of the reality that are often lost in the race to extreme precision (though an exhaustive review of fuzzy measures is still amiss, a through treatise of how fuzziness measures can be used in practice is the classical Springer textbook on Fuzzy measures [2]).

But measuring fuzziness, and with fuzziness, is not confined in the cramped quarters of hard sciences: just to hint at a limited sample of the possibilities, we have used a concept of Fuzzy distance, born in the field of artificial vision, to measure and compare the perceived complexity of paintings from different historical periods [3], as well as musical pieces played using different musical density [4]. We have employed again fuzzy measures born as controls in the evaluation of preferential choices in the perception of geometric visual illusions [5]. While different novelty

S. Greco et al. (Eds.): IPMU 2012, Part II, CCIS 298, pp. 62–67, 2012.
© Springer-Verlag Berlin Heidelberg 2012

measuring paradigms have come and go in literature, fuzziness measures are still trotting along fine after all these years, a success we maintain is not by chance, but due to the very nature of Fuzzy, as will be discussed in the following section.

The aim of the present paper is to investigate whether it is possible to shed some light on the specificity of the measures of fuzziness by relating its features to specific characteristics of the innovative aspects of the notion of fuzziness. With this intent in mind, in the following we will briefly discuss the unique nature of fuzziness (section 2), measuring with fuzziness (section 3), show a simple example of fuzziness measures applied to aesthetics (section 4), and try to draw some conclusions from this excursus into the past, present (and future) of fuzziness measures (section 5).

2   The Unique Nature of Fuzzy

The aptness of fuzziness measures in describing and representing the world is clearly demonstrated by countless research, but here we shall try to argue in favour of a simple notion. Namely, that such success history – and the criticism which have accompanied the birth and the development of Fuzzy Set Theory (and the connected notions and theories) – can be related to a very simple, immediate

Proposition 1: Fuzziness is not reducible to previous, different notions (the usual debate with probabilistic standard bearers comes to mind), but is a *truly* and *completely new concept*, and a *new scientific* concept.

This proposition comes with an unfortunately heavy load of bad consequences: as any fundamentally new concept, fuzziness has attracted in his now long history the critiques of the part of the establishment that sees anything new as a menace to the powers that are; the holier-than-thou stance of many from the "exact sciences" for fuzziness' attitude to embrace the various declinations of vagueness, concepts such as unsharp predicates, uncertainty, approximate and/or incomplete/inexact reasoning, partial knowledge and incomplete information, approximation, terms considered by them little more than swear words; a general holy war approach to the integration of fuzziness in other scientific endeavors, with an escalation from both parts involved which have not done any good to the whole field; and last but not least a real and true challenge to some consolidated attitudes of the scientific tradition. What's more, a significative part of these difficulties are not part of the past: long for being a rethorical way of celebrating these forty years, our insisting on the innovative characterization of fuzziness should also be taken as a put-forward warning about the very strong difficulties that such new and innovative concepts will continue to meet in the future.

But this list of grievances (past and future) won't impact the slightest the force represented by fuzziness as one of the significative new concepts in this century. Certainly Fuzziness is not the only innovative concept coming out in recent times: along the past century we have witnessed the emergence of a few other new, innovative notions. Just as an exemplification:

Complexity and chaos theory, for instance, comes to mind: another way at slicing reality that shows that not everything is clearly measurable or demonstrable, and "the crude data of sense", in Russell's words, needs more powerful characterization.

Computability, really represents a "unicum" in the history of science. We realize that - in a more direct way - if we present the classical Church-Turing thesis as equivalent to the fact that the notion of computability is such that the informal notion (the 'explicandum', in the sense of Carnap) coincides with all its proposed formalizations (the 'explicata', in Carnap's sense); but we also want to mention also the (strange) notion of

Complementarity, envisaged by Niels Bohr in order to reconcile incompatible descriptions of unusual properties of the microscopic world.

What we discuss here is not a thesis set in stone, but an attempt to help explicating - at a very general level - successes and problems that research in Fuzzy Sets Theory can face when proposing challenging questions. In order to do this, a fundamental question cannot be eluded: why fuzziness is innovative? As an opener to the discussion, we list four topics of interest, but let us add that this list is both tentative and open. New reasons could and must be added, and the proposed ones criticized and dissected.

Reason 1: there are fields in which fuzziness cannot be eradicated. It is, then, *ineliminable*.

Reason 2: fuzziness cannot be collapsed to other notions, aspects, concepts, conditions and so on in a "natural" way. It is, then, *irreducible*.

Reason 3: from the very beginning, it has been clear that the concept of precision does not coincide with the one of numerical accuracy.

Reason 4: the previous reason opens the way for taking into account, in the realm of scientifically affordable problems, the possibility that the same central variables can assume also non numerical values. As a matter of fact, "linguistic variables" make their appearance very early in the development of the theory.

The last two points, incidentally, naturally induce to reflect on the fact that developments along these lines could help in affording in a different way the debated old problem of the two cultures. In what follows, we shall briefly refer - for simplicity - only to two old and classical topics and to a couple of hot recent challenges. Of course a lot of other topics could be analyzed, studied and discussed along the same line of thought – fuzzy control is certainly among the candidates that immediately comes to the mind. The two classical examples which could be analyzed from the point of view outlined above are, respectively, the development of generalized logical connectives and the relationship between fuzziness and probability.

As regards generalized logical connectives, there obviously exists a very strong connection between fuzzy logic and the seminal ideas of Jan Łukasiewicz presented in the twenties of last Century. However we want to remark that the full exploitation of new mathematical tools in logic, historically happened only after the emergence of the visualization of "many truth values" as something "terrestrial". Secondly, it is a fact that no connections did emerge between the novelty of Łukasiewicz ideas and von Neumann observations on the features of logic and the analysis of "error". It is only inside the setting of the "agenda" posed by the presence of fuzziness that logical connectives more tuned with von Neumann's ideas emerged and were developed. It remains to be explored in more detail how many other suggestions provided by him can be developed.

Of course all the innovative developments along the years have been possible when taking seriously the problems both from a conceptual point of view and from the one of the adequacy of the technical solutions offered to the innovative aspects of the question asked. It is common experience that it does not suffice to find out uncritical "fuzzifications" of existing classical solutions, or to go on searching purely mathematical developments, however interesting they can be, which do not match conceptual requirements of innovative type.

3   Measuring Fuzziness

The theory of measures of fuzziness (and before the formal developments, the same idea of fuzzy entropy) has strong similarities with some aspects of Shannon's information theory. However the difference among them is not only the one based on probabilistic or non probabilistic concepts. It is the more general, conceptual context provided by the notion of fuzziness, which allows to envisage the fact that other measures can be put beside a fuzzy counterpart of Shannon's measure. We have a host of them: energy (weighted cardinality), specificity measures, dispersion measures as well as many variants of the measures of fuzziness (a variety which cannot be conceived inside Information theory). We have recently shown [6] how Shannon's entropy is not apt to the detection of global properties of an image that are not dependent by simple physical characteristics, such as aesthetics, a task at which fuzzy measures seem much more suited.

Many of these purely formal developments – although technically possible in a standard information-theoretical setting could have been scarcely conceived from a conceptual point of view. It is exactly all this conceptual flexibility that presumably could allow interesting applications of these notions outside classical problems in the engineering of trasmission of information. In the following section we report an example from the field of Aesthetic Theory in which fuzziness is shown to go beyond the acute criticism raised against straightforward applications of Information theory to aesthetic questions.

4   A Practical Example

The concept of unity in variety, a cornerstone of human judgment of beauty, is as old as the human interest in beauty and aesthetic values. George Birkhoff offered a breakthrough proposition in his pioneering 1932 book Aesthetic Measures [7]: for each subdomain of the artistic endeavor, the aesthetic value of an opus, or aesthetic measure, is a direct function of the ratio between its Order and its Complexity. This synthetic and yet comprehensive definition moves the gist of aesthetic evaluation from the original qualitative and subjective stance to the more rigorous problem of finding the parameters O and C which ratio yields the aesthetic measure of any object in the class.

Forty years after Birkhoff, Rudolf Arnheim returns to the topic by discussing the role of order (and disorder) in aesthetics [8]. Arnheim tackles the problem of defining order in contexts as diverse as art, philosophy, psychology, evolution, physics – a field from which he takes the original idea of entropy in order to extend it to the human side of the equation, and expresses a remark that seems mostly connected with the problem of aesthetic computation based on a order/complexity ratio: the idea that entropy defines order simply as an improbable arrangement of elements, regardless of the properties of the global arrangement. The concepts of order and entropy have no sense if they are not viewed in a framework where aesthetic values are not only generated by the components of a determined stimulus, but are also implicit in its global structure: numbers relative to order and complexity alone cannot describe aesthetics.

We think that Birkhoff's approach, incorporating Arnheim's critiques and moved away from the information bounded mindset on which computational esthetic based most of its analysis, may be usefully employed to help measure aesthetic content in a fuzzy framework. Both Shannon and Kolmogorov-Solomonoff measures of complexity and order are not sufficient to describe aesthetics [6], and need to be replaced by a more integrated approach built on specific image operators and fuzzy operators in order to include the intrinsic vagueness of the judgment. At that end we have create a mathematical model of visual complexity based on spatial parameters, local and global features. Global features (in our experiment Fuzzy Entropy) are suitable for deriving single values from the general properties of an image. Local features (we have used Pyramidal DST) are needed to take into account classical verbal explanations for the meaning of complexity. We have applied this process to well composed still life paintings from different periods in art history and derived a high aesthetic index regardless of the different pictorial techniques and skills employed.

5   Conclusions

The ample variety of technical instrument now available, all the different fuzziness measures already employed, an example of which we have shown in the previous section, and the interpretative possibilities hinted in this paper, corroborates the ideas presented here and elsewhere: the concept of fuzziness measures, the apparatus already offered by Fuzzy Sets Theory and a straight-on implementation of the measures based on this concepts and ideas are powerful tools, and their power is essentially derived by the strong originality and novelty shown by the fuzziness concept itself.

As fuzziness sails towards the future, new challenges come from Zadeh's proposals of "Computing with words" and "manipulations of perceptions". This research proposal, and its eventual implementation in term of new fuzziness measures proposes interesting and challenging questions which clash with very solid walls constructed by the classical scientific tradition. The first wall is represented by the so-called Church-Turing thesis. A few recent important efforts have tried to show that even this apparently so different model of computation is equivalent to classical models, and these results would be of the utmost importance, of course. However, we think that Zadeh's approach to the problem suggests that also a different and extremely more difficult road could be followed. One which takes seriously into account the fact that we could be in the presence of a new way of conceiving what a computation is. Something, which – of course – remains only a wishful thinking until we shall be able to define a model of effective procedure without necessarily make reference to the notion of numerical accuracy.

As far as the notion of perception based procedure is concerned, we should just observe that in itself, this proposal goes outside the traditional conceptual mainstream of scientific tradition, giving an unusual central role to the so-called secondary qualities and going nearer to Husserl than to Galileo, while preserving, however, the usual setting of western science.

Here's to the first forty years of fuzziness measure! We really think the best part of this lays ahead, and that in further developing fuzziness measures the fuzzy community is at the forefront of a very difficult enterprise. And of another very big (and great) challenge.

References

1. De Luca, A., Termini, S.: A definition of a nonprobabilistic entropy in the setting of fuzzy sets theory. Information and Control 20(4), 301–312 (1972)
2. Wang, Z., Klir, G.J.: Fuzzy measure theory. Plenum Press (1992)
3. Cardaci, M., Di Gesu, V., Petrou, M., Tabacchi, M.E.: A fuzzy approach to the evaluation of image complexity. Fuzzy Sets Syst. 160(10) (2009)
4. Carmeci, F., Tabacchi, M.E.: La Stima Temporale come Misura della Complessità Percettiva di Combinazioni di Stimoli Visivi-Uditivi. In: Atti del Quarto Convegno Nazionale Dell'Associazione Italiana Scienze Cognitive (2007)
5. Pinna, B., Tabacchi, M.E.: A Fuzzy Approach to the Role of Symmetry in Shape Formation: The Illusion of the Scalene Triangle. In: Di Gesù, V., Pal, S.K., Petrosino, A. (eds.) WILF 2009. LNCS, vol. 5571, pp. 197–204. Springer, Heidelberg (2009)
6. Tabacchi, M.E., Termini, S.: Measures of Fuzziness and Information: some challenges from reflections on aesthetic experience. In: Proceedings of WConSC 2011 (2011)
7. Birkhoff, G.: Aesthetic Measures. Kessinger Publishing Co. (1993)
8. Arnheim, R.: Entropy and Art. University of California Press (1969)

Understanding and Profiling User Requirements to Support the Conceptual Design of an Integrated Land Monitoring System

Maria Franca Norese and Chiara Novello

Politecnico di Torino,
Dipartimento di Ingegneria Gestionale e della Produzione, Turin, Italy
{mariafranca.norese,chiara.novello}@polito.it

Abstract. Acquiring and organizing knowledge and information elements can be essential not only to understand, but also to eliminate, reduce and control complexity and uncertainty. An integration of tools from different disciplines could systematically help in the construction of an agreed framework for problem formulation, above all when the situation is "new". An application was developed in relation to an industrial project, in order to propose profiles of the potential users of an innovative system and of their requirements, and to formally develop models that can orient analysis, decision and action. Some elements and results of this integrated application of "soft" and "hard" decision aid tools are here proposed as steps of an organizational learning cycle, which is a basic element of each innovation process.

Keywords: knowledge acquisition and representation, problem structuring methods, decision support, learning of profiles.

1   Introduction

Working with socio-technical systems, in which technological components are related to the complexity that is generated by individual and organizational actions and processes, can create several methodological problems. When an innovation process develops in a socio-technical system, many of the involved factors are not meaningfully quantifiable, since they are connected to technological, but also social, organizational, political and cognitive dimensions. Everything is connected to everything else and "what might seem to be the most marginal of factors can, under the right circumstances, become a dominating force of change" [1].

These innovation processes are characterized by multiple actors and perspectives, competitive or conflicting interests, constraints and uncertainties that (using the distinction proposed in [2]) can be connected to the working environment, the related decision fields and/or the guiding values. All these elements define what Rosenhead and Mingers [3] called "an unstructured problem".

Acquiring and organizing knowledge and information elements can be essential not only to understand, but also to eliminate, reduce or control complexity and uncertainty. "Traditional quantitative methods, mathematical (functional) modeling and

S. Greco et al. (Eds.): IPMU 2012, Part II, CCIS 298, pp. 68–77, 2012.
© Springer-Verlag Berlin Heidelberg 2012

simulation will simply not suffice in several cases" [1]. Sociological and psychological literature suggests approaches and methodological tools that can be used to identify and cope with complexity and uncertainty. Logical and structured procedures are also proposed in the Operations Research (OR) literature as "soft OR methods or problem structuring methods (PSM)", to facilitate a shared vision of the situation and to decide how complexities and uncertainties have to be controlled and improvement actions to be elaborated, evaluated, validated and implemented. PSM could be improved through an integrated and interdisciplinary approach, see for instance [4], that systematically helps in identifying or constructing an agreed framework for the problem formulation, above all when the situation is "new".

Actor network analysis and representation could be essential in problems that are characterized by multiple actors, perspectives, experiences and competing interests [5]. Actor analysis methods [6-9] can be used to analyze and understand the decision context, where the individual/organizational actors play a role (or multiple roles), and to reduce organizational complexity, but also to capture and represent differing readings of the situation that induce different problem formulations. Cognitive approaches and mapping techniques are proposed in literature (see, for instance, [10-11]) in order to acquire, synthesize, code and communicate all the elements that emerge from the different points of view of the actors who are, or could, be involved in cognitive processes, but also in decision or in innovation processes. Several types of map can be used to depict, structure and face complex issues [12].

An integration of actor analysis methods and cognitive mapping techniques could produce knowledge elements that are useful to clarify cognitive aspects and complete the vision of the situation. The knowledge elements that originate from the cognitive maps could also be used to improve the actor analysis, in order to propose, for example, new involved roles or actors, and related complex issues, that need to be analyzed, or contradictions between the actors' perceptions of some roles. At the same time, the actor network knowledge can facilitate the analysis of the actors' needs, when less clear or contradictory concepts are proposed and have to be analyzed by means of cognitive maps. The effectiveness of each method can be improved through the integration of a "complementary" method. When the main problems that are related to the situation are formulated, concepts and relationships that are structured and synthesized in actor networks and cognitive maps can be transformed into classical OR models (with actions, criteria and parameters, or objectives, variables, constraints and parameters) and OR methods can be applied, in order to elaborate possible solutions and compare them, or to modify the models and identify new aspects and points of view. An industrial research project and its aims are described together with an integrated application of some decision aid tools in the next sections.

2   The Problem Context

An industrial research project, SMAT-F1, was activated in January 2009 as the first phase of a global project for a new Advanced System to Monitor the Territory (hence the SMAT acronym) and it was financed by a public institution, the Piedmont Region.

The project involved several enterprises and some research units from the Politecnico di Torino and the University of Turin, under the leadership of Alenia Aeronautica, a company which is active in the military and civil aeronautical field.

One of the purposes of SMAT-F1 was to identify all the specific innovations that have to be introduced in order to guarantee the civil use of some Unmanned Aerial Vehicles (UAVs) working as an integrated monitoring system. SMAT-F1 was completed at the end of 2011 and the second phase, which is foreseen for the autumn of 2012, will implement innovations in the control station functions, and in some sensors, for specific data acquisition, and communication systems, as well as for data transmission, even in critical situations.

In the first phase of the project, the aim of our research unit was to identify the organisations that could become the clients of a new monitoring service and to analyse their monitoring needs, for the future phases of the SMAT project, in which the innovations have to be designed and implemented.

In aeronautics, where many years are required not only to create a new aircraft, but also to innovate some elements of a legacy system, a clear understanding of the points of view of the potential users of a new system is essential to identify and structure the requirements that orient the design. In this case, the key actors of the current land monitoring processes are some of the potential users of the SMAT technology, and recording and tracking their points of view could be important to understand the situation and also to involve some of them, in the future, in a decisional structure that could facilitate the design of both the innovative system and the new monitoring service. Several decisions in a design process are difficult or almost impossible without focusing attention on alternative ways of managing technical, political or structural uncertainty [2]. The nature of the prevailing uncertainty has to be identified and specific responses have to be developed to deal with it. Responses of a relatively technical nature can involve surveys, research investigations, or costing estimations, when there is a limited knowledge of the problem. Another kind of uncertainty calls for a more political response that might become an exercise in clarifying objectives and political or organizational constraints. There is often uncertainty about the structural relationships between the current decision and others that could be connected. A broader design perspective could be required and new time horizons and new actors should be considered. The points of view of the key actors in the current land monitoring processes should be acquired, and understanding and control of the main uncertainties that are present, in relation to the new technology, are essential. Conflicting objectives, interests, matters of concern or priorities of the key actors, i.e. their value systems, should be clarified and the nature of the operational relationships between the organizations that are involved in land monitoring processes should be investigated. Open interviews, starting from a framework of key questions, can be more useful than a questionnaire to underline and analyse these uncertainty elements and to obtain an idea of what the knowledge elements that have to be acquired and analysed are. The validity of the acquired knowledge (e.g. in terms of reliability, consistency, completeness) also has to be investigated.

At the start of the project, our research unit was requested to dedicate a period of four weeks to collecting as much information as possible about the present land monitoring needs. Due to limited time available, a local agency, the Turin Provincial Authority, was chosen as an organization-laboratory in which all the potential users of a new monitoring system were identified and interviewed. After these four weeks, and after the analysis and presentation of the first results, the time that was dedicated to this task was extended, and the inquiry was thus continued at a regional level, a territorial scale more consistent with the aims of the SMAT project.

Forty-nine potential users were identified and interviewed, in order to collect knowledge elements concerning any possible gaps between their present monitoring activities as well as the actual needs and their points of view in relation to the new system. Starting from the knowledge elements that the survey had proposed, an integrated procedure was activated with the characteristics of a PSM.

Cognitive mapping methods were used to deal with unstructured knowledge elements, in order to enrich the whole picture, to reduce the number of uncertain elements pertaining to the possible role of the innovation and to understand the nature of the new uncertainties the interviewees expressed. An integrated application of actor analysis and cognitive mapping methods allowed us to validate the collected information and to verify the reliability of the sources and their skills. Eventually, the main users and their requirements were identified and modelled, in relation to technological and organization factors that will need to be analyzed in the future design phases of the SMAT project.

3   Integrated Application of Decision Aid Tools

An integrated application of "soft" and "hard" decision aid tools was developed, to deal with the structured, partially structured and unstructured knowledge elements that were acquired during the interviews. Problem situations, that are above all connected to the uncertainties the interviewees expressed were identified, formulated and structured. Model frameworks and parameters were defined in order to facilitate communication, organizational learning and decision making.

The first analysis phase is related to the structured knowledge elements that emerged from the interviews. Their texts were analysed and all the structured knowledge elements (above all the characteristics of the current land monitoring activities, such as costs and required quality, and factors that should characterize the new monitoring activities) were acquired and organized in tables. A clustering approach was then applied to these elements and used to define land monitoring categories (or *macro activities*) and to assign all the expressed needs to these categories. At the same time, a data base, Monitoring activities, was elaborated from the literature and point of view of some experts. It was used to test the completeness of the set of macro activities and the consistency of the clustering approach, in which the proximity of the needs that were expressed during the interviews, in relation to the identified categories, was maximized and the number of the *basic activities* that synthesize similar needs was minimized. The last activity pertaining to the structured knowledge elements consisted of the definition of the main parameters that allow the basic activities to be described.

A second analysis phase, which is described in section 3.1, integrates cognitive mapping and actor analysis techniques. It was developed in relation to partially structured elements (e.g. actors who have been mentioned and indications about their role in the current processes) or unstructured knowledge elements (above all opinions about specific themes) with the aim of structuring all these elements, in order to highlight and visualize the complexity of the monitoring organization and to analyse the nature and structure of the proposed knowledge elements.

Actor networks, cognitive maps and model frameworks were created and used in this first phase of the project in order to reduce, or control, the uncertainty elements. The analysis of an actor network can reduce some of the uncertainties that are evident in a cognitive map. A map, that is, a model of action-orientated thinking, can be used to clarify the relationship between actors or an actor's role, through the understanding of current constraints on the acquisition and the use of data. Constraints, opportunities and preference systems can be used to generate model frameworks. The elaborated knowledge structures were created to activate a learning cycle, and to develop it in the subsequent phase of the SMAT project, where the possible problems can be analysed from different points of view and their (formal) representation could be changed, improved or shared in a decision context where the individual/organizational actors play a consistent role with the (visualized) decision space.

3.1   The Procedure

The organisations that develop monitoring activities (data acquisition, treatment, transfer or use) were considered potential users of SMAT in the industrial project.

A synthetic actor network was defined, as a first analysis step, on the basis of a first interview conduced with one of the directors of the Turin Provincial Authority. Each new interview allowed the actors who are involved in land monitoring processes with different roles to be added to the list of organizations that should be contacted. It was sometimes difficult to identify and understand the working relationships between these actors because the interviews were often not sufficiently clear. The actor network was frequently upgraded and analysed in order to understand how to complete the investigation, but also in order to have a better understanding of the actors' points of view. Many of the actors involved in the monitoring processes, both technicians with specific and various competencies and managers at different levels, were interviewed. They were required to describe the monitoring needs that a new technology could satisfy. They were also asked to describe their current monitoring activities in relation to different topics (agriculture, pollution, transport, waste, cartography, data updating, emergency situations, such as landslides and floods) and the main constraints that today limit some monitoring activities. But they also described the aspects that could positively or negatively affect the adoption of new procedures (expected benefits and perceived risks or criticalities) and doubts and uncertainties about any organizational change and some proposals to reduce these difficulties. Their points of view were sometimes contradictory and often unclear. The knowledge elements that emerged from the interviews sometimes presented interpretative uncertainties and lead to methodological questions.

As a second analysis step, a cognitive mapping approach can reduce these uncertainties. A specific cognitive mapping technique, Representation network, has been proposed in [6] and [13] and used in some different application contexts. The unstructured knowledge elements that emerge from the validated interviews are organized in statements, and then coded, synthesized in concepts, clustered and connected in representation networks or cognitive maps in which the logical relationships between the concepts can be analysed. A statement basically corresponds to a grammatical unit, or a sentence, of the interview and two elements are indicated for each statement: the source and a label in relation to the nature of the sentence (criticisms, proposals, wishes, but also aims, constraints and possible criteria, or specific information elements such as, in this case, actors that are or should be involved, their responsibility and specific relationships with other actors, as well as the nature and structure of the relationships) and/or to the related theme or subject (in this case, the control system, economic dimension, organization of a service), if it is clear enough. With this coding system, the statement that is taken out of a response is transformed into an information cell. All the information cells of the same nature, or which are related to a specific theme, are included in a list, with the original information (name of the proponent source, nature and theme). They are analysed together, in order to synthesize information into concepts (*concept identification*), *create clusters* of concepts pertaining to a theme and identify relationships between the concepts (*arcs of the representation network* with *concepts as nodes*). These networks are analysed in order to reduce interpretative uncertainties and improve knowledge reading and interpretation, to produce a whole vision of the problem components, to improve or complete an actor network or to extract the main elements of a model framework.

The third step is activated by analyzing the results from the actor network analysis and the cognitive mapping approach together. The representation networks in Figs.1a, 1b and 1c are cognitive maps that were developed during the project in relation to the "natural risk assessment, forecast, prevention and management" monitoring context. Each map proposes the different points of view of the interviewees in relation to a specific topic. All the nodes are concepts that were expressed during the interviews by a source who is indicated in brackets. The sources, who represent organizations that are connected to this specific context, are included in the network in Fig. 2. The links between the nodes are the result of a logical analysis of the concepts and their possible relationships and they define the knowledge structure that the involved sources propose. The relationships can be different (cause and effect, specification, exemplification, contradiction and so on). Some links are of an operational nature. They can make the need of new investigation activities explicit or connect a map with another representation network or suggest connections between concepts and possible elements of formal models, such as constraints, judgements, objectives, possible criteria, trade-off or the relative importance of the proposed aspects.

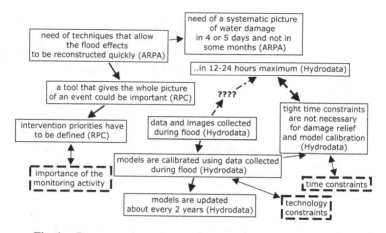

Fig. 1a. Representation network: *Compatibly with the event timing*

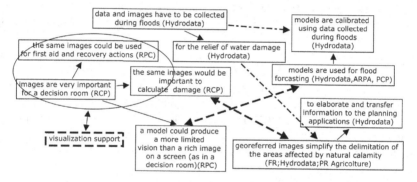

Fig. 1b. Representation network: *Data or Images?*

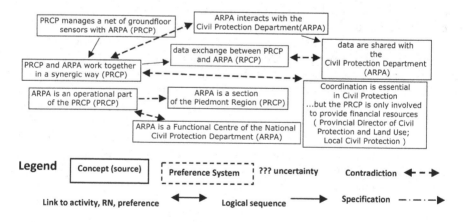

Fig. 1c. Representation network: *Role and Relationships of ARPA and PRCP*

The other relationships facilitate the cognitive analysis and are examined to clarify concepts that are considered too generic or to verify and better explain others that are too confused or to underline uncertainties and apparent contradictions that have to be analyzed in detail and reduced or understood. The map in Fig. 1a is related to the problem Compatibility with the event timing. It includes not only some time constraints, but also an uncertainty element and a possible contradiction between some expressions of these constraints. A contradiction between monitoring flood needs is present, and it is more evident in the representation network in Fig. 1b where the distinction "Data or images?" is not always clear and a possible misunderstanding emerges about the terminology or the actual nature of the need.   The integration of this knowledge structuring with the reliability analysis of the sources, whose roles and relationships are described by means of an actor network, could clarify these contradictions and reduce the uncertainty that has an impact on each attempt to size the demand of a new monitoring system. If also the actor network presents uncertainties, these have to be reduced by improving the analysis with new information.

Uncertainties emerged about two important actors involved in this context, ARPA Piedmont and the Piedmont Region Civil Protection (PRCP), from an analysis of the interviews, and clear contradictions between the concepts that synthesize the descriptions of the different roles and functions can be seen in the map in Fig. 1c (the concepts in the left part of the network are in contradiction with the others in the right part). Therefore, an analysis of the roles and relationships of these actors, and the others who are involved in the "natural risk assessment, forecast, prevention and management" context became crucial and an integration of the actor analysis and cognitive mapping approaches reduced uncertainty and explained some contradictions. The actor network in Fig. 2 includes all the knowledge sources (the interviewees) of this context and the other actors who were mentioned during the interviews as involved in these monitoring processes. All the technologies that were mentioned and described during the interviews (information systems, inventories, models, public registers, communication technologies and so on) are included in the network as *non human actors*, a terminology that was proposed in the Actor Network Theory [11] to define and analyse this kind of actor. Their role is important to understand which monitoring processes are currently activated and which organizations are operationally involved, in order to identify a market for SMAT and its characteristics. The arcs connect technology resources to the actors who are involved as users, developers or responsible organisations, or describe information exchange, the transfer of monetary resources, responsibility or specific actions, such as delegation. Some arcs in Fig. 2 show question marks that propose uncertainties in relation to the contradictions in Fig.1a. In order to limit these uncertainties and have a better understanding of the whole situation, a deeper analysis (with experts and using the Italian Civil Protection web site [14]) was conducted and this led to a new actor structure that clarified the situation.

The different Civil Protection organization levels (national, regional, provincial or local) and the roles of the actors in all the processes were analysed, not only in emergency conditions, but also in the prevision and prevention contexts. ARPA Piedmont (one of the main sources of the cognitive map shown in Fig. 1c and a crucial actor in Fig. 2) is described in the Italian Civil Protection web site as one of the few decentralized functional centres of the national Department of Civil Protection and as a Competence Centre. As far as the official Civil Protection processes are concerned, ARPA Piedmont is not an "operational part of the Regional Civil Protection" in Piedmont but it works closely with the national Department of Civil Protection. With this information, it was possible to understand some other apparent contradictions in the maps.

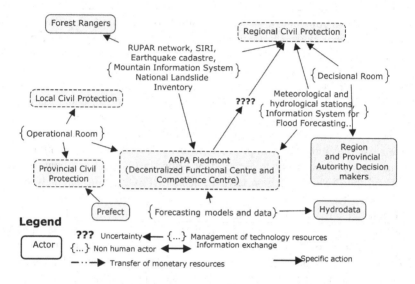

Fig. 2. Actors in the context of prevention, prevision and management of natural risks

4 Conclusive Remarks

"Cycling between modeling approaches gave benefits that could not have been attained by either hard or soft modeling in isolation" [15].

A sufficiently clear idea of some of the central problems in the SMAT project has been obtained through an integrated analysis of concepts and actor networks which identified the main constraints that currently limit several monitoring activities, the aspects that could positively or negatively affect the adoption of new procedures, the benefits that are expected and the main risks that are present in some situations, as well as the spaces of action of some potential users who should be involved as actors in the next phases of the project. Another integration of decision aid tools can be activated to transform concepts and relationships that are structured and synthesized by actor networks and cognitive maps into formal models (with actions and criteria, or objectives, variables and constraints) and to test the applicability of classical OR methods (in particular mathematical programming and multiple criteria decision analysis, as used in [16]), in order to elaborate possible solutions and compare them, also in relation to the end users' points of view.

The concepts of a representation network built in a cognitive mapping process can often be considered as elements of a "multi-actor" preference system that the interviewees have expressed. In a new decision space, with all the key actors of the concept design phase, an integrated analysis of the concepts and structures of the actors could be used to better define the uncertainties, constraints and expectations. These elements are essential to elaborate the components of formal decision aid models (such as structural dimensions and criteria, the importance of an aspect in relation to another one, goals and constraints, risks that cannot be accepted, and so on) and to evaluate and compare design alternatives that can be elaborated through the application of a mathematical programming method or proposed by the actors in the future design process phase. A sequence of "simulated" applications of the OR methods could be implemented, not as a problem solving approach, but to activate a new learning cycle, both at a technical and at an organization level, which could facilitate the conceptual design of an innovation.

References

1. Ritchey, T.: Problem Structuring using computer-aided morphological analysis. J. Oper. Res. Soc. 57, 792–801 (2006)
2. Friend, J.: The strategic choice approach. In: Rosenhead, J. (ed.) Rational Analysis for a Problematic World: Problem Structuring Methods for Complexity, Uncertainty and Conflict, pp. 71–100. Wiley, Chichester (1989)
3. Rosenhead, J., Mingers, J.: Rational Analysis for a Problematic World revisited. Wiley, Chichester (2001)
4. Eden, C., Ackermann, F.: Where next for problem structuring methods? J. Oper. Res. Soc. 57, 766–768 (2006)
5. Norese, M.F.: MACRAME: a problem formulation and model structuring assistant in multiactorial contexts. Eur. J. Oper. Res. 84, 25–34 (1995)
6. Ostanello, A., Tsoukias, A.: An explicative model of public interorganizational interactions. Eur. J. Oper. Res. 70, 67–82 (1993)
7. Bowen, K.: An experiment in Problem Formulation. J. Oper. Res. Soc. 34, 685–694 (1983)
8. Law, J.: Actor network theory and material semiotics. Ind. Law J. 35, 113–139 (2007)
9. Freeman, L.C.: Centrality in social networks: Conceptual clarification. Soc. Networks 1, 215–239 (1979)
10. Eden, C.: On the nature of cognitive maps. J. Manage. Stu. 29, 261–266 (1992)
11. Tegarden, D., Sheetz, S.: Group cognitive mapping: a methodology and system for capturing and evaluating managerial and organizational cognition. Omega 31, 113–125 (2003)
12. Novello, C.: An integrated use of tools to acquire and structure knowledge elements and to support decision in innovation processes. Ph.D Thesis in Production System and Industrial Design. Politecnico di Torino, Turin (2011)
13. Buffa, F., Marzano, G., Norese, M.F.: MACRAME: a modeling methodology in multiactor contexts. Decis. Support Syst. 17, 331–343 (1996)
14. Italian Civil Protection, http://ec.europa.eu/echo/civil_protection/vademecum/it/2-it-1.html
15. Ackermann, F., Eden, C., Williams, T.M.: A persuasive approach to delay and disruption using 'mixed methods'. Interfaces 27, 48–65 (1997)
16. Norese, M.F., Liguigli, E., Novello, C.: Integrated use of linear programming and multiple criteria methods in an engineering design process. In: Carrea, E., Greco, A., Penco, C. (eds.) Proceedings of the Fourth Workshop on Human Centered Processes, Placing Humans at the Center of Knowledge, Production and Interaction Networks, Genoa, pp. 10–16 (2011)

Dynamic Resampling Method for Classification of Sensitive Problems and Uneven Datasets

Marco Vannucci[1], Valentina Colla[1],
Marco Vannocci[1], and Leonardo M. Reyneri[2]

[1] TeCIP-PERCRO, Scuola Superiore Sant'Anna, Pisa, Italy
[2] Politecnico di Torino, Electronic Department, Turin, Italy

Abstract. In binary classification problems, in presence of unbalanced datasets, the detection of rare patterns is a difficult task due to several interacting factors which affect the performance of standard classifiers. In this paper a novel approach to this problem is presented. The described method tries to overcome the criticalities encountered by standard methods and by some systems expressly developed to face this problem by means of a dynamic resampling technique, which suitably resamples the training dataset by means of a feed–forward neural network counterbalancing the natural distribution of the dataset. The proposed method has been tested on literature and industrial datasets: the achieved encouraging results are presented and discussed in the paper.

1 Introduction

Many real world classification problems, coping with the so–called *uneven datasets*, deal with the identification of particular situations which are difficult to detect. Unfortunately, the correct identification of these situations is, in many cases, of utmost importance, such as it happens e.g. in industrial field [1] [2] for fault detection, or in the medical field [3], for diseases diagnosis. In this kind of applications the correct detection of the disease is more important than the correct identification of normal situations. On the other hand, the misclassification of patterns related to frequent situations (the so–called *false alarms*) is strongly preferable than the missed detection of rare ones. In binary classification problems, unbalanced datasets can be defined as those datasets where the rate of records belonging to the rare class (C_R) is far lower with respect to those belonging to the frequent class (C_F). The effect of class imbalance is highly detrimental for the predictive performance of standard classifiers, as they aim at maximizing the overall performance without paying particular attention to the rare, and more important, patterns [4]. Apart from rare cases, where there is a clear spatial distinction among patterns belonging C_R and C_F, the scarce number of samples in C_R prevents their correct characterization and makes the separation of the classes difficult for the any classifier. In facts, in [5] [6], the effect of the use of unbalanced dataset for training standard classifiers has been described, by also underlying that such undesirable effect does not depend upon the adopted classifier. In this paper a novel method for binary classification

S. Greco et al. (Eds.): IPMU 2012, Part II, CCIS 298, pp. 78–87, 2012.
© Springer-Verlag Berlin Heidelberg 2012

problems involving unbalanced datasets is presented, which is based on the dynamic resampling of training data during the learning phase of a standard Neural Network (NN). In Sec.2 common strategies for dealing with classification of unbalanced datasets are presented; in Sec.3 the proposed method is described in detail, the experimental setup is described in Sec.4. The method has been tested on real world and literature datasets and results are shown and compared in Sec.5. Finally in Sec.6 some conclusions are drawn and future perspectives of the proposed approach are discussed.

2   Background on Classification of Unbalanced Datasets

The methods for coping with uneven datasets within classification tasks are usually divided in two categories, namely *external* and *internal* approaches. The internal approaches include all those methods which are expressly designed for facing uneven datasets while the external methods resample the dataset in order to reduce the effect of the data unbalance and exploit standard classifiers. Many literature works deal with classification of unbalanced datasets through **internal methods**; among them it is worth to mention the method based on a variation of radial basis function, the Rectangular basis functions (RecBF) networks [7]. These networks have a special kind of neurons with hyper-rectangular activation functions in the hidden layer, which allow more precision in the detection of the boundary of the input space regions reserved to each class. Support Vector Machines (SVMs) and their evolutions have been tested on classification in imbalanced datasets as well: in [8], for instance, multiple SVMs (one for each class) is proposed, while in [9] a variation of SVM is employed for the identification of rare patterns within datasets. Another variation of SVM, the v-SVM proposed in [10], where it is used for the recognition of single-class patterns, as information on a single class is used for its training. Due to its peculiarity, v-SVM can be exploited to detect whether a pattern belongs to the rare ones. The TANN (Thresholded Artificial NN) method has achieved interesting results in several industrial problems concerning fault detection and product quality assessment [11]. The TANN consists of a traditional NN of the Multi-Layer Perceptron type with one single output neuron coupled with a threshold operator which activates this latter neuron when its natural activation overcomes a threshold τ. The determination of τ is automatic in a way to improve the sensitivity of the system to rare patterns whose detection is supported. A particular class of internal methods is based on the different weighting of misclassification errors [12] and emphasize the cost of the missed detection of rare patterns during the learning phase of the classifier through a suitable cost matrix, which compensates the class imbalance by establishing the misclassification costs according to application and distribution-driven criteria [14]. This approach can be coupled to several standard classification methods such as NNs or decision trees (DTs). For instance, the LASCUS method [13] combines the cost matrix approach to a self-organizing map and a fuzzy inference system obtaining very interesting results.

External methods are based on a focused reduction of the unbalance degree of the original dataset in order to avoid the classification problems encountered by standard methods. Due to its artificial nature, resampling modifies the original classes distribution and may lead to a loss of information; for this reason, in most of the cases, the dataset is not completely rebalanced but the frequency of rare events is suitably improved. This result can be obtained in two ways:

- **under-sampling** reduces the unbalance degree by removing samples belonging to the majority classe(s) until the desired unbalance ratio is reached;
- **over-sampling** replicates the samples representing the minority class that is already present in the original dataset.

Both these approaches show some potential drawbacks: undersampling can subtract interesting information from the dataset; oversampling can add misleading knowledge with detrimental effect, especially when classifying new patterns, not involved in the training phase. Moreover, an optimal unbalance ratio does not exist but is indeed dependent on the particular application and on the features of the original dataset, thus it is often estimated in a heuristic way or by trials. In order to overcome these limitations, some advanced techniques for a *smart* resampling have been developed e.g. in [18] and [4]: in these works under-sampling removes only frequent samples lying close to boundary regions of the input space while over-sampling replicates with higher probability the samples that are located close to the boundary with the majority class. The effect of this operation is the spread of the regions of the input space which is associated to the minority class by the classifier. Another oversampling method is the SMOTE algorithm [19], which synthetically creates new samples which are added to the database instead of replicating existing ones. Synthetic data are created by SMOTE and placed in the input space where they likely could be, in the neighborhood of original minority class samples. A deep review on the performance of external approaches can be found in [15] and in [17], where different methods are compared on several benchmark problems, and in [16], where they are coupled to a SVM ensemble.

3   Dynamic Resampling in Neural Networks Training

We propose an algorithm for creating a classifier for classification problems involving uneven datasets, whose target is not the achievement of the best overall performance in terms of correct classifications but the achievement of an optimal trade-off between the two kinds of misclassification errors, taking into account their different importance and meaning. In particular, the proposed classifier aims at improving mostrly the detection of unfrequent patterns when their identification is fundamental, despite the generation of some false alarms and/or the reduction of the overall classification performance. The proposed algorithm aims at overcoming the criticalities of standard methods through an hybrid internal-external approach mainly based on resampling. Basic resampling techniques suffer from a lack of clear and general strategies for planning a suitable resampling. Both oversampling and undersampling (and their combination) can produce undesirable side effects. Also the SMOTE approach creates new synthetic rare patterns close to existing rare ones but does not consider the presence of patterns belonging to the other classes, therefore eventually raising some conflicts. The basic idea behind the method proposed in this work is to employ a standard Feed–Forward NN (FFNN) as classifier, modifying the classic learning algorithm so as to perform a dynamic resampling of the training data of the NN through the generations. The resampling stage takes place during the training and creates, through the epochs, different undersampled versions of the original dataset. The characteristics of the designed classifier and learning algorithm are described as follows:

Classifier Architecture: a 2-layers FFNN is trained through the Levenberg Marquardt algorithm [20]. The number of hidden neurons depends on the dataset and the particular problem (several configurations are tested). Two output neurons are used, each one representing a class (C_R or C_F): an input pattern is associated to the class represented by the output neuron with higher activation.

Training Algorithm: the adopted algorithm is basically back–propagation with batch learning. The training is modified in order to meet the need of detecting a high number of rare patterns within the dataset. This operation is done by creating a different resampled version of the original training dataset for each epoch (or group of epochs) of the batch learning process. More in detail, the whole training process is planned as a *training campaign* which depicts the training as *blocks of epochs* where, for each block, a new training set is determined. A training campaign C^* is specified by an arbitrary number N of blocks, where each block refers to a sequence of training epochs: $C^* = B_1, B_2, .., B_N$. A training campaign defines a sequence of training sets $Tr_1, Tr_2, \ldots, Tr_N$. The rate of unbalance for each of the so–created training sets is kept constant and arbitrary determined according to the peculiarity of each problem and data distribution. The training campaign is arbitrarily set as well. Each training set Tr_i is formed by all the samples belonging to C_R and a subset of those belonging to C_F. The samples drawn from this latter subset are probabilistically selected in order to meet two different criteria: to favor the selection of previously less selected samples and to use the samples of C_F whose previous selection improved the classification performance of the system. To this second purpose a performance index, updated during the training process, has been associated to each frequent sample D_i. This index averages over the frequent samples the performance measure $m_i \in [0;1]$ that is proposed in [11], which is expressly designed for coping with unbalanced datasets classification tasks and promotes a satisfactory trade-off between detection of rare samples and generated false alarms:

$$m_i = \frac{\gamma UnfDet - FA}{Corr + \mu FA} \qquad (1)$$

where $Corr$ is the rate of overall correct classifications, FA is the false alarms rate and $UnfDet$ is the rate of correctly detected unfrequent samples, γ and μ are two empirically determined paramterer of the formula whose values is 0.7

and 0.3 respectively. Thus the probability of selecting a sample data $D_i \in C_F$, is calculated as follows by combining the two criteria in a balanced way (different combination weights have been tested but 0.5 is globally the best performing one) :

$$p_i = 0.5 \cdot \frac{N - S_i}{\sum_{j=1}^{N} N - S_j} + 0.5 \cdot m_i \qquad (2)$$

where S_i is the number of times the sample has been selected. The initial selection probability (adopted within block B_1) is uniform for each sample. This process affects the update of the NN weighs. In a batch training framework, the weights of the connections between neurons are updated at the end of each epoch aiming at reducing classification error on the employed dataset; when dealing with unbalanced datasets, the higher number of frequent samples supports the modifications of such weights toward the C_F class output. This effect is not achieved with the proposed algorithm as, at the end of each epoch, the weight update will reflect the classification performance of a *balanced* dataset.

This approach overcomes the criticalities of standard resampling methods since no undersampling is performed and, by consequence, no samples belonging to the C_F are deleted from the training dataset, thus there is no loss of information about the regions of the input space where data of F_C are located; furthermore, the criterion for the selection of frequent data to be included in the training set reduces the probability that some samples of F_C are never selected. On the other hand, no synthetic data are created, limiting the occurrence of conflicts in the areas of the input space.

4   Experimental Setup

The proposed approach has been tested on 4 binary classification problems where the databases are characterized by classes unbalance and the detection of rare events is of utmost importance: the first database belongs to the UCI database repository, the other ones come from the industrial world.

Wisconsin Breast Cancer DataBase (WBCDB). This database, extracted from the UCI repository, is very used for testing the efficiency of machine learning algorithms. It collects information on the analysis of biopsies conducted on patients suspected of breast cancer. The observations consist of 9 numerical features and of the classification of the tumor type, i.e. benign or malignant. The dataset is formed by 699 observations: 458 (65.5%) of them correspond to benign tumors, the remaining 241 (34.5%) to malignant ones. The importance of the detection of malignant tumors is straightforward.

Nozzle Occlusion in Steel Casting (NOST). This application concerns the detection of nozzle occlusion during the continuous casting of liquid steel. This phenomenon, called *clogging*, depends on the steel chemical composition and on the varying casting conditions. A classifier for clogging forecast is designed based on a dataset of 3800 records collecting information on process parameters and steel composition (6 variables). The rate of clogging-related observations is 1% and clogging detection is of utmost importance.

Metal Sheets Quality Control (MSQC). Within the manufacture of metal sheets, some surface controls are performed by means of a vision system to assess the product quality. A classification system exploiting the information extrapolated from the images provided by the vision system is designed to decide whether a product is marketable or not. The available database contains 1900 samples, 25% of which correspond to products classified as not-marketable; each observation includes 10 variables. The missed detection of a defective product is highly undesirable as it corresponds to the release on the market of a product which is not suitable to customer's requirements.

Surface Cleaning Monitoring System (SCMS). This problem is related to the monitoring of a process for the removal of surface defects from metal sheets by means of the use of a cleaning chemical solution which is applied on the product surface. If process parameters are not kept within safe ranges, the process does not work properly and the product is not suitable for the market. The detection of the defective products (about 0.3% of the total production) on the basis of process parameters is fundamental but difficult given the very small number of processes that led to the formation of defects.

The above-described datasets present different levels of unbalance and cover a wide range of real-world situations. The performance of the dynamic resampling approach achieved on the classification tasks has been compared to those of a set of different resampling approaches, in order to put into evidence the characteristics of the proposed algorithm. This set includes the standard FFNN, classic oversampling and undersampling methods and the SMOTE algorithm exploiting a NN as classifier. The use of the NN as a base classifier, combined with different resampling techniques, allows the characterization of the effect of the proposed method. These resampling techniques have been combined with the use of the creation of resampled datasets with different unbalance degree and to the use of asymmetric misclassification cost errors. Within the evaluation process, for each approach 100 tests have been performed, each one involving different training and validation databases, and the average results are presented.

5   Results

A table depicts the performance of various setup of the tested algorithm on each problem. Each table reports information on a representative subset of all the performed tests including the best performing ones. For each problem different setups of the method have been tested, varying the followingparameters: hidden units of the NN, unbalance rate, training epochs, cost matrix (when available). The information on the algorithm configuration include: training epochs (Ep), training campaign ($TR\ camp$), number of hidden units in the used NN (Hid), misclassification cost of rare patterns (with respect to frequent ones) (MW), unbalance rate ($Unb.\ rate$). The performance is expressed in terms of: overall correct classifications ($Corr$), rate of detection of unfrequent patterns ($Unf.$

Det) and false alarms (*FA*). . Tables 1, 2, 3 and 4 report the results on WBCDB,
NOST, MSQC, SCMS problems. On the WBCDB (see Tab.1) all the tested
methods perform generally well but, considering the sensitiveness of the problem, the achievement of even better performances in terms of malignant cancers
detected is extremely important. Thus the application of resampling techniques
to the original dataset leads to a performance improvement by using the standard over/under-sampling methods, i.e. the SMOTE and the dynamic resampling. The best results in this sense are achieved by the dynamic resampling,
which rises the rate of rare patterns detected to 99% and, in general, detects
more than 97% of them.

Table 1. Summary of results obtained on the WBCDB

Method	Ep.	TR camp.	Hid	MW	Unb. rate	Corr. (%)	Unf. Det (%)	FA (%)
FFNN	120	Na.	7	1	Na.	96	94	2
FFNN + Overs.	120	Na.	7	1	50%	96	96	3
FFNN + Overs.	120	Na.	7	1.2	50%	96	97	3
FFNN + Unders.	120	Na.	7	1	50%	96	96	3
FFNN + SMOTE	120	Na.	7	1	50%	96	96	3
Dynamic res.	120	60 x 2 Ep.	7	1	50%	96	99	1
Dynamic res.	120	30 x 4 Ep.	7	1	50%	96	98	2
Dynamic res.	120	60 x 2 Ep.	7	1.2	50%	96	97	3
Dynamic res.	120	60 x 2 Ep.	7	2	40%	96	97	3

Table 2. Results obtained on the nozzle occlusion detection problem

Method	Ep.	TR camp.	Hid	MW	Unb. rate	Corr. (%)	Unf. Det (%)	FA (%)
FFNN	100	Na.	6	1	Na.	99	3	0
FFNN + Overs.	100	Na.	8	1	25%	92	41	7
FFNN + Overs.	100	Na.	8	1.5	25%	90	40	9
FFNN + Unders.	100	Na.	6	1	25%	88	45	11
FFNN + Unders.	100	Na.	6	1.5	25%	83	55	16
FFNN + SMOTE	100	Na.	6	1	50%	86	53	13
FFNN + SMOTE	100	Na.	8	2	33%	76	67	24
Dynamic res.	100	20 x 5 Ep.	6	1	50%	77	67	22
Dynamic res.	60	30 x 2 Ep.	6	1	33%	88	56	12
Dynamic res.	100	20 x 5 Ep.	6	1.5	33%	83	61	15
Dynamic res.	80	10 x 8 Ep.	6	1	50%	74	72	26
Dynamic res.	80	10 x 8 Ep.	6	2	33%	79	65	21
Dynamic res.	100	20 x 5 Ep.	5	1	40%	82	65	18
Dynamic res.	100	20 x 5 Ep.	5	3	17%	85	62	14

As far as NOST is concerned, Tab.2 shows the efficiency of resampling techniques with respect to plain classifiers. The resampling based methods in facts,

drastically improve the rate of detected rare samples (67%), which are almost neglected by the standard FFNN approach (3%). It is particularly noticeable the performance of resampling methods combined with Asymmetric Cost Matrix (ACM). The SMOTE-based approach further raises the rate of unfrequented patterns detected but generates a high rate of FA. The overall performance of dynamic resampling are slightly better than those achieved by the other approaches: 65% of rare samples are correctly detected with an acceptable rate of false alarms. The MSQC problem is characterized by a not extreme rate of unbalance and thus the performance of standard classifier (see tab.3) with this problem are acceptable, with the detection of more than 60% of defective products. Nevertheless this application benefits from the use of specific techniques for the detection of rare patterns. The use of oversampling, undersampling and of the SMOTE algorithm raises the rate of defective products recognition to 70% (with a low FA rate) and, when combined with the ACM techniques, to 75%. In this case the use of the dynamic resampling technique leads to excellent results: the rate of recognition of defective sheets is raised to more than 70% for all the tested configurations and to 75% in the best case. In all these cases, considering the nature of the application, the rate of false alarms is satisfactory.

Table 3. Results obtained on the MSQC problem

Method	Ep.	TR camp.	Hid	MW	Unb. rate	Corr. (%)	Unf. Det (%)	FA (%)
FFNN	90	Na.	10	1	Na.	90	64	2
FFNN + Overs.	90	Na.	10	1	50%	88	70	4
FFNN + Overs.	90	Na.	8	3	25%	83	75	15
FFNN + Unders.	90	Na.	10	1	50%	89	69	4
FFNN + SMOTE	90	Na.	10	1	50%	89	68	4
FFNN + SMOTE	90	Na.	10	1	40%	87	72	7
Dynamic res.	90	30 x 3 Ep.	10	1	50%	88	71	3
Dynamic res.	90	10 x 9 Ep.	10	1	50%	88	70	5
Dynamic res.	90	10 x 9 Ep.	10	1.5	50%	86	74	9
Dynamic res.	90	6 x 15 Ep.	10	1.5	50%	85	73	9
Dynamic res.	90	30 x 3 Ep.	10	1.5	50%	85	73	8
Dynamic res.	100	20 x 5 Ep.	15	3	25%	89	75	5

The SCMS problem is characterized by a particularly unbalanced distribution of the target classes (0.3%). This unbalance heavily affects the performance of any classifier. According to Tab.4, the standard approach leads to complete neglection of rare patterns and the use of simple resampling technique slightly improves this performance. The combination of oversampling and ACM sensibly improves the classifier performance, which is comparable to the results obtained through SMOTE: Finally the use of the dynamic resampling by itself raises to satisfactory levels the rate of rare patterns detected but generates a high FA rate. Also in this case the use of this new approach combined with the ACM provides the best overall performance, with the highest rate of critical situations detected and a relatively low FA rate.

Table 4. Results obtained on the surface cleaning of steel monitoring system problem

Method	Ep.	TR camp.	Hid	MW	Unb. rate	Corr. (%)	Unf. Det (%)	FA (%)
FFNN	100	Na.	8	1	Na.	100	0	0
FFNN + Overs.	100	Na.	8	1	10%	98	9	1
FFNN + Overs.	100	Na.	8	4	20%	86	40	14
FFNN + Unders.	100	Na.	4	1	10%	98	4	1
FFNN + SMOTE	100	Na.	8	1	50%	79	52	21
FFNN + SMOTE	100	Na.	5	4	20%	82	52	18
Dynamic res.	90	30 x 3 Ep.	5	1	50%	67	62	33
Dynamic res.	60	30 x 2 Ep.	8	3	17%	84	44	16
Dynamic res.	90	30 x 3 Ep.	7	3	25%	78	60	22
Dynamic res.	90	30 x 3 Ep.	3	1.5	50%	62	71	38
Dynamic res.	60	6 x 10 Ep.	8	3.5	17%	83	54	17
Dynamic res.	90	30 x 3 Ep.	8	4	20%	77	59	23

6   Conclusions and Future Work

A novel method for facing binary classification problems in presence of uneven datasets has been described, which aims at overcoming the criticalities encountered by standard methods by modifying the training algorithm of a NN-based classifier: the training dataset is dynamically resampled through the epochs of the learning process in a *training campaign*, in accordance to the classifier performance and to suitably counterbalance the natural unbalance of the dataset. This method has been tested on several literature and industrial problems, which are characterized by different unbalance rates and by different needs. The performance of the dynamic resampling is encouraging as, within all the proposed problems, this approach improves the classification performance with respect to the standard approach and to other resampling techniques. Particularly good results are achieved, in some cases, combining this new technique to the use of ACM. Although the adoption of the method clearly improves the classifier performance, at the moment no general guideline can be extracted for the creation of an optimal training campaign, for the suitable combination of the method to the use of the ACM or for the exploitation of a particular unbalance rate. These aspects seems rather intrinsically related to the particular applications. In the future the idea at the basis of the dynamic resampling will be exploited with other classifiers, e.g. DTs or SVMs. The possibility of using some meta-heuristics for the creation of optimal training campaigns will be investigated.

References

1. Butler, K.L., Momoh, J.A.: A neural net based approach for fault diagnosis in distribution networks. In: Power Engineering Society Winter Meeting, vol. 2, pp. 1275–1278. IEEE (2000)

2. Shreekant, G., Bin, Y., Meckl, P.: Fault detection for nonlinear systems in presence of input unmodeled dynamics. In: 2007 IEEE/ASME International Conference on Advanced Intelligent Mechatronics, September 4-7, pp. 1–5 (2007)

3. Stepenosky, N., Polikar, R., Kounios, J., Clark, C.: Ensemble Techniques with Weighted Combination Rules for Early Diagnosis of Alzheimer's Disease. In: International Joint Conference on Neural Networks, IJCNN 2006 (2006)

4. Estabrooks, A.: A combination scheme for inductive learning from imbalanced datasets. MSC thesis. Faculty of computer science, Dalhouise university (2000)

5. Estabrooks, A., Japkowicz, N.: A multiple resampling method for learning from imbalanced dataset. Computational Intelligence 20(1) (2004)

6. Japkowicz, N.: The class imbalance problem: significance and strategies. In: Proceedings of the 2000 Intl. Conference on Artificial Intelligence (IC-AI 2000): Special Track on Inductive Learning, Las Vegas, Nevada (2000)

7. Soler, V., Prim, M.: Rectangular Basis Functions Applied to Imbalanced Datasets. In: de Sá, J.M., Alexandre, L.A., Duch, W., Mandic, D.P. (eds.) ICANN 2007. LNCS, vol. 4668, pp. 511–519. Springer, Heidelberg (2007)

8. Li, P., Chan, K.L., Fang, W.: Hybrid Kernel Machine Ensemble for Imbalanced Data Sets. In: 18th International Conference on Pattern Recognition. IEEE (2006)

9. Akbani, R., Kwek, S., Japkowicz, N.: Applying Support Vector Machines to Imbalanced Datasets. In: Boulicaut, J.-F., Esposito, F., Giannotti, F., Pedreschi, D. (eds.) ECML 2004. LNCS (LNAI), vol. 3201, pp. 39–50. Springer, Heidelberg (2004)

10. Scholkopf, B.: New support vector algorithms. Neural Computation 12, 1207–1245 (2000)

11. Vannucci, M., Colla, V., Sgarbi, M., Toscanelli, O.: Thresholded Neural Networks for Sensitive Industrial Classification Tasks. In: Cabestany, J., Sandoval, F., Prieto, A., Corchado, J.M. (eds.) IWANN 2009, Part I. LNCS, vol. 5517, pp. 1320–1327. Springer, Heidelberg (2009)

12. Pazzani, M., Marz, C., Murphy, P., Ali, K., Hume, T., Brunk, C.: Reducing misclassification cost. In: Proc. of the 11th Intl. Conf. on Machine Learning (1994)

13. Vannucci, M., Colla, V.: Novel classification methods for sensitive problems and uneven datasets based on neural networks and fuzzy logic. Applied Soft Computing 11, 2383–2390 (2011)

14. Elkan, C.: The foundations of cost–sensitive learning. In: Proc. of 17th Intl. Joint Conference on Artificial Intelligence, IJCAI 2001 (2001)

15. Estabrooks, A., Jo, T., Japkowicz, N.: A multiple resampling method for learning from imbalanced data sets. Computational Intelligence 20(1) (2004)

16. Liu, Y., An, A., Huang, X.: Boosting Prediction Accuracy on Imbalanced Datasets with SVM Ensembles. In: Ng, W.-K., Kitsuregawa, M., Li, J., Chang, K. (eds.) PAKDD 2006. LNCS (LNAI), vol. 3918, pp. 107–118. Springer, Heidelberg (2006)

17. Guo, H., Viktor, H.L.: Learning from imbalanced datasets with boosting and data generation: the databoost approach. SIGKDD Explorations 6 (2004)

18. Chawla, N.V.: C4.5 and imbalanced data sets: investigating the effect of sampling method, probabilistic estimate, and decision tree structure. In: Workshop on Learning from Imbalanced Dataset II, ICML, Washington, DC (2003)

19. Chawla, N.V., Bowyer, K.W., Hall, L.O., Kegelmeyer, W.P.: SMOTE: synthetic minority over-sampling technique. Journal of Artificial Intelligence Research 16, 321–357 (2002)

20. Marquardt, D.W.: An algorithm for least square estimation of non linear parameters. SIAM Journal of Applied Mathematics 11, 164–168

Handling Uncertain User Preferences in a Context-Aware System

Roberto Confalonieri[1], Hasier Iñan[2], and Manel Palau[2]

[1] Institut de Recherche en Informatique Toulouse (IRIT)
Universitè Paul Sabatier
118 Route de Narbonne
31062 Toulouse Cedex 9, France
roberto.confalonieri@irit.fr
[2] Tech Media Telecom Factory S.L. (TMT Factory)
Avda Diagonal 534, 6-2
E - 08006 Barcelona, Spain
{hasier.inan,manel.palau}@tmtfactory.com

Abstract. In context-aware systems, the representation of user profiles can greatly enhance the users' experience. User profiles often requires a compact and, at the same time, expressive language in order to represent conditional preferences, preference relations over the items they contain, and uncertainty labels. This paper presents the use of a possibilistic logic programming framework in a context-aware system to handle user profiles. The framework is able to capture and to process context-dependent preferences and qualitative uncertainty labels which are used to determine which set of preferences should be considered in a given context. Uncertainty labels are used both to select the most plausible preferences for content selection and to keep user profiles up-to-date.

1 Introduction

The appearance of ubiquitous systems such as smartphones and tablets has made it possible to convey information from different sources and to make it accessible to (almost) everyone at any time. One distinctive category of ubiquitous systems are the so-called context-aware systems [2]. A new trend on context-aware systems are Interactive Community Displays (ICDs) [7,19].

ICDs are multimedia information points that offer interactive services on the public thoroughfare in order to provide information to people living in or visiting a city. Some examples of ICDs are the *i-kiosks*[1] and *i+*[2] (respectively located in Aberdeen and Bristol). More recently, many other initiatives have been deployed in commercial malls and other public spaces such as *Punts BCN*, a Barcelona city council initiative to offer information public services.

However, current ICDs are often isolated or designed with predefined static sources and they do not actually exploit the benefits offered by the *Internet*

---

[1] http://www.aberdeencity.gov.uk/regeneration/ikiosk/reg_ikiosks.asp
[2] http://www.bristollegiblecity.info/projects/21/21.html

S. Greco et al. (Eds.): IPMU 2012, Part II, CCIS 298, pp. 88–97, 2012.
© Springer-Verlag Berlin Heidelberg 2012

of Things. Moreover, they usually do not distinguish users as individuals and they provide similar information to users who typically have different tastes and desires. As such, these systems are not capable of providing personalised content and of satisfying users who are looking for the most appropriate suggestions according to their *preferences* in a specific *context*.

A concrete way to achieve an effective personalisation is by means of *user profiles* [1]. Although user profiles represent a common practice to model users' preferences, they intrinsically bring several issues. First, preferences in an ICD depend on contextual information such as the kind of *petition*, the *time*, the *weather* and the *location* of users. Secondly, preferences can depend on incomplete information, that is, normally, one can have some preferences unless some exceptional conditions are met. Finally, user profiles often requires a compact and, at the same time, expressive language. These issues suggest that an enhancement of actual ICDs with a preference handling method can be valuable.

Preference handling is a rather new research topic in Artificial Intelligence (AI) [12,17]. Several specifications have been proposed for modeling user preferences such as Qualitative Choice Logic (QCL) [5], Conditional Preference Networks (CP-nets) [4], and Logic Programs with Ordered Disjunction (LPODs) [6]. Among them, LPODs is a logic programming framework that supports the specification of qualitative conditional preference statements and of preference relations by means of an ordered disjunction logical connective $\times$ (originally proposed in QCL). In this way, LPODs can be employed to represent and to process user profiles composed of preference rules such as: *normally, at lunch, I prefer to eat Italian food rather than tapas unless time is between 15 and 17* (encoded as *italian* $\times$ *tapas* $\leftarrow$ *lunch, not* $15-17h$).

Nevertheless, in real scenarios, preferences can be dynamic, that is, they can change over the time, and, in a given context, some preferences can be more certain than others, that is, they can have different certainty degrees [10]. Modeling uncertain information requires a qualitative representation. Indeed, when we refer to uncertain information, we commonly use statements such as "*I think that ...*", "*chances are ...* ", "*it is probable that ...* ", "*it is plausible that ...*" [20]. Moreover, numerical information is not always available for capturing certainty degrees of a statement and uncertainty is more qualitative in nature [15]. As such, a way to measure preference uncertainty in a qualitative way is another issue to be considered.

To this end, in [10], a possibilistic extension of LPODs was proposed which allows to associate preference rules with qualitative certainty labels. The framework, called Logic Programs with Possibilistic Ordered Disjunction (LPPODs), is able to represent and to reason about context-dependent preferences and to deal with certainty labels such as *fully-certain*, *quasi-certain*, *almost-certain*, *etc.* As a result, the LPPODs framework is able to represent uncertain context-dependent preferences rules such as: *I am fully certain that, at lunch, I prefer to eat Italian food rather than tapas* (encoded as **fully** $-$ **certain** : *italian* $\times$ *tapas* $\leftarrow$ *lunch*).[3]

---

[3] The LPPODs framework is presented in Section 4.2.

In this paper, we present the integration effort which brings the preference representation capabilities of LPPODs into an ICD in order to enhance its personalisation capabilities and to deal with users' preferences associated with certainty labels. We show how a logic programming-based preference handling method has been used to support a user profile adaptation process which allows the system to model and to keep user profiles up-to-date. In order to integrate the LPPODs framework into the system, a preference and profile ontology have been defined. The ontology is a means to bridge the gap between the well-structured data representation used by the system and the symbolic representation used by the LPPODs framework. A system prototype has been developed on the basis of the LPPODs framework. A video showing the main features of the prototype is accessible at http://research.tmtfactory.com/index.php/tmtresearch/projects/49/.

The rest of the paper is organised as follows. After providing a brief description of the use case considered (Section 2), in Section 3, we outline the user profile adaptation process we built upon the LPPODs framework. In Section 4, we present the preference and profile ontology and we describe how LPPODs is used to represent and to process uncertain context-dependent preferences. Section 5 discusses some related work in the literature. Finally, Section 6 concludes the paper.

2   Use Case

To exemplify our system, we will consider a typical ICD usage scenario. The scenario starts when a user interacts with the system's interface (the ICD). Initial interactions are processed in order either to load the corresponding user profile filled with user preferences provided by a registered user, or to assist a new user with the creation of an initial profile. New profiles are created by means of a drag-and-drop user interface which assist the user with the specification of an initial order between preferences. At the beginning, preferences are assumed to be fully certain. Then, the system presents a selection menu composed by several activity categories, such as cinemas, restaurants, and night venues. When the user asks for suggestions related to one of these activities, the system reasons about the most appropriate user preferences for that specific context, *i.e., petition, time, weather* and *location*. Since context-dependent preferences related to different activities can have different certainty degrees, information about available venues can be filtered using the most certain preferences. Once suggestions are provided, the user expresses some feedback by evaluating the suggestions. This feedback is processed by the system and the corresponding preferences are updated or new context-aware preferences are added. In the former case, for instance, a negative feedback in a recommendation about a restaurant venue for lunch, triggers a lowering of the certainty labels associated with the corresponding preference in the profile. When a certainty label reaches the minimum level, such preference becomes obsolete.

To address the above use case, and, generally speaking, to handle the user profiles created and maintained by the ICD, a multi-stage user profile adaptation process has been implemented.

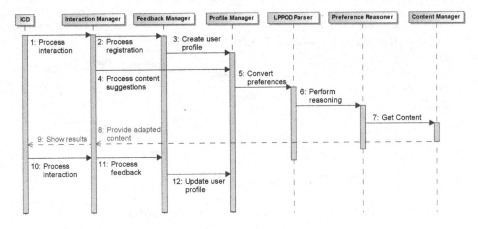

Fig. 1. User Profile Adaptation Process

3 User Profile Adaptation Process

An overview of the user profile adaptation process is shown in Figure 1. Different components are responsible to provide personalised content and to keep users' profiles up-to-date. The *Profile Manager* deals with the representation of user preferences. At the beginning, the creation of an initial user profile is assisted by the ICD's user interface. The profile is stored according to a *profile ontology* which contains a list of contextual preference relations. This abstract user profile representation is converted into the format of the *Preference Reasoner*, that is, the LPPODs syntax. This module collects the current context and reasons about uncertain context-aware preference rules. The result of the reasoner is an ordered list of preference items (associated with certainty degrees). These preferences are processed by the *Content Manager* which is in charge of querying the appropriate content to be provided. Finally, once the suggestions are provided, the user expresses some feedback. This feedback is processed by the *Feedback Manager* which, by interacting with the Profile Manager, updates the user profile.

4 Handling Uncertain Context-Dependent Preferences

In order to represent and process uncertain context-dependent preferences, we have used the logic programming framework of LPPODs [10]. The LPPODs framework supports (i) the creation and adaptation of user profiles by means of context-dependent preferences rules and necessity measures and (ii) the achievement of an order among the outcome of the encoded (user) preference model.

Since LPPODs admits text data, whereas the application works with well-structured data, we have specified a *user preference* and *profile ontology* upon which particular instances of user profiles can be created. This ontological representation allows to bridge the gap between the system and the LPPODs symbolic representation.

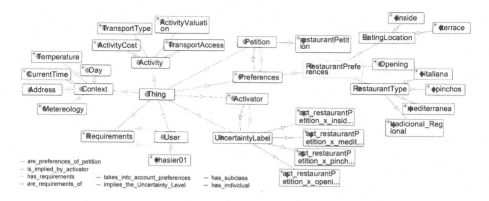

Fig. 2. Ontology overview including some instances

4.1   User Profile and Preference Ontology

User profiles are modeled according to an ontology which captures the relation between contexts and preferences by using the concept of a *possibilistic prefer-ence rule* (see Section 4.2). The *user profile* and *preference ontology* is shown in Figure 2, along with some individuals used in such classes and various rela-tions among users, their petitions and preferences. In order to keep preferences independent from the context, each preference rule is modeled involving several ontological concepts (see Figure 3) that contains a set of *Preferences* and an *Activator*. The set of rule's preferences is composed by several user preferences for a specific domain, and the activator of a rule is built by a *Context* and a *Peti-tion*. The *UncertaintyLabel* links *Preferences*, *Activity* (*i.e.*, preferences without domain) and *Activator*. It supports the representation of preferences in different contexts and domains and of certainty labels among preferences. This represen-tation abstractly represents context-aware preference rules which, at run-time, are converted into the symbolic representation of LPPODs.

4.2   Uncertain Preference Representation and Reasoning

At the symbolic level, user profiles are mapped into the syntax of LPPODs. LPPODs is a recently defined possibilistic logic programming framework able to represent and reason about uncertain context-dependent preferences [10].

An LPPOD is a logic program composed of a finite set of *possibilistic ordered disjunction rules* (preference rules for short) of the form:

$$\alpha : p_1 \times \ldots \times p_k \leftarrow c_1, \ldots, c_m, \; not \; c_{m+1}, \ldots, \; not \; c_{m+n} \qquad (1)$$

in which p_i's ($1 \leq i \leq k$) are preference literals, each c_j ($1 \leq j \leq m + n$) is a context literal and $\alpha \in \mathcal{S}$, where $\mathcal{S}$ is a finite linearly ordered scale made of $n + 1$ levels, *i.e.*, $\alpha_0 = \boldsymbol{impossible} < \alpha_1 < \ldots < \alpha_n = \boldsymbol{fully - certain}$. Each α_i denotes a qualitative label (a necessity measure according to possibilis-tic logic [13]) which measures the level of certainty of a preference rule. The

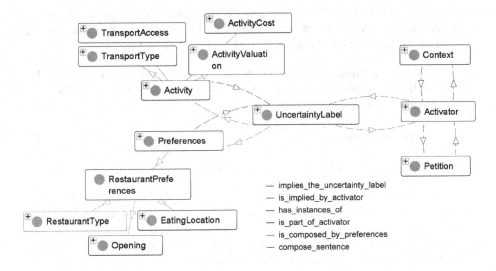

Fig. 3. The modeling of a preference rule

intuitive reading of an ordered disjunction rule is: *If possible, I prefer p_1, if p_1 is not possible, then p_2*, and so on. The certainty label α, by estimating the level of certainty of the rule, measures the importance of the rule, and, consequently of the preferences contained in the rule. For convention, we map the *head* of a rule, $p_1 \times \ldots \times p_k$, to an ordered disjunction of preferences related to the activities defined in the preference ontology. We map the *body* of a rule, $c_1, \ldots, c_m, not\ c_{m+1}, \ldots, not\ c_{m+n}$, to the context information needed to activate the rule. In such a way, we are able to represent that, in a given context, a user has an ordered set preferences with certainty α. We are also able to capture incomplete knowledge by means of negation as failure *not*.

The satisfaction of each rule depends on the presence of contextual information, *i.e.*, only the preferences of satisfied rules are taken into account in the reasoning process. As such, only those preferences - the user is contextually interested in - will appear as solutions of the program (in accordance to the LPPODs semantics definition [10]).

One of the distinctive characteristics of LPPODs is the possibility to specify an order among its solutions. The order among preferences depends on the position of the best satisfied preference literals and it is defined by a Pareto-based comparison criterion (see [10] for more details).

To exemplify the use of LPPODs in the modeling of user profiles, let us consider the following (simple) example.

Example 1. Let us imagine to have a user profile with the following preferences about restaurants: (i) *we are fully certain that she prefers to eat in an Italian restaurant over having "tapas" if time is not between 15 and 17*, otherwise (ii) *we are fully certain that she prefers tapas over italian food if time is between 15 and 17*. Then, (iii) *we are almost certain that she prefers to pay by Master Card over using her Visa* while (iv) *we are quasi certain that she prefers a restaurant accessible by metro line L1 rather than line L3.* This simple user profile can be encoded by means of the following LPPOD:

$$
\left\{
\begin{array}{llll}
r_1 = & \textbf{fully} - \textbf{certain} : & italian \times tapas & \leftarrow restaurant, not\ 15 - 17h. \\
r_2 = & \textbf{fully} - \textbf{certain} : & tapas \times italian & \leftarrow\ restaurant, 15 - 17h. \\
r_3 = & \textbf{almost} - \textbf{certain} : & masterCard \times visa \leftarrow & \top. \\
r_4 = & \textbf{quasi} - \textbf{certain} : & L1 \times L3 & \leftarrow \quad \top. \\
r_5 = & \textbf{fully} - \textbf{certain} : & restaurant & \leftarrow \quad \top.
\end{array}
\right\}
$$

with $\mathcal{S} = \{impossible < almost - certain < quasi - certain < fully - certain\}$.

Once user preferences have been modeled, the LPPODs semantics specifies a formal way to obtain the solutions of an LPPOD, that is, its possibilistic answer sets and to order them. The LPPODs semantics is computable and it has been implemented in the logic programming solver *posPsmodels* [11] (available at `http://github.com/rconfalonieri/posPsmodels/tarball/master`).

Returning to the example, the solver returns several possibilistic answer sets which represent all preference combinations (8), in which $\{(restaurant, fully - certain), (L1, quasi - certain), (masterCard, almost - certain), (italian, fully - certain)\}$ is the most preferred possibilistic answer set and $\{(restaurant, fully - certain), (tapas, fully - certain), (visa, almost - certain), (L3, quasi - certain)\}$ is the less preferred one. The labels associated with each preference allow the system to give priority to the most certain preferences when looking for suggestions and to update user profiles by means of the user feedback.

4.3   Content Filtering and Feedback

The retrieval of personalised suggestions for the user is left to the *Content Manager*. This modules is responsible to build preference queries and to map these queries into XPath expressions (the available information is XML-based). Concerning the preference queries, the generation works as follows. For each possibilistic answer set returned by the LPPODs solver, the Content Manager maps preference and context literals into query conditions. For instance, for the most preferred set in the previous example, that is, $\{(restaurant, fully - certain), (L1, quasi - certain), (masterCard, almost - certain), (italian, fully - certain)\}$, the generated query asks for a restaurant which offers *Italian* cuisine, is reachable by metro line *L1*, and accepts *Master Card*. Such restaurant may not exist. Therefore, certainty labels associated with preference literals are used to take into account only preferences with higher certainty. Hence, in our example, a bit less satisfactory result would be a restaurant which offers *Italian* food and it is reachable by metro line *L1*. In other words, the query can be relaxed by dropping less certain preferences. In our example, the preference about the payment method (*Master Card*) would be dropped from the query. In case that no items can be found, the query generation and execution is applied to less preferred possibilistic answer sets in a similar way.

Once the suggestions have been retrieved, they are visualised on an interactive city map. From this interface, the user can express his/her feedback about the results obtained. The feedback is processed by the Feedback Manager.

The *Feedback Manager* is responsible for adapting and updating user profiles by processing user interactions and valuations on provided suggestions. The valuation process follows two modes: (i) an explicit valuation by means of an explicit rating of the user on each suggestion; (ii) an implicit valuation by considering user's selections on provided suggestions as positive feedback.

Once the valuation is performed, the Feedback Manager receives a list of rankings for each preference rated. The module interacts with the Profile Manager to update or to create new preference rules based on a given context. During this interaction, two scenarios are possible. If the user profile already contains the preferences for the given context, those preferences are updated by increasing or decreasing their certainty labels (it may imply that some preferences can become obsolete); otherwise, if such preferences do not exist, a new preference rule is added to the user profile and the default certainty label is set.

5 Related Work

The reason for introducing LPPODs into the ICD was to enhance the system with a preference handling method in order to represent and to manage user profiles. The representation of user profiles has been done by considering contextual and incomplete information, as well as certainty label associated with preference rules. The process of retrieving personalised suggestions has been decoupled in a dedicate module (*i.e.,* the Content Manager) which is responsible to interpret preferences and associated certainty labels. This has been a design choice, since the information is collected from several Web services which are queried according to user preferences specified in the parameters of the service call. Instead, in some of the approaches that deal with user preferences, preference representation and preference queries are not decoupled. This is the case for the different lines of research in the literature which deal with preferences queries in databases and in possibilistic databases.

In the literature, the main reasons behind introducing preferences in the querying process are different. Main streamlines of research have focused on offering more expressive query languages and on providing preference relations for rank-ordering the retrieved items. These different points have been considered in approaches based on databases [18,8], on fuzzy set [14], and, more recently, on possibilistic logic [16] from different perspectives. In particular, works in the database community study and refine algorithms aiming at the efficient computation of non Pareto-dominated answers. Fuzzy set-based approaches use fuzzy set membership functions for describing the user profiles on each attribute domain involved in the query. This is especially convenient when dealing with numerical domains. A more effective approach to the handling of database preference queries, which takes its roots in the fuzzy set-based approaches, is offered by possibilistic logic [16]. Finally, preference queries have also been considered in the setting of possibilistic databases [3].

6   Concluding Remarks

In this paper, we have presented the enhancement of the personalisation capabilities of a context-aware system, an ICD, by means of user profiles. At knowledge level, we have represented user profiles according to a user profile and preference ontology. User profiles have then been translated, at symbolic level, into the logic programming specification of LPPODs. Indeed, LPPODs has proved to be a suitable specification in order to express user preferences which can depend both on contextual and incomplete information. Furthermore, preferences can be associated with certainty labels for expressing the preference importance. Such labels can be considered to relax preference conditions at the moment of retrieving personalised suggestions and to keep the user profile up-to-date. The experimental platform developed has shown in a real use case the advantages of handling uncertain user preferences in order to adapt the system behavior according to the changes in the environment and in the users' needs.

As future work, we aim at considering a more complex preference representation language. Right now, the syntax supported by LPPODs is quite limited, since it only allows to express alternatives between atomic preferences. However, one may need to encode more complex preference statements in the ICD. For instance, in the user profile about restaurants presented in Example 1, it can be valuable to capture more complex preference expressions in order to express equalities between options and/or combinations over alternatives. Indeed, the user may prefer to have *Italian* food over *tapas* over not having any of them, *i.e.*, expressions such as $italian \times tapas \times (not\ italian \wedge not\ tapas)$; or she may prefer to pay either by Master Card or by Visa over paying cash, *i.e.*, expressions such as $(MasterCard \vee Visa) \times cash$.

A first step towards an extension of LPPODs has been studied in [9] where a more general syntax, which allows the writing of nested preferences expressions built by means of connectives $\{\vee, \wedge, \neg, not, \times\}$, is proposed. To represent these formulas and to capture their semantics, an extension of the basic LPPODs syntax, called *Nested Logic Programs with Ordered Disjunction* (LPODs$^+$), is defined. The next step is to extend the LPODs$^+$ framework with possibilistic logic in order to associate preference rules with certainty labels.

References

1. Adomavicius, G., Tuzhilin, A.: Toward the Next Generation of Recommender Systems: A Survey of the State-of-the-Art and Possible Extensions. IEEE Transaction on Knowledge and Data Engineering 17(6), 734–749 (2005)
2. Baldauf, M., Dustdar, S., Rosenberg, F.: A survey on context-aware systems. International Journal of Ad Hoc and Ubiquitous Computing 2(4), 263–277 (2007)
3. Bosc, P., Pivert, O., Prade, H.: A Possibilistic Logic View of Preference Queries to an Uncertain Database. In: Proc. of 19th IEEE Int. Conf. on Fuzzy Systems (FUZZ-IEEE 2010), pp. 581–595 (2010)
4. Boutilier, C., Brafman, R.I., Domshlak, C., Hoos, H.H., Poole, D.: CP-nets: a tool for representing and reasoning with conditional ceteris paribus preference statements. Journal of Artificial Intelligence Research 21(1), 135–191 (2004)

5. Brewka, G., Benferhat, S., Le Berre, D.: Qualitative Choice Logic. Artificial Intelligence 157(1-2), 203–237 (2004)
6. Brewka, G., Niemelä, I., Syrjänen, T.: Logic Programs with Ordered Disjunction. Computational Intelligence 20(2), 333–357 (2004)
7. Ceccaroni, L., Codina, V., Palau, M., Pous, M.: PaTac: Urban, Ubiquitous, Personalized Services for Citizens and Tourists. In: Proc. of the 3rd Int. Conf. on Digital Society, pp. 7–12. IEEE Computer Society, Washington, DC (2009)
8. Chomicki, J.: Preference formulas in relational queries. ACM Transactions on Database Systems 28(4), 427–466 (2003)
9. Confalonieri, R., Nieves, J.C.: Nested Preferences in Answer Set Programming. Fundamenta Informaticae 113(1), 19–39 (2011)
10. Confalonieri, R., Nieves, J.C., Osorio, M., Vázquez-Salceda, J.: Possibilistic Semantics for Logic Programs with Ordered Disjunction. In: Link, S., Prade, H. (eds.) FoIKS 2010. LNCS, vol. 5956, pp. 133–152. Springer, Heidelberg (2010)
11. Confalonieri, R., Nieves, J.C., Vázquez-Salceda, J.: Towards the Implementation of a Preference- and Uncertain-Aware Solver Using Answer Set Programming. Tech. Rep. LSI-10-16-R, Universitat Politècnica de Catalunya, Barcelona, Spain (2010)
12. Domshlak, C., Hüllermeier, E., Kaci, S., Prade, H.: Preferences in AI: An overview. Artifical Intelligence 175(7-8), 1037–1052 (2011)
13. Dubois, D., Lang, J., Prade, H.: Possibilistic logic. In: Gabbay, D.M., Hogger, C.J., Robinson, J.A., Siekmann, J.H. (eds.) Handbook of Logic in Artificial Intelligence and Logic Programming, vol. 3, pp. 439–513. Oxford University Press, Inc., New York (1994)
14. Dubois, D., Prade, H.: Using fuzzy sets in flexible querying: Why and how? In: Flexible Query Answering Systems, pp. 45–60. Kluwer Academic Publishers, Norwell (1997)
15. Dubois, D., Prade, H.: Possibilistic logic: a retrospective and prospective view. Fuzzy Sets and Systems 144(1), 3–23 (2004)
16. HadjAli, A., Kaci, S., Prade, H.: Database Preferences Queries – A Possibilistic Logic Approach with Symbolic Priorities. In: Hartmann, S., Kern-Isberner, G. (eds.) FoIKS 2008. LNCS, vol. 4932, pp. 291–310. Springer, Heidelberg (2008)
17. Kaci, S.: Working with Preferences: Less Is More. Springer (2011)
18. Kießling, W.: Foundations of preferences in database systems. In: Proc. of the 28th Int. Conf. on Very Large Data Bases, pp. 311–322. Morgan Kaufmann (2002)
19. Palau, M., Ceccaroni, L., Gómez-Sebastià, I., Vázquez-Salceda, J., Nieves, J.C.: Coordination and Organisational Mechanisms Applied to the Development of a Dynamic, Context-aware Information Service. In: Filipe, J., Fred, A.L.N., Sharp, B. (eds.) Proc. of the Int. Conf. on Agents and Artificial Intelligence, ICAART 2010, vol. 2, pp. 88–95. INSTICC Press (2010)
20. Tversky, A., Kahneman, D.: Judgment under uncertainty: Heuristics and Biases. Science 185(4157), 1124–1131 (1974)

Allocation of Service Centers in the GIS with the Largest Vitality Degree

Alexander Bozhenyuk[1] and Igor Rozenberg[2]

[1] Scientific and Technical Center "Intech" of Southern Federal University, Taganrog, Russia
Avb002@yandex.ru
[2] Public Corporation "Research and Development Institute of Railway Engineers",
Moscow, Russia
I.rozenberg@gismps.ru

Abstract. In this paper the questions of the definition of the centers optimum allocation in the GIS are observed by the minimax criterion. It is supposed that the information received from GIS is presented like a fuzzy graph. In this case the task of the definition of the centers optimum allocation transforms into the task of the definition of the graph vitality fuzzy set. The method of the definition of the graph vitality fuzzy set is considered. The example of finding optimum allocation of centers in GIS for railway stations with the largest vitality degree is considered as well.

Keywords: Fuzzy graph, reachability degree, strong connection degree, vitality degree, fuzzy set of vitality.

1 Introduction

The large-scale increasing and versatile introduction of the geographical information system (GIS) is substantially connected with the necessity of perfection of the information systems providing decision-making. The GIS are applied practically in all spheres of human activity. Geographical information technologies have now reached an unprecedented level, offering a wide range of powerful functions such as information retrieval and display, analytical tools, and decision support [1, 2]. Unfortunately, geographical data are often analyzed and communicated amid a largely non-negligible uncertainty. Uncertainty exists in the whole process from the geographical abstraction, data acquisition, and geo-processing to the usage [3, 4]. One of the tasks solved the GIS is the task of the centers allocation [5]. The search of the optimal placing of hospitals, police stations, fire brigades, important enterprises and services on some sites of a considered territory is reduced to this task. In some cases the criterion of optimality can consist in the minimization of the journey time (or in the minimization of distances) from the service centre to the most remote service station. In other cases the criterion of optimality consists in the choice of such an allocation of the centers that the route from them to any other place of service is passed on the best way by some criterion. In other words the problem is the optimization of "the worst variant» [6]. However, the information represented in the

S. Greco et al. (Eds.): IPMU 2012, Part II, CCIS 298, pp. 98–106, 2012.
© Springer-Verlag Berlin Heidelberg 2012

GIS, has an approximate value or insufficiently authentic [7]. We consider that a certain railway system has n railway stations. There are k service centres, which may be placed into these railway stations. Each centre can serve several stations. The degree of a service station by a centre depends on a cyclic route which connects them.

It is necessary for the given number of centers to define the places of their best allocation. In other words, it is necessary to define the places of k centers into n railway stations so that the «control» of all territory (all railway stations) is carried out with the greatest possible degree of service.

2   Basic Concepts and Definitions

We suppose that the service degree of all stations is defined as the minimal value from the service degrees of each station. Taking into account that the service degree cannot always have the symmetry property, the model of such a task is the fuzzy directed graph $\tilde{G}=(X, \tilde{U})$ [8,9]. Here, set $X=\{x_i\}$, $i \in I=\{1,2,...,n\}$ is a set of vertices and $\tilde{U}=\{<\mu_U < x_i,x_j > / < x_i,x_j >> \},< x_i,x_j >\in X^2$ is a fuzzy set of directed edges with membership function $\mu_U:X^2\rightarrow[0,1]$. The membership function $\mu_U < x_i,x_j >$ of graph $\tilde{G} = (X,\tilde{U})$ defines the quality of a railway section from station i to station j.

We assume that the service degree has the property of transitivity, i.e. if the service centre is in area x_i and serves area x_j with degree $\mu_U(x_i,x_j)$, and if the service centre is in area x_j and serves area x_k with degree $\mu_U(x_j,x_k)$ then degree of service of area x_k from area x_i not less than $\mu_U(x_i,x_j) \& \mu_U(x_j,x_k)$. Here operation & is minimum operation.

The path of fuzzy graph $\tilde{l}(x_i,x_j)$ is called a direct sequence of fuzzy edges from vertex x_i to vertex x_j, in which the final vertex of any edge is the first vertex of the following edge [10]. The conjunctive strength of the path of a fuzzy graph is defined by the formula:

$$\mu_{\tilde{l}}(x_i,x_j)= \underset{<x_k,x_l>\in \tilde{l}(x_i,x_j)}{\&} \mu_U(x_k,x_l).$$

Let $\tilde{L}(x_i,x_j)$ be a family of the fuzzy graph paths from vertex x_i to vertex x_j. Then the value $\tau(x_i,x_j) = \underset{\tilde{l}\in\tilde{L}}{\max} \{\mu_l(x_i,x_j)\}$ defines the reachability degree of vertex x_j for vertex x_i.

We will consider the degree of fuzzy graph vitality as a degree of strong connection, so it will be defined by the formula [11, 12]:

$$V(\tilde{G}) = \underset{x_i\in X}{\&} \underset{x_j\in X}{\&} \tau(x_i,x_j).$$

It means there is a path between each pair of graph vertices with the conjunctive strength not less than value V.

For the allocation of service centers in a fuzzy graph we should consider the problem of the "optimal" placing in the sense that all (residual) vertices are served with the greatest vitality degree.

Let k be service center $(k<n)$, placed in the vertices of subset Y, $|Y|=k$, $Y \subset X$, and $\tau(x_i, x_j)$ is the reachability degree of vertex x_j from vertex x_i.

Definition 1. Value $V_{\tilde{G}}(Y) = \underset{\forall x_j \in X \setminus Y}{\&} (\underset{\forall x_i \in Y}{\vee} \tau(x_i, x_j) \& \tau(x_j, x_i))$ is the *vitality*

degree of fuzzy graph $\tilde{G}$ which is served by k-centers from vertex set Y.

Vitality degree $V_{\tilde{G}}(Y)$ determines the minimax strong connectivity value between each vertex from set $X \setminus Y$ and a center from set Y.

In other words, one can "leave" the vertex of subset Y, "reach" any vertex of the graph, "serve" it, return to the "initial" vertex while the conjunctive strength of the path will not be less than value $V_{\tilde{G}}(Y)$.

It is clear that value $V_{\tilde{G}}(Y) \in [0,1]$ depends either on the number of centers k, or the allocation of the centers on the vertices of graph $\tilde{G}$ (i.e. on the choice of set Y).

Thus, the problem of the allocation of k service centers $(k<n)$ on the fuzzy graph $\tilde{G}$ **is** reduced to determining such a subset of vertices $Y \subset X$, that the value of vitality degree $V_{\tilde{G}}(Y)$ reaches its maximum value, that is the value $V_{\tilde{G}}(k) = \underset{\substack{\forall Y \subset X \\ |Y|=k}}{\max}\{V_{\tilde{G}}(Y)\}$.

Definition 2. Fuzzy set $\tilde{V}_{\tilde{G}} = \{<V_{\tilde{G}}(1)/1>,<V_{\tilde{G}}(2)/2>,...,<V_{\tilde{G}}(n)/n>\}$, defined on vertex set X, is called the *fuzzy set of vitality* of graph $\tilde{G} = (X, \tilde{U})$. The fuzzy set of vitality $\tilde{V}_{\tilde{G}}$ determines the greatest vitality degrees of graph $\tilde{G}$ in the case that it is served by 1, 2,....., n centers.

Values $\tilde{V}_{\tilde{G}}(k)$ $(1 \leq k \leq n)$ signify that we can place k-centers in graph $\tilde{G}$ so that there is a path from at least one center to any vertex of graph $\tilde{G}$ and back. The conjunctive strength of the graph will be not less than $\tilde{V}_{\tilde{G}}(k)$.

Let's note some properties of fuzzy set of vitality.

Property 1. The equality of the form $V_{\tilde{G}}(1) = V(\tilde{G})$ is valid.

In other words, the vitality degree of the fuzzy graph when serving by a single center coincides with the vitality degree of the graph.

Property 2. The equality of the form $V_{\tilde{G}}(n) = 1$ is valid.

Otherwise, the vitality degree of the fuzzy graph when serving by n centers equals to 1.

Property 3. The statement of the form $(\forall k \in \overline{1,(n-1)})[V_{\tilde{G}}(k) \leq V_{\tilde{G}}(k+1)]$ is true.

Otherwise, the more service centers, the greater possible vitality degree of the fuzzy graph.

3   Method for Finding Service Centers

We will consider the method of finding a family of all service centers with the largest vitality degree. The given method is an analogue method for the definition of all minimal fuzzy dominating vertex sets [13] and it is a generalization of the Maghout's method for crisp graphs [14].

Let Y be a subset of vertices of fuzzy graph $\tilde{G} = (X, \tilde{U})$ in which the service centers are located and the vitality degree equals to V. Therefore, one of the two conditions for any vertex $x_i \in X$ can be satisfied:

a)   vertex x_i belongs to set Y;

b)   there is vertex x_j that belongs to set Y and inequalities $\tau(x_i, x_j) \geq V$ and $\tau(x_j, x_i) \geq V$ are encountered.

Using the notation quantifier form we can get the truth of the following formula:

$$(\forall x_i \in X)[x_i \in Y \vee (\exists x_j)(x_j \in Y \, \& \, \tau(x_i, x_j) \geq V \, \& \, \tau(x_j, x_i) \geq V)].$$

The logical variable p_i can be set in correspondence to each vertex $x_i \in X$. This logical variable possesses value 1 in the case of $x_i \in Y$ and 0, if otherwise. Fuzzy variable $\xi_{ij} = \tau(x_i, x_j)$ can be set in correspondence to expression $\tau(x_i, x_j) \geq V$. So we can get the truth of the logical formula:

$$\Phi_V = \underset{i=1,n}{\&} (p_i \vee \underset{j=1,n}{\vee} (p_j \, \& \, \xi_{ij} \, \& \, \xi_{ij})).$$

Let $\xi_{ii} = 1$ and equality $p_i \vee \underset{j}{\vee} p_i \, \& \, \xi_{ij} \, \& \, \xi_{ji} = \underset{j}{\vee} p_j \, \& \, \xi_{ij} \, \& \, \xi_{ji}$ hold for any x_i then:

$$\Phi_V = \underset{i=1,n}{\&} \underset{j=1,n}{\vee} (\xi_{ij} \, \& \, \xi_{ji} \, \& \, p_j). \tag{1}$$

Remove the brackets in formula (1) and collect the using rules of the fuzzy capture:

$$a \vee a \& b = a; \, a \& b \vee a \& \, \bar{b} = a; \, \xi' \& a \vee \xi'' \& a \& b, \text{ if } \xi' \geq \xi''. \tag{2}$$

Here, $a, b \in \{0, 1\}$ and $\xi', \xi'' \in [0, 1]$.

Consequently the formula (1) will be represented as:

$$\Phi_V = \underset{i=1,l}{\vee} (p_{1_i} \, \& \, p_{2_i} \, \& \, ... \, \& \, p_{k_i} \, \& \, V_i). \tag{3}$$

We may prove the following property:

Property 4. If further simplification in the formula (3) based on the rules (2) is not possible, then the totality of all vertices, conforming to variables, for each disjunctive term i gives the subset of vertices $Y \subseteq X$ with vitality degree V_i of fuzzy graph $\tilde{G} = (X, \tilde{U})$. Here subset Y is minimal in the sense that any subset of Y does not have this property.

The following method of finding a family of all service centers with the largest vitality degree may be suggested on the basis of Property 4:

- We write proposition (1) for given fuzzy graph $\widetilde{G}$;
- We simplify proposition (1) by proposition (2) and present it as proposition (3);
- We define all fuzzy bases, which correspond to the disjunctive members of proposition (3);
- We find a fuzzy set of vitality, which defines service centers with the largest vitality degree.

4   Example of Service Centers Finding

Let us consider a railway network limited by the stations Novosibirsk, Kemerovo, Barnaul and Novokuzneck. The network is presented in Fig. 1:

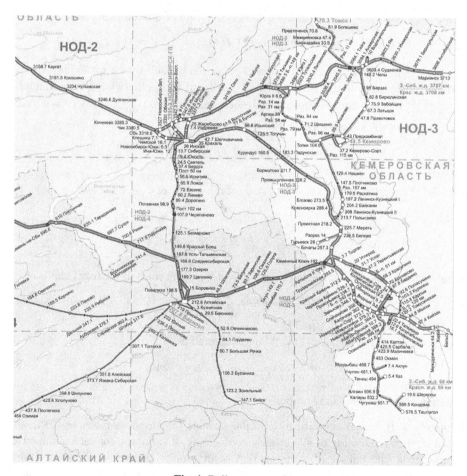

Fig. 1. Railway network

The fuzzy graph of this railway network, obtained from the GIS "Object Land" [15], is represented in Fig. 2:

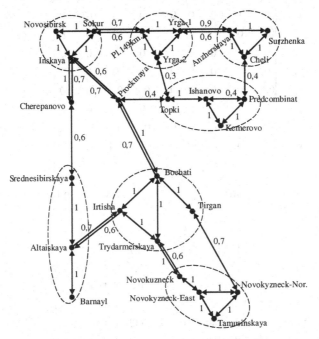

Fig. 2. Fuzzy graph of the railway network

It is necessary to find allocation of service centers with the largest vitality degree for this graph. For simplicity, we will present by one vertex, that all subgraphs with a strong connection degree equals to 1. As a result we will receive the aggregative fuzzy graph with $n=9$, which is represented in Fig. 3:

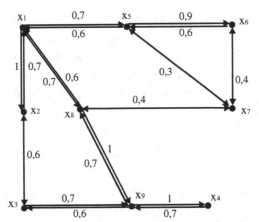

Fig. 3. Aggregative fuzzy graph $\widetilde{G}$ of the railway network

The vertex matrix for this graph has the following form:

$$R_X = \begin{array}{c} \\ x_1 \\ x_2 \\ x_3 \\ x_4 \\ x_5 \\ x_6 \\ x_7 \\ x_8 \\ x_9 \end{array} \begin{array}{ccccccccc} x_1 & x_2 & x_3 & x_4 & x_5 & x_6 & x_7 & x_8 & x_9 \\ \hline 0 & 1 & 0 & 0 & 0{,}7 & 0 & 0 & 0{,}7 & 0 \\ 0{,}7 & 0 & 0{,}6 & 0 & 0 & 0 & 0 & 0 & 0 \\ 0 & 0{,}6 & 0 & 0 & 0 & 0 & 0 & 0 & 0{,}7 \\ 0 & 0 & 0 & 0 & 0 & 0 & 0 & 0 & 0{,}7 \\ 0{,}6 & 0 & 0 & 0 & 0 & 0{,}9 & 0{,}3 & 0 & 0 \\ 0 & 0 & 0 & 0 & 0{,}6 & 0 & 0{,}4 & 0 & 0 \\ 0 & 0 & 0 & 0 & 0{,}3 & 0{,}4 & 0 & 0{,}4 & 0 \\ 0{,}6 & 0 & 0 & 0 & 0 & 0 & 0{,}4 & 0 & 0{,}7 \\ 0 & 0 & 0{,}6 & 1 & 0 & 0 & 0 & 0{,}7 & 0 \end{array}$$

We raise the contiguity matrix to 2, 3, ..., 9 powers. Uniting them, we find an accessible matrix:

$$N = \begin{array}{c} \\ x_1 \\ x_2 \\ x_3 \\ x_4 \\ x_5 \\ x_6 \\ x_7 \\ x_8 \\ x_9 \end{array} \begin{array}{ccccccccc} x_1 & x_2 & x_3 & x_4 & x_5 & x_6 & x_7 & x_8 & x_9 \\ \hline 1 & 1 & 0{,}7 & 0{,}7 & 0{,}7 & 0{,}7 & 0{,}4 & 0{,}7 & 0{,}7 \\ 0{,}7 & 1 & 0{,}6 & 0{,}7 & 0{,}7 & 0{,}7 & 0{,}4 & 0{,}7 & 0{,}7 \\ 0{,}6 & 0{,}6 & 1 & 0{,}7 & 0{,}6 & 0{,}6 & 0{,}4 & 0{,}7 & 0{,}7 \\ 0{,}6 & 0{,}6 & 0{,}6 & 1 & 0{,}6 & 0{,}6 & 0{,}4 & 0{,}7 & 0{,}7 \\ 0{,}6 & 0{,}6 & 0{,}6 & 0{,}6 & 1 & 0{,}9 & 0{,}4 & 0{,}6 & 0{,}6 \\ 0{,}6 & 0{,}6 & 0{,}6 & 0{,}6 & 0{,}6 & 1 & 0{,}4 & 0{,}6 & 0{,}6 \\ 0{,}4 & 0{,}4 & 0{,}4 & 0{,}4 & 0{,}4 & 0{,}4 & 1 & 0{,}4 & 0{,}4 \\ 0{,}6 & 0{,}6 & 0{,}6 & 1 & 0{,}6 & 0{,}6 & 0{,}4 & 1 & 1 \\ 0{,}6 & 0{,}6 & 0{,}6 & 1 & 0{,}6 & 0{,}6 & 0{,}4 & 0{,}7 & 1 \end{array}$$

The corresponding formula (1) for this graph has the following form:

$$\begin{aligned}
\Phi_B = &(1p_1 \vee 0{,}7p_2 \vee 0{,}6p_3 \vee 0{,}6p_4 \vee 0{,}6p_5 \vee 0{,}6p_6 \vee 0{,}4p_7 \vee 0{,}6p_8 \vee 0{,}6p_9) \,\& \\
&\& (0{,}7p_1 \vee 1p_2 \vee 0{,}6p_3 \vee 0{,}6p_4 \vee 0{,}6p_5 \vee 0{,}6p_6 \vee 0{,}4p_7 \vee 0{,}6p_8 \vee 0{,}6p_9) \,\& \\
&\& (0{,}6p_1 \vee 0{,}6p_2 \vee 1p_3 \vee 0{,}6p_4 \vee 0{,}6p_5 \vee 0{,}6p_6 \vee 0{,}4p_7 \vee 0{,}6p_8 \vee 0{,}6p_9) \,\& \\
&\& (0{,}6p_1 \vee 0{,}6p_2 \vee 0{,}6p_3 \vee 1p_4 \vee 0{,}6p_5 \vee 0{,}6p_6 \vee 0{,}4p_7 \vee 0{,}7p_8 \vee 0{,}7p_9) \,\& \\
&\& (0{,}6p_1 \vee 0{,}6p_2 \vee 0{,}6p_3 \vee 0{,}6p_4 \vee 1p_5 \vee 0{,}6p_6 \vee 0{,}4p_7 \vee 0{,}6p_8 \vee 0{,}6p_9) \,\& \\
&\& (0{,}6p_1 \vee 0{,}6p_2 \vee 0{,}6p_3 \vee 0{,}6p_4 \vee 0{,}6p_5 \vee 1p_6 \vee 0{,}4p_7 \vee 0{,}6p_8 \vee 0{,}6p_9) \,\& \\
&\& (0{,}4p_1 \vee 0{,}4p_2 \vee 0{,}4p_3 \vee 0{,}4p_4 \vee 0{,}4p_5 \vee 0{,}4p_6 \vee 1p_7 \vee 0{,}4p_8 \vee 0{,}4p_9) \,\& \\
&\& (0{,}6p_1 \vee 0{,}6p_2 \vee 0{,}6p_3 \vee 0{,}7p_4 \vee 0{,}6p_5 \vee 0{,}6p_6 \vee 0{,}4p_7 \vee 1p_8 \vee 0{,}7p_9) \,\& \\
&\& (0{,}6p_1 \vee 0{,}6p_2 \vee 0{,}6p_3 \vee 0{,}7p_4 \vee 0{,}6p_5 \vee 0{,}6p_6 \vee 0{,}4p_7 \vee 0{,}7p_8 \vee 1p_9).
\end{aligned}$$

Multiplying parentheses 1 and 2, parentheses 8 and 9, parentheses 3 and 4, parentheses 5 and 6, and using rules (2) we obtain:

$$\Phi_B = (0{,}7p_1 \vee 0{,}7p_2 \vee 0{,}6p_3 \vee 0{,}6p_4 \vee 0{,}6p_5 \vee 0{,}6p_6 \vee 0{,}4p_7 \vee 0{,}6p_8 \vee 0{,}6p_9 \vee 1p_1p_2) \&$$
$$\& \, (0{,}6p_1 \vee 0{,}6p_2 \vee 0{,}6p_3 \vee 0{,}7p_4 \vee 0{,}6p_5 \vee 0{,}6p_6 \vee 0{,}4p_7 \vee 0{,}7p_8 \vee 0{,}7p_9 \vee 1p_8p_9) \&$$
$$\& \, (0{,}6p_1 \vee 0{,}6p_2 \vee 0{,}6p_3 \vee 0{,}6p_4 \vee 0{,}6p_5 \vee 0{,}6p_6 \vee 0{,}4p_7 \vee 0{,}6p_8 \vee 0{,}6p_9 \vee$$
$$\vee 0{,}7p_3p_8 \vee 0{,}7p_3p_9 \vee 1p_3p_4) \&$$
$$\& \, (0{,}6p_1 \vee 0{,}6p_2 \vee 0{,}6p_3 \vee 0{,}6p_4 \vee 0{,}6p_5 \vee 0{,}6p_6 \vee 0{,}4p_7 \vee 0{,}6p_8 \vee 0{,}6p_9 \vee 1p_5p_6) \&$$
$$\& \, (0{,}4p_1 \vee 0{,}4p_2 \vee 0{,}4p_3 \vee 0{,}4p_4 \vee 0{,}4p_5 \vee 0{,}4p_6 \vee 1p_7 \vee 0{,}4p_8 \vee 0{,}4p_9)$$

Multiplying parentheses 1 and 2, parentheses 3 and 4 and using rules (2) we obtain:

$$\Phi_B = (0{,}6p_1 \vee 0{,}6p_2 \vee 0{,}6p_3 \vee 0{,}6p_4 \vee 0{,}6p_5 \vee 0{,}6p_6 \vee 0{,}4p_7 \vee 0{,}6p_8 \vee 0{,}6p_9 \vee$$
$$\vee 0{,}7p_1p_4 \vee 0{,}7p_1p_8 \vee 0{,}7p_1p_9 \vee 0{,}7p_2p_4 \vee 0{,}7p_2p_8 \vee 0{,}7p_2p_9 \vee 1p_1p_2p_8p_9) \&$$
$$\& \, (0{,}6p_1 \vee 0{,}6p_2 \vee 0{,}6p_3 \vee 0{,}6p_4 \vee 0{,}6p_5 \vee 0{,}6p_6 \vee 0{,}4p_7 \vee 0{,}6p_8 \vee 0{,}6p_9 \vee$$
$$\vee 0{,}7p_3p_8p_5p_6 \vee 0{,}7p_3p_5p_6p_9 \vee 1p_3p_4p_5p_6) \&$$
$$\& \, (0{,}4p_1 \vee 0{,}4p_2 \vee 0{,}4p_3 \vee 0{,}4p_4 \vee 0{,}4p_5 \vee 0{,}4p_6 \vee 0{,}4p_8 \vee 0{,}4p_9 \vee 1p_7).$$

Multiplying parentheses 1 and 2, and using rules (2) we obtain:

$$\Phi_B = (0{,}6p_1 \vee 0{,}6p_2 \vee 0{,}6p_3 \vee 0{,}6p_4 \vee 0{,}6p_5 \vee 0{,}6p_6 \vee 0{,}4p_7 \vee 0{,}8p_8 \vee 0{,}6p_9 \vee$$
$$\vee 0{,}7p_1p_3p_4p_5p_6 \vee 0{,}7p_1p_3p_5p_6p_8 \vee 0{,}7p_1p_3p_5p_6p_9 \vee 0{,}7p_2p_3p_4p_5p_6 \vee 0{,}7p_2p_3p_5p_6p_8 \vee$$
$$\vee 0{,}7p_2p_3p_5p_6p_9 \vee 1p_1p_2p_3p_4p_5p_6p_8p_9) \&$$
$$\& \, (0{,}4p_1 \vee 0{,}4p_2 \vee 0{,}4p_3 \vee 0{,}4p_4 \vee 0{,}4p_5 \vee 0{,}4p_6 \vee 0{,}4p_8 \vee 0{,}4p_9 \vee 1p_7).$$

Multiplying the parentheses, we finally obtain:

$$\Phi_B = \underline{0{,}4p_1} \vee 0{,}4p_2 \vee 0{,}4p_3 \vee 0{,}4p_4 \vee 0{,}4p_5 \vee 0{,}4p_6 \vee 0{,}4p_7 \vee 0{,}4p_8 \vee 0{,}4p_9 \vee$$
$$\vee \underline{0{,}6p_1p_7} \vee 0{,}6p_2p_7 \vee 0{,}6p_3p_7 \vee 0{,}6p_4p_7 \vee 0{,}6p_5p_7 \vee 0{,}6p_6p_7 \vee 0{,}6p_7p_8 \vee 0{,}6p_8p_9 \vee$$
$$\vee \underline{0{,}7p_1p_3p_4p_5p_6p_7} \vee 0{,}7p_1p_3p_6p_6p_7p_8 \vee 0{,}7p_1p_3p_5p_6p_7p_9 \vee 0{,}7p_2p_3p_4p_5p_6p_7 \vee$$
$$\vee 0{,}7p_2p_3p_5p_6p_7p_8 \vee 0{,}7p_2p_3p_5p_6p_7p_9 \vee \underline{1p_1p_2p_3p_4p_5p_6p_7p_8p_9}.$$

Graph $\tilde{G}$ has 24 subsets of vertices with the greatest vitality degree, which follows from the last equality, and the fuzzy set of vitality is defined as:

$$V(\tilde{G}) = \{<0{,}4/1>, <0{,}6/2>, <0{,}7/6>, <1/9>\}.$$

The fuzzy set of vitality defines the following optimum allocation of the service centres: if we have 9 service centres then we must place these centres into all vertices. The greatest vitality degree equals to 1. If we have 6 service centres then we must place these centres, for example, into vertices 1, 3, 4, 5, 6 and 7 (Inskaya, Barnaul, Novokuzneck, Yrga-2, Surzhenka, Kemerovo). In this case the greatest vitality degree equals to 0.7. If we have 2 service centres then we must place both centres, for example, into vertices 1 and 7 (Inskaya, Kemerovo). In this case the degree of service equals to 0.6. If we have only one service centre then we can place it in any vertex (for example, Inskaya). In the last case the degree of service equals to 0.4. The fuzzy set of vitality also indicates that, for example, there is no need to place 3, 4, or 5 centers. As in this case the greatest vitality degree will be as in the case of 2 centers.

5   Conclusion

We can begin to solve the problem of the "best" allocation of service centers after the implementation of the transition of the interrelation characteristics between objects and objects properties represented as membership functions. Then the basic definitions of strong connectivity and fuzzy graph vitality should be used. The present approach of finding a vitality fuzzy set enables us to solve either the problem of k-centers optimal allocation with the maximal vitality degree or the problem of selecting k-service center numbers.

Acknowledgements. This work has been supported by the Russian Foundation for Basic Research project № 11-01-00011a.

References

1. Clarke, K.: Analytical and Computer Cartography. Prentice Hall, Englewood Cliffs (1995)
2. Longley, P., Goodchild, M., Maguire, D., Rhind, D.: Geographic Information Systems and Science. John Wiley & Sons, Inc., New York (2001)
3. Zhang, J., Goodchild, M.: Uncertainty in Geographical Information. Taylor & Francis, Inc., New York (2002)
4. Goodchild, M.: Modelling Error in Objects and Fields. In: Goodchild, M., Gopal, S. (eds.) Accuracy of Spatial Databases, pp. 107–113. Taylor & Francis, Inc., Basingstoke (1989)
5. Kaufmann, A.: Introduction a la theorie des sous-ensembles flous. Masson, Paris (1977)
6. Christofides, N.: Graph theory. An algorithmic approach. Academic Press, London (1976)
7. Malczewski, J.: GIS and multicriteria decision analysis. John Willey and Sons, New York (1999)
8. Monderson, J.N., Nair, P.S.: Fuzzy Graphs and Fuzzy Hypergraphs. Physica-Verl., Heidelberg (2000)
9. Moreno Perez, J.A., Moreno-Vega, J.M., Verdegay, J.L.: In Location Problem on Fuzzy Graphs. Mathware & Soft Computing 8, 217–225 (2001)
10. Bershtein, L.S., Bozhenuk, A.V.: Fuzzy graphs and fuzzy hypergraphs. In: Dopico, J., de la Calle, J., Sierra, A. (eds.) Encyclopedia of Artificial Intelligence, Information SCI, Hershey, New York, pp. 704–709 (2008)
11. Bershtein, L.S., Bozhenyuk, A.V. Rozenberg, I.N.: Fuzzy Graph Vitality Degree Increase on the Base of Strong Connection. In: 12th Zittau Fuzzy Colloquium. Hochschule Zittau\Goerlitz, Zittau, pp. 309–312 (2005)
12. Bozhenyuk, A.V., Rozenberg, I.N., Starostina, T.A.: A Method of Increase of Vitality Degree of Fuzzy Graph. In: 13th Zittau Fuzzy Colloquium, Hochschule Zittau/Goerlitz, Zittau, September 13-15, pp. 235–240 (2006)
13. Bozhenyuk, A.V., Rozenberg, I.N., Starostina, T.A.: Analysis and Investigation of Flows and Vitality in Transportation Networks in Fuzzy Data. Scientific World, Moscow (2006)
14. Bershtein, L.S., Bozhenuk, A.V.: Maghout method for determination of fuzzy independent, dominating vertex sets and fuzzy graph kernels. J. General Systems. 30, 45–52 (2001)
15. Rozenberg, I.N., Gittis, C.A., Svyatov, D.C.: Geoinformation System Object Land. In: Proc. IPI RAN "Systems and Means of Informatics", Science, Moscow (2000)

Finding Memoryless Probabilistic Relational Policies for Inter-task Reuse⋆

Valdinei Freire da Silva, Fernando A. Pereira, and Anna Helena Reali Costa

Universidade de São Paulo, São Paulo, SP, Brazil
{valdinei.freire,fernando.pereira,anna.reali}@usp.br

Abstract. Relational representations let sequential decision problems be described through objects and relations, resulting in more compact, expressive, and domain-independent representations that make it possible to find and generalize solutions much faster than propositional representations. In this paper we propose a modified policy iteration algorithm (AbsProb-PI) for the infinite-horizon discounted-reward criterion; the algorithm finds a memoryless probabilistic relational abstract policy that abstracts well the solution from source problems so that it can be applied in new, similar problems. Experiments in robotic navigation validate our proposals and show that we can find effective and efficient abstract policies, outperforming solutions by inductive approaches in the literature.

Keywords: Relational MDP, Memoryless Probabilistic Relational Policies, Inter-task Reuse.

1 Introduction

In this paper we are interested in the following general question. Suppose an agent is confronted with a series of similar sequential decision problems in which she must display goal-seeking behaviors, such as a robot that must navigate to different target positions, in minimal time, in a given environment. The agent wishes to abstract the policy from source problems so as to have a reasonable abstract policy to be applied in new, similar problems. Our question is, How can the agent find this abstract policy, and how good can this abstract policy be?

In this paper we consider abstract policies that are encoded through relational representations, because many problems can be compactly described in terms of classes of domain objects. In seeking an abstraction for the solution of a sequential decision problem so that the result can be generalized and reused in other similar problems, we propose a two-stage architecture: a concrete level, in which a Markovian process is responsible for environment observations and interactions, and an abstract level, in which a non-Markovian process is activated by the concrete level and is responsible for the policy abstraction. In non-Markovian

---

⋆ This research was partially supported by FAPESP (Project LogProb 08/03995-5; Project CogBot 11/19280-8) and by CNPq (grant 305512/2008-0).

S. Greco et al. (Eds.): IPMU 2012, Part II, CCIS 298, pp. 107–116, 2012.
© Springer-Verlag Berlin Heidelberg 2012

processes, an agent's observation does not give complete information about the current state: different states might produce the same observation. We consider that each abstract state is an aggregation that consists of a set of concrete states. Hence, given only one abstract state in our model, we do not know which concrete state it represents, thereby constituting a non-Markovian process. In non-Markovian processes, *probabilistic* memoryless policies are quite interesting, since almost any such policy will be a satisficing policy, i.e., a policy whose total steps to goal is finite [11].

We introduce the AbsProb-PI algorithm, a policy iteration algorithm for the infinite-horizon discounted-reward criterion that finds a memoryless probabilistic relational policy that abstracts well the solution for source problems so that it can be applied in new, similar problems. A memoryless policy chooses actions only according to the current observation of the system, i. e., it simply maps observations into actions. Memoryless policies are often extremely compact and are in general applicable to many similar problems. Our experiments show that the proposed algorithm can find effective and efficient policies.

The paper is organized as follows. Section 2 reviews basic concepts of Markov decision processes (MDP) and Relational MDP, and reviews previous work. Section 3 presents our proposals for finding a memoryless probabilistic relational policy in the abstract level. Section 4 reports experiments that validate our proposals, and Section 5 summarizes our conclusions.

2   Background and Previous Work

Consider an agent interacting with the environment as follows. At each time step the agent observes the state of the system, chooses an action and moves to another state. This sequential decision problem can be modeled as a Markov Decision Process (MDP) [16]. For our purposes an MDP is a tuple $\langle \mathcal{S}, \mathcal{A}, T, r \rangle$, where $\mathcal{S}$ is a finite set of *states*; $\mathcal{A} = \bigcup_{s \in \mathcal{S}} \mathcal{A}^s$ is a finite set of *actions*, where $\mathcal{A}^s$ is the set of allowable actions in state $s \in \mathcal{S}$; $T : \mathcal{S} \times \mathcal{A} \times \mathcal{S} \mapsto [0, 1]$ is a *transition function* such that $T(s, a, s') = \mathbb{P}(s_{t+1} = s' | s_t = s, a_t = a)$; $r : \mathcal{S} \mapsto \mathbb{R}$ is a bounded *reward function*, such that $r_t = r(s)$ is the reward received when reaching state s at time t. We are particularly interested in a subclass of MDPs that is *episodic*: there is a set $\mathcal{G} \subset \mathcal{S}$ of goal states, and when the goal is reached the problem is restarted in some initial state chosen according to a probability distribution.

A Relational MDP (RMDP) [15] is a tuple $\langle \Sigma, BK, T, r \rangle$, where $\Sigma = D \cup P \cup A$ is a *relational alphabet* such that D is a set of *constants* representing the objects of the environment, P is a set of *predicates* used to describe relations and properties among objects, and A is a set of *action predicates*. *Background Knowledge BK* is a set of Horn Clauses. If $\mathsf{t}_1, \ldots, \mathsf{t}_n$ are *terms*, i.e. each one is a variable (represented with capital letters) or a constant (represented with lowercase letters), and if p/n is a predicate symbol with arity $n \geq 0$, then $\mathsf{p}(\mathsf{t}_1, \ldots \mathsf{t}_n)$ is an *atom*. A *conjunction* is a set of atoms. A term is called *ground* if it contains no variables; in a similar way we define ground atoms and ground conjunctions. The *Herbrand base* B_Σ is the set of all possible ground atoms that can be formed with the predicates and constants in Σ. The set of ground states S of the RMDP is a subset of the Herbrand base $B_{P \cup D}$ satisfying the integrity constraints imposed by BK. The set of ground actions is $A \subseteq B_{A \cup D}$. With S and A defined, T and r have the same meaning as described for MDPs. When S and A in an RMDP are ground sets, we call this a *concrete* RMDP. Note that a relational representation allows us to encode aggregate states and actions by using variables instead of constants in the predicate terms. In our discussion each variable in a conjunction will be implicitly assumed to be existentially quantified. A *substitution* θ is a set $\{X_1/t_1, \ldots, X_n/t_n\}$, binding each variable X_i to a term t_i; it can be applied to a term, atom or conjunction. If W and Y are conjunctions and there is a substitution θ such that $Y\theta \subseteq W$, we say that W is θ-*subsumed* by Y, denoted by $W \preceq_\theta Y$.

We call *abstract state* σ (and *abstract action* α) the representation in which the constants of the ground state s (and the ground action a) are replaced by variables. We denote by S_σ the set of ground states covered by σ, i.e., $S_\sigma = \{s \in S | s \preceq_\theta \sigma\}$. Similarly we define $A_\alpha = \{a \in A | a \preceq_\theta \alpha\}$. We also define S_{ab} and A_{ab} the set of abstract states and abstract actions in an RMDP, respectively. Suppose two ground states $s_1 = \{p_1(t_1), p_2(t_1, t_2)\}$ and $s_2 = \{p_1(t_3), p_2(t_3, t_4)\}$, $s_1, s_2 \in S$; an abstract state $\sigma \in S_{ab}$, $\sigma = \{p_1(X_1), p_2(X_1, X_2)\}$ subsumes s_1 with $\theta = \{X_1/t_1, X_2/t_2\}$, and subsumes s_2 with $\theta = \{X_1/t_3, X_2/t_4\}$. In this case σ represents an abstraction of both, s_1 and s_2. This fact is exploited in our work.

The task of the agent in an (R)MDP is to find a *policy*. An *optimal policy* π^* is a policy that maximizes some function R_t of the future rewards $r_t, r_{t+1}, r_{t+2}, \ldots$ A common definition, which we use, is to consider the sum of *discounted rewards* over an *infinite horizon* $R_t = \sum_{t=0}^{\infty} \gamma^t r_t$, where $0 < \gamma < 1$ is the *discount factor*. In a decision problem it is of interest to determine the most specific class of policies that guarantees optimality. It is known that in a concrete MDP, the set of deterministic stationary memoryless policies, $\pi : S \to A$, is sufficient for optimality [16],[11]. We define an *abstract policy* as $\pi_{ab} : S_{ab} \times A_{ab} \mapsto [0,1]$, with $\mathbb{P}(\alpha_i|\sigma) = \pi_{ab}(\sigma, \alpha_i)$, $\sigma \in S_{ab}$, $\alpha_i \in A_{ab}^\sigma$, $A_{ab}^\sigma \subseteq A_{ab}$, and A_{ab}^σ is the set of allowable abstract actions in abstract state $\sigma \in S_{ab}$.

Our interest here is to propose an algorithm that abstracts a policy π_{ab} from one or more source problems, and to transfer and reuse π_{ab} in a new similar problem. Several works have inspired our approach. All of them, one way or another, involve state abstraction. Li, Walsh and Littman [9] proposed a unified theory of state abstraction for MDPs, dividing the works into five classes: *(i)* a model-irrelevance abstraction that preserves the one-step model, i.e., for any ground action and any two ground states s_1 and s_2 aggregated in a unique abstract state σ, reward and transition functions for s_1 and s_2 should be the same, e.g. [6]; *(ii)* a Q^π-irrelevance abstraction that preserves the state-action value function for all policies; *(iii)* a Q^*-irrelevance abstraction that preserves the optimal state-action value function, e.g. [17]; *(iv)* a a^*-irrelevance abstraction that preserves the optimal action and its value, e.g. [14]; *(v)* a π^*-irrelevance abstraction that attempts to preserve the optimal action, e.g. [7]. Our work fits into the latter category, since we intend to define an optimal memoryless policy for an abstract RMDP by considering only conjunctions previously defined by the designer in the description of the MDP states. In this case, policy-search methods have a better chance of finding the optimal policy [9]. In addition, inductive methods [5],[4],[13] are more appropriate than deductive ones [1],[8] for finding abstract policies in our approach. Still, we interpret the abstract level of our approach as a case of partial observability of the state, once each abstract state σ maps to a set of ground states s in the corresponding concrete RMDP. In this case, probabilistic policies are more suitable. Due to this non-Markovian characteristic of the abstract RMDP, we seek inspiration in the works involving POMDPs [12],[11],[10] to define an appropriate inductive abstraction algorithm. We thus propose a policy iteration algorithm to solve our abstract RMDP by means of a memoryless probabilistic abstract policy, the AbsProb-PI algorithm.

3   Policy Iteration within Abstract States

The popular policy iteration (PI) algorithm produces optimal policies for MDPs, starting with an arbitrary policy π_0 and iterating through the following steps:

$$V^{\pi_i}(s) = \mathrm{E}\left[\sum_{t=0}^{\infty} \gamma^t r_t | \pi_i, s_0 = s\right] \forall s \in \mathcal{S}, \tag{1}$$

$$\pi_{i+1}(s) = \arg\max_{a \in \mathcal{A}}\left\{r(s) + \gamma \sum_{s \in \mathcal{S}} T(s, a, s') V^{\pi_i}(s')\right\} \forall s \in \mathcal{S}. \tag{2}$$

The PI algorithm converges to the optimal policy in finite steps, and it finishes when $\pi_{i+1}(s) = \pi_i(s)$, $\forall s \in \mathcal{S}$. The convergence is guaranteed because (i) it surely improves the current policy π_i if π_i is not optimal; and (ii) it iterates through the finite set of deterministic policies. If we attempt to use the PI algorithm with the set of abstracts states, we would need to guarantee both characteristics.

An abstract state σ is a set of underlying ground states $\mathcal{S}_\sigma$ and the value $V^\pi(\sigma)$ depends on such underlying ground states. If the execution of a policy π generates an ergodic process[1]; then we can define a steady-state distribution $b^\pi(s)$ over all ground states in $\mathcal{S}$, and we define:

$$V^\pi(\sigma) = \sum_{s \in \mathcal{S}_\sigma} b^\pi(s|\sigma) V^\pi(s), \tag{3}$$

where, for any $s \in \mathcal{S}_\sigma$, $b^\pi(s|\sigma) = \frac{b^\pi(s)}{\sum_{s \in \sigma} b^\pi(s)}$ is the probability of observing state s given that the policy π is executed and the abstract state σ is observed. The definition in Equation (3) has two important differences from Equation (1). First,

---

[1] A process is ergodic if its statistical properties can be deduced from a single, sufficiently long sample of the process.

it can only be defined under the ergodic condition when we aggregate ground states in an abstract state under the probability distribution $b^\pi(s)$. Second, the improvement step in Equation (2) can only be done because the transition function $T(s, a, s')$ is independent of the current policy π_i being performed; on the other hand, under the abstract state space, the transition function $T(\sigma, \alpha, \sigma')$ depends on the policy being executed in the corresponding concrete MDP, and $T(\sigma, \alpha, \sigma')$ cannot be defined independently from a steady-state distribution. Then the question is, How to improve a given policy in the abstract level?

The idea is to compare the current policy with another policy, and adopt the new policy if there is an improvement. Comparison between policies can be done through Perturbation Analysis (PA) [3]. Consider a matrix-vector representation of functions $r(s)$, $V^\pi(s)$ and $T^\pi(s, s') = \sum_{a \in \mathcal{A}} \pi(a|s)T(s, a, s')$: $\mathbf{r}$, $\mathbf{V}^\pi$ and $\mathbf{T}^\pi$, respectively. $\mathbf{V}^{\pi'} - \mathbf{V}^\pi = \gamma(\mathbf{I} - \gamma\mathbf{T}^{\pi'})^{-1}(\mathbf{T}^{\pi'} - \mathbf{T}^\pi)\mathbf{V}^\pi$ [3], with $\mathbf{I}$ the identity matrix.

In order to compare two policies π and π' we need the inverse $(\mathbf{I} - \gamma\mathbf{T}^{\pi'})^{-1}$ based on transition matrix $\mathbf{T}^{\pi'}$ of the policy π' and the value function $\mathbf{V}^\pi$ of the policy π, which is quite computationally expensive compared to the maximization in Equation (2). However, PA allows defining the gradient within a direction $\mathbf{Q} = \mathbf{T}^{\pi'} - \mathbf{T}^\pi$. Let $\pi^\delta = \pi + \delta(\pi' - \pi)$ and $\mathbf{T}^{\pi^\delta} = \mathbf{T}^\pi + \delta\mathbf{Q}$. The derivative of $\mathbf{V}^{\pi^\delta}$ is given by:

$$\frac{d\mathbf{V}^{\pi^\delta}}{d\delta} = \gamma(\mathbf{I} - \gamma\mathbf{T}^\pi)^{-1}\mathbf{Q}\mathbf{V}^\pi.$$

Since the derivative $\frac{d\mathbf{V}^{\pi^\delta}}{d\delta}$ depends on $\mathbf{T}^{\pi'}$ linearly (remember that $\mathbf{Q} = \mathbf{T}^{\pi'} - \mathbf{T}^\pi$), it can be used to choose the steepest direction of the improvement, i.e., to choose a direction $\mathbf{Q}$, and to improve the current policy by moving in such direction. We also need to define the step size of the movement, since moving to π' using an inappropriate step size may not improve the current policy π [10].

Cao and Tang [2] used gradient to find correlated deterministic optimal actions within subset of states, whereas Li, Yin and Xi [10] proposed an algorithm based on step size and PI to find memoryless probabilistic policies for POMDPs, both under the averaged reward evaluation. We adapt such ideas, and we contribute the AbsProb-PI algorithm that uses accumulated discount reward evaluation and abstract policies.

Remember that we evaluate policies based on the initial distribution $b^0(s)$, and that the abstract policy must be defined on the abstract state space. Let $\mathbf{b}^0$ be the vector representation of $b^0(s)$. The total derivative is given by $\mathbf{b}^0 \cdot \frac{d\mathbf{V}^{\pi^\delta}}{d\delta}$. For each abstract state $\sigma \in \mathcal{S}_{ab}$ we must choose the best direction (abstract action) to improve the total derivative. In order to do so, we must define the transition matrix $\mathbf{T}^{\pi_{ab}}$ of an abstract policy π_{ab}. An abstract policy π_{ab} can induce a policy π in a given concrete MDP. We propose to do so as follows. Given a ground state s, we find an abstract state σ such that $s \preceq_\theta \sigma$. We then have a set of abstract actions $\mathcal{A}_{ab}$ given by π_{ab}, with $\mathbb{P}(\alpha_i|\sigma)$ for each abstract action $\alpha_i \in \mathcal{A}_{ab}$.[2] An abstract action α_i is mapped into a set of concrete actions $\mathcal{A}_{\alpha_i}$ for the underlying concrete decision problem. To produce a particular concrete sequence of actions, we select an abstract action $\alpha_i \in \mathcal{A}_{ab}$ according to $\mathbb{P}(\alpha_i|\sigma)$, and again we select randomly (with uniform probability) a concrete action $a \in \mathcal{A}_{\alpha_i}$ from the set of concrete actions associated with the selected abstract action α_i. Then, considering that the set of abstract states $\mathcal{S}_{ab}$ makes a partition on the set of ground states $\mathcal{S}$, i.e., there exist a function $\sigma : \mathcal{S} \to \mathcal{S}_{ab}$, we define $\mathbf{T}^{\pi_{ab}}$ and $\mathbf{V}^{\pi_{ab}}$ by:

$$T^{\pi_{ab}}(s, s') = \sum_{\alpha \in \mathcal{A}_{ab}} \pi_{ab}(\alpha|\sigma(s)) \sum_{a \in \mathcal{A}_\alpha} \frac{1}{|\mathcal{A}_\alpha|} T(s, a, s'), \quad \mathbf{V}^{\pi_{ab}} = (\mathbf{I} - \gamma \mathbf{T}^{\pi_{ab}})^{-1} \mathbf{r}.$$

Similarly, we define the transition matrix $\mathbf{T}^{\alpha, \epsilon}$ that chooses abstract action α with probability $1 - \epsilon$ and chooses uniformly among all other abstract actions with probability ϵ.

Given the previous considerations, we define the AbsProb-PI algorithm:

1. Initiate the abstract probabilistic policy π_{ab} arbitrarily such that $\pi_{ab}(\sigma, \alpha) \geq \frac{\epsilon}{|\mathcal{A}_{ab}|}$ $\forall \sigma \in \mathcal{S}_{ab}, \alpha \in \mathcal{A}_{ab}$ and $\sum_{\alpha \in \mathcal{A}_{ab}} \pi_{ab}(\sigma, \alpha) = 1$ $\forall \sigma \in \mathcal{S}_{ab}$
2. At each iteration i
   a) Calculate the value function $\mathbf{V}^{\pi_{ab}}$;
   b) Calculate the product $\mathbf{C} = \gamma \mathbf{b}^{0\top} (\mathbf{I} - \gamma \mathbf{T}^{\pi_{ab}})^{-1}$;
   c) For each action $\alpha \in \mathcal{A}_{ab}$ calculate $\mathbf{\Delta}^{\alpha, \pi_{ab}} = (\mathbf{T}^{\alpha, \epsilon} - \mathbf{T}^{\pi_{ab}}) \mathbf{V}^{\pi_{ab}}$;
   d) For $\sigma \in \mathcal{S}_{ab}$ and $\alpha \in \mathcal{A}_{ab}$ calculate $W(\sigma, \alpha) = \sum_{s \in \mathcal{S}_\sigma} C(s) \Delta^{\alpha, \pi_{ab}}(s)$;
   e) For each $\sigma \in \mathcal{S}_{ab}$ find the best direction $\alpha_\sigma^* = \arg\max_{\alpha \in \mathcal{A}_{ab}} W(\sigma, \alpha)$;
   f) Choose a step size $\delta(i)$ and updates policy π_{ab} by:

$$\pi_{ab}(\sigma, \alpha) \leftarrow \begin{cases} (1 - \delta(i))\pi_{ab}(\sigma, \alpha) + \delta(i)\left(\frac{\epsilon}{|\mathcal{A}_{ab}|} + (1 - \epsilon)\right), & \text{if } \alpha = \alpha_\sigma^* \\ (1 - \delta(i))\pi_{ab}(\sigma, \alpha) + \delta(i)\frac{\epsilon}{|\mathcal{A}_{ab}|}, & \text{if } \alpha \neq \alpha_\sigma^*. \end{cases}$$

In this algorithm we must define the parameter $\epsilon > 0$ which guarantees that the policy converges at most to an ϵ-greedy policy; we must also choose the step size with the function $\delta(i)$. In our experiments we compare two different ways of choosing the step size: (i) decreasing step size, with $\delta(t) = \frac{1}{1 + \frac{t}{k_D}}$, and (ii) fixed step size, with $\delta(t) = k_F$; k_D and k_F are constants.

4   Experiments

We conducted experiments to evaluate our algorithm when finding the optimal abstract policy and using the abstract policy for inter-task reuse. Experiments were conducted on a simulated robotic navigation environment (Figure 1). We formulate different tasks by defining different goal positions in the environment.

---

[2] Without loss of generality, we simplify the notation by considering a set of abstract actions common to every abstract state, i.e., $\mathcal{A}_{ab}^\sigma = \mathcal{A}_{ab}$ for all $\sigma \in \mathcal{S}_{ab}$.

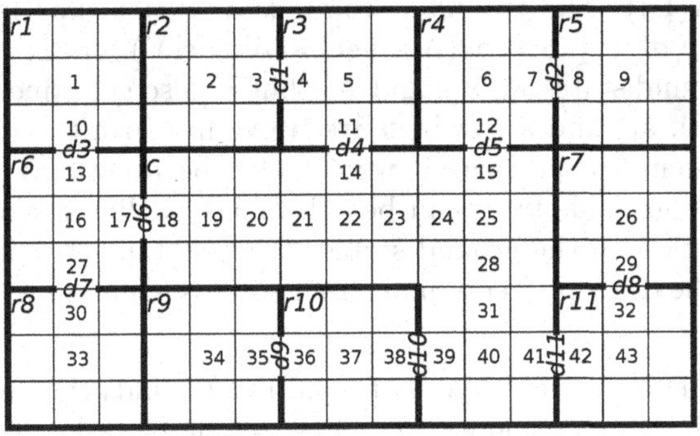

Fig. 1. The robotic-navigation environment

Navigation Domain. The environment is composed of three kinds of objects: rooms (ri), doors (di) and a corridor (c). The robot reaches some rooms ($r3$, $r4$, $r6$, $r10$ and $r11$) immediately from the corridor, and these rooms mediate the robot access to other ones ($r1$, $r2$, $r5$, $r7$, $r8$ and $r9$). A total of 43 discrete ground states describe the environment (states s_1, ..., s_{43}, represented by cell numbers in Figure 1) and the robot chooses among 4 ground actions (actions N, S, E and W) which moves the robot to the correspondent direction with probability 0.9 if there is a next ground state in that direction, and does not move otherwise. We defined 11 different tasks by choosing in each task a different room center as goal (ground states s_1, s_2, s_5, s_6, s_9, s_{16}, s_{26}, s_{33}, s_{34}, s_{37} and s_{43}).

We describe each ground state using the vocabulary $\Sigma = D \cup (P_E \cup P_G) \cup A$: D is the set of objects (rooms, corridor and doors). P_E describes predicates related to local observations, $P_E = \{$in_room(ri), in_corridor(ci), see_door_far(di), see_adj_room(ri), see_adj_corridor(di), see_empty_space$\}$; P_G describes predicates related to goal position, $P_G = \{$entity_app_goal(X), empty_app_goal, empty_away_goal, near_goal$\}$, where X can be a corridor, a room or a door; finally, A describes predicates related to actions and is defined by $A = \{$goto(X), goto_empty_app_goal, goto_empty_away_goal$\}$ where X can be a corridor, a room or a door.

Whereas semantics of some predicates are self evident, others require an explanation. The predicate see_door_far means the robot can see a door, but cannot see beyond it, whereas the predicate see_adj_corridor or see_adj_room means the robot is so close to a door that it can see the adjacent place through the door. The robot sees an empty (free) space (see_empty_space) if it does not see any other object in the next two locations. With regard to goals, the robot is near_goal if it is at a Manhattan distance of 5 to the goal. Finally, an object or an empty space can be perceived as taking the agent close to (app for approaching) or away from (away) the goal. As an example, consider the goal is located at ground state s_2 (position 2 in $r2$). Then, in a relational description, $s_{16} = \{$in_room($r6$), see_door_far($d6$), see_door_far($d3$), see_door_far($d7$), entity_app_goal($d3$), entity_app_goal($d6$)$\}$ and s_{16} is subsumed by the abstract state $\sigma = \{$in_room(X), see_door_far(Y), see_door_far(Z), entity_app_goal(Y)}. The ground state s_{37} is also subsumed by σ. Note that the abstract state $\sigma' = \{$in_room(X), see_door_far(Y), entity_app_goal(Y)$\}$ subsumes the ground states s_9, s_{43} and s_{33}, but σ' also subsumes ground states s_5 (near the goal), s_{16} and s_{37} (which are states in which the robot also see a door that, if chosen as a passage, it would take the robot to move away from the target). Since ground states can be subsumed by different abstract states, we create a partition on the ground states by considering that if a predicate is not included in the description of an abstract state, such predicate is universally denied.

Results. In order to evaluate how fast AbsProb-PI finds the optimal abstract probabilistic policy we considered the whole set of 11 tasks. Then, the agent considers the following: (*i*) a task is chosen randomly with uniform distribution; and (*ii*) an initial ground state is chosen randomly with uniform distribution. This scheme can be considered as a bigger MDP with 43×11 ground states. The agent receives a positive reward after accomplishing the task at hand and it must maximize the expected sum of discounted rewards ($\gamma = 0.999$). We compare both ways of choosing the step size function: $\delta_F(t)$ and $\delta_D(t)$. We first obtained empirically parameters $k_F = 0.10$ and $k_D = 1$ that present the best performance and compared them averaging over 50 runs of AbsProb-PI with random initial abstract policy. Figure 2–(Upper) shows the expected sum of discounted rewards obtained in each iteration while running AbsProb-PI. The function $\delta_D(t)$ makes the best trade-off between fast learning and better convergence because it can perform learning fast at the beginning of the process, and then it can tune a better policy at the end.

Our second experiment consists in transferring the knowledge among different tasks. We use the leave-one-out method in order to evaluate the transfer of knowledge, i.e., for each one of the 11 tasks we do the following: (*i*) take one task out; (*ii*) find the best policy among the other 10 left; and (*iii*) transfer the policy found to the task at hand. Figure 2–(Lower) compares the AbsProb-PI algorithm when making inter-task knowledge transfer (transfer AbsProp-PI curve in the figure) against three alternatives: (1) we consider the AbsProb-PI algorithm applied directly to the task at hand (local AbsProp-PI) — this represents a measure limiting the best possible performance to be achieved; we then consider a lifted probabilistic abstract policy obtained from grounded optimal solutions, (2) when defined from a set of source problems and then evaluated when applied to another task, and (3) when defined from and applied to the same task. The lifted policy was obtained as follows: (i) learn optimal ground policies for each task; (ii) experiment infinitely within every task; (iii) for each abstract state, count its occurrence and respectively chosen action; and (iv) defines a probabilistic policy according to such occurrences.

Using Figure 2–(Lower) we can understand some properties of the algorithm AbsProp-PI. First, AbsProp-PI can find probabilistic policies with a fair performance to find the goal even if the relational description and the task at hand do not allow a deductive approach to solve the problem. Second, when compared to methods that induce abstract policies, AbsProp-PI produces a better result.

The special property of our method is the trade-off between the ability to solve easy tasks and more difficult tasks. The traditional induction process (made by experiences from the application of ground optimal policies) imposes a higher probability value to the decisions taken in states near the goal, since they are relatively more visited, whereas our approach makes a better trade-off in the long run by evaluating the abstract policy directly.

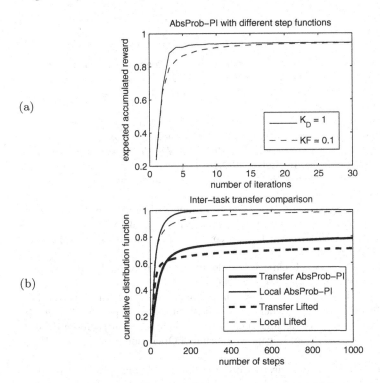

Fig. 2. (a) Different step functions within the AbsProb-PI algorithm. (b) Results for comparing learned AbsProb-PI policies against lifted policies.

5   Conclusions

The addition of structure to problem descriptions allows knowledge transfer amongst an extensive set of states or tasks. In our approach, we assume a relational description given by the designer, which partitions the ground state space. If the partition is too coarse, it may not help in finding a good generalization, whereas if the partition is too fine, it could be very computationally consuming to find an appropriate inter-tasks generalization. The AbsProb-PI algorithm finds a memoryless probabilistic abstract policy that can effectively generalize among many solutions from different problems. How to automatically define an appropriate compact set of predicates to describe states so that good abstractions could be made is a question for future research. We also assume that we are given a complete ground model of the problem; how to find optimal probabilistic policies based only on interaction experiences is another question for future research. Finally, while working directly in the space of ground states we can ensure convergence, working directly in the space of abstract states we can provide a faster learning and a broader generalization. Future research should provide appropriate conditions for the balanced use of both spaces.

References

1. Boutilier, C., Reiter, R., Price, B.: Symbolic dynamic programming for first-order MDPs. In: IJCAI, pp. 690–700. Morgan Kaufmann (2001)
2. Cao, X.R., Tang, H.T.: Gradient-based policy iteration: An example. In: 41st IEEE Conf. Decision Control, pp. 3367–3371 (2002)
3. Cao, X.R.: A sensitivity view of Markov decision processes and reinforcement learning. In: Modeling, Control and Optimization of Complex Systems
4. Cocora, A., Kersting, K., Plagemann, C., Burgard, W., De Raedt, L.: Learning relational navigation policies. In: IEEE/RSJ IROS (2006)
5. Džeroski, S., De Raedt, L., Driessens, K.: Relational reinforcement learning. Machine Learning 43(1/2), 7–52 (2001)
6. Givan, R., Dean, T., Greig, M.: Equivalence notions and model minimization in Markov decision processes. Artificial Intelligence 147, 163–223 (2003)
7. Jong, N.K., Stone, P.: State abstraction discovery from irrelevant state variables. In: IJCAI, pp. 752–757 (2005)
8. Kersting, K., Otterlo, M.V., Raedt, L.D.: Bellman goes relational. In: 21th Int. Conf. on Machine Learning, pp. 465–472 (2004)
9. Li, L., Walsh, T.J., Littman, M.L.: Towards a unified theory of state abstraction for MDPs. In: 9th Int. Symp. Artificial Int. and Mathematics, pp. 531–539 (2006)
10. Li, Y., Yin, B., Xi, H.: Finding optimal memoryless policies of pomdps under the expected average reward criterion. European Journal of Operational Research 211(3), 556–567 (2011)
11. Littman, M.L.: Memoryless policies: theoretical limitations and practical results. In: 3rd Int. Conf. on Simulation of Adaptive Behavior: from Animals to Animats, vol. 3, pp. 238–245 (1994)
12. Loch, J., Singh, S.: Using eligibility traces to find the best memoryless policy in partially observable Markov decision processes. In: 5th Int. Conf. Machine Learning, pp. 323–331 (1998)
13. Matos, T., Bergamo, Y.P., da Silva, V.F., Cozman, F.G., Costa, A.H.R.: Simultaneous abstract and concrete reinforcement learning. In: 9th Symp. Abstraction, Reformulation and Approximation, pp. 82–89. AAAI Press (2011)
14. McCallum, A.: Reinforcement Learning with Selective Perception and Hidden State. Ph.D. thesis, University of Rochester (1995)
15. van Otterlo, M.: Reinforcement learning for relational MDPs. In: Machine Learning Conf. of Belgium and the Netherlands, pp. 138–145 (2004)
16. Puterman, M.L.: Markov Decision Processes: Discrete Stochastic Dynamic Programming, 1st edn. John Wiley & Sons, New York (1994)
17. Sanner, S., Boutilier, C.: Practical solution techniques for first-order MDPs. Artificial Intelligence 173, 748–788 (2009)

Discovering Gene-Drug Relationships
for the Pharmacology of Cancer

Elisabetta Fersini, Enza Messina, and Alberto Leporati

University of Milano-Bicocca,
Viale Sarca, 336 - 20126 Milano, Italy
{fersini,messina,leporati}@disco.unimib.it

Abstract. The combined analysis of tissue microarray and drug response datasets has the potential of revealing valuable knowledge about the relationships between gene expression and drug activity of tumor cells. However, the amount and the complexity of biological data needs appropriate data mining and machine learning algorithms to uncover possible interesting patterns. In order to identify a suitable profile of cancer patients for revealing the link between gene expression profiles, drug activity responses and type of cancer, a learning framework based on three building blocks is proposed: p-Median based clustering, information gain feature selection and Bayesian Network prediction. The experimental investigation highlights three main findings: (1) the relational clustering approach is able to create groups of cell lines that are highly correlated both in terms of gene expression and drug response; (2) from a biological point of view, the gene selection performed on these clusters allows for the identification of a subset of genes that are strongly involved into several cancer processes; (3) the final prediction of drug responses, by using the patient profile obtained through clustering and gene selection, represents an initial step for predicting potential useful drugs.

1 Introduction

Microarray technologies, such as for example cDNA microarrays and affymetrix, have steadily established themselves as a standard tool in biological and biomedical research. Thanks to their recent progresses large amount of data have been collected, offering important opportunities for increasing the knowledge related to complex biological phenomena. One of the most challenging problems in biomedical research is related to the discovery of embedded relationships among human cancer, gene expression profile and drug response for enabling the definition of individual therapy driven by a specific gene profile. Several studies tried to integrate gene expression data with drug-response profiles in a sequential manner. A first gene-drug integrative analysis was presented in [5]. Authors developed a software, named "COMPARE", able to show that the growth inhibitory patterns against different cancer cell lines are well correlated with the mechanism of action of anticancer therapy. One of the most relevant alternative study into the pharmacology of cancer relates to [6], in which a hierarchical

S. Greco et al. (Eds.): IPMU 2012, Part II, CCIS 298, pp. 117–126, 2012.
© Springer-Verlag Berlin Heidelberg 2012

clustering algorithm, with several similarity metrics, has been used. Scherf et al. analyze: (1) cell-to-cell correlation on the basis of gene expression and drug activity profiles, (2) relationships between drug activity patterns and mechanisms of action, (3) gene-drug correlation on the basis of gene expression and drug activity profiles. In [1] and [2] the relationships between gene expression profiles and drug responses have been investigated by both unsupervised and supervised machine learning algorithms. In particular, while through the unsupervised Soft Topographic Vector Quantization algorithm [1] authors have shown that gene expression profiles are more related to the kind of cancer than to drug activity patterns, through the supervised Bayesian networks [1] [2] some biologically meaningful relationships among gene expression levels, drug activities, and cancer types have been revealed. An alternative approach to the traditional clustering and classification methods for discovering relationships among genes and drugs across different cell lines is represented by Biclustering algorithms. Kutalik et al. [4] applied the well known Iterative Signature Algorithm for uncovering co-modules, i.e. smaller building blocks that exhibit similar patterns across certain genes and drugs in some of the cell lines. The results of the above quoted papers and of a wide set of related approaches highlight three main interesting remarks:

1. Drug activity patterns are less related to the organ of origin compared to the gene expression profile. This suggests that the gene expression profile of a cell line plays a fundamental role, independently of the tissue of origin, to understand anticancer therapy responses.
2. The absence of a common pattern between gene expression profiles and drug response might be partly due to the activity of genes related to drug sensitivity and resistance. This idea has been supported by the fact that, as shown in [6], several cell lines with a relatively high expression level of those genes regulating multi-drug resistance have been clustered in the same group. This indicates that chemoresponse mechanisms are distributed across different tissues in the panel and that it should be possible to link drug response to gene expression profiles.
3. Learning Bayesian Networks reveals interesting relationships among subsets of genes, drugs and cancer types. This allows us to exploit Bayesian Networks not only for deductive purposes, but also for prediction issues.

Inspired by these remarks we propose a learning framework based on the following assumption: groups of cell lines homogeneous in terms of both gene expression profile and drug activity should be characterized by a subset of genes that explains the drug responses. The proposed framework consists of three main building blocks. The first component is aimed at performing a cluster analysis for creating groups of cell lines that are homogeneous with respect to gene expression profile and drug activity response. In particular a novel relational clustering algorithm based on a p-Median problem formulation has been investigated. The second building block exploits the output of the cluster analysis for identifying a subset of genes that characterizes each cluster, i.e. those subsets of genes that could be responsible of drug responses. Finally, the third component induces a (fixed structure) Bayesian Network (BN) to predict the response of a set of drugs given the selected genes. Computational results show that the proposed relational clustering formulation, combined with gene selection and BN inference engine, yields homogeneous clusters while guaranteeing good predictive power for inferring drug responses of a new cell line. A relevant evidence about the obtained results is represented by the biological evaluation performed on the selected genes. According to the existent literature the set of genes used to train BNs, which has been selected by using the groups of cell lines obtained by the proposed relational clustering approach, has shown to be biologically relevant from an oncological point of view.

The paper is organized as follows. In section 2 an overview of the dataset used in our investigation is outlined. In section 3 the proposed framework is described, focusing on cluster analysis (3.1), feature selection (3.2) and prediction (3.3). In section 4 the experimental investigation is presented, while conclusions and future work are detailed in section 5.

2   Data Source: NCI60 Dataset

The NCI60 dataset, established at the National Cancer Institute U.S.A., consists of 60 cell lines from 9 kinds of cancers, all extracted from human patients. The tumors considered in this panel derive from colorectal (8), renal (8), ovarian (6), breast (8), prostate (2), lung (8) and central nervous system (6) as well as leukemias (6) and melanomas (8) cancer tissues. The NCI60 dataset, presented in [6], can be viewed as a set Ω into the real vector space R^{m+n}:

$$\Omega = \{x | x = (x^G, x^D), x^G \in R^m, x^D \in R^n\} \tag{1}$$

where x is a cell line, x^G represents the gene expression level as a vector into the space R^m and x^D denotes the drug response as a vector into the space R^n. In particular, x^G has been derived by using the cDNA microarray and x^D by assessing the grown inhibition activities (GI_{50}) after 48 hours of drug treatment through Sulphorhodamine B. We can consequently define Ω^G and Ω^D as the set of cell lines represented through their gene expression profiles and their drug activity responses respectively:

$$\Omega^G = \{x^G | x = (x^G, x^D), x \in \Omega\} \tag{2}$$
$$\Omega^D = \{x^D | x = (x^G, x^D), x \in \Omega\} \tag{3}$$

In our investigation R^m, with $m = 1375$, includes genes selected from the original NCI60 dataset (characterized by 9073 genes) having 5 or fewer missing values and showing strong pattern of variation among the 60 cell lines. The space R^n, with $n = 1400$, includes drugs stated into the original dataset, where each compound has been tested one at time and independently. Missing values have been replaced by the average gene expression value (or the average drug activity) over the 60 cell lines.

3   The Proposed Framework

3.1   Cluster Analysis

Cluster analysis is aimed at discovering embedded patterns into a given dataset. This could be accomplished by partitioning data points into a pre-specified number of clusters through the optimization of a cost function related to a similarity/dissimilarity measure between data points. An important step in any clustering algorithm is to select a distance measure, which will determine how the similarity/dissimilarity of two data points is calculated. In order to perform a cluster analysis we chose one of the most used distance measures based on Pearson Correlation ($corr$):

$$d_{ik} = 1 - corr(x_i, x_k) \tag{4}$$

where x_i and x_k represent two cell lines and $corr(x_i, x_k)$ denotes the Pearson Correlation coefficient between x_i and x_k. The adoption of a correlation-based metric instead of the Euclidean distance is motivated by its sensitivity with respect to magnitude: Euclidean distance is sensitive to scaling and differences in average expression level, whereas correlation is not.

In the following subsections we present two different clustering approaches: p-Median and Relational p-Median. The main outcome expected by clustering is to create J mutually exclusive modules of cell lines (named also groups or clusters), with similar profiles of gene expression and drug response.

3.1.1   P-Median

The p-Median problem [3] was originally designed for facility location planning, where the location of P "facilities" relative to a set of "customers" has been formulated such that the sum of the shortest demand weighted distance between "customers" and "facilities" is minimized. In our investigation, the p-Median problem has been formulated as an assignment problem for creating groups of cell lines by using a "flat" representation of data, i.e. by representing each cell line as a vector in R^{m+n}. Given a cell line $x_i \in \Omega$ and J desired clusters, the clustering problem consists in assigning each x_i to a cluster C_j, represented by an existing cell line as centroid, such that the intra-cluster distance is minimized and the inter-cluster distance is maximized. If we define a matrix Z of dimension $|\Omega| \times |\Omega|$, as:

$$z_{ij} = \begin{cases} 1 \text{ if } x_i \in C_j \\ 0 \text{ otherwise} \end{cases} \tag{5}$$

where z_{ij} represents the assignment variable that indicates whether a cell line x_i is assigned to a cluster C_j, then the clustering problem can be formulated as:

$$\min F = \sum_{i=1}^{|\Omega|} \sum_{j=1}^{|\Omega|} z_{ij} d_{ij} \tag{6}$$

s.t:

$$\sum_{j=1}^{|\Omega|} z_{ij} = 1 \qquad \forall i \in \{1, 2, ..., |\Omega|\} \tag{7}$$

$$\sum_{j=1}^{|\Omega|} z_{jj} = J \tag{8}$$

$$z_{ij} - z_{jj} \leq 0 \qquad \forall i, j \in \{1, 2, ..., |\Omega|\} \tag{9}$$

According to this formulation, constraint (7) ensures that each cell line x_i is assigned to only one cluster, constraint (8) guarantees that there will be exactly J clusters and constraint (9) establishes that if a cell line x_i belongs to the cluster C_j then x_{jj} must be a centroid.

3.1.2 Relational P-Median

The clustering formulation presented in the previous subsection belongs to the category of distance-based approaches. In particular, the cost function is merely based on distance measures that do not take into account background information for constraining the cluster placement of data points. This weakness, joint with the remarks highlighted in section 1, led us to define of a relational p-Median formulation based on two steps: the first is aimed at determining groups of cell lines into the gene (or drug) space, whereas the second determines the clusters of cell lines into the drug (or gene) space, while constraining the optimal solution in order to take into account the assignment of the first step. This approach aims at finding a trade-off between gene expression and drug response profiles, by defining a sequence of two integer linear programming formulations. While the problem at the first step can be formulated as a traditional p-Median (in one of the two spaces, i.e. either gene or drug space), the second step leads to the definition of the following relational p-Median formulation:

$$\min F_r = \sum_{i=1}^{|\Omega|} \sum_{j=1}^{|\Omega|} z_{ij} d_{ij}^{(1)} \tag{10}$$

s.t:

$$\sum_{i=1}^{|\Omega|} \sum_{j=1}^{|\Omega|} z_{ij} d_{ij}^{(2)} \leq \mu \cdot \sum_{i=1}^{|\Omega|} \sum_{j=1}^{|\Omega|} z_{ij}^* d_{ij}^{(2)} \tag{11}$$

$$\sum_{j=1}^{|\Omega|} z_{ij} = 1 \qquad \forall i \in \{1, 2, ..., |\Omega|\} \tag{12}$$

$$\sum_{i=1}^{|\Omega|} z_{ii} = J \tag{13}$$

$$z_{ij} - z_{jj} \leq 0 \qquad \forall i, j \in \{1, 2, ..., |\Omega|\} \tag{14}$$

where z_{ij}^* denotes the solution of problem (6)-(9). This problem formulation consists in assigning each cell line x_i to a cluster C_j according to a distance measure computed in one space $d^{(1)}$ (for example the gene space). Constraints denoted by equations (12), (13) and (14) have the same role as in the traditional p-Median formulation, while equation (11) provides a constraint about the cluster assignment by taking into account the cluster placement occurred during the first step. Constraint (11) thus allows the new assignment z_{ij} to determine an intra-cluster distance that does not exceed the one obtained with the assignment z_{ij}^* at the first step. In particular, this constraint forces the clustering solution of the relational p-Median to maintain, according to a value μ and to the distance measure $d^{(2)} \neq d^{(1)}$ (for example the drug space), the solution found at the first step. The parameter μ tunes the effect of the solution that optimizes F, i.e. $\sum_{i=1}^{|\Omega|} \sum_{j=1}^{|\Omega|} z_{ij}^* d_{ij}^{(2)}$.
The parameter μ ranges between the lower bound $\mu = 1.0$ and an upper bound μ^* ($\mu < 1.0$ is not allowed because no admissible solution exists). $\mu = 1$ implies that the solution of the relational p-Median will generate the same assignment as the traditional p-Median solved at the first step. Increasing values of μ cause a decreasing effect of optimal assignment z_{ij}^* coming from the first phase (μ can be updated incrementally until the convergence criterion is satisfied, i.e. the solution of the relational p-Median doesn't change for increasing values of μ).

Algorithm 1. Iterative relational p-Median

1: $\mu \leftarrow 1.0$
2: $F \leftarrow$ p-Median on Ω^G (or Ω^D)
3: $F^*(\mu) \leftarrow$ p-Median on Ω^D (or Ω^G)
4: **repeat**
5:     $\mu_{old} \leftarrow \mu$
6:     $\mu \leftarrow \mu + 0.1$
7:     $F^*(\mu_{old}) \leftarrow F^*(\mu)$
8:     $F^*(\mu) \leftarrow$ p-Median on Ω^D (or Ω^G)
9: **until** $F^*(\mu) = F^*(\mu_{old})$

The pseudo-code reported in Algorithm 1 summarizes the iterative process for solving the relational p-Median until the convergence is achieved and therefore until the value of μ^* is found , i.e. until constraint (11) becomes redundant. For the sake of simplicity, we will denote with *relational p-Median (g-d)* the approach where at step 2 the set Ω^G is used and at steps 3 and 8 the set Ω^D is exploited. On the other hand, we will denote with *relational p-Median (d-g)* the approach where Ω^D is exploited at step 2, while at steps 3 and 8 the set Ω^G is used.

3.2   Feature Selection

In order to determine the most relevant genes that characterize a module (i.e. cluster) and therefore that can be responsible of drug response for the cell lines belonging to that module, a feature selection based on Information Gain has been applied. Information Gain measures the decrease in entropy when the feature is considered. According to this measure a "good" feature can contribute, independently of any other feature, to reduce the uncertainty of modules given the attribute values. Formally, given a cluster attribute C representing the obtained modules and a gene attribute A, denoting the expression level of a given gene, the Information Gain (IG) is computed as follows:

$$IG(C, A) = H(C) - H(C|A) \tag{15}$$

where

$$H(C) = \sum_{i=1}^{J} P(c_i) \log P\left(\frac{1}{c_i}\right) \tag{16}$$

$$H(C|A) = \sum_{i=1}^{J} \sum_{k=1}^{m} P(c_i, a_k) \log \frac{P(a_k)}{P(c_i, a_k)} \tag{17}$$

To compute the entropy in equation (17) a discretization has been applied for determining a_k nominal expression values. In particular, gene attributes have been discretized to down-, normo- and up-regulated according to the p-value $\rho = 0.05$. Genes down-regulated take values in the interval $(-\infty, -0.86]$, normo-regulated in $[-0.86, 0.86]$ and up-regulated in $[0.86, +\infty)$. Given the value of $IG(C, A)$ for each gene attribute, genes can be ranked accordingly. The top 10 genes have been selected as the most representative to train the predictive model described in the following subsection.

3.3   Prediction

The results obtained in the previous steps allow us to train a predictive model able to infer, for a new cancer patient, the drug response by using his/her gene expression profile of selected genes. Among the supervised approaches available in the literature, Bayesian Networks (BNs) represent a powerful model able to deal with both diagnostic and prognostic inference issues. BNs are probabilistic graphical models that compactly represent the joint probability distribution of S random variables, $Y = \{Y^1, Y^2, ..., Y^S\}$. The main assumption, captured graphically by a dependency structure, is that each variable is directly influenced by only few others. The joint probability distribution is represented as a directed acyclic graph (DAG) whose nodes represent random variables and whose edges denote direct dependencies between a node Y and its set of parents $Pa(Y)$. Formally, a BN asserts that each node is conditional independent of its non-descendants given its parents. This conditional independence assumption allows us to represent concisely the joint probability distribution. If we consider a distribution P over S features, it can be computed as the product of S conditional distributions:

$$P(y^1, y^2, ..., y^S) = \prod_{s=1}^{S} P(y^s | y^1, ..., y^{s-1}) = \prod_{s=1}^{S} P(y^s | Pa(y^s)) \tag{18}$$

where $P(y^s|Pa(y^s))$ is described by a conditional probability distribution (CPD). In equation (18) when $s = 1$, the joint probability distribution is estimated as $P(y^s|y^1, ..., y^{s-1}) = P(y^s)$. Figure 1 shows the BN dependency structure used for the prediction task. We could gain an insight that the expression pattern of genes influences the activity level of drugs through the module assignment. This structure of BN has been defined to train a probabilistic model able to predict the drug response of a new cell, only by providing its (selection of) gene expression profile. The upper part of the network, which comprises 10 nodes,

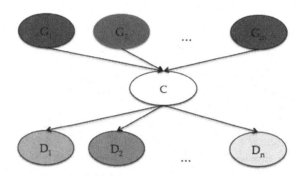

Fig. 1. NCI60 Bayesian Network. Given the observed values of the $m = 10$ genes of a cell line, the BN infers the most likely cluster C and consequently the corresponding $n = 1400$ drug responses.

represents the most relevant genes selected by the Information Gain policy. The central part of the network, which is composed of only one variable, denotes the module obtained by solving the clustering problems described in section 3.1. The bottom part, which comprises $n = 1400$ nodes, represents the drug responses to be predicted. These last variables have been discretized in order to train discrete CPDs and consequently a fully discrete BN. Also in this case the drug response attributes have been discretized according to the p-value $\rho = 0.05$. A drug is considered sensitive if it takes values in the interval $(-\infty, -0.8]$, intermediate in $[-0.8, 0.8]$ and resistant in $[0.8, +\infty)$. After this discretization process a BN is trained for predicting the response of n drugs given the expression of the 10 relevant genes.

4   Experimental Investigation

In order to evaluate the quality of the proposed framework, a two-fold analysis has been performed. The evaluation has been performed by setting $J = 9$ as the number of clusters to be obtained (which respects the number of tumor types considered by the NCI60 panel). The first analysis is concerned with the average Pearson Correlation Coefficient. Given the J modules obtained by solving the

clustering problem, the average Pearson Correlation Coefficient P is computed
as follows:

$$P = \sum_{j=1}^{J} \frac{n_j}{|\Omega|} \left[\frac{2}{n_j(n_j - 1)} \sum_{i<k} corr(x_i, x_k) z_{ij} z_{kj} \right] \quad (19)$$

where n_j is the cardinality of cluster j. More specifically, the coefficient P has
been computed with respect to the gene space and to the drug space, thus orig-
inating two correlation coefficients: P^G is computed considering the correlation
between instances represented by their gene expression profiles, while P^D is computed considering the correlation between instances represented by their drug
response profiles. In figure 2(a) a comparison in terms of correlation between the
traditional p-Median and the relational p-Median is depicted. For the relational
p-Median two series are reported, i.e. relational p-Median (g-d) and relational
p-Median (d-g). Each point of the series corresponds to a solution of a relational
approach obtained according to the parameter μ. The ordinate axis reports P^D
values, while the abscissae axis shows P^G values.

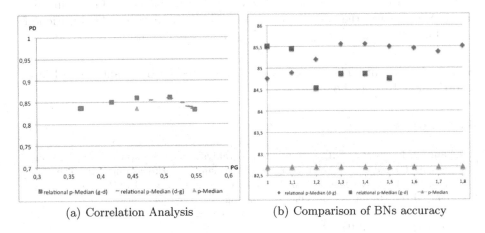

(a) Correlation Analysis   (b) Comparison of BNs accuracy

Fig. 2. Experimental Comparison

An interesting remark is related to the average correlation indices of the relational approach. All the solutions provided by the relational p-Median show a
slightly better average Pearson Coefficient than the traditional p-Median. This
implies that our approach leads to clusters that are more homogeneous both in
terms of gene expression and drug activity than the clusters obtained by the
traditional approach. Concerning the prediction challenge, in figure 2(b) a comparison in terms of accuracy (number of drugs correctly predicted) between the
investigated approaches is shown. Results are reported according to different
values of μ. The BN which performs better is the one trained on the clustering
solution obtained through the relational p-Median. The most important remark
to highlight is related to the set of genes used to train the BN with the highest

accuracy. The top ten genes, obtained by mining the clustering solution determined by the relational approach, have been characterized in the literature as biologically relevant. A remarkable evidence is provided by genes CDKN2A and DNAJA3 as tumor suppressors and gene POLR2F as tumor marker.

5   Conclusions and Ongoing Research

In this paper the problem of identifying a suitable profile of cancer patients by linking gene expression profiles, drug activity responses and type of cancer has been addressed. A learning framework based on three building blocks has been proposed. The experimental results highlight three main findings: (1) the relational clustering approach is able to create groups of cell lines that are highly correlated both in terms of gene expression and drug response; (2) from a biological point of view, the gene selection performed on these clusters allows for the identification of genes that are strongly involved in several cancer processes; (3) the prediction of drug responses, by using the patient profile obtained through clustering and gene selection, represents an initial step for predicting potential useful drugs. Concerning the ongoing research, several issues need to be investigated. Among them the next future work will be focused to the identification of a suitable number of clusters and the use of more selective discretization policies.

Acknowledgment. This work has been supported by the grant "Dote Ricercatori": FSE, Regione Lombardia.

References

1. Chang, J.H., Hwang, K.B., Zhang, B.T.: Analysis of gene expression profiles and drug activity patterns by clustering and Bayesian network learning. In: Methods of Microarray Data Analysis II, pp. 169–184. Kluwer Academic Publisher (2002)
2. Chang, J.H., Hwang, K.B., Oh, S.J., Zhang, B.: Bayesian network learning with feature abstraction for gene-drug dependency analysis. J. Bioinform. Comput. Biol. 3(1), 61–77 (2005)
3. Jarvinen, P., Rajala, J., Sinervo, H.: A branch and bound algorithm for seeking the pmedian. Operational Research 20, 173–178 (1972)
4. Kutalik, Z., Beckmann, J., Sven, B.: A modular approach for integrative analysis of large-scale gene-expression and drug-response data. Nat. Biotech. 26, 531–539 (2008)
5. Paull, K.D., Shoemaker, R.H., Hodes, L., Monks, A., Scudiero, D.A., Rubinstein, L., Plowman, J., Boyd, M.R.: Display and analysis of patterns of differential activity of drugs against human tumor cell lines: development of mean graph and COMPARE algorithm. J. Natl. Cancer Inst. 81, 1088–1092 (1989)
6. Scherf, U., Ross, D.T., Waltham, M., Smith, L.H., Lee, J.K., Tanabe, L., Kohn, K.W., Reinhold, W.C., Myers, T.G., Andrews, D.T., Scudiero, D.A., Eisen, M.B., Sausville, E.A., Pommier, Y., Botstein, D., Brown, P.O., Weinstein, J.N.: A gene expression database for the molecular pharmacology of cancer. Journal of Nature Genetics 66, 236–244 (2000)

Ontology-Based Management of Uncertain Preferences in User Profiles

Joan Borràs[1,2], Aïda Valls[2], Antonio Moreno[2], and David Isern[2]

[1] Science & Technology Park for Tourism and Leisure,
C/ Joanot Martorell, 15. 43480 Vila-Seca, Catalonia, Spain
joan.borras@pct-turisme.cat
[2] Intelligent Technologies for Advanced Knowledge Acquisition (ITAKA).
Departament d'Enginyeria Informàtica i Matemàtiques, Universitat Rovira i Virgili.
Av. Països Catalans, 26. 43007 Tarragona, Catalonia, Spain
{aida.valls,antonio.moreno,david.isern}@urv.cat

Abstract. Ontologies define a set of concepts related to a certain domain as well as the relationships among them. This structure may be exploited to represent and reason about the preferences of a user. The user profile stores the degrees of interest of the user on several concepts using membership functions. In this way, each concept in the ontology is a fuzzy set and any user belongs to this fuzzy set to a certain degree. To represent the uncertainty on this information, a degree of confidence on the membership value is also included. After an initial assignment of preferences, spreading algorithms that exploit the taxonomical information of the ontology are applied to propagate the information about the user's preferences (and their associated uncertainty) through the whole set of concepts. This framework for managing uncertain preferences has been successfully applied in a Tourism recommender system.

Keywords: Recommender systems, Ontologies, Learning user profiles.

1 Introduction

In the current context of information overload, people are daily confronted with many situations in which a decision must be taken in the presence of a wide set of alternatives defined on a large number of criteria or attributes. *Recommender systems* (RS) can be very helpful in these situations, because they can analyse automatically all the information available on the possible alternatives, compare it with the user preferences or interests, rate the alternatives and present to the user the most appropriate ones. Thus, a basic component of RS is the *user profile*, which stores the information about the domain preferences.

A current research trend is the design of *semantic recommender systems* (SRS), in which the semantic information about the domain, usually represented in the form of an ontology, is used to represent both the user profile and the recommendable items. As pointed out in [3], SRS provide the benefits of semantic richness (preferences are richer and more detailed than the standard ones based solely on keywords), hierarchical

S. Greco et al. (Eds.): IPMU 2012, Part II, CCIS 298, pp. 127–136, 2012.
© Springer-Verlag Berlin Heidelberg 2012

structure (allowing an analysis of preferences at different abstraction levels) and inference (the structure of the ontology may be used to reason about the preferences on all the domain concepts). As will be mentioned in the next section, some authors have already proposed works with ontology-based user profiles, and where the ontology components (especially the concepts and the taxonomic relationships between them) are used to spread preference information through the ontology, to compare users to form clusters of people with similar tastes (in collaborative filtering systems) or to match the user preferences with the representation of each item (in content-based RS). In those systems the user profile is usually built and maintained through explicit information provided by the users (filling forms, rating items) or implicit information related to the interaction of the user with the RS (saving items, deleting items). However, up to our knowledge, the uncertainty associated to these kinds of information has not been appropriately considered and incorporated into the management of the user profile. The work presented in this paper intends to fill this gap, by proposing a general framework that allows representing and reasoning about the uncertainty associated to preferences in ontology-based SRS.

The rest of the paper is structured as follows. Section 2 reviews some related work on SRS, and points out the lack of management of the uncertainty associated to the sources of information. Section 3 explains the representation of preferences and uncertainties in the proposed framework, detailing how preferences can be easily initialized and how this initial information may be propagated downwards the ontology. Once the user has interacted with some recommended activities, the spreading algorithms detailed in section 4 update the preference and uncertainty information on all the ontology concepts. This framework has already been applied to a specific system for recommendation of touristic activities, as described in section 5. The last section provides the final conclusions and outlines some points of future work.

2   Related Work

Recommender systems require a user profile that stores the degree of interest on each different criterion that describes an item [5]. *Semantic-based recommender systems* use the semantic knowledge stored in a domain ontology to improve the accuracy of the recommendations.

One possibility is to represent both the user preferences and the domain objects using the ontology concepts. Then, the relationships between them may be used to evaluate the similarities between the user interests and the recommendable items. For example, in [1] the user profile includes all the items that have been bought by the user, along with an interest between 0 and 1. This information is transferred to the concepts that are leaves of a domain ontology. In [3] both user preferences and items are represented as a set of weights between -1 and 1 associated to the concepts of an ontology. They also propose the idea of representing user stereotypes in the same way. The initial preferences are spread through the ontology by taking into account different kinds of semantic relationships between concepts. In [7] the initial user profile associates a weight 1 to each ontology concept. By analysing the documents with which the user interacts, the weights of the user profile are dynamically updated. This information is later spread through the ontology, by considering a particular pre-computed relationship weight between each pair of ontology concepts. A collaborative version of the same idea is applied in [8]. In [9] a content-based RS that crawls and clusters scientific papers according to their keywords is presented. The system matches those items with a personal ontology of concepts related to the user.

The use of an ontology to represent user profiles permits their comparison in collaborative filtering systems. As an example, in [4], the profile stores the tags employed by the user in a social network, which belong to a predefined taxonomy. By reasoning on the taxonomical relationships it is possible to compute the semantic similarity between users, and recommend to a user the items that similar users have tagged. In [3] the authors propose to identify communities of interest from the tastes and preferences expressed by users in personal ontology-based profiles. A user receives advertisements about items that have been positively valued by other users in the same cluster. Collaborative filtering using ontology-based user profiles is also applied in [6]. In this case, the authors propose to connect user profiles creating a social folksonomy and to provide a user with a recommendation of similar users in the network.

It is worth noting that, in all the works that represent user profiles through ontologies, the explicit management of uncertainty has not been considered (neither in the user profile representation nor in the propagation of this information through the ontology). The main novel component of the work proposed in this paper is the careful consideration of the explicit and implicit sources of information about the user preferences in order to store (and reason about) not only the preferences associated to each domain concept, but also their reliability.

3   A Fuzzy Approach to Store the User Profile in an Ontology

In a RS the domain ontology permits to classify the objects of recommendation. We consider that each object is an instance of one (or several) of the lowest level classes of the ontology (*i.e.* the leaves). Thanks to the taxonomical structure of the concepts in the ontology, we can reason about the objects at different levels of generality. We propose to use the domain ontology to represent the preferences of the users of the recommender system. In this way, the concepts are interpreted as subsets of the domain in which the user can be interested. As the interest degree can be different from one concept to another, the preferences are represented using fuzzy sets.

Proposition 1. Let us consider a fuzzy set for each concept c of the ontology, so that, for each user u, $\mu_c(u)$ gives the membership degree of u to the concept c.

This membership degree is personal for each user and represents his degree of interest in a certain concept c. If the user is completely interested in c, then $\mu_c(u)=1$. Oppositely, when $\mu_c(u)=0$, we assume user u is not interested at all in concept c.

When a certain user u needs a recommendation, we propose to find the values of $\mu_c(u)$ for all the concepts in the ontology. Once the ontology has been completely labelled with $\mu_c(u)$, the RS will be able to find the most appropriate items for this user, taking into account that each object is an instance of some of the concepts. The values of $\mu_c(u)$ will be calculated using explicit and implicit information elicited from the user interaction with the system. Due to this process of estimation, there is a strong uncertainty in the preference values. To manage this uncertainty, we will consider the following confidence degree:

Proposition 2. Let us consider a confidence level $CL_c(u)$ between 0 and 1 that quantifies the confidence associated to the estimation of the membership degree of u to the concept c, denoted as $\mu_c(u)$.

A large value of $CL_c(u)$ indicates that we can trust the value of $\mu_c(u)$ as the true degree of interest of the user u for the concept c, whereas a low value indicates that the estimation is not so reliable. In that way, not only the degree of membership to the concepts in the ontology is considered to select the best alternatives, but also the confidence on the estimation of those values is taken into account. For instance, the recommender system may decide to ignore the values with a low confidence level, because they have not achieved enough support.

In summary, the user personal profile consists on a copy of the ontology that stores the degree of interest of this user on each concept, as well as the related confidence levels. As an example, let us consider a recommender system for the members of a Hiking association. Fig. 1 shows a small portion of the domain ontology, which can be used to recommend events, news or conferences of interest to the association members. As said before, it is assumed that all the recommendable items are instances of the lowest level concepts (RuralRoutes, WineRoutes, CultureRoutes, Trekking, etc.). The instances do not belong to the profile; they are stored in a database.

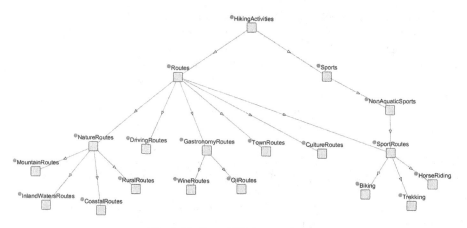

Fig. 1. Portion of Hiking ontology

3.1   Initialization of the Profile

Each ontology concept has an interest degree $\mu_c(u)$ estimated by the system, which is calculated from the collection of user information through the session, which can be extracted explicitly or implicitly. For the initialization of the user interests the application asks him to fill in a form where he can express the interest on some general domain aspects, represented by first-level ontology concepts (in the example shown in Fig. 1, those general concepts are Routes and Sports). Rating values range from 0.0 (no interest) to 1.0 (highest interest). The confidence level associated to these ratings is 1.0 because the value is fully reliable since it is given directly by the user.

3.2   Propagation of the Initial Preference and Certainty Values

The structure of the ontology may be exploited to transfer the preference information through the nodes through a *downwards propagation* of the initial preference and confidence values obtained for the first-level ontology concepts. Imagine that a user explicitly expresses a high interest in the first-level concept Routes ($\mu_{Routes}(u)=0.8$, $CL_{Routes}(u)=1.0$). This suggests an interest in different kinds of routes, which are represented by its descendants. Therefore, the system has to transfer the interest shown in the most general concept to its subclasses until the concepts in the lowest level (that are used to instantiate the items of recommendation) are reached. However, there is some level of uncertainty that the interest is equal in all its children, which increases as we propagate to deeper levels of the ontology. We propose to copy the membership degree of the user to the parent class to all its descendants, but decreasing the degree of confidence at each level by a factor α, which can be customized to the needs of the application and represents the decrease in certainty as we move down the ontology hierarchy, far from the general concepts that have been explicitly valued by the user.

Definition 1 (Downwards propagation of the initial preferences)
The preference associated to a concept c is calculated as an average of the preferences of his parents (χ^c), weighted by their confidence values. The confidence value associated to c is the average of the confidences in his parents, decremented by α:

$$\mu_c(u) = \frac{\sum_{i \in \chi^c} \mu_i(u)CL_i(u)}{\sum_{i \in \chi^c} CL_i(u)} \qquad CL_c(u) = \frac{\sum_{i \in \chi^c} CL_i(u)}{|\chi^c|} - \alpha \qquad (1)$$

4   Dynamic Refinement of the User Profile

During the execution of the recommender system, we can gather additional knowledge about the user's interests. The evidences provided by the different types of actions on the objects are used to modify both the membership degrees of the user to the related concepts and their confidence level. The information obtained about an object i affects the concepts which i is instantiating (which are leaves in the ontology).

We distinguish two main types of information that can be obtained from the interaction of the user with the recommender system:

A) Since each object is labelled with concepts at the lowest level of the ontology, we can learn about the interest of the user on these concepts by studying the actions he does on them, which can be either *positive* (*e.g.* saving a recommended item) or *negative* (*e.g.* removing a saved item). For this type of indirect feedback, the confidence level should be low.

B) Recommender systems may ask the user to rate some items shown to him. In this case, the rating values on the items can also be used to estimate the membership degree of the user to the lowest level concepts. The confidence level can be high because this is explicit information provided by the user.

Table 1 summarizes the scores s (between -1 and 1) and the weights w (between 0 and 1) associated to each user action. This feedback is useful to refine the estimation of the membership degree of the user by inferring his interests based on the behaviour of the user in front of the previously recommended objects.

Table 1. User actions collected by the system

User actions	Explicit	Implicit	s	w
Save recommended item		●	0.5	0.5
Remove recommended item		●	-0.5	0.5
Request detailed information about an item		●	0.1	0.2
Request item similar to the current one		●	0.15	0.3
Rate an item	●		[-1.0, 1.0]	1.0

Assume that we have observed a set of actions A_c on a group of objects that are instances of the concept c. The scores and weights associated to these actions are aggregated together as follows:

$$\Delta_c = \frac{\sum_{a \in A_c} s_a w_a}{\sum_{a \in A_c} w_a} \qquad CA_c = \frac{MIN(\lambda, \sum_{a \in A_c} w_a)}{\lambda} \qquad (2)$$

As can be seen in equation 2, the aggregated confidence of the actions is normalized using a parameter λ, which indicates the level above which a higher amount of evidence is not required to have a full aggregated confidence of 1. For instance, it could have a value of 2.4 if 3 good reviews (0.8*3) are considered enough to have a full confidence. If the aggregated confidence in the actions is higher than the current confidence level of the concept ($CA_c \geq CL_c$), then its preference and confidence values are updated as follows:

$$\mu_c = \begin{cases} if\,(\Delta_c > 0) & MIN(1, \mu_c + \beta \times \Delta_c) \\ else & MAX(0, \mu_c + \beta \times \Delta_c) \end{cases} \qquad CL_c = \beta \times CA_c + (1 - \beta) \times CL_c \qquad (3)$$

β is a parameter between 0 and 1 that graduates the level of change between the current values and the scores and weights given by the user actions. The higher its value, the bigger is the impact of the user actions on the concept information. For instance, if it is 0.75, the new confidence will be computed taking into account the confidence in the last action 3 times more (0.25) than the previous confidence.

4.1   Upwards Propagation

At this point, the feedback of the user has been used to modify the information stored at the lowest-level concepts of the ontology. After the system has collected a sufficiently large set of user actions, the values can be propagated through the ontology to update the values of other related concepts. In a first step, we make an *upwards propagation* to the ancestor concepts of the modified leaves. Again, the more distant an ancestor is, the more uncertainty we have.

Note that several children of the same concept may have been modified (e.g., the user may have interacted with instances of WineRoutes and OilRoutes, both children of GastronomyRoutes). Let us assume that φ^c is the set of concepts that are children of c and have confidence values higher than a certain threshold (concepts that don't have enough confidence should not influence on their parents). The aggregated preference and confidence values of the children of c may be computed as follows:

$$\Delta_c = \frac{\sum_{i \in \varphi^c} \mu_i CL_i}{\sum_{i \in \varphi^c} CL_i} \qquad CA_c = \frac{\sum_{i \in \varphi^c} CL_i}{|\varphi^c|} \tag{4}$$

If the aggregated confidence of the children of c, CA_c is higher than a threshold, then its preference and confidence values are updated as shown in equation 5. β is the parameter used in equation 3, which regulates the degree of change.

$$\mu_c = \frac{(1-\beta) \times \mu_c CL_c + \beta \times \Delta_c CA_c}{(1-\beta) \times CL_c + \beta \times CA_c} \qquad CL_c = \beta \times CA_c + (1-\beta) \times CL_c \tag{5}$$

4.2   Downwards Propagation

Once the upwards propagation has been completed, a second step propagates the preference and confidence values to the descendants of the updated nodes. For instance, if the preference of the user in SportRoutes has been modified due to the rating of some HorseRiding activities, a modification of the values for Biking and Trekking seems reasonable, due to their high semantic similarity with HorseRiding.

In this downwards propagation, the information of a concept c is modified according to the preference and confidence values of its parents, χ^c, as long as these confidence values exceed a given threshold. The aggregation of the information of the parents is done equivalently to the upwards case, as follows:

$$\Delta_c = \frac{\sum_{i \in \chi c} \mu_i CL_i}{\sum_{i \in \chi c} CL_i} \qquad CA_c = \frac{\sum_{i \in \chi c} CL_i}{|\chi c|} \tag{6}$$

If CA_c is higher than a given threshold and c has not been updated during the upwards propagation, its information is changed according to equation 5.

5   Recommendation of Touristic Activities

The ontology-based preference management framework presented in this paper has been implemented in a Web recommender system of tourist activities within the Catalan region of "Costa Daurada and Terres de l'Ebre", called SigTur. The architecture of the system and its main features are summarized in [2]. The systems considers the uncertainty associated to the transmission of general preferences down the ontology hierarchy and the uncertainty associated to the interpretation of the actions of the user.

A specific Tourism domain ontology, focused on the kind of activities available in this particular geographical area, has been manually built, following general guidelines of the World Tourism Organisation. It covers a wide variety of types of activities, which have been classified into nine main concepts that constitute the first level of the hierarchy (see Fig.2). There are 203 concepts in a 5-levels hierarchy.

1,300 activities have been catalogued in an external database, including a textual description, timetable, town and location coordinates, among others. Each activity is annotated with the lowest level concepts in the ontology to which it belongs. The initialization of the user profile is done with the information collected from the tourist with the application form shown in figure 2. In the initialization stage, these values are propagated downwards as explained in section 3.2.

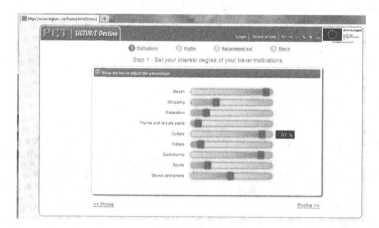

Fig. 2. Explicit user interests about generic kinds of tourist activities

Using this initial information, a first recommendation is done using both content-based and collaborative-based techniques [5]. The basic idea is that the RS considers the ontology leaves that have a certainty level above a certain threshold, and orders them according to their preference level. After that, the system builds a list of specific activities associated to the concepts of the top of this ranked list and shows them to the user. The system displays the activities and their localization on a map, as shown in Figure 3.The interaction of the user with the recommended items allows refining the user profile dynamically, as described in section 4. Users can select activities which are added to a travel planner, can ask for additional information and also rate the activity proposed. The refinement of the profile is applied after 10 user actions. Then, a new list of recommended activities is proposed to the user.

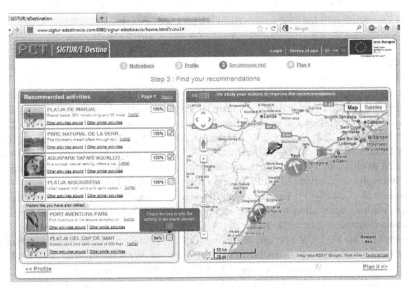

Fig. 3. SigTur graphical interface

6   Conclusions

The idea of using semantic domain knowledge to improve the accuracy of the recommendations provided by an intelligent system is compelling, and there are some works that have already suggested the use of ontologies to represent the user profile and the items of recommendation [1, 3, 7, 8]. However, those tools do not support the uncertainty associated to these preferences (both the one due to the lack of initial information and the one associated to the dynamic changes in the user profile induced from the user actions). This work suggests a first step in this direction, considering the maintenance of both preference and certainty information for each ontology concept. The framework is general enough to be usable in different applications, because the system actions (and their scores and weights) and the parameters for preference adaptation can be customized. Our future work includes a thorough analysis of the influence of these parameters in the dynamic change of the user preferences, the analysis of different aggregation procedures of the preferences coming from a set of children/parents, the study of different ways in which the information about preferences and certainties may be used by the RS, the estimation of the user satisfaction with the provided recommendations and the test of this general framework in other domains.

Acknowledgements. SigTur is a project funded by the FEDER European Regional Funds and the Government of the Province of Tarragona. Part of the work has been supported by the Universitat Rovira i Virgili (predoctoral grant of L.Marin), the Spanish Ministry of Science and Innovation (DAMASK project, Data mining algorithms with semantic knowledge, TIN2009-11005) and the Spanish Government (PlanE, Spanish Economy and Employment Stimulation Plan).

References

[1] Blanco-Fernández, Y., López-Nores, M., Pazos-Arias, J.J., García-Duque, J.: An improvement for semantics-based recommender systems grounded on attaching temporal information to ontologies and user profiles. Eng. Appl. Art. Intell. 24(8), 1385–1397 (2011)

[2] Borràs, J., de la Flor, J., Pérez, Y., Moreno, A., Valls, A., Isern, D., Orellana, A., Russo, A., Anton-Clavé, S.: SigTur/E-Destination: A System for the Management of Complex Tourist Regions. In: Proc. of International Conference on Information and Communication Technologies in Tourism, ENTER 2011, pp. 39–50. Springer, Innsbruck (2011)

[3] Cantador, I., Castells, P.: Extracting multilayered Communities of Interest from semantic user profiles: Application to group modeling and hybrid recommendations. Computers in Human Behavior 27(4), 1321–1336 (2011)

[4] Liang, H., Xu, Y., Li, Y., Nayak, R., Wang, L.T.: Personalized recommender systems integrating social tags and item taxonomy. In: Proc. of Web Intelligence and Intelligent Agent Technology, WI-IAT 2009, pp. 540–547. IEEE Press, Milano (2009)

[5] Montaner, M., López, B., de la Rosa, J.L.: A Taxonomy of Recommender Agents on the Internet. Artif. Intell. Rev. 19(3), 285–330 (2003)

[6] Nocera, A., Ursino, D.: An approach to providing a user of a "social folksonomy" with recommendations of similar users and potentially interesting resources. Know.-Based Syst. 24(8), 1277–1296 (2011)

[7] Sieg, A., Mobasher, B., Burke, R.: Learning Ontology-Based User Profiles: A Semantic Approach to Personalized Web Search. IEEE Intelligent Informatics Bulletin 8(1), 7–18 (2007)

[8] Sieg, A., Mobasher, B., Burke, R.: Improving the effectiveness of collaborative recommendation with ontology-based user profiles. In: Proc. of Information Heterogeneity and Fusion in Recommender Systems, HetRec 2010, pp. 39–46 (2010)

[9] Tang, X., Zeng, Q.: Keyword clustering for user interest profiling refinement within paper recommender systems. J. Syst. Soft. 85(1), 87–101 (2012)

Decreasing Uncertainty When Interpreting Profiles through the Traffic Lights Panel

Karina Gibert[1,2,*], Dante Conti[1,3], and Miquel Sànchez-Marrè[2,4]

[1] Dep. of Statistics and Operation Research,
Universitat Politècnica de Catalunya, Barcelona, Spain
[2] Knowledge Engineering and Machine Learning Group,
Universitat Politècnica de Catalunya, (Barcelona Tech), Spain
karina.gibert@upc.edu
[3] Dep. of Operations Research, Universidad de Los Andes, Mérida, Venezuela
[4] Dep. Software, Universitat Politècnica de Catalunya

Abstract. This paper describes Traffic Lights Panel (TLP) as a useful interpretation-oriented tool for clustering results, suitable for helping the domain experts to induce a conceptualization of the resulting profiles. Till now, the TLP is manually derived from the clustering results, but it has been well accepted by the domain experts of several real applications as a very helpful contribution to understand the classes' meaning and improve reliable decision-making. Here, a proposal to automatically construction of TLP is presented trying to mimic the real process that the analyst performs. Two criteria based on different central trend statistics of the variables inside a class are introduced, tested with a real case study in Neurorehabilitation field and compared. Finally, uncertainty concerning TLP is analyzed; the *annotated TLP* (aTLP) is proposed to visualize uncertainty associated to the decisions derived from TLP, thus enhancing robustness of TLP as a supporting tool in decision-making.

Keywords: Traffic Lights Panel, Clustering, Profiles Interpretation, KDD, Uncertainty, Decision-making, Neurorehabilitation. Post-processing.

1   Introduction

Nowadays it is well known that Knowledge Discovery (KDD) approach provides a good framework to analyze complex phenomena for getting novel and valid knowledge that can improve the background *corpus doctrinae* [3]. Fayyad's proposal marked the beginning of a new paradigm in KDD research: *"Most previous work on KDD has focused on [...] DM step. However, the other steps are of considerable importance for the successful application of KDD in practice"*, [3]. The approach included prior and posterior analysis tasks as well as the application of DM algorithms. These may in fact require great effort when dealing with real applications. Data cleaning, variable selection, transformation, selection of DM techniques and optimization of parameters (if required) are critical for a proper analysis and are often

---

* Corresponding author.

S. Greco et al. (Eds.): IPMU 2012, Part II, CCIS 298, pp. 137–148, 2012.
© Springer-Verlag Berlin Heidelberg 2012

time consuming and difficult, mainly because the processes should be tailored to each specific application and human interaction is required. Interpretation of results is also often time consuming and requires much human guidance [4].

Clustering techniques are one of the most frequently used KDD tasks in real applications [5]. In this work we are focusing on the process of post-processing the results of a clustering method as an integral part of a whole KDD process.

In this paper the *Traffic lights panel* (TLP) is presented as a symbolic postprocessing of the clustering results to help the expert to better understand the clusters and to be able to identify domain concepts referred to the discovered classes. The use of TLP has been proved extremely useful and well-accepted by domain experts in several real applications. However, till now, it has been built manually by data miners on the basis of a previous graphical representation of the classes, the Class Panel Graph (CPG), based on conditional distributions of the variables [6]. After defining the structure of the TLP, an initial proposal to build them in automatic way directly from the clustering results is presented. Two different alternatives are tested and compared here on the basis of a real case study from the neurorehabilitation field. Being this initial TLP approach a symbolic representation of the prototypical patterns characterizing the classes, uncertainty propagation to final decisions is involved by itself, since the prototypes describe central trend in the classes disregarding individual deviations from main patterns. In order to decrease this fact, a second TLP approach, called annotated TLP (aTLP) is introduced to enhance robustness of TLP as a supporting tool in decision-making processes.

On these premises, the paper has the following structure: In section 2, some techniques or facilities to interpret clustering are shown. In section 3, application domain and previous works are presented. Section 4 summarizes the TLP concept and shows a TLP derived from the case (neurorehabilitation) mentioned in section 3. Section 5 approaches the automatic building of TLP, while section 6 refers the evaluation uncertainty related to TLP and also presents the annotated TLP (aTLP) to reduce the uncertainty propagation involved in the initial approach of section 5. Finally, future works and conclusions are mentioned in section 7.

2   On Clustering Interpretation

Traditionally, the clustering results are expressed as a partition of the set of elements to be clustered (patients in this paper). So, several groups of objects are listed as final result. After that, the analyst is the responsible to identify the particularities of every group and to help the expert to discover the underlying clustering criteria that permits semantics interpretation of the results, obtaining effective valid and useful knowledge to increase the *corpus doctrinae*. Very often, basic statistics per group and some basic inference tests between groups are performed manually to understand the nature of the discovered profiles. When either the number of discovered classes and/or the number of variables to be considered is big, this is a very complex process and it becomes difficult and tedious to analyze basic statistics and decide which are the proper tests to be performed. Few works are specifically oriented to post-process clustering results with an interpretation support orientation. Some references address the problem from the structural point of view: in [10] fractal theory is used to post-process clusters and detect artificial divisions that can be merged; in [12] a method based on silhouettes is proposed to analyze the structure of the clusters; in [9] automatic interpretation of Self Organizing Maps (SOM) is done by approaching the contributions of the features to the classes. However, this do not guarantee interpretability of clusters. Only few references tackle the problem of finding the meaning of the clusters independently of the underlying clustering method. In [11] an interesting procedure in the field of image clustering is introduced: independent experts are asked to label the classes and common hyperonims of labels are then found; experts use the whole set of pictures for every cluster, which is not viable with non graphical data. In [3] Class panel graph (CPG) is introduced as tool to identify relevant variables in the classes based on conditional distributions. In [2] Traffic Light panel is proposed as an improvement to CPG. In [8] heat maps are used inside every clustering to find local relationships among variables is a health application. None of the works approaching understandability of clusters is proposing an automatic tool to support this process.

3   Application Domain and Previous Work

Neuropsychological rehabilitation seeks to reduce cognitive disability after acquired brain injury. However, there is not enough data yet to allow neuropsychological rehabilitation based on scientific evidence type I [13]. Although there is a considerable amount of comparative studies aimed to show strongest efficacy of rehabilitation versus other interventions, most of them remain inconclusive [14]. It is accepted by the international scientific community the difficulties for using standard methods as in other therapies or clinical trials in this field, mainly because the studied populations are highly heterogeneous and there is an important lack of knowledge about the natural evolution of the process for different patients, as well as for the "active" components of the treatments to be controlled [15].

On this premise, 71 patients with Traumatic Brain Injury (TBI) between 16 and 50 years, receiving neurorehabilitation treatment at the *Institut Guttmann-Hospital de Neurorehabilitació* were clustered to confirm results from [2]. All patients were administered the neuropsychological assessment at admission. Same evaluation was also performed at the end of the rehabilitation. Differences between pre- and post-treatment test scores were used to measure particular patient's improvements in brain functions related with attention, memory and executive functions. Neuropsychological assessment was based on the scales ordinary measured at the Institut Guttmann and covered the major cognitive domains [1]. A final set of 12 variables was considered to be relevant for the target problem: 3 attention scales, 4 memory and learning scales and 5 executive functions scales. A clustering process was run using the scores of 12 scales after the treatment plus the difference pre-post. This clustering provided 4 classes that were validated by the experts and reconfirmed the profiles found in [2] with a previous sample with a slightly different set of tests, see [2] for details on description: a single group of people already able to perform the tests before the treatment, which improve after treatment **Assessable** (labelled **C49** in Figure 1) and three groups of people with severe impairment before the treatment and different responses: **Global Improvement (C47)**, equals levels of assessable group after treatment, **DysExecutive (C46)**, still problems with executive functions after the treatment and **Resistant (C40)**, still severe impairment after the treatment, they do not respond to the treatment.

4 The Traffic Light Panels

Traffic lights panel (TLP) was introduced in [2] after realizing that the histograms or boxplots represented in the CPG could be perceived as too technical by some non-technical experts as environmental experts or medical experts, even if they appeared conveniently marked by the analyst with the relevant values of the variables. The TLP displays the qualitative dominant levels of a set of variables through a set of classes. It corresponds, in fact, to an abstraction of the information provided by the CPG, providing a more symbolic representation, which is closer to the interpretation codes of a non-technical expert, like a physician, biologist, chemical engineer or psychologist.

The analyst has to read the CPG, mark the characteristic values of the variables for the different classes and assign qualitative levels to those values. The dominant level of a variable in a given class can be determined in two ways: a) Identify the qualitative level of the mean or median of the variable in the class, b) Identify the qualitative level of the mode of the variable in the class.

When the variables have only 3 qualitative levels assigned, it is very interesting to assign the colours of a traffic light to those levels (red for the bad or negative value, yellow for the medium or neutral value and green for the good or positive value), being the *bad* values the higher or lower values of the variable depending on the variable's semantics. This is explaining the name of the graph. If more than 3 qualitative levels should be considered, intermediate colours should be included. But, it is important to keep red and green as non-verbal codes for *bad* and *good* values to connect with the expert's implicit codes for interpreting. An important property of the TLP is that, as the classes are well-constructed, they must be distinguishable, and they must represent different profiles. Thus, there should not be two rows of the graph with the same combination of colours.

For the application case presented in section 2, 4 classes with different kind of responses to treatment were found. Figure 1 shows the CPG of the 12 relevant variables after (POST) the treatment and also the differences (DIFE) between before and after the treatment scores. The column *Classe* indicates the class and the column n_c indicates the number of patients classified in every class.

The analyst was then marking the characteristic values of the variables over the CPG in the different classes and assigned qualitative levels and colours to every value. Instead of presenting the marked CPG to the expert, the TLP was build. Figure 2 shows in a graphical way how the TLP for the memory tests was constructed. For every variable it has been analyzed whether the high scores represented a good performance of the tests by the patient or a bad one and colours were assigned accordingly. The same procedure was used for the whole set of variables. Figure 3 shows the complete TLP presented to the expert. Upon that panel, the experts were able to clearly identify the type of treatment response represented by each profile and could conveniently conceptualize those prototypical response patterns as described in section 2. Therefore, the main idea of TLP could be described as a symbolic abstraction of the CPG providing information closer to the expert knowledge and making even easier the process of recognizing the concepts represented by the profiles. The final interpretation process is:

1. Perform the Class panel graph (CPG) of all the variables versus the discovered classes
2. Calculate the basic statistics per class
3. Using materials from steps 1 and 2 identify variables or combination of variables with specific ranges of values in a class that distinguish the class from the others.
4. Assign qualitative levels to the variables implied in step 3 by detecting the area where the mass of the distribution is placed.
5. Perform a TLP for the variables, using the qualitative values assigned in step 4
6. Show the Traffic lights panel to the expert and ask him to select a label for the class. The expert is conceptualizing the class in this step, on the basis of the Traffic lights panel
7. Perform significance tests assessing relevance of differences for the variables implied in step 6, for instance: ANOVA, Kruskall-Wallis or χ^2 independence tests depending on the item.

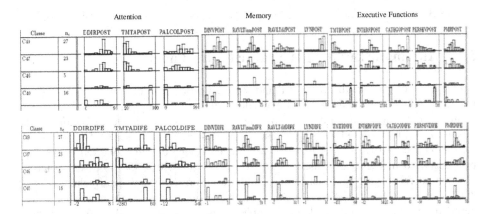

Fig. 1. Class Panel Graph for the whole set of tests (After the treatment "POST" and the score differences between pre and post treatment "DIFE"). Columns show conditional distribution of each variable against classes.

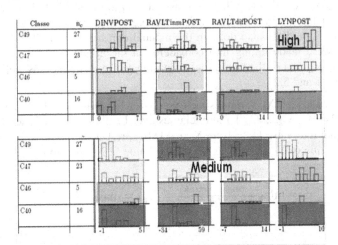

Fig. 2. Transformation of a Class panel graph in a Traffic lights panel (memory tests)

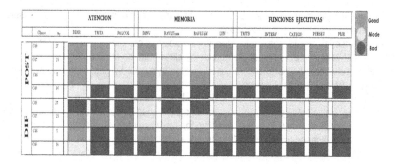

Fig. 3. Complete Traffic lights panel for the whole set of tests considered in the analysis

5   Automatic Building of Traffic Lights Panel

On the basis of the usefulness of TLP and the final process of interpretation described in the previous section, the next step would consist in finding robust criteria which addresses the problem of automatic building of TLP. In this work, we are dealing with this automation problem by trying to mimic the real process that the analyst performs for the TLP construction. For that reason, the percentage of cells coloured as the expert proposed in Figure 3 is used as quality index to evaluate the proposed criteria. Two initial criteria are approached here, both based on basic statistics (mean and median) related to the central trend of the variable inside a class. The main idea is focused on dividing the range of the variable in three equal intervals and establishes decision rules which allow automatic assignment of qualitative levels (LEFT "L", CENTERED "C" and RIGHT "R") to represent the area where the distribution of the variable concentrates inside every class. Further connection between qualitative levels and semantics of the variable will permit association to the traffic light colours in the correct sense, namely *direct colour coding* (red-yellow-green) or *reverse colour coding* (green-yellow-red) as also done in the manual construction of TLP. Some initial experiments were made taking into consideration the application case presented in Section 3. Description of the two initial criteria tested in this paper, as well as results are shown in 5.1 and 5.2.

Notation: Given a set o X_K variables measured over I individuals ($I = \{i_1, i_2,...,i_n\}$), a partition P ($P = \{C_1, C_2,....,C_m\}$) of m classes over I and the range of each X_k divided into three equal intervals, $D_k = [\min X_k, r_{k-}) \cup [r_{k-}, r_{k+}] \cup (r_{k+}, \max X_k]$ with min X_k as minimum value of X_k, max X_k as maximum value of X_k, r_{k-} and r_{k+} defined as follows:

$$r_{k-} = \min_k + \frac{(maxk - mink)}{3} \qquad r_{k+} = \max_k - \frac{(maxk - mink)}{3} \qquad (1)$$

5.1 Criterion 1: Automatic Construction of TLP Based on Equal Ranges and Conditional Mean

Since the most intuitive indicator for the central trend of a distribution is the mean, this first criterion uses the conditional mean of every variable in each class $\bar{X}_k|C$ to decide qualitative level of the TLP cell by following this decision rule:

> For each X_k
> For each C.
>> If $\bar{X}_k|C \in [\min X_k, r_{k-})$ then TLP cell is labelled as LEFT
>> If $\bar{X}_k|C \in [r_{k-}, r_{k+}]$ then TLP cell is labelled as CENTERED
>> If $\bar{X}_k|C \in (r_{k+}, \max X_k]$ then TLP cell is labelled as RIGHT
> End for
> End for

In fact, the effective induction of the TLP from data is not using the CPG as an input, but an initial table providing the conditional mean for each variable and class. Next, results obtained by the sample data used as a reference are provided. Table 1 shows the conditional means for each variable and class. From this information a new table with qualitative levels identifying the central trend of the variable is obtained (Table 2) by applying the decisional rules established above, and translated to colours according to the semantics of the variable to get the final TLP (figure 4).

From figure 4, using the proportion of cells coloured diversely than the expert did in Figure 3 as a quality indicator of the proposed TLP (Figure 3) a 79.17% of correctness is found with this criterion. However, although these figures could be more than acceptable for classical model fitting, being the TLP an interpretation oriented tool, we are interested in finding a new criterion with raises as much as possible the quality of the TLP.

Table 1. Conditional means of variables by classes

	ATTENTION			MEMORY				EXECUTIVE FUNCTIONS				
	DDIRPOST	TMTAPOST	PALCOLPOST	DINVPOST	RAVLTinmPOST	RAVLTdifPOST	LYNPOST	TMTBPOST	INTERFPOST	CATEGOPOST	PERSEVPOST	PMRPOST
Class 49	6,33	65,07	36,44	4,59	45,22	6,44	9,36	139,19	4,69	4,44	19,07	36,67
Class 47	5,57	79,48	30,00	3,61	37,87	4,87	7,29	171,48	0,44	3,83	17,13	31,70
Class 46	5,40	146,20	21,60	4,40	56,60	9,40	5,00	294,60	-8,49	5,00	14,40	28,40
Class 40	3,38	261,56	7,44	1,81	17,00	1,69	0,00	480,88	-19,71	0,31	47,63	7,81
Global Mean	5,35	119,73	26,77	3,63	37,28	5,07	7,23	237,59	-3,11	3,35	24,55	27,97
	DDIRDIFE	TMTADIFE	PALCOLDIFE	DINVDIFE	RAVLTinmDIFE	RAVLTdifDIFE	LYNDIFE	TMTBDIFE	INTERFDIFE	CATEGODIFE	PERSEVDIFE	PMRDIFE
Class 49	0,30	-49,70	5,96	0,67	7,78	1,11	1,64	-147,74	1,78	2,44	-12,30	10,93
Class 47	3,96	-212,26	25,91	2,48	25,00	3,17	6,57	-328,52	17,55	3,43	-23,13	16,09
Class 46	5,40	-3,00	1,20	4,40	56,60	9,40	5,00	-14,20	0,75	2,60	-19,60	6,80
Class 40	1,88	-37,81	4,88	0,94	8,69	0,50	0,00	-9,13	3,29	0,00	-0,44	-0,44
Global Mean	2,20	-96,39	11,85	1,58	17,00	2,23	3,14	-165,66	7,16	2,23	-13,65	9,75

Table 2. Qualitative levels induced by the equal ranges and conditional mean criterion

	ATTENTION			MEMORY				EXECUTIVE FUNCTIONS				
	DDIRPOST	TMTAPOST	PALCOLPOST	DINVPOST	RAVLTinmPOST	RAVLTdifPOST	LYNPOST	TMTBPOST	INTERFPOST	CATEGOPOST	PERSEVPOST	PMRPOST
Class 49	RIGHT	LEFT	CENTERED	CENTERED	CENTERED	CENTERED	RIGHT	LEFT	CENTERED	CENTERED	CENTERED	CENTERED
Class 47	CENTERED	LEFT	CENTERED	CENTERED	CENTERED	CENTERED	CENTERED	LEFT	CENTERED	CENTERED	CENTERED	CENTERED
Class 46	CENTERED	CENTERED	CENTERED	CENTERED	RIGHT	RIGHT	CENTERED	CENTERED	LEFT	RIGHT	LEFT	CENTERED
Class 40	CENTERED	RIGHT	LEFT	LEFT	LEFT	LEFT	LEFT	RIGHT	RIGHT	LEFT	RIGHT	LEFT
	DDIRDIFE	TMTADIFE	PALCOLDIFE	DINVDIFE	RAVLTinmDIFE	RAVLTdifDIFE	LYNDIFE	TMTBDIFE	INTERFDIFE	CATEGODIFE	PERSEVDIFE	PMRDIFE
Class 49	LEFT	RIGHT	LEFT	LEFT	CENTERED	CENTERED	LEFT	CENTERED	LEFT	CENTERED	CENTERED	CENTERED
Class 47	CENTERED	LEFT	CENTERED	CENTERED	CENTERED	CENTERED	RIGHT	LEFT	CENTERED	RIGHT	LEFT	CENTERED
Class 46	RIGHT	RIGHT	LEFT	RIGHT	RIGHT	RIGHT	CENTERED	RIGHT	LEFT	CENTERED	CENTERED	CENTERED
Class 40	CENTERED	RIGHT	LEFT	LEFT	CENTERED	CENTERED	LEFT	RIGHT	LEFT	LEFT	CENTERED	CENTERED

	ATTENTION			MEMORY				EXECUTIVE FUNCTIONS				
	DDIRPOST	TMTAPOST	PALCOLPOST	DINVPOST	RAVLTinmPOST	RAVLTdifPOST	LYNPOST	TMTBPOST	INTERFPOST	CATEGOPOST	PERSEVPOST	PMRPOST
Class 49												
Class 47												
Class 46												
Class 40												
	DDIRDIFE	TMTADIFE	PALCOLDIFE	DINVDIFE	RAVLTinmDIFE	RAVLTdifDIFE	LYNDIFE	TMTBDIFE	INTERFDIFE	CATEGODIFE	PERSEVDIFE	PMRDIFE
Class 49												
Class 47												
Class 46												
Class 40												

Fig. 4. Induced TLP by using the equal ranges and conditional mean criterion

5.2   Criterion 2: Automatic Construction of TLP Based on Equal Ranges and Conditional Median

As the results in section 4.1 points a low performance of the mean mainly due to its lack of robustness to the outliers presence, and taking into account that in many real applications highly skewed distributions may appear and outliers can also perturb the mean, a second criteria is tested here.

Therefore, a most robust central trend statistics, the conditional median of every variable in each class $Me_k|C$ is used to decide qualitative level of the TLP cell by following this decision rule:

For each X_k

        For each C

           If $Me_k|C \in [\min X_k, r_{k-})$ then TLP cell is labelled as LEFT

           If $Me_k|C$ (r_{k-}, r_{k+}) then TLP cell is labelled as CENTERED

           If $Me_k|C$ $(r_{k+}, \max X_k]$ then TLP cell is labelled as RIGHT

        End for

End for

Following the same remarks from criterion 1 but applied to conditional medians, results are shown in table 3 and figure 5.

Being the Median a robust indicator of the central trend of a distribution, which disregards skewnesses and outliers, the TLP obtained in this second case is replicating much better the criteria really used by the experts. The tax of correctness increases in more than 10 points in comparison with the results obtained in criterion 1and reaches a level of 91.67%. Hence, conditional medians criterion seems to be a better way to initialize the automatic building of TPL approached in this paper.

Table 3. Conditional medians of variables by classes

	ATTENTION			MEMORY				EXECUTIVE FUNCTIONS				
	DDIRPOST	TMTAPOST	PALCOLPOST	DINVPOST	RAVLTinmPOST	RAVLTdifPOST	LYNPOST	TMTBPOST	INTERFPOST	CATEGOPOST	PERSEVPOST	PMRPOST
Class 49	6	50	38	4	50	6	9	107	4	6	16	36
Class 47	6	53	30	4	43	6	8	132	0,81	5	17	30
Class 46	5	55	26	5	56	10	5	300	-3,29	6	9	30
Class 40	4	300	0	2	0	0	0	500	-25	0	50	0
Global Median	6	62	30	4	45	5	8	153	0,81	4	20	30
	DDIRDIFE	TMTADIFE	PALCOLDIFE	DINVDIFE	RAVLTinmDIFE	RAVLTdifDIFE	LYNDIFE	TMTBDIFE	INTERFDIFE	CATEGODIFE	PERSEVDIFE	PMRDIFE
Class 49	0	-10	4	1	4	1	1	-80	0	3	-12	7
Class 47	5	-247	26	3	31	3	6	-368	23,51	4	-28	21
Class 46	5	0	0	5	56	10	5	0	0	3	-14	0
Class 40	0,5	0	0	0	0	0	0	0	0	0	0	0
Global Median	1	-18	4	1	10	1	3	-80	0	0	-9	6

	ATTENTION			MEMORY				EXECUTIVE FUNCTIONS				
	DDIRPOST	TMTAPOST	PALCOLPOST	DINVPOST	RAVLTimmPOST	RAVLTdifPOST	LYNPOST	TMTBPOST	INTERFPOST	CATEGOPOST	PERSEVPOST	PMRPOST
Class 49												
Class 47												
Class 46												
Class 40												
	DDIRDIFE	TMTADIFE	PALCOLDIFE	DINVDIFE	RAVLTimmDIFE	RAVLTdifDIFE	LYNDIFE	TMTBDIFE	INTERFDIFE	CATEGODIFE	PERSEVDIFE	PMRDIFE
Class 49												
Class 47												
Class 46												
Class 40												

Fig. 5. Induced TLP by using the equal ranges and conditional mean criterion

6   Uncertainty Evaluation on Traffic Light Panels

In this paper, a particular application to the neurorehabilitation field has been presented, although the TLP has been used to conceptualize profiles in many other applications, like profiles of mental health systems in low and middle income countries, in collaboration with the World Health Organization, Borderline Personality Disorder profiles in collaboration with the Hospital Vall Hebrón in Barcelona, waste-water treatment plants profiles in collaboration with the LEQUIA (Spain) [7]. From this experiences we have seen that, being a symbolic representation of the prototypical patterns characterizing the classes only based on the central trends, the TLP involves an intrinsic ambiguity regarding the uncertainty propagated to the final conceptualization, and even getting a criteria producing 100% correct TLP, enrichment is still required to provide good decision-making support.

From the basic representation offered in section 3, it cannot be distinguished whereas a yellow cell is corresponding to:

1. A quite homogeneous class with elements concentrated in intermediate values (see PMRdife C49).
2. A very heterogeneous class with low elements in intermediate values and a high tax of elements in both low and high values (see DinvDife in C47).

This uncertainty is propagated to the final conceptualization, and has direct incidence to the reliability of the decisions or actions associated to the induced profiles.

A second contribution of this work is to propose the *annotated TLP* (aTPL), which is an enrichment of the original TLP including information about the variability of the classes. Variation coefficient ($VC = s_k / \overline{x}_k$,) of the variables conditioned to the classes (see Table 4) is used instead of classical standard deviation since VC is a normalized coefficient which is adimensional and its values have the same semantics for all the variables. This permits to establish a single gradation for all variables (low – medium and high variability). Thus, a darkening of the basic colour of every cell in the TLP will be applied to indicate decreasing in class purity. The degree of darkening can be calculated proportionally to the variation coefficient associated to the cell. Here a first approach is used where low variation (VC<0.30) implies basic colour and high variation (VC>0.90) implies hard darkening of basic colour and light darkening is for intermediate values. Results of a first *aTLP* applied to TLP (got by criterion 2) are shown in figure 6. It can be seen a considerable number of dark cells, what means quite high heterogeneity associated and uncertainty related to the final profiles derived. Experts will have to take into account that the induced profiles can involve high individual variability and decision-making should be corrected accordingly, in other words, strong decisions are only justified on the basic colour cells whereas major caution is required when decisions involve darker cells.

Table 4. Variation Coefficients of variables by classes

	ATTENTION			MEMORY				EXECUTIVE FUNCTIONS				
	DDIRPOST	TMTAPOST	PALCOLPOST	DINVPOST	RAVLTinmPOST	RAVLTdifPOST	LYNPOST	TMTBPOST	INTERFPOST	CATEGOPOST	PERSEVPOST	PMRPOST
Class 49	0,19	0,82	0,36	0,26	0,40	0,64	0,14	0,70	2,28	0,45	0,64	0,43
Class 47	0,33	0,96	0,49	0,36	0,52	0,70	0,32	0,71	26,19	0,66	0,89	0,69
Class 46	0,21	0,96	1,03	0,20	0,03	0,40	0,00	0,71	1,82	0,28	0,86	0,70
Class 40	0,73	0,32	1,89	0,73	1,34	1,98	0,00	0,12	0,51	2,79	0,14	1,82
Global VC	0,38	0,91	0,67	0,44	0,60	0,83	0,48	0,73	4,67	0,76	0,71	0,74
	DDIRDIFE	TMTADIFE	PALCOLDIFE	DINVDIFE	RAVLTinmDIFE	RAVLTdifDIFE	LYNDIFE	TMTBDIFE	INTERFDIFE	CATEGODIFE	PERSEVDIFE	PMRDIFE
Class 49	3,22	1,78	1,55	1,25	2,08	2,61	1,23	1,05	4,69	0,99	1,45	1,12
Class 47	0,64	0,39	0,66	0,78	0,85	0,96	0,33	0,37	0,74	0,74	0,85	1,72
Class 46	0,21	2,24	2,24	0,20	0,03	0,40	0,00	2,24	2,24	1,00	1,11	4,11
Class 40	1,21	2,19	2,23	1,38	1,68	2,53	0,00	5,98	2,18	1,00	24,55	31,63
Global VC	1,17	1,18	1,33	1,11	1,27	1,57	1,00	1,05	1,67	1,14	1,39	2,10

	ATTENTION			MEMORY				EXECUTIVE FUNCTIONS					VC < 0,30
	DDIRPOST	TMTAPOST	PALCOLPOST	DINVPOST	RAVLTinmPOST	RAVLTdifPOST	LYNPOST	TMTBPOST	INTERFPOST	CATEGOPOST	PERSEVPOST	PMRPOST	0,30<VC<0,90
Class 49													VC>0,90
Class 47													
Class 46													
Class 40													
	DDIRDIFE	TMTADIFE	PALCOLDIFE	DINVDIFE	RAVLTinmDIFE	RAVLTdifDIFE	LYNDIFE	TMTBDIFE	INTERFDIFE	CATEGODIFE	PERSEVDIFE	PMRDIFE	
Class 49													
Class 47													
Class 46													
Class 40													

Fig. 6. Induced annotated TLP (aTPL)

7   Conclusions and Future Works

The TLP has been confirmed as a powerful visual tool to support the conceptualization of a set of profiles obtained by some clustering methods, provided that the clustering results have been properly validated previously. In this work, preliminary results to find an effective way to build the TLP automatically are shown. Making a basic division of the range of variables in three equal-length intervals, a central trend indicator of the variables in every class is used to identify the qualitative level of the variable where the mass of the distribution is concentrated. These levels can easily be translated to traffic lights colours considering the codes provided by the user in relation to the semantics of the variable, and thus, decide a direct coding or a reverse coding into the TLP.

Two criteria have been tested using both mean and median as basic statistic. Results obtained for the application case allows pointing out that conditional median criterion has a better performance. Future works related to refine this criterion will be developed: Dividing the range of the variable not in equal intervals but using different values of quartiles, include bootstrapping techniques and use of non-parametric tests like U-Mann Whitney in the decisional rules are in progress.

The annotated TLP (aTLP) includes additional information about the variance of the conditional distributions of the variables in every class and this quantifies the uncertainty of the conceptualizations induced upon TLPs. New decision rules for automatic building of aTLP will be reviewed and studied. In this way the robustness of TLPs as supporting tool in decision making processes will be focalised to decrease uncertainty propagation to the decision-making.

Acknowledgements. This research has been partially financed by project TIN2004-01368 from the Comisión Interministerial de Ciencia y Tecnología, a project from the Secretaría de Estado de Servicios Sociales, Familia y Discapacidad del Ministerio de Trabajo y Asuntos Sociales. Thanks to the Institut Guttmann, hospital de neurore-habilitació, to Instituto de Salud Carlos III and to Agència d'Avaluació de Tecnolo-gies i Recerca Mèdiques de la Generalitat de Catalunya. Authors wants specially thanks the medical experts from Institut Guttmann directly implied in the application presented in the paper, Dr. José María Tormos, Dra. Teresa Roig-Rovira, Dra. Montse Bernabeu and very special thanks to Dr. Alberto García-Molina and Dr. Alejandro García-Rudolph.

References

1. Lezak, M.D.: Neuropsychological Assessment, 4th edn. Oxford University Press, New York (2004)
2. Gibert, K., et al.: Response to TBI-neurorehabilitation through an AI& Stats hybrid KDD methodology. Medical Archives 62(3), 132–135 (2008)
3. Fayyad, U.: Advances in Knowledge Discovery and Data Mining. MIT Press, Cambridge (1996)
4. Gibert, K., et al.: Data Mining for Environmental Systems. In: Environmental Modelling, Software and Decision Support. State of the art and New Perspectives. IDEA Series, vol. (3), pp. 205–228. Elsevier (2008)
5. Gibert, K., Sànchez-Marrè, M.: Outcomes from the iEMSs Data Mining in the Environmental Sciences Workshop Series. Environmental Modelling and Software (26), 983–985 (2011)
6. Gibert, K., Nonell, R., Velarde, J.M., Colillas, M.M.: Knowledge Discovery with clustering: impact of metrics and reporting phase by using KLASS. Neural Network World (04), 319–326 (2005)
7. Gibert, K., Rodríguez-Silva, G., Rodríguez-Roda, I.: Knowledge Discovery with Clustering based on rules by States: A water treatment application. Environmental Modelling and Software (25), 712–723 (2010)
8. Lindsey, J.C., Jacobson, D.L., Li, H., Houseman, E.A., Aldrovandi, G.M., Mulligan, K.: Using Cluster Heat Maps to Investigate Relationships Between Body Composition and Laboratory Measurements in HIV-Infected & HIV-Uninfected Children & Young Adults. J. of Acquired Immune Deficiency Syndromes 59(3), 325–338 (1999)
9. Siponen, M., Vesanto, J., Simula, O., Vasara, P.: An approach to automated interpretation of SOM. Advances in Self-Organising Maps, 89–94 (2001)
10. Yan, G., Li, Z.: Using cluster similarity to detect natural cluster hierarchies. In: Proceedings of Fourth International Conference on Fuzzy Systems and Knowledge Discovery, pp. 291–295 (2007)

11. Barnard, K., Duygulu, P., Forsyth, D.: Clustering art. In: Computer Vision and Pattern Recognition, vol. 2, pp. 434–441 (2001)
12. Trauwaert, T., Rouseew, P., Kauffman, L.: Some silhouette-based graphics for clustering interpretation. Belgian J. Operations Research, Statistics and Computer Science 29(3), 35–55
13. Rohling, M.: Effectiveness of Cognitive Rehabilitation Following Acquired Brain Injury: A Meta-Analytic Re-Examination of Cicerone et al.'s (2000, 2005) Systematic Reviews. Neuropsychology 23(1), 20–39 (2009)
14. ECRI, Cognitive Rehabilitation Therapy for Traumatic Brain Injury: What We Know and Don't Know about Its Efficacy, EDITORIAL NOTE 10/11/11: IOM.s New Report on Brain Injury Treatments Draws Conclusions Similar to ECRI Institute's Earlier Findings (2011)
15. Tormos (ed.): Desarrollo de Herramientas para evaluar el resultado de las tecnologías aplicadas al proceso rehabilitador. Estudio a partir de dos modelos concretos: Lesión Medular y Daño Cerebral Adquirido. Madrid: Plan de Calidad para el Sistema Nacional de Salud. Ministerio de Sanidad y Consumo. Agència d'avaluació de tecnologia i recerca mèdiques de Catalunya. Informes de evaluación de tecnologías sanitarias AATRM, n 2006/12 (2007)

Determining Affinity of Users in Social Networks Using Fuzzy Sets

Ronald R. Yager[1] and Marek Z. Reformat[2]

[1] Iona College, NY, USA
yager@panix.com
[2] University of Alberta, Edmonton, Canada
Marek.Reformat@ualberta.ca

Abstract. More and more often the web is perceived as a new social platform. The users exchange information and opinion about different items posted on the web. It is easily observed in one of the forms of web 2.0 called tagging. Tagging is a process of annotating (labeling) digital items – called resources – by users. A single user can describe a number of items using a number of different tags.

Users' signatures – created based on such activities – can be used to determine similarity between users, and give users a way to find new friends with similar interests and options. This concept is investigated here.

The paper describes a process of creating fuzzy-based users' signatures and comparing them for the purpose of finding similar users.

1   Introduction

The introduction of the web 2.0 "pushes" the web-based interaction among users – social contact – to even higher levels. It allows users to be more involved in the process of adding to the content of web and sharing it with others. With the web 2.0, the users can easily leave their observations and opinions on the web, and allow others to see them and express their own options about the same digital items, called hereafter web resources.

Popular social services on the web, like Delicious (*del.isio.us*), Furl (*furl.net*), Flickr (*flickr.com*), and CiteULike (*citeulike.org*), allow users to annotate and categorize web resources. The annotation processes performed by users means labeling resources with tags. Tags represent any strings that user consider appropriate as descriptions of resources on the web. Resources, on the other hand, could be any items that have been posted on the Internet, and are accessible by users. The process of labeling – annotating – resources performed by users is called *tagging* [1].

The changes happening to the web and easiness of utilizing it create new expectations among users. They see the web as a place that potentially can help them to find other individuals that are similar to them, or have similar sets of interests.

At the same time, users' activities on the web are easier to monitor. Analysis and processing of these activities can allow for determining users' characteristic features,

S. Greco et al. (Eds.): IPMU 2012, Part II, CCIS 298, pp. 149–160, 2012.
© Springer-Verlag Berlin Heidelberg 2012

and building users' profiles. In the case of tagging, these profiles are built based on a set of resources the user labelled, and a set of tags she used.

The fact that a single tag is associated with a number of resources, and a single resource is associated with a number of tags creates an opportunity to look at tags and resources from the perspective of fuzzy sets [2]. Once a tag fuzzy set and a resource fuzzy set are determined they can be combined to create fuzzy relation that represents a user. The concept of fuzzy representation of a single user – called here fuzzy signature of a user – is developed here. The fuzzy signatures of users are further used to determine a level of similarity between users.

2   Tag Clouds as User-Driven Resource Descriptors

2.1   Concepts and Example

A growing involvement of users in building repositories of digital items and being responsible for their maintenance brings a new approach to a process of describing resources. This new approach is called *tagging*. All items are described by anyone who "sees" them and wants to provide his/her description and/or comment. Experts are not required to provide category structures and their descriptions. This bottom-up approach becomes quite popular due to its simplicity, effectiveness, and enjoyableness [3].

Tagging becomes a source of information that is used for a number of research topics: for discovering changes in behavioral patterns of users [4], for inferring about global semantics fitting a bottom-up approach to semantic annotation of web resources [5]. There is also an interesting work targeting the issues of tag similarity and relatedness [6], as well as discovering regularities in user activities, tag frequencies, and kinds of tags used [7].

As an example let us take a look at the LibraryThing (*LibraryThing.com*) – a web site with descriptions of more than 15 millions of books, and with more than 200,000 users who used more than 20 millions tags. If we look for a book *One Hundred Years of Solitude* we obtain a list of related tags – keywords "attached" to this book by different users. Such tags are "Latin America", "latin american literature", "Colombia", "fiction", "magical realism", and "satire", Fig. 1.

1001 **20th century** classic classics **Colombia** Colombian Colombian literature Columbia family fantasy **fiction** Gabriel Garcia Marquez **Latin America** **latin american literature** literature **magical realism** marquez Nobel **Nobel Prize** **novel** own read Roman **South America** Spanish TBR to read translated translation unread

Fig. 1. Tags for *One Hundred Years of Solitude* (TBR stands for To Be Read)

This list represents a "user-based" description of the book. The tags express users' perception of the book, as well as the meanings and associations that the book brings to them. Some tags represent users' interests, for example "American literature", "historical fiction", "humor", "military", while some other ones represent users' ways of describing the book – "own", "to read", "unread".

The tags play the role of "hooks" for pulling information from other sites. In this case they can represent links to other resources, located anywhere on the web, that are "associated" with the same tags [3].

2.2   Tag-Clouds and Their Importance

A tagging process performed by multiple users means that many tags are used to annotate a single resource, and multiplicity of those tags can vary. A graphical representation of such scenario is called a tag-cloud. It is a way of presenting tags where more frequently assigned tags, to a given resource, are emphasized – usually in size or color. Tag clouds tell at a glance which tags are more popular.

The previously presented set of tags for *One Hundred Years of Solitude* (Fig. 1) is an example of such a tag-cloud. Each tag is of different size proportional to a number representing how many times a given tag was used by different users to label the resource. In our example, the book *One Hundred Years of Solitude* has been labeled with the tag "fiction" by 2,954 users, with the tag "magical realism" by 1,320 users, the "novel" by 610, the "Latin America" by 594, the "literature" by 504, the "Colombia" by 324 users, the "Spanish" by 309, the "latin american literature" by 307, and the "South America" by 303.

3   Tagging Definitions and Structure

3.1   General Overview

Following [Hotho06], a tagging system can be represented as a tuple. The formal definition is as follows:

Definition 1. A tagging system is a tuple TS=(U, T, R, Y) where U, T and R are finite sets with elements *users*, *tags* and *resources* respectively, while Y is a relation between the sets, i.e., Y is subset of U x T x R. A *post* is a triple (u, T_{ur}, r) with u $\in$ U, and r $\in$ R, and a non-empty set T_{ur} = {t $\in$ T| (u, t, r) from Y}.

The relation (u_k, t_i, r_j) means that the user u_k assigned the tag t_i to the resource r_j. Such definition allows us to define other quantities, for example, an occurrence.

Definition 2. An occurrence of a given tag t_i as a label for a resource r_j is given by the number of triples (u_k, t_i, r_j) where u_k is any user that belongs to U, i.e.,

$$occur_{i,j}(t_i, r_j) = card\{(u_k, t_i, r_j) \in Y \mid u_k \in U\} \tag{3.1}$$

3.2   Tags and Resources

Given a tagging system (U, T, R, Y), we define the Resource-Tag Graph – RTG – as a weighted undirected graph whose set of vertices is a union of sets T and R. A tag t_i

and a resource r_j are connected by an edge, iff there is at least one post (u_k, T_{ur}, r_j) where t_i is $\in T_{ur}$, and $u_k \in U$. The weight of this edge is given by the occurrence $occur_{i,j}(t_i, r_j)$.

An interesting representation of the tag-cloud, together with a bigger fragment of RTG containing this tag-cloud, is presented in Fig. 2. It contains three resources **r1**, **r2**, and **r3**, and a number of tags – from **t1** to **t10**. Each connection of this network is associated with a number representing how many times a given tag has been used in describing a given resource – $occur_{i,j}(t_i, r_j)$.

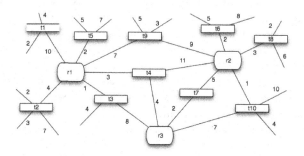

Fig. 2. A snippet of RTG with resources (**r1-3**) and tags (**t1-10**). The tags also label other resources not shown here. Numbers indicate how many times a tag was used to label a resource – occurrences.

4   Fuzzy Representation of User's Interests and Activities

4.1   User's Interests and Actions as Fuzzy Sets

Social networks users constantly interact with their peers, add new items and tags, as well as tag items they experienced. One of the ways of looking at this activity is a single slice of a <U,R,T> matrix that is related to a given user u_l. Such a slice could look like the one presented in Table 1 (the table contains also information about another user u_j, this information will be used later in the paper).

This two-dimensional matrix represents all information about activities of the user u_l. Any time she uses a tag to describe an item (resource), a trace is left in the matrix. A mark is put at the crossing of a specific tag and recourse to indicate user's interest in this tag and resource. If we sum up the cells (treating x as one) over a single row we obtain frequency of usage of a given tag – the column "tag frequency", if we sum them up over a column we obtain a number of tags used by the user to describe a resource – the row "tags/resource". See Table 1 for sample values.

A closer look at the row "tags/resource" in Table 1 allows us to think about these numbers as indicators of importance/attractiveness of resources for the user. The idea of building a fuzzy set "Resource Attractiveness" – *ResAttract* for short – seems to be natural. This is a set with membership functions representing a degree of attention the user commits to each of the resources. There are multiple ways of building such a fuzzy set. One of them is proposed below:

$$ResAttract_{u\_k}(r) = \{\frac{b_1}{r_1}, \frac{b_2}{r_2}, ... \frac{b_m}{r_m}, ... \frac{b_M}{r_M}\}$$

where

$$b_m = \frac{\text{\# of tags used for } r_m \text{ by } u_k}{\text{max \# of different tags used for a single resource by } u_k}$$

The values of the proposed membership function are determined as a ratio of a number of tags the user used for a given resource to a maximum number of tags the user used to label a single resource among all resources labelled by the user. In other words, the value assigned to a single resource expresses the user's degree of attention dedicated to this resource when compared to the most "popular" resource, i.e., the resource with the highest number of labels given by the user.

Table 1. A slice of <U, R, T> matrix representing activates of two users u_i and u_j

resource / tag	r1 ui/uj	r2 ui/uj	r3 ui/uj	r4 ui/uj	r5 ui/uj	r6 ui/uj	r7 ui/uj	r8 ui/uj	r9 ui/uj	r10 ui/uj	tag freq.
t1	x/x	x/x								-/x	2/3
t2		x/x	x/x					x/x			3/3
t3	-/x	-/x	x/-	x/x	x/x		x/x	x/-	-/x		5/6
t4	x/x			x/-	x/x		x/x	x/x	x/-	x/x	7/5
t5					x/x	x/x		-/x	x/x		3/4
t6	x/-	x/x						-/x	x/-	x/-	4/2
t7	x/x	-/x	x/x	x/x	x/x		-/x	-/x			4/7
t8			-/x		-/x	x/-					1/2
t9		x/x									1/1
t10				x/x			x/-	x/x	-/x		3/3
t11							x/x		x/-	x/x	3/2
t12					x/x		x/x	x/x		-/x	3/4
t13									x/x	x/-	2/1
t14							x/x			-/x	1/2
t15							x/-	x/x		-/x	2/2
t16							x/x			-/x	1/2
tags/resource	4/4	4/6	3/3	4/3	5/6	2/1	8/7	6/8	5/4	4/7	

A very similar procedure can be applied to the column "tag frequency" in Table 1. Here, we create a fuzzy set "Tag Popularity" – *TagPop* for short. The purpose of this fuzzy set is to assign to each tag a degree of its utilization, i.e., a value that represents how often the user uses it among all tags. The membership function is:

$$TagPop_{u\_k}(t) = \{\frac{a_1}{t_1}, \frac{a_2}{t_2}, \dots \frac{a_n}{t_n}, \dots \frac{a_N}{t_N}\}$$

where

$$a_n = \frac{\text{\# of times } t_n \text{ is used by } u_k}{\text{max \# of resources tagged by } u_k \text{ with a single tag}}$$

The procedure for calculating the values of a membership function a_n uses the maximum number of resources tagged with a single tag. In general, it is possible to use any reasonable number as the reference – for example, an average number of resources tagged by a single tag. In such case, we assume that any tag that is used above average will have a membership value of one. This would represent an "optimistic" approach to estimating tag popularity. In the example presented in the paper, we use the formula above – more "pessimistic" view.

4.2   Fuzzy Relation as User Representation

Both fuzzy sets defined in Section 4.1 describe user's activities – degrees of her interest in resources (higher degree of membership of a fuzzy set *ResAttract* more attention she dedicates to a resource) and degrees of her usage of labels (higher degree of membership of a fuzzy set *TagPop* more often a given tag is used).

In order to capture both aspects of user's typical usage of resources and tags we propose to build a fuzzy relation based on both sets. We will call this relation *UserSignature*:

$$UserSignature_{u\_k}(r,t) = ResAttract_{u\_k}(r) \times TagPop_{u\_k}(t)$$

For a single resource r_i and a single tag t_j the value of a relation is:

$$UserSignature_{u\_k}(r_i,t_j) = \min\{ResAttract_{u\_k}(r_i), \ TagPop_{u\_k}(t_j)\}$$

This relation is interpreted in the following way: high values of the relation indicate resources that are of interest for the user labeled with tags that the user likes. In other words, this relation has the highest values for the case of the most distinctive – unique for the user – resource/tag combinations.

Based on the definition presented above and the examples of fuzzy sets shown in Section 4.1 we can build such a relation. Its values are shown in Table 2.

In general, we can perform some simple analysis of this user's signature. For example, we can project it on one of the dimensions – resources or tags – and study user's interest in resources and tags' popularity once the influence of tags and resources has been taken care of (via building the relation). If additionally, we make α-cuts for different values of α, we can look at subsets of resources representing different degrees of user's interests, and subsets of tags representing different degrees of popularity.

Table 2. A fuzzy relation as a signature of the user u_i

resource / tag	r1	r2	r3	r4	r5	r6	r7	r8	r9	r10	TagPop
t1	0.29	0.29									2/7 (0.29)
t2		0.43	0.38					0.43			3/7 (0.43)
t3			0.38	0.5	0.63		0.71	0.71			5/7 (0.71)
t4	0.5			0.5	0.63		1.00	0.75	0.63	0.5	7/7 (1.00)
t5					0.43	0.25			0.43		3/7 (0.43)
t6	0.5	0.5							0.57	0.5	4/7 (0.57)
t7	0.5		0.38	0.5	0.57						4/7 (0.57)
t8						0.14					1/7 (0.14)
t9		0.14									1/7 (0.14)
t10				0.43			0.43	0.43			3/7 (0.43)
t11							0.43		0.43	0.43	3/7 (0.43)
t12				0.43			0.43	0.43			3/7 (0.43)
t13									0.29	0.29	2/7 (0.29)
t14							0.14				1/7 (0.14)
t15							0.29	0.29			2/7 (0.29)
t16							0.14				1/7 (0.14)
ResAttract	4/8 (0.5)	4/8 (0.5)	3/8 (0.38)	4/8 (0.5)	5/8 (0.63)	2/8 (0.25)	8/8 (1.0)	6/8 (0.75)	5/8 (0.63)	4/8 (0.5)	

5   Affinity between Two Users

5.1   Similarity of Users: Concept

The relations *UserSignature* created for each user constitute users' descriptions. Therefore, we assert that comparison of users is equivalent to comparison of their *UserSignature* relations. The relations *UserSignature* are two-dimensional fuzzy sets. We want to compare these fuzzy sets based on their number of elements. At the same time, we want to take into account elements' membership values. In order to address this, we have adapted one of the best-known similarity measures for sets – the Jaccard index:

$$usersAffinity(u_i, u_j) = \frac{|\,T(UserSignature_{u\_i}(r,t), UserSignature_{u\_j}(r,t))\,|}{|\,S(UserSignature_{u\_i}(r,t), UserSignature_{u\_j}(r,t))\,|}$$

where |.| represents set's cardinality, a T-norm is used to determine the union of sets, and the intersection is done using a T-conorm (S-norm). The presented equation requires cardinality of a fuzzy set. For the purpose of affinity estimation we propose a new approach for determining cardinality.

5.2   Cardinality of Fuzzy Sets

Cardinality of fuzzy sets is usually determined in a number of different ways [8]. For the fuzzy sets defined on the discrete universe of discourse, we propose a different way of determining cardinality of such fuzzy sets.

We "treat" cardinality as a fuzzy set called *Cardinality*. Let's assume we want to determine cardinality of a fuzzy set A. The set *Cardinality* is constructed by determining cardinalities of sets created by α-cuts of A for different values of α. The fuzzy set *Cardinality* is formed in the following way:

$$Cardinality(A) = \{\frac{\alpha_1}{card_{\alpha1}}, \frac{\alpha_2}{card_{\alpha2}}, \frac{\alpha_3}{card_{\alpha3}}, ... \frac{\alpha_N}{card_{\alpha N}}\}$$

where α_i represents a value used for an α_i-cut, and *card* is the cardinality of an α-cut set for a given α_i. In other words, the elements of the *Cardinality* set are the cardinality values for a given α-cut, and the values of α are their membership values.

In general, α can assume any value from 0 to 1. For example, if N is nine, α_1 is 0.1, α_2 is 0.2, and so on. If it happens that the same value of cardinality *card* is obtained for different α then, in order to preserve functional character of the fuzzy set, the maximum of these α's is "assigned" to this cardinality. For example,

$$Cardinality(A) = \{\frac{0.1}{14}, \frac{0.2}{11}, \frac{0.3}{11}, \frac{0.4}{9}, \frac{0.5}{6}, \frac{0.6}{4}, \frac{0.7}{4}, \frac{0.8}{2}, \frac{0.9}{1}\}$$

is modified, and the resulting fuzzy set is

$$Cardinality(A) = \{\frac{0.1}{14}, \frac{0.3}{11}, \frac{0.4}{9}, \frac{0.5}{6}, \frac{0.7}{4}, \frac{0.8}{2}, \frac{0.9}{1}\}$$

Let us take a closer look at the set *Cardinality* created for a given fuzzy set and try to interpret it: a value of 0.1 for α indicates that we are very liberal regarding set membership values and allow any element with a membership value at least 0.1 to be treated as a member of the set, and the cardinality obtained for such created set is a member of the *Cardinality* set to the degree of 0.1. On the other hand, the value of 0.9 means that we are very strict and only elements with high membership values – at least 0.9 – are considered as members of the set, the cardinality of such set has a membership value to the *Cardinality* set equal to 0.9.

Such understanding of the *Cardinality* set has led us to a novel process of "converting" it into a single cardinality values that we can "plug" into the Jaccard index. This process involves an input from the user - a quantity called **membership requirement**. This is a fuzzy set, called hereafter *MemberReq*, defined on the universe of discourse <0,1> representing user's perception of what membership values an element should have to be treated as a member of a set. Examples of three such sets: *Strict*, *Moderate* and *Relaxed* are shown in Fig. 3. The user does not need to understand the concept of fuzzy sets; she provides only a linguistic term representing her level of "strictness" in determining the level of similarity – the so-called similarity regime.

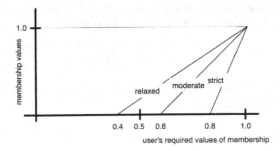

Fig. 3. Examples of fuzzy sets for membership requirement: *Relaxed, Moderate* and *Strict*

For the purpose of determining cardinality the above-defined fuzzy set *MemberReq* is "interpreted" in the following way: values from the universe of discourse of *MemberReq* are treated as values of α used for α-cuts. So, right now the set *Strict* indicates user's rigorous requirements regarding α values, i.e., the user considers as valid only α-cuts for α of 0.8 and higher. For example, the α=0.9 has a membership value of 0.5 and this means the user's level of acceptance of an α-cut for α=0.9 is equal to 0.5. Now, we represent *MemberReq* fuzzy sets in the following way:

$$MemberReq = \frac{\mu(\alpha_i)}{\alpha_i} \qquad \text{for } \alpha_i \in <0,1>$$

where $\mu(\alpha_i)$ represents a membership value of a given α_i value determined by the user's requirement regarding acceptable/desired values of α for an α-cut. One of the fuzzy sets illustrated in Figure 5.1 – *moderate* – can be presented in the following way:

$$MemberReq\_moderate = \{\frac{0.0}{0.0},...,\frac{0.0}{0.6},\frac{0.25}{0.7},\frac{0.5}{0.8},\frac{0.75}{0.9},\frac{1.0}{1.0}\}$$

Both fuzzy sets defined above are presented one more time below:

$$Cardinality(A) = \frac{\alpha_j}{card_{\alpha j}} \qquad MemberReq = \frac{\mu(\alpha_i)}{\alpha_i}$$

A closer look at both fuzzy sets allows us to merge them and create another fuzzy set that represents user's perception of cardinality in the context of user's acceptable levels of α's for α-cuts. When we perform the "merge" based on the values of α we obtain a new fuzzy set

$$Cardinality_{MemberReq}(A) = \frac{\mu(\alpha_i)}{card_{\alpha i}}$$

The interpretation of this set is as follows: it represents user's degrees of acceptance of cardinalities of α-cuts performed on a given fuzzy set taking into consideration values of α the user perceives as representative for cardinality determination.

Example. Let us illustrate this with a simple example. The user indicated values of α to be considered as suitable for determining cardinality as a fuzzy set *Moderate*

(Fig. 3). A fuzzy set *Cardinality* has been constructed performing α-cuts for α values from 0.1 to 1.0 with a step of 0.1. The set looks like this:

$$Cardinality(A) = \{\frac{0.1}{14}, \frac{0.3}{11}, \frac{0.4}{8}, \frac{0.5}{6}, \frac{0.6}{5}, \frac{0.7}{4}, \frac{0.8}{2}, \frac{0.9}{1}, \frac{1.0}{0}\}$$

"Merging" these two sets leads to the following *Cardinality* set modified by user's view on cardinality determination:

$$Cardinality_{Member \, \text{Re} \, q\_\text{mod} \, erate}(A) = \{\frac{0.0}{5}, \frac{0.25}{4}, \frac{0.5}{2}, \frac{0.75}{1}, \frac{1.0}{0}\}$$

Once the fuzzy set is determined a defuzzification is performed to obtain a single value representing cardinality based on user's preferences regarding acceptance of cardinalities for different α-cuts. For the example presented above, the cardinality of a fuzzy set with *Moderate* requirement (regarding cardinalities) is $|A|_{moderate} = 1.10$

5.3   Fuzzy-Based Determining of Affinity of Users

The affinity between users, as presented in Section 5.1, can be determined using the equation:

$$usersAffinity(u_i, u_j) = \frac{|T(UserSignature_{u\_i}(r,t), UserSignature_{u\_j}(r,t))|}{|S(UserSignature_{u\_i}(r,t), UserSignature_{u\_j}(r,t))|}$$

The cardinalities of both sets – $T(UserSignature_{u\_i}, UserSignature_{u\_j})$ and $S(UserSignature_{u\_i}, UserSignature_{u\_j})$ – are calculated with the user's input regarding her requirements about cardinalities. With that, we are able to determine affinity between users.

Example. In order to explain the steps required to determine affinity between users we include a simple illustration of the process. Let us assume that the user u_i wants to compare herself to the user u_j. She wants to know how "compatible" she is with u_j, and she wants to know that with three different levels of *similarity regimes*: being strict, moderate, and relaxed.

The activities of user u_i, i.e., her resources and labels, and how she uses them are presented in Table 1. Her *UserSignature* is shown in Table 2. The activities for the second user – u_j – are also presented in Table 1 (the values after the slash). The *UserSignature* of u_j is calculated based on these values.

The fuzzy sets obtained after performing T-norm and S-norm operations, let them be A_T and A_S respectively, are further processed to determine their cardinalities. It was indicated in the description of the example, the user wants to know the compatibility between herself and another user with three different levels of *similarity regimes*: being strict, moderate, and relaxed. Therefore, we need to calculate cardinality of T-norm and S-norm generated sets for these three regimens. The fuzzy set *cardinality* of A_T is:

$$Cardinality(A_T) = \{\frac{0.1}{33}, \frac{0.2}{28}, \frac{0.3}{22}, \frac{0.4}{17}, \frac{0.5}{9}, \frac{0.6}{5}, \frac{0.7}{3}, \frac{0.8}{0}, \frac{0.9}{0}, \frac{1.0}{0}\}$$

Similarly calculated, the fuzzy set *cardinality* of A_S is:

$$Cardinality(A_S) = \{\frac{0.1}{60}, \frac{0.2}{58}, \frac{0.3}{45}, \frac{0.4}{43}, \frac{0.5}{20}, \frac{0.6}{13}, \frac{0.7}{12}, \frac{0.8}{4}, \frac{0.9}{2}, \frac{1.0}{2}\}$$

For the similarity regime *strict* (Fig. 3), we obtain

$$usersAffinity(u_i, u_j)_{strict} = \frac{|A_T|_{strict}}{|A_S|_{strict}} = \frac{0.0}{1.5} = 0.0000.$$

While for the similarity regime *moderate*

$$usersAffinity(u_i, u_j)_{moderate} = \frac{|A_T|_{moderate}}{|A_S|_{moderate}} = \frac{0.30}{3.40} = 0.0882$$

and for the similarity regime *relaxed*

$$usersAffinity(u_i, u_j)_{relaxed} = \frac{|A_T|_{relaxed}}{|A_S|_{relaxed}} = \frac{1.33}{5.71} = 0.2329$$

As it can be observed, the values of similarity increase with the less dementing similarity regime. When inspecting cardinalities of A_T and A_S, the similarity for the regime *relaxed* is comparable with the similarity calculated based on the α-cut for $\alpha=0.7$. For the α-cuts with $\alpha>0.7$ the similarity is 0, and for $\alpha<0.7$ they are in the range from 0.38 to 0.55.

6   Conclusions

The utilization of the web for social purposes means we can look at the web as place of amplified interactions of users. More and more often the users want to find new individuals on the web, and want to connect to them. These new individuals should share similar interests and pursuits. The web 2.0, and especially tagging, creates environment suitable for achieving this.

This paper proposes a fuzzy-based approach to determine users' profiles in a social network with tagging. A fuzzy relation is built to capture user's activities regarding labeling web resources – which resources the user likes, and which tags the user prefers. Such a relation – called here *UserSignature* – is used to find users who have similar *UserSignatures*, i.e., similar activities regarding labeling web resources.

The proposed comparison of *UserSignatures* is based on the Jaccard index, and requires assessment of cardinality of fuzzy sets. A novel method of determining cardinality of fuzzy sets is proposed. The method requires the user to identify her preferred similarity regime, i.e., her membership requirement determining when elements are treated as members of a set. The approach allows for personalization of the search process.

References

[1] Hammond, T., Hannay, T., Lund, B., Scott, J.: Social Bookmarking Tools (I): A General Review. D-Lib Magazine 11 (2005),
http://www.dlib.org/dlib/april05/hammond/04hammond.html

[2] Zadeh, L.A.: Fuzzy sets. Information and Control 8, 338–353 (1965)

[3] Smith, G.: Tagging: People-Powered Metadata for the Social Web. New Riders (2008)

[4] Fu, W.-T., Kannampallil, T., Kang, R.: A Semantic Imitation Model of Social Tag Choices. In: 2009 Inter. Conf. on Computational Science and Engineering, pp. 66–73 (2009)

[5] Zhang, L., Wu, X., Yu, Y.: Emergent Semantics from Folksonomies: A Quantitative Study. In: Spaccapietra, S., Aberer, K., Cudré-Mauroux, P. (eds.) Journal on Data Semantics VI. LNCS, vol. 4090, pp. 168–186. Springer, Heidelberg (2006)

[6] Cattuto, C., Benz, D., Hotho, A., Stumme, G.: Semantic Grounding of Tag Relatedness in Social Bookmarking Systems. In: Sheth, A.P., Staab, S., Dean, M., Paolucci, M., Maynard, D., Finin, T., Thirunarayan, K. (eds.) ISWC 2008. LNCS, vol. 5318, pp. 615–631. Springer, Heidelberg (2008)

[7] Golder, S., Huberman, B.: The Structure of Collaborative Tagging Systems. Journal of Information Sciences 32, 198–208 (2006)

[8] Wygralak, M.: On the best scalar approximation of cardinality of a fuzzy set. International Journal of Uncertainty, Fuzziness and Knowledge-based Systems 56, 681–687 (1997)

Idempotent Copulas with Fractal Support

Wolfgang Trutschnig

Research Unit for Intelligent Data Analysis and Graphical Models
European Centre for Soft Computing
Edificio de Investigación
Calle Gonzalo Gutiérrez Quirós S/N
33600 Mieres (Asturias), Spain
wolfgang.trutschnig@softcomputing.es

Abstract. In [7] Fredricks et al. showed that certain Iterated Function Systems (IFS) can be used to construct copulas with fractal support. Since, firstly, the same construction also works with respect to the D_1-metric on the space of copulas which is much stronger than the uniform metric and, secondly, the star product of copulas is (jointly) continuous with respect to this metric the IFS approach can also be used to construct idempotent copulas with fractal support. The main result of the paper is that for each open interval $I \subseteq [1, 2]$ there exists an idempotent copula A such that the Hausdorff dimension of the support of A is contained in the interval I.

Keywords: Copula, Star product, Idempotence, Iterated Function System, Fractal.

1 Introduction

Since its introduction by Darsow et el. in 1992 (see [2]) the so-called star product of copulas has been studied in various papers. In 1996 Olsen et al. showed that the space $(\mathcal{C}, *)$ of (two-dimensional) copulas with the star product as binary operation and the space $(\mathcal{M}, \circ)$ of Markov operators with the composition as binary operation are isomorphic (see [12] and Section 2) and that every copula $A \in \mathcal{C}$ can be written in the form $A = B^t * C$ whereby B, C are so-called completely dependent (or, equivalently, left invertible) copulas (see [12]) and B^t denotes the transpose of a copula. Using the above mentioned isomorphism Sempi (see [14]) in 2002 showed that there is a one-to-one correspondence between the class of idempotent copulas $\mathcal{C}_i$ (i.e. copulas with $A * A = A$) and the subclass of $\mathcal{M}$ consisting of conditional expectations. In 2010 Darsow et al. answered the question posed in [2] whether idempotent copulas are necessarily symmetric and gave a complete characterization of $\mathcal{C}_i$.

  The main objective of the present paper is to construct some idempotent copulas with fractal support. In fact, we will show that for each open interval $I \subset [1, 2]$ there exists an element $A \in \mathcal{C}_i$ such that the Hausdorff dimension of the support of A lies in I. To do so we will use the fact that the construction of copulas with fractal support via special Iterated Function Systems (see [7])

S. Greco et al. (Eds.): IPMU 2012, Part II, CCIS 298, pp. 161–170, 2012.
© Springer-Verlag Berlin Heidelberg 2012

also works w.r.t. to the metric D_1 (which is a metrization of the strong operator topology on $\mathcal{M}$, see [15]) together with the fact that the star product is (jointly) continuous w.r.t. D_1.

The rest of the paper is organized as follows: Section 2 gathers some preliminaries and notations that will be used throughout the paper. The above mentioned fact that the set of Hausdorff dimensions of the supports of elements in $\mathcal{C}_i$ is dense in $[1, 2]$ and some concrete examples are the main content of Section 3. Finally, Section 4 discusses open points and future work.

2   Notation and Preliminaries

As already mentioned before $\mathcal{C}$ will denote the family of all *two-dimensional copulas*. Π will denote the product copula. For properties of copulas see [5] and [11]. $\mathcal{B}(\mathbb{R})$ denotes the Borel σ-field in $\mathbb{R}$, $\mathcal{B}([0, 1]^d)$ the Borel σ-field in $[0, 1]^d$, $d \geq 1$, λ the Lebesgue measure on $[0, 1]$, $\mathcal{P}([0, 1]^2)$ the family of all probability measures on $\mathcal{B}([0, 1]^2)$ and $\mathcal{P}_\mathcal{C}$ the subclass of doubly stochastic measures (i.e. probability measures whose corresponding distribution function is a copula).

A *Markov kernel* from $\mathbb{R}$ to $\mathcal{B}(\mathbb{R})$ is a mapping $K : \mathbb{R} \times \mathcal{B}(\mathbb{R}) \rightarrow [0, 1]$ such that $x \mapsto K(x, B)$ is measurable for every fixed $B \in \mathcal{B}(\mathbb{R})$ and $B \mapsto K(x, B)$ is a probability measure for every fixed $x \in \mathbb{R}$. Suppose that X, Y are real-valued random variables on a probability space $(\Omega, \mathcal{A}, \mathcal{P})$, then a Markov kernel $K : \mathbb{R} \times \mathcal{B}(\mathbb{R}) \rightarrow [0, 1]$ is called *regular conditional distribution of Y given X* if for every $B \in \mathcal{B}(\mathbb{R})$

$$K(X(\omega), B) = \mathbb{E}(\mathbf{1}_B \circ Y | X)(\omega) \tag{1}$$

holds $\mathcal{P}$-a.s. It is well know that for each pair (X, Y) of real-valued random variables a regular conditional distribution $K(\cdot, \cdot)$ of Y given X exists, that $K(\cdot, \cdot)$ is unique $\mathcal{P}^X$-a.s. (i.e. unique for $\mathcal{P}^X$-almost all $x \in \mathbb{R}$) and that $K(\cdot, \cdot)$ only depends on $\mathcal{P}^{X \otimes Y}$. Hence, given $A \in \mathcal{C}$ we will denote (a version of) the regular conditional distribution of Y given X by $K_A(\cdot, \cdot)$ and refer to $K_A(\cdot, \cdot)$ simply as *regular conditional distribution of A* or as *the Markov kernel of A*. Note that for every $A \in \mathcal{C}$, its conditional regular distribution $K_A(\cdot, \cdot)$, and a Borel set $G \in \mathcal{B}([0, 1]^2)$ we have

$$\int_{[0,1]} K_A(x, G_x) \, d\lambda(x) = \mu_A(G), \tag{2}$$

so in particular

$$\int_{[0,1]} K_A(x, F) \, d\lambda(x) = \lambda(F). \tag{3}$$

for every $F \in \mathcal{B}([0, 1])$.

On the other hand, every Markov kernel $K : [0, 1] \times \mathcal{B}([0, 1]) \rightarrow [0, 1]$ fulfilling (3) induces a unique element $\mu \in \mathcal{P}_\mathcal{C}$ via (2) (with K_A replaced by K and μ_A replaced by μ). For more details and properties of conditional expectation and regular conditional distributions see [8] and [9].

A copula A will be called *completely dependent* (see [10] and [15]) if there exists a λ-preserving transformation $S : [0,1] \to [0,1]$ such that $K(x, E) := 1_E(Sx) = \delta_{Sx}(E)$ is a regular conditional distribution of A.

A linear operator T on $L^1([0,1], \mathcal{B}([0,1]), \lambda)$ is called *Markov operator* (see [2] and [12]) if it fulfills the following three properties:

1. T is positive, i.e. $T(f) \geq 0$ whenever $f \geq 0$
2. $T(1_{[0,1]}) = 1_{[0,1]}$
3. $\int_{[0,1]} (Tf)(x) d\lambda(x) = \int_{[0,1]} f(x) d\lambda(x)$

As mentioned in the introduction $\mathcal{M}$ will denote the class of all Markov operators on $L^1([0,1], \mathcal{B}([0,1]), \lambda)$. It is straightforward to see that the operator norm of T is one, i.e. $\|T\| := \sup\{\|Tf\|_1 : \|f\|_1 \leq 1\} = 1$ holds. According to [2] and [12] *there is a one-to-one correspondence between $\mathcal{C}$ and $\mathcal{M}$* - in fact, the mappings $\Phi : \mathcal{C} \to \mathcal{M}$ and $\Psi : \mathcal{M} \to \mathcal{C}$, defined by

$$\Phi(A)(f)(x) := (T_A f)(x) := \frac{d}{dx} \int_{[0,1]} A_{,2}(x,t) f(t) d\lambda(t),$$

$$\Psi(T)(x,y) := A_T(x,y) := \int_{[0,x]} (T 1_{[0,y]})(t) d\lambda(t) \tag{4}$$

for every $f \in L^1([0,1])$ and $(x,y) \in [0,1]^2$ ($A_{,2}$ denoting the partial derivative w.r.t. y), fulfil $\Psi \circ \Phi = id_{\mathcal{C}}$ and $\Phi \circ \Psi = id_{\mathcal{M}}$. Note that in case of $f := 1_{[0,y]}$ we have $(T_A 1_{[0,y]})(x) = A_{,1}(x,y)$ λ-a.s. According to [15] the first equality in (4) can be simplified to

$$(T_A f)(x) = \mathbb{E}(f \circ Y | X = x) = \int_{[0,1]} f(y) K_A(x, dy) \qquad \lambda\text{-a.s.} \tag{5}$$

Expressing copulas in terms of their corresponding regular conditional distributions the metric D_1 on $\mathcal{C}$ can be defined as follows:

$$D_1(A, B) := \int_{[0,1]} \int_{[0,1]} |K_A(x, [0,y]) - K_B(x, [0,y])| d\lambda(x) d\lambda(y) \tag{6}$$

It can be shown that $(\mathcal{C}, D_1)$ is a complete metric space and that, given copulas $A, A_1, A_2 \ldots$ and their corresponding Markov operators $T_A, T_{A_1}, T_{A_2} \ldots$, the following two conditions are equivalent:

(a) $\lim_{n \to \infty} D_1(A_n, A) = 0$
(b) $\lim_{n \to \infty} \|T_{A_n} f - T_A f\|_1 = 0$ for every $f \in L^1([0,1], \mathcal{B}([0,1]), \lambda)$

i.e. D_1 is a metrization of the strong operator topology on $\mathcal{M}$ (see [15]). Given $A, B \in \mathcal{C}$ the star product $A * B \in \mathcal{C}$ is defined by (see [2], [4])

$$(A * B)(x,y) := \int_{[0,1]} A_{,2}(x,t) B_{,1}(t,y) d\lambda(t) \tag{7}$$

and fulfills

$$T_{A*B} = \Phi_{A*B} = \Phi(A) \circ \Phi(B) = T_A \circ T_B, \tag{8}$$

so the mapping Φ in (4) is an isomorphism (see [12]). Suppose now that $E \in \mathcal{B}([0,1])$, then, using (4) and (5), for λ-almost every $x \in [0,1]$ it follows that

$$K_{A*B}(x, E) = (T_A \circ T_B)(\mathbf{1}_E)(x) = T_A(K_B(\cdot, E))(x)$$
$$= \int_{[0,1]} K_B(y, E) K_A(x, dy).$$

In other words, the Markov kernel of $A * B$ is just the standard composition of the Markov kernels of A and B (for the composition of Markov kernels see [8] and [9]). Hence, in terms of conditional distributions, the star product can be seen as natural generalization of the multiplication of stochastic matrices in the discrete Markov chain setting and studying the star product means studying the composition of Markov kernels $K : [0,1] \times \mathcal{B}([0,1]) \to [0,1]$ fulfilling (3) and vice versa. Finally, the family of idempotent copulas, i.e. copulas fulfilling $A * A = A$, will be denoted by $\mathcal{C}_i$.

3   Idempotent Copulas with Fractal Support

We will follow the construction of copulas induced by special Iterated Function Systems described in [7] and make use of the D_1-related results in [15]. First we recall the definition of an Iterated Function System with probabilities and that of a transformation matrix (see [1] and [7] respectively):

Definition 1. *Suppose that* (Ω, d) *is a metric space and that* $n \in \mathbb{N}$. *A mapping* $w : \Omega \to \Omega$ *is called* contraction *if there exists a constant* $L < 1$ *such that* $d(w(x), w(y)) \leq L d(x, y)$ *holds for all* $x, y \in \Omega$. *A family* $(w_l)_{l=1}^n$ *of contractions on* Ω *together with a vector* $(p_l)_{l=1}^n \in [0,1]^n$ *fulfilling* $\sum_{l=1}^n p_l = 1$ *is called an* Iterated Function System with probabilities *(IFS for short). We will denote IFSs by* $\{(w_l)_{l=1}^n, (p_l)_{l=1}^n\}$.

Definition 2. *A matrix* $M = (t_{ij})_{i=1...n, j=1...m}$ *with* $n \geq 2$ *rows and* m *columns is called* transformation matrix *if it fulfills the following three conditions: (i) All entries are non-negative, (ii)* $\sum_{i,j} t_{ij} = 1$, *and (iii) no row or column has all entries 0. The class of all transformation matrices will be denoted by* $\mathcal{T}$.

Given $M \in \mathcal{T}$ we define the vectors $(a_j)_{j=0}^m, (b_i)_{i=0}^n$ of cumulative column and row sums by

$$a_0 = b_0 = 0$$
$$a_j = \sum_{j_0 \leq j} \sum_{i=1}^n t_{ij} \quad j \in \{1, \ldots, m\} \tag{9}$$
$$b_i = \sum_{i_0 \leq i} \sum_{j=1}^m t_{ij} \quad i \in \{1, \ldots, n\}.$$

Since M is a transformation matrix both $(a_j)_{j=0}^m$ and $(b_i)_{i=0}^n$ are strictly increasing. Consequently $R_{ji} := [a_{j-1}, a_j] \times [b_{i-1}, b_i]$ are compact non-degenerated rectangles for every $j \in \{1, \ldots, m\}$ and $i \in \{1, \ldots, n\}$. M induces the IFS $\{(w_{ji})_{j=1\ldots m, i=1\ldots n}, (t_{ij})_{j=1\ldots m, i=1\ldots n}\}$, whereby the contractions $w_{ji} : [0,1]^2 \to R_{ji}$ are defined by

$$w_{ji}(x,y) = \left(a_{j-1} + x(a_j - a_{j-1}), \; b_{i-1} + x(b_i - b_{i-1})\right).$$

It is straightforward to verify that the operator $V_M : \mathcal{P}([0,1]^2) \to \mathcal{P}([0,1]^2)$, defined by

$$V_M(\mu) := \sum_{j=1}^{m} \sum_{i=1}^{n} t_{ij} \, \mu^{w_{ji}}. \tag{10}$$

maps $\mathcal{P}_C$ into itself (see [7]) so we can also interpret it as operator on $\mathcal{C}$. Using Banach's fixed point theorem and completeness of $(\mathcal{C}, D_1)$ the following result can be proved:

Theorem 1 ([15]). *Suppose that M is a transformation matrix and let the operator V_M be defined according to (10). Then V_M is a contraction on the metric space $(\mathcal{C}, D_1)$ and there exists a unique copula $A^\star$ such that $V_M A^\star = A^\star$ and $\lim_{n\to\infty} D_1(V_M^n B, A^\star) = 0$ for every $B \in \mathcal{C}$.*

Given these results we will start with a small lemma and then construct a first idempotent copula whose support has Hausdorff dimension $\ln(5)/\ln(3)$.

Lemma 1. *$\mathcal{C}_i$ is closed in $(\mathcal{C}, D_1)$.*

Proof: First of all is easy to show that the star product is (jointly) continuous w.r.t. D_1: Suppose that $A, A_1, A_2, \ldots$ and $B, B_1, B_2, \ldots$ are copulas with $\lim_{n\to\infty} D_1(A_n, A) = \lim_{n\to\infty} D_1(B_n, B) = 0$. Then for every $f \in L^1([0,1])$, using the triangle inequality and that fact that Markov operators have operator norm 1, we get

$$\|T_{A_n} \circ T_{B_n} f - T_A \circ T_B f\|_1 \leq \|T_{B_n} f - T_B f\|_1 + \|T_{A_n} \circ T_B f - T_A \circ T_B f\|_1,$$

hence $\|T_{A_n} \circ T_{B_n} f - T_A \circ T_B f\|_1 \longrightarrow 0$ and $\lim_{n\to\infty} D_1(A_n * B_n, A * B) = 0$. Consequently, if $(A_n)_{n\in\mathbb{N}}$ is a sequence in $\mathcal{C}_i$ converging to $A \in \mathcal{C}$ w.r.t. D_1, then $(A_n)_{n\in\mathbb{N}}$ converges both to A and to $A * A$, so $A = A * A$ and $A \in \mathcal{C}_i$. ∎

Now consider the matrix $M = (t_{ij})_{i,j=1}^3 \in \mathcal{T}$ defined by

$$M = \begin{pmatrix} \frac{1}{6} & 0 & \frac{1}{6} \\ 0 & \frac{1}{3} & 0 \\ \frac{1}{6} & 0 & \frac{1}{6} \end{pmatrix}. \tag{11}$$

and set $N = (n_{ij})_{i,j=1}^3 = 3M$, then N is an idempotent doubly stochastic (hence symmetric) matrix. The first four iterates of the corresponding operator V_M applied to the product copula are depicted in Figure 1. According to Theorem 1 there exists a unique copula $A^\star$ such that for every starting copula $B \in \mathcal{C}$ we have $\lim_{n\to\infty} D_1(V_M^n B, A^\star) = 0$. Furthermore (see [7]) the support of $A^\star$ has Hausdorff dimension $\ln(5)/\ln(3)$. It remains to prove that $A^\star$ is also idempotent which can be done in three steps:

Step 1: We explicitly show how, for a given copula $B \in \mathcal{C}$, the kernel $K_{V_M B}$ can directly be calculated from K_B. For every $i \in \{1,2,3\}$ define functions $h_i : \mathbb{R} \to \mathbb{R}$ by $h_i(x) := 3x - (i-1)$ and extend the definition of the kernel K_B to whole $[0,1] \times \mathcal{B}(\mathbb{R})$ by setting $K_B(x,E) = 0$ whenever $E \cap [0,1] = \emptyset$. Fix $E \in \mathcal{B}([0,1])$ then we get

$$K_{V_M B}(x,E) = \begin{cases} \frac{1}{2} K_B\big(h_1(x), h_1(E)\big) + \frac{1}{2} K_B\big(h_1(x), h_3(E)\big) & \text{if } x \in \big[0, \frac{1}{3}\big] \\ K_B\big(h_2(x), h_2(E)\big) & \text{if } x \in \big(\frac{1}{3}, \frac{2}{3}\big) \\ \frac{1}{2} K_B\big(h_3(x), h_1(E)\big) + \frac{1}{2} K_B\big(h_3(x), h_3(E)\big) & \text{if } x \in \big[\frac{2}{3}, 1\big] \end{cases}$$

which implies

$$\begin{pmatrix} K_{V_M B}\big(h_1^{-1}(x), E\big) \\ K_{V_M B}\big(h_2^{-1}(x), E\big) \\ K_{V_M B}\big(h_3^{-1}(x), E\big) \end{pmatrix} = \underbrace{\begin{pmatrix} \frac{1}{2} & 0 & \frac{1}{2} \\ 0 & 1 & 0 \\ \frac{1}{2} & 0 & \frac{1}{2} \end{pmatrix}}_{N} \begin{pmatrix} K_B\big(x, h_1(E)\big) \\ K_B\big(x, h_2(E)\big) \\ K_B\big(x, h_3(E)\big) \end{pmatrix} \tag{12}$$

for every $x \in [0,1]$. Consequently, since the family of simple functions is dense in $L^1([0,1])$, it follows that for every $f \in L^1([0,1])$, every $i \in \{1,2,3\}$ and every $x \in [0,1]$ the following transformation formula holds:

$$\int_{[0,1]} f(z) \, K_{V_M B}(h_i^{-1}x, dz) = \int_{[0,1]} \sum_{j=1}^{3} n_{ij} f(h_j^{-1}(z)) \, K_B(x, dz) \tag{13}$$

Step 2: We show that for every $B \in \mathcal{C}_i$ the copula $V_M(B)$ is idempotent again: Equalities (12) and (13) together with the idempotence of N and $B \in \mathcal{C}_i$ imply that for every $i \in \{1,2,3\}$, every $x \in [0,1]$ and every $E \in \mathcal{B}([0,1])$ we have

$$\begin{aligned} K_{V_M B * V_M B}(h_i^{-1}(x), E) &= \int_{[0,1]} K_{V_M B}(z, E) K_{V_M B}(h_i^{-1}(x), dz) \\ &= \int_{[0,1]} \sum_{j=1}^{3} n_{ij} K_{V_M B}(h_j^{-1}(z), E) \, K_B(x, dz) \\ &= \int_{[0,1]} (n_{i1}, n_{i2}, n_{i3}) \, N \begin{pmatrix} K_B\big(z, h_1(E)\big) \\ K_B\big(z, h_2(E)\big) \\ K_B\big(z, h_3(E)\big) \end{pmatrix} K_B(x, dz) \\ &\stackrel{N \text{ ip}}{=} \int_{[0,1]} \sum_{j=1}^{3} n_{ij} K_B(z, h_j(E)) \, K_B(x, dz) \\ &\stackrel{B \in \mathcal{C}_i}{=} \sum_{j=1}^{3} n_{ij} K_B(z, h_j(E)) = K_{V_M B}(h_i^{-1}(x), E) \end{aligned}$$

which shows that $V_M B \in \mathcal{C}_i$.

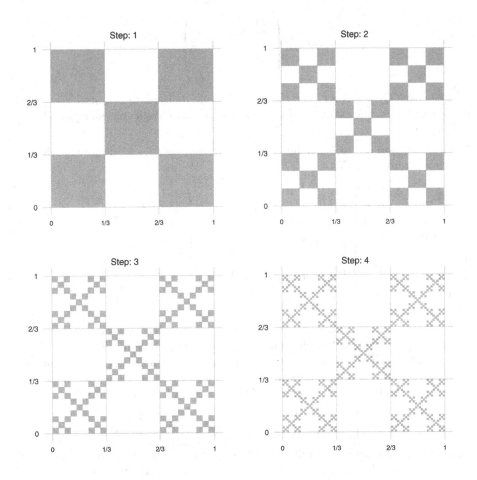

Fig. 1. Support of $V_M^n \Pi$ for $n \in \{1, 2, 3, 4\}$, M according to (11)

Step 3: Since we have $\lim_{n\to\infty} D_1(V_M^n B, A^\star) = 0$ for *every* $B \in \mathcal{C}$ we can choose $B = \Pi$ (so $B \in \mathcal{C}_i$) to construct a sequence $(V_M^n \Pi)_{n\in\mathbb{N}}$ of elements in $\mathcal{C}_i$ that converges to $A^\star$. Consequently, according to Lemma 1, $A^\star$ has to be idempotent too.

Note that the crucial point in proving that the limit $A^\star$ is idempotent was that the transformation matrix M, up to a scalar, is a doubly stochastic idempotent matrix (which, in particular, implies that all function w_{ji} are similarities). All doubly stochastic idempotent matrices are, however, well known in all dimensions since the 1960s - according to [6] and [13] the following theorem holds:

Theorem 2 ([13]). *Any idempotent doubly stochastic $d \times d$-matrix I is of the form $I = W^{-1}UW$ where W is a permutation matrix and U is a matrix of the form*

$$U = \begin{pmatrix} Q_1 & 0 & \dots & 0 \\ 0 & Q_2 & \dots & 0 \\ \vdots & \vdots & \ddots & \vdots \\ 0 & 0 & \dots & Q_s \end{pmatrix},$$

whereby each Q_i is a $r_i \times r_i$-matrix with all elements equal to $1/r_i$ and $\sum_{i=1}^{s} r_i = d$. Conversely, every matrix of this form is doubly stochastic and idempotent with rank equal to s.

Fix a dimension $d \geq 3$, consider one of the following $(d-2)$ doubly stochastic idempotent matrices N

$$\begin{pmatrix} \frac{1}{2} & \frac{1}{2} & 0 & 0 & \dots & 0 & 0 \\ \frac{1}{2} & \frac{1}{2} & 0 & 0 & \dots & 0 & 0 \\ 0 & 0 & 1 & 0 & \dots & 0 & 0 \\ 0 & 0 & 0 & 1 & \dots & 0 & 0 \\ \vdots & \vdots & \vdots & \vdots & \ddots & \vdots & \vdots \\ 0 & 0 & 0 & 0 & \dots & 1 & 0 \\ 0 & 0 & 0 & 0 & \dots & 0 & 1 \end{pmatrix} \begin{pmatrix} \frac{1}{3} & \frac{1}{3} & \frac{1}{3} & 0 & \dots & 0 & 0 \\ \frac{1}{3} & \frac{1}{3} & \frac{1}{3} & 0 & \dots & 0 & 0 \\ \frac{1}{3} & \frac{1}{3} & \frac{1}{3} & 0 & \dots & 0 & 0 \\ 0 & 0 & 0 & 1 & \dots & 0 & 0 \\ \vdots & \vdots & \vdots & \vdots & \ddots & \vdots & \vdots \\ 0 & 0 & 0 & 0 & \dots & 1 & 0 \\ 0 & 0 & 0 & 0 & \dots & 0 & 1 \end{pmatrix}, \dots, \begin{pmatrix} \frac{1}{d-1} & \frac{1}{d-1} & \frac{1}{d-1} & \frac{1}{d-1} & \cdots & \frac{1}{d-1} & 0 \\ \frac{1}{d-1} & \frac{1}{d-1} & \frac{1}{d-1} & \frac{1}{d-1} & \cdots & \frac{1}{d-1} & 0 \\ \frac{1}{d-1} & \frac{1}{d-1} & \frac{1}{d-1} & \frac{1}{d-1} & \cdots & \frac{1}{d-1} & 0 \\ \frac{1}{d-1} & \frac{1}{d-1} & \frac{1}{d-1} & \frac{1}{d-1} & \cdots & \frac{1}{d-1} & 0 \\ \vdots & \vdots & \vdots & \vdots & \ddots & \vdots & \vdots \\ \frac{1}{d-1} & \frac{1}{d-1} & \frac{1}{d-1} & \frac{1}{d-1} & \cdots & \frac{1}{d-1} & 0 \\ 0 & 0 & 0 & 0 & \dots & 0 & 1 \end{pmatrix}$$

$$(14)$$

and set $M := \frac{1}{d} N$. Then $M \in \mathcal{T}$ and, according to Theorem 1, there exists a unique copula $A^\star$ such that for every starting copula $B \in \mathcal{C}$ we have $\lim_{n \to \infty} D_1(V_M^n B, A^\star) = 0$. All corresponding contractions w_{ji} are similarities with contraction factor $\frac{1}{d}$, Morgan's open set condition is fulfilled so (again see [1] and [7]) the Hausdorff dimension of the support of $A^\star$ is contained in the set

$$H_d := \left\{ \frac{\ln(k(k-1)+d)}{\ln(d)} : k = 2, 3, \dots, d-1 \right\} \subseteq [1, 2].$$

Furthermore, analogously to Step 1 before, one can define functions $h_i : \mathbb{R} \to \mathbb{R}$ for every $i \in \{1, 2, \dots, d\}$ by $h_i(x) := dx - (i-1)$ and easily verify that for every $f \in L^1([0,1])$, every $i \in \{1, 2, \dots, d\}$, every $x \in [0,1]$ and every $B \in \mathcal{C}$

$$\int_{[0,1]} f(z) \, K_{V_M B}(h_i^{-1} x, dz) = \int_{[0,1]} \sum_{j=1}^{d} n_{ij} f(h_j^{-1}(z)) \, K_B(x, dz) \qquad (15)$$

holds. Having this it follows in completely the same manner (just replace dimension 3 by dimension d) that $A^\star$ is idempotent. Since $\bigcup_{d=3}^{\infty} H_d$ is dense in $[1, 2]$ we have proved the following result.

Theorem 3. *For every open interval $I \subseteq [1, 2]$ there exists an idempotent copula $A \in \mathcal{C}_i$ such that the Hausdorff dimension of the support of A is contained in I.*

Figure 2 depicts a the first four iterates of another operator V_M applied to the product copula whereby M is the matrix

$$M = \begin{pmatrix} \frac{1}{12} & \frac{1}{12} & 0 & \frac{1}{12} \\ \frac{1}{12} & \frac{1}{12} & 0 & \frac{1}{12} \\ 0 & 0 & \frac{1}{4} & 0 \\ \frac{1}{12} & \frac{1}{12} & 0 & \frac{1}{12} \end{pmatrix}. \qquad (16)$$

$N := 4\,M$ is a permutation of the second matrix in (14) for $d = 4$. The corresponding limit copula $A^\star$ is idempotent and the Hausdorff dimension of its support is $\ln(10)/\ln(4)$.

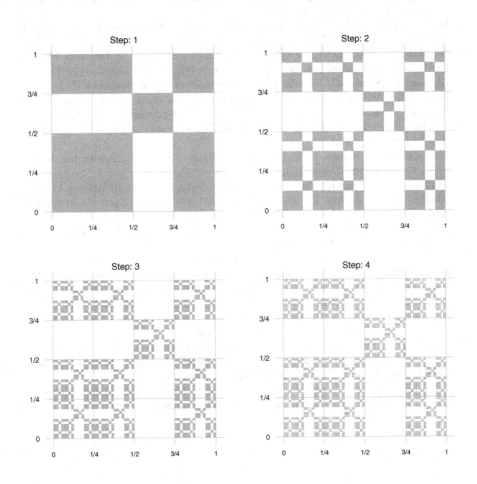

Fig. 2. Support of $V_M^n \Pi$ for $n \in \{1, 2, 3, 4\}$, M according to (16)

4   Open Points and Future Work

Given Theorem 3 the question naturally arises if for every $s \in [1, 2]$ there exists an element $A \in \mathcal{C}_i$ such that the Hausdorff dimension of the support of A is equal to s. To the best of the author's knowledge this question has not been answered yet. Apart from that there are various interesting questions concerning the star product (smoothing behaviour, etc.) that seem worth investing some work.

References

1. Barnsley, M.F.: Fractals everywhere. Academic Press, Cambridge (1993)
2. Darsow, W.F., Nguyen, B., Olsen, E.T.: Copulas and Markov processes. Ill. J. Math. 36(4), 600–642 (1992)
3. Darsow, W.F., Olsen, E.T.: Characterization of idempotent 2-copulas. Note Mat. 30(1), 147–177 (2010)
4. Durante, F., Klement, E.P., Quesada-Molina, J., Sarkoci, J.: Remarks on Two Product-like Constructions for Copulas. Kybernetika 43(2), 235–244 (2007)
5. Durante, F., Sempi, C.: Copula theory: an introduction. In: Jaworski, P., Durante, F., Härdle, W., Rychlik, T. (eds.) Copula Theory and its Applications. Lecture Notes in Statistics–Proceedings, vol. 198, pp. 1–31. Springer, Berlin (2010)
6. Farahat, H.K.: The semigroup of doubly-stochastic matrices. Proc. Glasgow Mat., Ass. 7, 178–183 (1966)
7. Fredricks, G.A., Nelsen, R.B., Rodríguez-Lallena, J.A.: Copulas with fractal supports. Insur. Math. Econ. 37, 42–48 (2005)
8. Kallenberg, O.: Foundations of modern probability. Springer, Heidelberg (1997)
9. Klenke, A.: Probability Theory - A Comprehensive Course. Springer, Heidelberg (2007)
10. Lancaster, H.O.: Correlation and complete dependence of random variables. Ann. Math. Stat. 34, 1315–1321 (1963)
11. Nelsen, R.B.: An Introduction to Copulas. Springer, New York (2006)
12. Olsen, E.T., Darsow, W.F., Nguyen, B.: Copulas and Markov operators. In: Proceedings of the Conference on Distributions with Fixed Marginals and Related Topics. IMS Lecture Notes. Monograph Series, vol. 28, pp. 244–259 (1996)
13. Schwarz, S.: A Note on the Structure of the Semigroup of Doubly-Stochastic Matrices. Mathematica Slovaca 17(4), 308–316 (1967)
14. Sempi, C.: Conditional Expectations and Idempotent Copulae. In: Cuadras, C.M., et al. (eds.) Distributions with Given Marginals and Statistical Modelling, pp. 223–228. Kluwer, Netherlands (2002)
15. Trutschnig, W.: On a strong metric on the space of copulas and its induced dependence measure. J. Math. Anal. Appl. 384, 690–705 (2011)

On a Class of Variolinear Copulas

Hans De Meyer[1], Bernard De Baets[2], and Tarad Jwaid[2]

[1] Department of Applied Mathematics and Computer Science, Ghent University,
Krijgslaan 281 S9, B-9000, Gent, Belgium
hans.demeyer@ugent.be
[2] Department of Mathematical Modelling, Statistics and Bioinformatics,
Ghent University, Coupure links 653, B-9000, Gent, Belgium
{bernard.debaets,tarad.jwaid}@ugent.be

Abstract. We construct variolinear copulas with a given diagonal section, i.e. copulas that are linear on line segments connecting points on the diagonal to points on the boundary of the unit square. These line segments cover the unit square, two line segments can only intersect at $(0,1)$ or $(1,0)$, and the line segments may have a varying angle w.r.t. the main diagonal. The class of variolinear copulas covers the subclasses of semilinear, ortholinear and biconic copulas, whose construction has been reported before. We restrict the analysis to the case of symmetric variolinear copulas and we focus on the situation where the variability of the line segments is governed by two linear functions. For that subclass we provide the necessary and sufficient conditions on a diagonal function to obtain a variolinear copula. Some examples are provided.

Keywords: biconic copula, copula, diagonal section, ortholinear copula, semilinear copula, symmetric copula, variolinear copula.

1 Introduction

Copulas are binary operations on the unit interval having 0 as absorbing and 1 as neutral element and satisfying the condition of 2-monotonicity [10], i.e. a copula C is a $[0,1]^2 \to [0,1]$ function having the following properties:

1. For all $x \in [0,1]$, it holds that $C(x,0) = C(0,x) = 0$ and $C(x,1) = C(1,x) = x$;
2. For all $x, x', y, y' \in [0,1]$ such that $x \leq x'$ and $y \leq y'$, it holds that

$$C(x,y) + C(x',y') - C(x,y') - C(x',y) \geq 0.$$

The diagonal section of a copula C is the function $\delta_C : [0,1] \to [0,1]$ defined by $\delta_C(x) = C(x,x)$. A diagonal function δ is a $[0,1] \to [0,1]$ function that satisfies the following conditions:

(i) $\delta(0) = 0$, $\delta(1) = 1$;
(ii) For all $x \in [0,1]$, it holds that $\delta(x) \leq x$;

S. Greco et al. (Eds.): IPMU 2012, Part II, CCIS 298, pp. 171–180, 2012.
© Springer-Verlag Berlin Heidelberg 2012

(iii) For all $x, x' \in [0, 1]$ such that $x \leq x'$, it holds that $0 \leq \delta(x') - \delta(x) \leq 2(x' - x)$.

If δ is differentiable on $[0, 1]$, then condition (iii) is equivalent to $0 \leq \delta'(x) \leq 2$ for all $x \in [0, 1]$. The diagonal section δ_C of a copula C is a diagonal function. Conversely, for any diagonal function δ there exists at least one copula C with diagonal section $\delta_C = \delta$.

The construction of copulas, given a diagonal function, was already briefly considered at the time copulas were introduced in statistics [11]. This topic recently regained full interest and was reinvestigated from different points of view. General construction methods have been proposed in [3,12], while simultaneously research efforts have been concentrated on constructing copulas with a given diagonal section that have special properties [2,5]. In particular, much focus has been put on the property of linearity on line segments. This led to the concept of semilinear copulas, i.e. copulas that are locally linear in at least one of their arguments, or, otherwise stated, copulas that are linear on line segments parallel to one of the boundaries of the unit square. Four types of semilinear copulas have been distinguished, depending on the orientation of the line segments above and below the diagonal [1,4]. The situation where besides the diagonal section also the opposite diagonal section is given, led us to define orbital semilinear copulas [7].

The concept of linearity on line segments offers much more perspectives than just the construction of semilinear copulas. Disregarding the requirement of a fixed diagonal, some of the present authors studied the so-called conic copulas, which are linear on line segments that connect the points on a zero-curve in the unit square to the upper-right corner point [6]. Moreover, the present authors have reported on the construction of copulas with a given diagonal section that are linear on line segments connecting the diagonal points to the upper-left and lower-right corner points. These are called biconic copulas [8]. Even more recently, we have investigated the construction of ortholinear copulas with a given diagonal section, i.e. copulas that are linear on line segments perpendicular to the main diagonal [9].

Instead of continuing to study more particular cases such as the ones mentioned above, we clearly should aim at developing a more general framework for the construction of copulas with a given diagonal section that are linear on given line segments in the unit square. In fact, the most general framework is that of copulas whose graphical representation in three dimensions is (part of) a ruled surface. However, the counterpart for allowing such a high degree of flexibility, is that the conditions the diagonal function should satisfy, may become very intricate. We believe that the concept of variolinear copulas, which we introduce in the present paper, is not only sufficiently general to cover all the situations mentioned before, but also leads to conditions on the diagonal function that are sufficiently simple to verify and to interpret.

The outline of the paper is as follows. In the next section, we briefly review the construction of semilinear, biconic and·ortholinear copulas with a given diagonal section. In section 3 we define the concept of variolinear copula and present some partial results on the existence of general variolinear copulas with a given diagonal section. Section 4 is concerned with the complete analysis of symmetric variolinear copulas that are linear on sections whose orientation is governed by two linear functions. We provide some examples in section 5.

2   Review of Semilinear, Biconic and Ortholinear Copulas

Recently, Durante et al. [3,4], De Baets et al. [1] and Jwaid et al. [7] have studied families of semilinear copulas with a given diagonal section. We briefly review these construction methods.

A first construction is based on linear interpolation on line segments connecting the diagonal to the left or lower boundary of the unit square; this yields the symmetric lower semilinear copulas [4]. The second construction is based on linear interpolation on line segments connecting the diagonal to the lower and upper boundary of the unit square, yielding the in general nonsymmetric vertical semilinear copulas [1]. The two construction methods are graphically illustrated in Fig. 1.

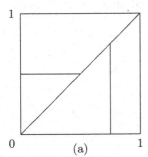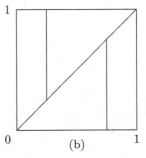

Fig. 1. Semilinear copulas with a given diagonal section. (a) lower semilinear copula: linear on horizontal line segments above and on vertical line segments below the diagonal, (b) vertical semilinear copula: linear on vertical line segments above and below the diagonal.

We recall the conditions on δ that guarantee the existence of a lower or vertical semilinear copula with diagonal section equal to δ.

Proposition 1. [4] For a diagonal function δ, let the function $C_\delta^l : [0,1]^2 \rightarrow [0,1]$ be defined by

$$
C_\delta^l(x,y) =
\begin{cases}
y\dfrac{\delta(x)}{x} & \text{, if } y \leq x\,, \\[2mm]
x\dfrac{\delta(y)}{y} & \text{, otherwise}\,,
\end{cases}
$$

where the convention $\frac{0}{0} := 0$ is adopted. Then C_δ^l is a copula, called the lower semilinear copula with diagonal section δ, if and only if the function $\lambda :]0,1] \to [0,1]$ defined by $\lambda(x) = \delta(x)/x$ is increasing and the function $\mu :]0,1] \to [1,\infty[$ defined by $\mu(x) = \delta(x)/x^2$ is decreasing.

Proposition 2. [1] For a diagonal function δ, let the function $C_\delta^v : [0,1]^2 \to [0,1]$ be defined by

$$C_\delta^v(x,y) = \begin{cases} y\dfrac{\delta(x)}{x} & \text{, if } y \le x, \\ \dfrac{x(y-x) + (1-y)\delta(x)}{1-x} & \text{, otherwise,} \end{cases}$$

where the convention $\frac{0}{0} := 1$ is adopted. Then C_δ^v is a copula, called the vertical semilinear copula with diagonal section δ, if and only if the function $\lambda :]0,1] \to [0,1]$ defined by $\lambda(x) = \delta(x)/x$ is increasing, the function $\bar{\lambda} : [0,1[\to [0,1]$ defined by $\bar{\lambda}(x) = (x - \delta(x))/(1-x)$ is increasing, and it holds for all $x \in [0,1]$ that $\delta(x) \ge x^2$.

A biconic copula with a given diagonal section is a copula that is linear on line segments connecting the diagonal points to the corner points (0,1) and (1,0). This defining property is graphically illustrated on the left square in Fig. 2.

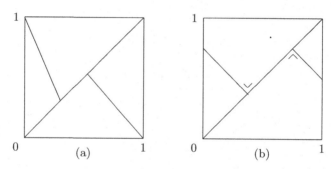

Fig. 2. (a) Biconic copula: linear on line segments connecting diagonal points to (0,1) above and to (1,0) below the diagonal; (b) ortholinear copula: linear on line segments that are perpendicular to the diagonal.

Proposition 3. [8] For a diagonal function δ, let the function $C_\delta^b : [0,1]^2 \to [0,1]$ be defined by

$$C_\delta^b(x,y) = \begin{cases} (1+y-x)\,\delta\left(\dfrac{y}{1+y-x}\right) & \text{, if } y \le x, \\ (1+x-y)\,\delta\left(\dfrac{x}{1+x-y}\right) & \text{, otherwise.} \end{cases}$$

Then C_δ^b is a symmetric copula, called the biconic copula with diagonal section δ, if and only if δ is convex.

Finally, ortholinear copulas with a given diagonal section are copulas that are linear on line segments perpendicular to the main diagonal of the unit square. This defining property is graphically illustrated on the right square in Fig. 2.

Proposition 4. [9] For a diagonal function δ, let the function $C_\delta^o : [0,1]^2 \rightarrow [0,1]$ be defined by

$$C_\delta^o(x,y) = C_\delta^o(y,x)$$
$$= \begin{cases} \dfrac{2x}{x+y}\, \delta\left(\dfrac{x+y}{2}\right) & , \text{ if } x \leq y, x+y \leq 1, \\[2ex] \dfrac{(y-x)(x+y-1)+2(1-y)\delta\left(\frac{x+y}{2}\right)}{2-x-y} & , \text{ if } x \leq y, x+y \geq 1. \end{cases}$$

Then C_δ^o is a symmetric copula, called the ortholinear copula with diagonal section δ, if and only if δ is convex.

3   Variolinear Copulas

We now want to bring in more flexibility in the choice of line segments on which we require the copula to be linear. We must allow for variability of the direction of these line segments. Furthermore, we want to cover the classes of lower semilinear copulas, biconic copulas and ortholinear copulas. To that aim, we propose to divide the unit square in six sectors, three above and three below the main diagonal, as shown in Fig. 3.

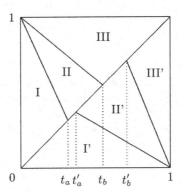

Fig. 3. Partitioning of the unit square in six sectors, three above and three below the diagonal

   In sector I, which on the diagonal extends from $(0,0)$ to (t_a, t_a), $0 \leq t_a \leq t_b$, the line segments connect the points (t,t) to the points $(0, \phi(t))$, $t \in [0, t_a]$, on the left boundary of the unit square, as is shown in Fig. 4(a). Hence, the direction of a line segment in sector I is completely governed by the function

$\phi : [0, t_a] \rightarrow [0, 1]$, which we assume to be continuous and strictly increasing on $[0, t_a]$. On sector I, the function C_I that is linear on the given line segments and for which it holds that $C_\mathrm{I}(0, y) = 0$ for all $y \in [0, 1]$ and $C_\mathrm{I}(t, t) = \delta(t)$ for all $t \in [0, t_a]$ is given by

$$C_\mathrm{I}(x, y) = x\lambda(t),$$

where t is the unique solution in $[0, t_a]$ of the implicit equation

$$y - x = \Phi(t)(t - x),$$

with $\lambda(t) = \delta(t)/t$ and $\Phi(t) = \phi(t)/t$.

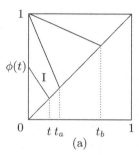
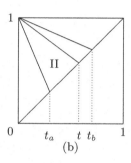
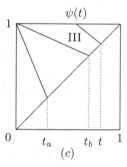

Fig. 4. (a) In sector I the line segments on which the copula is linear are determined by the function $\phi(t)$, $0 \le t \le t_a$; (b) In sector II the line segments on which the copula is linear have (0,1) as one endpoint and (t, t), $t_a \le t \le t_b$ as the other endpoint; (c) In sector III the line segments on which the copula is linear are determined by the function $\psi(t)$, $t_b \le t \le 1$.

In sector II, the line segments on which the copula should be linear connect the points (t, t) to the upper left corner $(0, 1)$ of the unit square for $0 \le t_a \le t \le t_b \le 1$ (see Fig. 3 and Fig. 4(b)). The function C_II defined on sector II which is linear on these line segments and for which it holds that $C_\mathrm{II}(t, t) = \delta(t)$ for all $t \in [t_a, t_b]$ is given by

$$C_\mathrm{II}(x, y) = (1 + x - y)\delta\left(\frac{x}{1 + x - y}\right).$$

In sector III, the line segments connect the points (t, t) to the points $(\psi(t), 1)$, $t \in [t_b, 1]$, on the upper boundary of the unit square, as is shown on Fig. 4(c). We assume the function $\psi : [t_b, 1] \rightarrow [0, 1]$ continuous and strictly increasing. On sector III, the function C_III that is linear on the given line segments and for which it holds that $C_\mathrm{III}(x, 1) = x$ for all $x \in [0, 1]$ and $C_\mathrm{I}(t, t) = \delta(t)$ for all $t \in [t_b, 1]$ is given by

$$C_\mathrm{III}(x, y) = x - (1 - y)\bar{\lambda}(t),$$

where t is the unique solution in $[t_b, 1]$ of the implicit equation

$$y - x = 1 - \Psi(t)(t - y),$$

with $\bar{\lambda}(t) = (t - \delta(t))/(1 - t)$ and $\Psi(t) = (1 - \psi(t))/(1 - t)$.

The line segments in sectors I', II' and III' are analogously defined as in sectors I, II and III. In sector I' (resp. III') the function $\rho : [0, t_a] \to [0, 1]$ (resp. $\sigma : [t_b, 1] \to [0, 1]$) plays the same role as ϕ (resp. ψ) in sector I (resp. III). The expressions for the corresponding functions C'_I, C'_{II} and C'_{III} are easily obtained. With the six functions $C_I, C_{II}, C_{III}, C'_I, C'_{II}, C'_{III}$, we compose on the unit square the variolinear function C associated with the four given functions ϕ, ψ, ρ, σ and the given diagonal function δ.

It is easily verified that we retrieve:

- for $t_a = t'_a = 1$, $\phi(t) = \rho(t) = t$, the lower semilinear function with diagonal section δ;

- for $t_b = 0$, $t'_a = 1$, $\psi(t) = \rho(t) = t$, the vertical semilinear function with diagonal section δ;

- for $t_a = t'_a = 0$, $t_b = t'_b = 1$, the biconic function with diagonal section δ;

- for $t_a = t_b = t'_a = t'_b = 1/2$, $\phi = \phi(t) = \rho(t) = 2t$, $\psi(t) = \sigma(t) = 2t - 1$, the ortholinear function with diagonal section δ.

We next want to find the conditions on ϕ, ψ, ρ, σ and δ such that the variolinear function C is a copula. By construction C satisfies the boundary conditions of a copula, there only remains to impose 2-monotonicity. For example, assuming that the second-order derivative of the functions ϕ and δ exists on $[0, 1]$, the condition of 2-monotonicity on sector I is equivalent to the condition that for all $x \in [0, t]$ and for all $t \in [0, t_a]$, it must hold that

$$x(\Phi(t) - 1)[p\lambda''(t) - q(t)\lambda'(t)] + p\lambda'(t)[t\Phi'(t) + \Phi(t)] \geq 0,$$

where

$$p = (t - x)\Phi'(t) + \Phi(t), \quad q = (t - x)\Phi''(t) + 2\Phi'(t).$$

Note that the left-hand side of the inequality condition is, in general, quadratic in x. The inequality necessarily must be satisfied for $x = 0$ and $x = t$. Hence, we obtain as necessary conditions that for all $t \in [0, t_a]$, it must hold that

$$\lambda'(t) \geq 0 \text{ and } [\phi(t) - t]\phi(t)\delta''(t) + t\lambda(t)'\phi'(t)[2t - \phi(t)] \geq 0.$$

Similarly, we can derive the necessary and sufficient conditions expressing the required 2-monotonicity of C on the other sectors and on the lines that separate the different sectors. As these conditions are rather intricate, we will report on them elsewhere. Instead, we further investigate the subclass of variolinear copulas that are associated with linear functions ϕ, ψ, ρ, τ.

4 Variolinear Copulas with Line Segments Governed by Linear Functions

Since semilinear, biconic and ortholinear copulas are types of variolinear copulas for which the line segments on which they are linear, are defined by means of functions ϕ, ψ, ρ and σ that are linear, we will analyze more deeply this special situation. We also restrict the present analysis to the symmetric case, hence we choose $\rho = \phi$ and $\sigma = \psi$. We define

$$\phi(t) = at, \quad a \geq 1; \quad \psi(t) = bt + 1 - b, \quad b \geq 1.$$

It follows that $t_a = 1/a$ and $t_b = 1 - 1/b$. Clearly it must hold that $t_a \leq t_b$, or, equivalently, that

$$\frac{1}{a} + \frac{1}{b} \leq 1,$$

while equality implies that sectors II and II' are void. The restrictions $a \geq 1$ and $b \geq 1$ imply that in sectors I and III we only accept line segments with negative slope. In the following proposition, we not only give the explicit expression of the variolinear function associated with the parametrized linear functions ϕ and ψ, but also the conditions to be imposed on the given diagonal function δ guaranteeing that the variolinear function is a (variolinear) copula.

Proposition 5. *For a diagonal function δ that is twice differentiable on $[0, 1]$, let the function $C_\delta^{vl} : [0, 1]^2 \to [0, 1]$ be defined by*

$$C_\delta^{vl}(x, y) = C_\delta^{vl}(y, x)$$
$$= \begin{cases} x \lambda \left(\dfrac{y + (a - 1)x}{a} \right) & \text{, if } x \leq y, y + (a - 1)x \leq 1, \\ x - (1 - y)\bar{\lambda} \left(\dfrac{x + (b - 1)y}{b} \right) & \text{, if } x \leq y, (b - 1)(1 - y) \leq x, \end{cases}$$

with $\lambda(t) = \delta(t)/t$ and $\bar{\lambda}(t) = (t - \delta(t))/(1 - t)$. Then C_δ^{vl} is a symmetric copula, called the variolinear copula with diagonal section δ, if and only if δ satisfies the following conditions:

(1) $\lambda'(t) \geq 0$ for $0 \leq t \leq 1/a$;

(1') $\bar{\lambda}'(t) \geq 0$ for $1 - 1/b \leq t \leq 1$;

(2) $(a - 1)\delta''(t) + (2 - a)\lambda'(t) \geq 0$ for $0 \leq t \leq 1/a$;

(2') $\delta''(t) \geq 0$ for $1/a \leq t \leq 1 - 1/b$;

(2") $(b - 1)\delta''(t) + (2 - b)\bar{\lambda}'(t) \geq 0$ for $1 - 1/b \leq t \leq 1$;

(3) $2\delta(t) - (2 - a)t\delta'(t) \geq 0$ for $0 \leq t \leq 1/a$;

(3') $2\delta(t) + (2 - b)(1 - t)\delta'(t) \geq 2(1 - b(1 - t))$ for $1 - 1/b \leq t \leq 1$.

One can easily verify that for the special cases of the lower semilinear copula ($a = 1$, only conditions (1) and (2) apply), the biconic copula (only condition (2') applies) and the ortholinear copula ($a = b = 2$, condition (2') is irrelevant), these conditions are in agreement with the previously derived conditions, provided one takes into consideration the assumption that δ is twice differentiable on $[0, 1]$. Also note that $\delta''(t) \geq 0$ on $[0, 1]$ implies that $\lambda'(t) \geq 0$ on $[0, 1]$ and $\bar{\lambda}'(t) \geq 0$ on $[0, 1]$, but the converse is in general not true.

·5   Examples

We will illustrate Proposition 5 with two types of examples. First we will give examples where δ is given and we investigate which linear functions ϕ and ψ can be used in order to obtain a copula. Secondly, we will give an example where the functions ϕ and ψ are given and we will investigate for which diagonal functions δ the resulting variolinear function is a copula.

Example 1. Consider the diagonal function δ defined by

$$\delta(t) = t^{1+\alpha}, \qquad 0 \leq \alpha \leq 1.$$

The restriction on the real parameter α guarantees that δ is indeed a valid diagonal function. For $\alpha = 0$ and $\alpha = 1$ it is immediately verified that all conditions of Proposition 5 are satisfied. For $0 < \alpha < 1$, it is more difficult but straightforward to prove that again all these conditions are satisfied. Hence, for diagonal functions δ that are a power of t and that are situated between the diagonal section of the min-copula M and the diagonal section of the product-copula Π, we find that any choice of two linear functions ϕ and ψ, leads to a variolinear copula with diagonal section equal to δ.

Example 2. Consider the diagonal function δ defined by

$$\delta(t) = t^2 + t^2(1 - t)^2.$$

It can be verified that δ is a valid diagonal function. It is a matter of direct verification to prove that all conditions of Proposition 5 are satisfied for any $a \geq 1$ and any $b \geq 1$.

Example 3. Consider the diagonal function δ defined by

$$\delta(t) = \frac{t}{2 - t}.$$

Note that this is the diagonal section of the Hamacher product [10] and therefore is a valid diagonal function. It is again a matter of direct verification to prove that all conditions of Proposition 5 are satisfied for any $a \geq 1$ and any $b \geq 1$.

Example 4. Let us fix the functions ϕ and ψ as follows. We choose $a = b = 3$. Hence, $t_a = 1/3$ and $t_b = 2/3$. Conditions (2) and (2") respectively become $2\delta''(t) - \lambda'(t) \geq 0$ and $2\delta''(t) - \bar{\lambda}'(t) \geq 0$. Condition (3) is trivially satisfied, whereas condition (3') becomes

$$2\delta(t) - (1 - t)\delta'(t) \geq 2(3t - 2), \qquad \frac{2}{3} \leq t \leq 1.$$

If Condition (1') is satisfied, i.e. $\bar{\lambda}'(t) \geq 0$, then taking into account that for any diagonal function δ it holds that $\delta(t) \geq 2t - 1$ (the r.h.s. is the diagonal section of the smallest copula W), the above inequality is indeed satisfied. In conclusion, the conditions to be imposed on the diagonal function δ can be summarized as follows:

$$\begin{cases} 0 \leq \dfrac{1}{2}\lambda'(t) \leq \delta''(t) \text{ , for } 0 \leq t \leq 1/3 \,, \\[2mm] 0 \leq \delta''(t) \qquad\quad\ \text{ , for } 1/3 \leq t \leq 2/3 \,, \\[2mm] 0 \leq \dfrac{1}{2}\bar{\lambda}'(t) \leq \delta''(t) \text{ , for } 2/3 \leq t \leq 1 \,. \end{cases}$$

It goes without saying that the diagonal functions from Examples 1–3 all satisfy these conditions.

References

1. De Baets, B., De Meyer, H., Mesiar, R.: Asymmetric Semilinear Copulas. Kybernetika 43, 221–233 (2007)
2. Durante, F., Jaworski, P.: Absolutely Continuous Copulas with Given Diagonal Sections. Communications in Statistics: Theory and Methods 37, 2924–2942 (2008)
3. Durante, F., Kolesárová, A., Mesiar, R., Sempi, C.: Copulas with Given Diagonal Sections, Novel Constructions and Applications. Internat. J. Uncertainty, Fuzziness and Knowledge-Based Systems 15, 397–410 (2007)
4. Durante, F., Kolesárová, A., Mesiar, R., Sempi, C.: Semilinear Copulas. Fuzzy Sets and Systems 159, 63–76 (2008)
5. Durante, F., Mesiar, R., Sempi, C.: On a Family of Copulas Constructed from the Diagonal Section. Soft Computing 10, 490–494 (2006)
6. Jwaid, T., De Baets, B., Kalická, J., Mesiar, R.: Conic Aggregation Functions. Fuzzy Sets and Systems 167, 3–20 (2011)
7. Jwaid, T., De Baets, B., De Meyer, H.: Orbital Semilinear Copulas. Kybernetika 45, 1012–1029 (2009)
8. Jwaid, T., De Baets, B., De Meyer, H.: Biconic Aggregation Functions. Information Sciences 187, 129–150 (2012)
9. Jwaid, T., De Baets, B., De Meyer, H.: Ortholinear Copulas. Kybernetika (submitted)
10. Nelsen, R.: An Introduction to Copulas. Springer, New York (2006)
11. Nelsen, R., Fredricks, G.: Diagonal Copulas. In: Beneš, V., Štěpán, J. (eds.) Distributions with given Marginals and Moment Problems, pp. 121–127. Kluwer Academic Publishers, Dordrecht (1977)
12. Nelsen, R., Quesada-Molina, J., Rodríguez-Lallena, J., Úbeda-Flores, M.: On the Construction of Copulas and Quasi-copulas with Given Diagonal Sections. Insurance: Math. Econ. 42, 473–483 (2008)

A Note on Exchangeable Copulas

Roberto Ghiselli Ricci

Department of Economia Istituzioni Territorio,
University of Ferrara,
Via Voltapaletto 11, I-44121 Ferrara, Italy
ghsrrt@unife.it

Abstract. This paper focuses on exchangeable copulas: some characterizing conditions are given and various examples are provided.

Keywords: Exchangeable copulas, 2-increasing property, semilinear copula.

1 Introduction

This paper focuses on exchangeable copulas. Let us introduce the following, basic notions.

Definition 1. *Let F be a real function defined on some domain $D \subseteq \mathbb{I}^2$, where $\mathbb{I} := [0,1]$. Let R be the rectangle $[u, u'] \times [v, v']$, for any $u, u', v, v' \in \mathbb{I}$ such that $u < u'$ and $v < v'$. Assume that $R \subseteq D$: we say that $V_F(R)$, given by*

$$V_F(R) = F(u', v') - F(u, v') - F(u', v) + F(u, v), \tag{1}$$

is the F-volume of the rectangle R.

Definition 2. *A (bivariate) copula is a function $C : \mathbb{I}^2 \to \mathbb{I}$ if, and only if, it satisfies:*

(a) *the* boundary conditions

$$C(u, 0) = C(0, u) = 0 \ \text{ and } \ C(u, 1) = C(1, u) = u \quad \text{for all } u \in \mathbb{I};$$

(b) *the 2-increasing property, i.e. $V_C(R) \geq 0$ for any rectangle $R \subseteq \mathbb{I}^2$.*

For more details, see [5].

Definition 3. *A copula C is* exchangeable *if $C(u, v) = C(v, u)$ for all u, v in $\mathbb{I}$.*

Copulas were introduced in a statistical context in order to join bivariate distribution functions (= d.f.'s) to their univariate marginal d.f.'s. In fact, according to *Sklar's theorem* (see [7]), for each random pair (X, Y) there is a copula $C = C_{X,Y}$ (uniquely defined whenever X and Y are continuous) such that the joint distribution function $F_{X,Y}$ of (X, Y) may be represented, for all $x, y \in \mathbb{R}$, under the form

$$F_{X,Y}(x, y) = C(F_X(x), F_Y(y)),$$

S. Greco et al. (Eds.): IPMU 2012, Part II, CCIS 298, pp. 181–185, 2012.
© Springer-Verlag Berlin Heidelberg 2012

where F_X and F_Y are the d.f.'s of the random variables X and Y, respectively. For this reason, copulas are popular in statistical applications, but they have proved useful in a variety of modeling situations, such as in the study of the relationships between dependence and aging for exchangeable random vectors (see [1]) or in fuzzy set theory (see, for instance, [2]).

Our purpose is to determine a result able to characterize exchangeable copulas and, at the same time, to allow an easy construction of families of such copulas. In one case, we will extend the class of semilinear copulas (see [4]).

2   Main Results

In this section we will exclusively deal with the class $\mathcal{C}_E$ of exchangeable copulas. Let us set $\mathcal{F} := \{F : \Delta \to \mathbb{R}\}$, where $\Delta := \{(x, y) \in \mathbb{I}^2 : y \leq x\}$: given any $F \in \mathcal{F}$, set $\delta_F(t) := F(t, t)$, for all $t \in \mathbb{I}$. Further, we denote by $D_1 F(x, y_0)$, whenever and wherever it exists, the partial derivative of F with respect to the first component, for any fixed $y_0 \in [0, 1[$, and analogously for $D_2 F(x_0, y)$ for any fixed $x_0 \in \,]0, 1]$. Now, let $\mathcal{F}_C$ be the subclass of $\mathcal{F}$ constituted by those mappings F such that

(i) $F(x, 0) = 0$ and $F(1, x) = x$ for all $x \in \mathbb{I}$;
(ii) $V_F(R) \geq 0$ for any rectangle $R \subset \Delta$;
(iii) $F(x, x) + F(y, y) \geq 2F(x, y)$ for any $(x, y) \in \Delta$.

Lemma 1. *There is a bi-univocal correspondence between $\mathcal{C}_E$ and $\mathcal{F}_C$.*

Let $\mathcal{F}_{QC}$ be the subclass of $\mathcal{F}$ formed by functions F satisfying property (i) and such that

(c) F is monotone increasing in each component;
(d) F is 1-*Lipschitz*, i.e.

$$F(x', y') - F(x, y) \leq x' - x + y' - y$$

for all $(x, y), (x', y') \in \Delta$ such that $y < y'$ and $x < x'$.

Next lemma states that every mapping $F \in \mathcal{F}_{QC}$ is a good candidate to be an exchangeable copula.

Lemma 2. *The class $\mathcal{F}_C$ is a proper subset of $\mathcal{F}_{QC}$.*

We emphasize that the two conditions (ii) and (iii) are independent of each other. Indeed, consider $F \in \mathcal{F}$ given by $F(x, y) = yx^2$. It is quite easy to show that such F verifies (i)-(ii), but, at the same time, (iii) fails, for instance, when $x = 1/2$ and $y = 2/5$. Conversely, let $F : \Delta \to \mathbb{R}$ be given by

$$F(x, y) = \begin{cases} y(x + y), & x + y \leq 1, \\ y, & \text{otherwise.} \end{cases}$$

Now, F trivially satisfies (i) and it is a simple task to check that also (iii) holds. However, $V_F(R^*) = -1/64$ when $R^* = [1/2, 3/4] \times [1/4, 3/8]$, so that (ii) fails.

Our purpose is to characterize properties (ii) and (iii) in differential form under the most general hypothesis. Note that, in the sequel, every property admitted by a mapping $F \in \mathcal{F}_{QC}$ almost everywhere (a.e.) is to be intended with respect to the Lebesgue measure.

Proposition 1. *Let $F \in \mathcal{F}_{QC}$. Assume that property* (iii) *holds. Then, the following inequality holds:*

$$\delta'_F(u) \geq 2 \cdot D_1^+ F(u, u) \quad \text{a.e. on } \mathbb{I}, \tag{2}$$

where $D_1^+ F(x, y)$, defined for any $(x, y) \in \Delta$ such that $x < 1$, is a right-side upper Dini derivative *with respect to the first place, given by*

$$D_1^+ F(x, y) = \limsup_{h \to 0^+} \frac{F(x + h, y) - F(x, y)}{h}.$$

Remark that eq. (2) is only a necessary condition, but not sufficient to guarantee that a certain $F \in \mathcal{F}_{QC}$ is a copula (see Example 2.1 in [6]). With regard to property (ii), we have a complete characterization.

Proposition 2. *Let $F \in \mathcal{F}_{QC}$. Then, $F \in \mathcal{F}_C$ if, and only if, the function $\nu \mapsto D_1 F(u, \nu)$, which is defined a.e. on $\mathbb{I}$ and exists for almost all $u \in \mathbb{I}$, is increasing.*

Remark 1. *In [3, Theorem 2.1], Durante et al. characterize the 2-increasing property by using the notion of Dini derivative. Note that their theorem may be applied to a wider class of functions than quasi-copulas, even if a Dini derivative requires a moderately more complicated calculation than an usual, partial derivative. In this sense, the only result from that paper directly comparable with Proposition 2 is Corollary 2.2.*

Based upon the previous results, we can provide a complete characterization of property (iii).

Proposition 3. *Let $F \in \mathcal{F}_{QC}$. Then, $F \in \mathcal{F}_C$ if, and only if, for almost all $u \in \mathbb{I}$ the function $\nu \mapsto D_1 F(u, \nu)$ is increasing on $\mathbb{I}$ and eq. (2) holds.*

Finally, the characterization conditions become particularly simple to check when F admits the first partial derivative with respect to the first (or second) place at almost all points of the main diagonal of the unit square.

Proposition 4. *Let F be in $\mathcal{F}_{QC}$. Assume that $D_1 F(u, u)$ exists a.e. on $\mathbb{I}$. Then, $F \in \mathcal{F}_C$ if, and only if, for almost all $u \in \mathbb{I}$ the function $\nu \mapsto D_1 F(u, \nu)$ is increasing on $\mathbb{I}$ and the following inequality holds:*

$$D_2 F(u, u) \geq D_1 F(u, u) \quad \text{a.e. on } \mathbb{I}. \tag{3}$$

3 An Application

In this section, we propose an example of construction of a very general class of exchangeable copulas, which allows a certain freedom and extends the semilinear ones.

In the sequel we will call A any mapping belonging to $\mathcal{F}$ defined as follows:

$$A(x, y) = y \cdot \frac{f(x) + g(y)}{f(1) + g(y)}, \tag{4}$$

where $f, g : \mathbb{I} \to [0, \infty[$, with $f(1) > 0$.

Remark 2. *Note that if $f \equiv c$, for any $c > 0$, A corresponds to $C(u, v) = \min\{u, v\}$.*

Remark 3. *Remark that if $g \equiv 0$, A reduces to*

$$A(x, y) = y \cdot \frac{\delta_F(x)}{x},$$

where $\delta_F(x) = xf(x)/f(1)$. By Proposition 1, one can get a very simple proof of Theorem 4 in [4], covering the particular case of semilinear copulas.

Remark 4. *It is easy to see that the requirement $A \in \mathcal{F}_{QC}$ implies the differentiability of both f and g a.e. on $\mathbb{I}$.*

Proposition 5. *Let $A \in \mathcal{F}_{QC}$. Then, eq. (3) holds if, and only if, the following inequality holds a.e. on $\mathbb{I}$:*

$$f(v) + g(v) + vg'(v)\frac{f(1) - f(v)}{f(1) + g(v)} \geq vf'(v). \tag{5}$$

Example 1. *Just for sake of simplicity in the construction of A, let us choose $f = g$. Then, eq. (5) reduces to $f(1) + f(v) \geq vf'(v)$ a.e. on $\mathbb{I}$. Consider, for instance, the class of mappings $f(x) = x^\alpha$, for any $\alpha > 0$. Then, eq. (5) is fulfilled if, and only if, $\alpha \leq 2$. Curiously, the same condition holds also for property (ii), according to Proposition 2, as shown in the next result.*

Proposition 6. *Let A be given by*

$$A(x, y) = y \cdot \frac{x^\alpha + y^\alpha}{1 + y^\alpha}, \quad \alpha > 0.$$

Then $A \in \mathcal{F}_C$ if, and only if, $\alpha \leq 2$.

References

1. Bassan, B., Spizzichino, F.: Bivariate survival models with Clayton aging functions. Insurance Math. Econom. 37, 6–12 (2005)
2. Diaz, S., De Baets, B.: Additive decomposition of fuzzy pre-orders. Fuzzy Sets and Systems 158, 830–842 (2007)

3. Durante, F., Jaworski, P.: A New Characterization of Bivariate Copulas. Communications in Statistics - Theory and Methods 39, 2901–2912 (2010)
4. Durante, F., Kolesarova, A., Mesiar, R., Sempi, C.: Semilinear copulas. Fuzzy Sets and Systems 159, 63–76 (2008)
5. Nelsen, R.B.: An introduction to copulas. Springer, New York (1999)
6. Nelsen, R.B., Quesada-Molina, J.J., Rodríguez-Lallena, J.A., Úbeda-Flores, M.: Quasi-copulas and signed measures. Fuzzy Sets and Systems 161, 2328–2336 (2010)
7. Sklar, A.: Fonctions de repartition a n dimensions et leurs marges. Publ. Inst. Statist. Univ. Paris 8, 229–231 (1959)

How Many Archimedean Copulæ Are There?

Carlo Sempi

Dipartimento di Matematica e Fisica "Ennio De Giorgi"
Università del Salento, 73100 Lecce, Italy

Abstract. Two algebraic notions, power of an associative binary function and nilpotency, are used in order to show that every bivariate Archimedean copula C is isomorphic to either the independence copula Π_2, if it is strict, or to the lower Fréchet–Hoeffding bound W_2, if it is nilpotent.

1 Introduction

Archimedean copulæ in dimension either $d = 2$ or $d > 2$ have been extensively studied both for their own sake and because of the ease in applications. Here we mention the references [23] and [22] for the case $d = 2$ and [19] for the case $d > 2$. The origin of the concept lies in the representation of triangular norms (t–norms for short in the sequel) given in Ling's seminal paper [18]. Since this origin and, above all, some of the consequences deriving from it seem to be unknown to the probability and statistics community, we begin by presenting a brief introduction to t–norms.

2 An Introduction to t-Norms

The notion of t–norm rests on that of associative function on an interval. For our purposes we shall always assume this interval to be $\mathbb{I} := [0, 1]$. For an extensive treatment of t–norms see [23,16,1]

Definition 1. *A binary operation T on $\mathbb{I}$, i.e., a function $\mathbb{I}^2 \to \mathbb{I}$, is said to be associative if, for all s, t and u in $\mathbb{I}$,*

$$T\left(T(s,t), u\right) = T\left(s, T(t, u)\right). \tag{1}$$

Notice that if T is associative, the pair $(\mathbb{I}, T)$ is a *semigroup*.

Definition 2. *The T–powers of an element $t \in \mathbb{I}$ under the associative function T are defined recursively by*

$$t^1 := t \qquad and \qquad t^{n+1} := T\left(t^n, t\right), \tag{2}$$

for every $n \in \mathbf{N}$. .When it is important to stress the t-norm T, the n–th power of the element x under T will be denoted by x_T^n.

S. Greco et al. (Eds.): IPMU 2012, Part II, CCIS 298, pp. 186–193, 2012.
© Springer-Verlag Berlin Heidelberg 2012

The following two conditions will also be required from the associative function T:

(T.1) T is isotone in each place, i.e.,

$$T(s_1, t_1) \leq T(s_2, t_2), \tag{3}$$

whenever $s_1 \leq s_2$ and $t_1 \leq t_2$;

(T.2) 1 is the identity of T:

$$T(1, t) = T(t, 1) = t. \tag{4}$$

for every $t \in \mathbb{I}$.

The following lemma is proved in Section 5.3 of [23].

Lemma 1. *If the associative function T satisfies properties* (T.1) *and* (T.2) *then it also satisfies the properties*

(T.3) 0 *is the null element of T, i.e.,*

$$T(0, t) = T(t, 0) = 0,$$

for every $t \in \mathbb{I}$;

(T.4) $T(s, t) \leq \min\{s, t\}$ *for all s and t in $\mathbb{I}$;*

(T.5) $\delta_T(t) := T(t, t) \leq t$ *for every $t \in \mathbb{I}$.*

Definition 3. *A* triangular norm, *or, briefly, a* t–norm *T is a function $T : \mathbb{I}^2 \to \mathbb{I}$ that is associative, commutative, isotone in each place, and such that $T(1, t) = t$ for every $t \in \mathbb{I}$.*

We now come to the definition of the word *Archimedean*.

Definition 4. *Let T be an associative function on $\mathbb{I}$ and let it satisfy conditions* (T.1) *and* (T.2)*; then T is said to be* Archimedean *if, for all s and t in $]0, 1[$, there is $n \in \mathbf{N}$ such that $s^n < t$.*

Before stating the important result of Lemma 2, further properties will be required of T:

(T.6) If there is $t \in \mathbb{I}$ such that $\ell^+ \delta_T(t) := \lim_{s \to t, s > t} \delta_T(s) = t$, then $\delta_T(t) = t$;
(T.7) if $T(t, t) = t$ then the functions $s \mapsto T(s, t)$ and $s \mapsto T(t, s)$ are continuous.

Lemma 2. *Let the associative function T satisfy conditions* (T.1)*,* (T.2)*,* (T.6) *and* (T.7)*. Then T is symmetric, i.e., $T(s, t) = T(t, s)$ for all s and t in $\mathbb{I}$ and the following statements are equivalent:*

(a) *T is Archimedean;*
(b) *$\delta_T(t) < t$ for every $\in]0, 1[$.*

The following representation originally proved by Ling ([18]) is of paramount importance. The weakest known form of the assumptions were given by G. Krause ([17]).

Theorem 1. *The following statements are equivalent for a t-norm T:*

(a) T *is continuous and Archimedean;*
(b) T *admits the representation*

$$T(x, y) = \varphi \left(\varphi^{(-1)}(x) + \varphi^{(-1)}(y) \right), \tag{5}$$

where $\varphi : \overline{\mathbb{R}}_+ := [0, +\infty] \to \mathbb{I}$ is continuous, strictly decreasing on $[0, x_0]$ if there exists $x_0 > 0$ such that $\varphi(x_0) = 0$, otherwise, strictly decreasing on $\mathbb{R}_+$, with $\varphi(0) = 1$, while $\varphi^{(-1)} : \mathbb{I} \to \overline{\mathbb{R}}_+$ is a quasi–inverse of φ that is continuous, strictly decreasing on $\mathbb{I}$ and such that $\varphi^{(-1)}(1) = 0$. If T is strictly increasing in each place on $\mathbb{I}^2$, then $\varphi(x) > 0$ for every $x > 0$ and $\lim_{x \to +\infty} \varphi(x) = 0$, so that $\varphi^{(-1)}$ is the inverse φ^{-1} of φ and, for all x and y in $\mathbb{I}$,

$$T(x, y) = \varphi \left(\varphi^{-1}(x) + \varphi^{-1}(y) \right). \tag{6}$$

The t–norm of eq. (5) is said to be *generated* by φ.

We formalize the notion of generator.

Definition 5. *A function $\varphi : \overline{\mathbb{R}}_+ \to \mathbb{I}$ is said to be an (outer additive) generator if it is continuous, decreasing and $\varphi(0) = 1$, $\lim_{t \to +\infty} \varphi(t) = 0$ and is strictly decreasing on $[0, t_0]$, where $t_0 := \inf\{t > 0 : \varphi(t) = 0\}$. If the function φ is invertible, or, equivalently, strictly decreasing on $\mathbb{R}_+$, then the generator is said to be* strict. *If φ is strict, then $\varphi(t) > 0$ for every $t > 0$ (and $\lim_{t \to +\infty} \varphi(t) = 0$).*

Whenever we speak of a generator, we always mean an outer additive generator[1]
   The following are examples of generators; it will be seen later (Section 4) why they are fundamental.

Example 1. The t–norm (and copula) Π_2 is Archimedean: take the generator $\varphi_{\Pi_2}(t) = e^{-t}$; this is strict since $\lim_{t \to +\infty} \varphi(t) = 0$ and $\varphi(t) > 0$ for every $t > 0$; then $\varphi^{-1}(t) = -\ln t$ and

$$\varphi \left(\varphi^{-1}(u) + \varphi^{-1}(v) \right) = \exp \left(-(-\ln u - \ln v) \right) = uv = \Pi_2(u, v).$$

Also the lower Fréchet–Hoeffding bound W_2 is Archimedean; in order to see this, it suffices to take the generator $\varphi_{W_2}(t) := \max\{1 - t, 0\}$. Since $\varphi_{W_2}(1) = 0$, it is not strict.

---

[1] The reader should be alerted to the fact that it is common in the literature on copulas to represent the copulas of the present section through their inner generators $\varphi^{(-1)}$ rather than by means of the outer generator φ as we are now doing following [19]. As usual the quasi–inverse of a generator φ will be denoted by $\varphi^{(-1)}$.

On the contrary, the upper Fréchet–Hoeffding bound defined by $M_2(u, v) := \min\{u, v\}$ is not Archimedean, since $\delta_{M_2}(t) = t$ for every $t \in \mathbb{I}$ (recall Lemma 2). One should also bear in mind that it was proved by Arnold ([2]) that there do not exist continuous (not necessarily monotone) functions f, g and h that represent M_2 in the form $f(g(x) + h(y))$. Later Ling ([18]) proved that M_2 cannot be represented in the form $f(g(x) + g(y))$ where f is a quasi–inverse of g and both are strictly monotone (but not necessarily continuous). ∎

Definition 6. *An element $a \in \,]0, 1[$ is said to be* nilpotent *for the t–norm T if there exists $n \in \mathbf{N}$ such that $a_T^{(n)} = 0$.*

Definition 7. *A t–norm T is said to be* strict *if it is continuous on $\mathbb{I}^2$ and is strictly increasing on $]0, 1[$; it is said to be* nilpotent *if it is continuous on $\mathbb{I}^2$ and every $a \in \,]0, 1[$ is nilpotent.*

The t–norms $\Pi_2(u, v) := uv$ and $W_2(u, v) := \max\{u + v - 1, 0\}$ provide examples of a strict and of a nilpotent t–norm, respectively. While it is immediately seen that Π_2 is strict, in order to see that W_2 is nilpotent, one easily calculates, for $a \in \,]0, 1[$,

$$a_{W_2}^n = \max\{na - (n - 1), 0\},$$

so that $a_{W_2}^n = 0$ for $n \geq 1/(1 - a)$.

Definition 8. *Given a t–norm T, the* serial iterates *of T are the functions $T^n :$ $\mathbb{I}^{n+1} \to \mathbb{I}$, $(n \in \mathbf{N})$ defined recursively by $T^1 := T$ and by*

$$T^n(x_1, \ldots, x_n, x_{n+1}) := T\left(T^{n-1}(x_1, \ldots, x_n), x_{n+1}\right).$$

3   Copulæ and t–Norms

We recall that a *d–dimensional copula* (shortly, a *d–copula*) ($d \geq 2$) is a *d*–dimensional d.f. on $\mathbb{I}^d$ whose univariate marginals are uniformly distributed on $\mathbb{I}$. The set of *d*–copulas will be denoted by $\mathcal{C}_d$.

It is easily recognized that a 2–copula C is a t–norm if, and only if, it is symmetric and associative. However, not every t–norm T is a (symmetric) copula, since T may fail to be 2–increasing. It is therefore important, in general, to recognize t–norms that are 2–copulæ. This question is answered in the following theorem ([21]).

Theorem 2. *For a t–norm T the following statements are equivalent:*

(a) *T is a 2–copula;*
(b) *T satisfies the Lipschitz condition:*

$$T(x', y) - T(x, y) \leq x' - x \tag{7}$$

for all x, x' and y in $\mathbb{I}$ with $x \leq x'$.

Example 2. Consider the t–norm T whose additive generator is given by $\varphi(t) = 2/(2+t)$, for $t \in [0,2]$, and by $\varphi(t) = 3/(2\,(t+1))$, for $t \in [2,+\infty[$. Then T is strict, stronger than W_2 (i.e., $T \geq W_2$), but not a 2–copula.   ∎

Example 3. The 2–copula C defined by

$$C(u,v) = uv + uv\,(1-u)\,(1-v)$$

is symmetric but not a t–norm, since it is not associative.   ∎

Now a question poses itself naturally: when is a t–norm T represented by eq. (5) a 2–copula, or, more generally, when is its d–th serial iterate

$$T_\varphi^{(d)}(\mathbf{u}) = \varphi\left(\sum_{j=1}^{d} \varphi^{(-1)}(u_j)\right), \tag{8}$$

a d–copula?

Notice that even when T as given by (5) is a copula, (8) need not be a d–copula. The characterization of the d–copulas represented by eq. (8) is given in [19, Theorem 2.2].

Theorem 3. *Let φ be a generator that has derivatives up to order d on $[0,+\infty[$. Then the following are equivalent:*

(a) *φ generates an Archimedean d–copula;*
(a) *φ is d–monotone, namely, $(-1)^k\,\varphi^{(k)}(x) \geq 0$ for $k = 1,2,\ldots,d$ for every $x \in [0,+\infty[$.*

Corollary 1. *The t–norm (5) is a 2–copula, if, and only if, φ is convex.*

Definition 9. *A d–copula C with $d \geq 2$ is said to be d–extended[2] if a generator φ exists such that*

$$C(\mathbf{u}) = \varphi\left(\varphi^{(-1)}(u_1) + \varphi^{(-1)}(u_2) + \ldots + \varphi^{(-1)}(u_d)\right) \qquad \mathbf{u} \in \mathbb{I}^d. \tag{9}$$

With reference to the generator, then the copula of eq. (8) is denoted by C_φ.

When φ is strict its quasi–inverse $\varphi^{(-1)}$ equals its inverse, $\varphi^{(-1)} = \varphi^{-1}$, and the copula C_φ is said to be strict; in this case, C_φ has the representation

$$C_\varphi(\mathbf{u}) = \varphi\left(\varphi^{-1}(u_1) + \ldots + \varphi^{-1}(u_d)\right). \tag{10}$$

Notice that if $C \in \mathcal{C}_2$ is represented by (5), then its d–th serial iterate according to Definition 8 is given by

$$C_\varphi^{(d)}(\mathbf{u}) = \varphi\left(\sum_{j=1}^{d} \varphi^{(-1)}(u_j)\right).$$

---

[2] The copulæ of the type (9) are usually called *Archimedean* in analogy with the 2–dimensional case; however, for $d \geq 3$ there is no clear algebraic justification of the name Archimedean. Therefore we have chosen to call them d–extended.

4 Isomorphisms of Generators

Let $\varphi : \mathbb{R}_+ \to \mathbb{I}$ be a generator (which now may well be called an *Archimedean generator*) and let ψ be a stricly increasing bijection on $\mathbb{I}$, so that, in particular, $\psi(0) = 0$ and $\psi(1) = 1$. Then $\psi \circ \varphi$ is also a generator.

If T_φ is the Archimedean t–norm generated by φ, then, as is immediately checked, $\psi \circ \varphi$ is the generator of the t–norm

$$T_{\psi \circ \varphi}(u, v) = (\psi \circ \varphi)\left(\varphi^{(-1)} \circ \psi^{-1}(u) + \varphi^{(-1)} \circ \psi^{-1}(v)\right), \tag{11}$$

which may also be written as

$$T_{\psi \circ \varphi}(u, v) == \psi\left(T_\varphi\left(\psi^{-1}(u), \psi^{-1}(v)\right)\right).$$

Definition 10. *Two generators φ_1 and φ_2 are said to be* isomorphic *if there exists a strictly increasing bijection $\psi : \mathbb{I} \to \mathbb{I}$ such that $\varphi_2 = \psi \circ \varphi_1$.*

Two t–norms T_1 and T_2 are said to be isomorphic *if there exists a strictly increasing bijection $\psi : \mathbb{I} \to \mathbb{I}$ such that, for all u and v in $\mathbb{I}$,*

$$T_2(u, v) = \psi\left(T_1\left(\psi^{-1}(u), \psi^{-1}(v)\right)\right).$$

One immediately proves the following result.

Theorem 4. *Two Archimedean t-norms T_1 and T_2 are isomorphic if, and only if, their generators φ_1 and φ_2 are isomorphic.*

The following results are proved in [16] (see Propositions 3.36 and 5.6 and Corollary 5.7).

Theorem 5. *For a function $T : \mathbb{I}^2 \to \mathbb{I}$, the following statements are equivalent:*

(a) *T is a strict t–norm;*
(b) *T is isomorphic to Π_2.*

Theorem 6. *For a function $T : \mathbb{I}^2 \to \mathbb{I}$, the following statements are equivalent:*

(a) *T is a nilpotent t–norm;*
(b) *T is isomorphic to W_2.*

Since every Archimedean 2–copula is a t–norm the previous two results and Example 1 imply the following theorems for copulas

Theorem 7. *For an Archimedean 2–copula $C \in \mathcal{C}_2$, the following statements are equivalent:*

(a) *C is strict;*
(b) *C is isomorphic to Π_2;*
(c) *every outer additive generator φ of C is isomorphic to φ_{Π_2}.*

Theorem 8. *For an Archimedean 2–copula $C \in \mathcal{C}_2$, the following statements are equivalent:*

(a) C *is nilpotent;*
(b) C *is isomorphic to* W_2;
(c) *every outer additive generator* φ *of* C *is isomorphic to* φ_{W_2}.

As a consequence of Theorems 7 and 8 and in view of Theorem 4, the generators φ_{Π_2} and φ_{W_2} of the copulas Π_2 and W_2, respectively, play the central rôle among all the possible outer additive generators, since every such generator is isomorphic to either one of them. In fact, any Archimedean copula $C \in \mathcal{C}_2$ or extended copula $C \in \mathcal{C}_d$, with $d \geq 3$, may be obtained from either φ_{Π_2} or φ_{W_2} through an isomorphism ψ, provided the resulting generator $\psi \circ \varphi_{\Pi_2}$ or $\psi \circ \varphi_{W_2}$ satisfies the requirements of Corollary 1, in the case $d = 2$, or of Theorem 3, when $d \geq 3$. The question posed in the title is now easily answered in the following way: there is a one–to–one correspondence between Archimedean copulas and stricly increasing bijections on $\mathbb{I}$ (with the required properties).

It would be possible to show that *all* the examples of Archimedean 2–copulas given in Table 4.1 in Chapter 4 of [22] have a generator that is isomorphic either to φ_{Π_2}, when it is strict, or to φ_{W_2}, when it is nilpotent. In the recent paper [20] the authors explicitly carry out this programme, but, lacking the theoretical support of Theorems 7 and 8, do so by using a third generator, that of the copula of Example 4 below, which we now show to be isomorphic to φ_{Π_2}.

Example 4. The copula
$$C(u, v) := \frac{uv}{u + v - uv} \, ,$$
usually denoted by $\Pi/(\Sigma - \Pi)$ in the literature, is strict; its generator is

$$\varphi(t) = \frac{1}{1 + t} \qquad (t \in \mathbb{R}_+).$$

The isomorphism with φ_{Π_2} is realized by the function $\psi : \mathbb{I} \to \mathbb{I}$ defined by

$$\psi(s) = \frac{1}{1 - \ln s} \, .$$

∎

References

1. Alsina, C., Frank, M.J., Schweizer, B.: Associative functions. Triangular norms and copulas. World Scientific, Singapore (2006)
2. Arnold, V.I.: Concerning nthe representability of functions of two variables in the form $\chi(\varphi(x) + \psi(y))$. Uspehi Mat. Nauk 12, 119–121 (1957)
3. Barnett, V.: Some bivariate uniform distributions. Comm. Statist. A—Theory Methods 9, 453–461 (1980)
4. Frank, M.J.: On the simultaneous associativity of $F(x,y)$ and $x + y - F(x,y)$. Aequationes Math. 19, 194–226 (1979)
5. Genest, C., Ghoudi, K.: Une famille de lois bidimensionnelle insolite. C. R. Acad. Sci Paris Sér. I Math. 318, 351–354 (1994)

6. Genest, C., MacKay, J.: The joy of copulas: bivariate distributions with uniform marginals. Amer. Statist. 40, 280–283 (1986)
7. Genest, C., MacKay, J.: Copules archimédienes et familles de lois bidimensionnelles dont les marges sont données. Canad. J. Statist. 14, 280–283 (1986)
8. Grabisch, M., Marichal, J.–L., Mesiar, R., Pap, E.: Aggregation functions. Encyclopedia of Mathematics and its Applications, vol. 127. Cambridge Univesity Press, New York (2009)
9. Gumbel, E.J.: Distributions à plusieurs variables dont les marges sont données. C. R. Acad. Sci. Paris 246, 2717–2719 (1958)
10. Gumbel, E.J.: Distributions à plusieurs variables dont les marges sont données. C. R. Acad. Sci. Paris 246, 2717–2719 (1960)
11. Hamacher, H.: Über logische Aggregationen nicht–binär explizierter Entscheidungskriterien. Rita G. Fischer Verlag (1978)
12. Hougaard, P.: A family of multivariate failure time distributions. Biometrika 73, 671–678 (1986)
13. Hutchinson, T.P., Lai, C.D.: Continuous bivariate distributions. Emphasising applications. Rumsby Scientific Publishing, Adelaide (1990)
14. Joe, H.: Parametric families of multivariate distributions with given marginals. J. Multivariate Anal. 46, 262–282 (1993)
15. Joe, H.: Multivariate models and dependence concepts. Chapman & Hall, London (1997)
16. Klement, E.P., Mesiar, R., Pap, E.: Triangular norms. Kluwer, Dordrecht (2000)
17. Krause, G.: A strengthened form of Ling's theorem on associative functions. Ph. D. Dissertation, Illinois Institute of Technology (1981)
18. Ling, C.H.: Representation of associative functions. Publ. Math. Debrecen 12, 189–212 (1965)
19. McNeil, A.J., Nešlehová, J.: Multivariate Archimedean copulas, d–monotone functions and l_1–norm symmetric distributions. Ann. Statist. 37, 3059–3097 (2009)
20. Michiels, F., De Schepper, A.: Understanding copula transforms: a review of dependence properties, Research paper 2009–012, Department of accounting and finance, University of Antwerp (2009)
21. Moynihan, R.: On τ_T–semigroups of probability distribution functions II. Aequationes Math. 17, 19–40 (1978)
22. Nelsen, R.B.: An introduction to copulas, 2nd edn. Lecture Notes in Statistics, vol. 139. Springer, New York (1999/2006)
23. Schweizer, B., Sklar, A.: Probabilistic Metric Spaces. North-Holland, New York (1983); reprinted, Dover, Mineola (2005)

Non-commutative Product Logic
and Probability of Fuzzy Events

Denisa Diaconescu

University of Bucharest,
Faculty of Mathematics and Computer Science,
Str. Academiei Nr. 14, Bucharest, Romania
ddiaconescu@fmi.unibuc.ro

Abstract. In this paper we develop the non-commutative product logic psΠL as the non-commutative analogue of the product logic ΠL introduced by Hájek, Godo and Esteva [10]. The investigation of this logical system is an open problem in Hájek [9]. We also introduce a probabilistic logic based on the non-commutative product logic capable to reason about the probability of fuzzy events.

Keywords: non-commutative logic, product logic, fuzzy events.

1 Introduction

The idempotence of a strong conjunction implies commutativity, therefore there is no non-commutative analogue of Gödel logic, but the development of the non-commutative generalizations of Łukasiewicz logic and product logic is left as an open problem by Hájek [9]. Non-commutative Łukasiewicz logic was developed by Leuştean [11] and it was among the first non-commutative logical systems that were investigated.

The goal of the present paper is to develop the non-commutative analogue of the product logic introduced by Hájek, Godo and Esteva [10], filling a gap in the theory of non-commutative many-valued logics.

We introduce the non-commutative product logic, denoted by psΠL in a direct way, by considering the non-commutative analogue of the axioms of the product logic and then we show that psΠL can also be defined as a schematic extension of the non-commutative logic psBL introduced by Hájek [8]. We prove that the logic psΠL is strongly complete with respect to pseudo-product algebras, algebraic structures introduced by DiNola, Georgescu and Iorgulescu [2] but without any consideration on the corresponding logic.

Since the logical deduction should be a reflection of the algebraic filter theory, we notice that, beside the usual notion of provability which allows all deduction rules to be used, we have to define a weaker notion of provability which restricts the usage of the deduction rules. As a logical reflection of normal filters, we introduce the notion of normal theories and the main achievement is a deduction theorem for this kind of theories, which is the standard deduction theorem for many-valued logics.

S. Greco et al. (Eds.): IPMU 2012, Part II, CCIS 298, pp. 194–205, 2012.
© Springer-Verlag Berlin Heidelberg 2012

Recently, states on non-commutative many-valued logic algebras were studied (see for example, Georgescu [6] and Dvurečenskij, Rachůnek and Šalounová [3]). The development of probabilistic logics based on non-commutative many-valued logics appears as a natural problem. In this paper we make some first attempts on this direction, introducing the logic SFP(psΠL, psΠL) which is a probabilistic logical system based on the non-commutative product logic psΠL capable to reason about the probability of fuzzy events. This logical system can be seen as an extension of the logic SFP(Ł, Ł) developed by Flaminio and Montagna [5] which has as underlying logic the Łukasiewicz logic.

2 Non-commutative Product Logic: Definitions and Properties

In this section we introduce the non-commutative product logic, denoted by psΠL. The language of the logic psΠL consists of denumerable many propositional variables (we denote by Var the set of all propositional variables), the primitive connectives $\rightarrow$, $\rightsquigarrow$, &, $\wedge$, $\vee$ and the constants $\overline{0}$ and $\overline{1}$. Further connectives are defined as follows: $\neg\varphi$ is $\varphi \rightarrow \overline{0}$, $\sim \varphi$ is $\varphi \rightsquigarrow \overline{0}$, $\varphi \leftrightarrow \psi$ is $(\varphi \rightarrow \psi)\&(\psi \rightarrow \varphi)$, $\varphi \leftrightsquigarrow \psi$ is $(\varphi \rightsquigarrow \psi)\&(\psi \rightsquigarrow \varphi)$. The formulas are defined by structural induction in the usual way and we denote by Form$_{psΠL}$ the set of all formulas of psΠL logic.

Definition 1. For any formula $\varphi \in$ Form$_{psΠL}$, we define $\varphi^\bullet$ by:

(1) if $\varphi \in$ Var, then $\varphi^\bullet$ is φ,

(2) if φ is $\overline{0}$ or $\overline{1}$, then $\varphi^\bullet = \varphi$,

(3) if φ is $\neg\psi$, then $\varphi^\bullet = \sim \psi^\bullet$,

(4) if φ is $\sim \psi$, then $\varphi^\bullet = \neg\psi^\bullet$,

(5) if φ is $\psi\&\chi$, then $\varphi^\bullet = \chi^\bullet\&\psi\bullet$,

(6) if φ is $\psi \rightarrow \chi$, then $\varphi^\bullet = \psi^\bullet \rightsquigarrow \chi^\bullet$,

(7) if φ is $\psi \rightsquigarrow \chi$, then $\varphi^\bullet = \psi^\bullet \rightarrow \chi^\bullet$,

(8) if φ is $\psi \leftrightarrow \chi$, then $\varphi^\bullet = \chi^\bullet \leftrightsquigarrow \psi^\bullet$,

(9) if φ is $\psi \leftrightsquigarrow \chi$, then $\varphi^\bullet = \chi^\bullet \leftrightarrow \psi\bullet$,

(10) if φ is $\psi \circ \chi$, then $\varphi^\bullet = \psi^\bullet \circ \chi^\bullet$, where $\circ \in \{\wedge, \vee\}$.

The formula $\varphi^\bullet$ just interchanges the two implications $\rightarrow$ and $\rightsquigarrow$ and reverses the arguments of the non-commutative conjunction &. It is straightforward to observe that $(\varphi^\bullet)^\bullet = \varphi$. Since we are dealing with the non-commutative counterpart of a logical system, we have to generalize the axioms of the logic ΠL for both implications, resulting an impressive number of axioms. We use the above concept in order to present the axioms of the logic psΠL in a more crisp fashion. Therefore, the axioms of psΠL are:

I. A formula which has one of the following form is an axiom

(psΠA1) $\varphi \to (\psi \to \varphi)$

(psΠA2) $(\varphi \to \psi) \rightsquigarrow ((\psi \to \chi) \rightsquigarrow (\varphi \to \chi))$

(psΠA3) $\varphi \to 1$ and $0 \to \varphi$

(psΠA4) $(\varphi \& (\psi \& \chi)) \to ((\varphi \& \psi) \& \chi)$

(psΠA5a) $(\varphi \to (\psi \to \chi)) \to ((\varphi \& \psi) \to \chi)$

(psΠA5b) $((\varphi \& \psi) \to \chi) \to (\varphi \to (\psi \to \chi))$

(psΠA6) $(\varphi \to \psi) \to ((\varphi \& \chi) \to (\psi \& \chi))$

(psΠA7) $\sim \neg \varphi \to (((\varphi \& \chi) \to (\psi \& \chi)) \to (\varphi \to \psi))$

(psΠA8) $(\chi \to \varphi) \to ((\chi \to \psi) \to (\chi \to (\varphi \wedge \psi)))$

(psΠA9) $(\varphi \to \chi) \to ((\psi \to \chi) \to ((\varphi \vee \psi) \to \chi))$

(psΠA10) $(\varphi \to \psi) \vee (\psi \to \varphi)$

(psΠA11) $(\varphi \wedge \neg \varphi) \to 0$

(psΠA12a) $(\varphi \wedge \psi) \to ((\varphi \to \psi) \& \varphi)$

(psΠA12b) $((\varphi \to \psi) \& \varphi) \to (\varphi \wedge \psi)$

(psΠA13a) $(\varphi \vee \psi) \to (((\varphi \rightsquigarrow \psi) \to \psi) \wedge ((\psi \rightsquigarrow \varphi) \to \varphi))$

(psΠA13b) $(((\varphi \rightsquigarrow \psi) \to \psi) \wedge ((\psi \rightsquigarrow \varphi) \to \varphi)) \to (\varphi \vee \psi)$

II. If φ is an axiom, then $\varphi^\bullet$ is also an axiom.

Let us comment a little on the above axioms. Hájek, Godo and Esteva [10] considered the formula $(\varphi \& \psi) \to (\psi \& \varphi)$ as an axiom for the logic ΠL, but since the logic psΠL has a non-commutative strong conjunction, we drop this axiom. Also, the axiom $((\varphi \& \psi) \& \chi) \to (\varphi \& (\psi \& \chi))$ for ΠL follows from (psΠA4$^\bullet$) in the case of psΠL. Axioms (psΠA12a), (psΠA12b), (psΠA13a) and (psΠA13b) are needed since the connectives $\wedge$ and $\vee$ are no longer defined from $\&$, $\to$ and $\rightsquigarrow$.

The deduction rules of the logic psΠL are the following:

$$(\text{MP1}) \; \frac{\varphi \quad \varphi \to \psi}{\psi} \qquad (\text{MP2}) \; \frac{\varphi \quad \varphi \rightsquigarrow \psi}{\psi} \qquad (\text{Impl1}) \; \frac{\varphi \to \psi}{\varphi \rightsquigarrow \psi} \qquad (\text{Impl2}) \; \frac{\varphi \rightsquigarrow \psi}{\varphi \to \psi}$$

A theory over psΠL is any set of formulas. Provability in a theory T is defined in the obvious way, using all the deduction rules. We denote by $T \vdash \varphi$ the fact that φ is a T-theorem and by $\text{Theor}_{\text{psΠL}}(T)$ the set of all T-theorems (we use the notation $\text{Theor}_{\text{psΠL}}$ when T is the empty set).

Proposition 1. *For any formula φ of psΠL and any theory T, $T \vdash \varphi$ iff $T \vdash \varphi^\bullet$.*

Proof. If $T \vdash \varphi$ and $\varphi_1, \ldots, \varphi_n = \varphi$ is a proof for φ, then it is straightforward that $\varphi_1^\bullet, \ldots, \varphi_n^\bullet$ is a proof for $\varphi^\bullet$. The converse implication follows similarly since $\varphi = (\varphi^\bullet)^\bullet$.

Therefore, if we prove a theorem over the logic psΠL, we can immediately derive others by using the deduction rules (Impl1) or (Impl2), or by interchanging $\to$ with $\rightsquigarrow$, $\leftrightarrow$ with $\leftrightsquigarrow$, $\neg$ with $\sim$ and reversing the arguments of $\&$ (if the initial theorem is denoted by (n), then the new theorem will be denoted by $(n^\bullet)$).

We introduced the logic psΠL in a direct way, by generalizing to the non-commutative case, in an appropriate way, the axioms of the logic ΠL given by Hájek, Godo and Esteva in [10]. Hájek [7] showed that the product logic ΠL is a schematic extension of the logic BL. This relationship is preserved in the non-commutative framework: the logic psΠL is an extension of the logic psBL introduced by Hájek [8] as it is shown by the following result:

Proposition 2. *The logic* psΠL *is the extension of the logic* psBL *by the following axioms:*

$$(ps\Pi 1) \sim \neg\varphi \rightarrow (((\varphi \& \chi) \rightarrow (\psi \& \chi)) \rightarrow (\varphi \rightarrow \psi))$$
$$(ps\Pi 2)(\varphi \wedge \neg\varphi) \rightarrow 0$$

and $(ps\Pi 1^{\bullet})$, $(ps\Pi 2^{\bullet})$.

Therefore, all theorems of the logic psBL are also theorems of psΠL. Below we recall some properties that are needed in the sequel:

Lemma 1. psΠL *proves the following:*

(1) $(\psi \rightarrow \chi) \rightarrow ((\varphi \rightarrow \psi) \rightarrow (\varphi \rightarrow \chi))$,
(2) $(\varphi \rightarrow (\psi \rightsquigarrow \chi)) \rightarrow (\psi \rightsquigarrow (\varphi \rightarrow \chi))$,
(3) $\varphi \rightarrow (\psi \rightsquigarrow \varphi)$,
(4) $\varphi \rightarrow \varphi$.

The corresponding algebraic structures for the logic psΠL were already introduced by DiNola, Georgescu and Iorgulescu [2] under the name of pseudo-product algebra, but without any considerations on the corresponding logic. Pseudo-product algebras are just the non-commutative generalizations of the product algebras introduced by Hájek, Godo and Esteva [10].

Definition 2. [2] A *pseudo-product algebra* is a psBL-algebra

$$A = (A, \vee, \wedge, \odot, \rightarrow, \rightsquigarrow, 0, 1)$$

which fulfils the following conditions:

(P1) $x \wedge x^- = 0$ and $x \wedge x^\sim = 0$,
(P2) $z^= \odot ((x \odot z) \rightarrow (y \odot z)) \leq x \rightarrow y$,
(P3) $z^\approx \odot ((z \odot x) \rightsquigarrow (z \odot y)) \leq x \rightsquigarrow y$,

where $z^- = z \rightarrow 0$ and $z^\sim = z \rightsquigarrow 0$.

The following is an example of a pseudo-product algebra arising from the theory of l-groups and it was introduced by DiNola, Georgescu and Iorgulescu [2]. This example generalizes to the non-commutative case one example of product algebra given by Cignoli and Torrens [1].

Example 1. [2] Let $(G, \vee, \wedge, +, -, 0)$ be an arbitrary l-group and let $\bot$ be a symbol distinct from the elements of G. If $G^- = \{x \in G \mid x \leq 0\}$, then we define on $G_L = \{\bot\} \cup G^-$ the following operations:

$$x \odot y = \begin{cases} x+y, & \text{if } x, y \in G^- \\ \bot, & \text{otherwise} \end{cases},$$

$$x \to y = \begin{cases} (y - x) \wedge 0, & \text{if } x, y \in G^- \\ \perp, & \text{if } x \in G^- \text{ and } y = \perp, \\ 0, & \text{if } x = \perp \end{cases}$$

$$x \rightsquigarrow y = \begin{cases} (-x + y) \wedge 0, & \text{if } x, y \in G^- \\ \perp, & \text{if } x \in G^- \text{ and } y = \perp. \\ 0, & \text{if } x = \perp \end{cases}$$

If we consider $\perp \leq x$, for any $x \in G_L$, then $(G_L, \geq)$ becomes a lattice with first element $\perp$ and last element 0. Therefore the structure

$$\mathbf{G_L} = (G_L, \vee, \wedge, \odot, \to, \rightsquigarrow, 0_L = \perp, 1_L = 0)$$

is a pseudo-product algebra.

For any theory T over psΠL, we define the Lindenbaum-Tarski algebra $\mathbf{L_T}$ of T as usual. $\mathbf{L_T}$ has elements of the form

$$[\varphi]_T = \{\psi \mid T \vdash \varphi \to \psi \text{ and } T \vdash \psi \to \varphi\},$$

for any formula φ. The operations on $\mathbf{L_T}$ are defined by representatives: $[\varphi]_T \odot [\psi]_T = [\varphi \& \psi]_T$, $[\varphi]_T \circ [\psi]_T = [\varphi \circ \psi]_T$, where $\circ \in \{\vee, \wedge, \to, \rightsquigarrow\}$, $0_T = [0]_T$ and $1_T = \text{Theor}_{\text{psΠL}}(T)$. We can define $[\varphi]_T \leq [\psi]_T$ if $T \vdash \varphi \to \psi$ or, equivalently, if $T \vdash \varphi \rightsquigarrow \psi$, and it is easy to remark that $\leq$ is an ordering on L_T.

Lemma 2. *If T is a theory over* psΠL, *then the following hold:*

(a) $T \vdash \varphi$ *iff* $[\varphi]_T = \text{Theor}_{\text{psΠL}}(T)$,
(b) *if* $T \vdash \varphi$, *then* $[\varphi \to \psi]_T = [\psi]_T$ *and* $[\varphi \rightsquigarrow \psi]_T = [\psi]_T$,
(c) *if* $T \vdash \varphi_2 \to \varphi_1$ *and* $T \vdash \psi_1 \to \psi_2$, *then* $T \vdash (\varphi_1 \to \psi_1) \rightsquigarrow (\varphi_2 \to \psi_2)$,
(d) *if* $T \vdash \varphi_1 \to \varphi_2$ *and* $T \vdash \psi_1 \to \psi_2$, *then* $T \vdash \varphi_1 \circ \psi_1 \to \varphi_2 \circ \psi_2$, *where* $\circ \in \{\&, \vee, \wedge\}$.

Proof. We prove only (a), since the other proofs are routine syntactical deductions. Suppose $T \vdash \varphi$. If $\psi \in \text{Theor}_{\text{psΠL}}(T)$, then $T \vdash \psi$. By Lemma 1 (3), we have $T \vdash \psi \to (\varphi \rightsquigarrow \psi)$ and $T \vdash \varphi \to (\psi \rightsquigarrow \varphi)$. Using (MP1), it follows that $T \vdash \varphi \rightsquigarrow \psi$ and $T \vdash \psi \rightsquigarrow \varphi$, therefore $\text{Theor}_{\text{psΠL}}(T) \subseteq [\varphi]_T$. Conversely, if $\psi \in [\varphi]_T$, then $T \vdash \varphi \to \psi$. Using again (MP1), we obtain that $T \vdash \psi$, therefore $\psi \in \text{Theor}_{\text{psΠL}}(T)$ and, moreover, $[\varphi]_T \subseteq \text{Theor}_{\text{psΠL}}(T)$. Suppose now that $[\varphi]_T = \text{Theor}_{\text{psΠL}}(T)$. Let α be an axiom. Then $\alpha \in \text{Theor}_{\text{psΠL}}(T)$, thus $\alpha \in [\varphi]_T$. Therefore $T \vdash \alpha$ and $T \vdash \alpha \to \varphi$, hence $T \vdash \varphi$ by (MP1). $\blacksquare$

Proposition 3. *For any theory T over* psΠL, $\mathbf{L_T} = (L_T, \vee, \wedge, \odot, \to, \rightsquigarrow, 0_T, 1_T)$ *is a pseudo-product algebra.*

Proof. $\mathbf{L_T}$ is well-defined by Lemma 2. The fact that $\mathbf{L_T}$ is a pseudo-product algebra follows immediately from the axioms of psΠL logic. $\blacksquare$

The semantics of psΠL is defined in the usual way. If A is pseudo-product algebra, then an A-evaluation is a map $e : \text{Var} \to A$ and its extension e_A to a truth evaluation of all formulas is defined in the obvious way.

Definition 3. Let T be a theory and φ be a formula over psΠL. For any pseudo-product algebra A, φ is a T-*tautology* with respect to A if

$$e(T) = \{e(\psi) \mid \psi \in T\} = \{1\} \text{ implies } e(\varphi) = 1,$$

for any A-evaluation $e : \text{Var} \to A$.

We denote by $T \models_A \varphi$ the fact that φ is a T-tautology with respect to A. The set of all T-tautologies with respect to A is denoted by $\text{Taut}_A(T)$. If T is empty, we are dealing with tautologies with respect to A and we denote this set by Taut_A. One can easily see that

$$\models_A \varphi \text{ iff } e(\varphi) = 1, \text{ for any A-evaluation } e : \text{Var} \to A.$$

Theorem 1 (Completeness). *Let T be a theory and φ be a formula over* psΠL. *Then*

$$T \vdash \varphi \text{ iff } T \models_A \varphi, \text{ for any pseudo-product algebra } A.$$

Proof. Suppose $T \vdash \varphi$ and let $\varphi_1, \ldots, \varphi_n = \varphi$ be a T-proof for φ. For any pseudo-product algebra A and for any A-evaluation e such that $e(T) = \{1\}$, it is easy to prove by induction that $e(\varphi_i) = 1$, for any $i \in [n]$. Conversely, suppose that $T \nvdash \varphi$. Let L_T be the Lindenbaum-Tarski algebra of T and define $e(p) = [p]_T$, for every propositional variable. It is easy to prove that $e_{\text{L}_\text{T}}(\alpha) = [\alpha]_T$, for any formula α. In particular, $e_{\text{L}_\text{T}}(T) = \{1_T\}$, but $e_{\text{L}_\text{T}}(\varphi) = [\varphi]_T \neq 1_T$ since $T \nvdash \varphi$.

Corollary 1. $\text{Theor}_{\text{psΠL}} = \bigcap \{\text{Taut}_A \mid A$ *is a pseudo-product algebra*$\}$.

3   Normal Theories and Deduction Theorem

The logical deduction should be a reflection of the algebraic filter theory. In any pseudo-product algebra, $\{1\}$ is a filter and the property

$$x \to y \in \{1\} \text{ iff } x \rightsquigarrow y \in \{1\}$$

is valid, but if F is an arbitrary filter, the property

$$x \to y \in F \text{ iff } x \rightsquigarrow y \in F$$

is in general not valid; it is true only in the case of normal filters as it was proved by DiNola, Georgescu and Iorgulescu [2]. Therefore we introduce another notion of provability in which the deduction rules (Impl1) and (Impl2) are allowed only to prove logical truths, not when proving from additional axioms.

Definition 4. A formula φ is ∘-*provable* in a theory T over psΠL if it has a ∘-proof in T, i.e. there exists a sequence of formulas $\varphi_1, \ldots, \varphi_n = \varphi$ and for each $i \in [n]$, φ_i is either a theorem in psΠL or an element of T or it follows from the previous ones by modus ponens for $\to$ or for $\rightsquigarrow$.

We denote by $T \vdash^\circ \varphi$ the fact that φ is $\circ$-provable in T and by $\mathrm{Theor}^\circ_{\mathrm{psIIL}}(T)$ the set of all $\circ$-provable formulas from T. The deduction $\vdash^\circ$ reflects at the logical level exactly the above situation on algebraic filter theory, while the deduction $\vdash$ does not. We mention that Hájek [9] defined a similar weak provability for the non-commutative logic psMTL.

For the deduction $\vdash^\circ$, it is a natural problem to investigate the logical counterparts of normal filters. Therefore we introduce the notion of normal theories and we investigate their properties using some ideas of Leuştean [11], where a similar investigation was done in the framework of non-commutative Łukasiewicz logic.

Definition 5 (Normal theory). A theory T is *normal* if for any $\varphi, \psi \in \mathrm{Form}_{\mathrm{psIIL}}$,

$$T \vdash^\circ \varphi \to \psi \text{ iff } T \vdash^\circ \varphi \rightsquigarrow \psi.$$

It follows immediately that $\emptyset$ and $\mathrm{Theor}_{\mathrm{psIIL}}$ are normal theories. Also, if T is a normal theory, then $\mathrm{Theor}^\circ_{\mathrm{psIIL}}(T) = \mathrm{Theor}_{\mathrm{psIIL}}(T)$.

Notations. If $n \geq 1$ is a natural number and $\varphi_1, \ldots, \varphi_n, \psi$ are formulas, then the formula $\varphi_1 \to (\ldots (\varphi_n \to \psi) \ldots)$ will be noted by $\varphi_1 \ldots \varphi_n \to \psi$ and by $\varphi \overset{+}{\to} \psi$, if $\varphi_1 = \ldots = \varphi_n = \varphi$. We make a similar notation for $\rightsquigarrow$.

The following lemmas reflect the behaviour of normal theories.

Lemma 3. *If T is a theory, we have the following:*

(a) *if $T \vdash^\circ \varphi_1 \ldots \varphi_n \to \varphi$ and $T \vdash^\circ \varphi \to \psi$, then $T \vdash^\circ \varphi_1 \ldots \varphi_n \to \psi$;*
(b) *if $T \vdash^\circ \varphi_1 \ldots \varphi_n \rightsquigarrow \varphi$ and $T \vdash^\circ \varphi \rightsquigarrow \psi$, then $T \vdash^\circ \varphi_1 \ldots \varphi_n \rightsquigarrow \psi$.*

Proof. (a) The proof is by induction on $n \geq 1$. For $n = 1$, the conclusion follows by (psIIA2) and (MP2). Suppose that (a) holds for some $n \geq 1$ and let us prove it for $n+1$. By hypothesis, $T \vdash^\circ \varphi_1 \ldots \varphi_{n+1} \to \varphi$, i.e. $T \vdash^\circ \varphi_1 \ldots \varphi_n \to (\varphi_{n+1} \to \varphi)$. Since $T \vdash^\circ \varphi \to \psi$, by Lemma 1 (1) and (MP1), we obtain $T \vdash^\circ (\varphi_{n+1} \to \varphi) \to (\varphi_{n+1} \to \psi)$. Using the induction hypothesis, we conclude the desired property.

(b) follows similarly, by (psIIA2$^\bullet$) and Lemma 1 (1$^\bullet$). $\qquad\blacksquare$

Proposition 4. *If T is a normal theory, we have the following:*

(a) *if $T \vdash^\circ \varphi_1 \ldots \varphi_n \to (\varphi \rightsquigarrow \psi)$, then $T \vdash^\circ \varphi \to (\varphi_1 \ldots \varphi_n \to \psi)$;*
(b) *if $T \vdash^\circ \varphi_1 \ldots \varphi_n \rightsquigarrow (\varphi \to \psi)$, then $T \vdash^\circ \varphi \rightsquigarrow (\varphi_1 \ldots \varphi_n \rightsquigarrow \psi)$;*
(c) *$T \vdash^\circ \varphi_1 \ldots \varphi_n \to \varphi$ iff $T \vdash^\circ \varphi_n \ldots \varphi_1 \rightsquigarrow \varphi$.*

Proof. (a) The proof is by induction $n \geq 1$. For $n = 1$, we have $T \vdash^\circ \varphi_1 \to (\varphi \rightsquigarrow \psi)$, so by Lemma 1 (2) and (MP1), it follows that $T \vdash^\circ \varphi \rightsquigarrow (\varphi_1 \to \psi)$. Since T is normal, we obtain that $T \vdash^\circ \varphi \to (\varphi_1 \to \psi)$. Suppose that (a) holds for some $n \geq 1$ and let us prove it for $n + 1$. By hypothesis, we have $T \vdash^\circ \varphi_1 \ldots \varphi_{n+1} \to (\varphi \rightsquigarrow \psi)$, i.e. $T \vdash^\circ \varphi_1 \ldots \varphi_n \to (\varphi_{n+1} \to (\varphi \rightsquigarrow \psi))$. By Lemma 1 (2), we have $T \vdash^\circ (\varphi_{n+1} \to (\varphi \rightsquigarrow \psi)) \to (\varphi \rightsquigarrow (\varphi_{n+1} \to \psi))$. Using Lemma 3 (a), we obtain that $T \vdash^\circ \varphi_1 \ldots \varphi_n \to (\varphi \rightsquigarrow (\varphi_{n+1} \to \psi))$. By the induction hypothesis we conclude that $T \vdash^\circ \varphi \to (\varphi_1 \ldots \varphi_n \to (\varphi_{n+1} \to \psi))$.

(b) and (c) can be proved similarly by induction on $n \geq 1$. $\qquad\blacksquare$

Proposition 5. *If T is a normal theory and $T \vdash^\circ \varphi_1 \ldots \varphi_n \to \varphi$, the following hold:*

(a) if $T \vdash^\circ \gamma_1 \ldots \gamma_k \to (\varphi \rightsquigarrow \psi)$, then $T \vdash^\circ \varphi_1 \ldots \varphi_n \gamma_1 \ldots \gamma_k \to \psi$;

(b) if $T \vdash^\circ \gamma_1 \ldots \gamma_k \to (\varphi \to \psi)$, then $T \vdash^\circ \gamma_1 \ldots \gamma_k \varphi_1 \ldots \varphi_n \to \psi$.

Proof. The proof of (a) follows immediately by induction on $k \geq 1$, using Proposition 4 (a), Lemma 1 (2) and Lemma 3 (a). Therefore we prove only (b). We can easily show the following property:

$(a^\bullet)$ if $T \vdash^\circ \varphi_1 \ldots \varphi_n \rightsquigarrow \varphi$ and $T \vdash^\circ \gamma_1 \ldots \gamma_k \rightsquigarrow (\varphi \to \psi)$, then
$$T \vdash^\circ \varphi_1 \ldots \varphi_n \gamma_1 \ldots \gamma_k \rightsquigarrow \psi.$$

By hypothesis and Proposition 4 (c), we obtain

$$T \vdash^\circ \varphi_1 \ldots \varphi_n \to \varphi \text{ implies } T \vdash^\circ \varphi_n \ldots \varphi_1 \rightsquigarrow \varphi.$$

$$T \vdash^\circ \gamma_1 \ldots \gamma_k \to (\varphi \to \psi) \text{ implies } T \vdash^\circ \gamma_k \ldots \gamma_1 \rightsquigarrow (\varphi \to \psi).$$

Using $(a^\bullet)$, it follows that $T \vdash^\circ \varphi_n \ldots \varphi_1 \gamma_k \ldots \gamma_1 \rightsquigarrow \psi$, thus, by Proposition 4 (c), we get $T \vdash^\circ \gamma_1 \ldots \gamma_k \varphi_1 \ldots \varphi_n \to \psi$.

The main result of this section is a deduction theorem for normal theories over the logic psΠL, which is the standard deduction theorem in the framework of many-valued logics.

Theorem 2 (Deduction theorem for normal theories). *If T is a normal theory and φ, ψ are formulas over psΠL, then the following are equivalent:*

(a) $T \cup \{\varphi\} \vdash^\circ \psi$;

(b) $T \vdash^\circ \varphi \overset{+}{\to} \psi$;

(c) $T \vdash^\circ \varphi \overset{+}{\rightsquigarrow} \psi$.

Proof. $(a) \Rightarrow (b)$. Suppose that $T \cup \{\varphi\} \vdash^\circ \psi$ and let $\psi_1, \ldots, \psi_k = \psi$ be a $\circ$-proof from $T \cup \{\varphi\}$ for ψ. We prove the following property:

(b') there exist $n \geq 1$ and $\varphi_1, \ldots, \varphi_n \in \text{Theor}^\circ_{\text{psΠL}}(T) \cup \{\varphi\}$ such that
$$T \vdash^\circ \varphi_1 \ldots \varphi_n \to \psi.$$

The proof of (b') is by induction on $1 \leq i \leq k$. For $i = 1$ we have two possibilities:

- if $\psi_1 \in \text{Theor}^\circ_{\text{psΠL}}$, then the conclusion follows by Lemma 1 (3) and (MP2);
- if $\psi_1 \in T \cup \{\varphi\}$, then we use Lemma 1 (4) and we obtain $T \vdash^\circ \psi_1 \to \psi_1$.

Thus, (b') is satisfied for $i = 1$. Let $1 < i \leq k$ and suppose that the result holds for all $j < i$. If $\psi_i \in \text{Theor}^\circ_{\text{psΠL}}$ or $\psi_i \in T \cup \{\varphi\}$, then the conclusion follows as above. Otherwise, there are two possible cases:

- there are $j, t < i$ such that ψ_t is $\psi_j \to \psi_i$. By induction hypothesis, there are $n, m \geq 1$ and $\chi_1, \ldots, \chi_n, \rho_1, \ldots, \rho_m \in \text{Theor}^\circ_{\text{psΠL}}(T) \cup \{\varphi\}$ such that $T \vdash^\circ \chi_1 \ldots \chi_n \to \psi_j$ and $T \vdash^\circ \rho_1 \ldots \rho_m \to \psi_t$. Since T is a normal theory, we apply Proposition 5 (b) and we obtain that $T \vdash^\circ \rho_1 \ldots \rho_m \chi_1 \ldots \chi_n \to \psi_i$;

– there are $j, t < i$ such that ψ_t is $\psi_j \leadsto \psi_i$. This case is proved similarly with the above one, but we make use of Proposition 5 (a).

The remaining step is to prove the following, for any $\theta \in \mathrm{Theor}^\circ_{\mathrm{psIIL}}(T)$:

(1) if $T \vdash^\circ \theta \to (\varphi \to \psi)$, then $T \vdash^\circ \varphi \to \psi$ (similar for $\leadsto$);
(2) if $T \vdash^\circ \varphi \to (\theta \to \psi)$, then $T \vdash^\circ \varphi \to \psi$ (similar for $\leadsto$).

The implications from (1) are straightforward by (MP1) and (MP2). In order to prove (2), assume that $T \vdash^\circ \varphi \to (\theta \to \psi)$. By Proposition 4 (c), we have $T \vdash^\circ \theta \leadsto (\varphi \leadsto \psi)$, so $T \vdash^\circ \varphi \leadsto \psi$ by (1). Since T is a normal theory, we obtain $T \vdash^\circ \varphi \to \psi$.

$(b) \Rightarrow (a)$. Suppose that $T \vdash^\circ \varphi \xrightarrow{+} \psi$. It is obvious that $T \cup \{\varphi\} \vdash^\circ \varphi$, so by using (MP1) repeatedly we obtain $T \cup \{\varphi\} \vdash^\circ \psi$.

The other implications are proved similarly, therefore the proof is complete.

For the weak deduction $\vdash^\circ$ it is an interesting problem when we can define the Lindenbaum-Tarski algebra of a theory. For any theory T and any formulas φ, ψ over psIIL, let us define the following:

$$\varphi \equiv_{\overrightarrow{T}} \psi \text{ iff } T \vdash^\circ \varphi \to \psi \text{ and } T \vdash^\circ \psi \to \varphi,$$
$$\varphi \equiv_{\overset{\leadsto}{T}} \psi \text{ iff } T \vdash^\circ \varphi \leadsto \psi \text{ and } T \vdash^\circ \psi \leadsto \varphi.$$

We remark immediately that the relations $\equiv_{\overrightarrow{T}}$ and $\equiv_{\overset{\leadsto}{T}}$ are equivalences on $\mathrm{Form}_{\mathrm{psIIL}}$ and that they do not necessarily coincide. The following result solves this problem:

Proposition 6. *For any normal theory T, the relations $\equiv_{\overrightarrow{T}}$ and $\equiv_{\overset{\leadsto}{T}}$ coincide.*

Proof. Straightforward by the definition of normal theories.

Therefore, if T is a normal theory, we use the notation $\equiv_T = \equiv_{\overrightarrow{T}} = \equiv_{\overset{\leadsto}{T}}$. Thus, in the context of the deduction $\vdash^\circ$, we can define the Linbenbaum-Tarski algebra only for normal theories. From this point the construction is the same as that described in Section 2. Moreover, notice that we can obtain strong completeness results for psIIL using the weak provability $\vdash^\circ$ only for normal theories.

4   Probabilistic Non-commutative Product Logic

States on algebraic structures for many-valued logics were deeply investigated in the last years and, in parallel, different probabilistic logics have been developed. Hájek [7] introduced a probabilistic many-valued logic FP(L) based on the Łukasiewicz logic. The logic FP(L) has a modality operator P, interpreted as "probably", and it was proved that it is suitable for the treatment of probability of classical events. On the semantics side, the probability of an event φ is interpreted as the truth value of the formula $P(\varphi)$.

Trying to generalize this idea for fuzzy events, Flaminio and Godo [4] developed another probabilistic many-valued logic FP(L, L), having as underling logic also Łukasiewicz logic, which is capable to treat probability of fuzzy events. This logical system was latter refined by Flaminio and Montagna [5] into a logic named SFP(Ł, Ł) by dropping down some restrictions on formulas, obtaining a language more expressive: in the logic SFP(Ł, Ł), $P(\varphi)$ is a formula whenever φ is a formula, while in the logic FP(Ł, Ł), $P(\varphi)$ is a formula if and only if φ is a formula without occurrence of P; moreover the logic FP(Ł, Ł) do not permit formulas of the form $\varphi \circ P(\psi)$, where $\circ$ is a connective of Łukasiewicz logic, while in the logic SFP(Ł, Ł) such constructions are allowed.

In this section we introduce the logic SFP(psΠL, psΠL) which is a probabilistic logical system based on the non-commutative product logic psΠL capable to reason about the probability of fuzzy events. The logic SFP(psΠL, psΠL) can be thought as a generalization of the logic SFP(Ł, Ł) of Flaminio and Montagna [5]. In this paper we only introduce the basic definitions and properties on this probabilistic logic, many investigations still need to be done in a future work for proving the strengths and the weaknesses of this logic.

The language of the logic SFP(psΠL, psΠL) is built over the language of the logic psΠL and has a new unary connective P, interpreted as "probably". The set of formulas is defined as usual by induction, but also using the new connective P. We denote this set by $\text{Form}_{\text{SFP(psΠL,psΠL)}}$. For any formula φ of the logic SFP(psΠL, psΠL) we define, as in Section 2, the formula $\varphi^\bullet$, where $P(\varphi)^\bullet = P(\varphi^\bullet)$.

The logic SFP(psΠL, psΠL) has the following axioms:

I. The axioms of the logic psΠL.
II. A formula which has one of the following form is an axiom
    $(P1)$ $P(\varphi \to \psi) \leftrightarrow P(\varphi) \to P(\varphi \wedge \psi)$
    $(P2a)$ $P(\varphi\&\psi) \leftrightarrow P(\varphi)\&P(\varphi \rightsquigarrow (\varphi\&\psi))$
    $(P2b)$ $P(\varphi\&\psi) \leftrightarrow P(\varphi \to (\varphi\&\psi))\&P(\varphi)$
    $(P3)$ $P(P(\varphi)\&P(\psi)) \leftrightarrow P(\varphi)\&P(\psi)$
    $(P4)$ $P(P(\varphi) \to P(\psi)) \leftrightarrow P(\varphi) \to P(\psi)$
    $(P5)$ $P(P(\varphi) \vee P(\psi)) \leftrightarrow P(\varphi) \vee P(\psi)$
III. If φ is a formula of the form $(P1)$ or $(P4)$, then $\varphi^\bullet$ is also an axiom.

The deduction rules of SFP(psΠL, psΠL) are the deduction rules of the logic psΠL plus the necessitation rule

$$(\text{NEC}) \ \frac{\varphi}{P(\varphi)}.$$

Provability in a theory T is defined in the obvious way, using all the deduction rules. We denote by $\text{Theor}_{\text{SFP(psΠL,psΠL)}}(T)$ the set of all T-theorems over the logic SFP(psΠL, psΠL).

Before introducing the algebraic semantics for the logic SFP(psΠL, psΠL), we recall the following definition from Dvurečenskij, Rachůnek and Šalounová [3]:

Definition 6. [3] If A is a bounded non-commutative Rl-monoid, then a *state-operator* on A is a function $\sigma : A \to A$ such that the following conditions are satisfied:

(1) $\sigma(0) = 0$,

(2) $\sigma(x \to y) = \sigma(x) \to \sigma(x \wedge y)$ and $\sigma(x \rightsquigarrow y) = \sigma(x) \rightsquigarrow \sigma(x \wedge y)$,

(3) $\sigma(x \odot y) = \sigma(x) \odot \sigma(x \rightsquigarrow x \odot y) = \sigma(y \to x \odot y) \odot \sigma(y)$,

(4) $\sigma(\sigma(x) \odot \sigma(y)) = \sigma(x) \odot \sigma(y)$,

(5) $\sigma(\sigma(x) \to \sigma(y)) = \sigma(x) \to \sigma(y)$ and $\sigma(\sigma(x) \rightsquigarrow \sigma(y)) = \sigma(x) \rightsquigarrow \sigma(y)$,

(6) $\sigma(\sigma(x) \vee \sigma(y)) = \sigma(x) \vee \sigma(y)$.

A pseudo-product algebra is a bounded non-commutative Rl-monoid (or a divisible residuated lattice) which satisfies in addition the pseudo-prelinearity condition, i.e. $(x \to y) \vee (y \to x) = (x \rightsquigarrow y) \vee (y \rightsquigarrow x) = 1$, and conditions (P1)-(P3) from Definition 2. Therefore we introduce the following definition:

Definition 7. A structure (A, σ) is a *pseudo-product algebra with internal state* (or, simply, *state pseudo-product algebra*) if A is a pseudo-product algebra and $\sigma : A \to A$ is a state-operator on A.

Example 2. If A is a linearly ordered pseudo-product algebra and $\sigma = id_A$ is the identity on A, then the structure (A, σ) is state pseudo-product algebra.

State pseudo-product algebras are the corresponding algebraic structures for the logic SFP(psΠL, psΠL). Finding other non-trivial examples of state pseudo-product algebras would lead to a better understanding of the semantics of the logic SFP(psΠL, psΠL).

In the rest of this section we will prove that SFP(psΠL, psΠL) is strongly complete with respect to state pseudo-product algebras. Notice that the axioms for the unary connective P are just a logical reflection of the conditions of a state-operator from Definition 6. These conditions are the usual one for a modality operator.

For any theory T over the logic SFP(psΠL, psΠL), we define $[\varphi]_T = \{\psi \mid T \vdash \varphi \to \psi$ and $T \vdash \psi \to \varphi\}$, for any formula φ and we denote by $L_T = \{[\varphi]_T \mid \varphi \in$ Form$_{SFP(psΠL,psΠL)}\}$. As in Section 2, we define the operations $\odot, \vee, \wedge, \to, \rightsquigarrow$ and the elements 0_T and 1_T on L_T. Furthermore, we define the operation

$$\sigma_T([\varphi]_T) = [P(\varphi)]_T.$$

The structure (L_T, σ_T) is the Lindenbaum-Tarski algebra of a theory T over the logic SFP(psΠL, psΠL). Using the axioms on the modality operator P, we can immediately prove the following result:

Proposition 7. *For any theory T over the logic* SFP(psΠL, psΠL), *the structure* (L_T, σ_T) *is a state pseudo-product algebra.*

The logic SFP(psΠL, psΠL) is strongly complete with respect to state pseudo-product algebras as it is proved by the following completeness results:

Theorem 3 (Completeness). *Let T be a theory and φ be a formula over* SFP(psΠL, psΠL). *The following are equivalent:*

(i) $T \vdash \varphi$,

(ii) for every evaluation e into a state pseudo-product algebra (A, σ), *if* $e(\psi) = 1$, *for every* $\psi \in T$, *then* $e(\varphi) = 1$.

Proof. If $T \vdash \varphi$, then the claim is proved by an easy induction on the length of the proof from T for φ. For the other implication, suppose that $T \nvdash \varphi$. We consider the Lindenbaum-Tarski algebra (L_T, σ_T) of the theory T. (L_T, σ_T) is a state pseudo-product algebra. As usual, we define the evaluation e into (L_T, σ_T) by $e(\psi) = [\psi]_T$. We obtain that $e(\psi) = 1_T$, for every $\psi \in T$, but $e(\varphi) < 1_T$, since φ is not provable from T.

Acknowledgements. The author is deeply grateful to the anonymous referees for their valuable remarks and suggestions which improved the final version of this paper.

References

1. Cignoli, R., Torrens, A.: An algebraic analysis of product logic. Multiple-Valued Logic 5, 45–65 (2000)
2. DiNola, A., Georgescu, G., Iorgulescu, A.: Pseudo-BL algebras -part II. Multiple-Valued Logic 8(5-6), 717–750 (2002)
3. Dvurečenskij, A., Rachůnek, J., Šalounová, D.: State operators on generalizations of fuzzy structures. Fuzzy Sets and Systems 187(1), 58–76 (2012)
4. Flaminio, T., Godo, L.: A logic for reasoning about the probability of fuzzy events. Fuzzy Sets and Systems 158, 625–638 (2007)
5. Flaminio, T., Montagna, F.: MV-algebras with internal states and probabilistic fuzzy logics. International Journal of Approximate Reasoning 50, 138–152 (2009)
6. Georgescu, G.: Bosbach states on fuzzy structures. Soft Computing 8, 217–230 (2004)
7. Hájek, P.: Metamathematics of Fuzzy Logic. Trends in Logic, vol. 4. Kluwer, Dordrecht (1998)
8. Hájek, P.: Fuzzy logics with non-commutative conjunctions. Journal of Logic and Computation 13, 469–479 (2003)
9. Hájek, P.: Observations on non-commutative fuzzy logic. Soft Computing 8, 38–43 (2003)
10. Hájek, P., Godo, L., Esteva, F.: A complete many-valued logic with product-conjunction. Arch. Math. Logic 35(3), 191–208 (1996)
11. Leuştean, I.: Non-commutative Łukasiewicz propositional logic. Arch. Math. Logic 45(2), 191–213 (2006)

Linear Representation of Residuated Lattices

Irina Perfilieva

Centre of Excellence IT4Innovations
Division of the University of Ostrava
Institute for Research and Applications of Fuzzy Modeling,
Ostrava, Czech Republic
Irina.Perfilieva@osu.cz

Abstract. We reconsider the notion of semilinear space and consider it as a couple of two semimodules connected by residuated scalar multiplications. We show that under certain conditions the semigroup of endomorphisms of a semilinear space is a residuated, commutative ℓ-monoid. By this, we obtain what can be regarded as a linear representation of a residuated, commutative ℓ-monoid.

Keywords: Residuated, commutative ℓ-monoid, residuated lattice, orbit, semiring, semimodule, semilinear space.

1 Introduction

The notion of commutative residuated ℓ-monoid has been introduced in [1] with the goal "to outline a common framework for a diversity of monoidal structures which constitute the basis of various papers in fuzzy set theory". This notion is a bit more general than the earlier introduced [2] notion of "residuated lattice" for an integral, residuated, commutative ℓ-monoid. Both papers became fundamental in the literature related to mathematical fuzzy logic [3–5], algebraic foundations of fuzzy systems [6], algebraic foundations of triangular norms [7], etc. Moreover, they had significant impact on intensive development of various residuated algebraic structures such as residuated ℓ-groupoids, residuated ℓ-semigroups, etc. (see, e.g. [8]).

The main purpose of the first part of this paper is to study conditions under which a commutative semigroup of residuated maps of a bounded lattice is a residuated, commutative ℓ-monoid. In the second part, we reconsider the notion of semilinear space which has been introduced in [9] with the purpose to serve as a theoretical background for the theory of fuzzy relation equations [10]. Being helpful in deciding solvability, this notion is not helpful in representation of solutions. Therefore, we propose to extend this notion and consider a semilinear space as a couple of two semimodules connected by residuated scalar multiplications. We show that under conditions formulated in the first part, the semigroup of endomorphisms of a semilinear space is a residuated, commutative ℓ-monoid. From this, we obtain what can be regarded as a linear representation of a residuated, commutative ℓ-monoid.

S. Greco et al. (Eds.): IPMU 2012, Part II, CCIS 298, pp. 206–215, 2012.
© Springer-Verlag Berlin Heidelberg 2012

2   Residuated, Commutative ℓ-monoid of Residuated Maps

Throughout this paper, let $(L, \leq)$ be a fixed bounded lattice where the join (meet) operation is denoted by $\vee$ ($\wedge$) and the bottom (top) element is denoted by $\perp$ ($\top$). By Res_L (Res_L^+) we will denote a set of residuated maps $h : L \to L$ (a corresponding set of residual maps such that $\mathrm{Res}_L^+ = \{h^+ \mid h^+ : L \to L, h \in \mathrm{Res}_L\}$). We refer to [8, 11] for the notion of residuated maps and their algebraic properties. It is known that $(\mathrm{Res}_L, \circ)$ and $(\mathrm{Res}_L^+, \circ)$ are semigroups which are not necessary residuated. In this section, we find conditions which specify a residuated, commutative ℓ-monoid on a certain set of residuated maps. Later on, they will be used in linear representation of a residuated, commutative ℓ-monoid.

2.1   Commutative Monoids $(H, \circ)$ and $(H^+, \circ)$ of Residuated Maps

Let H be a subsemigroup of $(\mathrm{Res}_L, \circ)$ and $e \in L$ be an element such that the following two conditions are fulfilled:

C1. the *orbit* of e relative to H is equal to L, i.e. $\{h(e) \mid h \in H\} = L$,
C2. for all $h', h'' \in H$, $h'(h''(e)) = h''(h'(e))$.

By H^+ we denote a subset of Res_L^+ which consists of all those maps which are residual to respective maps in H, i.e.

$$H^+ = \{h^+a \in \mathrm{Res}_L^+ \mid h_a \in H\}.$$

H^+ is a subsemigroup of $(\mathrm{Res}_L^+, \circ)$.

In the below given Theorem 1 , we will show that both semigroups $(H, \circ)$ and $(H^+, \circ)$ are commutative monoids.

Theorem 1. *Semigroups $(H, \circ)$ and $(H^+, \circ)$ are commutative monoids with the common unit element h_e. Moreover, for all $h_a, h_b \in H$ and all $h_a^+, h_b^+ \in H^+$,*

$$h_a \circ h_b = h_{h_a(b)}, \tag{1}$$
$$h_a^+ \circ h_b^+ = h_{h_a(b)}^+. \tag{2}$$

2.2   Residuated, Commutative ℓ-monoids $(H, \leq, \circ)$ and $(H^+, \leq^d, \circ)$ of Residuated Maps

Let $(L, \leq)$ be a bounded lattice, $H = \{h_a \mid a \in L\}$ be a subset of Res_L such that **C1 – C2** are fulfilled. Let $H^+ = \{h_a^+ \mid a \in L\}$. Obviously, H and H^+ are posets with respect to partial orders defined by

$$h_a \leq h_b \iff (\forall x \in L) \quad (h_a(x) \leq h_b(x)), \tag{3}$$

and

$$h_a^+ \leq^d h_b^+ \iff (\forall x \in L) \quad (h_a^+(x) \geq h_b^+(x)). \tag{4}$$

It can be shown that $(H, \leq)$ and $(H^+, \leq^d)$ are isomorphic lattices. Moreover, each of them is isomorphic to $(L, \leq)$.

Below, we will show that the following structures: $\mathscr{H} = (H, \leq, \circ)$, where $\circ$ is expressed by (1), and $\mathscr{H}^+ = (H^+, \leq^d, \circ)$, where $\circ$ is expressed by (2), are isomorphic residuated, commutative ℓ-monoids [1].

Let us recall [1] that $(L, \leq, *)$ is a residuated, commutative ℓ-monoid [1] if $(L, \leq)$ is a bounded lattice, $(L, *)$ is a commutative monoid (e is the unit element) and the operation $*$ is residuated, i.e. there exists a binary operation $\to$ on L such that for all $a, b, c \in L$,

$$a * b \leq c \iff b \leq a \to c.$$

Theorem 2.   (i) $\mathscr{H} = (H, \leq, \circ)$ is a residuated, commutative ℓ-monoid where the following binary operation

$$h_a \to h_b = h_{h_a^+(b)}, \tag{5}$$

is the residuum of $\circ$ given by (1).
(ii) $\mathscr{H}^+ = (H^+, \leq^d, \circ)$ is a residuated, commutative ℓ-monoid where the following binary operation

$$h_a^+ \to^d h_b^+ = h_{h_a^+(b)}^+, \tag{6}$$

is the residuum of $\circ$ given by (2).
(iii) Residuated, commutative ℓ-monoids $\mathscr{H}$ and $\mathscr{H}^+$ are isomorphic.

2.3 Representation Theorem for Residuated, Commutative ℓ-monoids

Let $(L, \leq)$, $H = \{h_a \mid a \in L\}$ and $H^+ = \{h_a^+ \mid a \in L\}$ be as above. Let us extend the lattice $(L, \leq)$ by the following two binary operations:

$$a * b = h_a(b), \tag{7}$$
$$a \to b = h_a^+(b), \tag{8}$$

and denote $\mathscr{L} = (L, \leq, *)$ the respective monoidal extension of $(L, \leq)$. It is easy to see that for all $a \in L$, the maps $h_a \in H$ and $h_a^+ \in H^+$ are left translations of the respective binary operations $*$ and $\to$, i.e. $h_a = a * (\cdot)$ and $h_a^+ = a \to (\cdot)$. Below we will prove that the monoidal extension $(L, \leq, *)$ is a residuated, commutative ℓ-monoid if and only if there exists a subsemigroup H of $(\mathrm{Res}_L, \circ)$ that fulfils **C1 – C2**.

Theorem 3. Let $(L, \leq)$ be a bounded lattice and a subsemigroup H of $(\mathrm{Res}_L, \circ)$ fulfil **C1 – C2**. Let $*$ and $\to$ be binary operations on L given by (7) and (8). Then

---

[1] If a residuated, commutative ℓ-monoid $(L, \leq, *)$ is integral, i.e. the greatest element of L is a unit with respect to $*$, then it is called [2] a "residuated lattice". In our paper, we distinguish these terms.

(i) $\mathscr{L} = (L, \leq, *)$ is a residuated, commutative ℓ-monoid,

(ii) $\mathscr{H} = (H, \leq, \circ)$ is a residuated, commutative ℓ-monoid of left translations of $*$,

(iii) $\mathscr{H}^+ = (H^+, \leq^d, \circ)$ is a residuated, commutative ℓ-monoid of left translations of $\rightarrow$,

(iv) residuated, commutative ℓ-monoids $\mathscr{L}$, $\mathscr{H}$ and $\mathscr{H}^+$ are isomorphic.

Let us show that the converse statement is also true.

Theorem 4. *Let $\mathscr{L} = (L, \leq, *)$ be a residuated, commutative ℓ-monoid where an adjoint to $*$ binary operation will be denoted by $\rightarrow$ and the unit of $*$ will be denoted by e. Then*

(i) *the set $H = \{h_a \mid h_a = a * (\cdot), a \in L\}$ of left translations of $*$ fulfils* **C1** – **C2**;

(ii) $\mathscr{H} = (H, \leq, \circ)$, *where H is ordered by (3), is isomorphic to $\mathscr{L}$*;

(iii) $\mathscr{H}^+ = (H^+, \leq^d, \circ)$, *where $H^+ = \{h_a^+ \mid h_a^+ = a \rightarrow (\cdot), a \in L\}$ is a set of left translations of $\rightarrow$ ordered by (4), is isomorphic to $\mathscr{L}$.*

The following two theorems are consequences of the two previous ones. They show necessary and sufficient conditions under which *(i)* a bounded lattice can be extended to residuated, commutative ℓ-monoid, or *(ii)* a commutative semigroup of residuated maps of a bounded lattice can be extended to residuated, commutative ℓ-monoid.

Theorem 5. *Every bounded lattice L with a non-empty semigroup $(Res_L, \circ)$ of residuated maps can be endowed with a structure of a residuated, commutative ℓ-monoid if and only if there exists a subsemigroup H of $(Res_L, \circ)$ and an element $e \in L$ such that $(H, \circ)$ is a commutative semigroup and the orbit of e relative to H is equal to L.*

Theorem 6. *Every commutative semigroup $(H, \circ)$, which consists of residuated maps of a bounded lattice L, is a residuated, commutative ℓ-monoid if there exists an element $e \in L$ such that the orbit of e relative to H is equal to L.*

3   Semimodules in Residuated, Commutative ℓ-monoid

Let us recall that a *semiring* is an algebraic structure with two associative operations which are connected by distributive laws (cf. [6, 12, 13]). In more details, a semiring $R = (R, +, \cdot, 0, e)$ is an algebraic structure with the following properties:

– $(R, +, 0)$ is a commutative monoid,

– $(R, \cdot, e)$ is a monoid,

– $a \cdot (b + c) = a \cdot b + a \cdot c$ and $(a + b) \cdot c = a \cdot c + b \cdot c$ hold for all $a, b, c \in R$.

A semiring is called *commutative* if $(R, \cdot, e)$ is a commutative monoid. An example of a commutative semiring, which will be used in the sequel, is as follows.

Example 1. Let $\mathscr{L} = (L, \leq, *)$ be a residuated, commutative ℓ-monoid. Then $\mathscr{R}_\vee^\mathscr{L} = (L, \vee, *, \bot, e)$, where $\bot$ is a bottom element of $(L, \leq)$ and e is the unit with respect to $*$, is a semiring reduct of $\mathscr{L}$. This easily follows from the fact that for every $a \in L$, the map $a * (\cdot) : L \to L$ is residuated and therefore, it preserves the join operation, i.e. for all $x, y \in L$, $a * (x \vee y) = (a * x) \vee (a * y)$ holds.

Let us give a definition of a (left) *R-semimodule*.

Definition 1. *Let R be a semiring. A (left) R-semimodule is an algebra $M = (M, +, 0, (h_a)_{a \in R})$, where $(M, +, 0)$ is a commutative monoid and each $h_a : M \to M$ is a unary operation so that the following properties are fulfilled:*

$$h_a(x + y) = h_a(x) + h_a(y), \tag{9}$$

$$h_{a+b}(x) = h_a(x) + h_b(x), \tag{10}$$

$$h_{a \cdot b}(x) = h_a(h_b(x)). \tag{11}$$

Let us remark that the above definition is different from those in [6, 12] where there are additional requirements on zero elements of R and M.

A right R-semimodule can be defined similarly. In our paper, we will be restricted to left semimodules only, so that we will refer to them as semimodules only. Commutative monoid $(M, +, 0)$ is called a *monoidal reduct* of an R-semimodule $M = (M, +, 0, (h_a)_{a \in R})$.

The unary operation h_a is usually considered as a (left) *scalar multiplication* by a. An R-semimodule is called *unital* (or *unitary*) if the unit element $e \in R$ determines the identical map on M, i.e. for all $x \in M$, $h_e(x) = x$.

Example 2. It is easy to see that if $R = (R, +, \cdot, 0, e)$ is a semiring then $M_R = (R, +, 0, (a \cdot (\cdot))_{a \in R})$ is a unital semimodule where $a \cdot (\cdot) : x \mapsto a \cdot x$. We will say that the semimodule $M_R = (R, +, 0, (a \cdot (\cdot))_{a \in R})$ is induced by a semiring $R = (R, +, \cdot, 0, e)$.

Example 3. Let $\mathscr{L} = (L, \leq, *)$ be a residuated, commutative ℓ-monoid and $\mathscr{R}_\vee^\mathscr{L} = (L, \vee, *, \bot, e)$ its semiring reduct. By Example 2, $(L, \vee, \bot, (a * (\cdot))_{a \in L})$ is a $\mathscr{R}_\vee^\mathscr{L}$-semimodule induced by the respective semiring.

4   Semi-linear Spaces

The notion of *semilinear space* has been introduced in [9] with the purpose to serve as a theoretical background for the theory of fuzzy relation equations [10]. This notion connects a semilinear space with a semimodule over a monoidal reduct of a lattice ordered residuated monoid. A series of theoretical results about solvability of systems of fuzzy relation equations was obtained on the basis of this formalism, see e.g.[14]. However, the introduced background is helpful in deciding solvability, but it is not helpful in representing solutions. Therefore, we propose to extend this notion and consider a semilinear space as a couple of two semimodules connected by residuated scalar multiplications. In this and subsequent sections, we introduce a definition of a semilinear space and show that under certain conditions the semigroup of endomorphisms of a semilinear space is a residuated, commutative ℓ-monoid. By this, we will obtain what is called below a linear representation of a residuated, commutative ℓ-monoid.

Definition 2. *Let $\mathscr{P} = (P, \leq, \bot, \top)$ be a bounded lattice and $\mathscr{R} = (R, +, \cdot, 0, e)$ be an idempotent commutative semiring. Assume that $\mathscr{P}_\vee = (P, \vee, \bot, r(\cdot)_{r \in R})$ and $\mathscr{P}_\wedge = (P, \wedge, \top, r\backslash(\cdot)_{r \in R})$ are unital left $\mathscr{R}$-semimodules where the respective unary operations (scalar multiplications) $p \mapsto rp$ and $p \mapsto r\backslash p$, $p \in P$, $r \in R$, are residuated, i.e.*

$$rp \leq q \iff p \leq r\backslash q,$$

and moreover, for all $p \in P$,

$$0p = \bot, \quad 0\backslash p = \top.$$

Then the couple $(\mathscr{P}_\vee, \mathscr{P}_\wedge)$ is called a left $\mathscr{R}$-semilinear space (or a left semilinear space over $\mathscr{R}$). The first component $\mathscr{P}_\vee$ is called an upper space, and the second component $\mathscr{P}_\wedge$ is called a lower space.

Let us remark that both upper and lower spaces in $(\mathscr{P}_\vee, \mathscr{P}_\wedge)$ are ordered by $\leq$, and unary operations $r(\cdot)$ are isotone and residuated. It is obvious that the corresponding set $\{r(\cdot) : P \to P \mid r \in R\}$ of residuated maps is a subsemigroup of $(\mathrm{Res}_P, \circ)$.

Semilattice $(P, \vee, \bot)$ (respectively, $(P, \wedge, \top)$) is called an *upper semilattice reduct* (respectively, *lower semilattice reduct*) of a semilinear space $(\mathscr{P}_\vee, \mathscr{P}_\wedge)$.

A *right $\mathscr{R}$-semilinear space* can be defined similarly. In what follows, we will fix an idempotent commutative semiring $\mathscr{R} = (R, +, \cdot, 0, e)$ with the support R and consider solely left $\mathscr{R}$-semilinear spaces. They will be called simply $(\mathscr{R})$-*semilinear spaces*.

Lemma 1. *Let $(\mathscr{P}_\vee, \mathscr{P}_\wedge)$ be a $\mathscr{R}$-semilinear space. Then for all $r \in R$,*

$$r\bot = \bot.$$

Let $(\mathscr{P}_\vee, \mathscr{P}_\wedge)$ be a $\mathscr{R}$-semilinear space where $\mathscr{R} = (R, +, \cdot, 0, e)$ is an idempotent commutative semiring. The set R can be ordered in such a way that

$$r \leq q \iff r + q = q. \tag{12}$$

Under this order, 0 is the least element of R and $\sup\{r, q\} = r + q$.

Definition 3. *Let $\mathscr{P} = (P, \leq, \bot, \top)$ and $\mathscr{Q} = (Q, \leq, \bot, \top)$ be bounded lattices, and $(\mathscr{P}_\vee, \mathscr{P}_\wedge)$ and $(\mathscr{Q}_\vee, \mathscr{Q}_\wedge)$ be two semilinear spaces over the same semiring $\mathscr{R}$. A map $H : P \to Q$ is a homomorphism of $(\mathscr{P}_\vee, \mathscr{P}_\wedge)$ into $(\mathscr{Q}_\vee, \mathscr{Q}_\wedge)$ if*

- *H is residuated with the residual $H^+ : Q \to P$,*
- *H commutes with unary operations $r(\cdot)$, $r \in R$, i.e. for all $p \in P$, $H(rp) = rH(p)$.*

Let $H : P \to Q$ be a homomorphism between $\mathscr{R}$-semilinear spaces $(\mathscr{P}_\vee, \mathscr{P}_\wedge)$ and $(\mathscr{Q}_\vee, \mathscr{Q}_\wedge)$ with the residual $H^+ : Q \to P$. Then H is a homomorphism between upper semilattice reducts $(P, \vee, \bot)$ and $(Q, \vee, \bot)$ and H^+ is a homomorphism of semilattice reduct $(P, \wedge, \top)$ into semilattice reduct $(Q, \wedge, \top)$. Moreover, H^+ commutes with unary operations $r\backslash(\cdot)$, i.e. for all $p \in P$, $r \in R$, $H^+(r\backslash p) = r\backslash H^+(p)$.

Lemma 2. *Assume that $H : P \to Q$ is a homomorphism of $\mathscr{R}$-semilinear space $(\mathscr{P}_\vee, \mathscr{P}_\wedge)$ into $\mathscr{R}$-semilinear space $(\mathscr{Q}_\vee, \mathscr{Q}_\wedge)$, and $H^+ : Q \to P$ is the residual of H. Then for any $r \in R$, the map $rH : p \mapsto (rH)(p)$ is a homomorphism of $(\mathscr{P}_\vee, \mathscr{P}_\wedge)$ into $(\mathscr{Q}_\vee, \mathscr{Q}_\wedge)$ as well.*

4.1   Semigroup of Endomorphisms

Let $(\mathscr{P}_\vee, \mathscr{P}_\wedge)$ be a semilinear space over $\mathscr{R}$ and $\mathscr{H} = \{H : P \to P\}$ be a set of endomorphisms of $(\mathscr{P}_\vee, \mathscr{P}_\wedge)$. The set $\mathscr{H}$ can be partially ordered in a usual way, i.e. if $H_1, H_2 \in \mathscr{H}$ then

$$H_1 \leq H_2 \iff (\forall p \in P)(H_1(p) \leq H_2(p)).$$

By routine technique, $\mathscr{H}$ is a bounded $\vee$-semilattice where the bottom element is $H_\bot$, $H_\bot(p) = \bot$, $p \in P$. Moreover, $(\mathscr{H}, \leq, \circ)$ is an ordered semigroup of residuated maps of the lattice $\mathscr{P}$,

5   Linear Representation of Residuated Commutative ℓ-monoid

The purpose of this section is to show that under certain conditions the semigroup $(\mathscr{H}, \circ)$ of endomorphisms of a $\mathscr{R}$-semilinear space $(\mathscr{P}_\vee, \mathscr{P}_\wedge)$ is a residuated, commutative ℓ-monoid. By this, we will obtain what is below called a linear representation of a residuated, commutative ℓ-monoid.

Definition 4. *A homomorphism of a residuated commutative ℓ-monoid $\mathscr{L}$ into a residuated commutative ℓ-monoid of endomorphisms of a $\mathscr{R}$-semilinear space $(\mathscr{P}_\vee, \mathscr{P}_\wedge)$ is called a linear representation of $\mathscr{L}$ over $\mathscr{R}$. $(\mathscr{P}_\vee, \mathscr{P}_\wedge)$ is a representation space.*

Below, we consider two particular cases where a linear representation is established.

5.1   Linear Representation by Endomorphisms with One Generator

In this section, we consider a general residuated, commutative ℓ-monoid $\mathscr{L}$ and put restrictions on a semilinear space which enable to construct a required subsemigroup of endomorphisms that is isomorphic to $\mathscr{L}$. This subsemigroup is generated by one specific endomorphism, see Example 4 below.

Lemma 3. *Let $(\mathscr{P}_\vee, \mathscr{P}_\wedge)$ be a $\mathscr{R}$-semilinear space, $p_0 \in P$. Let R_{p_0} be a subsemiring of $\mathscr{R}$ such that*

$$\{rp_0 \mid r \in R_{p_0}\} = P. \tag{13}$$

Then the semigroup reduct $(R_{p_0}, \cdot)$ of the respective semiring is a residuated, commutative ℓ-monoid.

Theorem 7. *Let $(\mathscr{P}_\vee, \mathscr{P}_\wedge)$ be a $\mathscr{R}$-semilinear space, $p_0 \in P$, and R_{p_0} a subsemiring of R such that (13) holds. Let $H \in \mathscr{H}$ be an endomorphism of $(\mathscr{P}_\vee, \mathscr{P}_\wedge)$ such that $H(p_0) = p_0$. Then the set $\mathscr{H}_{p_0} = \{rH \mid r \in R_{p_0}\}$ is a subsemigroup of $(\mathscr{H}, \circ)$ which fulfils **C1** – **C2**. Moreover, $(H_{p_0}, \circ)$ is a residuated, commutative ℓ-monoid.*

Example 4. Let $\mathscr{L} = (L, \leq, *)$ be a residuated, commutative ℓ-monoid and $\mathscr{R}_\vee^{\mathscr{L}} = (L, \vee, *, \bot, e)$ its semiring reduct where e is the unit with respect to $*$. Assume that $(\mathscr{P}_\vee, \mathscr{P}_\wedge)$ is a $\mathscr{R}_\vee^{\mathscr{L}}$-semilinear space, $p_0 \in P$, H is an endomorphism of $(\mathscr{P}_\vee, \mathscr{P}_\wedge)$ such that the assumptions of Theorem 7 are fulfilled and moreover, R_{p_0} coincides with L. Then the set of endomorphisms $\mathscr{H}_{p_0} = \{rH \mid r \in R_{p_0}\}$ is a linear representation of $\mathscr{L}$.

5.2 Linear Representation by Endomorphisms Induced by Vector Products

In this Section, we consider a direct product of residuated, commutative ℓ-monoids and show that it can be linearly represented by the respective semigroup of endomorphisms.

Lemma 4. *Let $\mathscr{R} = (R, +, \cdot, 0, e)$ be an idempotent commutative semiring ordered by (12). Assume that (12) is a lattice order and R has a top element. Let moreover, $P = R^n$, $n \geq 1$, and a partial order on P is induced by (12). Assume that $(\mathscr{P}_\vee, \mathscr{P}_\wedge)$ is a $\mathscr{R}$-semilinear space where the scalar multiplications $p \mapsto rp$ and $p \mapsto r \backslash p$ are defined componentwise, i.e. if $p = (r_1, \ldots, r_n)$ and $r, r_1, \ldots, r_n \in R$, then*

$$r(r_1, \ldots, r_n) = (r \cdot r_1, \ldots, r \cdot r_n),$$
$$r \backslash (r_1, \ldots, r_n) = (r \backslash r_1, \ldots, r \backslash r_n).$$

With every element $(q_1, \ldots, q_n) \in P$ we associate a map $H_{(q_1, \ldots, q_n)} : P \to P$ such that for any $(r_1, \ldots, r_n) \in P$,

$$H_{(q_1, \ldots, q_n)}(r_1, \ldots, r_n) = (q_1 \cdot r_1, \ldots, q_n \cdot r_n).$$

Then $H_{(q_1, \ldots, q_n)}$ is an endomorphism of $(\mathscr{P}_\vee, \mathscr{P}_\wedge)$.

Theorem 8. *Let the assumptions of Lemma 4 be fulfilled and $\mathscr{H} = \{H_{(q_1, \ldots, q_n)} \mid (q_1, \ldots, q_n) \in P\}$ be a set of endomorphisms of $(\mathscr{P}_\vee, \mathscr{P}_\wedge)$. Then $(\mathscr{H}, \circ)$ is a residuated, commutative ℓ-monoid.*

Example 5. Let $\mathscr{L} = (L, \leq, *)$ be a residuated, commutative ℓ-monoid and $\mathscr{R}_{\vee}^{\mathscr{L}} = (L, \vee, *, \bot, e)$ its semiring reduct where e is the unit with respect to $*$. Assume that $(\mathscr{P}_{\vee}, \mathscr{P}_{\wedge})$ is a $\mathscr{R}_{\vee}^{\mathscr{L}}$-semilinear space that fulfils assumptions of Lemma 4. Then the set of endomorphisms $\mathscr{H} = \{H_{(q_1, \ldots, q_n)} \mid (q_1, \ldots, q_n) \in P\}$ is a linear representation of $\mathscr{L}^n$.

6 Conclusion

In this paper, we studied conditions under which a commutative semigroup of residuated maps of a bounded lattice is a residuated, commutative ℓ-monoid. We reconsidered the notion of semilinear space with the purpose to make it helpful in representing solutions. We proposed to consider a semilinear space as a couple of two semimodules connected by residuated scalar multiplications. We showed that under conditions, which have been found in the first part, the semigroup of endomorphisms of a semilinear space is a residuated, commutative ℓ-monoid. By this, we obtained a linear representation of a residuated, commutative ℓ-monoid.

Acknowledgment. The authors acknowledge that they prepared this paper in connection with the project IT4Innovations Centre of Excellence, reg. no. CZ.1.05/1.1.00/02.0070.

References

[1] Höhle, U.: Commutative residuated l-monoids. In: Höhle, U., Klement, E.P. (eds.) Non-Classical Logics and Their Applications to Fuzzy Subsets. A Handbook of the Mathematical Foundations of Fuzzy Set Theory, pp. 53–106. Kluwer, Dordrecht (1995)

[2] Dilworth, R.P., Ward, M.: Residuated lattices. Trans. Amer. Math. Soc. 45, 335–354 (1939)

[3] Hájek, P.: Metamathematics of Fuzzy Logic. Kluwer, Dordrecht (1998)

[4] Novák, V., Perfilieva, I., Močkoř, J.: Mathematical Principles of Fuzzy Logic. Kluwer, Dordrecht (1999)

[5] Esteva, F., Godo, L.: Monoidal t-norm based logic: towards a logic for left-continuous t-norms. Fuzzy Sets and Systems 124, 271–288 (2001)

[6] Di Nola, A., Lettieri, A., Perfilieva, I., Novák, V.: Algebraic analysis of fuzzy systems. Fuzzy Sets and Systems 158, 1–22 (2007)

[7] Klement, E.P., Mesiar, R., Pap, E.: Triangular Norms. Kluwer, Dordrecht (2000)

[8] Galatos, N., Jipsen, P., Kowalski, T., Ono, H.: Residuated Lattices: an algebraic glimpse at substructural logics. Studies in Logics and the Foundations of Mathematics. Elsevier, Amsterdam (2007)

[9] Perfilieva, I.: Semi-linear spaces. In: In Noguchi, H., Ishii, H., et al. (eds.) Proc. of VIIth Czech-Japanese Seminar on Data Analysis and Decision Making under Uncertainty, Hyogo, Japan, pp. 127–130 (2004)

[10] Perfilieva, I.: Fuzzy Relation Equations in Semilinear Spaces. In: Hüllermeier, E., Kruse, R., Hoffmann, F. (eds.) IPMU 2010. CCIS, vol. 80, pp. 545–552. Springer, Heidelberg (2010)

[11] Blyth, T.S.: Lattices and Ordered Algebraic Structures. Springer, London (2005)
[12] Golan, J.S.: Semirings and their Applications. Kluwer Academic Pulishers, Dordrecht (1999)
[13] Gondran, M., Minoux, M.: Graphs, Dioids and Semirings. Springer, New York (2008)
[14] Perfilieva, I., Nosková, L.: System of fuzzy relation equations with inf → composition: complete set of solutions. Fuzzy Sets and Systems 159, 2256–2271 (2008)

An Extension of Gödel Logic for Reasoning under Both Vagueness and Possibilistic Uncertainty

Moataz El-Zekey[1] and Lluis Godo[2]

[1] Department of Basic Sciences, Faculty of Engineering, Benha University, Egypt
m_s_elzekey@hotmail.com
[2] IIIA-CSIC, Campus UAB - 08193 Bellaterra, Spain
godo@iiia.csic.es

Abstract. In this paper we introduce a logic called $FNG_{\sim}(\mathbb{Q})$ that combines the well-known Gödel logic with a strong negation, rational truth-constants and Possibilistic logic. In this way, we can formalize reasoning involving both vagueness and (possibilistic) uncertainty. We show that the defined logical system is useful to capture the kind of reasoning at work in the medical diagnosis system CADIAG-2, and we finish by pointing out some of its potential advantages to be developed in future work.

1 Introduction

In the field of uncertain reasoning, many formalisms (e.g., [6], [16], [18]) have been developed to deal with different measures of uncertainty. The most general notion of uncertainty is captured by monotone set functions with two natural boundary conditions. In the literature, these functions have received several names, like *Sugeno measures* [17], *plausibility measures* [12] or *capacities* [1]. In its simplest form, given a *Boolean algebra* of events $\wp = (U, \wedge, \vee, ', \bot, \top)$, a Sugeno measure is a mapping $\mu : U \to [0,1]$ satisfying $\mu(\top) = 1$ and $\mu(\bot) = 0$, and the monotonicity condition $\mu(x) \le \mu(y)$ whenever $x \le^{\wp} y$, where $\le^{\wp}$ is the lattice order in $\wp$. Many popular uncertainty measures, like probabilities [18], Dempster-Shafer plausibility and belief functions [16], or possibility and necessity measures [6], can be therefore seen as particular classes of Sugeno measures. In this paper, we focus on possibilistic models of uncertainty.

Recall that a *possibility measure* on a (finite) Boolean algebra of events $\wp = (U, \wedge, \vee, ', \bot, \top)$ is a Sugeno measure μ^* satisfiying the following $\vee$-decomposition property

$$\mu^*(u \vee v) = \max(\mu^*(u), \mu^*(v)),$$

while a *necessity measure* is a Sugeno measure μ_* satisfying the $\wedge$-decomposition property

$$\mu_*(u \wedge v) = \min(\mu_*(u), \mu_*(v)).$$

Actually, in presence of these decomposition properties, there is no need for the monotonicity condition since it easily follows from each one of them. Possibility

S. Greco et al. (Eds.): IPMU 2012, Part II, CCIS 298, pp. 216–225, 2012.
© Springer-Verlag Berlin Heidelberg 2012

and necessity measures are *dual* in the sense that if μ^* is a possibility measure, then the mapping $\mu_*(u) = 1 - \mu^*(u')$ is a necessity measure, and vice versa. If U is the power set of a (finite) set X, then any dual pair of measures (μ^*, μ_*) on U is induced by a *normalized possibility distribution*, namely a mapping $\pi : X \to [0, 1]$ such that $\sup_{x \in X} \pi(x) = 1$, and, for any $A \subseteq X$,

$$\mu^*(A) = \sup\{\pi(x)|x \in A\} \text{ and } \mu_*(A) = \inf\{1 - \pi(x)|x \notin A\}.$$

On the other hand, formal computational models of vague statements usually resort to some sort of fuzzy logic. Fuzzy logics rely on the idea that truth comes in degrees. The inherent vagueness in many real-life declarative statements makes it impossible to always claim either their full truth or full falsity. For this reason, propositions are taken as statements that can be potentially evaluated as being partially true.

Probably the most studied and developed many-valued systems related to fuzzy logic are those corresponding to logical calculi with the real interval $[0, 1]$ as set of truth-values and built up from a conjunction & and an implication $\to$, interpreted respectively by a continuous t-norm $*$ and its residuum $\Rightarrow$, and where the negation is defined as $\neg\varphi = \varphi \to \bar{0}$, with $\bar{0}$ being the truth-constant for falsity. In the framework of these logics, called *t-norm based fuzzy logics*, each continuous t-norm $*$ uniquely determines a semantical (propositional) calculus $PC(*)$ over formulas defined in the usual way from a countable set of propositional variables, connectives $\wedge$, & and $\to$ and truth-constant $\bar{0}$ [13]. Evaluations of propositional variables are mappings e assigning each propositional variable p a truth-value $e(p) \in [0, 1]$, which extend truth-functionally and univocally to compound formulas as follows:

$$e(\bar{0}) = 0$$
$$e(\varphi \& \psi) = e(\varphi) * e(\psi)$$
$$e(\varphi \to \psi) = e(\varphi) \Rightarrow e(\psi)$$

A formula φ is said to be a 1-tautology of $PC(*)$ if $e(\varphi) = 1$ for each evaluation e. The set of all 1-tautologies of $PC(*)$ will be denoted as $TAUT(*)$. For instance, the well-known *Gödel logic* G is one of the three outstanding t-norm based fuzzy logic calculi corresponding to the choice $* = *_G$, where

$$x *_G y = \min(x, y)$$
$$x \Rightarrow_G y = \begin{cases} 1, & \text{if } x \leq y \\ y, & \text{otherwise.} \end{cases}$$

The set $TAUT(*_G)$ is finitely axiomatizable, for instance, as the schematic extension of Hájek's BL with the idempotency axiom $\varphi \to \varphi \& \varphi$ [13].

In some situations, like in the medical diagnosis system CADIAG-2, one has to deal with statements referring to both uncertainty and vagueness (in the sense of gradual properties). CADIAG-2 consists of a knowledge base in the form of a set of if-then rules that relate medical entities (i.e., symptoms on the one hand and diagnoses on the other hand). The rules are defined along with a certain degree of confirmation which intuitively expresses the degree to which the antecedent confirms the consequent. CADIAG-2 considers statements about symptoms as being gradual, where grades refer to the intensity with which symptoms are observed. The second class of propositions in CADIAG-2 refers to diagnoses. It is often the case not, or not yet, possible to confirm or to exclude a diagnosis with certainty. Thus, to each diagnosis, a degree of certainty is associated.

CADIAG-2 also allows facts be qualified by degrees, providing a measure of certainty of crisp statements or a degree of presence of vague statements. Hence, CADIAG-2 shows a challenging feature, i.e., it combines notions of linguistic vagueness and uncertainty. The way those (certainty) values were interpreted and the compositional way they were handled by the inference procedures varied from one approach to another. Several approaches have been developed to provide a clear basis for CADIAG-2. However, in all of these approaches, there was a mismatch between the intended semantics of the (certainty) degrees and the way they were used. Indeed, in some approaches the certainty values were interpreted probabilistically (in some form or another), like in [14], but the propagation rules were either not sound or they were making too strong conditional independence assumptions. On the other hand, other approaches interpreted certainty degrees as truth degrees in a truth-functional many-valued of fuzzy logic setting (see, e.g. [3]). Here the problem was the misuse of partial degrees of truth as belief degrees. This kind of confusion was quite common, but Hájek (in his monograph [13]) had already clear this distinction in mind. He argues a very important issue to distinguish uncertainty measures and truth values in a logical setting, many-valued logics are truth functional but uncertainty measures are not.

Clearly, since uncertainty and vagueness are semantically quite different, it is important to have a unifying formalism for the medical expert system CADIAG-2, which allows us to deal with both uncertainty and vagueness. Any formalism disallowing a unified platform for handling both uncertainty and vagueness is therefore inapt to capture this knowledge and entails the danger of fallacies due to misplaced precision.

We propose an alternative framework for the medical expert system CADIAG-2. Our approach is guided by the idea to use a logical calculus that can deal with both uncertainty and vagueness, and to find an interpretation for CADIAG-2's rules within this unified formalization. In our approach, we make a strong distinction between degrees of uncertainty due to a state of incomplete knowledge and intermediary degrees of truth due to the presence of vague propositions. Our framework to deal with uncertainty is possibilistic logic. The reader is referred to [7] for an extensive overview on possibilistic logic. The proposed logic provides a satisfying conceptual framework for CADIAG-2.

2   The Logic $\text{FNG}_\sim(\mathbb{Q})$ and Its Possibilistic Semantics

Not surprisingly, the logic which we have in mind is an extension of the logic $G_\sim(\mathbb{Q})$, that is Gödel logic extended by the standard negation $\sim$ as well as with rational truth constants[1]. More precisely we will define a logic, called $FNG_\sim(\mathbb{Q})$, F for fuzzy and N for necessity, which will include an extension of possibilistic logic embedded inside the fuzzy logic $G_\sim(\mathbb{Q})$, where it is possible to express e.g. statements very close to the so-called *certainty fuzzy if-then rules* [4] of the form "the more φ is true, the more certain ψ holds "[2], where φ is a fuzzy proposition and ψ is Boolean proposition, as in "the younger a man, the more certainly he is single", or "the higher the fever, the more likely there is an infection".

Starting from the basic ideas exposed by Hájek in [13], various kinds of uncertainties can be studied by using various kinds of modal-fuzzy logics (see, e.g., [10,11]). The very basic idea allowing a treatment of the certainty of classical (crisp) events inside a fuzzy-logical setting consists of interpreting the certainty degree of a (classical) proposition ϕ as the truth value of a modal proposition $\Box\phi$ which reads "ϕ is certain".

Following the same approach, we define below the logic $FNG_\sim(\mathbb{Q})$ which combines in the same logic a formal treatment of fuzziness and uncertainty aspects, the latter under the possibilistic semantics of necessity measures.

Language. We start from a countable set of Boolean propositional variables $V_B = \{\delta_1, \delta_2, ...\}$ and a countable set $V_{MV} = \{\sigma_1, \sigma_2, ...\}$ of *many-valued propositional variables*. We assume that the two sets V_B and V_{MV} are disjoint. Then formulas of $FNG_\sim(\mathbb{Q})$ are defined as follows:

- The set BFm consists of *Boolean formulas* built from the countable set of propositional variables V_B using the classical logic connectives. $\top$ and $\bot$ will continue denoting the truth constants *true* and *false* respectively. Boolean formulas will be denoted by lower case greek letters $\varphi, \psi, \ldots$
- *Box-formulas* are formulas of the kind $\Box\varphi$, where $\varphi \in BFm$.
- General *FNG-formulas* are then built up from the countable set of many-valued propositional variables V_{MV} together with $\Box$-formulas (taken as new many-valued variables) using $G_\sim(\mathbb{Q})$ connectives ($\wedge, \to, \sim$) and rational truth constants $\bar{r}$ for every rational $r \in [0, 1]$. We shall denote them by lower case greek letters ζ, ξ, τ, η.

For instance, if ζ is a FNG-formula and $\varphi \in BFm$ is a Boolean formula, then $\overline{0.5} \to (\zeta \to \Box\varphi)$ is a FNG-formula, while $\overline{0.5} \to (\zeta \to \varphi)$ is not.

Note that, as in $G_\sim(\mathbb{Q})$, other connectives are definable, notably $\neg\zeta$ is $\zeta \to \bar{0}$ (Gödel negation), $\Delta\zeta$ is $\neg\sim\zeta$ (Monteiro-Baaz connective), $\zeta \vee \xi$ is $((\zeta \to \xi) \to \xi) \wedge ((\xi \to \zeta) \to \zeta)$ (max disjunction), and $\zeta \leftrightarrow \xi$ is $\zeta \to \xi) \wedge (\xi \to \zeta)$ (equivalence).

---

[1] Due to lack of space, we cannot include preliminaries on basic notions regarding Gödel logic and its expansions with truth-constants, with Monteiro-Baaz's operator Δ and with an involutive negation, that will be used throughout this section. Instead, the reader is referred to [13,8,9] for the necessary background.

[2] Informally interpreted as *truth-degree*(φ) $\leq$ *certainty-degree*(ψ).

Semantics. The intended possibilistic semantics is given by what we call *mixed possibilistic models.* A mixed possibilistic model is a pair

$$\mathbf{M} = (v, \langle W, e, \pi \rangle)$$

where $v : V_{MV} \rightarrow [0,1]$ is a $[0,1]$-valued interpretation of the many-valued propositional variables, and $\mathbf{M} = \langle W, e, \pi \rangle$ is a possibilistic Kripke model, where W is a non-empty set whose elements are called nodes (or states or possible worlds), $e : W \times V_B \rightarrow 0,1$ provides for each world w a $\{0,1\}$-evaluation of Boolean propositional variables, and $\pi : W \rightarrow [0,1]$ is a normalized possibility distribution on W, i.e π: is such that $\max_{w \in W} \pi(w) = 1$. In other words, π models a consistent belief state, in the sense that at least one possible world has to be fully plausible. An evaluation of Boolean propositional variables extends to an evaluation of Boolean formulas of BFm in the usual way. For each $\varphi \in BFm$, we shall write $[\varphi]$ to denote the set of worlds which are a model of φ, i.e. $[\varphi] = \{w \in W : e(w, \varphi) = 1\}$.

Given a mixed possibilistic model $\mathbf{M}$ for FNG$_\sim(\mathbb{Q})$ and a FNG-formula ζ, the truth value of ζ in $\mathbf{M}$, denoted by $\|\zeta\|_{\mathbf{M}}$, is inductively defined as follows:

- if ζ is a propositional variable from the set V_{MV}, then $\|\zeta\|_{\mathbf{M}} = v(\zeta)$,
- if ζ is a Box-formula $\Box\varphi$, where $\varphi \in BFm$, then $\|\zeta\|_{\mathbf{M}} = N([\varphi]|\pi)$, where $N(.|\pi)$ is the necessity measure induced by π on the power set of W, defined as $N([\varphi]|\pi) = \inf_{w \notin [\varphi]}(1 - \pi(w))$.
- if ζ is a compound FNG-formula, then its truth-value $\|\zeta\|_{\mathbf{M}}$ is computed using the truth functions of G$_\sim(\mathbb{Q})$.

The notions of *satisfaction* and *validity* of a formula are defined as usual, as well as the notion of *logical consequence* of a formula from a set of formulas, that we will denote by $\models_{FNG}$. For instance, it is very easy to check that $\overline{0.6} \rightarrow \Box\varphi$, saying that φ is certain at least to the degree 0.6, is a logical consequence of the set of FNG-formulas $\{\overline{0.8} \rightarrow \sigma_1, \overline{0.6} \leftrightarrow \sigma_2, \overline{0.7} \rightarrow (\sigma_1 \wedge \sigma_2 \rightarrow \Box\varphi)\}$, saying that σ_1 is true at least to the degree 0.8, σ_2 is true to the degree 0.6 and that, for every $r \in [0,1]$, if $\sigma_1 \wedge \sigma_2$ is true at least to the degree r, then φ is certain at least to the degree $\min(r, 0.7)$.

Axioms and rules. FNG$_\sim(\mathbb{Q})$ has the following axioms and rules:

- Axioms of classical propositional logic for BFm-formulas.
- Axioms and rules of G$_\sim(\mathbb{Q})$ for FNG-formulas.
- The following axiom schemata for the modality $\Box$:
  - (N1) $\sim\Box\bot$
  - (N2) $\Box(\varphi \rightarrow \psi) \rightarrow (\Box\varphi \rightarrow \Box\psi)$
  - (N3) $\Box(\varphi \wedge \psi) \leftrightarrow (\Box\varphi \wedge \Box\psi)$
- The *modus ponens* rule of (for BFm and FNG-formulas).
- The *necessitation* rule for $\Box$: from φ derive $\Box\varphi$, for any Boolean formula φ.

A theory Γ over $\text{FNG}_\sim(\mathbb{Q})$ is a set of FNG-formulas. We define a notion of proof (denoted by $\vdash_{FNG}$) from a theory in the usual way from the above axioms and rules.

Using standard techniques, it is not hard to prove that $\text{FNG}_\sim(\mathbb{Q})$ is indeed *sound and strongly complete* for deductions from finite theories with respect to the class of mixed possibilsitic models, i.e., for every finite theory T and formula ζ, it holds that $T \models_{FNG} \zeta$ iff $T \vdash_{FNG} \zeta$. Details of the completeness proof are to be found in a longer version of this manuscript in preparation.

3   CADIAG-2 and the Logic $\text{FNG}_\sim(\mathbb{Q})$

As we have already mentioned, CADIAG-2 is a knowledge-based system for medical diagnosis, whose (weighted) if-then rules may combine vague with uncertain knowledge. In this section we explain how the logic $\text{FNG}_\sim(\mathbb{Q})$ can represent CADIAG-2 if-then rules as well as the data associated to a patient. The latter is the data describing the state of the patient and it is the input of a particular run of CADIAG-2. We will specify how the input data and the rules translate to formulas of $\text{FNG}_\sim(\mathbb{Q})$. We will also compare the CADIAG-2 inference mechanism with proofs in the logic $\text{FNG}_\sim(\mathbb{Q})$. We will examine the situation from the theoretical side. Actually, instead of referring to CADIAG-2 system itself, we will usually refer to the formal calculus CadL defined in [3] (see also [2]) capturing its operational semantics in a logical framework.

A knowledge-base of CADIAG-2 (or a theory in CadL) basically deals with two kinds of basic information variables, corresponding to symptoms (including signs), and to diagnoses (diseases and therapies). Given a finite set $S = \{\sigma_1, \sigma_2, \ldots, \sigma_m\}$ of symptoms and a finite set $D = \{\delta_1, \delta_2, \ldots, \delta_n\}$ of diagnoses, propositions of CadL are built from the variables by means of three connectives "and" ($\wedge$), "or" ($\vee$) and "not" ($\neg$), and graded propositions are of the form (ζ, r), where ζ is a proposition and $r \in [0, 1]$. A graded if-then rule is represented in CadL as a pair $(\zeta \to \varphi, r)$ where ζ is a proposition, φ is a literal (a variable from $S \cup D$ or its negation), and $r \in [0, 1]$. Finally, an input for a run of the system is a set of graded atomic propositions $(\sigma_1, r_1), (\sigma_2, r_2) \ldots$ and $(\delta_1, d_1), (\delta_2, d_2) \ldots$ referring to the available data about the presence of a set of symptoms and diagnoses of a given patient. [3]

In order to define a translation of CadL formulas into $\text{FNG}_\sim(\mathbb{Q})$ formulas, first of all we make a formal distinction between symptoms and diagnoses because we formally distinguish between degrees of presence (for symptoms) and degrees of certainty (for diagnoses). Thus, we shall identify each symptom and diagnosis appearing in a CadL theory with a unique atomic proposition from the sets V_{MV} and V_B, respectively, of the language of $\text{FNG}_\sim(\mathbb{Q})$. In other words, we assume $S = \{\sigma_1, \sigma_2, \ldots, \sigma_m\} \subseteq V_{MV}$ and $D = \{\delta_1, \delta_2, \ldots, \delta_n\} \subseteq V_B$. Furthermore, let $Lit(D) = \{\delta, \neg\delta \mid \delta \in D\}$ where $\neg\delta$ is the negation of δ, and let $D^\square = \{\square\varphi : \varphi \in Lit(D)\}$. Recall that $\square\delta$ means we are certain that the disease δ is present, while

---

[3] For convenience, from now on we consider all weights being actually rational numbers from $[0, 1]$.

$\Box\neg\delta$ means we are certain that the disease δ is not present (or equivalently, the disease δ is impossible).

The translation of CadL propositions is done as follows. Consider the set M of FNG-formulas built from the set of many-valued propositional variables S and from Box-formulas $\Box\varphi$ for each $\varphi \in Lit(D)$, using the connectives $\wedge, \vee, \sim$ of FNG$_\sim(\mathbb{Q})$. Then, we shall also identify each compound entity in CadL with the respective many-valued formulas from the set M. For instance, assume that we are given the following compound proposition: $(\sigma_1 \vee \neg\delta_1) \wedge (\delta_2 \wedge \neg\sigma_2)$ where σ_1, σ_2 are symptoms and δ_1, δ_2 are diagnoses, then we translate it to the respective FNG formula $(\sigma_1 \vee \Box\neg\delta_1) \wedge \Box\delta_2 \wedge \sim\sigma_2$. We shall denote formulas from M by lower case greek letters ζ, ξ, τ, η.

Let us now consider the input of a specific run of CADIAG-2. It consists typically of weighted symptoms, but is also allowed to contain information about confirmed or excluded diagnoses. The two cases are to be distinguished.

- Assume that the graded proposition (σ_i, r) is provided, where $\sigma_i \in S$ is a symptom and r is its degree of presence. Hence, we translate it to the following FNG-formula $\bar{t} \leftrightarrow \sigma_i$. Note that, as particular cases, when $r = 1$ and $r = 0$ the FNG-formula $t \leftrightarrow \sigma_i$ is equivalent to σ_i and $\sim\sigma_i$, respectively.
- Assume that the graded proposition (δ_i, r) is provided, where $\delta_i \in D$ is a diagnosis and $r > 0$. In this case r expresses a degree of uncertainty; we translate it to the following FNG-formula $\bar{r} \to \Box\delta_i$, meaning that we are certain to a degree at least t that the disease δ_i is present. Note that the degree assigned to δ_i may be increased at a later point of a CadL run[4]. As a particular case, when $t = 1$, the FNG-formula $\bar{r} \to \Box\delta_i$ is equivalent to $\Box\delta_i$. However, in case that $t = 0$, the graded proposition $(\delta_i, 0)$ means in CadL that the diagnosis δ_i is excluded, and hence it will be translated to the following FNG-formula $\Box\neg\delta_i$.

We next turn to the translations of rules in the language of CadL. Rules contained in a knowledge base are classified as being of three types: (C), (me), and (ao). We consider first the rules of type (C). It is necessary to differentiate its contents. Namely, there are three kinds of rules that all belong to the type (C).

- First, there are the symptom-symptom rules, which are of the form $(\sigma_i \to \sigma_j, 1)$, where $\sigma_i, \sigma_j \in S$ denote symptoms. According to the manipulation rule (c) of CadL (see [3,2]), the above rule is to be interpreted as specifying that the degree of σ_j is at least as high as the one of σ_i. Hence, we translate that rule to the following FNG-formula $\sigma_i \to \sigma_j$.
- The second group of rules of type (C) are the diagnosis-diagnosis rules, which are of the form $(\delta_i \to \delta_j, 1)$, where $\delta_i, \delta_j \in D$ are diagnoses. These rules resemble the symptom-symptom rules and the translation of these rules is straightforward: $\Box\delta_i \to \Box\delta_j$.

---

[4] This is why we interpret r as a lower bound for the certainty degree on δ_i rather than an equality.

- The last group of rules of type (C) are the symptom-diagnosis rules, of the form ($\tau \to \delta, d$), where τ is a (compound) proposition and $\delta \in D$ refers to a diagnosis. These rules could be considered as the kernel of the inference of CadL and they express that δ is certain to the degree d given the proviso that τ is true. Again, according to the CadL manipulation rule (c) such a rule is to be interpreted as "we are certain that δ is true with a necessity degree at least equal to $\min\{\|\tau\|, d\}$, where $\|\tau\|$ is the truth value of τ. Therefore, the translation into a FNG formula is again straightforward:

$$\overline{d} \wedge \tau^* \to \Box \delta$$

where τ^* is the translation into its corresponding FNG formula of the CadL proposition τ. Due to the residuation property, equivalent translations would also be $\overline{d} \to (\tau^* \to \Box \delta)$ and $\tau^* \to (\overline{d} \to \Box \delta)$.

We finally turn to the rules of type (me) and (ao). They are of the form ($\tau \to \neg\delta, 1$) and ($\neg\tau \to \neg\delta, 1$), respectively, where τ is a possibly compound CadL proposition and $\delta \in D$ refers to a diagnosis. According to the CadL manipulation rules (me) and (ao), we translate these rules into the following FNG formulas

$$\triangle \tau^* \to \Box \neg \delta \qquad\qquad \triangle (\sim\tau^*) \to \Box \neg \delta$$

respectively, where again τ^* is the translation into its corresponding FNG formula of the CadL proposition τ. The role of Monteiro-Baaz's operator $\triangle$[5] in the translation of the rules of type (me) and (ao) is obvious, we just have to recall that a CadL rule (me) is applicable if the respective proposition τ is fully present (i.e., its truth value is 1), but not if it is present to any degree strictly smaller than 1. The case of rules (ao) is similar.

Rules of type (me) or (ao) are also used to express relationships between other kinds of entities, namely between two symptoms, or between two diagnoses. The translation of the rules is analogous, e.g., in the case of two symptoms, the translation of such rules is respectively:

$$\triangle \sigma_1 \to \sim\sigma_2, \qquad\qquad \triangle (\sim\sigma_1) \to \sim\sigma_2.$$

From the above, we conclude that the data processed by CadL is translated into a theory of FNG$_\sim(\mathbb{Q})$ in a way that preserves the contents. However, we have not yet addressed the question what CADIAG-2 (or CadL) on the one hand and FNG$_\sim(\mathbb{Q})$ on the other hand do with this information. In the following we will show that FNG$_\sim(\mathbb{Q})$ allows us to draw all possible conclusions in CadL. For this purpose, let us consider the inference rules of CadL (the reader is referred to [3,2] for details) and check that for every inference rule of CadL, we can specify a corresponding valid rule in the logic FNG$_\sim(\mathbb{Q})$. Indeed, for all FNG-formulas $\zeta, \tau \in M$, for all Boolean formulas $\delta \in D$ and all rational numbers $r, s, d \in (0, 1] \cap \mathbb{Q}$, we have that the following inferences are valid (and hence provable) in FNG$_\sim(\mathbb{Q})$:

---

[5] Recall that this operator is interpreted in a model **M** as follows : $\|\triangle\tau\|_\mathbf{M} = 1$ if $\|\tau\|_\mathbf{M} = 1$, $\|\triangle\tau\|_M = 0$ otherwise.

- $\Box\neg\delta \vdash \,\sim\Box\delta$
- $\Box\neg\delta \vdash \,\sim(\zeta \wedge \Box\delta)$
- $\sim\zeta \vdash \,\sim(\tau \wedge \zeta)$
- $\overline{r} \leftrightarrow \zeta, \ \overline{s} \leftrightarrow \tau \vdash \overline{\min(r,s)} \leftrightarrow (\zeta \wedge \tau)$
- $\overline{r} \leftrightarrow \zeta, \ \overline{s} \leftrightarrow \tau \vdash \overline{\max(r,s)} \leftrightarrow (\zeta \vee \tau)$
- $\overline{r} \rightarrow \zeta, \ \overline{s} \rightarrow \tau \vdash \overline{\min(r,s)} \rightarrow (\zeta \wedge \tau)$
- $\overline{r} \rightarrow \zeta, \ \overline{s} \rightarrow \tau \vdash \overline{\max(r,s)} \rightarrow (\zeta \vee \tau)$
- $\overline{r} \leftrightarrow \zeta \vdash \overline{1-r} \leftrightarrow \,\sim\zeta$
- $\overline{r} \leftrightarrow \zeta \vdash \overline{r} \rightarrow (\zeta \vee \tau)$
- $\overline{r} \rightarrow \zeta \vdash \overline{r} \rightarrow (\zeta \vee \tau)$
- $\overline{r} \rightarrow \zeta, \ \overline{d} \wedge \zeta \rightarrow \tau \vdash \overline{\min(d,r)} \rightarrow \tau$
- $\overline{r} \rightarrow \zeta, \ \overline{d} \wedge \zeta \rightarrow \Box\delta \vdash \overline{\min(d,r)} \rightarrow \Box\delta$
- $\triangle\tau \rightarrow \Box\neg\delta, \ \tau \vdash \Box\neg\delta$
- $\triangle\sim\tau \rightarrow \Box\neg\delta, \ \sim\tau \vdash \Box\neg\delta$
- $\overline{r} \rightarrow \zeta, \ \overline{s} \rightarrow \zeta \vdash \overline{\max(r,s)} \rightarrow \zeta$

Therefore we conclude that the logic $\text{FNG}_\sim(\mathbb{Q})$ can reproduce the inference of the CadL system. One difference is certainly present, $\text{FNG}_\sim(\mathbb{Q})$ is stricly stronger than CadL. In other words, $\text{FNG}_\sim(\mathbb{Q})$ can produce inferences that CadL cannot, for instance, the following rule concerning $\sim$ is also valid in $\text{FNG}_\sim(\mathbb{Q})$: $\overline{r} \rightarrow \zeta \vdash \zeta \rightarrow \overline{1-r}$, since if r is a lower bound for the truth value of ζ, then $1 - r$ is an upper bound of the truth value of ζ.

4 Final Remarks and Future Work

We end by addressing the special feature in CADIAG-2's inference engine, related to the particular role played by the truth value 0. It is a special feature of CADIAG-2 that sharp values dominate over intermediate ones. For example, a medical entity δ, where δ is a diagnosis, may be assigned the certainty value $r \in (0,1) \cap \mathbb{Q}$ at some step in the inference process and it may be the case that 0 is also assigned to it (that is to say, it is considered false with certainty or impossible) in a later step. Hence, according to CADIAG-2, the former value r of δ becomes obsolete once δ is assigned 0.

This means that in such a situation, both the FNG-formulas $\Box\neg\delta$ and $\overline{r} \rightarrow \Box\delta$, with $r > 0$, could be provable in the logic $\text{FNG}_\sim(\mathbb{Q})$ from a theory obtained by the translation of a CADIAG-2 knowledge base, expressing the constraints $N(\neg\delta) = 1$ and $0 < r \leq N(\delta)$. But having $\min(N(\delta), N(\neg\delta)) = r > 0$ is in conflict with the postulates of possibility theory, that stipulates $\min(N(\delta), N(\neg\delta)) = 0$ for any δ. Therefore, the particular role assigned to 0 in CADIAG-2 may lead to deal with theories with (partial) possibilistic inconsistencies, and thus being $\text{FNG}_\sim(\mathbb{Q})$-inconsistent as well.

Part of our future work will address non-monotonicity aspects arising when dealing with (partial) inconsistency in $\text{FNG}_\sim(\mathbb{Q})$ theories, either by adapting well-known techniques already used in Possibilistic logic [5], or by designing particular revision or inconsistency repairing mechanisms specially suited for the particular case of CadL in the line of [15] for the case of dealing with a probabilistic semantics.

Acknowledgments. The authors are grateful to the anonymous reviewers for their very helpful comments. This research has been partially supported by the Austrian WWTF grant WWTF016, the Spanish projects ARINF TIN2009-14704-C03-03 and AT CONSOLIDER-INGENIO 2010, as well as the FP7-PEOPLE-2009-IRSES project MaToMUVI (PIRSES-GA-2009-247584).

References

1. Choquet, G.: Theory of capacities. Annales de l'Institut Fourier (5), 131–295 (1953)
2. Ciabattoni, A., Picado Muiño, D., Vetterlein, T., El-Zekey, M.: Formal approaches to rule-based systems in medicine: the case of CADIAG-2 (submitted)
3. Ciabattoni, A., Vetterlein, T.: On the (fuzzy) logical content of CADIAG-2. Fuzzy Sets and Systems 161, 1941–1958 (2010)
4. Dubois, D., Esteva, F., Godo, L., Prade, H.: Fuzzy-set based logics - An history-oriented presentation of their main developments. In: Gabbay, D.M., Woods, J. (eds.) Handbook of the History of Logic. The many valued and nonmonotonic turn in logic, vol. 8, pp. 325–449 (2007)
5. Dubois, D., Lang, J., Prade, H.: Possibilistic logic. In: Gabbay, et al. (eds.) Handbook of Logic in Artificial Intelligence and Logic Programming. Nonmonotonic Reasoning and Uncertain Reasoning, vol. 3, pp. 439–513. Oxford University Press (1994)
6. Dubois, D., Prade, H.: Possibility theory: an approach to computerized processing of uncertainty. Plenum Press, New York (1988)
7. Dubois, D., Prade, H.: Possibilistic logic: a retrospective and prospective view. Fuzzy Sets and Systems 144, 3–23 (2004)
8. Esteva, F., Godo, L., Hájek, P., Navara, M.: Residuated fuzzy logics with an involutive negation. Archive for Mathematical Logic 39(2), 103–124 (2000)
9. Esteva, F., Gispert, J., Godo, L., Noguera, C.: Adding truth-constants to logics of a continuous t-norm: axiomatization and completeness results. Fuzzy Sets and Systems 158, 597–618 (2007)
10. Flaminio, T., Godo, L.: A logic for reasoning about the probability of fuzzy events. Fuzzy Sets and Systems 158(6), 625–638 (2007)
11. Flaminio, T., Godo, L., Marchioni, E.: On the Logical Formalization of Possibilistic Counterparts of States over n-Valued Lukasiewicz Events. Journal of Logic and Computation 21(3), 429–446 (2011)
12. Halpern, J.Y.: Reasoning about uncertainty. MIT Press, Cambridge (2003)
13. Hájek, P.: Metamathematics of fuzzy logic. Trends in Logic—Studia Logica Library, vol. 4. Kluwer Academic Publishers, Dordrecht (1998)
14. Picado-Muiño, D.: A probabilistic interpretation of the medical expert system CADIAG-2. Soft Computing 15(10), 2013–2020 (2011)
15. Picado-Muiño, D.: Measuring and repairing inconsistency in probabilistic knowledge bases. International Journal of Approximate Reasoning 52(6), 828–840 (2011)
16. Shafer, G.: A mathematical theory of evidence. Princeton University Press, Princeton (1976)
17. Sugeno, M.: Theory of Fuzzy Integrals and its Applications. PhD thesis, Tokyo Institute of Technology, Tokio, Japan (1974)
18. Walley, P.: Statistical reasoning with imprecise probabilities. Monographs on Statistics and Applied Probability, vol. 42. Chapman and Hall Ltd., London (1991)

State-Complete Riesz MV-Algebras and *L*-Measure Spaces

Ioana Leuştean

Faculty of Mathematics and Computer Science, University of Bucharest,
Academiei 14, C.P. 010014, Bucharest, Romania
ioana@fmi.unibuc.ro
http://fmi.unibuc.ro/ro/departamente/informatica/leustean_ioana/

Abstract. State-complete Riesz MV-algebras are a particular class of probability MV-algebras. We associate to any state-complete Riesz MV-algebra (A, s) a measure space (X, Ω, μ) such that (A, s) and $(L_1(\mu)_u, s_\mu)$ are isometrically isomorphic Riesz MV-algebras, where $L_1(\mu)_u$ is an interval of $L_1(\mu)$ and s_μ is the integral. This result can be seen as an analogue of Kakutani's concrete representation for L-spaces [10] and it leads to a categorical duality between Riesz MV-algebras and a special class of measure spaces (called L-measure spaces).

Keywords: Riesz MV-algebra, state, L-space, L-measure space.

1 Introduction

MV-algebras were introduced by Chang in 1958 [2] as the algebraic counterpart of ∞-valued Łukasiewicz propositional logic. Due to the categorical equivalence proved by Mundici in 1986 [14], the algebraic theory of MV-algebras is deeply connected with the theory of abelian lattice-ordered groups with strong unit.

Following Mundici's equivalence, any MV-algebra is, up to isomorphism, the unit interval of an abelian lattice-ordered group with strong unit (as defined in Example 1). If we consider Riesz spaces (vector lattices) with strong unit instead of lattice-ordered groups, then the unit interval is closed to the scalar multiplication with scalars from $[0, 1]$. *Riesz MV-algebras* are the structures obtained in this way, so they are MV-algebras endowed with a scalar multiplication with scalars form $[0, 1]$.

The theory of states(probabilities) defined on MV-algebra has its roots in the Boolean probability theory, as well as in the theory of states defined on lattice-ordered groups. The notion of *state* defined on an MV-algebra was introduced in [15] and it captures the notion of "average degree of truth" of a proposition. The state s induces a natural pseudo-metric ρ_s on A. A *state-complete* MV-algebra is a pair (A, s) where A is an MV-algebra, s is a state on A and (A, ρ_s) is a complete metric space. Note that any state-complete MV-algebra is a *probability MV-algebra*, as defined in [16].

In this paper we characterize state-complete Riesz MV-algebras as algebras of integrable functions. Our theorem is similar with Kakutani's concrete representation for L-spaces [10]. The representation result leads us to categorical duality

S. Greco et al. (Eds.): IPMU 2012, Part II, CCIS 298, pp. 226–234, 2012.
© Springer-Verlag Berlin Heidelberg 2012

between state-complete Riesz MV-algebras and a particular class of measure spaces.

2   Preliminaries

An *MV-algebra* is a structure $(A, \oplus, ^*, 0)$, where $(A, \oplus, 0)$ is an abelian monoid and the following identities hold for all $x, y \in A$:

$$(x^*)^* = x, \ 0^* \oplus x = 0^* \text{ and } (x^* \oplus y)^* \oplus y = (y^* \oplus x)^* \oplus x.$$

MV-algebras are the algebraic structures of Łukasiewicz ∞-valued logic. The real unit interval $[0, 1]$ equipped with the operations $x^* = 1 - x$ and $x \oplus y = \min(1, x + y)$ is the standard MV-algebra, i.e. an equation holds in any MV-algebra if and only if it holds in $[0, 1]$. We refer to [3] for the basic theory of MV-algebras and to [16] for advanced topics.

Every MV-algebra A is a bounded distributive lattice, where

$$x \vee y = x \oplus (x \oplus y^*)^* \text{ and } x \wedge y = (x^* \vee y^*)^* \text{ for any } x, y \in A.$$

We also set $x \odot y = (x^* \oplus y^*)^*$ and $x \ominus y = x \odot y^*$. Note that $\odot$ is the Łukasiewicz t-norm on $[0, 1]$. The distance function on A is $d(x, y) = (x \ominus y) \vee (y \ominus x)$.

An MV-algebra A is *Dedekind-MacNeille complete* if any set $X \subseteq A$ has supremum $\sup\{x | x \in X\} \in A$. An MV-algebra A is σ-*complete* if any sequence $(x_n)_n \subseteq A$ has supremum $\sup\{x_n | n \in \mathbb{N}\} \in A$.

A nonempty subset I of an MV-algebra A is an *ideal* if the following conditions are satisfied:

(i1) if $x \in I$ and $y \leq x$ then $y \in I$,
(i2) if $x, y \in I$ then $x \oplus y \in I$.

An ideal I is *proper* if $I \neq A$. An ideal I is *maximal* if it is a maximal element in the set of proper ideals, ordered by inclusion. An MV-algebra is *semisimple* if the intersection of maximal ideals is $\{0\}$. The semisimple MV-algebras are, up to isomorphism, algebras of $[0, 1]$-valued functions [15, Corollary 3.6.8].

Let A be an MV-algebra. A function $s : A \to [0, 1]$ is a *state* on A [14] if the following properties are satisfied:

(s1) $s(1) = 1$,
(s2) if $x \odot y = 0$ then $s(x) \odot s(y) = 0$ and $s(x \oplus y) = s(x) + s(y)$.
   The state s is *faithful* if $s(x) = 0$ implies $x = 0$.

One can see [16] for a detailed study of states defined on MV-algebras. For any state $s : A \to [0, 1]$, one can define a pseudo-metric by $\rho_s : A \times A \to [0, 1]$, $\rho_s(x, y) = s(d(x, y))$. If s is faithful, then (A, ρ_s) is a metric space.

A *state-complete MV-algebra* is a pair (A, s) where A is an MV-algebra and s is a state defined on A such that (A, ρ_s) is a complete metric space. The completion of an MV-algebra with respect to the metric induced by a state was studied in [11]. If (A, s) is a state-complete MV-algebra then A is a σ-complete

MV-algebra and s is a faithful σ-continuous state by [11, Theorem 4.2], so (A, s) is a *probability MV-algebra* [16, Definition 13.6].

Recall that a *lattice-ordered group* [1] is a structure $(G, +, \leq)$ such that $(G, +)$ is a group, $(G, \leq)$ is a lattice and every group translation is isotone, i.e. $x \leq y$ implies $x + z \leq y + z$ for any x, y, $z \in G$. The following example of an MV-algebra is fundamental.

Example 1. Let G be a lattice-ordered group and $g \geq 0$ in G then $([0, g], \oplus, {}^*, 0)$ is an MV-algebra, where $x \oplus y = (x + y) \wedge g$ and $x^* = g - x$ for any x, $y \in [0, g]$. Hence $x \odot y = (x + y - 1) \vee 0$ and $x \ominus y = (x - y) \vee 0$ for any x, $y \in [0, g]$.

A crucial result in the theory of MV-algebras is Mundici's categorical equivalence.

Theorem 1. *[14] MV-algebras are categorically equivalent with abelian lattice-ordered groups with strong unit.*

An element $u > 0$ of a lattice-ordered group G is a *strong unit* if for any $g \in G$ there exists $n \in \mathbb{N}$ such that $|g| \leq nu$. The functor Γ which establishes the equivalence is defined by $\Gamma(G, u) = ([0, u], \oplus, {}^*, 0)$ for any lattice ordered group with strong unit (G, u), where the operations are defined as in Example 1. Consequently, any MV-algebra is, up to isomorphism, the unit interval of an abelian lattice-ordered group with strong unit with the MV-algebraic operations defined as above.

A real vector space $(L, +, \cdot)$ is a *Riesz space* [4,12] if L is endowed with a partial order $\leq \subseteq L \times L$ such that:

(rs1) $(L, +, \leq)$ is a lattice-ordered group,
(rs2) if $x \leq y$ in L then $r \cdot x \leq r \cdot y$ for any $r \geq 0$ in $\mathbb{R}$.

If we consider Riesz spaces with strong unit instead of lattice-ordered groups, then the unit interval is closed to the scalar multiplication with scalars from $[0, 1]$. The structure obtained in this way, called *Riesz MV-algebra*, is axiomatized as follows.

Definition 1. *A* Riesz MV-algebra *is a structure* $(R, \cdot)$, *where R is an MV-algebra and* $\cdot : [0, 1] \times R \to R$ *is such that the following properties hold for any x, $y \in R$ and r, $q \in [0, 1]$:*

(1) $(r \cdot x) \odot (r \cdot y) = 0$ *and* $r \cdot (x \oplus y) = (r \cdot x) \oplus (r \cdot y)$ *whenever* $x \odot y = 0$,
(2) $(r \cdot x) \odot (q \cdot x) = 0$ *and* $(r \oplus q) \cdot x = (r \cdot x) \oplus (q \cdot x)$ *whenever* $r \odot q = 0$,
(3) $(r \cdot q) \cdot x = r \cdot (q \cdot x)$,
(4) $1 \cdot x = x$.

In the sequel we simply say than R is a Riesz MV-algebra and write rx for $r \cdot x$ for any $r \in [0, 1]$ and $x \in R$.

Remark 1. If R is an RMV-algebra and $I \subseteq R$ is an MV-ideal, then $rx \in I$ for any $r \in [0, 1]$ and $x \in I$ [6, Remark 3.15]. Hence, the MV-ideals and the

RMV-ideals coincide, i.e. the MV-algebra congruences are compatible with the scalar multiplication. If $f : R_1 \to R_2$ is an MV-algebra homomorphism then $f(rx) = rf(x)$ $r \in [0,1]$ and $x \in R_1$, so RMV-algebra homomorphisms are MV-algebra homomorphisms between RMV-algebras.

We specialize Mundici's categorical equivalence as follows.

Theorem 2. *[6] The category of RMV-algebras with MV-algebra homomorphisms is equivalent to the category of Riesz spaces with strong unit with unit preserving Riesz homomorphisms. As a consequence, for any RMV-algebra A there exists a Riesz space with strong unit (R, u) such that A is isomorphic with $\Gamma(R, u)$.*

Interpreting the product as scalar multiplication with scalars from $[0,1]$, the standard algebra $[0,1]$ generates the variety of Riesz MV-algebras. We refer to [7] as the main reference for Riesz MV-algebras.

Assume A is a Riesz MV-algebra. If $s : A \to [0,1]$ is a state on the MV-algebra reduct of A, then one can easily prove that $s(rx) = rs(x)$ for any $x \in A$ and $r \in [0,1]$.

In the following we study the *state-complete Riesz MV-algebras*, i.e. structures (A, s) where A is a Riesz MV-algebra, s is a state defined on A and (A, ρ_s) is a complete metric space.

3   Concrete Representation for State-Complete Riesz MV-Algebras

An ideal I of an MV-algebra (a Riesz MV-algebra) A is *closed* if for any $S \subset I$ we have $\sup(S) \in I$ whenever $\sup(S)$ exists in A.

By [5, Proposition 2.1] there is a bijective map between the closed ideals of A and the closed ideals of the corresponding lattice-ordered group with strong unit. Following Remark 1, when A is a Riesz MV-algebra, there is a bijective map between the closed ideals of A and the closed ideals of the corresponding Riesz space. Note that the closed ideals in Riesz spaces are called *bands* [4,12].

If R is a Riesz space, then a *lattice norm* on R is a norm $\|\cdot\|$ such that $\|x\| \leq \|y\|$ whenever $|x| \leq |y|$ in R, where $|x|$ is the absolute value of x. A *normed Riesz space* is a pair $(R, \|\cdot\|)$, where R is a Riesz space and $\|\cdot\|$ is a lattice norm on R. A *Banach lattice* is a normed Riesz space which is complete with respect to its norm [13].

An *L-space* [4,10,13] is a Banach lattice $(L, \|\cdot\|)$ such that

$$x \geq 0, y \geq 0 \text{ in } L \implies \|x + y\| = \|x\| + \|y\|.$$

A element $e > 0$ in L is a *weak unit* if the closed ideal generated by $\{e\}$ is L [4, Definition 15.7].

We establish a correspondence between state-complete Riesz MV-algebra and L-spaces. Note that, by [11, Theorem 4.2], every state-complete Riesz MV-algebra is σ-complete, hence it is semisimple by [15, Proposition 6.6.2].

Proposition 1. *A Riesz MV-algebra (A, s) is state-complete if and only if there is an L-space $(L, \|\cdot\|)$ with weak unit e such that (A, s) and $([0, e]_L, \|\cdot\|_e)$ are isometrically isomorphic Riesz MV-algebras, where $\|\cdot\|_e$ is the restriction of $\|\cdot\|$ to the interval $[0, e]$.*

Proof. One implication is obvious. For the other, assume that (A, s) is a state-complete Riesz MV-algebra. There is a Riesz-space with strong unit (R, e) and a Riesz MV-algebra isomorphism $\varphi_A : A \to [0, e]_R$. By [15, Theorem 2.4] there is a state $\widetilde{s} : R \to [0, \infty)$ such that $\widetilde{s}(\varphi_A(a)) = s(a)$ for any $a \in A$. Note that R is archimedean since A is semisimple and $\widetilde{s}$ is an additive seminorm on R. If $(L, \|\cdot\|)$ be the norm-completion of $(R, \|\cdot\|)$, then $(L, \|\cdot\|)$ is an L-space. Since (A, s) is state-complete, the interval $[0, e]_R$ is closed in R with respect to $\|\cdot\|$. It follows that $[0, e]_L = [0, e]_R$, so e is a weak unit in L. Moreover, $\|\varphi_A(a)\| = \widetilde{s}(\varphi_A(a)) = s(a)$ for any $a \in A$.

Corollary 1. *If (A, s) is a state-complete Riesz MV-algebra, then A is Dedekind-MacNeille complete.*

Proof. It follows by Proposition 1 and the fact that any L-space is Dedekind-MacNeille complete [8, 26B].

We introduce a particular class of measure spaces.

Definition 2. *The measure space (X, Ω, μ) is an L-measure space if the following properties are satisfied:*

(1) X is a Stonean space, i.e X is the Stone space of a Dedekind-MacNeille complete Boolean algebra,

(2) Ω it the Borel σ-algebra of X, i.e. the Boolean σ-algebra generated by the open sets of X,

(3) μ is a topological finite measure, i.e. μ is finite and the μ-negligible sets coincide with the meager subsets of X.

We recall that a subset W of X is meager *if there exists a countable sequence $W_1, W_2, \ldots$ of subsets of X such that $W \subseteq \bigcup_n W_n$ and every W_n is closed and has an empty interior [17, 20.6]. Condition (3) asserts that the measure-theoretical "small" sets coincide with the topological "small" sets.*

Let (X, Ω, μ) be a measure space and let $\mathcal{L}_1(\mu)$ denote the set of all real-valued μ-integrable functions defined on X. For $f, g \in \mathcal{L}_1(\mu)$ we define $f \sim g$ if $f = g$ μ-almost everywhere, and we denote by $\hat{f}$ the equivalence class of f with respect to $\sim$. We set $L_1(\mu) = \{\hat{f} \mid f \in \mathcal{L}_1(\mu)\}$. Hence $L_1(\mu)$ with componentwise operations is a Riesz space [9, 242C(d)]. In the following, we will sometimes identify a function $f \in \mathcal{L}_1(\mu)$ with its class $\hat{f} \in L_1(\mu)$.

Using the above notations, we write $L_1(\mu)_u$ for the interval $[\mathbf{0}, \mathbf{1}]$ of $L_1(\mu)$, where $\mathbf{0}$ and $\mathbf{1}$ are the constant functions 0 and 1, i.e.

$$L_1(\mu)_u = \{\hat{f} \in L_1(\mu) \mid \mathbf{0} \leq \hat{f} \leq \mathbf{1}\}.$$

Let $s_\mu : L_1(\mu)_u \to [0,1]$ be defined by $s_\mu(\hat{f}) = \int_X f d\mu$.

We recall a main result in the theory of L-spaces: the representation theorem of Kakutani.

Theorem 3. *[10] For any L-space L with weak unit e there exists a measure space (X, Ω, μ) such that L is isometrically Riesz isomorphic with $L^1(\mu)$ and the correspondence maps e to 1.*

Our version for state-complete Riesz MV-algebras is the following.

Theorem 4. *For any state-complete Riesz MV-algebra (A, s) there exists an L-measure space (X, Ω, μ) such that (A, s) and $(L_1(\mu)_u, s_\mu)$ are isometrically isomorphic Riesz MV-algebras.*

Proof. Let (A, s) be a state-complete Riesz MV-algebra and $(L, \|\cdot\|)$ the L-space from Proposition 1. Hence L has a weak unit e and (A, s) is isometrically isomorphic with $([0, e]_L, \|\cdot\|_e)$. We apply Kakutani theorem (Theorem 3) for L with weak unit e and we get a measure space (X, Ω, μ) such that (A, s) and $(L_1(\mu)_u, s_\mu)$ are isometrically isomorphic Riesz MV-algebras. The fact that (X, Ω, μ) can be chosen to be L-measure space follows by [4, Theorem 16.8]. $\quad\square$

We give a concrete description of isomorphism between (A, s) and $(L_1(\mu)_u, s_\mu)$.

From now on, $Cls(A)$ is the set of the closed ideals of A. If $a \subseteq A$, then $cl(a)$ is the closed ideal generated by $\{a\}$.

Proposition 2. *If A is a state-complete Riesz MV-algebra, then $Cls(A)$ is a Dedekind-MacNeille complete Boolean algebra.*

Proof. Since A is also Dedekind-MacNeille complete, the conclusion follows by [12, Theorems 30.2, 24.9]. $\quad\square$

By [4, Definition 15.7, Exercise 15.D], an element $e > 0$ of a Riesz space R is a weak unit if and only if $cl(e) = L$.

Remark 2. Assume (A, s) and $(L_1(\mu)_u, s_\mu)$ are the state-complete Riesz MV-algebras from Theorem 4. Following [4, Theorem 16.8] and [12, Definition 49.1, Theorem 50.1], $X = Max(Cls(A))$, the maximal ideal space of the Boolean algebra $Cls(A)$, and the isomorphism $\varphi_{(A,s)} : (A, s) \to (L_1(\mu)_u, s_\mu)$ is defined by $\varphi_{(A,s)}(a) = \hat{a}$,

$$\hat{a} : X \to \mathbb{R}, \quad \hat{a}(\mathfrak{m}) = \sup\{\alpha | cl((\alpha e) \ominus a) \in \mathfrak{m}\}$$

for any $a \in A$ and $\mathfrak{m} \in X$.

4   Duality for State-Complete Riesz MV-Algebras

If A and B are MV-algebras (Riesz MV-algebras), a homomorphism $h : A \to B$ is called *order-continuous* if $\sup(h(S))$ exists in B whenever $S \subseteq A$ such that $\sup(S)$ exists in A and, in this case, $h(\sup(S)) = \sup(h(S))$.

Let (X, Ω, μ) and (Y, Λ, ν) be measure spaces and $T : X \to Y$ a measurable transformation, i.e. $T^{-1}(\lambda) \in \Omega$ for any $\lambda \in \Lambda$. We say that T *preserves the negligible sets* if $\mu(T^{-1}(\lambda)) = 0$ whenever $\nu(\lambda) = 0$.

If A is a state-complete Riesz MV-algebra then, by Proposition 2, $Cls(A)$ is a Dedekind-MacNeille complete Boolean algebra. Consequently, the maximal ideal space $Max(Cls(A))$ is a Stonean space.

We write **StCoRMV** for the category of state-complete Riesz MV-algebras and order-continuous homomorphisms. We write **LMeasureSp** for the category of L measure spaces with measurable transformations that preserve the negligible sets.

The cofunctors **M** and **L** are defined as follows.

M : StCoRMV → LMeasureSp

- $\mathbf{M}(A, s) = (X, \Omega, \mu)$, where (X, Ω, μ) is given by Theorem 4.
- If (A, s), (C, p) are objects in **StCoRMV** and $h \colon A \to C$ is an order-continuous homomorphism of Riesz MV-algebras, then $\mathbf{M}(h) \colon Max(Cls(C)) \to Max(Cls(A))$ is defined by $\mathbf{M}(h)(\mathfrak{m}) = h^{-1}(\mathfrak{m})$ for any $\mathfrak{m} \in Max(Cls(C))$.

L : LMeasureSp → StCoRMV

- $\mathbf{L}(X, \Omega, \mu) = (L_1(\mu)_u, s_1)$, where $s_1(f) = \int_X f \, d\mu$ for any $f \in L_1(\mu)_u$.
- If (X, Ω, μ), (Y, Σ, ν) are objects in **LMeasureSp** and $T \colon X \to Y$ is a measurable transformation that preserves the negligible sets, then let $U_T \colon L_1(\nu) \to L_1(\mu)$ be the induced operator, i.e. $U_T(g) = g \circ T$ for any $g \in L_1(\nu)$. We define $\mathbf{L}(T) \colon L_1(\nu)_u \to L_1(\mu)_u$ by $\mathbf{L}(T)(f) = U_T(f) = f \circ T$ for any $f \in L_1(\nu)_u$.

Lemma 1. *The functors* **M** *and* **L** *are well defined.*

Proof. The functors are well defined on objects by Theorem 4. Order-continuous homomorphisms are mapped to measurable transformations that preserve the negligible sets by [9, 324B,324E, 361J].

Proposition 3. *The composite functor* **LM** *is naturally equivalent to the identity functor of* **StCoRMV**.

Proof. If (A, s) is an object in **StCoRMV** and $\mathbf{M}(A, s) = (X, \Omega, \mu)$, then $\mathbf{L}(\mathbf{M}(A, s)) = (L_1(\mu), s_1)$ defined as in Theorem 4 and $\varphi_{(A,s)} : (A, s) \to \mathbf{L}(\mathbf{M}(A, s))$ is defined as in Remark 2. We only have to prove that $\varphi : \mathbf{LM} \to \mathrm{Id}_{\mathbf{StCoRMV}}$ is a natural transformation, i.e. the diagram

$$
\begin{array}{ccc}
(A, s) & \xrightarrow{\ \ h\ \ } & (B, t) \\
\Big\downarrow{\varphi_{(A,s)}} & & \Big\downarrow{\varphi_{(B,t)}} \\
\mathbf{L}(\mathbf{M}(A, s)) & \xrightarrow{\mathbf{L}(\mathbf{M}(h))} & \mathbf{L}(\mathbf{M}(B, t))
\end{array}
$$

is commutative, where (A, s) and (B, t) are objects in **StCoRMV** and $h :$ $(A, s) \rightarrow (B, t)$ is an order-continuous homomorphism of Riesz MV-algebras. Note that h preserves the closed ideals, so

$$a \in h^{-1}(\mathfrak{m}) \Leftrightarrow h(a) \in \mathfrak{m} \text{ for any } \mathfrak{m} \in Max(Cls(B)) \text{ and } a \in A.$$

Hence $\hat{a} \circ h^{-1} = h(\hat{a})$ for any $a \in A$, which gives $\mathbf{L}(\mathbf{M}(h)) \circ \varphi_{(A,s)} = \varphi_{(B,t)} \circ h$.

If X is a set and $\omega \subseteq X$ then we write χ_ω for the characteristic function of ω.

Lemma 2. Let (X, Ω, μ) be an L-measure space. Then (X, Ω, μ) and $\mathbf{M}(\mathbf{L}(X, \Omega, \mu))$ are isomorphic objects in **LMeasureSp** and the isomorphism $\psi_{(X,\Omega,\mu)} : (X, \Omega, \mu) \rightarrow \mathbf{M}(\mathbf{L}(X, \Omega, \mu))$ is defined by

$$\psi_{(X,\Omega,\mu)}(x) = \{\chi_\omega | \omega \in \Omega, x \notin \omega\}$$

for any $x \in X$.

Proof. Let $(\mathfrak{A}, \bar{\mu})$ be the measure algebra of (X, Ω, μ). By [9, 365S(a)], $\mathfrak{A}$ and $Cls(L_1(\mu))$ are isomorphic Boolean algebras and the isomorphism is $\omega \mapsto \chi_\omega$. Note that we identify $\omega \in \Omega$ with its class in $\mathfrak{A}$ and χ_ω with its class in $L_1(\mu)$. Consequently, X and $Max(Cls(L_1(\mu)))$ are homeomorphic spaces and the homeomorphism is defined by $\psi_X(x) = \{\chi_\omega | \omega \in \Omega, x \notin \omega\}$. Moreover $\mu(\omega) = \int_X \chi_\omega d\mu = s_1(\chi_\omega)$ for any $\omega \in \Omega$. Hence $\psi_{(X,\Omega,\mu)}$ is a measure-preserving transformation.

Proposition 4. *The composite functor* $\mathbf{ML}$ *is naturally equivalent to the identity functor of* **LMeasureSp**.

Proof. Let (X, Ω, μ) be an object in **LMeasureSp** and $\psi_{(X,\Omega,\mu)}$ defined as in Lemma 2. We have to prove that $\psi : \mathbf{ML} \rightarrow Id_{\mathbf{LMeasureSp}}$ is a natural transformation, i.e. the diagram

$$
\begin{array}{ccc}
(X, \Omega, \mu) & \xrightarrow{\quad T \quad} & (Y, \Lambda, \nu) \\
\downarrow{\psi_{(X,\Omega,\mu)}} & & \downarrow{\psi_{(Y,\Lambda,\nu)}} \\
\mathbf{M}(\mathbf{L}(X, \Omega, \mu)) & \xrightarrow{\mathbf{M}(\mathbf{L}(T))} & \mathbf{M}(\mathbf{L}(Y, \Lambda, \nu))
\end{array}
$$

is commutative, where (Y, Λ, ν) is also an object in **LMeasureSp** and $T :$ $(X, \Omega, \mu) \rightarrow (Y, \Lambda, \nu)$ is a measure-preserving transformation. Note that, for any $\lambda \in \Lambda$, we have

$$\chi_\lambda \in \psi_{(Y,\Lambda,\nu)}(T(x)) \Leftrightarrow T(x) \notin \lambda \Leftrightarrow x \notin T^{-1}(\lambda) \Leftrightarrow x \notin U_T(\chi_\lambda)$$

$$\Leftrightarrow U_T(\chi_\lambda) \in \psi_{(X,\Omega,\mu)}(x) \Leftrightarrow \chi_\lambda \in U_T^{-1}(\psi_{(X,\Omega,\mu)}(x)).$$

This means that $\psi_{(Y,\Lambda,\nu)}(T(x)) = U_T^{-1}(\psi_{(X,\Omega,\mu)}(x))$ for any $x \in X$, so $\psi_{(Y,\Lambda,\nu)} \circ T = \mathbf{M}(\mathbf{L}(T)) \circ \psi_{(X,\Omega,\mu)}$.

Theorem 5. *The categories* **StCoRMV** *and* **LMeasureSp** *are dually equivalent.*

Proof. The functors **M** and **L** establish the dual equivalence.

Remark 3. If (A, s) and (B, p) are MV-algebras with states, an MV-algebra homomorphism $h: A \to B$ is *state-preserving* if $p \circ f = s$. One can easily see that the monomorphisms in **StCoRMV** are exactly the state-preserving homomorphisms.

Acknowledgments. The author was supported by the strategic grant POSDRU/89/1.5/S/58852 cofinanced by ESF within SOP HRD 2007-2013.

References

1. Bigard, A., Keimel, K., Wolfenstein, S.: Groupes et anneaux réticulés. Lecture Notes in Math., vol. 608. Springer, Berlin (1977)
2. Chang, C.C.: Algebraic analysis of many valued logics. Transactions of the American Mathematical Society 88, 467–490 (1958)
3. Cignoli, R., D'Ottaviano, I.M.L., Mundici, D.: Algebraic Foundations of many-valued Reasoning. Kluwer, Dordrecht (2000)
4. De Jonge, E., van Rooij, A.C.M.: Introduction to Riesz spaces. Mathematical Centre Tracs 78, Amsterdam (1977)
5. Di Nola, A., Georgescu, G., Sessa, S.: Closed Ideals of MV-algebras. Contemporary Mathematics 235, 99–112 (1999)
6. Di Nola, A., Flondor, P., Leuştean, I.: MV-modules. Journal of Algebra 267(1), 21–40 (2003)
7. Di Nola, A., Leuştean, I.: Riesz MV-algebras and their logic. In: Proceedings of EUSFLAT-LFA 2011, pp. 140–145 (2011) (to appear)
8. Fremlin, D.H.: Topological Riesz Spaces and Measure Theory. Cambridge University Press (1974)
9. Fremlin, D.H.: Measure Theory,
   http://www.essex.ac.uk/maths/people/fremlin/mt.htm
10. Kakutani, S.: Concrete representations of abstract (L)-spaces and the mean ergodic theorem. Annals of Mathematics 42, 523–537 (1941)
11. Leuştean, I.: Metric completions of MV-algebras with states. An approach to stochastic independence. Journal of Logic and Computation 21(3), 493–508 (2011)
12. Luxemburg, W.A.J., Zaanen, A.C.: Riesz Spaces I. North-Holland, Amsterdam (1971)
13. Meyer-Nieberg, P.: Banach Lattices. Universitext. Springer (1991)
14. Mundici, D.: Interpretation of AF C*-algebras in Łukasiewicz sentential calculus. J. Functional Analysis 65, 15–63 (1986)
15. Mundici, D.: Averaging the truth value Łukasiewicz logic. Studia Logica 55, 113–127 (1995)
16. Mundici, D.: Advanced Łukasiewicz calculus and MV-algebras. Trends in Logic, vol. 35. Springer (2011)
17. Schechter, E.: Handbook of Analysis and Its Foundations. Academic Press (1997)

On Finitely Valued Fuzzy Description Logics: The Łukasiewicz Case

Marco Cerami[1], Francesc Esteva[1], and Àngel García-Cerdaña[1,2]

[1] Artificial Intelligence Research Institute (IIIA - CSIC),
Campus de la UAB, 08193 Bellaterra, Catalonia, Spain
{cerami,esteva,angel}@iiia.csic.es
http://www.iiia.csic.es
[2] Departament de Lògica, Història i Filosofia de la Ciència,
Universitat de Barcelona, Montalegre 6, 08001 Barcelona, Catalonia, Spain
http://www.ub.edu

Abstract. Following the guidelines proposed by Hájek in [1], some proposals of research on Fuzzy Description Logics (FDLs) were given in [2]. One of them consists in the definition and development of a family of description languages, each one having as underlying fuzzy logic the expansion with an involutive negation and truth constants of the logic defined by a divisible finite t-norm. A general framework for finitely valued FDLs was presented in [3]. In the present paper we study the family of languages $\mathcal{ALC}_{\mathbf{L}_n^c}$ based on the finitely valued Łukasiewicz logics with truth constants. In addition, we provide an interpretation of these FDLs into fuzzy multi-modal systems. We also deal with the corresponding reasoning tasks and their relationships, and we report some results on decidability and computational complexity.

Keywords: Description Logics, Finitely Valued Description Logics, n-graded Łukasiewicz Description Logics.

1 Introduction

Description Logics (DLs) are knowledge representation languages particularly suited to specify ontologies, to create knowledge bases and to reason with them. A full reference manual of the field is [4]. The vocabulary of DLs consists of symbols for *individuals*, *concepts*, which denote sets of individuals, and *roles*, which denote binary relations among individuals. From atomic concepts and roles and by means of *constructors*, DL systems allow to build complex descriptions of both concepts and roles. These complex descriptions are used to describe a domain through a knowledge base (KB) containing the definitions of relevant domain concepts or some hierarchical relationships among them (*Terminological Box* or *TBox*) and a specification of properties of the domain instances (*Assertional Box* or *ABox*). One of the main issues of DLs is the fact that the semantics is given in a Tarski-style presentation and the statements in both *TBox* and *ABox* can be identified with formulas in first-order logic, and hence we can use reasoning to obtain implicit knowledge from the explicit knowledge in the KB.

S. Greco et al. (Eds.): IPMU 2012, Part II, CCIS 298, pp. 235–244, 2012.
© Springer-Verlag Berlin Heidelberg 2012

Nevertheless, the knowledge used in real applications is commonly imperfect and has to address situations of uncertainty, imprecision and vagueness. From a real world viewpoint, vague concepts like "patient with a high fever" and "person living near Paris" have to be considered. A natural generalization to cope with vague concepts and relations consists in interpreting DL concepts and roles as fuzzy sets and fuzzy relations, respectively. The initial proposals for Fuzzy Description Logics (FDLs) have been made (see [5,6,7]) mainly based on the earlier approaches to fuzzy logic. In recent times, fuzzy logics has evolved into what is known as Mathematical Fuzzy Logic (as a general reference for the field see [8]). The starting point is the book *Metamathematics of Fuzzy Logics* [9] where Hájek shows the connection between fuzzy logic systems and many-valued residuated logics based on continuous *t*-norms. Later on, in the paper *Making fuzzy description logic more general* [1], Hájek proposes to deal with FDLs taking as basis *t*-norm based fuzzy logics with the aim of enriching the expressive possibilities in FDLs. Following this line, we have developed the topic in [2,3]. Since real applications are mainly made using a finite number of values, we are interested in FDLs over finitely valued fuzzy logics. In the present paper we study FDLs based on finitely valued Łukasiewiz logics. In our proposal, description languages are restricted to constructors defined from logical connectives and the fuzzy versions of universal and existential quantifiers. We study the languages, reasoning tasks and their relationships, and decidability and complexity. Special mention is due to the modal translation section that, as far as we know, it is not already considered in the literature for the fuzzy case. Finally, let us mention the recent papers [10,11], which contain results related to our work.

2   The Finitely Valued Łukasiewicz Logic with Truth Constants

Given a positive integer $n \geq 2$, the algebra $\mathbf{L}_n$ is the structure $\langle L_n, \otimes, N, 0 \rangle$, where $L_n = \{0, \frac{1}{n-1}, \frac{2}{n-1}, \ldots, \frac{n-2}{n-1}, 1\}$, $\otimes$ is the *Łukasiewicz t-norm* defined as $a \otimes b := \max\{0, a + b - 1\}$, for each $a, b \in L_n$, and N is the negation associated to Łukasiewicz t-norm, defined as $N(a) = 1 - a$, for each $a \in L_n$.[1] Further operations are defined as follows:

$a \Rightarrow b$	$:=$	$N(a \otimes N(b))$	$\min\{0, 1 - a + b\}$
$a \wedge b$	$:=$	$a \otimes (a \Rightarrow b)$	$\min\{a, b\}$
$a \vee b$	$:=$	$(a \Rightarrow b) \Rightarrow b$	$\max\{a, b\}$
$a \oplus b$	$:=$	$N(N(a) \otimes N(b))$	$\min\{1, a + b\}$
1	$:=$	$N(0)$	1

Let us consider the set of formulas built from a countable set of *propositional variables* $\Phi = \{p_j : j \in J\}$ using the connectives & (strong conjunction), $\sim$ (involutive negation) and $\bar{0}$ (falsity truth constant). A *propositional evaluation* is a map $e : \Phi \to L_n$ which is extended to all $\langle \&, \sim, \bar{0} \rangle$-formulas by setting $e(\varphi \& \psi) = e(\varphi) \otimes e(\psi)$, $e(\sim \varphi) = N(e(\varphi))$, and $e(\bar{0}) = 0$. The *n*-valued

---

[1] In fact this is the unique involutive negation definable in L_n.

Łukasiewicz logic, which we denote by $\Lambda(\mathbf{L}_n)$ is obtained by putting for all sets $\Gamma \cup \{\varphi\}$ of $\langle \&, \sim, \bar{0} \rangle$-formulas, $\Gamma \models_{\mathbf{L}_n} \varphi$ if, and only if, for every evaluation e, if $e[\Gamma] \subseteq \{1\}$, then $e(\varphi) = 1$. As defined connectives we have *implication, biconditional, additive conjunction, additive disjunction, strong disjunction,* and *true truth constant:* $\varphi \rightarrow \psi := \sim(\varphi \& \sim \psi)$, $\varphi \leftrightarrow \psi := (\varphi \rightarrow \psi) \& (\psi \rightarrow \varphi)$, $\varphi \wedge \psi := \varphi \& (\varphi \rightarrow \psi)$, $\varphi \vee \psi := \sim(\sim \varphi \wedge \sim \psi)$, $\varphi \veebar \psi := \sim(\sim \varphi \& \sim \psi)$, $\bar{1} := \sim \bar{0}$. It is well known that this logic is finitely axiomatizable having Modus Ponens as the unique inference rule (cf. [12, p.171]; see also [13]). The logic $\Lambda(\mathbf{L}_n^c)$ is the expansion of $\Lambda(\mathbf{L}_n)$ with truth constants. It is obtained by adding to the language n *canonical* constants: one truth constant $\bar{r}$ for each $r \in L_n \backslash \{0\}$; the semantics of the constant $\bar{r}$ is its canonical value r. $\Lambda(\mathbf{L}_n^c)$ is finitely axiomatizable from an axiomatization of $\Lambda(\mathbf{L}_n)$ by adding the so-called *book-keeping* axioms:

$$(bk_1) \quad \bar{r} \& \bar{s} \leftrightarrow \overline{r \otimes s}$$
$$(bk_2) \quad \sim \bar{r} \leftrightarrow \overline{N(r)}$$

The predicate logic $\Lambda(\mathbf{L}_n^c)\forall$ is defined from $\Lambda(\mathbf{L}_n^c)$ as it is done for the fuzzy predicate logics introduced in [9, Chapter 5]. Let $\Sigma = \langle \mathcal{C}, \mathcal{P} \rangle$ be a first order signature (without functional symbols), $\mathcal{C}$ being a countable set of object constants and $\mathcal{P}$ a countable set of predicate symbols, each one with arity $k \geq 1$. An $\mathbf{L}_n^c$-*interpretation* for Σ is a tuple $\mathbf{M} = \langle M, \{a^{\mathbf{M}} : a \in \mathcal{C}\}, \{P^{\mathbf{M}} : P \in \mathcal{P}\} \rangle$, where 1) M is a non-empty set; 2) for each object constant $a \in \mathcal{C}$, $a^{\mathbf{M}}$ is an element of M; and 3) for each k-ary predicate symbol P, $P^{\mathbf{M}}$ is an n-graded k-ary relation defined on M, that is, a function $P^{\mathbf{M}} : M^k \rightarrow L_n$. Given an interpretation $\mathbf{M}$, a map v assigning an element $v(x) \in M$ to each variable x is called an *assignation of the variables in* $\mathbf{M}$. Given $\mathbf{M}$ and v, the *value of a term* t in $\mathbf{M}$, denoted by $\|t\|_{\mathbf{M},v}$, is defined as $v(x)$ when t is a variable x, and as $a^{\mathbf{M}}$ when t is a constant a. In order to emphasize that a formula α has its free variables in $\{x_1, \ldots, x_n\}$, we will denote it by $\alpha(x_1, \ldots, x_n)$. Let v be an assignation such that $v(x_1) = b_1, \ldots, v(x_n) = b_n$. The *truth value in* $\mathbf{M}$ *over* $\mathbf{L}_n^c$ *of the predicate formula* $\varphi(x_1, \ldots, x_n)$ *for the assignation* v, denoted by $\|\varphi\|_{\mathbf{M},v}$ or by $\|\varphi(b_1, \ldots, b_n)\|_{\mathbf{M}}$, is a value in L_n defined inductively as follows:

$$
\begin{array}{ll}
P^{\mathbf{M}}(\|t_1\|_{\mathbf{M},v}, \ldots, \|t_k\|_{\mathbf{M},v}), & \text{if } \varphi = P(t_1, \ldots, t_k); \\
r, & \text{if } \varphi = \bar{r} \in \{\bar{0}, \bar{r}_1, \ldots, \bar{r}_{n-1}\}; \\
1 - \|\alpha\|_{\mathbf{M},v}, & \text{if } \varphi = \sim \alpha; \\
\|\alpha\|_{\mathbf{M},v} \otimes \|\beta\|_{\mathbf{M},v}, & \text{if } \varphi = \alpha \& \beta; \\
\inf \{\|\alpha(a, b_1, \ldots, b_n)\|_{\mathbf{M}} : a \in M\}, & \text{if } \varphi = (\forall x)\alpha(x, x_1, \ldots, x_n).
\end{array}
$$

A $\mathbf{L}_n^c$-interpretation $\mathbf{M}$ is an $\mathbf{L}_n^c$-*model*, or simply a *model*, of a set of formulas Γ if, for each $\varphi \in \Gamma$, and each assignation v, $\|\varphi\|_{\mathbf{M},v} = 1$. The logic $\Lambda(\mathbf{L}_n^c)\forall$ is defined by a finite set of axioms. Moreover, we have the following result:[2]

Theorem 1. *The logic* $\Lambda(\mathbf{L}_n^c)\forall$ *is strongly complete with respect to interpretations over* $\mathbf{L}_n^c$.

---

[2] A direct proof of this theorem is easy since the unique subdirectly irreducible algebra of the variety corresponding to $\Lambda(\mathbf{L}_n^c)$ is $\mathbf{L}_n^c$.

3   The n-Valued Łukasiewicz Description Logics $\mathcal{ALC}_{\mathbf{Ł}_n^c}$

Description Logics based on finitely valued Łukasiewicz logics are built in the same way as in the classical case, but now we need a set of constructors that corresponds to the logical symbols existing in the setting of the first order logics $\Lambda(\mathbf{Ł}_n^c)\forall$ (cf. [3]).[3] To do so we introduce some symbols for new propositional constructors: $\boxtimes$ for *strong intersection*; $\boxplus$ for *strong union*; $\sqsupset$ for *residuated implication*, and a *constant* $\mathfrak{r}$ for every $r \in L_n$. Moreover, in our setting, we have the classical $\sqcup$ and $\sqcap$ as defined constructors. It is worth pointing out that $\mathcal{ALC}$-like DLs based on n-valued Łukasiewicz logics are analogous to the classical $\mathcal{ALC}$ in the sense that the basic relations between connectives remain true:

- complementation is involutive,
- both pairs of weak and strong intersection and union are dual w.r.t. complementation,
- the universal and the existential quantifications are inter-definable by means of complementation,
- implication is definable from complementation and strong intersection or from complementation and strong union.

Notice that the above relations are not satisfied in other finitely valued t-norm based predicate fuzzy logics.

Definition 1 (The attributive languages $\mathcal{ALC}_{\mathbf{Ł}_n^c}$). *Let us fix a description signature $\mathcal{D} = \langle N_I, N_A, N_R \rangle$, that is, a set of individual names N_I, a set N_A of concept names (the atomic concepts), and a set N_R of role names (the atomic roles). An $\langle \mathcal{ALC}_{\mathbf{Ł}_n^c}, \mathcal{D} \rangle$-description, or simply an $\mathcal{ALC}_{\mathbf{Ł}_n^c}$-description, is inductively defined in accordance with the following syntactic rules (we use the symbols C, C_1, C_2 as meta-variables for descriptions of concepts):*

$$
\begin{aligned}
C, C_1, C_2 \quad \rightsquigarrow \quad & A \mid & \textit{(atomic concept)} \\
& \bot \mid & \textit{(empty description)} \\
& \top \mid & \textit{(universal description)} \\
& \mathfrak{r} \mid & \textit{(constant description)} \\
& \neg C \mid & \textit{(strong complementary concept) } (\mathcal{C}) \\
& C_1 \boxplus C_2 \mid & \textit{(concept strong union)} \qquad (\mathcal{U}) \\
& C_1 \boxtimes C_2 \mid & \textit{(concept strong intersection)} \\
& \forall R.C \mid & \textit{(universal quantification)} \\
& \exists R.C \mid & \textit{(existential quantification)} \qquad (\mathcal{E}) \\
& R \mid & \textit{(atomic role)}
\end{aligned}
$$

Further constructors are defined as follows:

$$
\begin{aligned}
C_1 \sqsupset C_2 &:= \neg(C_1 \boxtimes \neg C_2) & \textit{(residuated implication)} \\
C_1 \sqcap C_2 &:= C_1 \boxtimes (C_1 \sqsupset C_2) & \textit{(weak intersection)} \\
C_1 \sqcup C_2 &:= \neg(\neg C_1 \sqcap \neg C_2) & \textit{(weak union)}
\end{aligned}
$$

---

[3] In [3] a new hierarchy of attributive languages adapted to the behavior of the connectives in the fuzzy setting is proposed.

The notion of *instance of a description* allows us to read description formulas of a given description signature $\mathcal{D}$ as predicate formulas of $\mathbf{\Lambda}(\mathbf{L}_n^c)\forall$ as it is done in Definition 2 following Hajék's paper [1]. From this notion, we can define the truth value of a description formula as the truth value of a first order formula.

Definition 2 (Instance of a description). *Given a description signature* $\mathcal{D} = \langle N_I, N_A, N_R \rangle$, *we define the first order signature* $\Sigma_{\mathcal{D}} = \langle \mathcal{C}_{\mathcal{D}}, \mathcal{P}_{\mathcal{D}} \rangle$, *where* $\mathcal{C}_{\mathcal{D}} = N_I$ *and* $\mathcal{P}_{\mathcal{D}} = N_A \cup N_R$. *We read each individual name in* N_I *as an object constant, each atomic concept in* N_A *as a unary predicate symbol, and each atomic role in* N_R *as a binary predicate symbol. We define as* instances *of an* $\langle \mathcal{ALC}_{\mathbf{L}_n}, \mathcal{D} \rangle$- *description the following formulas of* $\mathbf{\Lambda}(\mathbf{L}_n^c)\forall$:

- *The* instance *of a truth constant is defined as* $\bar{0}$ *for* $\bot$; $\bar{1}$ *for* $\top$; *and* $\bar{r}$ *for* $\mathfrak{r}$.
- *Given a term* t *and a concept* D, *the* instance $D(t)$ *of* D *is defined as*

$$
\begin{array}{ll}
A(t) & \text{if } D \text{ is an atomic concept } A, \\
{\sim}C(t) & \text{if } D = \neg C, \\
C_1(t) \veebar C_2(t) & \text{if } D = C_1 \boxplus C_2, \\
C_1(t)\&C_2(t) & \text{if } D = C_1 \boxtimes C_2, \\
(\forall y)(R(t,y) \rightarrow C(y)) & \text{if } D = \forall R.C, \\
(\exists y)(R(t,y)\&C(y)) & \text{if } D = \exists R.C.
\end{array}
$$

- *An* instance *of an atomic role* R *is any atomic first order formula* $R(t_1, t_2)$, *where* t_1 *and* t_2 *are terms*.

We can define the consequence relation $\models_{\mathcal{ALC}_{\mathbf{L}_n^c}}$ as the restriction of the consequence relation of the logic $\mathbf{\Lambda}(\mathbf{L}_n^c)\forall$ to instances of $\mathcal{ALC}_{\mathbf{L}_n^c}$-descriptions.

4 $\mathcal{ALC}_{\mathbf{L}_n^c}$ and Modal Finite-Valued Łukasiewicz Logics

It is known that there is a translation between classical $\mathcal{ALC}$ and multi-modal logical systems (cf. [4, Chapter 4]). In this section we show that a similar translation is also possible between $\mathcal{ALC}_{\mathbf{L}_n^c}$ and multi-modal finite-valued Łukasiewicz logics with truth constants.[4] The language of each one of these multi-modal systems, denoted by μ_m, is obtained by fixing a natural number m and expanding the language of $\mathbf{\Lambda}(\mathbf{L}_n^c)$ with m unary connectives $\Box_1, \ldots, \Box_m$ (m *necessity* operators).

Definition 3 (Kripke m-frames and m-models). *An* n-valued Kripke m- frame *is a tuple* $\mathfrak{F} = \langle W, R_1, \ldots, R_m \rangle$, *where* W *is a non-empty set (the set of* worlds*) and* $R_1, \ldots, R_m$ *are binary relations (the* accessibility relations*) valued in* L_n. *The Kripke frame is said to be* crisp *if the range of the relations* R_k *is included in* $\{0,1\}$. *The class of all* n-valued m-frames *will be denoted by* Fr *and the class of crisp* m-frames *by* CFr. *A Kripke* $\langle \mathbf{L}_n^c, m \rangle$-model *is a pair* $\mathfrak{M} = \langle \mathfrak{F}, V \rangle$, *where* $\mathfrak{F}$ *is an* n-valued Kripke m-frame *and* V *is a valuation assigning*

---

[4] Modal finite-valued Łukasiewicz logics –with and without truth constants– have been studied in [14].

to each variable in $\Phi = \{p_j : j \in J\}$ and each world in W a value in L_n. The map V can be uniquely extended to a map, which we also denote by V, assigning an element of L_n to each pair formed by a μ_m-formula φ and a world w in such a way that:

- $V(\varphi \& \psi, w) = V(\varphi, w) \otimes V(\psi, w)$, $V(\sim \varphi, w) = 1 - V(\varphi, w)$, $V(\bar{0}, w) = 0$;
- for each canonical constant $\bar{a}_i$, $i \in \{1, \ldots, n-1\}$, $V(\bar{a}_i, w) = a_i$;
- for each k, $1 \le k \le m$, $V(\Box_k \varphi, w) = \inf \{R_k(w, w') \Rightarrow V(\varphi, w') : w' \in W\}$.

Note that since the algebra of values is finite, we have that this infimum is always a minimum. Therefore, we are sure that we can compute the value of formulas with $\Box_k$. For each operator $\Box_k$, an operator of *possibility* is defined as follows: $\Diamond_k \varphi := \sim \Box_k \sim \varphi$. According with this definition it is easy to see that:

$$V(\Diamond_k \varphi, w) = \sup \{R_k(w, w') \otimes V(\varphi, w') : w' \in W\}.$$

Definition 4 (Validity, the set $\Lambda(\mathsf{K}, \mathbf{L}_n^c)$). *Let $\mathfrak{M} = \langle W, r_1, \ldots, r_m, V \rangle$ be a $\langle \mathbf{L}_n^c, m \rangle$-model. We will say that $w \in W$ satisfies a formula φ in $\mathfrak{M}$ whenever $V(\varphi, w) = 1$; then we write $\mathfrak{M}, w \models^1 \varphi$. And we write $\mathfrak{M} \models^1 \varphi$ whenever $\mathfrak{M}, w \models^1 \varphi$ for every $w \in W$. Then we say that φ is valid in $\mathfrak{M}$. We say that φ is valid in the frame $\mathfrak{F}$ when φ is valid in any Kripke model based on $\mathfrak{F}$. Then we write $\mathfrak{F} \models^1 \varphi$. Given a class K of frames, we write $\mathsf{K} \models^1 \varphi$ to mean that φ is valid in all frames in this class. The set of all the formulas that are valid in all the frames of a class K will be denoted by $\Lambda(\mathsf{K}, \mathbf{L}_n^c)$.[5]*

Definition 5 (The standard translation in the $\mathbf{L}_n^c$-valued framework). *Fix a positive natural number m and let us consider the propositional multi-modal language with constants μ_m. Let $\Phi = \{p_j : j \in J\}$ be a countable set of propositional letters. Let $\mathcal{L}_{\mu_m}(\Phi)$ be the first order language which has a unary predicate P_j for each propositional letter $p_j \in \Phi$, and a binary relation symbol R_k for every necessity operator $\Box_k$ from μ_m. Let x be a first order variable. We define the standard translation τ_x from μ_m-formulas to $\mathcal{L}_{\mu_m}(\Phi)$-formulas as follows:*

$$\begin{aligned}
\tau_x(p_j) &= P_j(x), \text{ for each } j \in J, \\
\tau_x(\varphi \& \psi) &= \tau_x(\varphi) \& \tau_x(\psi), \\
\tau_x(\sim \varphi) &= \sim \tau_x(\varphi), \\
\tau_x(\Box_k \varphi) &= (\forall y)(R_k(x, y) \rightarrow \tau_y(\varphi)), \ 1 \le k \le m, \\
\tau_x(\bar{0}) &= \bar{0}, \\
\tau_x(\bar{a}_i) &= \bar{a}_i, \ 1 \le i \le n-1.
\end{aligned}$$

Proposition 1. *Let $\mathfrak{M} = \langle W, r_1, \ldots, r_m, V \rangle$ be a $\langle \mathbf{L}_n^c, m \rangle$-model. From $\mathfrak{M}$ we define the $\mathcal{L}_{\mu_m}(\Phi)$-interpretation $\mathcal{I}_{\mathfrak{M}} = \langle W, (P_j^{\mathcal{I}_{\mathfrak{M}}})_{j \in J}, R_1^{\mathcal{I}_{\mathfrak{M}}}, \ldots, R_m^{\mathcal{I}_{\mathfrak{M}}} \rangle$, where $P_j^{\mathcal{I}_{\mathfrak{M}}} : W \to L_n$ such that $P_j^{\mathcal{I}_{\mathfrak{M}}}(w) = V(p_j, w)$, and $R_k^{\mathcal{I}_{\mathfrak{M}}} = r_k$. Then:*

1. *For every μ_m-formula φ and $w \in W$, $\|\tau_x(\varphi)(w)\|_{\mathcal{I}_{\mathfrak{M}}} = V(\varphi, w)$.*
2. *For every $w \in W$, $\mathfrak{M}, w \models^1 \varphi$ iff $\|\tau_x(\varphi)(w)\|_{\mathcal{I}_{\mathfrak{M}}} = 1$.*
3. *$\mathfrak{M} \models^1 \varphi$ iff $\|(\forall x)\tau_x(\varphi)\|_{\mathcal{I}_{\mathfrak{M}}} = 1$.*

---

[5] In [14, Section 4.2] finite axiomatizations for $\Lambda(\mathsf{K}, \mathbf{L}_n^c)$ are given when $\mathsf{K} \in \{\mathsf{Fr}, \mathsf{CFr}\}$.

Given a description signature $\mathcal{D}$ with $N_A = \{A_1, A_2, \ldots\}$ as the set of atomic concepts, and $N_R = \{R_1, \ldots, R_m\}$ as the set of atomic roles, the corresponding language $\mathcal{ALC}_{\mathbf{L}_n^c}$ can be seen as a propositional language built from the concept names $A \in N_A$ (seen as propositional letters) using $\boxtimes$ as binary connective, the unary connective $\neg$, a unary connective denoted by $\forall R.$ for every $R \in N_R$, and the constants $\bot, \mathfrak{r}_1, \ldots, \mathfrak{r}_{n-1}$. We have an isomorphism f between the set of $\mathcal{ALC}_{\mathbf{L}_n^c}$-formulas built from the generators $\{A_1, A_2, \ldots\}$ and the set of μ_m-formulas generated by a set of propositional letters $\{p_j : j \in J\}$ with the same cardinality as N_A:

$$f(A_j) = p_j, \text{ for each } j \in J,$$
$$f(C \boxtimes D) = f(C) \& f(D),$$
$$f(\neg C) = \sim f(C),$$
$$f(\forall R_k.C) = \Box_k f(C), \ 1 \le k \le m,$$
$$f(\bot) = \bar{0},$$
$$f(\mathfrak{r}_i) = \bar{a}_i, \ 1 \le i \le n-1.$$

This isomorphism is a preserving translation in the sense stated in the following proposition.

Proposition 2. *Let f be as above and let us consider the first order signature $\mathcal{L}(\mathcal{D}) = \langle (A_j)_{j \in J}, R_1, \ldots, R_m \rangle$ given by the description signature $\mathcal{D} = \langle N_A, N_R \rangle$. Let $\mathcal{I} = \langle W, (A_j^{\mathcal{I}})_{j \in J}, R_1^{\mathcal{I}}, \ldots, R_m^{\mathcal{I}} \rangle$ be an $\mathcal{L}(\mathcal{D})$-interpretation. From $\mathcal{I}$ we define a Kripke $\langle \mathbf{L}_n^c, m \rangle$-model $\mathfrak{M}_{\mathcal{I}} = \langle W, r_1^{\mathfrak{M}_{\mathcal{I}}}, \ldots, r_m^{\mathfrak{M}_{\mathcal{I}}}, V_{\mathfrak{M}_{\mathcal{I}}} \rangle$, where $r_j^{\mathfrak{M}_{\mathcal{I}}} = R_j^{\mathcal{I}}$, and $V_{\mathfrak{M}_{\mathcal{I}}} : \Phi \times W \to L_n$ such that $V_{\mathfrak{M}_{\mathcal{I}}}(p_j, w) = A_j^{\mathcal{I}}(w)$. Then:*

1. *For every concept C and every $w \in W$, $\|C(w)\|_{\mathcal{I}} = V_{\mathfrak{M}_{\mathcal{I}}}(f(C), w)$.*
2. *For every instance $C(x)$ and every $w \in W$, $\|C(w)\|_{\mathcal{I}} = 1$ iff $\mathfrak{M}_{\mathcal{I}}, w \models^1 f(C)$.*
3. *$\|(\forall x) C(x)\|_{\mathcal{I}} = 1$ iff $\mathfrak{M}_{\mathcal{I}}, \models^1 f(C)$.*

5   Reasoning

In this section we define firstly the graded axioms used to define knowledge bases for our n-graded DLs and after the equivalences between the corresponding reasoning tasks. Finally we report the state of the art of the research on the computational complexity of these reasoning tasks.

5.1   Knowledge Bases for $\mathcal{ALC}_{\mathbf{L}_n^c}$

To define knowledge bases (KBs) for the description logics $\mathcal{ALC}_{\mathbf{L}_n^c}$, we need the notion of *evaluated formula*. Given $r \in L_n$, an evaluated formula of the logic $\Lambda(\mathbf{L}_n^c)\forall$ is a formula of one of the forms $\bar{r} \to \varphi$, $\varphi \to \bar{r}$, or $\bar{r} \leftrightarrow \varphi$, where φ does not contain any occurrence of truth constants other than $\bar{0}$ or $\bar{1}$. In our framework, since we are interested in reasoning on partial truth of formulas, it seems reasonable to restrict ourselves to evaluated formulas for representing the knowledge contained in a knowledge base. Having truth constants in the language, we can handle graded inclusion axioms in addition to graded assertion axioms (see [2]), as usually done in FDLs (see [7,15]). Next we define these graded notions.

Let C, D be concepts without occurrences of any truth constant other than $\perp$ or $\top$, R be an atomic role and a, b be constant objects. Finally let $r \in L_n$.

A *graded concept inclusion axiom* is an expression of the form $\langle C \sqsubseteq D, \bar{r} \rangle$, whose corresponding evaluated first order sentence is $\bar{r} \to (\forall x)(C(x) \to D(x))$.

An *graded equivalence axiom* is an expression of the form $\langle C \equiv D, \bar{r} \rangle$, whose corresponding evaluated first order sentence is $\bar{r} \to (\forall x)(C(x) \leftrightarrow D(x))$.

A *graded concept assertion axiom* (or *graded assertion*) is an expression of the form $\langle C(a), \bar{r} \rangle$, whose corresponding evaluated first order sentence is $\bar{r} \to C(a)$.

Finally, *graded role assertion axioms* is an expression of the form $\langle R(a, b), \bar{r} \rangle$. Its corresponding evaluated first order sentence is $\bar{r} \to R(a, b)$.

A *TBox* for a graded DL language is a finite set of graded concept inclusion axioms. An *ABox* is a finite set of graded concept and role assertion axioms. A *knowledge base* (KB) is a pair $\mathcal{K} = \langle \mathcal{T}, \mathcal{A} \rangle$, where the first component is a *TBox* and the second one is an *ABox*.

5.2   Reasoning Tasks in $\mathcal{ALC}_{\mathbf{L}_n^c}$

Among the reasoning tasks that can be defined in a multi-valued framework we can find the usual ones, i.e, KB consistency, concept satisfiability and subsumption with respect to a (possibly empty) KB and entailment of an assertion axiom from a (possibly empty) KB (see [16]). In this framework we can define the following graded notions:

Definition 1 (Satisfiability). *A concept C is* satisfiable *w.r.t. a knowledge base $\mathcal{K}$ in a degree greater or equal than r iff there is an $\mathbf{L}_n^c$-model $\mathbf{M}$ of $\mathcal{K}$, and an individual $a \in M$ such that $\|C(a)\|_{\mathbf{M}} \geq r$. In particular, C is* positively satisfiable *when $r = \frac{1}{n}$ (strictly greater than 0) and* 1-satisfiable *when $r = 1$.*

Definition 2 (Subsumption). *A concept C is* subsumed *by a concept D in a degree greater or equal than r w.r.t. a KB $\mathcal{K}$ iff, for every $\mathbf{L}_n^c$-model $\mathbf{M}$ of $\mathcal{K}$, it holds that $\|(\forall x)(C(x) \to D(x))\|_{\mathbf{M}} \geq r$. In case C is subsumed by D in a degree greater or equal than 1, we will simply say that C is subsumed by D.*

In our language we only need the notions of 1 and positive satisfiability since, thanks to the expressive power given by the presence of the truth constants in the language, all other graded notions can be reduced to them in $\mathcal{ALC}_{\mathbf{L}_n^c}$.

Proposition 1. *Let $\mathcal{K}$ be a (possibly empty) knowledge base, C, D be $\mathcal{ALC}_{\mathbf{L}_n^c}$-concepts and $r \in L_n$, then the following equivalences hold:*

1. *C is satisfiable w.r.t. $\mathcal{K}$ in a degree greater or equal than r iff the concept $\bar{r} \sqsupset C$ is 1-satisfiable w.r.t. $\mathcal{K}$.*
2. *C is subsumed by D w.r.t. $\mathcal{K}$ in a degree greater or equal than r iff concept $\bar{r} \boxtimes C$ is subsumed by D in degree 1.*

3. *A concept C is subsumed in degree 1 by a concept D w.r.t. a knowledge base $\mathcal{K}$ iff $\mathcal{K} \cup \{C \boxtimes \sim D\}$ is not positively satisfiable.*

Notice that this last result is true only for the Łukasiewicz case and it is not achievable in the general framework of (finite) t-norm based FDLs presented in [2,3], where negation is not necessarily involutive.

5.3 Decidability and Complexity Issues

From results in [1] it is easy to prove that concept satisfiability for $\mathcal{ALC}$-like FDLs based on finite t-norms is a decidable problem. The method used in that paper, based on a recursive reduction to propositional satisfiability, can be also used to obtain decidability for the ABox consistency and the concept satisfiability w.r.t. an ABox. Moreover, in [11] it has been proved that concept satisfiability w.r.t. a general TBox for FDLs over finite lattices is EXPTIME-complete. From these results, we can easily obtain the following decidability results and complexity bounds for our finite-valued Łukasiewicz FDLs:

- TBox consistency is EXPTIME-complete.
- Entailment of an assertion from an ABox is decidable.
- Entailment of an inclusion axiom from a TBox is EXPTIME-complete.

Concept satisfiability can be seen as concept satisfiability w.r.t. the empty TBox, thus obtaining EXPTIME upper bound for this problem. Nevertheless, in [17] has been proved that finite-valued Łukasiewicz modal logic is PSPACE-complete and, since this logic can be seen as a notational variant of $\mathcal{ALC}_{\mathbf{Ł}_n^c}$, we obtain PSPACE-completeness of the concept satisfiability problem in $\mathcal{ALC}_{\mathbf{Ł}_n^c}$.

Another remarkable result is the one reported in [18], where a reduction from finitely valued fuzzy $\mathcal{ALCH}$ to classical $\mathcal{ALCH}$ is provided. Since, however, the reduction is not polynomial, it can only be used to obtain decidability of its reasoning tasks, but not to obtain their computational complexity. Finally, let us mention [10] where the authors show how to reason with a fuzzy extension of the description language $\mathcal{SROIQ}$ under finitely valued Łukasiewicz logics. They show that it is decidable by presenting a reasoning preserving procedure to obtain a crisp representation of the logics.

Acknowledgments. The authors acknowledge support of the Spanish MICINN projects MTM2011-25747, ARINF TIN2009-14704-C03-03, TASSAT TIN2010-20967-C04-01, the ESF Eurocores-LogICCC/MICINN project FFI2008-03126-E/FILO, the grants 2009-SGR-1433/1434 from the Generalitat de Catalunya, and the grant JAEPredoc, n.074 of CSIC. The authors also want to thank Carles Noguera for his helpful comments and suggestions.

References

1. Hájek, P.: Making fuzzy description logic more general. Fuzzy Sets and Systems 154(1), 1–15 (2005)

2. García-Cerdaña, À., Armengol, E., Esteva, F.: Fuzzy Description Logics and t-norm based fuzzy logics. International Journal of Approximate Reasoning 51(6), 632–655 (2010)
3. Cerami, M., García-Cerdaña, À., Esteva, F.: From classical description logic to n-graded fuzzy description logic. In: Proceedings of the FUZZ-IEEE 2010. WCCI 2010 IEEE World Congress on Computational Intelligence, pp. 1506–1513 (2010)
4. Baader, F., Calvanese, D., McGuinness, D.L., Nardi, D., Patel-Schneider, P.F. (eds.): The Description Logic Handbook: Theory, Implementation, and Applications. Cambridge University Press, New York (2003)
5. Yen, J.: Generalizing Term Subsumption Languages to Fuzzy Logic. In: Proc. of the 12th IJCAI, Sidney, Australia, pp. 472–477 (1991)
6. Tresp, C.B., Molitor, R.: A Description Logic for Vague Knowledge. Technical Report RWTH-LTCS Report 98-01. Aachen University of Technology (1998)
7. Straccia, U.: Reasoning within Fuzzy Description Logics. Journal of Artificial Intelligence Research 14, 137–166 (2001)
8. Cintula, P., Hájek, P., Noguera, C. (eds.): Handbook of Mathematical Fuzzy Logic. Studies in Logic, vol. 1,2. College Publications, London (2011)
9. Hájek, P.: Metamathematics of Fuzzy Logic. Trends in Logic. Studia Logica Library, vol. 4. Kluwer Academic Publishers, Dordrecht (1998)
10. Bobillo, F., Straccia, U.: Reasoning with the Finitely Many-valued Łukasiewicz Fuzzy Description Logic SROIQ. Information Sciences 181, 758–778 (2011)
11. Borgwardt, S., Peñaloza, R.: Description logics over lattices with multi-valued ontologies. In: Proceedings of the Twenty-Second International Conference on Artificial Intelligence, pp. 768–773 (2011)
12. Cignoli, R., D'Ottaviano, I., Mundici, D.: Algebraic Foundations of Many-Valued Reasoning. Trends in Logic—Studia Logica Library, vol. 7. Kluwer Academic Publishers, Dordrecht (2000)
13. Tuziak, R.: An Axiomatization of the Finite-Valued Łukasiewicz Calculus. Studia Logica 47(1), 49–55 (1988)
14. Bou, F., Esteva, F., Godo, L., Rodríguez, R.: On the Minimum Many-Valued Modal Logic over a Finite Residuated Lattice. Journal of Logic and Computation 21(5), 739–790 (2011)
15. Straccia, U., Bobillo, F.: Mixed Integer Programming, General Concept Inclusions and Fuzzy Description Logics. Mathware and Soft Computing 14(3), 247–259 (2007)
16. Baader, F., Horrocks, I., Sattler, U.: Description logics. In: van Harmelin, F., Lifshitz, V., Porter, B. (eds.) Handbook of Knowledge Representation, pp. 135–179. Elsevier (2008)
17. Bou, F., Cerami, M., Esteva, F.: Finite-valued Łukasiewicz Modal Logic is PSPACE-complete. In: Proceedings of the IJCAI 2011, pp. 774–779 (2011)
18. Bobillo, F., Straccia, U.: Finite fuzzy description logics: A crisp representation for finite fuzzy $\mathcal{ALCH}$. In: Bobillo, F., et al. (eds.) Proceedings of the 6th ISWC Workshop on Uncertainty Reasoning for the Semantic Web (URSW 2010). CEUR Workshop Proceedings, vol. 654, pp. 61–72 (November 2010)

Handling Context in Lexicon-Based Sentiment Analysis

Alejandro Moreo, Juan Luis Castro, and Jose Manuel Zurita

Dept. of Computer Sciences and Artificial Intelligence, University of Granada.
C/Periodista Daniel Saucedo Aranda s/n, E-18071, Granada, Spain
{moreo,castro,zurita}@decsai.ugr.es
http://decsai.ugr.es/

Abstract. Internet has evolved to the Web 2.0 allowing people all around the world to interact with each other and to speak freely about any relevant topic. This kind of user-generated content represents an unstructured knowledge source of undeniable interest in decision-making for both common people and organizations. However, given the high volume of data stored in the Web, performing a manual analysis of this information becomes (practically) impossible. In such a context, Sentiment Analysis aims to automatically summarize opinions expressed in texts providing understandable sentiment reports. However, the computational analysis of opinions is inevitably affected by inherent difficulties presented in natural language. Ambiguity, anaphora, and ellipsis, are examples of context-dependant problems attached to natural language. In this paper, we present a lexicon-based algorithm dealing with sentiment analysis that takes advantage of context analysis to provide sentiment summarization reports.

Keywords: Sentiment Analysis, Lexicon-based, Context-Awareness.

1 Introduction

The Web 2.0 has emerged after the arrival of the digital Era, allowing users from all over the world to interact with each other. Social networks, blogs, forums, or so on, encourage user communities to express their opinion on any relevant topic. As a result, large quantity of unstructured information, known as user-generated content, is continuously appearing. This information is undeniably interesting for both companies and customers decisions. Nonetheless, given the sheer quantity of opinions scattered throughout the Internet, it is very difficult, if not impossible, to manually analyze it all —automatic methods to summarize this information in an understandable manner are desired.

The computational study of opinions, sentiments, and emotions expressed in texts is known as Sentiment Analysis or Opinion Mining [10]. Usually this research area concerns the study of subjectivity, polarity (positive or negative sentiments) and strength (intensity of opinions). Generally, sentiment analysis operates on a document-level, classifying the entire document (overall sentiment). Optionally, another goal is to discover main topics (features) on which

S. Greco et al. (Eds.): IPMU 2012, Part II, CCIS 298, pp. 245–254, 2012.
© Springer-Verlag Berlin Heidelberg 2012

users express their opinions, and even consider their sentiment individually (feature mining or feature-based analysis). In this scenario, discerning what feature is attached to a certain opinion-bearing expression becomes a new challenge (Example 1). Furthermore, natural language (NL) presents several particularities that make its processing very complex. Besides the inherent characteristics of subjective expressions —imprecision, vagueness, and uncertainty—, there are other difficulties such as ambiguity, ellipsis, or anaphora, that should be addressed in order to carry out a feature-based analysis. For example, the feature *price* could be omitted since it is implicit in the expression *expensive* (Example 2). In Example 3, the polarity of the subjective expression *large* depends on the anaphoric expression *it*. Note that its sentiment would be positive if, for example, the opinion referred to a TV size, or negative if it referred to a mobile phone size.

Table 1. Examples of opinion-bearing sentences

	Sentences	Analysis
Example 1	The camera lens is amazing, but its price is quite expensive	Lens:positive Price:negative
Example 2	The camera is quite expensive	Price:negative
Example 3	It is large	TV size:positive OR Mobile phone size:negative

Examples above lead us to think that delimiting context is crucial to support the analysis of sentiment expressed in user comments. We thus propose Context-based Sentiment Analyzer (CSA) in this paper, a sentiment analysis algorithm that relies on a previous context analysis to summarize the sentiment expressed in a set of comments (Figure 1). As shall be seen, lexicon model is modularized, allowing the separate definition of knowledge and its maintenance (lexicon extensions).

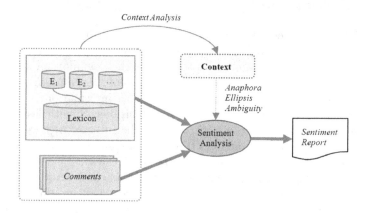

Fig. 1. CSA: Context-based Sentiment Analyzer algorithm

Earlier studies on Sentiment Analysis have focused on the classification of product reviews [5,8]. This research area helps companies to determine user affinity to their products instead of conducting costly market studies or customer satisfaction surveys. Most Sentiment Analysis techniques can be divided into machine-learning approaches and dictionary-based approaches. Even though machine-learning approaches have made significant advances [8,13] in sentiment classification, the compilation of labeled training data sets requires considerable time and effort. Dictionary-based approaches are usually based on lexicons such as MPQA lexicon [14] or SentiWordNet [3], that map words to their semantic value. Although these dictionaries are usually handmade, no further training data is required once they are built. Moreover, automatically expanding initial sets of "seed words" alleviates the cost of constructing the lexicon [4]. However, since most of them rely on WordNet, they are not able to handle technical terms or colloquial expressions, incurring in low accuracy in multi-domain scenarios [2].

The rest of this paper is organized as follows. Section 2 describes the structure of our knowledge model. The analysis of the context is outlined in Section 3. In Section 4 the Sentiment Analysis algorithm is discussed. Finally, Section 5 describes the experimental validation, and Section 6 concludes with a discussion of results and future research.

2   Extensible Knowledge Model: Lexicon

The lexicon represents the linguistic knowledge of the system. It consists of a structured dictionary of concepts along with their linguistic expressions. In this study we focus on defining a hierarchical and extensible model based on relations between entities.

2.1   Lexicon Structure

Lexicon model is structured as a taxonomy of objects and features. An *object* may be a person, an entity, a product, etc. hierarchically related through IS-A relations. The *features* are heritable characteristics of each object. For example, QUALITY and PRICE are some of the features of the PRODUCT object. Note that the object MOBILEPHONE inherits those features from PRODUCT, and may also have particular features such as COVERAGE, OPERATINGSYSTEM, or so on. For simplicity, we use the term *entity* to indistinctly refer both objects or features.

As discussed in [11], maintaining a universal lexicon for all application domains is (practically) impossible. Attempting to exhaustively store all possible expressions that users could employ to name entities would be unrealistic. Instead of trying to collect all sentiment knowledge in a static container, our intention is to define an extendible and modularized model. Only generic objects are defined in the lexicon and domain-dependant ones are defined in the lexicon extensions. Each concrete entity X defined in an extension is accompanied by an "extends Y" directive, indicating that X is a subclass of Y. In this way, the entity ARTIST, and its child node SINGER are defined in the general lexicon, and LAURAPAUSINI —offspring node of SINGER— is defined in a music extension. In order to identify new concrete entities to update the extensions some semiautomatic approaches such as [15] could be helpful. Besides inheriting the expressions associated with the parent object (e.g. *artist* or *singer*), new objective expressions, such as his name, and subjective expressions, such as his nicknames, should also be added.

2.2   Linguistic Expressions

A set of linguistic multi-word expressions (MWE) are also stored in the lexicon. Those MWE could be attached to an object (*mobile phone*) or to a feature of an object (*mobile coverage*). Also, expressions have an associated value $\nu \in [-1, 1]$ indicating its sentiment. Values $\nu > 0$ indicate positive sentiment, while values $\nu < 0$ indicate negative sentiment. Absolute value $|\nu|$ is related to strength of the sentiment. In this way, *subjective expressions* are associated to non-zero values while *objective expressions* (not expressing any opinion) are associated to zero values. Note also that subjective expressions could be attached to some object (or feature) indicating a valuation on that implicit object (*jalopy* referring to PRODUCT). Furthermore, child nodes inherit the expressions of their antecedent node, so that if *politician* is an expression for the object POLITICIAN, it is also an expression for its child node PRESIDENT. These set of expressions could be enhanced semiautomatically by using some techniques such as [7] to detect new objective expressions, or [9] to detect new subjective expressions. As shall be seen, MWE are used in a shallow parsing perspective in order to capture the sentiment of users' sentences and the entities references in the context.

Usually, sentiment values are manually specified by experts. However, to alleviate this task and expand a vaster language, several researches have been proposed. Since contextual valence shifters (e.g. negators, adverb intensifiers, etc.) play a key role in the improvement of the representation of subjective expressions [1], they have been incorporated in our model. Table 2 briefly shows some examples of how linguistic patterns display a larger language.

Table 2. Modifiers and linguistic rules

Modifier	Examples	Modification
VERY	*very, absolutely, extremely, ...*	$+\sqrt{\nu}$ iff $\nu \geq 0$ $-\sqrt{|\nu|}$ in other case
LESS	*a little bit, relatively, not quite, ...*	$+\nu^2$ iff $\nu \geq 0$ $-\nu^2$ in other case
NEG	*not, nothing, not at all, ...*	0 iff $|\nu| \geq 0.5^a$ $-\nu$ in other case
...	...	...

---

[a] For example *it is not perfect...* In this case it seems to be a subjective expression. However, since its polarity is not clear, considering neutral sentiment $\nu = 0$ is recommended.

3   Handling Context

As discussed below, NL presents several characteristics that difficult its processing. In this study, we plan to keep track of the context of comments in order to determine which entities are the object of valuations. Thus, context is defined here as the set of objects and features to which opinions are being expressed, and will be noted as C. This context helps to disambiguate the interpretation of subjective expressions (such as *large* in Example 3). Ellipsis and anaphora should be analyzed by searching the referenced antecedent. Inspecting previously referenced entities and taking advantage of the implicit hierarchical knowledge of the lexicon, several ambiguities could also be resolved.

In this section we first discuss the procedure to delimit C. Later, how C complements information in the lexicon to resolve ambiguities will be explained.

3.1   Delimiting the Context

The interpreting context C is initialized with every possible referenced entity in the document. However, since (i) multi-word expressions could be attached to several entities in the lexicon (*animal* could be an objective expression or a subjective expression referring to a "brutal person"), and (ii) hierarchical relations imply the propagation of expressions in a certain node to all its child nodes (hyponyms), C is likely to be too broad. In order to delimit the context we simultaneously conduct a two-fold filter: Frequency analysis (document-level), and Disambiguation analysis (comment-level), until there are no more changes to be made in C.

Frequency Analysis relies on the assumption that rarely referenced entities should not be taken into account to compute the global sentiment analysis summary. Low referenced entities could be caused by noisy linguistic interferences in the matching process of linguistic expressions. Furthermore, low referenced entities could be involved in user comments containing punctual arguments or exemplifications that actually lend support to an opinion on the main topics (for example named entity CAR in comment *It is shameful that even in crisis politicians have those private cars!*, concerning *Budget Deficit* issue). In any case, it does not make much sense to consider those entities in the final sentiment summary. Thus, those named entities e whose frequency of appearance in the document do not exceed a threshold are removed from the context (Equation 1).

$$C := C - \{e \in C : frec(e) \leqslant \gamma\} \tag{1}$$

In [12] it is suggested that frequency-based methods fail while selecting relevant terms for feature mining. However, our heuristic does not contradict this research since it is combined with a disambiguation analysis heuristic that modifies the frequency of candidate features in context.

Disambiguation Analysis uses the implicit knowledge contained in the hierarchical structure of the lexicon to tackle with the named entities co-reference. For example, consider that the only named entities in a comment are the followings: PRODUCT, MOBILEPHONE, and IPHONE. Since they are hierarchically related in the lexicon, this analysis replaces PRODUCT and MOBILEPHONE references with IPHONE label, because they are probably a co-reference (hypernym) of IPHONE. Note that if other particular mobile phone were also referenced, then this heuristic could only replace PRODUCT with MOBILEPHONE since it is the only valid co-reference to all other related entities. It should be pointed out that, since replacing references modifies their frequency, it is possible for the Frequency analysis to discard new named entities.

More formally, assuming the set of all named entities in the comment to be C_l, then the disambiguation analysis replaces a named entity e with its hyponym e' if e is in the set defined by Equation 2, where $desc(x)$ denotes the set of all the descending focuses of x in the lexicon hierarchy.

$$\{e \in C_l \mid \exists e' \in (desc(e) \cap C_l) : (desc(e) \cap C_l - \{e'\}) \subseteq desc(e')\} \qquad (2)$$

Figure 2 may serve to clarify the explanation above. Note that this heuristic deals with the ambiguity problem since it helps to precise references to hypernyms terms.

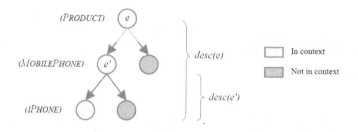

Fig. 2. Disambiguation heuristic

4   Sentiment Summary Report

After resolving possible ambiguities and discarding noisy references, the context is considered to be established. In this section we discuss how the context model supports the sentiment analysis in an attempt to solve some ellipsis and anaphora problems.

An anaphoric expression is an expressions referring to another one that is replaced by a deictic form. Ellipsis could be understood as a type of anaphora where the referred expression is not replaced but omitted. Anaphora resolution is a context-dependant task that implies the identification of the antecedent. On this study, we assume that each subjective expression evaluates certain object or feature that is already contained in the lexicon. Thus, we address the anaphora resolution problem by identifying previously mentioned entities in the discourse.

Firstly, comments and linguistic expressions in the lexicon are preprocessed by applying well-known techniques in natural language processing including word normalization and stemming to gain in generality. Later, a splitter is applied to separate sentences of the comments.

In the first step, named entities and subjective expressions are identified in each sentence. As commented in Section 2.2, every expression in the lexicon has a sentiment value and is optionally attached to an entity. In this case, only expressions attached to entities in their comment-context C_l are kept.

In the second step, all sentences containing subjective expressions that do not contain any named or implicit entity are identified as anaphoric sentences. Last referred entity (if any) in previous sentences is considered the antecedent and is linked to each subjective expression in the sentence. Note that the antecedent could appear in the previous comment. Only the three previous sentences are considered in the search.

Subjective expressions not attached to any entity are considered free-valuations. In the third step, these expressions are linked to the nearest referred entity in the sentence. After that, the sentiment of entities in each C_l is calculated as the average sentiment of linked valuations. Entities in C_l along with their sentiment average are considered the sentiment summary of that comment.

Finally, the overall sentiment summary report is generated (Figure 3). Entities in the context C represent the main discussion topics in the entire document. Each one is accompanied by (i) a linguistic label indicating its average sentiment score and (ii) a reliability measurement indicating the proportion of comments containing references to that entity on its C_l. Furthermore, not only the average sentiment is reported, but also the partial sentiments given to each entity. This allows the study of polarity distributions in the users' opinion.

```
Headline: "Alonso signs with Ferrari"
Overall Sentiment: POSITIVE (reliability=76.8%)
            VERY_POSITIVE: 57%
            POSITIVE:24%
            NEUTRAL:4%
            NEGATIVE:15%
            VERY_NEGATIVE:0%
FERRARI: VERY_POSITIVE (reliability=74.23%)
            VERY_POSITIVE:59%
            POSITIVE: 23%
            NEUTRAL: 12%
                    ...
```

Fig. 3. Fragment of sentiment report

5   Evaluation Performance

We have implemented[1] and contrasted the efficiency of CSA with: (i) Feature-Based Summarization [5], that performs feature mining and overall mining analyses by exploiting synonymy and antonymy relations in WordNet, and (ii) Pointwise Mutual Information-Information Retrieval (PMI-IR) [13], that is one of the most widely used algorithms in the literature to calculate the polarity of texts.

The experiments were performed on a set of 500 current news items randomly selected from *20 Minutos*[2]. These comments were read and manually labeled by 10 student volunteers. For each news item, students were requested to reflect the polarity of the entire document and the main discussion topics involved (a maximum of 5 topics) along with the estimation of their particular sentiment.

To construct the lexicon, 100 news items (different from testing ones) containing at least 50 comments were manually annotated by experts. Most recurrent discussion topics and a long variety of linguistic expressions were collected. As a result, various lexicon extensions including sports, politics, economy, society, and entertainment were created containing a total of about 2500 expressions. Approximately the same proportion of news items was involved in the creation of each lexicon extension.

We evaluated the overall sentiment analysis by means of Accuracy (Equation 3) and the featured-based analysis by means of F-measure metric (Equation 6). Accuracy considers the proportion of correctly classified news based on their polarity labeled while F-measure represents the weighted harmonic mean of Precision (Equation 4) and Recall (Equation 5).

$$Acc = \frac{\#\{successfully\ labeled\ news\}}{\#\{news\}} \tag{3}$$

$$Precision = \frac{\#(\{labeled\ focuses\} \cap \{retrieved\ focuses\})}{\#\{retrieved\ focuses\}} \tag{4}$$

$$Recall = \frac{\#(\{labeled\ focuses\} \cap \{retrieved\ focuses\})}{\#\{labeled\ focuses\}} \tag{5}$$

$$F - measure = 2 \cdot \frac{Precision \cdot Recall}{Precision + Recall} \tag{6}$$

Table 3 shows results in overall sentiment analysis experiment in comparison to PMI-IR and FBS algorithms. Global standard deviation in terms of Accuracy is 0.33 for CSA, 0.39 for PMI, and 0.43 for FBS. Table 4 shows the results in feature-based sentiment analysis compared to FBS algorithm. Global standard deviation in terms of F-measure is 0.23 for CSA, and 0.18 for FBS.

---

[1] We have implemented our method in Java HotSpotTM 1:6:0_11; Client VM 11.0-b16. We have used the GPL Library FreeLing 2.2 (http://nlp.lsi.upc.edu/freeling/) to implement the preprocessing, and XML notation to define the lexicon. An Intel(R) Core(TM)2 Quad Q8200 2.33GHz with 6GBytes RAM was used to carry out the tests.

[2] www.20minutos.es

Table 3. Overall Sentiment Analysis results

	News					
	Sports	Politics	Economy	Society	Entert.	Total
CSA	.65	.91	.98	.95	.92	.86
PMI	.43	.99	.98	.92	.88	.81
FBS	.54	.51	.77	.76	.64	.64

Table 4. Feature-based Sentiment Analysis results

	News																	
	Sports			Politics			Economy			Society			Entert.			Total		
	P	R	F_1	P	R	F_1	P	R	F_1	P	R	F_1	P	R	F_1	P	R	F_1
CSA	.85	.67	.75	.81	.59	.68	.93	.53	.68	.88	.53	.66	.90	.56	.69	.84	.58	.69
FBS	.61	.33	.75	.59	.38	.46	.63	.42	.50	.56	.35	.43	.76	.37	.50	.62	.36	.45

Results indicate that handling context contributes to a better performance in the analysis of sentiments expressed in user comments. Although constructing a lexicon is much more tedious than expanding initial sets of words through Word-Net, it seems that handling multi-word expressions and exploiting hierarchical relations between entities in the lexicon leads to a better performance. Furthermore, we have realized that in this kind of user-generated content, there are a plenty of colloquial subjective expressions that contain non-standard words.

In view of the results, it should be underlined that keeping track of context was a better approach even to the overall sentiment problem than performing a global calculation as PMI-IR does.

6 Conclusions and Future Works

In this paper, a Context-based Sentiment Analyzer (CSA) algorithm dealing with the summarization of sentiments expressed in texts is proposed. NL presents several particularities that difficult automatic processes to extract the sentiment of opinions. In this work we study how handling context could help to address the anaphora, ellipsis, and ambiguity problems.

One of the goals of this study was to provide a well-structured knowledge model to support the analysis. Our lexicon is structured as a hierarchy of objects and features, and it is based on multi-word expressions. It contains two types of knowledge sources: generic entities and domain extensions. Since knowledge is modularized, it can be easily maintained just by adding or modifying some of their objects, features, or hierarchical relations.

Furthermore, hierarchical structure of the lexicon provides implicit information that can be useful to resolve certain ambiguities. We take advantage of frequency analysis and semantic information in the lexicon to keep track of context. Handling context allows us to address the antecedent resolution in the anaphora problem. As a result, feature-based sentiment analysis is more reliable.

Some authors propose methods to detect and filter inappropriate comments [6]. In future researches, we plan to incorporate context information to the Opinion Spam Detection problem in order to identify noisy comments, such as advertising ones, by checking their consistency with main discussion topics. We also plan to improve our sentiment analysis module by incorporating a more fine-grained context analysis. That may allow us to achieve a more reliable sentiment analyzer in complex sentences including various named entities and various opinion-wearing expressions.

References

1. Choi, Y., Cardie, C.: Learning with compositional semantics as structural inference for subsentential sentiment analysis. In: Proceedings of the Conference on Empirical Methods in Natural Language Processing (EMNLP 2008), Stroudsburg, PA, USA, pp. 793–801 (2008)
2. Denecke, K.: Are sentiwordnet scores suited for multi-domain sentiment classification? In: International Conference on Digital Information Management (2009)
3. Esuli, A., Sebastiani, F.: Sentiwordnet: A publicly available lexical resource for opinion mining. In: Proceedings of the 5th Conference on Language Resources and Evaluation (LREC), Genova, Italy (2006)
4. Hatzivassiloglou, V., McKeown, K.R.: Predicting the semantic orientation of adjectives. In: Proceedings of 35th Meeting of the Association for Computational Linguistics, Madrid, Spain, pp. 174–181 (1997)
5. Hu, M., Liu, B.: Mining and summarizing customer reviews. In: Proceedings of the Tenth ACM SIGKDD International Conference on Knowledge Discovery and Data Mining, USA, Seattle, WA (August 2004)
6. Jindal, N., Liu, B.: Opinion spam and analysis. In: Proceedings of the Conference on Web Search and Web Data Mining (WSDM), Stanford, CA, pp. 219–230 (2008)
7. Lloyd, L., Mehler, A., Skiena, S.S.: Identifying Co-referential Names Across Large Corpora. In: Lewenstein, M., Valiente, G. (eds.) CPM 2006. LNCS, vol. 4009, pp. 12–23. Springer, Heidelberg (2006)
8. Mullen, T., Collier, N.: Sentiment analysis using support vector machines with diverse information sources. In: Proceedings of EMNLP, pp. 412–418 (2004)
9. Neviarouskaya, A., Prendinger, H., Ishizuka, M.: Sentiful: A lexicon for sentiment analysis. IEEE Transactions on Affective Computing 2(1), 22–36 (2011)
10. Pang, B., Lee, L.: Opinion mining and sentiment analysis. Foundations and Trends in Information Retrieval 2(1), 1–135 (2008)
11. Qiu, G., Liu, B., Bu, J., Chen, C.: Expanding domain sentiment lexicon through double propagation. In: Proceedings of the 21st International Joint Conferences on Artificial Intelligence, Pasadena, California, pp. 1199–1204 (2009)
12. Rafrafi, A., Gigue, V., Gallinari, P.: Pénalisation des mots fréquents pour la classification de sentiments. Les Cahiers du numérique 7(2), 1622–1494 (2011)
13. Turney, P.D.: Thumbs up or thumbs down?: semantic orientation applied to unsupervised classification of reviews. In: Proceedings of the 40th Annual Meeting on Association for Computational Linguistics, Philadelphia, Pennsylvania (July 2002)
14. Wilson, T., Wiebe, J., Hoffmann, P.: Recognizing contextual polarity in phrase-level sentiment analysis. In: Proceedings of the LT-EMNLP (2005)
15. Yi, J., Nasukawa, T., Bunescu, R., Niblack, W.: Sentiment analyzer: Extracting sentiments about a given topic using natural language processing techniques. In: Proceedings of the Third IEEE International Conference on Data Mining (November 2003)

Possibilistic Rules from Fuzzy Prototypes

Guanyi Li* and Jonathan Lawry

Intelligent System Lab
Department of Engineering Mathematics
University of Bristol
Bristol, UK
peerincle@gmail.com, J.Lawry@bristol.ac.uk

Abstract. A new interpretation of description labels in fuzzy rules is introduced based on the idea of fuzzy prototypes. For each label L_i in a description set we identify a fuzzy prototype resulting in a possibility distribution quantifying the possibility that L_i is the most appropriate label to describe a given input value. A rule induction algorithm is then proposed for learning *Takagi-Sugeno* style rules from data, within this label representation framework. Given an appropriate inference and defuzzification method we then demonstrate the potential of this approach by its application to a number of benchmark regression problems.

Keywords: Fuzzy prototype, label semantics, possibility measure, rule based learning.

1 Introduction

Using words to convey vague information as part of uncertain reasoning is a sophisticated human activity. Computing with words, based on fuzzy set theory, attempts to formally capture this human reasoning process. Furthermore, from the philosophical viewpoint of epistemic stance, Lawry proposed a functional calculus, label semantics, for computing with words [6,7,8,9]. In this framework, the subjective probabilities that a given set of labels is appropriate to describe a given instance are represented by mass functions, which encode the meaning of linguistic labels. Recently, Lawry and Tang [11,12] have developed the relationship between prototype theory for vague concepts and the label semantics framework. In this work, the meaning of linguistic labels can also be captured by the similarity between the underlying instances and the prototypes for linguistic labels.

Prototype theory has been proposed by Rosch as an alternative model of concepts in natural language. The fundamental idea is that concepts, instead of being defined by formal rules or mappings, are represented by a set of prototypical cases [10]. Prototypes may not simply correspond to actual perceptions of objects or experiences but instead particular points or a region of conceptual space may be identified [11]. In general prototype are subsets of conceptual space and proximity to this set quantifies the applicability of the concept in a particular case.

---

* Corresponding author.

S. Greco et al. (Eds.): IPMU 2012, Part II, CCIS 298, pp. 255–264, 2012.
© Springer-Verlag Berlin Heidelberg 2012

Given the empirical manner in which the use of concept labels is learnt in natural language, it is natural that a prototype model should allow for some level of uncertainty associated with the prototypes themselves. This semantic uncertainty can be partly modeled by defining prototypes as fuzzy subsets of the underlying conceptual space. Here we are adopting a random set interpretation of fuzzy sets allowing for us to represent the semantic uncertainty about prototype definitions in terms of a probability distribution over different possible set-values.

This paper introduces an extension of the label semantics framework so that it can incorporate fuzzy prototypes. This extended theory is then used as a representational framework for linguistic rules defined in terms of fuzzy labels. The underlying inference process is possibilistic, resulting in a possibility distribution on the output space for a given input. We propose a simple rule learning algorithm within this framework and demonstrate, its potential on a number of benchmark regression problems.

The outline of this paper is as follows. Section 2 introduces possibilistic rules generated from labels with fuzzy prototypes. Then Section 3 describes some experimental results obtained by applying the rule-based fuzzy prototype learning algorithm to benchmark data problems. Finally, we give some conclusion and discuss future work in Section 4.

2   Possibilistic Rules for Fuzzy Prototypes

In this section we outline how description labels can be defined in terms of prototypes corresponding to subsets of an underlying conceptual space. We then generalize this to the case where prototypes are bounded fuzzy sets [20]. This is related to the framework proposed by Lawry and Tang [18] except that in this case the uncertainty is regarding the prototypes themselves rather than a threshold distance from the prototype defining the region of space in which the given label can be appropriately applied.

In the following sub-section we first outline how description labels can be defined in terms of fuzzy prototypes. Then a new rule based learning method will be introduced in Section 2.2.

2.1   Fuzzy Prototype Based Semantic Labels

In our model, prototypes are defined as bounded subsets of an underlying conceptual space $\Omega = \mathbb{R}^k$ denoted by $p_i \subseteq \Omega$. A set of labels $LA = \{L_1, L_2, ..., L_m\}$ are then defined by prototypes $P = \{p_1, p_2, ..., p_m\}$.

In order to measure the appropriateness of label L_i to describe an element x, we need to define a distance measure between a prototype and a concept. The following are two well known lower and upper distance metrics for quantifying the distance between an element and a set, as follows:

$$d_{max}(x, p_i) = \sup\{d(x, y) : y \in p_i\}$$
$$d_{min}(x, p_i) = \inf\{d(x, y) : y \in p_i\}$$

Given two labels L_i and L_j we may want to determine which is most appropriate to describe an element x. Based on these two distance measures, we define the following relation between labels representing their possible relative appropriateness:

Definition 1 (Appropriateness Relation). *Given two labels L_i and L_j describing Ω. We say that label L_i is possibly more appropriate to describe an instance x than L_j if and only if :*

$$d_{min}(x, p_i) \leq d_{max}(x, p_j)$$

Based on this appropriateness relation between two labels, we can introduce a boolean possibility for a label being the most appropriate description for x, as follows:

Definition 2 (Boolean Possibility). *L_i is possibly the most appropriate description for instance x if and only if $\forall j \neq i$, $d_{min}(x, p_i) \leq d_{max}(x, p_j)$. Its boolean possibility is then given by:*

$$\Pi_{L_i}(x) = \begin{cases} 1 : & d_{min}(x, p_i) \leq d_{max}(x, p_j), \forall j \neq i \\ 0 : & otherwise \end{cases}$$

Notice, that there may be several labels where $\Pi_{L_i}(x) = 1$. This is due to the fact that in some cases L_i may be possibly more appropriate than L_j while L_j may also be possibly more appropriate than L_i according to the relation given in Definition 1. In the case that we have fuzzy prototypes for labels then definition 2 naturally generalises to a graded possibility distribution. First we give the definition of fuzzy prototype as follows:

Definition 3 (Fuzzy prototype). *A bounded fuzzy set [20] $\tilde{p}_i$ in $\mathbb{R}^n$ is characterized by a membership function $\tilde{p}_i(x)$ which associates with each point in $\mathbb{R}^n$ a real number in the interval [0, 1], with the value of $\tilde{p}_i(x)$ at x representing the grade of membership of x in $\tilde{p}_i$.*

Hence, based on definition 3, we give the possibility distribution that label L_i is the most appropriate to describe x as follows:

Definition 4 (Possibility Distribution). *Given a set of fuzzy prototypes $P = \{\tilde{p}_1, \tilde{p}_2, ..., \tilde{p}_m\}$ of labels $LA = \{L_1, L_2, .., L_m\}$. Then the possibility distribution value that L_i is the most appropriate label to describe x is given by:*

$$\Pi_{L_i}(x) = sup\{\alpha : d_{min}(x, (\tilde{p}_i)_\alpha) \leq d_{max}(x, (\tilde{p}_j)_\alpha), \forall j \neq i\}$$

where $(\tilde{p}_i)_\alpha$ is the $\alpha - cut$:

$$(\tilde{p}_i)_\alpha = \{x : \tilde{p}_i(x) \geq \alpha, x \in \mathbb{R}^n\}$$

2.2   Rule Based Learning Algorithm for Fuzzy Prototypes

Suppose we have an underlying functional mapping $f : \mathbb{R}^n \to \mathbb{R}$, where $X = (x_1, x_2, ..., x_n)$ is the input and y is the output i.e $y = f(X)$. Given a set of training data of the form $DB = \{(x_1^j, x_2^j, .., x_n^j, y^j) : j = 1, .., N\}$, we now consider how to use linguistic rules learnt from DB in order to approximate the functional mapping $y = f(X)$. In the following we proposed a simple rule induction method based on a weighted linear programming algorithm.

According to the proposed fuzzy prototype model of labels, it is natural to define the following Takagi-Sugeno style IF-THEN rules [16] from the training data set DB :

$$\text{IF } X \text{ is } L_i \text{ THEN } y = f_i(X)$$

where L_i is a label from label set $LA = \{L_1, ..., L_m\}$ defined on the input space and $f_i : \mathbb{R}^n \to \mathbb{R}$ is a linear function.

In general, the value m should not be too hight in such a case that computational costs are high for infering this rule set. Also, a large number of rules may result in over-fitting of the training data and consequently poor generalization.

The basic idea of our rule learning algorithm is to firstly partition DB using a standard clustering algorithm, and then to fit linear functions based on the clustering result and weighted according to the possibilistic model outlined in the previous section.

It is clear that the resulting rules depend on the partitioning of the training data set DB. Different partitioning results in different clusters and therefore a different linguistic rule-base. Here, we use the k-means clustering algorithm to partition the dataset into a set of clusters with centroids $\{c_i\}$. We then define a set of fuzzy prototypes as follows:

$$\tilde{p}_i(x) = \begin{cases} \frac{r_i - d(x, c_i)}{r_i} & d(x, c_i) \leq r_i \\ 0 & otherwise \end{cases}$$

where r_i is

$$r_i = \frac{min(d(c_i, c_j))}{\tau}, \forall j \neq i$$

The threshold $\tau \in (0, +\infty)$ regulates the degree to which each fuzzy prototype overlaps with its neighbours. In the sequel we have set $\tau \in [1, 4]$ as a compromise between over fitting and over generalisation. In order to determine linear functions for each label L_i, we identify the subset of the database $S_i = \{(X^j, y^j) : \Pi_{L_i}(X^j) > 0\}$. Each linear function can be described by:

$$f_i(X) = a_0 + \sum_{j=1}^{n} a_j \times x_j$$

where n is the number of dimensions of the input space.

In order to determine the coefficients $a_0, a_1, ..., a_n$, we applied a weighted least squared regression algorithm to minimize the following objective function

$$O = \sum_{X_j \in S_i} \Pi_{L_i}(X_j) \times (y^j - f_i(X_j))^2$$

This can be done by constraining the gradient so that $\frac{\partial O}{\partial A} = 0$ and $B \times A = C$ where:

$$B = \begin{pmatrix} \sum_{X_j \in S_i} \Pi_{L_i}(X_j) & \sum_{X_j \in S_i} \Pi_{L_i}(X_j)x_1^j & \cdots & \sum_{X_j \in S_i} \Pi_{L_i}(X_j)x_n^j \\ \sum_{X_j \in S_i} \Pi_{L_i}(X_j)x_1^j & \sum_{X_j \in S_i} \Pi_{L_i}(X_j)x_1^j x_1^j & \cdots & \sum_{X_j \in S_i} \Pi_{L_i}(X_j))x_1^j x_n^j \\ \vdots & \vdots & \ddots & \vdots \\ \sum_{X_j \in S_i} \Pi_{L_i}(X_j))x_n^j & \sum_{X_j \in S_i} \Pi_{L_i}(X_j)x_n^j x_1^j & \cdots & \sum_{X_j \in S_i} \Pi_{L_i}(X_j)x_n^j x_n^j \end{pmatrix}$$

$$A = \begin{pmatrix} a_0 & a_1 & \cdots & a_n \end{pmatrix}$$

$$C = \begin{pmatrix} \sum_{X_j \in S_{L_i}} \Pi_{L_i}(X_j)y^j & \sum_{X_j \in S_{L_i}} \Pi_{L_i}(X_j)x_1^j y^j & \cdots & \sum_{X_j \in S_{L_i}} \Pi_{L_i}(X_j)x_n^j y^j \end{pmatrix}^T$$

Using a well known weighted least square optimizing method [14] we can then obtain the linear function $y = f_i(X)$. Given our rule base we now consider how to estimate an output value $\hat{y}$ from a particular input value X. The algorithm generates a mass function on sets of labels. To connect this to a probability requires a possibility-probability transfer. Here we adopt the well known pignistic transform as proposed by Smiths. Justification for his approach can be found in [3].

Here we apply the pignistic possibility-probability transform to determine $P(L_i|X)$ from $\Pi_{L_i}(X)$ for $i = 1, 2, .., m$. The approximate value of the output is then given by:

$$\hat{y} = \sum_{\{\tilde{p}_i : \Pi_{L_i}(X) > 0\}} P(L_i|X) \times f_i(X)$$

3   Experimental Results

In this section, we present experimental results for a number of benchmark datasets to demonstrate the performance of our algorithms. Overall results on various regression problems show both good accuracy and transparency. An outline of this section is as follows. Section 3.1 gives a brief description of the different datasets used in our experiments. Section 3.2 then shows the test results of these datasets. Finally, the Sunspot prediction problem will be discussed in detail in section 3.3.

3.1   Data Set Distribution

In this section we give a brief description of the datasets we have used in our experiments.

Abalone and Boston Housing problem

These two datasets are taken from the UCI repository [1]. The Abalone database concerns the problem of predicting the age of Abalone from physical measurements. Abalones are a type of shellfish, the age of which can be accurately determined by cutting the shell through the cone, staining it, and counting the number of rings through a microscope, which is a laborious and time consuming task. Boston Housing problem contains data on housing values in the suburbs of Boston, USA. The data set contains 506 instances and 13 continuous attributes (including the target attribute) and one binary attribute.

   To test our prediction methods the Abalone data set of 4,177 examples was randomly split into a test set of 2,089 instances and a training set of 2,088 instances while for the Boston Housing problem we split the 506 examples into 253 training examples and 253 for testing at random. In each case we repeated the experiment 10 times with random splits of the data, so as to obtain information not just on the predictive accuracy but also the stability of the methods. The learning parameters were then set-up as follows: for Abalone, we set $\tau = 2.1$ and number of fuzzy prototypes $m = 9$ and for Boston Housing, we set $\tau = 2.1$ and $m = 12$.

Mackey-Glass

Mackey-Glass is a time series generated from the following time delay differential equation:

$$\dot{x}(t) = \frac{0.2x\,(t - \rho)}{1 + x^{10}\,(t - \rho)} - 0.1x(t)$$

This time series is chaotic, and so there is no clearly defined period. The series will not converge or diverge, and the trajectory is highly sensitive to initial conditions. This is a benchmark problem in the neural network and fuzzy modelling research communities [17,5,15].

   The data consisted of time series values at integer points, obtained by applying the fourth-order Runge-Kutta method in order to find the numerical solution to the above MG equation. Here we assumed that $x(0) = 1.2$, $\rho = 17$, and $x(t) = 0$ for $t < 0$.

   In this time series prediction the objective is to use known values of the time series up to the point in time t, in order to predict the future time point $t + 6$. For each t, the input training data for the model is a four dimensional vector of the form, $X(t) = \langle x(t - 18), x(t - 12), x(t - 6), x(t) \rangle$. The output training data corresponds to the trajectory prediction, $y(t) = x(t + 6)$. With t ranging from 118 to 1117, we obtain 1000 input/output data values. We use the first 500 data values for the training dataset DB, while the remaining values are used as test data. Here we set τ as 2.5 and the fuzzy prototype number is 55.

Sunspot prediction

This problem is taken from the Time Series Data Library [4]. Sunspots, which are often considerably larger than the earth, were first discovered in about 1610 shortly after the invention of the telescope, and have an average life time of about 11 years, although this can vary between 7 and 15 years. Sunspots numbers have been recorded since 1700 but no method has been found to accurately predict or determine when or why these events occur. It is known however, that Sunspot numbers are related to solar activity such as the magnetic field of the sun changing, which occurs about every 22 years. In this experiment we use Sunspot relative numbers between the years 1700 and 1979 which was organized as described in [13].We use 209 examples (1712-1920) as the training data, and 59 examples (1921-1979) as the test data. The input attributes were x_{t-12} to x_{t-1} and the output attribute was x_t (i.e. one-year-ahead). For sunspot prediction problem, we set $\tau = 1.8$ and prototype number is 13.

3.2   Summary of Results

In this section we present some experimental results for the Abalone , Boston housing, Mackey-Glass and Sunspot regression problems. We use Root Mean Squared Error (RMSE) to compare our algorithm with other learning algorithms. **Table 1.** presents the results of experiments by testing Boston Housing, Abalone, Macky-Glass and Sunspot Prediction problems.

Table 1. Comparison of results for different learning algorithms from the Boston Housing, Abalone, Mackey-Glass and Sunspot prediction problems

Learning algorithms	Boston Housing	Abalone	Macky-Glass	Sunspot
Regression Tree	4.6153	2.8889	0.0285	29.9144
Back. Pro. NN	4.3020	2.1765	0.02	32.0341
ϵ-SVR system	3.9260	2.1360	0.0979	20.4481
Fuzzy prototype rules	3.8194	2.1238	0.0032	14.9176

From Table 1 we can see that our algorithm has very good performance. Indeed it compares well with three other well known regression algorithm: these are ϵ-Support Vector Regression system (ϵ-SVR) [19], implemented in the Matlab Support Vector Machine Toolkit (Version 3.1) [2], Back Propagation Neural Network (Matlab Neural Network Toolbox) and the Matlab implemented regression tree.

3.3   Result of Sunspot Prediction

In this section we show more detailed results concerning the sunspot prediction problem. In particular, we will investigate how performance changes as τ and m vary.

Initially we set the $\tau = 2.5$ then vary the prototype number m from 1 to 20. Different initializations of k-$means$ can potentially result in different clusters so in order to reduce the effect of this we computed the results for 10 different runs of k-$means$ for both training and testing data. We then calculated the average RMSE across all of them. Secondly we set the prototype number to 10. Then, by varying τ between 0.2 to 6 and using a similar method we investigated the sensitivity of our results to these parameters. Fig. 1 shows that the optimal prototype number $m = 7$ with $\tau = 2.5$ and $\tau = 1.8$ with 10 prototypes.

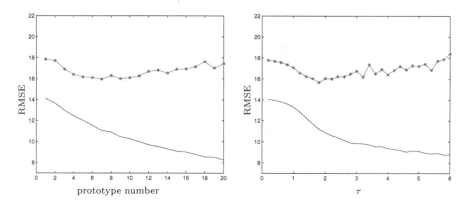

Fig. 1. RMSE against the prototype number m (left-hand figure) and RMSE against threshold τ (right-hand figure) for the Sunspot problem. The dotted line represents the result on test data and the solid line is result for the training data

Based on the experiments, we can see that with more prototypes the algorithm begins to over-fit test data resulting in diminished performance. Threshold τ determines the overlap size of a fuzzy prototype with its neighbours. In such a way that the overlap decreases as τ increases.

In order to avoid the over-fitting, we have adopted the heuristic that the number of prototypes should be approximately the same as the dimension of the input space i.e $m \approx n$. Similarity, setting τ to be close to 2 seems to provide a good level of overlap between a prototype and its neighbours.

For the final version of our algorithm, best performance was obtained with $\tau = 1.8$ and 13 prototypes. Using these parameters, we obtain a RMSE of 14.9176 on the test set, with only 13 linear rules. We plot the actual and predicted output for the training and the test sets as time series in Fig. 2. Then Fig. 3 shows the results as scatter plots of actual against predicted values.

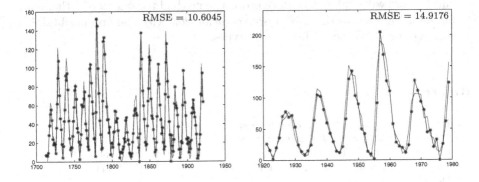

Fig. 2. Sunspots prediction result of the training data (left-hand figure) and on the test (right-hand figure) data with 13 rules: solid line is the actual output, dotted line is the predicted output.

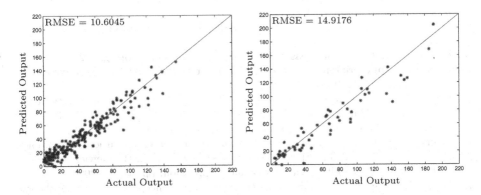

Fig. 3. Scatter plot showing the actual output vs. the predicted output of Sunspots training (left-hand figure) and test (right-hand figure) data with 13 rules.

4 Conclusion

In this paper we have introduce a new interpretation of fuzzy labels based on fuzzy prototypes. Within this representational framework we have proposed an algorithm for learning *Takagi-Sugeno* style IF-THEN rules for regression problems. We have then tested this new rule induction algorithm on a number of benchmark problems and compared its performance with that of a several well-know regression algorithms. Due to the transparency of the IF-THEN rules and the possibilistic distribution among fuzzified prototypes, our algorithm obtains better performance comparing with others.

Future work will explore the fuzzy prototype method together with other clustering methods such as the *EM clustering algorithm* with the aim of obtaining a more representative set of fuzzy prototypes.

References

1. Blake, C., Merz, C.J.: UCI machine learning repository,
   `http://www.ics.uci.edu/~mlearn/MLRepository.html`
2. Chang, C., Lin, C.: LIBSVM: A library for support vector machines. ACM Transactions on Intelligent Systems and Technology 2, 27:1–27:27 (2011)
3. Dezert, J., Smarandache, F., Daniel, M.: The Generalized Pignistic Transformation. Computing Research Repository, cs.OH/0409 (2004)
4. Hyndman, R., Akram, M.: Time series data library,
   `http://www-personal.buseco.monash.edu.au/hyndman/TSDL/index.htm`
5. Kim, D., Kim, C.: Forecasting time series with genetic fuzzy predictor ensemble. IEEE Transactions on Fuzzy Systems 5, 523–535 (1997)
6. Lawry, J.: A methodology for computing with words. International Journal of Approximate Reasoning 28, 51–89 (2001)
7. Lawry, J.: A Framework for Linguistic Modelling. Artificial Intelligence 155, 1–39 (2004)
8. Lawry, J.: Modelling and Reasoning with Vague Concepts. Springer (2006)
9. Lawry, J.: Appropriateness measures: An uncertainty model for vague concepts. Synthese 161, 255–269 (2008)
10. Lawry, J.: A Random Set and Prototype Theory Interpretation of Intuitionistic Fuzzy Sets. In: Hüllermeier, E., Kruse, R., Hoffmann, F. (eds.) IPMU 2010, Part I. CCIS, vol. 80, pp. 618–628. Springer, Heidelberg (2010)
11. Lawry, J., Tang, Y.: Relating prototype theory and label semantics. In: Dubois, D., Lubiano, M.A., Prade, H., Gil, M.A., Grzegorzewski, P., Hryniewicz, O. (eds.) Soft Methods for Handling Variability and Imprecision, pp. 35–42 (2008)
12. Lawry, J., Tang, Y.: Uncertainty modelling for vague concepts: A prototype theory approach. Artificial Intelligence 173, 1539–1558 (2009)
13. Randon, N.J.: Fuzzy and Random Set Based Induction Algorithms. PhD Thesis, University of Bristol (2004)
14. Ruppert, D., Wand, M.P.: Multivariate Locally Weighted Least Squares Regression. Annals of Statistics 22, 1346–1370 (1994)
15. Russo, M.: Genetic fuzzy learning. IEEE Transactions on Evolutionary Computation 4, 259–273 (2000)
16. Takagi, T., Sugeno, M.: Fuzzy identification of systems and its applications to modeling and control. IEEE Transactions on Systems, Man, and Cybernetics 15, 116–132 (1985)
17. Tang, Y., Xu, Y.: Application of fuzzy naive bayes and a real-valued genetic algorithm in identification of fuzzy model. Information Sciences 169, 205–226 (2005)
18. Tang, Y., Lawry, J.: Linguistic modelling and information coarsening based on prototype. International Journal of Approximate Reasoning 50, 1177–1198 (2009)
19. Vapnik, V.N.: The Nature of Statistical Learning Theory. Springer, New York (1995)
20. Zadeh, L.A.: Fuzzy sets. Information and Control 8, 338–353 (1965)

Extended Twofold-LDA Model
for Two Aspects in One Sentence

Nicola Burns, Yaxin Bi, Hui Wang, and Terry Anderson

University of Ulster
burns-n4@email.ulster.ac.uk,
{y.bi,h.wang,tj.anderson}@ulster.ac.uk

Abstract. The Latent Dirichlet Allocation (LDA) model has been recently used as a method of identifying latent aspects in customer reviews. In our previous work, we proposed Twofold-LDA to identify both aspects and positive or negative sentiment in review sentences. We incorporated domain knowledge (i.e. seed words) to produce more focused aspects and provided a user-friendly chart quantifying sentiment. Our previous work made an assumption that one sentence contains one aspect, but in this study we wish to extend our model to remove this assumption. Experimental results show that our extended model improves the performance for every aspect in the datasets. We also show the importance of seed words for identifying desired aspects.

Keywords: Aspect discovery, sentiment analysis, topic modeling.

1   Introduction

Online customer reviews has become a popular way of expressing opinions about products and seeking related information. Manufacturers may use reviews as a means of customer feedback. Automatically classifying the opinions expressed in reviews has been a popular research area [4][5][9]. In particular, reviews can be classified into different topics relating to the different aspects of products. For example, TV reviews can be split into topics related to sound, picture quality, etc.

Latent Dirichlet Allocation (LDA) [1] is an unsupervised generative (graphical) model used to discover latent topics in a set of unlabeled data. A topic could refer to an aspect of a product in customer reviews [7][13]. Our previous work proposed Twofold-LDA [3] which has the ability to identify both the aspect and sentiment in review sentences and display the results in a user friendly chart. It incorporates prior domain knowledge (i.e. seed words) to produce more focused aspects and also provides a graphical output quantifying positive and negative opinion for each aspect. The graphical output adds the advantage for end users to visually see the results. Recent research has approached this aspect discovery problem with the assumption that one sentence contains one aspect [7][2][15]. We propose an extension of the Twofold-LDA model to handle two aspects in one sentence. The extension will increase the accuracy of the results and therefore create a more meaningful representation of results. We chose to allow two aspects in one sentence as previous

S. Greco et al. (Eds.): IPMU 2012, Part II, CCIS 298, pp. 265–275, 2012.
© Springer-Verlag Berlin Heidelberg 2012

research using the LDA model started to work at document level [1], then went on to work at sentence level [7], we now want to consider multiple aspects in one sentence. We also look at how the seed words used can affect the performance of the results.

2   Related Work

To the best of our knowledge, identifying two aspects in one sentence has not been carried out in existing work. In this section, we explore research on aspect discovery and the use of LDAs to find latent aspects and sentiment in reviews.

A popular method for aspect discovery is to use association rules as a means of extracting noun phrases which are possible aspects. In [4][5], association rule mining is used to find frequent itemsets which are candidate aspects. Association rules are also used in [8] as a means of finding aspect and opinion words. A number of sentiment analysis systems have been developed which make use of part-of-speech tags to identify aspects, these include; Opinion observer [10] and OPINE [11].

In recent years, it has become popular to use the Latent Dirichlet Allocation (LDA) [1] model and variations of this model as means of finding aspects in a review text. Labelled LDA [12][6] maps identified concepts to latent aspects, it restricts the standard LDA to have a one-to-one correspondence between latent aspects and user tags. Our work also guides the output, as we incorporate predefined aspects and seed words into our model to improve the performance of the extended LDA model and facilitate to visualise our results.

In addition to the LDA model being used to extract aspects, it has also been used to extract both aspect and sentiment [14][7][13]. Aspect and Sentiment Unification Model (ASUM) [7] models aspect and sentiment together to identify the sentiment towards different aspects, this is done using pairs of {aspect, sentiment}. Latent Aspect Rating Analysis (LARA) [14] firstly identifies major aspects with a bootstrapping algorithm and then concludes aspect ratings using the review content and the overall rating. This differs from our work as we keep the two stages separate, running two LDAs for aspect and sentiment so as we can create our graphical output.

Seed words are important words describing different aspects. They can play a significant role in detecting aspects which relate to desired product features. They are a good source of prior knowledge as they are usually taken from the dataset on which experiments are carried out or from a dataset on a similar domain. A disadvantage to seed words is that they are quite time-consuming to produce. The main advantage, as we will show is that using seed words can not only produce better results but also more meaningful aspects. It is typically the case that seed words are incorporated into an algorithm to improve performance with prior knowledge. For example in [9], seed words are used to initialise word tokens to sentiment topic. When incorporating the prior information, results of the model significantly improve. In [7], seed words are also used to find sentiment topics. They use an asymmetric setting so positive words are not probable in negative comments and visa versa. Our work uses seed words for finding both aspect and its corresponding positive or negative sentiment as will be discussed later in the paper they are an important part of our model.

This paper presents an extension to our previous research [3] in order to improve the performance of our method. Previous research has proved that sentence level improves performance over document level so we make the assumption that multiple aspects in one sentence will improve performance over only identifying one aspect in a sentence. The Twofold-LDA model is shown in Figure 1, it runs two LDA's in parallel, one LDA is used for aspect assignment and one LDA is used for sentiment assignment. It uses seed words to direct the focus of the topics produced to aspects related to the domain. The main purpose of the Twofold-LDA is to use domain knowledge to produce more accurate results and to generate a graphical output which may be used by potential customers. An assumption made in our previous work is that one sentence contains only one aspect, but we now wish to improve our algorithm so that one sentence may contain two aspects. State of the art methods such as ASUM [7] and LARA [14] have addressed the problem of identifying aspects and sentiment. Our method differs in that we can produce a chart of findings which can benefit both customers and manufacturers and also the added extension means that we can produce more accurate results.

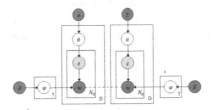

Fig. 1. Twofold-LDA model

3   Problem Statement

As discussed, previous work makes the assumption that one sentence contains one aspect [7][2][15]. Figure 2 shows an example of a hotel review taken from TripAdvisor. This review shows that sentences can contain none, one or many aspects. Using aspect seed words, we calculated that 80.27% of the TripAdvisor dataset contains one aspect seed word and the other 19.73% contains two or more different aspect seed words. Previous work has around the same ratios [15]. We therefore wish to extend the Twofold-LDA model to deal with two aspects in one sentence. The issues we consider are (a) how to automatically identify if a sentence has one or two aspects (Aspect Count), (b) how to calculate results (Alter Output).

"Immaculate, vintage hotel with personable staff—worth the price"

⊕⊕⊕⊕⊕ Reviewed 7 October 2008

This impeccably-restored, 1880's era hotel is clean and quiet and wonderfully located in a popular historic district near the waterfront. Our train was delayed and the night desk clerk cheerfully greeted us at 3 AM and even held the door for us. The breakfast, including hard-boiled eggs, various cereals and fresh batter with waffle-maker, was delicious. It is a bit pricey but we would stay there again in a heartbeat and recommend it highly.

Fig. 2. Example hotel review

4   Model Description

In this section, we describe our extension to Twofold-LDA, which incorporates two aspects in one sentence.

4.1   Aspect Count by Jaccard and Term Frequency – Inverse Document Frequency (Tf/Idf)

The first stage is to automatically investigate if a sentence contains one or two aspects by using similarity measures. Two measures have been employed in our studies, one is Jaccard and another is Tf-Idf. Jaccard is a method used in statistics to compare the similarity between sample sets.

The two sets we use are $d = \{w_1, w_2, ..., w_{|w|}\}$, where we refer to the words in a document (document refers to a sentence), and $S = \{s_1, s_2, ..., s_{|S|}\}$ refers to the seed words in an aspect seed set (there will be 7/5 aspects each having their own seed set i.e. list of seed words to describe the aspect). Using Jaccard we calculate if the words in the sentence are similar to the words in the seed set. If the similarity is over the threshold (threshold is set to > 0 i.e. if the sentence contains a seed word) then the sentence is said to contain that aspect. The sentence may now contain one or more aspects.

$$J(d, S) = \frac{|d \cap S|}{|d \cup S|} \tag{1}$$

With respect to Tf-Idf, we then use the Tf-Idf method to identify multiple aspects in a sentence. This calculates how important a word is to a document. The importance rises proportionally to the number of times a word appears in the document, however this is counterbalanced by the frequency of the word in the dataset.

By contrast, here we use the whole dataset to calculate similarity rather than just the sentence and seed words. The first part of the equation, $tf(w, d)$ calculates the word frequency, this is the importance of a word w in the document d. The 2nd half of the equation $idf(w)$ calculates the importance of the word. The total number of documents $|D|$ are divided by the number of documents in which the word appears $\{d : w \in d\}$, and then taking the logarithm of that measure. The seed words are incorporated into our model by calculating the proximity of seed words S and document d to identify the similarity between the two.

$$idf(w) = \log \frac{|D|}{\{d : w \in d\}} \tag{2}$$

$$tf - idf(w, d) = tf(w, d) \times idf(w) \tag{3}$$

4.2   Altering the Output

A further problem is then altering the output to incorporate two topics in one sentence. The two LDAs are run alongside each other, one LDA for assigning topics to sentences and one for assigning polarity. For the purpose of this research, we assume that one sentence has one sentiment but may contain one or two topics. We will only look at the aspect assignment side therefore, the generative process with the addition of how the results are output is as follows;

- For each document d, choose a distribution $\theta_d \sim Dirichlet\ (\alpha)$
- For each word w_i in the document d
    - Choose aspect $z_i \sim$ Multinomial (θ_d)
    - Generate word w_i from $p(w_i|z_i,\beta)$, a multinomial probablility conditioned on the aspect z_i

    Outputting Results:
- For each document d,
    - For each aspect z_i, if jaccard/tfidf.proximity(d, aspect seed words) > 0
        - Boolean z_i = true
    - If (Boolean $|z_i|$) >=2
        - Count top two topics
    - Else
        - Count top one topic

5   Experimental Results

In this section, we will first describe the dataset used then present and discuss the experimental results for both qualitative and quantitative analysis.

5.1   Datasets

We used hotel reviews from TripAdvisor. Reviewers provide ratings for the following aspects; *value, room, location, cleanliness, check in/front desk, service and business service*. We chose this dataset as our algorithm requires seed words for each aspect to be used in execution. In [14] the seed words have already been obtained for this dataset via a boot-strapping algorithm which can be reused for our algorithm. We also compare our results with a TV dataset which was created for a previous study [3]. The properties of the datasets are summarised in Table 1.

For the Tripadvisor dataset we followed the same process as [14], we discard all sentences which do not contain any seed words. Not all reviews contain comments on every aspect so to avoid missing aspects, reviews for each hotel are concatenated so as to provide one review for each hotel. There are a total of 1850 hotels. Due to the download of the TV dataset we could not concatenate reviews for each TV, thereby keeping the reviews separate, and discard sentences with no seed words.

Table 1. Properties of datasets

	Tripadvisor	TV
# reviews	1,850 (108.891)	13,923
# sentences	1,513,655	81,919
# words (pruned)	28,143,699 (10,961,805)	1,525,568 (574,676)
Avg. # sentences in review	13.90	5.88
Avg. # pruned words in review	100.67	41.28

5.2   Results

The Twofold-LDA model was run incorporating aspect seed words obtained from [14] and sentiment seed words (PARADIGM +) obtained from [7]. Symmetric hyperparameters $\alpha = 0.1$ and $\beta = 0.01$ were used and Markov chains run for 2000 samples. For the aspect assignment side we set Topics = 7 (Tripadvisor) and Topics = 5 (TV). For the polarity assignment side we set Topics = 6, one for positive, one for negative and four topics for neutral. We set neutral to four as 2/3 of the dataset does not contain any positive or negative seed words. For the purpose of this paper we are only examining the aspect assignment side.

Qualitative Evaluation

Firstly, to analyse our results we looked at individual sentences of reviews. We specifically look at two snippets from reviews taken from the Tripadvisor dataset. In Table 2, column one indicates if the sentence has one or two aspects (found using Jaccard and Tf/Idf). Column two shows the actual output from Extended Twofold-LDA, the topic which was assigned and the probability of that topic. The third column shows the sentence from the review. The final columns show using colour coding the topic(s) produced by the Extended Twofold-LDA (Two) model and the actual topics (Act) in the sentences (found using seed words).

Review 1 contains sentences that have both one and two aspects. Comparing the last two columns, in most cases the topic(s) produced corresponds that to the topics in the sentence, confirming that our method is effective. If we take a look at the sentences with one aspect, the topics produced match the seed words they contain. If we now take a look at sentences containing two aspects, the second sentence classifies both aspects correctly. For the last sentence, our model outputs *Value* and *Service* and the topics in the sentence indicate *Rooms* and *Service*. In this case, the LDA has wrongly interpreted this sentence as *Value*. Later in the paper we will perform quantitative testing to ensure these are not major problems.

Review 2 is a good example of sentences containing two aspects. In every case, the Twofold-LDA has classified the correct two topics corresponding to the seed words in the sentence. If we look closely at some of the sentences, the aspects also match the content of the sentence. Sentence one is classified as *Value* and *Location* and includes comments of the low price and fantastic location. This gives clear evidence that our model can accurately identify if a sentence contains one or two aspects and also correctly identify both aspects.

Table 2. Sentence comparison for Extended Twoldfold-LDA (*Value* = yellow, *rooms* = blue, *location* = pink, *checkin*= orange, *cleanliness* = green, *service* = light blue and *business* = red)

Aspects	Topic/Prob		Sentence	Two	Act
Review 1					
1	1	0.447	This is the place to stay at when visiting the historical		
	2	0.447	area of Seattle.		
2	2	0.483	Your right on the water front near the ferry's and		
	5	0.415	great sea food restraunts, and still with'in walking		
	4	0.075	distance for great blues and jazz music.		
2	0	0.445	We did'nt have to travel far to have a good cup of		
	5	0.445	"JOE" and a light meal to start our adventurous day		
	1	0.080	off into one of the most beautifull city's in america.		
Review 2					
2	0	0.551	Great hotel for a low price and fantastic location I		
	2	0.279	stayed at the Best Western Pioneer square for two		
	1	0.143	nights last month, and was very impressed.		
2	2	0.423	It was close to Safeco field and the other attractions		
	5	0.423	in the area as well as the best continental breakfast		
	6	0.113	I've ever had at a hotel.		
2	1	0.407	Rooms were very clean and comfortable.		
	3	0.407			

Quantitative Evaluation

We now quantitatively evaluate our results so we can calculate the improvement made by considering two aspects per sentence rather than one. We used the seed words to identify the sentences in the dataset with specific aspects, if the sentence contains multiple aspect seed words it is labelled to multiple aspects. A confusion matrix was then created for the original Twofold-LDA and another created for the extended Twofold-LDA. Jaccard and Tf/Idf produce the exact same results for both datasets. This is because when we are identifying if a sentence contains a seed word (i.e. threshold > 0), although both methods give a different answer we only want to know if a seed word present. Changing the threshold would mean that a sentence may need to contain more than one seed word in order for it to be classified as that particular topic and this is not how we want our model to work. As both these methods produce the same results, this confirms that our results are robust.

Tables 3a and 3b show the results for LDAs incorporating one and two aspect(s) per sentence for each of the 7 aspects for the Tripadvisor dataset. We first note that for every aspect of the results have been improved when our two aspect extension is used. *Cleanliness* and *Business* tend to have poor performance which will be examined later in the paper. We will now examine the empirical results in the form of precision and recall. Precision is a measure of presenting only relevant terms, the higher the precision the more relevant the results. Recall is the ability to retrieve as many relevant terms as possible. When comparing the original Twofold-LDA and extended Twofold-LDA, precision is high and has a modest increase ranging from 0.003(Checkin) - 0.098(*Cleanliness*) proving that we can return relevant results with our improved method. *Location* and *Rooms* have a slight decrease in precision but this is very small. In respect of the recall results, recall ranges from -0.001(*Checkin*) – 0.045(*Rooms*). Therefore, although our extended version may return slightly more additional results, it retrieves more relevant results.

Table 3a. 1 Aspect (Original Twofold-LDA)

	Value	*Rooms*	*Location*	*Cleanliness*	*Checkin*	*Service*	*Business*
Precision	0.537	0.977	0.907	0.420	0.902	0.954	0.223
Recall	0.894	0.705	0.781	0.868	0.817	0.761	0.815
F-measure	0.699	0.819	0.839	0.566	0.857	0.847	0.350

Table 3b. 2 Aspects (Extended Twofold-LDA)

	Value	*Rooms*	*Location*	*Cleanliness*	*Checkin*	*Service*	*Business*
Precision	0.599	0.976	0.906	0.518	0.905	0.960	0.269
Recall	0.894	0.750	0.798	0.890	0.816	0.783	0.839
F-measure	0.718	0.848	0.849	0.655	0.858	0.862	0.407

For the TV dataset 3 of the 5 aspects improve when our extension is used. When comparing the original and extended Twofold-LDA, precision ranges from - 0.003(*Value*) – 0.056(*Design*). Recall ranges from -0.002(*Value*) – 0.022(*Image*).

The F-measure combines precision and recall. We can clearly see from Figure 3a that in the Tripadvisor dataset the f-measure score is increased for every aspect when two aspects per sentence are considered. This proves that our extended version increases the performance of the model. *Rooms, Location, Checkin* and *Service* have the highest scores, with *Cleanliness* and *Business* having the lowest scores. Figure 3b shows that for the TV dataset the f-measure is increased for 3 of the 5 aspects. Again showing that our extended version can increase performance in most cases.

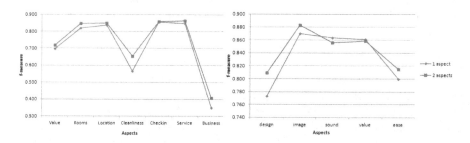

Fig. 3a. Comparison f-measure results (Tripadvisor dataset)   **Fig. 3b.** Comparison f-measure results (TV dataset)

Evaluation on Seed Words

To further analyse our results since our algorithm relies on seed words, we looked at the number of seed words used for each aspect. As the seed words may be used a different number of times we calculate the percentage of the dataset in which seed words are used for each aspect. Table 4 shows each group of aspect seed word values.

Table 4. Aspect seed word values (Tripadvisor dataset)

Aspects	Number of seed words	Number of times used	% whole dataset	% pruned dataset
Value	27	304709	0.591	2.780
Room	60	400011	0.776	3.649
Location	46	338842	0.657	3.091
Cleanliness	14	74334	0.144	0.678
Checkin	34	328608	0.638	2.998
Service	53	243931	0.473	2.225
Business	42	55324	0.107	0.505

From Table 4, we can see that the aspect with the least number of seed words, *Cleanliness*, has a poor performance. The aspect with the worst performance, *Business*, has 42 seed words which is a high number but if we look at the percentage of the dataset in which the seed words are used we can see that they are not used as often as other groups of seed words. The aspect seed words with the highest percentage of dataset have the highest performance. This illustrates a fact that the seed words greatly affect the performance of our algorithm. From our studies, it can be seen that the impact is not just the number of seed words but also the number of times the seed words are used in the datasets.

Table 5. Aspect seed word values (TV dataset)

Aspects	Number of seed words	Number of times used	% whole dataset	% pruned dataset
Design	15	13329	0.782	2.319
Image	31	46138	2.706	8.029
Sound	12	14499	0.850	2.523
Value	17	20375	1.195	3.545
Ease	12	9842	0.577	1.714

These results are confirmed with the TV dataset. All the results for each of the aspects in the TV dataset are good and if we take a look at Table 5, we can see that the percentage of the dataset ranges from 1.7-8.0% which is quite high for each aspect. Generally speaking, this provides evidence that a high percentage of seed words can improve performance.

6   Conclusion

In this paper, we proposed an extension to our previous research, Twofold-LDA model. The Twofold-LDA model uses seed words to influence LDA topics to relevant aspects and outputs the results in a user friendly chart with the assumption that one sentence contains one aspect. We then extended this model to incorporate sentences that may contain two aspects. Empirical analysis showed that our model works effectively and that the sentences relate to the topic they are assigned to. Quantitative analysis then gave us evidence that our extension is significantly better than our pervious Twofold-LDA model. For almost every aspect there was an improvement in performance. This supports the assumption made by our pervious work and other research can affect the performance of the results. Finally, we took a closer look at how the seed words affect our model. We found that the percentage of the dataset the seed words are used has an impact on our results, the more the seed words are used in the dataset the higher the performance (~1-8%).

The aim of this paper was to improve performance of the model and to remove the one aspect per sentence assumption. Experimental results has demonstrated that we have achieved this goal. The next stage of our will be to analyse and improve on the sentiment assignment side of the model and possibly to unify the model so it requires less time and effort.

References

1. Blei, D.M., Ng, Y.A., Jordan, M.I.: Latent Dirichlet Allocation. Journal of Machine Learning Research 3, 993–1022 (2003)
2. Brody, S., Elhadad, N.: An Unsupervised Aspect-Sentiment Model for Online Reviews. In: Proceedings of Human Language Technologies: The Annual Conference of the North American Chapter of the Association for Computational Linguistics, pp. 804–812. Association for Computational Linguistics, Stroudsburg (2010)
3. Burns, N., Bi, Y., Wang, H., Anderson, T.: A Twofold-LDA Model for Customer Review Analysis. In: Proceedings of Web Intelligence and Intelligent Agent Technology, pp. 253–256. ACM (2011)
4. Hu, M., Liu, B.: Mining opinion features in customer reviews. In: 19th National Conference on Artificial Intelligence, pp. 755–760. AAAI Press/The MIT Press (2004b)
5. Hu, M., Liu, B.: Mining and summarizing customer reviews. In: Proceedings of the 2004 ACM SIGKDD International Conference on Knowledge Discovery and Data Mining, pp. 168–177. ACM, New York (2004a)
6. Jin, F., Huang, M., Zhu, X.: Guided Structure-Aware Review Summarization. Journal of Computer Science and Technology 26(4), 676–684 (2011)
7. Jo, Y., Oh, A.: Aspect and Sentiment Unification Model for Online Review Analysis. In: Proceedings of the Fourth ACM International Conference on Web Search and Data Mining. ACM, New York (2011)
8. Kim, W., Ryu, J., Kim, K., Kim, U.: A Method for Opinion Mining of Product Reviews using Association Rules. In: Proceedings of the 2nd International Conference on Interaction Sciences: Information Technology, Culture and Human, pp. 270–274. ACM, New York (2009)

9. Lin, C., He, Y.: Joint Sentiment/Topic Model for Sentiment Analysis. In: Proceedings of the Conference on Information and Knowledge Management, pp. 375–384. ACM, New York (2009)

10. Liu, B., Hu, M., Cheng, J.: Opinion Observer: Analyzing and Comparing Opinions on the Web. In: Proceedings of the 14th International Conference on World Wide Web, pp. 342–351. ACM, New York (2005)

11. Popescu, A., Etzioni, O.: Extracting Product Features and Opinions from Reviews. In: Proceedings of the Conference on Human Language Technology and Empirical Methods in Natural Language Processing, pp. 339–346. Association for Computational Linguistics, Morristown (2005)

12. Ramage, D., Hall, D., Nallapati, R., Manning, C.D.: Labeled LDA: A supervised topic model for credit attribution in multi-labeled corpora. In: Proceedings of the 2009 Conference on Empirical Methods in Natural Language Processing, pp. 248–256. Association for Computational Linguistics, Stroudsburg (2009)

13. Titov, I., McDonald, R.: Modeling Online Reviews with Multi-Grain Topic Models. In: Proceeding of the 17th International Conference on World Wide Web, pp. 111–120. ACM, New York (2008)

14. Wang, H., Lu, Y., Zhai, C.: Latent Aspect Rating Analysis on Review Text Data: A Rating Regression Approach. In: Proceedings of the 16th International Conference on Knowledge Discovery and Data Mining, pp. 783–792. ACM, New York (2010)

15. Zhao, W.X., Jiang, J., Yan, H.L.: Jointly Modeling Aspects and Opinions with a MaxEnt-LDA Hybrid. In: Proceedings of the 2010 Conference on Empirical Methods in Natural Language Processing, pp. 56–65. Association for Computational Linguistics, Stroudsburg (2010)

Concept Identification in Constructing Multi-Document Summarizations

Daan Van Britsom, Antoon Bronselaer, and Guy De Tré

Department of Telecommunication and Information Processing,
Ghent University, Sint-Pietersnieuwstraat 41,
Ghent, Belgium
daan.vanbritsom@ugent.be

Abstract. This paper describes a way to influence the content identification process in automatically generating multi-document summarizations of a cluster of documents regarding the same topic. The proposed method uses the weighted harmonic mean between precision and recall and results in a multiset of concepts that we consider to be defining for a cluster. These concepts can be used for selecting the proper sentences from the original cluster of documents and thus generating the multi-document summarization.

Keywords: Concept identification, weighted harmonic mean, multi-document summarizations.

1 Introduction

The Multi-Document Summarization or MDS problem consists of the need for a system that summarizes multiple documents, typically concerning the same topic, automatically. In [5] we have introduced a technique to generate multi-document summarizations using sentence extraction for a set of documents, referred to as a cluster. The documents from a cluster were coreferent, meaning they regarded the same subject. For every cluster a set of concepts C that are considered to be defining for the cluster had been provided and the summarization process depended for a large part on these concepts. It is however clearly feasible to lose this dependency and be able to define the essential concepts of any cluster of coreferent documents automatically and formally. In [1] we have presented a framework for multiset merging and illustrated how it can be used for concept identification in constructing multi-document summarizations. The proposed method relies on the harmonic mean, between the precision, a measurement of correctness, and the recall, a measurement of completeness, the so-called f-value, of a possible solution compared to the original dataset. The f-optimal merge function returns the multiset resulting in the highest f-value, thus providing us with the set of concepts that resembles the dataset both correctly and completely. However, a perfect balance between precision and recall is not always the desired result. In this paper we propose a method to influence this concept identification process based on applying a preference towards precision

S. Greco et al. (Eds.): IPMU 2012, Part II, CCIS 298, pp. 276–284, 2012.
© Springer-Verlag Berlin Heidelberg 2012

or recall by using the weighted harmonic mean and weighted f_β-optimal merge functions. In Section 2 we recall some definitions regarding multisets and merge functions required to formally present our framework. In Section 3 we illustrate the result of these merge functions on textual data and how they can be used for constructing multi-document summarizations. In Section 4 we show how the concept identification process can be influenced by using the weighted harmonic mean and we illustrate this with an example. We end with concluding remarks on the proposed method in Section 5.

2   Preliminaries

2.1   Multisets

We briefly recall some important definitions regarding multisets [9]. Informally, a multiset is an unordered collection in which elements can occur multiple times. Many definitions have been proposed, but within the scope of this paper, we adopt the functional definition of multisets.

Definition 1 (Multiset). *A multiset M over a universe U is defined by a function:*

$$M : U \to \mathbb{N}. \tag{1}$$

For each $u \in U$, $M(u)$ denotes the multiplicity of u in M. The set of all multisets drawn from a universe U is denoted $\mathcal{M}(U)$.

The j-cut of a multiset M is a regular set, denoted as M_j and given as:

$$M_j = \{u | u \in U \wedge M(u) \geq j\}. \tag{2}$$

Whenever we wish to assign an index $i \in \mathbb{N}$ to a multiset M, we use the notation $M_{(i)}$, while the notation M_j is preserved for the j-cut of M. We adopt the definitions of Yager [9] for the following operators: $\cup, \cap, \subseteq$ and $\in$.

2.2   Merge Functions

The general framework of merge functions provides the following definition [2].

Definition 2 (Merge function). *A merge function over a universe U is defined by a function:*

$$\varpi : \mathcal{M}(U) \to U. \tag{3}$$

As explained in the introduction of this paper, we are interested in merge functions for (multi)sets rather than atomic elements. Therefore, we consider merge functions over a universe $\mathcal{M}(U)$ rather than a universe U. This provides us with functions of the following:

$$\varpi : \mathcal{M}\big(\mathcal{M}(U)\big) \to \mathcal{M}(U). \tag{4}$$

In order to avoid confusion, we shall denote S (a source) as a multiset over U and we shall denote M as a multiset over $\mathcal{M}(U)$ (a collection of sources). Thus, in general, M can be written as:

$$M = \{S_{(1)}, ..., S_{(n)}\}. \tag{5}$$

Finally, we shall denote $\mathscr{S} \in \mathcal{M}(U)$ as a general solution for a merge problem, i.e. $\varpi(M) = \mathscr{S}$. The most simple merge functions for multisets are of course the source intersection and the source union. That is, for any M:

$$\varpi_1(M) = \bigcap_{S \in M} \left(S \right) \tag{6}$$

$$\varpi_2(M) = \bigcup_{S \in M} \left(S \right). \tag{7}$$

Within this paper, we consider a solution relevant if it is a superset of the source intersection or a subset of the source union. Therefore, we call the source intersection the lower solution (denoted $\underline{\mathscr{S}}$) and the source union the upper solution (denoted $\overline{\mathscr{S}}$). To conclude this section, we introduce the family of f-optimal merge functions, which are merge functions that maximize the harmonic mean of a measure of solution correctness (i.e. precision) and a measure of solution completeness (i.e. recall). This objective is better known as the f-value [8]. To adapt the notion of precision and recall to the setting of multiset merging, we define two *local* (i.e. element-based) measures [1].

Definition 3 (Local precision and recall). *Consider a multiset of sources* $M = \{S_{(1)}, ..., S_{(n)}\}$. *Local precision and recall are defined by functions p^* and r^* such that:*

$$\forall u \in U : \forall j \in \mathbb{N} : p^*(u, j|M) = \frac{1}{|M|} \sum_{S \in M \wedge S(u) \geq j} M(S) \tag{8}$$

$$\forall u \in U : \forall j \in \mathbb{N} : r^*(u, j|M) = \frac{1}{|M|} \sum_{S \in M \wedge S(u) \leq j} M(S). \tag{9}$$

Definition 4 (f-optimal merge function). *Consider a multiset of sources* $M = \{S_{(1)}, ..., S_{(n)}\}$. *A merge function ϖ is f-optimal if it satisfies for any* $M \in \mathcal{M}(\mathcal{M}(U))$:

$$\varpi(M) = \underset{\mathscr{S} \in \mathcal{M}(U)}{\arg\max} f(\mathscr{S}|M) = \underset{\mathscr{S} \in \mathcal{M}(U)}{\arg\max} \left(\frac{2 \cdot p(\mathscr{S}|M) \cdot r(\mathscr{S}|M)}{p(\mathscr{S}|M) + r(\mathscr{S}|M)} \right) \tag{10}$$

constrained by:

$$\left(\max_{\mathscr{S} \in \mathcal{M}(U)} f(\mathscr{S}|M) = 0 \right) \Rightarrow \varpi(M) = \emptyset \tag{11}$$

and where, with T *a triangular norm, we have that:*

$$p(\mathscr{S}|M) = \underset{u \in \mathscr{S}}{\text{T}} \left(p^*(u, \mathscr{S}(u)|M) \right) \tag{12}$$

$$r(\mathscr{S}|M) = \underset{u \in \mathscr{S}}{\text{T}} \left(r^*(u, \mathscr{S}(u)|M) \right). \tag{13}$$

3   Multi-Document Summarization

One can apply the definition of a multiset to the problem of constructing Multi-Document Summarizations (MDS). The usefulness of multi-document summarizations has been shown in [6]. When considering every document as a multiset S of words, the universe U consists of the union of all the words of all the different documents. Thus the definition of a multiset (Definition 1) still applies.

Generating multi-document summarizations classically consists of two steps, content selection and content presentation [7] [4] sometimes referred to as the content planner and the linguistic component. The application of the technique proposed in this paper lies in the content selection step. Our system introduced in [1] identifies the key concepts of the cluster in a formally correct and objective manner without any pre-existing knowledge.

As an example a cluster of 27 articles and interviews were obtained from the websites of some of the most prominent international news agencies such as the BBC, the New York Times, the Guardian and several more. The only preprocessing that was performed was the elimination of about 650 different stop words such as 'the', 'it', 'he', thus avoiding their possible influence on the result. This resulted in a universe of 2859 words.

When we construct the multiset that provides the highest harmonic mean using the f-optimal merge function ϖ where precision and recall are calculated by means of the triangular norm T_M, thus optimizing the f-value as defined in Definition 4, we end up with the following solution $\mathscr{S}_{(opt)}$ paired with an f-value of $0.518518518\ldots$:

Example 1. $\mathscr{S}_{(opt)}$ = [obama:6, house:4, bill:4, economic:3, stimulus:3, president:3, senate:3, plan:3, tax:2, jobs:2, republicans:2, state:1, conference:1, congress:1, version:1, washington:1, government:1, time:1, money:1, country:1, tuesday:1, support:1, work:1, billion:1, final:1, american:1, republican:1, monday:1, democrats:1, federal:1, people:1, economy:1, news:1, 000:1, package:1, secretary:1, spending:1, create:1, crisis:1, public:1, barack:1, week:1, white:1, cuts:1]*

As introduced in [5] these concepts can be used to generate the summarization and therefore also cover the content presentation step. This will provide a score for each sentence in the initial set and to generate the summarization one can select sentences as described in [5]. In order to influence the length of the summarization all one can do at this point is select more or less sentences, based on the concepts extracted with the f-optimal merge function. If the user however wants to construct a briefer summarization odds are the user wants only the most important information in stead of a smaller amount of relatively important information. The same problem occurs when the user wants a larger summarization. If the user wants a more elaborate summarization one can assume the user wants a broader spectrum of information concerning the subject instead of twice as much sentences on the relatively important information. Therefore it would be feasible to select more/less concepts from the dataset in a formally correct manner.

4 Influencing the Content Selection

The f-optimal merge function as defined in Definition 4 doesn't allow one to influence the outcome $\mathscr{S} \in \mathcal{M}(U)$ of the merge function. Suppose one would want to select fewer concepts in order to show a preference to precision rather than recall. In order to do so one could take a subset of $\mathscr{S}$ but then one would no longer have a solution with an optimal f-value. The merge function becomes even more restricting if one would want more concepts as a solution, thus giving preference to recall rather than precision, for there is no option to gain more concepts. In order to influence the outcome of the f-optimal merge function we have chosen to use the weighted harmonic mean [3], and the merge function thus changes as follows.

Definition 5 (Weighted f_β-optimal merge function). *Consider a multiset of sources $M = \{S_{(1)}, ..., S_{(n)}\}$. A merge function ϖ is f_β-optimal if it satisfies for any $M \in \mathcal{M}(\mathcal{M}(U))$:*

$$\varpi(M) = \underset{\mathscr{S} \in \mathcal{M}(U)}{\arg\max} f_\beta(\mathscr{S}|M) = \underset{\mathscr{S} \in \mathcal{M}(U)}{\arg\max} \left(\frac{(1 + \beta^2) \cdot p(\mathscr{S}|M) \cdot r(\mathscr{S}|M)}{\beta^2 \cdot p(\mathscr{S}|M) + r(\mathscr{S}|M)} \right) \quad (14)$$

still constrained by (11), $\beta \in [0, \infty]$ and where, with T a triangular norm, (12) and (13) still apply.

The parameter β expresses how much more weight is given to recall as opposed to precision, more specifically, recall has a weight of β times precision. Thus, when $\beta = 1$ precision and recall are weighted the same and this results in the non-weighted f-optimal merge function as defined in Definition 4. When $\beta < 1$ a preference is given to precision, for example when $\beta = 0.5$ recall is given half the weight of precision. When $\beta > 1$ a preference is given to recall, for example when $\beta = 2$ recall is given twice the weight of precision. When $\beta = 0$ f_β returns the precision and when β approaches infinity f_β results in the recall.

For the sake of simplicity we shall for the remainder of the paper restrict ourselves to the case where $T = T_M$. In this specific case, it can be shown [1] that there exists a confined set of solutions $\{\mathscr{S}_{(1)} \ldots \mathscr{S}_{(l)}\}$ that satisfies:

$$\mathscr{S}_{(1)} = \underline{\mathscr{L}} \quad (15)$$
$$\mathscr{S}_{(l)} = \overline{\mathscr{S}} \quad (16)$$
$$\forall i \in [1, l[\; : \; \mathscr{S}_{(i)} \subseteq \mathscr{S}_{(i+1)} \quad (17)$$

Due to monotonicity we have that;

$$p(\mathscr{S}_{(i)}|M) \geq p(\mathscr{S}_{(i+1)}|M) \quad (18)$$
$$r(\mathscr{S}_{(i)}|M) \leq r(\mathscr{S}_{(i+1)}|M) \quad (19)$$

This is proven for the standard f-optimal merge function [1], but it still applies considering the weighted f_β-function is an isotonic function as well and this is the only factor that changes. This result provides us with an efficient algorithm, because the set of possible solutions is significantly smaller than the set of all possible solutions. To be more specific, the maximal number of possible solutions is:

$$\sum_{u \in \mathscr{S}} \left(\mathscr{S}(u) + 1 \right) \tag{20}$$

which means that the complexity is reduced from exponential to quadratic. This is the mean reason why T_M is of specific interest. We emphasize once more that this only holds for the case where $T = T_M$.

The use of the weighted f-optimal merge function enables one to influence the outcome of the algorithm a lot more. Let us consider the previous example.

Example 2. The original f-optimal merge function resulted in the following solution:

$\mathscr{S}_{(opt)}$ = *[obama:6, house:4, bill:4, economic:3, stimulus:3, president:3, senate:3, plan:3, tax:2, jobs:2, republicans:2, state:1, conference:1, congress:1, version:1, washington:1, government:1, time:1, money:1, country:1, tuesday:1, support:1, work:1, billion:1, final:1, american:1, republican:1, monday:1, demo-crats:1, federal:1, people:1, economy:1, news:1, 000:1, package:1, secretary:1, spending:1, create:1, crisis:1, public:1, barack:1, week:1, white:1, cuts:1]*

This coincides with a β value of 1 in the weighted f_β-optimal merge function. When we consider a few other values for β the resulting solutions are:

$\varpi_{\beta=0.1}(M)$ = *[obama:2, house:1, president:1, stimulus:1]*

$\varpi_{\beta=0.5}(M)$ = *[obama:4, house:3, economic:2, president:2, stimulus:2, bill:2, plan:2, barack:1, senate:1, tax:1, republicans:1, cuts:1, congress:1, economy:1, package:1, people:1, spending:1, jobs:1]*

$\varpi_{\beta=1.5}(M)$ = *[obama:7, bill:6, house:5, president:5, stimulus:4, senate:4, eco-nomic:3, plan:3, billion:3, congress:2, version:2, money:2, tax:2, republican:2, jobs:2, economy:2, package:2, republicans:2, white:2, state:1, conference:1, washington:1, government:1, time:1, legislation:1, country:1, local:1, tuesday:1, support:1, years:1, million:1, work:1, vote:1, final:1, administration:1, unem-ployment:1, american:1, financial:1, expected:1, monday:1, set:1, federal:1, democrats:1, told:1, people:1, news:1, 000:1, secretary:1, spending:1, create:1, crisis:1, public:1, barack:1, good:1, treasury:1, year:1, week:1, cuts:1, mea-sures:1, percent:1, congressional:1]*

$\varpi_{\beta=2.0}(M)$ = *[obama:9, house:6, bill:6, president:5, senate:5, economic:4, stimulus:4, plan:4, jobs:3, billion:3, tax:2, support:2, money:2, government:2, people:2, congress:2, white:2, washington:2, spending:2, economy:2, cuts:2, version:2, vote:2, republican:2, republicans:2, package:2, week:1, secretary:1, states:1, senators:1, state:1, indiana:1, health:1, representatives:1, governments:1, geithner:1, senator:1, measures:1, credit:1, news:1, part:1, congressional:1, final:1, bills:1, top:1, 3:1, private:1, administration:1, give:1, needed:1, democrats:1, years:1, country:1, florida:1, passed:1, good:1, year:1, bad:1, friday:1, banks:1, unemployment:1, democratic:1, rate:1, legislation:1, work:1, system:1, month:1, financial:1, time:1, million:1, recovery:1, told:1, treasury:1, education:1, federal:1, 000:1, monday:1, crisis:1, press:1, set:1, american:1, conference:1, majority:1, americans:1, days:1, aides:1, presidency:1, measure:1, barack:1, added:1, act:1, don:1, percent:1, road:1, start:1, create:1, high:1, expected:1, deal:1, local:1, negotiations:1, voted:1, public:1, votes:1, tuesday:1]*

As illustrated in Example 1 one can clearly see that when $\beta < 1$ the weighted f-optimal solution is a subset of the normal f-optimal solution and when $\beta > 1$ it is a superset. This can be proven formally:

Theorem 1. *Consider a set of sources* $M = \{S_{(1)}, \ldots, S_{(n)}\}$, *an* f-*optimal merge function* ϖ_1 *resulting in the solution* $\mathscr{S}_{(opt)}$ *and a weighted* f_β-*optimal merge function* ϖ_2 *resulting in* $\mathscr{S}_{\beta(opt)}$, *both under* T_M.

Then we have that:

$$\beta < 1 \Rightarrow \mathscr{S}_{\beta(opt)} \subseteq \mathscr{S}_{(opt)} \tag{21}$$

$$\beta > 1 \Rightarrow \mathscr{S}_{\beta(opt)} \supseteq \mathscr{S}_{(opt)} \tag{22}$$

Proof. We know there exists a set of candidate solutions $\Gamma = \{\mathscr{S}_{(1)}, \cdots \mathscr{S}_{(l)}\}$ *such that:*

$$\underline{\mathscr{L}} = \mathscr{S}_{(1)} \subseteq \ldots \subseteq \mathscr{S}_{(l)} = \overline{\mathscr{S}} \tag{23}$$

$$p(\mathscr{S}_{(i)}|M) \geq p(\mathscr{S}_{(i+1)}|M) \tag{24}$$

$$r(\mathscr{S}_{(i)}|M) \leq r(\mathscr{S}_{(i+1)}|M) \tag{25}$$

and we know that:

$$\mathscr{S}_{\beta(opt)} \in \Gamma \tag{26}$$

$$\mathscr{S}_{(opt)} \in \Gamma. \tag{27}$$

Let precision and recall of $\mathscr{S}_{(opt)} \in \Gamma$ *be* p_1 *and* r_1 *and for any solution* $\mathscr{S} \in \Gamma$ *let precision and recall be referred to as* p_2 *and recall* r_2, *we have that:*

$$\frac{2 \cdot p_1 \cdot r_1}{p_1 + r_1} \geq \frac{2 \cdot p_2 \cdot r_2}{p_2 + r_2} \tag{28}$$

$$\Leftrightarrow p_1 \cdot r_1 \cdot (p_2 + r_2) \geq p_2 \cdot r_2 \cdot (p_1 + r_1) \tag{29}$$

with $(p_1, r_1, p_2, r_2) \in [0,1]^4$

We restrict to proving that $\beta < 1 \Rightarrow \mathscr{S}_{\beta(opt)} \subseteq \mathscr{S}_{(opt)}$, proving that $\beta > 1 \Rightarrow$
$\mathscr{S}_{\beta(opt)} \supseteq \mathscr{S}_{(opt)}$ is completely equivalent.

$$\beta < 1 \Rightarrow \mathscr{S}_{\beta(opt)} \subseteq \mathscr{S}_{(opt)} \Leftrightarrow \tag{30}$$

$$\beta < 1 \Rightarrow \mathscr{S}_{\beta(opt)} \not\supseteq \mathscr{S}_{(opt)} \tag{31}$$

It is therefore sufficient to prove that no solution $\mathscr{S} \in \Gamma$ that is a superset of $\mathscr{S}_{(opt)}$ can have a higher f_β-value. This is the same as proving that:

$$\frac{(1 + \beta^2) \cdot p_1 \cdot r_1}{\beta^2 \cdot p_1 + r_1} \geq \frac{(1 + \beta^2) \cdot p_2 \cdot r_2}{\beta^2 \cdot p_2 + r_2} \tag{32}$$

with $p_1 \geq p_2$ and $r_1 \leq r_2$ due to the way the solutions were constructed as stated above.

This can be written as:

$$\Leftrightarrow \frac{p_1 \cdot r_1}{\beta^2 \cdot p_1 + r_1} \geq \frac{p_2 \cdot r_2}{\beta^2 \cdot p_2 + r_2} \tag{33}$$

$$\Leftrightarrow p_1 \cdot r_1 \cdot (\beta^2 \cdot p_2 + r_2) \geq p_2 \cdot r_2 \cdot (\beta^2 \cdot p_1 + r_1) \tag{34}$$

which we know to be true given (29), monotonicity of the multiplication and the fact that:

$$p_2 + r_2 - (\beta^2 \cdot p_2 + r_2) \leq p_1 + r_1 - (\beta^2 \cdot p_1 + r_1) \tag{35}$$

$$\Leftrightarrow p_2 + r_2 - \beta^2 \cdot p_2 - r_2 \leq p_1 + r_1 - \beta^2 \cdot p_1 - r_1 \tag{36}$$

$$\Leftrightarrow p_2 - \beta^2 \cdot p_2 \leq p_1 - \beta^2 \cdot p_1 \tag{37}$$

$$\Leftrightarrow (1 - \beta^2) \cdot p_2 \leq (1 - \beta^2) \cdot p_1 \tag{38}$$

$$\Leftrightarrow p_2 \leq p_1 \tag{39}$$

which we know to be true.

5   Conclusion

In this paper we have proposed a method to influence concept identification in order to generate multi-document summarizations. By using the weighted f_β-optimal merge functions, based upon the weighted harmonic mean, one is able to influence the outcome of the merge function by giving a preference to either precision or recall. We have illustrated this with an elaborate example to show the effect of the parameter β on the solution. By choosing a value for β smaller than 1 we select fewer concepts, a subset of the non weighted result, giving a preference to the correctness of the set of concepts. When we choose a value for β larger than 1 we select more concepts, a superset of the non weighted result, giving a preference to the completeness of the set of concepts. Naturally more testing is required in order to see which values for β are the most efficient for effectively generating summarizations. In the future we will be testing on the Document Understanding Conferences (DUC) datasets among others, but for now preliminary tests show promising results.

References

1. Bronselaer, A., Van Britsom, D., De Tré, G.: A framework for multiset merging. Fuzzy Sets and Systems 191(0), 1–20 (2012)
2. Bronselaer, A., De Tré, G., Van Britsom, D.: Multiset merging: the majority rule. In: Proceedings of the EUROFUSE 2011 Workshop (2011)
3. van Rijsbergen, C.J.: Information Retrieval. Butterworths, London (1979)
4. Lin, C.-Y., Hovy, E.: From single to multi-document summarization: A prototype system and its evaluation. In: ACL 2002 Proceedings of the 40th Annual Meeting of the Association for Computational Linguistics on Computational Linguistics, pp. 457–464 (2002)
5. Britsom, D.V., Bronselaer, A., De Tré, G.: Automatically generating multi-document summarizations. In: Proceedings of the 11th International Conference on Intelligent Systems Design and Applications, pp. 142–147. IEEE (2011)
6. McKeown, K., Passonneau, R., Elson, D., Nenkova, A., Hirschberg, J.: Do summaries help? a task based evaluation of multi document summarization. In: Proceedings of the 28th Annual International ACM SIGIR Conference on Research and Development in Information Retrieval, pp. 210–217 (2005)
7. Barzilay, R., McKeown, K.R., Elhadad, M.: Information fusion in the context of multi-document summarization. In: ACL 1999 Proceedings of the 37th Annual Meeting of the Association for Computational Linguistics on Computational Linguistics, pp. 550–557 (1999)
8. Baeza-Yates, R., Ribeiro-Neto, B.: Modern information retrieval. ACM Press (1999)
9. Yager, R.: On the theory of bags. International Journal of General Systems 13(1), 23–27 (1986)

Quality Assessment
in Linguistic Summaries of Data[*]

Rita Castillo-Ortega[1], Nicolás Marín[1],
Daniel Sánchez[1,2], and Andrea G.B. Tettamanzi[3]

[1] Dept. Computer Science and A.I., University of Granada, 18071, Granada, Spain
{rita,nicm,daniel}@decsai.ugr.es
[2] European Centre for Soft Computing, 33600, Mieres, Spain
daniel.sanchezf@softcomputing.es
[3] Università degli Studi di Milano, Milan, Italy
andrea.tettamanzi@unimi.it

Abstract. We study the problem of ordering linguistic summaries of data in terms of quality, and we propose a model of quality on the basis of four basic criteria. The importance of the user in the definition and the properties of ordering relations are stressed in this paper. We illustrate our approach in the specific setting of linguistic summaries of time series data.

Keywords: Quality, linguistic summaries of data, preorder.

1   Introduction

Linguistic summarization of data is one of the most important research areas in the field of Natural Language Generation, with an important commercial impact. Its objective is to provide an accurate textual description (*summary*) of a dataset satisfying certain users' needs. From a general point of view, we can consider that i) a data set d is a collection of data elements $\{e_1, ..., e_i, ..., e_{n_d}\}$ that use a formal representation model to express the result of the observation of a given reality, and ii) a linguistic summary is a collection of sentences, generated by some formal mechanism, that refer to aspects of the data that are relevant for the user.

One of the most important problems in linguistic summarization is that of assessing the quality of a summary. This is a key point, since the process of generating the summary is usually guided by the objective of obtaining a summary with high quality. However, determining the quality of a summary as well as trying to find the best summary in this sense are very difficult tasks because of several reasons:

---

[*] This work has been partially supported by the projects i) *Representación y Manipulación de Objetos Imperfectos en Problemas de Integración de Datos: Una Aplicación a los Almacenes de Objetos de Aprendizaje*, Junta de Andalucía, Consejería de Economía, Innovación y Ciencia (P07-TIC-03175), and ii) TIN2009-08296, Ministry of Science and Innovation, Spain.

S. Greco et al. (Eds.): IPMU 2012, Part II, CCIS 298, pp. 285–294, 2012.
© Springer-Verlag Berlin Heidelberg 2012

- Quality has many different facets, so in order to assess quality we have to identify and to assess all its aspects. However, there is no agreement about neither the set of aspects to consider, nor the way to evaluate them quantitatively.
- There is a strong interrelation between the different aspects of quality of a summary, with the important problem that they are most of the times opposite, contradictory, and/or have a negative correlation. This means that there is in general no such thing as the *optimum* or *best* summary for a given dataset. On the contrary, we are faced with a multiobjective optimization problem, in which there are several conflicting objectives.
- An important part of quality assessment is clearly subjective and context-dependent as a summary is intended to satisfy the needs of a certain user in a given context.
- The search space comprised of all the possible summaries expressed in a certain suitable subset of natural language (specified for a certain application and dependent on the dataset, user, and context) is usually enormously huge. Hence, the process of obtaining a summary for a certain dataset has a very high complexity.

There are several approaches to perform linguistic summarization of data, based on different data analysis and text generation technologies. In this paper, we face the study of quality independently of the approach employed. We study quality first by means of the properties of an abstract relation $\leq_Q$ meaning *having less quality than*. We also propose some quality criteria that form a multidimensional quality model.

One important group of summarization approaches are based on using fuzzy logic. Among other advantages, fuzzy logic allows us to represent the fuzzy boundaries that are common to most user's concepts, and provides a way to assess the degree of compatibility between linguistic statements and datasets. Different authors have studied the issue of quality of a linguistic summary in this fuzzy setting [9,7,6,10,4,8]. In order to illustrate our approach in a specific setting, we describe a fuzzy summarization model considering summaries consisting of a collection of fuzzy quantified sentences of the form *Q of D are A*, *Q* being a fuzzy quantifier (*Most, At least 80%*, etc.) and *D* and *A* being fuzzy subsets of a certain crisp set *X* induced by fuzzy concepts (e.g., *Most of the tall students are intelligent*). We propose concrete definitions of measures for the previously introduced criteria for these summaries.

2   Quality in Linguistic Summaries

2.1   The Concept of Quality

The main objective when studying the quality of linguistic summaries is to compare two summaries from the point of view of quality. This has led us to start the study of quality from the perspective of a binary order relation in the space of possible summaries of a certain dataset, that is, a binary relation fulfilling at least the reflexive and transitive properties. Let d be a dataset and S_d the set of all possible summaries for d, then we consider a quality relation defined on S_d, $\leq_Q$, verifying

- $\forall s \in S_d \ s \leq_Q s$ (reflexivity)
- $\forall s_1, s_2, s_3 \in S_d \ s_1 \leq_Q s_2 \wedge s_2 \leq_Q s_3 \rightarrow s_1 \leq_Q s_3$ (transitivity)

This kind of relation is called a *preorder*. The possibility that $\leq_Q$ is a more strict order depends on the fulfilment of additional properties such as the antisymmetric and comparability properties. These, on its turn, depend on the quality model employed for determining $\leq_Q$.

In this respect, one way to address the construction of $\leq_Q$ is to determine a criterion associated to quality and to define a measure for it. Under this approach, if the measure is defined for the whole set S_d, the comparability property is guaranteed. If in addition the measure is defined by an injective function, the antisymmetric property will hold as well, and we'll have a total order.

Unfortunately, as it is widely acknowledged in the literature, quality has different facets and hence, more than one criterion has to be considered. Even when it is possible to identify every criteria and to define measures for each one, the fact that these criteria have to be combined somehow (aggregation of measures, definition of orders between criteria, etc.) in a meaningful way, makes it difficult to keep the properties that lead to a total order, that will depend on the combination model.

The criteria associated to quality are many, usually conflicting, and always intimately related to the subjectivity of the user that is the ultimate receiver and the one that has requested and will use the summary. In this work we focus only on those criteria that, though affected also by the subjectivity of the user in their mathematical definition, can be calculated automatically from the dataset and the summary.

Following this idea, in the next section we propose a multidimensional model of quality comprised of four criteria that any "good" measure should intuitively satisfy.

2.2   A Multidimensional Model

In this section, a multidimensional model of quality is presented. A good summary has *to cover the data succinctly and certainly* according to user interest. This short definition of summary suggests some important concepts that have to be taken into account when assessing the quality of a given summary.

Let us first focus on the coverage.

Definition 1 (Coverage of a summary - $c_d(s)$). *Let us consider a dataset d that has to be linguistically summarized and s a given linguistic summary of d. The coverage of d by s, $c_d(s)$, can be defined as the extent to which all data elements $e_i \in d$ are considered in s.*

Whatever the way the coverage is computed, without loss of generality, we can assume that c_d is a normalized fuzzy measure on d. That is, if $d_s = \{e_i \in d \mid e_i$ is considered in s$\}$, then:

- If $d_s = \emptyset$, then $c_d(s) = 0$.
- If $d_s = d$, then $c_d(s) = 1$.
- $\forall s_1, s_2, d_{s_1} \subseteq d_{s_2} \rightarrow c_d(s_1) \leq c_d(s_2)$.

That is, if none of the data elements of d are considered in the summary s, then $c_d(s) = 0$. Conversely, when each and every data element in d is considered in s, then $c_d(s) = 1$. As the number of data elements considered in s increases, $c_d(s)$ also increases.

Table 1. Example dataset

Player	Height (cm)
P1	183
P2	194
P3	181
P4	190
P5	204
P6	211
P7	190
P8	189
P9	203
P10	204

For example, consider the following two summaries of the players' heights in the dataset of table 1:

- s_1: There are four players over 200 cms, three others within [190,200], and the other three are below 190.
- s_2: There are four players over 200 cms.

Summary s_1 considers all the players, while only four players are considered in summary s_2. Then, in this example, first summary s_1 covers more data than summary s_2 and, in this sense, $c_d(s_1)$ must be greater (or equal) than $c_d(s_2)$.

After the definition of coverage, and according to the initial sentence of the section (*to cover the data succinctly and certainly*), we can focus on the succinctness of the summary.

Definition 2 (Brevity of a summary - $b(s)$). *Let us consider a dataset d that has to be linguistically summarized and s a given linguistic summary of d. The brevity of s, $b(s)$, is the extent to which the summary is short.*

Without loss of generality, as we are working with computers with physical limitations that impose bounds on the length of a summary, we can assume that $b(s) \in [0, 1]$.

A value 1 of $b(s)$ means that the summary s is one of the shortest possible summaries; for instance, if we consider brevity in terms of number of sentences, the shortest summaries are those comprised by a single sentence. Of course, the higher the brevity, the better the summary under this criterion.

As an example, it is clear that $b(s_1)$ is less (or equal) than $b(s_2)$.

Finally, regarding whether the summary certainly describes the data, we can consider two main aspects, namely: specificity and accuracy.

Definition 3 (Specificity of a summary - $p(s)$). *Let us consider a dataset d that has to be linguistically summarized and s a given linguistic summary of d. The specificity of s, $p(s)$, is the extent to which concepts in the summary clearly define or identify the data.*

As we are considering datasets represented in computers, we can assume, without loss of generality, that $p(s) \in [0, 1]$.

The value 1 of $p(s)$ means the concepts in the summary clearly identify the involved data; that is, from a summary we can state the concerned data without any doubt. The higher the specificity, the better the summary under this criterion.

For example, consider the following two summaries of the players' heights in the dataset of table 1:

- s_1: There are four players over 200 cms, three others within [190,200], and the other three below 190.
- s_3: One player slightly exceeds 210 cms, three other players are within [200,205], three others within [190,195], and the other three are within [180,189].

In this example, the second summary s_3 uses concepts that give more specific information about the data than the concepts used in the first summary s_1. Thus, $p(s_3)$ must be greater (or equal) than $p(s_1)$.

Definition 4 (Accuracy of a summary - $a_d(s)$). *Let us consider a dataset d that has to be linguistically summarized and s a given linguistic summary of d. The accuracy of s, $a_d(s)$, is the extent to which what the summary says is true for all the covered data elements d_s.*

As in the case of coverage, whatever the way the accuracy is computed, and without loss of generality, we can assume that a_d is a normalized fuzzy measure on d_s. That is, if $t_s = \{e_i \in d_s|$ what s says about e_i is true$\}$, then:

- If $t_s = \emptyset$, then $a_d(s) = 0$.
- If $t_s = d_s$, then $a_d(s) = 1$.
- $\forall s_1, s_2, t_{s_1} \subseteq t_{s_2} \to a_d(s_1) \leq a_d(s_2)$.

A value 1 of accuracy means that what the summary says is true for each data point covered. The higher the accuracy, the better the summary in terms of this criterion.

For example, consider the following two summaries of the players' heights in the dataset of table 1:

- s_1: There are four players over 200 cms, three others within [190,200], and the other three below 190.
- s_4: Half of the players exceed 200 cms while the other half does not go below 180.

In this example, the accuracy of the first summary s_1 is greater than the accuracy of the second summary s_4. Notice that, in this example, $c_d(s_1) = c_d(s_4) = 1$.

These four criteria constitute a four-dimensional quality model defining a wide family of quality relations. The instantiation of this model into an specific order relation must take into consideration the intuition and interest of the user in two respects:

- The definition of suitable measures for each criterion taking into account the semantics and understanding of each criterion by the user.
- The combination of the four criteria in order to determine the final order relation, that must satisfy

$$\forall s_1, s_2 \in S, c(s_1) \leq c(s_2) \wedge b(s_1) \leq b(s_2) \wedge s(s_1) \leq s(s_2) \wedge a(s_1) \leq a(s_2) \rightarrow s_1 \leq_{Q_d} s_2$$

The lesser of the relations that verify the condition above is introduced in the next definition:

Definition 5 (Basic Quality Ordering Relationship - $\leq_{Q_d}^B$). *Let us consider a dataset d that has to be linguistically summarized and S_d be the universe of the summaries that can be built to describe d according to a given formal mechanism. The Basic Quality Ordering Relationship is defined as a binary relation $\leq_{Q_d}^B$ on S_d, as follows:*
$$\forall s_1, s_2 \in S_d, s_1 \leq_{Q_d}^B s_2 \Leftrightarrow c_d(s_1) \leq c_d(s_2) \wedge b(s_1) \leq b(s_2) \wedge s(s_1) \leq s(s_2) \wedge a(s_1) \leq a(s_2)$$

It can be easily seen that the following properties are fulfilled:

- $\forall s \in S_d, s \leq_{Q_d}^B s$ (Reflexivity)
- $\forall s_1, s_2, s_3 \in S_d, (s_1 \leq_{Q_d}^B s_2 \wedge s_2 \leq_{Q_d}^B s_3) \rightarrow s_1 \leq_{Q_d}^B s_3$ (Transitivity)

Thus, the Basic Quality Relationship $\leq_{Q_d}^B$ defines a preorder in S_d.

The use of this basic relationship has important consequences when trying to develop algorithmic techniques to linguistically summarize a given dataset d: we will have to deal with a set of good summaries which may not be comparable.

3   Illustrating the Model with Fuzzy Summarization of Time Series

We describe in this section an instantiation of the previous model and its application for a problem of linguistic summarization of time series data addressed by the authors in [1,2].

3.1   Quantified Sentences as a Tool to Summarize Data

In this example we consider time series data as the dataset, having the form $d = \{< t_1, v_1 >, ..., < t_m, v_m >\}$, where every v_i is a value of the basic domain D_V of a variable V. In order to linguistically describe the information of this time series, we have considered using fuzziness as follows:

- The basic domain of variable V under study is partitioned by a set of linguistic labels $A=\{A_1, ..., A_s\}$.
- The time dimension is hierarchically organized in n levels, namely, $L=L_1, ..., L_n$. Each level L_i has associated a partition $\{D_{i,1}, ..., D_{i,p_i}\}$ of the basic time domain.

We then consider linguistic summaries comprised of a set of fuzzy quantified sentences of the form "Q of D are A", where Q represents a fuzzy quantifier, and D and A are fuzzy subsets of the dataset induced by a fuzzy subset of the time dimension and A fuzzy subset of the domain of the values, respectively, as explained before. The fuzzy quantifier Q can be one of a collection in a totally ordered subset $\{Q_1, ..., Q_{qmax}\}$ of a coherent family of quantifiers $\mathfrak{Q}$ (see [3]). An example is the statement *Most of the days in winter the temperature is low or very low.*

3.2   An Instantiation of the Proposed Model

First of all, a suitable way of computing the quality measures is shown. After that, an example data set will be presented, and also summaries of that data set with the corresponding measures.

Brevity: Let $len(s)$ be the number of quantified sentences that make up the summary s. Then, the brevity of a linguistic summary will be $b(s) = 1/len(s)$.

Accuracy: The accuracy of a single sentence is computed based on the GD method (see [5] for further information). Then, the accuracy of the entire summary is obtained by averaging these accuracies as follows:

$$a_d(s) = \frac{\sum_{i=1}^{len(s)} GD(sen_i)}{len(s)}. \tag{1}$$

where sen_i is the i-th sentence in summary s.

Coverage: The coverage $c_d(s)$ is computed as the percentage of time points that are covered by sentences in the summary. We consider a point x is covered if there is a sentence sen_i having a set D induced by a fuzzy time interval D_j such that $D_j(x) > 0$.

Specificity: For each sentence in the summary,

$$imp(sen_i) = (area(Q) + area(A))/2, \tag{2}$$

where $area(Q), area(A) \in [0,1]$ are the relative area under the membership functions of fuzzy sets Q and A with respect to the membership function of their respective referential sets. Then

$$p(s) = 1 - \left(\frac{\sum_{i=1}^{len(s)} imp(sen_i)}{len(s)} \right). \tag{3}$$

3.3   Example

Figure 1 represents the patient inflow along a given year to a certain medical centre (365 measures). As we can see, the time dimension is hierarchically organized thanks to three fuzzy partitions of the time domain, namely: one based on approximate months (in order to avoid a strong dependence of the obtained summaries with respect to the crisp boundaries of conventional months) and two others based on a meteorological criteria with two levels of granularity. Fuzziness is specially useful in these two last partitions because transitions between periods are clearly fuzzy. A fuzzy partition of the inflow basic domain with five labels completes the example. The specific definition of all fuzzy sets can be found in [1].

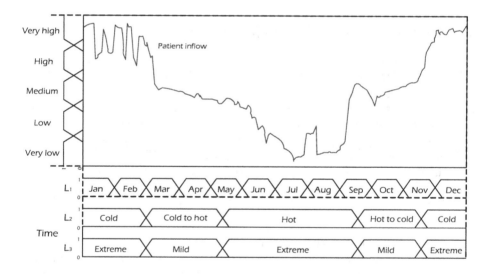

Fig. 1. Patient inflow data set

Among the different summaries that can describe the patient inflow data set, two of them have been selected to illustrate the Basic Quality Ordering Relationship (Definition 5).

Summary 1

Most of days, with cold weather, income is very high or high.
At least 70% of days, with hot weather, income is low or very low.
Most of days, with mild weather, income is medium.

Summary 2

Most of days, with cold weather, income is very high or high.
At least 70% of days, in May, income is medium or low.
Most of days, with hot to cold weather, income is medium.
At least 80% of days, in September, income is medium or very low.
At least 80% of days, with cold to hot weather, income is medium.
At least 70% of days, with hot weather, income is low or very low.

Table 2. Quality measures for summaries 1 and 2

Quality measures	Summary 1	Summary 2
Brevity	**1/3**	1/6
Accuracy	0.97549	**0.98774**
Coverage	1	1
Specificity	0.271667	**0.289167**

A comparison of the quality measures of both summaries, summary 1 and summary 2, is shown in Table 2. As can be seen, the coverage in both summaries reach the maximum value. So regarding this criterion, both summaries are equal. However, this equality does not apply in the other three criteria. With respect to brevity, summary 1 is better than summary 2, as it is comprised by less sentences. But, in terms of accuracy and specificity, summary 2 has better results. If we base the comparison in terms of quality on the Basic Quality Ordering Relationship $\leq^B_{Q_d}$, it cannot be said that one of the summaries is better than the other one, i.e., they are not comparable.

4   Conclusions and Further Work

In this paper we have proposed a multidimensional model for assessing the quality of linguistic summaries of data. Four criteria are considered which may be assessed by means of measures satisfying certain properties. The specific measures must be defined in accordance with the intuition of the user, since the ordering of summaries in terms of quality is always subject to user's interest. Because of the same reason, there are different ways in which these criteria may be combined in order to obtain a final quality relation. A basic one is proposed which verifies the required properties.

We have illustrated the usefulness of our proposal in the specific problem of summarizing time series data using quantified sentences, following an approach previously introduced by the authors. We have proposed here specific measures for the four criteria, and we have shown some results for a simple dataset.

The four criteria considered can be automatically calculated from the dataset and the summary. However, other user-dependent criteria are also important for the quality of summaries. As future work, we shall consider the extension of our model based on the inclusion of these criteria, for instance those studied in [8].

References

1. Castillo-Ortega, R., Marín, N., Sánchez, D.: A fuzzy approach to the linguistic summarization of time series. Journal of Multiple-Valued Logic and Soft Computing 17(2-3), 157–182 (2011)
2. Castillo-Ortega, R., Marín, N., Sánchez, D., Tettamanzi, A.: A multi-objective memetic algorithm for the linguistic summarization of time series. In: GECCO 2011 (2011)
3. Cubero, J., Medina, J., Pons, O., Vila, M.: The generalized selection: An alternative way for the quotient operations in fuzzy relational databases. In: Bouchon-Meunier, B., Yager, R., Zadeh, L. (eds.) Fuzzy Logic and Soft Computing. World Scientific Press (1995)
4. Díaz-Hermida, F., Ramos, A., Bugarín, A.: On the role of fuzzy quantified statements in linguistic summarization of data. In: Proceedings ISDA 2011 (2011)
5. Delgado, M., Sánchez, D., Vila, M.: Fuzzy cardinality based evaluation of quantified sentences. International Journal of Approximate Reasoning 23, 23–66 (2000)
6. Kacprzyk, J., Yager, R.: Linguistic summaries of data using fuzzy logic. International Journal of General Systems 30, 133–154 (2001)
7. Kacprzyk, J., Yager, R., Zadrozÿny, S.: A fuzzy logic based approach to linguistic summaries of databases. International Journal of Applied Mathematics and Computer Science 10, 813–834 (2000)
8. Pereira-Fariña, M., Eciolaza, L., Trivino, G.: Quality assessment of linguistic description of data. In: Proceedings ESTYLF 2012 (2012)
9. Yager, R.: A new approach to the summarization of data. Information Sciences 28, 69–86 (1982)
10. Yager, R., Petry, F.: A multicriteria approach to data summarization using concept ontologies. IEEE Transactions on Fuzzy Systems 14(6), 767–780 (2006)

Selection of the Best Suitable Sentences in Linguistic Descriptions of Data

Carlos Menendez[1] and Gracian Trivino[2]

[1] HC Energia,
[2] European Centre for Soft Computing,
Asturias, Spain

Abstract. We describe our results in the field of automatic linguistic description of data. Our goal is the design of a new generation of computational applications able to summarize in a few meaningful natural language sentences the meaning of huge amounts of available data about complex phenomena. As part of our research line in this field, we present our advances on selecting relevant sentences in Granular Linguistic Models of Phenomena. The concept is demonstrated using a practical application.

Keywords: Linguistic description of data, Computing with words and perceptions, Granular linguistic model of phenomena.

1 Introduction

Computational systems are able to store huge amounts of data about the phenomena in our environment. Nevertheless, their ability to extract relevant knowledge from this data and express it in understandable language remains limited.

Human cognition is based on the role of perceptions. While describing a phenomenon we use a collection of granular perceptions. Perception granulation abstract from individual observations of a phenomenon to view the phenomenon as a whole, improving understanding for problem solving [1].

In the research line of Computational Theory of Perceptions (CTP) [2][3], we have created the Granular Linguistic Model of a Phenomenon (GLMP). It is a data structure that allows computational systems to generate linguistic descriptions of input data. The linguistic description of a phenomenon is a summary of the available information where certain relevant aspects are remarked while other irrelevant aspects remain hidden.

In this paper, we explore, upon our previous research, the possibilities to automatically acquire constraints to reorganize the structure of an initial GLMP obtained from a defined input domain. We do so by a machine driven process of reorganization of the GLMP. The reorganization is performed by pruning non relevant perceptions and by aggregating related ones avoiding redundancy. The objective is to generate coherent and cohesive linguistic sentences, avoiding repetition and linking individual granular sentences.

We include a practical example to provide linguistic sentences about electricity consumption gathered at hourly periods.

S. Greco et al. (Eds.): IPMU 2012, Part II, CCIS 298, pp. 295–304, 2012.
© Springer-Verlag Berlin Heidelberg 2012

2   Granular Linguistic Model of Phenomena

CTP was introduced in the Zadeh's seminal paper "From computing with numbers to computing with words - from manipulation of measurements to manipulation of perceptions" [2] and further developed in subsequent papers, e.g., [3]. It grounds on the fact that human cognition is based on the role of perceptions, and the remarkable capability to granulate information in order to perform physical and mental tasks without any traditional measurements and computations.

In the research line of CTP, we have developed the GLMP. In this section, we introduce the components of GLMP for developing computational systems able to generate linguistic descriptions of data [4] [5] [6] [7] [8] .

Computational Perception (CP). A *CP* is the computational model of a unit of information acquired by the designer about the phenomenon to be modeled. In general, *CP*s correspond with specific parts of the phenomenon at certain degrees of granularity. A *CP* is a tuple (A, W, R) where:

$A = (a_1, a_2, \ldots, a_n)$ is a vector of linguistic expressions (sentences in NL) that represents the linguistic domain of the CP. Each a_i describes the value of the CP in each situation with specific degree of granularity. These sentences can be either simple, e.g., $a_i =$ *"The consumption in the morning is quite high"* or more complex, e.g., $a_i =$ *"Some days you could save a lot of money"*.

$W = (w_1, w_2, \ldots, w_n)$ is a vector of validity degrees $w_i \in [0, 1]$ assigned to each a_i in the specific context. The concept of validity depends on the application, i.e., it is a function of the truthfulness of each sentence for specific input data.

$R = (r_1, r_2, \ldots, r_n)$ is a vector of relevancy degrees $r_i \in [0, 1]$ assigned to each a_i in the specific context. The concept of relevancy depends on the application. During the initialization stage, these values are assigned by the designer of the computational system in function of specific requirements in the application context.

In this paper, as a contribution to this research line, we have increased the expressivity of *CP* by including the vector of relevancies R in its definition. It is used as complementary data to select the most suitable sentences.

For example, a computational perception that models the morning consumption $CP_1 = (A_1, W_1, R_1)$, could be instantiated as:
$a_1 =$"The consumption in the morning is high",$w_1 = 0, 7, r_1 = 0, 8$
$a_2 =$"The consumption in the morning is medium",$w_2 = 0, 3, r_2 = 0, 3$
$a_3 =$"The consumption in the morning is low",$w_3 = 0, r_3 = 0, 8$

Perception Mapping (PM). We use *PM*s to create and aggregate *CP*s. There are many types of *PM*s and this paper explores several of them. A *PM* is a tuple (U, y, g, T) where:

U is a vector of input *CP*s, $U = (u_1, u_2, \ldots, u_n)$, where $u_i = (A_i, W_i)$. In the special case of first order Perception Mappings (*1PM*s), these are the inputs

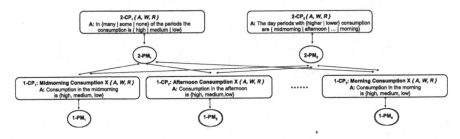

Fig. 1. Example of GLMP structure

to the GLMP and they are values $z \in R$ being provided either by a sensor or obtained from a database.

y is the output CP, $y = (A_y, W_y)$.

g is an aggregation function employed to calculate the vector of fuzzy degrees of validity assigned to each element in y, $W_y = (w_1, w_2, ..., w_{n_y})$, as a fuzzy aggregation of input vectors, $W_y = g(W_{u_1}, W_{u_2}, ..., W_{u_n})$, where W_{u_i} are the degrees of validity of the input perceptions. In Fuzzy Logic many different types of aggregation functions have been developed. For example g could be implemented using a set of fuzzy rules. In the case of *1PMs*, g is built using a set of membership functions as follows:

$$W_y = (\mu_{a_1}(z), \mu_{a_2}(z), \ldots, \mu_{a_{n_y}}(z)) = (w_1, w_2, \ldots, w_{n_y})$$

where W_y is the vector of degrees of validity assigned to each a_y, and z is the input data.

T is a text generation algorithm that allows generating the sentences in A_y. In simple cases, T is a linguistic template, e.g., *"The consumption of electricity is {high | medium | low}"*.

Structure of the GLMP. The *GLMP* consists of a network of *PM*s. Each *PM* receives a set of input *CP*s and transmits upwards a *CP*. We say that each output *CP* is *explained* by the *PM* using a set of input *CP*s. In the network, each *CP* covers specific aspects of the phenomenon with certain degree of granularity. In the example showed in Fig. 1, 1-CPs are obtained from input data, 2-CPs are calculated based on subordinate CPs, describing information at different levels of granularity.

Using different aggregation functions and different linguistic expressions, the paradigm *GLMP* allows the designer to model computationally his/her perceptions. Nevertheless, after being instantiated with a set of input data, the GLMP provides a structure of valid sentences that in medium size applications could include hundreds of sentences.

In a GLMP each PM spread upwards generating an ordered layout. The GLMP structure is organized by layers. Fig. 2 shows an example of a GLMP Linguistic expression instantiation, for simplicity only the sentences for each CP with the highest validity are showed.

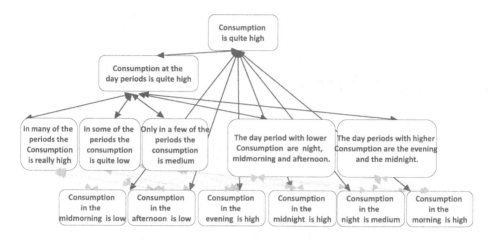

Fig. 2. Example of instantiation of linguistic expressions

The hierarchical structure in the GLMP allows to infer formal relations between perceptions providing cohesion as it is spread from bottom perceptions till top-level perceptions.

3   Text Generation

For each vector of linguistic expressions in a CP, individual expressions are selected or not in an output text based on its validity and relevance. Only those linguistic expressions with the highest degree of validity will remain in the resulting text, e.g., the degree of validity provided by the membership function and relevance defined by the relevancy weight is higher than a threshold value.

In order to generate linguistic descriptions, the text generator must be able to determine what information to communicate and how to organize this information to accomplish a communicative goal. We use a set of heuristics derived from an initial GLMP, that is used to decide what types of simple perceptions constitute a relevant linguistic description, as well as the ways in which simple sentences are combined into most complex ones. The aim for this reorganization is to avoid redundancy and provide cohesion. We do so by pruning non relevant perceptions instances and by aggregating and linking related perceptions instances. Our criteria for performing this task consisted of following the Gricean Maxims [9].

Maxim of Quality. It requires to analyze the candidate report from the viewpoint of its truth in the context current conditions. After instantiating the GLMP with input data, for each CP, each possible sentence a_i has associated a degree of validity w_i.

Maxim of Quantity. It requires evaluate if the quantity of statements used in the report are the right for expressing the relevant ideas or if there is redundancy in the text, i.e., if the report provides the adequate amount of information. The more branches of the GLMP are pruned, the shorter the report. The more sentences are fused the shorter the report.

Maxim of Relation Relevance. The relevance is very subjective, since it depends of the background of final user. The designer will assign to each sentence a_i a degree of relevance r_i in function of the application context.

Maxim of Manner. The candidate report must be evaluated considering if it uses the adequate vocabulary, if the order of the ideas is appropriate or if the used expressions are the right ones. The designer must choose linguistic expressions typically used by the final user, i.e., these sentences must belong to the domain of language of the final user in the application context. By the other hand, the aggregation of simple clauses to form complex sentences must follow an straight forward mechanism. For example, high order CPs can be explained by subordinate CPs using the conjunction "because".

4 Pruning

Pruning defines, in the instantiation, what information to communicate in order to provide relevant linguistic descriptions. While pruning, a suitable weight for each sentence is computed for afterwards excluding irrelevant ones.

We face the problem of selecting the most suitable sentences by calculating a weight of suitability S_i for each expression with three components, namely s_1 degree of validity, s_2 degree of relevancy and s_3 degree of covering.

The degree of validity, $s_1 = w_i$ determines the degree to which a sentence is valid as a basic criteria. It is performed in a first step during content planning, maintaining in the GLMP only those sentences with the highest degree of validity, e.g., the degree of validity specified by the membership function is higher than a threshold value.

The degree of relevancy $s_2 = r_i$ determines the importance of the sentence defined in the semantic context of the application. It applies to perception attribute and value pairs. For example, to speak about *efficiency* is relevant but it could be more relevant to speak about *very low efficiency* behaviour than to speak about *medium efficiency* behaviour.

The degree of covering s_3 is performed by assigning more importance to a summary than to individual perceptions and by identifying summaries with a low covering, avoiding local behavior without representativeness. For example, speak about overall daily consumption is considered more relevant because of its general covering than to speak about the consumption at 4:00 in the morning. It is computed as the number of subordinated CPs divided by the total number of CPs in the GLMP.

$$s_3 = \frac{CP_{GLMP_{childnodes}} w_i}{GLMP_{nodes} w_{i..n}}$$

Non relevant information among all the linguistic expressions in CPs are excluded using the suitability weight S_i, following a bottom-up strategy. The pruning algorithm starts from the leaves and go up until the root node is reached. Note

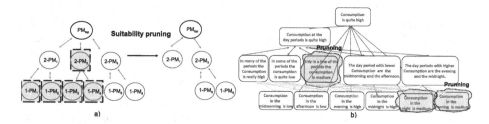

Fig. 3. Suitability Pruning Layout and Example of Sentence Instantiation

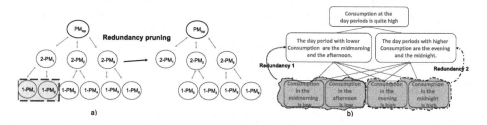

Fig. 4. Redundancy Pruning Layout and Example of Sentence Instantiation

that pruning is performed for each linguistic expression, and not over CPs. Pruning is performed for those sentences under an specific degree of validity, relevance, and coverage, e.g., perceptions with a suitability degree lower than a threshold value are pruned.

Conceptually, in Fig. 3.a is showed a generic GLMP structure and its suitability pruning. Independently in Fig. 3.b it is showed an example of a GLMP Linguistic expression suitability pruning, for simplicity only the sentences for each CP with the highest validity are showed, e.g., "Only in a few of the periods the consumption is medium" is pruned because of its low suitability.

A second pruning is performed following a top-down path, when parent perceptions are explained by the children ones, and therefore additional meaning is not deployed but redundancy.

Conceptually, in Fig. 4.a is showed a generic GLMP structure and its redundancy pruning. Independently in Fig. 4.b it is showed an example of a GLMP Linguistic expression redundancy pruning, for simplicity only the sentences for each CP with the highest validity are showed, e.g., "Consumption in the morning is low" is pruned because it is already expressed in its parent perception.

5   Aggregation

Aggregation provides, in the instantiation, cohesion to linguistic expressions. It merges linguistic expressions of different CPs if they can be expressed in a complex sentence. While aggregating, relations between perceptions sentences are computed by similarity, and if applies, clustered together using a connective. The

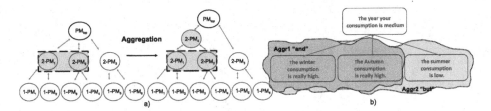

Fig. 5. GLMP Aggregation Layout and example of Sentence Instantiation

choice of the connective depends on the relations that hold between perceptions and their semantics, e.g., *additive "and" or adversative "but" conjunctions*.

Aditive aggregation is computed by the similarity of perceptions sentences and applied as shared participants, e.g. *"The Winter and Autum consumption is really high."* . Adversative aggregation is computed by dissimilarity of perceptions sentences and applied as shared structures, e.g. *"The Winter consumption is really high but the Summer consumption is low."*. Note that causal aggregation is already defined by IF-THEN rules in second order perceptions, e.g., *"The efficiency is low due to the high consumption and low efficiency devices"*.

Conceptually, in Fig. 5.a is showed a generic GLMP structure and the merging. Independently in Fig. 5.b it is showed an example of a GLMP Linguistic expression merging, for simplicity only the sentences for each CP with the highest validity are showed.

Aggregations are computed in order, first additive and later adversative at each GLMP layer. The algorithm decides for each CP, if a new parent CP should be created aggregating children or should remain. Note that parent perceptions are completely explain by children ones, that because of redundancy are pruned.

6   Application

In this section, we use a practical application to illustrate the details of our approach. The scope of this example is limited to a prototype for demonstrating the concept. The company HC Energia [10] launched the project "Ecofamilias", with the objective of providing useful information about electricity consumption to households. The consumption measures are retrieved by hourly meter devices.

In a previous article we proposed the navigation through the information stored in an GLMP schema [11]. Using a subset of the previous GLMP schema, it is defined the historical energy consumption database [11]. The dimensions associated with a query over the consumption measure are translated to computational perceptions. The definition of fuzzy Consumption measure has values $Consumption \in \{Really\ High,\ Quite\ high,\ Medium,\ Quite\ Low,\ Realy\ Low\}$. The dimensional fuzzy attributes for the Time dimension are defined as Time $\in \{Price\ Period, Day\ Period, Hour\}$ with values:
- $PricePeriod \in \{ChargedPeriod, ReducedPeriod\}$
- $Day\ Period \in \{Morning, \dots, Night\}$
- $Hour \in [1, 24] \in N$

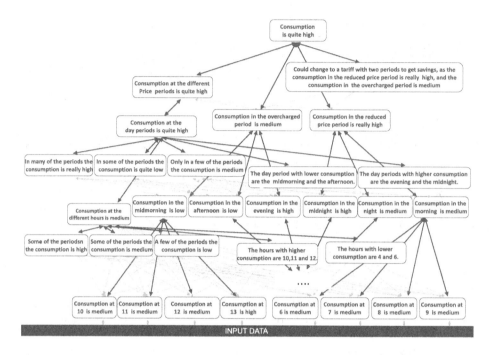

Fig. 6. Linguistic Expressions Instantiation

A *Summarizer* ∈ {*Only a few, Some, A lot, Most of*} and a maximizer and minimizer quantifiers *Max/Min* ∈ {*the highest, the lowest*} are defined and applied to fuzzy attributes. A second order perception based on if-then rules is generated for tariff advice to get savings, based on consumption in the overcharged and reduced price period, e.g. *"IF Consumption in ChargedPeriod is low AND Consumption in the ReducedPeriod is high THEN TwoPeriods Tariff"*.

The communicative objective is to identify relevant information as response to the query *"How is the consumption this year"*. Input data is retrieved from a query on *Time* dimension. The result is a table with the numeric value of the average consumption for each hour as it is the lower time hierarchy attribute, e.g. *as tuples (Hour-Consumption in wh) "H22 - 1.320, H23 - 1.796, H24 - 586,1 - 217, H2 - 131,3 - 97, H4 - 45, H5 - 65, H6 - 161, H7 - 129, H8 - 945, H9 - 1.243, H10 - 116, H11 - 145, H12 - 132, H13 - 87, H14 - 161, H15 - 129, H16 - 171, H17 - 131, H18 - 253, H19 - 275, H20 - 876, H21 - 934 "*

During GLMP definition, first order perceptions are computed from these input data for each lower level attribute values, e.g. *"Your consumption at 23 is quite high"*. Second order perceptions are spread upwards for each attribute value along the Time hierarchy till defining the overall GLMP structure.

	Degree of Validity	Degree of Relevancy	Degree of Covering	Suitability
Your consumption is quite high	1,000	0,625	1,000	0,850
You could change to a tariff with two periods	0,960	1,000	0,762	0,897
The consumption at the different price periods is quite high	0,973	0,625	0,952	0,826
The consumption in the reduced price period is really high	0,960	0,750	0,881	0,844
The consumption in the overcharged price period is medium	0,987	0,300	0,881	0,670
In many of the periods the consumption is really high	1,000	0,750	0,643	0,757
In some of the periods the consumption is medium	1,000	0,300	0,643	0,577
Only in a few of the periods the consumption is quite low	1,000	0,750	0,643	0,757
The day periods with higher consumption are the evening and midnight	0,900	0,750	0,571	0,709
The day period with lower consumption are the night, the midmorning and the	0,900	0,750	0,571	0,709
The consumption at the different day periods is quite high	0,973	0,625	0,524	0,654
The consumption in the midnight is really high.	0,917	0,750	0,095	0,521
The consumption in the night is quite low	0,962	0,625	0,095	0,480
The consumption in the morning is really high	1,000	0,750	0,095	0,538
The consumption in the midmorning is medium	0,962	0,300	0,095	0,350
The consumption in the afternoon is quite low	1,000	0,625	0,095	0,488
The consumption in the evening is really high	1,000	0,750	0,095	0,538
....				
The consumption at the different hours is quite high	1,000	0,625	0,286	0,564
The consumption at 00 is quite high	1,000	0,625	0,024	0,460
The consumption at 1 is medium	0,671	0,300	0,024	0,324
The consumption at 2 is quite low	1,000	0,625	0,024	0,460
The consumption at 3 is quite low	1,000	0,625	0,024	0,460
The consumption at 4 is really low	0,851	0,750	0,024	0,480
....				

Fig. 7. Suitability assignment for perception instances

The hierarchical layout is defined using the dimensional axis to generate the granular ordered structure, using the Time hierarchy. The resulting GLMP is showed on Fig. 6.

For sentences selection and pruning, it is performed the computation of suitability S_i, namely (1) the degree of validity, (2) the degree of relevancy and (3) the degree of covering. Here we have followed the simple criteria of using

$$S_i = \frac{1}{n}\sum_{i=1}^{n} s_i$$

Pruning represents the process of identification of relevant information among all the CPs instantiated in the GLMP. As defined in the model, perceptions with a suitability degree lower than 0,65 are pruned.Results are displayed on Fig. 7.

After pruning, remaining CPs are aggregated if their meaning can be expressed in an individual complex perception. The choice of connectives is based on relations that holds between perceptions and their semantics. First step is looking for similar perceptions, expressed by the "and" connective. Second aggregation is performed looking for opposed behavior expressed by a "but" connective.

The output text generated by the instantiation of the reorganized GLMP is as follows: *"Your consumption is quite high. You could change to a tariff with two periods to get savings, as your consumption in the reduced price period is really high and the consumption in the overcharged price period is medium. In many of the day periods the consumption is really high, but only in a few the consumption is quite low. The day periods with higher consumption are the evening and the midnight, whether day periods with lower consumption are the midmorning and the afternoon".*

7   Conclusions

In the context of generating linguistic descriptions using a GLMP, this paper focus the problem of choosing the more relevant sentences among a set of valid sentences. In general, the empirical rules of relevancy that must be applied to generate a specific linguistic report could be very complex. This paper shows some basic ideas about how to face an automatic solution to this challenging problem. The practical application demonstrates the possibilities of our approach.

Acknowledgements. The authors would like to thank HC Energia by the opportunity of applying this research in a practical project. This work has been funded by the Spanish government under project TIN2011-29827-C02-01.

References

1. Granular Computing An Introduction Bargiela, Andrzej, Pedrycz, Witold, 480p. (2002)
2. Zadeh, L.A.: From computing with numbers to computing with words- from manipulation of measurements to manipulation of perceptions. IEEE Transactions on Circuits and Systems 45(1) (1999)
3. Zadeh, L.A.: Toward human level machine intelligence - is it achievable? The need for a paradigm shift. IEEE Computational Intelligence Magazine (August 2008)
4. Mendez-Nunez, S., Trivino, G.: Combining semantic web technologies and computational theory of perceptions for text generation in financial analysis. In: Proceedings of the IEEE Fuzzy 2010, Barcelona, Spain (2010)
5. Trivino, G., Sanchez, A., Montemayor, A.S., Pantrigo, J.J., Cabido, R., Pardo, E.G.: Linguistic description of traffic in a roundabout. In: Proceedings of the IEEE Fuzzy 2010, Barcelona, Spain (2010)
6. Trivino, G., Alvarez, A., Bailador, G.: Application of the computational theory of perceptions to human gait pattern recognition. Pattern Recognition 43-7, 2572–2581 (2010)
7. Trivino, G., Sobrino, A.: Human perceptions versus computational perceptions in computational theory of perceptions. In: Proceedings of the International Fuzzy Systems Association World Congress, IFSA/EUSFLAT
8. Trivino, G., van der Heide, A.: An experiment on the description of sequences of fuzzy perceptions. In: Proceedings of the 8th International Conference on Hybrid Intelligent Systems (HIS 2008), Barcelona, Spain (September 2008)
9. Grice, P.: Studies on the way of words. Hardward University Press (1991)
10. HC ENERGIA, http://www.hcenergia.com
11. Menendez, C., Trivino, G.: OLAP navigation in the Granular Linguistic Model of a Phenomenon. In: Proceedings of the 5th IEEE International Symposium on Computational Intelligence and Data Mining (CIDM 2011), Paris, France, April 11-15, pp. 260–267 (2011)

Some Results on the Composition of L-Fuzzy Contexts

Cristina Alcalde[1], Ana Burusco[2], and Ramón Fuentes-González[2]

[1] Dpt. Matemática Aplicada, Escuela Universitaria Politécnica
UPV/EHU. Plaza de Europa, 1
20018 - San Sebastián, Spain
c.alcalde@ehu.es

[2] Dpt. Automática y Computación. Universidad Pública de Navarra
Campus de Arrosadía
31006 - Pamplona, Spain
{burusco,rfuentes}@unavarra.es

Abstract. In this work, we introduce and study the composition of two
L-fuzzy contexts that share the same attribute set. Besides studying its
properties, this composition allows to establish relations between the sets
of objects associated to both L-fuzzy contexts.

We also define, as a particular case, the composition of an L-fuzzy
context with itself.

In all the cases, we show some examples that illustrate the results.

Keywords: Formal contexts theory, L-fuzzy contexts, Contexts associated with a fuzzy implication operator.

1 Introduction

In some situations we have information that relates two sets X and Z to the same
set Y and we want to know if these relations allow us to establish connections
between X and Z. In the present work we will try to deal with the study of this
problem using as tool the L-fuzzy Concepts Theory.

The Formal Concept Analysis developed by Wille ([11]) tries to extract some
information from a binary table that represents a formal context (X, Y, R) with
X and Y two finite sets (of objects and attributes, respectively) and $R \subseteq X \times Y$. This information is obtained by means of the formal concepts which are
pairs (A, B) with $A \subseteq X$, $B \subseteq Y$ fulfilling $A^* = B$ and $B^* = A$ (where $*$ is
the derivation operator which associates to each object set A the set B of the
attributes related to A, and vice versa). A is the extension and B the intension
of the concept.

The set of the concepts derived from a context (X, Y, R) is a complete lattice
and it is usually represented by a line diagram.

In some previous works ([2],[3]) we defined the L-fuzzy context (L, X, Y, R),
with L a complete lattice, X and Y the sets of objects and attributes respectively
and $R \in L^{X \times Y}$ an L-fuzzy relation between the objects and the attributes, as

S. Greco et al. (Eds.): IPMU 2012, Part II, CCIS 298, pp. 305–314, 2012.
© Springer-Verlag Berlin Heidelberg 2012

an extension to the fuzzy case of the Wille's formal contexts when the relation between the objects and the attributes that we want to study takes values in a complete lattice L. When we work with these L-fuzzy contexts we use the derivation operators 1 and 2 defined by: For every $A \in L^X, B \in L^Y$

$$A_1(y) = \inf_{x \in X}\{I(A(x), R(x, y))\}, \quad B_2(x) = \inf_{y \in Y}\{I(B(y), R(x, y))\}$$

where I is a fuzzy implication [5] defined in $(L, \leq)$, $I : L \times L \longrightarrow L$, and A_1 represents, in a fuzzy way, the attributes related to the objects of A and B_2 the objects related to the attributes of B.

The information of the context is visualized by means of the L-fuzzy concepts which are pairs $(A, A_1) \in (L^X, L^Y)$ with $A \in \text{fix}(\varphi)$ the set of fixed points of the operator φ, being this one defined by the derivation operators 1 and 2 mentioned above as $\varphi(A) = (A_1)_2 = A_{12}$. These pairs, whose first and second components are the extension and the intension respectively, represent, in a vague way, the set of objects that share some attributes.

The set $\mathcal{L} = \{(A, A_1) : A \in \text{fix}(\varphi)\}$ with the order relation $\leq$ defined as:

$$(A, A_1), (C, C_1) \in \mathcal{L}, \quad (A, A_1) \leq (C, C_1) \text{ if } A \leq C$$

(or equiv. $C_1 \leq A_1$) is a complete lattice that is said to be the L-fuzzy concept lattice ([2],[3]).

On the other hand, given $A \in L^X$, (or $B \in L^Y$) we can obtain the derived L-fuzzy concept by applying the defined derivation operators. In the case of the use of the Lukasiewicz implication operator (as it holds in this work), the associated L-fuzzy concept is (A_{12}, A_1) (or (B_2, B_{21})).

Other extensions of the Formal Concept Analysis to the Fuzzy area are in [12], [10], [1], [6], [8], [9] and [4].

2   Composed Formal Contexts

The composition of formal contexts allows to establish relations between the elements of two sets of objects that share the same attribute set.

Definition 1. *Let $(X, Y, R1)$ and $(Z, Y, R2)$ be two formal contexts, the composed formal context is defined as the context $(X, Z, R1 \star R2)$, where $\forall (x, z) \in X \times Z$:*

$$R1 \star R2(x, z) = \begin{cases} 1 & \text{if } R2(z, y) = 1, \ \forall y \text{ such that } R1(x, y) = 1 \\ 0 & \text{in other case} \end{cases}$$

That is, the object x is related to z in the composed context if z shares all the attributes of x in the original contexts.

Proposition 1. *The relation of the composed context, $R1 \star R2$, can also be defined as:*

$$R1 \star R2(x, z) = \min_{y \in Y}\{\max\{R1'(x, y), R2(z, y)\}\} \quad \forall (x, z) \in X \times Z$$

where $R1'$ is the negation of the relation $R1$, that is, $R1'(x,y) = (R1(x,y))'$ $\forall(x,y) \in X \times Y$.

Remark 1. Given the formal contexts $(X,Y,R1)$ and $(Z,Y,R2)$, the relation of the composed context $R1 \star R2$ is not necessarily the opposed of the relation $R2 \star R1$, that is, there exists $(x,z) \in X \times Z$ such that $R1 \star R2(x,z) \neq R2 \star R1(z,x)$.

This property will be helpful in the following sections.

2.1 Particular Case: When a Formal Context Is Composed with Itself

Let us analyze a particular case where some interesting results are obtained.

Proposition 2. *Let (X,Y,R) be a formal context. If (X,Y,R) is composed with itself, then the obtained context is $(X,X,R \star R)$ where the sets of objects and attributes are coincident and the relation $R \star R$ is a binary relation defined on X as follows:*

$$R \star R(x_1,x_2) = \min_{y \in Y}\{\max\{R'(x_1,y),R(x_2,y)\}\} \ \forall(x_1,x_2) \in X \times X$$

Remark 2. The object x_1 is related to attribute x_2 in the composed context, if in the original contexts the object x_2 has at least the same attributes than x_1.

Proposition 3. *The relation $R \star R$ obtained by the composition of the formal context (X,Y,R) with itself is a preorder relation defined on the object set X.*

Proof. As a consequence of the definition, it is immediate to prove that:

1. The relation $R \star R$ is reflexive.
2. The relation $R \star R$ is transitive.

$\square$

Remark 3. It is a simple verification to see that:

- The relation $R \star R$ is not, in general, a symmetric relation. To be symmetric it is necessary that whenever an object x_2 in the original context (X,Y,R) has all the attributes of another object x_1, both objects have the same set of attributes.
- The relation $R \star R$ is not antisymmetric either. Therefore, $R \star R$ is not, in general, an order relation.

3 Extension to the *L*-Fuzzy Context Case

The expression given in proposition 1 can be extended to the fuzzy case substituting the maximum operator by a t-conorm S and taking a strong negation $'$. In this way, we can define the compositions of two L-fuzzy contexts as follows:

Definition 2. *Let $(L, X, Y, R1)$ and $(L, Z, Y, R2)$ be two L-fuzzy contexts, we define the composed L-fuzzy context $(L, X, Z, R1 \star R2)$, where:*

$$R1 \star R2(x, z) = \inf_{y \in Y} \{S(R1'(x, y), R2(z, y))\} \quad \forall (x, z) \in X \times Z$$

with S a t-conorm defined in the lattice L.

If we recall the definition of a fuzzy S-implication, the previous one can be expressed in this way:

Definition 3. *Let $(L, X, Y, R1)$ and$(L, Z, Y, R2)$ be two L-fuzzy contexts, and I an S-implication operator. We define the composed L-fuzzy context $(L, X, Z, R1 \star R2)$, where:*

$$R1 \star R2(x, z) = \inf_{y \in Y} \{I(R1(x, y), R2(z, y))\} \quad \forall (x, z) \in X \times Z$$

We can generalize this definition to any fuzzy implication as we will see next.

3.1   Composition of *L*-Fuzzy Contexts Associated with an Implication Operator

Definition 4. *Let $(L, X, Y, R1)$ and $(L, Z, Y, R2)$ be two L-fuzzy contexts, and let I be a fuzzy implication operator, we define the* composed *L-fuzzy context associated with the implication I as the L-fuzzy context $(L, X, Z, R1 \star_I R2)$, where:*

$$R1 \star_I R2(x, z) = \inf_{y \in Y} \{I(R1(x, y), R2(z, y))\} \quad \forall (x, z) \in X \times Z$$

Remark 4. If we remind the definition of the *triangle subproduct* operator ⊲ given by [7], one of the standard operators in the fuzzy relation theory, we can see that the composed relation defined here can be written as

$$R1 \star_I R2 = R1 \lhd (R2)^{op}$$

As can be observed, also in this case a similar result to the crisp case is obtained.

Proposition 4. *Let $(L, X, Y, R1)$ and $(L, Z, Y, R2)$ be two L-fuzzy contexts. Then, the relation of the composed L-fuzzy context $(L, X, Z, R1 \star_I R2)$ is not, in general, the opposite of the relation of the composed L-fuzzy context $(L, Z, X, R2 \star_I R1)$.*

$$(R1 \star_I R2)^{op} \neq R2 \star_I R1$$

That is, if we change the order of the composition, the obtained relation between the elements of X and Z is different.

Proof. Given two *L*-fuzzy contexts $(L, X, Y, R1)$ and $(L, Z, Y, R2)$, and a fuzzy implication operator I, the relation of the composed *L*-fuzzy context $(L, X, Z, R1 \star_I R2)$ is:

$$R1 \star_I R2(x, z) = \inf_{y \in Y} \{I(R1(x, y), R2(z, y))\} \quad \forall(x, z) \in X \times Z$$

On the other hand, the relation of the composed *L*-fuzzy context $(L, Z, X, R2 \star_I R1)$ is defined as:

$$R2 \star_I R1(z, x) = \inf_{y \in Y} \{I(R2(z, y), R1(x, y))\} \quad \forall(z, x) \in Z \times X$$

As, in general, given a fuzzy implication $I(a, b) \neq I(b, a)$, then these relations are not opposed.   □

Example 1. We have a company of temporary work in which we want to analyze the suitability of some candidates to obtain some offered employments. The company knows the requirements of knowledge to occupy each one of the positions, represented by means of the *L*-fuzzy context $(L, X, Y, R1)$, where the set of objects X is the set of employments, the attributes Y the necessary knowledge, and the relation among them appears in the Table 1 with values in the lattice L. In this case, to simplify the calculations, the chosen lattice is the chain $L = \{0, 0.1, 0.2, \ldots, 1\}$.

Table 1. The requirements of knowledge to obtain each one of the employments

R1	computer science	accounting	mechanics	cooking
domestic helper	0.1	0.3	0.1	1
waiter	0	0.4	0	0.7
accountant	0.9	1	0	0
car salesman	0.5	0.7	0.9	0

On the other hand, we have the knowledge of some candidates for these positions, represented by the *L*-fuzzy context $(L, Z, Y, R2)$ in which the objects are the different candidates to occupy the jobs, the attributes the necessary knowledge and the relation among them is given by Table 2.

A candidate will be suitable to obtain a job if he owns all the knowledge required in this position. Therefore, to analyze what candidate is adapted for each job, we would use the composed *L*-fuzzy context $(L, X, Z, R1 \star R2)$. The relation of this composed context, calculated using the Lukasiewicz implication operator, is the represented in Table 3.

To obtain the information of this *L*-fuzzy context we will use the ordinary tools of the *L*-fuzzy Concept Theory to analyze the associated *L*-fuzzy concepts. Thus, for example, if we want to find the best candidate to occupy the job of *waiter*, we will take as a departure set:

Table 2. Knowledge of the candidates

$R2$	computer science	accounting	mechanics	cooking
C1	0.5	0.8	0.3	0.6
C2	0.2	0.5	0.1	1
C3	0	0.2	0	0.3
C4	0.9	0.4	0.1	0.5
C5	0.7	0.5	0.2	0.1

Table 3. Suitability of each candidate for each position

$R1 \star R2$	C_1	C_2	C_3	C_4	C_5
domestic helper	0.6	1	0.3	0.5	0.1
waiter	0.9	1	0.6	0.8	0.4
accountant	0.6	0.3	0.1	0.4	0.5
car salesman	0.4	0.2	0.5	0.2	0.3

$$\{\text{domestic helper}/0, \text{waiter}/1, \text{accountant}/0, \text{car salesman}/0\}$$

and we will obtain the derived L-fuzzy concept, whose intension will be:

$$\{C_1/0.9, C_2/1, C_3/0.6, C_4/0.8, C_5/0.4\}$$

If we look at the attributes whose membership degrees stand out from the others, we can deduce that the most suitable candidate for the job of *waiter* is C_2, followed by C_1 and C_4.

If, for instance, we want to find the best person to be *accountant* in a restaurant that also could work as a *waiter*, we will take the departure set

$$\{\text{domestic helper}/0, \text{waiter}/1, \text{accountant}/1, \text{car salesman}/0\}$$

and the derived L-fuzzy concept will be

$$\{C_1/0.6, C_2/0.3, C_3/0.1, C_4/0.4, C_5/0.4\}$$

where we can see that the most suitable candidate is C_1.

On the other hand, if our interest is to analyze which of the jobs is the most suitable for each candidate, we will do the composition in the contrary order, obtaining the L-fuzzy context $(L, Z, X, R2 \star R1)$, where the composed relation is represented in Table 4.

We can see in this example that both compositions are different: A candidate can be the best to occupy a concrete job, but that job can not be the most appropriate for this candidate.

The following result will be of interest to study the L-fuzzy concepts associated to the objects of the composed L-fuzzy context.

Table 4. Suitability of each employment for each candidate

$R2 \star R1$	domestic helper	waiter	accountant	car salesman
C_1	0.5	0.5	0.4	0.4
C_2	0.8	0.7	0	0
C_3	0.3	0.2	0.2	0.7
C_4	0.2	0.1	0.5	0.5
C_5	0.4	0.3	0.8	0.8

Proposition 5. *If the implication operator I is residuated and we take as a departure set:*

$$A(x) = \begin{cases} 1 & \text{if } x = x_i \\ 0 & \text{in other case} \end{cases}$$

then, the intension of the L-fuzzy concept obtained in the composed L-fuzzy context $(L, X, Z, R1 \star_I R2)$ taking A as a departure set, is equal to the extension of the L-fuzzy concept obtained in $(L, Z, Y, R2)$ from the intension of the L-fuzzy concept obtained in $(L, X, Y, R1)$ taking A as a departure set. That is, we obtain the same fuzzy set Z applying the derivation operators twice (once in each one of the contexts that make up the composition), or once in the composed context.

Moreover, the membership degrees obtained are the values of the row of $R1 \star_I R2$ that corresponds to the object x_i.

That is, if the subscripts point out the derivation operators and the superscripts the L-fuzzy contexts where they are applied, then $A_1^{\circledcirc}$ is the derived set from A obtained in the composed L-fuzzy context, $A_1^{\circled{1}}$ is the derived set obtained in the L-fuzzy context $(L, X, Y, R1)$, and $(A_1^{\circled{1}})_2^{\circled{2}}$ the derived set of the last one in the L-fuzzy context $(L, Z, Y, R2)$, and it is verify that:

$$\forall z \in Z, \quad A_1^{\circledcirc}(z) = (A_1^{\circled{1}})_2^{\circled{2}}(z) = R1 \star_I R2(x_i, z)$$

Proof. Let be $A(x) = \begin{cases} 1 & \text{if } x = x_i \\ 0 & \text{in other case} \end{cases}$, the intension of the L-fuzzy concept

obtained from A in the context $(L, X, Y, R1)$ is the L-fuzzy subset of Y:

$$A_1^{\circled{1}}(y) = \inf_{x \in X} \{I(A(x), R1(x, y))\}, \quad \forall y \in Y.$$

As the implication I is residuated, $\forall a \in L$ it is verified that $I(0, a) = 1$ and $I(1, a) = a$, thus,

$$A_1^{\circled{1}}(y) = R1(x_i, y), \quad \forall y \in Y.$$

Taking now as a departure set $A_1^{\circled{1}}$, we obtain the derived L-fuzzy concept in the L-fuzzy context $(L, Z, Y, R2)$, the extension of which is:

$$(A_1^{\circled{1}})_2^{\circled{2}}(z) = \inf_{y \in Y} \{I(A_1^{\circled{1}}(y), R2(z, y))\} =$$

$$= \inf_{y \in Y} \{I(R1(x_i, y), R2(z, y))\} = R1 \star_I R2(x_i, z), \quad \forall z \in Z.$$

On the other hand, the intension of the obtained L-fuzzy concept in the composed L-fuzzy context from A is:

$$A_1^{\oplus}(z) = \inf_{x \in X} \{I(A(x), R1 \star_I R2(x,y))\} = R1 \star_I R2(x_i, z), \quad \forall z \in Z.$$

$\square$

3.2   Composition of an L-Fuzzy Context with Itself

The composition of an L-fuzzy context (L, X, Y, R) with itself will allow us to set up some relationships between the elements of the object set X.

Proposition 6. *If I is a residuated implication associated with a left continuous t-norm T, then the relation $R \star_I R$ that results of the composition of (L, X, Y, R) with itself, associated with the implication I, constitutes a preorder relation defined in the object set X.*

Proof.   − First, we prove that it is a reflexive relation, that is, the relation verifies:

$$\forall x \in X, \; R \star_I R(x, x) = 1.$$

By the definition of the composition associated with an implication operator, we have that $\forall x \in X, \; R \star_I R(x, x) = \inf_{y \in Y} \{I(R(x,y), R(x,y))\}$, and, as any residuated implication verifies that $I(a, a) = 1$, $\forall a \in L$, then

$$\forall x \in X, \quad R \star_I R(x, x) = 1.$$

− To see that $R \star_I R$ is a T-transitive relation, we have to prove that

$$\forall x, t, z \in X, \quad T(R \star_I R(x, t), R \star_I R(t, z)) \leq R \star_I R(x, z),$$

that is, the following inequality must be verified:

$$T\left(\inf_{\alpha \in Y} \{I(R(x, \alpha), R(t, \alpha))\}, \inf_{\beta \in Y} \{I(R(t, \beta), R(z, \beta))\}\right) \leq$$
$$\leq \inf_{\alpha \in Y} \{I(R(x, \alpha), R(z, \alpha))\}.$$

By the monotony of the t-norm, we have:

$$T\left(\inf_{\alpha \in Y} \{I(R(x, \alpha), R(t, \alpha))\}, \inf_{\beta \in Y} \{I(R(t, \beta), R(z, \beta))\}\right) \leq$$
$$\inf_{\alpha \in Y} \left\{T\left(I(R(x, \alpha), R(t, \alpha)), \inf_{\beta \in Y} \{I(R(t, \beta), R(z, \beta))\}\right)\right\} \leq$$
$$\inf_{\alpha \in Y} \{T(I(R(x, \alpha), R(t, \alpha)), I(R(t, \alpha), R(z, \alpha)))\}.$$

As the used t-norm T is left-continuous, we know that [5]

$$\forall a, b, c \in [0, 1], \; T(I(a, b), I(b, c)) \leq I(a, c),$$

and it is verified that:

$$T\left(\inf_{\alpha\in Y}\{I(R(x,\alpha),R(t,\alpha))\},\inf_{\beta\in Y}\{I(R(t,\beta),R(z,\beta))\}\right)\le$$
$$\le \inf_{\alpha\in Y}\{I(R(x,\alpha),R(z,\alpha))\}$$

□

Remark 5. The relation $R\star_I R$ is neither symmetric nor antisymmetric and then, is neither an equivalence nor an order relation.

Remark 6. If we are using a non residuated implication operator, not always a preorder relation is obtained.

The application of this composition can be very interesting in social or work relations as we can see next:

Example 2. There are four different manufacture processes in a factory and we want to organize the workers so that each of them is subordinate of another one if its capacity to carry out each one of the processes of manufacture is smaller.

To model this problem, we are going to take the L-fuzzy context (L, X, Y, R), where the set of objects X is formed by the workers $\{O_1, O_2, O_3, O_4, O_5\}$, the attributes are the different manufacture processes $\{P_1, P_2, P_3, P_4\}$, and the relation R represents the capacity of each one of the workers to carry out each one of the processes, in a scale of 0 to 1 (See Table 5(a)).

The L-fuzzy context that results of the composition of this context with itself allow us to define relations boss-subordinate between the workers so that the relation $R \star R(x, y)$ of the compound context (associated with the Lukasiewicz implication) gives the degree in which the worker x is subordinate of the worker y. (See Table 5(b)).

Table 5.

(a) Capacity of the workers for the different processes

R	P_1	P_2	P_3	P_4
O_1	0.7	1	0.3	0
O_2	0.3	0.8	0.9	0.4
O_3	0.1	0.2	1	0.5
O_4	0.5	0.3	0.2	0.4
O_5	1	0.5	0.8	1

(b) Relation "To be subordinate of".

$R \star R$	O_1	O_2	O_3	O_4	O_5
O_1	1	0.6	0.2	0.3	0.5
O_2	0.4	1	0.4	0.3	0.7
O_3	0.3	0.9	1	0.2	0.8
O_4	0.6	0.8	0.6	1	1
O_5	0	0.3	0.1	0.4	1

This will allow us, for example, to choose bosses in the group watching the columns of the obtained relation: In this case, we could choose as bosses of the workers to O_2 and O_5 because both have as subordinate O_3 and O_4 and the subordination degrees are the biggest values of the columns.

4 Conclusions and Future Work

This work constitutes the first approach to the problem of composition of L-fuzzy contexts. In future works we will use these results in the resolution of other problems that seem interesting: This composition will be useful to study the chained L-fuzzy contexts, that is, to find relations between two defined contexts where the set of attributes of the first context is the same that the set of objects of the second one. On the other hand, it will be useful to define the composition of L-fuzzy contexts in the interval-valued case in order to study certain situations.

Acknowledgements. This work has been partially supported by the Research Group "Intelligent Systems and Energy (SI+E)" of the Basque Government, under Grant IT519-10, and by the Research Group "Adquisicin de conocimiento y minera de datos, funciones especiales y mtodos numricos avanzados" of the Public University of Navarra.

References

1. Bělohlávek, R.: Fuzzy Galois connections and fuzzy concept lattices: from binary relations to conceptual structures. In: Novak, V., Perfileva, I. (eds.) Discovering the World with Fuzzy Logic, pp. 462–494. Physica-Verlag (2000)
2. Burusco, A., Fuentes-González, R.: The Study of the L-Fuzzy Concept Lattice. Mathware and Soft Computing 1(3), 209–218 (1994)
3. Burusco, A., Fuentes-González, R.: Construction of the L-Fuzzy Concept Lattice. Fuzzy Sets and Systems 97(1), 109–114 (1998)
4. Djouadi, Y., Dubois, D., Prade, H.: On the possible meanings of degrees when making formal concept analysis fuzzy. In: EUROFUSE Workshop on Preference Modelling and Decision Analysis, Pamplona, pp. 253–258 (September 2009)
5. Fodor, J., Roubens, M.: Fuzzy Preference Modelling and Multicriteria Decision Support. Kluwer Academic Publishers, Dordrecht (1994)
6. Jaoua, A., Alvi, F., Elloumi, S., Yahia, S.B.: Galois Connection in Fuzzy Binary Relations. In: Applications for Discovering Association Rules and Decision Making, RelMiCS, pp. 141–149 (2000)
7. Kohout, L.J., Bandler, W.: Use of fuzzy relations in Knowledge representation, acquisition, and processing. In: Zadeh, L., Kacprzyk, J. (eds.) Fuzzy Logic for Management of Uncertainty, pp. 415–435 (1992)
8. Krajči, S.: A generalized concept lattice. Logic J. IGPL 13(5), 543–550 (2005)
9. Medina, J., Ojeda-Aciego, M., Ruiz-Calviño, J.: On Multi-adjoint Concept Lattices: Definition and Representation Theorem. In: Kuznetsov, S.O., Schmidt, S. (eds.) ICFCA 2007. LNCS (LNAI), vol. 4390, pp. 197–209. Springer, Heidelberg (2007)
10. Pollandt, S.: Fuzzy Begriffe: Formale Begriffsanalyse unscharfer Daten. Springer (1997)
11. Wille, R.: Restructuring lattice theory: an approach based on hierarchies of concepts. In: Rival, I. (ed.) Ordered Sets, pp. 445–470. Reidel, Dordrecht (1982)
12. Wolff, K.E.: Conceptual interpretation of fuzzy theory. In: Proc. 6th European Congress on Intelligent Techniques and Soft Computing, vol. 1, pp. 555–562 (1998)

On a Generalization of Yager's Implications

Sebastià Massanet and Joan Torrens

Department of Mathematics and Computer Science
University of the Balearic Islands
07122 Palma de Mallorca, Spain
{s.massanet,dmijts0}@uib.es

Abstract. In this paper, a generalization of Yager's implications is proposed and the resulting new class of implications from f-generated implications with $f(0) < +\infty$ is studied. The generalization is based on considering a more general internal function than the product into their expression. In this particular case, this more general function has to be, in fact, a binary aggregation function and depending on its properties, the behaviour and additional properties of the generated implication are determined. Finally, we prove that this new class intersects some of the well-known classes, such as (S, N) and (U, N)-implications, among others.

Keywords: Fuzzy implication, Yager's f-generated implication, Yager's g-generated implication, aggregation function, exchange principle.

1 Introduction

Fuzzy implications, the generalization of the binary classical implication on fuzzy logic, have recently attracted the efforts of numerous researchers, as evidence the publication of the survey [12] and the book [1], entirely devoted to these operators. The growing interest on fuzzy implications comes from their wide range of applications. They have a key role in approximate reasoning, fuzzy control and other fields where these theories are applied.

All these applications have led to the necessity of using many different models to perform fuzzy implications. The main reason is because any "If-Then" rule is interpreted through one of these implications and so, depending on the context, and on the proper rule and its behaviour, different implications can be adequate in any case. Moreover, fuzzy implications are used to perform forward and backward inferences. Thus, the choice of the fuzzy implication cannot be made independently of the inference rule that is going to be applied. The importance of having so different models for fuzzy implications is also pointed out in [15], where it is proved that the meaning and the behaviour of each one of these models are crucial in their election.

Among these different models, the most usual ones are those obtained through t-norms and t-conorms via the so-called R and (S, N)-implications and QL and D-operations, see for instance [1]. These types have been extended and other

S. Greco et al. (Eds.): IPMU 2012, Part II, CCIS 298, pp. 315–324, 2012.
© Springer-Verlag Berlin Heidelberg 2012

aggregation functions have been used for this purpose. Thus, new classes of implications have been generated by copulas, quasi-copulas and even conjunctions in general ([7,17]), representable aggregation functions ([5]), and mainly uninorms ([2,6,11]). However, another approach to generate fuzzy implications is available through the use of univalued generators of aggregation functions. In this sense, Yager's f and g-generated implications ([16]) are generated from additive generators of Archimedean t-norms and t-conorms; h-generated implications ([3]), from multiplicative generators of Archimedean t-conorms and h-implications ([14]), from additive generators of representable uninorms.

Going deeper in this direction to obtain new classes of implications, here the main idea is to propose a generalization of Yager's implications preserving the use of an additive generator of an Archimedean t-norm or t-conorm but now, considering a more general internal function than the product. In this paper, we focus on the particular case of f-generated implications with $f(0) < +\infty$, proving that this more general function has to be a binary aggregation function in order to generate a fuzzy implication. After that, some intersections of the new class with the most usual classes of implications are presented. Finally, the properties of the new class of implications are determined depending on those satisfied by the aggregation function.

2   Preliminaries

To make this work self-contained, we recall here some of the concepts and results employed in the rest of the paper. First of all, the definition of fuzzy negation is given.

Definition 1. *(Definition 1.1 in [8]) A decreasing function $N : [0,1] \to [0,1]$ is called a fuzzy negation, if $N(0) = 1$, $N(1) = 0$. A fuzzy negation N is called*

(i) strict, if it is strictly decreasing and continuous.
(ii) strong, if it is an involution, i.e., $N(N(x)) = x$ for all $x \in [0,1]$.

Next, we recall the definition of fuzzy implications.

Definition 2. *(Definition 1.15 in [8]) A binary operator $I : [0,1]^2 \to [0,1]$ is said to be a fuzzy implication if it satisfies:*

(I1) $I(x,z) \geq I(y,z)$ *when* $x \leq y$, *for all* $z \in [0,1]$.
(I2) $I(x,y) \leq I(x,z)$ *when* $y \leq z$, *for all* $x \in [0,1]$.
(I3) $I(0,0) = I(1,1) = 1$ *and* $I(1,0) = 0$.

Note that, from the definition, it follows that $I(0,x) = 1$ and $I(x,1) = 1$ for all $x \in [0,1]$ whereas the symmetrical values $I(x,0)$ and $I(1,x)$ are not derived from the definition. We will denote by $\mathcal{FI}$ the set of all fuzzy implications. Special interesting properties for implication functions are:

– The *exchange principle*,

$$I(x, I(y,z)) = I(y, I(x,z)), \quad x,y,z \in [0,1]. \tag{EP}$$

- The *law of importation* with a t-norm T,

$$I(T(x,y),z) = I(x, I(y,z)), \quad x,y,z \in [0,1]. \tag{LI}$$

- The *weak law of importation* with a conjunctive, commutative and non-decreasing function $F : [0,1]^2 \rightarrow [0,1]$, (see [13])

$$I(F(x,y),z) = I(x, I(y,z)), \quad x,y,z \in [0,1]. \tag{WLI}$$

- The *left neutrality principle*,

$$I(1,y) = y, \quad y \in [0,1]. \tag{NP}$$

- The *ordering property*,

$$x \leq y \iff I(x,y) = 1, \quad x,y \in [0,1]. \tag{OP}$$

- The *identity principle*,

$$I(x,x) = 1, \quad x \in [0,1]. \tag{IP}$$

- The *contrapositive symmetry* with respect to a fuzzy negation N,

$$I(x,y) = I(N(y), N(x)), \quad x,y \in [0,1]. \tag{CP(N)}$$

Definition 3. *(Definition 1.4.15 in [1]) Let I be a fuzzy implication. The function N_I defined by $N_I(x) = I(x,0)$ for all $x \in [0,1]$, is called the natural negation of I.*

Next, we recall the definitions of Yager's f and g-generated implications.

Definition 4. *([16]) Let $f : [0,1] \rightarrow [0,\infty]$ be a strictly decreasing and continuous function with $f(1) = 0$. The function $I : [0,1]^2 \rightarrow [0,1]$ defined by*

$$I(x,y) = f^{-1}(x \cdot f(y)), \quad x,y \in [0,1]$$

with the understanding $0 \cdot \infty = 0$, is called an f-generated implication. The function f itself is called an f-generator of the I generated as above. In such a case, to emphasize the apparent relation we will write I_f instead of I.

Definition 5. *([16]) Let $g : [0,1] \rightarrow [0,\infty]$ be a strictly increasing and continuous function with $g(0) = 0$. The function $I : [0,1]^2 \rightarrow [0,1]$ defined by*

$$I(x,y) = g^{(-1)}\left(\frac{1}{x} \cdot g(y)\right), \quad x,y \in [0,1]$$

with the understanding $\frac{1}{0} = \infty$ and $\infty \cdot 0 = \infty$, is called a g-generated implication, where the function $g^{(-1)}$ is the pseudo-inverse of g given by

$$g^{(-1)}(x) = \begin{cases} g^{-1}(x) & \text{if } x \in [0, g(1)], \\ 1 & \text{if } x \in [g(1), \infty]. \end{cases}$$

The function g is called a g-generator of the function I. In this case, we will write I_g instead of I to emphasize the apparent relation.

3   Generalized Yager's Operations

If the definitions of Yager's implications are observed accurately, one can distinguish the use of the product function $F_P(x,y) = x \cdot y$ as internal function, i.e,

$$I_f(x,y) = f^{-1}(x \cdot f(y)) = f^{-1}(F_P(x, f(y))),$$
$$I_g(x,y) = g^{(-1)}\left(\frac{1}{x} \cdot g(y)\right) = g^{(-1)}\left(F_P\left(\frac{1}{x}, g(y)\right)\right).$$

So, the straightforward generalization that comes to mind is to consider a more general binary function F instead of F_P into these expressions.

Definition 6. *Let F be a binary function, f an f-generator and g a g-generator. The functions $I_{f,F}, I_{g,F} : [0,1]^2 \rightarrow [0,1]$ defined by*

$$I_{f,F}(x,y) = f^{-1}(F(x, f(y))), \quad x, y \in [0,1] \tag{1}$$

$$I_{g,F}(x,y) = g^{(-1)}\left(F\left(\frac{1}{x}, g(y)\right)\right), \quad x, y \in [0,1] \tag{2}$$

are called generalized f *and* g-generated operations, *respectively.*

Remark 1. Note that in order to obtain well-defined generalized f and g-generated operations, the image and the domain of the binary function F must be in accordance of the properties of the considered f and g-generators.

Remark 2. Obviously, not all binary functions F generate generalized f-generated and g-generated operations satisfying the necessary conditions, enumerated in Definition 2, in order to be a fuzzy implication. When this fact happens, we will use the terms *generalized f-generated and g-generated implications.*

3.1   Generalized f-Generated Operations with $f(0) < \infty$

In this work, we will focus on the particular case of generalized f-generated operations with $f(0) < +\infty$. In this case, using Theorem 3.1.4 in [1], f-generators are unique up to a positive multiplicative constant and therefore, it is enough to consider only f-generators with $f(0) = 1$ since we can take $f_1(x) = \frac{f(x)}{f(0)}$. Taking into account this fact, these f-generators are in fact, strict negations and we will restrict the study to f-generated operations with $f(0) = 1$, without any loss of generality. In addition, in order to obtain a well-defined generalized f-generated operation through expression (1), it is necessary to consider a binary function $F : [0,1]^2 \rightarrow [0,1]$. Let us study in this case which binary functions $F : [0,1]^2 \rightarrow [0,1]$ generate generalized f-generated implications with $f(0) = 1$.

Theorem 1. *Let $F : [0,1]^2 \rightarrow [0,1]$ be a binary function and f an f-generator with $f(0) = 1$. The generalized f-generated operation, $I_{f,F}$, is a fuzzy implication if and only if F is a binary aggregation function* [1] *with $F(1,0) = F(0,1) = 0$.*

---

[1] All the necessary results and notations on aggregation functions used throughout this paper can be found in [4] and more deeply in [9].

Proof. Let us determine which properties must satisfy the function F to obtain a generalized f-generated implication with $f(0) = 1$.

- $I_{f,F}(0,0) = 1 \Leftrightarrow f^{-1}(F(0, f(0))) = 1 \Leftrightarrow F(0,1) = 0$.
- $I_{f,F}(1,1) = 1 \Leftrightarrow f^{-1}(F(1, f(1))) = 1 \Leftrightarrow F(1,0) = 0$.
- $I_{f,F}(1,0) = 0 \Leftrightarrow f^{-1}(F(1, f(0))) = 0 \Leftrightarrow F(1,1) = 1$.
- Consider $x_1 \leq x_2$ and $y \in [0,1]$. We have that

$$I_{f,F}(x_1, y) \geq I_{f,F}(x_2, y) \Leftrightarrow f^{-1}(F(x_1, f(y))) \geq f^{-1}(F(x_2, f(y)))$$
$$\Leftrightarrow F(x_1, f(y)) \leq F(x_2, f(y)).$$

  Since f is continuous, we obtain that F has to be increasing in the first variable.
- Consider $y_1 \leq y_2$ and $x \in [0,1]$. We have that

$$I_{f,F}(x, y_1) \leq I_{f,F}(x, y_2) \Leftrightarrow f^{-1}(F(x, f(y_1))) \leq f^{-1}(F(x, f(y_2)))$$
$$\Leftrightarrow F(x, f(y_1)) \geq F(x, f(y_2)).$$

  Since f is a strictly decreasing continuous function and therefore, $f(y_1) \geq f(y_2)$, we obtain that F has to be increasing in the second variable.

Finally, note that using the increasingness of F and $F(0,1) = 0$, it is clear that $F(0,0) = 0$ and consequently, F must be a binary aggregation function. $\square$

Remark 3. The previous result shows a new way to obtain fuzzy implications from a binary aggregation function F with $F(1,0) = F(0,1) = 0$ and a strict negation N in the following way:

$$I_{N,F}(x, y) = N^{-1}(F(x, N(y))), \quad x, y \in [0,1].$$

Although this new class of implications is introduced to generalize Yager's implications, more classes of implications are encompassed by the generalized f-generated operations with $f(0) = 1$. Thus, taking different kinds of aggregation functions, we obtain different classes as the following example shows.

Example 1. – If we consider $F = T_P$, the product t-norm, we obtain Yager's f-generated implications with $f(0) < \infty$.
- If we consider $F = T$, a t-norm, we obtain (S, N)-implications with N a strict negation generated from $N = f^{-1}$ and the f-dual t-conorm of T, that is $S(x, y) = f^{-1}(T(f(x), f(y)))$, since

$$I_{T,f}(x, y) = f^{-1}(T(x, f(y))) = S(f^{-1}(x), y)) = S(N(x), y).$$

- If we consider $F = U$, a conjunctive uninorm, we obtain (U, N)-implications with N a strict negation generated from $N = f^{-1}$ and the f-dual disjunctive uninorm of U, that is $U'(x, y) = f^{-1}(U(f(x), f(y)))$, since

$$I_{U,f}(x, y) = f^{-1}(U(x, f(y))) = U'(f^{-1}(x), y)) = U'(N(x), y).$$

– If we consider $F = C$, a copula, and $f(x) = N_C(x) = 1 - x$, we obtain material implications $I_{D,N}(x,y) = D(N(x),y)$ from a co-copula $D(x,y) = 1 - C(1-x, 1-y)$ and $N = f$ (see [17]) since

$$I_{C,f}(x,y) = f^{-1}(C(x, f(y))) = 1 - C(x, 1-y) = D(1-x, y).$$

From now on, we want to study which additional properties can be satisfied by a generalized f-generated implication with $f(0) = 1$. These properties will be related to the ones of the binary aggregation function F and in some cases, we will be able to establish the class of aggregation functions needed to obtain a certain property.

(NP) and its counterpart for implications derived from uninorms, (NP$_e$), that is $I(e,y) = y$ for all $y \in [0,1]$ and for some $e \in (0,1)$, are related to a neutral element of the aggregation function.

Proposition 1. *Let F be an aggregation function with $F(1,0) = F(0,1) = 0$ and f an f-generator with $f(0) = 1$. The generalized f-generated implication, $I_{f,F}$, satisfies:*

(i) (NP) if and only if 1 is the neutral element of F, i.e., F is a semicopula.
(ii) (NP$_e$) if and only if e is the neutral element of F.

Proof. First, let us prove (i). Then we have

$$I_{f,F}(1,y) = y \Leftrightarrow f^{-1}(F(1, f(y))) = y \Leftrightarrow F(1, f(y)) = f(y).$$

Since f is continuous, 1 is the neutral element of F, i.e., F is a semicopula. Now, let us prove (ii). In this case, we have

$$I_{f,F}(e,y) = y \Leftrightarrow f^{-1}(F(e, f(y))) = y \Leftrightarrow F(e, f(y)) = f(y).$$

Using again the continuity of f, e is the neutral element of F.   □

At this point, we will use the concept of contour line introduced in [10] for the particular case of any aggregation function F satisfying $F(1,0) = F(0,1) = 0$.

Definition 7. *Let F be a binary aggregation function satisfying $F(1,0) = F(0,1) = 0$ and $a \in [0,1]$. The function C_F^a defined by*

$$C_F^a(x) = \sup\{y \in [0,1] \mid F(x,y) \le a\}$$

for all $x \in [0,1]$, is called the a-contour line of F.

It is clear that C_F^a is a decreasing function using the increasingness of the function F. Moreover, the two following results are immediate.

Proposition 2. *Let F be a binary aggregation function satisfying $F(1,0) = F(0,1) = 0$. The function C_F^0 is a fuzzy negation if and only if $F(1,y) > 0$ for all $y > 0$.*

Corollary 1. *Let F be a binary aggregation function satisfying $F(1,0) = F(0,1) = 0$ with a neutral element $e \in (0,1]$. Then C_F^0 is a fuzzy negation.*

Proof. Since $F(e,y) = y$ for all $y \in [0,1]$, we have that $F(1,y) \geq F(e,y) = y > 0$ for all $y > 0$ and the result follows using the previous proposition.   □

Note that the contour line C_F^0 when F is a t-norm is, in fact, the negation induced by F. The contour lines play an important role when analysing (OP), (IP) and their counterparts for implications derived from uninorms, (OP$_e$), that is $I(x,y) \geq e \Leftrightarrow x \leq y$ and (IP$_e$), that is $I(x,x) = e$, for some $e \in (0,1)$.

Proposition 3. *Let F be an aggregation function with $F(1,0) = F(0,1) = 0$ and f an f-generator with $f(0) = 1$. The generalized f-generated implication, $I_{f,F}$, satisfies:*

(i) *$I_{f,F}(x,y) = 1$ if and only if $f(y) \leq C_F^0(x)$. Moreover, $I_{f,F}$ satisfies (OP) if and only if $C_F^0 = f$.*

(ii) *$I_{f,F}(x,x) = 1$ if and only if $f(x) \leq C_F^0(x)$. Moreover, $I_{f,F}$ satisfies (IP) if and only if $f \leq C_F^0$.*

(iii) *$I_{f,F}(x,y) \geq e$ if and only if $f(y) \leq C_F^{f(e)}(x)$. Moreover, $I_{f,F}$ satisfies (OP$_e$) if and only if $C_F^{f(e)} = f$.*

(iv) *$I_{f,F}(x,x) = e$ if and only if $f(x) \leq C_F^{f(e)}(x)$. Moreover, $I_{f,F}$ satisfies (IP$_e$) if and only if $f \leq C_F^{f(e)}$.*

Proof. Let us prove (i). We obtain that

$$I_{f,F}(x,y) = 1 \Leftrightarrow f^{-1}(F(x,f(y))) = 1 \Leftrightarrow F(x,f(y)) = 0 \Leftrightarrow f(y) \leq C_F^0(x)$$
$$\Leftrightarrow y \geq f^{-1}(C_F^0(x)).$$

Moreover, note that $I_{f,F}$ satisfies (OP) if and only if this condition is equivalent to $y \geq x$, that is, only when $C_F^0 = f$.

Now, we will prove (ii). The first part is immediate taking $x = y$ in (i). Moreover, $I_{f,F}$ satisfies (IP) if and only if $f(x) \leq C_F^0(x)$ for all $x \in [0,1]$.

Finally, (iii) and (iv) are analogously proved taking now the $f(e)$-contour line instead of the 0-one.   □

The next studied properties are (EP) and (WLI). The relation between these two properties have been recently studied in [13], concluding that (WLI) is stronger than (EP).

Proposition 4. *Let F be an aggregation function with $F(1,0) = F(0,1) = 0$, f an f-generator with $f(0) = 1$ and $F^* : [0,1]^2 \to [0,1]$ a commutative and increasing function with $F^*(1,0) = 0$. The generalized f-generated implication, $I_{f,F}$, satisfies:*

(i) *(EP) if and only if $F(x,F(y,z)) = F(y,F(x,z))$. Further, if F is a commutative and associative function, $I_{f,F}$ satisfies (EP).*

(ii) *(WLI) with F^* if and only if $F(x, F(y, z)) = F(F^*(x, y), z)$. Further, if F is a commutative and associative function such that $F(\cdot, z_0)$ is one-to-one for some $z_0 \in (0, 1]$, $I_{f,F}$ satisfies (WLI) only with F.*

Proof. Let us start proving the result for (EP).

$$I_{f,F}(x, I_{f,F}(y, z)) = I_{f,F}(y, I_{f,F}(x, z))$$
$$\Leftrightarrow f^{-1}(F(x, F(y, f(z)))) = f^{-1}(F(y, F(x, f(z))))$$
$$\Leftrightarrow F(x, F(y, f(z))) = F(y, F(x, f(z))),$$

and the result follows. Moreover, if F is a commutative and associative function, we have that

$$F(x, F(y, z)) = F(F(x, y), z) = F(F(y, x), z) = F(y, F(x, z)).$$

So, $I_{f,F}$ satisfies (EP).
With respect to (WLI), we obtain

$$I_{f,F}(x, I_{f,F}(y, z)) = I_{f,F}(F^*(x, y), z)$$
$$\Leftrightarrow f^{-1}(F(x, F(y, f(z)))) = f^{-1}(F(F^*(x, y), f(z)))$$
$$\Leftrightarrow F(x, F(y, f(z))) = F(F^*(x, y), f(z)),$$

and the result follows. Moreover, if F is an associative function such that $F(\cdot, z_0)$ is one-to-one for some $z_0 \in (0, 1]$ and $I_{f,F}$ satisfies (WLI) with F^*, taking $z = z_0$ into the required property, we have

$$F(x, F(y, z_0)) = F(F^*(x, y), z_0) \Rightarrow F(F(x, y), z_0) = F(F^*(x, y), z_0)$$
$$\Rightarrow F(x, y) = F^*(x, y).$$

Finally, using the associativity and the commutativity of F, $I_{f,F}$ satisfies (WLI) with F $\qquad \square$

Corollary 2. *Let F be a semicopula and f an f-generator with $f(0) = 1$. The generalized f-generated implication, $I_{f,F}$, satisfies (EP) if and only if F is a t-norm.*

Proof. If $I_{f,F}$ satisfies (EP), then using the previous result, we have $F(x, F(y, z)) = F(y, F(x, z))$. Taking $z = 1$ in this equality, we obtain $F(x, y) = F(y, x)$ and consequently, F is commutative. In addition, it is associative since

$$F(F(x, y), z) = F(z, F(x, y)) = F(x, F(z, y)) = F(x, F(y, z)).$$

Thus, F is a t-norm.
The reciprocal holds straightforwardly using the previous result. $\qquad \square$

The next result deals with the natural negation of these implications.

Proposition 5. *Let F be an aggregation function with $F(1, 0) = F(0, 1) = 0$ and f an f-generator with $f(0) = 1$. The natural negation of the generalized f-generated implication, $I_{f,F}$, is given by $N_{I_{f,F}}(x) = f^{-1}(F(x, 1))$. Moreover,* *(i)* If the 1-section, $F(\cdot, 1)$ is continuous (and strictly increasing), $N_{I_{f,F}}$ is continuous (strict).

(ii) If $F(f^{-1}(F(x,1)),1) = f(x)$, $N_{I_{f,F}}$ is strong.

(iii) If 1 is the neutral element of F, $N_{I_{f,F}} = f^{-1}$ and it is strong when $f = f^{-1}$.

Proof. The expression of the natural negation is

$$N_{I_{f,F}}(x) = I_{f,F}(x,0) = f^{-1}(F(x,1)).$$

Then, from this fact, *(i)* is immediate. Let us prove *(ii)*,

$$N_{I_{f,F}}(N_{I_{f,F}}(x)) = x \Leftrightarrow f^{-1}(F(f^{-1}(A(x,1)),1)) = x$$
$$\Leftrightarrow F(f^{-1}(F(x,1)),1) = f(x).$$

Finally, *(iii)* is straightforward from the expression of the natural negation and *(ii)*.   □

Finally, let us study now (CP) and then, the continuity of these implications.

Proposition 6. *Let F be an aggregation function with $F(1,0) = F(0,1) = 0$, f an f-generator with $f(0) = 1$ and N a fuzzy negation. The generalized f-generated implication, $I_{f,F}$, satisfies (CP(N)) if and only if $F(x,f(y)) = F(N(y), f(N(x)))$.*

Proof.

$$I_{f,F}(x,y) = I_{f,F}(N(y),N(x)) \Leftrightarrow f^{-1}(F(x,f(y))) = f^{-1}(F(N(y),f(N(x))))$$
$$\Leftrightarrow F(x,f(y)) = F(N(y),f(N(x))).$$

Proposition 7. *Let F be an aggregation function with $F(1,0) = F(0,1) = 0$ and f an f-generator with $f(0) = 1$. The generalized f-generated implication, $I_{f,F}$, is continuous if and only if F is continuous.*

Proof. Immediate from the expression of these implications.   □

4   Conclusions and Future Work

In this paper, we have proposed a generalization of Yager's f and g-generated implications based on considering a more general internal function than the product. The generated new class of implications, called generalized f and g-generated implications, has been studied in the particular case of f-generators with $f(0) < +\infty$. This subclass is strongly connected with aggregation functions and depending on the properties of the considered aggregation function, we obtain implications satisfying important properties such as (EP), (OP) or (WLI). Furthermore, they contain not only f-generated implications with $f(0) < +\infty$ but also (S,N) and (U,N)-implications with N a strict negation, among others.

As a future work, we want to study the subclass of generalized f-generated implications with $f(0) = +\infty$ and the generalized g-generated implications. These classes clearly generalize the corresponding usual Yager's implications, but it is worth to study if they generalize other families of implications. Finally, we want to study some other possible generalizations of Yager's implications.

Acknowledgements. This paper has been partially supported by the Spanish Grant MTM2009-10320 with FEDER support.

References

1. Baczyński, M., Jayaram, B.: Fuzzy Implications. STUDFUZZ, vol. 231. Springer, Heidelberg (2008)
2. Baczyński, M., Jayaram, B.: (U,N)-implications and their characterizations. Fuzzy Sets and Systems 160, 2049–2062 (2009)
3. Balasubramaniam, J.: Contrapositive symmetrisation of fuzzy implications–revisited. Fuzzy Sets and Systems 157(17), 2291–2310 (2006)
4. Beliakov, G., Pradera, A., Calvo, T.: Aggregation Functions: A Guide for Practitioners. STUDFUZZ, vol. 221. Springer (2007)
5. Carbonell, M., Torrens, J.: Continuous R-implications generated from representable aggregation functions. Fuzzy Sets and Systems 161, 2276–2289 (2010)
6. De Baets, B., Fodor, J.C.: Residual operators of uninorms. Soft Computing 3, 89–100 (1999)
7. Durante, F., Klement, E., Mesiar, R., Sempi, C.: Conjunctors and their residual implicators: Characterizations and construction methods. Mediterranean Journal of Mathematics 4, 343–356 (2007)
8. Fodor, J.C., Roubens, M.: Fuzzy Preference Modelling and Multicriteria Decision Support. Kluwer Academic Publishers, Dordrecht (1994)
9. Grabisch, M., Marichal, J.-L., Mesiar, R., Pap, E.: Aggregation Functions, 1st edn. Encyclopedia of Mathematics and its Applications. Cambridge University Press, New York (2009)
10. Maes, K.C., De Baets, B.: On the structure of left-continuous t-norms that have a continuous contour line. Fuzzy Sets and Systems 158, 843–860 (2007)
11. Mas, M., Monserrat, M., Torrens, J.: Two types of implications derived from uninorms. Fuzzy Sets and Systems 158, 2612–2626 (2007)
12. Mas, M., Monserrat, M., Torrens, J., Trillas, E.: A survey on fuzzy implication functions. IEEE Transactions on Fuzzy Systems 15(6), 1107–1121 (2007)
13. Massanet, S., Torrens, J.: The law of importation versus the exchange principle on fuzzy implications. Fuzzy Sets and Systems 168(1), 47–69 (2011)
14. Massanet, S., Torrens, J.: On a new class of fuzzy implications: h-implications and generalizations. Information Sciences 181(11), 2111–2127 (2011)
15. Trillas, E., Mas, M., Monserrat, M., Torrens, J.: On the representation of fuzzy rules. Int. J. Approx. Reasoning 48(2), 583–597 (2008)
16. Yager, R.R.: On some new classes of implication operators and their role in approximate reasoning. Information Sciences 167, 193–216 (2004)
17. Yager, R.R.: Modeling holistic fuzzy implication using co-copulas. Fuzzy Optimization and Decision Making 5, 207–226 (2006)

Coimplications on Finite Scales

Juan Vicente Riera and Joan Torrens

University of Balearic Islands, Palma de Mallorca 07122, Spain
{jvicente.riera,dmijts0}@uib.es

Abstract. Co-implication functions are the dual connectives of fuzzy implications. In this paper co-implications defined on finite ordinal scales, called discrete co-implications, are introduced. In particular, strong co-implications derived from smooth t-norms and residual co-implications derived from smooth t-conorms are studied in detail. The structure of such co-implications is given and several properties are investigated.

Keywords: coimplication function,implication function, discrete setting.

1 Introduction

The study of logical connectives is a key point in the development of the theory of fuzzy sets and fuzzy logic. On one hand, t-norms and t-conorms are commonly used to model conjunctions and disjunctions respectively. In this context, t-norms and t-conorms are dual operators one of each other through strong negations, that usually perform complements in the fuzzy sets theory.

In this direction, one of the most important types of connectives in fuzzy logic are fuzzy implication functions. They are widely used in fuzzy control and approximate reasoning, because they are essential in modelling fuzzy conditionals as well as in the inference process. For this reason, implication functions have been extensively studied from both, the applicational and the theoretical points of view (see for instance [2], [11] and the references therein). Curiously, their dual operators, called co-implications, have been systematically forgotten in this study and just some works have dealt with them (see [7, 4, 18–20]).

When we deal with fuzzy logic the used scale is always the unit interval [0,1]. However, in many applications only a finite number of values is used and even only qualitative information is handled. For this reason, many authors have studied in last years operations defined on a finite chain L_n, usually called discrete operations. For instance, t-norms and t-conorms were characterized in [17], uninorms and nullnorms in [12], idempotent uninorms in [5], a non-commutative version of nullnorms in [6], weighted means in [10], smooth aggregation functions in [15], copulas in [16] and also implications functions in [13] and [14]. It is proved in [17] that only the number of elements of the finite chain L_n is relevant when we deal with monotonic operations on L_n, and so the finite chain used in many of the mentioned works is the most simple one $L_n = \{0, 1, \ldots, n\}$. As in the case of [0,1], two of the most usual ways to define fuzzy implications on the finite chain L_n are the so-called R and S-implications (see [13]).

S. Greco et al. (Eds.): IPMU 2012, Part II, CCIS 298, pp. 325–334, 2012.
© Springer-Verlag Berlin Heidelberg 2012

In this paper we want to study coimplication functions on L_n. In particular, the counterpart of R and S-implications for coimplications, that is, residual and model coimplications on L_n, respectively. We view that each one of these two types of coimplications are N-dual of their respective types of implications, where N is the only strong negation on L_n. From this duality many properties of these kinds of coimplications can be derived.

2   Preliminaries

We will suppose the reader to be familiar with the basic theory of logical connectives in both, the fuzzy and the discrete cases. For operators on $[0, 1]$ see [8] and for operators on finite scales see [17] and also [13]. Thus, we recall only some key definitions and results for the rest of the paper.

Since in our framework any finite chain with the same number of elements is equivalent (see for instance [17]) we will work with the most simple one with $n + 1$ elements:

$$L_n = \{0, 1, 2, \ldots, n\}.$$

Operators defined on L_n are usually called discrete operations and they have been studied by many authors (see [4, 10, 12–14, 17]). In these studies the following condition, generally used as a discrete counterpart of continuity, is considered.

Definition 1. *A function $f : L_n \to L_n$ is said to be smooth if it satisfies: $\mid f(x) - f(x - 1) \mid \le 1$ for all $x \in L_n$ with $x \ge 1$.*

Definition 2. *A binary operation $F : L_n^2 \to L_n$ is said to be smooth when each one of its vertical and horizontal sections ($F(x, .)$ and $F(., y)$, respectively) are smooth.*

Smooth discrete t-norms and t-conorms were characterized in [17]. There, it is also proved that there is one and only one strong negation on L_n which is given by

$$N(x) = n - x \quad \text{for all} \quad x \in L_n. \tag{1}$$

Discrete implication functions were studied in [13] and [14]. Two of the most usual ways to define implication functions on L_n are, for all $x, y \in L_n$,

$I_T(x, y) = \sup\{z \in L_n \mid T(x, z) \le y\}$ (Residual implications or R-implications)
$I_S(x, y) = S(N(x), y)$ (Strong implications or S-implications),

where T is a (smooth) t-norm, S a (smooth) t-conorm on L_n, and N is the strong negation given by (1). Note that in the framework of L_n the supremum in the definition of R-implications can be obviously replaced by maximum. Both kinds of discrete implications were studied and characterized in [13][1].

---

[1] In fact, S-implications were initially characterized in the more general framework of bounded partially ordered sets in [3], where they are introduced as *Model implications*.

Proposition 1. *([13], [3]) Let $I : L_n^2 \to L_n$ be an implication function. Then I is an S-implication if and only if I satisfies*

- *The* neutrality principle: $I(n, y) = y$ *for all* $y \in L_n$
- *The* exchange principle: $I(x, I(y, z)) = I(y, I(x, z))$ *for all* $x, y, z \in L_n$
- *The* contraposition law *(with respect to the negation N):* $I(n - y, n - x) = I(x, y)$ *for all* $x, y \in L_n$.

Proposition 2. *([13]) Let $I : L_n^2 \to L_n$ be an implication function. Then I is an R-implication if and only if I satisfies the neutrality principle, the exchange principle and*

- *The* ordering property $(I(x, y) = n \iff x \leq y)$.

With respect to coimplications functions, there are only some few works dealing with them. In the framework of $[0, 1]$ we can cite [7], [19] and [20], whereas in the framework of a bounded partially ordered set in general we can find [4]. However, nothing is currently done for discrete coimplications and this is the main goal of this paper.

3   Coimplications on Discrete Settings

From now on L_n will denote the finite chain $L_n = \{0, 1, \ldots, n\}$ and N the only strong negation on L_n given by equation (1). In this section, we study some properties of coimplication functions defined on L_n, similarly to the study given for implications in [13]). First of all recall that, while implications are the extensions of the Boolean implication $\implies$, where $p \implies q$ means that p is sufficient for q, coimplications are the extensions of the Boolean coimplication, $\not\Longleftarrow$, where $p \not\Longleftarrow q$ means that p is not necessary for q.

Let us begin by recalling the definition of a coimplication.

Definition 3. *([7], [4]) A coimplication function J on L_n or simply a discrete coimplication is a binary operator $J : L_n^2 \to L_n$ that is decreasing in the first variable, increasing in the second one and satisfies the corner conditions $J(0, 0) = 0, J(1, 1) = 0$ and $J(0, 1) = 1$.*

Remark 1. ([4]) Note that for any discrete coimplication it turns out that

$$J(n, \alpha) = J(\alpha, 0) = 0, \text{ for all } \alpha \in L_n$$

a property called the *absorption principle*.

A key point in the work is the fact that discrete implications and coimplications are N-dual one of each other as follows.

Proposition 3. *([4]) Let $I : L_n^2 \to L_n$ be a function. Then I is a discrete implications if and only if its N-dual I^*, given by*

$$I^*(x, y) = n - I(n - x, n - y) \quad \text{for all} \quad x, y \in L_n,$$

is a discrete coimplication. Similarly, a function $J : L_n^2 \to L_n$ is a discrete coimplication if and only if J^* is a discrete implicaton.

Note that, since N is involutive, it is $(I^*)^* = I$ for any function $I : L_n^2 \to L_n$. This duality allows to derive properties for coimplications directly from the properties of their dual implications. Next, we list some of the most usual properties of discrete implications jointly with their counterparts for coimplications. In the following table, I stands for an implication, J for a coimplication and $x, y \in L_n$.

$(I1)$ $I(n, y) = y$ $\qquad\qquad\qquad \to$ $(J1)$ $J(0, y) = y$

$(I2)$ $I(x, I(y, z)) = I(y, I(x, z))$ $\quad \to$ $(J2)$ $J(x, J(y, z)) = J(y, J(x, z))$

$(I3)$ $I(x, y) = I(n - y, n - x)$ $\quad\; \to$ $(J3)$ $J(x, y) = J(n - y, n - x)$

$(I4)$ $I(x, y) = n$ if and only if $x \le y \to$ $(J4)$ $J(x, y) = 0$ if and only if $x \ge y$

$(I5)$ $I(x, x) = n$ $\qquad\qquad\qquad\; \to$ $(J5)$ $J(x, x) = 0$

$(I6)$ $I(x, y) \ge y$ $\qquad\qquad\qquad \to$ $(J6)$ $J(x, y) \le y$

$(I7)$ $I(x, n - x) = n - x$ $\qquad\;\; \to$ $(J7)$ $J(x, n - x) = n - x$

It was proved in [19] that a fuzzy implication satisfies each one of these properties if and only if the dual coimplication satisfies it.

Proposition 4. *Let I be a discrete implication. For each $i = 1, 2, \ldots, 7$, I satisfies the property (Ii) if and only if I^* satisfies the property (Ji).*

Proof. The same proof as in the case of $[0, 1]$ applies here. Let us include only the proof corresponding to the property (I7) that is not included in [19]. We have $I^*(x, n - x) = n - x$ for all $x \in L_n$ if and only if $n - I(n - x, x) = n - x$. But, changing $n - x = y$, this is true if and only if $I(y, n - y) = n - y$. □

As it was mentioned in the previous section, two of the most usual ways to define implication functions on L_n are S-implications and R-implications. Thus, in the two next sections, we want to deal with the similar cases for coimplications on L_n. First, we recall the definitions of these types of binary functions.

Definition 4. *Let T be a discrete t-conorm on L_n. A discrete T-coimplication function is the binary operator J_T on L_n defined by*

$$J_T(x, y) = T(n - x, y) \quad \text{for all } x, y \in L_n.$$

Definition 5. *Let S be a discrete t-conorm on L. Then the discrete R-coimplication function derived from S is the binary operator J_S on L_n defined by*

$$J_S(x, y) = \min\{z \in L_n \mid S(x, z) \ge y\}.$$

3.1 T-Coimplications on Discrete Settings

In this section we deal with some interesting properties about these operators. We begin by giving their structure when they are derived from smooth t-norms (for the classification and expressions of smooth t-norms see [17]).

Theorem 1. *Let T be the smooth t-norm whose set of idempotent elements is $Idemp_T = \{0 = i_0 < i_1 < \ldots < i_m = n\}$. Then the corresponding T-coimplication is given by*

$$J_T(x, y) = \begin{cases} \max(i_k, n - x + y - i_{k+1}) & \text{if } (x, y) \in [n - i_{k+1}, n - i_k] \times [i_k, i_{k+1}] \\ \min(n - x, y) & \text{otherwise} \end{cases}$$

Proof. According to the definition,

$$J_T(x,y) = T(n-x,y)$$

Thus, taking into account the characterization of the smooth t-norm T (see [17], Theorem 7.3.8), we have:

i) If there is some $k \in \{0, \ldots, m-1\}$ such that $(x,y) \in [n-i_{k+1}, n-i_k] \times [i_k, i_{k+1}]$, then $(n-x,y) \in [i_k, i_{k+1}]^2$ and so

$$J_T(x,y) = T(n-x,y) = \max(i_k, n-x+y-i_{k+1})$$

ii) If there is no k in the conditions above, then $(n-x,y) \notin [i_k, i_{k+1}]^2$ for any k and so

$$J_T(x,y) = T(n-x,y) = \min(n-x,y).$$

□

The structure of coimplications derived from smooth t-norms can be viewed in Figure 1.

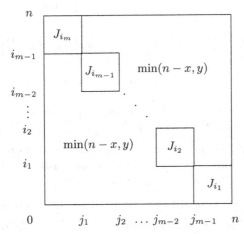

Fig. 1. General structure of the T-coimplication function obtained from the t-norm T with idempotent elements $Idemp_T = \{0, i_1, \ldots, i_{m-1}, n\}$, where $j_k = n - i_{m-k}$, and $J_{j_{k+1}}(x,y) = \max(i_k, n-x+y-i_{k+1})$ for each $k = 0, \cdots, m-1$

Remark 2. In particular, from the Łukasiewicz t-norm $T_{\mathbf{L}}$ the corresponding coimplication is given by

$$J_{T_{\mathbf{L}}}(x,y) = \max(0, y-x) = \begin{cases} y-x & \text{if } x < y \\ 0 & \text{otherwise.} \end{cases}$$

In the same way, from the minimum t-norm, we obtain $J_{\min}(x,y) = \min(n-x,y)$ for all $x, y \in L_n$.

On the other hand, a characterization for T-coimplications was given in [4] in the general case of bounded partially ordered sets and, consequently it applies in particular in our framework. So we have

Proposition 5. *[4] Let $J : L_n^2 \to L_n$ be a coimplication. Then there exists a discrete t-norm T on L_n such that $J = J_T$ if and only if J satisfies properties $(J1), (J2)$ and $(J3)$.*

Moreover, we can prove that the duality between implications and coimplications preserves this kind of operations. That is, the dual coimplication of an S-implications is in fact the T-coimplication derived from S^*, the dual t-norm of S, as it is proved in the following proposition.

Proposition 6. *Let $T : L_n^2 \to L_n$ be a t-norm on L_n. Then it is $J_T = (I_{T^*})^*$.*

Proof. It is clear since

$$(I_{T^*})^*(x, y) = n - I_{T^*}(n - x, n - y) = n - T^*(x, n - y) = T(n - x, y) = I_T(x, y).$$

$\square$

The previous proposition jointly with Proposition 4 allows us to derive all properties of T-coimplications from the already known properties of S-implications.

Proposition 7. *Let $T : L_n^2 \to L_n$ be a smooth t-norm on L_n. Then the following items hold,*

1. *J_T satisfies $(J4)$ if and only if T is the Łukasiewicz t-norm.*
2. *J_T satisfies $(J5)$ if and only if T is the Łukasiewicz t-norm.*
3. *J_T satisfies $(J7)$ if and only if T is the minimum t-norm.*
4. *J_T is smooth if and only if T is smooth.*

Proof. All items can be proven similarly. Let us prove the first one as an example. J_T satisfies $(J4)$ if and only if $(J_T)^* = I_{T^*}$ satisfies $(I4)$. By Proposition 6 in [13] this occurs if and only if T is the Łukasiewicz t-norm. $\square$

The following result deals with the dual result of the modus ponens.

Proposition 8. *Let S be a smooth t-conorm on L_n. Then, J_T satisfies the condition $T^*(x, J_T(x, y)) \geq y$ for all $x, y \in L_n$ if and only if T is the Łukasiewicz t-norm on L_n.*

Proof. Again the proof can be done by duality. Suppose that $T^*(x, J_T(x, y)) \geq y$ for all $x, y \in L_n$, then

$$n - T(n - x, n - J_T(x, y)) \geq y \quad \Longleftrightarrow \quad T(n - x, (J_T)^*(n - x, n - y)) \leq n - y,$$

and changing $a = n - x$ and $b = n - y$, we obtain

$$T(a, I_{T^*}(a, b)) \leq b \quad \text{for all} \quad a, b \in L_n. \tag{2}$$

Now, by applying Proposition 8 in [13], equation (2) implies that T must be the Łukasiewicz t-norm.

The converse is a simple calculation. $\square$

3.2 Residual Coimplications

In this section we make a similar study as in the section above for residual coimplications. Let us begin in this case by some properties that can be derived directly from the definition.

Proposition 9. *Let S be a a t-conorm on L_n and J_S its residual coimplication function. Then J_S satisfies properties $(J4), (J5), (J6)$, and also for all $x, y, z \in L_n$,*

- *$S(x, y) \geq z$ if and only if $J_S(x, z) \leq y$*
- *$S(x, J_S(x, z)) \geq z$.*

Proof. All properties are direct from the definition, taking into account that $J_S(x, z)$ is given by the minimum. □

Now, we want to find the structure of residual coimplications when they are derived from smooth t-conorms (for the classification and expressions of smooth t-conorms see [17]).

Theorem 2. *Let S be the smooth t-conorm on L whose set of idempotent elements is given by $Idemp_S = \{0 = i_0 \leq i_1 \leq \cdots \leq i_{m-1} \leq i_m = n\}$. Then,*

$$J_S(x, y) = \begin{cases} 0 & \text{if } y \leq x \\ i_k + y - x & \text{if } i_k \leq x < y \leq i_{k+1} \\ y & \text{otherwise} \end{cases}$$

Proof. According to Proposition 9 i) it follows that $J_S(x, y) = 0$ if $y \leq x$. Now, suppose that $y > x$. In this case, we consider two possibilities:

i) If there exists $i_k \in I$ such that $i_k \leq x < y \leq i_{k+1}$, according to Theorem 7.3.9 in [17],

$$S(x, y - x + i_k) = \min(i_{k+1}, x + y - x + i_k - i_k) = \min(i_{k+1}, y) = y$$

and then, $J_S(x, y) = \min\{z \in L \mid S(x, z) \geq y\} = i_k + y - x$.

ii) If $(x, y) \notin [i_k, i_{k+1}]^2$, applying again Theorem 7.3.9 in [17], $S(x, y) = \max(x, y) = y$ and so $J_S(x, y) = y$. □

The structure of residual coimplications derived from smooth t-conorms can be viewed in Figure 2.

Remark 3. In particular, from the Łukasiewicz t-conorm $S_{\mathbf{L}}$ the corresponding coimplication is given by

$$J_{S_{\mathbf{L}}}(x, y) = \begin{cases} y - x & \text{if } x < y \\ 0 & \text{otherwise.} \end{cases}$$

In the same way, from the maximum t-conorm, we obtain

$$J_{\max}(x, y) = \begin{cases} y & \text{if } x < y \\ 0 & \text{otherwise.} \end{cases}$$

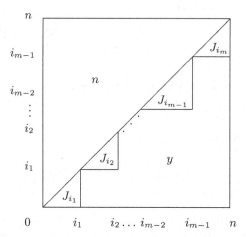

Fig. 2. General structure of the R-coimplication function obtained from the smooth conorm S with idempotent elements $Idemp_S = \{0 = i_0 \leq i_1 \leq \cdots \leq i_{m-1} \leq i_m = n\}$, where $J_{i_{k+1}}(x,y) = i_k + y - x$

In this case again the duality between implications and coimplications preserves this kind of operations. That is, the dual coimplication of the R-implications obtained from a t-norm T is in fact the R-coimplication derived from T^*, the dual t-conorm of T, as it is proved in the following proposition.

Proposition 10. *Let $T : L_n^2 \to L_n$ be a t-norm on L_n. Then it is $J_{T^*} = (I_T)^*$.*

Proof. It is clear since

$$(I_T)^*(x,y) = n - I_T(n-x, n-y) = n - \max\{z \in L_n \mid T(n-x,z) \leq n-y\}$$
$$= \min\{n - z \in L_n \mid T(n-x,z) \leq n-y\}.$$

whereas
$$(I_{T^*})(x,y) = \min\{z \in L_n \mid T^*(x,z) \geq y\}$$
$$= \min\{z \in L_n \mid n - T(n-x, n-z) \geq y\}$$
$$= \min\{z \in L_n \mid T(n-x, n-z) \leq n-y\}.$$

and the result follows.   □

The previous proposition jointly with Proposition 4 allows us to derive all properties of R-coimplications from the already known properties of R-implications. First we can derive an axiomatic characterization for discrete R-coimplications.

Proposition 11. *Let $J : L_n^2 \to L_n$ be a coimplication on L_n. Then there exists a t-conorm S such that $J = J_S$ if and only if J satisfies properties $(J1), (J2)$ and $(J4)$.*

Proof. There exists a t-conorm S such that $J = J_S$ if and only if there esists a t-norm S^* such that $J^* = (J_S)^* = I_{S^*}$. By Theorem 2 in [13], this occurs if and only if I_{S^*} satisfies properties $(I1), (I2)$ and $(I4)$. Now the result follows from Proposition 4.   □

Other properties that can be derived by duality are listed in the following proposition.

Proposition 12. *Let* $S : L_n^2 \to L_n$ *be a smooth t-conorm on* L_n. *Then the following items hold,*

1. J_S *is smooth if and only if* S *is the Łukasiewicz t-conorm.*
2. J_S *satisfies* $(J3)$ *if and only if* S *is the Łukasiewicz t-conorm.*
3. J_S *satisfies* $J_S(x, n) = n - x$ *if and only if* S *is the Łukasiewicz t-conorm.*
4. *Both coimplications* J_S *and* J_{S^*} *coindice if and only if* S *is the Łukasiewicz t-conorm.*

Proof. All items can be proven similarly. Let us prove item 4 which deals with the coincidence of R-coimplications and T-coimplications. Effectively, both coimplications J_S and J_{S^*} coindice if and only if the corresponding dual implications $(J_S)^* = I_{S^*}$ and $(J_{S^*})^* = I_S$ coincide. By Proposition 10 in [13] this occurs if and only if S^* is the Łukasiewicz t-norm and this ends the proof.   □

4   Conclusions

In this article we deal with co-implications defined on finite ordinal scales, called discrete co-implications. In particular, strong co-implications derived from smooth t-norms and residual co-implications derived from smooth t-conorms are characterized and their structure is given. On the other hand, the duality between discrete co-implications and discrete implications is pointed out and it is also used to derive some properties of co-implications from those already known for implications.

Acknowledgment. This work has been partially supported by the MTM2009-10962 and MTM2009-10320 project grants, both with FEDER support.

References

1. Aguiló, I., Suñer, J., Torrens, J.: Matrix representation of discrete quasi-copulas. Fuzzy Sets and Systems 159, 1658–1672 (2008)
2. Baczyński, M., Jayaram, B.: Fuzzy Implications. STUDFUZZ, vol. 231. Springer, Heidelberg (2008)
3. De Baets, B.: Model implicators and their characterization. In: Sreele, N. (ed.) Proceedings of the First ICSC International Symposium on Fuzzy logic, ICSC 1995, pp. A42–A49. Academic Press (1995)
4. De Baets, B.: Coimplicators: The forgotten connectives. Tatra Mountains 12, 229–240 (1997)

5. De Baets, B., Fodor, J., Ruiz-Aguilera, D., Torrens, J.: Idempotent uninorms on finite ordinal scales. International Journal of Uncertainty, Fuzziness and Knowledge-Based Systems 17, 1–14 (2009)

6. Fodor, J.C.: Smooth associative operations on finite ordinal scales. IEEE Trans. on Fuzzy Systems 8, 791–795 (2000)

7. Fodor, J., Roubens, M.: Fuzzy preference modelling and multicriteria decision support. Series D: System Theory, Knowledge Engineering and Problem Solving, vol. 14. Kluwer Academic Publishers (1994)

8. Klement, E.P., Mesiar, R., Pap, E.: Triangular Norms. Trends in Logic - Studi Logica Library, vol. 8. Kluwer Academic Publishers (2000)

9. Klir, G.J., Yuan, B.: Fuzzy sets and fuzzy logic (Theory and applications). Prentice-Hall (1995)

10. Kolesárová, A., Mayor, G., Mesiar, R.: Weighted ordinal means. Information Sciences 177, 3822–3830 (2007)

11. Mas, M., Monserrat, M., Torrens, J., Trillas, E.: A survey on Fuzzy Implications Functions. IEEE Transactions on fuzzy systems 15, 1107–1121 (2007)

12. Mas, M., Mayor, G., Torrens, J.: t-operators and uninorms on a finite totally ordered set. International Journal of Intelligent Systems 14, 909–922 (1999)

13. Mas, M., Monserrat, M., Torrens, J.: S-implications and R-implications on a finite chain. Kybernetica 40, 3–20 (2004)

14. Mas, M., Monserrat, M., Torrens, J.: On two types of discretes implications. International Journal of Approximate Resoning 40, 262–279 (2005)

15. Mas, M., Monserrat, M., Torrens, J.: Smooth Aggregation Functions on Finite Scales. In: Hüllermeier, E., Kruse, R., Hoffmann, F. (eds.) IPMU 2010. LNCS(LNAI), vol. 6178, pp. 398–407. Springer, Heidelberg (2010)

16. Mayor, G., Suñer, J., Torrens, J.: Copula-like operations on finite settings. IEEE Transactions on Fuzzy Systems 13, 468–477 (2005)

17. Mayor, G., Torrens, J.: Triangular norms on discrete settings. In: Klement, E.P., Mesiar, R. (eds.) Logical, Algebraic, Analytic, and Probabilistic Aspects of Triangular Norms, pp. 189–230. Elsevier, Netherlands (2005)

18. Oh, K., Kandel, A.: Coimplication and its applications to fuzzy expert systems. Information Sciences 56, 247–260 (1991)

19. Reixer, R., Bedregal, B.: Automorphisms acting on N-dual fuzzy functions: implications and coimplications. Anais do CNMAC 3, 229–235 (2010)

20. Ruiz, D., Torrens, J.: Residual implications and co-implications from idempotent uninorms. Kybernetika 40, 21–38 (2004)

Survival Implications

Przemysław Grzegorzewski[1,2]

[1] Systems Research Institute, Polish Academy of Sciences
ul. Newelska 6, 01-447 Warsaw, Poland
[2] Faculty of Mathematics and Information Science, Warsaw University of Technology
Plac Politechniki 1, 00-661 Warsaw, Poland
pgrzeg@ibspan.waw.pl, pgrzeg@mini.pw.edu.pl
http://www.ibspan.waw.pl/~pgrzeg

Abstract. A new family of implication operators, called survival implications, is discussed. It is shown that survival implications have some interesting properties, both in the field of fuzzy implications and in probability theory, connected with the dependence structure of the random environment. Moreover, survival S-implications are also considered.

Keywords: fuzzy implication, S-implication, copula, survival copula, conditional probability, approximate reasoning.

1 Introduction

Fuzzy implications play a key role in approximate reasoning and fuzzy control. They are interesting both because of the theoretical point and many diverse applications (see [1]). However, one should remember that uncertainty cannot always be reduced to imprecision. Sometimes it is rather an immanent effect of randomness. Therefore, another type of implication that takes into consideration both sources of uncertainty would be desirable. Such a construction, called probabilistic implications, was suggested in [4]. However, in many applications we are interested in the times to failure or lifetimes of individuals and there the most natural description of uncertainty is delivered by a survival function. And this very concept makes the background of the survival implication suggested in this contribution.

The paper is organized as follows. In Sec. 2 we recall basic information on fuzzy implications, probabilistic implications and related notions. In Sec. 3. we introduce a survival implication operator and examine its basic properties. Next in Sec. 4 we explore survival implications' connections with the underlying dependence structure revealed by copulas. Finally we propose another way for defining fuzzy implications based on survival function, called survival S-implications.

2 Fuzzy Implications

Although in classical logic an implication can be defined in many ways depending on the mathematical framework, physical nature or philosophical background in

S. Greco et al. (Eds.): IPMU 2012, Part II, CCIS 298, pp. 335–344, 2012.
© Springer-Verlag Berlin Heidelberg 2012

which it appears, it should satisfy the so-called truth table. Starting from different definitions and using diversity of methods we may obtain a great number of multi-valued implications, known in the literature as fuzzy implications. Anyway all of them should satisfy some fundamental requirements that generalize the classical truth table and hence define a fuzzy implication (see [1], [3]).

Definition 1. *A function* $I : [0,1]^2 \to [0,1]$ *is called a fuzzy implication if it satisfies the following conditions for all* $x, x_1, x_2, y, y_1, y_2 \in [0,1]$
(I1) if $x_1 \leq x_2$ *then* $I(x_1, y) \geq I(x_2, y)$
(I2) if $y_1 \leq y_2$ *then* $I(x, y_1) \leq I(x, y_2)$
(I3) $I(0,0) = 1$
(I4) $I(1,1) = 1$
(I5) $I(1,0) = 0$.

The theory of fuzzy implications is closely connected with the theory of fuzzy negations, conjunctions and disjunctions. Many researchers study both mathematical properties and possible applications of fuzzy implications. The literature devoted to that topic is quite broad but the most comprehensive treatise on fuzzy implications is the monograph [1]. Further on the family of all fuzzy implications will be denoted by $\mathcal{FI}$.

One has to be aware that uncertainty which appears in many systems originates not only from imprecision but may be caused by randomness. In particular, according to modus ponens inferential rule we may expect that provided A is "surely" true and the implication $A \to B$ is also "surely" true then B is true. However, in practice we may neither be completely sure that A nor that the the implication $A \to B$ is 100% true. We can only estimate the probability $P(A)$ that A is true and the probability $P(A \to B)$ that the implication $A \to B$ holds. Here the most natural approach is to interpret the probability of an implication as the conditional probability $P(B|A)$, i.e.

$$P(B|A) = \frac{P(B \cap A)}{P(A)}, \tag{1}$$

where $P(A) > 0$. Hence, if we know the probability of the premise A and the probability of the implication then we can find the probability that both B and A are true, i.e. $P(B \cap A) = P(B|A) \cdot P(A)$.

To reconcile the theory of fuzzy implications with the probabilistic interpretation based on the conditional probability Grzegorzewski [4] introduced the notion of so-called probabilistic implication. Since his construction is based on the copula, let us recall that notion first.

Definition 2. *A copula (specifically a 2-copula) is a function* $C : [0,1]^2 \to [0,1]$ *which satisfies the following conditions:*
(a) $C(u,0) = C(0,v) = 0$ *for every* $u, v \in [0,1]$
(b) $C(u,1) = u$ *for every* $u \in [0,1]$
(c) $C(1,v) = v$ *for every* $v \in [0,1]$
(d) for every $u_1, u_2, v_1, v_2 \in [0,1]$ *such that* $u_1 \leq u_2$ *and* $v_1 \leq v_2$

$$C(u_2, v_2) - C(u_2, v_1) - C(u_1, v_2) + C(u_1, v_1) \geq 0. \tag{2}$$

It can be shown that every copula is bounded by the so-called Fréchet-Hoeffding bounds, i.e. for any copula C and for all $u, v \in [0, 1]$ we have $W(u, v) \leq C(u, v) \leq M(u, v)$, where $W(u, v) = \max\{u + v - 1, 0\}$ and $M(u, v) = \min\{u, v\}$ are also copulas. For more information on copulas we refer the reader to [7].

The importance of the copulas is clarified by the Sklar theorem [9] showing that copulas link joint distribution functions to their one-dimensional margins, i.e. if X and Y are random variables with joint c.d.f. H and marginal c.d.f. F and G, respectively, then there exists a copula C such that

$$H(x, y) = C(F(x), G(y)) \tag{3}$$

for all $x, y \in \mathbb{R}$. If F and G are continuous, then C is unique. Conversely, if C is a copula and F and G are distribution functions, then the function H defined by (3) is a joint distribution function with margins F and G.

Let us now consider the following definition (see [4]):

Definition 3. *A function $I_C : [0, 1]^2 \rightarrow [0, 1]$ given by*

$$I_C(u, v) = \begin{cases} 1 & if \quad u = 0 \\ \frac{C(u, v)}{u} & if \quad u > 0, \end{cases} \tag{4}$$

*where C is a copula, is called a **probabilistic implication** (based on copula C).*

Grzegorzewski also discussed conditions when a probabilistic implication I_C is a fuzzy implication and examined basic properties of the probabilistic implications (see [4], [5]).

3   Survival Implication

In many applications we are interested in the lifetimes of individuals or elements of a population under study. The probability that a given object will survive beyond time x is characterized by the survival function (reliability function) $\overline{F}(x) = P(X > x)$. Of course, $\overline{F}(x) = 1 - F(x)$, where F denotes the c.d.f. of X.

For a pair (X, Y) of random variables with joint c.d.f H the joint survival function is $\overline{H}(x, y) = P(X > x, Y > y)$. There is a relationship between the joint survival function $\overline{H}$ and univariate marginal survival functions $\overline{F}$ and $\overline{G}$, analogous to that given by (3):

$$\overline{H}(x, y) = C^*(\overline{F}(x), \overline{G}(y)), \tag{5}$$

where C^* is called the **survival copula** and defined as

$$C^*(u, v) = u + v - 1 + C(1 - u, 1 - v). \tag{6}$$

Let us now consider the conditional probability (1) for the following events $A = \{\omega : X(\omega) > x\}$ and $B = \{\omega : Y(\omega) > y\}$ of surviving beyond time x and y, respectively. Assuming $P(X > x) > 0$ and adopting previous notation we get

$$P(Y > y | X > x) = \frac{P(X > x, Y > y)}{P(X > x)} = \frac{\overline{H}(x, y)}{\overline{F}(x)} = \frac{C^*(\overline{F}(x), \overline{G}(y))}{\overline{F}(x)} \quad (7)$$

$$= \frac{C^*(u, v)}{u} = \frac{u + v - 1 + C(1 - u, 1 - v)}{u},$$

where $u = \overline{F}(x)$ and $v = \overline{G}(y)$. These intuitions lead to the following definition.

Definition 4. *A function* $I_C^* : [0, 1]^2 \to [0, 1]$ *given by*

$$I_C^*(u, v) = \begin{cases} 1 & if \quad u = 0 \\ \frac{u + v - 1 + C(1 - u, 1 - v)}{u} & if \quad u > 0, \end{cases} \quad (8)$$

*where C is a copula, is called a **survival implication** (based on copula C).*

Now let us examine some basic properties of the function I_C^*.

Lemma 1. *For any copula C a survival implication $I_C^* : [0, 1]^2 \to [0, 1]$ based on C satisfies the following conditions:*
(i) $I_C^*(0, 0) = 1$
(ii) $I_C^*(1, 1) = 1$
(iii) $I_C^*(1, 0) = 0$
(iv) if $v_1 \le v_2$ then $I_C^*(u, v_1) \le I_C^*(u, v_2)$.

Proof: Property (i) holds by definition, since according to (8) $I_C^*(0, v) = 1$ for each v, hence in particular $I_C^*(0, 0) = 1$. Next two properties are simply direct conclusions from Def. 2. Actually, condition (a) in Def. 2 states that $C(0, 0) = 0$. Thus $I_C^*(1, 1) = 1$ and hence (ii) holds. Similarly, property (iii) is fulfilled because of condition (b) in Def. 2. Since $C(1 - u, 1) = 1 - u$ for every $u \in [0, 1]$ then $I_C^*(1, 0) = 0$.

Now let us prove (iv) that $I_C^*(u, \cdot)$ is increasing. Thus we have to show that $v_1 \le v_2$ implies $I_C^*(u, v_1) \le I_C^*(u, v_2)$ for any $u \in [0, 1]$. If $u = 0$ then $I_C^*(u, v_1) = 1 = I_C^*(u, v_2)$. If $u > 0$ and $v_1 \le v_2$ then we get

$$I_C^*(u, v_2) - I_C^*(u, v_1)$$
$$= \frac{u + v_2 - 1 + C(1 - u, 1 - v_2)}{u} - \frac{u + v_1 - 1 + C(1 - u, 1 - v_1)}{u}$$
$$= \frac{1}{u} [1 - v_1 - (1 - v_2) - C(1 - u, 1 - v_1) + C(1 - u, 1 - v_2)]$$
$$= \frac{1}{u} [C(1, 1 - v_1) - C(1, 1 - v_2) - C(1 - u, 1 - v_1) + C(1 - u, 1 - v_2)] \ge 0$$

according to property (2). This completes the proof.   □

Lemma 1 states that our function I_C^* fulfills requirements (I2)-(I5) specified in Def. 1 of a fuzzy implication. Thus an immediate question is whether $I_C^*(\cdot, v)$ is decreasing for any copula C, i.e. if $u_1 \le u_2$ then $I_C^*(u_1, v) \ge I_C^*(u_2, v)$. If

$u_1 = u_2 = 0$ it is obvious by (8). Unfortunately, if $0 < u_1 < u_2$ then I_C^* may not be decreasing. Consider, e.g. the lower Fréchet-Hoeffding bound W. Suppose $u_1 = 0.3 < u_2 = 0.6$ and $v = 0.8$. Then $I_W^*(u_1, v) = \frac{1}{3} < I_W^*(u_2, v) = \frac{2}{3}$ which shows that I_W^* is not decreasing. Hence survival implications are not, in general, fuzzy implications. However, we can formulate the following theorem.

Theorem 1. *A survival implication I_C^* based on a copula C is a fuzzy implication if and only if*

$$C(1 - u_1, 1 - v)u_2 - C(1 - u_2, 1 - v)u_1 \geq (1 - v)(u_2 - u_1) \qquad (9)$$

for every $u_1, u_2, v \in [0, 1]$ such that $u_1 \leq u_2$.

Proof: By Lemma 1 function I_C^* fulfills requirements (I2)-(I5) specified in Def. 1 for any copula C. Condition (9) assures that $I_C^*(\cdot, v)$ is decreasing. Actually, if $0 < u_1 < u_2$ then (9) is equivalent to

$$C(1 - u_1, 1 - v)u_2 + (v - 1)u_2 \geq C(1 - u_2, 1 - v)u_1 + (v - 1)u_1$$

which after dividing both sides by $u_2 u_1$ gives us

$$\frac{v - 1 + C(1 - u_1, 1 - v)}{u_1} - \frac{v - 1 + C(1 - u_2, 1 - v)}{u_2} \geq 0.$$

Hence also $1 + \frac{v-1+C(1-u_1,1-v)}{u_1} - (1 + \frac{v-1+C(1-u_2,1-v)}{u_2}) \geq 0$, i.e. $I_C^*(u_1, v) - I_C^*(a_2, v) \geq 0$, which means that $I_C^*(\cdot, v)$ is decreasing, i.e. (I1) is also satisfied and hence I_C^* is a fuzzy implication, i.e. $I_C^* \in \mathcal{FI}$. $\qquad \square$

The following equivalent criteria may also be useful.

Theorem 2. *A survival implication I_C^* based on a copula C is a fuzzy implication if and only if*

$$I_C^*(u, v) \geq 1 - \frac{\partial C(1 - u, 1 - v)}{\partial u} \qquad (10)$$

for almost all $u \in [0, 1]$.

Proof: Each function I_C^* given by (8) satisfies requirements (I2)-(I5) specified in Def. 1 for any copula C. Hence, it is enough to prove that condition (10) is equivalent to (9), i.e. (10) assures that $I_C^*(\cdot, v)$ is decreasing.

First of all let us notice that the existence of the partial derivative $\frac{\partial C(u,v)}{\partial u}$ is obvious because monotone functions are differentiable almost everywhere. Function $I_C^*(\cdot, v)$ is decreasing if and only if $\frac{\partial I_C^*(u,v)}{\partial u} \leq 0$. However, simple calculations show that for $u > 0$ we get

$$\frac{\partial I_C^*(u, v)}{\partial u} = \frac{\partial}{\partial u} \left(\frac{u + v - 1 + C(1 - u, 1 - v)}{u} \right)$$

$$= \frac{1}{u^2} \left((1 - \frac{\partial C(1 - u, 1 - v)}{\partial u})u - (u + v - 1 + C(1 - u, 1 - v)) \right)$$

$$= \frac{1}{u^2} \left(1 - v - u\frac{\partial C(1 - u, 1 - v)}{\partial u} - C(1 - u, 1 - v) \right).$$

Hence $\frac{\partial I_C(u,v)}{\partial u} \leq 0$ if and only if $1 - v - u\frac{\partial C(1-u,1-v)}{\partial u} - C(1-u,1-v) \leq 0$.
However, the last inequality is equivalent to $1 - \frac{\partial C(1-u,1-v)}{\partial u} \leq \frac{u+v-1+C(1-u,1-v)}{u}$,
i.e. $1 - \frac{\partial C(1-u,1-v)}{\partial u} \leq I_C^*(u,v)$, which is equivalent to (10).   □

Example 1

Let us consider Farlie-Gumbel-Morgenstern's family of copulas given by

$$C_\theta(u,v) = uv + \theta uv(1-u)(1-v). \tag{11}$$

Here, parameter $\theta \in [-1,1]$ is responsible for the dependence structure. In particular, for $\theta = 0$ we obtain the product copula, i.e. $C_\theta(u,v)|_{\theta=0} = uv = \Pi(u,v)$. A survival implication based on the Farlie-Gumbel-Morgenstern copula is then

$$I_{FGM(\theta)}^*(u,v) = \begin{cases} 1 & \text{if} \quad u = 0 \\ v + \theta v(1-u)(1-v) & \text{if} \quad u > 0. \end{cases} \tag{12}$$

Now let us check whether survival implication based on the Farlie-Gumbel-Morgenstern copula is a fuzzy implication. Substituting (11) into (9) we get

$$C(1 - u_1, 1 - v)u_2 - C(1 - u_2, 1 - v)u_1 - (1 - v)(u_2 - u_1)$$
$$= \theta u_1 u_2 v(u_2 - u_1)(1 - v) \geq 0$$

which is nonnegative for every $u_1, u_2, v \in [0,1]$ such that $u_1 \leq u_2$ if and only if if $\theta \geq 0$. Therefore, we may conclude that $I_{FGM(\theta)}^* \in \mathcal{FI} \Leftrightarrow \theta \geq 0$, i.e. the survival implication (12) based on the Farlie-Gumbel-Morgenstern copula is a fuzzy implication not for all possible values of parameter θ but only for $\theta \geq 0$.   ■

It is worth noting (see [4], [5]) that we have obtained the same result for the probabilistic implication based on the Farlie-Gumbel-Morgenstern copula. And it should not be surprising since for this very family of copulas we have

$$C_\theta^*(u,v) = u + v - 1 + C_\theta(1-u,1-v)$$
$$= u + v - 1 + ((1-u)(1-v) + \theta(1-u)(1-v)uv)$$
$$= uv + \theta uv(1-u)(1-v) = C_\theta(u,v)$$

and hence also $I_{FGM(\theta)}^*(u,v) = I_{FGM(\theta)}(u,v)$. This observation leads to the more general conclusion

Lemma 2. *If $C^*(u,v) = C(u,v)$ for each $u,v \in [0,1]$ then the survival implication based on C is equal to the probabilistic implication based on the same copula, i.e. $I_C^* = I_C$.*

The proof of this lemma is straightforward.

Example 2

As the immediate consequence of that lemma we may conclude e.g. that the survival implication based on the upper Fréchet-Hoeffding bound M is the Goguen implication $I_{GG}(u,v)$. Obviously, $M^*(u,v) = u + v - 1 + M(1-u,1-v) = u + v - 1 + \min\{1-u,1-v\} = \min\{u,v\}$ and therefore $I_M^*(u,v) = \frac{\min\{u,v\}}{u} = I_M(u,v) = I_{GG}(u,v)$ (see also [4], [5]).   ■

4   Survival Implications and the Dependence Structure

Survival implications as other fuzzy implications might be considered and developed in a formal way without any reference to probability theory. However, since they are based on copulas which describe a dependence structure between underlying random variables, it seems that the probabilistic context may get a deeper insight into the nature of these implications. Let us start by recalling of some basic types of dependence (see [2]).

Definition 5. *Let X and Y be random variables. Then*

- *X and Y are positively quadrant dependent (PQD) if $P(X \leq x, Y \leq y) \geq P(X \leq x)P(Y \leq y)$ for all $(x,y) \in \mathbb{R}^2$*
- *Y is left tail decreasing in X [denoted by $LTD(Y|X)$] if $P(Y \leq y|X \leq x)$ is a decreasing function of x for all y*
- *Y is right tail increasing in X [denoted by $RTI(Y|X)$] if $P(Y > y|X > x)$ is a increasing function of x for all y*
- *Y is stochastically increasing in X [denoted by $SI(Y|X)$] if $P(Y > y|X = x)$ is a increasing function of x for all y*
- *X and Y having join density function(or, in the discrete case, join probability mass function) $h(x,y)$ are totally positive of order 2 [denoted by TP_2] if $h(x_1,y_1)h(x_2,y_2) \geq h(x_2,y_1)h(x_1,y_2)$ for all $x_1, x_2, y_1, y_2 \in \overline{\mathbb{R}}$ such that $x_1 \leq x_2$ and $y_1 \leq y_2$.*

As it is known, there are relationships among dependence concepts mentioned above which form the following hierarchy (see [2]):

$$TP_2 \Longrightarrow SI(Y|X) \Longrightarrow LTD(Y|X) \Longrightarrow PQD \tag{13}$$
$$TP_2 \Longrightarrow SI(Y|X) \Longrightarrow RTI(Y|X) \Longrightarrow PQD.$$

Further on we say that if X and Y denote two random variables with copula C then a survival implication I_C^* based on the such copula C is said to be generated by X and Y.

Theorem 3. *A survival implication I_C^* is a fuzzy implication if and only if it is generated by (X, Y) such that Y is right tail increasing in X.*

Proof: By Def. 4 and all further discussion we know that a survival implication I_C^* is a fuzzy implication provided $I_C^*(\cdot, v)$ is decreasing. However, if $I_C^*(u,v) = \frac{u+v-1+C(1-u,1-v)}{u} = 1 + \frac{v-1+C(1-u,1-v)}{u}$ is decreasing in u thus $\frac{v-1+C(1-u,1-v)}{u}$ is also decreasing in u for any $v \in [0,1]$. Substituting $u := 1 - u$ and $v := 1 - v$ we get that $\frac{-v+C(u,v)}{1-u}$ is also increasing in u for any $v \in [0,1]$. Hence $\frac{v-C(u,v)}{1-u}$ is decreasing in u for any $v \in [0,1]$. In other words, $I_C^*(\cdot, v)$ is decreasing if and only if $\frac{v-C(u,v)}{1-u}$ is decreasing in u for any $v \in [0,1]$.

It can be shown that the criteria given in Def. 5 for Y being right tail increasing in X is equivalent to the following: Y is $RTI(Y|X)$ iff $\frac{v-C(u,v)}{1-u}$ is decreasing in u for any $v \in [0,1]$ (see [7]). Therefore, combining these two facts we obtain immediately the desired conclusion that I_C^* is a fuzzy implication iff Y is right tail increasing in X which proves the theorem.   □

It is worth noting that this result corresponds to the theorem given in [5]:

Theorem 4. *A probabilistic implication I_C is a fuzzy implication if and only if it is generated by (X, Y) such that Y is left tail decreasing in X.*

By (13) we can also prove the following properties:

Theorem 5. *If X and Y are totally positive of order 2 then a survival implication generated by X and Y is a fuzzy implication.*

Theorem 6. *If Y is stochastically increasing in X then a survival implication generated by X and Y is a fuzzy implication.*

5   Survival S-Implications

The conditional probability is not the only way that combines implication with randomness. According to classical logic

$$p \rightarrow q \equiv \neg p \vee q. \tag{14}$$

Hence the other formalization interprets the probability of implication $A \rightarrow B$ as the probability that either B occurs or A does not occur, i.e. $P(A' \cup B)$, where A' is the complement of A. Starting from this perspective Grzegorzewski [6] suggested the definition of the probabilistic S-implication.

Definition 6. *A function $\widetilde{I}_C : [0,1]^2 \rightarrow [0,1]$ given by*

$$\widetilde{I}_C(u,v) = C(u,v) - u + 1 \tag{15}$$

*where C is a copula, is called a **probabilistic S-implication** (based on C).*

The origin of that definition goes back to simple transformations of the above mentioned probability $P(A' \cup B)$ related to (14). For more details we refer the reader to [6]. Let us make some calculations on probabilities also here to obtain a survival S-implication. Consider a probabilistic space $(\Omega, \mathcal{F}, P)$ and any two events $A, B \in \mathcal{F}$. Then we have

$$P(A' \cup B) = P(A') + P(B) - P(A' \cap B) = P(A') + P(A \cap B). \tag{16}$$

Since $P(A') = 1 - P(A)$ hence (16) reduces to

$$P(A' \cup B) = P(A \cap B) - P(A) + 1. \tag{17}$$

Now, assuming as in Sec. 2, that $A = \{\omega : X(\omega) > x\}$ and $B = \{\omega : Y(\omega) > y\}$ and adopting previous notation for H as the joint cumulative probability function of (X, Y) with margins F and G corresponding to X and Y, respectively, and C for the corresponding copula, we may rewrite (17) as

$$P(X \leq x \text{ or } Y > y) = P(X > x, Y > y) - P(X > x) + 1$$
$$= \overline{H}(x, y) - \overline{F}(x) + 1 = C^*(\overline{F}(x), \overline{G}(y)) - \overline{F}(x) + 1$$
$$= C^*(u, v) - u + 1 = u + v - 1 + C(1 - u, 1 - v) - u + 1$$
$$= v + C(1 - u, 1 - v)$$

where $u = \overline{F}(x)$ and $v = \overline{G}(y)$. The reasoning given above shows motivations for the following definition.

Definition 7. *A function* $\widetilde{I}_C^* : [0, 1]^2 \to [0, 1]$ *given by*

$$\widetilde{I}_C^*(u, v) = v + C(1 - u, 1 - v), \tag{18}$$

*where C is a copula, is called a **survival S-implication** (based on copula C).*

As we remember not all survival implications are fuzzy implications but some additional requirements are necessary to ensure that $I_C^* \in \mathcal{FI}$. Now let us consider whether the same situation holds for survival S-implications.

Theorem 7. *For any copula C a survival S-implication $\widetilde{I}_C^*$ given by (18) is a fuzzy implication.*

Proof: We have to show that for any copula C function $\widetilde{I}_C^*$ satisfies requirements (I1)-(I5) specified in Def. 1. Boundary conditions (I3)-(I5) are easily seen. Actually, $\widetilde{I}_C^*(0, 0) = 0 + C(1, 1) = 1$, $\widetilde{I}_C^*(1, 1) = 1 + C(0, 0) = 1$ and $\widetilde{I}_C^*(1, 0) = 0 + C(0, 1) = 0$. Now let us assume that $u_1, u_2 \in [0, 1]$ and $u_1 \leq u_2$. Then for any $v \in [0, 1]$ we get

$$\widetilde{I}_C^*(u_1, v) \geq \widetilde{I}_C^*(u_2, v) \equiv v + C(1 - u_1, 1 - v) \geq v + C(1 - u_2, 1 - v)$$
$$\Leftrightarrow C(1 - u_1, 1 - v) \geq C(1 - u_2, 1 - v)$$

which holds since by Def. 2 function $C(y, \cdot)$ is increasing. Hence $\widetilde{I}_C^*$ is decreasing with respect to the first argument and thus (I1) holds.

If $v_1 \leq v_2$ then we get

$$\widetilde{I}_C(u, v_2) - \widetilde{I}_C(u, v_1) = v_2 + C(1 - u, 1 - v_2) - v_1 - C(1 - u, 1 - v_1)$$
$$= 1 - v_1 - (1 - v_2) - C(1 - u, 1 - v_1) + C(1 - u, 1 - v_2)$$
$$= C(1, 1 - v_1) - C(1, 1 - v_2) - C(1 - u, 1 - v_1) + C(1 - u, 1 - v_2) \geq 0$$

which by eq. (2) holds for any $u \in (0, 1]$ for any copula. Of course, if $u = 0$ then we get immediately $\widetilde{I}_C^*(0, v_2) = \widetilde{I}_C^*(0, v_1)$. Therefore, $\widetilde{I}_C^*$ is increasing with respect to the second argument (i.e. (I2) holds) which completes the proof. □

In other words, each survival S-implication, contrary to survival implications, is a fuzzy implication without any further conditions. We should also note that

Lemma 3. *If $C^*(u,v) = C(u,v)$ for each $u,v \in [0,1]$ then the survival S-implication based on C is equal to the probabilistic S-implication based on the same copula, i.e. $\widetilde{I}^*_C = \widetilde{I}_C$.*

Proof: It is easily seen that $C^*(u,v) = C(u,v)$ for each $u,v \in [0,1]$ then $C(u,v) = C^*(u,v) = u+v-1+C(1-u,1-v)$ and hence $\widetilde{I}^*_C(u,v) = v+C(1-u,1-v) = C(u,v)-u+1 = \widetilde{I}_C(u,v)$ which proves our lemma.

6 Conclusions

Survival implications (and survival S-implications) together with probabilistic implications (and probabilistic S-implications) form a promising link between probability theory and the theory of fuzzy implications that might be useful in approximate reasoning. They open a new perspective for developing their analytic and algebraic properties and for discovering connections between these new families and the well-known structures deeply recognized in the theory of fuzzy implications. However, what seems that even more interesting and promising is their straightforward relationship with the dependence structure between corresponding random variables. Actually, knowing more about underlying stochastic environment we may get a deeper insight into the reasoning schemes modeled through corresponding fuzzy implications and, on the other hand, some results obtained for fuzzy implications might also be fruitful for examining and interpreting the behavior of some stochastic events.

References

1. Baczynski, M., Jayaram, B.: Fuzzy Implications. Springer (2008)
2. Barlow, R.E., Proschan, F.: Statistical Theory of Reliability and Life Testing. Rinehart and Winston, Inc., Holt (1975)
3. Fodor, J.C., Roubens, M.: Fuzzy Preference Modelling and Multicriteria Decision Support. Kluwer, Dordrecht (1994)
4. Grzegorzewski, P.: Probabilistic implications. In: Proc. 7th Conf. European Society for Fuzzy Logic and Technology, pp. 254–258. Atlantis Press (2011)
5. Grzegorzewski, P.: On the Properties of Probabilistic Implications. In: Melo-Pinto, P., Couto, P., Serôdio, C., Fodor, J., De Baets, B. (eds.) Eurofuse 2011. AISC, vol. 107, pp. 67–78. Springer, Heidelberg (2011)
6. Grzegorzewski, P.: Probabilistic implications and their properties (submitted, 2012)
7. Nelsen, R.B.: An Introduction to Copulas. Springer, New York (1999)
8. Nguyen, H.T., Mukaidono, M., Kreinovich, V.: Probability of implication, logical version of Bayes' theorem, and fuzzy logic operations. In: Proceedings of the FUZZ-IEEE 2002, Honolulu, Hawaii, pp. 530–535 (2002)
9. Schweizer, B., Sklar, A.: Probabilistic Metric Spaces. Elsevier, New York (1983)

Generated Implications Revisited

Dana Hliněná[1], Martin Kalina[2], and Pavol Kráľ[3]

[1] Dept. of Mathematics FEEC Brno Uni. of Technology
Technická 8, Cz-616 00 Brno, Czech Republic
hlinena@feec.vutbr.cz
[2] Department of Mathematics, Slovak Technical University
Radlinského 11, Sk-813 68 Bratislava, Slovakia
kalina@math.sk
[3] Dept. of Quantitative Methods and Information Systems, Matej Bel University
Tajovského 10, Sk-975 90 Banská Bystrica, Slovakia
pavol.kral@umb.sk

Abstract. In this paper we generalize f-generated fuzzy implications introduced by Yager. Further we generalize I_f and I_N^g implications introduced by Smutná and RU-implications, studied by De Baets and Fodor, as well as (U, N)-implications. We study basic properties of these newly proposed fuzzy implications.

Keywords: fuzzy implication, fuzzy negation, generated implication, t-norm, uninorm.

1 Introduction and Preliminaries

A fuzzy implication is a mapping $I : [0, 1]^2 \to [0, 1]$ that generalizes the classical implication to fuzzy logic case in a similar way as t-norms (t-conorms) generalize the classical conjunction (disjunction). It is well known that there exist many ways how to construct them (see e.g., [2,3,4,5,6,10,12,15,17,18]). Fuzzy implications, in some cases, can be represented in the form $h^{(-1)}(f(x) * g(y))$, where h, f, g are appropriate one variable functions and $*$ a suitable arithmetic operation, e.g. a t-norm, a uninorm, ordinary arithmetic operations $+, \cdot$ etc. We will propose some new fuzzy implications and study their basic properties with respect to a chosen operation $*$ and/or with respect to properties of a chosen triple of functions (f, g, h). Particularly, we will study the case when the chosen operation is a t-norm (Section 2) and $+$ in combination with triples of increasing functions (f, g, h) (Section 3).

Definition 1. (see, e.g., [7]) *A decreasing function $N : [0, 1] \to [0, 1]$ is called a fuzzy negation if $N(0) = 1, N(1) = 0$. A fuzzy negation N is called*

1. *strict if it is strictly decreasing and continuous in $[0, 1]$,*
2. *strong if it is an involution, i.e., if $N(N(x)) = x$ for all $x \in [0, 1]$.*

Example 1. ([2]) The standard negation $N_C(x) = 1 - x$ and the fuzzy negation $N(x) = \sqrt{1 - x^2}$ are strong. The fuzzy negation $N(x) = 1 - x^2$ is strict, but

S. Greco et al. (Eds.): IPMU 2012, Part II, CCIS 298, pp. 345–354, 2012.
© Springer-Verlag Berlin Heidelberg 2012

not strong. The Gödel negation N_{D_1} is the least fuzzy negation and dual Gödel negation N_{D_2} is the greatest fuzzy negation, both are non-continuous. More examples of fuzzy negations can be found in [7].

$$N_{D_1} = \begin{cases} 1 & \text{if } x = 0, \\ 0 & \text{if } x > 0, \end{cases} \qquad N_{D_2} = \begin{cases} 1 & \text{if } x < 1, \\ 0 & \text{if } x = 1. \end{cases}$$

Definition 2. (see, e.g., [16]) A triangular norm T (t-norm for short) is a commutative, associative, monotone binary operator on the unit interval $[0, 1]$, fulfilling the boundary condition $T(x, 1) = x$, for all $x \in [0, 1]$.

Remark 1. Note that, for a strict negation N, the N-dual operation to a t-norm T defined by $S(x, y) = N^{-1}(T(N(x), N(y)))$ is called t-conorm. For more information, see, e.g., [11].

Uninorms were introduced by Yager and Rybalov in 1996 [19] as a generalization of triangular norms and conorms.

Definition 3. *An associative, commutative and increasing operation $U : [0, 1]^2 \to [0, 1]$ is called a uninorm, if there exists $e \in [0, 1]$, called the neutral element of U, such that*

$$U(e, x) = U(x, e) = x \quad \text{for all } x \in [0, 1].$$

Fodor et al. [8] characterized the so-called representable uninorms.

Proposition 1. *([8]) A uninorm U with neutral element $e \in]0, 1[$ is representable if and only if there exists a strictly increasing and continuous function $h : [0, 1] \to [-\infty, \infty]$ such that $h(0) = -\infty$, $h(e) = 0$, $h(1) = \infty$. The uninorm U is in that case given by*

$$U(x, y) = h^{-1}(h(x) + h(y)) \quad \text{for } x, y \in [0, 1],$$

where the value $\infty - \infty$ can be defined as ∞ or $-\infty$.

For each function h we have two possibilities how to define the corresponding representable uninorm. These two possibilities are the disjunctive (in case $\infty - \infty = \infty$) and conjunctive (in case $\infty - \infty = -\infty$) ones. In literature, we can find several definitions of fuzzy implications. In this paper we will use the following one, which is equivalent to the definition introduced by Fodor and Roubens in [7]. For more details one can consult [1] or [12].

Definition 4. *A function $I : [0, 1]^2 \to [0, 1]$ is called a fuzzy implication if it satisfies the following conditions:*

(I1) I is decreasing in its first variable,
(I2) I is increasing in its second variable,
(I3) $I(1, 0) = 0$, $I(0, 0) = I(1, 1) = 1$.

Next we list some important properties of fuzzy implications. For more information one can consult [9], [13] and [14].

Definition 5. *A fuzzy implication* $I : [0,1]^2 \to [0,1]$ *satisfies:*

(NP) *the left neutrality property, or is called left neutral, if*

$$I(1,y) = y; \quad y \in [0,1],$$

(EP) *the exchange principle if*

$$I(x, I(y,z)) = I(y, I(x,z)) \text{ for all } x, y, z \in [0,1],$$

(IP) *the identity principle if*

$$I(x,x) = 1; \quad x \in [0,1],$$

(OP) *the ordering property if*

$$x \le y \iff I(x,y) = 1; \quad x, y \in [0,1],$$

(CP) *the contrapositive symmetry with respect to a given fuzzy negation N if*

$$I(x,y) = I(N(y), N(x)); \quad x, y \in [0,1].$$

(LI) *the law of importation with respect to a t-norm T if*

$$I(T(x,y), z) = I(x, I(y,z)); \quad x, y, z \in [0,1].$$

(WLI) *the weak law of importation with respect to a commutative and increasing function $F : [0,1]^2 \to [0,1]$ if*

$$I(F(x,y), z) = I(x, I(y,z)); \quad x, y, z \in [0,1].$$

Definition 6. *Let $I : [0,1]^2 \to [0,1]$ be a fuzzy implication. The function N_I defined by $N_I(x) = I(x,0)$ for all $x \in [0,1]$, is called the natural negation related to I.*

(S,N)-implications, which are based on t-conorms S and fuzzy negations N, form one of the well-known classes of fuzzy implications. They are defined as

$$I_{S,N}(x,y) = S(N(x), y), \quad \text{for } x, y \in [0,1].$$

Remark 2. Similarly also (U,N)-implications are defined for disjunctive uni-norms U (i.e., if 1 is annihilator of U) as $I_{U,N}(x,y) = U(N(x), y)$.

Theorem 1. (Baczyński and Jayaram [1], Theorem 5.1) *For a function $I : [0,1]^2 \to [0,1]$, the following statements are equivalent:*

- *I is an (S,N)-implication generated from some t-conorm and some continuous (strict, strong) fuzzy negation N.*
- *I satisfies (I2), (EP) and N_I is a continuous (strict, strong) fuzzy negation.*

Another way of extending the classical binary implication operator to the unit interval $[0, 1]$ is based on the residuation operator with respect to a left-continuous triangular norm T

$$I_T(x, y) = \sup\{z \in [0, 1]; T(x, z) \le y\},$$

where $\sup \emptyset = 0$. Elements of this class are known as R-implications.

Example 2. For left-continuous t-norms T_M, T_P a T_L we get the following residual implications:

- $I_{T_M}(x, y) = \begin{cases} 1, & \text{if } x \le y, \\ y, & \text{otherwise,} \end{cases}$
- $I_{T_P}(x, y) = \min\left(\frac{y}{x}, 1\right),$ (Goguen implication)
- $I_{T_L}(x, y) = \min(1 - x + y, 1).$ (Łukasiewicz implication)

Note that the natural negations of I_{T_M} and I_{T_P} are the same and they are equal to the Gödel negation N_{D_1}. The natural negation of I_{T_L} is the standard negation.

Theorem 2. (Fodor and Roubens [7], Theorem 1.14) *For a function* $I : [0, 1]^2 \to [0, 1]$, *the following statements are equivalent:*

- *I is an R-implication based on some left-continuous t-norm* T.
- *I satisfies (I2), (OP), (EP), and* $I(x, .)$ *is right-continuous for any* $x \in [0, 1]$.

Analogously to R-implications with respect to t-norms, also residual implications with respect to uninorms were defined.

Definition 7. *A function* $I : [0, 1]^2 \to [0, 1]$ *is called an RU-operation, if there exists a uninorm* U *such that*

$$I(x, y) = \sup\{t \in [0, 1]; U(x, t) \le y\}, \text{ for all } x, y \in [0, 1].$$

If I is an RU-operation generated from a uninorm U then we will often denote it by I_U. An important technical notion is the following.

Definition 8. (see e.g., [11]) *Let* $f : [0, 1] \to [0, \infty]$ *be a decreasing function. Then* $f^{(-1)} : [0, \infty] \to [0, 1]$ *defined by*

$$f^{(-1)}(x) = \sup\{z \in [0, 1]; f(z) > x\},$$

is called the pseudo-inverse of f, *with the convention* $\sup \emptyset = 0$.

Definition 9. (see e.g., [7]) *Let* $g : [0, 1] \to [0, \infty]$ *be an increasing function. The function* $g^{(-1)}$ *which is defined by*

$$g^{(-1)}(x) = \sup\{z \in [0, 1]; g(z) < x\},$$

is called the pseudo-inverse of g, *with the convention* $\sup \emptyset = 0$.

2 $I_{T,f}$ Implications

Yager [18] introduced a new family of fuzzy implications, called f-generated fuzzy implications.

Proposition 2. ([18]) *If $f : [0,1] \rightarrow [0,\infty]$ is a strictly decreasing and continuous function with $f(1) = 0$, then the function $I : [0,1]^2 \rightarrow [0,1]$ defined by*

$$I(x,y) = f^{-1}(x \cdot f(y)), \tag{1}$$

with the understanding $0 \cdot \infty = 0$, is a fuzzy implication.

Note that if $\mathrm{rng}(f) = [0,1]$, we can write formula (1) in the following way

$$I(x,y) = f^{-1}(T_P(x, f(y))), \quad \text{for } x,y \in [0,1]. \tag{2}$$

Since implication is only a binary operation, we do not have to care about associativity. This means that instead of strictly decreasing functions we can consider also functions $f : [0,1] \rightarrow [0,1]$ which are not strictly decreasing, and the product t-norm T_P can be substituted by an arbitrary t-norm T.

Definition 10. *We say that a function $f : [0,1] \rightarrow [0,1]$ is admissible, if it fulfils the following properties:*

f *is a decreasing function,* $f(1) = 0,$ $f(0) = 1$ *and* $f(x) > 0$ *for $x < 1$.*

Proposition 3. *Let f be an admissible function. Further, let $T : [0,1]^2 \rightarrow [0,1]$ be an arbitrary t-norm. Then the function $I : [0,1]^2 \rightarrow [0,1]$ defined by*

$$I_{T,f}(x,y) = f^{(-1)}(T(x, f(y))), \tag{3}$$

is a fuzzy implication.

Example 3. For t-norm T_M and admissible functions $f_1(x) = 1 - x$, $f_2(x) = 1 - x^2$ and $f_3(x) = \begin{cases} 1 - x & \text{if } x \in [0, \frac{1}{2}] \\ \frac{1-x}{2} & \text{if } x \in]\frac{1}{2}, 1] \end{cases}$ we get the following implications:

- $I_{T_M,f_1} = \max(1 - x, y) = I_{S_M}$, (Kleenn-Dienes implication)
- $I_{T_M,f_2} = \max(\sqrt{1 - x}, y)$,
- $I_{T_M,f_3} = \begin{cases} 1 - 2x & \text{if } x \in [0, \frac{1}{4}] \text{ and } 2x + y \leq 1, \\ \frac{1}{2} & \text{if } (x,y) \in [\frac{1}{4}, \frac{1}{2}] \times [0, \frac{1}{2}], \\ 1 - x & \text{if } x \in]\frac{1}{2}, 1] \text{ and } x + y \leq 1, \\ y & \text{otherwise.} \end{cases}$

Note that the natural negations of these implications are equal to pseudo-inverses of the functions f_1, f_2 and f_3, respectively.

Proposition 4. *Let f be an admissible function. Further, let $T : [0,1]^2 \rightarrow [0,1]$ be an arbitrary t-norm. The natural negation related to $I_{T,f}$ is $N_{I_{T,f}}(x) = f^{(-1)}(x)$.*

Definition 11. ([1]) *Let T be a t-norm. A function $N_T : [0,1] \to [0,1]$ defined as*

$$N_T(x) = \sup\{y \in [0,1]; T(x,y) = 0\} \quad \text{for } x \in [0,1],$$

is called the natural negation of T, or the negation induced by T.

Note that the pseudo-inverse of a strictly decreasing function f is a continuous function. For simplicity, conditions under which $I_{T,f}$-implications possess some of the properties from Definition 5 are briefly listed in Table 1.

Table 1. Properties of f, T and the corresponding properties of $I_{T,f}$-implications

Properties of f	Properties of T	$I_{T,f}$-implications
strictly decreasing admissible	arbitrary	(NP)
continuous admissible	arbitrary	(EP)
admissible, $T(x, f(x)) = 0$	nilpotent	(IP)
admissible, $f(x) = N_T(x)$	nilpotent, left-continuous	(OP)

Directly from the properties listed in Table 1 and Theorem 1 we get for implications $I_{T,f}$:

Proposition 5. *Let f be a continuous strictly decreasing admissible function, and $T : [0,1]^2 \to [0,1]$ be an arbitrary t-norm. Then, for the fuzzy negation $N = f$ and the t-conorm S which is N-dual to T, the fuzzy implication $I_{T,f}$ is an (S, N^{-1})-implication.*

3   Generalizations of (U, N)- and RU-Implications

Smutná in [17] introduced two types of implications denoted as I_f and I_N^g.

Proposition 6. [17] *Let $f : [0,1] \to [0,\infty]$ be a strictly decreasing function such that $f(1) = 0$. Then the function $I_f(x,y) : [0,1]^2 \to [0,1]$ which is given by*

$$I_f(x,y) = \begin{cases} 1 & \text{if } x \leq y, \\ f^{(-1)}(f(y^+) - f(x)) & \text{otherwise,} \end{cases} \quad (4)$$

is an implication, where $f(y^+)$ is the right-side limit at y.

Proposition 7. ([17]) *Let $g : [0,1] \to [0,\infty]$ be a strictly increasing function such that $g(0) = 0$ and $N : [0,1] \to [0,1]$ be a fuzzy negation. Then the function $I_N^g(x,y) : [0,1]^2 \to [0,1]$ which is given by*

$$I_N^g(x,y) = g^{(-1)}(g(N(x)) + g(y)), \quad (5)$$

is an implication.

De Baets and Fodor in [4] introduced RU-implications and proved the following characterization.

Proposition 8. ([4]) *Let* $U : [0,1]^2 \rightarrow [0,1]$ *be a representable uninorm and* $h : [0,1] \rightarrow [-\infty, \infty]$ *be its additive generator. Then its residual implication is given by*

$$I_U(x,y) = \begin{cases} 1 & \text{if } x = y = 0 \text{ or } x = y = 1, \\ h^{-1}(h(y) - h(x)) & \text{otherwise.} \end{cases} \tag{6}$$

We can generalize these three approaches from Propositions 6, 7 and 8, as well as (U, N)-implications. As in the previous section, we do not need the associativity and commutativity of uninorm. This means that we can consider increasing and non-constant functions $f : [0,1] \rightarrow [-\infty, \infty]$, $g : [0,1] \rightarrow [-\infty, \infty]$ and $h : [0,1] \rightarrow [-\infty, \infty]$. Via the triple $\mathcal{F} = (f, g, h)$ we define an arithmetic operation by the following formula

$$x *_{\mathcal{F}} y = h^{(-1)}(f(x) + g(y)) \quad \text{with convention } \infty - \infty = \infty. \tag{7}$$

Proposition 9. *Let* $\mathcal{F} = (f, g, h)$ *be a triple of increasing and non-constant functions. Assume that h is in a left-neighbourhood of 1 strictly increasing. Then*

$$I_{\mathcal{F}}(x,y) = h^{(-1)}(g(y) - f(x)) \quad \text{with convention } \infty - \infty = \infty, \tag{8}$$

is a fuzzy implication if and only if the following conditions are fulfilled

$$h(0^+) \geq g(0) - f(1), \quad h(1^-) \leq \min\{g(1) - f(1), g(0) - f(0)\}.$$

Lemma 1. *Let* $\mathcal{F} = (f, g, h)$ *be a triple of increasing and non-constant functions, such that $I_{\mathcal{F}}$, given by formula (8), is a fuzzy implication. Let $*_{\mathcal{F}}$ be the operation defined by formula (7). Then*

$$I_{\mathcal{F}}(x,y) = \sup\{z \in [0,1]; x *_{\mathcal{F}} z \leq y\}$$

if and only if $h(x) = g(x)$ for all $x \in]0, 1[$ and h is continuous in $]0, 1[$.

The fuzzy implication defined by formula (8) will be called $I_{*_{\mathcal{F}}}$-implication.

Proposition 10. *Let* $\mathcal{F} = (f, g, h)$ *be a triple of increasing and non-constant functions and $*_{\mathcal{F}}$ be an operation defined by formula (7). Assume that h is in a left-neigbourhood of 1 strictly increasing. Further we assume that N is an arbitrary negation. Then*

$$I_{*_{\mathcal{F}}, N}(x,y) = N(x) *_{\mathcal{F}} y \tag{9}$$

is a fuzzy implication if and only if

$$h(1^-) \leq \min\{f(1) + g(0), f(0) + g(1)\}, \quad h(0^+) \geq f(0) + g(0),$$

with the convention $\infty - \infty = \infty$.

The fuzzy implication defined by formula (9) will be called $(*_{\mathcal{F}}, N)$-implication. In fact, an operation $*_{\mathcal{F}}$ fulfilling conditions from Proposition 10, is a commutative disjunction. Implications mentioned in Lemma 1 and Proposition 10 are particular cases of R- and S-implications like operators, presented in [15].

Example 4. Take the triples $\mathcal{F}_1 = (f_1, g_1, h_1)$ and $\mathcal{F}_2 = (f_2, g_2, h_2)$ such that

$$f_1(x) = \begin{cases} 0, & \text{for } x \in [0, \tfrac{1}{2}], \\ x - \tfrac{1}{2}, & \text{for } x \in]\tfrac{1}{2}, 1[, \\ 1, & \text{for } x = 1, \end{cases} \qquad g_1(x) = h_1(x) = \begin{cases} 2x - \tfrac{1}{2}, & \text{for } x \in [0, \tfrac{1}{4}], \\ 0, & \text{for } x \in]\tfrac{1}{4}, \tfrac{3}{4}[, \\ 2x - \tfrac{3}{2}, & \text{for } x \in]\tfrac{3}{4}, 1], \end{cases}$$

$$f_2(x) = g_2(x) = h_2(x) = \begin{cases} 2x - 1, & \text{for } x \in]0, 1[, \\ -\infty, & \text{for } x = 0, \\ \infty, & \text{for } x = 1. \end{cases}$$

Then

$$h_1^{(-1)}(x) = \begin{cases} \tfrac{1}{2}x + \tfrac{1}{4}, & \text{for } x \in [-\tfrac{1}{2}, 0], \\ \tfrac{1}{2}x + \tfrac{3}{4}, & \text{for } x \in]0, \tfrac{1}{2}], \\ 0, & \text{for } x < -\tfrac{1}{2}, \\ 1, & \text{for } x > \tfrac{1}{2}, \end{cases} \qquad h_2^{(-1)}(x) = \begin{cases} \tfrac{1}{2}x + \tfrac{1}{2}, & \text{for } x \in [-1, 1], \\ 0, & \text{for } x < -1, \\ 1, & \text{for } x > 1. \end{cases}$$

Let $N = N_C$. Then for the triple $\mathcal{F}_1$ we get a fuzzy implication $I_{*_{\mathcal{F}_1}, N_C}$, sketched on Figure 1 (note that $I_{\mathcal{F}_1}$ is not a fuzzy implication since, e.g., $I_{\mathcal{F}_1}(1,1) = 0$), and for the triple $\mathcal{F}_2$ we get a fuzzy implication $I_{*_{\mathcal{F}_2}, N_C} = I_{\mathcal{F}_2}$, sketched on Figure 2. Due to the convention in formulas (7) and (8) we have that $I_{*_{\mathcal{F}_2}, N_C}(x, 0) = I_{*_{\mathcal{F}_2}, N_C}(1, y) = 0$ for all $x \in]0, 1]$ and $y \in [0, 1[$. Further, $I_{*_{\mathcal{F}_2}, N_C}(\tfrac{1}{2}, y) = y$ for all $y \in [0, 1]$.

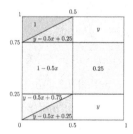

Fig. 1. Fuzzy implication $I_{*_{\mathcal{F}_1}, N_C}$

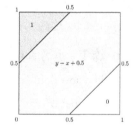

Fig. 2. Fuzzy implication $I_{*_{\mathcal{F}_2}, N_C}$

Lemma 2. *Let $\mathcal{F} = (f, g, h)$ be a triple of increasing and non-constant functions and let $\tilde{\mathcal{F}} = (k \cdot f, k \cdot g, k \cdot h)$ for a $k > 0$. Then $I_{*_{\mathcal{F}}, N} = I_{*_{\tilde{\mathcal{F}}}, N}$ and $I^{\mathcal{F}} = I^{\tilde{\mathcal{F}}}$.*

Because of lack of space we skip a deep analysis of conditions under which $(*_{\mathcal{F}}, N)$- and $I_{*_{\mathcal{F}}}$-implications possess properties from Definition 5. We just briefly list them in tables. We will need an operation $*_f[0,1]^2 \rightarrow [0,1]$ given by

$$x *_f y = f^{(-1)}(f(x) + f(y)).$$

In Table 2 we assume that the triple of increasing functions $\mathcal{F} = (f, g, h)$ is such that $I_{*_\mathcal{F}, N}$ is a fuzzy implication. Instead of (NP) property we consider (NPe) meaning $I_{*_\mathcal{F}, N}(e, y) = y$ for an $e \in]0,1]$.

Table 2. Properties of $\mathcal{F}$ and N, and the corresponding properties of $(*_\mathcal{F}, N)$-implications

Properties of $\mathcal{F}$ and N	$(*_\mathcal{F}, N)$-implications
$g = h$ are continuous in $]0,1[$, N arbitrary	(EP)
$g = h$, all continuous, N strict	(WLI) w.r.t. $*_f$
$f = g = h$ continuous, N strong	(CP) w.r.t. N
$g = h$ strictly increasing, $f(e) = 0$, if $e \neq 1$ then $N(e) = e$	(NPe)
f or g unbounded and $N = N_{G_2}$	(IP)
$f, g \geq 0$ bounded, all continuous and strictly increasing, N strict such that $f(N(x)) + g(x) = h(1)$	(IP), (OP)

In Table 3 we assume that the triple of increasing functions $\mathcal{F} = (f, g, h)$ fulfils the conditions from Proposition 9.

Table 3. Properties of h and the corresponding properties of $I_{*_\mathcal{F}}$-implications

Properties of $\mathcal{F}$	$I_{*_\mathcal{F}}$-implications
$g = h$ continuous	(EP)
all continuous, $g = h$	(WLI) w.r.t. $*_f$
$g = h$ continuous and $f(e) = 0$	(NPe)
$h(1) \leq \inf\limits_{x \in [0,1]} (g(x) - f(x))$	(IP)
$f = g$ strictly increasing, $h(x) < 0$, $h(1^-) = 0$	(IP), (OP)

4   Conclusions

In the paper we have presented new classes of implications generated via an appropriate function of one variable – $I_{T,f}$, and generated via a triple of increasing functions $\mathcal{F}$ – $I_{*_\mathcal{F}}$-implications and $(*_\mathcal{F}, N)$-implications. We studied their properties and relationship between them and the well-known R- and (S, N)-implications.

Acknowledgements. Dana Hliněná has been supported by project FEKT-S-11-2(921). Martin Kalina has been supported from the Science and Technology Assistance Agency under contract No. APVV-0073-10, and from the VEGA grant agency, grant numbers 1/0143/11 and 1/0297/11. Pavol Král' acknowledges the support from the grant 1/0297/11 provided by VEGA grant agency. Finally, we would like to thank the anonymous referees for their valuable suggestions helping us to improve the paper.

References

1. Baczyński, M., Jayaram, B.: Fuzzy implications. STUDFUZZ, vol. 231. Springer, Berlin (2008)
2. Baczyński, M., Jayaram, B.: (S,N)- and R-implications: A state-of-the-art survey. Fuzzy Sets and Systems 159(14), 1836–1859 (2008)
3. Baczyński, M., Jayaram, B.: QL-implications: Some properties and intersections. Fuzzy Sets and Systems 161(2), 158–188 (2010)
4. De Baets, B., Fodor, J.: Residual operators of uninorms. Soft Computing 3, 89–100 (1999)
5. Biba, V., Hliněná, D.: Generated fuzzy implications and known classes of implications. Acta Univ. M. Belii, Ser. Math. 16, 25–34 (2010)
6. Biba, V., Hliněná, D., Kalina, M., Král', P.: Implicators generated by strictly decreasing functions and known classes of implicators. Information Sciences (2011) (submitted, manuscript)
7. Fodor, J., Roubens, M.: Fuzzy preference modelling and multicriteria decision support. Kluwer Academic Publishers (1994)
8. Fodor, J., Yager, R.R., Rybalov, A.: Structure of uninorms. International Journal of Uncertainty, Fuzziness and Knowledge-Based Systems 5, 411–422 (1997)
9. Hájek, P.: Mathematics of Fuzzy Logic. Kluwer, Dordrecht (1998)
10. Jayaram, B.: Yager's new class of implications jf and some classical tautologies. Information Sciences 177(3), 930–946 (2007)
11. Klement, E.P., Mesiar, R., Pap, E.: Triangular Norms, 1st edn. Springer (2000)
12. Mas, M., Monserrat, J., Torrens, M.: E Trillas. A survey on fuzzy implication functions. IEEE T. Fuzzy Systems 15(6), 1107–1121 (2007)
13. Massanet, S., Torrens, J.: The law of importation versus the exchange principle on fuzzy implications. Fuzzy Sets and Systems 168(1), 47–69 (2011)
14. Novák, V., Perfilieva, I., Močkoř, J.: Mathematical Principles of Fuzzy Logic. Kluwer, Boston (1999)
15. Ouyang, Y.: On fuzzy implications determined by aggregation operators. Information Sciences 193, 153–162 (2012)
16. Schweizer, B., Sklar, A.: Probabilistic Metric Spaces. North Holland, New York (1983)
17. Smutná, D.: On many valued conjunctions and implications. Journal of Electrical Engineering 50, 8–10 (1999)
18. Yager, R.R.: On some new classes of implication operators and their role in approximate reasoning. Information Sciences 167(1-4), 193–216 (2004)
19. Yager, R.R., Rybalov, A.: Uninorm aggregation operators. Fuzzy Sets and Systems 80, 111–120 (1996)

Fuzzy Negation and Other Weak Fuzzy Connectives

Anna Król

Institute of Mathematics, University of Rzeszów,
al. Rejtana 16A, 35-310 Rzeszów, Poland
annakrol@univ.rzeszow.pl

Abstract. This paper deals with some dependencies between fuzzy negations and other fuzzy connectives. The generalized laws of contradiction and excluded middle are considered. Methods for generating fuzzy negation from fuzzy conjunction, disjunction or fuzzy implication together with another fuzzy negation are also presented. In the case of a fuzzy conjunction and disjunction only border conditions and monotonicity are assumed. The results are illustrated by examples of weak fuzzy connectives.

Keywords: Fuzzy negation, fuzzy conjunction, fuzzy disjunction, fuzzy implication, law of contradiction, law of excluded middle.

1 Introduction

Fuzzy set theory introduced by L.A. Zadeh [10] brought new applications of multivalued logic and new directions in examination of logical connectives. After the contribution of B. Schweizer and A. Sklar [9] the notions of the triangular norm and conorm have played the role of a fuzzy conjunction and disjunction. J. Fodor and M. Roubens [5], M. Baczyński and B. Jayaram [1] examined families of multivalued connectives based on triangular norms and conorms. However, some authors (e.g. I. Batyrshin and O. Kaynak [2], F. Durante et al. [4]) underline that the assumptions made on these multivalued connectives are sometimes too strong and difficult to obtain. Thus, some of the conditions are omitted.

A fuzzy negation can be generated from a fuzzy implication by means of the equation $N_I(x) = I(x,0), x \in [0,1]$ (considered by J. Lukasiewicz [8]). Such dependency was lately discussed (e.g ([1], p. 13, [7]). In this paper some other dependencies between a fuzzy negation and other fuzzy connectives are considered.

The generalized law of contradiction and law of excluded middle have been examined in the literature in the case when the conjunction and disjunction are a triangular norm and conorm, respectively ([1], p. 52). The ways of generating fuzzy negations from fuzzy conjunctions and disjunction in the case of t-norms and t-conorms can be found in ([6], p. 233, [1], p. 49). Such dependencies are considered in this paper in the case when only border conditions and monotonicity are required for fuzzy conjunctions and disjunctions (Sections 3 and 4). In

S. Greco et al. (Eds.): IPMU 2012, Part II, CCIS 298, pp. 355–364, 2012.
© Springer-Verlag Berlin Heidelberg 2012

Section 5 another way of generating a fuzzy negation (from a fuzzy implication and a fuzzy negation) is taken into account.

2   Basic Definitions

In this section the definitions and examples of fuzzy connectives used in the sequel are presented. First, the notion of a fuzzy negation is recalled.

Definition 1 ([1], p. 14). *A decreasing function* $N \colon [0,1] \to [0,1]$ *is called a fuzzy negation if*

$$N(0) = 1, \qquad N(1) = 0. \tag{1}$$

A fuzzy negation is called:
- a strict negation if it is continuous and strictly decreasing,
- a strong negation if it an involution,
- a non-vanishing negation, if $N(x) = 0 \Leftrightarrow x = 1$, $x \in [0,1]$,
- a non-filling negation, if $N(x) = 1 \Leftrightarrow x = 0$, $x \in [0,1]$.

Remark 1. Strict and strong negations are continuous functions. A strong negation is a strict one. A strict or a strong negation is both non-vanishing and non-filling.

Example 1 (cf. [1], p. 15). The classical fuzzy negation $N_S(x) = 1 - x$ for $x \in [0,1]$ belongs to all four classes of fuzzy negations mentioned above.

Example 2. A fuzzy negation is called a threshold negation, if it has one of the forms

$$N_t(x) = \begin{cases} 1, & \text{if } x < t \\ 0, & \text{if } x \geq t \end{cases}, \quad t \in (0,1], \quad x \in [0,1],$$

$$N^t(x) = \begin{cases} 1, & \text{if } x \leq t \\ 0, & \text{if } x > t \end{cases}, \quad t \in [0,1), \quad x \in [0,1].$$

A threshold negation is neither strong nor strict. The only threshold negation, which is non-vanishing is the greatest fuzzy negation N_1. The only threshold negation, which is non-filling is the least fuzzy negation N^0, where

$$N^0(x) = \begin{cases} 1, & \text{if } x = 0 \\ 0, & \text{if } x > 0 \end{cases}, \qquad N_1(x) = \begin{cases} 1, & \text{if } x < 1 \\ 0, & \text{if } x = 1 \end{cases}.$$

Now, the definition of a fuzzy conjunction is presented.

Definition 2 ([3]). *An operation* $C : [0,1]^2 \to [0,1]$ *is called a fuzzy conjunction if it is increasing with respect to each variable and*

$$C(1,1) = 1, \quad C(0,0) = C(0,1) = C(1,0) = 0.$$

Corollary 1. *A fuzzy conjunction has a zero element* 0.

Example 3. Consider the following family of fuzzy conjunctions for $\alpha \in [0, 1]$

$$C^\alpha(x, y) = \begin{cases} 1, & \text{if } x = y = 1 \\ 0, & \text{if } x = 0 \text{ or } y = 0 \\ \alpha & \text{otherwise} \end{cases}.$$

Operations C^0 and C^1 are the least and the greatest fuzzy conjunction, respectively. The following are the other examples of fuzzy conjunctions. The well-known triangular norms are denoted in the traditional way.

$C_2(x, y) = \begin{cases} y, & \text{if } x = 1 \\ 0, & \text{if } x < 1 \end{cases}$	$T_M(x, y) = \min(x, y)$
$C_3(x, y) = \begin{cases} x, & \text{if } y = 1 \\ 0, & \text{if } y < 1 \end{cases}$	$T_P(x, y) = xy$
$C_4(x, y) = \begin{cases} 0, & \text{if } x + y \leqslant 1 \\ y, & \text{if } x + y > 1 \end{cases}$	$T_L(x, y) = \max(x + y - 1, 0)$
$C_5(x, y) = \begin{cases} 0, & \text{if } x + y \leqslant 1 \\ x, & \text{if } x + y > 1 \end{cases}$	$T_D(x, y) = \begin{cases} x, & \text{if } y = 1 \\ y, & \text{if } x = 1 \\ 0 & \text{otherwise} \end{cases}$

Next, the notion of a fuzzy disjunction is recalled.

Definition 3 ([3]). *An operation* $D : [0, 1]^2 \to [0, 1]$ *is called a fuzzy disjunction if it is increasing with respect to each variable and*

$$D(0, 0) = 0, \quad D(0, 1) = D(1, 0) = D(1, 1) = 1.$$

Corollary 2. *A fuzzy disjunction has a zero element* 1.

Example 4. Consider the following family of fuzzy disjunctions for $\alpha \in [0, 1]$

$$D^\alpha(x, y) = \begin{cases} 0, & \text{if } x = y = 0 \\ 1, & \text{if } x = 1 \text{ or } y = 1 \\ \alpha & \text{otherwise} \end{cases}.$$

Operations D^0 and D^1 are the least and the greatest fuzzy disjunction, respectively. The following are other examples of fuzzy disjunctions. The well-known triangular conorms are denoted in the traditional way.

$D_2(x,y) = \begin{cases} y, & \textit{if } x = 0 \\ 1, & \textit{if } x > 0 \end{cases}$	$S_M(x,y) = \max(x,y)$
$D_3(x,y) = \begin{cases} x, & \textit{if } y = 0 \\ 1, & \textit{if } y > 0 \end{cases}$	$S_P(x,y) = x + y - xy$
$D_4(x,y) = \begin{cases} 1, & \textit{if } x + y \geqslant 1 \\ y, & \textit{if } x + y < 1 \end{cases}$	$S_L(x,y) = \min(x + y, 1)$
$D_5(x,y) = \begin{cases} 1, & \textit{if } x + y \geqslant 1 \\ x, & \textit{if } x + y < 1 \end{cases}$	$S_D(x,y) = \begin{cases} x, & \textit{if } y = 0 \\ y, & \textit{if } x = 0 \\ 1 & \textit{otherwise} \end{cases}$

Finally, the notion of a fuzzy implication is recalled.

Definition 4 ([1], p. 2). *A binary operation* $I \colon [0,1]^2 \to [0,1]$ *is called a fuzzy implication if it is decreasing with respect to the first variable and increasing with respect to the second variable and*

$$I(0,0) = I(0,1) = I(1,1) = 1, \quad I(1,0) = 0.$$

Example 5. Consider the following family of fuzzy implications for $\alpha \in [0,1]$

$$I^\alpha(x,y) = \begin{cases} 0, & \text{if } x = 1, y = 0 \\ 1, & \text{if } x = 0 \text{ or } y = 1 \,. \\ \alpha & \text{otherwise} \end{cases}$$

Operations I^0 and I^1 are the least and the greatest fuzzy implication, respectively.

3   Laws of Contradiction and Excluded Middle

On the pattern of the law of contradiction and the law of excluded middle in the classical propositional calculus, that is

$$\sim (p \wedge \sim p) \quad \text{and} \quad p \vee \sim p,$$

some relationships between fuzzy negation and conjunction, or an disjunction can be defined. These relationships are considered in the literature, where C is a triangular norm, D triangular conorm and N strict negation ([5]) or without additional assumptions about N ([1]). Let us start from the generalization of the first of these laws. Because the commutativity of a fuzzy conjunction and disjunction is not required, the generalization consists of two conditions.

Definition 5 (cf. [1], p. 55). *Let* N, C *be a fuzzy negation and conjunction, respectively. We say that the pair* (C, N) *fulfils the law of contradiction (LC) if both*

$$C(N(x), x) = 0, \quad x \in [0,1] \tag{LC1}$$

and

$$C(x, N(x)) = 0, \quad x \in [0,1]. \tag{LC2}$$

Example 6. For an arbitrary fuzzy negation N the pair (C^0, N) fulfils (LC). Indeed, for $C = C^0$ conditions (LC1) and (LC2) hold if and only if $N(1) \neq 1$ which is true for any fuzzy negation N.

The following statements characterize a negation (or conjunction) fulfilling (LC) with the other fixed fuzzy connective.

Theorem 1. *Let N be a fuzzy negation and C fuzzy conjunction without zero divisors. Then, the pair (C, N) fulfils (LC1) ((LC2)) if and only if $N = N^0$.*

Proof. Let $x \in [0, 1]$. Consider condition (LC1). On the assumption about the conjunction one obtains

$$C(N(x), x) = 0 \Leftrightarrow N(x) = 0 \vee x = 0 \Leftrightarrow N(x) = \begin{cases} 1, & \text{if } x = 0 \\ 0, & \text{if } x \neq 0 \end{cases} \Leftrightarrow N(x) = N^0(x),$$

which was to be demonstrated. The proof of (LC2) is analogous.

Theorem 2. *Let C be a fuzzy conjunction. The pair (C, N_1) fulfils (LC) if and only if $C = C^0$.*

Proof. Let $x \in [0, 1]$. One has

$$C(N_1(x), x) = \begin{cases} C(0, 1), & \text{if } x = 1 \\ C(1, x), & \text{if } x \neq 1 \end{cases} = \begin{cases} 0, & \text{if } x = 1 \\ C(1, x), & \text{if } x \neq 1 \end{cases},$$

$$C(x, N_1(x)) = \begin{cases} C(1, 0), & \text{if } x = 1 \\ C(x, 1), & \text{if } x \neq 1 \end{cases} = \begin{cases} 0, & \text{if } x = 1 \\ C(x, 1), & \text{if } x \neq 1 \end{cases}.$$

Thus, conditions (LC1) and (LC2) are fulfilled if and only if $C(x, 1) = C(1, x) = 0$ for $x \in [0, 1)$. From the monotonicity of the conjunction C it follows that the last condition is equivalent to the condition $C = C^0$, which ends the proof.

Similarly as the law of contradiction one can generalize the law of excluded middle.

Definition 6 (cf. [1], p. 52). *Let N and D be a fuzzy negation and disjunction, respectively. We say that the pair (D, N) fulfils the law of excluded middle (LEM) if both*

$$D(N(x), x) = 1, \quad x \in [0, 1], \tag{LEM1}$$

and

$$D(x, N(x)) = 1, \quad x \in [0, 1]. \tag{LEM2}$$

Example 7. For an arbitrary fuzzy negation N the pair (D^1, N) fulfils (LEM). Indeed, for $D = D^1$ conditions (LEM1) and (LEM2) hold if and only if $N(0) \neq 0$ which is true for any fuzzy negation N.

The next theorems characterize a negation (or disjunction) fulfilling (LEM) with the other fixed fuzzy connective.

Theorem 3. *Let N be a fuzzy negation and D fuzzy disjunction without zero divisors $(z = 1)$. The pair (D, N) fulfils (LEM1) ((LEM2)) if and only if $N = N_1$.*

Proof. Let $x \in [0, 1]$. Consider condition (LEM1). On the assumption on the disjunction one obtains

$$D(N(x), x) = 1 \Leftrightarrow N(x) = 1 \vee x = 1 \Leftrightarrow N(x) = \begin{cases} 0, & \text{if } x = 1 \\ 1, & \text{if } x \neq 1 \end{cases} \Leftrightarrow N(x) = N_1(x),$$

which was to be demonstrated. For condition (LEM2) the proof of is analogous.

Theorem 4. *Let D be a fuzzy disjunction. The pair (D, N^0) fulfils (LEM) if and only if $D = D^1$.*

Proof. Let $x \in [0, 1]$. One has

$$D(N^0(x), x) = \begin{cases} D(1, 0), & \text{if } x = 0 \\ D(0, x), & \text{if } x \neq 0 \end{cases} = \begin{cases} 1, & \text{if } x = 0 \\ D(0, x), & \text{if } x \neq 0 \end{cases},$$

$$D(x, N^0(x)) = \begin{cases} D(0, 1), & \text{if } x = 0 \\ D(x, 0), & \text{if } x \neq 0 \end{cases} = \begin{cases} 1, & \text{if } x = 0 \\ D(x, 0), & \text{if } x \neq 0 \end{cases}.$$

Thus, conditions (LEM1) and (LEM2) are fulfilled if and only if $D(x, 0) = D(0, x) = 0$ for $x \in (0, 1]$. By the monotonicity of the disjunction D it follows that the last condition is equivalent to the condition $D = D^1$, which ends the proof.

4   Negation Generated from Conjunction or Disjunction

The relationship between a fuzzy negation and a fuzzy conjunction (or disjunction) may be expressed in other way, which indicates how to define a fuzzy negation from a given fuzzy conjunction (or disjunction). Such a negation is examined for example in [1] in the case when the generator is a triangular norm (or conorm) and is called a natural negation of a t-norm (or t-conorm). Because of the lack of assumption about commutativity of a fuzzy conjunction and disjunction, there exist two analogous methods of generating a fuzzy negation from each of the two binary connectives.

Theorem 5. *Let C be a fuzzy conjunction. The function $N_C \colon [0, 1] \to [0, 1]$,*

$$N_C(x) = \sup\{y \in [0, 1] : C(x, y) = 0\}, \quad x \in [0, 1]$$

is a fuzzy negation if and only if $C(1, y) > 0$ for $y \in (0, 1]$.

Proof. First, observe that a set

$$R(x) := \{y \in [0, 1] : C(x, y) = 0\}$$

is nonempty for any $x \in [0,1]$. Indeed, by Corollary 1 it follows that $C(x,0) = 0$, so $0 \in R(x)$. Thus, $\sup R(x) \in [0,1]$. Let us check the border conditions (1). Again, by Corollary 1 one obtains

$$N_C(0) = \sup\{y \in [0,1] : C(0,y) = 0\} = \sup\{y \in [0,1] : 0 = 0\} = 1.$$

Consider $N_C(1) = \sup\{y \in [0,1] : C(1,y) = 0\}$. Observe, that $N_C(1) = 0$ if and only if $C(1,y) > 0$ for $y \in (0,1]$.

Now, let $x_1, x_2 \in [0,1]$, $x_1 \leqslant x_2$. By the monotonicity of the conjunction C one has $C(x_1,t) \leqslant C(x_2,t)$ for all $y \in [0,1]$. Hence,

$$\{y \in [0,1] : C(x_1,y) = 0\} \supset \{y \in [0,1] : C(x_2,y) = 0\},$$
$$\sup\{y \in [0,1] : C(x_1,y) = 0\} \geqslant \sup\{y \in [0,1] : C(x_2,y) = 0\},$$
$$N_C(x_1) \geqslant N_C(x_2).$$

Thus, function N_C is decreasing.

Similarly as Theorem 5 one can prove

Theorem 6. *Let C be a fuzzy conjunction. The function $N_C^* \colon [0,1] \to [0,1]$,*

$$N_C^*(x) = \sup\{y \in [0,1] : C(y,x) = 0\}, \quad x \in [0,1]$$

is a fuzzy negation if and only if $C(y,1) > 0$ for $y \in (0,1]$.

Obviously, if a conjunction C is commutative, then $N_C^* = N_C$. Observe, that commutativity of the conjunction C is not a necessary condition for $N_C^* = N_C$.

Theorem 7. *Let C be a fuzzy conjunction without zero divisors. Then $N_C = N^0$ and $N_C^* = N^0$.*

Proof. The conjunction C has no zero divisors, so $C(x,y) = 0 \Leftrightarrow x = 0 \vee y = 0$ for $x, y \in [0,1]$. Thus,

$$N_C(x) = \begin{cases} \sup[0,1], & \text{if } x = 0 \\ \sup\{0\}, & \text{if } x \neq 0 \end{cases} = \begin{cases} 1, & \text{if } x = 0 \\ 0, & \text{if } x \neq 0 \end{cases} = N^0(x)$$

for all $x \in [0,1]$. Similarly, one can prove the case N_C^*.

In the same way one may consider statements which allow to generate a fuzzy negation from a fuzzy disjunction.

Theorem 8. *Let D be a fuzzy disjunction. The function $N_D \colon [0,1] \to [0,1]$,*

$$N_D(x) = \inf\{y \in [0,1] : D(x,y) = 1\}, \quad x \in [0,1]$$

is a fuzzy negation if and only if $D(0,y) < 1$ for $y \in [0,1)$.

Theorem 9. *Let D be a fuzzy disjunction. The function* $N_D^*: [0,1] \to [0,1]$,

$$N_D^*(x) = \inf\{y \in [0,1] : D(y,x) = 1\}, \quad x \in [0,1]$$

is a fuzzy negation if and only if $D(y,0) < 1$ *for* $y \in [0,1)$.

Theorem 10. *Let D be a fuzzy disjunction without zero divisors. Then* $N_D=N_1$ *and* $N_D^*=N_1$.

Proof. On the assumption about the disjunction D it follows that $D(x,y) = 1 \Leftrightarrow x = 1 \vee y = 1$ for $x, y \in [0,1]$. Hence,

$$N_D(x) = \begin{cases} \inf[0,1], & \text{if } x = 1 \\ \inf\{1\}, & \text{if } x \neq 1 \end{cases} = \begin{cases} 0, & \text{if } x = 1 \\ 1, & \text{if } x \neq 1 \end{cases} = N_1(x)$$

for all $x \in [0,1]$. The proof for N_D^* is analogous.

Example 8. The following table shows fuzzy negations together with their generators: fuzzy conjunctions C and disjunctions D. The symbol „–" denotes that for a given generator the negation does not exist.

C	N_C	N_C^*	D	N_D	N_D^*
C^α, $\alpha \in (0,1)$	N^0	N^0	D^α, $\alpha \in (0,1)$	N_1	N_1
C^0	–	–	D^0	–	–
C^1	N^0	N^0	D^1	N_1	N_1
C_2	N_1	–	D_2	N^0	–
C_3	–	N_1	D_3	–	N^0
C_4	N_S	N_S	D_4	N_S	N_S
C_5	N_S	N_S	D_5	N_S	N_S
T_M	N^0	N^0	S_M	N_1	N_1
T_P	N^0	N^0	S_P	N_1	N_1
T_{LK}	N_S	N_S	S_{LK}	N_S	N_S
T_{FD}	N_S	N_S	S_{FD}	N_S	N_S
T_D	N_1	N_1	S_D	N^0	N^0

5   Negation Generated by Implication and Negation

Fuzzy negations can be generated from fuzzy implications and fuzzy negations by means of generalizations of the following laws od propositional calculus

$$\sim p \Leftrightarrow (1 \Rightarrow \sim p), \quad \sim p \Leftrightarrow \sim (1 \Rightarrow p).$$

First, observe the following dependency.

Proposition 1. *Let I be a fuzzy implication fulfilling the neutral property, that is* $I(1,y) = y$ *for* $y \in [0,1]$. *For each fuzzy negation N the following equations are fulfilled*

$$N(x) = I(1, N(x)), \quad x \in [0,1], \tag{2}$$

$$N(x) = N(I(1,x)), \quad x \in [0,1]. \tag{3}$$

Example 9. Consider the Rescher implication $I_{RS}(x,y) = \begin{cases} 1, & \text{if } x \leqslant y \\ 0, & \text{if } x > y \end{cases}$ that

does not fulfil the neutral property. For any $x \in [0,1]$ one has

$$I_{RS}(1, N(x)) = \begin{cases} 1, & \text{if } N(x) = 1 \\ 0, & \text{if } N(x) < 1 \end{cases}.$$

Thus, N fulfils (2) if and only if N is a threshold negation. Moreover, for any $x \in [0,1]$ one has

$$N(I_{RS}(1, x)) = \begin{cases} 0, & \text{if } x = 1 \\ 1, & \text{if } x < 1 \end{cases} = N_1(x).$$

Hence, N fulfils (3) if and only if $N = N_1$.

From the above example it follows that for certain fuzzy implications equations (2) and (3) are not fulfilled by any fuzzy negation. Besides, for a given fuzzy implication they are not equivalent. This is why these equations can be used for generating fuzzy negations.

Theorem 11. *Let N and I be a fuzzy negation and implication, respectively. The functions $N_{N,I}^*$ and $N_{N,I}^{**}$, where*

$$N_{N,I}^*(x) = I(1, N(x)), \qquad N_{N,I}^{**}(x) = N(I(1, x))$$

for $x \in [0,1]$ are fuzzy negations.

Proof. Observe, that

$$N_{N,I}^*(0) = I(1, N(0)) = I(1,1) = 1, \quad N_{N,I}^*(1) = I(1, N(1)) = I(1,0) = 0,$$
$$N_{N,I}^{**}(0) = N(I(1,0)) = N(0) = 1, \quad N_{N,I}^{**}(1) = N(I(1,1)) = N(1) = 0.$$

Moreover, the functions $N_{N,I}^*$ and $N_{N,I}^{**}$ are decreasing as the composition of the increasing and decreasing functions.

Example 10. Consider a fuzzy implication not fulfilling the neutral property

$$I(x,y) = \begin{cases} 0, & \text{if } x > 0, \ y = 0 \\ 1 & \text{otherwise} \end{cases}, \quad x, y \in [0,1].$$

Then

$$N_{N,I}^*(x) = I(1, N(x)) = \begin{cases} 0, & \text{if } N(x) = 0 \\ 1, & \text{if } N(x) > 0 \end{cases}, \quad x \in [0,1].$$

Thus, $N_{N,I}^* = N$ only in the case when N is a threshold negation. Moreover, if N is a non-vanishing negation then $N_{N,I}^* = N_1$. Besides

$$N_{N,I}^{**}(x) = N(I(1,x)) = \begin{cases} 1, & \text{if } x = 0 \\ 0, & \text{if } x > 0 \end{cases} = N^0(x), \quad x \in [0,1].$$

Example 11. Consider the family of fuzzy implications I^α and the standard negation N_S. One has

$$N^*_{N_S, I^\alpha}(x) = \begin{cases} 0, & \text{if } N_S(x) = 0 \\ \alpha, & \text{if } 0 < N_S(x) < 1 \\ 1, & \text{if } N_S(x) = 1 \end{cases} = \begin{cases} 0, & \text{if } x = 1 \\ \alpha, & \text{if } 0 < x < 1 \\ 1, & \text{if } x = 0 \end{cases}$$

and

$$N^{**}_{N_S, I^\alpha}(x) = \begin{cases} N_S(1), & \text{if } x = 1 \\ N_S(\alpha), & \text{if } 0 < x < 1 \\ N_S(0), & \text{if } x = 0 \end{cases} = \begin{cases} 0, & \text{if } x = 1 \\ 1 - \alpha, & \text{if } 0 < x < 1 \\ 1, & \text{if } x = 0 \end{cases}.$$

6   Conclusions

In this contribution the generalized law of contradiction (Definition 5) and the generalized law of excluded middle (Definition 6) are considered. Besides, the methods of generating fuzzy negation from a fuzzy conjunction (Theorems 5 and 6), disjunction (Theorems 8 and 9) or both implication and negation (Theorem 11) are presented.

Acknowledgement. This work is partially supported by the Ministry of Science and Higher Education Grant Nr N N519 384936.

References

1. Baczyński, M., Jayaram, B.: Fuzzy implications. Springer, Berlin (2008)
2. Batyrshin, I., Kaynak, O.: Parametric classes of generalized conjunction and disjunction operations for fuzzy modelling. IEEE Trans. Fuzzy Syst. 7, 586–595 (1999)
3. Drewniak, J., Król, A.: A survey of weak connectives and the preservation of their properties by aggregations. Fuzzy Sets Syst. 161, 202–215 (2010)
4. Durante, F., Klement, E.P., Mesiar, R., Sempi, C.: Conjunctors and their residual implicators: characterizations and construction methods. Mediterr. J. Math. 4, 343–356 (2007)
5. Fodor, J., Roubens, M.: Fuzzy preference modelling and multicriteria decision support. Kluwer, Dordrecht (1994)
6. Klement, E.P., Mesiar, R., Pap, E.: Triangular norms. Kluwer, Dordrecht (2000)
7. Król, A.: Dependencies between fuzzy negation, disjunction and implication. In: Atanassov, K.T., Baczyński, M., Drewniak, J., Kacprzyk, J., Krawczyk, M., Szmidt, E., Wygralak, M., Zadrożny, S. (eds.) Recent Advances in Fuzzy Sets, Intuitionistic Fuzzy Sets, Generalized Nets and Related Topics. Fundations, vol. I, pp. 113–121. SRI PAS, Warsaw (2011)
8. Łukasiewicz, J.: Interpretacja liczbowa teorii zdań. Ruch Filozoficzny 7, 92–93 (1923); translated In: Borkowski, L. (ed.) Jan Łukasiewicz Selected Works, pp. 129–130. North Holland, Amsterdam (1970)
9. Schweizer, B., Sklar, A.: Probabilistic metric spaces. North Holland, New York (1983)
10. Zadeh, L.A.: Fuzzy sets. Inform. Control 8, 338–353 (1965)

Fuzzy Implications: Novel Generation Process and the Consequent Algebras

Nageswara Rao Vemuri and Balasubramaniam Jayaram

Department of Mathematics,
Indian Institute of Technology Hyderabad,
Yeddumailaram - 502 205, India
ma10p001@iith.ac.in, jbala@iith.ac.in

Abstract. In this work we present novel methods of generating fuzzy implications from the given ones. We show that these methods lead to various and much richer algebraic structures on the set of all fuzzy implications than obtained in the literature so far.

Keywords: Fuzzy logic connectives, Fuzzy implications, Generation Methods, Algebras, Semigroup, Monoid, Semiring, Lattice.

1 Introduction

Fuzzy implications are generalizations of the classical (boolean) implications to the multi valued setting. They play an important role in approximate reasoning, fuzzy control, decision theory, control theory, expert systems, etc, see for example [7],[8] or the recent monograph exclusively devoted to fuzzy implications [2]. Hence, there is always a need for a panoply of fuzzy implications satisfying different properties that make them valuable in the appropriate context.

The different ways of obtaining fuzzy implications found in the literature, so far, can be largely categorized based on the underlying operators from where they are generated: (i) from other fuzzy logic connectives (ii) from monotone functions over the unit interval $[0, 1]$ and (iii) from given fuzzy implications. The last of these generation processes also has an interesting fall out: Considering fuzzy implications as real functions on $[0, 1]^2$, this process defines an operation on the set of all fuzzy implications, which will be denoted by $\mathcal{FI}$. Thus, this process allows us to study the algebraic structures that arise on $\mathcal{FI}$.

In the literature we can find very few methods of obtaining fuzzy implications from fuzzy implications, see Chapter 6 in [2]. For instance, lattice operations generate newer fuzzy implications as well as produce a complete, completely distributive lattice structure on $\mathcal{FI}$. Among all the existing methods, the richest algebraic structure known so far is that of a semigroup on a subset of $\mathcal{FI}$ and under some assumptions, see Baczyński et. al [1]. For more details on this topic, see Chapter 6 in [2].

In this work, our aim is two-fold. On the one hand, we are interested in generating newer fuzzy implications from existing fuzzy implications and propose

S. Greco et al. (Eds.): IPMU 2012, Part II, CCIS 298, pp. 365–374, 2012.
© Springer-Verlag Berlin Heidelberg 2012

a few novel ways of doing the same. On the other hand, we also study the ensuing algebraic structures on $\mathcal{FI}$. We show that through the generation process proposed in this work, we obtain far richer structures on $\mathcal{FI}$ than previously known.

2 Fuzzy Implications: Definition and Basic Properties

In this section we give the main definitions and properties related to fuzzy implications only. For the definitions of other basic fuzzy logic connectives, viz., t-norms, t-conorms, negation, aggregation operators and classical algebra, viz., semigroup, monoid, etc, we refer the readers to, for instance, [4–6].

Definition 1 ([2]). *A binary function I on $[0,1]$ is called a fuzzy implication (FI) if it is such that*

- *I is decreasing in the first variable and increasing in the second variable,*
- *$I(0,0) = I(1,1) = I(0,1) = 1$ and $I(1,0) = 0$.*

Table 1 lists the basic fuzzy implications (see [2]).

In the following we list a few of the most important properties of fuzzy implications [2]. They are a generalization of the corresponding properties of the classical implication.

A fuzzy implication I is said to satisfy

(i) the left neutrality property (NP) if

$$I(1,y) = y, \qquad y \in [0,1] . \tag{NP}$$

(ii) the ordering property (OP), if

$$x \leq y \iff I(x,y) = 1 . \tag{OP}$$

(iii) the identity principle (IP), if

$$I(x,x) = 1, \qquad x \in [0,1] . \tag{IP}$$

(iv) the exchange principle (EP), if

$$I(x, I(y,z)) = I(y, I(x,z)), \qquad x,y,z \in [0,1] . \tag{EP}$$

(v) the law of contraposition w.r.t a fuzzy negation N, CP(N), if

$$I(x,y) = I(N(y), N(x)), \qquad x,y \in [0,1] . \tag{CP(N)}$$

(vi) the law of importation (LI) w.r.t a t-norm T, if

$$I(x, I(y,z)) = I(T(x,y), z), \qquad x,y,z \in [0,1] . \tag{LI}$$

By $\mathcal{FI}$ we denote the set of all fuzzy implications. We reserve $\mathcal{FI}_P$ for the set of all fuzzy implications satisfying the property P from the list above.

Table 1. Examples of basic fuzzy implications

Name	Formula
Lukasiewicz	$I_{\mathbf{LK}}(x,y) = \min(1, 1 - x + y)$
Gödel	$I_{\mathbf{GD}}(x,y) = \begin{cases} 1, & \text{if } x \leq y \\ y, & \text{if } x > y \end{cases}$
Reichenbach	$I_{\mathbf{RC}}(x,y) = 1 - x + xy$
Kleene-Dienes	$I_{\mathbf{KD}}(x,y) = \max(1 - x, y)$
Goguen	$I_{\mathbf{GG}}(x,y) = \begin{cases} 1, & \text{if } x \leq y \\ \frac{y}{x}, & \text{if } x > y \end{cases}$
Rescher	$I_{\mathbf{RS}}(x,y) = \begin{cases} 1, & \text{if } x \leq y \\ 0, & \text{if } x > y \end{cases}$
Yager	$I_{\mathbf{YG}}(x,y) = \begin{cases} 1, & \text{if } x = 0 \text{ and } y = 0 \\ y^x, & \text{if } x > 0 \text{ or } y > 0 \end{cases}$
Weber	$I_{\mathbf{WB}}(x,y) = \begin{cases} 1, & \text{if } x < 1 \\ y, & \text{if } x = 1 \end{cases}$
Fodor	$I_{\mathbf{FD}}(x,y) = \begin{cases} 1, & \text{if } x \leq y \\ \max(1 - x, y), & \text{if } x > y \end{cases}$
Least FI	$I_0(x,y) = \begin{cases} 1, & \text{if } x = 0 \text{ or } y = 1 \\ 0, & \text{if } x > 0 \text{ and } y < 1 \end{cases}$
Largest FI	$I_1(x,y) = \begin{cases} 1, & \text{if } x < 1 \text{ or } y > 0 \\ 0, & \text{if } x = 1 \text{ and } y = 0 \end{cases}$

3 FIs from FIs and Structures on $\mathcal{FI}$

As noted earlier, we are interested in generating newer fuzzy implications from existing ones. In the literature only a few such generating methods are known. In this section, we briefly review the existing methods and the algebraic structure they produce on $\mathcal{FI}$. For more details please see [2].

3.1 Lattice of Fuzzy Implications

Theorem 1 ([2]). *The family* $(\mathcal{FI}, \leq)$ *is a complete, completely distributive lattice with the lattice operations*

$$(I \,\varovee\, J)(x,y) = \max(I(x,y), J(x,y)), \qquad I, J \in \mathcal{FI}\,, \qquad \text{(Latt-Max)}$$
$$(I \,\varowedge\, J)(x,y) = \min(I(x,y), J(x,y)), \qquad I, J \in \mathcal{FI}\,. \qquad \text{(Latt-Min)}$$

In fact, as will be seen later, we enrich the above lattice structure on $\mathcal{FI}$ to a semiring structure.

3.2   Convex Classes of Fuzzy Implications

We know that fuzzy implications are basically functions on $[0,1]$. So, we can define convex combinations of the fuzzy implications in the usual manner.

Definition 2. *Convex combination of two fuzzy implications I, J is defined as*

$$K(x,y) = \lambda I(x,y) + (1 - \lambda)J(x,y), \qquad x, y \in [0,1], \ \lambda \in [0,1] .$$

Theorem 2 ([2]). *Convex combination of any two fuzzy implications is also a fuzzy implication. Thus the set of all fuzzy implications is a convex set.*

3.3   Conjugacy Classes of Fuzzy Implications

Let Φ denote the set of all increasing bijections on $[0,1]$.

Definition 3. *For any $\varphi \in \Phi$ and $I \in \mathcal{FI}$, we define the Φ-conjugate of I by,*

$$I_\varphi(x,y) = \varphi^{-1}\left(I(\varphi(x),\varphi(y))\right), \qquad x, y \in [0,1] .$$

Theorem 3 ([2]). *For every $I \in \mathcal{FI}$, the function $I_\varphi \in \mathcal{FI}$, for every $\varphi \in \Phi$.*

Definition 4. *([2]) A fuzzy implication I is called* self-conjugate *or* invariant *if $I_\varphi = I$, for all $\varphi \in \Phi$. $\mathcal{FI}_{inv}$ denotes the set of all invariant fuzzy implications.*

Theorem 4 ([2],[3]). *$\mathcal{FI}_{inv}$ is a distributive lattice and it contains only 18 fuzzy implications.*

3.4   Compositions of Fuzzy Implications

Definition 5 ([1],[2]). *Let $I, J \in \mathcal{FI}$ and $*$ be a t-norm. Then* sup-$*$ *composition of I, J is given as follows:*

$$(I \overset{*}{\circ} J)(x,y) = \sup_{t \in [0,1]} (I(x,t) * J(t,y)), \forall x, y \in [0,1] . \qquad \text{(COMP)}$$

Theorem 5 ([1],[2]). *Let $*$ be a t-norm. If $I, J \in \mathcal{FI}$, then $(I \overset{*}{\circ} J) \in \mathcal{FI} \Longleftrightarrow (I \overset{*}{\circ} J)(1,0) = 0$.*

Theorem 6. *If $*$ is a left continuous (l.c.) t-norm, then $\overset{*}{\circ}$ is associative. Thus $(\mathcal{FI}, \overset{*}{\circ})$ is a semigroup.*

Note that while (COMP) gives a nice algebraic structure, namely, semigroup, the condition in Theorem 5 shows that the algebra is on a subset of $\mathcal{FI}$. So far no other algebraic structure has been proposed on whole of $\mathcal{FI}$.

4   Novel Generation Methods and Algebras on $\mathcal{FI}$

Note that all the operations in Section 3 do the following:

(i) Give rise to new fuzzy implications from the existing ones,
(ii) Determine an algebraic structure on a subset of $\mathcal{FI}$.

Hence, in this section, our aim is two-fold, viz.,

(i) On the one hand, we propose an operation that generates a new fuzzy implication from the given ones. We then study both the new and inherited properties of these fuzzy implications.
(ii) On the other hand, instead of looking at them as operations on [0,1] we view them as operations on the set $\mathcal{FI}$ and investigate the algebraic structure imposed by them on $\mathcal{FI}$.

4.1   Semigroup of Fuzzy Implications

In this section, we propose an operation $\triangledown$ on $\mathcal{FI}$ that makes it a semigroup.

Definition 6. $I, J \in \mathcal{FI}$. *Define the function* $(I \triangledown J)$ *as*

$$(I \triangledown J)(x, y) = I(J(y, x), J(x, y)), \qquad x, y \in [0, 1] . \tag{1}$$

Theorem 7. $I \triangledown J$ *is an implication on* $[0, 1]$, *i.e.,* $I \triangledown J \in \mathcal{FI}$.

Theorem 8. $(\mathcal{FI}, \triangledown)$ *forms a semigroup.*

Proof. It suffices to discuss the associativity. For $I, J, K \in \mathcal{FI}$ and $x, y \in [0, 1]$,

$$\begin{aligned}
(I \triangledown (J \triangledown K))(x, y) &= I((J \triangledown K)(y, x), (J \triangledown K)(x, y)) \\
&= I(J(K(x, y), K(y, x)), J(K(y, x), K(x, y))) \\
&= (I \triangledown J)(K(y, x), K(x, y)) \\
&= ((I \triangledown J) \triangledown K)(x, y) .
\end{aligned}$$

Thus $\triangledown$ is associative in $\mathcal{FI}$ and $(\mathcal{FI}, \triangledown)$ is a semigroup.

Theorem 9. $\mathcal{FI}_{NP}, \mathcal{FI}_{IP}, \mathcal{FI}_{OP}, \mathcal{FI}_{inv}$ *are subsemigroups of* $(\mathcal{FI}, \triangledown)$.

Proof. It suffices to show that the above subsets are closed w.r.t $\triangledown$. We show this only for $\mathcal{FI}_{OP}$, since the proof for the other subsets can also be obtained in a straightforward manner.

Let $I, J \in \mathcal{FI}_{OP}$. On the one hand, $x \leq y$, implies

$$(I \triangledown J)(x, y) = I(J(y, x), J(x, y)) = I(J(y, x), 1) = 1.$$

On the other hand, let $(I \triangledown J)(x, y) = 1$. Suppose $x > y$. Then $(I \triangledown J)(x, y) = I(J(y, x), J(x, y)) = I(1, J(x, y))$, by (OP) of J. Again by (OP) of I we have $J(x, y) = 1$ which implies $x \leq y$, a contradiction to $x > y$. Thus $x \leq y$ and $I \triangledown J \in \mathcal{FI}_{OP}$.

4.2   Monoid of Fuzzy Implications

While in the previous section we made $\mathcal{FI}$ into a semigroup, here we propose an operation $\circledast$ on $\mathcal{FI}$ that not only makes it a semigroup but also has a unit element thus making $\mathcal{FI}$ into a monoid.

Definition 7. *For any two fuzzy implications* I, J *we define* $(I \circledast J)$ *as*

$$(I \circledast J)(x, y) = I(x, J(x, y)), \qquad x, y \in [0, 1] . \tag{2}$$

Theorem 10. *The function* $I \circledast J$ *is an implication on* $[0, 1]$, *i.e.,* $I \circledast J \in \mathcal{FI}$.

Theorem 11. $(\mathcal{FI}, \circledast)$ *forms a monoid, whose identity element is given by*

$$I^{\circledast}(x, y) = \begin{cases} 1, & if \ x = 0 , \\ y, & otherwise . \end{cases}$$

Theorem 12. *The subsets* $\mathcal{FI}_{NP}, \mathcal{FI}_{inv}$ *are submonoids of* $(\mathcal{FI}, \circledast)$, *while* $\mathcal{FI}_{IP}$ *is a subsemigroup of* $(\mathcal{FI}, \circledast)$.

4.3   Powers of Fuzzy Implications w.r.t $\circledast$ and $\triangledown$

The main families of fuzzy implications are as follows: (S, N)-, R-, QL-, f- and g-implications, which are obtained either from the basic fuzzy operations of t-norms T, t-conorms S, negation N and or the generators of T, S. Once again, for definitions and properties of these families please see, for instance, [2]. Also, see Definition 8 below.

In general, if I, J are, say, (S, N)-implications with different S and N, then neither $I \triangledown J$ nor $I \circledast J$ will again be an (S, N)-implication. So is the case with the other families.

However, since the operations $\circledast$ and $\triangledown$ are binary on $\mathcal{FI}$, we could, in fact, derive new implications from a single $I \in \mathcal{FI}$. In the following, we present some results pertaining to whether this approach generates newer implications for ever or does it saturate, in which case the limit of such sequences are also given.

Firstly, note that by the associativity of $\circledast$ and $\triangledown$, for $n \geq 2$, we obtain:

$$I_{\circledast}^{[n]}(x, y) = I\left(x, I_{\circledast}^{[n-1]}(x, y)\right) = I_{\circledast}^{[n-1]}\left(x, I(x, y)\right) ,$$

$$I_{\triangledown}^{[n]}(x, y) = I\left(I_{\triangledown}^{[n-1]}(y, x), I_{\triangledown}^{[n-1]}(x, y)\right) = I_{\triangledown}^{[n-1]}\left(I(y, x), I(x, y)\right) .$$

In the following, we present a generalization of the established families of fuzzy implications and discuss their closure w.r.to the powers of $\circledast, \triangledown$.

Definition 8. *A fuzzy implication* I *is called*

(i) *a* generalized (S, N)-implication *if there exist a t-conorm* S, *a fuzzy negation* N *such that*

$$I(x, y) = S\left((N(x))_S^{[n]}, y\right)$$

for some $n \in \mathbb{N}$, *where* $t_S^{[n]} = S(t, t_S^{[n-1]})$ *and* $t_S^{[1]} = t$, *for any* $t \in [0, 1]$.

Table 2. Closures of $\circledast$ and $\triangledown$ w.r.to different properties and some generalised families

Property	I, J	$I \circledast J$	$I \triangledown J$
IP	✓	✓	✓
OP	✓	✗	✓
NP	✓	✓	✓
EP	✓	✗	✗
CP(N)	✓	✗	✓
Self conjugate	✓	✓	✓
Continuous	✓	✓	✓

Implication I	$I \circledast I$	$I \triangledown I$
Gen (S,N)-imp	✓	✗
Gen R-imp from l.c. T	✓	✓
Gen f-imp	✓	✗
Gen g-imp with $g(1) = \infty$	✓	✗

(ii) a generalized *R-implication, if there exists a t-norm T such that*

$$I(x, y) = \sup \left\{ t \in [0,1] \ \middle| \ T(x_T^{[n]}, t) \leq y \right\}.$$

(iii) a generalized *f-implication if there exists a strictly decreasing, continuous function $f \colon [0,1] \to [0,\infty]$ with $f(1) = 0$ and $h \in \Phi$ such that*

$$I(x, y) = f^{-1}(h(x) \cdot f(y)).$$

(iv) a generalized *g-implication if there exists a strictly increasing continuous function $g \colon [0,1] \to [0,\infty]$ with $g(0) = 0$ and a strictly decreasing function $k \colon [0,1] \to [1,\infty]$ with $k(1) = 1$ such that*

$$I(x, y) = g^{(-1)}\left(k(x) \cdot g(y)\right),$$

where $g^{(-1)}$ is called the pseudo-inverse of g and is given by

$$g^{(-1)}(x) = \begin{cases} g^{-1}(x), & \text{if } x \in [0, g(1)], \\ 1, & \text{if } x \in [g(1), \infty]. \end{cases}$$

Theorem 13. *If I is a generalized (S, N)-implication (a generalized R-, f- or g-implication with $g(1) = \infty$, resp.), then $I \circledast I$ is also a generalized (S, N)-implication (a generalized R-, f- or g-implication with $g(1) = \infty$, resp.).*

Table 2 summarises the results pertaining to the closures of $\circledast$ and $\triangledown$ w.r.to different properties and families. Further, Table 3 gives the expressions for the powers of I from these main families w.r.to both $\circledast$ and $\triangledown$, while Table 4 presents the limit of the generated sequences when I is one of the basic fuzzy implications (see Table 1). Please note that $I_{\mathbf{FD}}^2$ is given by

$$I_{\mathbf{FD}}^2(x, y) = \begin{cases} 1, & \text{if } x \leq y \text{ or } x \in [0, 0.5], \\ \max(1 - x, y), & \text{otherwise}. \end{cases}$$

Table 3. Powers of main families of fuzzy implications w.r.t $\circledast$ and $\triangledown$

Implication	$I^{[n]}_{\circledast}$	$I^{[n]}_{\triangledown}$
(S,N)-imp	$I\left((N(x))^{[n]}_S, y\right)$	$I\left(I\left(I^{n-2}_{\triangledown}(x,y),0\right), I\left(I^{n-1}_{\triangledown}(y,x), I\left(I^{n-2}_{\triangledown}(y,x),0\right)\right)\right)$
R-imp from $l.c.\ T$	$I\left(x^{[n]}_T, y\right)$	I
f-imp	$I\left(x^n, y\right)$	$I\left(x \cdot \prod_{i=1}^{n-1} I^{[i]}_{\triangledown}(y,x), y\right)$
g-imp with $g(1) = \infty$	$I\left(x^n, y\right)$	$I\left(x \cdot \prod_{i=1}^{n-1} I^{[i]}_{\triangledown}(y,x), y\right)$

Table 4. Powers of the basic fuzzy implications under $\circledast$ and $\triangledown$

Implication	$\lim\limits_{n\to\infty} I^{[n]}_{\circledast}$	$\lim\limits_{n\to\infty} I^{[n]}_{\triangledown}$
I_{RC}	I_{WB}	I_{WB}
I_{KD}	I_{KD}	I_{KD}
I_{FD}	I^2_{FD}	I_{FD}
I_{GD}	I_{GD}	I_{GD}
I_{GG}	I_{WB}	I_{GG}
I_{RS}	I_{RS}	I_{RS}
I_{LK}	I_{WB}	I_{LK}
I_{WB}	I_{WB}	I_{WB}
I_{YG}	I_{WB}	I_{WB}
I_1	I_1	I_1
I_0	I_0	I_1

Theorem 14. *Let* $I \in \mathcal{FI}$ *satisfy* (LI) *w.r.t a t-norm* T.

(i) *Then* $I^{[n]}_{\circledast}(x,y) = I(x^{[n]}_T, y)$.

(ii) *Further, if* T *is Archimedean, then* $\lim\limits_{n\to\infty} I^{[n]}_{\circledast}(x,y) = \begin{cases} 1, & \text{if } x < 1, \\ I(x,y), & \text{if } x = 1. \end{cases}$

(iii) *Moreover, if* $I \in \mathcal{FI}_{\mathcal{NP}}$ *then* $\lim\limits_{n\to\infty} I^{[n]}_{\circledast} = I_{WB}$.

Proof.

(i) Let $x, y \in [0,1]$. Then $I^{[2]}_{\circledast}(x,y) = I(x, I(x,y)) = I(T(x,x), y)$, since I satisfies (LI). Thus $I^{[2]}_{\circledast}(x,y) = I(x^{[2]}_T, y)$. By induction, $I^{[n]}_{\circledast}(x,y) = I(x^{[n]}_T, y)$.

(ii) Let $\epsilon > 0$ and $x < 1$. Since T is Archimedean, for any $\epsilon > 0$, there exists an $m \in \mathbb{N}$ s.t. $x^{[m]}_T < \epsilon$. Thus for $y \in [0,1], I^{[n]}_{\circledast}(x,y) = I(x^{[n]}_T, y) \to I(0,y)$, as

$n \to \infty$. Thus in this case $\lim_{n \to \infty} I_{\circledast}^{[n]}(x,y) = 1$. Now if $x = 1$ then $I_{\circledast}^{[2]}(1,y) = I(1, I(1,y)) = I(T(1,1),y) = I(1,y)$. In general, $I_{\circledast}^{[n]}(1,y) = I(1,y)$.

(iii) Follows from (i) and (ii).

5   Commutative Algebras on Fuzzy Implications

So far, we have discussed some new methods of generating fuzzy implications from fuzzy implications. However, since a fuzzy implication is not commutative, towards obtaining a commutative algebra on $\mathcal{FI}$ we take the help of other fuzzy logic connectives. In the following sections, this line of approach is explored.

5.1   Commutative Monoids of Fuzzy Implications

In this section we propose an operation that gives us a commutative monoid structure on the set of all fuzzy implications.

Definition 9. *Let A be an aggregation function on [0,1] and $I, J \in \mathcal{FI}$. We define $(I \odot_A J)$ as*

$$(I \odot_A J)(x,y) = A(I(x,y), J(x,y)), \qquad x,y \in [0,1] . \tag{3}$$

Clearly, $I \odot_A J \in \mathcal{FI}$. When we take a t-norm or a t-conorm instead of a general aggregation A in (3), we get much richer algebras on $\mathcal{FI}$. Let T be a t-norm and S a t-conorm. Let us define for $I, J \in \mathcal{FI}$,

$$(I \odot_T J)(x,y) = T(I(x,y), J(x,y)), \qquad x,y \in [0,1] ,$$
$$(I \odot_S J)(x,y) = S(I(x,y), J(x,y)), \qquad x,y \in [0,1] .$$

Theorem 15. *The set $(\mathcal{FI}, \odot_T)\big((\mathcal{FI}, \odot_S), resp.\big)$ is a commutative monoid with $I_1, \big(I_0, resp.\big)$ being the neutral element.*

If $T(x,y) = \min(x,y)$ and $S(x,y) = \max(x,y)$ then $\odot_T = \oslash$ and $\odot_S = \obslash$.

Theorem 16. *$\mathcal{FI}_{IP}, \mathcal{FI}_{OP}$ are commutative subsemigroups of both $(\mathcal{FI}, \odot_T)$, $(\mathcal{FI}, \odot_S)$. $\mathcal{FI}_{NP}$ is also a commutative subsemigroup of both $(\mathcal{FI}, \oslash), (\mathcal{FI}, \obslash)$.*

5.2   Semirings of Fuzzy Implications

It is interesting to note that with $\circledast$, as defined in (2), acting as the multiplication, we get an even richer structure on $\mathcal{FI}$, viz., that of a semiring.

Theorem 17. *$(\mathcal{FI}, \oslash, \circledast)$ forms a positive semiring, in fact, a band. Further, it is a complete, idempotent dioid.*

Corollary 1. *$\mathcal{FI}_{NP}, \mathcal{FI}_{inv}$ are subsemirings of $(\mathcal{FI}, \oslash, \circledast)$.*

5.3   Commutative Semirings of Fuzzy Implications

Theorem 18. $(\mathcal{FI}, \odot_T, \odot_S)$ *is a commutative semiring iff either T is the minimum t-norm or S is the maximum t-conorm.*

Lemma 1. $(\mathcal{FI}, \oslash, \odot_S)$ *is a commutative semiring as well as a band.*

Lemma 2. $\mathcal{FI}_{IP}, \mathcal{FI}_{OP}$ *are commutative subsemirings of* $(\mathcal{FI}, \oslash, \odot_S)$.

Theorem 19. *The commutative semiring $(\mathcal{FI}, \oslash, \odot_S))$ is a complete, idempotent dioid. Moreover if S is cancellative, then so is $(\mathcal{FI}, \oslash, \odot_S)$.*

Similar results also hold for $(\mathcal{FI}, \oslash, \odot_T)$.

6   Concluding Remarks

In this work we have presented a few novel methods of generating fuzzy implications from given ones and have shown that these methods lead to various and much richer algebraic structures on the set of all fuzzy implications than obtained in the literature so far.

In fact, considering the set $\mathcal{FI}$ as a poset (w.r.to pointwise ordering), some of the proposed operations give further connectives on this poset. For instance, $\odot_T, \odot_S$ form a t-norm, t-conorm on $\mathcal{FI}$, by inheritance. Further, independently, if we define,

$$(I \diamond J)(x, y) = J(I(y, x), J(x, y)), \qquad x, y \in [0, 1] \,,$$

then $\diamond$ defines a fuzzy implication on $\mathcal{FI}$. Of course, $I \diamond J \in \mathcal{FI}$ too. This line of study is already underway and the results will be presented in a future work.

Acknowledgements. This work was partially supported by the Department of Science and Technology, INDIA, project SERB/F/2862/2011-12 and is gratefully acknowledged.

References

1. Baczyński, M., Drewniak, J., Sobera, J.: Semigroups of fuzzy implications. Tatra Mt. Math. Publ. 21, 61–71 (2001)
2. Baczyński, M., Jayaram, B.: Fuzzy implications. STUDFUZZ, vol. 231. Springer, Berlin (2008)
3. Drewniak, J.: Invariant fuzzy implications. Soft Comput 10, 506–513 (2006)
4. Fodor, J.C., Roubens, M.: Fuzzy preference modelling and multicriteria decision support. Kluwer Academic Publishers, Dordrecht (1994)
5. Hungerford, T.: Algebra. Springer Science (1973)
6. Klement, E.P., Mesiar, R., Pap, E.: Triangular norms. Kluwer Academic Publishers, Dordrecht (2000)
7. Yager, R.R.: On some new classes of implication operators and their role in approximate reasoning. Inf. Sci. 167, 193–216 (2004)
8. Zadeh, L.A.: Outline of a new approach to the analysis of complex systems and decision process. IEEE Trans. on Syst. Man and Cyber. 3, 28–44 (1973)

A Note on the Distributivity
of Fuzzy Implications over Representable
Uninorms

Michał Baczyński

Institute of Mathematics, University of Silesia,
40-007 Katowice, ul. Bankowa 14, Poland
michal.baczynski@us.edu.pl

Abstract. Recently, in [1] we have presented the solutions of the following two distributive equations $I(x, U_1(y, z)) = U_2(I(x, y), I(x, z))$ and $I(U_1(x, y), z) = U_2(I(x, z), I(y, z))$, when U_1, U_2 are given representable uninorms and I is an unknown function, in particular a fuzzy implication. Unfortunately, we have realized that results presented for the second equation, in section 6, are incorrect. Our mistake arises from the absence of the proofs in this section – we have incorrectly considered the vertical section instead of horizontal section. In this paper we will show the correct results and will also present the sketches of proofs. We would like to note that all other results presented in article [1] are correct.

Keywords: Fuzzy connectives, Fuzzy implication, Functional Equations, Uninorm.

1 Introduction

Recently, in [1] we have investigated the following two distributive equations:

$$I(x, U_1(y, z)) = U_2(I(x, y), I(x, z)), \qquad \text{(D1)}$$

$$I(U_1(x, y), z) = U_2(I(x, z), I(y, z)), \qquad \text{(D2)}$$

by characterizing functions I (in particular fuzzy implications), which satisfy the above equations for all $x, y, z \in [0, 1]$, when U_1 and U_2 are given representable uninorms. The correct solutions for the first Eq. (D1) we have presented with the proofs in section 5 of that article. Unfortunately, the solutions presented in [1, Section 6] for the second Eq. (D2) are incorrect. They have been presented without the proofs and our mistake follows from the fact that we have incorrectly considered the vertical section instead of horizontal section.

It should be noted that Eq. (D2) was studied independently by Ruiz-Aguilera and Torrens in [9] for the major part of known classes of uninorms with continuous underlying t-norm and t-conorm and for strong implications derived from uninorms, while in [10], they also studied (D2), but with the assumption that I is a residual implication derived from a given uninorm.

S. Greco et al. (Eds.): IPMU 2012, Part II, CCIS 298, pp. 375–384, 2012.
© Springer-Verlag Berlin Heidelberg 2012

2   Preliminaries

We assume that the reader is familiar with the classical results concerning uni-norms, so we only recall basic definitions and facts which will be useful in the sequel. In the literature we can find several diverse definitions of fuzzy implications. In this article we will use the following one, which is equivalent to the well accepted definition proposed by Fodor, Roubens [6, Definition 1.15] (see also Kitainik [8, p. 50], Bustince et al. [3] and Baczyński, Jayaram [2]).

Definition 2.1. *A function $I: [0,1]^2 \to [0,1]$ is called a* fuzzy implication *if it satisfies the following conditions:*

$$I \text{ is decreasing in the first variable,} \tag{I1}$$

$$I \text{ is increasing in the second variable,} \tag{I2}$$

$$I(0,0) = 1, \quad I(1,1) = 1, \quad I(1,0) = 0. \tag{I3}$$

Uninorms were introduced by Yager and Rybalov in 1996 (see [11]) as a generalization of triangular norms and conorms. For the recent overview of this family of operations see [4].

Definition 2.2. *An associative, commutative and increasing operation $U: [0,1]^2 \to [0,1]$ is called a* uninorm, *if there exists $e \in [0,1]$, called the neutral element of U, such that $U(e,x) = U(x,e) = x$, for all $x \in [0,1]$.*

Remark 2.3. (i) If $e = 0$, then U is a t-conorm and if $e = 1$, then U is a t-norm.
(ii) The neutral element e corresponding to a uninorm U is unique.
(iii) For any uninorm U we have $U(0,0) = 0$ and $U(1,1) = 1$ and $U(0,1) \in \{0,1\}$. A uninorm U such that $U(0,1) = U(1,0) = 0$ is called *conjunctive* and if $U(0,1) = U(1,0) = 1$, then it is called *disjunctive*.

In the literature one can find several different classes of uninorms (see [7]). Uninorms that can be represented as in Theorem 2.4 are called *representable uninorms*.

Theorem 2.4 (Fodor et al. [7, Theorem 3]). *For a function $U: [0,1]^2 \to [0,1]$ the following statements are equivalent:*

(i) U is a strictly increasing and continuous on $]0,1[^2$ uninorm with the neutral element $e \in]0,1[$ such that U is self-dual, except in points $(0,1)$ and $(1,0)$, with respect to a strong negation N with the fixed point e, i.e.,

$$U(x,y) = N(U(N(x),N(y))), \qquad x,y \in [0,1]^2 \setminus \{(0,1),(1,0)\}.$$

(ii) U has a continuous additive generator, i.e., there exists a continuous and strictly increasing function $h: [0,1] \to [-\infty,\infty]$, such that $h(0) = -\infty$, $h(e) = 0$ for $e \in]0,1[$ and $h(1) = \infty$, which is uniquely determined up to a positive multiplicative constant, such that either, for all $x,y \in [0,1]$,

$$U(x,y) = \begin{cases} 0 & \text{if } (x,y) \in \{(0,1),(1,0)\}, \\ h^{-1}(h(x) + h(y)), & \text{otherwise,} \end{cases} \tag{1}$$

when U is conjunctive, or

$$U(x,y) = \begin{cases} 1 & \text{if } (x,y) \in \{(0,1),(1,0)\}, \\ h^{-1}(h(x) + h(y)), & \text{otherwise,} \end{cases} \qquad (2)$$

when U is disjunctive.

It should be noted that research connected with representable uninorms are still conducted. For example, the very recent characterizations of this class of uninorms can be found in [5].

Remark 2.5. One can easily observe that if a representable uninorm U is conjunctive, then the representation $U(x,y) = h^{-1}(h(x) + h(y))$ holds for all $x, y \in [0,1]$ with the assumption that

$$(-\infty) + \infty = \infty + (-\infty) = -\infty. \qquad \text{(A-)}$$

Similarly, if a representable uninorm U is disjunctive, then $U(x,y) = h^{-1}(h(x) + h(y))$ holds for all $x, y \in [0,1]$ with the assumption that

$$(-\infty) + \infty = \infty + (-\infty) = \infty. \qquad \text{(A+)}$$

We have two important results connected with the distributivity of fuzzy implications over uninorms.

Lemma 2.6 ([1, Lemma 3.1]). *Let a function $I: [0,1]^2 \to [0,1]$ satisfy (I3) and also (D1) with some uninorms U_1, U_2. Then U_1 is conjunctive if and only if U_2 is conjunctive.*

Lemma 2.7 ([1, Lemma 3.2]). *Let a function $I: [0,1]^2 \to [0,1]$ satisfy (I3) and also (D2) with some uninorms U_1, U_2. Then U_1 is conjunctive if and only if U_2 is disjunctive.*

By the above results it is enough, in our context, to consider the functional equation (D1) only when both uninorms U_1, U_2 are either conjunctive or disjunctive uninorms, and the functional equation (D2) only when either U_1 is conjunctive and U_2 is disjunctive, or U_1 is disjunctive and U_2 is conjunctive.

3 Cauchy Functional Equations on Real Extended Lines

In paper [1] we have obtained the following results, which will be useful in the next main section.

Proposition 3.1 ([1, Proposition 4.5]). *Let $X = Y = [-\infty, \infty]$. For a function $f: X \to Y$ the following statements are equivalent:*

(i) f satisfies the additive Cauchy functional equation

$$f(x+y) = f(x) + f(y), \qquad x, y \in X, \qquad \text{(C)}$$

with the assumption (A-), i.e., $(-\infty) + \infty = \infty + (-\infty) = -\infty$ in the set X and the assumption (A+), i.e., $(-\infty) + \infty = \infty + (-\infty) = \infty$ in the set Y.

(ii) Either $f = -\infty$, or $f = 0$, or $f = \infty$, or f has the form

$$f(x) = \begin{cases} -\infty, & \text{if } x = -\infty, \\ 0, & \text{if } x \in]-\infty, \infty], \end{cases} \tag{3}$$

or

$$f(x) = \begin{cases} \infty, & \text{if } x = -\infty, \\ 0, & \text{if } x \in]-\infty, \infty], \end{cases} \tag{4}$$

or

$$f(x) = \begin{cases} -\infty, & \text{if } x \in \mathbb{R}, \\ \infty, & \text{if } x \in \{-\infty, \infty\}, \end{cases} \tag{5}$$

or

$$f(x) = \begin{cases} \infty, & \text{if } x = -\infty, \\ -\infty, & \text{if } x \in]-\infty, \infty], \end{cases} \tag{6}$$

or there exists a unique additive function $g \colon \mathbb{R} \to \mathbb{R}$ such that f has the form

$$f(x) = \begin{cases} -\infty, & \text{if } x \in \{-\infty, \infty\}, \\ g(x), & \text{if } x \in \mathbb{R}, \end{cases} \tag{7}$$

or

$$f(x) = \begin{cases} \infty, & \text{if } x \in \{-\infty, \infty\}, \\ g(x), & \text{if } x \in \mathbb{R}, \end{cases} \tag{8}$$

or

$$f(x) = \begin{cases} \infty, & \text{if } x = -\infty, \\ g(x), & \text{if } x \in \mathbb{R}, \\ -\infty, & \text{if } x = \infty. \end{cases} \tag{9}$$

Proposition 3.2 ([1, Proposition 4.7]). *Let $X = Y = [-\infty, \infty]$. For a function $f \colon X \to Y$ the following statements are equivalent:*

(i) f satisfies the additive Cauchy functional equation (C) for all $x, y \in X$, with the assumption (A+), i.e., $(-\infty) + \infty = \infty + (-\infty) = \infty$ in the set X and the assumption (A-), i.e., $(-\infty) + \infty = \infty + (-\infty) = -\infty$ in the set Y.

(ii) Either $f = -\infty$, or $f = 0$, or $f = \infty$, or f has the form

$$f(x) = \begin{cases} -\infty, & \text{if } x \in \{-\infty, \infty\}, \\ \infty, & \text{if } x \in \mathbb{R}, \end{cases} \tag{10}$$

or

$$f(x) = \begin{cases} 0, & \text{if } x \in [-\infty, \infty[, \\ -\infty, & \text{if } x = \infty, \end{cases} \tag{11}$$

or

$$f(x) = \begin{cases} 0, & \text{if } x \in [-\infty, \infty[, \\ \infty, & \text{if } x = \infty, \end{cases} \tag{12}$$

or

$$f(x) = \begin{cases} \infty, & \text{if } x = -\infty, \\ -\infty, & \text{if } x \in]-\infty, \infty], \end{cases} \tag{13}$$

or there exists a unique additive function $g \colon \mathbb{R} \to \mathbb{R}$ *such that* f *has the form* (7), *or* (8), *or* (9).

4 The Revised Solutions on Eq. (D2) for Representable Uninorms

As we have already mentioned, solutions for the Eq. (D2) have been presented in [1, Section 6]. But main results presented there, i.e. Theorem 6.1 and Theorem 6.2 are incorrect. To see our mistake, let us consider the following example.

Example 4.1. Let U_1 be any conjunctive representable uninorm with the neutral element $e_1 \in]0,1[$ and U_2 be any disjunctive representable uninorm with the neutral element $e_2 \in]0,1[$. Let us assume that we are using the vertical sections described in [1, Theorem 6.1]. Assume that for $x = 0$ the vertical section is $I(0, \cdot) = 0$, while for $x = 1$ the vertical section is $I(1, \cdot) = 1$. Now, let us calculate the left-hand side of Eq. (D2) for $x = 0$, $y = 1$ and any $z \in [0,1]$:

$$I(U_1(x,y), z) = I(U_1(0,1), z) = I(0, z) = 0.$$

We have used here the assumption that U_1 is conjunctive. Now, let us calculate the right-hand side of Eq. (D2) for the same variables:

$$U_2(I(x,z), I(y,z)) = U_2(I(0,z), I(1,z)) = U_2(0,1) = 1.$$

We have used here the assumption that U_2 is disjunctive. Thus, these functions do not satisfy Eq. (D2).

Fortunately, our mistake can be easily corrected. The main idea is to consider horizontal sections instead of vertical sections. Below we will present the correct results with the sketch of proof.

Theorem 4.2 (cf. [1, Theorem 6.1]). *For a conjunctive representable uninorm* U_1 *with the neutral element* $e_1 \in]0,1[$, *disjunctive representable uninorm* U_2 *with the neutral element* $e_2 \in]0,1[$ *and a function* $I \colon [0,1]^2 \to [0,1]$ *the following statements are equivalent:*

(i) The triple of functions U_1, U_2, I *satisfies the functional equation* (D2) *for all* $x,y,z \in [0,1]$.

(ii) There exist continuous, strictly increasing functions $h_1, h_2 \colon [0,1] \to [-\infty, \infty]$ *with* $h_1(0) = h_2(0) = -\infty$, $h_1(e_1) = h_2(e_2) = 0$ *and* $h_1(1) = h_2(1) = \infty$, *which are uniquely determined up to positive multiplicative constants, such that* U_1 *admit the representation* (1) *with* h_1, U_2 *admit the representation* (2) *with* h_2 *and for every fixed* $x \in [0,1]$, *the horizontal section* $I(\cdot, y)$ *has, for all* $x \in [0,1]$, *one of the following forms:*

$$I(x,y) = 0, \tag{14}$$

$$I(x,y) = e_2, \tag{15}$$

$$I(x,y) = 1, \tag{16}$$

$$I(x,y) = \begin{cases} 0, & \text{if } x = 0, \\ e_2, & \text{if } x \in]0,1], \end{cases} \tag{17}$$

$$I(x,y) = \begin{cases} 1, & \text{if } x = 0, \\ e_2, & \text{if } x \in]0,1], \end{cases} \tag{18}$$

$$I(x,y) = \begin{cases} 0, & \text{if } x \in]0,1[, \\ 1, & \text{if } x = 0 \text{ or } x = 1, \end{cases} \tag{19}$$

$$I(x,y) = \begin{cases} 1, & \text{if } x = 0, \\ 0, & \text{if } x \in]0,1], \end{cases} \tag{20}$$

$$I(x,y) = \begin{cases} 0, & \text{if } x = 0 \text{ or } x = 1, \\ h_2^{-1}\left(g_y(h_1(x))\right), & \text{if } x \in]0,1[, \end{cases} \tag{21}$$

$$I(x,y) = \begin{cases} 1, & \text{if } x = 0 \text{ or } x = 1, \\ h_2^{-1}\left(g_y(h_1(x))\right), & \text{if } x \in]0,1[, \end{cases} \tag{22}$$

$$I(x,y) = \begin{cases} 1, & \text{if } x = 0, \\ h_2^{-1}\left(g_y(h_1(x))\right), & \text{if } x \in]0,1[, \\ 0, & \text{if } x = 1, \end{cases} \tag{23}$$

with a unique additive function $g_y \colon \mathbb{R} \to \mathbb{R}$.

Proof. $(ii) \Longrightarrow (i)$ The proof in this direction can be checked by a direct substitution.

$(i) \Longrightarrow (ii)$ Let us assume that uninorms U_1, U_2 and a function I are solutions of the functional equation (D2) satisfying the required properties. By the characterization of representable uninorms, U_1, U_2 admit the representations (1) and (2) for some continuous, strictly increasing functions $h_1, h_2 \colon [0,1] \to [-\infty, \infty]$ with $h_1(0) = h_2(0) = -\infty$, $h_1(e_1) = h_2(e_2) = 0$ and $h_1(1) = h_2(1) = \infty$. Moreover, both generators are uniquely determined up to positive multiplicative constants. Now, by Remark 2.5, the equation (D2) becomes,

$$I(h_1^{-1}(h_1(x) + h_1(y)), z) = h_2^{-1}(h_2(I(x,z)) + h_2(I(y,z))), \qquad x, y, z \in [0,1],$$

with the assumption (A-) in the codomain of h_1 and with the assumption (A+) in the codomain of h_2.

Let $z \in [0,1]$ be arbitrarily fixed. Define a function $I^z \colon [0,1] \to [0,1]$ by the formula

$$I^z(a) = I(a,z), \qquad a \in [0,1].$$

Thus, our equation can be written in the following form

$$I^z(h_1^{-1}(h_1(x) + h_1(y))) = h_2^{-1}(h_2(I^z(x)) + h_2(I^z(y))), \qquad x, y \in [0,1],$$

By standard substitutions, $f^z = h_2 \circ I^z \circ h_1^{-1}$, $u = h_1(x)$, $v = h_1(y)$, for $x, y \in [0,1]$, we obtain the following additive Cauchy functional equation

$$f^z(u+v) = f^z(u) + f^z(v), \qquad u, v \in [-\infty, \infty],$$

where $f^z \colon [-\infty, \infty] \to [-\infty, \infty]$ is an unknown function, with the assumption (A-) in its domain and the assumption (A+) in its codomain. Now, Proposition 3.1 describes all solutions f^z. Because of the definition of the function f^z we get all our 10 formulas.

Consequently, [1, Remark 6.2] is also incorrect – there are infinite number of solutions which are fuzzy implications. It should be noted that with this assumption only the horizontal sections (16), (18), (20) and (23) are possible, while for $y = 1$ the horizontal section should be (16). We should also remember that a fuzzy implication is decreasing in the first variable while it is increasing in the second one.

Example 4.3. (i) If U_1 is a conjunctive representable uninorm and U_2 is a disjunctive representable uninorm, then the least solution of Eq. (D2) which is a fuzzy implication is the least fuzzy implication (see [2]):

$$I_0(x,y) = \begin{cases} 1, & \text{if } x = 0 \text{ or } y = 1, \\ 0, & \text{otherwise.} \end{cases}$$

The horizontal sections are the following: for $y \in [0, 1[$ it is the solution (20) and for $y = 1$ it is the solution (16) in Theorem 4.2. One can easily check, by considering several easy cases, that I_0 indeed satisfy Eq. (D2) with the appropriate uninorms.

The similar (in fact the same) counterexample as in Example 4.1 can be presented for [1, Theorem 6.3].

Example 4.4. Let U_1 be any disjunctive representable uninorm with the neutral element $e_1 \in]0,1[$ and U_2 be any conjunctive representable uninorm with the neutral element $e_2 \in]0,1[$. Let us assume that we are using the vertical sections described in [1, Theorem 6.3]. Assume that for $x = 0$ the vertical section is $I(0, \cdot) = 0$ while for $x = 1$ the vertical section is $I(1, \cdot) = 1$. Now, let us calculate the left-hand side of Eq. (D2) for $x = 0$, $y = 1$ and any $z \in [0,1]$:

$$I(U_1(x,y), z) = I(U_1(0,1), z) = I(1, z) = 1.$$

We have used here the assumption that U_1 is disjunctive. Now, let us calculate the right-hand side of Eq. (D2) for the same variables:

$$U_2(I(x,z), I(y,z)) = U_2(I(0,z), I(1,z)) = U_2(0,1) = 0.$$

At the end we have used the assumption that U_2 is conjunctive. Thus, these functions do not satisfy Eq. (D2).

Theorem 4.5 (cf. [1, Theorem 6.3]). *For a disjunctive representable uninorm U_1 with the neutral element $e_1 \in {]}0,1[$, conjunctive representable uninorm U_2 with the neutral element $e_2 \in {]}0,1[$ and a function $I\colon [0,1]^2 \to [0,1]$ the following statements are equivalent:*

(i) *The triple of functions U_1, U_2, I satisfies the functional equation (D2) for all $x, y, z \in [0,1]$.*
(ii) *There exist continuous, strictly increasing functions $h_1, h_2\colon [0,1] \to [-\infty, \infty]$ with $h_1(0) = h_2(0) = -\infty$, $h_1(e_1) = h_2(e_2) = 0$ and $h_1(1) = h_2(1) = \infty$, which are uniquely determined up to positive multiplicative constants, such that U_1 admit the representation (2) with h_1, U_2 admit the representation (1) with h_2 and for every fixed $x \in [0,1]$, the horizontal section $I(\,\cdot\,,y)$ has, for all $x \in [0,1]$, one of the following forms:*

$$I(x,y) = 0, \tag{24}$$

$$I(x,y) = e_2, \tag{25}$$

$$I(x,y) = 1, \tag{26}$$

$$I(x,y) = \begin{cases} 0, & \text{if } x = 0 \text{ or } x = 1, \\ 1, & \text{if } x \in {]}0,1[, \end{cases} \tag{27}$$

$$I(x,y) = \begin{cases} e_2, & \text{if } x \in [0,1[, \\ 0, & \text{if } x = 1, \end{cases} \tag{28}$$

$$I(x,y) = \begin{cases} e_2, & \text{if } x \in [0,1[, \\ 1, & \text{if } x = 1, \end{cases} \tag{29}$$

$$I(x,y) = \begin{cases} 1, & \text{if } x = 0, \\ 0, & \text{if } x \in {]}0,1], \end{cases} \tag{30}$$

$$I(x,y) = \begin{cases} 0, & \text{if } x = 0 \text{ or } x = 1, \\ h_2^{-1}\left(g_y(h_1(x))\right), & \text{if } x \in {]}0,1[, \end{cases} \tag{31}$$

$$I(x,y) = \begin{cases} 1, & \text{if } x = 0 \text{ or } x = 1, \\ h_2^{-1}\left(g_y(h_1(x))\right), & \text{if } x \in {]}0,1[, \end{cases} \tag{32}$$

$$I(x,y) = \begin{cases} 1, & \text{if } x = 0, \\ h_2^{-1}\left(g_y(h_1(x))\right), & \text{if } x \in {]}0,1[, \\ 0, & \text{if } x = 1, \end{cases} \tag{33}$$

with a unique additive function $g_y\colon \mathbb{R} \to \mathbb{R}$.

Proof. $(ii) \Longrightarrow (i)$ The proof in this direction can be checked by a direct substitution.

$(i) \Longrightarrow (ii)$ Let us assume that uninorms U_1, U_2 and a function I are solutions of the functional equation (D2) satisfying the required properties. By the characterization of representable uninorms, U_1 and U_2 admit the representation (2) and (1) for some continuous, strictly increasing functions $h_1, h_2\colon [0,1] \to [-\infty, \infty]$

with $h_1(0) = h_2(0) = -\infty$, $h_1(e_1) = h_2(e_2) = 0$ and $h_1(1) = h_2(1) = \infty$. Moreover, both generators are uniquely determined up to positive multiplicative constants. Now, by Remark 2.5, the equation (D2) becomes,

$$I(h_1^{-1}(h_1(x) + h_1(y)), z) = h_2^{-1}(h_2(I(x, z)) + h_2(I(y, z))), \qquad x, y, z \in [0, 1],$$

with the assumption (A+) in the codomain of h_1 and with the assumption (A-) in the codomain of h_2.

Let $z \in [0, 1]$ be arbitrarily fixed. Define a function $I^z : [0, 1] \to [0, 1]$ by the formula

$$I^z(a) = I(a, z), \qquad a \in [0, 1].$$

Thus, our equation can be written in the following form

$$I^z(h_1^{-1}(h_1(x) + h_1(y))) = h_2^{-1}(h_2(I^z(x)) + h_2(I^z(y))), \qquad x, y \in [0, 1],$$

By standard substitutions, $f^z = h_2 \circ I^z \circ h_1^{-1}$, $u = h_1(x)$, $v = h_1(y)$, for $x, y \in [0, 1]$, we obtain the following additive Cauchy functional equation

$$f^z(u + v) = f^z(u) + f^z(v), \qquad u, v \in [-\infty, \infty],$$

where $f^z : [-\infty, \infty] \to [-\infty, \infty]$ is an unknown function, with the assumption (A+) in its domain and the assumption (A-) in its codomain. Now, Proposition 3.2 describes all solutions f^z. Because of the definition of the function f^z we get all our formulas.

Consequently, [1, Remark 6.4] is also incorrect – there are infinite number of solutions which are fuzzy implications. It should be noted that with this assumption only the horizontal sections (26), (20) and (33) are possible, while for $y = 1$ the horizontal section should be (26).

Example 4.6. If U_1 is a disjunctive representable uninorm and U_2 is a conjunctive representable uninorm, then the least solution of Eq. (D2) which is a fuzzy implication is also the least fuzzy implication I_0. In this case the horizontal sections are the following: for $y \in [0, 1[$ it is the solution (30) and for $y = 1$ it is the solution (26) in Theorem 4.5.

5   Conclusion

In this paper we have shown that some results presented in the article [1] are incorrect. In particular all results in Section 6 are written incorrectly by using the vertical sections of unknown function I. With the help of the correct facts from that article we have improved all the results by describing the horizontal sections of the solution. We have also presented the examples which show that also for the second distributive equation for implications and uninorms, namely for Eq. (D2), there exist solutions which are fuzzy implications. In our future work we will describe the solutions which have some regular properties (like continuity) and we will also consider distributive equations for other classes of uninorms.

Acknowledgment. This work has been partially supported by the Polish Ministry of Science and Higher Education Grant Nr N N519 384936.

The author would like to thank anonymous reviewers for their valuable comments and corrections.

References

1. Baczyński, M.: On the distributivity of fuzzy implications over representable uninorms. Fuzzy Sets and Systems 161, 2256–2275 (2010)
2. Baczyński, M., Jayaram, B.: Fuzzy implications. STUDFUZZ, vol. 231. Springer, Heidelberg (2008)
3. Bustince, H., Burillo, P., Soria, F.: Automorphisms, negation and implication operators. Fuzzy Sets and Systems 134, 209–229 (2003)
4. Fodor, J., De Baets, B.: Uninorm Basics. In: Wang, P.P., Ruan, D., Kerre, E.E. (eds.) Fuzzy Logic: A Spectrum of Theoretical and Practical Issues. STUDFUZZ, vol. 215, pp. 49–64. Springer, Heidelberg (2007)
5. Fodor, J., De Baets, B.: A single-point characterization of representable uninorms. Fuzzy Sets and Systems (2011), doi: 10.1016/j.fss.2011.12.001
6. Fodor, J., Roubens, M.: Fuzzy Preference Modelling and Multicriteria Decision Support. Kluwer, Dordrecht (1994)
7. Fodor, J., Yager, R.R., Rybalov, A.: Structure of uninorms. Int. J. Uncertainty Fuzziness Knowledge-Based Syst. 5, 411–427 (1997)
8. Kitainik, L.: Fuzzy Decision Procedures with Binary Relations. Kluwer, Dordrecht (1993)
9. Ruiz-Aguilera, D., Torrens, J.: Distributivity of strong implications over conjunctive and disjunctive uninorms. Kybernetika 42, 319–336 (2005)
10. Ruiz-Aguilera, D., Torrens, J.: Distributivity of residual implications over conjunctive and disjunctive uninorms. Fuzzy Sets and Systems 158, 23–37 (2007)
11. Yager, R.R., Rybalov, A.: Uninorm aggregation operators. Fuzzy Sets and Systems 80, 111–120 (1996)

Bandler-Kohout Subproduct
with Yager's Classes of Fuzzy Implications

Sayantan Mandal and Balasubramaniam Jayaram

Department of Mathematics,
Indian Institute of Technology Hyderabad,
Yeddumailaram-502205, India
{ma10p002,jbala}@iith.ac.in

Abstract. In this work we discuss the Bandler-Kohout Subproduct (BKS) relational inference system with the fuzzy implication interpreted as the Yager's classes of implications which do not form a residuated lattice structure on $[0, 1]$. We show that many of the desirable properties, viz., interpolativity, continuity, robustness and computational efficiency, that are known for BKS with residuated implications are also available under this framework, thus expanding the choice of operations available to practitioners.

Keywords: Bandler-Kohout Subproduct, Fuzzy implications, f-implications, g-implications, Relational Inference, Interpolativity, Continuity and Robustness of inference.

1 Introduction

An Inference mechanism in Appriximate Reasoning (AR) is a function which gives a meaningful output from often imprecise inputs. Fuzzy sets have been widely used for this type of purpose. Among many types of inference mechanisms proposed in AR using fuzzy logic, Relational Inference Mechanisms and Similarity Based Reasoning are very common in the literature. Zadeh's Compositional Rule of Inference (CRI) [14], and Bandler-Kohout Subproduct (BKS) [2], [9], are the two well-established relational inference mechanisms.

1.1 Measures of 'goodness' of a Fuzzy Inference Mechanism

While dealing with fuzzy inference mechanisms (FIM), choosing the operators employed in it is flexible. However, the question that arises is whether an FIM with a particular choice of operators is good. Once again, the 'goodness' of an FIM itself can be measured against different parameters. In the literature, some measures of goodness proposed against which an FIM is compared and contrasted are as follows: (i) interpolativity, (ii) continuity, (iii) robustness, (iv) approximation capability and (v) efficiency, see [12] and the references therein.

Perfilieva and Lehmke [10] studied the continuity and interpolativity of CRI with SISO multiple rules and showed that a fuzzy relation R is a correct model

S. Greco et al. (Eds.): IPMU 2012, Part II, CCIS 298, pp. 385–394, 2012.
© Springer-Verlag Berlin Heidelberg 2012

of the given rulebase if and only if it is also a continuous model and thus have shown the equivalence between continuity and interpolativity. The robustness of CRI was dealt with by Klawonn and Castro [5]. Later on Štěpnička and Jayaram [12] have undertaken a similar study for the BKS inference mechanism.

1.2 Motivation for the Work

Note that in all the above works the underlying fuzzy logic operations on $[0, 1]$ were obtained from a left-continuous conjunction and hence turned the unit interval into a rich residuated lattice structure possessing very many properties that were employed extensively in the proofs of the results. However, when a non-residuated implication is employed in the BKS inference, no such study has been undertaken.

In this work, we study the above properties of the BKS inference mechanism when the Yager's class of implication operators [13], i.e, f- and g-implications - which do not give rise to a residuated structure on $[0, 1]$ - are employed. Note that f- and g-implications satisfy the law of importation (see (LI)) w.r.to the product t-norm and hence an equivalent hierarchical model of inference can be given making it computationally efficient. However, the other desirable properties have not been rigorously studied - which forms the motivation for this work.

Under this framework, firstly, we derive some necessary and sufficient conditions for interpolativity. After defining continuity suitably, we have shown that continuity is equivalent to interpolativity. Finally, we show that robustness is also available to us, thus adding more choice of operations under the BKS scheme.

2 Fuzzy Implications

Fuzzy implications are a generalization of the classical implications. In this section we give the main definitions and properties related to fuzzy implications only. For the definitions of other basic fuzzy logic connectives, please see, for instance, [4].

Definition 1 ([1]). *A function $I: [0, 1]^2 \to [0, 1]$ is called a* fuzzy implication *if it is decreasing in the first variable, increasing in the second variable and $I(0, 0) = 1$, $I(1, 1) = 1$, $I(1, 0) = 0$. We will often denote I by $\longrightarrow$.*

Definition 2. *A fuzzy implication I is said to satisfy*

(i) the left neutrality property, *if*

$$I(1, y) = y , \qquad y \in [0, 1] , \tag{NP}$$

(ii) the Law Of Importation *w.r.to a t-norm T, if*

$$I(x, I(y, z)) = I(T(x, y), z) , \qquad x, y, z \in [0, 1] . \tag{LI}$$

2.1   Yager's Families of Fuzzy Implications

Yager [13] introduced two families of fuzzy implications based on strictly monotonic functions on $[0, 1]$.

Definition 3 ([1]). *Let* $f \colon [0, 1] \to [0, \infty]$ *be a strictly decreasing and continuous function with* $f(1) = 0$. *The function* $I_f \colon [0, 1]^2 \to [0, 1]$ *defined by*

$$I_f(x, y) = f^{-1}\left(x \cdot f(y)\right), \qquad x, y \in [0, 1], \tag{1}$$

with the understanding $0 \cdot \infty = 0$, *is a fuzzy implication and called an* f-*implication. The function* f *itself is called an* f-*generator of the* I_f *generated as in* (1). *We will often write* $\longrightarrow_f$ *instead of* I_f.

Definition 4 ([1]). *Let* $g \colon [0, 1] \to [0, \infty]$ *be a strictly increasing and continuous function with* $g(0) = 0$. *The function* $I_g \colon [0, 1]^2 \to [0, 1]$ *defined by*

$$I_g(x, y) = g^{(-1)}\left(\frac{1}{x} \cdot g(y)\right), \qquad x, y \in [0, 1], \tag{2}$$

with the understanding $\frac{1}{0} = \infty$ *and* $\infty \cdot 0 = \infty$, *is a fuzzy implication and called a* g-*implication, where the function* $g^{(-1)}$ *in* (2) *is the pseudo-inverse of* g *[1].*

Note that both I_f and I_g satisfy (NP) and (LI) with the product t-norm, $T_{\mathbf{P}}(x, y) = xy$. Both the Yager's families of fuzzy implications satisfy the following:

Proposition 1. *Let* $\mathcal{I}$ *be any index set. For any* $x, y, x_i, y_i \in [0, 1]$, *with* $\longrightarrow$ *being* f-*implication or* g-*implication, i.e.,* $\longrightarrow = \longrightarrow_f \ / \ \longrightarrow_g$, *we have*

$$x \longrightarrow \bigwedge_{i \in \mathcal{I}}(y_i) = \bigwedge_{i \in \mathcal{I}}(x \longrightarrow y_i), \tag{3}$$

$$\bigvee_{i \in \mathcal{I}}(x_i) \longrightarrow y = \bigwedge_{i \in \mathcal{I}}(x_i \longrightarrow y). \tag{4}$$

2.2   Generalised Fuzzy Implication

In this section we define a generalised implication from $[0, \infty]^2 \to [0, 1]$, which when its domain is restricted to $[0, 1]^2$ will be the usual fuzzy implication.

Definition 5. *A function* $I^* \colon [0, \infty]^2 \to [0, 1]$ *is called a* generalised fuzzy implication *if it is decreasing in the first variable, increasing in the second variable and* $I^*(0, 0) = 1$, $I^*(1, 1) = 1$, $I^*(1, 0) = 0$. *We will often denote* I^* *by* $\overset{*}{\longrightarrow}$.

Our interest is specially on the following generalised fuzzy implication, which has a formula similar to that of the Goguen implication, the residual of the product t-norm. In the sequel, this function plays an important role in giving crisp expressions to many results and properties and hence we define it here and present some of its important properties, without proof.

Definition 6. *(i) The function* $I_{\mathbf{GG}}^* : [0, \infty]^2 \to [0, 1]$ *defined as*

$$I_{\mathbf{GG}}^*(x, y) = \begin{cases} 1, & \text{if } x \le y \\ \dfrac{y}{x}, & \text{if } x > y \end{cases}, \qquad x, y \in [0, \infty], \tag{5}$$

is called the Generalised Goguen *implication. We will also denote* $I_{\mathbf{GG}}^*$ *by* $\overset{*}{\longrightarrow}_{\mathbf{G}}$ *for better readability in proofs.*

(ii) The biimplication [8] obtained from $I_{\mathbf{GG}}^*$ *is defined and denoted as follows:*

$$x \overset{*}{\longleftrightarrow}_{\mathbf{G}} y = (x \overset{*}{\longrightarrow}_{\mathbf{G}} y) \wedge (y \overset{*}{\longrightarrow}_{\mathbf{G}} x). \tag{6}$$

Proposition 2. *Let* $a, b, a_i, b_i, c, d \in [0, \infty]$, $i \in \mathcal{I}$, *an index set. Then, the following inequalities are true:*

$$\left(\bigvee_{i \in \mathcal{I}} a_i \right) \overset{*}{\longleftrightarrow} \left(\bigvee_{i \in \mathcal{I}} b_i \right) \ge \bigwedge_{i \in \mathcal{I}} \left(a_i \overset{*}{\longleftrightarrow} b_i \right), \tag{7}$$

$$\left(a \overset{*}{\longleftrightarrow}_{\mathbf{G}} b \right) \cdot \left(c \overset{*}{\longleftrightarrow}_{\mathbf{G}} d \right) \le (a \cdot c) \overset{*}{\longleftrightarrow}_{\mathbf{G}} (b \cdot d). \tag{8}$$

3   Fuzzy Inference Mechanism

Let X be a non-empty classical set. Let $\mathcal{F}(X)$ denote the set of all fuzzy sets on X. Given two non-empty classical sets X, Y, a multiple Single Input Single Output (SISO) rule base of n rules is of the form:

$$\textbf{IF } \tilde{x} \text{ is } A_i \textbf{ THEN } \tilde{y} \text{ is } B_i, \text{ (Multiple SISO)} \tag{9}$$

where $\tilde{x}, \tilde{y}$ are the linguistic variables and $A_i, B_i, i = 1, 2, \ldots n$ are the linguistic values taken by the linguistic variables. These linguistic values are represented by fuzzy sets in their corresponding domains.

Now, given any input " $\tilde{x}$ is A' ", the main objective of an inference mechanism is to find B' such that " $\tilde{y}$ is B' ".

3.1   Bandler-Kohout Subproduct

Pedrycz [9] proposed an inference mechanism based on the Bandler-Kohout Subproduct composition. For a given SISO rule base (9), the Bandler-Kohout Subproduct (BKS) inference mechanism is denoted as :

$$B' = A' \triangleleft R, \tag{10}$$

where $A' \in \mathcal{F}(X)$ is the input, the relation $R : X \times Y \to [0, 1]$ i.e, $R \in \mathcal{F}(X \times Y)$ represents the rule base, B' is the obtained output and $\triangleleft$ is the mapping $\triangleleft \colon \mathcal{F}(X) \times \mathcal{F}(X \times Y) \to \mathcal{F}(Y)$ given as :

$$B'(y) = \bigwedge_{x \in X} [A'(x) \longrightarrow R(x, y)], \qquad y \in Y, \tag{BKS-R}$$

with $\longrightarrow$ interpreted as a fuzzy implication. The operator $\triangleleft$ is also known as the inf $-I$ composition where I is a fuzzy implication.

3.2 BK-Subproduct with Yager's Classes of Fuzzy Implications

In this work, we consider the BKS inference mechanism, where the fuzzy implication is one of the Yager's classes of implications. Essentially, we interpret the $\longrightarrow$ in (BKS-R) as an f- or g-implication and denote the modified BKS inference mechanism as $\lhd_f$ and $\lhd_g$, where $\lhd_f = \inf - I_f$ and $\lhd_g = \inf - I_g$ respectively.

Further, we limit our study to the implicative form of rules with the implication being an f- or g-implication, i.e., the relation R representing the rule base is given as:

$$\hat{R}_f(x,y) = \bigwedge_{i=1}^{n} (A_i(x) \longrightarrow_f B_i(y)), \qquad x \in X, y \in Y . \tag{Imp-$\hat{R}_f$}$$

4 BKS with f-Implications: Its Suitability

Firstly, we derive some necessary and sufficient conditions for interpolativity. After defining continuity suitably, we show that continuity is equivalent to interpolativity. Finally, we show that robustness is also available to us, thus adding more choice of operations under the BKS scheme.

4.1 Interpolativity of BKS with f-Implications

Interpolativity is one of the most fundamental properties of an inference mechanism. A system is interpolative if an antecedent of a rule is given as the input then the corresponding consequent should be the inferred output, i.e.,

$$B_i = A_i \lhd R, \qquad i = 1, 2 \dots n., \ A_i \in \mathcal{F}(X), \ R \in \mathcal{F}(X \times Y).$$

Interpolativity pertains to the solvability of the fuzzy relational equations corresponding to the system. See Di Nola [3] for the results pertaining to CRI and Nosková [6], [7], Nosková and Perfilieva [11] for BKS inference.

Perfilieva and Lehmke [10] studied the continuity and interpolativity of CRI with SISO multiple rules and showed that a fuzzy relation R is a correct model of the given rulebase if and only if it is also a continuous model and thus have shown the equivalence between continuity and interpolativity. Later on Štěpnička and Jayaram [12] have undertaken a similar study for the BKS inference mechanism with R-implications.

The following result gives a necessary and sufficient condition for interpolativity for a BKS inference mechanism with an f-implication.

Theorem 1. *Let A_i for $i = 1 \dots n$ be normal. A necessary and sufficient condition for $\hat{R}_f$ to be a solution to $B_i = A_i \lhd_f R$ is as follows: For any $i, j \in \{1 \dots n\}$,*

$$\bigvee_{x \in X} (A_i(x) \cdot A_j(x)) \leq \bigwedge_{y \in Y} \left(f\left(B_i(y)\right) \overset{*}{\longleftrightarrow}_{\mathbf{G}} f\left(B_j(y)\right) \right) , \tag{11}$$

where " $\overset{*}{\longleftrightarrow}_{\mathbf{G}}$ " is the generalised Goguen biimplication and f is the generator function of the corresponding f-implication.

Proof. Since the system has interpolativity, we have, for any $y \in Y$, $i \in \mathbb{N}_n$

$$\left(A_i \lhd_f \hat{R}_f\right)(y) = B_i(y),$$

$$\Longleftrightarrow \bigwedge_{x \in X} \left(A_i(x) \longrightarrow_f \bigwedge_j \left(A_j(x) \longrightarrow_f B_j(y)\right)\right) = B_i(y),$$

$$\Longleftrightarrow A_i(x) \longrightarrow_f \left(A_j(x) \longrightarrow_f B_j(y)\right) \geq B_i(y), \qquad (\forall j, \forall x),$$

$$\Longleftrightarrow \left(A_i(x) \cdot A_j(x)\right) \longrightarrow_f B_j(y) \geq B_i(y), \qquad (\forall j, \forall x), \ (by\ (LI)),$$

$$\Longleftrightarrow f^{-1}\left(A_i(x) \cdot A_j(x) \cdot f\left(B_j(y)\right)\right) \geq B_i(y), \qquad (\forall j, \forall x),$$

$$\Longleftrightarrow A_i(x) \cdot A_j(x) \cdot f\left(B_j(y)\right) \leq f\left(B_i(y)\right), \qquad (\forall j, \forall x),$$

$$\Longleftrightarrow A_i(x) \cdot A_j(x) \leq \frac{f(B_i(y))}{f(B_j(y))}, \qquad (\forall j, \forall x).$$

Since i, j are arbitrary, interchanging them in the above inequality, we have,

$$A_j(x) \cdot A_i(x) \leq \frac{f(B_j(y))}{f(B_i(y))} .$$

Now from the above inequalities we see,

$$A_i(x) \cdot A_j(x) \leq \min\left\{\frac{f(B_i(y))}{f(B_j(y))}, \frac{f(B_j(y))}{f(B_i(y))}\right\} \qquad (\forall i, j)(\forall x, y),$$

$$\Longleftrightarrow \bigvee_{x \in X} \left(A_i(x) \cdot A_j(x)\right) \leq \bigwedge_{y \in Y} \min\left\{\frac{f(B_i(y))}{f(B_j(y))}, \frac{f(B_j(y))}{f(B_i(y))}\right\} \qquad (\forall i, j).$$

$$\square$$

4.2   Continuity of BKS with f-Implications

We call a model *correct* if interpolativity is present in the model. Štěpnička and Jayaram [12] have dealt with the continuity of the BKS inference mechanism. Since we are dealing with a non-residuated lattice structure we define continuity suitably and show that continuity is equivalent to the correctness of the model.

Definition 7. *A fuzzy relation $R \in \mathcal{F}(X \times Y)$ is said to be a continuous model of fuzzy rules (9) in a BKS inference mechanism with f-implications, if for each $i \in I$ and for each $A \in \mathcal{F}(X)$, the following inequality holds :*

$$\bigwedge_{y \in Y} \left[f\left(B_i(y)\right) \overset{*}{\longleftrightarrow}_{\mathbf{G}} f\left((A \lhd_f R)(y)\right)\right] \geq \bigwedge_{x \in X} \left[A_i(x) \overset{*}{\longleftrightarrow}_{\mathbf{G}} A(x)\right] . \qquad (12)$$

Theorem 2. *Let us consider a BKS inference mechanism with f-implications. The fuzzy relation $\hat{R}_f \in \mathcal{F}(X \times Y)$ is a correct model of fuzzy rules (9) if and only if it is a continuous model of these rules.*

Proof. Let $\hat{R}_f$ be a continuous model of the fuzzy if-then rules (9). So by **Definition 7**, the inequality (12) is valid for all $i = 1, 2, \ldots n$ and arbitrary $A \in \mathcal{F}(X)$. Now putting $A = A_i$ in (12), we have

$$\bigwedge_{y \in Y} \left[f(B_i(y)) \overset{*}{\longleftrightarrow}_{\mathbf{G}} f\left(\left(A_i \lhd_f \hat{R}_f \right)(y) \right) \right] \geq 1, \qquad (\forall i),$$

$$\implies f(B_i(y)) \overset{*}{\longleftrightarrow}_{\mathbf{G}} f\left(\left(A_i \lhd_f \hat{R}_f \right)(y) \right) = 1, \qquad (\forall i, y),$$

$$\implies f(B_i(y)) = f\left(\left(A_i \lhd_f \hat{R}_f \right)(y) \right), \qquad (\forall i, y),$$

$$\implies \left(A_i \lhd_f \hat{R}_f \right)(y) = B_i(y), \qquad (\forall i, y).$$

Thus we have interpolativity starting from continuity.

Now let us assume that the model has interpolativity. Towards proving (12), for arbitrary $y \in Y$, note that the following is true for any $i = 1, 2, \ldots n$:

$$f\left(\left(A \lhd_f \hat{R}_f \right)(y) \right) \overset{*}{\longleftrightarrow}_{\mathbf{G}} f(B_i(y))$$

$$= f\left(\left(A \lhd_f \hat{R}_f \right)(y) \right) \overset{*}{\longleftrightarrow}_{\mathbf{G}} f\left(\left(A_i \lhd_f \hat{R}_f \right)(y) \right), \quad \text{(Since } (A_i \lhd_f \hat{R}_f)(y) = B_i(y))$$

$$= f\left(\bigwedge_{x \in X} \left[A(x) \longrightarrow_f \hat{R}_f(x,y) \right] \right) \overset{*}{\longleftrightarrow}_{\mathbf{G}} f\left(\bigwedge_{x \in X} \left[A_i(x) \longrightarrow_f \hat{R}_f(x,y) \right] \right)$$

$$= f\left\{ \bigwedge_{x \in X} f^{-1}\left[A(x) \cdot f\left(\hat{R}_f(x,y) \right) \right] \right\} \overset{*}{\longleftrightarrow}_{\mathbf{G}} f\left\{ \bigwedge_{x \in X} f^{-1}\left[A_i(x) \cdot f\left(\hat{R}_f(x,y) \right) \right] \right\}$$

$$= \bigvee_{x \in X} \left[A(x) \cdot f\left(\hat{R}_f(x,y) \right) \right] \overset{*}{\longleftrightarrow}_{\mathbf{G}} \bigvee_{x \in X} \left[A_i(x) \cdot f\left(\hat{R}_f(x,y) \right) \right]$$

$$\geq \bigwedge_{x \in X} \left[A(x) \cdot f\left(\hat{R}_f(x,y) \right) \overset{*}{\longleftrightarrow}_{\mathbf{G}} A_i(x) \cdot f\left(\hat{R}_f(x,y) \right) \right] \qquad (\text{Using}(7))$$

$$\geq \bigwedge_{x \in X} \left(\left[A(x) \overset{*}{\longleftrightarrow}_{\mathbf{G}} A_i(x) \right] \cdot \left[f(\hat{R}_f(x,y)) \overset{*}{\longleftrightarrow}_{\mathbf{G}} f(\hat{R}_f(x,y)) \right] \right) \qquad (\text{Using}(8))$$

$$= \bigwedge_{x \in X} \left[A(x) \overset{*}{\longleftrightarrow}_{\mathbf{G}} A_i(x) \right] .$$

from which we obtain (12). $\qquad \square$

4.3 Robustness of BKS with f-Implications

Similar to the equivalence relation in classical set theory, similarity relation or fuzzy equivalence relation has been proposed. Similarity relations have been used to characterize the inherent indistinguishability in a fuzzy system [5].

Definition 8 ([5], Definition 2.5). *A similarity relation $E \colon X \times X \to [0,1]$ with respect to the t-norm $\star$ on X is a fuzzy relation over $X \times X$ which satisfies the conditions :*

- $E(x, x) = 1.$ *(Reflexivity)*
- $E(x, y) = E(y, x).$ *(Symmetry)*
- $E(x, y) \star E(y, z) \leq E(x, z).$ *($\star$ -Transitivity)*

We denote a fuzzy equivalence relation by $(E, \star)$.

Definition 9 ([5], Definition 2.7). *A fuzzy set $A \in \mathcal{F}(X)$ is called extensional with respect to a fuzzy equivalence relation E on X if,*

$$A(x) \star E(x, y) \leq A(y), \qquad x, y \in X.$$

Definition 10 ([5], Definition 2.8). *Let $A \in \mathcal{F}(X)$ and $(E, \star)$ be a fuzzy equivalence relation on X. The fuzzy set,*

$$\hat{A}(x) = \bigvee \{C : A \leq C \text{ and } C \text{ is extensional w.r.to } E\},$$

is called the extensional hull of A. By $A \leq C$ we mean that for all $x \in X, A(x) \leq C(x)$, i.e, ordering in the sense of inclusion.

Proposition 3 ([5], Proposition 2.9). *Let $A \in \mathcal{F}(X)$ and $(E, \star)$ be a fuzzy equivalence relation on X. Then*

$$\hat{A}(x) = \bigvee \{A(y) \star E(x, y) \mid y \in X\} .$$

The robustness of CRI was dealt with by Klawonn and Castro [5]. Later on Štěpnička and Jayaram [12] have undertaken a similar study for BKS inference mechanism with R-implications. Here we present a result on the robustness of BKS with f-generated implications.

Theorem 3. *Let us consider the rule base (9). Let $(E, \cdot)$ w.r.to product t-norm be a fuzzy equivalence relation on X w.r.to which every A_i is extensional for $i = 1, 2, \ldots n$. Then for any fuzzy set $A' \in \mathcal{F}(X)$,*

$$A' \vartriangleleft_f \hat{R}_f = \hat{A}' \vartriangleleft_f \hat{R}_f .$$

Proof. Let $R \in \mathcal{F}(X \times Y)$. Now by definition of $\hat{A}'$ we have the following:

$$\hat{A}' \geq A' \Longrightarrow \hat{A}' \longrightarrow_f \hat{R}_f \leq A' \longrightarrow_f \hat{R}_f \Longrightarrow \hat{A}' \vartriangleleft_f \hat{R}_f \leq A' \vartriangleleft_f \hat{R}_f .$$

Since $\hat{R}_f$ is given by (Imp-$\hat{R}_f$), we have

$$\hat{A}' \vartriangleleft_f \hat{R}_f = \bigwedge_{x \in X} \left[\hat{A}'(x) \longrightarrow_f \bigwedge_{i=1}^{n} \left(A_i(x) \longrightarrow_f B_i(y) \right) \right], \qquad y \in Y.$$

Since every A_i is extensional with respect to E, for any $x, x' \in X$ and for any $i = 1, 2, \ldots n$, we have,

$$A_i(x') \geq A_i(x) \cdot E(x, x')$$
$$\Longrightarrow A_i(x') \longrightarrow_f B_i(y) \leq [A_i(x) \cdot E(x, x')] \longrightarrow_f B_i(y), \qquad y \in Y. \qquad (13)$$

Now for any $x \in X$,

$$\hat{A}'(x) \longrightarrow_f \bigwedge_{i=1}^{n} (A_i(x) \longrightarrow_f B_i(y))$$

$$= \left(\bigvee_{x' \in X} [A'(x') \star E(x,x')] \right) \longrightarrow_f \bigwedge_{i=1}^{n} (A_i(x) \longrightarrow_f B_i(y)), \qquad \text{(Using Proposition 3)}$$

$$= \bigwedge_{x' \in X} \left([A'(x') \star E(x,x')] \longrightarrow_f \bigwedge_{i=1}^{n} (A_i(x) \longrightarrow_f B_i(y)) \right), \qquad \text{(Using (4))}$$

$$= \bigwedge_{i=1}^{n} \bigwedge_{x' \in X} ([A'(x') \star E(x,x')] \longrightarrow_f (A_i(x) \longrightarrow_f B_i(y))), \qquad \text{(Using (3))}$$

$$= \bigwedge_{i=1}^{n} \bigwedge_{x' \in X} (A'(x') \longrightarrow_f [E(x,x') \longrightarrow_f (A_i(x) \longrightarrow_f B_i(y))]), \qquad \text{(By (LI)}$$

$$= \bigwedge_{i=1}^{n} \bigwedge_{x' \in X} (A'(x') \longrightarrow_f [(E(x,x') \star A_i(x)) \longrightarrow_f B_i(y)]), \qquad \text{(By (LI)}$$

$$\geq \bigwedge_{i=1}^{n} \bigwedge_{x' \in X} (A'(x') \longrightarrow_f [A_i(x') \longrightarrow_f B_i(y)]) \qquad \text{(Using (13))}$$

$$= (A' \lhd_f \hat{R}_f)(y) .$$

Thus $\hat{A}' \lhd_f \hat{R}_f \geq A' \lhd_f \hat{R}_f$ and the result follows. $\qquad \square$

5   BKS with g-Implications

In this section we consider the BKS inference mechanism with g-implication and we repeat the above analysis. Once again, we employ the implicative model of rules with the relation $\hat{R}_g$ which is obtained from (Imp-$\hat{R}_f$) with $\longrightarrow = \longrightarrow_g$. Due to space constraints we state only the results without the proofs.

Theorem 4. *Let A_i for $i = 1, 2, \ldots n$ be normal. A necessary and sufficient condition for $\hat{R}_g$ to be a solution to $B_i = A_i \lhd_g R$ is as follows: For any $i, j \in \{1, 2, \ldots n\}$,*

$$\bigvee_{x \in X} (A_i(x) \cdot A_j(x)) \leq \bigwedge_{y \in Y} (g(B_i(y)) \overset{*}{\longleftrightarrow}_{G} g(B_j(y))) .$$

where 'g' is the generator function of the corresponding g-implication.

Definition 11. *A fuzzy relation $R \in \mathcal{F}(X \times Y)$ is said to be a continuous model of fuzzy rules (9) in a BKS inference mechanism with g-implications, if for each $i \in I$ and for each $A \in \mathcal{F}(X)$, the following inequality holds :*

$$\bigwedge_{y \in Y} \left[g(B_i(y)) \overset{*}{\longleftrightarrow}_{G} g((A \lhd_g R)(y)) \right] \geq \bigwedge_{x \in X} \left[A_i(x) \overset{*}{\longleftrightarrow}_{G} A(x) \right] .$$

Theorem 5. *Let us consider a BKS inference mechanism with g-implications. The fuzzy relation $\hat{R}_g \in \mathcal{F}(X \times Y)$ is a correct model of fuzzy rules (9) if and only if it is a continuous model of these rules.*

Theorem 6. *Let us consider the rule base (9). Let E w.r.to product t-norm be a fuzzy equivalence relation on X w.r.to which every A_i is extensional for $i = 1 \ldots n$. Then for any fuzzy set $A' \in \mathcal{F}(X)$,*

$$A' \lhd_g \hat{R}_g = \hat{A}' \lhd_g \hat{R}_g.$$

6   Concluding Remarks

In this work, we have shown that the properties like interpolativity, continuity and robustness which are available for the BKS inference mechanism with residuated implications are also available when we employ the Yager's classes of fuzzy implications.

References

1. Baczyński, M., Jayaram, B.: Fuzzy Implications. STUDFUZZ, vol. 231. Springer, Heidelberg (2008)
2. Bandler, W., Kohout, L.J.: Semantics of implication operators and fuzzy relational products. Internat. J. Man-Mach. Stud. 12, 89–116 (1979)
3. Di Nola, A., Sessa, S., Pedrycz, W., Sanchez, E.: Fuzzy Relational Equations and their Applications to Knowledge Engineering. Kluwer Academic Publishers, Boston (1989)
4. Klement, E.P., Mesiar, R., Pap, E.: Triangular norms. Kluwer, Dordrecht (2000)
5. Klawonn, F., Castro, J.L.: Similarity in fuzzy reasoning. Mathware and Soft Computing 2, 197–228 (1995)
6. Nosková, L.: Systems of fuzzy relation equation with $inf \rightarrow$ composition: solvability and solution. J. of Electrical Eng. 12(s), 69–72 (2005)
7. Nosková, L.: Systems of fuzzy relation equations: Criteria of Solvability. In: Proceedings of IPMU (2006)
8. Novák, V., Perfilieva, I., Močkǒr, J.: Mathematical Principles of Fuzzy Logic. Kluwer Academic Publishers, Boston (1999)
9. Pedrycz, W.: Application of fuzzy relational equations for methods of reasoning in presence of fuzzy data. Fuzzy Sets and Syst. 16, 163–175 (1985)
10. Perfilieva, I., Lehmke, S.: Correct models of fuzzy if-then rules are continuous. Fuzzy Sets and Syst. 157, 3188–3197 (2006)
11. Perfilieva, I., Nosková, L.: Systems of fuzzy relation equation with $inf \rightarrow$ composition: complete set of solution. Fuzzy Sets and Syst. 159, 2256–2271 (2008)
12. Štěpnička, M., Jayaram, B.: On the suitability of the Bandler-Kohout subproduct as an inference mechanism. IEEE Trans. on Fuzzy Syst. 18, 285–298 (2010)
13. Yager, R.R.: On some new classes of implication operators and their role in approximate reasoning. Inform. Sci. 167, 193–216 (2004)
14. Zadeh, L.A.: Outline of a new approach to the analysis of complex systems and decision processes. IEEE Trans. on Syst. Man and Cyber. 3, 28–44 (1973)

Solving General Fuzzy Relation Equations Using Property-Oriented Concept Lattices*

Juan Carlos Díaz, Jesús Medina**, and Rafael Rodríguez

Department of Mathematics, University of Cádiz
{juancarlos.diaz,jesus.medina,rafael.rodriguez}@uca.es

Abstract. A generalization of the classical fuzzy relation equations has been introduced in order to consider any residuated conjunctor. Moreover, these equations can be solved using the theory of a general property-oriented concept lattice.

Keywords: Fuzzy relation equations, Galois connection, property-oriented concept lattice.

1 Introduction

In the 70's, fuzzy relation equations were introduced by E. Sanchez [20], and they are associated with the composition of fuzzy relations. These equations have been used to investigate theoretical and applicational aspects of fuzzy set theory [8], e.g., approximate reasoning, time series forecast, decision making, fuzzy control, as an appropriate tool for handling and modeling of non-probabilistic form of uncertainty, etc. Solving these kind of equations is an important goal and it has been investigated in several papers, e.g., in [1,7,8,18].

This paper presents a generalization of the classical fuzzy relation equations [17,20] in order to consider any residuated conjunctor, and that provides more flexibility in order to relate the variables considered in the system. Moreover, these equations can be solved using the theory of a general property-oriented concept lattice. Specifically, the existence of solutions of a system of general fuzzy relation equations is given using concept lattices theory. Furthermore, if this system has a solution, the largest solution has been related to a concept of a property-oriented concept lattice and more solutions have been obtained in this concept lattice environment.

The relation introduced provides important properties for systems of fuzzy relation equations, which can be given from the results proved, such as in [2,12,19]. Furthermore, in order to obtain the solutions of these kinds of systems, the algorithms developed, for example, in [3,4,14], can be applied.

---

* Partially supported by the Spanish Science Ministry TIN2009-14562-C05-03 and by Junta de Andalucía project P09-FQM-5233.
** Corresponding author.

S. Greco et al. (Eds.): IPMU 2012, Part II, CCIS 298, pp. 395–404, 2012.
© Springer-Verlag Berlin Heidelberg 2012

2 Fuzzy Property-Oriented Concept Lattices

This section recalls a fuzzy generalization of the property-oriented concept lattices presented in [15]. Adjoint triples are the basic operators in this environment, which are formed by three mappings: a non-commutativity conjunctor and two residuated implications [13], that satisfy the well-known adjoint property.

Definition 1 ([16]). *Let* $(P_1, \leq_1)$, $(P_2, \leq_2)$, $(P_3, \leq_3)$ *be posets and* $\&\colon P_1 \times P_2 \to P_3$, $\swarrow\colon P_3 \times P_2 \to P_1$, $\nwarrow\colon P_3 \times P_1 \to P_2$ *be mappings, then* $(\&, \swarrow, \nwarrow)$ *is* an *adjoint triple* with respect to P_1, P_2, P_3 *if:*

1. $\&$ *is order-preserving in both arguments.*
2. $\swarrow$ *and* $\nwarrow$ *are order-preserving on the first argument[1] and order-reversing on the second argument.*
3. $x \leq_1 z \swarrow y$ *iff* $x \& y \leq_3 z$ *iff* $y \leq_2 z \nwarrow x$, *where* $x \in P_1$, $y \in P_2$ *and* $z \in P_3$.

Example of adjoint triples are the Gödel, product and Łukasiewicz t-norms together with their residuated implications.

Example 1. Since the Gödel, product and Łukasiewicz t-norms are commutative, the residuated implications satisfy that $\swarrow^G = \nwarrow_G$, $\swarrow^P = \nwarrow_P$ and $\swarrow^L = \nwarrow_L$. Therefore, the Gödel, product and Łukasiewicz adjoint triples are defined on $[0,1]$ as:

$$\&_P(x,y) = x \cdot y \qquad\qquad z \nwarrow_P x = \begin{cases} 1 & \text{if } x \leq z \\ z/x & \text{otherwise} \end{cases}$$

$$\&_G(x,y) = \min\{x,y\} \qquad z \nwarrow_G x = \begin{cases} 1 & \text{if } x \leq z \\ z & \text{otherwise} \end{cases}$$

$$\&_L(x,y) = \max\{0, x+y-1\} \quad z \nwarrow_L x = \min\{1, 1-x+z\}$$

More general examples of adjoint triples can be given.

Example 2. Let $[0,1]_m$ be a regular partition of $[0,1]$ in m pieces, for example $[0,1]_2 = \{0, 0.5, 1\}$ divide the unit interval in two pieces.

A discretization of the Gödel t-norm is, e.g., the operator $\&_G^*\colon [0,1]_{20} \times [0,1]_8 \to [0,1]_{100}$ defined, for each $x \in [0,1]_{20}$ and $y \in [0,1]_8$, as:

$$x \&_G^* y = \frac{\lceil 100 \cdot \min\{x,y\} \rceil}{100}$$

where $\lceil \_ \rceil$ is the ceiling function.

For this operator, the corresponding residuated implication operators $\swarrow_G^*$ $\colon [0,1]_{100} \times [0,1]_8 \to [0,1]_{20}$ and $\nwarrow_G^*\colon [0,1]_{100} \times [0,1]_{20} \to [0,1]_8$ are defined as:

$$b \swarrow_G^* a = \frac{\lfloor 20 \cdot (b \swarrow^G a) \rfloor}{20} \qquad\qquad b \nwarrow_G^* c = \frac{\lfloor 8 \cdot (b \nwarrow_G a) \rfloor}{8}$$

where $\lfloor \_ \rfloor$ is the floor function.

---

[1] Note that the antecedent will be evaluated on the right side, while the consequent will be evaluated on the left side, as in logic programming framework.

The triple $(\&_G^*, \diagup_G^*, \diagdown_G^*)$ is an adjoint triple, although the operator $\&_G^*$ is neither commutative nor associative.

The basic structure, which fixes the triplet of lattices and the adjoint triple, is the fuzzy property-oriented frame.

Definition 2. *Given two complete lattices* $(L_1, \preceq_1)$ *and* $(L_2, \preceq_2)$, *a poset* $(P, \leq)$ *and one adjoint triple with respect to* P, L_2, L_1, $(\&, \diagup, \diagdown)$, *a fuzzy property-oriented frame is the tuple*

$$(L_1, L_2, P, \preceq_1, \preceq_2, \leq, \&)$$

Fuzzy property-oriented context is defined analogously to the one given in [16].

Definition 3. *Let* $(L_1, L_2, P, \&)$ *be a fuzzy property-oriented frame. A context is a tuple* (A, B, R) *such that* A *and* B *are non-empty sets (usually interpreted as attributes and objects, respectively),* R *is a* P-*fuzzy relation* $R \colon A \times B \to P$

From now on, we will fix a fuzzy property-oriented frame $(L_1, L_2, P, \&)$ and context (A, B, R). The mappings $^{\uparrow \pi} \colon L_2^B \to L_1^A$ and $^{\downarrow^N} \colon L_1^A \to L_2^B$ are defined as

$$g^{\uparrow \pi}(a) = \sup\{R(a, b) \& g(b) \mid b \in B\}$$

$$f^{\downarrow^N}(b) = \inf\{f(a) \diagdown R(a, b) \mid a \in A\}$$

These definitions generalize the classical possibility and necessity operators [11]. Moreover, $(^{\uparrow \pi}, ^{\downarrow^N})$ is an isotone Galois connection and $^{\uparrow \pi \downarrow^N} \colon L_2^B \to L_2^B$ is a closure operator and $^{\downarrow^N \uparrow \pi} \colon L_1^A \to L_1^A$ is an interior operator.

A concept, in this environment, is a pair of mappings $\langle g, f \rangle$, with $g \in L^B, f \in L^A$, such that $g^{\uparrow \pi} = f$ and $f^{\downarrow^N} = g$, which will be called *fuzzy property-oriented concept*. In that case, g is called the *extent* and f, the *intent* of the concept. The set of all these concepts will be notated as $\mathcal{F}_{\pi N}$.

Definition 4. *A* fuzzy property-oriented concept lattice *is the set*

$$\mathcal{F}_{\pi N} = \{\langle g, f \rangle \mid g \in L_2^B, f \in L_1^A \text{ and } g^{\uparrow \pi} = f, f^{\downarrow^N} = g\}$$

in which the ordering is defined by $\langle g_1, f_1 \rangle \preceq \langle g_2, f_2 \rangle$ *iff* $g_1 \preceq_2 g_2$ *(or equivalently* $f_1 \preceq_1 f_2$*).*

The pair $(\mathcal{F}_{\pi N}, \preceq)$ is a complete lattice [15], which generalizes the concept lattice introduced in [6] to a fuzzy environment.

3   General Fuzzy Relation Equations

A generalization of the classical fuzzy relation equations [20] will be introduced in this section, which was proposed in [9]. For that, we will consider adjoint triples as generalization of the sup-∗-composition, introduced in [21], and inf-→-composition, introduced in [1]. From now on, two lattices $(L_1, \preceq_1)$, $(L_2, \preceq_2)$, a poset $(P, \preceq)$ and an adjoint triple $(\&, \nearrow, \diagdown)$ will be fixed.

Let $U = \{u_1, \dots, u_m\}$ and $V = \{v_1, \dots, v_n\}$ be two universes, $R \in L_2^{U \times V}$ an unknown fuzzy relation, and $K_1 \dots, K_n \in P^U$, $D_1, \dots, D_n \in L_1^V$ as arbitrarily chosen fuzzy subsets of respective universes.

A *system of fuzzy relation equations with sup-&-composition* is the following system of equations

$$\bigvee_{u \in U} (K_i(u) \,\&\, R(u,v)) = D_i(v) \tag{1}$$

for all $i \in \{1, \dots, n\}$.

If an element v of V is fixed and for each $i \in \{1, \dots, n\}$, $j \in \{1, \dots, m\}$, $K_i(u_j) = k_{ij}$, $R(u_j, v) = x_j$, $D_i(v) = d_i$, then System (1) can be written as

$$
\begin{aligned}
k_{11} \,\&\, x_1 \vee \cdots \vee k_{1m} \,\&\, x_m &= d_1 \\
\vdots \quad \vdots \qquad \quad \vdots \quad \vdots \\
k_{n1} \,\&\, x_1 \vee \cdots \vee k_{nm} \,\&\, x_m &= d_n
\end{aligned}
\tag{2}
$$

Hence, for each $v \in V$, if we solve System (2), then we obtain a "column" of R (i.e. the elements $R(u_j, v)$, with $j \in \{1, \dots, m\}$). Thus, solving n similar systems, one for each $v \in V$, the unknown relation R is obtained.

On the other hand, we can assume equations with an implication as operator. A *system of fuzzy relation equations with inf-$\diagdown$-composition*, that is

$$\bigwedge_{v \in V} (R(u,v) \diagdown K_j^*(v)) = E_j(u) \tag{3}$$

for all $j \in \{1, \dots, m\}$, that is considered with respect to unknown fuzzy relation $R \in L_1^{U \times V}$, and where $K_1^*, \dots, K_m^* \in P^V$ and $E_1, \dots, E_m \in L_2^U$.

If an element $u \in U$ is fixed, fuzzy subsets $K_1^*, \dots, K_m^* \in P^V$, $E_1, \dots, E_m \in L_2^U$ are assumed, such that $K_j^*(v_i) = k_{ij}$, $R(u, v_i) = y_i$ and $E_j(u) = e_j$, for each $i \in \{1, \dots, n\}$, $j \in \{1, \dots, m\}$, then System (3) can be written as

$$
\begin{aligned}
y_1 \diagdown k_{11} \wedge \cdots \wedge y_n \diagdown k_{n1} &= e_1 \\
\vdots \qquad \quad \vdots \qquad \quad \vdots \quad \vdots \\
y_1 \diagdown k_{1m} \wedge \cdots \wedge y_n \diagdown k_{nm} &= e_m
\end{aligned}
\tag{4}
$$

Therefore, for each $u \in U$, we obtain a "row" of R (i.e. the elements $R(u, v_i)$, with $i \in \{1, \dots, n\}$), consequently, solving m similar systems, the unknown relation R is obtained.

Systems (2) and (4) have the same aim, searching for the unknown relation R although the mechanism is different.

3.1   Solving General Fuzzy Relation Equations

This section shows that Systems (2) and (4) can be interpreted as a fuzzy property-oriented concept lattice, and so, the properties given to the isotone

Galois connection $(\uparrow_\pi, \downarrow^N)$, as well as to the complete lattice $\mathcal{F}_{\pi N}$ can be used in the resolution of these systems. Hence, the environment given to define Systems (2) and (4) is assumed.

Now, two mappings will be introduced which provide the relation between both environments, the fuzzy property-oriented concept lattice framework and the general fuzzy relation equations given above. The first one is $C_K \colon L_2^m \to L_1^n$, where $C_K(\bar{x})$ has n components $C_K(\bar{x})_i$, and which is defined as:

$$C_K(\bar{x})_i = k_{i1} \,\&\, x_1 \vee \cdots \vee k_{im} \,\&\, x_m \tag{5}$$

for each $i \in \{1,\dots,n\}$ and $\bar{x} = (x_1,\dots,x_m) \in L_2^m$. The other mapping is $I_{K^*} \colon L_1^n \to L_2^m$ that has m components $I_{K^*}(\bar{y})_j$, and it is defined as

$$I_{K^*}(\bar{y})_j = y_1 \nwarrow k_{1j} \wedge \cdots \wedge y_n \nwarrow k_{nj} \tag{6}$$

for each $j \in \{1,\dots,m\}$ and $\bar{y} = (y_1,\dots,y_n) \in L_1^n$.

If we assume a system of fuzzy relation equations with sup-&-composition, a fuzzy context (A, B, S) can be considered, where $A = \{a_1,\dots,a_n\}$ is a set of arbitrary attributes with the same cardinality of V, set $B = \{b_1,\dots,b_m\}$ is formed by arbitrary objects with the same cardinality of U, and $S \colon A \times B \to P$ is defined as $S(a_i, b_j) = k_{ij}$, for all $i \in \{1,\dots,n\}$, $j \in \{1,\dots,m\}$. In this framework, the following result holds.

Proposition 1. *For each $\bar{x} \in L_2^m$ and $\bar{y} \in L_1^n$, there exist $\mu \in L_2^B$ and $\lambda \in L_1^A$, such that $\mu^{\uparrow_\pi}(a_i) = C_K(\bar{x})_i$, $\lambda^{\downarrow^N}(b_j) = I_{K^*}(\bar{y})_j$, for all $i \in \{1,\dots,n\}$ and $j \in \{1,\dots,m\}$.*

As a consequence, the mappings $C_K \colon L_2^m \to L_1^n$ and $I_{K^*} \colon L_1^n \to L_2^m$ are equivalent to the mappings $\uparrow_\pi \colon L_2^B \to L_1^A$ and $\downarrow^N \colon L_1^A \to L_2^B$, respectively.

Since (C_K, I_{K^*}) is an isotone Galois connection, any result in order to solve one system of fuzzy relation equations has its dual counterpart in the other system, which can be obtained by replacing C_K with I_{K^*}, $\leq$ with $\geq$, $\vee$ with $\wedge$, respectively. The following result explains when these systems can be solved and how a solution can be obtained.

Theorem 1. *Given the above environment to define Systems (2) and (4), we have that System (2) can be solved if and only if $I_{K^*}(\bar{d})$ is a solution. In this case, $I_{K^*}(\bar{d})$ is the largest solution.*

Moreover, System (4) can be solved if and only if $C_K(\bar{e})$ is a solution, which is the smallest solution.

Considering the environment needed to define Systems (2) and (4), there exists a context (A, B, S) such that to solve System (2) is equivalent to obtaining a mapping $\mu \in L_2^B$, which verifies

$$\mu^{\uparrow_\pi} = \lambda_{\bar{d}} \tag{7}$$

where $\lambda_{\bar{d}} \in L_1^A$ is defined as $\lambda_{\bar{d}}(a_i) = d_i$, for all $i \in \{1,\dots,n\}$. Similarly, there exists a context (A, B, S) such that System (4) can be solved if and only there exists a mapping $\lambda \in L_1^A$, which satisfies

$$\lambda^{\downarrow^N} = \mu_{\bar{e}} \tag{8}$$

where $\mu_{\bar{e}} \in L_2^B$, defined as $\mu_{\bar{e}}(b_j) = e_j$, for all $j \in \{1, \ldots, m\}$. Consequently, Theorem 1 can be rewritten as follows:

Lemma 1. *Given the above environment, we obtain that System (2) can be solved if and only if $\lambda_{\bar{d}}^{\downarrow^N \uparrow_\pi} = \lambda_{\bar{d}}$.*

Similarly, System (4) can be solved if and only if $\mu_{\bar{e}}^{\uparrow_\pi \downarrow^N} = \mu_{\bar{e}}$.

From Lemma 1 and the definition of fuzzy property-oriented concept lattice $\mathcal{F}_{\pi N}$, the following consequence can be stabilized.

Theorem 2. *System (2) can be solved if and only if $\langle \lambda_{\bar{d}}^{\downarrow^N}, \lambda_{\bar{d}} \rangle$ is a concept of $\mathcal{F}_{\pi N}$. Furthermore, System (4) can be solved if and only if $\langle \mu_{\bar{e}}, \mu_{\bar{e}}^{\uparrow_\pi} \rangle$ is a concept of $\mathcal{F}_{\pi N}$.*

The relation introduced above provides more important properties for Systems (2) and (4), which can be proved from the results given, for example, in [2,12,19], applying Theorem 2. Furthermore, in order to obtain the solutions of Systems (2) and (4), the algorithms developed, for example, in [3,4,14], can be applied.

Example 3. In this example, we will consider one given in [5], in which the authors assume a fuzzy relational equation and they look for (minimal) solutions. Here, we will assume this fuzzy relation equation, together with other equations in order to form a system of fuzzy relational equations, and we will prove that the system has a solution and we will attain the largest solution.

Let $U = \{u_1, u_2, u_3, u_4\}$ and $V = \{v_1, v_2, v_3, v_4, v_5\}$ be two universes, $R \in [0,1]^{U \times V}$ an unknown fuzzy relation, which is represented by the matrix $R = (R(u_i, v_j))$ and $K_1, K_2, K_3, K_4, K_5 \in [0,1]^U$, $D_1, D_2, D_3, D_4, D_5 \in [0,1]^V$ fuzzy sets in U and V, defined by the following matrices K and D

$$K = \begin{pmatrix} 0.3 & 0.2 & 0.7 & 0.8 \\ 0.5 & 0.4 & 0.4 & 0.9 \\ 0.7 & 0.3 & 0.2 & 0.7 \\ 0.9 & 0.6 & 0.1 & 0.2 \\ 0.8 & 0.5 & 0.6 & 0.4 \end{pmatrix} \qquad D = \begin{pmatrix} 0.7 & 0.3 & 0.3 & 0.5 & 0.8 \\ 0.4 & 0.4 & 0.4 & 0.5 & 0.9 \\ 0.4 & 0.3 & 0.3 & 0.7 & 0.7 \\ 0.3 & 0.4 & 0.6 & 0.9 & 0.5 \\ 0.6 & 0.4 & 0.5 & 0.8 & 0.6 \end{pmatrix}$$

as $K_i(u_j) = K(i,j)$ and $D_i(v_j) = D(i,j)$. Therefore, the mappings K_i and D_i are given by the rows of K and D, respectively.

The goal will be to obtain a matrix R, such that $K \odot R = D$, where $\odot$ is the *sup-&-composition* and the conjunctor & is the minimum, $\&(x,y) = min(x,y)$. Hence, the fuzzy property-oriented frame considered will be $([0,1], [0,1], [0,1], \&)$, and the context (A, B, S) will be $A = \{a_1, a_2, a_3, a_4, a_5\}$, $B = \{b_1, b_2, b_3, b_4\}$, and $S \in [0,1]^{A \times B}$ defined as $S(a_i, b_j) = k_{ij}$. The fuzzy property-oriented concept lattice associated to the frame and context above will be denoted as $\mathcal{F}_{\pi N}$.

Note that the number of attributes is equal to the cardinality of V and the number of objects is equal to the cardinality of U.

Following the steps given by the theoretical results, we need to consider the fuzzy subsets $\lambda_1, \lambda_2, \lambda_3, \lambda_4, \lambda_5 \in [0,1]^A$ associated to the columns of the matrix D, that is, for λ_1 we have $\lambda_1(a_1) = 0.7$, $\lambda_1(a_2) = 0.4$, $\lambda_1(a_3) = 0.4$, $\lambda_1(a_4) = 0.3$, $\lambda_1(a_5) = 0.6$. Therefore, $\lambda_j(a_i) = D(i,j)$, for all $i, j \in \{1,\ldots,5\}$.

Now, we need to check whether the fuzzy subsets of attributes $\lambda_1, \lambda_2, \lambda_3, \lambda_4, \lambda_5$ are the intent of a concept in $\mathcal{F}_{\pi N}$.

For that, first of all, it is necessary to compute the fuzzy subsets of objects $\lambda_1^{\downarrow^N}, \lambda_2^{\downarrow^N}, \lambda_3^{\downarrow^N}, \lambda_4^{\downarrow^N}, \lambda_5^{\downarrow^N}$. The mappings $\lambda_i^{\downarrow^N}$ will be given as a list of values.

$$\lambda_1^{\downarrow^N} = (0.3, 0.3, 1, 0.4) \qquad \lambda_2^{\downarrow^N} = (0.3, 0.4, 0.3, 0.3)$$
$$\lambda_3^{\downarrow^N} = (0.3, 1, 0.3, 0.3) \qquad \lambda_4^{\downarrow^N} = (1, 1, 0.5, 0.5)$$
$$\lambda_5^{\downarrow^N} = (0.5, 0.5, 1, 1)$$

Now, we apply the mapping $\uparrow^\pi$ to these subsets and, finally, we must check the following equality:

$$\lambda_j^{\downarrow^N \uparrow^\pi} = \lambda_j$$

for all $j \in \{1,\ldots,5\}$.

As these equalities are verified, then the system $K \odot R = D$ is solvable and the largest solution is given by the matrix R in which each element of the matrix $R(i,j)$ is $\lambda_j^{\downarrow^N}(b_i)$, for all $i \in \{1,\ldots,4\}$ and $j \in \{1,\ldots,5\}$.

$$R = \begin{pmatrix} 0.3 & 0.3 & 0.3 & 1 & 0.5 \\ 0.3 & 0.4 & 1 & 1 & 0.5 \\ 1 & 0.3 & 0.3 & 0.5 & 1 \\ 0.4 & 0.3 & 0.3 & 0.5 & 1 \end{pmatrix}$$

Note that the system associated to the first column of D has a solution and this solution (the vector $(0.3, 0.3, 1, 0.4)$) is equal to the one obtained in [5] but now using a fuzzy concept lattice framework and an algorithm developed in this mathematical environment.

Thus, we have a new tool in order to prove the existence of solutions of the equations $K \odot R = D$, where R is an unknown matrix. Moreover, fuzzy property-oriented concept lattices theory is used to obtain the largest solution.

3.2   Set of Solutions

Another important goal in fuzzy relation equation is to obtain minimal solutions. In this section we have given a first step in this direction. We have shown that a subset of solutions of a system is given by the mappings between the extents of two concepts, the one given by the largest solution and a lower neighbor of it, $\langle g_0, f_0 \rangle \in \mathcal{F}_{\pi N}$, that is, $\langle g_0, f_0 \rangle$ satisfies $\langle g_0, f_0 \rangle \prec \langle \lambda_{\bar{d}}^{\downarrow^N}, \lambda_{\bar{d}} \rangle$ and that there is not $\langle g_1, f_1 \rangle \in \mathcal{F}_{\pi N}$, such that $\langle g_0, f_0 \rangle \prec \langle g_1, f_1 \rangle \prec \langle \lambda_{\bar{d}}^{\downarrow^N}, \lambda_{\bar{d}} \rangle$.

Theorem 3. *Considered the environment needed to define Systems (2) and (4) and a lower neighbor concept $\langle g_0, f_0 \rangle$ of $\langle \lambda_{\bar{d}}^{\downarrow^N}, \lambda_{\bar{d}} \rangle$. Given $g \in L_2^B$ verifying $g_0 \prec_2 g \prec_2 \lambda_{\bar{d}}^{\downarrow^N}$, we obtain that g is a solution of System (2).*

The minimal solutions are the minimal elements of the set of mappings $\{g \in L_2^B \mid g^{\uparrow_\pi \downarrow^N} = \lambda_{\bar{d}}^{\downarrow^N}\}$. Hence, by the previous theorem we have the following result.

Proposition 2. *Given* $\langle g_1, f_1 \rangle, \langle g_2, f_2 \rangle, \ldots, \langle g_n, f_n \rangle \in L_2^B$ *lower neighbors of the largest solution of System 2,* $\langle \lambda_{\bar{d}}^{\downarrow^N}, \lambda_{\bar{d}} \rangle$, *if an element* $g_m \in L_2^B$ *is a minimal solution of System 2 then* g_m *is a minimal element of the set* $\{g \in L_2^B \mid g_i \prec_2 g \preceq_2 \lambda_{\bar{d}}^{\downarrow^N}, i \in \{1, \ldots, n\}\}$ *or* g_m *is incomparable with* g_i, *for all* $i \in \{1, \ldots, n\}$.

Example 4. In Example 3, in order to apply the algorithm given in [4,10], we will consider the regular partition in 10 pieces of the unit interval, $[0,1]_{10} = \{0.0, 0.1, \ldots, 1.0\}$, instead of the unit interval $[0,1]$. Note that, considering the

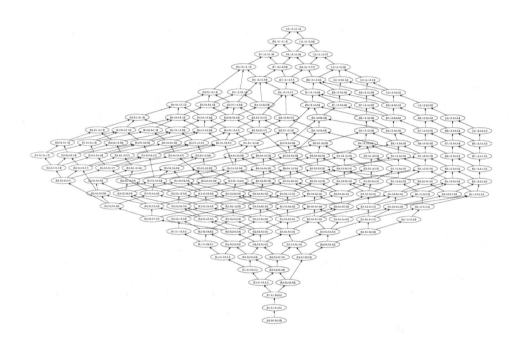

Fig. 1. The Hasse diagram of $(\mathcal{F}_{\pi N}, \preceq)$

environment in Example 3, the number of mappings between the set of objects and $[0,1]_{10}$ is $10^4 = 10\,000$. Moreover, the number of fuzzy property-oriented concepts $\mathcal{F}_{\pi N}$ is 179, which is a considerable set of concepts. Figure 1 is the Hasse diagram of the property-oriented concept lattice $(\mathcal{F}_{\pi N}, \preceq)$. In order to obtain the concepts of $(\mathcal{F}_{\pi N}, \preceq)$, we have used an implementation of the necessity and possibility operators in *Python* programming language and the fast algorithm given in [4].

The adjoint triple assumed will be a discretization of the Gödel t-norm, similar to the one given in Example 2. Assuming the system in [5], that is the system

$KX = \lambda_1$, where X is the unknown matrix, we computed in Example 3 that the largest solution is $\lambda_1^{\downarrow^N} = (0.3, 0.3, 1.0, 0.4)$. As can be checked in Figure 2, the extents of the lower neighbor concepts of the concept $\langle \lambda_1^{\downarrow^N}, \lambda_1 \rangle$, are $g_0^1 = (0.2, 0.2, 1.0, 0.4)$, $g_0^2 = (0.3, 0.3, 0.6, 0.4)$ and $g_0^3 = (0.3, 0.3, 1.0, 0.3)$. Therefore, by Theorem 3, solutions of the system $KX = \lambda_1$ are:

- From the inequality $g_0^1 \leq \lambda_1^{\downarrow^N}$, we obtain the solutions: $g_s^1 = (0.3, 0.2, 1.0, 0.4)$ and $g_s^2 = (0.2, 0.3, 1.0, 0.4)$.
- The inequality $g_0^2 \leq \lambda_1^{\downarrow^N}$ gives $g_s^5 = (0.3, 0.3, 0.7, 0.4)$ as a solution. Moreover, $g_s^4 = (0.3, 0.3, 0.8, 0.4)$, $g_s^5 = (0.3, 0.3, 0.9, 0.4)$ are also solutions.
- Finally, any more solution is obtained from the inequality $g_0^3 \leq \lambda_1^{\downarrow^N}$, since there is not a mapping g verifying $g_0^3 < g < \lambda_1^{\downarrow^N}$.

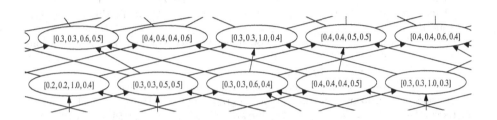

Fig. 2. Concept $\langle \lambda_1^{\downarrow^N}, \lambda_1 \rangle$ and its neighbors

4 Conclusions and Future Work

Fuzzy relation equations have been generalized using adjoint triples. Moreover, both environments, fuzzy property-oriented concept lattice framework and this general fuzzy relation equations, have been related to obtain solutions of systems of these kind of equations. Properties provided, e.g. in [2,12,19], can be applied to obtain additional characteristics of these systems. Furthermore, fuzzy property-oriented lattice framework has been used to find more solutions of this kind of systems.

In the future, we will compare the actual methods to obtain solutions of classical fuzzy relation equations to the one proposed in this paper, and especially those methods looking for minimal solutions using the covering problem. Moreover, more properties and advantages of the proposed method will be studied.

References

1. Bandler, W., Kohout, L.: Semantics of implication operators and fuzzy relational products. Int. J. Man-Machine Studies 12, 89–116 (1980)
2. Bělohlávek, R.: Concept lattices and order in fuzzy logic. Annals of Pure and Applied Logic 128, 277–298 (2004)

3. Belohlavek, R., De Baets, B., Outrata, J., Vychodil, V.: Lindig's Algorithm for Concept Lattices over Graded Attributes. In: Torra, V., Narukawa, Y., Yoshida, Y. (eds.) MDAI 2007. LNCS (LNAI), vol. 4617, pp. 156–167. Springer, Heidelberg (2007)

4. Bělohlávek, R., De Baets, B., Outrata, J., Vychodil, V.: Computing the lattice of all fixpoints of a fuzzy closure operator. IEEE Transactions on Fuzzy Systems 18(3), 546–557 (2010)

5. Chen, L., Wang, P.P.: Fuzzy relation equations (i): the general and specialized solving algorithms. Soft Computing - A Fusion of Foundations, Methodologies and Applications 6, 428–435 (2002)

6. Chen, Y., Yao, Y.: A multiview approach for intelligent data analysis based on data operators. Information Sciences 178(1), 1–20 (2008)

7. De Baets, B.: Analytical solution methods for fuzzy relation equations. In: Dubois, D., Prade, H. (eds.) The Handbooks of Fuzzy Sets Series, vol. 1, pp. 291–340. Kluwer, Dordrecht (1999)

8. Di Nola, A., Sanchez, E., Pedrycz, W., Sessa, S.: Fuzzy Relation Equations and Their Applications to Knowledge Engineering. Kluwer Academic Publishers, Norwell (1989)

9. Díaz, J., Medina, J., Rodríguez, R.: Solutions of systems of fuzzy relation equations as concepts of a formal context. In: XVI Congreso Español sobre Tecnologías y Lógica Fuzzy, ESTYLF 2012, pp. 156–162 (2012)

10. Díaz, J., Medina, J., Rodríguez, R.: Un algoritmo rápido para obtener retículos de conceptos utilizando el lenguaje de programación PYTHON. In: XVI Congreso Español sobre Tecnologías y Lógica Fuzzy, ESTYLF 2012, pp. 14–19 (2012)

11. Gediga, G., Düntsch, I.: Modal-style operators in qualitative data analysis. In: Proc. IEEE Int. Conf. on Data Mining, pp. 155–162 (2002)

12. Georgescu, G., Popescu, A.: Non-dual fuzzy connections. Arch. Math. Log. 43(8), 1009–1039 (2004)

13. Hájek, P.: Metamathematics of Fuzzy Logic. Trends in Logic. Kluwer Academic (1998)

14. Lindig, C.: Fast concept analysis. In: Stumme, G. (ed.) Working with Conceptual Structures-Contributions to ICCS 2000, pp. 152–161 (2000)

15. Medina, J.: Towards Multi-adjoint Property-Oriented Concept Lattices. In: Yu, J., Greco, S., Lingras, P., Wang, G., Skowron, A. (eds.) RSKT 2010. LNCS (LNAI), vol. 6401, pp. 159–166. Springer, Heidelberg (2010)

16. Medina, J., Ojeda-Aciego, M., Ruiz-Calviño, J.: Formal concept analysis via multi-adjoint concept lattices. Fuzzy Sets and Systems 160(2), 130–144 (2009)

17. Pedrycz, W.: Fuzzy relational equations with generalized connectives and their applications. Fuzzy Sets and Systems 10(1-3), 185–201 (1983)

18. Perfilieva, I., Nosková, L.: System of fuzzy relation equations with inf-→ composition: Complete set of solutions. Fuzzy Sets and Systems 159(17), 2256–2271 (2008)

19. Radzikowska, A.M., Kerre, E.E.: A comparative study of fuzzy rough sets. Fuzzy Sets and Systems 126(2), 137–155 (2002)

20. Sanchez, E.: Resolution of composite fuzzy relation equations. Information and Control 30(1), 38–48 (1976)

21. Zadeh, L.A.: The concept of a linguistic variable and its application to approximate reasoning I, II, III. Information Sciences 8-9, 199–257, 301–357, 43–80 (1975)

Teacher Support for Theatrical Learning Support in Lectutainment

Seeing through Students Using Augmented Reality

Hiroyuki Mitsuhara[1], Katsuhiko Moriya[1], Kazumoto Tanaka[2],
Junko Kagawa[1], Kazuhide Kanenishi[1], and Yoneo Yano[1]

[1] The University of Tokushima, Tokushima, Japan
mituhara@is.tokushima-u.ac.jp
[2] Kinki University, Hiroshima, Japan

Abstract. Lectutainment aims at increasing student learning motivation in a lecture. Specifically, it makes unusual lecture atmosphere by executing audiovisual effects as theatrical learning support. A support function is necessary for a teacher to provide audiovisual effects. Our fundamental idea for the teacher support function is to superimpose information about the students onto the teacher's view in a lecture. In other words, it is to enable the teacher to see through the students using augmented reality.

Keywords: Lecture, entertainment, learning motivation, audiovisual effect.

1 Introduction

Nowadays, digital technologies are introduced in many lecture rooms to diversify lectures. For example, teaching with digital slideshow is becoming a common lecture style. Furthermore, advanced learning/teaching support systems are introduced in some lecture rooms. For example, an active learning support system of Liao et al. enables a teacher and students to annotate digital slides through the intuitive handwriting interface on tablet PCs [1]. A ubiquitous learning support system of Mitsuhara et al. provides personalized quiz materials on a student's PDA after automatic attendance check using RFID [2]. Patry reported that handled wireless responders (a commercial system called "Clicker") helped university students to understand course material in a large lecture [3]. Previously, such introductions have aimed at increasing learning efficiency and efficacy from pedagogical viewpoints.

In contrast, we aim at increasing learning motivation in a lecture from an entertainment computing viewpoint. Learning motivation is indispensable for successful lectures and therefore has been actively investigated [4]. For example, Keller [5] proposed the ARCS model, which consisted of the four categories for increasing learning motivation: "attention", "relevance", "confidence", and "satisfaction". Malone and Lepper [6] identified the four factors of intrinsic learning motivation: "challenge", "curiosity", "control", and "fantasy".

S. Greco et al. (Eds.): IPMU 2012, Part II, CCIS 298, pp. 405–414, 2012.
© Springer-Verlag Berlin Heidelberg 2012

Our idea is "Lectutainment"—a coined term from "lecture" and "entertainment". It is to regard a lecture room as a theater and make atmosphere like a theatrical performance (stage show) in the lecture by executing audiovisual effects. In other words, it is theatrical learning support that focuses on accomplishment, exaltation (excitement), joy, relaxation, tension, etc. We developed a Lectutainment prototype system and conducted a preliminary experiment. The results of the experiment indicated that the Lectutainment could increase university student learning motivation [7].

However, the prototype system does not have enough support for teachers who provide the theatrical learning support. Therefore, we have to design and implement functions of the theatrical learning support.

2   Lectutainment

2.1   Learning Motivation Model

The Lectutainment aims at increasing student learning motivation, which may be ambiguous and difficult to be universalized. First of all, therefore, we should indicate our learning motivation model.

Our proposed model represents stepwise learning motivation in a lecture and consists of three layers (Fig. 1).

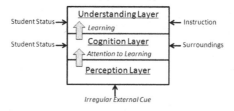

Fig. 1. Proposed learning motivation model

(1) Perception Layer
This layer is positioned at the model's bottom and handles whether a student pays attention to the lecture by an irregular external cue that stimulates his/her perception (e.g., ears and eyes). For example, when suddenly a teacher begins to explain in a loud voice, the student will be surprised and pay attention to the teacher. This layer can be associated partly with "attention" in the ARCS model.

(2) Cognition Layer
This layer is positioned at the model's middle and handles whether the student's attention transitions to learning actions (e.g., listening to the teacher's explanation and note-taking). In this layer, the student recognizes his/her internal states (e.g., understanding level) and surrounding situations (e.g., other students' learning attitudes) and then judges whether he/she takes a learning action.

(3) Understanding Layer

This layer is positioned at the model's top and handles whether the student can understand the lecture as a result of his/her learning actions. Here, his/her understanding depends on his/her internal states and the teacher's instruction. This layer can be associated partly with "confidence" and "satisfaction" in the ARCS model.

2.2   Theatrical Learning Support

In realizing the Lectutainment, we focus on the perception layer abovementioned and "fantasy" in the Malone and Lepper's identification [6]. The fantasy, which indicates that learning activities that do not actually occur in everyday life provide meaningful imagination, can be easily stimulated with an entertainment computing approach. This is because both the fantasy and the entertainment (computing) deal with unusuality to cause a certain kind of surprise, which will start from human perception.

Our belief behind the Lectutainment is that a lecture atmosphere different than usual influences students evenly and their learning motivation will be increased. In other words, unusuality in a lecture is available for increasing learning motivation independently of learning topics. The lecture atmosphere may not be the core issue in education but should not be ignored in terms of learning motivation.

We think that a lecture room resembles a theater and therefore a lecture resembles a theatrical performance. For example, black/white boards and screens, room lights and speakers, a teacher, and students can be associated with stage backdrops, stage equipments, a performer, and audience, respectively. From the resemblance between the two, we think that methods for making a theatrical performance more dramatic can be applied to increasing learning motivation in a lecture. In the theater, audiovisual effects (e.g., background music, sound effect, and light) are indispensable for a dramatic theatrical performance. Therefore we propose theatrical learning support, which executes audiovisual effects in a lecture to increase student learning motivation.

2.3   Prototype System

The prototype system consists of three subsystems: effect manager (EM for short), effect executor (EE for short) and effect bank (EB for short). Fig. 2 shows the system composition. The typical equipments necessary for the Lectutainment (the lecture room) are digital projectors, speakers (including directional speakers), a wireless network router, an EM-installed computer, EE-installed computers, PDAs, and RFID readers.

(1) Effect Manager

As the preliminary preparation for executing audiovisual effects, the EM receives an effect execution plan from the EB and distributes the plan to every EE. In the plan, conditions for effect execution (to whom, what, and when) are written in XML.

Teachers and students carry RFID cards containing their own ID codes. The EM-installed computer, which communicates with the EE and the EB via the wireless network, is connected to an RFID reader embedded in the door to check whether a teacher is allowed to attend the lecture. If he/she is the allowed teacher, the EM informs every EE of the teacher attendance by sending the teacher ID code. A PDA, which equips an RFID reader and a wireless network interface, is put on every student desk to check whether a student is allowed to attend the lecture—he/she has to put his/her RFID card on the reader when having a seat. If he/she is the allowed student, the EM sends the student ID code and the seat ID code (PDA's ID code) to every EE. From these two codes, the EM (and the EE) recognizes which seat the student has.

When the teacher requests effect execution at an arbitrary time, the EM sends the request to a corresponding EE.

(2) Effect Executer

Each EE-installed computer is connected to one projector and one set of speakers. When receiving the effect execution plan, each EE downloads digital material files (e.g., PPT/PPS, MPEG, and MP3) used for the audiovisual effects from the EB. The EE waits for the ID code or the request from the EM and simultaneously it checks the timing for effect execution at a regular interval. When the current situation matches a condition in the effect execution plan (e.g., when the current time matches the execution time of an effect), the EE executes the corresponding effect immediately.

(3) Effect Bank

The EB working on a server stores effect execution plans, digital material files, the spatial information of lecture rooms (e.g., the dimensions of a lecture room and seat positions), and fundamental settings of lectures (e.g., starting and ending time) registered by teachers.

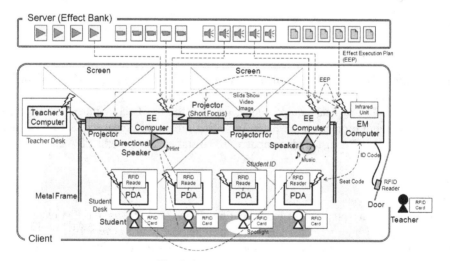

Fig. 2. System composition

2.4   Examples of Theatrical Learning Support

This section introduces two examples of theatrical learning support (audiovisual effects) in a lecture (Fig. 3). When the teacher requests a student to answer a quiz (question), a spotlight is cast on the student. The student has to answer the quiz under tension (pressure) created by the spotlight effect. At the same time, many of the other students will look at the student, also feel tension, and get motivated to learn more seriously. Some students will dislike this effect and decrease their learning motivation. However, we believe that many students can overcome such tension and continually increase their learning motivation with positive senses (e.g., accomplishment and joy). Therefore, we regard such an effect as theatrical learning support.

When the quiz is difficult for the student (answerer), a verbal hint is given to the student in a synthesized whisper that only he/she can hear. To realize this effect, the EE computer is connected to directional speakers (parametric speakers1) whose directions are adjusted to the student position by controlling two servo motors (pitching and yawing). The directional speakers can be also used to give warning (alarm) to a specific student taking unwanted behaviors during a lecture (e.g., talking, sleeping, and using a mobile phone). The verbal hint and warning are converted from the text sentences inputted by the teacher to the synthesized whisper and then sent to the student.

Fig. 3. Spotlight effect (left) and a directional speaker on the jointed motors (right)

3   Teacher Support

A support function is necessary for a teacher to provide effective theatrical learning support (audiovisual effects) in Lectutainment. Especially concerning the audiovisual effects for a specific student (e.g., the spotlight and the verbal hint), the teacher should extemporarily choose the student to increase his/her learning motivation maximally by an audiovisual effect—it is ideal that as many students as possible can increase their learning motivation simultaneously by the audiovisual effect. Therefore, we aim at the

---

[1] A parametric speaker transmits audible sound through ultrasonic and therefore has high directionality.

function that enables the teacher to see information about the students (e.g., their attendance rates, understanding levels and interests) without disturbing the lecture.

3.1   Fundamental Idea

Our fundamental idea for the teacher support function is to superimpose information about the students onto the teacher's view in a lecture. In other words, it is to enable the teacher to see through the students using AR (augmented reality). Fig. 4 shows the overview of the function.

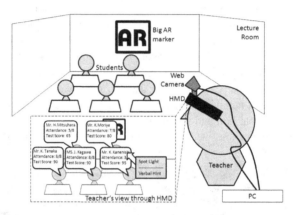

Fig. 4. Overview of AR-based teacher support function

The teacher wears a HMD (head-mounted display) with a web camera. A big AR marker(s) is put on the back wall of the lecture room. The Lectutainment prototype system can recognize which seat a student has from the RFID-based student identification (attendance check). The spatial positions of the seats are inputted previously by a teacher or a university officer—he/she can input the positions using a Web system (See 3.2). Therefore, the function can recognize where the students are on the plane coordinates in the lecture room. If the spatial (three-dimensional) calibration between the AR marker and the seats is fit, the function can work as intended.

3.2   Web System for Preparing Theatrical Learning Support

We developed a Web system where users can input the following information necessary for executing the audiovisual effects. We suppose that this system will be integrated in the EB. Fig. 5 shows a user interface of the system.

(1) Lecture Room Information
Currently, the lecture room is limited to rectangular-shaped rooms. A user inputs horizontal and vertical sizes of the lecture room and adjusts the sizes by mouse operation. The lecture room inputted is visualized as a simple frame on the user interface.

(2) Student Seat Information
The user arranges student seats inside the frame by mouse operation (drag and drop) or activates automatic arrangement, and then adjusts the size of each seat (including student desk) by clicking on an arranged seat and inputting its size.

(3) Projector Information
For visual effects, information of projectors (and screens) is necessary. Especially for the spotlight effect, the projection area of each projector should be precisely determined. The user arranges projectors and adjusts the projection areas covering the arranged seats by mouse operation.

(4) Directional Speaker Information
For the verbal hint, three-dimensional positions, original directions, and motion ranges of directional speakers should be precisely determined. The function for inputting this information has not been implemented yet.

(5) Connection Information
The user arranges the EE-installed computers and inputs information about them (e.g., computer ID, IP address, and pixel resolution). Then, the user sets the connection information of computer-projector and computer-speaker to execute the audiovisual effects.

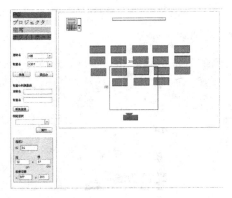

Fig. 5. User interface of Web system for preparing theatrical learning support

3.3   Superimposed Information

The superimposed information should consist of some levels depending on the teacher's intention. Currently we suppose the two levels: (1) overall information about all the students and (2) information about a specific student.

In the level of (1), the information is vaguely represented (visualized) and the teacher provides not a specific student but all the students with theatrical learning support. When many students have not understood the previous lecture, for example, a dark-colored filter is superimposed onto the teacher's view. Due to the dark view, the teacher will regard this situation as "bad atmosphere" and execute an audiovisual effect for all the students (e.g., playing an inspiring music) or mention the previous lecture. Such a filter is more advantageous than text information in that the teacher's view is not hindered.

In the level of (2), the information is represented for each student and the teacher provides a specific student with the support. When executing the spotlight effect, for example, the teacher can see the students' past test scores to choose a student who can answer a quiz successfully. Due to the students' past test scores, the teacher can also directly advise students who have not understood enough.

3.4   Prototype Function

We tentatively implemented a prototype function of the teacher support, focusing on the level of (2) described in 3.3. The prototype function is based on ARToolKit [8].

For the operation verification, we made a big AR marker (approximately 1 x 1 m) and put the marker on the back wall of the lecture room (approximately 10 x 20 m). Then, we laid out the experimental situation where a student had a seat right in front of the marker and a teacher wearing a binocular HMD stood on a platform. Fig. 6 shows an example of the teacher's view displayed in the HMD. In this figure, the student's name, past test score (mean score), and number of answering a quiz are superimposed near the student.

Fig. 6. Teacher's view with superimposed information (partially extracted and zoomed)

3.5   Discussion

Through the experimental use of the prototype function, we are concerned with the following practical difficulties in a real lecture (room).

(1) Overcrowded Information

If student seats are arranged without enough spaces and many students have the seats, the teacher's view will become crowded with the superimposed information. Although supposing the levels of the superimposed information to remove the overcrowded information, we should discuss whether the combination of AR and HMD is the best. A binocular HMD currently we use is too heavy to be of practical use in a lecture and uncomfortable to wear for a long lecture. Furthermore, the teacher's view is narrowed inside the HMD and formed by secondary images with delay. On the other hand, a see-through monocular HMD (e.g., "AiRScouter" by Brother International Corporation, Japan) can overcome these disadvantages—but it is still too expensive to be introduced in educational facilities.

A possible solution for the overcrowded information is that we do not use AR. For example, information about each student is displayed, linked with his/her seat visualized on the teacher's PC. This solution will be easy to be introduced in terms of cost-effectiveness and enable the teacher to choose a specific student more easily. However, we think that the teacher should choose a specific student, looking at information about the students and their faces at the same time. Therefore, we believe that the combination of AR and HMD will be the best for the teacher support.

(2) Inaccurate Position Adjustment

In the experimental use, we had difficulty in adjusting the position between the AR marker and the student seat. A larger lecture room will cause a larger margin of positional error. The positional error may become pronounced in the case where just one marker is used. Solution of such inaccurate position adjustment (geometric registration) is a high-priority issue in AR-based systems.

A possible solution is that every student has a unique AR marker. Miura and Nakada developed a responder system using fiducial (AR) markers [9]. In the lecture where the system is introduced, every student has a unique marker and hold up the maker when the teacher asks a single-choice question. The system recognizes each student's answer from the markers' rotation angles. In the possible solution, however, there is concern that the AR markers are often hidden fortuitously by obstacles (e.g., other students' bodies). Therefore, we attempt to make the position adjustment more accurate using as few AR markers as possible.

(3) How to Collect Information about Students

For the successful teacher support, it is important to collect as much as possible of information about students. For example, information of student attendance is easy to be collected by the Lectutainment system (RFID-based student identification). On the other hand, student knowledge level may be difficult to be collected precisely in a lecture.

A possible solution is that the Lectutainment system (the EB) should be extended to a learning management system including a computer-based test function in order to collect students' knowledge levels precisely.

4   Summary

This paper outlined the teacher support in Lectutainment. The support function is based on ARToolKit and superimposes information about students onto the teacher's view using a binocular HMD. We implemented the prototype function and checked through the experimental use that the teacher support will be able to be realized.

Our future work includes conceptual sophistication and workable implementation of the teacher support function. In addition, we have to examine the implemented function more strictly from technological viewpoints (e.g., the visibility of the AR marker, the three-dimensional resolution in information presentation, and the pixel resolution of the HMD) and practical viewpoints (e.g., usability, teacher's burden, and learning effectiveness).

Acknowledgments. This study was supported in part by 22650202 from the Japan Society for the Promotion of Science.

References

1. Liao, C., Guimbretière, F., Anderson, R., Linnell, N., Prince, C., Razmov, V.: PaperCP: Exploring the Integration of Physical and Digital Affordances for Active Learning. In: Baranauskas, C., Abascal, J., Barbosa, S.D.J. (eds.) INTERACT 2007, Part II. LNCS, vol. 4663, pp. 15–28. Springer, Heidelberg (2007)
2. Mitsuhara, H., Kanenishi, K., Yano, Y.: Handheld Review: Ubiquitous Technology-Based Method to Bridge Class and e-Learning. In: Proc. of the 18th International Conference on Computers in Education (ICCE 2008), pp. 635–642 (2008)
3. Patry, C.: Clickers in Large Classes: From Student Perceptions Towards an Understanding of Best Practices. International Journal for the Scholarship of Teaching and Learning 3(2) (2009)
4. Svinicki, M.D.: New directions in learning and motivation. New Directions for Teaching and Learning 1999(80), 5–27 (1999)
5. Keller, J.M.: Motivational Design for Learning and Performance: The ARCS Model Approach. Springer (2009)
6. Malone, T.W., Lepper, M.R.: Making Learning Fun: A Taxonomy of Intrinsic Motivations for Learning. In: Aptitude, Learning and Instruction, Hillsdale, NJ, pp. 223–253 (1987)
7. Mitsuhara, H., Moriya, K., Kagawa, J., Kanenishi, K., Yano, Y.: Lectutainment: An Entertainment Computing Approach to Motivating Students in Classroom Lecture. In: Proc. of IADIS International Conference e-Society 2012, pp. 35–43 (2012)
8. Kato, H., Billinghurst, M., Poupyrev, I., Imamoto, K., Tachibana, K.: Virtual Object Manipulation on a Table-Top AR Environment. In: Proc. of the International Symposium on Augmented Reality (ISAR 2000), pp. 111–119 (2000)
9. Miura, M., Nakada, T.: Device-Free Personal Response System based on Fiducial Markers. In: Proc. of the 7th IEEE International Conference on Wireless, Mobile, and Ubiquitous Technologies in Education (WMUTE 2012), pp. 87–91 (2012)

Students' Posture Sequence Estimation Using Spatio-temporal Constraints

Masayuki Mukunoki, Kota Yoshitsugu, and Michihiko Minoh

Kyoto University, 6068501 Japan
mukunoki@media.kyoto-u.ac.jp

Abstract. We propose a method for estimating the students' posture sequence in classroom from video footage by computer automatically. A posture sequence is a time-series of student's postures during a lecture and a posture of a student is described by a set of his head, body trunk (torso) and hands/arms states, which we call the body part states. The detection of body parts from video footage has many errors. To cope with the errors, we introduce spatio-temporal constraints, in which we propagate the belief of postures through a given time interval with considering the confidence of observation. Through this propagation, we can revise the erroneous detection results and estimate an appropriate posture sequence. In the experiment, we apply our proposed method to a real lecture, and show that our method can improve the accuracy of posture sequence estimation.

Keywords: posture estimation, students' behavior, spatio-temporal constraints, belief and confidence.

1 Introduction

In recent years, lectures have been analyzed as a part of Faculty Development. Many studies regard the lecture as the communication between an instructor and students and analyze it in the context of discourse analysis or interaction analysis [1–4]. In these studies, pedagogic researchers observe the lecture or lecture video and record the behavior of the instructor and students manually. This imposes heavy tasks on pedagogic researchers. For the instructor, we can use special sensor devices, e.g. motion captures or position sensors, and it is relatively easy to record his behavior[5]. On the other hand, there are many students in a classroom and it is not realistic to arrange a special sensor device, e.g. Kinect[6], on each student for recording his behavior. So, it is desired to estimate the students' behavior in classroom from video footage by computer automatically.

On the other hand, pedagogic researchers who analyze lectures use several kinds of behaviors depending on the discourse model or interaction model they employ for analysis. Since these models use different behavior set for analysis one by one, if a behavior estimation method adopts a behavior set, it is not useful for other behavior sets. Considering the versatility of the estimation method, we need to use a common scheme for describing many kinds of behaviors.

S. Greco et al. (Eds.): IPMU 2012, Part II, CCIS 298, pp. 415–424, 2012.
© Springer-Verlag Berlin Heidelberg 2012

In this paper, we introduce more primitive criterion than behavior, which is called *posture sequence* and propose a method for estimating the students' *posture sequence* in classroom from video footage by computer automatically. A posture sequence is a time-series of student's postures during a lecture and a posture of a student is described by a set of his head, body trunk (torso) and hands/arms states, which we call the body part states. A behavior can be defined as a specific part of the posture sequence. Thus, once the posture sequence is estimated from lecture video, pedagogic researchers can map the estimation results to his behavior set. Furthermore, since the posture sequence is based on body parts position, the result is objective and quantitative data for characterize the lecture. There is new possibility to analyze the lecture quantitatively using the results of the students' posture sequence.

In order to estimate the posture sequence, we can use computer vision technology. There are several studies on posture estimation from video footage[7–9]. However, since students in classroom show small action and their body parts often overlap in the observed videos, the results of posture estimation tend to include many errors even if we use the state-of-the-art method.

To cope with this problem, we introduce the spatio-temporal constraints of body parts and postures. We call these constraints *posture model* and *transition model*. The posture model is the spatial constraints between body parts and applied in estimating the posture of each moment. The transition model is the temporal constraints between postures. Using these a prior knowledge, we give the confidence of sensor and the belief of posture at each moment. During the posture sequence estimation process, the belief of posture is propagated through some interval and the posture sequence is gradually revised through the interval. Finally, our method complements the erroneous postures by the confident observation and outputs appropriate estimation results.

2 Definition of Terms

2.1 Posture Sequence

We define the posture sequence based on the position of body parts. Terms used in this paper are defined as follows:

Body part. *Head, torso* and *hands/arms.*
Body part position. Detected 2D position of a body part in the observed video frame.
Body part state. Estimated class of quantized position for the body part in 3D space.
Posture. Combination of body parts states for a student at a moment.
Posture sequence. Sequence of postures along the time order.
Behavior. Giving a meaning to some period of posture sequence.

We assume that each student sits down on a fixed seat and is observed by a video camera in front and above the classroom(Fig. 1). The lower half of the student's body is hidden by the table and the upper half of it is observed. Thus, we only take account of head, torso and hands/arms as the body part. We also assume that the area observed a student for each seat is given. The body part position is expressed with the normalized coordinates relative to the given seat area. From the body part position, we estimate the 3D position of it. The 3D position for each body part is quantized in several classes and expressed as the state. The detail is described in the next subsection. A posture of a student is expressed as the tuple of body parts states, that is, the combination of head, torso and hands/arms states. The posture sequence is simply the list of the posture of a student along the time. So, if we can obtain the precise posture of the student at each moment, the list of the posture estimation results can be used as the posture sequence. However, the original posture estimation results include many errors. In our method, we try to correct such errors on the posture sequence.

Fig. 1. An example of lecture video

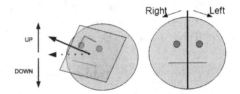

Fig. 2. Body part state of head

2.2 Body Part State

Body part state is the basic element for expressing the posture, posture sequence and behavior. It should be enough general to describe many kinds of behaviors. At the same time, it should be enough capacity to express many kinds of postures observed in classroom. Based on the observation of lecture videos and considering the generality and capacity of the description, we define the following body part states for head, torso and hands/arms.

For the head body part (Fig.2), students frequently show up and down actions and sometimes cock their heads. Thus, we combine the head direction of up-and-down and right-and-left and employ 4 states: *Up Right*, *Up Left*, *Down Right* and *Down Left*.

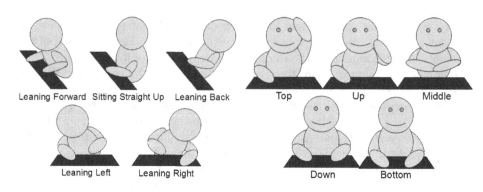

Fig. 3. Body part state of torso   **Fig. 4.** Body part state of hands/arms

For the torso body part (Fig.3), students lean their torso in several direction. Thus, we employ 5 states: *Leaning Forward, Leaning Backward, Leaning Left, Leaning Right* and *Sitting Straight Up.*

Finally for the hands/arms body part (Fig.4), students frequently shows the following actions: touch their hair or face, fold their arms, take notes with putting their arms on the table and take a rest with putting their elbow on the table. Thus, we employ 5 states: *Hand Top, Hand Up, Hand Middle, Hand Down* and *Hand Bottom.*

Since the posture of a student is expressed by the combination of his body parts states, we can express $4 \times 5 \times 5 = 100$ kinds of postures using our body part state. Table 1 shows the summary of the body part states for all body parts.

Table 1. Summary of body part state

Hands/Arms	Torso	Head
Hand Top	Sitting Straight Up	Up Left
Hand Up	Leaning Forward	Up Right
Hand Middle	Leaning Back	Down Left
Hand Down	Leaning Right	Down Right
Hand Bottom	Leaning Left	

2.3 Spatio-temporal Constraints

It is difficult to estimate the posture of a human from a given video footage. There are several studies challenging this issue in the computer vision research field. However, the estimation results are not enough when we apply the methods to the lecture videos even if we use the state-of-the-art. This is because the property of the students' posture observed in classroom. Most estimation methods use the edge, contour and texture to detect human from the image. If these elements can be extracted stably, the estimation results will be fairly good. However, students in classroom do not show exaggerated gestures and usually hands and arms are beside the torso. Thus, these body parts are overlapped in the observed videos and the edge, contour and texture of the body parts are not extracted stably. Furthermore, the overlap between the before and behind students in the videos gets the problem more difficult. As the result, the posture estimation results typically includes the following errors:

- Accidental error while the student keeps same posture
- Unstable changes while the student keeps same posture and the student behind him/her take some action
- Unstable several changes while the student only change from one posture to another

These kinds of unstableness tend to be eliminated by complementing the posture estimation results between the successive estimated postures. However, when the errors occur frequently in some time period, we cannot judge which result is correct and which result is wrong.

To cope with that, we introduce a prior knowledge about the posture and transition of postures. In classroom, students show some postures frequently and show other postures very seldom. Similarly, some transition of postures are shown frequently and others not. The *"posture model"* represents the spatial relationship between body part states of a student. For example, students tend to put their hands on the table when they lean forward their torso. The posture model expresses the spatial constraints between body parts and contains the knowledge on frequently appearing posture. The *"transition model"* represents the temporal transition between successive postures. For example, students tend to keep the same posture or to change only the head direction comparing to other posture changes. The transition model contains this kind of knowledge.

Once the body part positions are extracted from video footage using the posture estimation technology, we estimate the *"confidence"* of all body part states for each body part. Applying our posture model in this stage, we give precedence to the postures frequently shown in classroom. Then we calculate the *"belief"* of posture as the combination of confidence on body part states. After that, we propagate the belief within some time interval. The frequently observed posture transition is emphasized during this propagation by applying our transition model. In this way, relying on the observation of frequently appearing postures, we complement errors and estimate the posture sequences.

3   Posture Sequence Estimation

3.1   Procedure

Our posture sequence estimation procedure goes as follows:

1. Detect the body part position.
2. Assign the confidence of body part states using the "posture model."

3. Calculate and propagate belief of posture applying the "transition model" within a given time interval K.
4. Iterate step 1 to 3 for each moment along the time order.
5. After the procedure finished, the posture which has the most belief at each moment is adopted as the final result.

This procedure is inspired by Bayesian Network[10]. In Bayesian Network, conditional dependency of random variables is expressed by a directed acyclic graph. Once values of some variables are given (observed), the belief of the other variables can be calculated along paths in the graph. In our method, once the body part position is detected, the confidence of the detection is calculated and the belief of the posture is propagated through a given time interval. As the result, we can gradually revise the erroneous observation using the a prior knowledge.

3.2   Detection of Body Parts

We use Ferrari's method[7] for detecting body parts. This program is available on the Web [11]. The results of body parts detection include large errors, especially in the position of hands. When the detected position of the forearms far away from the detected upper arm position, we search the skin color region from the image and if the region exists in the fixed length away from the detected upper arm position, we revise the hand position to the detected skin region (Fig.5).

Ferrari's method can detect the head position, but in our body parts states we need the head direction. For detecting that, we use OKAO Vision[13] toolkit. When we cannot detect the head, we assume that the head direction is down.

Fig. 5. Detected body parts and Revised body parts

Fig. 6. An example of distribution: Hand Up

3.3   Confidence of Body Part States

After we detect the body parts positions, we estimate the confidence of all body part states for each body part. The set of state for each body part S_{head}, S_{torso}, S_{hands} is given as shown in Table 1. For the body part $n \in \{head, torso, hands\}$

and its state $s_n \in S_n$, the confidence at the moment t is denoted as $C_{parts}(s_n, t)$. The assignment of confidence is achieved by giving the mapping between position and confidence value for each body state. They are expressed by Gaussian distribution in the image. An example of distribution on "Hand Up" is shown in Fig.6.

Then we apply posture model to reflect the spatial constraints. Posture model is the relationship between states of two body parts. It is expressed by conditional probability $P(s_m | s_n)$, where s_m, s_n are the states of body part $m, n \in \{head, torso, hands\}$, respectively. The confidence of body part state is calculated using the following equation:

$$C_{pos}(s_m, t) = \sum_{s_n \in \{S_{head}, S_{torso}, S_{hands}\}} P(s_m | s_n) C_{parts}(s_n, t).$$

Note that the conditional probability between the same state of the same body part $P(s_m | s_m)$ is set to be 1.0.

3.4   Belief of Posture

Combining the confidence of body part states, we calculate the belief of all possible postures at the moment t. A posture $\lambda \in \Lambda$ is expressed by the tuple of head, torso and hands/arms state, where Λ is the posture set

$$\Lambda = \{(s_{head}, s_{torso}, s_{hands}) | s_{head} \in S_{head}, s_{torso} \in S_{torso}, s_{hands} \in S_{hands}\}.$$

The number of possible postures is 100 in our body part state set.

The belief of the posture $\lambda = (s_{head}, s_{torso}, s_{hands})$ at the moment t is the product of the confidence of the body parts and calculated by

$$B_{pos}(\lambda, t) = C_{pos}(s_{arm}, t) C_{pos}(s_{torso}, t) C_{pos}(s_{head}, t).$$

Then we propagate the belief of posture at the moment t applying the transition model. The transition model is the relationship between two time successive postures. It is express by conditional probability $P(\lambda_p | \lambda_q)$ and $P(\lambda_q | \lambda_p)$, where $\lambda_p, \lambda_q \in \Lambda$ are the posture at the current and its previous moment, respectively.

We propagate the belief through a given time interval K. Propagation of the belief for the posture has two phases. In the first phase, the belief $B_{rev}(\lambda_p, t) := B_{pos}(\lambda_p, t)$ is propagated along previous time direction:

$$B_{rev}(\lambda_q, t - k - 1) = \sum_{\lambda_p \in \Lambda} P(\lambda_q | \lambda_p) B_{rev}(\lambda_p, t - k)$$

in the order $k = 0, \ldots, K$. In the second phase, the belief $B_{trans}(\lambda_p, t - K) := B_{rev}(\lambda_p, t - K)$ is propagated to subsequent time direction:

$$B_{trans}(\lambda_p, t - k) = \sum_{\lambda_q \in \Lambda} P(\lambda_p | \lambda_q) B_{trans}(\lambda_q, t - k - 1)$$

in the order $k = K-1, \ldots, 0$. We consider all possible postures in Λ and calculate the belief for all postures.

4   Experiments

In this experiment, we apply our proposed method to a real lecture and evaluate the performance by comparing the results with the manually given ground truth. The lecture video is captured by a camera in front and above students (Fig.7). The resolution of the video is 1280×960 and the frame rate is 10 fps. For the experiments, we extract 1800 frames (3 minutes) of the video clip from a 90 minutes long lecture video. We select 9 students from the video, 7 from the front seat in the classroom (marked by red circles in Fig. 7) and 2 from the rear seat (marked by blue circles in Fig. 7), and give the ground truth of the postures of these students manually.

We observe several lecture videos and gives the posture model and the transition model. For the posture model, we found that the following three cases appear frequently.

- Hand Down and Leaning Forward
- Hand Bottom and Leaning Forward
- Hand Middle and Leaning Back

We give a larger probability (0.8, 0.8 and 0.7, respectively) to these combinations of body part states and give a probability of 0.0 to the other combinations. For the transition model, we give the larger probability to the following transitions:

- Transition to the same posture (prob. 0.001)
- Transition between the postures head UP and Down while the other body part states are unchanged (prob. 0.0009)

We give a probability of 0.00001 to the other transitions. These probability values are decided heuristically. Once we give these values, we normalize the probability so that the sum of the probability will be equal to 1.0.

The results of body part states and posture estimation for the students are shown in Table 2. The columns of "Original" denote the result without applying posture model and transition model, and the columns of "Proposed" denote the result of our method. We use the time interval for the belief propagation $K = 10$.

The results show that the accuracy of estimation are improved applying our method. We achieve the remarkable improvement for the students A and B and a certain amount of improvement for the students C, D, E and G, while for the student F the accuracy is decreased in estimating hand states. The degree of improvement depends on whether the student's posture matches the posture and transition model or not. Since the student F shows different postures from the other students, the accuracy is not improved. However, even in this case, the decline of accuracy is relatively small and the accuracy of the other body part state is improved. This shows that our propagation method, which gradually revises the postures, produces fewer side effects to the posture estimation.

For the students H and I, who sit on rear seats in the classroom, we cannot achieve obvious improvement for the estimation. Since the students in rear seats are observed with low resolution in the video, we cannot detect the body parts correctly and the estimation errors continue stationary. In this case, the complement using the spatio-temporal constraints does not work efficiently.

Fig. 7. Configuration of the experiment

Table 2. Accuracy of posture estimation

Student	Hands/Arms		Torso		Head		Posture	
	Original	Proposed	Original	Proposed	Original	Proposed	Original	Proposed
A	5.7%	67.3%	9.1%	59.7%	53.2%	53.5%	0.8%	38.4%
B	34.7%	80.2%	11.7%	98.8%	62.6%	62.3%	1.6%	52.5%
C	92.9%	92.6%	37.1%	46.9 %	77.6%	78.1%	20.1%	34.0%
D	41.0%	51.7%	27.8%	52.5 %	72.3%	72.4%	6.2%	15.0%
E	12.2%	13.9%	37.1%	55.3%	79.9%	80.2%	0.1%	12.3%
F	30.5%	19.0%	38.8%	69.6%	85.5%	85.8%	0.0%	10.1%
G	18.2%	49.2%	17.3%	76.9%	90.5%	91.1%	8.6%	26.1%
H	3.5%	7.6%	17.7%	36.6%	50.4%	50.7%	0.1%	0.5%
I	54.1%	55.2%	52.3%	55.7%	42.4%	45.0%	31.2%	35.2%

5   Conclusion

We proposed a method to improve the posture estimation by spatio-temporal constraints and obtain reasonable posture sequence automatically. The posture sequence is a primitive description scheme for human behavior and it has a possibility applicable to wider range of applications. The experimental results show that our method can indeed improve the accuracy of posture sequence estimation.

However, the absolute values of accuracy for posture estimation are not so high. The error may be co-opted when mapping the posture sequence into behavior. This is left as a future work.

Acknowledgements. This work was supported by KAKENHI(22500919 and 23300311).

References

1. Luke, A.: Text and Discourse in Education: An Introduction to Critical Discourse Analysis. Review of Research in Education 21, 3–48 (1996)
2. Eder, D.: Ability Grouping as a Self-Fulfilling Prophecy: A Micro-Analysis of Teacher-Student Interaction. Sociology of Education 54(3), 151–162 (1981)

3. Herring, M., Wahler, R.G.: Children's Cooperation at School: The Comparative Influences of Teacher Responsiveness and the Children's Home-Based Behavior. Journal of Behavioral Education 12(2), 119–130 (2003)
4. Hadwin, A., Wozney, L., Pontin, O.: Scaffolding the Appropriation of Self-regulatory Activity: A Socio-cultural Analysis of Changes in Teacher-student Discourse about a Graduate Research Portfolio. Instructional Science 33(5), 413–450 (2005)
5. Ukida, H., Kaji, S., Tanimoto, Y., Yamamoto, H.: Human Motion Capture System Using Color Markers and Silhouette. In: Proc. of IEEE Instrumentation and Measurement Technology Conference (IMTC), pp. 151–156 (2006)
6. Kinect- XBox.com, http://www.xbox.com/kinect
7. Ferrari, V., Marin-Jimenez, M., Zisserman, A.: Progressive Search Space Reduction for Human Pose Estimation. In: Proc. of IEEE CVPR, pp. 1–8 (2008)
8. Pellegrini, S., Iocchi, L.: Human posture tracking and classification through stereo vision and 3D model matching. Journal on Image and Video Processing (7), 1–12 (2008)
9. Agarwal, A., Triggs, B.: Recovering 3D Human Pose from Monocular Images. IEEE Trans. on PAMI 28(1), 44–58 (2006)
10. Bayesian Network, http://en.wikipedia.org/wiki/Bayesian_network
11. 2D articulated human pose estimation software, http://www.vision.ee.ethz.ch/~calvin/articulated_human_pose_estimation_code/
12. Ramanan, D.: Learning to parse images of articulated bodies. In: Proc. of NIPS, pp. 1129–1136 (2006)
13. OKAO Vision, http://www.omron.co.jp/ecb/products/mobile/

Investigation of a Method to Estimate Learners' Interest Level for Agent-Based Conversational e-Learning

Kazuaki Nakamura[1], Koh Kakusho[2], Tetsuo Shoji[3], and Michihiko Minoh[4]

[1] Graduate School of Law, Kyoto University, Kyoto, 606-8501 Japan
`nakamura@mm.media.kyoto-u.ac.jp`
[2] School of Science and Technology, Kwansei Gakuin University,
Hyogo, 669-1337 Japan
[3] Faculty of Sociology, Nara University, Nara, 631-0803 Japan
[4] Academic Center for Computing and Media Studies, Kyoto University, Kyoto,
606-8501 Japan

Abstract. A method for recognizing or estimating learners' affective state plays a key role for realizing agent-based conversational e-Learning. In this paper, we focus on the learners' interest level as an example of the important affective state, and investigate a method for estimating it from their nonverbal behaviors. In conversational situations, the sense of the nonverbal behaviors will vary depending on the contexts of the conversations. Therefore we do not use the nonverbal behaviors themselves but use the occurrence frequencies of the nonverbal behaviors as inputs for estimation mechanism. In the result of our experiment, the proposed method could estimate whether the learners' interest level is "High" or "Low" with the accuracy of more than 70%.

Keywords: agent-based e-Learning, interest level, nonverbal behaviors, human-agent interactions.

1 Introduction

In recent years, many universities and other educational institutions have incorporated e-Learning into their curriculums with development and spread of ICT technologies. While e-Learning has a variety of its types today, the earliest one called WBT (Web Based Training) is still one of the most typical types of e-Learning, in which learners individually access to course materials on a web server and learn the materials by themselves on their own convenient time and location. However, WBT has a problem that the learners easily lose their motivations and dropout from the learning [1].

In conventional face-to-face classes, the role of an instructor is not limited to presenting a content of learning; they also need to consider the learners' affective state such as motivation and satisfaction [2]. To achieve this, the instructor actively has a conversation with the learners during classes, and then, through the conversation, the instructor estimates the learner affective states and reflects

S. Greco et al. (Eds.): IPMU 2012, Part II, CCIS 298, pp. 425–433, 2012.
© Springer-Verlag Berlin Heidelberg 2012

them in his/her teaching activities. In contrast, in e-Learning, it is difficult for both the learners and the instructor to have such kind of conversations. This is just the reason that the above problem arises.

To cope with this problem, several researchers have attempted to introduce a conversational agent into e-Learning [3–5]. Matsuura et al. have proposed Agent-based Virtual Classroom system called AVC for short, in which two types of agents, "lecturer agent" and "learner agent," can give a comment to human learners [3]. In this system, the human learners also can make comments, so that they can have a kind of conversation with the agents. However, the agents' comments are basically given to the learners at scheduled timings. This means that the agents do not consider the learner affective states at all. Unlike the system of Matsuura et al., Neji et al. have proposed the Agent-based e-Learning Framework which can consider the learner affective states [5]. They have considered Ekman's six universal emotions as the learner affective states and tried to recognize the emotions from the learners' facial expressions. Then, based on the recognized emotions, their proposed agents choose their actions adaptively.

As pointed out in the work of Neji et al. [5], a technique for recognizing or estimating a learner's affective state plays a key role for realizing e-Learning systems with conversational agents. In this paper, we focus on a learner's interest level, which can be reflected in the learning (or teaching) activities more directly than the Ekman's six emotions, and investigate a method for estimating it from their nonverbal behaviors including facial expressions, eye gaze, postures, hand gestures, and so on.

2   Related Works

There are some previous works which have focused on e-Learning and tried to estimate the learners' interest level from various kinds of information. For instance, Mota et al. have tried to estimate the learners' interest level from their postural behaviors obtained by a chair with two matrices of pressure sensors [6]. Nosu et al. also have tried to estimate the learner affective states including interest level from their facial expressions as well as biometrical signals such as pulse rate, breathing rate and finger temperature [7]. Fujisawa et al. have used "face approach" behavior for estimating the learners' interest level, which is the action of the learners to move their face closely to the monitor they used [8]. The face approach behaviors have obtained by a webcam in that research. However, all of these previous works have focused only on the conventional WBT type of e-Learning. They have not considered the agent-based conversational e-Learning.

In a natural conversation between two people, the role of each person changes periodically; he/she becomes sometimes a speaker and sometimes a listener. In addition, the context of the conversation also changes momentarily. These changes will influence the relations between the person's affective state and his/her nonverbal behaviors; in other words, the sense of the person's nonverbal behaviors will vary depending on his/her role and the conversational context. For example, the person's "leaning head" action could mean "lack of confidence

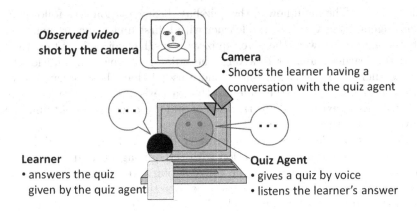

Fig. 1. Quiz-based conversational e-Learning environment

of his/her own opinion" when he/she is a speaker, although the same action could mean "disagreement with the other person" when he/she is a listener. This will be also the case in conversations between a human and an agent. Nevertheless the above previous works have assumed that a same behavior or a same behavioral pattern is always related to same affective state and tried to model the relation between the learners' behaviors themselves and their affective state, because the assumption is suitable for the learners learning in WBT environment. However the assumption will not hold in the agent-based conversational e-Learning environment.

Based on the above discussion, we do not focus on the learners' nonverbal behaviors themselves but focus on the sets of the nonverbal behaviors performed in a duration of certain (relatively longer) length, and try to model the relation between the learners' interest level and the sets of their nonverbal behaviors in this paper.

3   Investigation of a Method for Estimating Interest Level

3.1   Data Collection

To examine the idea described in the previous section, we first observed several learners having an actual conversation with an agent and obtained their videos, from which we collected data for analyzing the relation between the learners' interest level and their nonverbal behaviors.

(1) Observed conversation environment

The conversational e-Learning environment used in this research is shown in Figure 1. In this environment, the learners have a quiz-based conversation with a quiz agent, who has a function for giving quizzes to the learners with artificial voices. The main flow of the quiz-based conversation is as follows: First, the quiz agent gives a quiz to the learner with a first hint using artificial voices. Next, the learner answers the given quiz with his/her voices based on the first hint. If the learner's answer is wrong, the quiz agent gives an additional hint to the learner. The additional hint is more useful than those given before, for ordinary learners. On the other hand, if the learner's answer is correct, then the quiz agent gives next quiz. Thus the learner and the quiz agent continually have a conversation with their voices.

We instructed 5 learners (whom we refer to as A, B, C, D, and E in this paper) to have the above conversation with the quiz-agent, and observed them with a camera. Each learner has the conversation seven times. The time spent in the conversation is around 12 minutes per one time. We refer to the learners' videos obtained here as "obtained videos" simply in the remainder of this paper.

(2) Collecting data of interest level

We showed the *observed videos* of the 5 learners to themselves right after they finished the quiz-based conversations, and instructed them to evaluate their own interest level in 2 levels, "Low" or "High," for each frame of their *observed videos*. Thus we collected the data of the learners' interest level. We refer to these self-evaluated values for each frame t as $m(t) \in \{$Low, High$\}$ in the remainder of this paper.

(3) Collecting data of nonverbal behaviors

As for the data of the learners' nonverbal behaviors, we first defined a behavior set targeted in this research as Table 1, which consists of 17 nonverbal actions. We describe each of the 17 nonverbal actions as a *"unit action,"* and refer to each *unit action* as the symbol U_k ($k = 1, 2, \cdots, 17$) in this paper.

Most of the 17 *unit actions* have been targeted in many previous works for interaction analysis [6, 8–10]. Only U_6 and U_{17} have not been analyzed so much in the previous works, however they were often seen on our *observed videos*. On the other hand, although the learners can behave freely in e-Learning environments and therefore their nonverbal behaviors are not exclusive to the *unit actions* listed in Table 1, behaviors other than the 17 *unit actions* were seldom seen on our *observed videos*. From these facts, the 17 *unit actions* listed in Table 1 are considered to be appropriate as a target set of nonverbal behaviors for analyzing the relation between the learners' interest level and their nonverbal behaviors.

We collected the data of each *unit action* as follows: First, we showed the *observed videos* to the third person who is different from all of the 5 learners. Then we instructed the third person to mark up the start frame t_k^s and finish frame t_k^f of the learners' each *unit action* U_k on each *observed video*. In the remainder of this paper, we represent the collected data of each U_k by a variable u_k whose value is 1 while and only while each learner is performing the *unit action* U_k; that is,

Table 1. Targeted nonverbal behavior set consisting of 17 *unit actions*

symbol	*unit actions*
U_1	leaning head
U_2	looking away to the upside
U_3	looking away to the downside
U_4	looking away to the upside right before/after looking downside
U_5	wandering eyes
U_6	reading a sentence of a quiz
U_7	leaning upper body forward
U_8	leaning upper body backward
U_9	adjusting posture of upper body
U_{10}	touching chin with hands
U_{11}	touching face with hands
U_{12}	touching hair with hands
U_{13}	nodding
U_{14}	shaking head
U_{15}	smiling
U_{16}	furrowing eyebrows
U_{17}	shutting eyes

$$u_k(t) = \begin{cases} 1 & \text{if } t_k^{\text{s}} \leq t \leq t_k^{\text{f}} \\ 0 & \text{otherwise} \end{cases}. \tag{1}$$

Of course the learners can perform 2 or more *unit actions* at a same time. In fact, there were some learners who were nodding with a smile at a certain frame t on the *observed videos*. In such case, both the value of $u_{13}(t)$ and that of $u_{15}(t)$ simultaneously become 1.

3.2 Relation between Interest Level and Nonverbal Behaviors

Using the collected data $m(t)$ and $u_k(t)$, we analyzed the relation between the learners' interest level and their nonverbal behaviors as follows: We first calculated the values of $p(u_k = 1|m = \text{Low})$ and $p(u_k = 1|m = \text{High})$, and then we compared these two values, where $p(u_k = 1|m = x)$ ($x \in \{\text{Low, High}\}$) is the ratio of the number of frame t satisfying $u_k(t) = 1$ and $m(t) = x$ divided by the total number of frame t satisfying only $m(t) = x$; in other words, the $p(u_k = 1|m = x)$ means occurrence probability of the *unit action* U_k under the condition that the learners are highly interested (or not interested at all) in the content of the conversations.

Figure 2 and 3 show the results of this analysis for the learner B and D respectively, who are two of the 5 learners. From these results, the following three facts can be found: First, most of the *unit actions* were actually performed regardless of whether the learners' interest level is "high" or "low." This indicates that the learners' interest level cannot be estimated so accurately only using the *unit actions* themselves. Second, for several *unit actions* such as U_3, U_4, and

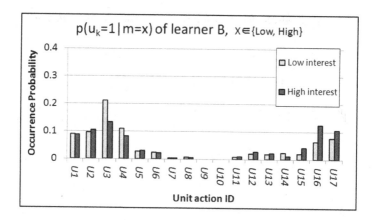

Fig. 2. Conditional occurrence probability of each *unit action* U_k for the learner B

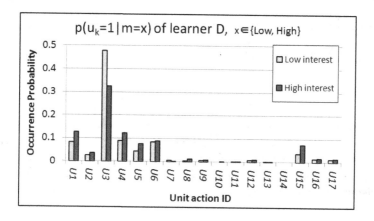

Fig. 3. Conditional occurrence probability of each *unit action* U_k for the learner D

U_{15}, the values of the probabilities $p(u_k = 1|m = \text{Low})$ and $p(u_k = 1|m = \text{High})$ are relatively different from each other. This indicates the possibility that the occurrence frequencies of the *unit actions* are effective for estimating the learners' interest level. Third, the relation between the interest level and the occurrence frequencies of the *unit actions* will vary depending on each individual learner. The first fact supports the idea described in Section 2.

3.3 Proposing Frequency-Based Estimation Method

Based on the result of the analysis, we propose the following method for estimating the learners' interest level: We use the occurrence frequencies of the *unit actions* in a duration of certain length as the input features for an estimation mechanism. In addition, we use a machine learning technique for coping with the problem of the individual-dependency; that is, we independently train a two-class classifier for each individual learner to estimate whether his/her interest level is "High" or "Low" from the input features, using a machine learning technique.

4   Experiment and Results

We examined the effectiveness of the proposed method by an experiment.

In this experiment, we first extracted two sets of continued video frame sequences $\{T_j^{\mathrm{L}}\}$ and $\{T_j^{\mathrm{H}}\}$ from the *observed videos* for each learner so that each of the sequences T_j^x ($x = $ L, H) satisfies the following condition:

$$\forall t \in T_j^{\mathrm{L}} \ m(t) = \mathrm{Low} \quad \text{and} \quad \forall t \in T_j^{\mathrm{H}} \ m(t) = \mathrm{High}, \tag{2}$$

where j denotes the index of each extracted sequence. Because of the condition (2), the learners' interest level for each sequence T_j^x can be defined as

$$m(T_j^{\mathrm{L}}) = \mathrm{Low} \quad \text{and} \quad m(T_j^{\mathrm{H}}) = \mathrm{High}. \tag{3}$$

The lengths of all the sequences were exactly same with each other; that is, when a length of a sequence T is denoted as $l(T)$, the following conditions are satisfied:

$$\forall T \in \{T_j^{\mathrm{L}}\} \cup \{T_j^{\mathrm{H}}\} \ l(T) = \tau, \tag{4}$$

where τ is a positive constant. Only fewer number of sequences can be extracted with longer τ because $l(T)$ has an upper limit depending on how long each learner continually keeps his/her interest level high or low. In this experiment, the parameter τ is set at less than 900 frames as described below, which made the total numbers of the sequences in the two sets $\{T_j^{\mathrm{L}}\}$ and $\{T_j^{\mathrm{H}}\}$ be around 30 for each learner, respectively.

Next, we calculated the occurrence frequency of each *unit action* U_k in the duration of each sequence $T \in \{T_j^{\mathrm{L}}\} \cup \{T_j^{\mathrm{H}}\}$. More specifically, we calculated the total number of frame t which satisfies $u_k(t) = 1$ and $t \in T$, for each $T \in \{T_j^{\mathrm{L}}\} \cup \{T_j^{\mathrm{H}}\}$. Let $h_k(T)$ be the occurrence frequency of the *unit action* U_k in the duration of the sequence T. Using the $h_k(T)$, we defined the feature vector $\boldsymbol{h}(T) \in \Re^{17}$, each of whose elements was identical to $h_k(T)$. Regarding $m(T) \in \{\mathrm{Low}, \mathrm{High}\}$ as a class label, we created the following single data set:

$$\mathcal{D} = \big\{ \big(\boldsymbol{h}(T_j^{\mathrm{L}}), \mathrm{Low} \big) \big\}_{j=1}^{30} \cup \big\{ \big(\boldsymbol{h}(T_j^{\mathrm{H}}), \mathrm{High} \big) \big\}_{j=1}^{30}. \tag{5}$$

Then we performed LOOCV on the data set $\mathcal{D}$ by using SVM, and evaluated the estimation accuracy of the learners' interest level.

We repeated the above procedure 9 times, setting the parameter τ as 100, 200, 300, $\cdots$, and 900 frames, respectively (The length of 900 frames is equal to 60

Table 2. Estimation accuracy of the learners' interest level by the proposed method

		\multicolumn{9}{c}{length of the sequences, τ iframesj}
		100	200	300	400	500	600	700	800	900
	A	66.0%	65.4%	69.7%	64.8%	68.1%	75.4%	71.4%	67.5%	70.6%
	B	55.9%	58.3%	58.5%	57.0%	57.8%	72.6%	64.4%	62.0%	66.7%
learner ID	C	71.2%	72.9%	74.2%	80.3%	81.6%	78.1%	87.9%	92.6%	91.7%
	D	69.3%	70.8%	74.2%	76.2%	81.0%	84.1%	78.2%	85.1%	84.2%
	E	45.7%	48.6%	51.6%	52.2%	60.8%	51.2%	58.8%	60.7%	77.8%
avg.		61.6%	63.2%	65.6%	66.1%	69.9%	**72.3%**	**72.1%**	**73.6%**	**78.2%**

seconds in this experiment because of 15 fps of the video frame rate). The results are shown in Table 2. The learners' interest level were averagely estimated with higher accuracy by the longer τ. This is because the variance of the conditional distribution $p(\boldsymbol{h}|m)$ can get smaller by prolonging τ for all $m \in \{\text{Low}, \text{High}\}$, according to the law of large numbers.

On the misestimated data, the occurrence frequencies h_k of some *unit actions* U_k have an anomalous property which is opposed to many other cases. For instance, although the learner B performed the "smiling" action (U_{15}) more frequently when he felt "High interest" in most cases, sometimes he performed the same action even under his feelings of "Low interest." This would be because that he had a wry smile at continued boring topics of given quizzes. In such cases, the proposed method could not estimate the learner's interest level correctly.

5   Conclusion

In this paper, we investigated a method for estimating the learners' interest level from their nonverbal behaviors, which will play a key role for realizing agent-based conversational e-Learning. In a natural conversation between two people, the senses of their nonverbal behaviors will vary depending on the context of the conversation. Therefore, we did not use the nonverbal behaviors themselves, rather we proposed to use the occurrence frequencies of the nonverbal behaviors as inputs for the estimation mechanism. In the result of our experiment using SVM, the proposed method could estimate the learners' interest level with the accuracy of more than 70%. Note that we tried to estimate the learners' interest level as two-class classification task whose class labels are "High interest" and "Low interest" in this experiment.

One of the future works is to estimate the learners' interest level as multi-class (more than 2 classes) classification task or regression task for further contributing the realization of actual agent-based e-Learning. Another future work is to use nonverbal behaviors as well as some other information such as voice or speech information simultaneously for estimating the learners' interest level more accurately.

Acknowledgements. This paper is based on the work supported by NTT Communication Science Laboratories. We would like to express our deep appreciation to them for their great help in the experiment.

References

1. Xenos, M., Pierrakeas, C., Pintelas, P.: A survey on student dropout rates and dropout causes concerning the students in the course of informatics of the hellenic open university. Computers and Education 39(4), 361–377 (2002)
2. Danchak, M.M.: Bringing Affective Behavior to e-Learning. The Technology Source (September/October 2002)
3. Matsuura, K., Ogata, H., Yano, Y.: Supporting Asynchronous Communication in an Agent-based Virtual Classroom. Int'l Journal of Continuing Engineering Education and Lifelong Learning 12(5-6), 433–447 (2002)
4. Mahmood, A.K., Ferneley, E.: Embodied Agents in E-Learning Environments: An Exploratory Case Study. Journal of Interactive Learning Research 17(2), 143–162 (2006)
5. Neji, M., Ammar, M.B.: Agent-based Collaborative Affective e-Learning Framework. The Electronic Journal of e-Learning 5(2), 123–134 (2007)
6. Mota, S., Picard, R.W.: Automated posture analysis for detecting learner's interest level. In: Proc. of the Conf. on CVPR Workshop, p. 49 (2003)
7. Nosu, K., Kurokawa, T.: A multi-modal emotion diagnosis system to support e-learning. In: Proc. of the 1st Int'l Conf. on Innovative Computing, Information and Control, vol. 2, pp. 274–278 (2006)
8. Fujisawa, K., Aihara, K.: Estimation of user interest from face approaches captured by webcam. In: Shumaker, R. (ed.) VMR 2009. LNCS, vol. 5622, pp. 51–59. Springer, Heidelberg (2009)
9. Morris, D.: Bodytalk: The Meaning of Human Gestures. Crown Publishers (1995)
10. Peters, C., Pelachaud, C., Bevacqua, E., Mancini, M., Poggi, I.: A Model of Attention and Interest Using Gaze Behavior. In: Panayiotopoulos, T., Gratch, J., Aylett, R.S., Ballin, D., Olivier, P., Rist, T. (eds.) IVA 2005. LNCS (LNAI), vol. 3661, pp. 229–240. Springer, Heidelberg (2005)

Application of Fuzzy Relations to Test Theory

Michael Wagenknecht[1], Oleksandr Sokolov[2], and Olga Molchanova[2]

[1] Univ. Appl. Sc., Zittau/Goerlitz, Germany
m.wagenknecht@hs-zigr.de
[2] National Aerospace Univ., Kharkiv, Ukraine
oleksandr_sokolov@yahoo.com

Abstract. Unlike the classical probability-based approach we consider the ge-neration and evaluation of tests based on a fuzzy approach. This leads to tasks which can be solved within the frame of fuzzy relational equations. Sever-al ex-amples illustrate the usefulness of our approach.

Keywords: Test theory, generation and evaluation of tests, fuzzy relational equations.

1 Generation of Tests with Desired Properties

Tests are one of the powerful means in modern educational systems [2]. The structure of a test is determined by items which are characterized by complexity, discrimina-tion, correlation to the test and so on. Items are usually collected into so-called item banks that can be used for the generation of different tests. The test has to be designed from items that have desired characteristics according to test specification. The test examines the knowledge of a testee with respect to some subject, the latter being cha-racterized by units of knowledge (UOK). Obviously, each item can be interrelated with a set of UOK.

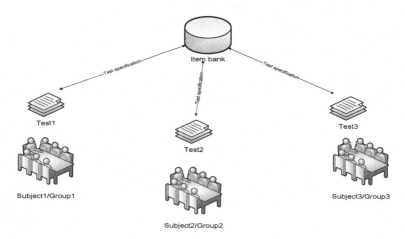

Fig. 1. Working with item bank

S. Greco et al. (Eds.): IPMU 2012, Part II, CCIS 298, pp. 434–440, 2012.
© Springer-Verlag Berlin Heidelberg 2012

One of the problems of test developers is the generation of a test from the item bank that has certain statistical characteristics (according to test specification) as well as a desired unit of knowledge (according to the subject that is assessed). There may be situations when it is necessary to design the tests from one subject but for different groups with different levels of knowledge (Fig.1).

The problem of choosing items is complex, because the bank of items may contain up to some thousands objects that are collected at universities or national centers of assessment. The scheme of test generation is shown in Fig.2.

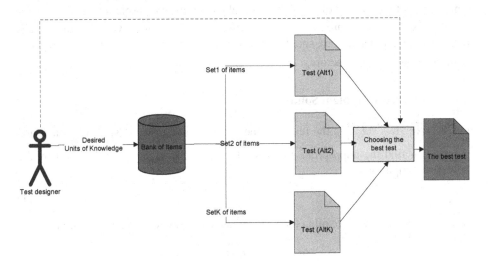

Fig. 2. Procedure of test generation

2   Formalization of the Task and Problem Formulation

Let us consider an item bank containing N items $T = \{I_1, I_2, ..., I_N\}$ from some subject (e.g., mathematics). Moreover, we have M UOK $U = \{U_1, U_2, ..., U_M\}$ describing this subject (e.g., numbers, sets, functions, statistics, geometry,...). Let R express the quantification of the relation between the items and the UOK reflecting the fitness of the items with respect to these units:

$$R = \begin{pmatrix} r_{11} & r_{12} & \cdots & r_{1M} \\ r_{21} & r_{22} & \cdots & r_{2M} \\ \cdots & \cdots & \cdots & \cdots \\ r_{N1} & r_{N2} & \cdots & r_{NM} \end{pmatrix}.$$

The elements r_{ij} may be from the unit interval (i.e., R can be interpreted as fuzzy relation) expressing the truth degree of the fitness. Sometimes, however, it is useful to have the r_{ij} from a lattice, e.g. from set $\{0, 1, ..., S\}$. In this case the matrix elements estimate the level of correspondence of fitness. In what follows, however, we assume the unit [0,1] as basis for evaluation.

There are at least two problems to consider. First, one has to find the underlying set of UOK U^* when the testee has performed his test T^* and got the results as truth levels of answers with respect to the items. Hence, we answer the question which UOK does the testee know well. This is the *direct* problem. Second, one may be faced with the question how to choose the set of items T^* from the item bank (i.e., the test) if we want to test some subset U^* of UOK. It is clear that we may get different tests which assess the same set of UOK. This is called the *inverse* problem.

The sets T^* and U^* are supposed to be fuzzy sets on their universes T and U. The memberships are denoted by small letters and for simplicity we equate the fuzzy sets with their membership vectors, i.e. $T^* = \left(i_1^*,...,i_N^*\right)$, $U^* = \left(u_1^*,...,u_N^*\right)$.

2.1   The Direct Problem Solution

Let $T^* = \left\{i_1^*, i_2^*, ..., i_N^*\right\}$ is the result of the test for some testee. Using relation R and T^* we can find the appropriate fuzzy set for the UOK successfully handled by the testee by computing

$$U^* = T^* \circ R \tag{1}$$

where "$\circ$" means the max-min composition law for fuzzy relations and sets, i.e.

$$u_j^* = \max_{k \in \{1,...,N\}} \min\left(i_k^*, r_{kj}\right), j \in \{1,...,M\}. \tag{2}$$

Example 1. Let us consider a test in mathematics containing of 10 items assessing the following units of knowledge: u_1 - Algebra, u_2 - Numbers and Expressions, u_3 - Equations and Inequalities, u_4 - Functions, u_5 - Combinatorial Calculus and Probabilities, u_6 - Statistics, u_7 - Geometry, u_8 - Plane Geometry, u_9 - Stereometry.

Moreover, we have the relation R (obtained from experts) between items and units of knowledge

$$R = \begin{pmatrix} 1 & 1 & 0 & 0 & 0 & 0 & 0 & 0 & 0 \\ 0 & 1 & 1 & 0 & 1 & 0 & 0 & 0 & 0 \\ 1 & 0 & 1 & 0 & 0 & 1 & 0 & 0 & 0 \\ 0 & 0 & 0 & 1 & 0 & 0 & 1 & 1 & 0 \\ 0 & 0 & 0 & 0 & 0 & 0 & 1 & 0 & 1 \\ 0 & 0 & 1 & 0 & 1 & 0 & 0 & 0 & 0 \\ 0 & 0 & 0 & 1 & 0 & 0 & 1 & 0 & 1 \\ 0 & 0 & 1 & 1 & 0 & 0 & 0 & 0 & 0 \\ 1 & 1 & 0 & 0 & 0 & 1 & 0 & 0 & 0 \\ 0 & 0 & 0 & 1 & 0 & 1 & 0 & 0 & 0 \end{pmatrix}.$$

Assume that the testee has obtained the following result: $\left(i_1^*, i_2^*, \ldots, i_{10}^*\right) =$
$= (1,0,1,1,0,0,0,1,0,0)$. Then computation (2) yields $U* = (1,1,1,1,0,1,1,1,0)$. It means that the testee knows $u_1 - u_4$ and $u_6 - u_8$, but he does not know u_5 and u_9.

Now let the answers be evaluated from a 5-degrees scale, e.g. from the set $\{0, 0.25, 0.5, 0.75, 1\}$ and suppose that the testee got the following result: $\left(i_1^*, \ldots, i_{10}^*\right) =$

$= \left(0.75, 0, 0.75, 1, 0.25, 0, 0.25, 0.5, 0.25, 0.25\right)$.

According to (2) we find $U* = (0.75, 0.75, 0.75, 1, 0, 0.75, 1, 1, 0.25)$. This means that the testee does not know only u_5 and knows the remaining units at different levels.

2.2   The Inverse Problem

The inverse problem consists in the determination of T^* with known R, U^* in (1). That is we want to know which tests might have led to the evaluation U^*. This task is much harder to solve (in comparison to the direct problem) and we may be faced with infinitely many solutions or no solution at all. It is a classical problem in the theory of fuzzy relation equations [3,5,7]. In the case of solveability the maximal (in the sense of fuzzy inclusion) solution $\hat{T} = \left(\hat{i}_1, \ldots, \hat{i}_N\right)$ is given by

$$\hat{T} = R\alpha U^* \qquad (3)$$

Where $\left(R\alpha U^*\right)_k = \min_{1 \le j \le M} r_{kj} \, \alpha u_j^*$, and the well-known α-operation (Goedel implication) is defined as

$$a\alpha b = \begin{cases} 1 \text{ for } a \le b, \\ b \text{ otherwise.} \end{cases}$$

There may be, however, a large number of minimal solutions [7] the calculation of which is not trivial for larger N (typical in test theory).

Example 2. Let us consider the test with 10 items and relation from Example 1. Now we want to find the assessment of answers to items if we are given the UOK by $U^* = (0.75, 0.75, 0.75, 1, 0, 0, 0.75, 1, 1, 0.25)$. We obtain the maximal solution $\hat{T} = (0.75, 0, 0.75, 1, 0.25, 0, 0.25, 0.75, 0.75, 0.75)$ and the four minimal solutions
$T_1^{\min} = (0.75, 0, 0.75, 1, 0, 0, 0, 0, 0, 0)$, $T_2^{\min} = (0.75, 0, 0, 1, 0, 0, 0, 0.75, 0, 0)$,
$T_3^{\min} = (0, 0, 0.75, 1, 0, 0, 0, 0, 0.75, 0)$, $T_4^{\min} = (0, 0, 0, 1, 0, 0, 0, 0.75, 0.75, 0)$.

2.3   Inverse Problems with Restrictions

Often the tester is not interested in the whole solution set of (1), but solutions with special properties are desired, as mentioned in Section 1. We distinguish two approaches: individual and global.

2.3.1 Individual Approach

In this case, we search at least one solution of (1) with T individual restrictions on the member values in each element I_j leading to the following task: Search T^* fulfilling

$$U^* = T^* \circ R$$

$$\underline{T} \subseteq T^* \subseteq \overline{T} \tag{4}$$

where $\underline{T}, \overline{T}$ are fuzzy sets on T and "$\subseteq$" means the inclusion of fuzzy sets. This situation occurs for example if we want to get a solution T^* where certain items are surpressed and other items are to be in the solution set with high evaluation.

In practice one is often faced with the problem to search for solutions with a special structure. Suppose, one has to determine a test $T = \{I_1, I_2, ..., I_N\}$ where item I_j takes part with probability p_j, i.e. T is characterized by a probability distribution P. This restriction can be transformed into a fuzzy set T_P^* using corresponding methods [4,6]. Due to a certain ambiguity in the choice of the transformation method and accounting that the p_j may be imprecise it seems to be more appropriate to include T_P^* in bounds, i.e. $\underline{T}_P \subseteq T_P^* \subseteq \overline{T}_P$ and we are led to task (4). The following statement enables the determination of a solution of (4) in an efficient way.

Statement 1. *Denote the solution set of (4) by* Γ. *Moreover let* $\tilde{T} = \hat{T} \cap \overline{T}$ *with* $\hat{T} = R \alpha U^*$ *(see (3)). Then* $\Gamma \neq \varnothing$ *iff* $\tilde{T} \in \Gamma$.

The proof follows from [9] where a more general situation is considered.

Example 3. Let U^* given as in Example 2. Suppose, we are interested in item solutions with evaluations of at least 0.5 for items I_1, I_4, I_8, I_9. Items I_2, I_7, I_{10} are irrelevant and items I_3, I_5, I_6 should be excluded from consideration. This leads the restrictions $\underline{T} = (0.5, 0, 0, 0.5, 0, 0, 0, 0.5, 0.5, 0)$, $\overline{T} = (1,1,0,1,0,0,1,1,1)$. One sees that $\tilde{T} = (0.75, 0, 0, 1, 0, 0, 0.25, 0.75, 0.75, 0.75)$ fulfills the restrictions and it is a solution, because $T_2^{\min} \subseteq \tilde{T} \subseteq \hat{T}$.

2.3.2 Global Approach

It may be of interest to globally confine the memberships of T^* to a given (crisp) subset $\Omega \subseteq [0,1]$. This situation is typical when Boolean solutions are desired $(\Omega = \{0,1\})$ or solutions where the membership of each item i should be below a level or above another one $(\Omega = [0, \underline{\omega}] \cup [\overline{\omega}, 1]$ with $0 \leq \underline{\omega} \leq \overline{\omega} \leq 1)$. Formally this means that we search a T^* with

$$U^* = T^* \circ R \tag{5}$$

$$i_j^* \in \Omega \text{ for } j = 1,...,N.$$

For the analysis of (5) we apply results given in [1]. Therefore define a function $\varphi_\Omega : [0,1] \rightarrow [0,1]$ by

$$\varphi_\Omega(a) = \sup_{\substack{b \in \Omega \\ b \leq a}} b. \tag{6}$$

Remark 1. a) For $\Omega = \{0,1\}$ (Boolean case) we obtain $\varphi_\Omega(a) = \begin{cases} 1 \text{ for } a=1, \\ 0 \text{ otherwise.} \end{cases}$

b) For $\Omega = [0,\underline{\omega}] \cup [\overline{\omega},1]$ as above we have $\varphi_\Omega(a) = \begin{cases} a \text{ for } a \in \Omega, \\ \underline{\omega} \text{ otherwise.} \end{cases}$

A solution of (5) can be found by the following

Statement 2. *Denote the solution set of (5) by* Ψ_Ω *and let* Ω *be closed. Set* $\hat{T} = \varphi_\Omega(\hat{T})$ *(i.e.* φ_Ω *applied elementwise). Then* $\Psi_\Omega \neq \varnothing$ *iff* $\hat{T} \in \Psi_\Omega$.

Example 4. Suppose U^* to be like in Example 2. We want to determine a solution with evaluations not lower than 0.5. Otherwise we exclude the item from further consideration. That is, $\Omega = \{0\} \cup [0.5,1]$. A solution fulfilling the constraints is $\hat{T} = (0.75, 0, 0.75, 1, 0, 0, 0, 0.75, 0.75, 0.75)$, and obviously $T_1^{\min} \subseteq \hat{T} \subseteq \hat{T}$.

3   Conclusion

The proposed approach of analysis and the formation of tests based on fuzzy relations opens up prospects for the automation of test generation based on the matrix elements of knowledge regarding the relationship and bank of items. Taking into account that in real test systems the item bank may contain hundreds of items, the problem of determining an optimal set of items is important. However, the demand for exact solvability may be too restrictive (i.e. Γ or Ω may be empty). Then one might search for approximative solutions (e.g. by transforming U^* into an interval-valued fuzzy set, see [8]). This will be the topic of future research.

References

1. Bartl, E., Belohlavek, R., Vychodil, V.: Bivalent and Other Solutions of Fuzzy Relational Equations via Linguistic Hedges. Fuzzy Sets and Systems 187, 103–112 (2012)
2. Crocker, L., Algina, J.: Introduction to Classical and Modern Test Theory. Thompson Wadsworth (2006)
3. Czogala, E., Drewniak, J., Pedrycz, W.: Fuzzy Relation Equations on a Finite Set. Fuzzy Sets and Systems 7, 89–101 (1982)
4. Dubois, D., Prade, H., Sandri, S.: On Possibility/Probability Transformations. In: Proc. 4th IFSA Conf. (1993)
5. Higashi, M., Klir, G.J.: Resolution of Fuzzy Relation Equations. Fuzzy Sets and Systems 13, 65–82 (1984)
6. Mouchaweh, M.S., Billaudel, P.: Variable Probability-Possibility Transformation for the Diagnosis by Pattern Recognition. Int. Journal Comp. Intelligence 1, 9–21 (2006)
7. Peeva, K., Kyosev, Y.: Fuzzy Relation Calculus. Theory, Applications and Software. Scientific Publishing Co. (2004)
8. Wagenknecht, M., Hartmann, K.: Application of Fuzzy Sets of Type 2 to the Solution of Fuzzy Equations Systems. Fuzzy Sets and Systems 25, 183–190 (1988)
9. Wagenknecht, M.: On the Controllability of Fuzzy Multistage Systems. Fuzzy Sets and Systems 35, 251–252 (1990)

A Recommender System with Uncertainty on the Example of Political Elections*

Krzysztof Dyczkowski and Anna Stachowiak

Faculty of Mathematics and Computer Science
Adam Mickiewicz University
Umultowska 87, 61-614 Poznań, Poland
{chris,aniap}@amu.edu.pl

Abstract. The article presents a system of election recommendation in which both candidate's and voter's preferences can be described in an imprecise way. The model of the system is based on IF-set theory which can express hesitation or lack of knowledge. Similarity measures of IF-sets and linguistic quantifiers are used in the decision-making process.

Keywords: recommender systems, intuitionistic fuzzy sets (IF-sets), similarity of IF-sets, linguistic quantifiers.

1 Introduction

Recommender systems have been proposed as an answer to the problem of "information overload". When search engines are not sufficient to deal with a vast amount of online information, recommender systems try to guess what kind of information or what goods and services we really need. They have not only become an important component of e-commerce systems, but are helpful in discriminating between relevant and irrelevant documents, and suggesting a new relationship or cultural event. Every (personalized) recommender system must know a user profile which, for example, contains the user's preferences. This profile can be acquired *implicitly* by analyzing past user behavior, or *explicitly* by asking the user about his or her preferences. Recommender systems that take into account a community of users are often referred as *collaborative* approaches, while those based on item description are called *content-based* ([1]). The second approach is strongly rooted in information retrieval and information filtering. The user preferences and items descriptions are somehow compatible, so that it is possible to compare them and to find an item matching the user preferences. For a brief review of different recommender systems algorithms, see [2].

One of the core issues for recommender systems is how to model and then compare user preferences and item descriptions in a flexible and natural way. Obviously, user preferences as well as item description can be imprecise, incomplete, subjective and of different importance. One approach, adopted by Yager

* Research supported by Ministry of Science and Higher Education Grant N N519 384936.

© Springer-Verlag Berlin Heidelberg 2012

in [3], is based on the use of fuzzy set theory. Another approach, which utilizes fuzzy clustering as a tool for recommendation, was presented in [4]. In this paper we would like to propose an IF-set based approach and to focus on an aspect of incomplete knowledge about item description and a way to cope with it.

In the following sections we introduce an example of a recommender system for elections, and we define a model for expressing user preferences and items descriptions. Next we show how to find a recommendation using linguistic quantifiers and a similarity measure of IF-sets.

2   Description of the Problem

During political (e.g. parliamentary or presidential) elections, voters are required to take a decision as to which candidate to choose. This decision has become particularly difficult recently, when much more attention is paid to personalities, images and campaign events than to party manifestos and policy issues.

A set of internet applications often called voting advice applications (VAA) has been created to help voters in this decision by finding a candidate or a party that stands closest to their preferences. The general idea of such systems consists in asking candidates a series of questions on different political issues. Next, a voter answers the same questions. Finally, those answers are compared and for each voter a list of matching candidates is found.

During the last parliamentary elections in Poland a group from the Center For Citizenship Education (see [5]) created such a system under the name "Latarnik Wyborczy". Twenty questions were prepared and then put to five electoral committees. Examples of the questions are:

- Should Poland cease to involve the armed forces in international military operations?
- Should the retirement age of women and men be equated at a level of 65 years or more as soon as possible?
- Should financing of political parties not be done from the state budget?

In this paper we consider a content-based recommender system for recommending a candidate to an elector. In our project we use data (i.e. a set of 20 questions and set of answers from 5 electoral committees) from [6] as test data. What distinguishes our system is the fact that we take into consideration the possibility that the candidate intentionally did not answer some questions or tried to blur his or her real beliefs. What is more we propose an alternative method of finding the final solution. We draw on a natural human way of reasoning based on linguistic quantifiers - we assume that when a voter is trying to find the best candidate he is searching for one such that the following statement is true:

(S1) "*Most* of the questions *important* to the voter were answered in a *similar* way by the candidate".

Note the words in *italics*, whose nature is imprecise. We will concentrate on them in later parts of this paper.

Our further discussion will be based on the following example. Each candidate and a voter are supposed to answer a set of questions using one out of six possible answers: Agree (A), Rather Agree (RA), Neutral (N), Rather Disagree (RD), Disagree (D), No Answer (NA). Additionally a voter is asked to set the importance of each question by choosing one of: Very important (VI), Important (I), Average (A), Not Important (NI), Totally not Important (TI).

For reasons of space, we reduce our example to 5 candidates and 8 questions. Answers given by the candidates and a voter are presented in Tables 1 and 2.

Table 1. The candidates' answers

	q_1	q_2	q_3	q_4	q_5	q_6	q_7	q_8
c_1	D	RD	A	A	RD	D	D	A
c_2	A	A	RA	A	RD	NA	RA	N
c_3	A	A	RD	RA	RA	RA	RD	NA
c_4	RA	A	NA	A	D	D	RA	RA
c_5	D	A	D	A	D	D	D	D

Table 2. The voter's answers and importance weights

	q_1	q_2	q_3	q_4	q_5	q_6	q_7	q_8
Answers	RA	RA	A	N	RA	RA	RA	RD
Importance	I	A	A	NI	A	A	VI	NI

In the following sections we will describe in detail the individual elements of our method, i.e. a model for answers and weights, a similarity measure, and a quantifier-based solution.

3   Modeling the Elements of a Recommender System

Here we describe the elements of our recommender system in more formal terms.

A content-based recommender system for recommending a candidate to a voter in an election includes:

- $C = \{c_1, \ldots, c_m\}$ - a set of m candidates in a political election (these are items to be recommended);
- $P = \{p_1, \ldots, p_n\}$ - a set of n questions in a questionnaire (these are attributes describing the items);

- $A_{c_k} = [a_1, \ldots, a_n]$ - a vector of encoded answers given by a candidate c_k to questions P; details will be described later (this vector describes an item);
- u - a voter (this is an active user for whom a recommendation is generated);
- $A_u = [a_1, \ldots, a_n]$ - a vector of encoded answers given by a voter u to questions P;
- $w = [w_1, \ldots, w_n]$ - a vector of weights assigned by a voter to each question, to indicate the subjective importance of the question (the vector of answers and the vector of weights together constitute the profile of the voter).

We now focus on the representation of answers encoded in vectors $A_{c_1}, \ldots, A_{c_m}$. We would like the following requirements to be fulfilled:

- only the answers "Agree" and "Disagree" are considered complete, i.e. they carry full knowledge about the candidate's beliefs;
- consequently, the answers "Rather Agree", "Rather Disagree" and "Neutral" indicate uncertainty about what the candidate really thinks about an issue (from the point of view of a voter);
- "No Answer" is an option for those candidates who want to hide their opinion about some issue that is controversial, for example; it is doubtful that the candidate really does not have an opinion.

Summing up, we want to emphasize that the uncertainty factor in the presented example is not of an immanent nature, but results from lack of knowledge or from the conscious decision of a candidate to hide his or her preferences. It reflects an uncertainty of a voter about a real preferences of a candidate. Yet when it comes to voting only Yes and No options are available.

We find that an adequate method to model candidate's answers and to maintain the described conditions is IF-set theory (Atanassov's intuitionistic fuzzy sets theory, see [7], [8]). We briefly recall some basic facts. An IF-set $\mathcal{A}$ is a triple:

$$\mathcal{A} = (A^+, A^-, A^?),$$

where A^+ is a fuzzy set of elements that belong to $\mathcal{A}$, and A^- is a fuzzy set of elements that do not belong to $\mathcal{A}$. This theory, in contrast with fuzzy set theory, incorporates uncertainty about the membership of an element, as A^- is not necessarily a negation of A^+, but $A^- \subset (A^+)^c$ where the complement of fuzzy set A is defined as $A^c(x) = 1 - A(x)$ for each x (for a generalized definition of IF-set with a use of a complement generated by an arbitrary strong negation, see e.g. [9]). Therefore, the value $A^?(x) = 1 - A^+(x) - A^-(x)$ reflects the uncertainty or hesitation about membership of an element x in an IF-set $\mathcal{A}$.

Applying this theory to our problem, we propose the IF-valuation of answers presented in Table 3.

We pay special attention to the uncertainty factor $A^?$. Let us notice that it changes from 0 to 1. As we stated before, the only two options with no uncertainty are "Agree" and "Disagree". When we move away from these strict

Table 3. IF-valuation of possible answers

	A^+	A^-	$A^?$
Agree:	1	0	0
Rather Agree:	0.75	0	0.25
Neutral:	0.25	0.25	0.5
Rather Disagree:	0	0.75	0.25
Disagree:	0	1	0
No Answer:	0	0	1

Table 4. Importance valuation

	weight
Very important:	1
Important:	0.75
Average:	0.5
Not important:	0.25
Totally Not important:	0

answers, the uncertainty increases. It is equal to 0.25 for "Rather Agree" or "Rather Disagree", because from a voter point of view it is not perfectly clear how a candidate would vote on a question about which he "Rather Agree". Next, uncertainty is 0.5 for Neutral, and it takes the largest value (1) for No Answer, as in this case a voter does not know anything about the candidate's preferences. We believe that this representation is consistent with intuition and, moreover, it gives a unified method to express all "Yes-No" answers, "Rather" answers and lack of answer. The uncertainty factor plays a significant role in this representation as well as in the calculation of similarity (which will be discussed in next section).

A similar model may be used to encode the answers of a voter. Additionally, a voter can rate the importance of a question, using fuzzy weights, and in particular can give a question a weight of 0 (Totally Not Important) (see Table 4).

At the end of this process we obtain a set of IF-preference vectors, one for each candidate and one for a voter. An example is shown in Tables 5 and 6.

Table 5. Vectors of the candidates' answers with IF-sets valuation

	q_1	q_2	q_3	q_4	q_5	q_6	q_7	q_8
c_1	(0,1,0)	(0,0.75,0.25)	(1,0,0)	(1,0,0)	(0,0.75,0.25)	(0,1,0)	(0,1,0)	(1,0,0)
c_2	(1,0,0)	(1,0,0)	(0.75,0,0.25)	(1,0,0)	(0,0.75,0.25)	(0,0,1)	(0.75,0,0.25)	(0.25,0.25,0.5)
c_3	(1,0,0)	(1,0,0)	(0,0.75,0.25)	(0.75,0,0.25)	(0.75,0,0.25)	(0.75,0,0.25)	(0,0.75,0.25)	(0,0,1)
c_4	(0.75,0,0.25)	(1,0,0)	(0,0,1)	(1,0,0)	(0,1,0)	(0,1,0)	(0.75,0,0.25)	(0.75,0,0.25)
c_5	(0,1,0)	(1,0,0)	(0,1,0)	(1,0,0)	(0,1,0)	(0,1,0)	(0,1,0)	(0,1,0)

Table 6. Voter's answers and weights valuation

	q_1	q_2	q_3	q_4	q_5	q_6	q_7	q_8
Answer	(0.75,0,0.25)	(0.75,0,0.25)	(1,0,0)	(0.25,0.25,0.5)	(0.75,0,0.25)	(0.75,0,0.25)	(0.75,0,0.25)	(0,0.75,0.25)
Importance	0.75	0.5	0.5	0.25	0.5	0.5	1	0.25

4 Determining Similarity between a Candidate's and Voter'S Answers

The next step of the algorithm involves determining the degree of similarity between a candidate and a voter, that is between two IF-sets.

The similarity measure is based on the notion of a distance - the smaller the distance (of any kind) between objects, the greater the similarity between them. The concept of calculating distance in the context of IF-sets arouses some controversy. In the literature we can find two approaches to this problem - one in which the distance is calculating using two terms only (membership and non-membership degree), and a second using all three terms (membership, non-membership and uncertainty degree). Although mathematically both methods are correct, it has been shown that the three-term approach is more appropriate, as it does not lose important information about the uncertainty factor (for a detailed discussion, see e.g. [10,11,12,13]).

Thus we propose to calculate the similarity between a candidate's and voter's answers using three term Hausdorff distance based on the Hamming metric as used in [13]. Note that we do not calculate the similarity between a candidate and voter but between each of their answers separately, because overhusty aggregation might blur the differences between candidates.

The Hausdorff distance is described as the maximum distance of a set to the nearest point in the other set. As both of the sets we wish to compare (i.e. answers to a question) have one element only, we use formula (1) to determine the Hausdorff distance:

$$H(A, B) = max\left\{|A^+ - B^+|, |A^- - B^-|, |A^? - B^?|\right\} \tag{1}$$

and formula (2) to calculate similarity:

$$Sim(A, B) = 1 - H(A, B). \tag{2}$$

Assuming six possible answers, we can construct a matrix of similarity of each pair of answers, as presented in Table 7.

Table 7. Similarity valuation

		A (1,0,0)	RA (0.75,0,0.25)	N (0.25,0.25,0.5)	RD (0,0.75,0.25)	D (0,1,0)	NA (0,0,1)
A	(1,0,0)	1	0.75	0.25	0	0	0
RA	(0.75,0,0.25)	0.75	1	0.5	0.25	0	0.25
N	(0.25,0.25,0.5)	0.25	0.5	1	0.5	0.25	0.5
RD	(0,0.75,0.25)	0	0.25	0.5	1	0.75	0.25
D	(0,1,0)	0	0	0.25	0.75	1	0
NA	(0,0,1)	0	0.25	0.5	0.25	0	1

The result of this step is a set of vectors of fuzzy values indicating similarity degree between a candidate and a voter in the context of a particular question. These vectors are collected in Table 8. The advantage of the chosen similarity measure is its simplicity and the ability to easily compare the results. Although this measure is fuzzy, it is influenced by uncertainty - e.g. according to this measure a certain information like (0.5, 0.5, 0) would be more similar to another certain information (0.3, 0.7, 0) than to uncertain one like (0.3, 0.3, 0.4) (notice that this would not be true if we used a similarity measure based on membership and nonmembership only).

Table 8. Vectors of similarity between the answers of candidate c_k and of a voter u

	q_1	q_2	q_3	q_4	q_5	q_6	q_7	q_8
c_1	0	0.25	1	0.25	0.25	0	0	0
c_2	0.75	0.75	0.75	0.25	0.25	0.25	1	0.5
c_3	0.75	0.75	0	0.5	1	1	0.25	0.25
c_4	1	0.75	0	0.25	0	0	1	0.25
c_5	0	0.75	0	0.25	0	0	0	0.75

5   Linguistic Quantifier in Calculating Recommendation

A final recommendation is made by a valuation of the sentence (S1). (S1) can be formalized in the following way:

$$Q \, Imp \, x \quad \text{are} \quad Sim \tag{3}$$

where Q is a linguistic quantifier of "most" type (see [14]) and a set of questions P forms a universe of discourse, $x \in P$, with two fuzzy sets defined: Imp - "important questions" (with importance expressed by a vector w) and Sim - "similar questions" (questions answered in a similar way by candidate c_k and a voter). Thus the degree of truth of (S1) is calculated as the relative scalar cardinality of those two fuzzy sets, i.e.:

$$[\![Q \, Imp \, x \quad \text{are} \quad Sim]\!] = Q(\sigma_f(Sim|Imp)) = Q\left(\frac{\sigma_f(Sim \cap_T Imp)}{\sigma_f(Imp)}\right). \tag{4}$$

An intersection of two fuzzy sets $A \cap_T B$ is generated by a t-norm T, where the two most common ones are the minimum t-norm $aTb = a \wedge b$ and the algebraic t-norm: $a \, T_a \, b = a \cdot b$. Moreover, σ_f is a generalized scalar cardinality of fuzzy set A defined as

$$\sigma_f(A) = \sum_{x \in supp(A)} f(A(x))$$

with a cardinality pattern f, where $f : [0,1] \rightarrow [0,1]$ is a non-decreasing function, $f(0) = 0$ and $f(1) = 1$ (for more details see e.g. [15]). The simplest example of cardinality pattern is the identity function, which will be used during our further considerations.

In previous sections we have discussed our approaches to modeling importance and similarity. We have constructed fuzzy set of important questions(Imp), presented in Table 6, and a fuzzy sets of similar answers(Sim), presented in Table 8. Now we come to the final solution for our example, obtained by calculating a degree of truth of (S1) according to formula (2), for each candidate $k = 1, 2, \ldots, m$. We take $f = id$, $T = T_a$ and:

$$Q(x) = \begin{cases} 1, & \text{if } x \geq 0.8, \\ 2x - 0.6, & \text{if } x \in (0.3, 0.8), \\ 0, & \text{if } x \leq 0.3. \end{cases}$$

As a result we obtain a list of candidates with an assigned degree specifying fulfillment of (S1), i.e. a list of candidates similar to a voter in terms of political beliefs. For the recommendation we naturally choose the one with the highest degree. Table 9 presents the final ranking of candidates. Candidate c_2 seems to be the best one.

Table 9. Ranking of candidates

pos.	cand.	degree
1.	c_2	0,96
2.	c_3	0,61
3.	c_4	0,32
4.	c_1	0
5.	c_5	0

Note that alternatively to (S1) we can formulate a sentence like (S2): "Not too many important questions are not similar", or others.

6   Conclusions

In this paper we have developed the successive parts of a system for recommending a candidate to a voter in a political election. The main observation is that IF-set theory can adequately model incomplete knowledge about a candidate's political views, and make it possible to operate successfully on such information. In the recommending process we have used a similarity measure of IF-sets and linguistic quantifier. The system can be customized by choosing a proper quantifier Q and a suitable cardinality pattern and t-norms. As part of this work an implementation of a recommender system was developed. This is a Web application that is intended to be a universal platform for creating recommender systems for elections for everyone who needs it, in an easy way. In our further research we would like to apply and compare different similarity measures of IF-sets.

References

1. Jannach, D., Zanker, M., Felfernig, A., Friedrich, G.: Recommender Systems: An Introduction. Cambridge University Press (2010)
2. Vozalis, E., Margaritis, K.G.: Analysis of recommender systems algorithms. In: Proceedings of The Sixth Hellenic European Conference on Computer Mathematics and its Applications, HERCMA 2003 (2003)
3. Yager, R.R.: Fuzzy logic methods in recommender systems. Fuzzy Sets and Systems 136, 133–149 (2003)
4. Terán, L., Meier, A.: A Fuzzy Recommender System for eElections. In: Andersen, K.N., Francesconi, E., Grönlund, Å., van Engers, T.M. (eds.) EGOVIS 2010. LNCS, vol. 6267, pp. 62–76. Springer, Heidelberg (2010)
5. WWW: Center for Citizenship Education, http://www.ceo.org.pl/
6. WWW: Web service "Latarnik wyborczy" (Eng. Election Lighthouse), http://latarnik.nq.pl/
7. Atanassov, K.: Intuitionistic fuzzy sets. Fuzzy Sets and Systems 20, 87–96 (1986)
8. Atanassov, K.: Intuitionistic fuzzy sets: Theory and Applications. Springer (1999)
9. Pankowska, A., Wygralak, M.: On Hesitation Degrees in IF-Set Theory. In: Rutkowski, L., Siekmann, J.H., Tadeusiewicz, R., Zadeh, L.A. (eds.) ICAISC 2004. LNCS (LNAI), vol. 3070, pp. 338–343. Springer, Heidelberg (2004)
10. Szmidt, E., Kacprzyk, J.: Distances between intuitionistic fuzzy sets. Fuzzy Sets and Systems 114, 505–518 (2000)
11. Szmidt, E., Kacprzyk, J.: A Similarity Measure for Intuitionistic Fuzzy Sets and Its Application in Supporting Medical Diagnostic Reasoning. In: Rutkowski, L., Siekmann, J.H., Tadeusiewicz, R., Zadeh, L.A. (eds.) ICAISC 2004. LNCS (LNAI), vol. 3070, pp. 388–393. Springer, Heidelberg (2004)
12. Szmidt, E., Kacprzyk, J.: Analysis of Similarity Measures for Atanassov's Intuitionistic Fuzzy Sets. In: Proccedings of IFSA-EUSFLAT 2009, pp. 1416–1421 (2009)
13. Szmidt, E., Kacprzyk, J.: Intuitionistic fuzzy sets two and three term representations in the context of a hausdorff distance. Acta Universitatis Matthiae Belii 19, 53–62 (2011)
14. Yager, R.R.: Interpreting linguistically quantified propositions. International Journal of Intelligent Systems 9, 541–569 (1994)
15. Wygralak, M.: Cardinalities of fuzzy sets. Springer, Heidelberg (2003)

Generation of Interval-Valued Intuitionistic Fuzzy Implications from K-Operators, Fuzzy Implications and Fuzzy Coimplications

Renata Reiser[1], Benjamín Bedregal[2],
Humberto Bustince[3], and Javier Fernandez[3]

[1] Centro de Desenvolvimento Tecnológico, Universidade Federal de Pelotas
Rua Gomes Carneiro, 1, Centro, 96010/610 Pelotas, Brazil
reiser@inf.ufpel.edu.br
[2] Depto. de Informática e Matemática Aplicada,
Universidade Federal do Rio Grande do Norte
Campus Universitário s/n, 59072-970 Natal, Brazil
bedregal@dimap.ufrn.br
[3] Depto. de Automática y Computación, Universidad Pública de Navarra
Campus Arrosadia s/n, 31006 Pamplona, Spain
{bustince,fcojavier.fernandez}@unavarra.es

Abstract. The interval-valued intuitionistic fuzzy implications which are generated from interval-valued fuzzy implications and coimplications and from K-operators are introduced, extending the main properties of fuzzy implication and exploring the class of interval-valued intuitionistic S-implications.

Keywords: interval-valued intuitionistic fuzzy logic, fuzzy implications, K-operators.

1 Introduction

In Bustince et al. [7], in order to construct interval connectives (shortly IV-connectives) such as t-norms, t-conorms and fuzzy negations, it makes use of K-operators, enabling an interval approach for the fuzzy connectives based on the concept of interval amplitudes. In [12], starting with preliminary definitions of interval representations and fuzzy negations, recalling the $K_\alpha-$operator, the conditions in which IV-implications and their conjugates satisfy the main properties of fuzzy implications are studied. Following both approaches, this paper shows that interval-valued intuitionistic fuzzy implications (shortly IVI implications), as conceived by Atanassov [1], can be generated from K-operators. The class of IVI S-implications is also considered.

This paper is organized as follows: in Sect. 3, focussing not only on IV-implications, but also on their dual structure named IV-coimplications, their main properties and canonical representation are reported. In particular, Sect. 3.1 explores K-representable S-(co)implications which are interval S-(co)implications obtained from the action of K-operators and a dual pair of an S-implication and an S-coimplication, and therefore from interval t-(co)norms and interval strong fuzzy negations. Via the generalized Atanassov's operator, in Sect. 4, the more general class of IVI-implications obtained from IV-(co)implications and K-operators is defined. Our study also considers,

S. Greco et al. (Eds.): IPMU 2012, Part II, CCIS 298, pp. 450–460, 2012.
© Springer-Verlag Berlin Heidelberg 2012

in Sect. 4.1, the K-representable intuitionistic S-implications, showing that they are preserved by such generalized structure. We conclude with main results and further work.

2 Preliminaries

2.1 Interval Representations

Consider the real unit interval $U = [0,1] \subseteq \Re$ and let $\mathbb{U}$ be the set of all subintervals of U, that is, $\mathbb{U} = \{[a,b] \mid 0 \le a \le b \le 1\}$. The projection-functions $l, r : \mathbb{U} \to U$, defined as $l([a,b]) = a$ and $r([a,b]) = b$. For an arbitrary $X \in \mathbb{U}$, $l(X)$ and $r(X)$ will be denoted by $\underline{X}$ and $\overline{X}$, respectively. For each $x \in U$, the interval $[x,x]$ is called a degenerate interval and will be denoted by x. Among different relations on interval-valued fuzzy sets, the partial order that is considered in this paper is the component-wise *Kulisch-Miranker order* (also called *product order*), given by:

$$X \le_{\mathbb{U}} Y \Leftrightarrow \underline{X} \le \underline{Y} \wedge \overline{X} \le \overline{Y}, \ \forall X, Y \in \mathbb{U}. \tag{1}$$

Thus, $\mathbf{0} = [0,0] \le_{\mathbb{U}} X \le_{\mathbb{U}} \mathbf{1} = [1,1] \in \mathbb{U}$, for all $X \in \mathbb{U}$.

A function $F : \mathbb{U}^n \to \mathbb{U}$ is an **interval representation** of a function $f : U^n \to U$ if, for each $\mathbf{X} \in \mathbb{U}^n$ and $\mathbf{x} \in \mathbf{X}$, $f(\mathbf{x}) \in F(\mathbf{X})$ [14]. An interval function may be seen as a representation of a subset of real numbers. An interval function $F : \mathbb{U}^n \to \mathbb{U}$ is a *better interval representation* of $f : U^n \to U$ than $G : \mathbb{U}^n \to \mathbb{U}$, denoted by $G \sqsubseteq F$, if, for each $\mathbf{X} \in \mathbb{U}^n$, $F(\mathbf{X}) \subseteq G(\mathbf{X})$. And, the **canonical representation of a real function** $f : U^n \to U$, is the interval function $\widehat{f} : \mathbb{U}^n \to \mathbb{U}$ defined by

$$\widehat{f}(\mathbf{X}) = [\inf\{f(\mathbf{x}) : \mathbf{x} \in \mathbf{X}\}, \sup\{f(\mathbf{x}) : \mathbf{x} \in \mathbf{X}\}]. \tag{2}$$

The interval function $\widehat{f}$ is well defined and for any other interval representation F of f, $F \sqsubseteq \widehat{f}$. It also returns a narrower interval than any other interval representation of f. Thus, $\widehat{f}$ has the *optimality property* of interval algorithms [10].

2.2 Interval-Valued Fuzzy Negation and Interval-Valued Triangular (Co)norms

A function $N : U \to U$ is a *fuzzy negation* if, for all $x, y \in U$, it holds that:

N1 : $N(0) = 1$ and $N(1) = 0$;   **N2** : If $x \ge y$ then $N(x) \le N(y)$.

Moreover, fuzzy negations verifying the involutive property, **N3**:$N(N(x)) = x, \forall x \in U$, are called strong fuzzy negations (SFN in short). So, $N_S : U \to U, N_S(x) = 1 - x$, called the standard negation, is SFN function on U. A fuzzy negation N is a *strict* one if it also verifies the next two properties [11], [N3]: N is continuous; and [N4]: If $x < y$ then $N(x) > N(y), \forall x, y \in U$. And, each strong fuzzy negation is a strict fuzzy negation.

An interval function $\mathbb{N} : \mathbb{U} \to \mathbb{U}$ is an **interval fuzzy negation** (IVFN, shortly) if, for any X, Y in $\mathbb{U}$, the following properties hold:

$\mathbb{N}1$: $\mathbb{N}(\mathbf{0}) = \mathbf{1}$ and $\mathbb{N}(\mathbf{1}) = \mathbf{0}$; $\mathbb{N}2$: If $X \ge_{\mathbb{U}} Y$ then $\mathbb{N}(X) \le_{\mathbb{U}} \mathbb{N}(Y)$.

When $\mathbb{N}$ meets the interval extension of involutive property, $\text{N3} : \mathbb{N}(\mathbb{N}(X)) = X$, for all $X \in \mathbb{U}$, then $\mathbb{N}$ is a strong IVFN. An IVFN is a *strict* function if it also verifies the properties: [N3a]: $\mathbb{N}$ is Moore continuous; [N3b]: $\mathbb{N}$ is Scott continuous; and [N4]: $\mathbb{N}(Y) <_{\mathbb{U}} \mathbb{N}(X)$, if $X <_{\mathbb{U}} Y$. And, from **N2** and Eq.(2), a formula for $\widehat{N}$ is given by:

$$\widehat{N}(X) = [N(\overline{X}), N(\underline{X})]. \tag{3}$$

Theorem 1. *[5, Theorem 4.2] When $N : U {\to} U$ is a SFN function, $\widehat{N}$ is a strong IVFN.*

A triangular (co)norm (t-(co)norm, for short) is a function $(S)T : U^2 \to U$ satisfying commutativity, associativity and monotonicity properties and has $(0)1$ as the neutral element. An N-dual t-(co)norm $(S)T$ is a (t-norm) t-conorm $(S_N)T_N : U^2 {\to} U$ given by:

$$(S_N(x,y) = N(S(N(x),N(y)))) \quad T_N(x,y) = N(T(N(x),N(y))). \tag{4}$$

When N is a SFN on U, $((S, S_N))\,(T, T_N)$ is a pair of mutual dual functions [11].

An interval t-(co)norm $(\mathbb{S})\mathbb{T} : \mathbb{U}^2 {\to} \mathbb{U}$ verifies the interval extension of these properties, which means, it satisfies the commutativity, associativity and monotonicity properties and has $(\mathbf{0})\mathbf{1}$ as the neutral element. In a dual approach, according with [4], $(\mathbb{S}_N)\mathbb{T}_N : \mathbb{U}^2 {\to} \mathbb{U}$ is an interval (t-norm) t-conorm given as:

$$(\mathbb{S}_{\mathbb{N}}(X,Y) = \mathbb{N}(\mathbb{S}(\mathbb{N}(X),\mathbb{N}(Y)))) \quad \mathbb{T}_{\mathbb{N}}(X,Y) = \mathbb{N}(\mathbb{T}(\mathbb{N}(X),\mathbb{N}(Y))). \tag{5}$$

When $\mathbb{N}$ is involutive on $\mathbb{U}$, $((\mathbb{S}, \mathbb{S}_{\mathbb{N}}))\,(\mathbb{T}, \mathbb{T}_{\mathbb{N}})$ is a pair of mutual dual interval functions.

2.3 K-Operators

Based on [7, Def. 2], when $M_A : \mathcal{X} \to \mathbb{U}$ is a membership function on the universe $\mathcal{X} \neq \emptyset$, an interval-valued fuzzy set A (IVFS A in short) on $\mathcal{X}$ is defined by $A = \{(x, M_A(x)) : x \in \mathcal{X}\}$. An IVFS A can also be viewed as a fuzzy set in $L{-}$Goguen's sense, in the complete lattice $(\mathbb{U}, \leq_{\mathbb{U}})$, for all $X \in \mathbb{U}$ such that $\mathbf{0} \leq_{\mathbb{U}} X \leq_{\mathbb{U}} \mathbf{1}$. Introduced by Atanassov, a **K$-$operator** is a family of function to associate each FS to IVFS, see [2] and [1]. From definition of a K-operator, IV connectives can be generated.

Definition 1. *[7, Def. 3] A family of functions $(K_\alpha : \mathbb{U}{\to}\mathbb{U})_{\alpha \in U}$ is a **K$-$operator** if it satisfies the next properties:*

K1 $K_\alpha(\mathbf{x}) = x$, *for all $x \in U$;*
K2 $K_0(X) = \underline{X}$, $K_1(X) = \overline{X}$, *for all $X \in \mathbb{U}$;*
K3 *If $X \leq Y$ then $K_\alpha(X) \leq K_\alpha(Y)$, for all $X, Y \in \mathbb{U}$ and $\alpha \in U$;*
K4 $\alpha \leq \beta$ *iff $K_\alpha(X) \leq K_\beta(X)$, for all $X \in \mathbb{U}$ and $\alpha, \beta \in U$.*

For notational simplicity we will use $K_{\alpha \in U}$ instead of $(K_\alpha : \mathbb{U} \to U)_{\alpha \in U}$. Thus, K_α denotes the α element of the $K_{\alpha \in U}$ family.

Proposition 1. *[12, Prop. 1] Let $\alpha \in U$ and W_X be the amplitude of the interval X, i.e. $W_X = \overline{X} - \underline{X}$. Then, the family of functions $A_{\alpha \in U}(A^{\alpha \in U}) : \mathbb{U} \to U$ expressed by Eq. (6) in the following, are K-operators.*

$$A_\alpha(X) = A_0(X) + \alpha W_X \quad (A^\alpha(X) = A_1(X) - \alpha W_X). \tag{6}$$

A_α is called the Atanassov's operator, known as weighted arithmetic mean (or convex combination). The role of W_X in Eq. (6) is to guarantee that $A_\alpha(X), A^\alpha(X) \in X$.

Proposition 2. *[7, Theorem 21] When $\mathbb{N}$ is an IVFN and $K_{\alpha \in U}$ is a K-operator then*

$$W_X = W_{\mathbb{N}(X)} \quad iff \quad \mathbb{N}(X) = [N_S(K_1(X)), N_S(K_0(X))]. \tag{7}$$

Concluding this section, an N_S-dual K-operator is introduced.

Proposition 3. *The family $(A_{\alpha,N} : \mathbb{U} \to U)_{\alpha \in U}$ where for each $\alpha \in U$*

$$A_{\alpha N}(X) = N_S(A_{N_S(\alpha)}(\mathbb{N}_S(X))), \forall X \in \mathbb{U}, \tag{8}$$

*is a K-operator, called as the $\mathbb{N}_S$-**dual K-operator** of an $A_{\alpha \in U}$ family,*

Proof. Based on results of Prop. 1, Eq.(6) and Prop.2, Eq.(7), $A_{\alpha N}$ is well defined:

$$A_{N_S(\alpha)}(\mathbb{N}_S(X)) = A_0(\mathbb{N}_S(X)) + N_S(\alpha)W_{\mathbb{N}_S(X)} = N_S(A_1(X)) + N_S(\alpha)W_X.$$

Therefore, $A_{N_S(\alpha)}(\mathbb{N}_S(X)) = N_S(A_0(X)) + \alpha W_X = N_S(A_\alpha(X))$. In addition, $A_{\alpha N}$ also verifies the K-operator's properties:

K1 $A_{\alpha N}(\mathbf{x}) = N_S(A_{N(\alpha)}(\mathbb{N}_S(\mathbf{x}))) = N_S(N_S(x)) = x$, for all $x \in U$;

K2 $A_{0N}(X) = N_S(A_1(\mathbb{N}_S(X))) = \underline{X}$, $A_{1N}(X) = N_S(A_0(\mathbb{N}_S(X))) = \overline{X}, \forall X \in \mathbb{U}$;

K3 If $X \leq Y$, $A_{\alpha N}(\mathbb{N}_S(X)) \geq A_{\alpha N}(\mathbb{N}_S(Y))$ iff $N_S(A_{\alpha N}(\mathbb{N}_S(X))) \leq N_S(A_{\alpha N}(\mathbb{N}_S(Y)))$, and so, $A_{\alpha N}(X) \leq K_{\alpha N}(Y), \forall X, Y \in \mathbb{U}, \alpha \in U$;

K4 $\alpha \leq \beta$ iff $N_S(A_{\alpha N}(\mathbb{N}_S(X))) \leq N_S(A_{\beta N}(\mathbb{N}_S(X)))$ iff $A_{\alpha N}(X) \leq A_{\beta N}(X)$, for all $X \in \mathbb{U}$ and $\alpha, \beta \in U$.

Proposition 4. *An $\mathbb{N}_S$-dual K-operator of an $A_{\alpha \in U}$ family can be given as*

$$A_{\alpha N}(X), = A^\alpha(X), \forall \alpha \in U, \forall X \in \mathbb{U}. \tag{9}$$

Proof. By Eq. (6), $N_S(A_\alpha(\mathbb{N}_S(X)) = N_S(N_S(A_1(X)) + \alpha(N_S(A_0(X)) - N_S(A_1(X))))$, which means, $N_S(A_\alpha(\mathbb{N}_S(X)) = A_1(X) - \alpha W_X = A^\alpha(X)$. So, $A_{\alpha N}(X) = A^\alpha(X)$.

Proposition 5. *[7, Theorems 8,10] Let $\alpha, \beta \in U$, $\alpha < \beta$ and $(S_a, S_b)T_a, T_b:U^2 \to U$ be t-(co)norms such that $(S_a \leq S_b)\ T_a \leq T_b$. A function $(\mathbb{S}_{S_a, S_b}), \mathbb{T}_{T_A, T_b}:\mathbb{U}^2 \to \mathbb{U}$, given as*

$$\mathbb{S}_{S_a, S_b}(X, Y) = [S_a(K_\alpha(X), K_\alpha(Y)), S_b(K_\beta(X), K_\beta(Y))]; \tag{10}$$

$$\mathbb{T}_{T_a, T_b}(X, Y) = [T_a(K_\alpha(X), K_\alpha(Y)), T_b(K_\beta(X), K_\beta(Y))], \tag{11}$$

is an interval t-(co)norm iff $K_\alpha(X) = K_0(X)$ and $K_\beta(X) = K_1(X)$, for all $X, Y \in \mathbb{U}$.

By [9, Def. 5], when $\alpha = 0$ and $\beta = 1$, (Eq. (10)) Eq. (11) characterizes an IV t-(conorm) $(\mathbb{S})\mathbb{T}$ as a t-representable t-(co)norm. Moreover, by [7, Def.7], an interval t-(co)norm $(\mathbb{S}_{S_a, S_b})\mathbb{T}_{T_a, T_b}:\mathbb{U}^2 \to \mathbb{U}$ is said to be representable iff there exist $(S_a, S_b)T_a, T_b: U^2 \to U$ such that, for all $X, Y \in \mathbb{U}$, it holds that:

$$K_0(\mathbb{S}_{S_a, S_b}(X, Y)) = S_a(K_0(X), K_0(Y)), K_1(\mathbb{S}_{S_a, S_b}(X, Y)) = S_b(K_1(X), K_1(Y)); \tag{12}$$

$$K_0(\mathbb{T}_{T_a, T_b}(X, Y)) = T_a(K_0(X), K_0(Y)), K_1(\mathbb{T}_{T_a, T_b}(X, Y)) = T_b(K_1(X), K_1(Y)). \tag{13}$$

3 Interval-Valued Fuzzy (Co)implications

The agreement over several definitions of fuzzy implications and of their dual construction named fuzzy coimplications (see [3,8] and [16]) is that they should have the same behavior as the classical ones for the crisp case. Thus, a function $(J)I : U^2 \to U$ is a *fuzzy (co)implication* if $(J)I$ meets the boundary conditions:

I1 : $I(1,1) = I(0,1) = I(0,0) = 1$ and $I(1,0) = 0$.
J1 : $J(1,1) = J(1,0) = J(0,0) = 0$ and $J(0,1) = 1$.

Several other properties may be required for fuzzy implications:

J2: if $x \leq z$ then $J(x,y) \geq J(z,y)$; **I2**: if $x \leq z$ then $I(x,y) \geq I(z,y)$;
J3: if $y \leq t$ then $J(x,y) \leq J(x,t)$; **I3**: if $y \leq t$ then $I(x,y) \leq I(x,t)$;
J4: $J(1,y) = 0$;   **I4**: $I(0,y) = 1$;
J5: $J(x,0) = 0$;   **I5**: $I(x,1) = 1$;
J6: $J(0,y) = y$;   **I6**: $I(1,y) = y$;
J7: $J(x,J(y,z)) = J(y,J(x,z))$;   **I7**: $I(x,I(y,z)) = I(y,I(x,z))$;
J8: $J(x,y) = 0$ iff $x \geq y$;   **I8**: $I(x,y) = 1$ iff $x \leq y$;
J9: $J(x,y) \leq y$;   **I9**: $I(x,y) \geq y$;
J10: $J(x,x) = 0$;   **I10**: $I(x,x) = 1$;
J11: $J(x,y) = J(N(y),N(x))$;   **I11**: $I(x,y) = I(N(y),N(x))$.

An N-dual (co)implication $(J_N)I_N:U^2 \to U$ is a (implication) coimplication given by:

$$(J_N(x,y) = N(J(N(x),N(y)))) \quad I_N(x,y) = N(I(N(x),N(y))). \tag{14}$$

When N is a SFN on U, $((J, J_N))$ (I, I_N) is a pair of mutual dual functions.

For an interval (co)implication $(\mathbb{J})\mathbb{I} : \mathbb{U}^2 \to \mathbb{U}$ the following conditions hold:

I1: $\mathbb{I}(1,1) = \mathbb{I}(0,0) = \mathbb{I}(0,1) = 1$ and $\mathbb{I}(1,0) = 0$.
J1: $\mathbb{J}(1,1) = \mathbb{J}(0,0) = \mathbb{J}(1,0) = 0$ and $\mathbb{J}(0,1) = 1$.

In addition, a corresponding $\mathbb{N}$-dual (co)implication $(\mathbb{J_N})\mathbb{I_N}:\mathbb{U}^2 \to \mathbb{U}$ is given by:

$$(\mathbb{J_N}(X,Y) = \mathbb{N}(\mathbb{J}(\mathbb{N}(X),\mathbb{N}(Y)))), \quad \mathbb{I_N}(X,Y) = \mathbb{N}(\mathbb{I}(\mathbb{N}(X),\mathbb{N}(Y))). \tag{15}$$

When $\mathbb{N}$ is a strong IVFN, $((\mathbb{J}, \mathbb{J_N}))$ $(\mathbb{I}, \mathbb{I_N})$ is a pair of mutual dual interval functions. And so, their related properties can be naturally extended to the interval approach [9]. Those properties, from **(J2)** **I2** to **(J11)I11** in $(U, \leq)$ can be applicable to $(\mathbb{U}, \leq_U)$, and their related extensions will be denoted by **(J2)** **I2** ... **(J11)** **I11** in the following.

Proposition 6. *[6, Prop. 21] [13, Prop. 3.7] A fuzzy (co)implication $(J)I : U^2 \to U$ satisfies* **(J2)** **I2** *and* **(J3)** **I3** *iff its canonical representation $(\widehat{J})\widehat{I}$, can be expressed as*

$$\widehat{I}(X,Y) = [I(\overline{X},\underline{Y}), I(\underline{X},\overline{Y})]; \quad \widehat{J}(X,Y) = [J(\overline{X},\underline{Y}), J(\underline{X},\overline{Y})].$$

Proposition 7. *[12, Prop.4] Let $K_{\alpha \in U}$ be a K-operator, and $\alpha, \beta \in U$ such that $\alpha \leq \beta$ and $(J_a, J_b)I_a, I_b : U^2 \to U$ be fuzzy (co)implications satisfying* **(J2, J3)** **I2, I3** *such that $(J_b \leq J_a)$ $I_a \leq I_b$. Thus, $(\mathbb{J}_{J_a,J_b})\mathbb{I}_{I_a,I_b} : \mathbb{U}^2 \to \mathbb{U}$ is an IV-(co)implication given by:*

$$\mathbb{I}_{I_a,I_b}(X,Y) = [I_a(K_\beta(X), K_\alpha(Y)), I_b(K_\alpha(X), K_\beta(Y))], \tag{16}$$

$$\mathbb{J}_{J_a,J_b}(X,Y) = [J_b(K_\beta(X), K_\alpha(Y)), J_a(K_\alpha(X), K_\beta(Y))]; \tag{17}$$

According with conditions stated in Prop. 7, an interval (co)implication $(\mathbb{J}_{J_a,J_b})\mathbb{I}_{I_a,I_b}$ generated by $(J_a, J_b)I_a, I_b$ and K_α, K_β operators is said to be K-**representable**.

Proposition 8. *[12, Prop. 5] Let $(\mathbb{J}_{J_a,J_b})\mathbb{I}_{I_a,I_b} : \mathbb{U}^2 \to \mathbb{U}$ be a K-representable (co)implication given by (Eq. (16)) Eq. (17)), as stated in Prop. 7. When $K_\alpha = K_0$, $K_\beta = K_1$ and $(J)I : U \to U$ satisfies $(\mathbf{J_2}, \mathbf{J_3})\mathbf{I_2}, \mathbf{I_3}$, then $(\mathbb{J}_{J,J} = \widehat{J})\,\mathbb{I}_{I,I} = \widehat{I}$.*

Proposition 9. *Let $K_{\alpha \in U}$ be a K-operator, and $\alpha, \beta \in U$ such that $\alpha \leq \beta$ and $(J_a, J_b)I_a, I_b : U^2 \to U$ be fuzzy (co)implications satisfying $(\mathbf{J2})\,\mathbf{I2}$ and $(\mathbf{J3})\,\mathbf{I3}$ and such that $(J_b \leq J_a)\,I_a \leq I_b$. When $\mathbb{N} = \widehat{N_S}$ and $N = N_S$ such that $N_S(\alpha) = \beta$, then the $\mathbb{N}_S$-dual construction of an IV-implication $\mathbb{I}_{I_a,I_b}$ is an IV-(co)implication given by:*

$$\mathbb{I}_{I_a,I_b\mathbb{N}}(X,Y) = [I_{bN}(K_\beta(X), K_\alpha(Y)), I_{aN}(K_\alpha(X), K_\beta(Y))]; \tag{18}$$

$$\mathbb{J}_{J_a,J_b\mathbb{N}}(X,Y) = [J_{aN}(K_\beta(X), K_\alpha(Y)), J_{bN}(K_\alpha(X), K_\beta(Y))]. \tag{19}$$

Proof. We prove the former, the latter is analogously done. So, taking $\mathbb{N} = \mathbb{N}_S$, $N = N_S$ and $N_S(\alpha) = \beta$, it holds that:

$$\mathbb{I}_{I_a,I_b\mathbb{N}_S}(X,Y) = \mathbb{N}(\mathbb{I}_{I_a,I_b}(\mathbb{N}(X), \mathbb{N}(Y))) \text{ by Eq.(15)}$$
$$= \mathbb{N}([I_a(K_\beta(\mathbb{N}(X)), K_\alpha(\mathbb{N}(Y))), I_b(K_\alpha(\mathbb{N}(X)), K_\beta(\mathbb{N}(Y)))]) \text{ by Eq.(16)}$$
$$= \mathbb{N}([I_a(N(K_\alpha(X)), N(K_\beta(Y))), I_b(N(K_\beta(X)), N(K_\alpha(Y)))])\text{by Eq.(8)}$$
$$= [I_{bN_S}(K_\beta(X), K_\alpha(Y)), I_{aN_S}(K_\alpha(X), K_\beta(Y))] \text{ by Eqs.(3),(14).}$$

Necessary conditions are presented, in addition to the constrains stated in Prop. 7.

Proposition 10. *A K-representable IV-(co)implication $(\mathbb{J}_{J_a,J_b})\,\mathbb{I}_{I_a,I_b}$ satisfies the property $(\mathbf{J}k)\,\mathbb{I}k$ if $(J_a, J_b)I_a, I_b$ satisfy the property $(\mathbf{J}k)\mathbf{I}k$ such that*

(i) $K_\alpha \leq K_\beta$, for $k \in \{1, \ldots, 5\}$;
(ii) $K_\beta = K_1$ and $K_\alpha = K_0$, for $k \in \{6, 7, 9\}$;
(iii) $K_\alpha = K_\beta$ and $K_\alpha(X) \leq K_\alpha(Y)$ implies that $X \leq_U Y$, for $k \in \{8, 10\}$;
(iv) $K_\alpha = N_S \circ K_\beta$, when $k = 11$ and $\mathbb{N} = \mathbb{N}_S$.

Proof. We prove the former, the latter related to IV-coimplications is analogously done. Items (i), (ii) and (iii) follow from Props. 6, 7 and 8 in [12], respectively. For item (iv), take $K_\alpha = N_S \circ K_\beta$ and I_a, I_b verifying $\mathbf{I}11$. So, by Eqs. (8,16), if $\mathbb{N} = \mathbb{N}_S$, we have:

$$\mathbb{I}_{I_a,I_b}(\mathbb{N}_S(Y), \mathbb{N}_S(X)) = [I_a(K_\beta(\mathbb{N}_S(Y)), K_\alpha(\mathbb{N}_S(X))), I_b(K_\alpha(\mathbb{N}_S(Y)), K_\beta(\mathbb{N}_S(X)))]$$
$$= [I_a(N_S(K_\alpha(Y)), N_S(K_\beta(X))), I_b(N_S(K_\alpha(Y)), N_S(K_\beta(X)))]$$
$$= [I_a(K_\beta(X), K_\alpha(Y)), I_b(K_\beta(Y), K_\alpha(X))] = \mathbb{I}_{I_a,I_b}(X,Y).$$

3.1 $\mathbb{S}$-Implications

Let T (S) be a t-norm (t-conorm) and N be a fuzzy negation. A fuzzy (co)implication $(J_{(T,N)})I_{(S,N)} : U^2 \to U$, called (S, N)-**(co)implication**, is defined as

$$I_{(S,N)}(x,y) = S(N(x),y), \quad J_{(T,N)}(x,y) = T(N(x),y). \tag{20}$$

And, if N is strong, it is a strong (co)implication, called S-**(co)implication**.

Proposition 11. *[15, Theorem 3.2] A function $I_S : U^2 \to U$ is an S-implication iff it satisfies the Properties: I2, I3, I6, I7 and I11.*

Based on dual Trillas and Valverde's characterization, an S-coimplication also verifies the Properties: **J2, J3, J6, J7** and **J11**.

Let $\mathbb{T}$ ($\mathbb{S}$) be an interval t-norm (t-conorm) and $\mathbb{N}$ be an interval fuzzy negation. An interval function $(\mathbb{J}_{(\mathbb{T},\mathbb{N})})\mathbb{I}_{(\mathbb{S},\mathbb{N})} : \mathbb{U}^2 \to \mathbb{U}$ is an interval (co)implication, called $((\mathbb{T}, \mathbb{N})$-coimplication) $(\mathbb{S}, \mathbb{N})$-implication, defined as

$$\mathbb{J}_{(\mathbb{T},\mathbb{N})}(X, Y) = \mathbb{T}(\mathbb{N}(X), Y), \quad \mathbb{I}_{(\mathbb{S},\mathbb{N})}(X, Y) = \mathbb{S}(\mathbb{N}(X), Y). \quad (21)$$

And, if $\mathbb{N}$ is strong, $(\mathbb{J}_{(\mathbb{T},\mathbb{N})})\mathbb{I}_{(\mathbb{S},\mathbb{N})}$ is a strong IV (co)implication, called $\mathbb{S}$-(co)implication.

Proposition 12. *[6, Theorem 29] [13, Prop 3.17] An interval function $\mathbb{J}_{(\mathbb{T},\mathbb{N})}, \mathbb{I}_{(\mathbb{S},\mathbb{N})} : \mathbb{U}^2 \to \mathbb{U}$ is a $\mathbb{S}$-(co)implication iff it satisfies the properties ($\mathbb{J}2, \mathbb{J}3, \mathbb{J}6, \mathbb{J}7$ and $\mathbb{J}11$) $\mathbb{I}2, \mathbb{I}3, \mathbb{I}6, \mathbb{I}7$ and $\mathbb{I}11$.*

In addition, when $\mathbb{N}$ is an interval SFN and taking $(\mathbb{T}, \mathbb{S} = \mathbb{T}_\mathbb{N})$ as a pair of N-dual functions, then $(\mathbb{I}_{(\mathbb{S},\mathbb{N})}, \mathbb{J} = \mathbb{I}_{(\mathbb{S},\mathbb{N})_\mathbb{N}})$ also defines a pair of mutual dual functions on $\mathbb{U}^2$. Hereinafter, we present the proof for the implication case, the dual case is analogous.

Proposition 13. *Let $N = N_S$ and (J_a, J_b) I_a, I_b be S-(co)implications. An IV-(co)implication $(\mathbb{J}_{J_a,J_b})\mathbb{I}_{I_a,I_b} : \mathbb{U}^2 \to \mathbb{U}$, given by (Eq. (17)) Eq. (16) and verifying conditions stated in Prop. 7, is an $\mathbb{S}$-(co)implication iff $K_\alpha = K_0$, $K_\beta = K_1$ and $\mathbb{N} = \mathbb{N}_S$.*

Proof. ($\Rightarrow$) By Prop. 11, when I_a and I_b are (S, N)-implications, both verify **I2, I3, I6, I7** and **I11**. Taking $K_\alpha = K_0$, $K_\beta = K_1$ and $\mathbb{N} = \mathbb{N}_S$, by Props. 10 and 5, it is equivalent to say that $\mathbb{I}_{I_a,I_b}$ verifies Properties $\mathbb{I}2$ and $\mathbb{I}3$, $\mathbb{I}6$, $\mathbb{I}7$ including $\mathbb{I}11$, respectively. Therefore, $\mathbb{I}_{I_a,I_b}$ is an $\mathbb{S}$-implication. ($\Leftarrow$) It is proved in a similar way.

Proposition 14. *Let $(J_a, J_b) I_a, I_b : U^2 \to U$ be (S, N_S)-(co)implications. An IV-function $(\mathbb{J}_{J_a,J_b})\mathbb{I}_{I_a,I_b} : \mathbb{U}^2 \to \mathbb{U}$, given by (Eq. 16) Eq. 17 and verifying conditions stated in Prop. 7, is a K-representable (S, N_S)-(co)implication iff $K_\alpha = K_0$ and $K_\beta = K_1$.*

Proof. ($\Rightarrow$) Let $S_a, S_b : U^2 \to U$ be t-conorms and N be a fuzzy negation related to S-implications $I_{(S_a,N)}, I_{(S_b,N)} : U^2 \to U$, which are given by $I_{(S_a,N)}(x, y) = S_a(N(x), y)$ and $I_{(S_b,N)}(x, y) = S_b(N(x), y)$, respectively. By Prop. 7, it follows that:

$$\mathbb{I}_{I_{(S_a,N)},I_{(S_b,N)}}(X,Y) = [I_{(S_a,N)}(K_\beta(X), K_\alpha(Y)), I_{(S_b,N)}(K_\alpha(X), K_\beta(Y))] \text{ by Eq.(16)}$$

$$= [S_a(N(K_\beta(X)), K_\alpha(Y)), S_b(N(K_\alpha(X)), K_\beta(Y))] \text{ by Eq.(20)}$$

$$= [S_a(K_\alpha(\mathbb{N}_S(X)), K_\alpha(Y)), S_b(K_\beta(\mathbb{N}_S(X)), K_\beta(Y))] \text{ by Eq.(8).}$$

So, by Prop. 5, $\mathbb{I}_{I_{(S_a,N)},I_{(S_b,N)}} = \mathbb{S}_{S_a,S_b} \circ \mathbb{N}$, when $\mathbb{N} = \mathbb{N}_S$, which means, it is a K-representable (S, N_S)-implication. ($\Leftarrow$) The converse is proved similarly.

Corollary 1. *A canonical representation of an (S, N)-(co)implication is an interval representable $(\mathbb{S}, \mathbb{N})$-(co)implication expressed as*

$$\widehat{I_{(S,N)}}(X, Y) = \mathbb{I}_{I_{(S,N)}}(X, Y) = [I_{(S,N)}(K_1(X), K_0(Y)), I_{(S,N)}(K_0(X), K_1(Y))],$$

$$\widehat{J_{(T,N)}}(X, Y) = \mathbb{J}_{J_{(T,N)}}(X, Y) = [J_{(T,N)}(K_1(X), K_0(Y)), J_{(T,N)}(K_0(X), K_1(Y))].$$

Proof. Straightforward from Props. 6, 13 and 14.

Example 1. Let N_S, S_M and $\mathbb{T}_M$ be the standard negation, the maximum t-conorm, the minimum t-conorm and consider their corresponding K-representable functions: $\mathbb{N}_S(X) = [N(\overline{X}), N(\underline{X})]$, $\mathbb{S}(X,Y) = [\max(K_0(X), K_0(Y)), \max(K_1(X), K_1(Y))]$ and $\mathbb{T}(X,Y) = [\min(K_0(X), K_0(Y)), \min(K_1(X), K_1(Y))]$. Based on [7, Prop. 5 and Lemma 11], taking $a = b$, $K_\alpha = K_0$ and $K_\beta = K_1$ in Eq.(16), the Kleene-Dienes implication is given by $I_{S_M, N_S}(x, y) = S_M(N_S(x), y) = \max(N(x), y)$. Dually, its coimplication is given by $J_{T_M, N_S}(x, y) = T_M(N_S(x), y) = \min(N(x), y)$. So, a K-representable $\mathbb{S}$-(co)implication, denoted by $(\mathbb{J}_{T_M, N_S})\, \mathbb{I}_{S_M, N_S}$, is given as:

$$\mathbb{I}_{S_M, N_S}(X, Y) = [\max(N(K_1(X)), K_0(Y)), \max(N(K_0(X)), K_1(Y))], \quad (22)$$

$$\mathbb{J}_{T_M, N_S}(X, Y) = [\min(N(K_1(X)), K_0(Y)), \min(N(K_0(X)), K_1(Y))]. \quad (23)$$

4 Interval-Valued Intuitionistic Fuzzy Implications

This section considers the study of IVI fuzzy implications, introduced by Atanassov and conceived as an extension of the intuitionistic fuzzy implications by the integration of concepts of IV membership functions which are not necessarily $\mathbb{N}_S$-dual constructions of non-membership functions.

As the main contribution, a general expression of an IVI fuzzy implication generated by K-operators and a pair of mutual dual functions, named IV-implication and IV-coimplication, is presented following the approach in [7]. Such construction, related to the Atanassov's operator, provides interpretation to these fuzzy connectives based on K-operators acting on interval values of truth and of non-truth in logical propositions.

IVI fuzzy sets, their main concepts and properties are now, briefly studied. For that, let $\tilde{U} = \{\tilde{X} = (X_1, X_2) | (X_1, X_2) \in U^2 \text{ and } X_1 + X_2 \leq 1\}$ be the set of all IVI-fuzzy membership degrees, such that, for all $\tilde{X}, \tilde{Y} \in \tilde{U}$:
(i) $\tilde{X} \leq_{\tilde{U}} \tilde{Y} \Leftrightarrow X_1 \leq Y_1 \text{ and } X_2 \geq Y_2$; (ii) $\tilde{0} = (0, 1) \leq_{\tilde{U}} \tilde{X} \text{ and } \tilde{1} = (1, 0) \geq_{\tilde{U}} \tilde{X}$.
An IVI-set has two projections $l_{\tilde{U}}, r_{\tilde{U}} : \tilde{U} \to U$, defined by $l_{\tilde{U}}(\tilde{X}) = X_1$ and $r_{\tilde{U}}(\tilde{X}) = X_2$, for all $\tilde{X} = (X_1, X_2) \in \tilde{U}$. An IVI-negation $\mathcal{N} : \tilde{U} \to \tilde{U}$ verifies the conditions:
$\mathcal{N}1 : \mathcal{N}(\tilde{0}) = \tilde{1}$ and $\mathcal{N}(\tilde{1}) = \tilde{0}$; $\mathcal{N}2 :$ If $\tilde{X} \geq_{\tilde{U}} \tilde{Y}$ then $\mathcal{N}(\tilde{X}) \leq_{\tilde{U}} \mathcal{N}(\tilde{Y}), \forall \tilde{X}, \tilde{Y} \in \tilde{U}$.

IVI negations satisfying the involutive property are called *strong* IVI-negations:
$\mathcal{N}3 : \mathcal{N}(\mathcal{N}(\tilde{X})) = \tilde{X}, \forall \tilde{X} \in \tilde{U}$. In addition, when $\mathbb{N} : U \to U$ is a strong IV-negation, $\mathcal{N} : \tilde{U} \to \tilde{U}$ given by $\mathcal{N}(\tilde{X}) = \mathcal{N}(X_1, X_2) = (\mathbb{N}(\mathbb{N}_S(X_2)), \mathbb{N}(\mathbb{N}_S(X_1)))$ is a strong IVI-negation. So, if $\mathbb{N} = \mathbb{N}_S$: $\mathcal{N}(\tilde{X}) = (\mathbb{N}_S(\mathbb{N}_S(X_2)), \mathbb{N}_S(\mathbb{N}_S(X_1))) = (X_2, X_1)$.

A function $(\mathcal{S})\mathcal{T} : \tilde{U}^2 \to \tilde{U}$ is an IVI fuzzy triangular (co)norm, if it is commutative, associative and increasing operator with neutral element $(\tilde{0})\, \tilde{1}$. In the following, a K-representable t-(co)norm is presented, based on results of Prop. 5.

Proposition 15. *Let* $(\mathbb{S}_{S_a, S_b}) \mathbb{T}_{T_a, T_b} : U^2 \to U$ *be a representable t-(conorm) verifying conditions of Eq.(12) such that* $\mathbb{T}_{T_a, T_b}(X, Y) \leq \mathbb{N}_S(\mathbb{S}_{S_a, S_b}(\mathbb{N}_S(X), \mathbb{N}_S(Y)))$. *Then, for all* $\tilde{X} = (X_1, X_2), \tilde{Y} = (Y_1, Y_2) \in \tilde{U}$, *an IVI t-(co)norm is defined as*

$$\mathcal{S}(\tilde{X}, \tilde{Y}) = (\mathbb{S}_{S_a, S_b}(X_1, Y_1), \mathbb{T}_{T_a, T_b}(X_2, Y_2)); \mathcal{T}(\tilde{X}, \tilde{Y}) = (\mathbb{T}_{T_a, T_b}(X_1, Y_1), \mathbb{S}_{S_a, S_b}(X_2, Y_2)). \quad (24)$$

Definition 2. *An IVI-implication* $\mathcal{I} : \tilde{U}^2 \to \tilde{U}$ *is a function verifying the conditions:*
$\mathcal{I}1 : \mathcal{I}(\tilde{0}, \tilde{0}) = \mathcal{I}(\tilde{0}, \tilde{1}) = \mathcal{I}(\tilde{1}, \tilde{1}) = \tilde{1}$ *and* $\mathcal{I}(\tilde{1}, \tilde{0}) = \tilde{0}$.

The corresponding properties of fuzzy implications reported in Section 3 can be naturally extended to the bounded lattice $(\tilde{U}, \leq_{\tilde{U}})$, and will be denoted by $\mathcal{I}2, \ldots \mathcal{I}11$.

Definition 3. *Let* $K_{\alpha \in U}$ *be a* K-*operator,* $(J)I : U^2 \to U$ *be a (co)implications satisfying* $(J2, J3)$ $I2, I3$ *and* $(\mathbb{J}_J)\mathbb{I}_I$ *be its* K-*representable fuzzy (co)implication. When* (I, J) *is a pair of dual functions, a function* $\mathcal{I}_{I,J} : \tilde{U}^2 \to \tilde{U}$ *given by:*

$$\mathcal{I}_{I,J}(\tilde{X}, \tilde{Y}) = (\mathbb{I}_I(\mathbb{N}(X_2), Y_1), \mathbb{J}_J(\mathbb{N}(X_1), Y_2)), \forall \tilde{X}, \tilde{Y} \in \tilde{U} \qquad (25)$$

is a K**-representable intuitionistic fuzzy implication,** *whose projections are given as:*

$$(l_{\tilde{U}} \circ \mathcal{I}_{I_a, J_a})(\tilde{X}, \tilde{Y}) = [I(K_1(\mathbb{N}(X_2)), K_0(Y_1)), I(K_0(\mathbb{N}(X_2)), K_1(Y_1))];$$
$$(r_{\tilde{U}} \circ \mathcal{I}_{I,J})(\tilde{X}, \tilde{Y}) = [J(K_1(\mathbb{N}(X_1)), K_0(Y_2)), J(K_0(\mathbb{N}(X_1)), K_1(Y_2))].$$

Theorem 2. *A* K-*representable intuitionistic fuzzy implication* $\mathcal{I}_{I,J} : \tilde{U}^2 \to \tilde{U}$ *defined by conditions of Def. 3 is an IVI-implication.*

Proof. Since I_a satisfies $I2, I3$ and by Prop. 7 and Eq.(25), it follows both inequalities:

(i) $X_1 \leq_U \mathbb{N}_S(X_2)$ implies $K_1(\mathbb{N}_S(X_2)) \geq_U K_1(X_1) = N_S(K_0(\mathbb{N}_S(X_1))$; and
(ii) $Y_1 \leq_U \mathbb{N}_S(Y_2)$ implies $K_0(Y_1) \leq N_S(K_1(Y_2))$. Therefore, it holds that:

$I(K_1(\mathbb{N}_S(X_2)), K_0(Y_1)) \leq_U I(\mathbb{N}_S(K_0(\mathbb{N}_S(X_1))), \mathbb{N}_S(K_1(Y_2)))$. So, we can also state that $I(K_1(\mathbb{N}_S(X_2)), K_0(Y_1)) \leq_U \mathbb{N}_S(J(K_0(\mathbb{N}_S(X_1))), K_1(Y_2))$. Analogously, we have that $I(K_0(\mathbb{N}_S(X_2)), K_1(Y_1)) \leq_U \mathbb{N}_S(J(K_1(\mathbb{N}_S(X_1))), K_0(Y_2))$. So, $\mathcal{I}_{I,J}$ is well defined. In addition, the next boundary conditions are also verified:

$$\mathcal{I}_{I,J}(\tilde{0}, \tilde{0}) = (\mathbb{I}_I(0, 0), \mathbb{J}_J(1, 1)) = \tilde{1}; \quad \mathcal{I}_{I,J}(\tilde{1}, \tilde{1}) = (\mathbb{I}_I(1, 1), \mathbb{J}_J(0, 0)) = \tilde{1};$$
$$\mathcal{I}_{I,J}(\tilde{0}, \tilde{1}) = (\mathbb{I}_I(0, 1), \mathbb{J}_J(1, 0)) = \tilde{1}; \quad \mathcal{I}_{I,J}(\tilde{1}, \tilde{0}) = (\mathbb{I}_I(1, 0), \mathbb{J}_J(0, 1)) = \tilde{0}.$$

The next Props. 16 and 17 follow from Def. 3, Prop. 9 and Prop. 10, respectively.

Proposition 16. *Let* $\mathcal{I}_{I,J} : \tilde{U}^2 \to \tilde{U}$ *be a* IVI_K-*implication defined by conditions of Def. 3 such that* $(\mathbb{I}_I, \mathbb{J}_J)$ *is a pair of mutual* $\mathbb{N}$-*dual IV-functions. Then, the projections of* $\mathcal{I}_{I,J}$ *can be expressed as* $(l_{\tilde{U}} \circ \mathcal{I}_{I,J})(\tilde{X}, \tilde{Y}) = (\mathbb{N} \circ r_{\tilde{U}} \circ \mathcal{I}_{I,J})(\tilde{X}, \tilde{Y})$.

Proposition 17. *Consider* $I, J : U^2 \to U$. *A* K-*representable intuitionistic fuzzy implication* $\mathcal{I}_{I,J} : \tilde{U}^2 \to \tilde{U}$ *given by Def. 3, satisfies the property* $\mathcal{I}k$ *if* I *and* J_a *satisfy* $\mathbf{I}k$ *and* $\mathbf{J}k$, *respectively, such that*

(i) *for all* $k \in \{1, \ldots, 5\}$; (ii) $K_\beta = K_1$ *and* $K_\alpha = K_0$, *for all* $k \in \{6, 7, 9\}$;
(iii) $K_\alpha = K_\beta$, $K_\alpha(X) \leq K_\alpha(Y)$ *implies that* $X \leq_U Y$, *for all* $k \in \{8, 10\}$;
(iv) $K_\alpha(X) = N_S \circ K_\beta(X)$, *when* $k = 11$ *and* $N = N_S$.

4.1 Interval-Valued Intuitionistic Fuzzy S-Implications

Definition 4. *Let* $(S)\mathcal{T} : \tilde{U}^2 \to \tilde{U}$ *be an IVI t-(co)norm and* $\mathcal{N}$ *be an IVI-negation. An interval-valued intuitionistic* $(S, \mathcal{N})$*-implication is a function* $\mathcal{I}_{(S,\mathcal{N})} : \tilde{U}^2 \to \tilde{U}$ *defined by*

$$\mathcal{I}_{(S,\mathcal{N})}(\tilde{X}, \tilde{Y}) = S(\mathcal{N}(\tilde{X}), \tilde{Y}), \text{ for all } \tilde{X}, \tilde{Y} \in \tilde{U}. \tag{26}$$

Proposition 18. *A* K*-representable intuitionistic implication* $\mathcal{I}_{I_S, J_S} : \mathcal{U}^2 \to \mathcal{U}$ *is a strong IVI* $\mathbb{S}$*-implication iff it satisfies the properties* $\mathcal{I}2, \mathcal{I}3, \mathcal{I}6, \mathcal{I}7$ *and* $\mathcal{I}11$.

Proof. Straightforward from Defs. 4 and 3 and Prop. 10.

Proposition 19. *A* K*-representable intuitionistic implication* $\mathcal{I}_{I,J} : \tilde{U}^2 \to \tilde{U}$, *verifying conditions of Def. 3, is an IVI* S*-implication iff* $J : U^2 \to U$ *is the corresponding* S*-coimplication of the* S*-implication* $I : U^2 \to U$.

Proof. Let $I : U^2 \to U$ be an S-implication defined as $I(x, y) = S(N_S(x), y)$ and, in the same approach, $J : U^2 \to U$ be an S-coimplication defined as $J(x, y) = T(N_S(x), y)$. Then, by Def. 3, Props. 2, 5 and 15 and Eq. 24, it holds that:

$$
\begin{aligned}
\mathbb{I}_I(\mathbb{N}(X_2), Y_1) &= [I(K_1(\mathbb{N}(X_2)), K_0(Y_1)), I(K_0(\mathbb{N}(X_2)), K_1(Y_1))] \\
&= [S(N_S(K_1(\mathbb{N}(X_2))), K_0(Y_1)), S(N_S(K_0(\mathbb{N}(X_2))), K_1(Y_1))] \\
&= [S(K_0(X_2), K_0(Y_1)), S(K_1(X_2), K_1(Y_1))] = \mathbb{S}_S(X_2, Y_1);
\end{aligned}
$$

In the same way, we can show that $\mathbb{J}_J(\mathbb{N}(X_1), Y_2) = \mathbb{T}_T(X_1, Y_2)$. So, it holds that $\mathcal{I}_{I,J}((\tilde{X}, \tilde{Y})) = (\mathbb{S}_S(X_2, Y_1), \mathbb{T}_T(X_1, Y_2)) = S(\mathcal{N}(\tilde{X}), \tilde{Y})$, which means $\mathcal{I}_{I,J}$ is an S-implication. Analogously, the converse proof can be obtained.

Example 2. Cf. Example 1, the IVI implication introduced by K. Atanassov and G. Gargov can be obtained by K-operators and the pair $(\mathbb{I}, \mathbb{I}_{N_S})$ defined by Kleene-Dienes implication and coimplication in Eqs.(23) and (22), respectively. Applying Prop. 16, we obtain the folowing expressions of related projections of such IVI implication:

$$l_{\tilde{U}} \circ \mathbb{I}_I(\tilde{X}, \tilde{Y}) = \mathbb{I}(Max(X_1, \mathbb{N}_S(X_2)), Min(Y_1, \mathbb{N}_S(Y_2))) = Max(X_2, Y_1); \text{ and}$$

$$r_{\tilde{U}} \circ \mathbb{I}_I(\tilde{X}, \tilde{Y}) = \mathbb{I}_{\mathbb{N}_S}(Max(\mathbb{N}_S(X_1), X_2), Min(\mathbb{N}_S(Y_1), Y_2)) = Max(X_1, Y_2)$$

5 Conclusion and Final Remarks

As the main contribution, this work introduces the K-representable intuitionistic fuzzy implication (Def.3) shown as a IVI-implication (Theorem 2), discussing under which conditions the generation of IVI-implications from fuzzy (co)implications and from K-operators preserve the main properties of implications (Prop. 16 and Prop. 17). We also focussed on the extension of such approach in order to study the K-representable S-implication and the K-representable intuitionistic S-implications (Sect. 4.1).

Further work continues such investigations on K-representability of fuzzy implication and intuitionistic fuzzy implications, extending to R-implications, QL-implications and D-implications. It also includes the action of interval automorphisms which preserve main properties from such classes of corresponding fuzzy connectives.

Acknowledgment. This work is supported by CNPq (under the process number 480832/2011-0) and FAPERGS (under the process number 11/1520-1 of Edital PqG 02/2011). We are grateful to the referees for their valuable suggestions.

References

1. Atanassov, K.: Intuitionistic Fuzzy Sets. Fuzzy Sets and Systems 20, 87–96 (1986)
2. Atanassov, K.: Intuitionistic Fuzzy Sets, Theory and Applications. Physica-Verlag, Heilderberg (1999)
3. Baczyński, M.: Residual Implications Revisited, Notes on the Smets-Magrez Theorem. Fuzzy Sets and Systems 145(2), 267–277 (2004)
4. Bedregal, B., Takahashi, A.: The Best Interval Representation of T-Norms and Automorphisms. Fuzzy Sets and Systems 157(24), 3220–3230 (2006)
5. Bedregal, B., Takahashi, A.: Interval-Valued Versions of T-conorms, Fuzzy Negations and Fuzzy Implications. In: IEEE Proc. of the Int. Conf. on Fuzzy Systems, pp. 1981–1987. IEEE Press, Vancouver (2006)
6. Bedregal, B., Dimuro, G., Santiago, R., Reiser, R.: On Interval Fuzzy S-implications. Inf. Sci. 180(8), 1373–1389 (2010)
7. Bustince, H., Barrenechea, E., Pagola, M.: Generation of Interval-valued Fuzzy and Atanassov's Intuitionistic Fuzzy Connectives from Fuzzy Connectives and from K_α Operators: Law of Conjunctions and Disjunctions, Amplitude. Int. J. Intell. Syst. 23(6), 680–714 (2008)
8. Fodor, J.C., Roubens, M.: Fuzzy Preference Modelling and Multicriteria Decision Support. Kluwer Publisher, Dordrecht (1994)
9. Cornelis, C., Deschrijver, G., Kerre, E.: Implications in Intuitionistic Fuzzy and Interval-Valued Fuzzy Set Theory: Construction, Classification and Application. Int. J. of Approximate Reasoning 35, 55–95 (2004)
10. Hickey, T., Ju, Q., Emdem, M.: Interval Arithmetic: from Principles to Implementation. J. of the ACM 48(5), 1038–1068 (2001)
11. Klement, E.P., Mesiar, R., Pap, E.: Triangular Norms. Kluwer, Dordrecht (2000)
12. Reiser, R.H.S., Bedregal, B.R.C.: Generation of Interval-Valued Fuzzy Implications from K_α Operators. In: Fanelli, A.M., Pedrycz, W., Petrosino, A. (eds.) WILF 2011. LNCS (LNAI), vol. 6857, pp. 41–49. Springer, Heidelberg (2011)
13. Reiser, R., Bedregal, B., Reis, G.: Interval-Valued Fuzzy Coimplications. Journal of Computer and System Sciences, 1–32 (to be published)
14. Santiago, R., Bedregal, B., Acióly, B.: Formal Aspects of Correctness and Optimality in Interval Computations. Formal Asp. of Comput. 18(2), 231–243 (2006)
15. Trillas, E., Valverde, L.: On Implication and Indistinguishability in the Setting of Fuzzy Logic. In: Kacprzyk, J., Yager, R. (eds.) Management Decision Support Systems using Fuzzy Sets and Possibility Theory, pp. 198–212. Verlag TUV Rheinland, Cologne (1985)
16. Yager, R.R.: On Some New Classes of Implication Operators and Their Role in Approximate Reasoning. Inf. Sci. 167(1-4), 193–216 (2004)
17. Zadeh, L.A.: Fuzzy sets. Information and Control 8(3), 338–353 (1965)

Ranking of Bipolar Satisfaction Degrees

Tom Matthé and Guy De Tré

Department of Telecommunications and Information Processing,
Ghent University,
Sint-Pietersnieuwstraat 41, B-9000 Ghent, Belgium
{Tom.Matthe,Guy.DeTre}@UGent.be

Abstract. Flexible querying and fuzzy querying of regular databases
have been highly discussed topics in database literature for many years.
The main goal is to allow the user to express his/her query in a more
flexible way, thereby retrieving more human consistent results for the
query. Ranking of these results is also an important issue in flexible and
fuzzy querying. Users must be able to identify the results which are best
suited for him/her, according to the query he/she formulated. In this
paper, ranking results of the special case of bipolar querying will be
dealt with, within a framework of bipolar satisfaction degrees, where,
besides a satisfaction degree, also an independent dissatisfaction degree
is used, which makes that the ranking cannot be solved in a linear way,
i.e., final ranking is influenced by both independent degrees.

Keywords: fuzzy querying, bipolar querying, ranking.

1 Introduction

Since many years, research on flexible querying of regular databases aims at making database systems better accessible, and this by allowing queries to be formulated in a more flexible, human consistent, manner. An important subtopic of flexible database querying is fuzzy querying [2–4, 8, 12, 15]. In fuzzy querying, 'a more flexible way' means that the constraints in the query can be approximately specified, hereby allowing to better reflect human reasoning. Approximations are modeled using fuzzy set theory [14]. This implies that the constraint satisfaction can be a matter of degree, according to the users preferences. Usually, this constraint satisfaction, and more general the query satisfaction, is modeled by means of a *satisfaction degree* s which takes values in the unit interval $[0, 1]$ [13], and which indicates the degree to which a particular database record satisfies the (flexible) constraints in the users query.

However, this last assumption does not always hold in general. In human reasoning, user preferences are often given in several forms, independently of each other. On the one hand, users can state preferences indicating what is favorable, satisfactory, mandatory, etc. (i.e. *positive* information, or information referring to things the user wants), while on the other hand users can state preferences indicating what is unfavorable, dissatisfactory, forbidden, etc. (i.e. *negative* information, or information referring to things the user doesn't want). This is what

S. Greco et al. (Eds.): IPMU 2012, Part II, CCIS 298, pp. 461–470, 2012.
© Springer-Verlag Berlin Heidelberg 2012

is called the *bipolar* nature of human reasoning. It is important to notice that positive and negative information can be given at the same time, independent of each other and that in human reasoning it is not always the case that what is favorable and unfavorable to the user are exactly the opposite of each other. E.g. when a user states that he doesn't want a black car, it is not necessarily the case that he/she will be equally satisfied with any other color. When this is taken into account, one speaks of *heterogeneous* bipolarity [5, 7], and we can no longer assume that the extent to which a database record, which satisfies a constraint with satisfaction degree s, does not satisfy the given constraint, is equal to $1 - s$. The reason for this is that the user can have some indifference about whether some attribute values are satisfactory or not. Therefore, a semantical richer modeling technique is required for the handling of heterogeneous bipolarity. Several approaches exist to deal with this heterogeneous bipolarity in flexible querying and multicriteria decision making [4–6, 9–11, 16, 17]. In this paper, a framework based on Bipolar Satisfaction Degrees (BSDs), first introduced in [11], will be used.

In fuzzy querying, it is important to also present the results in a human consistent manner to the user. This means that the user must be able to easily identify the result(s) which match the best with the query, making it necessary to be able to rank the results according to the query satisfaction. In this paper, several possible ranking functions for BSDs will be introduced and discussed.

The remainder of this paper is organized as follows. In the next section, some preliminaries on BSDs will be given. The ranking of these BSDs will be discussed in section 3. Finally, section 4 states some conclusions of the presented work.

2   Bipolar Satisfaction Degrees

Query satisfaction degrees $s \in [0, 1]$ in regular 'fuzzy' querying do not allow it to explicitly distinguish between heterogeneous satisfaction and dissatisfaction in query evaluation. Due to the fact that in standard approaches the negation operator is usually treated as an involutive operator (most often, $\neg x = 1 - x$), it is explicitly assumed that a record with satisfaction degree s does not satisfy the query to an extent $1 - s$. This assumption does not generally hold when dealing with heterogeneous bipolar query criteria specifications. If we consider negation as no longer being involutive, i.e., the negation of a positive criterion is not generally implying the negative counterpart of that criterion, then we need a semantical richer framework that allows to explicitly and independently keep track of query dissatisfaction. Reconsidering the case where a user does not want to buy a black car, we can meaningfully assume that not all cars that are not black will be accepted by the user. There could be other car colours, although not explicitly specified, which could also be rejected by the user. Reversely, if the user is stating that he or she wants to buy a blue car, we can for similar reasons not exclude to the same extent all cars that are not blue. There could be other car colours, although not explicitly specified, which could also be acceptable for the user. To explicitly cope with this heterogeneous bipolarity in query criteria evaluation and handling, a logical framework based on *Bipolar Satisfaction Degrees* has been proposed [11].

2.1 Definition and Basic Characteristics

By definition, a Bipolar Satisfaction Degree (BSD) is a pair $(s, d), s, d \in [0, 1]$ where s is called the satisfaction degree and d is called the dissatisfaction degree. Both s and d take their values in the unit interval [0,1] and are independent of each other: they independently denote to which extent the BSD respectively represents 'satisfied' and 'dissatisfied'. Extreme values for s and d are 0 ('not at all') and 1 ('fully'). As such and as special cases, the BSD $(1,0)$ represents 'fully satisfied, not dissatisfied at all', whereas $(0,1)$ represents 'not satisfied at all, fully dissatisfied'. The set of all possible BSDs will be denoted by $\tilde{\mathbb{B}}$, i.e., $\tilde{\mathbb{B}} = \{(s, d)|s, d \in [0, 1]\}$.

From a semantical point of view, BSDs are closely related to Atanassov intuitionistic fuzzy sets (AIFS) [1], except that it is explicitly assumed that there is no consistency condition for BSDs, i.e., a condition like $0 \le s + d \le 1$ is missing. Indeed, because s and d are considered to be completely independent of each other, it is allowed that $s + d > 1$. The motivation for this is that BSDs try to reflect heterogeneous bipolarity in human reasoning, and that human reasoning can sometimes be inconsistent. Three cases are distinguished:

- $s + d < 1$: the BSD is *underspecified*. In the context of the evaluation of a query criterion, this means that there is an amount, $1 - s - d$, of indifference (or hesitation, as it is called in the case of AIFSs) about whether the criterion is satisfied or not.
- $s + d = 1$: the BSD is *fully specified*. In fact, in this case it holds that $d = 1 - s$, so this is the case of regular, involutive query satisfaction modeling. One also speaks of symmetric bipolarity.
- $s + d > 1$: the BSD is *overspecified* and denotes an amount, $s + d - 1$, of conflict.

2.2 Bipolar Query Conditions

The advantage of using a framework of bipolar satisfaction degrees, is that users can specify bipolar query conditions in their query. Under bipolar query conditions, it is understood that the user can state both what is desired as well as what is undesired. This is especially useful when the user doesn't have complete control over the domain, or when the domain is too large to completely specify the satisfaction and dissatisfaction degree for every value in the domain. In that case, it is often easier to state what is undesired than to state what is satisfactory. E.g. it is easier to say "I don't want a blue car" than to say "I want a car where the color is red or green or yellow or black or ...".

In general, a bipolar query condition can specify both a satisfaction degree ($\in [0, 1]$) and a dissatisfaction degree ($\in [0, 1]$) for every value in the domain. In the presented framework, a bipolar query condition c_i is defined by means of an AIFS, with the relaxation of the consistency condition:

$$c_i = \{(x, \mu_{c_i}(x), \nu_{c_i}(x)) | x \in dom_{a_i}\}$$

that is defined over the set dom_{a_i} of valid values for attribute a_i and is fully determined by the two functions

$$\mu_{c_i}, \nu_{c_i} : dom_{a_i} \rightarrow [0, 1]$$

The function μ_{c_i} is called the membership function and defines the satisfaction curve, i.e., the membership grade $\mu_{c_i}(x)$ associated with a domain value $x \in dom_{a_i}$ denotes to what extent x is considered to be satisfactory with respect to attribute a_i. The other function ν_{c_i} is called the non-membership function and defines the dissatisfaction curve, i.e., the non-membership grade $\nu_{c_i}(x)$ associated with a domain value $x \in dom_{a_i}$ thus denotes to what extent x is considered to be unsatisfactory. The relaxation of the consistency condition means that it must not necessarily hold that $0 \leq \mu_{c_i}(x) + \nu_{c_i}(x) \leq 1, \forall x \in dom_{a_i}$

Three cases can be distinguished for the formulation of bipolar query conditions:

- The user gives both positive and negative information. This is the most general case where both a membership function and a non-membership function are declared.
- The user gives only positive information, by declaring a membership function μ_{c_i}. Because, in this case, the user does not explicitly state his/her dissatisfaction curve, it can be assumed that the non-membership function will be the inverse of the membership function: $\forall x \in dom_{a_i} : \nu_{c_i}(x) = 1 - \mu_{c_i}(x)$.
- The user gives only negative information, by declaring a non-membership function ν_{c_i}. Analogously to the previous case, it can be assumed that the membership function will be the inverse of the non-membership function: $\forall x \in dom_{a_i} : \mu_{c_i}(x) = 1 - \nu_{c_i}(x)$.

2.3   Evaluation

In general, a bipolar flexible query will consist of several individual bipolar query conditions, interconnected by logical operators. This subsection presents the evaluation of such individual bipolar query conditions, while in the next subsection, the aggregation of several individual conditions will be handled. In general, the evaluation of a database record R against a bipolar query condition c_i over attribute a_i will result in a BSD, which is calculated as follows (R_{a_i} is the value of record R for attribute a_i):

$$(s_{c_i}^R, d_{c_i}^R) = (\mu_{c_i}(R_{a_i}), \nu_{c_i}(R_{a_i})) \tag{1}$$

with $s_{c_i}^R$ and $d_{c_i}^R$ the satisfaction degree, respectively dissatisfaction degree, of record R for condition c_i.

If only positive information is given by the user (μ_{c_i}), this is reduced to $(s_{c_i}^R, d_{c_i}^R) = (\mu_{c_i}(R_{a_i}), 1 - \mu_{c_i}(R_{a_i}))$. Analogously, when only negative information is given (ν_{c_i}), this is reduced to $(s_{c_i}^R, d_{c_i}^R) = (1 - \nu_{c_i}(R_{a_i}), \nu_{c_i}(R_{a_i}))$

2.4   Aggregation of BSDs

When evaluating flexible queries, the results of the evaluation of the individual query conditions must be combined to come up with a result for the entire query, on the basis of which a decision can be made about the appropriateness of a particular record for the given query. The same holds for bipolar flexible queries: first all individual bipolar query conditions $c_i, i = 1, 2, \ldots, n$ must be evaluated for a particular record R, resulting in a list of BSDs $(s_{c_i}^R, d_{c_i}^R), i = 1, 2, \ldots, n$. To calculate a global BSD for the entire query, this list needs to be aggregated into a single result (s^R, d^R). Some basic aggregation techniques have been introduced in [11], and are summarized below.

Conjunction. The result of the conjunction of two query conditions c_1 and c_2 is the intersection of the set of records satisfying c_1 with the set of records satisfying c_2. For the conjunction to be satisfactory, both conditions must be satisfactory. Therefore the minimum of both individual satisfaction degrees can be taken. On the other hand, for the conjunction to be unsatisfactory, one of both conditions must be unsatisfactory. Therefore the maximum of both individual dissatisfaction degrees can be taken. So, the BSD of a record R for the conjunction of conditions c_1 and c_2, $(s_{c_1 \wedge c_2}^R, d_{c_1 \wedge c_2}^R)$, can be calculated as follows:

$$(s_{c_1 \wedge c_2}^R, d_{c_1 \wedge c_2}^R) = (\min(s_{c_1}^R, s_{c_2}^R), \max(d_{c_1}^R, d_{c_2}^R)) \tag{2}$$

This approach is not exactly the same as in [6], where positive information is treated as mere desires and the fulfillment of one desire is enough for the whole to be desirable, which would mean taking also the maximum for the calculation of the satisfaction degree.

Besides minimum and maximum, other aggregation operators, based on triangular (co-)norms, can also be used if a reinforcement effect is needed or desired.

Disjunction. The disjunction of two query conditions c_1 and c_2 can be treated dually to the conjunction. For a disjunction to be satisfactory, one of both conditions must be satisfactory. Therefore the maximum of both individual satisfaction degrees can be taken. On the other hand, for a disjunction to be unsatisfactory, both conditions must be unsatisfactory. Therefore the minimum of both individual satisfaction degrees can be taken. So, the BSD of a record R for the disjunction of conditions c_1 and c_2, $(s_{c_1 \vee c_2}^R, d_{c_1 \vee c_2}^R)$, can be calculated as follows:

$$(s_{c_1 \vee c_2}^R, d_{c_1 \vee c_2}^R) = (\max(s_{c_1}^R, s_{c_2}^R), \min(d_{c_1}^R, d_{c_2}^R)) \tag{3}$$

Negation. The BSD of a record R for the negation of condition c, $(s_{\neg c}^R, d_{\neg c}^R)$, can be obtained by switching the satisfaction degree and dissatisfaction degree of the BSD of the initial condition c:

$$(s_{\neg c}^R, d_{\neg c}^R) = (d_c^R, s_c^R) \tag{4}$$

This formula is based on the negation operator for AIFSs, where the membership degree and the non-membership degree are also switched when negating. In fact, the same effect of negation can also be achieved by just switching the membership and non-membership function expressing the query condition.

Remark that this is not the same as taking the inverse of the satisfaction degree and dissatisfaction degree of the BSD of the initial condition c. This would lead to $(s^R_{\neg c}, d^R_{\neg c}) = (1 - s^R_c, 1 - d^R_c))$, but gives the result of the case of total indifference (BSD $(0,0)$) and the case of total conflict (BSD $(1,1)$) being each others negation. This is incorrect since the negation of total indifference should still be total indifference (and the same for total conflict).

3   Ranking of BSDs

When all (bipolar) query conditions have been evaluated and aggregated for all possible query results, every resulting record R_i will have a calculated global BSD (s^{R_i}, d^{R_i}), representing the global (dis)satisfaction of the record with respect to the formulated query. In order to provide useful results to the end user, this list of records R_i needs to be ordered, according to their global (dis)satisfaction for the formulated query. This means that, also on the list of BSDs attached to the database records R_i, an ordering must be imposed. Since BSDs consist of two individual, and independent, components, this ordering, can not be performed in a linear way, unless the two independent degrees are aggregated into one value. Below, several options for ranking BSDs will be presented.

A suitable ranking function r_i for BSDs must meet following requirements:

1. $0 \le r_i(x, y) \le 1$, with (x, y) a BSD, i.e. $r_i : \tilde{\mathbb{B}} \to [0, 1]$
2. $r_i(1, 0) = 1$, i.e. the BSD with full satisfaction and no dissatisfaction should be ranked the highest.
3. $r_i(0, 1) = 0$, i.e. the BSD with full dissatisfaction and no satisfaction should be ranked the lowest.
4. $\forall x, y \in [0, 1] : r_i(x, x) = r_i(y, y)$, i.e. for all BSDs with equal satisfaction degree and dissatisfaction degree, the ranking should also be equal. The reason is that, ranking wise, it is impossible to make a sensible distinction between the cases of total indifference (i.e. BSD $(0, 0)$) and total conflict (i.e. BSD $(1, 1)$), and also all other intermediate BSDs (x, x) (i.e. where $s = d$).

These requirements eliminate the use of ranking functions which solely rank on either the satisfaction degree s or the dissatisfaction degree d, and use the other degree (d or s respectively) only as a 'tiebreaker', because they would violate the fourth requirement. These ranking functions, also known as lexicographical ordering [6], might be useful in some cases, but will not be used here because of the assumed total independence between the satisfaction degree and dissatisfaction degree.

A list of examples of possible ranking functions which will be further discussed, is given below:

$$r_1 = \frac{s + (1 - d)}{2} \tag{5}$$

$$r_2 = \frac{s}{s + d} \tag{6}$$

$$r_3 = \frac{1 - d}{(1 - s) + (1 - d)} \tag{7}$$

$$r_4 = \frac{s}{s + d} \cdot \frac{1 - d}{(1 - s) + (1 - d)} \tag{8}$$

$$r_5 = \max\{0, s - d\} \tag{9}$$

$$r_6 = \min\{1 + s - d, 1\} \tag{10}$$

The plots of these functions with their course in the unit cube can be found in Figure 1. Their boundary conditions ($s = d$, $s = 0$, $d = 1$, $s = 1$, $d = 0$) are given in Table 1. Remark that functions r_2, r_3 and r_4 might cause a division by 0 when $s = d = 0$ (for r_2 and r_4) or $s = d = 1$ (for r_3 and r_4). In that case, taking a limit leads to the results found in Table 1 for $s = d$.

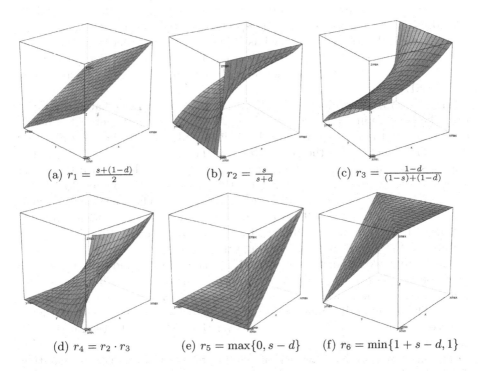

(a) $r_1 = \frac{s + (1 - d)}{2}$ (b) $r_2 = \frac{s}{s + d}$ (c) $r_3 = \frac{1 - d}{(1 - s) + (1 - d)}$

(d) $r_4 = r_2 \cdot r_3$ (e) $r_5 = \max\{0, s - d\}$ (f) $r_6 = \min\{1 + s - d, 1\}$

Fig. 1. Ranking functions

Table 1. Boundary properties of the ranking functions

	$s = d$	$s = 0$	$d = 1$	$s = 1$	$d = 0$
r_1	$r_1 = 0.5$	$0 \leq r_1 \leq 0.5$	$0 \leq r_1 \leq 0.5$	$0.5 \leq r_1 \leq 1$	$0.5 \leq r_1 \leq 1$
r_2	$r_2 = 0.5$	$r_2 = 0$ (when $d \neq 0$)	$0 \leq r_2 \leq 0.5$	$0.5 \leq r_2 \leq 1$	$r_2 = 1$ (when $s \neq 0$)
r_3	$r_3 = 0.5$	$0 \leq r_3 \leq 0.5$	$r_3 = 0$ (when $s \neq 1$)	$r_3 = 1$ (when $d \neq 0$)	$0.5 \leq r_3 \leq 1$
r_4	$r_4 = 0.25$	$r_4 = 0$ (when $d \neq 0$)	$r_4 = 0$ (when $s \neq 1$)	$0.5 \leq r_4 \leq 1$ (when $d \neq 1$)	$0.5 \leq r_4 \leq 1$ (when $s \neq 0$)
r_5	$r_5 = 0$	$r_5 = 0$	$r_5 = 0$	$0 \leq r_5 \leq 1$	$0 \leq r_5 \leq 1$
r_6	$r_6 = 1$	$0 \leq r_6 \leq 1$	$0 \leq r_6 \leq 1$	$r_6 = 1$	$r_6 = 1$

The first ranking function, r_1 (Fig. 1(a)), takes the average (arithmetic mean) of the satisfaction degree and the inverse of the dissatisfaction degree. This function gives equal importance to both the satisfaction degree and the dissatisfaction degree, and has a continuous course in the entire unit cube. A consequence of this ranking function is that elementary query conditions cannot be seen as strict restrictions, but only as preferences or desires. This means that records of which the evaluation leads to a dissatisfaction degree $d = 1$, or dually a satisfaction degree of $s = 0$, should not a priori be excluded. Indeed, e.g., the BSDs $(0.5, 1)$ and $(0, 0.5)$, although having $d = 1$ (respectively $s = 0$), both have ranking 0.25 and hence should not be catalogued as being totally unsatisfactory.

Remark that other averaging function, like the geometric or harmonic mean, can not be used because they do not meet the fourth requirement (equal ranking for all BSDs where $s = d$).

The second ranking function, r_2 (Fig. 1(b)), is built to make hard constraints from the positive information in the query. With 'hard constraints', it is meant that, if $s = 0$, the ranking will also be 0 (unless also $d = 0$), i.e. $r_2(0, d) = 0$ if $d \neq 0$. This function has the advantage over the arithmetic mean that you can impose some true constraints (i.e. the constraints have to be fulfilled to at least a certain degree), but has the drawback that it is discontinuous in BSD $(0, 0)$. E.g. $r_2(0, 0) = 0.5$ while $r_2(0, 0.01) = 0$. Moreover it also has the drawback that, when $d = 0$, the ranking will always be 1 (unless also $s = 0$). This is probably not desired, because this would mean that other BSDs than $(1, 0)$ might also be mapped to the highest possible ranking value.

The third ranking function, r_3 (Fig. 1(c)), is dual to r_2 and is built to make hard constraints from the negative information in the query. This means that, if $d = 1$, the ranking will always be 0 (unless also $s = 1$), i.e. $r_3(s, 1) = 0$ if $s \neq 1$. This function has more or less the same drawback as r_2, namely that it is discontinuous in BSD $(1, 1)$, and moreover that, when $s = 1$, the ranking will always be 1 (unless also $d = 1$).

The most important drawback of ranking functions r_2 and r_3 is that they map other BSDs than $(1, 0)$ to the highest ranking, i.e. 1. E.g. irrespective of the value of s (except $s = 0$), $r_2(s, 0) = 1$, and dually for r_3, irrespective of the value of d (except $d = 1$), $r_2(1, d) = 1$. Therefore, the fourth ranking function,

r_4 (Fig. 1(d)), is built as the combination of r_2 and r_3, by taking their product. The result is that now both the positive and negative information in the query can be treated as hard constraints, in the sense that, if $s = 0$ or $d = 1$, the ranking will also be 0 (unless also $d = 0$ or $s = 1$ respectively), i.e. $r_4(0, d) = 0$ if $d \neq 0$ and $r_4(s, 1) = 0$ if $s \neq 1$. Moreover, this function also solves the issue of other BSDs than $(1, 0)$ being mapped to the highest ranking. This function still has the drawback though of being discontinuous, this time in 2 points, i.e. the 2 boundary BSDs $(0, 0)$ and $(1, 1)$.

Another approach to aggregate the two degrees of a BSD into a single ranking value r_i, would be to take a t-norm $i(x, y)$ or t-conorm $u(x, y)$ to combine them (with $x = s$ and $y = 1 - d$). Taking a t-norm would calculate the ranking mostly based on the worst of the two degrees $(i(s, 1 - d) \leq \min(s, 1 - d))$, while taking a t-conorm would calculate the ranking mostly based on the best of the two degrees $(u(s, 1 - d) \geq \max(s, 1 - d))$. The problem with this approach is that most t-(co)norms violate the fourth requirement (equal ranking for all BSDs where $s = d$), so that they can not be used as ranking functions for BSDs. A t-norm and t-conorm that does fulfill this requirement though, is the Łukasiewicz t-(co)norm. So, opposed to the other t-(co)norms, this one can be used as ranking function for BSDs, leading to the ranking functions $r_5(s, d) = i_{Luk}(s, 1 - d)$ (Fig. 1(e)) and $r_6(s, d) = u_{Luk}(s, 1 - d)$ (Fig. 1(f)). It can immediately be noticed that for these ranking functions, half of the BSDs spectrum is mapped on the same ranking value $(r_5(s, d) = 0)$ if $s \leq d$, and $r_6(s, d) = 1$ if $s \geq d$. This property doesn't make them a good candidate for a ranking function for BSDs, because a lot of BSDs will be mapped to the same value, making them indistinguishable. Moreover, they follow more or less the same course as r_1, the arithmetic mean. Indeed, r_1 can be seen as a rescaling from the function $s - d$ to the unit interval, while r_5 and r_6 are cropped versions of $s - d$ and $1 + s - d$ respectively.

When looking at all presented ranking functions, it can be concluded that two ranking functions can be seen as 'the best', namely r_1 and r_4. Ranking function r_1 is fairly easy to calculate, has continuous course, and gives equal importance to both the satisfaction degree s and the dissatisfaction degree d. However, as pointed out above, when using this ranking function, elementary query conditions cannot be seen as strict restrictions, but only as mere desires.

Ranking functions r_4 on the other hand is harder to calculate but also gives equal importance to both the satisfaction degree s and the dissatisfaction degree d (when looking at the plot (Fig. 1(d)), it can be noticed that this function is symmetrical over the diagonal $(0, 1) - (1, 0)$), and has the advantage over r_1 that you can impose some true constraints (i.e. the constraints have to be fulfilled to at least a certain degree). This function is discontinuous though in the boundary BSDs $(0, 0)$ and $(1, 1)$.

4   Conclusions

In this paper, ranking of Bipolar Satisfaction Degrees (BSDs), which are a result of evaluating and aggregating bipolar query conditions, is discussed. This ranking is necessary in order to deliver good quality results to the end user for his/her query, because this user must be able to identify the best results for the query he/she formulated. Because these BSDs are constructed by means of two values, an independent pair of a satisfaction degree and a dissatisfaction degree, the ranking must take into account both independent degrees. Several possible ranking functions are given in the paper.

References

1. Atanassov, K.: Intuitionistic fuzzy sets. Fuzzy Sets and Systems 20, 87–96 (1986)
2. Bordogna, G., Pasi, G. (eds.): Recent Issues on Fuzzy Databases. Physica-Verlag, Heidelberg (2000)
3. Bosc, P., Pivert, O.: Some approaches for relational databases flexible querying. International Journal of Intelligent Information Systems 1, 323–354 (1992)
4. De Tré, G., De Caluwe, R., Kacprzyk, J., Zadrożny, S.: On flexible querying via extensions to fuzzy sets. In: Proc. of the EUSFLAT 2005 and LFA 2005 Joint Conference, Barcelona, Spain, pp. 1225–1230 (2005)
5. Dubois, D., Kaci, S., Prade, H.: Bipolarity in reasoning and decision – an introduction. the case of the possibility theory framework. In: Proc. of the IPMU 2004 Conference, Perugia, Italy, pp. 959–966 (2004)
6. Dubois, D., Prade, H.: Bipolarity in Flexible Querying. In: Andreasen, T., Motro, A., Christiansen, H., Larsen, H.L. (eds.) FQAS 2002. LNCS (LNAI), vol. 2522, pp. 174–182. Springer, Heidelberg (2002)
7. Dubois, D., Prade, H.: Handling bipolar queries in Fuzzy Information Processing. In: Galindo, J. (ed.) Handbook of Research on Fuzzy Information Processing in Databases, pp. 97–114. Information Science Reference, New York (2008)
8. Galindo, J., Medina, J.M., Pons, O., Cubero, J.C.: A Server for Fuzzy SQL Queries. In: Andreasen, T., Christiansen, H., Larsen, H.L. (eds.) FQAS 1998. LNCS (LNAI), vol. 1495, pp. 164–174. Springer, Heidelberg (1998)
9. Grabisch, M., Greco, S., Pirlot, M.: Bipolar and bivariate models in multicriteria decision analysis: Descriptive and constructive approaches. International Journal of Intelligent Systems 23(9), 930–969 (2008)
10. Lin, L., Yuan, X.H., Xia, Z.Q.: Multicriteria fuzzy decision-making methods based on intuitionistic fuzzy sets. Journal of Computer and System Sciences 73, 84–88 (2007)
11. Matthé, T., De Tré, G.: Bipolar query satisfaction using satisfaction and dissatisfaction degrees: bipolar satisfaction degrees. In: Proc. of the ACM Symposium on Applied Computing, ACM SAC 2009, Honolulu, Hawaii, pp.1699–1703(2009)
12. Prade, H., Testemale, C.: Generalizing database relational algebra for the treatment of incomplete or uncertain information and vague queries. Information Sciences 34, 115–143 (1984)
13. Tahani, V.: A conceptual framework for fuzzy query processing: a step toward very intelligent database systems. Information Processing and Management 13, 289–303 (1977)
14. Zadeh, L.A.: Fuzzy sets. Information and Control 8(3), 338–353 (1965)
15. Zadrożny, S., Kacprzyk, J.: Fquery for access: towards human consistent querying user interface. In: Proc. of the 1996 ACM Symposium on Applied Computing, SAC 1996, Philadelphia, USA, pp. 532–536 (1996)
16. Zadrożny, S., Kacprzyk, J.: Bipolar queries and queries with preferences. In: Proc. of the DEXA 2006 Conference, pp. 415–419, Kraków, Poland (2006)
17. Zadrożny, S., Kacprzyk, J.: Bipolar queries: An approach and its various interpretations. In: Proc. of the 2009 IFSA/EUSFLAT Conference, pp. 1288–1293 (2009)

Additive Generators Based on General Arithmetic Operators in Interval-Valued Fuzzy Set Theory

Glad Deschrijver

Fuzziness and Uncertainty Modelling Research Unit,
Department of Applied Mathematics and Computer Science,
Ghent University,
Krijgslaan 281(S9), B–9000 Gent, Belgium
Glad.Deschrijver@UGent.be

Abstract. In this paper we discuss additive generators of t-norms in interval-valued fuzzy set theory or, equivalently, Atanassov's intuitionistic fuzzy set theory. We make use of the arithmetic operators which are axiomatically defined on the underlying lattice of interval-valued fuzzy set theory. We give a complete characterization of continuous additive generators which map exact values (that are intervals with only one element) on exact values. We investigate under which conditions for the addition operator, such a generator actually generates a t-norm.

Keywords: interval-valued fuzzy set, Atanassov's intuitionistic fuzzy set, t-norm, additive generator, arithmetic operator on $\mathcal{L}^I$, representable.

1 Introduction

Triangular norms on $([0, 1], \leq)$ were introduced in [20] and play an important role in fuzzy set theory (see e.g. [10, 13, 15] for more details). Generators are very useful in the construction of t-norms: any generator on $([0, 1], \leq)$ can be used to generate a t-norm. Generators play also an important role in the representation of continuous Archimedean t-norms on $([0, 1], \leq)$. Moreover, some properties of t-norms which have a generator can be related to properties of their generator. See e.g. [9, 14–16, 18] for more information about generators on the unit interval.

Interval-valued fuzzy set theory [12, 19] is an extension of fuzzy theory in which to each element of the universe a closed subinterval of the unit interval is assigned which approximates the unknown membership degree. Another extension of fuzzy set theory is intuitionistic fuzzy set theory introduced by Atanassov [1–3]. In [7] it is shown that intuitionistic fuzzy set theory is equivalent to interval-valued fuzzy set theory and that both are equivalent to L-fuzzy set theory in the sense of Goguen [11] w.r.t. a special lattice $\mathcal{L}^I$. In [4] we introduced additive and multiplicative generators on $\mathcal{L}^I$ based on a special kind of addition introduced in [5]. In [8] another addition was introduced and many more additions can be introduced. Therefore, in this paper we will investigate additive generators on $\mathcal{L}^I$ independently of the

S. Greco et al. (Eds.): IPMU 2012, Part II, CCIS 298, pp. 471–480, 2012.
© Springer-Verlag Berlin Heidelberg 2012

addition. For some special additions we will investigate which t-norms can be generated by continuous additive generators which are a natural extension of an additive generator on the unit interval.

2   The Lattice $\mathcal{L}^I$

The underlying lattice $\mathcal{L}^I$ of interval-valued fuzzy set theory is given as follows.

Definition 1. *We define $\mathcal{L}^I = (L^I, \leq_{L^I})$, where*

$$L^I = \{[x_1, x_2] \mid (x_1, x_2) \in [0, 1]^2 \text{ and } x_1 \leq x_2\},$$

$$[x_1, x_2] \leq_{L^I} [y_1, y_2] \iff (x_1 \leq y_1 \text{ and } x_2 \leq y_2), \text{ for all } [x_1, x_2], [y_1, y_2] \text{ in } L^I.$$

Similarly as Lemma 2.1 in [7] it is shown that $\mathcal{L}^I$ is a complete lattice.

Definition 2. [12, 19] *An interval-valued fuzzy set on U is a mapping $A : U \to L^I$.*

Definition 3. [1–3] *An intuitionistic fuzzy set on U is a set*

$$A = \{(u, \mu_A(u), \nu_A(u)) \mid u \in U\},$$

where $\mu_A(u) \in [0, 1]$ denotes the membership degree and $\nu_A(u) \in [0, 1]$ the nonmembership degree of u in A and where for all $u \in U$, $\mu_A(u) + \nu_A(u) \leq 1$.

An intuitionistic fuzzy set in the sense of Atanassov A on U can be represented by the L-fuzzy set A in the sense of Goguen [11] given by

$$A : U \to L^I :$$
$$u \mapsto [\mu_A(u), 1 - \nu_A(u)], \quad \forall u \in U.$$

In Fig. 1 the set L^I is shown. Note that to any element $x = [x_1, x_2]$ of L^I there corresponds a point $(x_1, x_2) \in [0, 1]^2$.

In the sequel, if $x \in L^I$, then we denote its bounds by $x_1 = \mathrm{pr}_1(x)$ and $x_2 = \mathrm{pr}_2(x)$, i.e. $x = [x_1, x_2]$. The smallest and the largest element of $\mathcal{L}^I$ are given by $0_{\mathcal{L}^I} = [0, 0]$ and $1_{\mathcal{L}^I} = [1, 1]$. The hypotenuse of the triangle corresponds to the set $D = \{[x_1, x_1] \mid x_1 \in [0, 1]\}$ of values in L^I about which there is no indeterminacy and can be identified with the unit interval $[0, 1]$ from (classical) fuzzy set theory. The elements of D are called the *exact elements* of the lattice $\mathcal{L}^I$. Note that, for x, y in L^I, $x <_{L^I} y$ is equivalent to "$x \leq_{L^I} y$ and $x \neq y$", i.e. either $x_1 < y_1$ and $x_2 \leq y_2$, or $x_1 \leq y_1$ and $x_2 < y_2$. We denote by $x \ll_{L^I} y$: $x_1 < y_1$ and $x_2 < y_2$. We define for further usage the sets

$$\bar{L}^I = \{[x_1, x_2] \mid (x_1, x_2) \in \,]-\infty, +\infty[^2 \text{ and } x_1 \leq x_2\},$$
$$\bar{D} = \{[x_1, x_1] \mid x_1 \in \,]-\infty, +\infty[\},$$
$$\bar{L}^I_+ = \{[x_1, x_2] \mid (x_1, x_2) \in [0, +\infty[^2 \text{ and } x_1 \leq x_2\},$$
$$\bar{D}_+ = \{[x_1, x_1] \mid x_1 \in [0, +\infty[\},$$
$$\bar{L}^I_{\infty,+} = \{[x_1, x_2] \mid (x_1, x_2) \in [0, +\infty]^2 \text{ and } x_1 \leq x_2\},$$
$$\bar{D}_{\infty,+} = \{[x_1, x_1] \mid x_1 \in [0, +\infty]\}.$$

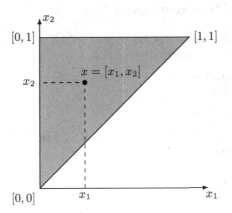

Fig. 1. The grey area is L^I

Definition 4. *A t-norm on $\mathcal{L}^I$ is a commutative, associative, increasing mapping $\mathcal{T} : (L^I)^2 \rightarrow L^I$ which satisfies $\mathcal{T}(1_{\mathcal{L}^I}, x) = x$, for all $x \in L^I$.*

A t-conorm on $\mathcal{L}^I$ is a commutative, associative, increasing mapping $\mathcal{S} : (L^I)^2 \rightarrow L^I$ which satisfies $\mathcal{S}(0_{\mathcal{L}^I}, x) = x$, for all $x \in L^I$.

Definition 5. *A t-(co)norm $\mathcal{T}$ ($\mathcal{S}$) on $\mathcal{L}^I$ is called t-representable if there exist t-(co)norms T_1 and T_2 (S_1 and S_2) on $([0,1], \leq)$ such that $T_1(x, y) \leq T_2(x, y)$ ($S_1(x, y) \leq S_2(x, y)$), for all x, y in $[0, 1]$, and such that, for all x, y in L^I,*

$$\mathcal{T}(x, y) = [T_1(x_1, y_1), T_2(x_2, y_2)]$$
$$(\mathcal{S}(x, y) = [S_1(x_1, y_1), S_2(x_2, y_2)]).$$

Then T_1 and T_2 (S_1 and S_2) are called the representants of $\mathcal{T}$ ($\mathcal{S}$), and $\mathcal{T}$ ($\mathcal{S}$) is denoted by $\mathcal{T}_{T_1, T_2}$ ($\mathcal{S}_{S_1, S_2}$).

A t-(co)norm $\mathcal{T}$ ($\mathcal{S}$) on $\mathcal{L}^I$ is called pseudo-t-representable if there exists a t-(co)norm T (S) on $([0, 1], \leq)$ such that, for all x, y in L^I,

$$\mathcal{T}(x, y) = [T(x_1, y_1), \max(T(x_1, y_2), T(x_2, y_1))]$$
$$(\mathcal{S}(x, y) = [\min(S(x_1, y_2), S(x_2, y_1)), S(x_2, y_2)]).$$

Then T (S) is called the representant of $\mathcal{T}$ ($\mathcal{S}$), and $\mathcal{T}$ ($\mathcal{S}$) is denoted by $\mathcal{T}_T$ ($\mathcal{S}_S$).

If for a mapping f on $[0, 1]$ and a mapping F on L^I it holds that $F(D) \subseteq \bar{D}$, and $F([a, a]) = [f(a), f(a)]$, for all $a \in L^I$, then we say that F is a natural extension of f to L^I. E.g. $\mathcal{T}_{T,T}$ and $\mathcal{T}_T$ are natural extensions of T to L^I.

Example 1. Using the Łukasiewicz t-norm T_W and t-conorm S_W on the unit interval, we define

$$\mathcal{T}_{T_W}(x, y) = [\max(0, x_1 + y_1 - 1), \max(0, x_1 + y_2 - 1, x_2 + y_1 - 1)],$$
$$\mathcal{S}_{S_W}(x, y) = [\min(1, x_1 + y_2, x_2 + y_1), \min(1, x_2 + y_2)].$$

3   Arithmetic Operators on $\bar{L}^I$

We start from two arithmetic operators $\oplus : (\bar{L}^I)^2 \to \bar{L}^I$ and $\otimes : (\bar{L}_+^I)^2 \to \bar{L}^I$ satisfying the following properties (see [6]),

(ADD-1) $\oplus$ is commutative,
(ADD-2) $\oplus$ is associative,
(ADD-3) $\oplus$ is increasing,
(ADD-4) $0_{\mathcal{L}^I} \oplus a = a$, for all $a \in \bar{L}^I$,
(ADD-5) $[\alpha, \alpha] \oplus [\beta, \beta] = [\alpha + \beta, \alpha + \beta]$, for all α, β in $\mathbb{R}$,
(MUL-1) $\otimes$ is commutative,
(MUL-2) $\otimes$ is associative,
(MUL-3) $\otimes$ is increasing,
(MUL-4) $1_{\mathcal{L}^I} \otimes a = a$, for all $a \in \bar{L}_+^I$,
(MUL-5) $[\alpha, \alpha] \otimes [\beta, \beta] = [\alpha\beta, \alpha\beta]$, for all α, β in $[0, +\infty[$.

The conditions (ADD-1)–(ADD-4) and (MUL-1)–(MUL-4) are natural conditions for any addition and multiplication operators. The conditions (ADD-5) and (MUL-5) ensure that these operators are natural extensions of the addition and multiplication of real numbers to $\bar{L}^I$.

Sometimes we will assume that $\oplus$ and $\otimes$ satisfy the following conditions instead of (ADD-5) and (MUL-5):

(ADD-5') $[\alpha, \alpha] \oplus b = [\alpha + b_1, \alpha + b_2]$, for all $\alpha \in \mathbb{R}$ and $b \in \bar{L}^I$,
(MUL-5') $[\alpha, \alpha] \otimes b = [\alpha b_1, \alpha b_2]$, for all $\alpha \in [0, +\infty[$ and $b \in \bar{L}_+^I$.

These conditions ensure that adding or multiplying an interval with an exact element (an interval with only one element, in other words an interval which does not contain any uncertainty) does not modify the amount of uncertainty in the interval, except in the case of a multiplication with $[0, 0]$ for which we obtain the expected result $[0, 0]$.

The properties of these operators are studied in [6].

Example 2. We give some examples of arithmetic operators satisfying the conditions (ADD-1)–(ADD-4) and (MUL-1)–(MUL-4).

- In the interval calculus (see e.g. [17]) the following operators are defined: for all x, y in $\bar{L}^I$,

$$x \oplus y = [x_1 + y_1, x_2 + y_2],$$
$$x \otimes y = [x_1 y_1, x_2 y_2], \quad \text{if } x, y \text{ in } \bar{L}_+^I.$$

  It is easy to see that these operators satisfy (ADD-1)–(ADD-4) and (MUL-1)–(MUL-4).

- In [5] the following operators are defined: for all x, y in $\bar{L}^I$,

$$x \oplus_{\mathcal{L}^I} y = [\min(x_1 + y_2, x_2 + y_1), x_2 + y_2],$$
$$x \otimes_{\mathcal{L}^I} y = [x_1 y_1, \max(x_1 y_2, x_2 y_1)], \quad \text{if } x, y \text{ in } \bar{L}_+^I.$$

  It was proven in [5] that these operators satisfy (ADD-1)–(ADD-4) and (MUL-1)–(MUL-4).

The following theorem shows that under a certain condition, a t-conorm can be constructed using any addition operator on $\mathcal{L}^I$ using a similar expression as for the Łukasiewicz t-conorm on the unit interval.

Theorem 1. *The mapping* $\mathcal{S}_\oplus : (L^I)^2 \to L^I$ *defined by, for all* x, y *in* L^I,

$$\mathcal{S}_\oplus(x, y) = \inf(1_{\mathcal{L}^I}, x \oplus y), \tag{1}$$

is a t-conorm on $\mathcal{L}^I$ *if and only if* $\oplus$ *satisfies the following condition:*

$$(\forall (x, y, z) \in (L^I)^3)$$
$$\Big(\big((\inf(1_{\mathcal{L}^I}, x \oplus y) \oplus z)_1 < 1 \text{ and } (x \oplus y)_2 > 1 \big) \tag{2}$$
$$\implies (\inf(1_{\mathcal{L}^I}, x \oplus y) \oplus z)_1 = (x \oplus \inf(1_{\mathcal{L}^I}, y \oplus z))_1 \Big).$$

Furthermore $\mathcal{S}_\oplus$ *is a natural extension of* S_W *to* L^I.

Theorem 1 shows that in order to check whether a mapping $\mathcal{S}_\oplus$ given by (1) is a t-conorm, it is sufficient to check the associativity for all x, y, z in L^I such that $(\inf(1_{\mathcal{L}^I}, x \oplus y) \oplus z)_1 < 1$ and $(x \oplus y)_2 > 1$.

4   Additive Generators on $\mathcal{L}^I$

Definition 6. [10, 14, 15] *A mapping* $f : [0, 1] \to [0, +\infty]$ *satisfying the following conditions:*

(ag.1) f *is strictly decreasing;*
(ag.2) $f(1) = 0$;
(ag.3) f *is right-continuous in 0;*
(ag.4) $f(x) + f(y) \in \mathrm{rng}(f) \cup [f(0), +\infty]$, *for all* $x, y \in [0, 1]$, *where* $\mathrm{rng}(f)$ *denotes the range of the function* f;

is called an additive generator on $([0, 1], \leq)$.

Definition 7. [14, 15] *Let* $f : [0, 1] \to [0, +\infty]$ *be a strictly decreasing function. The pseudo-inverse* $f^{(-1)} : [0, +\infty] \to [0, 1]$ *of* f *is defined by, for all* $y \in [0, +\infty]$,

$$f^{(-1)}(y) = \sup(\{0\} \cup \{x \mid x \in [0, 1] \text{ and } f(x) > y\}).$$

We extend these definitions to L^I as follows.

Definition 8. [4] *Let* $\mathfrak{f} : L^I \to \bar{L}^I_{\infty,+}$ *be a strictly decreasing function. The pseudo-inverse* $\mathfrak{f}^{(-1)} : \bar{L}^I_{\infty,+} \to L^I$ *of* $\mathfrak{f}$ *is defined by, for all* $y \in \bar{L}^I_{\infty,+}$,

$$\mathfrak{f}^{(-1)}(y) = \begin{cases} \sup\{x \mid x \in L^I \text{ and } \mathfrak{f}(x) \gg_{L^I} y\}, & \text{if } y \ll_{L^I} \mathfrak{f}(0_{\mathcal{L}^I}); \\ \sup(\{0_{\mathcal{L}^I}\} \cup \{x \mid x \in L^I \text{ and } (\mathfrak{f}(x))_1 > y_1 \\ \quad \text{and } (\mathfrak{f}(x))_2 \geq (\mathfrak{f}(0_{\mathcal{L}^I}))_2\}), & \text{if } y_2 \geq (\mathfrak{f}(0_{\mathcal{L}^I}))_2; \\ \sup(\{0_{\mathcal{L}^I}\} \cup \{x \mid x \in L^I \text{ and } (\mathfrak{f}(x))_2 > y_2 \\ \quad \text{and } (\mathfrak{f}(x))_1 \geq (\mathfrak{f}(0_{\mathcal{L}^I}))_1\}), & \text{if } y_1 \geq (\mathfrak{f}(0_{\mathcal{L}^I}))_1. \end{cases}$$

Note that if $\mathfrak{f}(0_{\mathcal{L}^I}) \in \bar{D}_{\infty,+}$, then, for all $y \in \bar{L}^I_{\infty,+}$,

$$\mathfrak{f}^{(-1)}(y) = \sup \Phi_y,$$

where

$$\Phi_y = \begin{cases} \{x \mid x \in L^I \text{ and } \mathfrak{f}(x) \gg_{L^I} y\}, \text{ if } y \ll_{L^I} \mathfrak{f}(0_{\mathcal{L}^I}); \\ \{0_{\mathcal{L}^I}\} \cup \{x \mid x \in L^I \text{ and } (\mathfrak{f}(x))_1 > y_1 \\ \quad \text{and } (\mathfrak{f}(x))_2 = (\mathfrak{f}(0_{\mathcal{L}^I}))_2\}, \text{ if } y_2 \geq (\mathfrak{f}(0_{\mathcal{L}^I}))_2. \end{cases} \quad (3)$$

Definition 9. [4] *A mapping* $\mathfrak{f} : L^I \to \bar{L}^I_{\infty,+}$ *satisfying the following conditions:*

(AG.1) $\mathfrak{f}$ *is strictly decreasing;*
(AG.2) $\mathfrak{f}(1_{\mathcal{L}^I}) = 0_{\mathcal{L}^I}$;
(AG.3) $\mathfrak{f}$ *is right-continuous in* $0_{\mathcal{L}^I}$;
(AG.4) $\mathfrak{f}(x) \oplus \mathfrak{f}(y) \in \mathcal{R}(\mathfrak{f})$, *for all* x, y *in* L^I, *where*

$$\mathcal{R}(\mathfrak{f}) = \text{rng}(\mathfrak{f}) \cup \{x \mid x \in \bar{L}^I_{\infty,+} \text{ and } [x_1, (\mathfrak{f}(0_{\mathcal{L}^I}))_2] \in \text{rng}(\mathfrak{f}) \text{ and } x_2 \geq (\mathfrak{f}(0_{\mathcal{L}^I}))_2\}$$
$$\cup \{x \mid x \in \bar{L}^I_{\infty,+} \text{ and } [(\mathfrak{f}(0_{\mathcal{L}^I}))_1, x_2] \in \text{rng}(\mathfrak{f}) \text{ and } x_1 \geq (\mathfrak{f}(0_{\mathcal{L}^I}))_1\}$$
$$\cup \{x \mid x \in \bar{L}^I_{\infty,+} \text{ and } x \geq_{L^I} \mathfrak{f}(0_{\mathcal{L}^I})\};$$

(AG.5) $\mathfrak{f}^{(-1)}(\mathfrak{f}(x)) = x$, *for all* $x \in L^I$;

is called an additive generator on $\mathcal{L}^I$.

If $\mathfrak{f}(0_{\mathcal{L}^I}) \in \bar{D}_{\infty,+}$, then

$$\mathcal{R}(\mathfrak{f}) = \text{rng}(\mathfrak{f}) \cup \{x \mid x \in \bar{L}^I_{\infty,+} \text{ and } [x_1, (\mathfrak{f}(0_{\mathcal{L}^I}))_2] \in \text{rng}(\mathfrak{f}) \text{ and } x_2 \geq (\mathfrak{f}(0_{\mathcal{L}^I}))_2\}$$
$$\cup \{x \mid x \in \bar{L}^I_{\infty,+} \text{ and } x \geq_{L^I} \mathfrak{f}(0_{\mathcal{L}^I})\}.$$

In [4] the following three properties are shown. Since their proofs do not involve (AG.4), they are also valid for the current definition of additive generator.

Lemma 1. [4] *Let* $\mathfrak{f} : L^I \to \bar{L}^I_{\infty,+}$ *be a mapping satisfying (AG.1), (AG.2), (AG.3) and (AG.5). Then, for all* $x \in L^I$ *such that* $x_1 > 0$, *it holds that* $(\mathfrak{f}(x))_2 < (\mathfrak{f}(0_{\mathcal{L}^I}))_2$ *and* $(\mathfrak{f}(x))_1 < (\mathfrak{f}(0_{\mathcal{L}^I}))_1$.

Lemma 2. [4] *Let* $\mathfrak{f} : L^I \to \bar{L}^I_{\infty,+}$ *be a mapping satisfying (AG.1), (AG.2), (AG.3) and (AG.5). Then* $(\mathfrak{f}([0,1]))_1 = (\mathfrak{f}(0_{\mathcal{L}^I}))_1$ *or* $(\mathfrak{f}([0,1]))_2 = (\mathfrak{f}(0_{\mathcal{L}^I}))_2$.

Corollary 1. [4] *Let* $\mathfrak{f} : L^I \to \bar{L}^I_{\infty,+}$ *be a mapping satisfying (AG.1), (AG.2), (AG.3), (AG.5) and* $\mathfrak{f}(D) \subseteq \bar{D}_{\infty,+}$. *Then* $(\mathfrak{f}([0,1]))_2 = (\mathfrak{f}(0_{\mathcal{L}^I}))_2$.

Lemma 3. *Let* f_1 *be an additive generator on* $([0,1], \leq)$ *and let* $\mathfrak{f} : L^I \to \bar{L}^I_{\infty,+}$ *be a mapping satisfying (AG.1), (AG.2), (AG.3), (AG.5) and, for all* $x \in L^I$,

$$(\mathfrak{f}(x))_1 = f_1(x_2). \quad (4)$$

Then, for all $y \in \bar{L}^I_{\infty,+}$,

$$(\mathfrak{f}^{(-1)}(y))_2 = f_1^{(-1)}(y_1). \quad (5)$$

Lemma 4. *Let f_2 be an additive generator on $([0,1], \leq)$ and let $\mathfrak{f} : L^I \to \bar{L}^I_{\infty,+}$ be a mapping satisfying (AG.1), (AG.2), (AG.3), (AG.5), $\mathfrak{f}(D) \subseteq \bar{D}_{\infty,+}$ and, for all $x \in L^I$,*

$$(\mathfrak{f}(x))_2 = f_2(x_1). \tag{6}$$

Then, for all $y \in \bar{L}^I_{\infty,+}$,

$$(\mathfrak{f}^{(-1)}(y))_1 = f_2^{(-1)}(y_2). \tag{7}$$

Theorem 2. *Let f be an additive generator on $([0,1], \leq)$ and let $\mathfrak{f} : L^I \to \bar{L}^I_{\infty,+}$ the mapping defined by, for all $x \in L^I$,*

$$\mathfrak{f}(x) = [f(x_2), f(x_1)]. \tag{8}$$

Then, for all $y \in \bar{L}^I_{\infty,+}$,

$$\mathfrak{f}^{(-1)}(y) = [f^{(-1)}(y_2), f^{(-1)}(y_1)]. \tag{9}$$

Lemma 5. *Let $\mathfrak{f} : L^I \to \bar{L}^I_{\infty,+}$ be a continuous mapping satisfying (AG.1), (AG.2), (AG.3), (AG.5) and $\mathfrak{f}(D) \subseteq \bar{D}_{\infty,+}$. Then there exists a continuous additive generator f on $([0,1], \leq)$ such that $(\mathfrak{f}(x))_1 = f(x_2)$, for all $x \in L^I$.*

Corollary 2. *Let $\mathfrak{f} : L^I \to \bar{L}^I_{\infty,+}$ be a continuous mapping satisfying (AG.1), (AG.2), (AG.3), (AG.5) and $\mathfrak{f}(D) \subseteq \bar{D}_{\infty,+}$. Then $\mathfrak{f}([0,1]) = [0, (\mathfrak{f}(0_{\mathcal{L}^I}))_2]$.*

Lemma 6. *Let $\mathfrak{f} : L^I \to \bar{L}^I_{\infty,+}$ be a continuous mapping satisfying (AG.1), (AG.2), (AG.3), (AG.5) and $\mathfrak{f}(D) \subseteq \bar{D}_{\infty,+}$. Then there exists a continuous additive generator f on $([0,1], \leq)$ such that $(\mathfrak{f}(x))_2 = f(x_1)$, for all $x \in L^I$.*

Lemma 7. *Let $\mathfrak{f} : L^I \to \bar{L}^I_{\infty,+}$ be a continuous mapping satisfying (AG.1), (AG.2), (AG.3), (AG.5) and $\mathfrak{f}(D) \subseteq \bar{D}_{\infty,+}$. Then there exists a continuous additive generator f on $([0,1], \leq)$ such that, for all $x \in L^I$,*

$$\mathfrak{f}(x) = [f(x_2), f(x_1)].$$

Lemma 8. *Let $\mathfrak{f} : L^I \to \bar{L}^I_{\infty,+}$ be a continuous mapping satisfying (AG.1), (AG.2), (AG.3), (AG.5) and $\mathfrak{f}(D) \subseteq \bar{D}_{\infty,+}$. Then $\mathcal{R}(\mathfrak{f}) = \bar{L}^I_{\infty,+}$ and $\mathfrak{f}$ satisfies (AG.4).*

Theorem 3. *A mapping $\mathfrak{f} : L^I \to \bar{L}^I_{\infty,+}$ is a continuous additive generator on $\mathcal{L}^I$ for which $\mathfrak{f}(D) \subseteq \bar{D}_{\infty,+}$ if and only if there exists a continuous additive generator f on $([0,1], \leq)$ such that, for all $x \in L^I$,*

$$\mathfrak{f}(x) = [f(x_2), f(x_1)]. \tag{10}$$

Theorem 3 shows that no matter which operator $\oplus$ satisfying (ADD-1)–(ADD-4) is used in (AG.4), a continuous additive generator $\mathfrak{f}$ on $\mathcal{L}^I$ for which $\mathfrak{f}(D) \subseteq \bar{D}_{\infty,+}$ can be represented using an additive generator on $([0,1], \leq)$.

Theorem 4. *Let f be an additive generator on $([0,1], \leq)$. Then the mapping $\mathfrak{f} : L^I \to \bar{L}^I_{\infty,+}$ defined by, for all $x \in L^I$,*

$$\mathfrak{f}(x) = [f(x_2), f(x_1)],$$

is an additive generator on $\mathcal{L}^I$ associated to $\oplus$ if and only if, for all x, y in L^I,

$$\mathfrak{f}(x) \oplus \mathfrak{f}(y) \in (\mathrm{rng}(f) \cup [f(0), +\infty])^2.$$

5   Additive Generators and Triangular Norms on $\mathcal{L}^I$

Lemma 9. *Let $\mathfrak{f}$ be an additive generator on $\mathcal{L}^I$ associated to $\oplus$. Then the mapping $\mathcal{T}_{\mathfrak{f}} : (L^I)^2 \to L^I$ defined by, for all x, y in L^I,*

$$\mathcal{T}_{\mathfrak{f}}(x, y) = \mathfrak{f}^{(-1)}(\mathfrak{f}(x) \oplus \mathfrak{f}(y)),$$

is commutative, increasing and $\mathcal{T}_{\mathfrak{f}}(1_{\mathcal{L}^I}, x) = x$, for all $x \in L^I$.

Theorem 5. *Let $\mathfrak{f}$ be a continuous additive generator on $\mathcal{L}^I$ associated to $\oplus$ for which $\mathfrak{f}(D) \subseteq \bar{D}_{\infty,+}$. The mapping $\mathcal{T}_{\mathfrak{f}} : (L^I)^2 \to L^I$ defined by, for all x, y in L^I,*

$$\mathcal{T}_{\mathfrak{f}}(x, y) = \mathfrak{f}^{(-1)}(\mathfrak{f}(x) \oplus \mathfrak{f}(y)),$$

is a t-norm on $\mathcal{L}^I$ if and only if $\oplus$ satisfies the following condition:

$$(\forall(x, y, z) \in A^3)$$
$$\left(\left((\inf(\alpha, x \oplus y) \oplus z)_1 < \alpha_1 \text{ and } (x \oplus y)_2 > \alpha_1 \right) \right. \tag{11}$$
$$\left. \Longrightarrow (\inf(\alpha, x \oplus y) \oplus z)_1 = (x \oplus \inf(\alpha, y \oplus z))_1 \right),$$

where $\alpha = \mathfrak{f}(0_{\mathcal{L}^I})$ and $A = \{x \mid x \in \bar{L}^I_{\infty,+} \text{ and } x \leq_{L^I} \mathfrak{f}(0_{\mathcal{L}^I})\}$.

The condition (11) is very similar to (2). In the following lemma we show that in some cases both conditions are equivalent.

Lemma 10. *Let for all $\alpha \in \bar{D}_+ \setminus \{0_{\mathcal{L}^I}\}$,*

$$P_\alpha \iff (\forall(x, y, z) \in A_\alpha^3)$$
$$\left(\left((\inf(\alpha, x \oplus y) \oplus z)_1 < \alpha_1 \text{ and } (x \oplus y)_2 > \alpha_1 \right) \right. \tag{12}$$
$$\left. \Longrightarrow (\inf(\alpha, x \oplus y) \oplus z)_1 = (x \oplus \inf(\alpha, y \oplus z))_1 \right),$$

where $A_\alpha = \{x \mid x \in \bar{L}^I_+ \text{ and } x \leq_{L^I} \alpha\}$. Assume that

(ADDMULDISTR) $[c, c] \otimes (x \oplus y) = ([c, c] \otimes x) \oplus ([c, c] \otimes y)$, *for all $c \in]0, +\infty[$ and x, y in $\bar{L}^I_+$.*

Then, for any α, β in $\bar{D}_+ \setminus \{0_{\mathcal{L}^I}\}$, $P_\alpha \iff P_\beta$.

The following theorem shows that there is a close relationship between t-norms generated by a continuous additive generator and $\mathcal{S}_\oplus$.

Theorem 6. *Let $\mathfrak{f}$ be a continuous additive generator on $\mathcal{L}^I$ associated to $\oplus$ for which $\mathfrak{f}(D) \subseteq \bar{D}_{\infty,+}$ and $\mathfrak{f}(0_{\mathcal{L}^I}) \in \bar{L}_+^I$. Define the mappings $\mathcal{T}_\mathfrak{f}, \mathcal{S}_\oplus : (L^I)^2 \to L^I$ by, for all x, y in L^I,*

$$\mathcal{T}_\mathfrak{f}(x, y) = \mathfrak{f}^{(-1)}(\mathfrak{f}(x) \oplus \mathfrak{f}(y)),$$
$$\mathcal{S}_\oplus(x, y) = \inf(1_{\mathcal{L}^I}, x \oplus y).$$

If (ADDMULDISTR) *holds, then $\mathcal{T}_\mathfrak{f}$ is a t-norm on $\mathcal{L}^I$ if and only if $\mathcal{S}_\oplus$ is a t-conorm on $\mathcal{L}^I$.*

We now give an easier sufficient condition for additive generators to generate a t-norm. First we give a lemma.

Lemma 11. *Let $\mathfrak{f}$ be an additive generator on $\mathcal{L}^I$ associated to $\oplus$. Assume that $\oplus$ satisfies the following conditions:*

$$(\forall (x, y) \in \bar{L}_+^I \times A)$$
$$\Big(\big(([x_1, \alpha_2] \oplus y)_1 < \alpha_1 \text{ and } x_2 \in]\alpha_2, 2\alpha_2]\big) \implies ([x_1, \alpha_2] \oplus y)_1 = (x \oplus y)_1\Big), \tag{13}$$

$$(\forall (x, y) \in \bar{L}_+^I \times A)$$
$$\Big(\big(([\alpha_1, x_2] \oplus y)_2 < \alpha_2 \text{ and } x_1 \in]\alpha_1, 2\alpha_1]\big) \implies ([\alpha_1, x_2] \oplus y)_2 = (x \oplus y)_2\Big), \tag{14}$$

where $\alpha = \mathfrak{f}(0_{\mathcal{L}^I})$ and $A = \{x \mid x \in \bar{L}_{\infty,+}^I \text{ and } x \leq_{L^I} \mathfrak{f}(0_{\mathcal{L}^I})\}$. Then, for all $x \in L^I$ and $y \in \mathcal{R}(\mathfrak{f})$ such that $y \leq_{L^I} \mathfrak{f}(0_{\mathcal{L}^I}) \oplus \mathfrak{f}(0_{\mathcal{L}^I})$,

$$\mathfrak{f}(x) \oplus \mathfrak{f}(\mathfrak{f}^{(-1)}(y)) \in \mathcal{R}(\mathfrak{f}), \text{ and}$$
$$\mathfrak{f}^{(-1)}(\mathfrak{f}(x) \oplus \mathfrak{f}(\mathfrak{f}^{(-1)}(y))) = \mathfrak{f}^{(-1)}(\mathfrak{f}(x) \oplus y). \tag{15}$$

Using Lemma 11, the following theorem can be shown.

Theorem 7. *Let $\mathfrak{f}$ be an additive generator on $\mathcal{L}^I$ associated to $\oplus$. If $\oplus$ satisfies (13) and (14), then the mapping $\mathcal{T}_\mathfrak{f} : (L^I)^2 \to L^I$ defined by, for all x, y in L^I,*

$$\mathcal{T}_\mathfrak{f}(x, y) = \mathfrak{f}^{(-1)}(\mathfrak{f}(x) \oplus \mathfrak{f}(y)),$$

is a t-norm on $\mathcal{L}^I$.

Theorem 3 and Theorem 2 show that no matter which operator $\oplus$ is used in (AG.4), a continuous additive generator $\mathfrak{f}$ on $\mathcal{L}^I$ satisfying $\mathfrak{f}(D) \subseteq \bar{D}_{\infty,+}$ is representable and has a representable pseudo-inverse. Therefore it depends on the operator $\oplus$ which classes of t-norms on $\mathcal{L}^I$ can have continuous additive generators that extend additive generators on $([0, 1], \leq)$. Theorem 7 gives a sufficient condition under which the additive generator and the used addition operator on $\mathcal{L}^I$ actually yield a t-norm. Theorem 6 shows that the additive generator and the addition operator can be used to construct a t-norm if and only if the addition operator can be used to define a t-conorm on $\mathcal{L}^I$ which extends the Łukasiewicz t-conorm on the unit interval.

References

1. Atanassov, K.T.: Intuitionistic fuzzy sets. VII ITKR's Session, Sofia (deposed in Central Sci.-Technical Library of Bulg. Acad. of Sci. (1697/1984) (1983) (in Bulgarian)
2. Atanassov, K.T.: Intuitionistic fuzzy sets. Fuzzy Sets and Systems 20(1), 87–96 (1986)
3. Atanassov, K.T.: Intuitionistic fuzzy sets. Physica-Verlag, Heidelberg (1999)
4. Deschrijver, G.: Additive and multiplicative generators in interval-valued fuzzy set theory. IEEE Transactions on Fuzzy Systems 15(2), 222–237 (2007)
5. Deschrijver, G.: Arithmetic operators in interval-valued fuzzy set theory. Information Sciences 177(14), 2906–2924 (2007)
6. Deschrijver, G.: Generalized arithmetic operators and their relationship to t-norms in interval-valued fuzzy set theory. Fuzzy Sets and Systems 160(21), 3080–3102 (2009)
7. Deschrijver, G., Kerre, E.E.: On the relationship between some extensions of fuzzy set theory. Fuzzy Sets and Systems 133(2), 227–235 (2003)
8. Deschrijver, G., Vroman, A.: Generalized arithmetic operations in interval-valued fuzzy set theory. Journal of Intelligent and Fuzzy Systems 16(4), 265–271 (2005)
9. Faucett, W.M.: Compact semigroups irreducibly connected between two idempotents. Proceedings of the American Mathematical Society 6, 741–747 (1955)
10. Fodor, J.C., Roubens, M.: Fuzzy preference modelling and multicriteria decision support. Kluwer Academic Publishers, Dordrecht (1994)
11. Goguen, J.A.: L-fuzzy sets. Journal of Mathematical Analysis and Applications 18(1), 145–174 (1967)
12. Gorzałczany, M.B.: A method of inference in approximate reasoning based on interval-valued fuzzy sets. Fuzzy Sets and Systems 21(1), 1–17 (1987)
13. Hájek, P.: Metamathematics of fuzzy logic. Kluwer Academic Publishers, Dordrecht (1998)
14. Klement, E.P., Mesiar, R., Pap, E.: Quasi- and pseudo-inverses of monotone functions, and the construction of t-norms. Fuzzy Sets and Systems 104(1), 3–13 (1999)
15. Klement, E.P., Mesiar, R., Pap, E.: Triangular norms. Kluwer Academic Publishers, Dordrecht (2000)
16. Ling, C.-H.: Representation of associative functions. Publ. Math. Debrecen. 12, 189–212 (1965)
17. Moore, R.E.: Interval arithmetic. Prentice-Hall, Englewood Cliffs (1966)
18. Mostert, P.S., Shields, A.L.: On the structure of semigroups on a compact manifold with boundary. Annals of Mathematics 65, 117–143 (1957)
19. Sambuc, R.: Fonctions Φ-floues. Application à l'aide au diagnostic en pathologie thyroidienne. Ph.D. thesis, Université de Marseille, France (1975)
20. Schweizer, B., Sklar, A.: Probabilistic metric spaces. Elsevier, North-Holland (1983)

Certain Aspects of Decision Making Model: Intuitionistic Fuzzy Preference Relations

Barbara Pękala

Institute of Mathematics, University of Rzeszów
Rejtana 16a, 35-310 Rzeszów, Poland
bpekala@univ.rzeszow.pl

Abstract. The goal of this paper is to consider preference property of intuitionistic fuzzy relations and preservation of a preference relation by some operations, composition and Atanassov's operators like $F_{\alpha,\beta}$, $P_{\alpha,\beta}$, $Q_{\alpha,\beta}$, where $\alpha, \beta \in [0,1]$ are studied. Moreover, transitivity property is considered. We study assumptions under which composition and powers or some Atanassov's operators of intuitionistic fuzzy relations fulfil transitivity property. In all these cases, if possible, characterizations of adequate conditions are given.

Keywords: Atanassov's intuitionistic fuzzy relations, Atanassov's operators, intuitionistic fuzzy preference relations.

1 Introduction

We deal with Atanassov's intuitionistic fuzzy relations which were introduced by Aranassov [1] as a generalization of the concept of a fuzzy relation defined by Zadeh [16]. Fuzzy sets and relations have applications in diverse types of areas, for example in data bases, pattern recognition, neural networks, fuzzy modelling, economy, medicine, multicriteria decision making. Similarly, intuitionistic fuzzy sets and relations are widely applied, for example in multiattribute decision making [8]. If it comes to the composition of intuitionistic fuzzy relations the effective approach to deal with decision making in medical diagnosis was proposed.

In the paper intuitionistic fuzzy preference relations are taken into account. These relations are applied in group decision making problems where a solution from the individual preferences over some set of options should be derived. The concept of a preference relation was considered by many authors, in the crisp case for example in [11] and in the fuzzy environment in [4]. The first authors who generalized the concept of preference from the fuzzy case to the intuitionistic fuzzy one, were Szmidt and Kacprzyk [12]. Preference relations are of great interest nowadays because of their applications [6], [7], [14]. Many other papers were devoted to this topic, for example [13], [15] and diverse problems were considered. In this paper we study properties of the composition of Atanassov's intuitionistic fuzzy relations. Consideration of diverse properties of the composition is interesting not only from a theoretical point of view but also for the applications, since the composition of interval-valued fuzzy relations has proved

S. Greco et al. (Eds.): IPMU 2012, Part II, CCIS 298, pp. 481–490, 2012.
© Springer-Verlag Berlin Heidelberg 2012

to be useful in several fields, see for example, performance evaluation, genetic algorithm, approximate reasoning and what is most important in decision making or in other.

Firstly, some concepts and results useful in further considerations are recalled (section 2). Next, results connected with the preservation of a preference relation by some operations, composition and Atanassov's operators are given (section 3). Finally, transitivity property is considered and its dependence with composition and some Atanassov's operators (section 4).

2   Basic Definitions

Now we recall some definitions which will be helpful in our investigations.

Definition 1 ([1]). *Let* $X, Y \neq \emptyset$, R, $R^d : X \times Y \to [0,1]$ *be fuzzy relations fulfilling the condition*

$$R(x,y) + R^d(x,y) \leq 1, \quad (x,y) \in (X \times Y). \tag{1}$$

A pair $\rho = (R, R^d)$ *is called an Atanassov's intuitionistic fuzzy relation. The family of all Atanassov's intuitionistic fuzzy relations described in the given sets* X, Y *is denoted by* $AIFR(X \times Y)$. *In the case* $X = Y$ *we will use the notation* $AIFR(X)$.

Basic operations for $\rho = (R, R^d)$, $\sigma = (S, S^d) \in AIFR(X \times Y)$ are the union and the intersection, respectively

$$\rho \vee \sigma = (R \vee S, R^d \wedge S^d), \ \rho \wedge \sigma = (R \wedge S, R^d \vee S^d). \tag{2}$$

Similarly, for arbitrary set $T \neq \emptyset$

$$(\bigvee_{t \in T} \rho_t)(x,y) = (\bigvee_{t \in T} R_t(x,y), \bigwedge_{t \in T} R_t^d(x,y)),$$

$$(\bigwedge_{t \in T} \rho_t)(x,y) = (\bigwedge_{t \in T} R_t(x,y), \bigvee_{t \in T} R_t^d(x,y)).$$

Moreover, the order is defined by

$$\rho \leq \sigma \Leftrightarrow (R \leq S, \ S^d \leq R^d). \tag{3}$$

The pair $(AIFR(X \times Y), \leq)$ is a partially ordered set. The boundary elements in $AIFR(X \times Y)$ are $\mathbf{1} = (1,0)$ and $\mathbf{0} = (0,1)$, where $0, 1$ are the constant fuzzy relations. Operations $\vee, \wedge$ are the binary supremum and infimum in the family $AIFR(X \times Y)$, respectively. The family $(AIFR(X \times Y), \vee, \wedge)$ is a complete, distributive lattice. Now, let us recall the notion of the composition in its standard form

Definition 2 (cf. [5],[3]). *Let* $\sigma = (S, S^d) \in AIFR(X \times Y)$, $\rho = (R, R^d) \in AIFR(Y \times Z)$. *By the composition of relations* σ *and* ρ *we call the relation* $\sigma \circ \rho \in AIFR(X \times Z)$,

$$(\sigma \circ \rho)(x, z) = ((S \circ R)(x, z), (S^d \circ' R^d)(x, z)),$$

where

$$(S \circ R)(x, z) = \bigvee_{y \in Y} (S(x, y) \wedge R(y, z)), \tag{4}$$

$$(S^d \circ' R^d)(x, z) = \bigwedge_{y \in Y} (S^d(x, y) \vee R^d(y, z)). \tag{5}$$

In a semigroup $(AIFR(X), \circ)$ we can consider the powers of its elements, i.e. relations ρ^n for $\rho \in AIFR(X)$, $n \in \mathbb{N}$.

By the powers of a relation $\rho = (R, R^d) \in AIFR(X)$ we call Atanassov's intuitionistic fuzzy relations

$$\rho^1 = \rho, \ \rho^{m+1} = \rho^m \circ \rho, \ m = 1, 2, \ldots .$$

The fuzzy relation $\pi_\rho \colon X \times Y \to [0, 1]$ is associated with each Atanassov's intuitionistic fuzzy relation $\rho = (R, R^d)$, where

$$\pi_\rho(x, y) = 1 - R(x, y) - R^d(x, y), \qquad x \in X, y \in Y. \tag{6}$$

The number $\pi_\rho(x, y)$ is called an index of an element (x, y) in an Atanassov's intuitionistic fuzzy relation ρ. It is also described as an index (a degree) of hesitation whether x and y are in the relation ρ or not. This value is also regarded as a measure of non-determinacy or uncertainty (see [9]) and is useful in applications. Intuitionistic fuzzy indices allow to calculate the best final result and the worst one that may be expected in a process leading to a final optimal decision (see [9]).

If we consider decision making problems in the intuitionistic fuzzy environment we deal with the finite set of alternatives $X = \{x_1, \ldots, x_n\}$ and an expert who needs to provide his/her preference information over alternatives. In the sequel, we will consider a preference relation on a finite set $X = \{x_1, \ldots, x_n\}$. In this situation intuitionistic fuzzy relations may be represented by matrices.

Definition 3 ([14], cf. [12]). *Let* $\overline{\overline{X}} = n$. *An intuitionistic fuzzy preference relation* ρ *on the set* X *is represented by a matrix* $\rho = (\rho_{ij})_{n \times n}$ *with* $\rho_{ij} = (R(i, j), R^d(i, j))$, *for all* $i, j = 1, \ldots, n$, *where* ρ_{ij} *is an intuitionistic fuzzy value, composed by the degree* $R(i, j)$ *to which* x_i *is preferred to* x_j, *the degree* $R^d(i, j)$ *to which* x_i *is non-preferred to* x_j, *and the uncertainty degree* $\pi(i, j)$ *to which* x_i *is preferred to* x_j. *Furthermore,* $R(i, j), R^d(i, j)$ *satisfy the following characteristics for all* $i, j = 1, \ldots, n$:

$$0 \leq R(i, j) + R^d(i, j) \leq 1,$$

$$R(i, j) = R^d(j, i), \ R(i, i) = 0.5.$$

From this Definition 3 it follows that $\pi(i, j) = \pi(j, i)$ for all $i, j = 1, \ldots, n$.

3 Operations on Preference Relations

The composition in the family $AIFR(X)$ do not preserve a preference relation, i.e. if ρ and σ are intuitionistic fuzzy preference relations, then their compositions need not have this property.

Example 1. Let $card\ X = 2$ and $\rho = (R, R^d), \sigma = (S, S^d) \in AIFR(X)$ be preference relations represented by the matrices:

$$\rho = \begin{bmatrix} (0.5, 0.5) & (0.3, 0.6) \\ (0.6, 0.3) & (0.5, 0.5) \end{bmatrix}, \sigma = \begin{bmatrix} (0.5, 0.5) & (1, 0) \\ (0, 1) & (0.5, 0.5) \end{bmatrix}.$$

Then according to (2), (3), (4), (5), we obtain

$$\rho \circ \sigma = \begin{bmatrix} (0.5, 0.5) & (0.5, 0.5) \\ (0.5, 0.5) & (0.6, 0.3) \end{bmatrix}, \rho \circ \rho = \begin{bmatrix} (0.5, 0.5) & (0.3, 0.6) \\ (0.5, 0.5) & (0.5, 0.5) \end{bmatrix}.$$

We see that none of the relations $\rho \circ \sigma$, $\rho \circ \rho$ is a preference relation.

By adequate assumptions we obtain preference relation of the composition.

Theorem 1. *Let* $\rho, \sigma \in AIFR(X)$, $\rho = (R, R^d)$, $\sigma = (S, S^d)$. *If* ρ, σ *are intuitionistic fuzzy preference relations and* $(S \circ' R)(x, y) = (R \circ S)(x, y)$ *and* $R(x, y) \wedge S(y, x) \leq \frac{1}{2}$, $R^d(x, y) \vee S^d(y, x) \geq \frac{1}{2}$ *for all* $(x, y) \in X \times X$, *then* $\rho \circ \sigma$ *is a preference relation.*

Proof. By assumptions: ρ, σ are intuitionistic fuzzy preference relations, i.e. $R^d(y, z) = R(z, y), S^d(z, x) = S(x, z)$ and $R(x, x) = R^d(x, x) = \frac{1}{2}, S(x, x) = S^d(x, x) = \frac{1}{2}$, moreover by $(S \circ' R)(x, y) = (R \circ S)(x, y)$ we obtain:

$$(R^d \circ' S^d)(y, x) = \bigwedge_{z \in X} (R^d(y, z) \vee S^d(z, x)) = \bigwedge_{z \in X} (R(z, y) \vee S(x, z)) = \bigwedge_{z \in X} (S(x, z) \vee R(z, y)) = (S \circ' R)(x, y) = (R \circ S)(x, y).$$

Now by assumptions: $R(x, y) \wedge S(y, x) \leq \frac{1}{2}$, $R^d(x, y) \vee S^d(y, x) \geq \frac{1}{2}$ we have

$$(R \circ S)(x, x) = \bigvee_{z \in X} (R(x, z) \wedge S(z, x)) = (R(x, x) \wedge S(x, x)) \vee \bigvee_{z \neq x, z \in X} (R(x, z) \wedge S(z, x)) = \frac{1}{2} \vee \bigvee_{z \neq x, z \in X} (R(x, z) \wedge S(z, x)) = \frac{1}{2},$$

$$(R^d \circ' S^d)(x, x) = \bigwedge_{z \in X} (R^d(x, z) \vee S^d(z, x)) = (R^d(x, x) \vee S^d(x, x)) \wedge \bigwedge_{z \neq x, z \in X} (R^d(x, z) \vee S^d(z, x)) = \frac{1}{2} \wedge \bigwedge_{z \neq x, z \in X} (R^d(x, z) \vee S^d(z, x)) = \frac{1}{2}.$$

So $\rho \circ \sigma$ is a preference relation.

However, if we consider some other operations on relations from the family $AIFR(X)$ we obtain preservation of a preference property.

Definition 4 ([2], p. 9). *Let* $\rho, \sigma \in AIFR(X)$, $\rho = (R, R^d)$, $\sigma = (S, S^d)$. *We consider the following operations:*

$$\rho @ \sigma = (\frac{R + S}{2}, \frac{R^d + S^d}{2}), \quad \rho \diamond \sigma = (\sqrt{RS}, \sqrt{R^d S^d}).$$

Proposition 1. *If $\rho, \sigma \in AIFR(X)$, $\rho = (R, R^d)$, $\sigma = (S, S^d)$ are intuitionistic fuzzy preference relations, then $\rho@\sigma$ and $\rho\diamondsuit\sigma$ are also intuitionistic fuzzy preference relations.*

Proof. Let $\rho = (R, R^d)$, $\sigma = (S, S^d)$ be intuitionistic fuzzy preference relations, i.e. $0 \leq R + R^d \leq 1$ and $0 \leq S + S^d \leq 1$. Then we obtain

$$0 \leq \frac{R+S}{2} + \frac{R^d + S^d}{2} \leq 1, \ \ 0 \leq \sqrt{RS} + \sqrt{R^d S^d} \leq 1.$$

Let $x, y \in X$. If $R(x,x) = R^d(x,x) = \frac{1}{2}$ and $S(x,x) = S^d(x,x) = \frac{1}{2}$, then

$$\frac{R+S}{2}(x,x) = \frac{R(x,x)+S(x,x)}{2} = \frac{1}{2} = \frac{R^d(x,x)+S^d(x,x)}{2} = \frac{R^d + S^d}{2}(x,x)$$

and

$$\sqrt{RS}(x,x) = \sqrt{R(x,x)S(x,x)} = \frac{1}{2} = \sqrt{R^d(x,x)S^d(x,x)} = \sqrt{R^d S^d}(x,x).$$

If $R(x,y) = R^d(y,x)$ and $S(x,y) = S^d(y,x)$, then

$$\frac{R+S}{2}(x,y) = \frac{R(x,y)+S(x,y)}{2} = \frac{R^d(y,x)+S^d(y,x)}{2} = \frac{R^d + S^d}{2}(y,x).$$

Moreover,

$$\sqrt{RS}(x,y) = \sqrt{R(x,y)S(x,y)} = \sqrt{R^d(y,x)S^d(y,x)} = \sqrt{R^d S^d}(y,x).$$

Thus relations @ and $\diamondsuit$ preserve preference property.

Now we put definitions of some Atanassov's operators

Definition 5 ([2]). *Let $\rho \in AIFR(X \times Y)$, $\rho = (R, R^d)$, α, $\beta \in [0,1]$, $\alpha + \beta \leq 1$. The operators $F_{\alpha,\beta}, P_{\alpha,\beta}, Q_{\alpha,\beta} : AIFR(X \times Y) \rightarrow AIFR(X \times Y)$ are defined as follows*

$$F_{\alpha,\beta}(\rho(x,y)) = (R(x,y) + \alpha\pi_\rho(x,y), R^d(x,y) + \beta\pi_\rho(x,y)),$$

$$P_{\alpha,\beta}(\rho(x,y)) = (\max(\alpha, R(x,y)), \min(\beta, R^d(x,y))),$$

$$Q_{\alpha,\beta}(\rho(x,y)) = (\min(\alpha, R(x,y)), \max(\beta, R^d(x,y))).$$

We examine whether Atanassov's operators preserve intuitionistic fuzzy preference relations.

Proposition 2. *Let $\rho \in AIFR(X)$, α, $\beta \in [0,1]$, $\alpha + \beta \leq 1$ and $\rho = (R, R^d)$ be an intuitionistic fuzzy preference relation.*

- $F_{\alpha,\beta}(\rho)$ *is an intuitionistic fuzzy preference relation if and only if $\alpha = \beta$;*
- $P_{\alpha,\beta}(\rho)$ *is an intuitionistic fuzzy preference relation if and only if $\alpha \leq R(i,j) \leq \beta$ for all $i, j = 1, ..., n$;*
- $Q_{\alpha,\beta}(\rho)$ *is an intuitionistic fuzzy preference relation if and only if $\beta \leq R(i,j) \leq \alpha$ for all $i, j = 1, ..., n$.*

Proof. First we consider operation $F_{\alpha,\beta}(\rho)$ and we observe for $1 \leq i,j \leq n$ that

$$F_{\alpha,\beta}(\rho_{ii}) = (R(i,i) + \alpha\pi_\rho(i,i), R^d(i,i) + \beta\pi_\rho(i,i)) = (R(i,i), R^d(i,i)) = (0.5, 0.5).$$

Moreover $R(i,j) + \alpha\pi_\rho(i,j) = R^d(j,i) + \beta\pi_\rho(j,i)$,
because $R(i,j) = R^d(j,i)$ and $\pi_\rho(i,j) = \pi_\rho(j,i)$.
Thus $F_{\alpha,\beta}(\rho)$ preserves the preference property if and only if $\alpha = \beta$.

Now we will examine operator $P_{\alpha,\beta}$. For $\alpha \leq R(i,j) \leq \beta$ we have

$$\max(\alpha, R(i,j)) = R(i,j) = R^d(j,i) = \min(\beta, R^d(j,i)).$$

This proves that $P_{\alpha,\beta}(\rho)$ preserves the preference property.

If $P_{\alpha,\beta}(\rho)$ and ρ are intuitionistic fuzzy preference relations, then

$$P_{\alpha,\beta}(\rho_{ii}) = (\max(\alpha, R(i,i)), \min(\beta, R^d(i,i))) = (\max(\alpha, 0.5), \min(\beta, 0.5)) = (0.5, 0.5).$$

As a result $\alpha \leq 0.5 = R(i,i)$ and $\beta \geq 0.5 = R^d(i,i)$. For $i \neq j$ we obtain

$$\max(\alpha, R(i,j)) = \min(\beta, R^d(j,i)) = \min(\beta, R(i,j)).$$

This condition is true only for $\alpha \leq R(i,j) \leq \beta$, so these inequalities are also true. The case of $Q_{\alpha,\beta}(\rho)$ can be proven in a similar way.

4   Transitivity Property

Now, we examine very interesting property, namely transitivity. This property is of the large interest for example in economy where it is applied in valuation of supply and demand.

In this section we consider some properties of intuitionistic fuzzy relations and intuitionistic fuzzy preference relations. First, we recall the concept of a partially included relation in which the $sgn : \mathbb{R} \to \mathbb{R}$ function occurs, where

$$sgn(t) = \begin{cases} 1, & t > 0 \\ 0, & t = 0 \\ -1, & t < 0 \end{cases}.$$

Definition 6 (cf. [3]). *An intuitionistic fuzzy relation $\rho = (R, R^d) \in AIFR(X)$ is partially included, if for all $x, y, z \in X$*

$$sgn(R(x,y) - R(y,z)) = sgn(R^d(y,z) - R^d(x,y)). \tag{7}$$

Definition 7. *An intuitionistic fuzzy relation $\rho = (R, R^d) \in AIFR(X)$ is transitive, if $\rho \circ \rho \leq \rho$ ($\rho^2 \leq \rho$).*

Thus we have

Lemma 1 (cf. [10]). *Let $\rho \in AIFR(X)$, $\alpha, \beta \in [0,1]$, $\alpha + \beta \leq 1$. If ρ is partially included and transitive, then $F_{\alpha,\beta}(\rho)$ is transitive.*

By Lemma 1 and by condition: $\rho_{ij} + \rho_{ji} = (1,1)$, which means that $R(i,j) + R(j,i) = 1$ and $R^d(i,j) + R^d(j,i) = 1$, we obtain the following

Proposition 3. *Let $\rho \in AIFR(X)$, $\overline{\overline{X}} = n$ and $\alpha, \beta \in [0,1]$. If $\rho = (R, R^d)$ is an intuitionistic fuzzy preference relation fulfilling the property $\rho_{ij} + \rho_{ji} = (1,1)$ for all $i,j = 1,...,n$ and the transitivity property, then $F_{\alpha,\beta}(\rho)$ $(F_{\alpha,\alpha}(\rho))$ is also an intuitionistic fuzzy transitive relation (intuitionistic fuzzy transitive preference relation).*

Proof. If $\rho_{ij} + \rho_{ji} = (1,1)$, then for an intuitionistic fuzzy preference relation $(R(i,j) + R(j,i) = 1) \Leftrightarrow (R^d(i,j) + R^d(j,i) = 1)$.

So ρ is partially included:

$$sgn(R(i,j) - R(j,k)) = sgn(1 - R(j,i) - (1 - R(k,j))) =$$
$$sgn(R(k,j) - R(j,i)) = sgn(R^d(j,k) - R^d(i,j)).$$

By Lemma 1 we see that $F_{\alpha,\beta}(\rho)$ is transitive, moreover by Proposition 2, $F_{\alpha,\beta}(\rho)$ for $\alpha = \beta$ is an intuitionistic fuzzy transitive preference relation.

We also obtain

Lemma 2. *Let $\rho \in AIFR(X)$, $\alpha, \beta \in [0,1]$ and $\alpha + \beta \leq 1$. If ρ is partially included and $F_{\alpha,\beta}(\rho)$ is transitive, then ρ is also transitive.*

Proof. We must prove that $F_{\alpha,\beta}^2(\rho) \leq F_{\alpha,\beta}(\rho) \Rightarrow \rho^2 \leq \rho$. Thus we assume

$$(R^2 + \alpha\pi_{\rho^2}, (R^d)^2 + \beta\pi_{\rho^2}) \leq (R + \alpha\pi_\rho, R^d + \beta\pi_\rho).$$

We consider the following cases:

1. If $\pi_{\rho^2} = \pi_\rho$, then by (3) we obtain $R^2 \leq R$ and $(R^d)^2 \geq R^d$.
2. If $\pi_{\rho^2} > \pi_\rho$, then $R + \alpha\pi_{\rho^2} > R + \alpha\pi_\rho \geq R^2 + \alpha\pi_{\rho^2}$ so $R^2 \leq R$ and $R - R^2 \geq \alpha(\pi_{\rho^2} - \pi_\rho)$. Moreover, by $R - R^2 \geq 0$ and

$$\alpha(\pi_{\rho^2} - \pi_\rho) \geq 0 \Leftrightarrow R - R^2 + R^d - (R^d)^2 \geq 0,$$

we have $R^d - (R^d)^2 \leq 0$, i.e. $R^d \leq (R^d)^2$. This means $\rho^2 \leq \rho$.
3. If $\pi_{\rho^2} < \pi_\rho$, then $R^d + \beta\pi_{\rho^2} < R^d + \beta\pi_\rho \leq (R^d)^2 + \beta\pi_{\rho^2}$, so $R^d \leq (R^d)^2$, i.e. $(R^d)^2 - R^d \geq 0$. Moreover,
$\beta(\pi_\rho - \pi_{\rho^2}) > 0 \Leftrightarrow R^2 - R + (R^d)^2 - R^d > 0$ and
$\beta(\pi_\rho - \pi_{\rho^2}) \leq (R^d)^2 - R^d$.
We have $R^2 - R \leq 0$, i.e. $R^2 \leq R$. This finishes the proof.

From the above lemma we obtain, similarly to Proposition 3, the following theorem

Corollary 1. *Let $\rho \in AIFR(X)$, $\overline{\overline{X}} = n$ and $\alpha, \beta \in [0,1]$. If $\rho = (R, R^d)$ is an intuitionistic fuzzy preference relation and $F_{\alpha,\beta}(\rho)$ $(F_{\alpha,\alpha}(\rho))$ is an intuitionistic fuzzy transitive relation (intuitionistic fuzzy transitive preference relation), then ρ is also transitive.*

Moreover, the following Atanassov's operators preserve transitivity, what we may prove from the Definition 5 and lattice properties

Proposition 4. *Let $\rho \in AIFR(X)$, $\alpha, \beta \in [0,1]$, $\alpha + \beta \leq 1$. If ρ is transitive, then*

$$P_{\alpha,\beta}(\rho), \quad Q_{\alpha,\beta}(\rho)$$

are transitive.

Proof. We prove for example the first condition. Let $x, y \in X$ and $\rho \in AIFR(X)$ be transitive.

$$P_{\alpha,\beta}^2(\rho)(x,y) = (\bigvee_{z \in X} (\max(\alpha, R(x,z)) \wedge (\max(\alpha, R(z,y)))),$$

$$\bigwedge_{z \in X} (\min(\beta, R^d(x,z)) \vee (\min(\beta, R^d(z,y))))))$$

and by absorption law and distributivity $\vee$ and $\wedge$ we obtain

$$(\alpha \vee \bigvee_{z \in X} (R(x,z) \wedge R(z,y)), \beta \wedge \bigwedge_{z \in X} (R^d(x,z) \vee R^d(z,y))) =$$

$$(\alpha \vee R^2(x,y), \beta \wedge (R^d)^2(x,y)) \leq (\alpha \vee R(x,y), \beta \wedge R^d(x,y)) = P_{\alpha,\beta}(\rho)(x,y),$$

so $P_{\alpha,\beta}(\rho)$ is transitive. The case of $Q_{\alpha,\beta}(\rho)$ can be proven in a similar way.

Now we consider composition of transitive Atanassov's intuitionistic fuzzy relations.

Theorem 2. *Let $\rho, \sigma \in AIFR(X)$, $\rho = (R, R^d)$, $\sigma = (S, S^d)$. If ρ, σ are intuitionistic fuzzy transitive relations and $\rho \circ \sigma = \sigma \circ \rho$, then $\rho \circ \sigma$ is transitive relation.*

Proof. By assumption:

$\rho \circ \sigma = \sigma \circ \rho \Leftrightarrow (R \circ S, R^d \circ' S^d) = (S \circ R, S^d \circ' R^d) \Leftrightarrow R \circ S = S \circ R, \ R^d \circ' S^d = S^d \circ' R^d$ and
$\rho^2 \leq \rho \Leftrightarrow (R^2 \leq R, (R^d)^2 \geq R^d)$, and $\sigma^2 \leq \sigma \Leftrightarrow (S^2 \leq S, (S^d)^2 \geq S^d)$ and by isotonicity of sup-min composition of intuitionistic fuzzy relations we obtain

$$(\rho \circ \sigma)^2 = ((R \circ S)^2, (R^d \circ' S^d)^2) = (R \circ S \circ R \circ S, R^d \circ' S^d \circ' R^d \circ' S^d) =$$
$$(R^2 \circ S^2, R^{d^2} \circ' S^{d^2}) \leq (R \circ S, R^d \circ' S^d) = \rho \circ \sigma.$$

Thus $\rho \circ \sigma$ have transitivity property.

Moreover we observe the following connection between transitivity and powers of intuitionistic fuzzy relation and composition.

Proposition 5. *Let $\rho \in AIFR(X)$. If ρ is subidempotent, then ρ^n is also subidempotent for $n \in \mathbb{N}$.*

Proof. By $\rho^2 \leq \rho$ and isotonicity of composition we have

$$(\rho^n)^2 \leq \dots \leq \rho^n \leq \dots \leq \rho^3 \leq \rho^2 \leq \rho.$$

So ρ^n is subidempotent.

Proposition 6. *Let* $\rho, \sigma \in AIFR(X)$. *If* $\rho \circ \sigma = \sigma \circ \rho$, *then*

$$\forall_{n \in \mathbb{N}} (\rho \circ \sigma)^n = \rho^n \circ \sigma^n. \tag{8}$$

Proof. The given equality may be proved by mathematical induction. First, for $\rho \circ \sigma = \sigma \circ \rho$ we obtain commutativity of powers, i.e.

$$\rho^k \circ \sigma^p = \sigma^p \circ \rho^k, \quad k, p \in \mathbb{N}. \tag{9}$$

Let $k, p \in \mathbb{N}$. We consider the following cases:
1. By mathematical induction we have

$$\forall_{k \in \mathbb{N}} \rho^k \circ \sigma = \sigma \circ \rho^k. \tag{10}$$

a) For $k = 1$ (10) is true.
b) By assumption that (10) is true for $k = n$ we obtain this equality for $k = n+1$, i.e.

$$\forall_{k \in \mathbb{N}} \rho^{n+1} \circ \sigma = \sigma \circ \rho^{n+1}. \tag{11}$$

The induction assumption and associativity of composition implies:

$$\rho^{n+1} \circ \sigma = (\rho^n \circ \rho) \circ \sigma = \rho^n \circ (\rho \circ \sigma) = \rho^n \circ (\sigma \circ \rho) =$$

$$(\rho^n \circ \sigma) \circ \rho = (\sigma \circ \rho^n) \circ \rho = \sigma \circ (\rho^n \circ \rho) = \sigma \circ \rho^{n+1},$$

which finishes the proof (10).
2. Similarly we may prove

$$\forall_{p \in \mathbb{N}} \rho \circ \sigma^p = \sigma^p \circ \rho. \tag{12}$$

By 1 and 2 we obtain (9). Now by this equality and mathematical induction we obtain (8).

5 Conclusion

We observed that transitivity is preserved by some operations and Atanassov's operators. We can also consider other Atanassov's operators and other properties. In our further considerations we want to study other transitivity properties of intuitionistic fuzzy preference relations. We can also consider preservation of transitive property by lattice operation and other operations. Moreover, we can examine more general form of composition of Atanassov's intuitionistic fuzzy relations by adequate additional assumptions for $\star$ and $\star'$ and apply in group decision making problems.

Acknowledgments. This paper is partially supported by the Ministry of Science and Higher Education Grant Nr N N519 384936.

References

1. Atanassov, K.T.: Intuitionistic fuzzy sets. Fuzzy Sets Syst. 20, 87–96 (1986)
2. Atanassov, K.: Intuitionistic Fuzzy Sets: Theory and Applications. Springer, Heidelberg (1999)
3. Burillo, P., Bustince, H.: Intuitionistic Fuzzy Relations. Effect of Atanassov's Operators on the Properties of the Intuitionistic Fuzzy Relations. Math. Soft Comp. 2, 117–148 (1995)
4. Chiclana, F., Herrera-Viedma, E., Alonso, S., Pereira, R.A.M.: Preferences and consistency issues in group decision making. In: Bustince, H., et al. (eds.) Fuzzy Sets and Their Extensions: Representation, Aggregation and Models, pp. 219–237. Springer, Berlin (2008)
5. Goguen, A.: L-Fuzzy Sets. J. Math. Anal. Appl. 18, 145–174 (1967)
6. Gong, Z.-W., Li, L.-S., Zhou, F.-X., Yao, T.-X.: Goal programming approaches to obtain the priority vectors from the intuitionistic fuzzy preference relations. Computers Industrial Eng. 57, 1187–1193 (2009)
7. Gong, Z.-W., Li, L.-S., Forrest, J., Zhao, Y.: The optimal priority models of the intuitionistic fuzzy preference relation and their application in selecting industries with higher meteorological sensitivity. Expert Syst. Appl. 38, 4394–4402 (2011)
8. Li, D.-F.: Multiattribute decision making models and method using intuitionistic fuzzy sets. J. Comput. Syst. Sci. 70, 73–85 (2005)
9. Lin, L., Yuan, X.-H., Xia, Z.-Q.: Multicriteria fuzzy decision-making methods based on intuitionistic fuzzy sets. J. Comput. Syst. Sci. 73, 84–88 (2007)
10. Pękala, B.: Properties of Interval-Valued Fuzzy Relations, Atanassov's Operators and Decomposable Operations. In: Hüllermeier, E., Kruse, R., Hoffmann, F. (eds.) IPMU 2010. CCIS, vol. 80, pp. 647–655. Springer, Heidelberg (2010)
11. Roubens, M., Vincke, P.: Preference Modelling. Springer, Berlin (1985)
12. Szmidt, E., Kacprzyk, J.: Using intuitionistic fuzzy sets in group decision making. Control Cybern. 31, 1037–1053 (2002)
13. Szmidt, E., Kacprzyk, J.: Atanassov's Intuitionistic Fuzzy Sets as a Promising Tool for Extended Fuzzy Decision Making Models. In: Bustince, H., et al. (eds.) Fuzzy Sets and Their Extensions: Representation, Aggregation and Models, pp. 335–355. Springer, Heidelberg (2008)
14. Xu, Z.: Intuitionistic preference relations and their application in group decision making. Inform. Sci. 17, 2363–2379 (2007)
15. Yager, R.R., Xu, Z.: Intuitionistic and interval-valued intuitionistic fuzzy preference relations and their measures of similarity for the evaluation of agreement within a group. Fuzzy Optim. Decis. Making 8, 123–139 (2009)
16. Zadeh, L.A.: Fuzzy Sets. Inform. Control 8, 338–353 (1965)

Local IF-Divergences

Ignacio Montes[1], Vladimir Janiš[2], and Susana Montes[1]

[1] University of Oviedo, Spain
{imontes,montes}@uniovi.es
[2] Matej Bel University, Slovak Republic
Vladimir.Janis@umb.sk

Abstract. In this work a particular type of measure of comparison of intuitionistic fuzzy sets is introduced: the local IF-divergences. This measure appears as a generalization of the local divergences for fuzzy sets. Some properties of this concept are introduced. In particular, we show that two methods used to build divergences from IF-divergences, and conversely IF-divergence from divergences, preserve the local property.

1 Introduction

Fuzzy set theory was introduced by Zadeh ([14]) in order to model situations in which classical set theory does not represent all the available information. However, there are situations in which the model provided by the fuzzy set theory can be improved. For this aim, Atanassov ([1,2]) introduced the theory of intuitionistic fuzzy sets (IF-sets, for short). These sets allow two freedom degrees: the membership and the non-membership degrees. Consequently, they allow us to take into account the possible lack of information.

Nowadays IF-set theory has become very popular, and in particular, several authors have focused in the comparison of IF-sets. For this aim, some measures of comparison between IF-sets can be found in the literature, like IF-dissimilarities and IF-distances.

In previous works ([8,9]) we introduced a new measure: IF-divergence, that generalizes the well-known divergences for fuzzy sets ([10]). We have already studied the relationships between the different measures of comparison of IF-sets, and we have introduced interesting properties of this new concept.

In this work we focus on a particular type of IF-divergences, those that satisfy a local property. We show a characterization of these measures, and we study some interesting properties. In particular, we consider two methods that allow us to build IF-divergences from divergences and, conversely, divergences from IF-divergences, and we investigate which condition must be imposed in order to preserve the local property.

This work is organized as follows: Section 2 is devoted to introduce the most basic notions of the theory of IF-sets. Then, the usual measures of comparison of IF-sets are introduced in Section 3. In Section 4 we focus on the local property of IF-sets. First of all we introduce its definition and its characterization and then we show several properties of these measures. Finally, we present some concluding remarks in Section 5.

S. Greco et al. (Eds.): IPMU 2012, Part II, CCIS 298, pp. 491–500, 2012.
© Springer-Verlag Berlin Heidelberg 2012

2   Intuitionistic Fuzzy Sets

Since Zadeh introduced the theory of fuzzy sets (see [14]), they became very popular to model situations in which uncertainty is present. However, there are situations in which the model provided by fuzzy sets can be improved. Atanassov introduced the theory of intuitionistic fuzzy sets as a generalization of fuzzy sets that allow two freedom degrees: a degree of membership and a degree of non-membership of every point to the set (see [1,2]). Formally, in an universe Ω, an IF-set A is given by:

$$A = \{(\omega, \mu_A(\omega), \nu_A(\omega)) \mid \omega \in \Omega\},$$

where $\mu_A, \nu_A : \Omega \to [0,1]$ satisfy $\mu_A(\omega) + \nu_A(\omega) \leq 1$ for every $\omega \in \Omega$. In this way $\mu_A(\omega)$ (respectively $\nu_A(\omega)$) can be interpreted as the degree in which the element ω belongs (respectively, does not belong) to the set A or the degree in which it satisfies (respectively, does not satisfy) the property defined by A. That is, $\mu_A(\omega)$ and $\nu_A(\omega)$ are the membership and non-membership degrees of ω in A. From these functions the intuitionistic fuzzy index, or hesitation index, can by defined by:

$$\pi_A(\omega) = 1 - \mu_A(\omega) - \nu_A(\omega),$$

and it measures the lack of knowledge of whether ω belongs to A or not.

In this sense, it is obvious that every fuzzy set A, with membership function $A(\omega)$, is in particular an IF-set, since it can be equivalently represented by:

$$A = \{(\omega, A(\omega), 1 - A(\omega)) \mid \omega \in \Omega\},$$

where the hesitation index π_A always takes the value zero. Then, if $FS(\Omega)$ denotes the set of all fuzzy sets defined on Ω, and $IFSs(\Omega)$ denotes the set of all IF-sets defined on Ω, it holds that $FS(\Omega) \subseteq IFSs(\Omega)$.

In the fuzzy set theory, operations like intersections, unions and complements and the inclusion relation can be defined. They can also be extended to the case of IF-sets as follows:

– The intersection and union of $A, B \in IFSs(\Omega)$ are defined by:

$$A \cap B = \{(\omega, \mu_{A \cap B}(\omega), \nu_{A \cap B}(\omega) \mid \omega \in \Omega\},$$
$$A \cup B = \{(\omega, \mu_{A \cup B}(\omega), \nu_{A \cup B}(\omega) \mid \omega \in \Omega\},$$

where

$$\mu_{A \cap B}(\omega) = \min(\mu_A(\omega), \mu_B(\omega)), \quad \nu_{A \cap B}(\omega) = \max(\nu_A(\omega), \nu_B(\omega)).$$
$$\mu_{A \cup B}(\omega) = \max(\mu_A(\omega), \mu_B(\omega)), \quad \nu_{A \cup B}(\omega) = \min(\nu_A(\omega), \nu_B(\omega)).$$

– For every $A \in IFSs(\Omega)$, its complement, A^c, is defined by:

$$A^c = \{(\omega, \nu_A(\omega), \mu_A(\omega)) \mid \omega \in \Omega\}.$$

– Given two IF-sets A and B, A is included in B, denoted by $A \subseteq B$, if:

$$\mu_A(\omega) \leq \mu_B(\omega) \text{ and } \nu_A(\omega) \geq \nu_B(\omega) \text{ for every } \omega \in \Omega.$$

Note that we are considering the initial definitions of intersection and union given by Atanassov ([1,2]), since they are the most usually considered in the literature. Nevertheless, these operations can be defined by means of a t-norm and its dual t-conorm (see [3]).

3   Measures of Comparison of IFS

The comparison of fuzzy sets is an interesting topic of research, and several measures have been proposed during last years, like distances, dissimilarities ([7]) and divergences ([10]). With the increasing popularity of the theory of IF-sets, these measures were generalized to the comparison of IF-sets. In this section we introduce some usual measures of comparison of IF-sets, IF-distances, IF-dissimilarities and IF-divergences, and we explain the relationships among these four notions.

Let us begin by recalling the most usual measure of comparison we can find in the literature, the distances for IF-sets (IF-distances, for short). An IF-distance is a map $d : IFSs(\Omega) \times IFSs(\Omega) \to \mathbb{R}$ satisfying the following properties:

IF-Dist.1: $d(A, B) \geq 0$ for every $A, B \in IFSs(\Omega)$.
IF-Dist.2: $d(A, B) = d(B, A)$ for every $A, B \in IFSs(\Omega)$.
IF-Dist.3: $d(A, B) = 0$ if and only if $A = B$.
IF-Dist.4: $d(A, C) \leq d(A, B) + d(B, C)$ for every $A, B, C \in IFSs(\Omega)$.

Properties from IF-Dist.1 to IF-Dist.4 are usually called non-negativity, identity of indiscernibles, symmetry and triangle inequality.

Other well known measures of comparison of IF-sets are IF-dissimilarities. They are functions $D : IFSs(\Omega) \times IFSs(\Omega) \to \mathbb{R}$ satisfying the following axioms:

IF-Diss.1: $D(A, A) = 0$ for every $A \in IFSs(\Omega)$.
IF-Dist.2: $D(A, B) = D(B, A)$ for every $A, B \in IFSs(\Omega)$.
IF-Diss.3:   For every $A, B, C \in IFSs(\Omega)$ such that $A \subseteq B \subseteq C$ it holds that $D(A, C) \geq \max(D(A, B), D(B, C))$.

The notion of IF-dissimilarity extends the dissimilarity measures used for the comparison of fuzzy sets (see [7]). However, dissimilarities for fuzzy sets impose an additional property that is not required in the intuitionistic framework:

Diss.4: $D(C, C^c) = \max(D(A, B) \mid A, B \in FS(\Omega))$ for every $C \in \mathcal{P}(\Omega)$.

Let us also note that some authors (see [5,6,13]) replace axiom IF-Diss.1 by a stronger condition, axiom IF-Dist.1. However, we consider the original definition since it is the most usual in the literature.

Recently, we extended one of the most usual measure of comparison of fuzzy sets, the divergences (see [10]), for the comparison of IF-sets. Let us recall that divergences for fuzzy sets are measures of comparison of fuzzy sets satisfying:

- The divergence between two sets is non-negative.
- The divergence between a set and itself must be zero.
- The divergence between two sets A and B is the same as the divergence between B and A.
- The "more similar" two sets are, the lower is the divergence between them.

Formally, a divergence for fuzzy sets is a map $D : FS(\Omega) \times FS(\Omega) \to \mathbb{R}$ satisfying the following properties:

Div.1: $D(A, A) = 0$ for every $A \in FS(\Omega)$.
Div.2: $D(A, B) = D(B, A)$ for every $A, B \in FS(\Omega)$.
Div.3: $D(A \cap C, B \cap C) \leq D(A, B)$ for every $A, B, C \in FS(\Omega)$.
Div.4: $D(A \cup C, B \cup C) \leq D(A, B)$ for every $A, B, C \in FS(\Omega)$.

Divergences can be easily extended to the comparison of IF-sets: an IF-divergence is a function $D_{\mathrm{IF}} : IFSs(\Omega) \times IFSs(\Omega) \to \mathbb{R}$ satisfying the following axioms:

IF-Diss.1: $D_{\mathrm{IF}}(A, A) = 0$ for every $A \in IFSs(\Omega)$.
IF-Dist.2: $D_{\mathrm{IF}}(A, B) = D_{\mathrm{IF}}(B, A)$ for every $A, B \in IFSs(\Omega)$.
IF-Div.3: $D_{\mathrm{IF}}(A \cap C, B \cap C) \leq D_{\mathrm{IF}}(A, B)$ for every $A, B, C \in IFSs(\Omega)$.
IF-Div.4: $D_{\mathrm{IF}}(A \cup C, B \cup C) \leq D_{\mathrm{IF}}(A, B)$ for every $A, B, C \in IFSs(\Omega)$.

We have introduced three different measures of comparison of IF-sets. Consequently, we shall investigate the possible relationships among them.

Theorem 1. *[9] If we consider IF-distances, IF-dissimilarities and IF-divergences, it holds that:*

- *IF-divergence $\Rightarrow$ IF-dissimilarity, and the converse implication does not hold in general.*
- *Even if the measure is also a distance, the converse implication of the previous item does not hold in general.*
- *There is not a general relationship of inclusion between distances and IF-dissimilarities or IF-distances and IF-divergences.*

Thus, IF-divergences impose stronger conditions than IF-dissimilarities. However, sometimes it can be an advantage, since the more restrictive the conditions, the more "robust " the measures is, in the sense that it is difficult to find counterintuitive examples.

4   Local Property of the IF-Divergences

We have already commented that some measures of comparison were introduced for the comparison of fuzzy sets. In particular, we recall a type of divergences: those that satisfy the local property. Let us recall that from now on we consider finite universes.

Definition 1. *A divergence measure for fuzzy sets D is a local divergence, or it satisfies the local property, if for every $A, B \in FS(\Omega)$ and every $\omega_i \in \Omega = \{\omega_1, \ldots, \omega_n\}$ it holds that:*

$$D(A, B) - D(A \cup \{\omega_i\}, B \cup \{\omega_i\}) = h(A(\omega_i), B(\omega_i)).$$

This means that the variation of the divergence only depends on what has been changed. Montes et al. ([10]) provided the following characterization of local divergences:

Theorem 2. *A map $D : FS(\Omega) \times FS(\Omega) \to \mathbb{R}$ is a local divergence if and only if there is a function $h : [0, 1] \times [0, 1] \to \mathbb{R}$ such that:*

$$D(A, B) = \sum_{i=1}^{n} h(A(\omega_i), B(\omega_i)), \quad and$$

loc.1 $h(x, y) = h(y, x)$ *for every* $(x, y) \in [0, 1]^2$.
loc.2 $h(x, x) = 0$ *for every* $x \in [0, 1]$.
loc.3 $h(x, z) \geq \max(h(x, y), h(y, z))$ *for every* $x, y, z \in [0, 1]$
       such that $x < y < z$.

In addition to this characterization, Montes et al. (see [10]) studied some properties of this particular type of divergences.

In this section our aim is to extend the local property for IF-divergences and to analyze the properties of this notion.

4.1   Local IF-Divergences

Let us consider a universe $\Omega = \{\omega_1, \ldots, \omega_n\}$ and an IF-divergence D_{IF}. If A and B are two IF-sets, and we consider $\omega_i \in \Omega$, applying axiom IF-Div.3 we know that $D(A \cup \{\omega_i\}, B \cup \{\omega_i\}) \leq D_{\text{IF}}(A, B)$. Moreover, we could suppose that the difference lies on the $i - th$ component. When this happens, we call the IF-divergence local.

Definition 2. *Let D_{IF} be an IF-divergence. It is called local (or it is said to satisfy the local property) when for every $A, B \in IFSs(\Omega)$ and every $\omega \in \Omega$ it holds that:*

$$D_{\text{IF}}(A, B) - D_{\text{IF}}(A \cup \{\omega\}, B \cup \{\omega\}) = h_{\text{IF}}(\mu_A(\omega), \mu_B(\omega), \nu_A(\omega), \nu_B(\omega)).$$

Theorem 2 characterizes local divergences for fuzzy sets. In a similar way, we can also characterize local IF-divergences.

Theorem 3. *A map $D_{\text{IF}} : IFSs(\Omega) \times IFSs(\Omega) \to \mathbb{R}$ on a finite universe $\Omega = \{\omega_1, \ldots, \omega_n\}$ is a local IF-divergence if and only if there is a function $h_{\text{IF}} : [0, 1]^4 \to \mathbb{R}$ such that for every $A, B \in IFSs(\Omega)$ it holds that:*

$$D_{\text{IF}}(A, B) = \sum_{i=1}^{n} h_{\text{IF}}(\mu_A(\omega_i), \mu_B(\omega_i), \nu_A(\omega_i), \nu_B(\omega_i)), \tag{1}$$

where $\mathcal{D}$ denotes the set $\mathcal{D} = \{(t, z) \in [0, 1]^2 \mid t + z \leq 1\}$ and h_{IF} satisfies the following properties:

IF-loc.1: $h_{\mathrm{IF}}(x, x, y, y) = 0$ for every $(x, y) \in \mathcal{D}$.

IF-loc.2: $h_{\mathrm{IF}}(x_1, y_1, x_2, y_2) = h_{\mathrm{IF}}(y_1, x_1, y_2, x_2)$ for every
$(x_1, x_2), (y_1, y_2) \in \mathcal{D}$.

IF-loc.3:   For every $(x_1, x_2), (y_1, y_2), (z_1, z_2) \in \mathcal{D}$ such that
$x_1 \leq z_1 \leq y_1$ and $x_2 \leq z_2 \leq y_2$, it holds that:
$\max(h_{\mathrm{IF}}(x_1, z_1, x_2, z_2), h_{\mathrm{IF}}(y_1, z_1, y_2, z_2)) \leq h_{\mathrm{IF}}(x_1, y_1, x_2, y_2)$.

IF-loc.4:   If $(x_1, x_2), (y_1, y_2) \in \mathcal{D}$, $z \in [0, 1]$ and $x_1 \leq z \leq y_1$,
it holds that $h_{\mathrm{IF}}(x_1, y_1, x_2, y_2) \geq h_{\mathrm{IF}}(x_1, z, x_2, y_2)$.
Moreover, if $\max(x_2, y_2) + z \leq 1$, it holds that:
$h_{\mathrm{IF}}(x_1, y_1, x_2, y_2) \geq h_{\mathrm{IF}}(z, y_1, x_2, y_2)$.

IF-loc.5:   If $(x_1, x_2), (y_1, y_2) \in \mathcal{D}$, $z \in [0, 1]$ and $x_2 \leq z \leq y_2$,
it holds that $h_{\mathrm{IF}}(x_1, y_1, x_2, y_2) \geq h_{\mathrm{IF}}(x_1, y_1, x_2, z)$.
Moreover, if $\max(x_1, y_1) + z \leq 1$, it holds that:
$h_{\mathrm{IF}}(x_1, y_1, x_2, y_2) \geq h_{\mathrm{IF}}(x_1, y_1, z, y_2)$.

IF-loc.6:   If $(x_1, x_2), (y_1, y_2) \in \mathcal{D}$ and $z \in [0, 1]$, then:
$h_{\mathrm{IF}}(z, z, x_2, y_2) \leq h_{\mathrm{IF}}(x_1, y_1, x_2, y_2)$ if $\max(x_2, y_2) + z \leq 1$ and
$h_{\mathrm{IF}}(x_1, y_1, z, z) \leq h_{\mathrm{IF}}(x_1, y_1, x_2, y_2)$ if $\max(x_1, y_1) + z \leq 1$.

This theorem allows us to characterize local IF-divergences by means of a function h_{IF} that satisfies conditions from IF-loc.1 to IF-loc.6. Thus, given a function $D : IFSs(\Omega) \times IFSs(\Omega) \to \mathbb{R}$, in order to check if it is or not a local IF-divergence, it is enough to prove if it can be expressed as in Equation 1 and if it satisfies such conditions.

Example 1. Let consider the Hamming and the Hausdorff distances, denoted by l_{IFS} and d_{H}, respectively. These measures of comparison of IF-sets can be frequently found in the literature, as for example in a recent paper of Szmidt and Kacprzyk ([12]). They are defined by:

$$l_{\mathrm{IFS}}(A, B) = \sum_{i=1}^{n} |\mu_A(\omega_i) - \mu_B(\omega_i)| + |\nu_A(\omega_i) - \nu_B(\omega_i)| + |\pi_A(\omega_i) - \pi_B(\omega_i)|.$$
$$d_{\mathrm{H}}(A, B) = \sum_{i=1}^{n} \max(|\mu_A(\omega_i) - \mu_B(\omega_i)|, |\nu_A(\omega_i) - \nu_B(\omega_i)|).$$

We have already proved (see [8]) that both measures are IF-divergences. In fact, if we consider the functions

$$h_{l_{\mathrm{IFS}}}(x_1, y_1, x_2, y_2) = |x_1 - y_1| + |x_2 - y_2| + |x_1 + x_2 - y_1 - y_2|;$$
$$h_{d_{\mathrm{H}}}(x_1, y_1, x_2, y_2) = \max(|x_1 - y_1|, |x_2 - y_2|);$$

then Hamming and Hausdorff distances can be expressed by:

$$l_{\mathrm{IFS}}(A, B) = \sum_{i=1}^{n} h_{l_{\mathrm{IFS}}}(\mu_A(\omega_i), \mu_B(\omega_i), \nu_A(\omega_i), \nu_B(\omega_i)).$$
$$d_{\mathrm{H}}(A, B) = \sum_{i=1}^{n} h_{d_{\mathrm{H}}}(\mu_A(\omega_i), \mu_B(\omega_i), \nu_A(\omega_i), \nu_B(\omega_i)).$$

Thus, both Hamming and Hausdorff distances are local IF-divergences.

4.2 Properties of the Local IF-Divergences

In this section we investigate some properties that local divergences satisfy. First of all, let us introduce a property that some IF-divergences may satisfy:

IF-Div.5: $D_{\mathrm{IF}}(A, B) = D_{\mathrm{IF}}(A^c, B^c)$ for every $A, B \in IFSs(\Omega)$.

This property becomes important since, if it is satisfied, axioms IF-Div.3 and IF-Div.4 are equivalent.

Proposition 1 ([8]). *Let $D_{\mathrm{IF}} : IFSs(\Omega) \times IFSs(\Omega) \to \mathbb{R}$ be a function satisfying IF-Diss.1, IF-Dist.2 and IF-Div.5. Then it satisfies IF-Div.3 if and only if it satisfies IF-Div.4.*

Consequently, if a function D_{IF} satisfies IF-Diss.1, IF-Dist.2 and IF-Div.5, in order to prove that it is an IF-divergence it is enough to check whether it satisfies either IF-Div.3 or IF-Div.4.

In the case of local IF-divergences, condition IF-Div.5 can be written in terms of the function h_{IF}.

Proposition 2. *Let D_{IF} be a local IF-divergence. Then D_{IF} satisfies property IF-Div.5 if and only if*

$$h_{\mathrm{IF}}(x_1, y_1, x_2, y_2) = h_{\mathrm{IF}}(x_2, y_2, x_1, y_1) \tag{2}$$

for every $(x_1, x_2), (y_1, y_2) \in \mathcal{D} = \{(x, y) \in [0, 1]^2 \mid x + y \le 1\}$.

In Example 1 we showed that both Hamming and Hausdorff distances are local. In fact, we know that both satisfy axiom IF-Div.5 (see [8]), but we can also prove it by means of the previous result, since the functions $h_{l_{\mathrm{IFS}}}$ and $h_{d_{\mathrm{H}}}$ satisfy Equation 2.

In previous works we proved a method that is useful to build IF-divergences from other IF-divergences. It is based on a non-decreasing function ϕ that satisfies $\phi(0) = 0$. In such a case, if D_{IF} is an IF-divergence, the function

$$D_{\mathrm{IF}}^{\phi}(A, B) = \phi(D_{\mathrm{IF}}(A, B))$$

is also an IF-divergence. In this case, although D_{IF} is a local IF-divergence, D_{IF}^{ϕ} may not be local. However, it is possible to prove a similar result.

Proposition 3. *Let D_{IF} be a local IF-divergence, and let $\phi : [0, \infty) \to [0, \infty)$ be a non-decreasing function satisfying $\phi(0) = 0$. In such a case, the function D_{IF}^{ϕ}, defined by:*

$$D_{\mathrm{IF}}^{\phi}(A, B) = \sum_{i=1}^{n} \phi(h_{\mathrm{IF}}(\mu_A(\omega_i), \mu_B(\omega_i), \nu_A(\omega_i), \nu_B(\omega_i)))$$

is a local IF-divergence.

To conclude this section, we relate local IF-divergences and real distances, in a similar way to the results established by Montes et al. in [10]. They proved that if d is a distance in $\mathbb{R}$ such that:

$$x < y < z \Rightarrow \max(d(x,y), d(y,z)) \leq d(x,z), \tag{3}$$

then the function D defined by:

$$D(A,B) = \sum_{i=1}^{n} \phi(d(A(\omega_i), B(\omega_i)), \text{ for every } A, B \in IFSs(\Omega),$$

is a local divergence for fuzzy sets, where ϕ is a non-decreasing function such that $\phi(0) = 0$. We next generalize this result.

Proposition 4. *Consider a distance $d : \mathbb{R} \times \mathbb{R} \to \mathbb{R}$ satisfying Equation 3. Then, for every non-decreasing function $\phi : [0,\infty) \times [0,\infty) \to [0,\infty)$ such that $\phi(0,0) = 0$, the function $D_{\text{IF}} : IFSs(\Omega) \times IFSs(\Omega) \to \mathbb{R}$ defined by on the following equation is a local IF-divergence:*

$$D_{\text{IF}}(A,B) = \sum_{i=1}^{n} \phi(d(\mu_A(\omega_i), \mu_B(\omega_i)), d(\nu_A(\omega_i), \nu_B(\omega_i))). \tag{4}$$

Example 2. Consider the distance d defined by $d(x,y) = |x - y|$, and the non-decreasing function $\phi(x,y) = \frac{x+y}{2n}$ that satisfies $\phi(0,0) = 0$. Then, applying the previous result, the function D_{IF} defined by Equation 4 is a local IF-divergence. In fact, if we input the values of ϕ and d, D_{IF} becomes:

$$D_{\text{IF}}(A,B) = \frac{1}{2n} \sum_{i=1}^{n} |\mu_A(\omega_i) - \mu_B(\omega_i)| + |\nu_A(\omega_i) - \nu_B(\omega_i)|. \tag{5}$$

We have obtained the IF-dissimilarity (that is, in fact, an IF-divergence) defined by Hong and Kim ([4]).

4.3   IF-Divergences and Divergences

In [9] we introduced a method that allows us to build IF-divergences from divergences and, conversely, divergences from IF-divergences. In this subsection our aim is to investigate whether these methods preserve or not the local property.

First of all, let us study the method that is valid to build IF-divergences from divergences.

Proposition 5 ([9]). *Let D_1 and D_2 be two divergences for fuzzy sets. If $f : [0,\infty) \times [0,\infty) \to [0,\infty)$ is a non-decreasing function in each component satisfying $f(0,0) = 0$, the following function is an IF-divergence:*

$$D_{\text{IF}}(A,B) = f(D_1(\mu_A, \mu_B), D_2(\nu_A, \nu_B)).$$

Let us now study what happens with the local property.

Proposition 6. *If in the conditions of the previous proposition D_1 and D_2 are two local divergences, then D_{IF} is a local IF-divergence if and only if f can be expressed by $f(x, y) = \alpha x + \beta y$, for some $\alpha, \beta \geq 0$. In such a case, if h_1 and h_2 are the associated function to D_1 and D_2, then $h_{IF}(x_1, x_2, y_1, y_2) = \alpha h_1(x_1, x_2) + \beta h_2(y_1, y_2)$.*

Let us now explain the method that, conversely, allows us to build divergences from IF-divergences.

Proposition 7 ([9]). *If D_{IF} is an IF-divergence, a divergence for fuzzy sets can be defined by $D(A, B) = D_{IF}(A, B)$ for every $A, B \in FS(\Omega)$.*

With respect to the locality, we obtain the following result.

Proposition 8. *If in the conditions of the previous proposition D_{IF} is a local function, defined through the function h_{IF}, then D is also a local divergence with function $h(x, y) = h_{IF}(x, y, 1 - x, 1 - y)$.*

To conclude this section we show an example of the application of these results.

Example 3. Let us consider the local IF-divergence of Hong and Kim defined on Equation 5. On one hand, if we apply Proposition 7 we obtain the following divergence:

$$D(A, B) = D_{IF}(A, B) = \frac{1}{n} \sum_{i=1}^{n} |A(\omega_i) - B(\omega_i)|.$$

This divergence is known as the Hamming distance for fuzzy sets (see [11]). Moreover, as the Hong and Kim IF-divergence satisfies the local property, applying Proposition 8 the Hamming distance for fuzzy sets is also a local divergence.

On the other hand, if we consider the function $f(x, y) = \frac{x+y}{2}$ and we apply Proposition 5 to the Hamming distance for fuzzy sets we obtain the following IF-divergence:

$$D_{IF}^*(A, B) = f(D(\mu_A, \mu_B), D(\nu_A, \nu_B)) = \frac{D(\mu_A, \mu_B) + D(\nu_A, \nu_B)}{2} = D(A, B).$$

That is, we obtain the original IF-divergence. We already know that it is local. However, we could also derive it from the fact that D is a local divergence for fuzzy sets and f is a linear function with positive parameters.

5   Conclusions

In the framework of the comparison of IF-sets, several measures can be found in the literature, like IF-distances and IF-dissimilarities. In previous works we introduced a different alternative, IF-divergences, a concept that imposes stronger conditions than IF-dissimilarities.

In this work we introduce a particular type of IF-divergence, those that satisfy the local property, that assures that the difference between $D_{IF}(A, B)$ and $D_{IF}(A \cup \{\omega_i\}, B \cup \{\omega_i\})$ lies on the $i - th$ component.

We have investigated some of the properties of this type of IF-divergences. In particular, we have considered two methods that allow us to build divergences from IF-divergences and, conversely, IF-divergences from divergences, and we have studied if these methods preserve the locality.

As future works we would like to study the possible applications of IF-divergences, and in particular of local IF-divergences, both to multicretiria decision making and pattern recognition.

Acknowledgements. The research in this paper is partly supported by the grant 1/0297/11 provided by Slovak grant agency VEGA, the Science and Education Ministry FPU grant AP2009-1034, by the Agency of the Slovak Ministry of Education for the Structural Funds of the EU, under project ITMS:26220120007 and the Spanish Ministry of Science and Innovation grant MTM2010-17844.

References

1. Atanassov, K.: Intuitionistic fuzzy sets. In: Proceedings of VII ITKR, Sofia (1983)
2. Atanassov, K.: Intuitionistic fuzzy sets. Fuzzy Sets and Systems 20, 87–96 (1986)
3. Deschrijver, G., Kerre, K.: A generalization of operators on intuitionistic fuzzy sets using triangular norms and conorms. Notes on IFS 1, 19–27 (2002)
4. Hong, D.H., Kim, C.: A note on similarity measures between vague sets and between elements. Information Sciences 115, 83–96 (1999)
5. Hung, W.L., Yang, M.S.: Similarity measures of intuitionistic fuzzy sets based on l_p metric. Int. Journal of Approximate Reasoning 46, 120–136 (2007)
6. Li, Y., Olson, D.L., Qin, Z.: Similarity measures between intuitionistic fuzzy (vague) sets: A comparative analysis. Pattern Recognition Letters 28, 278–285 (2007)
7. Lui, X.: Entropy, distance measure and similarity measure of fuzzy sets and their relations. Fuzzy Sets and Systems 52, 305–318 (1992)
8. Montes, I., Janiš, V., Montes, S.: An axiomatic definition of divergence of intuitionistic fuzzy sets. In: Proceedings of the 2011 EUSFLAT Conference (2011)
9. Montes, I., Janiš, V., Montes, S.: On the study of some measures of comparison of if-sets. In: Proceedings of XVI ESTYLF Conference (2012)
10. Montes, S., Couso, I., Gil, P., Bertoluzza, C.: Divergence measure between fuzzy sets. Int. Journal of Approximate Reasoning 30, 91–105 (2002)
11. Szmidt, E., Kacprzyk, J.: Analysis of Similarity measures for Atanassov's Intuitionistic Fuzzy Sets, pp. 1416–1421 (2009)
12. Szmidt, E., Kacprzyk, J.: Intuitionistic fuzzy sets - two and three term representations in the context of a hausdorff distance. ACTA Universitatis Matthiae BelII, Series Mathematics 19, 53–62 (2011)
13. Xu, Z.: Some similarity measures of intuitionistic fuzzy sets and their applications to multiple attribute decision making. Fuzzy Optimization and Decision Making 6, 109–121 (2007)
14. Zadeh, L.A.: Fuzzy sets. Information Control 8, 338–353 (1965)

Distributivity of Implication Operations over T-Representable T-Norms Generated from Continuous and Archimedean T-Norms

Michał Baczyński

Institute of Mathematics, University of Silesia,
40-007 Katowice, ul. Bankowa 14, Poland
michal.baczynski@us.edu.pl

Abstract. During previous IPMU 2010 conference we have started investigations connected with finding all solutions of the distributive equation of implications $\mathcal{I}(x, \mathcal{T}_1(y, z)) = \mathcal{T}_2(\mathcal{I}(x, y), \mathcal{I}(x, z))$ over t-representable t-norms in interval-valued fuzzy sets theory, i.e., when t-representable t-norms $\mathcal{T}_1$ and $\mathcal{T}_2$ on the lattice $\mathcal{L}^I$ are generated from continuous, Archimedean t-norms T_1, T_2 and T_3, T_4 on $[0, 1]$, respectively. In [2] we have presented solutions when $T_1 = T_2 = T_3 = T_4$ is a strict t-norm, in [3] we have discussed the solutions when $T_1 = T_2$ is a nilpotent t-norm and $T_3 = T_4$ is a strict t-norm, while in [4] we have showed the solutions when $T_1 = T_2$ and $T_3 = T_4$ are nilpotent t-norms. In this article we will present the solutions for the last possible case for continuous Archimedean t-norms, i.e. when $T_1 = T_2$ is a strict t-norm and $T_3 = T_4$ is a nilpotent t-norm. As a byproduct result we show all solutions of some functional equation related to this case.

Keywords: Interval-valued fuzzy sets; Intuitionistic fuzzy sets; Fuzzy implication; Triangular norm; Distributivity; Functional equations.

1 Introduction

Distributivity of fuzzy implications over different fuzzy logic connectives has been studied in the recent past by many authors (see [16], [6], [14], [15], [5], [1]). These equations have a very important role to play in efficient inferencing in approximate reasoning, especially fuzzy control systems (see [7]).

Recently, in [2], [3] and [4] we have discussed the distributive equation of implications $\mathcal{I}(x, \mathcal{T}_1(y, z)) = \mathcal{T}_2(\mathcal{I}(x, y), \mathcal{I}(x, z))$ over t-representable t-norms generated from continuous Archimedean t-norms, in interval-valued fuzzy sets theory. In these articles, as a byproduct, we have obtained the solutions for each of the following functional equations, respectively:

$$f(u_1 + v_1, u_2 + v_2) = f(u_1, u_2) + f(v_1, v_2),$$
$$g(\min(u_1 + v_1, a), \min(u_2 + v_2, a)) = g(u_1, u_2) + g(v_1, v_2),$$
$$h(\min(u_1 + v_1, a), \min(u_2 + v_2, a)) = \min(h(u_1, u_2) + h(v_1, v_2), b),$$

S. Greco et al. (Eds.): IPMU 2012, Part II, CCIS 298, pp. 501–510, 2012.
© Springer-Verlag Berlin Heidelberg 2012

where $a, b > 0$ are fixed real numbers, $f \colon L^\infty \to [0, \infty]$, $g \colon L^a \to [0, \infty]$, and $h \colon L^a \to [0, b]$ are unknown functions. The above we use the following notation $L^\infty = \{(u_1, u_2) \in [0, \infty]^2 \mid u_1 \ge u_2\}$, $L^a = \{(u_1, u_2) \in [0, a]^2 \mid u_1 \ge u_2\}$. In this paper we continue these investigations, but for t-norms generated from strict and nilpotent t-norms. In particular, we will present all solutions of the following equation:

$$f(u_1 + v_1, u_2 + v_2) = \min(f(u_1, u_2) + f(v_1, v_2), b), \tag{B}$$

where $f \colon L^\infty \to [0, b]$ is an unknown function. Such theoretical developments connected with solutions of different functional equations can be also useful in other topics like fuzzy mathematical morphology or similarity measures.

We assume that the reader is familiar with the notion of intuitionistic (by Atanassov) fuzzy sets theory and interval-valued fuzzy sets theory (in [8] it is shown that both theories are equivalent from the mathematical point of view). Since we are limited in number of pages, in this article we discuss main results in the language of interval-valued fuzzy sets, but they can be easily transformed to the intuitionistic fuzzy case. Let us define

$$L^I = \{(x_1, x_2) \in [0, 1]^2 \ : \ x_1 \le x_2\},$$
$$(x_1, x_2) \le_{L^I} (y_1, y_2) \Longleftrightarrow x_1 \le y_1 \wedge x_2 \le y_2.$$

In the sequel, if $x \in L^I$, then we denote it by $x = [x_1, x_2]$. One can easily observe that $\mathcal{L}^I = (L^I, \le_{L^I})$ is a complete lattice with bounds $0_{\mathcal{L}^I} = [0, 0]$ and $1_{\mathcal{L}^I} = [1, 1]$. An interval-valued fuzzy set on X is a mapping $A \colon X \to L^I$.

2 Basic Fuzzy Connectives

We assume that the reader is familiar with the classical results concerning basic fuzzy logic connectives, but we briefly mention some of the results employed in the rest of the work.

Definition 2.1 (cf. [12]). *Let $\mathcal{L} = (L, \le_L)$ be a complete lattice. An associative, commutative operation $T \colon L^2 \to L$ is called a t-norm if it is increasing and $1_{\mathcal{L}}$ is the neutral element of T.*

We have many important classes of t-norms. In this article we will use the following two classes of t-norms on the unit interval.

Definition 2.2. *A t-norm T on $([0, 1], \le)$ is said to be strict, if it is continuous and strictly monotone, i.e., $T(x, y) < T(x, z)$ whenever $x > 0$ and $y < z$.*

Definition 2.3. *A t-norm T on $([0, 1], \le)$ is said to be nilpotent, if it is continuous and if each $x \in (0, 1)$ is a nilpotent element of T, i.e., if there exists $n \in \mathbb{N}$ such that $x_T^{[n]} = 0$, where $x_T^{[n]} := \begin{cases} x, & \text{if } n = 1, \\ T(x, x_T^{[n-1]}), & \text{if } n > 1. \end{cases}$*

The following characterizations of nilpotent and strict t-norms are well-known in the literature.

Theorem 2.4 (see [12]).

(i) *A function $T\colon [0,1]^2 \to [0,1]$ is a nilpotent t-norm if and only if there exists a continuous, strictly decreasing function $t\colon [0,1] \to [0,\infty)$ with $t(1) = 0$, which is uniquely determined up to a positive multiplicative constant, such that*
$$T(x,y) = t^{-1}(\min(t(x) + t(y), t(0))), \quad x,y \in [0,1].$$

(ii) *A function $T\colon [0,1]^2 \to [0,1]$ is a strict t-norm if and only if there exists a continuous, strictly decreasing function $t\colon [0,1] \to [0,\infty]$ with $t(1) = 0$ and $t(0) = \infty$, which is uniquely determined up to a positive multiplicative constant, such that*
$$T(x,y) = t^{-1}(t(x) + t(y)), \quad x,y \in [0,1].$$

In our article we shall consider the following special class of t-norms.

Definition 2.5 (see [9]). *A t-norm $\mathcal{T}$ on $\mathcal{L}^I$ is called t-representable if there exist t-norms T_1 and T_2 on $([0,1], \leq)$ such that $T_1 \leq T_2$ and*
$$\mathcal{T}([x_1, x_2], [y_1, y_2]) = [T_1(x_1, y_1), T_2(x_2, y_2)], \quad [x_1, x_2], [y_1, y_2] \in L^I.$$

It should be noted that not all t-norms on $\mathcal{L}^I$ are t-representable (see [9]).

One possible definition of an implication on $\mathcal{L}^I$ is based on the well-accepted notation introduced by Fodor and Roubens [11] (see also [10] and [13]).

Definition 2.6. *Let $\mathcal{L} = (L, \leq_L)$ be a complete lattice. A function $\mathcal{I}\colon L^2 \to L$ is called a fuzzy implication on $\mathcal{L}$ if it is decreasing with respect to the first variable, increasing with respect to the second variable and fulfills the following conditions: $\mathcal{I}(0_{\mathcal{L}}, 0_{\mathcal{L}}) = \mathcal{I}(1_{\mathcal{L}}, 1_{\mathcal{L}}) = \mathcal{I}(0_{\mathcal{L}}, 1_{\mathcal{L}}) = 1_{\mathcal{L}}$ and $\mathcal{I}(1_{\mathcal{L}}, 0_{\mathcal{L}}) = 0_{\mathcal{L}}$.*

3   Some New Results Pertaining to Functional Equations

In this section we show one new result related to functional equations, which will be crucial in obtaining main results. Firstly, we will remind one result which will use in main proof.

Proposition 3.1 ([1, Proposition 3.4]). *Fix real $b > 0$. For a function $f\colon [0,\infty] \to [0,b]$ the following statements are equivalent:*

(i) *f satisfies the functional equation*
$$f(x+y) = \min(f(x) + f(y), b), \quad x,y \in [0,\infty].$$

(ii) *Either $f = b$, or $f = 0$, or $f(x) = \begin{cases} 0, & \text{if } x = 0, \\ b, & \text{if } x > 0, \end{cases}$ or $f(x) = \begin{cases} 0, & \text{if } x < \infty, \\ b, & \text{if } x = \infty, \end{cases}$ or there exists a unique constant $c \in (0,\infty)$ such that $f(x) = \min(cx, b)$, for all $x \in [0,\infty]$.*

Proposition 3.2. *Fix real $b > 0$. Let $L^\infty = \{(u_1, u_2) \in [0, \infty]^2 \; : \; u_1 \geq u_2\}$.*
For a function $f \colon L^\infty \to [0, b]$ the following statements are equivalent:

(i) f satisfies the functional equation (B) for all $(u_1, u_2), (v_1, v_2) \in L^a$.
(ii) Either

$$f = 0, \tag{S1}$$

or

$$f = b, \tag{S2}$$

or

$$f(u_1, u_2) = \begin{cases} 0, & \text{if } u_2 = 0, \\ b, & \text{if } u_2 > 0, \end{cases} \tag{S3}$$

or

$$f(u_1, u_2) = \begin{cases} 0, & \text{if } u_2 < \infty, \\ b, & \text{if } u_2 = \infty, \end{cases} \tag{S4}$$

or

$$f(u_1, u_2) = \begin{cases} 0, & \text{if } u_1 = 0, \\ b, & \text{if } u_1 > 0, \end{cases} \tag{S5}$$

or

$$f(u_1, u_2) = \begin{cases} 0, & \text{if } u_1 = u_2 < \infty, \\ b, & \text{if } u_2 = \infty \text{ or } u_1 > u_2, \end{cases} \tag{S6}$$

or

$$f(u_1, u_2) = \begin{cases} 0, & \text{if } u_2 = 0 \text{ and } u_1 < \infty, \\ b, & \text{if } u_2 > 0 \text{ or } u_1 = \infty, \end{cases} \tag{S7}$$

or

$$f(u_1, u_2) = \begin{cases} 0, & \text{if } u_1 < \infty, \\ b, & \text{if } u_1 = \infty, \end{cases} \tag{S8}$$

or there exists unique $c \in (0, \infty)$ such that

$$f(u_1, u_2) = \min(cu_2, b), \tag{S9}$$

or

$$f(u_1, u_2) = \begin{cases} \min(cu_1, b), & \text{if } u_1 = u_2, \\ b, & \text{if } u_1 > u_2, \end{cases} \tag{S10}$$

or

$$f(u_1, u_2) = \begin{cases} \min(cu_2, b), & \text{if } u_1 < \infty, \\ b, & \text{if } u_1 = \infty, \end{cases} \tag{S11}$$

or

$$f(u_1, u_2) = \begin{cases} \min(cu_1, b), & \text{if } u_2 = 0, \\ b, & \text{if } u_2 > 0, \end{cases} \tag{S12}$$

or

$$f(u_1, u_2) = \begin{cases} c(u_1 - u_2), & \text{if } u_2 < \infty, \\ \infty, & \text{if } u_2 = \infty, \end{cases} \qquad \text{(S13)}$$

or

$$f(u_1, u_2) = cu_1, \qquad \text{(S14)}$$

or there exist unique $c_1, c_2 \in (0, \infty)$, $c_1 \neq c_2$ such that

$$f(u_1, u_2) = \begin{cases} c_1(u_1 - u_2) + c_2 u_2, & \text{if } u_2 < \infty, \\ \infty, & \text{if } u_2 = \infty, \end{cases} \qquad \text{(S15)}$$

for all $(u_1, u_2) \in L^\infty$.

Proof. $(ii) \implies (i)$ It is a direct calculation that the above functions satisfy (B).
$(i) \implies (ii)$ Let a function $f \colon L^\infty \to [0, b]$ satisfy equation (B) for all (u_1, u_2), $(v_1, v_2) \in L^\infty$. Setting $u_1 = v_1 = \infty$ in (B) we get

$$f(\infty, u_2 + v_2) = \min(f(\infty, u_2) + f(\infty, v_2), b), \qquad u_2, v_2 \in [0, \infty].$$

Let us denote $f_\infty(x) := f(\infty, x)$, for $x \in [0, \infty]$. Therefore, we get

$$f_\infty(u_2 + v_2) = \min(f_\infty(u_2) + f_\infty(v_2), b), \qquad u_2, v_2 \in [0, \infty].$$

For this equation we can use solutions described in Proposition 3.1. We have 5 possible cases for the function f_∞.

1. If $f_\infty = 0$, then putting $u_1 = u_2 = \infty$ in (B) we have

$$f(\infty, \infty) = \min(f(\infty, \infty) + f(v_1, v_2), b), \qquad (v_1, v_2) \in L^\infty,$$

   thus $0 = \min(0 + f(v_1, v_2), b)$, hence $f(v_1, v_2)$ we get first possible (S1).

2. If $f_\infty(x) = \begin{cases} 0, & \text{if } x = 0 \\ b, & \text{if } x > 0 \end{cases}$, then putting $u_1 = \infty$ in (B) we have

$$f(\infty, u_2 + v_2) = \min(f(\infty, u_2) + f(v_1, v_2), b), \qquad (v_1, v_2) \in L^\infty.$$

   If we take $u_2 = v_2 = 0$ above, then we get $0 = \min(0 + f(v_1, 0), b)$, thus $f(v_1, 0) = 0$ for all $v_1 \in [0, \infty]$. If we take $u_2 = 0$ and $v_2 > 0$ above, then we get $f(\infty, v_2) = \min(f(\infty, 0) + f(v_1, v_2), b)$, hence $b = \min(0 + f(v_1, v_2), b)$, thus $f(v_1, v_2) = b$. In summary, we get the solution (S3).

3. If $f_\infty(x) = \begin{cases} 0, & \text{if } x < \infty \\ b, & \text{if } x = \infty \end{cases}$, then putting $u_1 = \infty$ and $u_2 = 0$ in (B) we have $f(\infty, v_2) = \min(f(\infty, 0) + f(v_1, v_2), b)$, thus $f(\infty, v_2) = \min(f(v_1, v_2), b)$. Since $f(v_1, v_2) \leq b$, we obtain $f(\infty, v_2) = f(v_1, v_2)$, so we get the solution (S4) in this case.

4. If $f_\infty(x) = \min(cx, b)$ with some real $c > 0$, then putting $u_1 = \infty$ and $u_2 = 0$ in (B) we have $f(\infty, v_2) = f(v_1, v_2)$, so we get the solution (S9) in this case.

Therefore, we need to solve our equation with the assumption that $f_\infty = b$. Setting now $u_2 = v_2 = 0$ in (B) we get

$$f(u_1 + v_1, 0) = \min(f(u_1, 0) + f(v_1, 0), b), \qquad u_1, v_1 \in [0, \infty].$$

Let us denote $f^0(x) := f(x, 0)$, for $x \in [0, \infty]$. Hence, we obtain

$$f^0(u_1 + v_1) = \min(f^0(u_1) + f^0(v_1), b), \qquad u_1, v_1 \in [0, \infty].$$

For this equation we again can use solutions described in Proposition 3.1. We have 5 possible cases for the function f^0.

1. If $f^0 = 0$, then $f(\infty, 0) = 0$, which contradicts our assumption $f_\infty = b$.
2. If $f^0 = b$, then putting $u_1 = u_2 = 0$ in (B) we have

$$f(v_1, v_2) = \min(f(0, 0) + f(v_1, v_2), b), \qquad (v_1, v_2) \in L^\infty,$$

thus $f(v_1, v_2) = \min(b + f(v_1, v_2), b)$, hence $f(v_1, v_2) = b$ and we get the solution (S2).

3. If $f^0(x) = \begin{cases} 0, & \text{if } x = 0 \\ b, & \text{if } x > 0 \end{cases}$, then putting $u_2 = 0$ in (B) we have

$$f(u_1 + v_1, v_2) = \min(f(u_1, 0) + f(v_1, v_2), b), \qquad u_1 \in [0, \infty], (v_1, v_2) \in L^\infty.$$

Let us assume that $u_1 > 0$ and $v_1 = v_2$ above. Then we get

$$f(u_1 + v_2, v_2) = \min(f(u_1, 0) + f(v_2, v_2), b), \qquad u_1 \in (0, \infty], v_2 \in [0, \infty].$$

hence

$$f(u_1 + v_2, v_2) = b, \qquad u_1 \in (0, \infty], v_2 \in [0, \infty].$$

Since $u_1 + v_2 \in (v_2, \infty]$, we have obtained the result that $f(x_1, x_2) = b$ for any $(x_1, x_2) \in L^\infty$ such that $x_1 > x_2$.

Let us take now $u_2 = u_1$ and $v_2 = v_1$ in (B). Then we have

$$f(u_1 + v_1, u_1 + v_1) = \min(f(u_1, u_1) + f(v_1, v_1), b), \qquad u_1, v_1 \in [0, \infty].$$

Let us denote $g(x) := f(x, x)$, for $x \in [0, \infty]$. Therefore, we get

$$g(u_1 + v_1) = \min(g(u_1) + g(v_1), b), \qquad u_1, v_1 \in [0, \infty].$$

For this equation we again can use solutions described in Proposition 3.1. We have 5 possible cases for the function g.

(a) If $g = 0$, then $f(\infty, \infty) = 0$, which contradicts our assumption $f_\infty = b$.
(b) If $g = b$, then $f(0, 0) = b$, which contradicts our assumption 3. on function f^0.

(c) If $g(x) = \begin{cases} 0, & \text{if } x = 0 \\ b, & \text{if } x > 0 \end{cases}$, then we get the solution (S5) in this case.

(d) If $g(x) = \begin{cases} 0, & \text{if } x < \infty \\ b, & \text{if } x = \infty \end{cases}$, then we get the solution (S6) in this case.

(e) If $g(x) = \min(cx, b)$ with some $c > 0$, then we get the solution (S10) in this case.

4. If $f^0(x) = \begin{cases} 0, & \text{if } x < \infty \\ b, & \text{if } x = \infty \end{cases}$, then putting $u_2 = 0$ and $v_1 = v_2$ in (B) we get $f(u_1 + v_1, v_1) = \min(f(u_1, 0) + f(v_1, v_1), b)$. Let us assume that $u_1 < \infty$ above. Then $f(u_1+v_1, v_1) = \min(0 + f(v_1, v_1), b)$, so $f(u_1+v_1, v_1) = f(v_1, v_2)$ whenever $u_1 < \infty$. Of course we know that $f(\infty, x) = b$ for any $x \in [0, \infty]$. Therefore it is enough to find solution for diagonal of function f. So let assume now that $u_2 = u_1$ and $v_2 = v_1$ in (B). Then we have

$$f(u_1 + v_1, u_1 + v_1) = \min(f(u_1, u_1) + f(v_1, v_1), b), \qquad u_1, v_1 \in [0, \infty].$$

Let us denote $g(x) := f(x, x)$, for $x \in [0, \infty]$. Therefore, we get

$$g(u_1 + v_1) = \min(g(u_1) + g(v_1), b), \qquad u_1, v_1 \in [0, \infty].$$

For this equation we again can use solutions described in Proposition 3.1. We have 5 possible cases for the function g.

(a) If $g = 0$, then $f(\infty, \infty) = 0$, which contradicts our assumption $f_\infty = \infty$.
(b) If $g = b$, then $f(0, 0) = \infty$, which contradicts our assumption 4. on function f^0.
(c) If $g(x) = \begin{cases} 0, & \text{if } x = 0 \\ b, & \text{if } x > 0 \end{cases}$, then taking into account all previous calculations we get the solution (S7).
(d) If $g(x) = \begin{cases} 0, & \text{if } x < \infty \\ b, & \text{if } x = \infty \end{cases}$, then taking into account all assumptions we get the solution (S8).
(e) If $g(x) = \min(cx, b)$ with some $c > 0$, then we get the solution (S11) in this case.

5. Let $f^0(x) = \min(c_1 x, b)$, with some real $c_1 > 0$ for $x \in [0, \infty]$. Putting $u_2 = 0$ and $v_1 = v_2$ in (B) we get

$$f(u_1 + v_1, v_1) = \min(\min(c_1 u_1, b) + f(v_1, v_1), b). \tag{1}$$

Now, let us put $u_2 = u_1$ and $v_2 = v_1$ in (B). In this case we again get

$$f(u_1 + v_1, u_1 + v_1) = \min(f(u_1, u_1) + f(v_1, v_1), b), \qquad u_1, v_1 \in [0, \infty].$$

Let us denote $g(x) := f(x, x)$, for $x \in [0, \infty]$. Therefore, we get

$$g(u_1 + v_1) = \min(g(u_1) + g(v_1), b), \qquad u_1, v_1 \in [0, \infty].$$

For this equation we again can use solutions described in Proposition 3.1. We have 5 possible cases for the function g.

(a) If $g = 0$, then $f(\infty, \infty) = 0$, which contradicts our assumption $f_\infty = b$.
(b) If $g = b$, then $f(0,0) = \infty$, which contradicts our assumption 5. on function f^0.
(c) If $g(x) = \begin{cases} 0, & \text{if } x = 0 \\ \infty, & \text{if } x > 0 \end{cases}$, then in (1) we get

$$f(u_1 + v_2, v_2) = \min \left(\min(c_1 u_1, b) + \begin{cases} 0, & \text{if } v_2 = 0 \\ b, & \text{if } v_2 > 0 \end{cases}, b \right)$$

which implies that

$$f(u_1 + v_2, v_2) = \min \left(\begin{cases} \min(c_1 u_1, b), & \text{if } v_2 = 0 \\ \min(c_1 u_1, b) + b, & \text{if } v_2 > 0 \end{cases}, b \right)$$

It is obvious that we have

$$f(u_1 + v_2, v_2) = \begin{cases} \min(c_1 u_1, b), & \text{if } v_2 = 0 \\ b, & \text{if } v_2 > 0 \end{cases}$$

for any $u_1, v_2 \in [0, \infty]$. Therefore, this solution can be written as (S12).

(d) If $g(x) = \begin{cases} 0, & \text{if } x < \infty \\ b, & \text{if } x = 0 \end{cases}$, then in (1) we get

$$f(u_1 + v_2, v_2) = \min \left(\min(c_1 u_1, b) + \begin{cases} 0, & \text{if } v_2 < \infty \\ b, & \text{if } v_2 = \infty \end{cases}, b \right)$$

which implies that

$$f(u_1 + v_2, v_2) = \min \left(\begin{cases} \min(c_1 u_1, b), & \text{if } v_2 < \infty \\ \min(c_1 u_1, b) + b, & \text{if } v_2 = \infty \end{cases}, b \right)$$

It is obvious that we get

$$f(u_1 + v_2, v_2) = \begin{cases} \min(c_1 u_1, b), & \text{if } v_2 < \infty \\ b, & \text{if } v_2 = \infty \end{cases}$$

for any $u_1, v_2 \in [0, \infty]$. Therefore, this solution can be written as (S13).

(e) If $g(x) = \min(c_2 x, b)$ with some real $c_2 > 0$, then in (1) we get

$$f(u_1 + v_2, v_2) = \min(\min(c_1 u_1, b) + \min(c_2 v_2, b), b), \qquad u_1, v_2 \in [0, \infty].$$

If $c_1 = c_2$, then $f(u_1 + v_2, v_2) = \min(c_1(u_1 + v_2), b)$, therefore this solution can be written as (S14). If $c_1 \neq c_2$, then we get the solution (S15) in this case.   □

4   Distributive Equation for T-Representable T-Norms

In this section we will show how we can use solutions presented in Proposition 3.2 to obtain all solutions of our main distributive equation

$$\mathcal{I}(x, T_1(y, z)) = T_2(\mathcal{I}(x, y), \mathcal{I}(x, z)), \qquad x, y, z \in L^I, \tag{D1}$$

where $\mathcal{I}$ is an unknown function and t-norms T_1 and T_2 on $\mathcal{L}^I$ are t-representable and generated from strict t-norms T_1, T_2 and nilpotent t-norms T_3, T_4, respectively. In [2] we have shown that if T_1 and T_2 on $\mathcal{L}^I$ are t-representable, then

$$g^1_{[x_1,x_2]}([T_1(y_1, z_1), T_2(y_2, z_2)]) = T_3(g^1_{[x_1,x_2]}([y_1, y_2]), g^1_{[x_1,x_2]}([z_1, z_2])),$$

$$g^2_{[x_1,x_2]}([T_1(y_1, z_1), T_2(y_2, z_2)]) = T_4(g^2_{[x_1,x_2]}([y_1, y_2]), g^2_{[x_1,x_2]}([z_1, z_2])),$$

where $[x_1, x_2] \in L^I$ is fixed and $g^1_{[x_1,x_2]}, g^2_{[x_1,x_2]} \colon L^I \to L^I$ are defined by

$$g^1_{[x_1,x_2]}(\cdot) := pr_1 \circ \mathcal{I}([x_1, x_2], \cdot), \qquad g^2_{[x_1,x_2]}(\cdot) := pr_2 \circ \mathcal{I}([x_1, x_2], \cdot).$$

Let us assume that $T_1 = T_2$ is a strict t-norm generated from additive generator t_1 and $T_3 = T_4$ is a nilpotent t-norm generated from additive generator t_3. Using the representation theorems of strict and nilpotent t-norms (see Theorem 2.4) we can transform our problem to the following equation (for a simplicity we deal only with g^1 now):

$$g^1_{[x_1,x_2]}([t_1^{-1}(t_1(y_1) + t_1(z_1)), t_1^{-1}(t_1(y_2) + t_1(z_2))])$$
$$= t_3^{-1}(\min(t_3(g^1_{[x_1,x_2]}([y_1, y_2])) + t_3(g^1_{[x_1,x_2]}([z_1, z_2])), t_3(0))).$$

Let us put $t_1(y_1) = u_1$, $t_1(y_2) = u_2$, $t_1(z_1) = v_1$ and $t_1(z_2) = v_2$. Of course $u_1, u_2, v_1, v_2 \in [0, \infty]$. Moreover $[y_1, y_2], [z_1, z_2] \in L^I$, thus $y_1 \leq y_2$ and $z_1 \leq z_2$. The generator t_1 is strictly decreasing, so $u_1 \geq u_2$ and $v_1 \geq v_2$. If we put

$$f_{[x_1,x_2]}(a, b) := t_3 \circ pr_1 \circ \mathcal{I}([x_1, x_2], [t_1^{-1}(a), t_1^{-1}(b)]), \qquad a, b \in [0, \infty], \, a \geq b,$$

then we get the following functional equation

$$f_{[x_1,x_2]}(u_1 + v_1, u_2 + v_2) = \min(f_{[x_1,x_2]}(u_1, u_2) + f_{[x_1,x_2]}(v_1, v_2), t_3(0)), \tag{2}$$

where $(u_1, u_2), (v_1, v_2) \in L^\infty$ and $f_{[x_1,x_2]} \colon L^\infty \to [0, t_3(0)]$ is an unknown function. In a same way we can repeat all the above calculations, but for the function g^2, to obtain the following functional equation

$$f^{[x_1,x_2]}(u_1 + v_1, u_2 + v_2) = \min(f^{[x_1,x_2]}(u_1, u_2) + f^{[x_1,x_2]}(v_1, v_2), t_3(0)), \tag{3}$$

where $f^{[x_1,x_2]}(a, b) := t_3 \circ pr_2 \circ \mathcal{I}([x_1, x_2], [t_1^{-1}(a), t_1^{-1}(b)])$. Observe that (2) and (3) are exactly our functional equation (B). Therefore, using solutions of Proposition 3.2, we are able to obtain the description of the vertical section $\mathcal{I}([x_1, x_2], \cdot)$ for a fixed $[x_1, x_2] \in L^I$. Since in this proposition we have 15 possible solutions, we should have 225 different solutions of (D1). Observe now that some of these solutions are not good, since the range of $\mathcal{I}$ is L^I. Finally, we need to notice that not all obtained vertical solutions in $\mathcal{L}^I$ can be used for obtaining fuzzy implication on $\mathcal{L}^I$ in the sense of Definition 2.6. We will investigate this problem in our future works.

Acknowledgment. This work has been supported by the Polish Ministry of Science and Higher Education Grant Nr N N519 384936.

References

1. Baczyński, M.: On the distributivity of fuzzy implications over continuous and Archimedean triangular conorms. Fuzzy Sets and Systems 161, 1406–1419 (2010)
2. Baczyński, M.: On the Distributivity of Implication Operations over t-Representable t-Norms Generated from Strict t-Norms in Interval-Valued Fuzzy Sets Theory. In: Hüllermeier, E., Kruse, R., Hoffmann, F. (eds.) IPMU 2010. CCIS, vol. 80, pp. 637–646. Springer, Heidelberg (2010)
3. Baczyński, M.: On the distributive equation for t-representable t-norms generated from nilpotent and strict t-norms. In: Galichet, S., Montero, J., Mauris, G. (eds.) Proc. EUSFLAT-LFA 2011, Aix-Les-Bains, France. Advances in Intelligent Systems Research, vol. 1, pp. 540–546. Atlantis Press, Amsterdam (2011)
4. Baczyński, M.: Distributivity of Implication Operations over t-Representable T-Norms Generated from Nilpotent T-Norms. In: Petrosino, A. (ed.) WILF 2011. LNCS(LNAI), vol. 6857, pp. 25–32. Springer, Heidelberg (2011)
5. Baczyński, M., Jayaram, B.: On the distributivity of fuzzy implications over nilpotent or strict triangular conorms. IEEE Trans. Fuzzy Systems 17, 590–603 (2009)
6. Balasubramaniam, J., Rao, C.J.M.: On the distributivity of implication operators over T- and S-norms. IEEE Trans. Fuzzy Systems 12, 194–198 (2004)
7. Combs, W.E., Andrews, J.E.: Combinatorial rule explosion eliminated by a fuzzy rule configuration. IEEE Trans. Fuzzy Systems 6, 1–11 (1998)
8. Deschrijver, G., Kerre, E.E.: On the relationship between some extensions of fuzzy set theory. Fuzzy Sets and Systems 133, 227–235 (2003)
9. Deschrijver, G., Cornelis, C., Kerre, E.E.: On the representation of intuitionistic fuzzy t-norms and t-conorms. IEEE Trans. Fuzzy Systems 12, 45–61 (2004)
10. Deschrijver, G., Cornelis, C., Kerre, E.E.: Implication in intuitionistic and interval-valued fuzzy set theory: construction, classification and application. Internat. J. Approx. Reason. 35, 55–95 (2004)
11. Fodor, J., Roubens, M.: Fuzzy preference modelling and multicriteria decision support. Kluwer, Dordrecht (1994)
12. Klement, E.P., Mesiar, R., Pap, E.: Triangular norms. Kluwer, Dordrecht (2000)
13. Mas, M., Monserrat, M., Torrens, J., Trillas, E.: A survey on fuzzy implication functions. IEEE Trans. Fuzzy Systems 15, 1107–1121 (2007)
14. Ruiz-Aguilera, D., Torrens, J.: Distributivity of strong implications over conjunctive and disjunctive uninorms. Kybernetika 42, 319–336 (2005)
15. Ruiz-Aguilera, D., Torrens, J.: Distributivity of residual implications over conjunctive and disjunctive uninorms. Fuzzy Sets and Systems 158, 23–37 (2007)
16. Trillas, E., Alsina, C.: On the law $[p \wedge q \rightarrow r] = [(p \rightarrow r) \vee (q \rightarrow r)]$ in fuzzy logic. IEEE Trans. Fuzzy Systems 10, 84–88 (2002)

Dual Connectives in Fuzzy Reasoning

Józef Drewniak

Institute of Mathematics,
University of Rzeszów,
ul. Rejtana 16a, 35-959 Rzeszów, Poland
jdrewnia@univ.rzeszow.pl

Abstract. Paper concerns applications of Duality Principle in fuzzy algebra, fuzzy logics and approximate reasoning. Examples of important dual notions from lattice theory to relation theory and from fuzzy logic to fuzzy relational equations are presented. In particular properties of dual connectives of multi-valued logic are described and properties of dual relation compositions are summarized. Finally, residuated lattices are used for description of L-valued approximate reasoning.

Keywords: Duality Principle, lattice duality, dual implication, dual relation composition, dual fuzzy systems, fuzzy reasoning.

1 Introduction

Approximate reasoning in fuzzy environment initiated by Zadeh [23] is a motivation of many algebraical and logical research. In particular, algebra of fuzzy relations [12] or fuzzy relation equations [15] provide answers for diverse questions of fuzzy reasoning. Similarly, axiomatizations of fuzzy connectives by Baldwin and Pilsworth [2] or Magrez and Smets [20] were based on needs of inference rules.

Duality is a fundamental notion of lattice theory [4]. However, diverse versions of duality appear in many other domains. Recently, approximate reasoning with interval-valued fuzzy sets [16] and intuitionistic fuzzy sets [5] needs attention to dual operations and properties of fuzzy algebra and fuzzy logic (cf. [18], [19]). We pay special attention to applications of Duality Principle in fuzzy algebra, fuzzy logics and soft computing.

2 Duality in Lattices

Let $(L, \leqslant) = (L, \vee, \wedge, 0, 1)$ be a bounded distributive lattice. Duality in lattices is connected with an isomorphism between semilattices $(L, \vee, 0, \leqslant)$ and $(L, \wedge, 1, \geqslant)$.

Theorem 1 (Duality Principle, cf. [4], pp. 3, 6). *Let $(L, \vee, \wedge, 0, 1)$ be a bounded lattice. Replacing '$\leqslant$' by '$\geqslant$', '$\vee$' by '$\wedge$', '0' by '1', and conversely in a lattice statement, we obtain the equivalent one.*

S. Greco et al. (Eds.): IPMU 2012, Part II, CCIS 298, pp. 511–520, 2012.
© Springer-Verlag Berlin Heidelberg 2012

This principle is a very useful tool in mathematical considerations because many proofs can be omitted as dual. Simultaneously, in applications we need precise definitions, theorems and examples, and many people try to deduce omitted statements.

Example 1. Besides primary dual pairs $(\leqslant, \geqslant)$, $(\vee, \wedge)$, $(0, 1)$ from Duality Principle, we have many secondary dual pairs such as: (above, below), (left, right), (maximum, minimum), (full, empty), (positive, negative), (odd, even), (upper bound, lower bound), (supremum, infimum), (maximal element, minimal element), (the greatest element, the least element), (upper semi-continuity, lower semi-continuity), (left continuity, right continuity) etc.

Now we consider more general case with an additional binary operation.

Definition 1 ([12]). *Let* $(L, \vee, \wedge, *, 0, 1)$ *be a complete lattice with an additional binary operation* $* : L^2 \to L$ *and* $T \neq \emptyset$ *be any index set.*
• *The operation* $*$ *is infinitely* sup *−distributive if*

$$\underset{a, b_t \in L}{\forall} \ a * (\sup_{t \in T} b_t) = \sup_{t \in T}(a * b_t), \qquad \underset{a, b_t \in L}{\forall} \ (\sup_{t \in T} b_t) * a = \sup_{t \in T}(b_t * a). \qquad (1)$$

• *The operation* $*$ *is infinitely* inf *−distributive if*

$$\underset{a, b_t \in L}{\forall} \ a * (\inf_{t \in T} b_t) = \inf_{t \in T}(a * b_t), \qquad \underset{a, b_t \in L}{\forall} \ (\inf_{t \in T} b_t) * a = \inf_{t \in T}(b_t * a). \qquad (2)$$

Corollary 1. *Let* L *be a complete lattice with an additional binary operation* $*$. *If the operation* $*$ *is infinitely* sup *−distributive (*inf *−distributive), then it is distributive with respect to* $\vee$ *(*$\wedge$*). In both the above cases the operation* $*$ *is increasing.*

According to [10], p. 25, in the case $L = [0, 1]$ we have

Lemma 1. *An operation* $* : [0, 1]^2 \to [0, 1]$ *is infinitely* sup *−distributive if and only if it is increasing and left-continuous. Dually, it is infinitely* inf *−distributive if and only if it is increasing and right-continuous.*

3   Duality between Fuzzy Conjunctions and Disjunctions

Definition 2 (cf. [7]). *Two operations* $C, D : [0, 1]^2 \to [0, 1]$ *are called dual if* $D = C'$, *where* $C'(x, y) = 1 - C(1 - x, 1 - y)$, $x, y \in [0, 1]$.

• *The operation* C *is called a fuzzy conjunction if it is increasing with respect to each argument and* $C(1, 1) = 1$, $C(0, 0) = C(0, 1) = C(1, 0) = 0$.
• *The operation* D *is called a fuzzy disjunction if it is increasing with respect to each argument and* $D(0, 0) = 0$, $D(0, 1) = D(1, 0) = D(1, 1) = 1$.
• *A fuzzy conjunction* C *is called a triangular norm (conjunctive uninorm) if it is associative, commutative with the neutral element* $e = 1$ $(e \in (0, 1])$;
• *A fuzzy disjunction* D *is called a triangular conorm (disjunctive uninorm) if it is associative, commutative with the neutral element* $e = 0$ $(e \in [0, 1))$.
Similarly, we can consider L-*fuzzy conjunctions and disjunctions* $C, D : L^2 \to L$.

Example 2. The most important dual pairs of fuzzy conjunctions and disjunctions are (lattice, product, Łukasiewicz, drastic and Fodor) triangular norms T and conorms S (respectively), where $T' = S$(cf. [14]):

$$T_M(x,y) = \min(x,y),\ T_P(x,y) = xy,\ T_L(x,y) = \max(x+y-1,0),$$
$$S_M(x,y) = \max(x,y),\ S_P(x,y) = x+y-xy,\ S_L(x,y) = \min(x+y,1),$$

$$T_D(x,y) = \begin{cases} 0, & \text{if } x,y < 1 \\ \min(x,y), & \text{otherwise} \end{cases},\quad S_D(x,y) = \begin{cases} 1, & \text{if } x,y > 0 \\ \max(x,y), & \text{otherwise} \end{cases},$$

$$T_{FD}(x,y) = \begin{cases} \min(x,y), & \text{if } x+y > 1 \\ 0, & \text{otherwise}, \end{cases},\quad S_{FD}(x,y) = \begin{cases} \max(x,y), & \text{if } x+y < 1 \\ 1, & \text{otherwise}, \end{cases},$$

for $x,y \in [0,1]$, where T_P, S_P are strictly increasing in $(0,1)^2$ and T_L, T_D, S_L, S_D have zero divisors.

A good example of fuzzy conjunction and disjunction gives geometric mean

$$G(x,y) = \sqrt{xy},\ G'(x,y) = 1 - \sqrt{(1-x)(1-y)},\ x,y \in [0,1].$$

Other examples can be obtained by convex combination of triangular norms (conorms)

$$C(x,y) = \lambda xy + (1-\lambda)\min(x,y),\ C'(x,y) = \lambda(x+y-xy) + (1-\lambda)\max(x,y),$$

where $\lambda, x, y \in [0,1]$. As examples of conjunctive and disjunctive uninorms for fixed $e \in (0,1)$ we consider the least uninorm $\underline{U_e}$ and the least idempotent uninorm $U_e^{\min}$ (cf. [11]) with their dual operations (the greatest uninorm and the greatest idempotent uninorm with neutral element $1 - e$), where

$$\underline{U_e} = \begin{cases} 0 & \text{in } [0,e)^2 \\ \max & \text{in } [e,1]^2 \\ \min & \text{otherwise} \end{cases},\quad \underline{U_e}' = \overline{U_{1-e}} = \begin{cases} 1 & \text{in } (1-e,1]^2 \\ \min & \text{in } [0,1-e]^2 \\ \max & \text{otherwise} \end{cases},$$

$$U_e^{\min} = \begin{cases} \max & \text{in } [e,1]^2 \\ \min & \text{otherwise} \end{cases},\quad (U_e^{\min})' = U_{1-e}^{\max} = \begin{cases} \min & \text{in } [0,1-e]^2 \\ \max & \text{otherwise} \end{cases}.$$

For the boundary case $e = 1$ we obtain $\underline{U_1} = T_D$, $\overline{U_0} = S_D$ and $U_1^{\min} = T_M$, $U_0^{\max} = S_M$.

Duality properties of fuzzy conjunctions and disjunctions are commonly known (cf. de Morgan Triples in [1], pp. 55-56). In particular we get

Theorem 2. *The dual operation of a fuzzy conjunction, triangular norm, or conjunctive uninorm is a fuzzy disjunction, triangular conorm, or disjunctive uninorm, respectively (and vice versa).*

4   Duality between Fuzzy Implications and Coimplications

Definitions and examples of fuzzy implications are based mainly on the recent monograph by Baczyński and Jayaram [1].

Definition 3 (cf. [1]). *Let function* $I\colon [0,1]^2 \to [0,1]$ *be decreasing with respect to the first variable and increasing with respect to the second one.*

- I *is called fuzzy implication if* $I(0,0) = I(0,1) = I(1,1) = 1$, $I(1,0) = 0$;
- I *is called fuzzy coimplication if* $I(0,0) = I(1,0) = I(1,1) = 0$, $I(0,1) = 1$.

A fuzzy implication I *is said to satisfy:*
- *(NP), the left neutral property, if* $I(1,y) = y$, $y \in [0,1]$,
- *(EP), the exchange principle, if* $I(x, I(y,z)) = I(y, I(x,z))$, $x,y,z \in [0,1]$,
- *(IP), the identity principle, if* $I(x,x) = 1$, $x \in [0,1]$,
- *(OP), the ordering property, if* $I(x,y) = 1 \Leftrightarrow x \leqslant y$, $x,y \in [0,1]$,
- *(CP), the law of contraposition, if* $I(x,y) = I(1-y, 1-x)$, $x,y \in [0,1]$.

Similarly, we can consider L-fuzzy implication, dual implication $I, I' \colon L^2 \to L$.

Example 3. Examples of fuzzy implications I (cf. [1]) with their dual operations I' (Łukasiewicz, Rescher, Gödel, Goguen and Fodor implications, respectively):

$$I_{LK}(x,y) = \min(1 - x + y, 1), \qquad I'_{LK}(x,y) = \max(0, y - x)$$

$$I_{RC}(x,y) = 1 - x + xy, \qquad I'_{RC}(x,y) = (1 - x)y,$$

$$I_{GD}(x,y) = \begin{cases} 1, & \text{if } x \leqslant y \\ y, & \text{if } x > y \end{cases}, \qquad I'_{GD}(x,y) = \begin{cases} 0, & \text{if } x \geqslant y \\ y, & \text{if } x < y \end{cases},$$

$$I_{GG}(x,y) = \begin{cases} 1, & \text{if } x \leqslant y \\ \frac{y}{x}, & \text{if } x > y \end{cases}, \qquad I'_{GG}(x,y) = \begin{cases} 0, & \text{if } x \geqslant y \\ \frac{y-x}{1-x}, & \text{if } x < y \end{cases},$$

$$I_{FD}(x,y) = \begin{cases} 1, & \text{if } x \leqslant y \\ \max(1 - x, y), & \text{if } x > y \end{cases}, \qquad I'_{FD}(x,y) = \begin{cases} 1, & \text{if } x \geqslant y \\ \max(1 - x, y), & \text{if } x < y \end{cases},$$

$x, y \in [0,1]$.

Theorem 3. *Let* $I'(x,y) = 1 - I(1 - x, 1 - y)$, $x, y \in [0,1]$.

- *The dual of a fuzzy implication is a coimplication and vice versa.*
- *Fuzzy implications fulfil (EP) or (CP) with their dual operations.*
- *If fuzzy implication* I *fulfils (NP), then* $I'(0,y) = y$, $y \in [0,1]$.
- *If fuzzy implication* I *fulfils (IP), then* $I'(x,x) = 0$, $y \in [0,1]$.
- *If fuzzy implication* I *fulfils (OP), then* $I'(x,y) = 0 \Leftrightarrow x \geqslant y$, $x, y \in [0,1]$.

5   Residuation Principle

According to [3] we consider residuated lattices.

Definition 4. *An algebraic system* $(L, *, \to, \leqslant, 0, 1)$ *is called a residuated lattice, if* $(L, \leqslant, 0, 1)$ *is a bounded lattice,* $(L, *, 1)$ *is a monoid and binary operations* $*$, $\to$ *fulfil the residuation principle:*

$$x * y \leqslant z \Leftrightarrow y \leqslant x \to z, \; x, y, z \in L. \tag{3}$$

Similarly, system $(L, *, \leftarrow, \geqslant, 1, 0)$ *is a dually residuated lattice, if* $(L, \geqslant, 1, 0)$ *is a bounded lattice,* $(L, *, 0)$ *is a monoid and binary operations* $*$, $\leftarrow$ *fulfil the dual residuation principle:*

$$x * y \geqslant z \Leftrightarrow y \geqslant x \leftarrow z, \ x, y, z \in L. \tag{4}$$

The residuated lattice is called complete if $(A, \leqslant)$ *is a complete lattice.*

Example 4. In the case of $L = [0, 1]$ the residuation principle is realized by the following pairs from Examples 2, 3: (T_M, I_{GD}), (T_P, I_{GG}), (T_L, I_{LK}), (T_{FD}, I_{FD}). Similarly, the dual residuation principle is realized by: (S_M, I'_{GD}), (S_P, I'_{GG}), (S_L, I'_{LK}), (S_{FD}, I'_{FD}). Thus we get diverse residuated lattices on $L = [0, 1]$.

Lemma 2 ([3], pp. 28-34). *If* $(L, *, \rightarrow, \leqslant, 0, 1)$ *is a residuated lattice, then*

$$x \leqslant y \rightarrow x, \ y \leqslant x \rightarrow x * y, \ (x \rightarrow y) * x \leqslant y, \ (x * y) \rightarrow z \Rightarrow x \rightarrow (y \rightarrow z),$$
$$x \leqslant y \Rightarrow (x * z \leqslant y * z, \ y \rightarrow z \leqslant x \rightarrow z, \ z \rightarrow x \leqslant z \rightarrow y).$$
$$x * y \leqslant x \wedge y, \ 1 \rightarrow y = y, \ x \leqslant y \Leftrightarrow x \rightarrow y = 1$$
$$x \rightarrow 1 = 1, \ 0 \rightarrow y = 1, \ x \rightarrow x = 1 \ for \ x, y, z \in L.$$

Similarly to Definitions 2 and 4 we can consider an associative, commutative L-fuzzy conjunction $*$ with neutral element 1, and an L-fuzzy implication $\rightarrow$, which additionally has properties (NP), (EP), (IP) and (OP). Dually we get properties of dual L-fuzzy conjunction $*$ and dual L-fuzzy implication $\leftarrow$.

Lemma 3. *If* $(L, *, \leftarrow, \geqslant, 1, 0)$ *is a dually residuated lattice, then*

$$x \geqslant y \leftarrow x, \ y \geqslant y \leftarrow x * y, \ (x \leftarrow y) * x \geqslant y, \ (x * y) \leftarrow z \Rightarrow x \leftarrow (y \leftarrow z),$$
$$x \leqslant y \Rightarrow (x * z \leqslant y * z, \ y \leftarrow z \leqslant x \leftarrow z, \ z \leftarrow x \leqslant z \leftarrow y),$$
$$x * y \geqslant x \vee y, \ 0 \leftarrow y = y, \ x \geqslant y \Leftrightarrow x \leftarrow y = 0,$$
$$x \leftarrow 0 = 0, \ 1 \leftarrow y = 0, \ x \leftarrow x = 0 \ for \ x, y, z \in L.$$

6   Dual Relation Compositions

Let $X, Y \neq \emptyset$ and $L = (L, \vee, \wedge, 0, 1)$ be a complete lattice. An L–fuzzy relation between sets X and Y is an arbitrary mapping $R : X \times Y \rightarrow L$ (a fuzzy relation for $L = [0, 1]$). In the case $X = Y$ we say about L–fuzzy relation on a set X. The family of all L–fuzzy relations on X is denoted by $LR(X)$ ($FR(X)$ for fuzzy relations). For $R, S \in LR(X)$ we use the induced order and the lattice operations:

$$R \leqslant S \quad \Leftrightarrow \quad \mathop{\forall}_{x,y \in X} (R(x, y) \leqslant S(x, y)), \tag{5}$$

$$(R \vee S)(x, y) = R(x, y) \vee S(x, y), \ (R \wedge S)(x, y) = R(x, y) \wedge S(x, y), \ x, y \in X. \tag{6}$$

Usually these operations are considered as the simplest version of inclusion, sum and intersection of fuzzy relations, respectively (cf. [22]). However, the most important operation on fuzzy relations is their composition.

Definition 5 ([12]). *Let L be a complete lattice and $* : L^2 \to L$. By $\sup -*$ composition of $L-$fuzzy relations R, S we call the $L-$fuzzy relation $R \circ S$, where*

$$(R \circ S)(x, z) = \sup_{y \in X}(R(x, y) * S(y, z)), \quad x, y \in X. \tag{7}$$

Similarly, inf $-*$ *composition (dual composition) is defined by*

$$(R \circ' S)(x, z) = \inf_{y \in X}(R(x, y) * S(y, z)), \quad x, y \in X. \tag{8}$$

Properties of composition $\circ$ depend on properties of operation $*$, what was examined in details in the paper [6] in the case $L = [0, 1]$. We recall here some of these results.

Theorem 4 ([6]). *Let $* : [0, 1]^2 \to [0, 1]$.*

- *Monotonicity of the operation $*$ (it is increasing or decreasing with respect to the first or to the second argument) is equivalent to the suitable property of the composition $\circ$.*
- *The operation $*$ has (left, right) zero element $z \in [0, 1]$ if and only if the composition $\circ$ has suitable zero element $Z(x, y) = z$, $x, y \in X$.*
- *If the operation $*$ is increasing, then the composition $\circ$ is distributive over $\vee$ and sub-distributive over $\wedge$, i.e.*

$$T \circ (R \vee S) = T \circ R \vee T \circ S, \ (R \vee S) \circ T = R \circ T \vee S \circ T, \ R, S, T \in FR(X).$$

$$T \circ (R \wedge S) \leqslant T \circ R \wedge T \circ S, \ (R \wedge S) \circ T \leqslant R \circ T \wedge S \circ T, \ R, S, T \in FR(X).$$

- *The operation $*$ is infinitely sup-distributive if and only if the composition $\circ$ is infinitely sup-distributive, i.e.*

$$R \circ (\sup_{t \in T} S_t) = \sup_{t \in T}(R \circ S_t), \quad (\sup_{t \in T} S_t) \circ R = \sup_{t \in T}(S_t \circ R),$$

where $R, S_t \in FR(X), t \in T$ for any index set $T \neq \emptyset$.
- *Let the operation $*$ be infinitely sup-distributive. The operation $*$ is associative in $[0, 1]$ if and only if the composition $\circ$ is associative in $FR(X)$.*
- *Let $z = 0$ be the zero element of the operation $*$. The operation $*$ has (left, right) neutral element $e \in (0, 1]$ if and only if the composition $\circ$ has suitable neutral element $E \in FR(X)$, where*

$$E(x, y) = \begin{cases} e, & x = y \\ 0, & x \neq y, \end{cases}, \quad x, y \in X. \tag{9}$$

Let us observe that in the case of relation composition based on a conjunctive uninorm $*$, we get change of the identity fuzzy relation onto relation (9). Directly from Theorem 4 and Lemma 1 we get

Corollary 2. *Let an operation $* : [0, 1]^2 \to [0, 1]$ be increasing.*

- *If the operation $*$ is left-continuous in $[0, 1]$, then the composition $\circ$ is infinitely sup-distributive in $FR(X)$.*
- *If the operation $*$ is left-continuous and associative in $[0, 1]$, then the composition $\circ$ is associative in $FR(X)$.*

Definition 6 ([13]). *Let the composition* $\circ$ *be associative. Powers of fuzzy relation* R *are defined by the recurrence:*

$$R^1 = R, \ R^{m+1} = R^m \circ R, \ m = 1, 2, \ldots$$

Additionally we consider the closure $R^\vee$ *and kernel* $R^\wedge$ *of* R:

$$R^\vee = \sup_{k \in \mathbb{N}} R^k, \ R^\wedge = \inf_{k \in \mathbb{N}} R^k.$$

Dual powers, closure and kernel are denoted by $R^{\bullet n}$, $R^{\bullet \vee}$ *and* $R^{\bullet \wedge}$, *respectively.*

Theorem 5 ([8]). *Let* $R, S \in FR(X)$. *If the operation* $*$ *is increasing, associative and left-continuous in* $[0, 1]$, *then*

$$(R \vee S)^n \geqslant R^n \vee S^n, \ (R \wedge S)^n \leqslant R^n \wedge S^n,$$

$$(R \vee S)^\vee \geqslant R^\vee \vee S^\vee, \ (R \vee S)^\wedge \geqslant R^\wedge \vee S^\wedge, \ (R \wedge S)^\vee \leqslant R^\vee \wedge S^\vee,$$

$$(R \wedge S)^\wedge \leqslant R^\wedge \wedge S^\wedge, \ R^n \circ R^\vee = R^\vee \circ R^n = (R^\vee)^{n+1},$$

$$(R^\vee)^n = \bigvee_{k=n}^{\infty} R^k \geqslant (R^n)^\vee, (R^\wedge)^{n+1} \leqslant \left\{ \begin{array}{l} R^n \circ R^\wedge \\ R^\wedge \circ R^n \end{array} \right. \leqslant \bigwedge_{k=n+1}^{\infty} R^k \leqslant (R^{n+1})^\wedge.$$

$$(R^\vee)^\vee = R^\vee, (R^\wedge)^\wedge \leqslant R^\wedge, (R^\wedge)^\vee \leqslant (R^\vee)^\wedge, \ n = 1, 2, \ldots$$

Using Duality Principle, the above results can be reformulated also for dual composition $\circ'$ in $FR(X)$. By direct verification we get

Theorem 6 (cf. [9], Theorem 2). *Compositions* $\sup -*$ *and* $\inf -*'$ *are connected by the formula*

$$\inf_{y \in X} (R(x, y) *' S(y, z)) = 1 - \sup_{y \in X} (1 - (R(x, y)) * (1 - S(y, z)), \ x, z \in X.$$

Moreover, if the operation $*$ *is increasing, left-continuous and associative, then*

$$R^{\bullet n} = 1 - (1 - R)^n, \ R^{\bullet \wedge} = 1 - (1 - R)^\vee, \ R^{\bullet \vee} = 1 - (1 - R)^\wedge \text{ for } R \in FR(X).$$

Theorem 7. *Let* $* : [0, 1]^2 \to [0, 1]$.

• *Monotonicity of the operation* $*$ *is equivalent to the suitable property of the composition* $\circ'$.
• *The operation* $*$ *has (left, right) zero element* $z \in [0, 1]$ *if and only if the composition* $\circ'$ *has suitable zero element* $Z'(x, y) = 1 - z$, $x, y \in X$.
• *If the operation* $*$ *is increasing, then the composition* $\circ'$ *is super-distributive over* $\vee$ *and distributive over* $\wedge$.
• *The operation* $*$ *is infinitely inf-distributive if and only if the composition* $\circ'$ *is infinitely inf-distributive.*
• *Let the operation* $*$ *be infinitely inf-distributive. The operation* $*$ *is associative in* $[0, 1]$ *if and only if the composition* $\circ'$ *is associative in* $FR(X)$.

• *Let $z = 1$ be the zero element of the operation $*'$. The operation $*$ has (left, right) neutral element $e \in (0,1]$ if and only if the composition $\circ'$ has suitable neutral element $E' \in FR(X)$, where*

$$E'(x,y) = \begin{cases} 1-e, & x = y \\ 1, & x \neq y \end{cases}, \quad x,y \in X.$$

Corollary 3. *Let an operation $* : [0,1]^2 \to [0,1]$ be increasing.*

• *If the operation $*$ is right-continuous in $[0,1]$, then the composition $\circ'$ is infinitely inf-distributive in $FR(X)$.*
• *If the operation $*$ is right-continuous and associative in $[0,1]$, then the composition $\circ'$ is associative in $FR(X)$.*

Theorem 8. *Let $R, S \in FR(X)$ If the operation $*'$ is increasing, associative and right-continuous in $[0,1]$, then*

$$(R \vee S)^{\bullet n} \geqslant R^{\bullet n} \vee S^{\bullet n}, \ (R \wedge S)^{\bullet n} \leqslant R^{\bullet n} \wedge S^{\bullet n},$$

$$(R \vee S)^{\bullet \vee} \geqslant R^{\bullet \vee} \vee S^{\bullet \vee}, \ (R \vee S)^{\bullet \wedge} \geqslant R^{\bullet \wedge} \vee S^{\bullet \wedge}, \ (R \wedge S)^{\bullet \vee} \leqslant R^{\bullet \vee} \wedge S^{\bullet \vee},$$

$$(R \wedge S)^{\bullet \wedge} \leqslant R^{\bullet \wedge} \wedge S^{\bullet \wedge}, \ R^{\bullet n} \circ' R^{\bullet \wedge} = R^{\bullet \wedge} \circ' R^{\bullet n} = (R^{\wedge})^{\bullet (n+1)},$$

$$(R^{\bullet \wedge})^{\bullet n} = \bigwedge_{k=n}^{\infty} R^{\bullet k} \leqslant (R^{\bullet n})^{\bullet \wedge},$$

$$(R^{\bullet \vee})^{\bullet (n+1)} \geqslant \begin{cases} R^{\bullet n} \circ' R^{\bullet \vee} \\ R^{\bullet \vee} \circ' R^{\bullet n} \end{cases} \geqslant \bigvee_{k=n+1}^{\infty} R^{\bullet k} \geqslant (R^{\bullet (n+1)})^{\bullet \vee}.$$

$$(R^{\bullet \vee})^{\bullet \vee} \geqslant R^{\bullet \vee}, (R^{\bullet \wedge})^{\bullet \wedge} = R^{\bullet \wedge}, (R^{\bullet \wedge})^{\bullet \vee} \leqslant (R^{\bullet \vee})^{\bullet \wedge}, n = 1, 2, \dots$$

Let $A \in [0,1]^{m \times n}$ and $b \in [0,1]^m$. Dual fuzzy systems of equations $A \circ x = b$ and $A \circ' x = b$ have dual properties.

Theorem 9 **([15]).** *Let $* : [0,1]^2 \to [0,1]$, $* \leqslant \min$ and $x *' y = 1 - (1-x) * (1-y)$ for $x, y \in [0,1]$, where the operation $*$ is increasing, left continuous and $1 * 0 = 0$.*

• *If the system $A \circ x = b$ is solvable, uniquely solvable or unsolvable, then the dual system has the same properties.*
• *The greatest solution u and the least solution u' have dual formulas:*

$$u_j = \bigwedge_{i=1}^{m} (a_{ij} \overset{*}{\to} b_i), \ u'_j = \bigvee_{i=1}^{m} (a_{ij} \overset{*'}{\leftarrow} b_i), \ j = 1, \dots, n.$$

• *If the system $A \circ x = b$ has minimal solutions, then the dual system has the same number of maximal solutions.*
• *If the system $A \circ x = b$ has the least solution, then the dual system has the greatest solution.*

7   L-Valued Fuzzy Reasoning

Let $A, A' : X \to L$, $B, B' : Y \to L$ be L-fuzzy sets, where $(L, *, \to, \leqslant, 0, 1)$ is a complete residuated lattice and $X, Y \neq \emptyset$. In the L-valued case, the Generalized Modus Ponens (cf. [23]) can be described as

$$Premises : \text{IF } x \text{ is } A \text{ THEN } y \text{ is } B \text{ AND } x \text{ is } A'$$
$$Conclusion : y \text{ is } B',$$

and the Generalized Modus Tollens is described as

$$Premises : \text{IF } x \text{ is } A \text{ THEN } y \text{ is } B \text{ AND } y \text{ is } B'$$
$$Conclusion : x \text{ is } A'.$$

Usually the 'IF – THEN' rule is described by fuzzy implication, and 'AND' is described by fuzzy conjunction, what can be applied in suitable form of Compositional Rule of Inference (cf. [23]). In L-valued case we use the implication $\to$ and the conjunction $*$ and putting $R(x, y) = A(x) \to B(y)$ (the greatest solution of relation equation $A \circ X = B$), we can describe the conclusion by

$$B'(y) = (A' \circ R)(y) = \sup_{x \in X}(A'(x) * R(x, y)) = \sup_{x \in X}(A'(x) * (A(x) \to B(y))).$$

Similarly we get

$$A'(x) = (R \circ B')(x) = \sup_{y \in Y}(R(x, y) * B'(y)) = \sup_{y \in Y}((A(x) \to B(y)) * B'(y)).$$

Properties of these conclusions under additional assumptions are discussed in many papers (cf. e.g. [16], [17] with additional bibliography).

8   Concluding Remarks

We listed here diverse consequences of Duality Principle which have applications in fuzzy logic, fuzzy algebra, soft computing, approximate reasoning and decision making. Such survey of duality properties can be useful during considerations of the above domains. Simultaneously, the presented properties and notions can be a subject of further examination, specification or generalization. For example, paper [18] describes interval extensions of dual implications generated from aggregation functions. More about approximate reasoning with uninorms can be found in [21].

Acknowledgement. This work is partially supported by the Ministry of Science and Higher Education Grant Nr N N519 384936.

References

1. Baczyński, M., Jayaram, B.: Fuzzy Implications. STUDFUZZ, vol. 231. Springer, Berlin (2008)
2. Baldwin, J.F., Pilsworth, B.W.: Axiomatic approach to implication for approximate reasoning with fuzzy logic. Fuzzy Sets Syst. 3, 193–219 (1980)
3. Bělohlávek, R.: Fuzzy Relational Systems. Kluwer, New York (2002)
4. Birkhoff, G.: Lattice Theory. AMS Coll. Publ. 25. AMS, Providence (1967)
5. Bustince, H., Burillo, P., Mohedano, V.: A method for inference in approximate reasoning based on normal intuitionistic fuzzy sets. Notes IFS 1, 51–55 (1995)
6. Drewniak, J., Kula, K.: Generalized compositions of fuzzy relations. Internat. J. Uncertain. Fuzziness Knowledge-Based Systems 10, 149–164 (2002)
7. Drewniak, J., Król, A.: A survey of weak connectives and the preservation of their properties by aggregations. Fuzzy Sets Syst. 161(2), 202–215 (2010)
8. Drewniak, J., Pękala, B.: Properties of powers of fuzzy relations. Kybernetika 43(2), 133–142 (2007)
9. Fan, Z.T.: A note on power sequence of a fuzzy matrix. Fuzzy Sets Syst. 102, 281–286 (1999)
10. Fodor, J.C., Roubens, M.: Fuzzy Preference Modelling and Multicriteria Decision Support. Kluwer, Dordrecht (1994)
11. Fodor, J.C., Yager, R.R., Rybalov, A.: Structure of uninorms. Internat. J. Uncertainty, Fuzzines Knowledge-Based System 5, 411–427 (1997)
12. Goguen, J.A.: L-fuzzy sets. J. Math. Anal. Appl. 18, 145–174 (1967)
13. Kaufmann, A.: Introduction to the Theory of Fuzzy Subsets. Academic Press, New York (1975)
14. Klement, E.P., Mesiar, R., Pap, E.: Triangular Norms. Kluwer, Dordrecht (2000)
15. Li, P., Fang, S.: A survey on fuzzy relational equations. Fuzzy Optim. Decis. Making 8, 179–229 (2009)
16. Liu, H.: Fully implicational methods for approximate reasoning based on interval-valued fuzzy sets. J. Syst. Eng. Electr. 21, 224–232 (2010)
17. Perfilieva, I., Lehmke, S.: Correct models of fuzzy IF–THEN rules are continuous. Fuzzy Sets Syst. 157, 3188–3197 (2006)
18. Reiser, R.H.S., Bedregal, B.C.: Obtaining representable coimplications from aggregation and dual operators. In: EUSFLAT-LFA 2011, pp. 238–245 (2011)
19. Ruiz, D., Torrens, J.: Residual implications and coimplications from idempotent uninorms. Kybernetika 40, 21–38 (2004)
20. Smets, P., Magrez, P.: Implication in fuzzy logic, Internat. J. Approx. Reason. 1, 327–347 (1987)
21. Takács, M.: Approximate reasoning in fuzzy systems based on pseudo-analysis and uninorm residuum. Acta Polytechnica Hungarica 1(2), 49–62 (2004)
22. Zadeh, L.A.: Fuzzy sets. Inform. Control 8, 338–353 (1965)
23. Zadeh, L.A.: Outline of a new approach to the analysis of complex systems and decision processes. IEEE Trans. Syst. Man Cyber. 3, 28–44 (1973)

New Types of Compositions of Intuitionistic Fuzzy Relations in Decision Making Problems

Paweł Drygaś

Institute of Mathematics,
University of Rzeszów,
ul. Rejtana 16a, 35-959 Rzeszów, Poland
paweldr@univ.rzeszow.pl

Abstract. We propose the use of intuitionistic fuzzy sets as a tool for reasoning under imperfect facts and imprecise knowledge.

We suggest applications of diverse types of composition of intuitionistic fuzzy relations to this problem. In particular, we will use composition of fuzzy relation in the sense of Goguen.

Keywords: Atanassov's intuitionistic fuzzy sets, composition of relation, decision making problem, medical diagnosis.

1 Introduction

In this paper we propose the use of inuitionistic fuzzy sets as a tool for reasoning under imperfect facts and imprecise knowledge. Since it is possible to give the connections between patients and symptoms, and symptoms and diagnosis by intuitionistic fuzzy relations, a composition of fuzzy relations is a natural way which allows to obtain connections between patients and diagnosis. The idea of this paper is to use diverse types of composition of intuitionistic fuzzy relations for this problem. In particular, we will use the composition of fuzzy relations in the sense of Goguen. At the end of this paper we put open problems which are connected with our consideration.

2 Basic Definitions

Now we recall some definitions which will be helpful in our investigations. One of the possible generalizations of a fuzzy set in X and a fuzzy relation in $X \times Y$ is given by Atanassov's intuitionistic fuzzy sets or relations which assign to each element of the universe not only a membership degree but also a non-membership degree.

Definition 1 ([1]). *Let $X \neq \emptyset$ be a given set. An Atanassov's intuitionistic fuzzy set in X is a triplet given by*

$$\mathcal{A} = (x, A, A^d),$$

S. Greco et al. (Eds.): IPMU 2012, Part II, CCIS 298, pp. 521–528, 2012.
© Springer-Verlag Berlin Heidelberg 2012

satisfying the following condition:

$$0 \leq A(x) + A^d(x) \leq 1, \quad \forall x \in X.$$

The characteristic functions $A, A^d : X \rightarrow [0,1]$ *define respectively the degree of membership and the degree of non-membership of the element* x *in* $\mathcal{A}$. *When the equality on the right side holds, i.e. when* $A(x) + A^d(x) = 1$ *for every* $x \in X$, *the set* $\mathcal{A}$ *is a fuzzy set. The family of all Atanassov's intuitionistic fuzzy sets described in the given set* X *is denoted by* $AIFS(X)$.

Definition 2 ([1]). *Let* $X, Y \neq \emptyset$ *be a given sets. An Atanassov's intuitionistic fuzzy relation from* X *to* Y *is an Atanassov's intuitionistic fuzzy set in* $X \times Y$, *i.e. a triplet given by* $\rho = ((x,y), R, R^d)$, *where* $R, R^d : X \times Y \rightarrow [0,1]$ *satisfy the condition*

$$0 \leq R(x,y) + R^d(x,y) \leq 1, \forall (x,y) \in X \times Y.$$

The family of all Atanassov's intuitionistic fuzzy relations described in the given sets X, Y *is denoted by* $AIFR(X,Y)$. *In the case* $X = Y$ *we will use the notation* $AIFR(X)$.

The boundary elements in $AIFR(X,Y)$ are

$$\mathbf{1} = ((x,y), 1, 0) \ and \ \mathbf{0} = ((x,y), 0, 1),$$

where $0, 1$ are the identities fuzzy relations.

The union, the intersection and the complement for Atanassov's intuitionistic fuzzy relations are defined as follows (see [2], Definition 1.4): let $\rho = ((x,y), R, R^d)$ and $\rho = ((x,y), P, P^d)$ are in $AIFR(X,Y)$, then

- $\rho \cup \sigma = ((x,y), R \vee P, R^d \wedge P^d)$;
- $\rho \cap \sigma = ((x,y), R \wedge P, R^d \vee P^d)$;
- $co\rho = ((x,y), R^d, R)$;

Moreover, we can compare elements of $AIFR(X,Y)$. In fact, if we define for all $\rho, \sigma \in AIFR(X,Y)$,

$$\rho \leq \sigma \ \Leftrightarrow \ (R \leq P, \ P^d \leq R^d),$$

then $(AIFR(X,Y), \leq)$ is a complete lattice.

The fuzzy relation $\pi_\rho : X \times Y \rightarrow [0,1]$ is associated with each Atanassov's intuitionistic fuzzy relation $\rho = ((x,y), R, R^d)$, where

$$\pi_\rho(x,y) = 1 - R(x,y) - R^d(x,y), \quad x \in X, \ y \in Y.$$

The number $\pi_\rho(x,y)$ is called an index of an element (x,y) in an Atanassov's intuitionistic fuzzy relation ρ. It is described as an index (a degree) of hesitation whether x and y are in the relation ρ or not. This value is also regarded as a measure of non-determinacy or uncertainty and is useful in applications.

The generalization of these two concepts are L-fuzzy sets and L-fuzzy relations

Definition 3 ([9]). *An L-fuzzy set $\mathcal{A}$ in a universe X is a function $\mathcal{A} : X \to L$, where L is a complete lattice.*

Definition 4 ([9]). *An L-fuzzy relation $\mathcal{R}$ in $X \times Y$ is a L-fuzzy set $\mathcal{R}$ in a universe $X \times Y$.*

Let us define
$$L^* = \{(x_1, x_2) \in [0, 1]^2 : x_1 + x_2 \leq 1\},$$
with order
$$(x_1, x_2) \leq_{L^*} (y_1, y_2) \Leftrightarrow x_1 \leq y_1 \text{ and } x_2 \geq y_2.$$
$(L^*, \leq_{L^*})$ is a complete lattice.

Equivalently, this lattice can also be defined as an algebraic structure $(L^*, \wedge, \vee)$, where the meet operator $\wedge$ and the join operator $\vee$ are defined as follows,

$$(x_1, x_2) \wedge (y_1, y_2) = (\min(x_1, y_1), \max(x_2, y_2));$$
$$(x_1, x_2) \vee (y_1, y_2) = (\max(x_1, y_1), \min(x_2, y_2)).$$

This lattice has the greatest element $1_{L^*} = (1, 0)$ and the least element $0_{L^*} = (0, 1)$.

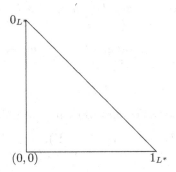

Fig. 1. Lattice L^*

Using this lattice, it can be easily seen that with every Atanassov's intuitionistic fuzzy set $\mathcal{A} = (x, A, A^d)$ corresponds an L^*-fuzzy set in the sense of Goguen, i.e. a mapping $\mathcal{A} : X \to L^*$. In the sequel we will use the same notation for an Atanassov's intuitionistic fuzzy set and its associated L^*-fuzzy set. So, for the Atanassov's intuitionistic fuzzy set $\mathcal{A}$ we will also use the notation $\mathcal{A}(x) = (A(x), A^d(x))$. Interpreting Atanasov's intuitionistic fuzzy sets as L^*-fuzzy sets gives way to a greater flexibility in calculating with membership and non-membership degrees, since the pair formed by the two degrees is an element of L^*, and often allows to obtain significantly more compact formulas. Moreover, some operators that are defined in the fuzzy case, such as triangular norms and conorms, can be extended to the Atanassov's intuitionistic fuzzy case by using the lattice $(L^*, \leq_{L^*})$.

Definition 5. *A triangular norm $\mathcal{T}$ is an increasing, commutative, associative operation $\mathcal{T} : (L)^2 \to L$ with neutral element 1_L. A triangular conorm $\mathcal{S}$ is an increasing, commutative, associative operation $\mathcal{S} : (L)^2 \to L$ with neutral element 0_L.*

Example 1. If $L = [0,1]$, then we obtain t-norms on $[0,1]$ (cf. [10]). Well-known t-norms and t-conorms are:

$$T_M(x,y) = \min(x,y), \quad S_M(x,y) = \max(x,y),$$

$$T_P(x,y) = x \cdot y, \quad S_P(x,y) = x + y - xy,$$

$$T_L(x,y) = \max(x + y - 1, 0), \quad S_L(x,y) = \min(x + y, 1),$$

Example 2. There are examples of triangular operation on L^*:

$$\inf(x,y) = (\min(x_1,y_1), \max(x_2,y_2)), \quad \sup(x,y) = (\max(x_1,y_1), \min(x_2,y_2)), \tag{1}$$

$$\mathcal{T}(x,y) = (\max(0, x_1+y_1-1), \min(1, x_2+y_2)), \quad \mathcal{T}(x,y) = (x_1 y_1, x_2 + y_2 - x_2 y_2).$$

Definition 6 ([6]). *A triangular norm $\mathcal{T}$ on L^* is called t-representable if there exist a triangular norm T and a triangular conorm S on $[0,1]$ such that, for all $x, y \in L^*$ $\mathcal{T}(x,y) = (T(x_1,y_1), S(x_2,y_2))$. A triangular conorm $\mathcal{S}$ on L^* is called t-representable if there exist a triangular norm T and a triangular conorm S on $[0,1]$ such that, for all $x, y \in L^*$ $\mathcal{S}(x,y) = (S(x_1,y_1), T(x_2,y_2))$.*

Example 3. All operations in Example 2 are t-representable operations. The following t-norm (called Łukasiewicz t-norm) is not t-representable:

$$\mathcal{T}_W(x,y) = (\max(0, x_1 + y_1 - 1), \min(1, x_2 + 1 - y_1, y_2 + 1 - x_1)) \tag{2}$$

Now, let us recall the notion of composition in its standard form

Definition 7 (cf. [3]). *Let $\sigma \in AIFR(X,Y)$, $\rho \in AIFR(Y,Z)$. Let denote $\sigma = (P, P^d)$, $\rho = (R, R^d)$. By the composition of relations σ and ρ we call the relation $\sigma \circ \rho \in AIFR(X,Z)$,*

$$(\sigma \circ \rho)(x,z) = ((P \circ R)(x,z), (P^d \circ' R^d)(x,z)), \tag{3}$$

where

$$(P \circ R)(x,z) = S_{y \in Y} T(P(x,y), R(y,z)),$$

$$(P^d \circ' R^d)(x,z) = T_{y \in Y} S(P^d(x,y), R^d(y,z)).$$

According to [3], Proposition 1 we obtain that the following condition holds

$$0 \le (P \circ R)(x,z) + (P^d \circ' R^d)(x,z) \le 1, \quad (x,z) \in X \times Z.$$

Looking at the definition of composition of relations, we see that it has a similar structure as t-representable operations. Therefore, we try to apply the general definition of the composition of relations in the lattice L^* - the Goguen's definition, which allow us to take into account also the value of hestitation degree (as it is considered in distance method used in paper [11]). It should be noted here that by the application the Definition 7 the hestitation function is not considered.

Definition 8 (cf. [9]). *Let $\sigma \in AIFR(X,Y)$, $\rho \in AIFR(Y,Z)$. By the composition of relations σ and ρ we call the relation $\sigma \circ \rho \in AIFR(X,Z)$,*

$$(\sigma \circ \rho)(x,z) = S_{y \in Y} T(\sigma(x,y), \rho(y,z)), \tag{4}$$

If we use t-representable operations in (4) then we obtain composition in the form (3).

3   Medical Diagnosis

We should pay attention to the fact that intuitionistic fuzzy relations we can use in medical diagnosis. As we know, the approach presented in [4] involves the following three steps:

1) Determination of symptoms.
A set of n patients is considered. For each patient p_i, $i = 1, 2, ..., n$, a set of symptoms S is given. As a result, an intuitionistic fuzzy relation Q is between the set of patients and the set of symptoms S.

2) Formulation of medical knowledge expressed by intuitionistic fuzzy relations.
It is assumed that another intuitionistic fuzzy relation R is given - from a set of symptoms S to the set of diagnoses D (medical knowledge).

3) Determination of diagnosis on the basic of a max-min composition of intuitionistic fuzzy relations.
The composition C of intuitionistic fuzzy relations R and Q describes the state of a patient given in terms of a membership function $C(p_i, d_k)$ and non-membership function $C^d(p_i, d_k)$, for each patient p_i and diagnosis d_k.
There exist Atanassov's intuitionistic fuzzy relations which are not comparable. So we consider a fuzzy relation which will allow to obtain a diagnosis.
   We generalize this method to diverse compositions and we compare the results.

Example 4. Let there be set of patients: $\mathcal{P} = \{A, B, C, D\}$. The set of considered symptoms is $S = \{$Temperature, Headache, Stomach pain, Cough, Chest pain$\}$. The intuitionistic fuzzy relation $Q = (q, q^d)$ is given in the Table 1 that contains description of symptoms for a group of patients.

Table 1.

Q	Temperature	Headache	Stomach pain	Cough	Chest pain
A	(0.3, 0)	(0.9, 0)	(0.7, 0.3)	(0.7, 0)	(0, 1)
B	(0.3, 0.4)	(0.7, 0.3)	(0.5, 0.2)	(0.3, 0.7)	(0.5, 0)
C	(0.3, 0.7)	(0.4, 0.1)	(0.5, 0.5)	(0.3, 0.6)	(0.4, 0.5)
D	(0.3, 0.5)	(0.4, 0.2)	(0.2, 0.3)	(0.2, 0.6)	(0.4, 0.2)

Let us consider the set of diagnosis $\mathcal{D} =$ {Viral fever, Malaria, Typhoid, Stomach problem, Chest problem}.

The intuitionistic fuzzy relation $\mathcal{R} = (r, r^d)$ (the medical data describing dependencies between the symptoms and a diagnosis, as expert knowledge [4]) is given in the Table 2

Table 2.

$\mathcal{R}$	Viral fever	Malaria	Typhoid	Stomach problem	Chest problem
Temperature	(0.4, 0)	(0.7, 0)	(0.3, 0.3)	(0.1, 0.7)	(0.1, 0.8)
Headache	(0.3, 0.5)	(0.2, 0.6)	(0.6, 0.1)	(0.2, 0.4)	(0, 0.8)
Stomach pain	(0.1, 0.7)	(0, 0.9)	(0.2, 0.7)	(0.8, 0)	(0.2, 0.8)
Cough	(0.4, 0.3)	(0.7, 0)	(0.2, 0.6)	(0.2, 0.7)	(0.2, 0.8)
Chest pain	(0.1, 0.7)	(0.1, 0.8)	(0.1, 0.9)	(0.2, 0.7)	(0.8, 0.1)

Similarly as the mentioned authors we use the (max-min, min-max) composition and we obtain the relation $\mathcal{C} = (c, c^d)$ between the patients and the diagnosis given in the Table 3, where for all $i \in \mathcal{P}$, $j \in \mathcal{D}$ (see (3))

$$\mathcal{C}(i,j) = (\mathcal{Q} \circ \mathcal{R})(i,j) = \left(\bigvee_{k \in \mathcal{S}} (q(i,k) \wedge r(k,j)), \bigwedge_{k \in \mathcal{S}} (q^d(i,k) \vee r^d(k,j)) \right).$$

Table 3.

$\mathcal{C}$	Viral fever	Malaria	Typhoid	Stomach problem	Chest problem
A	(0.4, 0)	(0.7, 0)	(0.6, 0.1)	(0.7, 0.3)	(0.2, 0.8)
B	(0.3, 0.4)	(0.3, 0.4)	(0.6, 0.3)	(0.5, 0.2)	(0.5, 0.1)
C	(0.3, 0.5)	(0.3, 0.6)	(0.4, 0.2)	(0.5, 0.4)	(0.4, 0.5)
D	(0.3, 0.5)	(0.3, 0.5)	(0.4, 0.2)	(0.2, 0.3)	(0.4, 0.2)

Moreover, to compare the obtained results we construct the relation

$$S_{\mathcal{C}} = c - c^d \pi_{\mathcal{C}}. \tag{5}$$

Table 4.

$S_{\mathcal{C}}$	Viral fever	Malaria	Typhoid	Stomach problem	Chest problem
A	0.4	0.7	0.57	0.7	0.2
B	0.18	0.18	0.57	0.44	0.46
C	0.2	0.24	0.32	0.46	0.35
D	0.2	0.2	0.32	0.05	0.32

The greatest element in each row points out the diagnosis for a given patient. For example, we can see that patient B has typhoid, but for A we obtain the same value in two columns. Thus, we observe that this method doesn't give always the diagnosis.

This is why we consider another types of compositions.

First we apply $\sup -T_W$ composition and we obtain the relation $\mathcal{C} = (c, c^d)$ between the patients and the diagnosis given in the Table 5, where for all $i \in \mathcal{P}$, $j \in \mathcal{D}$ (see (4), (1), (2))

$$\mathcal{C}(i, j) = (\mathcal{Q} \circ \mathcal{R})(i, j) = \bigvee_{k \in \mathcal{S}} T_W(\mathcal{Q}(i, k), \mathcal{R}(k, j)).$$

Table 5.

$\mathcal{C}$	Viral fever	Malaria	Typhoid	Stomach problem	Chest problem
A	(0.2, 0.6)	(0.4, 0.3)	(0.5, 0.2)	(0.5, 0.3)	(0, 0.8)
B	(0, 0.7)	(0, 0.7)	(0.3, 0.4)	(0.3, 0.4)	(0.3, 0.2)
C	(0, 0.7)	(0, 0.7)	(0, 0.6)	(0.3, 0.5)	(0.2, 0.7)
D	(0, 0.7)	(0, 0.7)	(0, 0.6)	(0, 0.5)	(0.2, 0.4)

Using the formula (5) to Table 5 we obtain the diagnosis different from the ones in the $(\max - \min, \min - \max)$ composition.

Table 6.

$S_{\mathcal{C}}$	Viral fever	Malaria	Typhoid	Stomach problem	Chest problem
A	0.08	0.31	0.45	0.44	-0.16
B	-0.21	-0.21	0.18	0.18	0.2
C	-0.21	-0.21	-0.24	0.2	0.13
D	-0.21	-0.21	-0.24	-0.25	0.04

So, we obtain the solutions to the previously not solved case A.

As a result $\sup -T_W$ composition seems to be the best of the the considered compositions.

4   Conclusions

On the basis of our observations we want to put the following problems:

- Which operations we should use in the formula (4)?
- Which type of compositions we should consider instead of $\sup -T_W$ composition?
- Is it possible to use another method of comparison of results than the formula (5)?
- Which properties of composition are important in our considerations?

Acknowledgments. This paper is partially supported by the Ministry of Science and Higher Education Grant Nr N N519 384936.

References

1. Atanassov, K.T.: Intuitionistic fuzzy sets. Fuzzy Sets and Systems 20, 87–96 (1986)
2. Atanassov, K.: Intuitionistic Fuzzy Sets: Theory and Applications. Springer (1999)
3. Burillo, P., Bustince, H.: Intuitionistic Fuzzy Relations. Effect of Atanassov's Operators on the Properties of the Intuitionistic Fuzzy Relations. Mathware and Soft Computing 2, 117–148 (1995)
4. De, S.K., Biswas, R., Roy, A.R.: An application of intuitionistic fuzzy sets in medical diagnosis. Fuzzy Sets and Systems 117, 209–213 (2001)
5. Deschrijver, G., Kerre, E.E.: On the relationship beetwen some extensions of fuzzy set theory. Fuzzy Sets and Systems 133, 227–235 (2003)
6. Deschrijver, G., Cornelis, C., Kerre, E.E.: On the Representation of Intuitonistic Fuzzy t-Norms and t-Conorms. IEEE Transactions on Fuzzy Syst. 12, 45–61 (2004)
7. Drygaś, P., Pękala, B.: Properties of decomposable operations on same extension of the fuzzy set theory. In: Atanassov, K.T., Hryniewicz, O., Kacprzyk, J., Krawczak, M., Nahorski, Z., Szmidt, E., Zadrony, S. (eds.) Advances in Fuzzy Sets, Intuitionistic Fuzzy Sets, Generalized Nets and Related Topics. Foundations, vol. I, pp. 105–118. EXIT, Warszawa (2008)
8. Drygaś, P., Pękala, B.: Decision making problem on intuitionistic fuzzy relations (submitted)
9. Goguen, A.: L-fuzzy sets. Journal of Mathematical Analysis and Applications 18, 145–174 (1967)
10. Klement, E.P., Mesiar, R., Pap, E.: Triangular norms. Kluwer Acad. Publ., Dordrecht (2000)
11. Szmidt, E., Kacprzyk, J.: Distances between intuitionistic fuzzy sets. Fuzzy Sets and Systems 114, 505–518 (2005)

A New Approach to Principal Component Analysis for Intuitionistic Fuzzy Data Sets

Eulalia Szmidt[1,2] and Janusz Kacprzyk[1,2]

[1] Systems Research Institute, Polish Academy of Sciences,
ul. Newelska 6, 01–447 Warsaw, Poland
[2] Warsaw School of Information Technology,
ul. Newelska 6, 01-447 Warsaw, Poland
{szmidt,kacprzyk}@ibspan.waw.pl

Abstract. We propose a new approach to Principal Component Analysis (PCA) for Atanassov's intuitionistic fuzzy sets (A-IFSs). We are mainly concerned with the dimension reduction for data represented as the A-IFSs, and provide an illustrative example.

1   Introduction

Principal component analysis (PCA) (Jolliffe [9]) is one of the best known and widely employed techniques for the reduction of dimensionality of a data set. It was first introduced by Pearson (1901) [13], and developed independently by Hotelling (1933). The reduction of dimensionality of data sets is important not only from the numerical point of view but also is crucial for the ability to discover and understand hidden phenomena in the data.

The reduction of dimensionality of a data set, in which there are lots of interrelated variables, is performed by transforming the source set to a new set of uncorrelated variables (the principal components, or PC, for short) to summarize features of the original data. The approach is relevant in many fields though a different terminology is used. For instance, in statistics, the term "variable" is used whereas in machine learning and computer science instead of "variable", the terms "feature" and "attribute" are employed.

PCA is a useful technique that has found applications in many fields – Jolliffe [10] cites many books and papers discussing applications in agriculture, biology, chemistry, climatology, demography, ecology, economics, food research, genetics, geology, meteorology, oceanography, psychology, quality control, etc. PCA is also, just to give an example, used in face recognition and image compression, as a common technique for finding patterns in data of high dimension.

Although PCA is not a new approach, it is still a topic of much research interest. For example, Ding and He [6] have shown that principal components (PCs) are continuous (relaxed) solutions of the cluster membership indicators in the k-means clustering.

In this paper we propose a new approach to PCA for data sets expressed in terms of Atanassov's intuitionistic fuzzy sets (A-IFSs) (Atanassov [1], [2]) in which data are described in terms of the membership values, non-membership values, and hesitation margins expressing the lack of knowledge (cf. Section 2). Since the A-IFSs become more and more widely applied in diverse fields, exemplified by image processing

S. Greco et al. (Eds.): IPMU 2012, Part II, CCIS 298, pp. 529–538, 2012.
© Springer-Verlag Berlin Heidelberg 2012

(cf. Bustince et al. [3], [4]), classification of imbalanced and overlapping classes (cf. Szmidt and Kukier [36], [37], [38]), group decision making, negotiations, voting and other situations (cf. Szmidt and Kacprzyk papers), the dimensionality reduction of data given as the A-IFSs is of utmost interest, too.

We demonstrate how to find the PCs for the A-IFS data. The PCs are the eigenvectors of data correlation matrices, with the first PC being the eigenvector corresponding to the largest eigenvalue. For most data sets the first few PCs capture most of the data variability, so the first PCs summarize and represent the most important features of the data. Although the procedure of finding PCs seems to be familiar, to obtain effective and efficient tools and techniques it is necessary to devise proper techniques and their numerical implementations for the calculation of correlation matrices (cf. Szmidt and Kacprzyk [35]) for A-IFSs (Section 3). For illustration, we present how PCA works for A-IFS data on a well known example by Quinlan [15].

2   A Brief Introduction to Intuitionistic Fuzzy Sets

One of the possible generalizations of a fuzzy set in X (Zadeh [39]), given by

$$A^{'} = \{< x, \mu_{A'}(x) > | x \in X\} \tag{1}$$

where $\mu_{A'}(x) \in [0, 1]$ is the membership function of the fuzzy set $A^{'}$, is Atanassov's intuitionistic fuzzy set (Atanassov [2]) A:

$$A = \{< x, \mu_A(x), \nu_A(x) > | x \in X\} \tag{2}$$

where: $\mu_A : X \rightarrow [0, 1]$ and $\nu_A : X \rightarrow [0, 1]$ such that $0 \leq \mu_A(x) + \nu_A(x) \leq 1$, and $\mu_A(x), \nu_A(x) \in [0, 1]$ denote the degree of membership and a degree of non-membership of $x \in A$, respectively, and the *hesitation margin* of $x \in A$ is:

$$\pi_A(x) = 1 - \mu_A(x) - \nu_A(x) \tag{3}$$

The $\pi_A(x)$ expresses a lack of knowledge of whether x belongs to A or not (Atanassov [2]); obviously, $0 \leq \pi_A(x) \leq 1$, for each $x \in X$.

The hesitation margin turns out to be important while considering the distances (Szmidt and Kacprzyk [18], [20], [27], entropy (Szmidt and Kacprzyk [22], [29]), similarity (Szmidt and Kacprzyk [30]) for the A-IFSs, etc. i.e., the measures that play a crucial role in virtually all information processing tasks. The hesitation margin is shown to be indispensable also in the ranking of intuitionistic fuzzy alternatives as it indicates how reliable (sure) information represented by an alternative is (cf. Szmidt and Kacprzyk [31], [32]).

The use of A-IFSs instead of fuzzy sets implies the introduction of additional degrees of freedom (non-memberships and hesitation margins) into the set description. Such a generalization of fuzzy sets gives us an additional possibility to represent imperfect knowledge which may lead to describing many real problems in a more adequate way. This is confirmed by successful applications of A-IFSs to image processing (cf. Bustince et al. [3], [4]), group decision making, negotiations, voting and other situations are presented in Szmidt and Kacprzyk [17], [19], [21], [23], [24], [25], [26], [28], [33], Szmidt and Kukier [36], [37].

3   Correlation

Obviously, the (degree of) correlation between variables is crucial, a prerequisite for further analysis. In the case of crisp or even fuzzy [7], [11], [16] (in our context, the non-A-IFS-type data), the problem is clear and solved. Unfortunately, the very essence of the A-IFSs, in which 3 degrees (of membership, non-membership and hesitation) characterize information conveyed, the problem of correlation between such types of data is not obvious. An effective and efficient approach, which takes a full advantage of the very essence of the A-IFSs has been proposed by the authors, cf. Szmidt and Kacprzyk [35] in which a new concept of the Pearson's correlation coefficient between two A-IFS-type data was introduced.

To briefly recall, the correlation coefficient (Pearson's r) between two variables is a measure of the linear relationship between them. The correlation coefficient is 1 in the case of a positive (increasing) linear relationship, -1 in the case of a negative (decreasing) linear relationship, and some value between -1 and 1 in all other cases. The closer the coefficient is to either -1 or 1, the stronger the correlation between the variables.

3.1   Correlation between the Crisp Sets

Let $(X_1, Y_1), (X_2, Y_2), \ldots, (X_n, Y_n)$ be a random sample of size n from a joint probability density function $f_{X,Y}(x, y)$, let $\overline{X}$ and $\overline{Y}$ be the sample means of variables X and Y, respectively, then the sample correlation coefficient $r(X, Y)$ is given as (e.g., [14]):

$$r(X, Y) = \frac{\sum\limits_{i=1}^{n} (x_i - \overline{X})(y_i - \overline{Y})}{(\sum\limits_{i=1}^{n} (x_i - \overline{X})^2 \sum\limits_{i=1}^{n} (y_i - \overline{Y})^2)^{0.5}} \tag{4}$$

where: $\overline{X} = \frac{1}{n} \sum\limits_{i=1}^{n} x_i, \quad \overline{Y} = \frac{1}{n} \sum\limits_{i=1}^{n} y_i.$

3.2   Correlation between the Fuzzy Sets

Suppose that we have a random sample $x_1, x_2, \ldots, x_n \in X$ with a sequence of paired data $(\mu_A(x_1), \mu_B(x_1)), (\mu_A(x_2), \mu_B(x_2)), \ldots, (\mu_A(x_n), \mu_B(x_n))$ which correspond to the membership values of fuzzy sets A and B defined on X, then the correlation coefficient $r_f(A, B)$ is given as ([5]):

$$r_f(A, B) = \frac{\sum\limits_{i=1}^{n} (\mu_A(x_i) - \overline{\mu_A})(\mu_B(x_i) - \overline{\mu_B})}{(\sum\limits_{i=1}^{n} (\mu_A(x_i) - \overline{\mu_A})^2)^{0.5} (\sum\limits_{i=1}^{n} (\mu_B(x_i) - \overline{\mu_B})^2)^{0.5}} \tag{5}$$

where: $\overline{\mu_A} = \frac{1}{n} \sum\limits_{i=1}^{n} \mu_A(x_i), \quad \overline{\mu_B} = \frac{1}{n} \sum\limits_{i=1}^{n} \mu_B(x_i).$

3.3 Correlation between the A-IFSs

A correlation coefficient for two A-IFSs, A and B should express not only a relative strength but also a positive or negative relationship between A and B (Szmidt and Kacprzyk [35]). Next, all three terms describing an A-IFSs (membership, non-membership values and the hesitation margins) should be taken into account because each of them influences the results (Szmidt and Kacprzyk [35]). The above assumptions make the difference between our approach and those from the literature (the arguments for our approach are in (Szmidt and Kacprzyk [35]).

Suppose that we have a random sample $x_1, x_2, \ldots, x_n \in X$ with a sequence of paired data $[(\mu_A(x_1), \nu_A(x_1), \pi_A(x_1)), (\mu_B(x_1), \nu_B(x_1), \pi_B(x_1))], [(\mu_A(x_2), \nu_A(x_2), \pi_A(x_2)), (\mu_B(x_2), \nu_B(x_2), \pi_B(x_2))], \ldots, [(\mu_A(x_n), \nu_A(x_n), \pi_A(x_n)), (\mu_B(x_n), \nu_B(x_n), \pi_B(x_n))]$ which correspond to the membership values, non-memberships values and hesitation margins of A-IFSs A and B defined on X, then the correlation coefficient $r_{A-IFS}(A, B)$ is given by Definition 1.

Definition 1. The correlation coefficient $r_{A-IFS}(A, B)$ between two A-IFSs, A and B in X, is:

$$r_{A-IFS}(A, B) = \frac{1}{3}(r_1(A, B) + r_2(A, B) + r_3(A, B)) \tag{6}$$

where

$$r_1(A, B) = \frac{\sum_{i=1}^{n} (\mu_A(x_i) - \overline{\mu_A})(\mu_B(x_i) - \overline{\mu_B})}{(\sum_{i=1}^{n} (\mu_A(x_i) - \overline{\mu_A})^2)^{0.5}(\sum_{i=1}^{n} (\mu_B(x_i) - \overline{\mu_B})^2)^{0.5}} \tag{7}$$

$$r_2(A, B) = \frac{\sum_{i=1}^{n} (\nu_A(x_i) - \overline{\nu_A})(\nu_B(x_i) - \overline{\nu_B})}{(\sum_{i=1}^{n} (\nu_A(x_i) - \overline{\nu_A})^2)^{0.5}(\sum_{i=1}^{n} (\nu_B(x_i) - \overline{\nu_B})^2)^{0.5}} \tag{8}$$

$$r_3(A, B) = \frac{\sum_{i=1}^{n} (\pi_A(x_i) - \overline{\pi_A})(\pi_B(x_i) - \overline{\pi_B})}{(\sum_{i=1}^{n} (\pi_A(x_i) - \overline{\pi_A})^2)^{0.5}(\sum_{i=1}^{n} (\pi_B(x_i) - \overline{\pi_B})^2)^{0.5}} \tag{9}$$

where: $\overline{\mu_A} = \frac{1}{n} \sum_{i=1}^{n} \mu_A(x_i)$, $\overline{\mu_B} = \frac{1}{n} \sum_{i=1}^{n} \mu_B(x_i)$, $\overline{\nu_A} = \frac{1}{n} \sum_{i=1}^{n} \nu_A(x_i)$,

$\overline{\nu_B} = \frac{1}{n} \sum_{i=1}^{n} \nu_B(x_i)$, $\overline{\pi_A} = \frac{1}{n} \sum_{i=1}^{n} \pi_A(x_i)$, $\overline{\pi_B} = \frac{1}{n} \sum_{i=1}^{n} \pi_B(x_i)$,

The proposed correlation coefficient (6) depends on two factors: the amount of information expressed by the membership and non-membership degrees (7)–(8), and the reliability of information expressed by the hesitation margins (9).

Remark: analogously as for the crisp and fuzzy data, $r_{A-IFS}(A, B)$ makes sense for A-IFS variables whose values vary. If, for instance, the temperature is constant and the amount of ice cream sold is the same, then it is impossible to conclude anything about their relationship (as, from the mathematical point of view, we avoid zero in the denominator).

The correlation coefficient $r_{A-IFS}(A, B)$ (6) fulfills the following properties:

1. $r_{A-IFS}(A, B) = r_{A-IFS}(B, A)$

2. If $A = B$ then $r_{A-IFS}(A, B) = 1$

3. $|r_{A-IFS}(A, B)| \leq 1$

The above properties are not only fulfilled by the correlation coefficient $r_{A-IFS}(A, B)$ (6) but also by all of its components (7)–(9).

Remark: It is should be emphasized that $r_{A-IFS}(A, B) = 1$ occurs not only for $A = B$ but also in the cases of a perfect linear correlation of the data (the same concerns each component (7)–(9)).

In Szmidt and Kacprzyk [35] there are examples showing that each component may play an important role when considering correlation between A-IFSs. On the other hand, (6) which aggregates (7)–(9)) plays an important role as a bird-eye-view revision of the correlation – in extreme cases, i.e., for the values: -1. 0, and 1 we have exact summarized information about the correlation. For other cases (6) suffers from the same drawbacks each aggregation measure does.

4 Principal Component Analysis for the A-IFS Data

Principal component analysis (PCA), i.e., the reduction of dimensionality of a data set in which there are lots of interrelated variables, is performed by transforming the source set of data to a new set of uncorrelated variables/features/attributes (the principal components PC) to summarize the features of the original data. Principal components (PCs) are ordered such that the k-th PC has the k-th largest variance among all PCs. The k-th PC points out the direction that maximizes the variation of the projections of the data points such that it is orthogonal to the first $(k - 1)$-th PCs. Traditionally, the first few PC are used in data analysis (they capture most of the variation in the original data set).

Principal component analysis (PCA) is one of the best known and widely used linear dimension reduction technique Jackson [8], Jolliffe [9], Marida et al. [12] in the sense of mean-square error. It is a well known procedure for crisp data (e.g. Jolliffe [10]) so that we will omit the formulas for that context, and will demonstrate the successive steps on an example expressed in terms of the A-IFSs.

The steps of PCA for crisp sets (Jolliffe [10], Jackson [8]) are:

– find the correlation matrix,
– find the eigenvectors and eigenvalues of the correlation matrix,
– rearrange the eigenvectors and eigenvalues in the order of decreasing eigenvalues,
– select a subset of the eigenvectors as the basis vectors,
– convert the source data into the new basis.

To demonstrate how PCA works, i.e. how the reduction of the dimensionality of a data set expressed in terms of the A-IFSs proceeds, we recall a well known example

Table 1. The "Saturday Morning" data in terms of the A-IFSs

No.	Attributes				Class
	Outlook	Humidity	Windy	Temperature	
1	$(0, 0.33, 0.67)$	$(0, 0.33, 0.67)$	$(0.2, 0, 0.8)$	$(0, 0.33, 0.67)$	N
2	$(0, 0.33, 0.67)$	$(0, 0.33, 0.67)$	$(0, 0.33, 0.67)$	$(0, 0.33, 0.67)$	N
3	$(1, 0, 0)$	$(0, 0.33, 0.67)$	$(0.2, 0, 0.8)$	$(0, 0.33, 0.67)$	P
4	$(0.2, 0.11, 0.69)$	$(0, 0.33, 0.67)$	$(0.2, 0, 0.8)$	$(0, 0, 1)$	P
5	$(0.2, 0.11, 0.69)$	$(0.6, 0, 0.4)$	$(0.2, 0, 0.8)$	$(0.4, 0.11, 0.49)$	P
6	$(0.2, 0.11, 0.69)$	$(0.6, 0, 0.4)$	$(0, 0.33, 0.67)$	$(0.4, 0.11, 0.49)$	N
7	$(1, 0, 0)$	$(0.6, 0, 0.4)$	$(0, 0.33, 0.67)$	$(0.4, 0.11, 0.49)$	P
8	$(0, 0.33, 0.67)$	$(0, 0.33, 0.67)$	$(0.2, 0, 0.8)$	$(0, 0, 1)$	N
9	$(0, 0.33, 0.67)$	$(0.6, 0, 0.4)$	$(0.2, 0, 0.8)$	$(0.4, 0.11, 0.49)$	P
10	$(0.2, 0.11, 0.69)$	$(0.6, 0, 0.4)$	$(0.2, 0, 0.8)$	$(0, 0, 1)$	P
11	$(0, 0.33, 0.67)$	$(0.6, 0, 0.4)$	$(0, 0.33, 0.67)$	$(0, 0, 1)$	P
12	$(1, 0, 0)$	$(0, 0.33, 0.67)$	$(0, 0.33, 0.67)$	$(0, 0, 1)$	P
13	$(1, 0, 0)$	$(0.6, 0, 0.4)$	$(0.2, 0, 0.8)$	$(0, 0.33, 0.67)$	P
14	$(0.2, 0.11, 0.69)$	$(0, 0.33, 0.67)$	$(0, 0.33, 0.67)$	$(0, 0, 1)$	N

considered by Quinlan [15]. The Quinlan's example, the so-called "Saturday Morning" example, considers the classification with nominal data. This example is small enough and illustrative, yet is a challenge to many classification and machine learning methods. The main idea of solving the example by Quinlan was to select the best attribute to split the training set (Quinlan used a so-called *Information Gain* which was a dual measure to Shannon's entropy). Quinlan obtained 100% accuracy, and the optimal solution (the minimal possible tree) involved three (of four) attributes.

We will verify if PCA gives satisfying results while considering the problem formulated by Quinlan [15] but expressed in terms of the A-IFSs.

The limitation of space does not let us discuss the Quinlan example [15] and its A-IFS counterpart (Table 1) in detail and we refer the reader to Szmidt and Kacprzyk [34]; we only present here the final results.

We begin by computing the correlation matrices (the components of which are calculated from (7)–(9)) between the attributes. The results are given in Tables 2–5. Although most of the correlation coefficients in Tables 2–5 are small in the absolute value, there are also nontrivial ones. In Table 2 it is correlation between Humidity and Temperature (0.63), the same in Table 4 (0.45), and Table 5 (0.4).

Having the correlation matrices, we calculate their eigenvectors and eigenvalues.

A property of the eigenvalue decomposition is that the total variation is equal to the sum of eigenvalues of the correlation matrix. The fraction of the first k eigenvalues gives the cumulative proportion of the variance explained by the first k PCs. In our example we have the following situation:

– Eigenvalues for the correlation matrix with respect to the membership values of the attributes considered (Table 2) are: 1.6, 1, 0.99, 0.36, so that the three first eigenvalues explain 91% [(1.6+1+0.99)/(1.6+1+0.99+0.36)=0.91] of the overall variation.

Table 2. Evaluation of the correlation components (7) (with respect to the membership values) of the "Saturday Morning" data

Attribute	Outlook	Humidity	Windy	Temperature
Outlook	1	0.03	-0.01	0.01
Humidity	0.03	1	0	0.63
Windy	-0.01	0	1	-0.1
Temperature	0.01	0.63	-0.1	1

Table 3. Evaluation of the correlation components (8) (with respect to the non-membership values) of the "Saturday Morning" data

Attribute	Outlook	Humidity	Windy	Temperature
Outlook	1	0.12	-0.07	0.01
Humidity	0.12	1	0	0.12
Windy	-0.07	0	1	-0.22
Temperature	0.01	0.12	-0.22	1

Table 4. Evaluation of the correlation components (9) (with respect to the hesitation margins) of the "Saturday Morning" data

Attribute	Outlook	Humidity	Windy	Temperature
Outlook	1	-0.005	0.09	0.015
Humidity	-0.005	1	0	0.45
Windy	0.09	0	1	-0.1
Temperature	0.15	0.45	-0.1	1

Table 5. Evaluation of the total correlation coefficients (6) of the "Saturday Morning" data

Attribute	Outlook	Humidity	Windy	Temperature
Outlook	1	0.05	-0.002	0.06
Humidity	0.05	1	0	0.4
Windy	-0.002	0	1	-0.14
Temperature	0.06	0.4	-0.14	1

– Eigenvalues for the correlation matrix with respect to the non-membership values of the attributes considered (Table 3) are: 1.28, 1.1, 0.93, 0.7, so the three first eigenvalues explain 83% of the overall variation.

– Eigenvalues for the correlation matrix with respect to the hesitation margins of the attributes considered (Table 4) are: 1.48, 1.1, 0.92, 0.51, so the three first eigenvalues explain 87% of the overall variation.

Finally, the eigenvalues for the aggregated correlation matrix (Table 5 – due to (6)) are: 1.4, 1, 0.98, 0.6, so that, again, the three first eigenvalues explain 85% of the overall variation.

Table 6. Principal components based on the correlation matrices with respect to the membership values, non-membership values, and the hesitation margins (counterparts of the first three eigenvalues) of the "Saturday Morning" data

Attribute	PCs "membership"			PCs "non-membership"			PCs "hesitation"		
	1	2	3	1	2	3	1	2	3
Outlook	0.1	0.7	-0.1	0.3	0.4	-0.6	0.2	0.7	-0.1
Humidity	0.7	0.1	0.7	-0.6	-0.6	-0.4	0.7	-0.1	0.7
Windy	0.7	0.1	0.67	0.7	-0.6	-0.4	0.6	-0.4	-0.7
Temperature	-0.02	0.7	-0.1	-0.3	0.4	-0.6	0.3	0.6	-0.2

To summarize, the first three eigenvalues explain most of variability of the data, and summarize the most important features of the data. The obtained result is consistent in a sense with the original result Quinlan gives [15] who has indicated that the optimal tree that classifies correctly all data consists of three attributes only which means that the data reduction is quite justified here.

The eigenvalues are obtained for the ordering of the eigenvectors of covariance matrices. The set of ordered eigenvectors of the covariance matrices point out the directions which characterize the data. The results indicate that we can only consider the first three eigenvectors. In Table 6 there are the three first eigenvectors of the correlation matrices with respect to the membership values, non-membership values, and hesitation margins (the values are rounded to the second place).

The final step, i.e., the "reduction" of the original data is obtained by multiplying the transposed eigenvectors by the transposed original data. In our case we multiply the 3×4 and 4×14 matrices. In this way we obtain a reduced description of the problem, in three instead of four dimensions. The procedure is repeated three times , for the membership and non-membership values, and the hesitation margins. Clearly, feature reduction makes sense for large problems (very many features) and then the reduction is usually considerable. Our example is just for illustration.

5   Conclusions

We presented a novel approach to principal component analysis (PCA) for data expressed by the A-IFSs, using all three terms describing A-IFSs, i.e. the degree of membership, non-membership and hesitation margin. Such a three-term representation has been shown in our previous works to be of utmost importance for the calculation of correlation coefficients in the case of A-IFSs. We hope that the new approach to PCA for A-IFS-type data can be important because, on the one hand, A-IFSs gain a wider and wider importance as a tool for data representation and processing in more and more areas. On the other hand, PCA is one of the most relevant techniques in data analysis, and it can considerably profit for an extension into a new type of data, expressed by the A-IFSs, hence making it possible to tackle more difficult real world problems.

Acknowledgment. Partially supported by the Ministry of Science and Higher Education Grant Nr N N519 384936.

References

1. Atanassov, K.: Intuitionistic Fuzzy Sets. VII ITKR Session. Sofia (Centr. Sci.-Techn. Libr. of Bulg. Acad. of Sci. 1697/1984) (1983) (in Bulgarian)
2. Atanassov, K.: Intuitionistic Fuzzy Sets: Theory and Applications. Springer (1999)
3. Bustince, H., Mohedano, V., Barrenechea, E., Pagola, M.: An algorithm for calculating the threshold of an image representing uncertainty through A-IFSs. In: IPMU 2006, pp. 2383–2390 (2006)
4. Bustince, H., Mohedano, V., Barrenechea, E., Pagola, M.: Image thresholding using intuitionistic fuzzy sets. In: Atanassov, K., Kacprzyk, J., Krawczak, M. (eds.) Issues in the Representation and Processing of Uncertain and Imprecise Information. Fuzzy Sets, Intuitionistic Fuzzy Sets, Generalized Nets, and Related Topics. EXIT, Warsaw (2005)
5. Chiang, D.-A., Lin, N.P.: Correlation of fuzzy sets. Fuzzy Sets and Systems 102, 221–226 (1999)
6. Ding, C., He, X.: K-means Clustering via Principal Component Analysis. In: Proc. 21st Int. Conf. Machine Learning, Banff, Canada, pp. 21–30 (2004)
7. Fang, Y.-C., Tzeng, Y.-F., Li, S.-X.: A Taguchi PCA fuzzy-based approach for the multiobjective extended optimization of a miniature optical engine. Journal of Physics D: Applied Physics 41(17), 175–188 (2008)
8. Jackson, J.E.: A User's Guide to Principal Components. John Wiley and Sons, New York (1991)
9. Jolliffe, I.T.: Principal Component Analysis. Springer (1986)
10. Jolliffe, I.T.: Principal Component Analysis, 2nd edn. Springer (2002)
11. Xia, L., Zhao, C.: The application of PCA-fuzzy probability analysis on risk evaluation of construction schedule of highway. In: IEEE 2010 Int. Conf. on Logistics Systems and Intelligent Management, pp. 1230–1234 (2010)
12. Mardia, K.V., Kent, J.T., Bibby, J.M.: Multivariate Analysis. In: Probability and Mathematical Statistics. Academic Press (1995)
13. Pearson, K.: On lines and planes of closest fit to systems of points in space. Phil. Mag. 6(2), 559–572 (1901)
14. Rodgers, J.L., Nicewander, W.A.: Thirteen Ways to Look at the Correlation Coefficient. The American Statistician 42(1), 59–66 (1988)
15. Quinlan, J.R.: Induction of decision trees. Machine Learning 1, 81–106 (1986)
16. Sebzalli, Y.M., Wang, X.Z.: Knowledge discovery fromprocess operational data using PCA and fuzzy clustering. Engineering Applications of Artifcial Intelligence 14, 607–616 (2001)
17. Szmidt, E., Kacprzyk, J.: Remarks on some applications of intuitionistic fuzzy sets in decision making. Notes on IFS 2(3), 22–31 (1996c)
18. Szmidt, E., Kacprzyk, J.: On measuring distances between intuitionistic fuzzy sets. Notes on IFS 3(4), 1–13 (1997)
19. Szmidt, E., Kacprzyk, J.: Group Decision Making under Intuitionistic Fuzzy Preference Relations. In: IPMU 1998, pp. 172–178 (1998)
20. Szmidt, E., Kacprzyk, J.: Distances between intuitionistic fuzzy sets. Fuzzy Sets and Systems 114(3), 505–518 (2000)
21. Szmidt, E., Kacprzyk, J.: On Measures on Consensus Under Intuitionistic Fuzzy Relations. In: IPMU 2000, pp. 1454–1461 (2000)
22. Szmidt, E., Kacprzyk, J.: Entropy for intuitionistic fuzzy sets. Fuzzy Sets and Systems 118(3), 467–477 (2001)
23. Szmidt, E., Kacprzyk, J.: Analysis of Consensus under Intuitionistic Fuzzy Preferences. In: Proc. Int. Conf. in Fuzzy Logic and Technology, pp. 79–82. De Montfort Univ. Leicester, UK (2001)

24. Szmidt, E., Kacprzyk, J.: Analysis of Agreement in a Group of Experts via Distances Between Intuitionistic Fuzzy Preferences. In: Proc. 9th Int. Conf. IPMU 2002, pp. 1859–1865 (2002a)
25. Szmidt, E., Kacprzyk, J.: An Intuitionistic Fuzzy Set Based Approach to Intelligent Data Analysis (an application to medical diagnosis). In: Abraham, A., Jain, L., Kacprzyk, J. (eds.) Recent Advances in Intelligent Paradigms and Applications, pp. 57–70. Springer (2002b)
26. Szmidt, E., Kacprzyk, J.: An Intuitionistic Fuzzy Set Based Approach to Intelligent Data Analysis (an application to medical diagnosis). In: Abraham, A., Jain, L., Kacprzyk, J. (eds.) Recent Advances in Intelligent Paradigms and Applications, pp. 57–70. Springer (2002c)
27. Szmidt, E., Kacprzyk, J.: Distances Between Intuitionistic Fuzzy Sets: Straight forward Approaches may not work. In: IEEE IS 2006, pp. 716–721 (2006)
28. Szmidt, E., Kacprzyk, J.: An Application of Intuitionistic Fuzzy Set Similarity Measures to a Multi-criteria Decision Making Problem. In: Rutkowski, L., Tadeusiewicz, R., Zadeh, L.A., Żurada, J.M. (eds.) ICAISC 2006. LNCS (LNAI), vol. 4029, pp. 314–323. Springer, Heidelberg (2006)
29. Szmidt, E., Kacprzyk, J.: Some Problems with Entropy Measures for the Atanassov Intuitionistic Fuzzy Sets. In: Masulli, F., Mitra, S., Pasi, G. (eds.) WILF 2007. LNCS (LNAI), vol. 4578, pp. 291–297. Springer, Heidelberg (2007)
30. Szmidt, E., Kacprzyk, J.: A New Similarity Measure for Intuitionistic Fuzzy Sets: Straight forward Approaches may not work. In: 2007 IEEE Conf. on Fuzzy Systems, pp. 481–486 (2007a)
31. Szmidt, E., Kacprzyk, J.: A new approach to ranking alternatives expressed via intuitionistic fuzzy sets. In: Ruan, D., et al. (eds.) Computational Intelligence in Decision and Control, pp. 265–270. World Scientific (2008)
32. Szmidt, E., Kacprzyk, J.: Amount of Information and Its Reliability in the Ranking of Atanassov's Intuitionistic Fuzzy Alternatives. In: Rakus-Andersson, E., Yager, R.R., Ichalkaranje, N., Jain, L.C. (eds.) Recent Advances in Decision Making. SCI, vol. 222, pp. 7–19. Springer, Heidelberg (2009)
33. Szmidt, E., Kacprzyk, J.: Ranking of Intuitionistic Fuzzy Alternatives in a Multi-criteria Decision Making Problem. In: Proceedings of the Conference: NAFIPS 2009, Cincinnati, USA, June 14-17. IEEE (2009) ISBN: 978-1-4244-4577-6
34. Szmidt, E., Kacprzyk, J.: Dealing with typical values via Atanassov's intuitionistic fuzzy sets. Int. J. of General Systems 39(5), 489–506 (2010)
35. Szmidt, E., Kacprzyk, J.: Correlation of Intuitionistic Fuzzy Sets. In: Hüllermeier, E., Kruse, R., Hoffmann, F. (eds.) IPMU 2010. LNCS(LNAI), vol. 6178, pp. 169–177. Springer, Heidelberg (2010)
36. Szmidt, E., Kukier, M.: Classification of Imbalanced and Overlapping Classes using Intuitionistic Fuzzy Sets. In: IEEE IS 2006, London, pp. 722–727 (2006)
37. Szmidt, E., Kukier, M.: A new approach to classification of imbalanced classes via Atanassov's intuitionistic fuzzy sets. In: Wang, H.-F. (ed.) Intelligent Data Analysis: Developing New Methodologies Through Pattern Discovery and Recovery, pp. 65–102. Idea Group (2008)
38. Szmidt, E., Kukier, M.: Atanassov's intuitionistic fuzzy sets in classification of imbalanced and overlapping classes. In: Chountas, P., Petrounias, I., Kacprzyk, J. (eds.) Intelligent Techniques and Tools for Novel System Architectures. SCI, vol. 109, pp. 455–471. Springer, Heidelberg (2008)
39. Zadeh, L.A.: Fuzzy sets. Information and Control 8, 338–353 (1965)

RFID Data Monitoring and Cleaning Using Tensor Calculus

Roberto De Virgilio and Franco Milicchio

Università Roma Tre, Rome, Italy
{dvr,milicchio}@dia.uniroma3.it

Abstract. In current trends of supply chains governance, RFID is a promising infrastructure-less technology. Nevertheless the unreliability of RFID data streams and the relevant amount of generated data in a supply chain pose significant challenges of monitoring and cleaning (i.e. to be processed on the fly). Current approaches provide hard-coded solutions, with high consumption of resources; moreover, these exhibit very limited flexibility dealing with multidimensional queries, at various levels of granularity and complexity.

In this paper we propose a general model for RFID data monitoring and cleaning based on the first principles of linear algebra, in particular on *tensorial calculus*. Leveraging our abstract algebraic framework, our technique allows quick decentralized on-line processing and logic analysis, according to needs and requirements of supply chain actors. Experimental results show how our approach can process analysis and maintenance of RFID data efficiently.

1 Introduction

In supply chain management, Radio-Frequency IDentification (RFID) is a promising infrastructure-less technology. One of the primary factors limiting the widespread adoption of RFID technology is the unreliability of the data streams produced by RFID readers. In particular, since such data are generated in high volume, significant error rates are introduced making RFID data streams useless for the purpose of higher-level applications. In this manuscript, we address the challenging problem of efficiently *monitoring* and *cleaning* large amount of raw data streams (*e.g.*, tera-data per day), generated by RFID applications (cf. [1,2,3], and [4]), focusing on stay records as the basic block to compress and store RFID data. We refer to *monitoring query* as real-time analysis on a supply chain that should monitor the correct traversing of products (*e.g.* if the transport of products has an unexpected delay, or any property exceeds a threshold value). Such analysis allows to detect error rates and to clean RFID readings, consequently. Usually state-of-the-art approaches introduce RFID *middleware systems* (*e.g.* [5] and [6]) between the readers and the logical application(s) in order to correct and clean RFID readings before processing business analysis. All of these approaches present limited flexibility dealing multidimensional queries at varying levels of granularity and complexity. To exploit the compression mechanism,

S. Greco et al. (Eds.): IPMU 2012, Part II, CCIS 298, pp. 539–549, 2012.
© Springer-Verlag Berlin Heidelberg 2012

such proposals have to fix the dimensions of analysis in advance and implement *ad-hoc* data structures to be maintained. It is not known in advance whether objects are sorted and grouped, and therefore, it is problematic to support different kinds of high-level queries efficiently. Moreover monitoring, cleaning and business analysis are distinct phases implemented in heterogeneous environments.

In this paper we propose a novel approach based on first principles derived from the linear algebra field. Matrix operations are invaluable tools in several fields, from engineering and design, graph theory, or networking. Standard matrix approaches focus on a standard two-dimension space, while we extend the applicability of such techniques with the more general definition of *tensors*, a generalization of linear forms, usually represented by matrices. We may therefore take advantage of the vast literature, both theoretic and applied, regarding tensor calculus. Our manuscript is organized as follows. In section 2 we will briefly recall the available literature. The general supply chain model, accompanied by a formal tensorial representation is supplied in Section 3, subsequently put into practice in Section 4. In Section 5 we benchmark our approach with several test beds. Finally, Section 6 sketches conclusion and future work.

2   Related Work

In a real scenario, great lapse and huge amounts of data are generated. There exists two main approaches to the management of RFID data. The former is based on processing data streams at run-time (cf. [2,5,6], and [7]). In the latter, the processing is performed off-line, once RFID data are aggregated, compressed and stored. For additional information, we refer the reader to [3] and [4]. If we consider RFID data as a stream, the main issues are event processing and data cleaning. Wang et al. have proposed a conceptualization of RFID events based on an extension of the ER model [7]. Based on such conceptual model, data streams are analyzed with respect to temporal aspects. Bai et al. have studied the limitations of using SQL to detect temporal events and have presented an SQL-like language to query such events in an efficient way [2]. The inaccuracy of RFID tags readings causes irregularities in the processing of data. Jeffery (cf. [5] and [6]) has proposed a general technique for the cleaning of data stream based on the definition of time and space metrics. This technique is improved and enriched using an adaptive filter called SMURF. Bai et al. [8] exploits a noise threshold to read noise readings with count of distinct tag EPC values below that threshold. Such approach preserves the original order of the readings and filter the duplicates but does not give the cleaning method for false negative reading. Moreover it does not mention how to confirm the threshold. Finally, Lee et al. have proposed an effective path encoding approach to represent the data flow representing the movements of products [4]. In a path, a prime number is assigned to each node and a path is encoded as the product of the number associated with nodes. Mathematical properties of prime numbers guarantee the efficient access to paths. A major limitation of the majority of these approaches have to fix the dimensions of analysis in advance to exploit *ad-hoc* data structures to be maintained. It follows that, in many application scenario the compression loses its effectiveness and the size of tables does not be reduced significantly.

3   RFID Data Modeling

This section is devoted to the definition of a general model capable of representing all aspects of a given supply chain.

3.1   A General Model

Let us define the set $\mathcal{E}$ as the set of all EPCs, with $\mathcal{E}$ being finite. A *property* of an EPC is defined as an application $\pi : \mathcal{E} \rightarrow \Pi$, where Π represents a suitable property codomain. Therefore, we define the application of a property $\pi(e) := \langle \pi, e \rangle$; a property is a surjective mapping between an EPC and its corresponding property value. A *supply chain* $\mathcal{S}$ is defined as the product set of all EPCs, and all the associated properties. Formally, let us introduce the family of properties π_i, $i = 1, \ldots, k + d < \infty$, and their corresponding sets Π_i:

$$\mathcal{S} = \mathcal{E} \times \Pi_1 \times \ldots \times \Pi_{k-1} \times \Pi_k \times \ldots \times \Pi_{k+d} . \tag{1}$$

The reader should notice as we divided explicitly the first k spaces $\mathcal{E}, \Pi_1, \ldots, \Pi_{k-1}$, from the remaining ones. As a matter of fact, properties may be split into two different categories: *countable* and *uncountable* ones. Such distinction will be described, and hence utilized, in Section 3.3. By definition, a set A is *countable* if there exists a function $f : A \rightarrow \mathbb{N}$, with f being injective; for example, every subset of natural numbers $U \subseteq \mathbb{N}$ is countable (possibly infinite), and relative and rational sets, $\mathbb{Z}$ and $\mathbb{Q}$, respectively, are countable (while $\mathbb{R}$ is uncountable).

3.2   Properties

In the following we will model some codomains Π and their associated features.

Location. Let us briefly model the *location* associated to an EPC.
Definition 1 (Location) *Let $\mathcal{L}$ be the set of ordered tuples $\ell := (\ell_1, \ell_2, \ell_3)$, with $\ell_1, \ell_2, \ell_3 \in \mathbb{R}$. We name $\mathcal{L}$ as* location set, *ℓ_1, ℓ_2 and ℓ_3 as* location coordinates.

A commonly employed coordinate system is the GPS location, *i.e.*, latitude and longitude, with an additional altitude coordinate. Other representations prefer to employ a simple mapping between locations and a subset of natural numbers, representing the *location identifier*. Which representation is more suitable to an application, is a matter of choice with respect to the domain of the problem, and therefore beyond the scope of this manuscript.

Time. In order to model a temporal interval relative to a product (EPC), we resort to an ordered couple of elements from the ring of real numbers. This suffices to specify the *entry* and *exit* time of a product from a given location.

Definition 2 (Time) *Let $\mathcal{T}$ be the set of ordered couples $\tau := (t_i, t_o)$, with $t_i, t_o \in \mathbb{R}$, and that are the* incoming *and* outcoming *timestamps, respectively.*

We highlight the fact that time spaces need not to be modeled as real numbers: in fact, subsets of $\mathbb{R}$ such as natural numbers, may also be suitable within a particular context, *e.g.*, employing UNIX timestamps. However, our model aims at generality, and therefore the real ring is the most appropriate choice, being the natural numbers set a proper subset of the real numbers ring.

Definition 3 (Inner sum) *Let us define the* inner sum *of two time elements* $\tau_1 = (t_i^1, t_o^1)$, $\tau_2 = (t_i^2, t_o^2)$ *as the operator* $\oplus : \mathcal{T} \times \mathcal{T} \to \mathcal{T}$:

$$\tau_1 \oplus \tau_2 := \big(\min(t_i^1, t_i^2), \max(t_o^1, t_o^2) \big) \ .$$

Such operation allows us to rigorously model the "addition of products", as in a product assembly line: a paint bucket, for instance, is the addition of the metallic container and liquid dye, hence the above definition of time summation.

Definition 4 (Lifetime) *We define as* lifetime *the linear form* $\lambda : \mathcal{T} \to \mathbb{R}$
$$\langle \lambda, \tau \rangle := t_o - t_i, \quad \tau = (t_i, t_o) \in \mathcal{T} \ .$$
Due to the linearity, we are allowed to construct equivalence classes in $\mathcal{T}$ as $[\tilde{\tau}] := \{\tau \in \mathcal{T} : \langle \lambda, \tau \rangle = \langle \lambda, \tilde{\tau} \rangle\}$. The *canonical representative* elements of the above equivalence classes are defined as $(0, t_o)$, with $t_o \in \mathbb{R}$.

Definition 5 (Admissible time) *Given a time element* $\tau \in \mathcal{T}$, *we say that* $\tau = (t_i, t_o)$ *is* admissible *iff* $\langle \lambda, \tau \rangle > 0$, *with* $t_i, t_o > 0$

3.3   Tensorial Representation

Let us now introduce a formal *tensorial framework* capable of grasping all properties related to a supply chain, as proposed in Section 3.1. As previously outlined, we divide properties into two categories, *countable* and *uncountable* spaces. This separation allows us to represent countable spaces with natural numbers, therefore mapping their product space to $\mathbb{N}^k$, while leaving the product space of all uncountable properties into a collective space $\mathbb{U}$:

$$\mathcal{S} = \underbrace{\mathcal{E} \times \Pi_1 \times \ldots \times \Pi_{k-1}}_{\mathbb{N}^k} \times \underbrace{\Pi_k \times \ldots \times \Pi_{k+d}}_{\mathbb{U}} \ . \tag{2}$$

Such mapping will introduce a family of injective functions called *indexes*:

$$\mathrm{idx}_i : \Pi_i \longrightarrow \mathbb{N}, \qquad i = 1, \ldots, k-1 \ . \tag{3}$$

When considering the set $\mathcal{E}$, we additionally define a supplemental index, the *EPC index function* $\mathrm{idx}_0 : \mathcal{E} \to \mathbb{N}$, consequently completing the map of all countable sets of a supply chain $\mathcal{S}$ to natural numbers. Therefore we have:

Definition 6 (Tensorial Representation) *The* tensorial representation *of a supply chain* $\mathcal{S}$, *as introduced in equation* (1), *with countability mapping as in* (2) *is a multilinear form*

$$\Sigma : \mathbb{N}^k \longrightarrow \mathbb{U} \ . \tag{4}$$

A supply chain can be therefore rigorously denoted as a rank-k tensor with values in $\mathbb{U}$, mapping countable to uncountable product space.

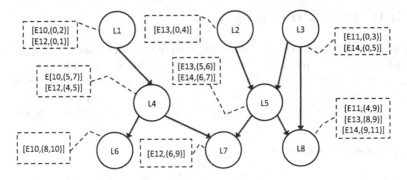

Fig. 1. An example supply chain represented by a directed graph. Callouts represent lists of tuple constituted by an EPC with the associated time (t_i, t_o).

3.4 Implementation

Our treatment is general, representing a supply chain with a tensor, *i.e.*, with a multidimensional matrix. A matrix-based representation need not to be *complete*. Supply chain rarely exhibit completion: practical evidence [9] suggests that products, identified by their EPC, for example, seldom present themselves in every location. The same consideration applies also to other properties, in particular, to countable properties. As a consequence, we are considering sparse matrices [10], *i.e.*, storing only non-zero elements.

Notation. A sparse matrix may be indicated with different notations (cf. [10] and [11]), however, for simplicity's sake, we adopt the *tuple notation*. This particular notation declares the components of a tensor $M_{i_1 i_2 \ldots i_k}(\mathbb{U})$ in the form $\mathcal{M} = \left\{ \{i_1 i_2 \ldots i_k\} \to u \neq 0 \,, u \in \mathbb{U} \right\}$, where we implicitly intended $u \neq 0 \equiv 0_{\mathbb{U}}$. For instance, consider a vector $\delta_4 \in \mathbb{R}^5$: its sparse representation will be therefore constituted by a single tuple of one component with value 1, *i.e.*, $\{ \{4\} \to 1 \}$.

Example 1. Let us consider the supply chain pictured in Fig. 1, described tensorially by $\Sigma : \mathbb{N}^2 \to \mathcal{T}$, whose representative matrix is as follows:

$$\begin{pmatrix} (0,2) & \cdot & \cdot & (5,7) & \cdot & (8,10) & \cdot & \cdot \\ \cdot & \cdot & (0,3) & \cdot & \cdot & \cdot & \cdot & (4,9) \\ (0,1) & \cdot & \cdot & (4,5) & \cdot & \cdot & (6,9) & \cdot \\ \cdot & (0,4) & \cdot & \cdot & (5,6) & \cdot & \cdot & (8,9) \\ \cdot & \cdot & (0,5) & \cdot & (6,7) & \cdot & \cdot & (9,11) \end{pmatrix}$$

where, for typographical simplicity, we omitted $0_{\mathcal{T}} = (0,0)$, denoted with a dot. We outline the fact that Σ is a rank-2 tensor with dimensions 5, 8. Hence:

$$\mathcal{E} = \{E10, E11, E12, E13, E14\} \,, \Pi_1 = \{L1, L2, L3, L4, L5, L6, L7, L8\} \,.$$

where $\mathrm{idx}_0(E10) = 1, \ldots, \mathrm{idx}_0(E14) = 5$, and $\mathrm{idx}_1(L1) = 1, \ldots, \mathrm{idx}_1(L8) = 8$. In the sparse representation we have $\{\{1,1\} \to (0,2), \ldots, \{5,8\} \to (9,11)\}$.

4   RFID Data Processing

This section is devoted to apply our conceptual method for analyzing RFID data. Referring to the example in Section 3, in the following we simplify our notation, employing two countable sets, EPC $\mathcal{E}$ and location $\mathcal{L}$ indexes, in that order, and the uncountable time set $\mathcal{T}$, *i.e.*, a matrix M_{ij}: i refers to EPCs, and j is the index of locations. We have no limitations on the generality of our approach.

4.1   Monitoring Queries

Real-time analysis on a supply chain should monitor the correct traversing of products. We would control if RFID readers are producing incorrect data, *e.g.*, $t_i > t_o$, or if the transport of products has an unexpected delay, or any property exceeds a threshold value. We call such analysis a *monitoring query*.

Tracking Query. A *tracking query* finds the movement history for a given tag identifier $e \in \mathcal{E}$. We can comfortably perform the query efficiently, using the model described in Section 3, by applying the tensor application. Therefore, given $i = \text{idx}(e)$, we build a Kroneker vector as a vector δ_i, with $|\delta_i| = |\mathcal{E}|$, and finally apply of the rank-2 tensor represented by M_{ij} to δ_i, *i.e.*: $r = M_{ij}\delta_i$. For instance, referring to the example pictured in Fig. 1, let us consider the tag $E13$, we have $i = \text{idx}(E13) = 4$, and therefore our vector will be $\delta_4 = \{\{4\} \rightarrow 1\}$. Consequently, the resulting vector will be $r = M_{ij}\delta_4 = \{2\} \rightarrow (0,4), \{5\} \rightarrow (5,6), \{8\} \rightarrow (8,9)\}$, or in another notation, $L2 \rightarrow L5 \rightarrow L8$.

Lifetime Admissibility. First of all, we introduce the *admissibility test*, selecting all EPCs whose time is not admissible (cf. Definition 5 in Section 3): $\text{map}(\langle \lambda, \cdot \rangle < 0, M_{ij})$. The reader should notice a shorthand notation for an implicit boolean function: as for all descendant of the C programming language, such definition yields 1 if the condition is met, *i.e.*, the time associated to an element of the tensor is not valid, 0 otherwise. For instance, let us suppose the triples $tpl_1 : (E15, L3, 3)$ and $tpl_2 : (E15, L3, 2)$ where tpl_1 is generated before than tpl_2. The compression will result $(E15, L3, 3, 2)$ that does not satisfy the admissibility test (*i.e.* an error will be detected instantly).

Delay. The *delay test* chooses all EPCs whose time surpasses an expected interval. In our framework, given two times τ_1 and τ_2, *i.e.* the bounds of the interval, we would return all EPCs whose time τ excesses the inner sum $\tau_3 = \tau_1 \oplus \tau_2$ (cf. Definition 3 in Section 3): $\text{map}((t_i(\cdot) > t_i(\tau_3)) \wedge (t_o(\cdot) < t_o(\tau_3)), M_{ij})$. As an example, let us consider $\tau_1 = (7,8)$ and $\tau_2 = (9,10)$, and hence $\tau_3 = \tau_1 \oplus \tau_2 = (7,10)$: in this case the delay test will return $E13$. In the same way, it is straightforward to extend similar analysis on other properties of a product.

Last Location. We may introduce the *last location* query, which shows, for a given EPC with index value i, the last known location. This is comfortably formalized in our framework as $\max_{t_i}(M_{ij}\delta_i)$, that is we select the location with the maximum value of t_i for the given EPC (*e.g.* for $E13$ we have $L8$).

Common Location. Additionally, we may supervise some properties regarding diverse locations or EPCs. We mention in passing a *common test*, that given two locations $L1$ and $L2$, finds all the common EPCs: given $j = \text{idx}(L1)$ and

$k = \text{idx}(L2)$, the result is given by $M_{ij}\delta_j \circ M_{ik}\delta_k$. As an example, let us consider $L4$ and $L6$ as in Fig. 1, with indexes 4 and 6, respectively. The common EPCs are therefore given by $M_{ij}\delta_4 \circ M_{ij}\delta_6$, hence $\{\{1\} \to (5,7), \{3\} \to (4,5)\} \circ \{\{1\} \to (8,10)\}$, which selects only $E10$ with index 1.

4.2   Error Detection Queries

Detecting errors is a major objective of RFID data monitoring. We may easily spot in the previous paragraph a simple error detection query in the admissibility test. Such examination, in fact, shows all readings that yield an incorrect lifespan, *e.g.*, a reading where an EPC has moved outside a location before entering in it.

General Admissibility. It is straightforward to generalize the *admissibility test* for any given EPC property. Let us substitute the lifetime pairing $\langle \lambda, \cdot \rangle$ with a suitable given function $\langle \text{threshold} : \mathbb{U} \times \mathbb{R}^k \longrightarrow \mathbb{R} \rangle$, where $\mathbb{R}^k$ allows the definition of complex spaces and conditions, *e.g.*, $\mathbb{R}^2$.

Path Consistency. Path-focused errors are more arduous to be detected. A *path consistency* query recognizes, for a given EPC, if the followed path is consistent with timings, *i.e.*, if it accesses a location prior to departing the previous one. Let us introduce the path-consistency function $\mathcal{P}$ defined as $\mathcal{P} : \mathcal{T} \times \mathcal{T} \longrightarrow \mathbb{R}$, that yields an invalid time value if two successive times $\tau_1, \tau_2 \in \mathcal{T}$ are not consistent as previously stated. Formalizing the definition, we have

$$\mathcal{P}(\,(t_i, t_o)^1, (t_i, t_o)^2\,) = \begin{cases} (t_i, t_o)^1, & t_o^1 \leq t_i^2\,, \\ (-\infty, +\infty), & \text{otherwise}\,. \end{cases} \tag{5}$$

For example, let us show a valid time comparison, *e.g.*, $\mathcal{P}(\,(1,5), (6,10)\,) = (1,5)$. The purpose of such definition will be clear in the following paragraph. Hence, given $i = \text{idx}(e)$, being $e \in \mathcal{E}$ the elected EPC, in order to control whether e followed a consistent path, let us find all the relative locations *sorted* by their incoming timestamp t_i: $\text{sort}_{t_i}(M_{ij}\delta_i)$. Therefore, by successive application of the $\mathcal{P}$ function on the preceding result, itself being a sparse matrix, we attain the objective of detecting path inconsistency. We underline the fact that $\mathcal{P}$ is an *associative* function, without the commutativity property. The result will consequently be obtained by *folding* the function $\mathcal{P}$ on the sorted sparse partial solution followed by the time $\tau_\infty = (+\infty, -\infty)$:

$$\text{fold}\left(\,\mathcal{P}, \text{sort}_{t_i}(M_{ij}\delta_i) \cup \{(+\infty, -\infty)\}\,\right)\,. \tag{6}$$

The *fold* or *accumulation* is a higher-order function that, given a function and a (non empty) list, recursively iterates over the list elements, applying the input function to each element and the preceding partial result; a comprehensive formalization of folding is beyond the scope of this manuscript, being such function a cornerstone of functional programming; for more information we refer the reader to [12] and [13]. Consequently, given Equation (6), the folding proceeds:

$$\mathcal{P}((t_i, t_o)_1\,, \mathcal{P}((t_i, t_o)_2\,, \ldots, \mathcal{P}((t_i, t_o)_n\,, (+\infty, -\infty))\ldots)))\,.$$

The above computation is advantageously visualized as a *computation binary tree*, where leaves contain a list element, and intermediate nodes indicate the folded function:

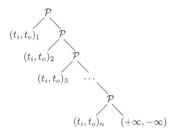

In order to illustrate the *path consistency* query, we should focus on EPC $E13$ from the example pictured in Fig. 1. The result of the sort on S is $S := \{\{2\} \rightarrow (0,4), \{5\} \rightarrow (5,6), \{8\} \rightarrow (8,9)\}$. Finally, we need to apply recursively $\mathcal{P}$ to $\mathcal{S}$ via *folding*:

$$\text{fold}(\mathcal{P}, S) = \mathcal{P}((0,4), \mathcal{P}((5,6), \mathcal{P}((8,9), (+\infty, -\infty)))) = \mathcal{P}((0,4), \mathcal{P}((5,6), (8,9)))$$
$$= \mathcal{P}((0,4), (5,6)) = (0,4) \,.$$

Let us consider now an invalid path $\widetilde{S}$, where $E13$ enters location 8 with timestamp 5, *i.e.*, $\{8\} \rightarrow (5,9)$. The computation will therefore yield an invalid value:

$$\text{fold}(\mathcal{P}, \widetilde{S}) = \mathcal{P}((0,4), \mathcal{P}((5,6), \mathcal{P}((5,9), (+\infty, -\infty)))) = \mathcal{P}((0,4), \mathcal{P}((5,6), (5,9)))$$
$$= \mathcal{P}((0,4), (-\infty, +\infty)) = (-\infty, +\infty) \,.$$

4.3 Cleaning Queries

In our framework cleaning queries can be considered as *insertion* and *deletion* operations on the matrix. This allows us not only to express EPCs and their properties within a theoretically sound mathematical model, but also to implicitly discarding duplicate records from diverse RFID readers. Moreover, by making use of tensor representations, we exploit the underlying computational capabilities of modern processors, natively designed for integer and floating point operations. In order to eliminate duplicates, and removing erroneous data, *e.g.*, inconsistent paths, insertion and deletion queries are pivotal functions that must be implemented. As a matter of fact, in our computational framework these procedures are reflected by *assigning values* in a given tensor. Removing a value is comfortably implemented by assigning the null value to an element, *i.e.*, $M_{ij} = 0_{\mathcal{T}}$, when referring to our example (cf. Fig. 1), and analogously, inserting or modifying a value is attained via a simple operation $M_{ij} = (t_i, t_o)$. Hence when a stream (e, l, t) is generated if e does not exist in l, we insert a new record (e, l, t, t), *i.e.* a *basic insertion*, otherwise, we update the t_o value of e in l with t, *i.e.* an *update*.

5   Experiments

We performed a series of experiments aimed at evaluating the performance of our approach (denoted as T), reporting the main results in the present section.

Table 1. Test queries for decentralized query execution

Q1/Q6	EPC = 17281	Q5	L_1 = L16 and L_2 = L628
Q2	map($\langle t_o, \cdot \rangle < 320, M_{ij}$)	Q7	*basic insertion*
Q3	$\tau_1 = (0, 5)$ and $\tau_2 = (4, 10)$	Q8	*update*
Q4	*last*(17281)	Q9	*delete*

Environment. Our benchmarking system is a dual core 2.66 GHz Intel with 2 GB of main memory running on Linux, where we implemented our framework as a Java application and linked to the Mathematica 8.0 computational environment. Our results have been tested against a generated synthetic RFID data in terms of raw data to compress in stay records, and considering products moving together in small groups or individually. Such behavior was called *IData* in [4]: data production followed the same guidelines on a supply chain of 100 locations and 8 levels. The simulation considers 100 raw data arriving per second to compress into our system. As discussed in Section 4: we insert (update), monitor and delete (clean) the readings, sequentially. We obtain five compressed datasets: 10^5, $5 \cdot 10^5$, 10^6, $5 \cdot 10^6$, and 10^7 stay records.

Results. Performances have been measured with respect to data loading and querying. Referring to the former, the main advantage of our approach is that we are able to perform loading without any particular relational schema, such as in [4], where a schema coupled with appropriate indexes have to be maintained by the system. In this case loading execution times are 0.9, 11, and 113 seconds, for sets of 10^5, 10^6, and 10^7 stay records, respectively. Another significant advantage of T relies in memory consumption: we need 13, 184, and 1450 MB to import the above mentioned sets; as a side-note, we highlight the fact that the 10^7 set required a division in smaller blocks, *e.g.*, 10^6, due to the limited memory at disposal. With respect to query execution, T presents a similar behavior and advantages, for both time and memory consumption. We performed *cold-cache* experiments, *i.e.*, dropping all file-system caches before restarting the systems and running the queries, and repeated all the tests three times, reporting the average execution time. As shown in Table 1, we formulated 9 queries to test the system. In brief, Q1/Q6 is a tracking/path consistency query, Q2 and Q3 are delay and admissibility tests, respectively, Q4 performs the last location, Q5 the common test, Q7 a basic insertion, Q8 an update and Q9 a deletion. All these queries were executed as the generation of synthetic data was running. In other words, using the same supply chain of the massive analysis, at periodic times we executed the queries on the data generated so far. Fig. 2.(a) shows the average query performance times in microseconds (μs) -logarithmic scale- for each query with respect to 10^5, 10^6 and 10^7 stay records. T executes such queries as tensor applications: the monitoring queries (*i.e.* Q1-Q5) has to traverse the sparse matrix, location-by-location, while the path consistency query (*i.e.* Q6) has to traverse the matrix for each EPC, that is the most complex operation. The most trivial operations are the cleaning (*i.e.* Q7-Q9). On average, T performs in the range $[0.006, 87]$ *msec*. Also in this case, another strong point of T is a very low consumption of memory, due to the *sparse matrix* representation of tensors and vectors. Fig. 2.(b) illustrates the main memory consumption of each query with respect to 10^5, 10^6, and 10^7 stay records. On the average, the queries require very few bytes of memory for any dataset, *i.e.* few KBytes. Results demonstrate how our approach can be used in a wide range of applications (e.g. also devices with limited calculus resources may process large amount of data efficiently).

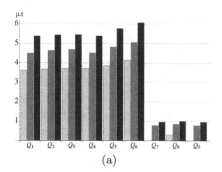
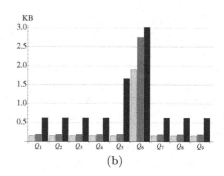

Fig. 2. (a) Query performances in microseconds (logarithmic scale) and (b) Main memory consumption in kilobytes for each query: black bars refer to 10^5, dark gray to 10^6, and light gray to 10^7 data size.

6   Conclusion and Future Work

We have presented an abstract algebraic framework for the efficient and effective analysis of RFID data in supply chain management. Our approach leverages tensorial calculus, proposing a general model that exhibits a great flexibility with multidimensional queries, at diverse granularity and complexity levels. Experimental results proved our method efficient, yielding the requested outcomes in memory constrained architectures. For future developments we are investigating massive centralized business logic analysis and the introduction of reasoning capabilities, along with a deployment in highly distributed Grid environments.

References

1. Angeles, R.: Rfid technologies: supply-chain applications and implementation issues. Information Systems Management 22(1), 51–65 (2005)
2. Bai, Y., Wang, F., Liu, P., Zaniolo, C., Liu, S.: Rfid data processing with a data stream query language. In: ICDE (2007)
3. Gonzalez, H., Han, J., Li, X., Klabjan, D.: Warehousing and analyzing massive rfid data sets. In: ICDE, p. 83 (2006)
4. Lee, C.H., Chung, C.W.: Efficient storage scheme and query processing for supply chain management using rfid. In: SIGMOD, pp. 291–302 (2008)
5. Jeffery, S.R., Garofalakis, M.N., Franklin, M.J.: Adaptive cleaning for rfid data streams. In: VLDB, pp. 163–174 (2006)

6. Jeffery, S.R., Alonso, G., Franklin, M.J., Hong, W., Widom, J.: A pipelined framework for online cleaning of sensor data streams. In: ICDE, p. 140 (2006)
7. Wang, F.-S., Liu, S., Liu, P., Bai, Y.: Bridging Physical and Virtual Worlds: Complex Event Processing for RFID Data Streams. In: Ioannidis, Y., Scholl, M.H., Schmidt, J.W., Matthes, F., Hatzopoulos, M., Böhm, K., Kemper, A., Grust, T., Böhm, C. (eds.) EDBT 2006. LNCS, vol. 3896, pp. 588–607. Springer, Heidelberg (2006)
8. Bai, Y., Wang, F., Liu, P.: Efficiently filtering rfid data streams. In: CleanDB - ICDE Workshop, pp. 50–57 (2006)
9. Derakhshan, R., Orlowska, M.E., Li, X.: Rfid data management: Challenges and opportunities. In: IEEE Int. Conf. on RFID, RFID 2007, pp. 175–182 (2007)
10. Davis, T.A.: Direct Methods for Sparse Linear Systems. SIAM (2006)
11. Osterby, O., Zlatev, Z.: Direct Methods for Sparse Matrices. LNCS, vol. 157. Springer, Heidelberg (1983)
12. Iverson, K.: A programming language. In: AFIPS Computer Conference (1962)
13. Kleene, S.C.: Introduction to Metamathematics. Van Nostrand Rheinhold (1952)

Prediction of Coronary Arteriosclerosis in Stable Coronary Heart Disease

Jan G. Bazan[1,3], Stanislawa Bazan-Socha[2], Sylwia Buregwa-Czuma[1],
Przemyslaw Wiktor Pardel[1,3], and Barbara Sokolowska[2]

[1] Institute of Computer Science, University of Rzeszów
Dekerta 2 Str., 35 - 030 Rzeszów, Poland
[2] II Dept. of Internal Medicine,
Jagiellonian University Medical College
Skawinska 8 Str., 31-066 Krakow, Poland
[3] Institute of Mathematics, Warsaw University
Banacha 2 Str., 02-097 Warsaw, Poland

Abstract. The aim of the study was to assess the usefulness of classification methods in recognizing cardiovascular pathology. From the medical point of view the study involves prediction of coronary arteriosclerosis presence in patient with stable angina using clinical data and electrocardiogram (ECG) Holter monitoring records. On the grounds of these findings the need for coronary interventions is determined. An approach to solving this problem has been found in the context of rough set theory and methods. Rough set theory introduced by Zdzisław Pawlak during the early 1980s provides the foundation for the construction of classifiers. From the rough set perspective, classifiers presented in the paper are based on a decision tree calculated on the basis of the local discretization method. The paper includes results of experiments that have been performed on medical data obtained from II Department of Internal Medicine, Jagiellonian University Medical College, Krakow, Poland.

Keywords: rough sets, discretization, classifiers, stable angina pectoris, morbus ischaemicus cordis, ECG Holter.

1 Introduction

Coronary heart disease (CHD) touches people all over the world and is caused by atherosclerosis, affecting coronary arteries. One of CHD's manifestation - angina pectoris is chest pain due to ischemia of the heart muscle. Acute angina, called unstable refers to acute coronary syndrome (ACS), and when its course is chronic, it is called stable. Coronary angiography enables assessment of coronary arteries anatomy and localization of stenosis, thus permits determination of therapeutic plan and prognosis. In the case of unaltered coronary flow the pharmacological treatment is applied, otherwise there is also a need for angioplasty or surgical treatment. In some cases the catheterization cannot be carried out. These cases involve health centers with limited access to diagnostic procedures or tight budget and patients with allergy to contrast medium and other

S. Greco et al. (Eds.): IPMU 2012, Part II, CCIS 298, pp. 550–559, 2012.
© Springer-Verlag Berlin Heidelberg 2012

contraindications to angiography. In this situation other methods assessing coronary arteries lesions are needed.

We propose application of clinical data together with electrocardiogram (ECG) Holter recordings as prospective candidate data for coronary artery stenosis prediction. The proposed method helps to determine the management of patients with stable angina, including the need for coronary intervention, without performing invasive diagnostic procedure that angiography is. It could also work as a screening tool for all patients with CHD. The problem appears considerable because angina is one of the most often cardiovascular disease (CVD) and according to WHO (World Health Organization) CVDs are leading cause of death globally and CHD kills more than 7 million people each year (see [10]).

The presented subject is concerned with substantial computation problem. It employs classifiers building for temporal data sets, where a *classifier* is an algorithm which enables us forecasting repeatedly on the basis of accumulated knowledge in new situations (see, *e.g.*, [2] for more details). Many approaches have been proposed to construct classifiers. Among them we would like to mention classical and modern statistical techniques, neural networks, decision trees, decision rules and inductive logic programming (see, *e.g.*, [2] for more details). Classifiers were constructed also for temporal data (see, *e.g.*, [2,7]). In the paper, an approach to solving problem has been found in the context of rough set theory and methods. Rough set theory introduced by Zdzisław Pawlak during the early 1980s provides the foundation for the construction of classifiers also for temporal data sets (see [14,4,3,2]).

We present a method of classifier construction that is based on features aggregating time points (see, *e.g.*, [2]). The patients are characterized by parameters (sensors), measured in time points for some period, called *a time window*. In the ECG recordings context, the exemplary parameters are number of QRS complexes, ST interval elevations and lowerings or total power of the heart rate variability (HRV) spectrum. The aggregation of time points is performed by special functions called *temporal patterns* (see, *e.g.*, [2]), that are numerical characterization of values of selected sensor from the whole time window. We assume that computing temporal pattern's value uses a formula defined by an expert. Having computed patterns, a classifier is constructed approximating a temporal concept. In studied subject, the temporal concept means the presence of coronary arteriosclerosis. The classification is performed using a decision tree that is calculated on the basis of the local discretization (see, *e.g.*, [13,4]).

To illustrate the method and to verify the effectiveness of presented classifiers, we have performed several experiments with the data sets obtained from Second Department of Internal Medicine, Collegium Medicum, Jagiellonian University, Krakow, Poland (see Section 4).

2   Stable Coronary Heart Disease

Stable angina pectoris is a common and disabling clinical syndrome. In the majority of European countries, 20 000–40 000 individuals of the population per million suffer from it (see [8]). Because of population ageing and increased frequency of risk factors the incidence of angina is still increasing.

2.1 Diagnosis

Diagnosis and assessment of angina involves history, physical examination, laboratory tests and specific cardiac investigations. Non-invasive standard investigations include a resting 12-lead ECG, ECG stress testing, echocardiography, ECG Holter monitoring. Invasive techniques used in coronary anatomy assessment are: coronary arteriography and intravascular ultrasound.

Holter ECG monitoring is a continuous recording of the ECG, done over a period of 24 hours or more. Holter software carries out an integrated automatic analysis process providing information about heart beat morphology, interval measurements, HRV and rhythm overview. There are numerous systems analyzing ECG recordings. They enable processing and aggregation of data by means of existing signal analyzing methods.

Coronary arteriography is a diagnostic invasive procedure that requires the percutaneous insertion of a catheter into the vessels and heart. Injected dye (contrast medium - CM) allows to identify the presence, localization and degree of stenosis in the coronary arteries. Coronary arteriography is considered a relatively safe procedure, but in same patients complications arise. Most of them are minor, of no long-term consequence. The risk of major complications is determined to be up to 2% (see [1]). Reactions to CM are relatively common, occurring in 1 to 12% of patients (see [5]) and most of them are mild. Moderate reactions occur in 1% of people receiving CM and frequently require treatment. Severe, life-threatening reactions are reported in 0,03 to 0,16% of patients, with an expected death rate of 1 to 3 per 100 000 contrast administrations (see [6]).

There are no routine noninvasive diagnostic procedures to assess coronary flow disturbances and when there is no opportunity to perform coronary angiography, alternative solutions to the problem are needed. Application of proposed method may select potential candidates for myocardial revascularization.

2.2 Treatment

The aim of CHD treatment is to prevent myocardial infarction and death. Pharmacological treatment should reduce plaque progression, stabilize plaque by reducing inflammation and by preventing thrombosis when endothelial failure or plaque rupture occurs. There are two methods of revascularization: surgical revascularization - coronary artery bypass graft (CABG) and percutaneous coronary intervention (PCI). PCI may denote balloon catheter angioplasty with or without implantation of stents or atherectomy. With appropriate management, the symptoms usually can be controlled and the prognosis improved.

3   Automated Prediction of Coronary Atherosclerosis Presence

Forecasting coronary stenosis in patients without performing angiography requires construction of classifier, which on the basis of available knowledge assigns objects (patients) to defined decision classes. Considered decision classes are: *patients with unaltered arteries who do not need invasive treatment* (decision class: *NO*) and *patients with coronary atherosclerosis who may need angioplasty* (decision class: *YES*). Classification thus permits decision making about coronary stenosis and therapy management.

The problem of forecasting coronary atherosclerosis presence can be treated as an example of a concept approximation problem, where the term *concept* means *mental picture of a group of objects*. Such problems often can be modeled by systems of complex objects and their parts changing and interacting over time. The objects are usually linked by some dependencies, sometimes can cooperate between themselves and are able to perform flexible autonomous complex actions (operations, changes). Such systems are identified as *complex dynamical systems* or *autonomous multiagent systems* (see [2] for more details). For example, in the problem of coronary stenosis prediction, a given patient can be treated as an investigated complex dynamical system, whilst diseases of this patient are treated as complex objects changing and interacting over time.

Concepts and methods of their approximation are usually useful tools for an efficient monitoring of complex dynamic system (see [2]). Any concept can be understand as a way to represent some features of complex objects. An approximation of such concepts can be made using parameters (sensor values) registered for a given set of complex objects. However, a perception of composite features of complex objects requires observation of objects over a period called a *time window*. Such features are often represented by *temporal patterns*. In this paper, we consider temporal patterns as a numerical characterization of values of selected sensors from a time window (e.g., the minimal, maximal or mean value of a selected sensor, initial and final values of selected sensor, deviation of selected sensor values).

One can see that any temporal pattern is determined directly by values of some sensors. For example, in case of the coronary disease one can consider temporal patters such as minimal heart rate and estimated QT dispersion within a time window. We assume that any temporal pattern ought to be defined by a human expert using domain knowledge accumulated for the given complex dynamical system.

The temporal patterns can be treated as new features that can be used to approximate more complex concepts. We call them *temporal concepts*. We assume that temporal concepts are specified by a human expert. Temporal concepts are usually used in queries about the status of some objects in a particular temporal window. The approximation of temporal concepts can be defined by classifiers, which are usually constructed on the basis of decision tables. Hence, if we want to apply classifiers for approximation of temporal concepts, we have to construct a suitable decision table called a *temporal pattern table* (PT) (see Figure 1).

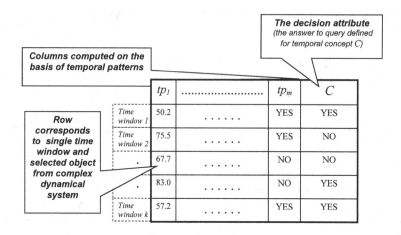

Fig. 1. The scheme of the temporal pattern table (PT)

A temporal pattern table is constructed from a table T consisting of registered information about objects (patients) occurring in a complex dynamical system. Any row of table T represents information about parameters of a single object registered in a time window. Assume, for example, that we want to approximate a temporal concept C using table (data set) T. Initially, we construct a temporal pattern table PT as follows:

- Construct table PT with the same objects as contained in table T.
- Any condition attribute of table PT is computed using temporal patterns defined by a human expert for the approximation of concept C,
- Values of the decision attribute (the characteristic function of concept C) are proposed by the human expert.

We assume that for any temporal pattern a formula for computing its value is given by an expert. Next, we can construct a classifier for table PT that can approximate temporal concept C. The most popular method for classifiers construction is based on learning rules from examples (see, e.g., [14,4,3,2]). Unfortunately, the decision rules constructed in this way can often be not appropriate to classify unseen cases. For instance, if we have a decision table where the number of values is high for some attributes, then there is a very low chance that a new object is recognized by rules generated directly from this table, because the attribute value vector of a new object will not match any of these rules. Therefore for decision tables with such numeric attributes some discretization strategies are built to obtain a higher quality classifiers. This problem is intensively studied and we consider discretization methods developed by Hung S. Nguyen (see [13,4]). In this paper we use local strategy of discretization (see [4]). One of the most important notion of this strategy is the notion of *a cut*. Formally, the cut is a pair (a, c) defined for a given *decision table* $\mathbf{A} = (U, A \cup \{d\})$ in Pawlak's sense (see [14]), where $a \in A$ (A is a set of attributes or columns in the data set) and c, defines a partition of V_a into *left-hand-side* and *right-hand-side interval* (V_a is a set of values of the attribute a). In other words, any cut (a, c) is associated with a new binary attribute (feature) $f_{(a,c)} : U \to \{0, 1\}$ such that for any $u \in U$:

$$f_{(a,c)}(u) = \begin{cases} 0 & \text{if } a(u) < c \\ 1 & \text{otherwise} \end{cases} \tag{1}$$

Moreover, any cut (a, c) defines two templates, where a template we understand as a description of some set of objects. The first template defined by a cut (a, c) is a formula $T = (a(u) < c)$, while the second pattern defined by a cut (a, c) is a formula $\neg T = (a(u) \geq c)$.

In this paper, the quality of a given cut is computed as a number of objects pairs discerned by this cut and belonging to different decision classes. It is worth noticing that such quality can be computed for a given cut in $O(n)$ time, where n is the number of objects in the decision table (see, e.g., [4]). The quality of cuts may be computed for any subset of a given set of objects.

In local strategy of discretization, after finding the best cut and dividing the object set into two subsets of objects (matching to both templates mentioned above for a given cut), this procedure is repeated for each object set separately until some stop condition holds. In this paper, we assume that the division stops when all objects from the current set of objects belong to the same decision class. Hence, the local strategy can be realized by using *decision tree* (see [4] and Figure 2).

The decision tree computed during local discretization can be treated as a classifier for the concept C represented by decision attribute from a given decision table $\mathbf{A}$. Let u be a new object and $\mathbf{A}(T)$ be a subtable containing all objects matching to template T defined by the cut from the current node of a given decision tree (at the beginning of algorithm work T is the template defined by the cut from the root). We classify object u starting from the root of the tree as follows:

Algorithm. *Classification by decision tree* (see [4])
Step 1 If u matches template T found for $\mathbf{A}$
           then: go to subtree related to $\mathbf{A}(T)$
           else: go to subtree related to $\mathbf{A}(\neg T)$.
Step 2 If u is at the leaf of the tree then go to 3
           else: repeat 1-2 substituting $\mathbf{A}(T)$ (or $\mathbf{A}(\neg T)$) for $\mathbf{A}$.
Step 3 Classify u using decision value attached to the leaf

Figure 2 presents a decision tree computed for the problem of forecasting coronary atherosclerosis presence on the basis of medical data set (see Section 4).

Sample application of the tree is classification of real life objects. For example, for a patient with maximal ULF, i.e. power in ultra low frequency equal to 112 ms^2 and maximal VLF (very low frequency) equal 256, we follow from the root of the tree, down to the right subtree, as the patient suits a template $MAX\_ULF < 248$. Then, in the next step we tread again a right tree, which consists of one node, called leaf, where we stop. The fitting path indicates that

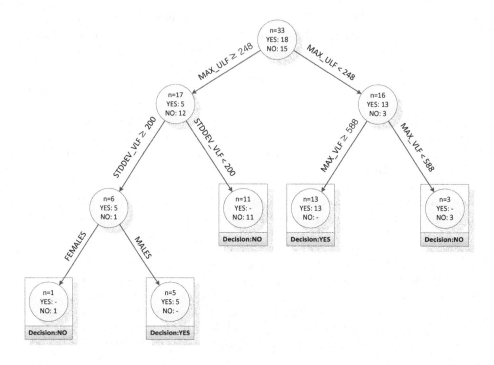

Fig. 2. The decision tree in CHD

the coronary arteries of that patient are not narrowed by atherosclerosis. For a man with maximal ULF equal to 605 and standard deviation of VLF equal 509.6, we anticipate, relaying the classifier, the atherosclerotic coronary arteries stenosis presence.

4   Experimental Results

To verify the effectiveness of classifiers based on behavioral patterns, we have implemented the algorithms from the library RSH-lib, which is an extension of the RSES-lib library forming the kernel of the RSES system [3].

The experiments have been performed on the medical data set obtained from Second Department of Internal Medicine, Collegium Medicum, Jagiellonian University, Krakow, Poland. The data were collected between 2006 and 2009. Two part 48-hour Holter ECG recordings were performed using Aspel's HolCARD 24W system. There was coronary angiography after first part of Holter ECG (after first 24-hour recording). In the paper, we report results of experiments performed for the first part of Holter ECG recordings. The data set includes a detail description of clinical status (age, sex, diagnosis), coexistent diseases, pharmacological management, the laboratory tests outcomes (level of cholesterol, troponin I, LDL - low density lipoproteins) and various Holter-based indices such as: ST interval deviations, HRV, arrythmias or QT dispersion. Moreover, for Holter-based indices a data aggregation was performed resulting in points describing one hour of recording. Our group of 33 patients with normal rhythm, underwent coronary angiography and 24.2% of them required additional angioplasty, whereas 24.2% were qualified for CAGB.

All data were imported into Infobright Community Edition (ICE) environment (see [9]). ICE is an open source software solution designed to deliver a scalable data warehouse, optimized for analytic queries (data volumes up to 50TB, market-leading data compression, from 10:1 to over 40:1). After internal preprocessing in the ICE environment (e.g., a data aggregation of Holter-based indices as was mentioned above) for further processing data have been imported into Java environment.

The aim of conducted experiments was to check the effectiveness of the algorithm described in this paper in order to predict atherosclerosis in coronary arteries. Here we present the experimental results of presented method. For testing quality of classifiers we applied leave-one-out (LOO) technique, that is usually employed when the size of a given data set is small. The LOO technique involves a single object from the original data set as the validation data, and the remaining observations as the training data. This is repeated such that each observation in the sample is used once as the validation data. As a measure of classification success (or failure) we use the following parameters well known from literature: the accuracy, the coverage, the accuracy for positive examples (Sensitivity, SN or recall), the coverage for positive examples, the precision for positive examples (Positive Predictive Value, PPV), the accuracy for negative examples (Specificity, SP), the coverage for negative examples and the precision for negative examples, also called Negative Predictive Value, NPV (see, *e.g.*, [2]).

Table 1 shows the results of applying the considered algorithm for the concept related to presence of coronary atherosclerosis in patients with stable angina.

Table 1. Results of experiments for coronary stenosis in CHD

Decision class	Accuracy	Coverage	Precision
Yes	0.778	1.0	0.778
No	0.733	1.0	0.733
All classes (Yes + No)	0.758	1.0	-

The method correctly identifies 77.8% of all patients with stenosis (SN), that's why a negative result would suggest the absence of disease. 73,3% of those who did not have stenosis (SP) were correctly identified, so a positive result means a high probability of the presence of disease. With PPV value equal 77.8%, a positive screen test is good at confirming coronary stenosis, however a negative result is also good as a screening tool at affirming that a patient does not have stenosis (NPV = 73.3%).

It is worth noticing that during LOO procedure, the most of generated trees revealed the same topology as final decision tree preserving siblings and ancestors order. The topology of the rest of trees was similar, that is, there were some differences in case of attribute values in the tree nodes and sometimes in attributes in the lower levels of generated trees. It shows that the method is quite robust to noise in data.

In Table 2 we give the results of experiments in applying other classification methods to our data. Those methods were developed in the following systems well known from literature: WEKA [15], RSES [3], and ROSE2 [12] (we used an early implementation of ModLEM algorithm [11] that is available in ROSE2). The coverage of all tested methods was equal 1.0 (every object was classified).

Table 2. Comparison results of alternative classification systems

	Accuracy			Precision	
Method	All classes	Yes	No	Yes	No
C4.5 (WEKA)	0.545	0.611	0.467	0.579	0.500
NaiveBayes (WEKA)	0.394	0.611	0.133	0.458	0.222
SVM (WEKA)	0.545	0.611	0.467	0.579	0.500
k-NN (WEKA)	0.667	0.833	0.467	0.652	0.700
RandomForest (WEKA)	0.515	0.722	0.267	0.542	0.444
Multilayer Perceptron (WEKA)	0.548	0.611	0.467	0.579	0.500
Global discretization + all rules (RSES)	0.667	0.611	0.733	0.733	0.611
Local discretization + all rules (RSES)	0.758	0.778	0.733	0.778	0.733
ModLEM (ROSE2)	0.576	0.556	0.600	0.625	0.529

Experimental results showed that the presented method of atherosclerosis prediction in coronary arteries gives good results and the results are comparable with results of another systems.

5 Conclusion

Presented methods were useful for development of new interesting observation and experience. We conclude that experimental outcomes showed that the proposed prediction method gives good results, also in the opinion of medical experts (compatible enough with the medical experience). But we realize that applying them in medical practice as a supporting tool for patients suffering from CHD needs clinical verification.

Acknowledgement. This work was supported by the grant N N516 077837 from the Ministry of Science and Higher Education of the Republic of Poland, the Polish National Science Centre (NCN) grant 2011/01/B/ST6/03867 and by the Polish National Centre for Research and Development (NCBiR) grant No. SP/I/1/77065/10 in frame of the strategic scientific research and experimental development program: "Interdisciplinary System for Interactive Scientific and Scientific-Technical Information".

References

1. ACC/AHA Guidelines for Coronary Angiography: Executive Summary and Recommendations. A Report of the American College of Cardiology/American Heart Association Task Force on Practice Guidelines. Circulation 99, 2345–2357 (1999)
2. Bazan, J.G.: Hierarchical Classifiers for Complex Spatio-temporal Concepts. In: Peters, J.F., Skowron, A., Rybiński, H. (eds.) Transactions on Rough Sets IX. LNCS, vol. 5390, pp. 474–750. Springer, Heidelberg (2008)
3. Bazan, J.G., Szczuka, M.: The Rough Set Exploration System. In: Peters, J.F., Skowron, A. (eds.) Transactions on Rough Sets III. LNCS, vol. 3400, pp. 37–56. Springer, Heidelberg (2005)
4. Bazan, J.G., Nguyen, H.S., Nguyen, S.H., Synak, P., Wróblewski, J.: Rough set algorithms in classification problems. In: Polkowski, L., Lin, T.Y., Tsumoto, S. (eds.) Rough Set Methods and Applications: New Developments in Knowledge Discovery in Information Systems. STUD FUZZ, vol. 56, pp. 49–88. Physica-Verlag, Heidelberg (2000)
5. Canter, L.M.: Anaphylactoid reactions to radiocontrast media. Allergy and Asthma Proceedings 26, 199–203 (2005)
6. Cochran, S.T.: Anaphylactoid reactions to radiocontrast media. Current Allergy and Asthma Reports 5, 28–31 (2005)
7. Douzal-Chouakria, A., Amblard, C.: Classification trees for time series. Pattern Recognition 45(3), 1076–1091 (2011)
8. Guidelines on the management of stable angina pectoris: executive summary. The Task Force on the Management of Stable Angina Pectoris of the European Society of Cardiology. European Heart Journal 27, 1341–1381 (2006)
9. The Infobright Community Edition (ICE), http://www.infobright.org/
10. Mackay, J., Mensah, G.A.: The Atlas of Heart Disease and Stroke. World Health Organization (2004)
11. Napierała, K., Stefanowski, J.: Argument Based Generalization of MODLEM Rule Induction Algorithm. In: Szczuka, M., Kryszkiewicz, M., Ramanna, S., Jensen, R., Hu, Q. (eds.) RSCTC 2010. LNCS, vol. 6086, pp. 138–147. Springer, Heidelberg (2010)
12. The Rough Sets Data Explorer (ROSE2), Homepage, http://idss.cs.put.poznan.pl/site/rose.html
13. Nguyen, H.S.: Approximate Boolean Reasoning: Foundations and Applications in Data Mining. In: Peters, J.F., Skowron, A. (eds.) Transactions on Rough Sets V. LNCS, vol. 4100, pp. 334–506. Springer, Heidelberg (2006)
14. Pawlak, Z., Skowron, A.: Rudiments of rough sets. Information Sciences 177, 3–27 (2007)
15. The Weka 3 - Data Mining Software in Java (WEKA), http://www.cs.waikato.ac.nz/ml/weka/

Framework for the Establishment of Resource-Aware Data Mining Techniques on Critical Infrastructures

Miguel Ángel Abad and Ernestina Menasalvas*

Universidad Politecnica de Madrid,Facultad de Informatica, Spain
miguel.abad.arranz@alumnos.upm.es, emenasalvas@fi.upm.es

Abstract. Nowadays, the development of modern societies is based on the availability of essential services by means of industrial control systems or SCADA[1] systems which form part of what has come to be known as *critical infrastructures*. SCADA systems are usually implemented in a distributed manner, in which some remote terminal units (RTU) are in charge of compiling all of the information from the sensors in the field. The implementation of any efficient protection mechanism in these RTUs demands a "context" and "resource aware" behavior, through the development of intelligent methods that in an efficient way could allow the device to react in a proactive way. However, RTUs are characterized by computational and storage limitations which make it difficult to provide the "intelligence" necessary to develop new decentralized protection systems, which could be useful for the early incident detection based on data mining techniques. This work deals with the problem of executing a classification algorithm in a device with limited computational possibilities. The design presented is characterized by its modularity, adaptability to the available resources, together with its capacity to be reused in other systems with similar characteristics. Results of the experiments carried out are also presented.

1 Introduction

SCADA systems are a type of Industrial Control Systems (ICS) dedicated to the supervision, monitoring and management of industrial processes. In order to carry out the aforementioned tasks, they use acquisition, interpretation, validation and evaluation techniques on the data coming from the different elements present in the architecture, which are also those that facilitate its correct working. The industrial processes upon which SCADA systems operate are present, for example, in the monitoring and automation of the manufacturing processes; generation, transmission and distribution of energy; treatment and distribution of water; airport management, smart buildings, . . .

Bearing in mind that SCADA systems are in many cases crucial for the provision of certain essential services, they usually are the backbone of critical infrastructures [4]. Thus, given the risks implied by the unlikely malfunctioning of or interruption in the activities that must carry out, their security and correct working should be key at the time of undertaking its design, management, operation and maintenance.

---

* Project partially financed by Project TIN2008-05924.

[1] SCADA stands for Supervisory Control and Data Acquisition.

S. Greco et al. (Eds.): IPMU 2012, Part II, CCIS 298, pp. 560–569, 2012.
© Springer-Verlag Berlin Heidelberg 2012

Historically, given the specialization of SCADA systems, these were characterized by being available in closed systems and highly controlled in areas in which there is no way of interconnection between the different platforms, thus guaranteeing the independence of the technological platforms that would impede the communication even between devices made by different manufacturers.

Over the years and as a result of the proliferation of interconnections between devices, together with the appearance of standard communication protocols for the development of the Internet, the industrial control systems went on to become platforms that would also allow the interconnection of other networks and devices. All of this would bring with it the possibility of managing SCADA systems remotely; an aspect that is known as telemetry. However, the need for SCADA systems to be capable of operating in an almost uninterruptible manner makes it difficult to apply most of the security measures used in "common" information and communication technologies.

In this way, this work presents a framework to facilitate the implementation of classification techniques, which in the area of data mining allows its autonomous and local execution and adaptation, making it suitable in each case for the computational requirements of the device. The local execution of those algorithms in the device would provide a greater device autonomy, avoiding the overload of its communication links because of the transmission of data used in that process, as it would occur in a distributed execution model. Furthermore, in the context of SCADA systems, this work can be used for the reduction of risk against intentional attacks that might affect their operability,

The possibility of executing data mining techniques in a local and efficient way, regarding the resource consumption, allows the development of new protection mechanisms based on data mining techniques, that could fit into RTUs of SCADA system. For instance, some of the intrusion detection systems (IDS) are based upon data mining techniques in order to improve its detection effectiveness [11], being this aspect one of the research areas that remains opened in the scope of the critical infrastructure protection [6].

Therefore, this work has the main objective of presenting a framework for the improvement of the protection of the remote units existing in the architectures of SCADA systems, by means of the efficient execution of the data mining algorithms. Those data mining algorithms will use context information limited to the degree of availability of the resources of the devices in which the corresponding algorithm is executed, with the following characteristics: i) The data mining components **will be designed to be executed in devices with limits as regards the available resources**, achieving a compromise between the precision of the model and the consumption of resources; ii) the data mining models generated with the aforementioned components will be trained using **local data**, that is, there will not exist a priori any form of communication between devices in order to undertake the data mining process. Furthermore, the data mining components should be **independent of the final device** in which they are executed.

In order to comply with all of these objectives, the inclusion of a module is proposed dedicated to acting as a "dispatcher", in such a way that starting from the resources of the corresponding device, the most appropriate data mining model can be chosen in each case. The existence of a module of this type contributes a sufficient flexibility for it to be reused in any environment. However it should be necessary to verify that the resources consumption of this proposed module will not affect the already possibly reduced computing capacity of the devices in which it is being executed. With the aim of evaluating the cost as regards the resources consumption of a module of this type, the results of an experiment carried out using the different implementations are presented, at the same time setting out the existence of other alternatives.

The rest of this work has been structured in the following manner: section 2 presents the work related to the environment of SCADA systems and the data mining, so that later, in section 3 the solution proposed for the execution of the data mining algorithms is presented which is dependent on the state of the resources. For this reason, subsection 3.1 details the scenario together with the different options for tackling the problem, establishing in subsection 3.2 the architecture chosen upon which an implementation of the system in subsection 3.3 is developed. Section 4 contains an analysis of the data obtained following the execution of a battery of the aforementioned tests. Finally, section 5 sets out the conclusions of the work together with the possible lines of research deriving from them.

2   Related Work

Application of data mining in SCADA systems have focused more on the computational point of view [2,7] than on the problems associated to the execution in constraint devices. In [14] it is presented the development of a platform for the execution of data mining processes over telemetry data, although it is not based on the local execution in the devices, establishing the need of a central data base. In this way, at the moment most of the data mining systems developed in environments with limited resources devices present an aggregation of centralized results [1], which makes difficult the task of keeping the device context information. As a result of this, a new area of research has appeared dedicated to covering the need to have "intelligent" components available. Those components could become proactive and acceptable to the context and the resources of the system [9].

For the case of network vulnerabilities, it is normal to have preventative measures available in the form of intrusion detection systems, which are usually based on data mining techniques [10]. Within this environment, work has been carried out both in the area of classification [15,5] (supervised data mining) and in clustering [17] (unsupervised data mining). However, most of the solutions proposed to date require a human expert with sufficient knowledge to participate actively in the process [12], in which there is no complete automation [16]. Furthermore, although some work has been developed in order to propose efficient systems [8], none of the solutions proposed in this area take into account the resources available in order to adapt their behavior to them.

3   Proposed Solution

3.1   Analysis

We assume a scenario in which the execution of a model of data mining will be required from among those available at a given moment in accordance with the state of the resources of the device in which it is executed. In this scenario, the following premises are defined:

- A data mining model is understood as a series of data mining algorithms grouped together for the achievement of a certain objective. Specific data mining algorithms can be added or eliminated transparently, without affecting the behavior of the system.
- Data are assumed to be preprocessed, so the preprocessing tasks with data remain outside the remit of this work.
- The existence and correct working of a component dedicated to the reading and sending of the resources of a device is assumed.

In this scenario, and with the premises expounded, there are different design options to undertake the stated objectives: i)to adapt source codes of the algorithms, so that they themselves modify their behavior at the time of execution in accordance with the resources available at all times; ii) by means of the inclusion of an independent component which would be responsible for receiving the consumption of resources of the system, with the objective of selecting the most appropriate data mining model. Although the first option could become the most optimal for a particular known and controlled case, it does not provide sufficient flexibility for it to be easily reusable in other operation environments. All of this is due to the fact that all of the algorithms should be modified so that they would be capable of responding suitably in accordance with the available resources. However, the second proposed option provides the flexibility lacking in the first one, but all of this at the cost of requiring previous knowledge of what the expected consumption would be for each of the data mining models available.

Casting aside the first option as a result of its inefficiency as regards its maintenance, the present work centers on the establishment of a component like that set out in the second option. However, another question to be resolved arises at this moment: How can the association of the envisaged consumption for each of the models be represented and managed? In order to provide an answer to this question, two new options arise:

1. A (human) expert directly associates what the suitable execution parameters should be for the different specific values or ranges of resource consumption values. This option would require the participation of the expert for the inclusion of new inputs for each data mining model, as well as for each value or range of resource values. This would make its treatment enormously difficult as it would increase the number of algorithms and/or resources to be evaluated. The benefit of this alternative would be however that it would not require any type of additional computing.
2. The other alternative would be the implementation of a system of meta-knowledge that, based on the record of all of the executions at all times during the data mining, is able to determine the relationship between the consumption of resources and the execution parameters of each algorithm. This alternative, although it would require a minimum computational capacity to manage the meta-knowledge system, would provide a greater flexibility and trust. Its main disadvantage is that it is necessary to have an already trained model, so that to guarantee its precision it would be necessary to have a sufficient number of historical data on the executions, which is not always possible. However, once the model is available, the inclusion of new resources only requires its retraining.

As regards what has already been said, this present work provides a solution based on the implementation of an independent component as a "dispatcher" for the selection of the most appropriate data mining model in accordance with the available resources, which leads to a flexible and scalable system which facilitates the inclusion of new data mining models. As regards the methods of representation and management of the estimated consumption for each model, an experiment is presented with the two afore-mentioned alternatives.

In this way it is guaranteed that the information on the context, in this case the level of consumption of the resources, will determine the ideal type of execution for each sit-uation. With this, we move towards the establishment of a non-intrusive system against the normal operability of the system, which is an aspect of great importance especially in the area of critical infrastructures characterized by the existence of certain industrial systems and with operations in real time, where the existence of elements that might perturb the usual behavior could lead to incidents with serious consequences for both the economy or society together.

In short, it would be the information on the context that would determine the ideal type of execution for each case. For example, in critical systems that require an answer in real time, perhaps communication with a central system may not be feasible for the generation of data mining; in other cases, maybe this communication does not exist. Therefore it is essential to have a new layer of local processing that determines the type of execution to be carried out, all of which will be transparent and will have the least possible repercussions on the resource load of the device.

3.2 Architecture

The architecture that is proposed is presented schematically in Fig.1, and consists of the following components:

1. A central component or "dispatcher", as responsible for accessing the existing data mining models. Once the level of consumption is received, it is capable of choosing the most convenient in each case.
2. A module specialized in the definition and management of the available data mining models stored in the system. This module will be crucial in order to ensure that the "dispatcher" is capable of obtaining the models available in order to choose the most suitable one in accordance with the available resources.
3. A component for the management of sources of information needed for the execu-tion of the data mining models.
4. A component for reading the levels of consumption of the hardware resources of the device.
5. A component for the management of the usual data mining processes, such as: the treatment and validation of data, filtering, the execution of algorithms and the representation of the results.

In this work we focus on the central component or "dispatcher" and on the component for the management of data mining models. In any case, the architecture proposed is completely flexible, given that it allows the inclusion of new data mining algorithms in new models or based on already existing ones; in the same way, it admits the inclusion of

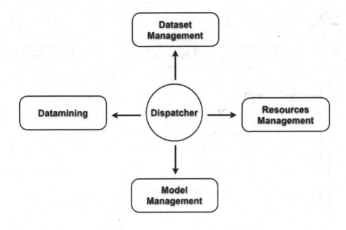

Fig. 1. System modules

new sources of data on which the new necessary data mining techniques are applied. It also allows an efficient management of the processes of knowledge management, such as preprocessing tasks, filtering, validation, the execution and presentation of the results. Finally, it allows the simple use of any mechanism for reading the resources level of consumption, all of which are transparent for the overall behavior of the system. Fig.2 shows a sequence diagram, in which it can be seen how the process data mining model selection is carried out: it begins with the execution in a device of data mining training in a certain context. Once the process has started, the "dispatcher" requests the sending of the levels of consumption of the resources of a device, in order to determine what would be the most appropriate data mining model in this situation. Then the execution of the chosen algorithm will be requested, which would involve the execution of all of the algorithms that make it up. The benefits of the proposed architecture are basically as follows:

- The system for the definition of the data mining models allows the inclusion of new models and/or algorithms transparently. It is not therefore necessary any type of modification of its behavior in order to do this task.
- The system, in turn, allows the inclusion of the measurement of the new resources of the device, although in order to obtain a complete integration it will be necessary to include a reference to them in the data mining models which may be affected.
- The modular design of the system allows the specialization of the process with the inclusion of new components.

3.3   Implementation

As regards the architecture proposed in section 3.2, the implementation of a prototype with the following characteristics has been carried out:

1. The data mining must be carried out locally in the devices.

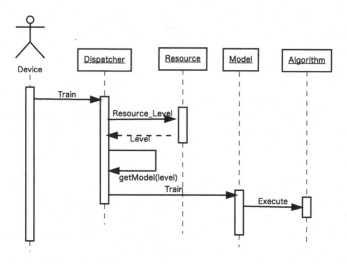

Fig. 2. Sequence diagram of the proposed system

2. The data mining process that is simulated in the device is focused on the training of a model based on the C4.5 algorithm. That is, the central module or "dispatcher" is focused on choosing the appropriate training parameters for that algorithm in accordance with the resources.
3. The representation of the different training options of the algorithms in accordance with the available resources, can be carried out by means of a direct mapping stored in a file, or by means of meta-knowledge models (decision tree, multilayer perceptron, Bayesian network, ...).
4. The resources information that will be handled will be the available memory and the consumption of the CPU. As regards the representation of the consumption of resources, a scale of values from 1 to 10 has been established; a value of 1 means the minimum computational load, and a value of ten being the maximum.

For the implementation of the described system, the *WEKA* [13] library and the *JAVA* programming language have been used, with the aim of facilitating the communication with the *WEKA* library on the one hand, and on the other hand to establish a multi-platform system capable of being implemented easily in small devices.

4   Experimentation Results

In order to show an estimation of the computational cost that the implementation of a central component as presented in this work would imply, a series of tests have been developed made up of the different types of execution. The main difference lies on the way in which the central component implements the relationships between the execution of the data mining algorithms with some determined parameters and the associated computational cost:

- Executions based on a central component which implements the relationships between the associated models and cost by means of files that contain this type of fixed relationship. In this way, this type of representation requires the establishment of the resources used in each corresponding execution model. Assuming that it works on a scale from 1 to 10 in order to measure the consumption of resources, the file should contain 10^x entries; x being the number of different inputs. Test files used have contained 5, 20, 100 and 200 different entries.
- Executions based on a central component which implements the relationships between the associated models and cost by means of the use of techniques based on meta-knowledge. Thus, by means of the use of an already trained classification model (based on synthetic data which simulates an execution history), it is possible to obtain the most suitable execution model in accordance with the level of available resources. Models based on decision trees, multilayer perception and a Bayesian network have been implemented during the tests.

As a result of the carrying out of the battery of tests described, the following conclusions have been reached:

- As regards the consumption of the memory of the "dispatcher", both the decision tree and the multilayer perceptron have a similar occupation at the moment of calculating the optimum model. The Bayesian network presents a lower occupation than the previous ones (see table 1), similar to the occupation of the use of a file with 100 inputs which contain the associations between available resources and the model to be executed in a fixed and predetermined manner. It is also important to highlight that the consumption of a component implemented by means of a file of this type grows as its content does (see table 2).
- As regards the consumption of the CPU of the "dispatcher" during the selection of the optimum model, both the implementation by means of multilayer perception or by means of a Bayesian network present a similar consumption, which is greatly reduced (some 30 times less) with the implementation by means of a decision tree. Table 3 reflects the said situation in the method known as the *"SelectModel()"* method. As regards the implementation by means of a file, just as would occur with the consumption of memory, that of the CPU also expands as does the size of the file. However, the most reduced file of those used (5 inputs) does not manage to be more efficient than the implementation by means of a decision tree trained with 100 instances (see table 3).

Table 1. Use of the memory heap: Bayesian network (left) and a multilayer perceptron (right)

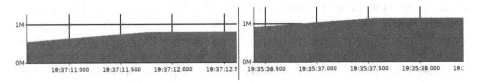

Table 2. use of the memory heap:file with 5 inputs (left) and 200 inputs (right)

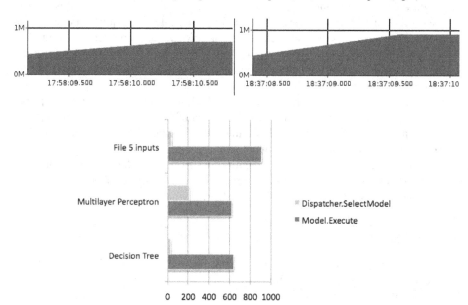

Fig. 3. CPU Consumption

5   Conclusions and Future Lines of Research

With the need to draw up a framework in which local data mining processes can be executed by taking into account the information on resources and context in constraint devices, this work has proposed a flexible and extendable model which allows the inclusion of any type of transparent data mining algorithm.

All of this takes into account that it is a question of a framework that could be applicable for the implementation of preventative protection measures such as intrusion detection systems in the remote units (RTU) of SCADA systems which are widely used in critical infrastructures, although the analysis of the actual impact of an application of the proposed model in this type of system would be a line for future research, bearing in mind that the tests performed in this work were carried out on a PC.

With the results presented, the critical nature of an optimum implementation has become clear in such a way that the central module ("dispatcher") is capable of obtaining the most suitable data mining models in accordance with the consumption of resources of the device, in the face of obtaining an efficient and flexible solution. In this sense, work is currently taking place on providing the flexibility of this module depending on the device in which it is being executed. Focuses based on ontologies similar to those presented in [3] have been analyzed, but with the inclusion of the parameters dedicated to the estimated consumption of resources as well as in flexible meta-knowledge mechanisms, which allow the estimation of the consumption of resources to be obtained starting from previous execution histories.

References

1. Bandyopadhyay, S., Giannella, C., Maulik, U., Kargupta, H., Liu, K., Datta, S.: Clustering distributed data streams in peer-to-peer environments. Inf. Sci. 176(14), 1952–1985 (2006)
2. Barkhuus, L., Dey, A.K.: Is context-aware computing taking control away from the user? Three levels of interactivity examined. In: Dey, A.K., Schmidt, A., McCarthy, J.F. (eds.) UbiComp 2003. LNCS, vol. 2864, pp. 149–156. Springer, Heidelberg (2003)
3. Bernstein, A., Provost, F.: An intelligent assistant for the knowledge discovery process. Information Systems Working Papers Series (2001)
4. Krutz, R.L.: Securing SCADA systems, pp. 4–16. Wiley Publishing, Inc. (2006)
5. Linda, O., Vollmer, T., Manic, M.: Neural network based intrusion detection system for critical infrastructures. In: Proceedings of the 2009 International Joint Conference on Neural Networks, IJCNN 2009, pp. 102–109. IEEE Press, Piscataway (2009)
6. Lopez, J., Alcaraz, C., Roman, R.: On the Protection and Technologies of Critical Information Infrastructures. In: Aldini, A., Gorrieri, R. (eds.) FOSAD 2007. LNCS, vol. 4677, pp. 160–182. Springer, Heidelberg (2007)
7. Saitta, L., May, M.: Blueprint in Ubiquitous Knowledge Discovery (2007)
8. Mahmood, A.N., Hu, J., Tari, Z., Leckie, C.: Critical infrastructure protection: Resource efficient sampling to improve detection of less frequent patterns in network traffic. J. Network and Computer Applications 33(4), 491–502 (2010)
9. Menasalvas, E., Eibe, S., Gomes, J., Zanda, A.: Context-aware recommendations in ubiquitous devices (2008)
10. Ning, P., Jajodia, S.: Intrusion Detection Basics. In: Bidgoli, H, ed. (2006)
11. Scarfone, K., Mell, P.: Intrusion detection and prevention systems. In: Handbook of Information and Communication Security, pp. 177–192 (2010)
12. Shih, Y.S., Lim, T.S., Loh, W.Y.: A comparison of prediction accuracy, complexity, and training time of thirty-three old and new classification algorithms. Machine Learning 40, 203–228 (2000)
13. Witten, I.H., Frank, E.: Data Mining: Practical machine learning tools and techniques, 2nd edn. Morgan Kaufmann (2005)
14. Wu, C.H., Yang, C.H., Lo, S.C., Vichare, N., Rhem, E., Pecht, M.: Automatic data mining for telemetry database of computer systems. Microelectronics Reliability (October 2010)
15. Yu, Z., Tsai, J.J.P., Weigert, T.: An adaptive automatically tuning intrusion detection system. ACM Transactions on Autonomous and Adaptive Systems 3 (August 2008)
16. Yu, Z., Tsai, J.J.P., Weigert, T.: An adaptive automatically tuning intrusion detection system. ACM Trans. Auton. Adapt. Syst. 3, 10:1–10:25 (2008)
17. Zhang, J., Zulkernine, M.: Anomaly based network intrusion detection with unsupervised outlier detection. In: 2006 IEEE International Conference on Communications, pp. 2388–2393 (2006)

Rough SQL – Semantics and Execution

Dominik Ślęzak[1,2], Piotr Synak[2], Graham Toppin[3],
Jakub Wróblewski[2], and Janusz Borkowski[2]

[1] Institute of Mathematics, University of Warsaw
ul. Banacha 2, 02-097 Warsaw, Poland
[2] Infobright Inc., Poland
ul. Krzywickiego 34, lok. 219, 02-078 Warsaw, Poland
[3] Infobright Inc., Canada
47 Colborne St., Suite 403, Toronto, ON M5E1P8 Canada
{slezak,synak,toppin,jakubw,januszb}@infobright.com

Abstract. We introduce *rough query*, which is a new approach to defining and computing SQL approximations. Rough query results are reported by means of simple metadata of attributes in an information system that would be a result of a standard `select` statement. The proposed approach is already available as an SQL extension in both Infobright Community and Enterprise Editions. Rough queries are computed practically in real time by basing on the statistical information layer, which was used so far only for the standard query optimization.

Keywords: Analytic RDBMS Solutions, Approximate SQL, Rough SQL.

1 Introduction

In such areas as business intelligence and web analytics there is an ongoing debate whether the answers to SQL statements have to exact in all cases. Of special importance are analytic sessions of advanced users who explore the data using various types of telescoping queries (where the form of each of queries depends on the results of the previous ones), trying to look around the data prior to specifying the final requests. The same question occurs in a case of SQL-based machine learning algorithms, which are often based on heuristics, randomness and inexactness anyway [1,2].

Approximate SQL can be understood in many ways. One can, e.g., generalize SQL operators to provide users with more flexible answers [3,4]. Another way is to keep the standard meaning of SQL but speed up an execution or decrease the size of outcomes by answering with not fully accurate/complete results. Motivation for SQL approximations may be related to complexity of queries and data sources, dynamically changing data with a limited access (e.g., for sensory data and data streams), but also to huge data sets for which there is a need to monitor convergence of a query execution over time, regardless of whether the final answers are to be standard or approximate [5,6].

In this paper, we discuss *rough query* (or *rough SQL*), which is an extension of the standard SQL available in the Infobright Community and Enterprise Editions (abbreviated as ICE and IEE, respectively[1]). Query results are approximated by using Infobright's *knowledge grid* (statistical summaries of horizontally and vertically partitioned

---

[1] www.infobright.org; www.infobright.com

S. Greco et al. (Eds.): IPMU 2012, Part II, CCIS 298, pp. 570–579, 2012.
© Springer-Verlag Berlin Heidelberg 2012

data pieces). Let us treat an answer to a `select` statement as an information system [7,8] with attributes corresponding to the items after `select` (e.g.: a and `count(*)` in `select a, count(*) from T group by a;`) and objects corresponding to the result's tuples (e.g.: distinct values of a). Approximation of an answer is specified as metadata of such an information system. Thus, rough query produces a kind of a knowledge grid of the query result by using the input metadata.

Rough SQL execution is orders of magnitude faster than in the standard case. Users obtain approximate results of all types of `select` statements practically in real time. In the current implementation, rough queries are free from *false positives*, i.e., their results are always guaranteed to approximate outputs of the corresponding standard queries in a valid way. This leads to a number of interesting applications. In particular, Infobright's users can improve the current knowledge-grid-based execution of standard SQL [9,10] by building their own scripts involving rough SQL.

The paper is organized as follows. Section 2 outlines the related work. Section 3 recalls Infobright's architecture. In Section 4, we introduce rough SQL and discuss examples of its use in practice. Section 5 categorizes possible future extensions of the current rough query's implementation. Section 6 concludes the paper.

2   Related Work

The proposed rough SQL is a specific example of an approximate query framework, as it supports users with fast approximate answers to `select` statements. Therefore, let us outline some relevant aspects of the research on approximate querying.

First of all, there are techniques based on estimating actual answers by executing queries against data samples [11]. Another trend is to rely on various types of data summaries [12]. One may interpret Infobright's knowledge grid as a kind of data summary layer, although it is used to support the query execution more deeply than in other RDBMS technologies. In the future, our knowledge grid may be also applied for efficient identification of data pieces that form statistically representative data samples.

In [3], the answer to a `select *` query is approximated as not bigger or not smaller than the standard one, dependent on whether lower or upper rough set approximations [8] are in use. This idea is partially analogous to rough query proposed in this paper, although the underlying algorithmic framework is different. Also, the ability to use the approach proposed in [3] for large data sets is limited, and semantics of approximate results is not provided for all types of `select` statements.

In [6], a framework for time-constrained SQL is proposed, where users can specify an upper bound for a query processing time and an acceptable nature of answers. Similar idea was presented earlier in [5]. An analogous framework can be designed in the future for Infobright by approximating a query result basing on the knowledge grid and then refining it gradually by accessing heuristically selected data pieces.

In [13], we investigate how to extend Infobright's knowledge grid in order to reduce the required data access, even if it leads to slightly inexact outcomes. Unfortunately, the proposed method requires tuning of a number of parameters, which is a general problem of approximate SQL methods. Another issue with our approach reported in [13] is an insufficiently clear interpretation of approximate answers to arbitrary `select` statements. Rough SQL proposed in this paper is far more straightforward, although further research on practically useful semantics of query results is still needed. With this in mind, one may seek for inspiration also beyond the database solutions [14].

3   Infobright's Architecture

Infobright's RDBMS is based on the principles of data compression and columnar storage that are widely known in database research and industry [15], in combination with the elements of rough sets and rough computing [8] that provide fast execution of unexpected analytic SQL statements over huge amounts of data.

Rows loaded into a data table are partitioned onto *blocks*, each consisting of 2^{16} of rows. Each block is partitioned onto *packs*, each consisting of 2^{16} values of a column. Various types of statistics are computed for each of the packs. Finally, the packs are compressed and written on a disk. For each data table, there is a *rough information system* with objects corresponding to blocks and attributes corresponding to the above-mentioned statistics. Such systems are stored in Infobright's knowledge grid.

In [9], we showed how to use the knowledge grid to speed up various types of data operations. Let us recall how it is applied in order to classify packs into three categories that are analogous to *positive*, *negative*, and *boundary regions* known from the theory of rough sets: *Relevant (R) packs* with all data elements relevant for further execution; *Irrelevant (I) packs* with no data elements relevant for further execution; *Suspect (S) packs* that cannot be R/I-classified based on the knowledge grid.

Also in [9], we presented the following case study: Consider table T with 350,000 rows and columns a and b. We have six blocks: (A1,B1) corresponds to rows 1-65,536, (A2,B2) – to rows 65,537-131,072, etc., until (A6,B6) corresponding to rows 327,681-350,000. Consider an example of *min/max statistics* that contain the minimum and maximum values for each separate pack, as displayed in Figure 1a. For simplicity, assume there are no nulls in T and ignore all other types of statistics gathered in Infobright's knowledge grid. The SQL statement of interest is as follows:

```
select max(a) from T where b > 15;
```

According to the min/max statistics for the column b, packs B1, B2, B3, B6 are S, B4 is R, and B5 is I (Figure 1b). According to the min/max statistics for the column a, we obtain the following approximation: max(a) subject to b > 15 is between 18 and 25. Thus, after re-classifying packs and their corresponding blocks, only (A1,B1) and (A3,B3) require further investigation (Figure 1c). The maximum in A1 is higher than in A3. Thus, (A1,B1) is the first one to be processed. Depending on the analysis of its rows, (A3,B3) will become I or will need the exact processing too (Figure 1d).

Figure 1 shows that one can interpret our query execution as an approximation process. It begins with the knowledge grid and then gradually steps down to the level of exact data. In the above example, the first approximation equals to $\langle 18, 25 \rangle$, and the second one would be obtained after decompressing (A1,B1). This also illustrates how rough set regions (corresponding to the R/S/I pack statuses) can change over time. In general, Infobright's approach to the query execution may be an interesting practical model for researchers studying the theory of rough sets (see also Section 5.3).

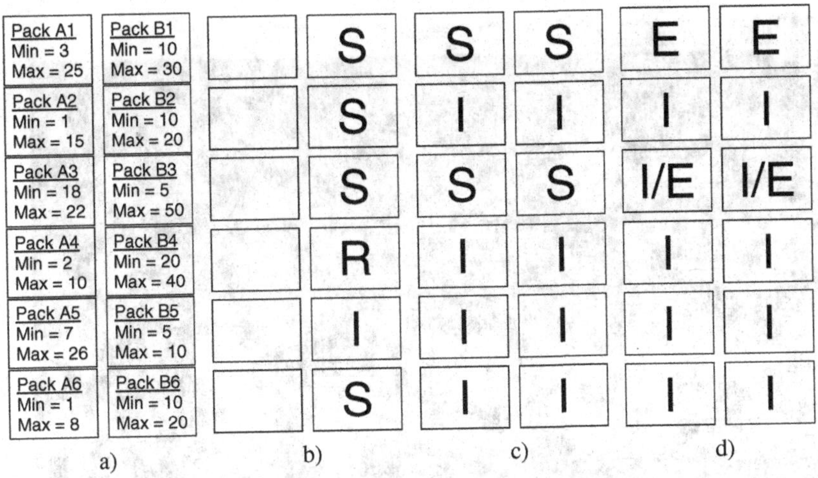

Pack A	Pack B					
Pack A1 Min = 3 Max = 25	Pack B1 Min = 10 Max = 30		S	S	E	E
Pack A2 Min = 1 Max = 15	Pack B2 Min = 10 Max = 20	S	I	I	I	I
Pack A3 Min = 18 Max = 22	Pack B3 Min = 5 Max = 50	S	S	S	I/E	I/E
Pack A4 Min = 2 Max = 10	Pack B4 Min = 20 Max = 40	R	I	I	I	I
Pack A5 Min = 7 Max = 26	Pack B5 Min = 5 Max = 10	I	I	I	I	I
Pack A6 Min = 1 Max = 8	Pack B6 Min = 10 Max = 20	S	I	I	I	I
a)			b)		c)	d)

Fig. 1. An illustration for Section 3: (a) Min/max statistics; (b,c,d) Execution stages. R, S and I denote Relevant, Suspect and Irrelevant packs, respectively. E means the need of exact processing.

4 Rough Query

4.1 Current Layout

In its current implementation, rough query's result is given as a range $\langle lower, upper \rangle$ approximating a result of the corresponding standard query. Every standard `select` statement returns a set of tuples labeled with the values of some attributes – a kind of an information system, as noted in Section 1. Consider the following example:

```
select min(a), sum(a), b
   from T where b > 1 group by b;
```

min(a)	sum(a)	b
2	3	2
2	2	6
null	null	5
1	3	3

The above query computes aggregations `min(a)` and `sum(a)` with respect to the column b. The resulting tuples correspond to the groups induced by b and there are three attributes: `min(a)`, `sum(a)` and b. Now, consider an analogous rough query:

```
select roughly min(a), sum(a), b
   from T where b > 1 group by b;
```

min(a)	sum(a)	b
1	2	2
2	3	6

Such query computes ranges for two aggregations and the grouping column. Query's outcome tells us that for each resulting tuple, if its value of `min(a)` is not `null`, then it is for sure between 1 and 2. Similarly, `sum(a)` is in $\langle 2, 3 \rangle$, and b is in $\langle 2, 6 \rangle$.

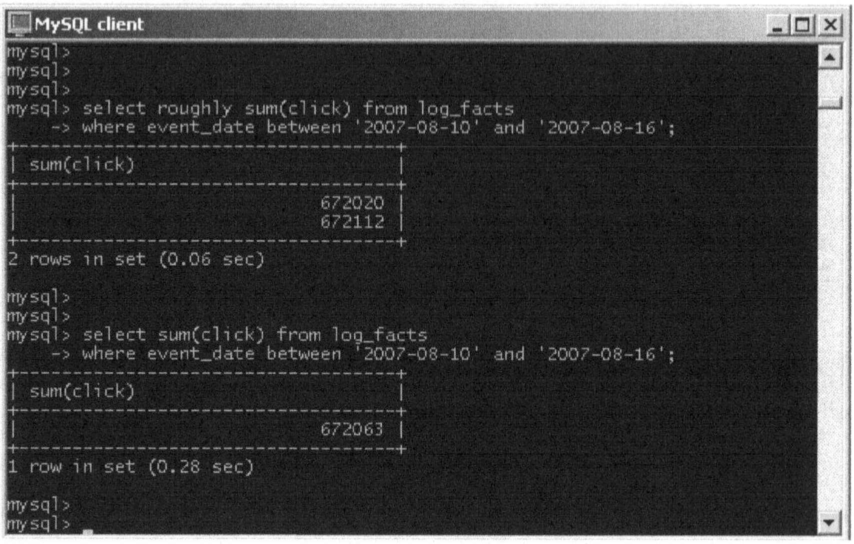

Fig. 2. Two versions of the same query executed on a standard PC against a table `log_facts` with 15 billion rows. The rough query runs in 0.06 sec. An analogous standard query runs in 0.28 sec. A usage of the MySQL client is possible thanks to leveraging the MySQL framework for storage engines (with some changes related to Infobright-specific query optimization [9]).

4.2   Solution Components

The architecture of rough SQL may be considered by means of the following layers: 1) the query execution algorithms, 2) the internal format of result, and 3) the methods that interpret, report, aggregate, and visualize that result.

The algorithms executing rough queries are based entirely on Infobright's knowledge grid, without accessing any packs of exact data. They do not construct explicitly the standard result as an intermediate stage. We implemented a number of techniques specific for particular stages of an execution of `select` statements. All of them are based on heuristics analogous to the mechanisms of dynamic approximation of standard query outcomes, as shown in Section 3. The speed of rough SQL implemented this way is illustrated by Figure 2. The obtained approximations are often not perfectly precise, e.g., it can happen that $\langle lower, upper \rangle$ for `sum(a)` in the example from Section 4.1 is $\langle 0, 4 \rangle$. We continue our work on improving this kind of precision.

The internal rough query algorithms have been used in our RDBMS for a longer time in order to speed up correlated subqueries [10]. Surely, one can adopt here some well-known methods of the correlated subquery optimization. However, the nested part of a query may still need to be processed for a huge amount of rows of an external table. Fast production of query approximations may eliminate the need of a standard computation at least for a subset of such rows. For instance, for the `select` statement from Figure 3, such a standard computation is avoided, if `clicks + 5000` is less than $lower$ of `(select ...)` for a given row of `user_campaign`.

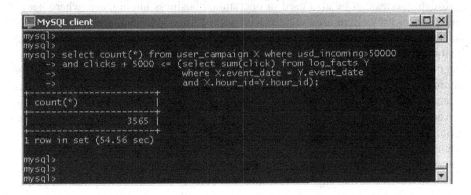

Fig. 3. An analytic SQL with a correlated subquery. It runs in 54.56 sec for the same data (and on the same machine) as in the case of Figure 2. With internal rough-query-based optimizations of correlated subqueries [10] turned off, the execution time increases to 1 min 47 sec.

There are some analogies between rough SQL introduced in Section 4.1 and the above rough optimization of correlated subqueries. In both cases, the aim is to increase query performance and to avoid already mentioned false positives, i.e., the situations when the $\langle lower, upper \rangle$ intervals are not valid approximations of the actual results. In the latter case the reason is obvious: invalid approximations might lead to invalid results of select statements. With regard to the former case, we noticed that fully valid approximations are, at least for now, easier to use by our customers.

A significant difference between externally exposed rough SQL and the methods hidden inside the database engine is the requirement of a comprehensive semantic of the output. As claimed in Section 1, a rough query result might take a form of the know-ledge grid describing an outcome of the corresponding standard statement. However, the statistical structures present in Infobright's knowledge grid would be totally unclear for users. This is why we postulate separation of two already-mentioned layers related to the internal output format and its external simplified interpretation. Our ultimate goal is to have the same algorithms and internal output formats for all kinds of a rough query usage, with a difference at the level of external result delivery.

In the current implementation, for the sake of clarity, we simplified not only the semantics of rough query results but also the rough query syntax. In the future, one may enrich it with additional parameters responsible, e.g., for a tradeoff between the speed and precision of execution. We discuss it in more details in Section 5.

4.3 Usage Examples

Our main motivation for introducing rough SQL is to run queries in (nearly) real time, as stated in Section 1. Rough queries can be executed, e.g., in order to narrow down the search space before executing regular SQL statements. This way, the time-consuming analytic queries become better focused thanks to the intermediate procedures, which are based on faster rough SQL. Such an approach, further referred to as the telescoping, can be useful in investigative analytics and data exploration.

Rough queries can be also used in operational business intelligence, where heavy aggregates or projections are executed with ad-hoc filters. For instance, in telecommunication applications, often the goal is to troubleshoot issues in the field and determine the trends of errors. The bulk of the corresponding queries generated by support engineers can return no results, and yet they are executed each time over huge data sets. By running rough SQL, one can anticipate such cases, reducing both, the time to arrive at an answer and the overhead associated with the speculative queries.

Another application of rough SQL relates to using Infobright as a pre-staging repository aimed at producing data sets for further analysis. Queries leading toward the required data sets can be very time-consuming as well. Moreover, prior to query execution, there is no guarantee that the outcome is going to satisfy given analytical requirements. In this scenario, rough SQL results can quickly provide descriptions of output data sets prior to their materialization. Basing on such descriptions, users can decide whether the underlying queries need further modifications.

The execution speed may not be the only practically meaningful advantage of rough SQL. Let us note that result sizes of rough queries are often orders of magnitude smaller than in the case of their corresponding standard `select` statements. It may be important, e.g., if an outcome of a complex multi-column `group by` is to be sent to users or third-party applications. Thus, when discussing possible extensions in Section 5, we should remember about a compactness of rough query outputs.

The last use case reported in this section may be a bit surprising as it relates to a usage of rough SQL in order to improve performance of standard queries. Let us consider the following type of analytic statements as an example:

```
select distinct a from T where F order by a desc limit L;
```

Let us refer to the above query as to $Q1$. Assume that a is a numeric column of T, L is a positive integer and filter F may be any combination of conditions, which often happens in an ad-hoc exploratory querying. Consider the following $Q2$:

```
select distinct a from T
          where F and a > X order by a desc limit L;
```

Our task is to come up with a procedure of a heuristic search for a threshold X such that $Q2$ leads to the same outcome as $Q1$, by itself or in combination with procedure's intermediate results. $Q2$ is supposed to execute faster than $Q1$. Also, execution of the search for X should be significantly faster than in the case of both $Q1$ and $Q2$.

Algorithm 1 illustrates how to use rough SQL not only to find the above-mentioned X but also to narrow down the filter and limit conditions in $Q2$. In the following, we denote by $result$ the set of intermediately extracted values of a that would be for sure included in the outcome of $Q1$. By $\langle lower, upper \rangle$, we denote ranges of the most-recently-executed rough query. In this case, the applied rough queries always refer to single numeric values, so parameters $lower$ and $upper$ should be interpreted as numeric values approximating the actual value from below and above, respectively. If N equals to 0 by the end of execution of Algorithm 1, then $result$ is the final answer to $Q1$ and no additional standard `select` statement is necessary. Otherwise, $result$ should be merged with the output of the following modification of $Q2$:

```
select distinct a from T
      where F and a > X and a < Y order by a desc limit N;
```

Algorithm 1 Rough pre-execution of $Q1$

Input: T, a, F, L; Output: X, Y, *result*, N

   X $\leftarrow$ $+\infty$, Y $\leftarrow$ $+\infty$, $B \leftarrow 1$, $M \leftarrow 0$, N $\leftarrow$ L, *result* $\leftarrow \emptyset$

  while $M < $ L **do**

     `select roughly max(a) from T where F and a < X;`

     X $\leftarrow$ *lower*

     if $B = 1$ **then**

       if *lower* $=$ *upper* **then**

         Y $\leftarrow$ X, *result* $\leftarrow$ *result* $\cup \{$X$\}$, N $\leftarrow$ N $- 1$

       else

         $B \leftarrow 0$

       end if

     end if

     `select roughly count(distinct a) from T where F and a > X;`

     $M \leftarrow$ *lower*

  end while

One may claim that the above mechanism should be rather implemented as one more internal method for improving the query execution. Actually, we intend to do it. However, there may be numerous other ways of using the knowledge grid that will need to wait for their implementation for a longer time. Rough SQL enables users to explore such methods by themselves, without waiting for the next Infobright's releases.

5 Further Extensions

5.1 Execution Internals

As already mentioned, rough queries work in their current form without accessing any packs of data. Precision of obtained $\langle lower, upper \rangle$ ranges depends on a *quality* of Infobright's knowledge grid, which intuitively corresponds to how *crisply* the packs' contents are described by their statistics (e.g. how close are the *min* and *max* values in the case of min/max statistics discussed in Section 3).

As emphasized in Section 4.2, we will continue developing algorithms producing better rough query outputs based on the knowledge grid. On the other hand, additional data access may not necessarily lead to a dramatic slowdown of a rough SQL execution. For instance, it is worth noting that Infobright caches recently used data packs in a memory. Integration of information residing within the knowledge grid with such packs may significantly improve a precision of results. Also, as one might notice in Section 3, Infobright's knowledge grid and information acquired from data accessed at a particular execution stage can be employed for heuristic selection of the very next packs that are likely to mostly contribute to narrowing down the $\langle lower, upper \rangle$ ranges.

The above ideas can be applied in many ways. For instance, one may think about introducing a threshold for the overall execution time, which would yield a percentage of mostly useful data packs that can be analyzed at the exact level. We can also consider a design of Infobright-specific incremental querying (see Section 2). However, this would also require appropriate extensions of query syntax and user interfaces.

5.2 Semantics of Results

Interpretation of approximate results is quite natural for queries that return a single vector of values (e.g.: $[\min(a),\sum(a)]$ in the case of `select min(a), sum(a) from T where b > 1;`). The problems start for multi-tuple outputs (e.g. the query considered in Section 4.1). In the case of `group by` statements, if cardinality of the grouping columns is known to be small enough, one may report approximations for each of grouping values separately [5]. For queries with a known upper bound for the number of resulting tuples (e.g. queries with `limit`), one can still try to do the same but without a guarantee that the output approximations will describe the right tuples [13]. However, for complex queries with large amounts of output tuples there is a need to work simultaneously with approximations of all attributes defining the result.

Of course, more advanced users may find the currently implemented rough query results as not sufficiently informative. In some sense, we treat the whole output of a corresponding standard query counterpart as a single block of output tuples and we annotate it with very simple statistics. One of possible extensions is to consider a number of more fine-grained blocks and report statistics for each of them. One can compare it, to some extent, with the result grouping methods in Web search engines [14]. One can also define an optimization problem of clustering the output tuples in such a way that statistics of obtained blocks are maximally informative (see [16] where we considered an analogous task for loading data). However, it is crucial to remember that in the case of rough querying, statistics of output blocks need to be approximated well enough without (or almost without) explicit creation of the blocks themselves.

5.3 Inexact Querying

In the literature, approximate queries are usually supposed to terminate with tuples being almost the same as tuples resulting from the corresponding standard queries, sometimes with some additional confidence intervals. In [13], we followed this path by enriching Infobright's knowledge grid and the corresponding database engine functions in order to compute *degrees of (ir)relevance* of particular packs at different levels of a query execution. Then, basing on some analogies to extensions of rough sets and rough computing [8], we loosened the criteria for R/I pack status, i.e., we treated *almost not suspect* packs as if they were truly (ir)relevant. This way, we created a framework for computing inexact query outputs with a lower need for a data access.

In its current implementation, rough SQL is in some sense exact, i.e., there is 100% of certainty that actual results would drop into their approximations. However, depending on the future user requirements (compare with Section 4.2), we can extend our framework toward approximate queries resulting with crisper (e.g. by means of shorter ⟨*lower, upper*⟩ intervals) but not always fully accurate answers.

From this point of view, it is important to emphasize that all the above extensions can be introduced complementarily to each other. For instance, inexact ⟨*lower, upper*⟩ ranges can be used to describe output blocks introduced in Section 5.2. Also, our above-mentioned experiences with enriching the knowledge grid and new ways of its interaction with data can be combined with mechanisms proposed in Section 5.1.

6   Conclusions

We outlined the functionality and performance of rough SQL, which is available as an extension of standard SQL in Infobright's RDBMS. We discussed applications of rough queries in exploratory data analysis and processing, operational business intelligence, as well as in additional optimization of standard `select` statements.

We intend to continue collecting and categorizing practical use cases of rough SQL. We will also consider extending its current implementation according to the directions formulated in Section 5. Last but not least, we will attempt to integrate our rough query layer with some data mining and approximate reporting solutions [1,12].

References

1. Nguyen, H.S., Nguyen, S.H.: Fast Split Selection Method and Its Application in Decision Tree Construction from Large Databases. International Journal of Hybrid Intelligent Systems 2(2), 149–160 (2005)
2. Sarawagi, S., Thomas, S., Agrawal, R.: Integrating Association Rule Mining with Relational Database Systems: Alternatives and Implications. Data Mining and Knowledge Discovery 4(2/3), 89–125 (2000)
3. Naouali, S., Missaoui, R.: Flexible Query Answering in Data Cubes. In: Tjoa, A.M., Trujillo, J. (eds.) DaWaK 2005. LNCS, vol. 3589, pp. 221–232. Springer, Heidelberg (2005)
4. Zadrożny, S., Kacprzyk, J.: Issues in the Practical Use of the OWA Operators in Fuzzy Querying. Journal of Intelligent Information Systems 33(3), 307–325 (2009)
5. Hellerstein, J.M., Haas, P.J., Wang, H.J.: Online Aggregation. In: SIGMOD, pp. 171–182 (1997)
6. Hu, Y., Sundara, S., Srinivasan, J.: Supporting Time-constrained SQL Queries in Oracle. In: VLDB, pp. 1207–1218 (2007)
7. Pawlak, Z.: Information Systems - Theoretical Foundations. Information Systems 6, 205–218 (1981)
8. Pawlak, Z., Skowron, A.: Rudiments of Rough Sets. Information Sciences 177(1), 3–27 (2007)
9. Ślęzak, D., Wróblewski, J., Eastwood, V., Synak, P.: Brighthouse: An Analytic Data Warehouse for Ad-hoc Queries. Proceedings of VLDB Endowment 1(2), 1337–1345 (2008)
10. Ślęzak, D., Synak, P., Borkowski, J., Wróblewski, J., Toppin, G.: A Rough-columnar RDBMS Engine-A Case Study of Correlated Subqueries. IEEE Data Engineering Bulletin 35(1), 34–39 (2012)
11. Chaudhuri, S., Das, G., Narasayya, V.: Optimized Stratified Sampling for Approximate Query Processing. ACM Transactions on Database Systems 32(2), 9 (2007)
12. Cuzzocrea, A., Serafino, P.: LCS-Hist: Taming Massive High-dimensional Data Cube Compression. In: EDBT, pp. 768–779 (2009)
13. Ślęzak, D., Kowalski, M.: Towards Approximate SQL – Infobright's Approach. In: Szczuka, M., Kryszkiewicz, M., Ramanna, S., Jensen, R., Hu, Q. (eds.) RSCTC 2010. LNCS, vol. 6086, pp. 630–639. Springer, Heidelberg (2010)
14. Carpineto, C., Osiński, S., Romano, G., Weiss, D.: A Survey of Web Clustering Engines. ACM Computing Surveys 41, 1–38 (2009)
15. White, P., French, C.: Database System with Methodology for Storing a Database Table by Vertically Partitioning all Columns of the Table. US Patent 5,794,229 (1998)
16. Ślęzak, D., Kowalski, M., Eastwood, V., Wróblewski, J.: Method and System for Database Organization. US Patent Application 2009/0106210 A1 (2009)

Polynomial Asymptotic Complexity of Multiple-Objective OLAP Data Cube Compression

Alfredo Cuzzocrea[1] and Marco Fisichella[2]

[1]ICAR-CNR and University of Calabria, Italy
cuzzocrea@si.deis.unical.it
[2] L3S Research Center, Germany
fisichella@L3S.de

Abstract. In this paper, we complement previous research results provided in [8], where the *multiple-objective OLAP data cube compression paradigm* has been introduced. This paradigm pursues the idea of *compressing OLAP data cubes in the dependence of multiple requirements* rather than only one, like in traditional approaches. Here, we provide a comprehensive description of algorithm computeMQHist, the main algorithm of the framework [8], which allows us to obtain compressed data cubes that adhere to the multiple-objective computational paradigm, and we prove that computeMQHist has a *polynomial asymptotic complexity*.

1 Introduction

In [8] we introduced a novel computational paradigm for advanced OLAP applications, the so-called *multiple-objective OLAP data cube compression*. Contrary to state-of-the-art research, this paradigm pursues the idea of *compressing OLAP data cubes in the dependence of multiple requirements* rather than only one. Traditional approaches, in fact, aim at compressing OLAP data cubes via the satisfaction of one requirement only, such as the minimization of the *query error* associated to a fixed query-workload (e.g., [3,10]), or the accomplishment of super-imposed *probabilistic guarantees* (e.g., [5,10]), or making adaptive the *degree of approximation* of the retrieved answers (e.g., [6,7]).

Integrating multiple-objective paradigms into Data Warehouse and OLAP processing, with particular regards to query processing issues, has recently captured the interest of a wide community of researchers. Several proposals exist in literature, which span from *multiple-query optimization for view selection* (e.g., [19]) to *multiple-query based data integration* (e.g., [11]), and from *multiple-objective query processing* in database (e.g., [17,2]), OLAP (e.g., [14]) and data stream management (e.g., [20,18]) systems to *skyline queries* (e.g., [15]), and so forth. In line with these initiative, [8] extends the problem to the more probing setting that deals with OLAP data cube compression methodologies, and proposes an innovative approach that supports the multiple-objective compression of data cube under the simultaneous evaluation of *Hierarchical Range Queries* (HRQ) [9]. HRQ are tree-like OLAP queries such that each node stores a classical aggregate (OLAP) query (e.g., SUM- or

S. Greco et al. (Eds.): IPMU 2012, Part II, CCIS 298, pp. 580–593, 2012.
© Springer-Verlag Berlin Heidelberg 2012

COUNT-based) and queries associated to intermediate nodes (of the tree) are *holistic* in nature [5]. Overall, the approach [8] proposes building the innovative *hierarchical multidimensional histogram* MQ-Hist($\mathcal{L}$) which, based on a *greedy algorithm*, is capable of finally generating an "intermediate" multidimensional representation (i.e., the compressed data cube) that accommodates, as much as possible, the different objectives deriving from evaluating multiple HRQ against the input data cube. In addition to this, in [8] we also prove the effectiveness and the efficiency of the histogram MQ-Hist($\mathcal{L}$) via assessing it against both benchmark and real-life data cubes, and in comparison with state-of-the-art approaches. In this paper, we further extends the results provided in [8] by means of the following contributions: (*i*) we provide a more detailed and comprehensive description of algorithm `computeMQHist`, the algorithm that computes the histogram MQ-Hist($\mathcal{L}$) starting from the input data cube (Section 2); (*ii*) we prove that `computeMQHist` has a *polynomial asymptotic complexity*, which is the most relevant result of this paper (Section 3).

2   Algorithm `computeMQHist`: Principles, Methods and Case Studies

In this Section, we present in detail our main algorithm `computeMQHist` that allows us to compress multidimensional data cubes under simultaneous multiple HRQ [8]. Given the input data cube $\mathcal{L}$, our main idea is that of finally obtaining an "intermediate" compressed representation of $\mathcal{L}$ that is able to accommodate, as much as possible, the different and even-heterogeneous requirements posed by evaluating multiple HRQ simultaneously against $\mathcal{L}$.

We are given: (*i*) an N-dimensional data cube $\mathcal{L}$ having P hierarchical levels; (*ii*) the set of M HRQ that must be evaluated against $\mathcal{L}$ simultaneously, $S_{HRQ} = \{Q_{H_0}, Q_{H_1}, ..., Q_{H_{M-1}}\}$ (recall that, for the sake of simplicity, we assume that HRQ in S_{HRQ} have the same depth, P, which is also equal to the number of hierarchical levels of $\mathcal{L}$); (*iii*) the storage space $\mathcal{B}$ available for housing the compressed representation of $\mathcal{L}$, $\tilde{\mathcal{L}}$, which is implemented by the histogram MQ-Hist($\mathcal{L}$). The multiple-query data cube compression technique we propose is implemented by the greedy algorithm `computeMQHist`, which basically realizes the following multi-step approach: (*i*) for each level ℓ of $\mathcal{L}$, such that ℓ belongs to [0, P-1], starting from the bottom level 0 (i.e., according to a *bottom-up strategy*), generate, for each dimension d of $\mathcal{L}_\ell$, the *ordered union* of range bounds of (range) queries (modeled as multidimensional points in the $\mathcal{L}_\ell$ ($\equiv \mathcal{L}$) multidimensional space) at level ℓ of HRQ in S_{HRQ} along d, thus obtaining the so-called *Multiple Range* (MR) for the dimension d at level ℓ, denoted by $MR_{\ell,d}$ – first step finally generates, for each cuboid $\mathcal{L}_\ell$ of $\mathcal{L}$, the set of N MR, denoted by $\mathcal{MR}(\mathcal{L}_\ell) = \{MR_{\ell,0}, MR_{\ell,1}, ..., MR_{\ell,N-1}\}$, and, overall, the whole set of P MR associated to $\mathcal{L}$, denoted by $\mathcal{MR}(\mathcal{L}) = \{\mathcal{MR}(\mathcal{L}_0), \mathcal{MR}(\mathcal{L}_1), ..., \mathcal{MR}(\mathcal{L}_{P-1})\}$, is determined; (*ii*) for each level ℓ of $\mathcal{L}$, generate a *Generalized Partition* (GP) of the cuboid $\mathcal{L}_\ell$ at level ℓ, denoted by $\mathcal{G}(\mathcal{L}_\ell)$, such that buckets in $\mathcal{G}(\mathcal{L}_\ell)$ are obtained via projecting, for each dimension d of $\mathcal{L}_\ell$, axes along points of MR in $\mathcal{MR}(\mathcal{L}_\ell)$ – the collection of GP (one for each level ℓ of $\mathcal{L}$), denoted by GP-Coll($\mathcal{L}$) = { $\mathcal{G}(\mathcal{L}_0)$, $\mathcal{G}(\mathcal{L}_1)$, ..., $\mathcal{G}(\mathcal{L}_{P-1})$}, constitutes the "sketch" of the histogram MQ-Hist($\mathcal{L}$), meaning that the histogram is finally obtained starting from GP-Coll($\mathcal{L}$); (iii) for each level ℓ of $\mathcal{L}$, obtain from the GP $\mathcal{G}(\mathcal{L}_\ell)$ of GP-Coll($\mathcal{L}$) the so-called *Multiple-Query Partition* (MQP) of the cuboid $\mathcal{L}_\ell$, denoted by $\mathcal{P}(\mathcal{L}_\ell)$, via (i) *meaningfully merging buckets* in $\mathcal{G}(\mathcal{L}_\ell)$ with the criterion that $\mathcal{P}(\mathcal{L}_\ell)$ must be able to fit, *at level* ℓ, all the different query requirements of HRQ in S_{HRQ}, and (ii) storing the SUM-based aggregations of items they contain – the collection of MQP (one for each level ℓ of $\mathcal{L}$) is denoted by MQP-Coll($\mathcal{L}$) = { $\mathcal{P}(\mathcal{L}_0)$, $\mathcal{P}(\mathcal{L}_1)$, ..., $\mathcal{P}(\mathcal{L}_{P-1})$}; (iv) return MQ-Hist($\mathcal{L}$) via hierarchically combining the P MQP $\mathcal{P}(\mathcal{L}_\ell)$ in MQP-Coll($\mathcal{L}$).

ALGORITHM buildMultipleRangeDim

Input: The data cube $\mathcal{L}$; the set of HRQ S_{HRQ}; a dimension d of $\mathcal{L}$; an integer ℓ.
Output: The set MR$_{\ell,d}$.

import *Sets.*;*
import *OLAPTools.*;*

Begin
    MR$_{\ell,n} \leftarrow \varnothing$;
    $m \leftarrow 0$;
    $M \leftarrow$ *Sets.getSize*(S_{HRQ});
    $Q_H \leftarrow \varnothing$;
    $k \leftarrow$ *OLAPTools.getDimensionIndex*($\mathcal{L},d$);
    $l \leftarrow 0$;
    rangeQuerySet $\leftarrow \varnothing$;
    $L \leftarrow 0$;
    $Q \leftarrow \varnothing$;
    queryRange $\leftarrow \varnothing$;
    while ($m < M$) **do**
        $Q_H \leftarrow$ *Sets.getItem*(S_{HRQ},m);
        $l \leftarrow 0$;
        rangeQuerySet $\leftarrow Q_H$.*getRangeQuerySet*(ℓ);
        $L \leftarrow$ *Sets.getSize*(*rangeQuerySet*);
        while ($l < L$) **do**
            $Q \leftarrow$ *Sets.getItem*(*rangeQuerySet,l*);
            queryRange $\leftarrow Q$.*getQueryRange*(k);
            MR$_{\ell,n} \leftarrow$
                Sets.orderedUnion(MR$_{\ell,d}$,*queryRange*);
            $l \leftarrow l + 1$;
        end
        $m \leftarrow m + 1$;
    end
    return MR$_{\ell,d}$;
End;

Fig. 1. Algorithm buildMultipleRange-Dim

ALGORITHM buildGeneralizedPartitionSet

Input: The data cube $\mathcal{L}$; the set of HRQ S_{HRQ}.
Output: The set of GP GP-Coll($\mathcal{L}$).

import *OLAPTools.*;*
import *Sets.*;*
import *HistogramTools.*;*

Begin
    GP-Coll $\leftarrow \varnothing$;
    $\ell \leftarrow 0$;
    $P \leftarrow$ *OLAPTools.getHierarchyDepth*($\mathcal{L}$);
    $\mathcal{L}_\ell \leftarrow \varnothing$;
    $\mathcal{G}_\ell \leftarrow \varnothing$;
    $k \leftarrow 0$;
    $N \leftarrow$ *OLAPTools.getDimensionNumber*($\mathcal{L}$);
    MR$_{\ell,n} \leftarrow \varnothing$;
    $\mathcal{MR}_\ell \leftarrow \varnothing$;
    while ($\ell < P$) **do**
        $\mathcal{L}_\ell \leftarrow$ *OLAPTools.getCuboid*(ℓ);
        $\mathcal{G}_\ell \leftarrow \varnothing$;
        $k \leftarrow 0$;
        while ($k < N$) **do**
            MR$_{\ell,n} \leftarrow$
                buildMultipleRangeDim($\mathcal{L},S_{HRQ},k,\ell$);
            $\mathcal{MR}_\ell \leftarrow$ *Sets.add*($\mathcal{MR}_\ell$,MR$_{\ell,d}$);
            $k \leftarrow k + 1$;
        end
        $\mathcal{G}_\ell \leftarrow$
        HistogramTools.buildPartitionByProjection($\mathcal{L}_\ell,\mathcal{MR}_\ell$);
        GP-Coll $\leftarrow$ *Sets.add*(GP-Coll,$\mathcal{G}_\ell$);
        $\ell \leftarrow \ell + 1$;
    end
    return GP-Coll;
End;

Fig. 2. Algorithm buildGeneralized-PartitionSet

The first step of our technique is implemented by algorithm `buildMultiple-Range` (see Figure 1), which takes as input the data cube $\mathcal{L}$ and the set of HRQ S_{HRQ}, and returns as output the set $\mathcal{MR}(\mathcal{L})$. `buildMultipleRange` makes use of a baseline algorithm, namely `buildMultipleRangeDim` (see Figure 1), which is in charge of generating the MR for a given dimension d at a given level ℓ of the data cube, having fixed the set of HRQ S_{HRQ}.

Algorithm `buildGeneralizedPartitionSet` (see Figure 2) implements the second step of our multiple-query data cube compression technique. `buildGeneralizedPartitionSet` takes as input the data cube $\mathcal{L}$ and the set of HRQ S_{HRQ}, and returns as output the set GP-Coll($\mathcal{L}$) via exploiting algorithm `buildMultipleRangeDim` (see Figure 1). We introduce algorithm `buildGeneralizedPartitionSet` throughout a meaningful example, where we also show how MR, sets of MR and GP are generated in practice. For the sake of simplicity, consider the following OLAP scenario: (i) a $|d_0| \times |d_1|$ two-dimensional cuboid $\mathcal{L}_\ell$, such that the domain of d_0 is $Dom(d_0) = \{a, b, c, d, e, f, g, h, i, l, m, n, o, p, q\}$, and the domain of d_1 is equal to that of d_0 (i.e., $Dom(d_1) = Dom(d_0)$), being the common-intended lexicographical ordering defined on both of these domains; (ii) three range queries, $Q_{i,\ell}$, $Q_{j,\ell}$, and $Q_{k,\ell}$ of *distinct* HRQ defined on $\mathcal{L}_\ell$, defined as follows: $Q_{i,\ell} = \langle [b, d], [c, f] \rangle$, $Q_{j,\ell} = \langle [d, e], [d, g] \rangle$, and $Q_{k,\ell} = \langle [h, i], [m, m] \rangle$. According to our multiple-query compression technique, we finally obtain the following configuration: (i) the MR of the dimension d_0, $MR_{\ell,0}$, is: $MR_{\ell,0} = \{b, d, e, h, i\}$; (ii) the MR of the dimension d_1, $MR_{\ell,1}$, is: $MR_{\ell,1} = \{c, d, f, g, m\}$; (iii) the set of MR of $\mathcal{L}_\ell$ is: $\mathcal{MR}(\mathcal{L}_\ell) = \{\{b, d, e, h, i\}, \{c, d, f, g, m\}\}$; (iv) the GP of $\mathcal{L}_\ell$, $\mathcal{G}(\mathcal{L}_\ell)$, is that depicted in Figure 3.

From Figure 3, note that the so-generated buckets of $\mathcal{G}(\mathcal{L}_\ell)$ are all the buckets that would allow us to provide, *at level* ℓ, approximate answers having the *highest accuracy* for *all* HRQ in S_{HRQ} at level ℓ. The same for the other GP of GP-Coll($\mathcal{L}$). Obviously, it is not possible to materialize *all* the buckets of *all* the GP of GP-Coll($\mathcal{L}$), due to the storage space constraint posed by the input bound $\mathcal{B}$. If this would be the case, we finally would obtain the histogram MQ-Hist($\mathcal{L}$) as corresponding to GP-Coll($\mathcal{L}$) directly, i.e. as a *full materialization* of GP-Coll($\mathcal{L}$). Being this impossible for reasonable configurations of the input parameters, we adopt the strategy of *obtaining*, for each level ℓ of $\mathcal{L}$, *the* MQP $\mathcal{P}(\mathcal{L}_\ell)$ *via meaningfully merging buckets* in the GP $\mathcal{G}(\mathcal{L}_\ell)$, thus reducing the overall final size of $\mathcal{P}(\mathcal{L}_\ell)$ and, as a consequence, the overall final size of MQ-Hist($\mathcal{L}$), keeping in mind the priority goal of accommodating, as much as possible, the multiple-query constraints posed by HRQ in S_{HRQ}. According to the guidelines given in Section 1, overall this strategy allows us to finally compute $\mathcal{P}(\mathcal{L}_\ell)$ as a *sub-optimal partition* of $\mathcal{G}(\mathcal{L}_\ell)$. Figure 4 shows a *possible* MQP $\mathcal{P}(\mathcal{L}_\ell)$ for the cuboid $\mathcal{L}_\ell$ of the running example.

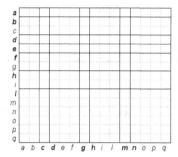

Fig. 3. The GP $\mathcal{G}(\mathcal{L}_t)$ of the running example

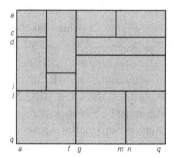

Fig. 4. A possible corresponding $\mathcal{P}(\mathcal{L}_t)$ for the GP $\mathcal{G}(\mathcal{L}_t)$ of Figure 3

The third step of our multiple-query data cube compression technique is implemented by algorithm `buildMultipleQueryPartitionSet` (see Figure 5), which takes as input the set GP-Coll($\mathcal{L}$), the storage space $\mathcal{B}$ and a threshold value V_U (described next), and returns as output the set MQP-Coll($\mathcal{L}$). To this end, `buildMultipleQueryPartitionSet` introduces a *global strategy* and a *local strategy*. The first one deals with the problem of how to explore the overall hierarchical search (bucket) space represented by GP-Coll($\mathcal{L}$). The second one deals with the problem of how to explore the planar search (bucket) space represented by a given $\mathcal{G}(\mathcal{L}_t)$.

First, consider the local strategy of `buildMultipleQueryPartitionSet`, which properly realizes the main greedy criterion used to obtain a MQP $\mathcal{P}(\mathcal{L}_t)$ from a given GP $\mathcal{G}(\mathcal{L}_t)$. In our approach, we adopt a strategy that is inspired by the one adopted by traditional multidimensional histograms (e.g., *MinSkew* [1] and *MHist* [16]), i.e. *obtaining final buckets storing as more uniform data as possible via minimizing the skewness* among buckets themselves. This, in turn, has beneficial effects on the accuracy of approximate answers computed against the histogram, as widely recognized (e.g., see [4]). The difference with respect to our approach lies in the fact that traditional histograms operate on the original data cube directly, whereas MQ-Hist($\mathcal{L}$) is built starting from the bucket space defined by GP-Coll($\mathcal{L}$), and, in turn, by each $\mathcal{G}(\mathcal{L}_t)$ (with respect to this particular aspect, our proposal is reminiscent of *GenHist* histograms [12]). According to these guidelines, in the local computation of `buildMultipleQueryPartitionSet`, given the GP $\mathcal{G}(\mathcal{L}_t)$, *we greedily select the most uniform bucket*, said b_U, among buckets of the overall bucket space of $\mathcal{G}(\mathcal{L}_t)$, and then we explore the *neighboring buckets* of b_U in search for buckets having a homogeneity close to that of b_U, having fixed a threshold value V_U that limits the maximum difference between the homogeneity of b_U and that of its neighboring buckets. To meaningfully support this task, given a bucket b_k of $\mathcal{G}(\mathcal{L}_t)$, we adopt as homogeneity definition the *greatest quadratic distance* from the average value of *outliers* in b_k, meaning that the less is such a distance, the more is the homogeneity of b_k. This approach is modeled by the function *unif*(b_k), defined as follows:

$$unif(b_k) = \frac{1}{\max\limits_{i \in Out(b_k)} \{0, |b_k[i] - \mathsf{AVG}(b_k)|^2\}} \qquad (1)$$

such that: (i) $Out(b_k)$ is the set of outliers of b_k, (ii) $b_k[i]$ is the value of the i-th item of b_k, and (iii) $\mathsf{AVG}(b_k)$ is the average value of items in b_k. Note that we make use of the second power to ensure the convergence of (1). Outlier detection (e.g., [10]) is a non-trivial engagement. Without going into detail, in our approach this task can be implemented by means of any of the method proposed in literature (conventional or not), so that this aspect of our work is orthogonal to the main contribution. On the other hand, defining a "good" metrics of homogeneity of a given data domain (e.g., a bucket) is probing as well. Experience acquired by us in the context of outlier management for efficient query answering against compressed data cubes [10] suggests us the validity of function $unif(\bullet)$, despite its apparent simplicity. Also, it should be noted that being the bucket merging process dependent on the threshold value V_U, different instances of this process can be easily tuned on the basis of particular application requirements.

When a set of neighboring buckets is detected and must be merged in a singleton bucket, said b_M, we impose the criterion of obtaining b_M as a *hyper-rectangular bucket* instead of an arbitrary bucket (i.e., a bucket with irregular shape). This reasonably follows the geometry of typical range queries against data cubes for BI, which in the domain of OLAP are typically rectangular, whereas in the domain of GIS can also have arbitrary shapes, e.g. *polygonal* ones. In doing this, based on geometrical issues, we simply "throw away" protruding parts of merged neighboring buckets in such a way as to obtain a "maximal", "internal" hyper-rectangular bucket. In turn, the protruding bucket parts are then materialized as new buckets of the GP $G(\mathcal{L}_\ell)$, and then the same task is iterated again on the *remaining* bucket set of $G(\mathcal{L}_\ell)$. Comparing with *STHoles* [3], we observe that [3] proposes a "total" *hierarchical strategy* for merging buckets, whereas we propose a *planar strategy* for merging buckets, but applied to each level of our hierarchical search (bucket) space due to the hierarchical nature of GP-Coll($\mathcal{L}$). Obviously, the underlying greedy criterion is different in the two proposals.

Once the MQP $\mathcal{P}(\mathcal{L}_\ell)$ at level ℓ is determined, SUM-based aggregations over final buckets of $\mathcal{P}(\mathcal{L}_\ell)$ are computed. These aggregations will be finally stored, along with the necessary indexing information, within the histogram MQ-Hist($\mathcal{L}$).

For what regards the second aspect of buildMultipleQueryPartitionSet (i.e., the global strategy), we adopt an *in-depth visit* of GP-Coll($\mathcal{L}$) starting from the aggregation ALL (i.e., from the corresponding GP at level P, $G(\mathcal{L}_\ell)$), when a merged bucket b_M is obtained in the GP $G(\mathcal{L}_\ell)$ at level ℓ, we hierarchically *move down* to the GP $G(\mathcal{L}_{\ell+1})$ at level $\ell + 1$, and consider the collection of buckets of $G(\mathcal{L}_{\ell+1})$ contained by the region defined by b_M over $G(\mathcal{L}_{\ell+1})$, and so forth. When aggregation $\varnothing$ is reached (i.e., the corresponding GP at level 0, $G(\mathcal{L}_0)$, is reached), we re-start again from the aggregation ALL. As said before, the whole process is bounded by the consumption of the available storage space $\mathcal{B}$.

Basically, the above-described one defines a *top-down* approach in the computation of MQ-Hist($\mathcal{L}$). Without going into details, it should be noted that the in-depth visit approach is in favor of the idea of accommodating a large family of range queries embedded in HRQ rather than range queries referred to a *particular* level of the logical hierarchy underlying the input data cube $\mathcal{L}$. The rationale of this way to do comes from arguing that, in a typical OLAP scenario, client applications are mainly interested in querying OLAP data at granularities different from the lowest one [13]. To become convinced of this, consider a repository $\mathcal{R}$ of census data (which are particularly suitable to be processed and analyzed by means of OLAP technology) and a data cube $\mathcal{L}$ defined on top of $\mathcal{R}$ such that $\mathcal{L}$ includes, among all, the dimension *Time* with hierarchy $\mathcal{H}_{Time}$. Also, suppose that $\mathcal{H}_{Time}$ is organized as follows: *Year* → *Quarter* → *Month* → *Day*. Even if census data are available in *all* the defined temporal granularities (i.e., *Year*, *Quarter*, *Month*, and *Day*), OLAP client applications typically access and query data at the granularities *Month* or *Quarter* or *Year* mostly, and rarely consider the aggregations at the granularity *Day* [13]. This evidence, combined with (*i*) the need of accommodating a large family of queries, and (*ii*) the presence of a bounded storage space (i.e., $\mathcal{B}$), gives raise to our top-down approach.

Algorithm computeMQHist (see Figure 6) implements our proposed multiple-query data cube compression technique via exploiting algorithms buildGeneralizedPartitionSet (see Figure 2) and buildMultipleQueryPartitionSet (see Figure 5). computeMQHist takes as input the data cube $\mathcal{L}$, the set of HRQ S_{HRQ}, the storage space $\mathcal{B}$ and a threshold value V_U, and returns as output the hierarchical multidimensional histogram MQ-Hist($\mathcal{L}$) built over $\mathcal{L}$. Also, computeMQHist makes use of the procedure buildHierarchicalReferences, belonging to the utility package HistogramTools, which takes as input a set of MultipleQueryPartition objects MQP-Coll($\mathcal{L}$) and returns as output the histogram MQ-Hist($\mathcal{L}$) via hierarchically combining the MQP $\mathcal{P}(\mathcal{L}_\ell)$ in MQP-Coll($\mathcal{L}$).

Finally, it should be noted that MQ-Hist($\mathcal{L}$) implicitly defines a *multi-level R-tree based partitioning scheme* of the input data cube $\mathcal{L}$, with the novelty that bounds of rectangular buckets at different levels are obtained by meaningfully handling and reasoning on the multiple-query scheme imposed by the multiple-objective OLAP scenario investigated in this paper. This data engineering model is perfectly able to capture the hierarchical nature of the compression process of $\mathcal{L}$, and, at the same time, efficiently answer SUM-based HRQ, which, as stated in Section 1, are the class of queries of interest for our research work. Obviously, this approach can be straightforwardly extended as to deal with different classes of HRQ, i.e. HRQ based on different kinds of SQL aggregate operators, with slight modifications of the approximate query answering engine. Also, note that the MQ-Hist($\mathcal{L}$) approach is in a clear opposition to other proposals where the data cube partition is obtained according to a pre-fixed scheme, such as quad-tree based partitions, which look at the data domain of the data cube rather than to its *information and knowledge content* in terms of schemas (e.g., data cube logical schemas) and models (e.g., OLAP queries and hierarchies).

ALGORITHM buildMultipleQueryPartitionSet

Input: The set of GP GP-Coll($\mathcal{L}$); the storage space $\mathcal{B}$; the threshold value V_U.

Output: The set of MQP MQP-Coll($\mathcal{L}$).

import *HistogramTools.*;*
import *Regs.*;*
import *Sets.*;*

Begin

    MQP-Coll($\mathcal{L}$) ← ∅; ℓ ← 0;
    $\mathcal{G}_\ell$ ← ∅;   *visitedBucketSet* ← ∅;
    $\mathcal{P}_\ell$ ← ∅; b_U ← ∅; b_k ← ∅;
    b_M ← ∅;   *mergeBucketSet* ← ∅;
    boundingMDRegion ← GP-Coll($\mathcal{L}$).*get*(0);
    newBucketSet ← ∅;
    while ($\mathcal{B}$ > 0) **do**
        $\mathcal{G}_\ell$ ← GP-Coll($\mathcal{L}$).*get*(ℓ);
        b_U ←
    HistogramTools.findMaxUnifBucket($\mathcal{G}_\ell$,*visitedBucketSet*);
        if (b_U = ∅) **then**
            b_U ←
                Regs.getRandomBucket($\mathcal{G}_\ell$,*visitedBucketSet*);
        end
        mergeBucketSet ← *Sets.add*(*mergeBucketSet*,b_U);
        visitedBucketSet ← *Sets.add*(*visitedBucketSet*,b_U);
        b_k ←
    Regs.getNextNeighBucket(b_U,*boundingMDRegion*,*visitedBucketSet*);
        while (b_k <> ∅ && *abs*(*unif*(b_k) − *unif*(b_U)) ≤ V_U) **do**
            mergeBucketSet ← *Sets.add*(*mergeBucketSet*,b_k);
            visitedBucketSet ← *Sets.add*(*visitedBucketSet*,b_k);
            b_k ←
    Regs.getNextNeighBucket(b_U,*boundingMDRegion*,*visitedBucketSet*);
        end;
        b_M ← *Regs.mergeBucketSet*(*mergeBucketSet*);
        if (MQP-Coll($\mathcal{L}$) <> ∅) **then**
            $\mathcal{P}_\ell$ ← MQP-Coll($\mathcal{L}$).*get*(ℓ);
        end
        $\mathcal{P}_\ell$ ← *Sets.add*($\mathcal{P}_\ell$,b_M);
        newBucketSet ←
    Regs.generateNewBucketSet(b_M,$\mathcal{G}_\ell$,*visitedBucketSet*);
        if (*Sets.getSize*(*newBucketSet*) > 0) **then**
            $\mathcal{G}_\ell$ ← *Sets.add*($\mathcal{G}_\ell$,*newBucketSet*);
        end
        $\mathcal{P}_\ell$ ←
                HistogramTools.computeSUMAggregations($\mathcal{P}_\ell$);
        MQP-Coll($\mathcal{L}$).*add*($\mathcal{P}_\ell$);
        $\mathcal{B}$ ←
    $\mathcal{B}$ − *HistogramTools.computeOccupancy*(MQP-Coll($\mathcal{L}$));
        ℓ ← ℓ + 1;
        if (ℓ ≥ *Sets.getSize*(GP-Coll($\mathcal{L}$)) **then**
            ℓ ← 0;
            boundingMDRegion ← GP-Coll($\mathcal{L}$).*get*(0);
        else
            boundingMDRegion ←
                Regs.project(b_M,GP-Coll($\mathcal{L}$).*get*(ℓ));
        end;
    end
    return MQP-Coll($\mathcal{L}$);
End;

ALGORITHM computeMQHist

Input: The data cube $\mathcal{L}$; the set of HRQ S_{HRQ}; the storage space $\mathcal{B}$; threshold value V_U.

Output: The histogram MQ-Hist($\mathcal{L}$).

import *HistogramTools.*;*

Begin

    MQ-Hist ← ∅;
    GP-Coll ←
    buildGeneralizedPartitionSet($\mathcal{L}$,S_{HRQ});
    MQP-Coll($\mathcal{L}$) ←
    buildMultipleQueryPartitionSet(GP-Coll,$\mathcal{B}$,V_U);
    MQ-Hist ←
    HistogramTools.buildHierachicalReferences(MQP-Coll($\mathcal{L}$));
        return MQ-Hist;
End;

Fig. 6. Algorithm computeMQHist

Fig. 5. Algorithm buildMultipleQuery-PartitionSet

3   The Polynomial Asymptotic Complexity of Algorithm computeMQHist

In this Section, we provide the complexity analysis and results of the multiple-query data cube compression technique we propose throughout algorithm computeMQ-Hist. In this analysis, we will make use of the well-known O *notation*, which is a well-known formalism to model and reason on the complexity of algorithms in the dependence on the input parameters, and in terms of their *worst case execution*, i.e. that execution for which the target algorithm exposes the *higher complexity*.

Consider the structure of algorithm computeMQHist (see Section 2). Given the input N-dimensional data cube $\mathcal{L}$ having P hierarchical level, the set of M HRQ S_{HRQ} each of one having depth equal to P and the storage space available to house the final histogram MQ-Hist($\mathcal{L}$), $\mathcal{B}$, we can recognize four main modules of computeMQ-Hist, which are related to the four main steps of our multi-query data cube compression technique, and, in turn, to the four algorithms presented in Section 2: (*i*) **buildMR**, which returns the set $\mathcal{MR}(\mathcal{L})$; (*ii*) **buildGP**, which returns the set GP-Coll($\mathcal{L}$); (*iii*) **buildMQP**, which returns the set MQP-Coll($\mathcal{L}$); (*iv*) **buildMQHist**, which returns the histogram MQ-Hist($\mathcal{L}$). Let O_H denote the complexity of algorithm computeMQHist. Since computeMQHist is a multi-step algorithm, its complexity can be determined in the dependence on the complexities of its underlying modules, as follows:

$$O_H = O_{MR} \oplus O_{GP} \oplus O_{MQP} \oplus O_{MQH} \tag{2}$$

such that: (*i*) O_{MR} denotes the complexity of **buildMR**, (*ii*) O_{GP} denotes the complexity of **buildGP**, (*iii*) O_{MQP} denotes the complexity of **buildMQP**, (*iv*) O_{MQH} denotes the complexity of **buildMQH**, (*v*) $\oplus$ denotes the sum operator in the domain of complexities. In the following, we separately provide closed formulas for characterizing the complexity of each module of computeMQHist. Then, starting from these complexities we finally derive the closed formula modeling the complexity of computeMQHist.

The complexity of **buildMR**, O_{MR}, is given by the following formula:

$$O_{MR} = O\left(N \cdot \sum_{m=0}^{M-1} \sum_{\ell=0}^{P-1} |\text{queries}_m(\ell)|\right) \tag{3}$$

such that $queries_m(\ell)$ denotes the set of range queries embedded in the HRQ Q_{H_m} at level ℓ (see Section 2).

(3) is due to noticing that, in order to build the set $\mathcal{MR}(\mathcal{L})$, in the worst case we have to access and manage, for each dimension d of *all* the N dimensions of $\mathcal{L}$, *all* the range queries embedded in *all* the P levels of *all* the M HRQ in S_{HRQ}. Note that, given two ordered set S_i and S_j, the complexity of obtaining the ordered union $S_h = S_i \cup S_j$ is $O(|S_i| + |S_j|)$ in the worst case in which all the items in S_i and S_j are different, i.e. S_i and S_j are disjointed ($S_i \cap S_j = \varnothing$). Since OLAP dimensions and ranges of queries are ordered [13], the complexity of generating the ordered union of M query ranges at a

given level ℓ_p is: $O\left(\sum_{m=0}^{M-1}|\text{queries}\ _m(\ell_p)|\right)$. Since this operation must be performed for each level of the data cube hierarchy and for each dimension of the data cube, we finally obtain (3) as characterizing the complexity of **buildMR**.

The complexity of **buildGP**, O_{GP}, is given by the following formula:

$$O_{GP} = O\left(\sum_{\ell=0}^{P-1}\sum_{n=0}^{N-1}|\text{MR}\ _{\ell,n}|\right) \tag{4}$$

(4) is due to observing that, in order to build the set GP-Coll($\mathcal{L}$), in the worst case we have to access and manage, for each dimension d of *all* the N dimension of $\mathcal{L}$, *all* the multidimensional points of *all* the N MR contained in *all* the P $\mathcal{MR}(\mathcal{L}_\ell)$ of $\mathcal{MR}(\mathcal{L})$. Also, note that, in the worst case, the cardinality of the each MR $\text{MR}_{\ell,d}$ at level ℓ along d is *equal* to the cardinality of *each* set **queries**$_m(\ell)$ at the *same* level ℓ, for each HRQ Q_{H_m} in S_{HRQ} (i.e., this means that, in the worst case, *all* the multidimensional points in the MR are *equal* to all the corresponding members in the query ranges of the HRQ, thus different one each other). Therefore, (4) can be re-written as follows:

$$O_{GP} = O\left(N \cdot \sum_{\ell=0}^{P-1}\sum_{m=0}^{M-1}|\text{queries}\ _m(\ell)|\right) \tag{5}$$

The complexity of **buildMQP**, O_{MQP}, is given by the following formula:

$$O_{MQP} = \sum_{\ell=0}^{P-1} O\left(N \cdot B_\ell^2\right) \tag{6}$$

such that B_ℓ denotes the number of buckets generated by **buildMQP** in the MQP $\mathcal{P}(\mathcal{L}_\ell)$ at level ℓ. Note that, in turn, the number of buckets B_ℓ can be expressed as a function of the input storage space $\mathcal{B}$, denoted by $\phi_\ell(\mathcal{B})$, as the *effective* number of buckets generated by **buildMQP** finally depends on $\mathcal{B}$. Therefore, (6) can be re-written as follows:

$$O_{MQP} = \sum_{\ell=0}^{P-1} O\left(N \cdot \phi_\ell(\mathcal{B})^2\right) \tag{7}$$

ϕ_ℓ models the way final buckets are mapped in secondary memory. The simplest expression for ϕ_ℓ one can think of is the following:

$$\phi_\ell(b_{\ell,k}) = \varphi_{DATA}(b_{\ell,k}) + \varphi_{INDEX}(b_{\ell,k}), \forall\ b_{\ell,k} \in \mathcal{P}(\mathcal{L}_\ell) \tag{8}$$

such that: (*i*) $b_{\ell,k}$ denotes a bucket belonging to the MQP $\mathcal{P}(\mathcal{L}_\ell)$ at level ℓ; (*ii*) φ_{DATA} is a function that, applied to a bucket $b_{\ell,k}$ of $\mathcal{P}(\mathcal{L}_\ell)$, returns the occupancy of data stored in $b_{\ell,k}$ in secondary memory; (*iii*) φ_{INDEX} is a function that, applied to a bucket $b_{\ell,k}$ of $\mathcal{P}(\mathcal{L}_\ell)$, returns the occupancy of index indexing $b_{\ell,k}$ in secondary memory. A conventional implementation for ϕ_ℓ is the following:

$$\phi_\ell(b_{\ell,k}) = 32 + \varphi_{INDEX}(b_{\ell,k}), \forall\ b_{\ell,k} \in \mathcal{P}(\mathcal{L}_\ell) \tag{9}$$

(9) states that, in secondary memory, data stored in $b_{\ell,k}$, $\varphi_{DATA}(b_{\ell,k})$, occupies 32 bits, as integer sums (which models the SUM-based aggregations of items $b_{\ell,k}$ contains – see Section 2) can be represented by this amount of bits in conventional computer architectures. For what regards the amount of bits needed to represent the index on $b_{\ell,k}$, $\varphi_{INDEX}(b_{\ell,k})$, we cannot enforce constant values, as the index depends on the particular data engineering solution adopted by the compressed data structure in this respect.

(7) is due to noticing that, in order to build the set MQP-Coll($\mathcal{L}$), we basically have to execute, for each level ℓ of the data cube hierarchy, the greedy bucket merge procedure on the MQP $\mathcal{P}(\mathcal{L}_\ell)$. The complexity of this task, which can be reasonably intended as the baseline operation of **buildMQP**, is similar to the complexity of constructing classical histograms (such as *MinSkew* [1]) that depends linearly on the data cube dimensionality, N, and quadratically on the (input) desired bucket number, B. Note that, contrary to classical proposals, in our approach we consider as input parameter the storage space $\mathcal{B}$ available to house the histogram rather than the desired number of buckets to be stored within the histogram. There parameters are, obviously, correspondent.

Finally, the complexity of **buildMQP**, O_{MQP}, is given by the following formula:

$$O_{GP} = O(P) \qquad (10)$$

(10) is due to observing that, in order to finally obtain the histogram MQ-Hist($\mathcal{L}$), we have to build the hierarchical multidimensional references among the P MQP of MQP-Coll($\mathcal{L}$). This requires a complexity that linearly depends on P.

Based on the previous results, (2) can be re-written as follows:

$$O\left(N \cdot \sum_{m=0}^{M-1} \sum_{\ell=0}^{P-1} |\text{ queries }_m(\ell)|\right) + O\left(N \cdot \sum_{\ell=0}^{P-1} \sum_{m=0}^{M-1} |\text{ queries }_m(\ell)|\right) + \sum_{\ell=0}^{P-1} O\left(N \cdot \phi_\ell(\mathcal{B})^2\right) + O(P) \qquad (11)$$

where the operator $\oplus$ of (2) is replaced by the native sum operator used in closed formulas, $+$.

In the following, we will provide the asymptotic analysis of (11) in order to derive the final complexity formula, which constitutes one of the main contributions of this research.

Consider the complexity of **buildMR** (3). (3) can be asymptotically reduced to the formula expressing the most costing operation it represents. In (3), this operation is given by the ordered union that involves the set of range queries having the *greatest cardinality* among those of all the range query sets of HRB in S_{HRQ}, denoted by queries $_{m*}^{MAX}(\ell*)$, with $m* \in [0, M-1]$ and $\ell* \in [0, P-1]$. Let O_{MR*} denote the latter complexity. O_{MR*} is given by the following formula:

$$O_{MR*} \approx O\left(N \cdot M \cdot P \cdot |\text{ queries }_{m*}^{MAX}(\ell*)|\right) \qquad (12)$$

Consider the complexity of **buildGP** (5). On the basis of similar reasons given for (12), (5) can be asymptotically reduced to the *same* formula (12), as follows:

$$O_{GP*} \approx O\left(N \cdot P \cdot M \cdot | \text{ queries } {}_{m*}^{MAX} (\ell*) | \right) \tag{13}$$

Consider the complexity of **buildMQP** (7). (7) cannot be asymptotically reduced, as its baseline operation (i.e., the greedy bucket merge procedure) must be performed for each level of the data cube hierarchy necessarily. In this case, we can only achieve a more compact formulation of (7) at a formal/theoretical point of view, just supposing that the cost of the baseline operation is the *same* for each level of the data cube hierarchy. Hence, we can express (7) in terms of a singleton level, $\ell*$. Under this assumption, (7) can be re-written as follows:

$$O_{MQP*} \approx O\left(P \cdot N \cdot \phi_{\ell*}(\mathcal{B})^2\right) \tag{14}$$

Consider the complexity of **buildMQP** (10). (10) cannot be asymptotically reduced, as it is already expressed in terms of a complexity that linearly depends on the depth of the data cube hierarchy, P.

Based on the analysis above, (11) can be asymptotically reduced as follows:

$$O_{H*} \approx$$
$$O\left(N \cdot M \cdot P \cdot | \text{ queries } {}_{m*}^{MAX} (\ell*) | \right) + O\left(N \cdot P \cdot M \cdot | \text{ queries } {}_{m*}^{MAX} (\ell*) | \right) + O\left(P \cdot N \cdot \phi_{\ell*}(\mathcal{B})^2\right) + O(P) \tag{15}$$

i.e.:

$$O_{H*} \approx 2 \cdot O\left(N \cdot M \cdot P \cdot | \text{ queries } {}_{m*}^{MAX} (\ell*) | \right) + O\left(P \cdot N \cdot \phi_{\ell*}(\mathcal{B})^2\right) + O(P) \tag{16}$$

From the study of (16), it clearly follows that the more costing complexity term in (16) is $O\left(P \cdot N \cdot \phi_{\ell*}(\mathcal{B})^2\right)$. Therefore, (11) can be *further* asymptotically reduced by disregarding the other terms in (16), i.e. $O\left(N \cdot M \cdot P \cdot | \text{ queries } {}_{m*}^{MAX} (\ell*) | \right)$ and $O(P)$, as follows:

$$O_{H*} \approx O\left(P \cdot N \cdot \phi_{\ell*}(\mathcal{B})^2\right) \tag{17}$$

or, in a more compact way:

$$O_{H*} \approx O\left(P \cdot N \cdot \mathcal{B}^2\right) \tag{18}$$

Intuitively enough, (18) makes sense perfectly, as, essentially, (18) expresses a complexity that it is equal to the complexity of constructing classical histograms (such as *MinSkew* [1]) multiplied by the depth of the data cube hierarchy, P. Particularly, the presence of the factor P is due to top-down nature of the multiple-query data cube compression technique we propose (see Section 2). Finally, (18) gives raise to Theorem 1, which constitutes the main contribution of this research, clearly proves that algorithm `computeMQHist` has a polynomial asymptotic complexity.

Theorem 1. *Given an N-dimensional data cube $\mathcal{L}$ having P hierarchical levels, a set of M HRQ S_{HRQ} having depth equal to P, and an amount of storage space $\mathcal{B}$, the histogram* $MQ\text{-}Hist(\mathcal{L})$ *that is able to accommodate, as much as possible, the multiple-query constraints posed by evaluating HRQ in S_{HRQ} against $\mathcal{L}$ simultaneously, and that fits within $\mathcal{B}$, is computed by algorithm* computeMQHist *in time* $O(P \cdot N \cdot \mathcal{B}^2)$.

4   Conclusions and Future Work

Starting from our previous research result provided in [8], where the principles, models and algorithms of the multiple-objective OLAP data cube compression framework has been introduced and experimentally assessed, in this paper we have provided further, significant extensions to the results [8] by means of a comprehensive descriptions of main algorithm computeMQHist and, mostly, proving that its complexity is asymptotically polynomial. Future work is mainly oriented to extend the theoretical results presented here as to make them more robust in order to cover the following two "difficult" OLAP data cube compression scenarios of the main framework [8]: (*i*) *multi-resolution OLAP data cube compression across suitable dimensional hierarchies*; (*ii*) *the presence of more complex setting parameters*, such as super-imposing *preferences* on the compression ratio of particular multidimensional ranges of the input OLAP data cube.

References

[1] Acharya, S., Poosala, V., Ramaswamy, S.: Selectivity Estimation in Spatial Databases. In: Proceedings of the 1999 ACM International Conference on Management of Data, pp. 13–24 (1999)

[2] Balke, W.-T., Güntzer, U.: Multi-Objective Query Processing for Database Systems. In: Proceedings of the 30th International Conference on Very Large Data Bases, pp. 936–947 (2004)

[3] Bruno, N., Chaudhuri, S., Gravano, L.: STHoles: A Multidimensional Workload-Aware Histogram. In: Proceedings of the 2001 ACM International Conference on Management of Data, pp. 211–222 (2001)

[4] Cuzzocrea, A.: Overcoming Limitations of Approximate Query Answering in OLAP. In: Proceedings of the 9th IEEE International Database Engineering and Applications Symposium, pp. 200–209 (2005)

[5] Cuzzocrea, A.: Providing Probabilistically-Bounded Approximate Answers to Non-Holistic Aggregate Range Queries in OLAP. In: Proceedings of the 8th ACM International Workshop on Data Warehousing and OLAP, pp. 97–106 (2005)

[6] Cuzzocrea, A.: Improving Range-Sum Query Evaluation on Data Cubes via Polynomial Approximation. Data & Knowledge Engineering 56, 85–121 (2006)

[7] Cuzzocrea, A.: Accuracy Control in Compressed Multidimensional Data Cubes for Quality of Answer-based OLAP Tools. In: Proceedings of the 18th IEEE International Conference on Scientific and Statistical Database Management, pp. 301–310 (2006)

[8] Cuzzocrea, A.: Top-Down Compression of Data Cubes in the Presence of Simultaneous Multiple Hierarchical Range Queries. In: Proceedings of the 17th International Symposium on Methodologies for Intelligent Systems, pp. 361–374 (2008)

[9] Cuzzocrea, A., Saccà, D., Serafino, P.: Semantics-aware Advanced OLAP Visualization of Multidimensional Data Cubes. International Journal of Data Warehousing and Mining 3(4), 1–30 (2007)

[10] Cuzzocrea, A., Wang, W.: Approximate Range-Sum Query Answering on Data Cubes with Probabilistic Guarantees. Journal of Intelligent Information Systems 28(2), 161–197 (2007)

[11] Doan, A., Levy, A.Y.: Efficiently Ordering Plans for Data Integration. In: Proceedings of the IEEE 18th International Conference on Data Engineering, pp. 393–402 (2002)

[12] Gunopulos, D., Kollios, G., Tsotras, V.J., Domeniconi, C.: Selectivity Estimators for Multidimensional Range Queries over Real Attributes. VLDB Journal 14(2), 137–154 (2005)

[13] Han, J., Kamber, M.: Data Mining: Concepts and Techniques. Morgan Kauffmann Publishers (2000)

[14] Kalnis, P., Papadias, D.: Multi-Query Optimization for On-Line Analytical Processing. Information Systems 28(5), 457–473 (2003)

[15] Papadias, D., Tao, Y., Fu, G., Seeger, B.: Progressive Skyline Computation in Database Systems. ACM Transactions on Database Systems 30(1), 41–82 (2005)

[16] Poosala, V., Ioannidis, Y.: Selectivity Estimation Without the Attribute Value Independence Assumption. In: Proceedings of the 25th International Conference on Very Large Data Bases, pp. 486–495 (1997)

[17] Roy, P., Seshadri, S., Sudarshan, S., Bhobe, S.: Efficient and Extensible Algorithms for Multi-Query Optimization. In: Proceedings of the 2000 ACM International Conference on Management of Data, pp. 249–260 (2000)

[18] Wang, S., Rundensteiner, E.A., Ganguly, S., Bhatnagar, S.: State-Slice: A New Paradigm of Multi-Query Optimization of Window-Based Stream Queries. In: Proceedings of the 32nd International Conference on Very Large Data Bases, pp. 619–630 (2006)

[19] Xu, W., Theodoratos, D., Zuzarte, C.: Computing Closest Common Sub-Expressions for View Selection Problems. In: Proceedings of the 9th ACM International Workshop on Data Warehousing and OLAP, pp. 75–82 (2006)

[20] Zhang, R., Koudas, N., Ooi, B.C., Srivastava, D.: Multiple Aggregations over Data Streams. In: Proceedings of the 2005 ACM International Conference on Management of Data, pp. 299–310 (2005)

Author Index